A HISTORY OF
NARRATIVE FILM

A HISTORY OF
NARRATIVE FILM
SECOND EDITION

David A. *Cook*

Emory University

W · W · Norton & Company · New York · London

Copyright © 1990, 1981 by W. W. Norton & Company, Inc.
All rights reserved.
Printed in the United States of America.

This book is composed in Sabon.
Composition by Vail Ballou.
Manufacturing by The Maple-Vail Book Manufacturing Group.

Library of Congress Cataloging-in-Publication Data

Cook, David A.
    A history of narrative film / David A. Cook. —2nd ed.
        p.   cm.
    Bibliography: p.
    Includes index.
    1. Motion pictures—History.   I. Title.
    PN1993.5.A1C65   1990
    791.43'09—dc19   88-33274

ISBN 0-393-95553-2

W. W. Norton & Company, Inc., 500 Fifth Avenue, New York, N.Y. 10110
W. W. Norton & Company Ltd., 37 Great Russell Street, London WC1B 3NU

2 3 4 5 6 7 8 9 0

For my family,
for the journey

Contents

Preface

We spend much of our waking lives surrounded by moving photographic images. They have come to occupy such a central position in our experience that it is unusual to pass even a single day without encountering them for an extended period of time, through either film or television. In short, moving photographic images have become part of the total environment of modern industrial society. Both materially and psychologically, they have a shaping impact on our lives. And yet few people in our society have been taught to understand precisely how they work. Most of us, in fact, have extremely vague notions about how moving images are formed and how they are structured to create the multitude of messages sent out to us by the audiovisual media on an almost continual basis. If we made an analogy with verbal language, we should be forced to consider ourselves barely literate—able to assimilate the language form without fully comprehending it. We would, of course, be appalled to find ourselves living in a culture whose general verbal literacy level corresponded to that of a three-year-old child. Most persons living in such a culture would, like small children, be easy prey to whoever could manipulate the language. They would be subject to the control of any minority that understood the language from the inside out and could therefore establish an authority of knowledge over them, just as verbally literate adults establish authority over children. Such a situation would be unthinkable in the modern industrial world, of course, and our own culture has made it a priority to educate its children in the institutions of human speech so that they can participate in the community of knowledge that verbal literacy sustains.

Imagine, though, that a new language form came into being at the turn of the twentieth century, an audiovisual language form that first took the shape of cinema and became in time the common currency of modern television. Imagine that because the making of statements in this language depended upon an expensive industrial process, only a handful of elite specialists were trained to use it. Imagine, too, that although public anxiety about the potentially corrupting influence of the new language was constant from its birth, it was *perceived* not as a language at all but as a medium of popular entertainment—that in this guise the language was gradually allowed to colonize us, as if it were the vernacular speech of some conquering foreign power. Finally, imagine waking up one day in the last quarter of the twentieth century to discover that we had mistaken language for a mode of dreaming and in the process become massively illiterate in a primary language form, one that had not only surrounded us materially but that, as language forms tend to do, had invaded our minds as well. What would we do if that happened? We could choose to embrace our error and lapse into the anarchic mode of consciousness characteristic of preliterate societies, which might be fun but would most certainly be dangerous in an advanced industrial society. Or we could attempt to reinstruct ourselves in the language form from the ground up and from the inside out. We could try to learn as much of its history, technology, and aesthetics as possible. We could trace the evolution of its syntactic and semantic forms from their birth through their present stages of development, and try to forecast the shapes they might take in the future. We could, finally, bring the apparatus of sequential logic and critical analysis to bear on the seemingly random structures of the language in order to read them in new and meaningful ways.

This scenario conforms quite accurately, I believe, to our present situation in the modern world. The language of the moving photographic image has become so pervasive in our daily lives that we scarcely notice its presence. And yet it *does* surround us, sending us messages, taking positions, making statements, and constantly redefining our relationship to material reality. We can choose to live in ignorance of its operations and be manipulated by those who presently control it. Or we can teach ourselves to read it, to appreciate its very real and manifold truths, to recognize its equally real and manifold deceptions. As a lifelong student and teacher of language forms, both verbal and audiovisual, I believe that most intelligent and humane persons in our culture will opt for the latter. it is for them that I have written this book.

Preface to the Second Edition

The second edition of *A History of Narrative Film* is different from the first in several ways. It contains new material on virtually every period and cinema discussed in the first, not merely an updating of information and/or scholarship but a deemphasis of the so-called "masterpiece" model of film history that often plagues works such as this one. I still believe that art is created primarily by human beings, regardless of their instruments; but the weighing of all other factors serves to reemphasize the importance of the human, and several chapters have been rewritten in this light. There are completely new sections on science fiction; on the cinemas of Australia, New Zealand, India, China, the nations of Latin America, and Africa; and on the history of color technology, amplified by an eight-page color insert. There are also approximately three hundred new black-and-white stills to illustrate the new material, and, of course, all sections are expanded and updated at least through mid-1989. Where full coverage of a new national or regional cinema could not be achieved in the text—as in the cases of Belgium, the Scandinavian countries, Spain, the Philippines, Ireland, Scotland, East Germany, and the Netherlands—it is carried on through a system of footnotes.

The most extraordinary thing that has happened since the first edition of this book is the availability on video of nearly every title discussed in it, and this cannot be a bad thing. But we need to remind ourselves that film exists most essentially as the product of a photochemical process that video replicates but feebly and that can be tampered with—by colorizers and time-compressers, for example—quite cavalierly. Video is a wonderful tool for teaching and researching our filmic heritage, but we must never forget the critical importance of experiencing and preserving that heritage in a manner as close to its original form as possible.

Acknowledgments

The revision of this book for its second edition took place actively over a four-year period from 1985 to 1989, and I have incurred numerous intellectual debts in the process. Limits of time and space permit me to acknowledge only the most crucial among them. First, I want to thank the three evaluators of the first edition—Allan Casebier of the University of Southern California, Bruce Kawin of the University of Colorado, and Timothy Lyons of the University of Dayton. Their thoughtful comments resulted in what I believe to be significant improvements to the text. It happened that Kawin was at work simultaneously on his own book *How Movies Work* (New York: Macmillan, 1987), and he shared many valuable insights from that project with me. Equally generous with their expertise were Douglas Gomery of the University of Maryland, Steven P. Hill of the University of Illinois–Urbana, and Charles Musser, editor of the Edison Papers, all of whom read relevant sections of the new material in manuscript and offered numerous constructive suggestions. I should also like to thank my colleagues and students in the Department of Theater and Film Studies at Emory University for their continuing support, and Mr. Robert Troutman of Atlanta for providing us with access to his extraordinary collection of classic films on videocassette. Finally, I thank my editor, Carol Stiles Bemis at W. W. Norton & Company, for a broad range of collaborative efforts and skills throughout the process of putting the revised edition together.

A Note on Method

For reasons that will become apparent in the course of this book, I believe that the history of film as we have experienced it to date is the history of a narrative form. Many of the greatest films ever made were created by artists seeking to break the constraints of this form as it defined itself at different points in time, and there is much evidence to suggest that since the 1950s the cinema has been moving in an increasingly non-narrative direction. But the fact remains that the language common to the international cinema from the last decade of the nineteenth century through the present has been narrative in both aspiration and structural form. For this reason, I have excluded documentary cinema, animated cinema, and the experimental avant-garde from consideration in this book except where they have influenced narrative form to a demonstrable and significant extent. This is not to suggest that any of these excluded forms is unimportant, but rather that each is important and distinctive enough to warrant a separate history of its own (several of which, in fact, already exist).

A Note on Supplementary Material

The endnotes for this volume are gathered in Part III of the Instructor's Manual. They are both documentary and substantive in nature, and instructors should note that some of the stills appearing in the latter chapters of the text are discussed therein.

A Note on the Color Insert

For discussions of the films illustrated in this insert and their use of color, the reader should consult the appropriate pages of the Index.

Color is used variously in motion pictures including, for example, historical spectacle (*The Adventures of Robin Hood, Gone with the Wind, Henry V, The Ten Commandments, Il gattopardo (The Leopard), Dr. Zhivago,* and *Ludwig*); fantasy and romance (*The Wizard of Oz, Fantasia, Meet Me in St. Louis, Kismet, South Pacific,* and *Indiana Jones and the Temple of Doom*); historical realism (*She Wore a Yellow Ribbon, The African Queen, Dr. Zhivago, 2001: A Space Odyssey, The Wild Bunch, McCabe and Mrs. Miller, The Godfather, The Godfather, Part II,* and *Heaven's Gate*); psychological and expressive realism (*Vertigo, Fahrenheit 451, Belle de jour, Il conformista (The Conformist), Morte a Venezia (Death in Venice), The Passenger, Picnic at Hanging Rock, My Life as a Dog,* and *Manhunter*); and exoticism, otherness, and horror (*Black Narcissus, Kwaidan, Fellini Satyricon, The Shining, Poltergeist, The Year of Living Dangerously,* and *Legend*).

A Note on Dates, Titles, and Stills

Wherever possible, the date given for a film is the year of its theatrical release in its country of origin. Unless otherwise noted (as in the case of intermittent production or delayed release), the reader may assume a lapse of six months between the start of production and the date of release. This is important in correlating the history of film with the history of human events (for instance, many American films with the release date of 1942 went into production and were completed before the Japanese attack on Pearl Harbor on December 7, 1941).

As for the titles of films in languages other than English, those in French, Italian, Spanish, Portuguese, and German are given in the original language, followed, in parentheses, by a literal English translation (and an alternate English-language release title, if one exists), followed by the date of release. After the initial reference, the original foreign-language title is used, except in the case of a film that is best known in the English-speaking world by its English title (for example, Jean-Luc Godard's *Breathless* [*A bout de souffle*, 1959]). For Scandinavian, Eastern European, Asian, and African languages the convention is reversed: the initial reference is given in English, followed by the original title in parentheses (a transliteration is supplied if the original title is in an alphabet other than our own). All subsequent references use the English title, unless the film is best known here by its foreign-language title (as in the case, for instance, of Akira Kurosawa's *Ikiru* [*Living / To Live*, 1952] and *Yojimbo* [*The Bodyguard*, 1961]). In the case of films for which the original foreign-language title was unavailable, only the English title is given.

The photographs used to illustrate the book represent a combination of production stills and frame enlargements. Since they are taken on the set by professional photographers, production stills yeild a higher quality of reproduction; but since they are made intially for the purpose of publicity, they sometimes "beautify" the shots they are intended to represent to the point of distortion. Frame enlargments, on the other hand, are blown-up photographically from 16mm prints of the films themselves, so that they represent the actual images as composed and shot by the film-makers. Their quality of reproduction is often lower than that of production stills, since several extra steps of photographic transference are involved in printing them, but their correspondence with the film images is exact. Whenever shot sequences have been reproduced for discussion or when lengthy analysis accompanies an individual image or series of images, I have tried to use frame enlargements. When less analytical procedures are involved, I have used production stills. (Many films of the fifties and most films of the sixties, seventies, and eighties were shot in some type of widescreen process, with aspect ratios varying from 255:1 to 1.85:1. For reasons of typography and design, most of the stills in this volume have been reproduced in the 1.33:1 aspect ratio of the Academy frame.) Though photographs can never replicate cinema, lacking as they do the essential component of motion, they can be made to represent it. Throughout the book, I have attempted to integrate the stills with the written text in a manner that will provide for maximum delivery of information. The reader is therefore encouraged to regard both photographic and verbal information as part of the same critical fabric, although neither, finally, can substitute for the audiovisual information contained in the films themselves.

The illustrations in this book were obtained from the Museum of Modern Art's Film Stills Archive with the following exceptions (and excluding frame enlargements supplied by the author):

The Academy of Motion Picture Arts and Sciences: 10.30.

Cinema 5: 18.43.

Cinemabilia: 10.24, 10.26.

Howard Cramer: 2.7.

The Library of Congress: 1.12, 1.13, 1.21 (a), 2.1, 2.2.

New Line Cinema: 18.40, 18.41.

The New York Film Festival: 18.48.

New Yorker Films: 18.39, 18.46.

Jerry Ohlinger's Movie Material Store: Insert illustrations for *The Adventures of Robin Hood; Gone with the Wind; The Wizard of Oz; Fantasia; The African Queen; Kismet; The Ten Commandments; South Pacific, Il gattapardo (The Leopard); Kwaidan; Dr. Zhivago; Fahrenheit 451; 2001: A Space Odyssey; The Wild Bunch; Fellini Satyricon; McCabe and Mrs. Miller; The Godfather; The Godfather, Part II; The Passenger; Days of Heaven; Heaven's Gate; The Shining; Poltergeist; The Year of Living Dangerously; Indiana Jones and the Temple of Doom; Legend; My Life as a Dog; Manhunter.*

Superstock International, Inc.: Insert illustrations for *Meet Me in St. Louis; Henry V; Black Narcissus; She Wore a Yellow Ribbon; Vertigo; Belle de jour; Il conformista (The Conformist); Morte a Venezia (Death in Venice); Ludwig; Picnic at Hanging Rock.*

Unifilm: 18.1, 18.4, 18.5, 18.15, 18.16, 18.21, 18.22, 18.23

Origins

OPTICAL PRINCIPLES

The beginning of film history is the end of something else: the successive stages of technological development throughout the nineteenth century whereby simple optical devices used for entertainment grew into sophisticated machines which could convincingly represent empirical reality in motion. Both toys and machines were dependent for their illusions upon interactive optical phenomena known as **persistence of vision** and the *phi phenomenon*. The former is a characteristic of human perception, known to the ancient Egyptians but first described scientifically by Peter Mark Roget in 1824, whereby the brain retains images cast upon the retina of the eye for approximately one-twentieth to one-fifth of a second beyond their actual removal from the field of vision. The latter, whose operation was discovered by the Gestalt psychologist Max Wertheimer in 1912, is the phenomenon which causes us to see the individual blades of a rotating fan as a unitary circular form or the different hues of a spinning color wheel as a single, homogeneous color. Together, persistence of vision and the *phi* phenomenon allow us to see a succession of static images as a single unbroken movement and permit the illusion of continuous motion upon which **cinematography** is based. Persistence of vision prevents us from seeing the dark space between the film frames by causing "flicker fusion" when the frequency with which the projection light is broken approaches 50 times per second; without this effect, our eyes would perceive the alternation of light and dark on the screen as each projected image succeeded the next, as, in fact, was the case in the earliest days of the movies, which became known colloquially as "flickers" or "flicks" for this very reason. The phi phenomenon, also known as the "stroboscopic effect," creates apparent movement from frame to frame at optimal projection speeds of 12 to 24 fps. This much is known, but perceptual psychologists still understand very little about the neural and cognitive processes involved in the perception of motion.

The **frames** of a strip of film are a series of individual still photographs which the motion-picture camera, as it was perfected by the Edison Laboratories in 1892 and as it exists today, imprints a single frame at a time. The succession of frames recorded in the camera, when projected at the same or similar speeds, creates the illusion of continuous motion essential

1.1　The Thaumatrope.

1.2　The Phenakistoscope.

1.3　The Zoetrope.

to the cinema. (Individual frames are actually held longer before the projector's lens than before the camera's, but the movement *between* frames is more rapid in projection, so that the speeds of both instruments remain synchronized.)

Illusion is the operative term here. Most motion-picture cameras today expose individual frames at the rate of 24 frames per second (fps), with an exposure time of about one-forty-eighth of a second per frame (the other forty-eighth of a second allows time for the film to move from one exposure to the next). The illusion of continuous motion can be induced in our brains at rates as low as 12 frames per second, yet speeds have traditionally been set at about 16 frames per second for silent film and 24 for sound. On the film strip itself, these frames are separated by thin, unexposed frame lines, but in projection a rotating **shutter** obscures the intervals between the frames and flashes each frame upon the **screen** twice to eliminate the flicker we would otherwise perceive by their movement. When we "watch" a film in a theater, we actually spend as much as 50 percent of the time in darkness, with the projector's shutter closed and nothing before us on the screen. Thus the continuity of movement and light that seems to be the most palpable quality of the cinema exists only in our brains, making cinema the first communications medium to be based upon psycho-perceptual illusions created by machines.* The second, of course, is television.

Persistence of vision and the phi phenomenon were exploited for the purpose of optical entertainment for many years before the invention of photography. A popular child's toy of the early nineteenth century was the Thaumatrope (from the Greek for "magical turning"), a paper disk with strings attached to either side so that it could be twirled between finger and thumb. A different image was imprinted on each face, and when the disk was spun the images seemed to merge into a single unified picture (a rider would mount a horse, a parrot enter his cage, etc.). Between 1832 and 1850, hundreds of optical toys were manufactured which used rotating "phase drawings" of things in motion to produce a crude form of animation. Drawings representing successive phases of an action would be mounted on a disk or cylinder and rotated in conjunction with some type of shutter apparatus (usually a series of slots in the disk or cylinder itself) to produce the illusion of motion. Joseph Plateau's Phenakistoscope (from the Greek for "deceitful view"—1832) and George Horner's Zoetrope ("live turning"—1834) were among the most popular of these toys, which reached increasing stages of refinement as the century progressed. When still photography was invented by Louis Jacques Mandé

---

* It might be argued that photography and telephony are no less illusory. But when we look at a photograph, there *is* a materially real, light-encoded representation of reality before us, and when we use the telephone, there *is* a materially real human voice behind the electronic pulses transmitting it through the wire. When we watch a film in a theater, on the other hand, the movement we perceive on the screen does not exist materially on the screen but solely in our heads. The only empirically real movement in the "movies" is the motion of the film strip through the camera and projector. Television compounds this illusion by dematerializing the screen and relocating it *inside* our heads, so that neither movement nor screen are materially "there" before us.

1.4 Muybridge's glass-plate series photographs.

Daguerre (1789–1851) in 1839* and perfected throughout the next decade, it was a relatively simple step to replace the phase drawings in the motion-simulation devices with individually posed "phase photographs," as Plateau began to do in 1849. At this point, live action could be *simulated photographically*, but not *recorded spontaneously and simultaneously as it occurred.* This required the drastic reduction in photographic **exposure** time from fifteen minutes to one one-thousandth of a second that was achieved by the replacement of collodion wet plates with gelatine dry plates between 1876 and 1881, and the introduction of "series photog-

---

*The very first photographs were actually made by Daguerre's business associate Joseph Nicéphore Niépce (1765–1833) in 1826 using a camera obscura. This device, whose name literally means "dark room," was invented during the Renaissance and consisted of a sealed chamber or box with a tiny hole in one wall. The hole acted as a lens to focus light from the outside (and therefore the image of the objects before the hole) onto the opposite wall. This is the simple optical principle on which all photography is based. Niépce added the final step by fixing the image thus projected on a pewter plate covered with chemical emulsions. But the exposure time for Niépce's process was eight hours, and he died in 1833 without making further innovations. Daguerre's contribution was the introduction of silvered copper plates, which reduced the exposure time to fifteen minutes and made photography a practical reality. Daguerreotypy popularized photography throughout Western Europe, but its prints were positive and therefore could not be reproduced. A rival process developed by the Englishman William Henry Fox Talbot (1800–1877) during the 1840s imprinted photographic images on negative paper stock coated with silver chloride, from which an infinite number of positive paper prints could be reproduced. Although his initial exposure time was three minutes, Talbot ultimately replaced his paper negatives with collodion film stock and by mid-century had reduced the exposure time to one-hundredth of a second, giving photography its modern form.

raphy" by the Anglo-American photographer Eadweard Muybridge (1830–1904).

SERIES PHOTOGRAPHY

In 1872 Muybridge was hired by Leland Stanford, a former California governor and wealthy businessman, to prove that at some point in its gallop a racehorse lifts all four hooves off the ground (a convention of nineteenth-century graphic illustration required that running horses always be pictured with at least one foot on the ground). After several years of abortive experiments, Muybridge accomplished this in the summer of 1877 by setting up a battery of twelve electrically operated cameras (later studies used twenty-four) along a Sacramento racetrack and stretching wires across it which would trip the cameras' shutters. As a horse came down the track, its hooves tripped each shutter individually and caused the cameras to photograph it in successive stages of motion during the gallop. Muybridge demonstrated his results in 1879 on a mechanism he called the zoopraxiscope. This special kind of "magic lantern"* projected colored, hand-drawn images that were based on these photographs and placed along the outer rim of a circular glass disk. Muybridge devoted the rest of his life to refining his process of series photography, but he was not "the man who invented moving pictures," as a recent biography proclaims. He recorded live action continuously for the first time in history, but he did so with a series of twelve or more cameras; until the separate functions of these machines could be incorporated into a single instrument, the cinema could not be born.

It was the French physiologist Étienne-Jules Marey (1830–1904) who recorded the first series photographs of live action in a single camera which, as it happens, was also portable. Marey, a specialist in animal locomotion, invented the "chronophotographic gun" in 1882 in order to take series pictures of birds in flight. This instrument was a camera shaped like a rifle which took twelve instantaneous photographs of a movement per second and imprinted them on a rotating glass plate. A year later Marey switched from the cumbersome plates to paper roll film, which had the effect of introducing the film strip to **cinematography.** But, like most of his contemporaries, Marey was not interested in cinematography as such. In his view, he had invented a machine for the dissection of motion similar to Muybridge's apparatus but more flexible, and he never intended to project his results. (In 1892, however, after the idea of projection had gained currency, Marey did attempt to design a projector that used celluloid roll film on a continuous belt; he was unsuccessful.)

1.5 A seventeenth-century illustration showing the magic lantern.

1.6 Marey's chronophotographic gun.

---

* The optical, or magic, lantern was a simple projection device invented in the seventeenth century, consisting of a light source and a magnifying lens. It enjoyed great popularity as a projector of still transparencies (or slides) throughout the eighteenth and nineteenth centuries and became a major component in subsequent motion-picture projection. Prefiguring this invention in the 1870s was the introduction of slides with movable parts which could be manipulated by lever during projection.

The next step was taken in 1887 in Newark, New Jersey, when an Episcopalian minister named Hannibal Goodwin first used celluloid roll film as a base for light-sensitive **emulsions.** Goodwin's idea was appropriated by the American entrepreneur George Eastman (1854–1932), who in 1889 began to mass-produce and market celluloid roll film on what would soon become an international scale.* Neither Goodwin nor Eastman was initially interested in motion pictures, but it was the introduction of a *plastic* recording medium (in the generic sense of both durable and flexible), coupled with the technical breakthroughs of Muybridge and Marey, that enabled the Edison Laboratories in West Orange, New Jersey, to invent the **Kinetograph,** the first true motion-picture camera.

MOTION PICTURES

Like his predecessors, Thomas Alva Edison was not interested in cinematography in and of itself. Rather, he wished to provide a visual accompaniment for his vastly successful phonograph, and in June 1889 he assigned a young laboratory assistant named William Kennedy Laurie Dickson (1860–1935) to help him develop a motion-picture camera for that purpose. Edison, in fact, envisioned a kind of "coin-operated / entertainment machine," in which motion pictures made by the Kinetograph would illustrate the sound from the phonograph.† This aspect of the Kinetograph's genesis is important for two reasons. In the first place, it

---

* This resulted in the first major patent infringement suit in film history, *Goodwin Film & Camera Company v. Eastman Kodak Company,* which was decided in Goodwin's favor in 1898 but for which claims litigation continued for another sixteen years. (I am indebted to Dan Greenberg for pointing this out to me.) Celluloid, a derivative of the carbohydrate cellulose, was invented in 1869 by the printer John Wesley Hyatt (1837–1920) as a substitute for ivory in the manufacture of billiard balls, then in great demand. Celluloid was the first synthetic plastic to receive wide commercial use, and the range of products made from it by the turn of the century extended from false teeth, to piano keys, to industrial taps and valves (and, of course, motion-picture film and billiard balls). Celluloid's one drawback for all applications was its high flammability.

† Perhaps Edison's most original invention, the phonograph was a combined product of certain principles of telegraphy (invented in 1839) and telephony (invented in 1876), although until very recently phonographic technology was mechanical rather than electrical. Edison discovered the technique of phonographic reproduction while attempting to design an automatic telegraph which would inscribe Morse code signals by needle onto continuously moving rolls of paper tape. In the process, he discovered the technology of voice and sound transcription, in which sound waves are recorded as physical vibrations in the grooves of a revolving wax cylinder or disk and redeemed as sound by a vibrating stylus and diaphragm in the phonographic performance. Like the motion-picture camera, the phonograph was a mechanical rather than an electrical invention: its sound was amplified by a simple horn, its power provided by a hand-turned crank. Edison patented the phonograph on December 15, 1877, and he initially conceived of it as a dictating machine. But it was as a home-entertainment device that the phonograph enjoyed its first great success. (In fact, it was the so-called phonograph craze of 1878 that first brought Edison to international attention.) By the 1890s, however, sophisticated coin-operated phonographs had become extremely popular and lucrative, and it was in this context that Edison conceived of the Kinetograph camera and the coin-operated viewing device which predated the projector by several years.

shows that the idea of making motion pictures was never divorced from the idea of recording sound. The movies were intended to talk from their inception, so that in some sense the silent cinema represents a thirty-year aberration from the medium's natural tendency toward a total representation of reality. More significant is the fact that the first viable motion-picture camera was invented as an accessory to a sound recording device and not for its own sake. The advent of the Kinetograph thus completes a pattern which has been emerging throughout this chapter and which should now be apparent: cinema was born as an independent medium only *after* the cinema machines had been evolved for purposes other than the establishment of such a medium. That is, the invention of the machines preceded any serious consideration of their documentary or aesthetic potential; and this relationship has remained constant throughout the history of film because the cinema at its material base is a technological form—one in which technological innovation precedes the aesthetic impulse (i.e., no artist can express him- or herself in cinema in ways which would *exceed* the technological capabilities of the machines).

Dickson "invented" the first motion picture camera in a brilliant synthesis of already existing principles and techniques which he had learned from studying the work of Muybridge, Marey, and others. After some ineffectual attempts to record photographic images microscopically on phonograph-like cylinders, Dickson began to experiment with the use of celluloid roll film in a battery-driven camera* similar to Marey's chronophotographic gun, and he arrived at the Kinetograph in late 1891. The machine incorporated what have come to be recognized as the two essentials of motion-picture camera and projector engineering: 1) a stop-motion device to insure the intermittent but regular motion of the film strip through the camera (at first, at the rate of 40 fps, but ultimately, at 16 and 24 fps for silent and sound film respectively), and 2) a perforated celluloid film strip consisting of four **sprocket** holes on the bottom edge of each frame on a three-quarter-inch-wide strip (subsequently one-and-three-eighths inch, the industry standard for 35mm still in use today).† The former, adapted by Dickson from the escapement mechanism of a watch, permits the unexposed film strip in its rapid transit through the camera to be stopped for a fraction of a second (usually twice the fps rate, to allow time for the movement of the film between frames—one thirty-second, one forty-eighth, etc.) before the lens while the shutter opens to *admit* light from the photographed object and expose the individual frames. In projection, the process is exactly reversed: each frame, now developed, is held intermittently before the projection lamp while the shutter opens to

1.7 W. K. L. Dickson (with violin) recording sound for an early Kinetophone experiment.

* Edison's faith in electricity notwithstanding, hand-cranked cameras proved the most popular and efficient of the silent era, since their operators could vary the speed of the film strip and rewind it at will to create special effects such as dissolves (the simultaneous fading out of one image and fading in of another). Hand-cranked cameras were also much lighter and more reliable than their counterparts.

† The original Kinetograph had a horizontal feed system, somewhat like that of 16mm cameras today. In October 1892, this was replaced by the now-standard vertical feed system, which employs a double set of sprocket holes, one on either side of the frame.

emit light through the lens and project the film image onto the screen. (In subsequent practice, the projection beam is broken once per frame by a rotating two-blade [for sound speed] or three-blade [for silent speed] shutter; this provides a shutter frequency of at least 48 "exposures" per second and eliminates the flicker effect through "flicker fusion.") Without a stop-motion device in both camera and projector, the film image would blur. The **synchronization** of film strip and shutter (which insures the exact regularity of this discontinuous movement) and the synchronization of the camera and projector is accomplished by means of the regular perforations in the film strip—inspired by the perforated paper of the Edison automatic telegraph—which is pulled through both machines by a system of clawed gears.

But Edison was not interested in projection. He mistakenly believed that the future of moving pictures lay in individual exhibition, so he commissioned Dickson to perfect the small viewing machine he had already designed for private use in the laboratory. The first moving pictures recorded in the Kinetograph were viewed by the public individually through the magnifing lens of a box-like peep-show machine in which a continuous forty- to fifty-foot film loop ran on spools between an electric lamp and a shutter. This device was dubbed the **Kinetoscope.** True to Edison's original intention, Dickson had attempted to design both viewer and camera so that sound and image could be synchronized and recorded simultaneously. But in fact, accurate synchronization proved impossible, and the very few Kinetoscope films (called "Kinetophones") made with sound employed asynchronous musical accompaniment. Furthermore, when speculative emphasis shifted to projection a few years later, the reproduction of sound became doubly infeasible because there was as yet no means of amplifying it for a large audience. (It would remain so until amplification and recording technologies were invented in the Bell Laboratories early in the twentieth century.) Edison applied for patents on his new machines in 1891 but decided against paying the extra $150 to secure an international copyright, realizing that the Europeans had done so much of the essential mechanical invention of the apparatus that patent claims against them would not hold up. Soon after patents were granted in 1893, Edison began to market Kinetoscopes through several companies. The leading domestic sales agency, headed by Norman C. Raff and Frank R. Gammon, bought them from Edison for $200 apiece and sold them for $350 (as the novelty faded, the price fell to roughly half these figures). The Edison Manufacturing Company went into the filmmaking business by establishing its own Kinetograph studio at West Orange, New Jersey.

On April 14, 1894, a Canadian entrepreneur named Andrew Holland opened the first Kinetoscope parlor in a converted shoe store at 1155 Broadway, in New York City. Holland charged twenty-five cents per person for access to a row of five Edison peep-show viewers,* each of which

1.8 The Edison Kinetoscope.

1.9 Peter Bacigalupi's Kinetoscope parlor, which opened in San Francisco in June 1894.

1.10 The "Black Maria."

---

* In 1894, twenty-five cents was a skilled worker's hourly wage, so admission could also be had at the rate of five cents per standard single view (fifty feet) or ten cents per fight film (150 feet). On recreation and entertainment patterns at the turn of the century, see Larry

contained a single film loop shot with the Kinetograph, and he became the first man in history to make a living from the movies. Others followed his lead, and soon Kinetoscope parlors were opened across the country, all supplied with fifty-foot shorts produced for them exclusively by the Edison Company's West Orange studio at the rate of ten to fifteen dollars outright per print. This first motion-picture studio had been constructed by Dickson in 1893 for just over six hundred dollars; it was an unusual edifice, to say the least. Called the "Black Maria" (after contemporary slang for what was later known as a "paddy wagon") because it was covered with protective tar-paper strips, Dickson's studio was a single room measuring about twenty-five by thirty feet. A section of its roof could be opened to admit the sunlight—then the cinema's only effective lighting source—and the whole building could be rotated on a circular track to follow the sun's course across the sky. Here, from 1893 to April 1895, Dickson was the producer, director, and cameraman for hundreds of brief films distributed by the Edison Company to the Kinetoscope parlors. (Both in the process of invention and production, Dickson worked closely with his assistant, William Heise, who was the camera operator on most early Edison films; Dickson left Edison in June 1895 to form the American Mutoscope and Biograph Company with four other partners [see pp. 63–64].)

These first films seem extremely primitive today in both content and form. The fifty-foot maximum format (approximately sixteen seconds at a speed of 40 fps; sixty at the later standard rate of 16) militated strongly against the construction of narratives but was eminently suitable for recording quick vaudeville turns, **slapstick** comedy skits, and other kinds of brief performance. Some characteristic titles are *Chinese Laundry, The Gaiety Girls Dancing, Trained Bears, Blacksmith Scene, Dentist Scene, Bucking Broncos,* and *Highland Dance.* Taken together, the earliest Kinetoscope shorts preserve a series of standard theatrical routines whose only requisite content is motion. Structurally, the films are even cruder, consisting of continuous, unedited footage of what occurred before the lens of Dickson's stationary camera. This stasis was partially the result of technological limitations—especially the small enclosure of the Black Maria studio and the cumbersomeness of the Kinetograph, which resembled a small icebox in shape and size and initially weighed over five hundred pounds. But it was also the result of a natural ignorance of the ways in which the cinema machines might be used. The first impulse was simply to turn the camera on some interesting subject, staged or real, and let it run. So in terms of structure, the earliest films, like Edison's shorts and those of his Continental counterparts the Lumière brothers, are simply brief recordings of entertaining or amusing subjects in which the camera was made to obey the laws of empirical reality. That is, it was treated as an unblinking human eye, and there was no concept of editing because

May, *Screening Out the Past: The Birth of Mass Culture and the Motion Picture Industry* (New York: Oxford University Press, 1980), pp. 3–42, and Garth S. Jowett, "The First Motion Picture Audiences," in John L. Fell, ed., *Film before Griffith* (Berkeley: University of California Press, 1983), pp. 196–206.

1.11 Original film strips of Strongman Sandow and the dancer Carmencita shot in the Black Maria, 1894. The handwriting and (inaccurate) dating are Dickson's. Reproduced to scale.

1.12 Typical Vitascope fare: *Parisian Dance* and *Black Diamond Express No. 1* (both 1897).

reality cannot be edited by the human eye. At this point in the history of film, the camera was never permitted to record more than could be seen by a single individual standing in one fixed spot and focusing on a single event for a given length of time.

PROJECTION: EUROPE AND AMERICA

Eadweard Muybridge's well-publicized presentations of his zoopraxiscope (in both Europe and America) during the 1880s did much to stimulate interest in perfecting the projection of a series of photographs. The basic requirements of projection engineering were 1) the enlargement of the images for simultaneous viewing by large groups and 2) a means of ensuring the regular but intermittent motion of the developed film strip as it passed between the projection lamp and the shutter (which would correspond with the discontinuous movement of the strip through the camera). The first requirement was easily and rapidly met by applying the principle of magic-lantern projection to film; the second proved more difficult but was eventually fulfilled by a variety of cams, shutters, and gears—and ultimately by the Maltese-cross system used in most projectors today. This system was perfected by the German film pioneer Oskar Messter (see pp. 110; 253); as indicated by the diagram, it has two basic parts: a) a gear in the shape of a Maltese cross connected directly to the sprocket wheels which pull the film through the projector, and b) a cir-

1.13 One of the most popular films made in the Black Maria, *Corbett and Courtney Before the Kinetograph* (1894).

1.14 A contemporary drawing (c. 1894) of a motion picture being made in the Black Maria, showing the bulk and awkwardness of the Kinetograph.

cular disk attached to the projector's drive mechanism, which carries a metal pin at its outer edge.

1.15 The Lumière Cinématographe in operation, c. 1895.

The disk rotates continuously and the pin is so located that it enters one slot of the cross per cycle and propels it through a quarter of a revolution; but when the disk makes contact again with the edge of the cross itself, the gear is tightly locked until the pin rotates around to the next slot. This ensures the regular stop-and-go motion of the film strip through the projector.*

Many of the people credited with having perfected the first workable projectors through these means left no concrete proof of their endeavors. The English inventor William Friese-Green (1855–1921) is supposed to have invented a combined camera and projector in 1887, but it never took or showed a sufficient number of frames to effectively create an illusion of movement. Similarly, a French scientist named Louis Aimé Augustin Le Prince (1842–1890?) patented a camera projector in 1888 and apparently did project moving pictures for French government officials at the Paris Opera in 1890, but he disappeared two months later and was never heard from again. It was actually the year 1895 which witnessed the most significant developments in projection technology, and these occurred almost simultaneously in every country in Western Europe, and in the United States. Ironically, the majority of projection devices brought forth in that year were modeled (quite legally and ethically, since there was no European copyright) upon the Kinetoscope, which the syndicate of Maguire and Baucus had marketed throughout Europe.

By far the most important of these devices was perfected by two brothers, Auguste and Louis Lumière (1862–1954; 1864–1948), who operated a factory for the manufacture of photographic equipment in Lyon, France—and whose family name was, appropriately, the French word for "light." After a thorough study of the workings of the Edison machine, the Lumières invented an apparatus which could serve as camera, projector, and film printer and which was finally patented as the **Cinématographe,** thus coining the term which attaches to the medium of film to this day.† (It is generally acknowledged today that only the youngest

1.16 *La Sortie des ouvriers de l'usine Lumière* (Lumières, 1895).

1.17 *L'Arroseur arrosée* (Lumières, 1895).

* Today, the Maltese cross appears as the imprimatur of the AFL-CIO in the credits of every American film produced with union labor.

† One distinct advantage of the Cinématographe was its portability. Whereas the Kinetograph was battery-driven and weighed several hundred pounds, the hand-cranked Lumière machine weighed just under sixteen. This and the Cinématographe's treble function as camera, projector, and printer freed it from the studio confinement of the Kinetograph and enabled Lumière cameramen to travel all over the world to film "local *actualitès.*" See Robert C. Allen, "Vitascope / Cinématographe: Initial Patterns of American Film Practice," *Journal of the University Film Association* 31, 2 (Spring 1979): 13–18; rpt. Gorham Kindem, ed., *The American Movie Industry: The Business of Motion Pictures* (Carbondale, Ill.: Southern Illinois University Press, 1982), pp. 3–11, and Fell, *Film before Griffith,* pp. 144–52.

Lumière, Louis, was responsible for the actual design and construction of the machine.) The Cinématographe was built to run at a speed of 16 fps and established the standard for silent film.* On March 22, 1895, the Lumière brothers projected their first film to a private audience in Paris. Many film historians designate *La Sortie des ouvriers de l'usine Lumière* (*Workers Leaving the Lumière Factory*) as the world's first moving picture;† certainly this was the first effective theatrical projection of a film made specifically for that purpose. On December 28, 1895, the Lumières rented a basement room in the Grand Café, on the Boulevard des Capucines in Paris, to project a program of about ten films for the first time to a paying audience. Some of the titles from that program were *L'Arrivé d'un train en gare* (*Arrival of a Train at a Station*), which dramatically marked the beginning of the cinema's long obsession with that particular icon of the Industrial Revolution; *Le Répas de bébé* (*Baby's Lunch*), a record of brother Auguste feeding his infant daughter; and *L'Arroseur arrosée* (*The Sprinkler Sprinkled*), a bit of slapstick in which a young boy steps on a hose which then squirts a gardener in the face when he peers at the nozzle. *L'Arrivé* was a visual tour de force, and audiences are said to have stampeded at the sight of the locomotive barreling toward them from a distant prospect into the foreground on the screen. Due to its relative lightness, the Cinématographe could be taken out of doors more easily than the Kinetograph, and for this reason the early Lumière films have a much higher **documentary** content than do Edison's (the Lumières called their films "*actualités*," or documentary views).** Structurally, however, the Lumière and Edison films are precisely the same—the camera and point of view are static and the action continuous from beginning to end, as if editing "reality" was unthinkable to their makers.

Admission to the Lumière program was one franc per customer, and the receipts for the first day totaled only thirty-five francs. But within a month the Cinématographe showings were earning an average of seven

1.18 *L'Arrive d'un train en gare* (Lumières, 1895).

1.19 **A poster advertising an early Ciné-matographe projection, c. 1895.**

---

* Sixteen frames per second (fps) was the *intended* standard for silent films, but the speed was hardly universal. As Kevin Brownlow points out in "Silent Film: What Was the Right Speed?" (*Sight and Sound* 49, 3 [Summer 1980]: 164–67), exhibitors would frequently speed up or slow down projection to accommodate their schedules, and cameramen would overcrank or undercrank during shooting for a variety of reasons, including, most prominently, the absence of speed indicators from cameras until well into the twenties. In practice, speeds among and even within silent films could vary by as much as 10 fps, from 14 to 24. (Indeed, several sequences in D. W. Griffith's *The Birth of a Nation* [1915] were so undercranked by Billy Bitzer that they could only be projected at 12 fps.) For practical purposes, then, 16 fps should be thought of as the *average* and not the uniform speed of silent film recording and projection. The motorization of cameras in the late twenties made it possible for sound speed to be internationally standardized at 24 fps. Since one reel of 35mm film contains just under 1,000 feet and runs about 60 feet per minute at 16 fps, a reel of silent film lasts approximately 16 minutes; at sound speed, or 24 fps, film runs at the standard rate of 90 feet per minute, so that a reel lasts 11 minutes.

† The oldest known print of *La Sortie des ouvriers*, dating from 1895, was discovered beneath the floorboards of a bank building in Perth, Australia, in October 1979. Twelve Lumière films were found in all, including three which previously had been unknown.

** By the turn of the century, both firms were competing heatedly for both markets, Edison turning his attention to Lumière-like *actualités* on the American subcontinent and the Lumières shooting studio-bound domestic stage performances.

thousand francs a week, and motion pictures had become, overnight, an extremely lucrative commercial enterprise. The most important aspect of the Cinématographe projections, however, was that they marked the end of the period of technological experimentation which began with Muybridge's series photography in 1872: the two machines upon which the cinema is founded had been perfected at last. In Germany, the Skladanowsky brothers, Max and Émile (1863–1939; 1859–1945) developed almost simultaneously with the Lumières a projector for celluloid film strips called the "Bioskop" or Bioscope (a common term for many early cameras and projectors) and projected films of their own making in a public performance at the Berlin Wintergarten on November 1, 1895. Projection reached England immediately thereafter, in 1896, when a manufacturer of scientific instruments named Robert W. Paul (1869–1943) patented the Theatrograph (later renamed the Animatograph), a projector based on the Kinetoscope*—although the Lumière Cinématographe was soon to capture both the British and the Continental markets.

Edison became aware of the vastly promising financial future of projection through the success of the Cinématographe at about the same time that Kinetoscope installations had reached saturation point in the United States (all told, just over nine hundred of them were sold), and he commissioned the invention of a projection device in the summer of 1895. In September of that year, however, Edison learned through Raff and Gammon that two aspiring inventors named C. Francis Jenkins (1867–1934) and Thomas Armat (1866–1948) had projected a program of Kinetograph shorts at the Cotton States Exposition in Atlanta, Georgia, with an electrically powered machine which incorporated a stop-motion mechanism superior to anything then under patent.† Their projector also made use of a small but extremely important device employed earlier in the year by the Latham family (brothers Gray and Otway, along with their father Woodville). The Lathams, who had made money showing fight films with Edison's Kinetoscope, formed the Lambda Company to make motion pictures of prize fights and other sporting events, and then project these on the screen. Their contribution, the **Latham loop,** merits special consideration here.

One of the chief practical problems of early motion-picture production and exhibition was that of film breakage. At lengths of greater than fifty to one hundred feet, the inertia of the take-up reel would frequently cause the film strip to tear or snap in the projector. Assisted by the engineer-

---

* Birt Acres (1854–1918), Paul's former partner in the invention of England's first camera and the making of the first British films (*Oxford and Cambridge University Boat Race, The Derby, Rough Sea at Dover*—all 1895), demonstrated a projection device called the Kineopticon several months before Paul, but it was apparently never produced commercially. Acres also invented the first home movie camera, patented as the "Birtac" in 1898, which took fifty-foot reels of 17.5mm film and would function as a projector by reversing its lens.

† An improved version of the Phantascope, developed by Jenkins and Armat in 1894. (The Kinetoscope, unlike the Kinetograph, ran continuously rather than intermittently.)

inventors Enoch Rector and Eugene Augustin Lauste (see p. 255), the Lathams had discovered that by placing a small loop in the film strip just above and below the projection lens, and maintaining it with an extra set of sprockets, the stress could be redistributed in such a manner as to permit films of greater length in the magazine. This relatively simple technological innovation had far-reaching aesthetic consequences, since without it the cinema could never have evolved as an art form. Obviously, there can be very little creative potential in a medium whose basic form is the one-minute short subject. The "Latham loop" is yet another dramatic example of the way in which technology and art are inextricably wed in cinema. Here, as so often in film history, the meeting of a rather minor technological exigency created a whole new aesthetic dimension for the medium.

Edison was so impressed with the features of Armat's machine that he abandoned his own research project and bought the apparatus outright under a scandalous agreement whereby Edison would himself manufacture the machine and take full credit for its invention while Armat would be allowed a small plate on the back crediting him with "design." Edison dubbed the new machine the Vitascope and gave it its first public exhibition on April 23, 1896, at the popular Koster and Bial's Music Hall in New York City, where it received top billing as "Edison's latest marvel." Some representative titles from the program of twelve short films were *Sea Waves; Butterfly Dance* (apparently the first color-tinted print); *The Barber Shop; A Boxing Bout; Venice—Showing Gondolas; Kaiser Wilhelm—Reviewing His Troops; Skirt Dance;* and *The Bar Room.* Like their predecessors, Edison's Vitascope films (some of which had originally been produced for the Kinetoscope, some of which had been illegally copied from the Lumières and the Birt Acres-Robert Paul collaboration) offered nothing more than unmediated glimpses of real action as it unfolded before the camera from a single point of view; but these rather crude "living pictures," as they were soon labeled, proved novel and engaging enough to satisfy the public's taste for several years to come. After all, the world had never seen their like before.

For example, a writer for *La Poste* commented on the Cinématographe projections of December 28, 1895: "The beauty of the invention resides in the novelty and ingenuity of the apparatus. When these apparatuses are made available to the public, everybody will be able to photograph those who are dear to them, no longer as static forms but with their movements, their actions, their familiar gestures, capturing the speech on their very lips. Then, death will no longer be absolute."* The original audiences for motion pictures did not perceive them as we do—as a succession of images linked together in a continuity of meaning—but rather as a series of discontinuous "animated photographs." Conditioned by lantern slide shows, comic strips, and other serial presentations of images, these audiences saw individual scenes as self-contained and did not infer meaning from one scene to the next. The shift in conscious-

1.20 The "Latham loop," as illustrated in the Armat patent application, 1901.

1.21 A poster and publicity sketches for an Edison Vitascope projection in a music hall, c. 1896.

---

* *La Poste,* December 30, 1895, quoted in Georges Sadoul, *Louis Lumière* (Paris: Editions Seghers, 1964), p. 119.

ness from films as animated photographs to films as continuous narratives began around the turn of the century.

The Vitascope and Cinématographe projections mark the culmination of the cinema's prehistory. By 1896, all the basic technological principles of film recording and projection had been discovered and incorporated into existing machines—which, with certain obvious exceptions like the introduction of light-sensitive sound, have remained essentially unchanged from that day to this. Conversely, the history of cinema as an art form begins with these events, for if our understanding of the machines was sophisticated, knowledge of how to use them was primitive indeed. In fact, the kind of documentary recording practiced by Edison and the Lumières was to become the mainstream tendency of the cinema until the turn of the century because there was as yet no notion that the camera might be used to tell a story—i.e., to *create* a **narrative** reality rather than simply *record* some real or staged event which occurred before its lens. It is true that during this period films were able to grow in length to one thousand feet, or approximately sixteen minutes, thanks to the Latham device, but they remained static in terms of form until their narrative dimension was discovered and articulated on the screen. Nevertheless, by the late 1890s cinema was already on its way toward becoming a mass medium with the then unimaginable power to communicate without print or speech.

THE EVOLUTION OF NARRATIVE: GEORGES MÉLIÈS

During the 1890s, near the end of the decade, exhibitors often created multishot narratives that focused on such subjects as a fire rescue or the Spanish-American War. (Programs of unrelated, miscellaneous scenes also remained popular.) The showmen developed these stories by purchasing various one-shot films from production companies, then putting them in an order and delivering a narration, often combined with **sound effects** and lantern slides. Creative responsibility was thus divided between producer and exhibitor. By the turn of the century, however, producers were beginning to assume this editorial responsibility by making multishot films on their own. In the process, filmmakers assumed greater control over the narrative, allowing for greater specificity in the story line. In many respects, therefore, the producers began to resemble modern-day filmmakers. Such a development is most clearly apparent in the work of Georges Méliès (1861–1938), a professional magician who owned and operated the Théâtre Robert-Houdin in Paris. Méliès had been using magic-lantern projections in his conjuring acts for years, and when he attended the first Cinématographe programs in 1895 he immediately recognized the vast illusionist possibilities of the "living pictures." Accordingly, in early 1896 he attempted to buy a Cinématographe from the Lumières for ten thousand francs but was promptly refused, since the brothers recognized potential competition when they saw it. Méliès, however, who had also been a mechanic, an actor, an illustrator, a photographer, and a stage designer, was not easily discouraged. Several months later, he bought an Animatograph projector from the English inventor Robert W. Paul for one thousand francs and simply reversed its mechanical principle to design his own camera, which was constructed for him by the instrument-maker Lucien Korsten.* By April 1896, Méliès was showing his own productions in his own theater. In time, he would become the cinema's first important narrative artist as well, but not before he had done some apprentice work in the manner of the Lumières and Edison by filming a series of *actualités*, comic episodes, and staged conjurer's tricks for projection in his theater.

One afternoon in the fall of 1896, while Méliès was filming a Parisian street scene, his camera jammed in the process of recording an omnibus as it emerged from a tunnel. When he got the machine working again, a funeral hearse had replaced the omnibus, so that in projection the omnibus seemed to change into the hearse.† By this accident, Méliès came to recognize the possibilities for the manipulation of real time and real space inherent in the editing of exposed film. He had discovered that film need not obey the laws of empirical reality, as his predecessors had supposed, because film was in some sense a separate reality with structural laws of its own. Unfortunately, Méliès put his discovery to only limited use. Although he went on to make hundreds of delightful narrative films, his model for them was the narrative mode of the legitimate theater since it was what he knew best. That is, he conceived all of his films in terms of dramatic **scenes** played out from beginning to end rather than in terms of **shots,** or individual visual perspectives on a scene; the only editing, therefore, aside from that used in optical illusions of disappearance and conversion, occurs *between* scenes rather than *within* them. The scenes themselves are composed of single shots taken with a motionless camera from a fixed point of view, that of a theater spectator sitting in the orchestra center aisle with an excellent eye-level view of the action; and the actors move across the film frame from left to right and right to left as if it were the proscenium arch** of a stage. A viewer experiences no more narrative manipulation within a Méliès film than in watching a stage play of the same action; one sees a significant amount of stage illusion, of course, but changes in time and space coincide precisely with changes in scene, and the narrative point of view is rigidly static.

---

*The machine was procured for Méliès by fellow magician David Devant (1868–1941), who then became the exclusive Star Film agent in England until 1900, when British sales were taken over by Charles Urban (1871–1942; see Chapter 8). Devant himself made several conjuring films and appeared in four for Paul performing some of his most famous acts, which were also frequently reconstructed in film by Méliès.

†According to Paul Hammond, in his authoritative study *Marvelous Méliès* (London: Gordon Fraser, 1974), this frequently recounted incident derives from Méliès' notoriously unreliable *Mes Mémoires* (Rome, 1938) and may well be apocryphal (p. 34). But if the tale was fabricated, it at least suggests that Méliès was consciously aware of his own inventiveness.

**In a theater, the part of the stage in front of the curtain (sometimes including the curtain). The proscenium provides a static framing device for the action on stage and marks the borders between stage illusion and the real world.

1.22 The interior of Méliès' studio at Montreuil.

Méliès was nevertheless the cinema's first narrative artist. By adapting certain techniques of still photography, theater spectacle, and magic-lantern projection to the linear medium of the film strip, he innovated significant narrative devices like the **fade-in,** the **fade-out,** the overlapping, or "lap," **dissolve,** and **stop-motion photography.** To put his discoveries into effect, Méliès, in late 1896, organized the Star Film Company, and, by the spring of 1897, he had constructed a small production studio on the grounds of his house in the Paris suburb of Montreuil. The building measured fifty-five by twenty feet and was glass-enclosed like a greenhouse to admit maximum sunlight, the cinema's only effective lighting source until the advent of mercury-vapor lamps in 1908. Here Méliès produced, directed, photographed, and acted in some five hundred films* between 1897 and 1913, when, like so many other film pioneers, he was forced out of business by his competitors (principally Charles Pathé; see pp. 49–51) because he had lost touch with the rapid development of both the medium and the industry. Representative titles, in translation, are *The Cabinet of Mephistopheles* (1897), *Cinderella* (1899), *The Man with the India-Rubber Head* (1901), *A Trip to the Moon* (1902), *The Palace of the Arabian Nights* (1905), *Twenty Thousand Leagues Under the Sea* (1907), and *The Conquest of the Pole* (1912). Although he also made many films based on historical and contemporary events (*actualités reconstituées,* or "reconstructed newsreels," he called them—see, e.g., *The Dreyfus Affair* [1899], his first multi-scene film), Méliès' most memorable productions concern the fantastic and bizarre and are acted out before lush, phantasmagoric backgrounds which he himself designed and painted. Many were released in color, since at the height of his very substantial success Méliès employed twenty-one women at the studio of Madame Tuillier to hand-tint his films individually, frame by frame (a practice apparently initiated by Edison for the first Vitascope projection and continued with some regularity throughout the early silent period. For a thorough discussion of color processes see pp. 327–49.) Although Méliès went bankrupt in 1923 due to his ruin at the hands of Pathé Frères and other rivals, his films had immense popular appeal at the turn of the century. Indeed, by 1902 Star Film had become one of the world's largest suppliers of motion pictures, with offices in New York, London, Barcelona, and Berlin, and had nearly driven the Lumières out of production.

By far the most successful and influential film Méliès made at Montreuil was *Le Voyage dans la lune* (*A Trip to the Moon*). Produced in 1902, this film achieved international circulation within months of its completion, albeit through unethical distribution of "dupes" by rival concerns as much as through Méliès' own sales.† *Le Voyage dans la lune,*

---

* Fewer than 140 of these survive today. Four hundred films were requisitioned by agents of the French army in 1917 and melted down to produce a chemical necessary in the manufacture of boot heels. When he went bankrupt in the summer of 1923, Méliès himself destroyed a batch of negatives and sold his own stock of prints by the kilo to a second-hand film dealer.

† These were maverick times for the small but burgeoning film industry. The status of copyright had yet to be clearly established in the courts and virtually no foreign films were

loosely adapted by Méliès from the Jules Verne novel of the same title, was 825 feet long (a little under fourteen minutes at the average silent speed of 16 fps), or three times the average length of the contemporary Edison and Lumière products (one of Méliès' achievements was increasing the standard length of fiction films). Utterly characteristic of both the strengths and weaknesses of Méliès' theatrical narrative mode, the film is composed of thirty separate scenes,* which he appropriately called *"tableaux,"* all photographed from the same angle and connected by means of lap dissolves. The scenes are arranged in precise chronological sequence, as follows:

1. The scientific congress at the Astronomic Club.
2. The planning of the trip itself.
3. The construction of the projectile in the factory.
4. The factory rooftop at night, with chimneys belching smoke in the background.
5. The boarding of the projectile by the astronomers.
6. The loading of the cannon (complete with female "Marines" in short pants and tights).
7. The firing of the cannon.
8. The flight of the projectile through space.
9. The landing in the eye of the moon (an action overlapped in the next shot).
10. The projectile landing, moonside, and the astronomers disembarking.
11. A view of the moon's topography.
12. The astronomers' dream (visions of the Pleiades and Zodiac signs).
13. A snowstorm on the moon.

---

copyrighted in United States before 1903 (although, when they were, copyright was *generally* respected in the United States because the threat of legal action was real). Despite massive distribution of "dupes" (a term referring to duplicate prints, usually made without the authorization of the picture's producer), however, *A Trip to the Moon* was so popular that Méliès made a fortune during its first year of distribution—a fact explained by the circumstance that films were not leased to exhibitors but sold to them outright until the advent of the first permanent theaters, the nickelodeons.

To prevent further piracy and to promote his films abroad, Méliès established an American branch of Star Film in New York in 1903 under the management of his older brother Gaston (1852–1915), who began to copyright Méliès "Star" films in mid-1903. Gaston founded his own production company and joined the Motion Picture Patents Company in 1908; between 1909 and 1913 he produced over 150 one-reel films—most of them Westerns and war "epics"—at the Star Film Ranch in San Antonio, Texas, and at Santa Paula, California, on the Pacific coast. Before going out of business in 1913, Gaston Méliès employed as directors both Wallace C. McCutcheon, the son of Biograph's Wallace McCutcheon (see p. 64), and Francis Ford, John Ford's eldest brother, who later convinced him to go into the motion picture business (see pp. 209; 325). For more, see Patrick McInroy, "The American Méliès," *Sight and Sound* 48, 4 (Autumn 1979): 250–54.

* These are the "scenes" as listed by Méliès in the *Star Film Catalogue* of 1903. In fact, many are not separate scenes at all but successive episodes within the same *tableau*. Most circulating prints today contain only fifteen *tableaux*, corresponding to *Star Catalogue* "scenes" 1–2, 3, 4, 5–6, 7, 8–9, 10–14, 15–17, 18–19, 20, 21, 22, 23, 24, and 25, as listed above. The missing episodes 26–30 represent a single concluding *tableau*.

14. The astronomers' descent into a crater.
15. A grotto of giant mushrooms in the interior of the moon.
16. Encounter with the moon creatures, or Selenites (acrobats from the Folies-Bergère).
17. The astronomers taken prisoner.
18. The astronomers brought before the King of the Moon and his Selenite army.
19. The astronomers' escape.
20. The Selenites' pursuit.
21. The astronomers' departure in the projectile.
22. The projectile falling vertically through space.
23. The projectile splashing into the sea.
24. The projectile at the bottom of the ocean.
25. The rescue and return to land.
26. The astronomers' triumphal return.
27. The decoration of the heroes.
28. Procession of "Marines."
29. The erection of the commemorative statue.
30. Public rejoicing.

As the description suggests, the whole film very much resembles a photographed stage play, save for the inclusion of some of the optical tricks which were a Méliès trademark. Some of these, such as the disappearance of the Selenites in a puff of smoke when they are struck by the astronomers' umbrellas, were accomplished cinematically, through the use of stop-motion photography, but are not terribly important in terms of narrative. Many others, however, the product of nineteenth-century stage illusion pure and simple, serve to illustrate how very far Méliès really was from tapping the full potential of the medium. The classic example of Méliès lack of vision in this respect is that when he wished to show the astronomers' projectile crashing dramatically into the face of the moon (shot 9), he moved the papier-mâché moon on a dolly into the lens of the camera rather than moving the camera into the moon.

Méliès, in fact, never moved his camera once in any of his more than five hundred films. Neither did he alternate the point of view within scenes or even between them by changing camera angles. His films were, as he once called them, "artificially arranged scenes," or "moving *tableaux*," and his camera functioned as the inert eye of a theater spectator from the beginning to the end of his career. Yet Méliès discovered, if he did not exploit, the enormous potential inherent in the editing of exposed film, and through his influence on contemporary filmmakers he pointed the cinema well on its way toward becoming an essentially narrative rather than a documentary medium, as Edison and Lumière cameramen had originally conceived it. Furthermore, Méliès was an artist of unique and individual talent, and his films endure every bit as much for their distinctive imaginative power as for their contributions to cinematic form. He had stumbled into the narrative dimensions of the cinema very much as cinema had stumbled into being—arbitrarily, almost by accident—and

1.23 Frames from twelve of the original *tableaux* in *Le Voyage dans la lune* (Georges Méliès, 1902). Frames 1–2, 5–6, 8–9, 10–14, 11–12, and 18–19 represent separate episodes from the same *tableaux;* there are no perceptible splices between these frames in the film itself.

1.24 A drawing (c. 1896) illustrating the way in which Méliès simulated camera movement in his films.

he had appropriated a conventional and unimaginative narrative model because it was what he knew best; yet those who came after him would understand. Charlie Chaplin called him "the alchemist of light," but D. W. Griffith, at the end of his own monumental career in 1932, put it best when he said of Méliès, "I owe him everything."*

EDWIN S. PORTER: DEVELOPING A CONCEPT OF CONTINUITY EDITING

Méliès ultimately lost his audience to the practitioners of a more sophisticated narrative style whose origins are closely associated with the work of Edwin S. Porter (1870–1941). Porter had worked as a Vitascope projectionist in 1896, helping to set up the landmark Koster and Bial's projection of April 23, and he subsequently operated his own equipment in such mainline theaters as the Eden Musee in New York City. In 1900 Porter joined the Edison Manufacturing Company as a mechanic and in early 1901 became production head of its new skylight studio on East Twenty-first Street, where for the next few years he served as director / cameraman for much of the company's output. His first films were one-shot skits and *actualités,* such as *Kansas City Saloon Smashers* and *New York City in a Blizzard* (both 1901) and brief multi-scene narratives based on political cartoons and contemporary events (*The Sampson-Schley Controversy,* 1901; *The Execution of Czolgosz,* 1901). Porter also filmed the extraordinary *Pan-American Exposition by Night* (1901), which used **time-lapse photography** to create a circular panorama of the illuminated fairgrounds, by modifying his camera to expose a single frame every ten seconds.

By 1901, Porter had encountered the films of Méliès and those of the two British pioneers George Albert Smith (1864–1959) and James Williamson (1855–1933). Smith, a portrait photographer, and Williamson, a lanternist, had constructed their own motion-picture cameras and, between 1896 and 1898, had begun to produce trick films featuring superimpositions (*The Corsican Brothers* [Smith, 1897]) and interpolated **close-ups** (*Grandma's Reading Glass* [Smith, 1897]; *The Big Swallow* [Williamson, 1901]). Smith would later develop the first commercially successful photographic color process (Kinemacolor, c. 1906–1908, with Charles Urban), while Williamson apparently experimented with intercutting between the interior and exterior of a building as early as 1901 in *Fire!* By 1902, both Smith and Williamson had built studios in their native Brighton, and, with their associates, came to be known as mem-

---

* The contemporary avant-garde also owes him a considerable debt. The American experimentalist Stan Brakhage (b. 1933), for example, has written, "I took my first senses of the individual frame life of a film from Méliès" (*Art Forum,* January 1973, p. 76). For a brilliant appreciation and revaluation of this aspect of Méliès' singular artistry, see Paul Hammond's *Marvelous Méliès,* cited n. p. 15. See also the feature-length compilation film, *Méliès et ses contemporains* (1983), prepared under the supervision of Franz Schmitt at the French State Film Archive in Bois d'Arcy.

bers of the "Brighton school," although they did not really constitute the coherent movement that such a term implies. Some historians (notably Georges Sadoul, Kenneth Macgowan, and Barry Salt) have credited the Brighton school with making major contributions to narrative form between 1902 and 1908, which is difficult to prove given the low survival rate of the era's films. Yet it seems certain that Porter saw some of the earlier Brighton work, since it was occasionally sold by Edison; and he may also have seen that of the Yorkshire-based filmmakers James Bamforth (*A Kiss in the Tunnel,* 1900) and Frank Mottershaw (*Daring Daylight Burglary,* 1903). (The influence was mutual: several later Brighton productions were clearly influenced by the continuity editing of Porter's *The Great Train Robbery* [1903], as was the work of London filmmaker Cecil Hepworth [1873–1953], whose *Rescued by Rover* [1905] is considered to be one of the most skillfully edited narratives before Griffith.)

Yet it may have been Porter's experience as a projectionist at the Eden Musee in the late 1890s that led him to the practice of continuity editing in the period 1901–1903. As he moved from exhibition to production, Porter began to apply many of the editorial skills he had learned to filmmaking. He was also clearly influenced by Méliès' story films. Thus *Jack and the Beanstalk* (1902) shows a strong debt to Méliès' *Bluebeard* (1902). By his own admission, Porter was powerfully influenced by Méliès' *A Trip to the Moon* (1902), which he came to know well in the process of duplicating it for distribution (again, illegal) by Edison in October 1902. Years later, he claimed that it was the Méliès film that had given him the idea for "telling a story in continuity form" which resulted in *Life of an American Fireman,* produced in late 1902 and released in January 1903.* The subject of this film—the dramatic rescue of a woman and child from a burning building by firemen—was a popular one, having been featured in lantern slide shows and other films for years before. What was unusual was Porter's idea of combining **stock footage** from the Edison archive with staged scenes of the rescue to create a uniquely cinematic form: a fiction constructed from recordings of empirically real events (which is, of course, a good definition of cinema itself). About the sequencing of these events, however, there has been much controversy. On the basis of the standard print distributed by the Museum of Modern Art (MoMA) Department of Film, it was long thought that in the final sequence of the film Porter intercut, or cut together, interior shots of a blazing room with exterior shots of a fireman climbing a ladder to rescue its occupants, creating a radically innovative effect—the illusion of separate but simultaneous and **parallel actions,** which was to become a basic structural element of cinematic narrative. But *Life of an American Fireman* was a lost film until 1944, when MoMA acquired a 35mm nitrate print from

---

*In a newspaper interview some years after *Life of an American Fireman,* Porter said: "From laboratory examination of some of the popular films of the French pioneer director, George Méliès—trick films like 'A Trip to the Moon'—I came to the conclusion that a picture telling a story in continuity form might draw the customers back to the theatres and set to work in this direction" (quoted in Musser, "The Early Cinema of Edwin S. Porter," p. 25).

1.25 The editing sequence of Porter's *The Life of an American Fireman* (1903).

Pathé News, Inc. Although MoMA has never claimed that this print, known today as the "Cross-Cut Version," was the original, it conforms in principle to the editing continuity of the original as it has been described by American film historians from Terry Ramsaye (*A Million and One Nights* [1926]) through Lewis Jacobs (*The Rise of the American Film* [1939]) and beyond. Ramsaye's description was based either on memory or on Porter's own account of the film (more recently set forth by Budd Schulberg in *Variety*, May 9, 1979). Jacobs' description was based on a combination of Ramsaye's version, the *Edison Catalogue* description, and a sequence of production stills made for copyright purposes by the Edison Company, which seem to suggest intercutting at the film's climax.

The Cross-Cut Version, which still has wide circulation, is 378 feet long (just over six minutes at the average silent speed of 16 fps) and consists of twenty separate* shots linked together by dissolves or straight cuts as follows:

1. The fire chief asleep, dreaming of his wife and child, who appear in a circular vignette at the upper right-hand corner of the screen, later called the "dream balloon"

2. Close-up of a fire-alarm box and an anonymous hand pulling its lever (Porter's first close-up to be completely integrated with its narrative context). All other shots in the film are **long shots.**

3. Interior of the firemen's dormitory, with the men first asleep, then waking in response to the alarm—a slight temporal overlap from shot 2—dressing, and sliding down the pole.

4. Interior ground floor of the firehouse, actually an outdoor set, with the pole in the center upon which no one has yet appeared; workers harness the horses to the engines, and the firemen finally slide down the pole from above at the conclusion of the scene, as the engine races off to the right. There is a significant temporal overlap and redundancy of action between shots 3 and 4, clearly establishing narrative space and time.

5. Exterior of the firehouse as the doors are flung open and the engines charge out, overlapping the action of shot 4.

6. Suburban street scene: eight engines rush past the camera from right to left, passing a crowd of bystanders (stock footage apparently, since it's snowing in this scene but nowhere else in the film).

7. Street scene: four engines rush past the camera, which pans (moves horizontally on its vertical axis) slightly to follow the fourth and comes to rest on the front of a burning house.

8. Interior of the house: mother and child in an upstairs room filled with smoke.

9. Exterior of the house: the mother approaches an upstairs window and calls for help.

10. Interior: the woman collapses on a bed.

11. Exterior: a fireman enters the front door.

12. Interior: the same fireman runs into the room through a door at the right and breaks the window (which was open in shots 9 and 11, but closed in 8 and 10).

---

* MoMA currently distributes the original or "Copyright" version, which contains only nine shots (see p. 24).

13. Exterior: firemen on the ground place a ladder against the broken window.
14. Interior: the fireman carries the woman to the ladder, which has appeared at the window.
15. Exterior: the fireman and the woman descend the ladder.
16. Interior: the fireman enters the window by the ladder and picks up the child.
17. Exterior: the woman becomes hysterical.
18. Interior: the fireman exits through the window with the child.
19. Exterior: the fireman descends the ladder with the child and reunites it with the mother.
20. Interior: firemen enter the room through the window to extinguish the fire with a hose.

By **crosscutting** (or, synonymously, **intercutting**) seven shots of an interior with seven shots of an exterior to depict parallel actions occurring simultaneously, Porter seemed to have achieved—for the first time in motion-picture history—the unique kind of narrative omniscience which only the cinema among all art forms is capable of sustaining. No other medium permits the rapid alternation of multiple perspectives without destroying point of view. (There were precedents for parallel editing, or crosscutting, of course, in late-nineteenth–century melodrama, fiction, magic-lantern projections, stereopticon slide shows, and newspaper comic strips.)

In recent years, however, another print of *Life of an American Fireman* has come to light which is based on the paper print filed for copyright at the Library of Congress by the Edison Company in 1903. This so-called Copyright Version is 400 feet long, and it simply repeats the entire interior sequence (shots 8, 10, 12, 14, 16, 18, and 20) and the entire exterior sequence (shots 9, 11, 15, 17, and 19) continuously without intercutting them at all. Intercutting these sequences, as the Cross-Cut Version does, creates the illusion of simultaneous actions occurring from simultaneously accessible points of view. The Copyright Version, which shows the entire rescue first from the inside and then from the outside, involves a returning to an early period of time, almost an "instant replay" from a new point of view. In fact, this use of temporal repetitions and overlapping action can be found in such comtemporaneous Porter films as *How They Do Things on the Bowery* (October 1902). Thanks primarily to the scholarship of Charles Musser, the Copyright Version has recently been established as the original, and in the restored print circulated by MoMA since 1985, the two concluding scenes repeat the same rescue operation from interior and exterior points of view, depicting it as two completely autonomous actions.*

---

* Like so many other issues of early film history, this one is complicated by these factors: 1) producers sometimes filed prints for copyright with the scenes spliced together in the order in which they had been shot rather than as they were edited for final release, and 2) after 1910 the public demand for films became so great that distributors and pirates would frequently re-edit older film to conform with contemporary tastes and redistribute them as completely new productions.

We know today that early filmmakers often overlapped events across their splices—as here and in the rocket landing in *A Trip to the Moon*—to establish spatial, temporal, and narrative relationships between shots. Yet, while this kind of overlapping continuity clearly defines spatial relationships, it leaves temporal ones underdeveloped and, to modern sensibilities, confused. Where, for example, in *Life of an American Fireman,* have the firemen been between the time they slide down the pole from their dormitory in shot 3 and appear on the pole on the ground floor in shot 4? Why, in *A Trip to the Moon,* does the rocket seem to land twice, once in shot 9 and again in shot 10? For a while, at least, these questions did not trouble contemporary audiences. Conditioned by lantern slide shows, stereopticon presentations, and even comic strips, they understood a sequence of motion-picture shots as a series of individual moving photographs, each of which was self-contained within its frame. If actions overlapped from shot to shot, it didn't matter since the temporal relationship between shots was assumed to be alinear—there was no assumption that time moved forward when **cutting** from one scene to the next. But spatial relationships in such pre-existing forms as slide shows were clear because their only medium *was* space. Motion added the dimension of time, and the major problem for early filmmakers would soon become the establishment of linear continuity from one shot to the next. Modern continuity editing, on which the classical Hollywood system is based, began when they discovered that action could be made to seem continuous from shot to shot, and, conversely, that two or more shots could be made to express a single unit of meaning.

It was Porter himself who first moved toward this discovery in *The Great Train Robbery* (December 1903), which exists in a single authoritative version and is widely acknowledged to be his finest achievement. Although its interior scenes were shot at the Edison studios in New York City and its exteriors near the Edison laboratory in Orange, New Jersey, *The Great Train Robbery* was simultaneously the cinema's first Western and, as Kenneth Macgowan has observed, the first film to exploit the violence of armed crime. The most significant thing about the film for us, however, is its editing continuity. Although *The Great Train Robbery* contains no intercutting *within* scenes, Porter cut *between* his scenes without dissolving or fading and—most important—*without playing them out to the end.* In Méliès, and in early Porter for that matter, all scenes are played out to their logical dramatic conclusion and all new scenes are begun in the studied and gradual manner of nineteenth-century theater. There are no ellipses in the action of a scene once it has begun, just as there would and could be none on the legitimate stage. But Porter discovered that a filmmaker could in fact cut away from one scene before it was dramatically or logically complete and simultaneously cut into another after it had already begun. This practice contains the rudiments of a truly cinematic narrative language, because it posited that the basic signifying unit of film—the basic unit of cinematic meaning—was not the *scene,* as in Méliès, and not the continuous unedited film strip, as in the earliest Edison and Lumière shorts, but rather the *shot,* of which, as Griffith would later demonstrate, there may be a virtually limitless number within

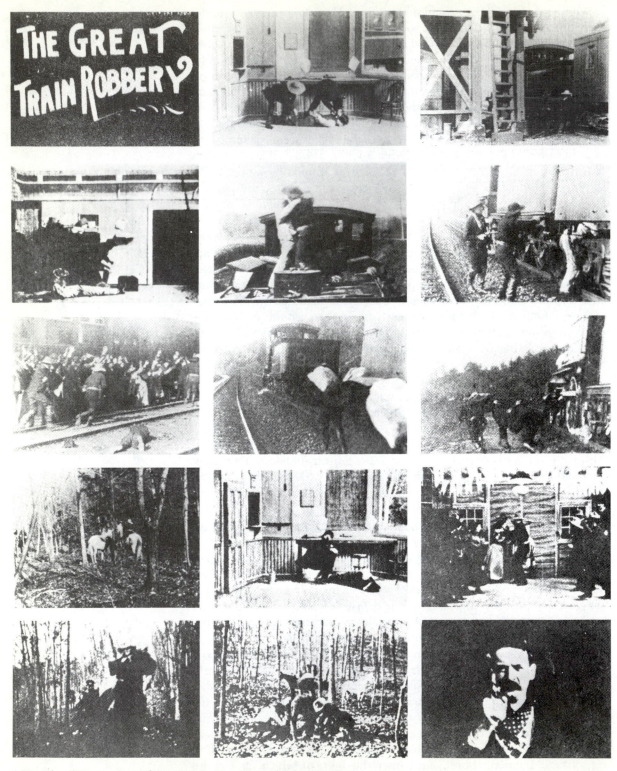

1.26 The editing sequence of Porter's *The Great Train Robbery* (1903).

any given scene. In this respect, it also looks forward to the formulation of the classical Hollywood editing style.

Written, directed, photographed, and edited by Porter, *The Great Train Robbery* is 740 feet long (a little over twelve minutes at the average standard silent speed of 16 fps) and consists of fourteen separate nonoverlapping *shots*—not scenes—of actions which are themselves dramatically incomplete. These are connected by straight cuts in the following **sequence:**

1. Interior of the railroad telegraph office: two bandits enter and bind and gag the operator while the moving train, visible through the office window, comes to a halt.
2. Railroad water tower: the other members of the gang board the train secretly as it takes on water.
3. Interior of the mail car with scenery rushing by through an open door; the bandits break in, kill a messenger, seize valuables from a strongbox, and leave.
4. Coal tender and interior of the locomotive cab: the bandits kill the fireman after a fierce struggle, throw his body off the train, and compel the engineer to stop.
5. Exterior shot of the train coming to a halt and the engineer uncoupling the locomotive.
6. Exterior shot of the train as the bandits force the passengers to line up along the tracks and surrender their valuables; one passenger attempts to escape, runs directly into the camera lens, and is shot in the back.
7. The bandits board the engine and abscond with the loot.
8. The bandits stop the engine several miles up the track, get off, and run into the woods as the camera tilts slightly to follow them.
9. The bandits scramble down the side of a hill and across a stream to mount their horses; the camera follows them in a sweeping vertical movement, or panning shot.
10. Interior of the telegraph office: the operator's daughter arrives and unties her father, who then runs out to give the alarm.
11. Interior of a crowded dance hall: a "tenderfoot" is made to "dance," as six-guns are fired at his feet; the telegraph operator arrives and a posse is formed.
12. Shot of the mounted bandits dashing down the face of a hill with the posse in hot pursuit; both groups move rapidly toward the camera; one of the bandits is killed as they approach.
13. Shot of the remaining bandits examining the contents of the stolen mail pouches; the posse approaches stealthily from the background and kills them all in a final shoot-out.
14. Medium close-up (a shot showing its subject from the mid-section up) of the leader of the bandits firing his revolver point blank into the camera (and, thus, the audience), a shot which, according to the Edison Catalogue, "can be used to begin or end the picture."

In addition to cutting away from scenes (or shots) before they were dramatically concluded and avoiding temporal overlap, *The Great Train Robbery* contained other innovations. Although the interior sequences were shot in the conventional manner of Méliès, the camera placement in many of the exterior sequences was fresh and dynamic. Several shots, for example, were staged in depth: in shot 4, the camera looks down on the action in the engine cab from the coal tender as the train plunges through space, and in shot 6 an actor moves diagonally across the frame into the camera lens rather than horizontally across it—a major departure from the frontally composed, theatrical staging of Méliès. There is what seems to be an effective use of in-camera matting* in shot 1 (the moving train coming to a halt, seen through the telegraph office window) and shot 3 (the landscape rushing past the express car door), but is more likely double exposure or double printing. More significant, there are two authentic **panning shots**—a rather perfunctory tilt following the bandits as they dismount the engine in shot 8, and an impressively cinematic pan following the sweep of their flight through the woods in shot 9.† Finally, there is a suggestion of parallel editing reminiscent of the Cross-Cut Version of *Life of an American Fireman* when Porter cuts from the bandits' getaway back to the bound telegraph operator in shot 10.

Nevertheless, aside from its contributions to the medium, *The Great Train Robbery* is not a great film. All of the interior scenes are photographed in the stage-like fashion of Méliès, with the actors moving from left to right, or vice versa, across the "proscenium" of the frame, and the actors' gestures are exaggerated and stilted. Furthermore, Porter never uses more than one camera angle or position in any one setting, and, like those of Méliès, most of his shots are long shots showing the actors at full length. On the other hand, by building up a continuity of dramatic action out of thirteen separate shots, not counting the final close-up, Porter had shown that the narrative structure of cinema need not be that of *scenes* arranged according to the dicta of the legitimate stage, which must observe the unities of time and place, but could and should be that of *shots* arranged according to the laws which film generates for itself. It remained for D. W. Griffith and others to elaborate these laws, but Porter had hit upon the absolutely essential fact that cinematic narrative depends not upon the *arrangement of objects or actors within a scene* (as does the theater and, to a large extent, still photography) but upon the *arrangement of shots in relation to one another*. As we shall see, it is the creative arrangement of the infinitely variable relationships among shots that makes later films like *The Birth of a Nation* (1915) and *Potemkin* (1925) great cinema over and above anything beautiful or moving in the specific content of their frames, however great this may be as well.

Contemporary audiences understood none of this, but they loved the

---

* Blacking out the window and door spaces on the first exposure and then double-exposing the film to imprint the projected sequence. See Raymond Fielding, *The Technique of Special Effects Cinematography* [New York, 1972], and John Brosnan, *Movie Magic: The Story of Special Effects in the Cinema* [New York, 1976].

† Panning was a relatively difficult operation before the introduction of the geared pan head for the camera tripod later in the decade. Charles Musser, however, points out that the technique had a long-established precedent in the photographic panoramas of the nineteenth century ("The Early Cinema of Edwin Porter," p. 17).

dramatic excitement generated by Porter's editing and by what amounted at the time to his **"special effects,"** including bursts of hand-tinted orange-yellow smoke during the gun fights. So spectacular was the commercial success of *The Great Train Robbery* that the film was studied and imitated by filmmakers all over the world. It is frequently credited with establishing the realistic narrative, as opposed to Méliès-style fantasy, as the dominant cinematic form from Porter's day to our own and with temporarily standardizing the length of that form at a single reel—one thousand feet, or ten to sixteen minutes, depending on the speed of projection (as pointed out earlier in this chapter, films could grow in narrative sophistication only in proportion to their growth in length). Furthermore, *The Great Train Robbery* probably did more than any film made before 1912 to convince investors that the cinema was a money-making proposition, and it was directly instrumental in the spread of permanent movie theaters, popularly called **nickelodeons** or "store theaters," across the country.

1.27 *The Dream of a Rarebit Fiend* (Edwin S. Porter, 1906).

More than fifty of Porter's subsequent films have survived. These display a richness of storytelling within the representational system that he had helped to establish. He continued to practice overlapping action in such conventional productions as *Uncle Tom's Cabin* (1903), a filmed play in fourteen "tableaux" linked together by descriptive intertitles (which he may, however, have been the first to use), complete with painted backdrops and a cakewalk, and in the social justice melodramas *The Ex-Convict* (1904) and *The Kleptomaniac* (1905), which are notable at least for their themes. Some of Porter's later work has modest technical interest—he matched camera angles from shot to shot in *Maniac Chase* (1904), employed dramatic, one-source lighting in *The Seven Ages* (1905), used panning shots in *The White Caps* (1905), and experimented with model animation in *Dream of a Rarebit Fiend* (1906) and *Teddy Bears* (1907), as well as animating the title sequences of a number of his other films (in fact, the titles of *How Jones Lost His Roll* [1905] are the earliest extant examples of American animation).

1.28 The original "Nickelodeon," Pittsburgh, 1905.

But Porter could not adapt to the new methods of filmmaking and the emerging system of representation that developed in response to the rampant growth of the nickelodeons, which by 1907 were drawing one million patrons per day. Their popularity had created a public demand for story films that forced the rationalization of production, which in his managerial capacity, at any rate, Porter initially encouraged. But as production became ever more hierarchical and rigorous, he left Edison to form his own production company. This eventually became the independent Rex Film, which he sold in 1912 to join Adolph Zukor as director-general of the Famous Players Film Company; there he supervised the entire output and directed such conventionally successful filmed plays as *The Prisoner of Zenda* (1913), *The Count of Monte Cristo* (1913), *Tess of the Storm Country* (1914), and *The Eternal City* (1915), until he left the business in 1916.* Like Méliès, Porter had a genius for constructing

---

* Always mechanically inclined, Porter spent a good deal of his time at Famous Players experimenting with sound recording, color and wide-screen cinematography, and even

narratives that communicated with early audiences at a certain crucial point in their developing relationship with the screen. The overlapping continuities of *How They Do Things on the Bowery* (1902) and *Life of an American Fireman* (1903), *The Kleptomaniac* (1905) and *Rescued from an Eagle's Nest* (1908) told their stories in ways their audiences could comfortably understand.

Ironically, it was the work of Porter as much as any other filmmaker that had created the nickelodeon boom. Before the rise of these nickelodeon theaters (1905–6), exhibitions were carried out in a wide variety of sites: vaudeville theaters, summer parks, small specialized storefront theaters, lecture halls, churches, saloons, between acts of plays by repertory companies touring the nation's opera houses. With vaudeville theaters in the major cities paying the largest fees and giving the greatest visibility to motion pictures, fierce competition existed among such houses by the turn of the century. These theaters hired and advertised the name of the exhibition service as much as or more than the films ("The Cinematographe," "The Biograph," etc.). During the novelty period (1895–97), the major exhibitors either made their own films (Lumière's Cinematographe) or were closely affiliated with a production company (Raff and Gammon's Vitascope with the Edison Manufacturing Company). The exhibition service would supply the theater with an "operator" and a short (eight to fifteen minutes) program of films. At this point, then, the film industry functioned as a unit, with the producers leasing a complete film service of projector, projectionist, and shorts to the vaudeville houses as a self-contained "act." By 1897, this pattern changed as producers began to sell projectors and films outright to itinerant exhibitors, who would travel with their shows from one temporary location— theaters, fairgrounds, circuses, lyceums, and the like—to the next, as the novelty of their programs wore off. Itinerant exhibition separated that function from production for the first time and gave the exhibitor a large degree of control over early film form, since he was responsible for arranging the one-shot films purchased from producers into coherent, crowd-pleasing programs. This process, which often involved the addition of narration, music, and **sound effects,** was effectively a form of editing, and the itinerant projectionists of the period 1897–1904 may be properly regarded as the first "authors" of motion pictures (some, like Porter, of course, became directors in the modern sense after the industry had stabilized in the first decade of the twentieth century).

Yet the practice of selling prints outright, which encouraged itinerant exhibition, simultaneously discriminated against the owners of permanent sites and inhibited their future growth. In 1903, in response to this situation, Harry J. and Herbert Miles, operating between offices in New York and San Francisco, functioned as middlemen between producers and exhibitors, buying prints from the former and leasing them to the

---

3-D projection. When he left, he founded the Precision Machine Corporation to manufacture the Simplex projector, a product of his own invention, which became the industry standard until the company was wiped out in the crash of 1929.

latter for 25 percent of the purchase price. Later, rental fees would be set according to production costs and admission returns per film, but the exchange system of distribution quickly caught on because it handsomely profited everyone concerned. The new film brokers, or "distributors," literally made fortunes by renting the same prints to different exhibitors over and over again; exhibitors found that they could vary their programs without financial risk and reduce overhead at the same time; and producers ultimately experienced a surge in demand so enormous that it forced the wholesale industrialization of production previously described. (For example, Robert C. Allen claims that between November 1906 and March 1907, producers increased their weekly output from 10,000 to 28,000 feet, and still could not meet demand.)

The most immediate effect of the rapid formation and rise of the distribution sector was the "nickelodeon boom," in which the number of permanent theaters in the United States mushroomed from a mere handful in 1904 to between eight and ten thousand by 1908. There had been such theaters in the United States since 1896, but few survived more than two or three years. Many had much briefer life spans. Thomas L. Tally opened his Electric Theater in Los Angeles in 1902 but closed it the following year to become a traveling exhibitor.* Storefront theaters did not become very profitable over the long term until the exchange system of distribution created an economic context for them and gave birth to the nickelodeons. Named for the original "Nickelodeon" (ersatz Greek for "nickel theater") opened in Pittsburgh in 1905, these were makeshift exhibition sites lodged in converted storefronts which showed from ten minutes to sixty minutes worth of shorts for an admission price of five to ten cents, depending on the amenities, such as piano accompaniment and cushioned seats, and the location. Although they were originally associated with working-class audiences, nickelodeons appealed increasingly to segments of the middle class as the decade wore on, becoming identified in the public mind with narrative; and their rapid spread across the country forced the standardization of film length at one reel, or 1,000 feet about sixteen minutes at the average silent speed of 16 fps (see note p. 11n), to facilitate new economies of production, distribution, and exhibition.

This was the industrial system that Porter resisted and ultimately rejected, but before he left Edison in 1909, he did something which, by circumstance, was to prove immensely important to the history of cinema. His otherwise undistinguished melodrama *Rescued from an Eagle's Nest* (1908—see pp. 63–64) provided a needy young actor named David Wark Griffith with his first leading role in films and marked the beginning of a career which was to last forty years and bring the embryonic narrative cinema to a high point of development.† Before he came to Porter, Grif-

---

* Musser to author, 4 / 14 / 88.

† The film was actually co-directed by J. Searle Dawley (?–1950). Following contemporary practice, Porter had hired Dawley in late 1907 as his collaborator. Dawley worked with him on scripts and directed the actors while Porter remained in charge of cinematography and editing, and ran the studio. As a former actor and playwright, Dawley had theatrical

1.29 D. W. Griffith in Porter's *Rescued from an Eagle's Nest* (1907).

THE FIRST MONSTER MOVIE ?

fith had tried his hand at almost everything, from hop picking to selling the *Encyclopedia Britannica* door-to-door, but he wanted most desperately to become a writer. A chain of rejected stories and failed plays had led him inexorably to the door of the Edison Corporation studios with a scenario based upon a work by the French playwright Victorien Sardou (1831–1908), *La Tosca*. This Porter flatly rejected as having too many scenes, but he offered Griffith a salary of five dollars a day to appear in a wildly improbable little film of his own. In it, Griffith, who was more than a little ashamed to have accepted work as a film actor, played a heroic woodcutter who rescues his infant child from the mountain aerie of a large and vicious eagle, wrestling the bird to its death in the process. (Appropriately, the struggle was emblematic of Griffith's simplistic vision of human experience, which he depicted in his own films as one long, arduous battle between the forces of darkness and the forces of light.) When *Rescued from an Eagle's Nest* first appeared on the screen in early 1908, Porter had already abdicated his position of creative leadership in film, but the technology of cinema had long been born and the rudiments of its narrative language evolved. The cinema now awaited its first great narrative artist, who would refine that language, elaborate it, and ultimately transcend it.

experience in staging which Porter lacked, while Porter possessed state-of-the-art skills in cinematography, and they worked together as a team until 1908, when Dawley was placed in charge of his own production unit. Even after Porter left Edison, Dawley stayed on, directing more than three hundred one-reelers for the company, until 1912, when he joined Porter at Famous Players as his executive assistant and creative consultant. There, he ultimately became a successful director of features, working with such stars as Mary Pickford and John Barrymore, until his retirement from the industry in the early twenties. See Charles Musser, *The Cinema of Edwin S. Porter*, Ph.D. diss. (New York University, 1985).

International Expansion, 1907–1918

AMERICA

The Early Industrial Production Process

By 1908 the cinema had risen from the status of a risky commercial venture to that of a permanent and full-scale, if not yet a major and respectable, industry. In that year, there were ten thousand nickelodeons and one hundred film exchanges operating in the United States, and they were supplied by about twenty "manufacturers" who churned out films at the rate of one to two one-reelers per director per week. A similar situation existed on the Continent and in Britain, and by the time Griffith entered the cinema, the studios or "factories" of the Western world could scarcely keep up with the public demand for new films. Furthermore, the novelty of the medium was such that almost anything the studios could produce, regardless of quality, was gobbled up by the international network of distribution and exchange. Although the introduction of mercury-vapor lamps encouraged several companies to construct indoor studios as early as 1903, films were generally shot out of doors in a single day on budgets of two hundred to five hundred dollars and rigorously limited to one reel of about one thousand feet in length, with a running time of ten to sixteen minutes, depending on projection speed. Nearly all of them were put together on an assembly-line basis following the stage-bound narrative conventions of Méliès and the overlapping continuities of Porter, with natural backgrounds and few, if any, retakes. Not surprisingly, industry emphasis on speed and quantity of production militated against creative experiment and demanded the detailed division of labor described by Lewis Jacobs in *The Rise of the American Film:*

Action was divided into scenes, and these were photographed in consecutive order. The number of scenes was limited to seven or eight, each 100 to 150 feet long, in order to keep the story within the 1,000-foot length in which the raw film came. ... Increased production necessitated more people and a division of duties to speed the output. By 1908 directing, acting, photographing, writing, and laboratory work were separate crafts, all of equal status. Each worker regarded himself as a factory hand, lacking only a time-clock ritual for concrete evidence of his position. No one received any screen credit for the work he did, for, as the employers realized, a public reputation would mean higher wages. Besides, most of the directors, actors, and cameramen who had come to the movies were more or less ashamed of their connection with them; they stayed in their jobs because they needed work,

2.1   The exterior and interior of a typical nickelodeon, c. 1909.

2.2   The Searchlight, a strorefront theater in Tacoma, Washington, c. 1900.

2.3   J. Stuart Blackton's rooftop studio in New York City, c. 1899.

2.4   British film pioneer G. A. Smith's studio in Brighton, c. 1900.

and they gave little thought to the medium's possibilities or opportunities. Nearly everyone still regarded movie making as a shabby occupation.

Jacob's last point is an important one: most early filmmakers felt that they were doing little more than grinding out cheap entertainment—a perception that on an economic plane was entirely true; hence the serious development of the medium was retarded for nearly a decade. As so often happened in the history of the cinema, the rigors and banalities of the production system itself forced these people to take a workaday attitude toward their craft, which—with notable exceptions—inhibited stylistic innovation and the free exchange of ideas. There was none of the intellectual excitement and creative ferment which we might expect to find at the birth of an art form, because no one was yet equipped to acknowledge that birth, and so between 1903 and 1912 the industry's level of artistic and technical competence scarcely ever rose above the marginally adequate.

Nevertheless, financial competition among rival production companies was fierce and frequently lawless. Though Thomas Edison claimed ownership of essential patents for the motion-picture camera, many companies were using versions of his machines without paying royalties. Hundreds of suits and countersuits were filed by Edison and his competitors during this renegade period of rampant growth. At the other end of the industry, relationships between distributors and exhibitors became increasingly strained. Since copyright law for motion pictures was still being defined by the courts and legislatures and, in any case, most production companies did not bother to copyright their pictures, the majority of films were more or less in the public domain, and prints were often stolen, pirated, and illicitly duplicated, just as books had been before 1893. Theoretically, of course, what a production company made it owned, even if its

2.5 The interior of the Edison studio (c. 1912), showing the shooting of several separate films.

product had been made with pirated equipment, but legal and professional standards for the film industry during this period of rapid international expansion were ill-defined, and their enforcement was difficult.

None of this should surprise us, since the same problems of ownership and duplication rights have arisen in our own day in connection with magnetic audio and video recording. The dispute over film patents and copyrights was perhaps more ruthless because it was conditioned by the mercenary social Darwinism of the Gilded Age, which operated on the principle that might makes right. The period 1880 to 1904 was the era of the great American "robber barons," and it is not in the least incongruous that Edison spies like Joseph McCay were engaged in industrial espionage against rival production companies during the same years that witnessed bloody strikebreaking by police, National Guardsmen, and Pinkertons all over the country, as well as race riots and lynchings. As one might expect, however, it took a counterforce of considerable intensity to turn the young industry from the anarchic competitiveness of laissez-faire capitalism toward a more orderly pursuit of profit.

This counterforce was provided by attacks from what were to become the American cinema's two classical antagonists: organized religion and the political Right. These institutions had tolerated "living pictures" so long as they promised to be a short-lived novelty, but when it became clear that the cinema was well on its way to becoming a major social and economic force in the nation, they took the offensive. In early 1907, for example, an editorial appeared in the conservative and influential *Chicago Tribune*, accusing the "Five Cent Theatre" of "ministering to the lowest passions of children" and being "wholly vicious." "Proper to suppress them at once," the editorial said. "They cannot be defended. They are hopelessly bad." The question basically was and is the ancient one,

2.6 *The Starving Artist* (Vitagraph, 1907).

2.7 The office staff of the Selig Polyscope Company, Western Avenue, Chicago, c. 1906. (The staff members frequently doubled as extras.)

dating from Plato's *Republic,* of the state's right of censorship. But the fact that film is a mass medium of popular entertainment as well as an art form—and a medium which bypasses language to communicate directly with the senses through moving photographic images of the apparently real—makes the issue more complex than perhaps it has ever been in Western culture.* There was no complexity as far as the *Tribune* and its allies were concerned; between 1907 and 1909 it became obligatory in many parts of the country for ministers, businessmen, and politicians to inveigh against the movies as a corrupter of youth and a threat to public morality. Yet the issue at this point was perhaps less ideological than economic; in becoming a major entertainment industry overnight, the movies suddenly threatened the very substantial revenues of churches, saloons, and vaudeville theaters from coast to coast. The situation was not unlike the sudden emergence of television as a formidable rival to the movies in the late forties, for in both cases the older institutions sought to take social and economic sanctions against the newer ones and fell on their faces in the process. Like television, the movies came to stay, and no amount of mud-slinging or moralizing was going to change that fact.

The Motion Picture Patents Company

Vilified by contemporary reformers and riven by internecine war, the most powerful American production companies banded together under joint Edison-Biograph leadership in a protective trade association called the Motion Picture Patents Company, or the MPPC, on December 18, 1908.† To insure their continued dominance of the market, Edison, Biograph, Vitagraph, Essanay, Kalem, Selig Polyscope, Lubin, Star Film, Pathé Frères, and Kleine Optical (the largest domestic distributor of foreign films) pooled the sixteen most significant U.S. patents for motion-picture technology and entered into an exclusive contract with Eastman-Kodak for the supply of raw **film stock**. The MPPC, also known simply as the "Trust" (which it was, Arthur Knight points out, "in the full Rooseveltian sense"), sought to control every segment of the industry through issuing licenses and assessing royalties therefrom. The use of its patents was granted only to licensed equipment manufacturers, and film stock could be sold only to licensed producers; licensed producers and importers were required to fix rental prices at a minimum level and set quotas for foreign footage to reduce competition; MPPC films could be sold only to licensed distributors, who could lease them only to licensed exhibitors; and only licensed exhibitors had the right to use MPPC projectors and rent Company films. To this seemingly airtight system was added the

---

*The superabundance of moving photographic images made possible by television and other video delivery systems in our own day further compounds the problem.

†In the year prior, Edison had headed its own "trust," the Association of Edison Licensees, which Biograph resisted by forming an association with a group of foreign producers on the basis of its own patents. It was Biograph's ability to survive the Edison initiative that led to a pooling of their interests in late 1908 in the MPPC. (Charles Musser to author, 1/22/88.)

General Film Company, which integrated the licensed distributors into a single corporate entity in 1910—the same year in which motion-picture attendance in the United States rose to 26 million persons a week.

Though it was clearly monopolistic in practice and intent, the MPPC helped to stabilize the American film industry during a period of unprecedented growth and change by standardizing exhibition practice, increasing the efficiency of distribution, and regularizing pricing in all three sectors. Furthermore, in the days when clarity of image and synchronization of camera and projector were still highly unreliable, Patents Company producers made the best films in the business because of their monopoly on the best equipment and film stock. MPPC films were generally static, stolid, and unimaginative in narrative terms, but they guaranteed their viewers a degree of technical competence that few other manufacturers could match. For this reason, and because General Film could guarantee national distribution, many foreign distributors who were immune to the coercive machinery of the Patents Company did business with it of their own volition. Had things gone according to plan, the MPPC would have completely monopolized the film industry of the United States and a large part of the Western world by 1911 or 1912. But the collusive nature of the "Trust" also provoked a reaction against it that ultimately destroyed it and gave the industry its modern form.

In a sense, the MPPC's iron-clad efforts to eliminate competition merely fostered it. Almost from the outset, there was widespread resistance to the MPPC from independent distributors (numbering ten or more in early 1909) and exhibitors (estimated at 2,000 to 2,500); and in January 1909 they formed their own trade association, the Independent Film Protective Association—reorganized that fall as the National Independent Moving Picture Alliance—to provide financial and legal support against the Trust. A more effective and powerful anti-Trust organization was the Motion Picture Distributing and Sales Company, which began operations in May 1910, three weeks after the inception of General Film, and which eventually came to serve forty-seven exchanges in twenty-seven cities. For nearly two years, independents were able to present a united front through the Sales Company, which finally split into two rival camps in the spring of 1912: the Mutual Film-Supply Company, which distributed for the independent producers Thanhouser, Gaumont, American Film Manufacturing, Great Northern, Reliance, Eclair, Solax, Majestic, Lux, and Comet, at the rate of about twenty reels per week; and Universal Film Manufacturing Company, which distributed for New York Motion Picture Company, Independent Motion Picture Company (IMP), Powers, Rex, Champion, Republic, and Nestor. By imitating MPPC practices of combination and licensing, the early independents were able to compete effectively against the Trust: in the Trust's first three years, the independents netted about 40 percent of all American film business. Their product, the one-reel **short,** and their modes of operation were fundamentally the same. But the later independents, such as William Fox (1879–1952) of the Greater New York Film Rental Company, and Adolph Zukor (1873–1976) of the Famous Players Film Company, would revolutionize the industry by adopting the multiple-reel film as their basic product, a move which caused the MPPC to embrace the one-reeler with a vengeance and hastened its demise.

Film length had originally been standardized at one reel out of a conviction that the public had a negligible attention span and would not sit still for more. It is true, of course, that a majority of early filmgoers were untutored laborers, many of them non-English-speaking immigrants, lacking sophisticated verbal skills; but the processes of verbal and visual cognition are quite distinct from one another (recent scientific research, in fact, has demonstrated them to be functions of separate hemispheres of the brain). Furthermore, there are few things more compelling in human perceptual experience than the cinematic image in projection. Nevertheless, the entire MPPC system was geared toward the production of one-reelers, and its licensees were expressly forbidden to make or to distribute films of greater length. Since the chief sources of story material for early films were novels and plays, this dictum produced such anomalies as one-reel versions of fifteen Shakespearian plays, including *King Lear* (1909) and *The Tempest* (1911); five Dickens novels; three Wagner operas; and *The Scarlet Letter* (1909), *Vanity Fair* (1911), and *Ben Hur* (1907), although most production during this period featured more popular subjects. When films like J. Stuart Blackton's five-reel *The Life of Moses*

BUT THEY ARE LINKED IN READING

2.8 A typical advertisement by independent Carl Laemmle from the trade journal *Motion Picture World* attacking the Patents Company's monopoly on the industry.

(1909) and D. W. Griffith's two-reel *His Trust* (1910) were produced by Patents Company members (Vitagraph and Biograph respectively), they were released to exhibitors in serial fashion at the rate of one reel a week, which seriously damaged their continuity. In open revolt against this practice, many exhibitors began to hold up the first reel of a multi-reel film until they had received the others and could show them sequentially on the same bill—a procedure which ultimately forced the MPPC to release Griffith's second two-reeler, *Enoch Arden* (1911), as a single film.

The Advent of the Feature Film

The multiple-reel film—which came to be called a **feature,** in the vaudevillian sense of a headline attraction—had gained general acceptance in 1911 with the release of two European imports, *The Crusaders* (four reels) and *Dante's Inferno* (aka *Inferno,* five reels). But it was the smashing success of the three-and-one-half-reel French film *Queen Elizabeth (La Reine Elizabeth* [Louis Mercanton, 1912]), starring the celebrated stage actress Sarah Bernhardt, that convinced the industry of the feature's commercial viability in America. Produced for the Histrionic Film Company, *Queen Elizabeth* was a laborious "filmed play" in the worst sense of the term (for a discussion of the narrative defects of such *films d'art,* see pp. 54–57), but it proved so profitable for importer Adolph Zukor that he was able to found the independent Famous Players production company with its returns (reportedly, eighty thousand dollars on an investment of eighteen thousand).

Even more persuasive was the huge American success of the nine-reel Italian superspectacle *Quo vadis?* in the spring of 1913. Directed by Enrico Guazzoni (1876–1949) for the Cines Company, this film contained vast crowd scenes and lavish **special effects** which kept audiences entranced throughout its running time of more than two hours, and it proved to American producers beyond question that the future of cinema lay at least in part in the feature film. *Quo vadis?* also established another important precedent: it was shown exclusively in first-class legitimate theaters rather than nickelodeons (a policy which Griffith would later adopt for his features) and thus attracted a more prosperous and sophisticated audience than the American cinema had enjoyed at any time since its birth. The international success of *Quo vadis?* was so great that it permitted Italy to capture a large share of the world market until the outbreak of the war, and the film was followed in early 1914 by a twelve-reel historical blockbuster, Giovanni Pastrone's (1883–1959) masterly *Cabiria.* In its liberal camera movement, elaborate **sets,** and skillfully constructed narrative, *Cabiria* anticipated the great epics of Griffith; in fact, Griffith probably saw the Italian films while he was working on *Judith of Bethulia* (1913) and *The Birth of a Nation* (1915), respectively.

A substantial portion of the film-going public had also been affected by the Italian spectacles, and soon a feature craze was sweeping the country and the industry, challenging the MPPC's conservative leadership and the very existence of its one- and two-reel films. At first, there were difficulties in distributing features, since the exchanges associated with both

2.9 Vitagraph's one-reel *Romeo and Juliet* (1908).

2.10 The original offices of Zukor's Famous Players Company, New York City, c. 1912.

2.11 An "arty" advertisement for an early American feature, from a 1912 issue of the *New York Dramatic Mirror*.

the Patents Company and the independents were geared toward cheaply made one-reel shorts. Owing to their more elaborate production values, features had relatively higher negative costs, and were disadvantaged by a system that charged a uniform price per foot. By 1914, however, national feature distribution alliances were organized which correlated pricing with a film's negative cost and box-office receipts (among the first were Adolph Zukor and Jesse L. Lasky's Paramount, Warners' Features, and Lou Selznick's World Film Company), and these new exchanges demonstrated the economic advantage of multiple-reel films over shorts. Exhibitors quickly learned that features could command higher admission prices and longer runs; single-title packages were also cheaper and easier to advertise than programs of multiple titles. On the manufacturing side, producers found that the higher expenditure for features was readily amortized by high-volume sales to distributors, who in turn were eager to share in the higher admission returns from the theaters. Soon the whole industry would reorganize itself around the economics of the multiple-reel film, and the effects of this restructuring gave motion pictures their characteristic modern form in almost every sense.

The feature film (arbitrarily defined in this era as any film of four or more reels) made motion pictures respectable for the middle class by providing a format analogous to that of the legitimate theater and suitable for the adaptation of middle-class novels and plays. The production companies of the century's first decade saw themselves as manufacturers of cheap entertainment for a generally uneducated mass public, and the MPPC had rigidly systematized this conception of filmmaking in its five-year domination of the industry. Audiences who aspired to more than short, simple action stories or comedies were unlikely to find it on the screen, so they stayed home and read or went to the theater instead, and their absence was felt by the small but growing number of filmmakers within the system—most notably D. W. Griffith—who were coming to regard their medium as a serious mode of expression. The advent of the feature, however, opened up the possibility of more complicated narratives and offered filmmakers a form commensurate with serious artistic endeavor. Features also placed a new premium on the quality of production as well as its quantity by demanding higher standards of verisimilitude. Longer films had to be made more slowly, with larger budgets and greater care than one- and two-reelers, and once the feature was popularly accepted, high technical standards and elaborate production values became a new focus of competition within the industry.

To accommodate the new films and their new audiences, a new kind of movie theater sprang up across the country, the first of which was the thirty-three-hundred-seat Strand opened by Mitchell L. Marks in the heart of the Broadway theater district of Manhattan in 1914. No longer converted storefronts with sawdust floors and hard seats, the new theaters were the earliest of the big, comfortable, and elegantly appointed urban "dream palaces" which came to be controlled by the major Hollywood studios in the 1920s. The Strand, for example, featured a two-story gilt and marble interior hung with tapestries and crystal chandeliers, plush pile carpeting, numerous lounges, a thirty-piece orchestra, and a monumental Wurlitzer organ—all for the respectably expensive admission price of twenty-five cents. Owing to their luxuriance, these houses required the regular showing of features to attract large audiences at premium prices, and by 1916 there were over twenty-one thousand such new or remodeled film theaters in the country. Their arrival signaled the close of the nickelodeon era and the beginnings of the Hollywood studio system.

The Rise of the Star System

The MPPC's attempt to monopolize the film industry through patents pooling and licensing was based on Edison's experience with the phonograph, and it failed to anticipate the unique volatility of the motion-picture market, especially the widespread resistance of the independents and the enormous potential of the feature film. Another issue that the Patents Company misjudged badly was the power of the marketing strategy which has come to be known as the "star system." Borrowed from the theater industry, this system involves the creation and management of publicity about key performers, or stars, to stimulate demand for their films. Initially, MPPC producers feared that using the real names of its actors, actresses, and directors in screen credits or advertisements would enable them to acquire a public following and demand higher salaries. Thus, for years the most popular of early performers were known to audiences only by the names of the characters they played (Mary Pickford was "Little Mary") or the companies in whose films they appeared (Florence Lawrence was "the Biograph girl"), even though producers were constantly deluged with requests for information about their leading players. In 1909, however, articles about personalities such as Ben Turpin, Pearl White, and Mary Pickford began to appear in trade journals; and in 1910, Carl Laemmle (1876–1939) of IMP lured Florence Lawrence away from Biograph and, through a series of media stunts, promoted her into national stardom.

Immediately after hiring Lawrence, Laemmle circulated anonymous press reports of her death, using her real name in public for the first time.* Then he undertook an extensive advertising campaign to denounce the story as a "black lie" spread by the Patents Company to conceal the fact that Miss Lawrence had come over to IMP; and, as proof of her continued existence, Laemmle promised that King Baggott, IMP's leading man (also named publicly for the first time), would escort Miss Lawrence to St. Louis on the day that their first IMP picture together opened in that city. There was a near riot as what seemed to be half of St. Louis crowded into the train station to get a glimpse of the former Biograph girl's still earthly presence, and the star system was born. Laemmle's publicization

2.12 "Dream palace" architecture in the twenties: the auditoriums of the Ambassador Theater, St. Louis, and the Oriental Theater, Chicago.

---

* In *Stardom: The Hollywood Phenomenon* (New York: Stein and Day, 1970), Alexander Walker maintains that Miss Lawrence had *already* been dismissed from Biograph for publicizing herself and had been blacklisted by all other licensed film companies when Laemmle hired her, which, if true, only serves to heighten the spectacular opportunism of the producer's coup.

2.13 A Laemmle advertisement in *Motion Picture World*.

of players like Florence Lawrence and King Baggott proved so successful that other independent producers soon adopted star policies of their own. Even MPPC members began to use this kind of publicity, although never as flamboyantly as their rivals, and by 1911, Vitagraph, Lubin, and Kalem had all begun to publicize their performers. Biograph resisted this change the longest, and it was not until 1913 that it began to advertise the names of its actors and its chief director—D. W. Griffith, who would soon join the ranks of the independents in any case. The production companies now suddenly subjected their audiences to a publicity blitz of photographs, posters, postcards, and fan magazines featuring their favorite stars; and stardom rapidly began to acquire the mythic dimensions which would make it the basis of production policy in the American cinema for the next fifty years.

The Move to Hollywood

Those fifty years were spent almost exclusively in the Los Angeles suburb (originally a small industrial town) called Hollywood—the result of a mass migration of production companies from the East which occurred between 1907 and 1913. The reasons why a full-scale Eastern-based industry moved its entire operation to Southern California during these years have never been completely clear, but the general contours of the phenomenon are obvious enough. In the wake of the nickelodeon boom, as exhibitors had begun to require as many as twenty to thirty new films per week, it became necessary to put production on a systematic year-round schedule. Since most shooting still occurred out-of-doors in available light, such schedules could not be maintained in the vicinities of New York and Chicago, where the industry had originally located itself to take advantage of trained theatrical labor pools; and, as early as 1907, producers such as Selig Polyscope began to dispatch production units in winter to warmer climates. It was soon clear that what producers required was a new industrial center—one with warm weather, a temperate climate, a variety of scenery, and other qualities (such as access to acting talent) essential to their highly unconventional form of manufacturing. Various companies experimented with location shooting in Jacksonville, Florida; San Antonio, Texas; Sante Fe, New Mexico; and even Cuba, but the ultimate site of the American film industry became Hollywood. It is

2.14 Hollywood, c. 1915 and 1919.

2.15 A Selig Polyscope Company stage, Hollywood, 1913. Note the compartmentalized sets and muslin sun diffusers overhead.

generally thought that Southern California's distance from the MPPC's headquarters in New York and proximity to the Mexican border made it an attractive sanctuary for independents, but by 1911 MPPC members such as Selig, Kalem, Biograph, and Essanay had also established facilities there in response to the region's other attractions. These included the very type of temperate climate required for year-round production (the U.S. Weather Bureau estimated that an average of 320 days per year were sunny and/or clear, so that even interiors could be shot outdoors if muslin sheets were placed overhead to soften the shadows) and a wide range of topography within a fifty-mile radius of Hollywood, including mountains, valleys, lakes, islands, woodland, seacoast, and desert—the Mediterranean could be simulated on the Pacific coastline, and Griffith Park could stand in for the Alpine forests of central Europe. Other attractions were the status of Los Angeles as a professional theatrical center, the existence of a low tax base, and the presence of cheap and plentiful labor and land. This latter factor enabled the newly arrived production companies to buy up tens of thousands of acres of prime real estate on which to locate their studios, standing sets, and **back lots.** Between 1908 and 1912, many of the independents moved permanently to Hollywood, and several Patents Company members began to shoot films there on a seasonal basis. D. W. Griffith, for example, first took his Biograph crew west for the winter in 1910, and he continued this practice until he left Biograph in 1913 to work in Southern California year-round with the independent Mutual Film Company.

The New Studio Chiefs and Industry Realignment

By 1915, there were approximately fifteen thousand workers employed by the motion picture industry in Hollywood and over 60 percent of

American production was centered there. In that same year, *Variety* reported that capital investment in American motion pictures—the business of artisanal craftsmen and fairground operators only a decade before—had exceeded 500 million dollars. Owing to its poor business practices, the MPPC had been functionally inoperative since 1914 (it would be formally dissolved in 1918 as the result of an antitrust suit initiated by the Wilson administration in 1912). Thus, the most powerful companies in the new film capital were the independents, flush with cash from their conversion to feature production: the Famous Players-Lasky Corporation (to become Paramount Pictures, 1935), formed by a merger of Adolph Zukor's Famous Players Company, Jesse L. Lasky's Feature Play Company, and the Paramount distribution exchange in 1916; Universal Pictures, founded by Carl Laemmle in 1912 by merging IMP with Powers, Rex, Nestor, Champion, and Bison; Goldwyn Pictures, founded in 1916 by Samuel Goldfish (later "Goldwyn") and Archibald Selwyn; Metro Pictures and Louis B. Mayer Productions, founded by Louis B. Mayer in 1915 and 1917 respectively; and the Fox Film Corporation (to become 20th Century–Fox, 1935), founded by William Fox in 1915. After World War I, these players were joined by Loew's, Inc. (parent corporation of MGM, by merger of Metro, Goldwyn, and Mayer companies just cited, 1924), a national exhibition chain organized by Marcus Loew and Nicholas Schenck in 1919; First National Pictures, Inc., a circuit of independent exhibitors who established their own production facilities at Burbank in 1922; Warner Bros. Pictures, incorporated by Harry, Albert ("Abe"), Sam, and Jack Warner in 1923 but active in the industry for at least a decade before; and Columbia Pictures, incorporated in 1924 by Harry and Jack Cohn. As their names indicate, these organizations were to become the backbone of the Hollywood studio system, and the men who controlled them shared several important common traits. For one thing, they were all independent exhibitors and distributors who had outwitted the Trust and clawed their way to the top through a genius for financial manipulation in the post-nickelodeon feature boom, merging production companies, organizing national distribution networks, and ultimately acquiring vast theater chains. They saw their business as basically a retailing operation modeled on the practice of Woolworth's and Sears. (Or, as Marcus Loew, then board chairman of MGM, put it to a business group in the mid-twenties, "Chain-store methods in the movies are just like what you have in railroads, telephones, and automobiles.") And yet most of these men had been small tradesmen who had gambled on the movie business in the anarchic first decade of the cinema, hoping to turn a quick profit. From penny-arcade showmen and nickelodeon operators they became "manufacturers" of their own films, then producer-distributors, and finally Hollywood studio chiefs—the temporary custodians of the twentieth century's most influential and culturally significant art form. Not incidentally, these men were all first-generation Jewish immigrants, most of them with little formal education, from Eastern Europe, while the audience they served—which came to call them "**moguls**," after the barbarian conquerors of the Indian empire—was 90 percent Protestant and Catholic. This circumstance would become an issue during the twenties, when the movies became a mass medium that was part of the life of every American citizen and when Hollywood became the chief purveyor of American culture to the world.*

The year 1914 was a crucial one for the American film industry. The feature film had by this time triumphed almost completely over the one- and two-reeler, or short, which survived only in the cartoon, newsreel, and serial installment (and, until the mid-twenties, as the vehicle for some of America's greatest comic talent as will be seen in Chapter 6); and this development coincided with a general economic boom created by the outbreak of war in Europe. Profits soared, along with costs, and the industry expanded rapidly in all directions, making and breaking fortunes in the process. Those companies—most notably Paramount—which had placed their faith in feature films became prosperous and powerful, while those which had cast their lot with the shorts were destroyed. The pioneers—Kalem, Star Film, General Film, Biograph, the Edison Company itself—were all wiped out by the new public hunger for feature films, and the MPPC dwindled to insignificance during the war years, finally succumbing in 1918 to the federal antitrust suit previously mentioned. Vitagraph, Lubin, Selig, and Essanay survived temporarily by merging as VLSE, and the independents Mutual, Reliance, and Keystone combined to form the short-lived but important Triangle Film Corporation, which simultaneously employed the talents of the American cinema's three top directors—D. W. Griffith, Thomas H. Ince, and Mack Sennett (whose careers will be explored in Chapters 3 and 6). Meanwhile, Paramount—and, to a lesser extent, Universal and Fox—had begun to produce features as never before. Jacobs estimates that by 1915 Paramount alone was releasing three to four features *per week* to some five thousand theaters across the nation.

The vast new market for feature-length films produced far-reaching changes in both the structure and scale of the industry. As films quintupled in length, and star salaries and screen-rights payments increased dramatically, production costs rose from between five hundred and one thousand dollars per film to between twelve thousand and twenty thousand—and the figures would triple in the postwar years. Production profits were ensured during this period through promotion of the star system and through advertising on a grand scale to increase demand, but producers also sought some means of national distribution to multiply the return on their increasingly large investments. As usual, it was Adolph Zukor who led the way.

---

* For example, before his ouster as head of the corporation in 1930, William Fox personally approved every picture released by Fox Film: "No picture ever produced by the Fox Film Corporation was permitted to be viewed by the general public, until every title it contained had been approved and passed by me, and I don't remember a single picture ever made by the company that the titles contained therein were not corrected, edited, and rewritten by me" (quoted in Upton Sinclair, *Upton Sinclair Presents William Fox* [Los Angeles: Upton Sinclair, 1933], p. 5). Fox had quit school at the age of eleven in order to help support his family.

The "Block Booking" Dispute and the Acquisition of Theaters

In 1916, Zukor merged his Famous Players Company with the Paramount distribution exchange and twelve smaller companies to form the Famous Players–Lasky Corporation (later Paramount Pictures)* which briefly came to dominate the industry by inventing the practice of block **booking.** The block-booking system of distribution forced exhibitors to accept a production company's films in large groups, or "blocks," tied to several particularly desirable titles (usually prestigious star vehicles) in advance of production. This all-or-nothing distribution policy quite obviously favored the producer, who was provided with a constant outlet for his films regardless of their quality, and soon every production company in the business had adopted it. Within a year's time, however, the practice of block booking had led to such abuses that the nation's leading exhibitors rebelled against the Hollywood-based production companies in much the same way that independents like Zukor had only several years earlier rebelled against the Patents Company monopolists.

In 1917, executives of twenty-six of the largest first-run exhibition chains established the First National Exhibitors Circuit, whose purpose was to challenge Paramount Famous Players–Lasky Corporation by producing and/or distributing its own features. It was an attempt to gain control over the means of film production and distribution, just as block booking represented an attempt on the part of producers to gain control over the means of distribution and exhibition. In short, both parties to the struggle, like Edison before them, recognized that whoever controlled distribution controlled the industry. Under the skillful management of W. W. Hodkinson, who had originally founded the Paramount exchange in 1914, First National was able to eliminate block booking temporarily by 1918 and to acquire sole distribution rights to the films of the industry's number one star, Charlie Chaplin. In retaliation, Paramount Famous Players–Lasky Corporation in 1919 entered the theater business and bought up first-run houses and exhibition circuits all over the country. Zukor's

---

* Paramount Pictures Corporation was founded as a feature distribution organization by W. W. Hodkinson (1881–1971) and other independent exhibitors on May 8, 1914. It financed and distributed the features of Zukor's Famous Players Film Company and Jesse L. Lasky's Feature Play Company (whose six-reel *The Squaw Man* [Cecil B. DeMille, 1914] was the first important feature made in Hollywood), among those of other producers, and in May 1916 Zukor and Lasky bought a controlling share of Paramount's stock. With Zukor as president, their Famous Players–Lasky Corporation was incorporated on June 19, 1916, but Paramount was kept as the company's trade name until 1927. From 1927 to 1930, the company was called Paramount Famous Lasky Corporation, and in 1930, with the acquisition of the huge Publix theater chain, it became the Paramount Publix Corporation. When the firm went bankrupt in 1933, Lasky (1880–1958) was forced out, and it was reorganized as Paramount Pictures, Inc., which name it retains today as a wholly owned subsidiary of Gulf and Western Industries (Paramount Communications, Inc., since 1989). In the text, I refer to Zukor's production-distribution-exhibition conglomerate of the teens and twenties as Paramount Famous Players–Lasky (or simply Paramount, as it was commonly known during the twenties), although each component was separately incorporated in a bid (ultimately unsuccessful as will be seen in Chapter 11) to avoid antitrust suits.

campaign to acquire exhibition outlets was as aggressive and ruthless as the MPPC's war against the independent producers had been a decade before. His agents became known as "the wrecking crew" and "the dynamite gang" among independent theater owners from New England to Texas to Colorado, and by 1921 Paramount Famous Players–Lasky owned 303 theaters compared to First National's 639. Its war with First National—and, later, Loew's, Inc.—for control of distribution and exhibition extended well into the twenties, culminating in Paramount's bankruptcy and First National's absorption by Warner Brothers. Before that occurred, however, First National had become a major power in its own right, and Fox, Goldwyn, and Universal had all joined Zukor in the race for theater acquisition.*

This race, which naturally required huge capital for real estate investment over and above normal production costs, was financed by the great Wall Street banking houses: Kuhn, Loeb, and Company were backing Paramount Famous Players–Lasky; the Du Ponts and the Chase National Bank stood behind Goldwyn; Fox was supported by the John F. Dryden–Prudential insurance group and Universal by Shields and Company. Stock issues were floated for the production companies and listed on the New York Exchange for public investment, and trained financiers began to assume managerial positions within the industry to protect their own investments. The continuing involvement of American big business in motion pictures had begun, and, less than a decade after the demise of the storefront theater, the cinema had become a large-scale industry. By the arrival of sound in the late twenties, it had become, by some accounts (largely those of its own publicists—see final footnote p. 251), the fourth largest in the nation.

The Rise of Hollywood to International Dominance

Hollywood's rise to power was assured by the First World War, which temporarily eliminated the European competition (mainly French and Italian) and gave America dominion over the world film market for the next fifteen years (and even after, though the configuration of the market changed with the coming of sound). Before August 1914, the American film industry had been forced to compete on the open market with all of

---

* Despite temporary victories, block booking persisted into later decades in one form or another until it was declared illegal as part of the Supreme Court's 1948 Paramount decision, as will be discussed in Chapters 8 and 11, and there is still a tendency for producer/distributors to coerce exhibitors (including, since the sixties, television networks) into accepting their less desirable titles as part of package deals. In the mid-seventies, the film companies instituted the practice of "blind bidding," whereby first-run exhibitors are required to put up a lump-sum rental fee for a major film four to eight months in advance of its release (the revenues, in fact, are often used to finance the film's production). Like block booking, blind bidding insures a profitable rate of return for the producer/distributor regardless of a film's box office success, and leaves the exhibitor with a disproportionate burden of financial risk. In 1979, the National Association of Theater Owners (NATO), a trade organization representing eight thousand U.S. exhibitors, crafted an anti-blind-bidding bill for introduction in about thirty state legislatures; but it was not widely adopted and the practice continues in most parts of the country.

the major European industries and for some years had actually lagged behind those of Italy and France. Just prior to the war, however, France's market position had slipped, and Italy's world-famous spectacles were losing their audience to American competition. But in America, the arrival of the big-budget feature had resulted in a considerable rise in the standards of motion-picture production in the immediate prewar years, and the audience had been growing rapidly. In some sectors, the American film was even gaining respectability as an art form: serious books were written about it (for example, the poet Vachel Lindsay's *The Art of the Moving Picture* [1915] and the philosopher Hugo Münsterberg's *The Film: A Psychological Study* [1916]), and newspapers established regular columns for "photoplay" reviews.

When war broke out on the Continent late in the summer of 1914, the European industries were virtually shut down since the same chemicals used in the production of celluloid were needed to manufacture gun powder, but the American cinema prospered throughout the war in unchallenged economic and political security. Jacobs estimates that while in 1914 the United States produced just a little over one half of the world's motion pictures, by 1918 it was making nearly all of them. Thus, for four years America exercised complete control over the international market and set up a formidable worldwide distribution system, and between 1914 and 1918 the world at large, including Asia and Africa (but excepting the belligerent Germany), saw nothing but American films if it saw films at all. In 1919, immediately following the Treaty of Versailles, 90 percent of all films screened in Europe were American, and the figure for South America was, and would remain for years, nearly 100 percent. During the twenties, of course, the European figures would decline significantly as Germany and the Soviet Union became major powers in world cinema and as other nations attempted to shield their industries with protective laws. Nevertheless, World War I had placed the American film industry in a position of undisputed economic and artistic leadership—a position it would maintain until the coming of sound and in some respects forever after.

EXPANSION ON THE CONTINENT

The German and Scandinavian film industries were still embryonic when war came to Europe in 1914,* and the British cinema, after taking an

---

* An exception was Denmark's Nordisk Films Kompagni, founded in 1906 and still in existence (making it the world's oldest production company), which was well organized and actively competitive in the world market, largely due to the international popularity of its leading lady, Asta Nielsen (1882–1972), and the narrative prescience of such talented directors as Vigo Larsen (also company founder; 1880–1957), Robert Dinesen (1874–1940), August Blom (1869–1947), Urban Gad (1879–1947), and Benjamin Christensen (1879–1959; q.v.). During the period 1911–16, Nordisk led the world in feature production and is credited with having invented both the figure of the "vamp" and the sensationalistic "social problem" film described in Chapter 6. World War I irreparably damaged the company by causing the loss of its non-German markets, and most of Nordisk's key personnel went to work for other industries after 1919. See Ebbe Neergaard, *The Story of*

early lead through the work of the Brighton school (see pp. 20–21), had failed to evolve industrially at all. But the industries of France and Italy had reached fairly advanced states of development in the first decade of the century, and together they led the world cinema commercially and artistically until the American industry usurped them.

The Empire of Pathé Frères

From 1898 to 1904, the French cinema was dominated by Georges Méliès, whose stagebound fantasies became so widely popular that all other producers were forced to imitate his techniques in order to compete with him. This meant that trick photography and the static camera became key features of French films until about 1905. Nevertheless, Méliès' commercial influence began to decline in the latter half of the decade as his Star Film Company, basically a small-scale artisanal business, was driven into competition with the ruthless and monopolistic Pathé Frères, founded in 1896 by the former phonograph manufacturer Charles Pathé (1863–1957).

The French film historian Georges Sadoul has called Charles Pathé "the Napoleon of the cinema," because in just over a decade he created a vast industrial empire which gave France control of the international film market until the eve of the war. Financed by some of France's largest corporations, Pathé acquired the Lumiére patents in 1902 and commissioned the design of an improved studio camera which soon dominated the market on both sides of the Atlantic (it has been estimated that, before 1918, 60 percent of all films were shot with a Pathé). Pathé also manufactured his own film stock, and in 1902 established a vast production facility at Vincennes where films were turned out on an assembly-line basis. The following year, he began to open foreign sales agencies, which rapidly developed into full-blown production companies—Hispano Film (1906), Pathé-Russe, Moscow (1907), Film d'Arte Italino (1909), Pathé-Britannia, London (1909), and Pathé-America (1910)—and soon there were Pathé agents all over the world. (Indeed, Pathé Frères are credited with pioneering the film industries of Australia, Japan, India, and Brazil.) Pathé also acquired permanent exhibition sites in every part of Europe, building in 1906 the world's first luxury cinema in Paris (the Omnia-Pathé), and by 1908 the company dominated distribution on the Continent. Thus, while he did not totally eliminate his competition, Charles Pathé realized within the structure of a single organization what Edison was unable to achieve through the conglomerate MPPC (of which Pathé and Star formed the Continental wing)—a complete vertical monopoly over every aspect of the industry. In 1908 Pathé marketed twice as many films in the United States as all the American production companies put together, and by 1909 the same situation existed in Great Britain.

With Pathé's profits fifty to one hundred times the cost of making its negatives, the company was able to become Méliès' distributor for sev-

---

Danish Film, trans. Elsa Guess (Copenhagen: The Danish Institute, 1962), and John Gillet, "Scandinavian Panorama," *Sight and Sound* 56, 1 (Winter 1986/87): 50–51.

eral stormy years between 1911 and 1913, after which the "alchemist of light" abandoned his alchemy altogether. In 1923, Méliès was forced to sell his negatives for the chemical value of the celluloid (the reason that less than 140 of his five hundred films survive—see note, p. 16), and in 1929 he was found operating a gift kiosk in a Paris Métro station*—like so many of the cinema's great pioneers, utterly forgotten. Happily, though, Méliès spent the remaining nine years of his life in the relative comfort of a rent-free apartment provided by Mutuelle du Cinéma, a rest home for retired cinematographers, and had the satisfaction of seeing his achievements revaluated by the first real historians of the cinema in the thirties.

The director-general of Pathé's huge studios at Vincennes was Ferdinand Zecca (1864–1947), a former music-hall singer whose canny instincts for what the public would pay to see contributed fundamentally to his employers' enormous financial success. Like Méliès, Zecca specialized in story films, and he was thoroughly conversant with the former magician's cinematic tricks, but in most of his productions Zecca broke away from the Méliès tradition of filmed theater by shooting out-of-doors and occasionally panning his camera to follow an action. His first films were realistic one-reel melodramas of the lower classes such as *L'Histoire d'un crime* (1901) and *Les victimes d'l'Alcoolisme* (1902—a five-minute version of Émile Zola's novel *L'Assommoir*), but he went on to become a master of many genres, including the historical romance, fantasy, farce, religious spectacle, and the highly popular *actualité reconstituée*, or "reconstructed newsreel," innovated by Méliès. Furthermore, borrowing freely from the chase films of England's Brighton school, Zecca developed a uniquely Gallic version of the type—the *course comique* ("comic chase"), in which cutting for parallel action was combined with trick photography *à la Méliès* to achieve not suspense but laughter. With titles like *Dix femmes pour un mari* (*Ten Wives for One Husband*), *La Course à la perruque* (*The Pursuit of the Wig*), *La Course aux tonneaux* (*The Pursuit of the Beer Barrels*)—all 1905—most of these films were shot in the streets of Paris and had a vitality and inventiveness which impressed the young Mack Sennett, among others, who found in them the model for his own Keystone Kops (see pp. 210–11).

Zecca remained with Pathé until its dissolution in 1939† but never evolved beyond an intelligent synthesizer of the discoveries of others. Like his German counterpart Oskar Messter (see p. 110), he is best remembered as an authentic primitive who upgraded and varied the content of his nation's films and who worked toward the refinement of the medium generally, without making any unique personal contributions.

2.16 Pathé's *La Passion* (Ferdinand Zecca and Lucien Nonguet, 1903).

2.17 Max Linder as Pathé's "Max."

---

* This story may also be apocryphal, deriving as it does from Méliès' now-discredited *Mes Mémoires*.

† The company was revived in 1944—sans Charles Pathé, who had sold his interest in the business to Bernard Natan in 1929—as the Société Nouvelle Pathé-Cinéma, which today specializes mainly in distribution (see Charles Pathé, *De Pathé Frères à Pathé Cinéma* [Lyons, 1970]).

Another Pathé talent was the comedian Max Linder (1883–1925), who became world famous for his subtle impersonation of an elegant but disaster-prone man-about-town in prewar Paris. Linder wrote and directed most of his four hundred films and had a profound influence upon the work of Charlie Chaplin in the next decade (see pp. 211–16). Finally, it should be remarked that in 1910 Pathé inaugurated the first regular weekly newsreel, the "Pathé Gazette," which acquired an international following in the years before the war.

Louis Feuillade and the Rise of Gaumont

Pathé's only serious rival on the Continent at this time was Gaumont Pictures, founded by the engineer-inventor Léon Gaumont (1864–1946) in 1895. Though never more than a quarter of the size of Pathé, Gaumont followed the same pattern of expansion, manufacturing its own equipment and mass-producing films under a supervising director (through 1906, Alice Guy [1875–1968], the cinema's first woman director; afterwards, Louis Feuillade [1873–1925]). Like Pathé, Gaumont opened foreign offices and acquired theater chains, and for nearly a decade after their construction in 1905 its studios at La Villette were the largest in the world. From 1914 to 1920,* Gaumont was able to dominate the French cinema, largely through the popular success of Feuillade. Formerly a scriptwriter for Pathé, Feuillade had begun his career at Gaumont in 1906 by directing comic shorts and chase films in the manner of Zecca. He made hundreds of narrative films over the next few years and finally came into his own with the serial detective film *Fantômas*, shot in five episodes of four to six parts each between 1913 and 1914. This type of film had been originated by Victorin Jasset (1862–1913), an ex-sculptor directing for the Eclair company, in the *Nick Carter* series of 1908. Feuillade brought to the form a sense of plastic beauty and visual poetry which allowed his serials to achieve the status of an art.

Fantômas was based on the popular serial novel by Pierre Souvestre and Marcel Allain about the adventures of the mysterious French super-criminal Fantômas, "Master of Terror," and the attempts of a ratiocinating police detective named Juve to track him down. The incredible exploits of Fantômas and his pursuer are all beautifully photographed on location in the streets, houses, sewers, and suburbs of prewar Paris and offer a strangely lyrical blend of naturalism and fantasy. Feuillade's other detective serials—the ten-episode *Les Vampires* (1915–16),† the twelve-episode *Judex* (1916), *La Nouvelle mission de Judex* (1917), *Tih Minh*

2.18 A poster for *Fantômas*, c. 1914.

2.19 *Fantômas* (Louis Feuillade, 1913–14): composition in depth.

---

* The outbreak of World War I in August 1914 temporarily paralyzed the French industry, as general mobilization drained the studios of both personnel and equipment. Production by major companies resumed in 1915 but fell considerably below prewar levels, forcing the French to rely heavily on American films and ultimately to lose control of their own market.

† Recently restored by the Cinémathèque Française, with long-missing intertitles reinserted by Feuillade's grandson Jacques Champreux. See the feature-length documentary history *Mille et une Marguerites* (*A Thousand and One Daisies*) [Pierre Phillipe, 1988]) made to celebrate Gaumont's ninetieth anniversary.

2.20 *Les Vampires* (Louis Feuillade, 1914–15): density and depth.

2.21 *Judex* (Louis Feuillade, 1916).

2.22 Pearl White in Pathé's *The Perils of Pauline* (Louis Gasnier, 1914).

(1918), and *Barabbas* (1919)—all manifest this same combination of mystery and the quotidian real, and their atmospheric beauty had a direct and continuing influence upon French film in the work of Jean Durand, Abel Gance, Jacques Feyder, and René Clair (see pp. 377–88).

Yet Feuillade was a conservative in terms of cinematic structure. As David Robinson has very aptly pointed out, Feuillade consistently rejected serially arranged shots (or **montage,** made famous by D. W. Griffith, whose work will be explored in Chapter 3.) in favor of *tableaux* elaborately composed in depth. This circumstance makes Feuillade not only a legitimate heir to Méliès but the progenitor of **mise-en-scène*** (literally, "putting-in-the-scene") aesthetics, first articulated after World War II by the French film theorist André Bazin and the young critics of *Cahiers du cinéma* (see pp. 550–52), which puts major emphasis on the creative use of movement and space *within* the shot rather than upon the relationship *between* shots, as does montage. At the height of his fame during World War I, Feuillade was recognized as a genius. Extremely successful with audiences all over the world, his serials were also admired by contemporary intellectuals—especially the surrealists André Breton, Louis Aragon, and Guillaume Apollinaire, who saw in his skillful amalgamation of realistic detail, dense poetic imagery, and pure fantasy an analogue for their own attempts to "re-spiritualize" modern art. But because montage aesthetics dominated film theory from the era of Griffith and Eisenstein (see pp. 179–86) until the writings of Bazin began to appear in the late forties, Feuillade's reputation was in total eclipse from 1918 to this latter date, when the *Cahiers* critics (who would later become the *auteurs* ["authors," or directors with a personal style] of the French New Wave) finally recognized Feuillade as the first great *metteur-en-scène* (practitioner of *mise-en-scène* aesthetics), as seminal to their theory of film art as Griffith was to montage.

---

* In theater, the arrangement of actors, scenery, and props in preparation for a performance. In cinema, that which occurs before the lens of the camera, as opposed to the effects created by editing.

The success of Feuillade's serials led to widespread acceptance of the form throughout the world: *Fantômas* is the father of the American *Perils of Pauline* series (actually directed for Pathé by the French director Louis Gasnier), Britain's *Ultus,* Germany's *Homunculus,* and Italy's *Tigris,* all well received in their day. And their popularity allowed Gaumont to succeed Pathé as the most powerful French studio of the century's second decade, although by 1914 France's monopoly on the international market was doomed. In 1910 approximately 60 to 70 percent of all imported films in the West derived from French studios, making France's domination of world cinema as nearly complete as Hollywood's was to be. When the war began, however, France lost much of its market at a time when the rate of Hollywood production was multiplying almost monthly.

The Gaumont studio commanded the talents not only of Feuillade but of his protégé Jean Durand (1882–1946), whose comedy series *Onesime, Calino* (originated by Roméo Bosetti, c. 1909), and *Zigoto,* made between 1907 and 1914 with his comic troupe "Les Pouics," influenced the work of both Mack Sennett and René Clair (see pp. 210–11 and 388–90). Gaumont also had under contract the former Alice Guy, Alice Guy-Blaché* (*La Vie du Christ* [*The Life of Christ,* 1906]; *Fanfan la Tulipe* [Fanfan the Tulip, 1907]), and the cartoonist Émile Cohl (1857–1938), who applied the principle of stop-motion photography to the drawing board and became the father of modern animation. The practice of animating concrete objects by photographing them one frame at a time and changing their position between frames was popularized by the American director J. Stuart Blackton (1875–1941) in such Vitagraph films as *A Mid-Winter's Night Dream* (1906) and *The Haunted Hotel* (1907) and was already known in France as *mouvement américain* when Cohl began to refine it near the end of the decade. In cartoons like the *Fantoche* series and *Les Joyeaux Microbes* (*The Jolly Germs,* 1909), Cohl pioneered the frame-by-frame animation of line drawings, puppets, and natural objects, and also became the first director to combine large-scale animation with live action. Finally, despite the French cinema's fall from international preeminence, Gaumont was able to establish a large production studio and exhibition circuit in England, called Gaumont-British, which remained under French control until 1922 and had a substantial impact on the development of British film (many of Alfred Hitchcock's first films, for example, were shot for Gaumont-British).†

* In 1907, Guy married Herbert Blaché (?–1953), a Gaumont cameraman and later, director. The couple came to New York in 1910 and founded the Solax Company, for which Alice was director-general until its dissolution in 1914. She continued to direct independent features in the United States through 1920; Herbert directed through 1929, although they divorced in 1922, when Alice returned with their two children to France.

† Léon Gaumont retired in 1928, selling his distribution and theater chains to MGM. The production company became part of the Gaumont-Franco Film-Aubert consortium, which went bankrupt in the early thirties, but the Gaumont name persists today in the Société Nouvelles des Établissements Gaumont, an international producer/distributor. Gaumont-British prospered independently under the stewardship of the producer Michael Balcon until he left in 1936 (see pp. 309–10), when it collapsed as a production/distribution firm. The exhibition chain was absorbed by the J. Arthur Rank Organization in the late forties, but newsreels continued to be made under the Gaumont-British logo until 1959.

Le Gaumont Palace

Le Plus Grand Cinema du Monde

2.23 Advertisements for the Gaumont Palace Theatre and the Gaumont studio, c. 1912.

2.24 *Les Joyeaux microbes* (Émile Cohl, 1909).

The Société Film d'Art

The most influential phenomenon to occur in French cinema during the period of international expansion, however, came in the first decade of the century and was only remotely connected with a major production company (Pathé had partial control of the venture). This was the work of the Société Film d'Art, founded by the Parisian financiers Frères Lafitte in 1908 for the purpose of transferring prestigious stage plays starring famous performers to the screen. The idea was to attract the theater-going middle classes to the cinema by increasing its aesthetic and intellectual appeal—a revolutionary notion at a time in which the medium had only just emerged from the nickelodeon and the fairground tent.

The film historian Kenneth Macgowan has called Film d'Art "the first highbrow motion picture movement," and that description applies in both its positive and negative senses. On the one hand, the company used the best creative talent of the stage to mount its productions, commissioning original plays from members of the esteemed Académie Française and employing stars of the Comédie Française to act in them. Leading composers wrote original scores for these plays and eminent stage directors were contracted to direct them. From a literary and dramatic perspective, in fact, the credentials of Film d'Art were impeccable. From the standpoint of cinema, on the other hand, the Film d'Art productions were regressive in the extreme.

For all their intellectual pedigree (and perhaps because of it), the lavishly staged productions of the Société Film d'Art were merely photographed plays; their directors made no concessions whatever to the filmic medium. Like a theater spectator in an orchestra seat, the camera occupied a central position with regard to the action and remained rigidly static throughout, so that the film frame assumed the function of a proscenium arch. All takes were long or medium-long shots which permitted the players to appear at full length on the screen, just as they would on the stage. Each shot was made to correspond to an entire dramatic scene played out from beginning to end, and the acting itself was full of wild gesticulation and bombast. Finally, as if to assure the spectators that they were indeed watching a "high-art film" (as American distributors billed the product), and not just an ordinary "living picture," Film d'Art sets were constructed of papier-mâché and plaster, and the backgrounds were painted canvas. As cinematic narratives, then, the Film d'Art productions were more primitive than the films of Méliès and considerably less imaginative. Nevertheless, for several years they enjoyed an immense popular success and were imitated throughout the Western world.

The screening of the first Film d'Art production, *L'Assassinat du duc de Guise* (*The Assassination of the Duc de Guise*), on November 17, 1908, met with nearly universal acclaim. Directed by Charles Le Bargy and André Calmettes of the Comédie Française, with a script by Académician Henri Lavédan and a score by Camille Saint-Saëns, *L'Assassinat du duc de Guise* was hailed by France's leading intellectual journals as a great cultural landmark; and one drama critic wrote that its premiere would prove as significant to the history of film as the first Cinémato-

2.25 *L'Assassinat de duc de Guise* (Charles Le Bargy and André Calmettes, for the Société Film d'Art, 1908).

graphe projection on December 28, 1895. In subsequent years, the Société Film d'Art filmed plays by Edmond Rostand, Francois Coppée, and Victorien Sardou, as well as versions of Dickens' novel *Oliver Twist, Madame Sans-Gêne* (a play by Sardou and Moreau), and Goethe's novel *The Sorrows of Young Werther,* before the company was killed off by the introduction of sound. In its prime, however, the Société Film d'Art had so many imitators in France, Italy, Great Britain, Germany, Denmark, and ultimately the United States that it could scarcely compete with them. France, for example, had not only the Société Cinématographiques des Auteurs et Gens de Lettres but the Série d'Art Pathé, Gaumont's Film Esthétique, Éclair's Association Cinématographique des Auteurs Dramatiques, and two independent companies, Film d'Auteurs and Théatro-Film.

For several years, the rage for lengthy adaptations of "classical" novels and plays—now known generically as **films d'art**—swept across Western Europe, stifling experiment and enshrouding the new medium of film in the literary orthodoxies of the past century. For a while it seemed as if everything written, sung, or danced (for filmed ballet and opera formed a large part of the *films d'art* corpus too) in Western Europe from the Renaissance to 1900 found its way into these stagebound and pretentious productions. Shakespeare, Goethe, Dumas *père* and *fils,* Hugo, Dickens, Balzac, Wagner, and Bulwer-Lytton, even the tragedies of Sophocles, were all represented, side by side with the "modern classics" of contemporary authors like Antole France and Henrik Sienkiewicz. Even Eastern Europe was affected: David Robinson maintains that the great Russian vogue for historical costume films, which reached its aesthetic peak in Eisenstein's two-part *Ivan the Terrible* (1944–46), was born during this period, as was the Hungarian cinema's permanent fascination with literary subjects, as will be seen in Chapters 5 and 16.

Although the *film d'art* vogue died out almost as rapidly as it had come into being, the movement's financial success had revealed a vast new audience which preferred serious screen stories to comic chases and vaudeville acts, convincing producers all over the world to upgrade the content of their films. Not surprisingly, when directors like Griffith and Feuillade began to cast serious stories into visually sophisticated form through montage on the one hand and *mise-en-scène* on the other, *film d'art* productions rapidly lost their audience, and the topsy-turvy state into which World War I threw the international market helped to accelerate the process.

Still, the *film d'art* movement had made the medium socially and intellectually respectable for the first time in its brief history, and had heightened the respect of the industry for itself. It also made a number of people—again, notably Griffith and Feuillade—aware of the necessity for developing a unique style of film acting which would eschew the broad gestures and facial grimaces of nineteenth-century theater in favor of a more subtle and restrained kind of playing. These contortions were important components of the grand theatrical style, appropriate and even necessary on a stage that is distant from its audience and fixed in space. In the cinema, however, a fixed distance between the figures on the screen and the audience cannot be maintained because spatial relationships are in a constant state of flux due to editing and camera movement. Furthermore, even in the most conservative of filmed plays—those photographed in long shot from a single camera angle and edited only between scenes—the figures in the arranged *tableaux* appear much larger on the screen than they would on the legitimate stage, and theatrical gestures easily become exaggerated to the point of absurdity. In short, by attempting to impersonate the eye of a theater spectator, the *film d'art* camera taught a generation of filmmakers how very little like an eye it really was. The human eye sees, but it also distorts, compensates, and errs. The scrutiny of the camera lens, however, is mercilessly accurate: it records all blemishes and is capable of magnifying the slightest facial mannerism to grotesque proportions on the screen. For this reason, film acting has had to develop conventions of its own in recognition of the perverse thoroughness with which the camera records certain aspects of reality, and it might well be said that *film d'art* performances provided a negative model for these conventions.

Finally, *film d'art* productions were directly responsible for increasing the standard length of films from a single reel to five reels and more. As *films d'art* grew increasingly popular, they turned to ever weightier source material and grew proportionally in length. *L'Assassinat du duc de Guise* had been only 921 feet, or a little less than fifteen minutes long at standard silent speed. One of the last and most prestigious *films d'art,* Louis Mercanton's *La Reine Elizabeth* (*Queen Elizabeth,* 1912), ran three and one-half reels, or about fifty minutes. The story of how Adolph Zukor imported *Queen Elizabeth* into the United States and proved to the MPPC that Americans would sit through a film above a single reel in length (and

2.26 Sarah Bernhardt in *La Reine Elizabeth* (Louis Mercanton, for Histrionic Films, 1912).

pay a dollar each for the experience) has already been told. But it should be pointed out that the success of *film d'art* productions was also responsible for increasing film length in Great Britain, France, Italy, Germany, and Scandinavia, where the industries were less rigidly controlled than in America but equally conservative with regard to length. Thus, it fell to the *film d'art* movement to inaugurate the feature-length film in the West, though its advent had probably been inevitable since the invention of the Latham loop.

The Italian Superspectacle

No country was more responsible for the rapid rise of the feature film than Italy, whose lavishly produced costume spectacles brought its cinema to international prominence in the years immediately preceding World War I. The Italian film industry may be said to have begun with the construction of the Cines studios in Rome, 1905–6, by the former inventor Filotea Alberini (1865–1937). This firm gave the Italian cinema its first costume film, *La presa di Roma* (*The Capture of Rome* [1905]), but devoted most of its first years to the production of short comedies in the French vein and modishly "decadent" melodramas starring the archetypal *femme fatale* Lyda Borelli (1884–1959—the model for America's own definitive vamp Theda Bara [1890–1955]). As major Italian financiers became increasingly interested in the film business, however, rival production companies began to proliferate. When Ambrosio Films of Turin released Luigi Maggi's (1867–1946) *Gli ultimi giorni di Pompei* (*The Last Days of Pompeii*) in 1908, Cines once again turned its attention to historical themes, producing Mario Caserini's (1874–1920) feature-length *Catilina* and *Beatrice Cenci* in 1909, and his *Lucrezia Borgia* and *Mes-*

2.27 The chariot race from Enrico Guazzoni's *Quo vadis?* (1913).

2.28 Giovanni Pastrone's *Cabiria* (1914).

salina in 1910. Concurrently, Pathé founded Film d'Art Italiana in Milan to produce historical costume dramas on its own, and suddenly the boom was on.

The years 1909–11 saw a flood of historical films with titles like *Giulio Cesare* (*Julius Caesar* [Giovanni Pastrone, 1909]), *La caduta di Troia* (*The Fall of Troy* [Giovanni Pastrone, 1910]), *Bruto* (*Brutus* [Enrico Guazzoni, 1910]), and *San Francisco* (*Saint Francis*[Enrico Guazzoni,

1911]); but 1913 witnessed the advent of the Italian superspectacle in a ten-reel remake of Maggi's *Gli ultimi giorni di Pompei,* directed by Mario Caserini for Ambrosio).* As Vernon Jarratt points out, however, this film is entitled to its designation as the first of the great **blockbusters** only by virtue of its length and its cast of one thousand extras. It was actually the nine-reel *Quo vadis?,* directed by Enrico Guazzoni for Cines in early 1913, that established the conventions of the superspectacle and captured the world market for the Italian cinema. Adapted from the novel by the Nobel laureate Henryk Sienkiewicz, *Quo vadis?* featured enormous three-dimensional sets designed by Guazzoni, crowd scenes with five thousand extras, a real chariot race, a real fire representing the burning of Rome, and a Coliseum full of real lions to devour the Christians. In terms of narrative, the film was a series of arranged scenes, but its spectacle properly made it an international hit, returning its producers twenty times their very substantial investment of 480,000 lire (about $48,000 in the currency of the period). So phenomenal was the success of *Quo vadis?* that the Cines technical staff was forced to work in twenty-four-hour shifts for some months to keep up with the worldwide demand for prints.

The successor to *Quo vadis?* was a film of even greater extravagance, grandeur, and distinction—the Italia Company's *Cabiria,* directed in 1914 by Giovanni Pastrone (under the name of Piero Fosco) and produced for the staggering sum of over one million lire (about $100,000 in the currency of the period). Pastrone wrote the script himself after twelve months of research in the Louvre and paid the famous Italian novelist Gabriele d'Annuzio 50,000 lire in gold to lend his name to it and to write the titles. Shot in Turin over a period of six months amid the most monumental and elaborate three-dimensional sets yet created for a motion picture, with exteriors filmed on location in Tunisia, Sicily, and the Alps, *Cabiria* is an epic saga of the Second Punic War between Rome and Carthage; it has been called by Vernon Jarratt "the dizziest peak of the Italian cinema." Its twelve reels develop a dramatically sophisticated narrative against a historical reconstruction of the entire struggle from the burning of the Roman fleet at Syracuse (accomplished through some of the best special effects to appear on the screen for the next twenty years) to Hannibal crossing the Alps and the sack of Carthage.

Spectacle aside, *Cabiria* contains some important innovations in film technique which may very well have influenced directors like Cecil B. DeMille and Ernst Lubitsch, as well as D. W. Griffith (see Chapter 6, p. 234). The film is most notable for its use of extended, slow-moving **tracking** (or traveling) **shots,** which permitted the camera to roam about freely among the vast sets, moving in to isolate the characters in close-up and moving out again to re-frame the shifting action. Pastrone and his innovative Spanish cameraman Segundo de Chomón (1871–1929) improvised a dolly (which Pastrone patented) and a primitive crane to achieve

---

*A rival version directed by the actor Enrico Vidali was produced in the same year by Ernesto Pasquali (1883–1919) for his own company, Pasquali Films, Turin.

these shots. Although Griffith was to use this process much more dynamically in *The Birth of a Nation* (1915) and *Intolerance* (1916), there is no question that Pastrone was the first director anywhere to attempt it on such a grand scale, and, for a while, slow tracking about a set became known in the industry as "*cabiria* movement." *Cabiria*'s other significant innovations were its systematic use of artificial (electrical) lighting to create dramatic effects, its use of careful and convincing process photography, its relatively restrained acting, and its painstaking reconstruction of period detail (subsequently a hallmark of Griffith's and Lubitsch's historical films).

Released on the eve of the war and overshadowed by the recent international triumph of the much less distinguished *Quo vadis?*, *Cabiria* was not the financial success for which its producers had hoped. Indeed, the Italian cinema's brief period of commercial and aesthetic dominance was abruptly ended by World War I, and the nation's subsequent descent into Fascism prevented a renaissance until after World War II. Nevertheless, it seems clear today that this last and greatest of the Italian superspectacles provided DeMille and Lubitsch with the model for their postwar historical spectacles and substantially influenced the narrative form of Griffith's epic masterworks. In fact, Griffith spoke of seeing both *Quo vadis?* and *Cabiria* while *The Birth of a Nation* was still in the planning stages, and there can be little doubt of their impact upon his development at a time when he was searching for an appropriate cinematic form into which to cast his epic vision of American history.*

---

* By some accounts, Griffith is said to have purchased his own print of *Cabiria* and studied it intensively during the shooting of *The Birth of a Nation*.

3

D. W. *Griffith and the Consummation of Narrative Form*

The achievement of David Wark Griffith (1875–1948) is unprecedented in the history of Western art, much less Western film. In the brief span of six years, between directing his first one-reeler in 1908 and *The Birth of a Nation* in 1914, Griffith established the narrative language of the cinema as we know it today and turned an aesthetically inconsequential medium of entertainment into a fully articulated art form. He has been called, variously, and, for the most part, accurately, "the father of film technique," "the man who invented Hollywood," "the cinema's first great **auteur**," and "the Shakespeare of the screen." Yet in the sixty years since his most important work was completed, Griffith's stature as an artist has been the subject of continuous debate among film scholars, and his critical reputation has suffered more fluctuation than that of any other major figure in film history. The problem is that Griffith was essentially a figure of paradox. He was unquestionably the seminal genius of the narrative cinema and its first great visionary artist, but he was also a provincial southern romantic with pretensions to high literary culture and a penchant for sentimentality and melodrama that would have embarrassed Dickens. Griffith was the film's first great technical master and its first legitimate poet, but he was also a muddleheaded racial bigot, incapable of abstract thought, who quite literally saw all of human history in the black-and-white terms of nineteenth-century melodrama. In one sense, Griffith presents the paradox of a nineteenth-century man who founded a uniquely twentieth-century art form, and this tension between ages accounts for many disparities of taste and judgment that we find in his films today. But there is another contradiction in Griffith which is less easy to rationalize and which raises issues central to the nature of film art itself, and that is the very existence of such staggering cinematic genius side by side with the intellectual and emotional shallowness described above. Given the peculiar limitations of his vision, Griffith was never dishonest or hypocritical, but he was intellectually narrow to an alarming degree for a major artist in any medium.

3.1 D. W. Griffith during his Biograph years.

61

FORMATIVE INFLUENCES

David Wark Griffith, the seventh child of a Confederate Army colonel, Civil War hero, and local character, Jacob "Roaring Jake" Griffith, was born in a rural district of Kentucky near the Indiana border in 1875. Never affluent, the Griffiths had been impoverished by the Reconstruction, but they clung to the ideals of the past, and David Wark grew up steeped in the romantic mythology of the Old South, with its codes of honor, chivalry, and purity intact. This regionalism combined well with Griffith's penchant for the more popular Victorian poets and novelists to produce a set of naïvely romantic values which the young man was never to outgrow. When Jacob Griffith died in 1885,* Griffith's mother moved the family to Louisville, where she attempted to operate a boardinghouse with scant success, adding urban poverty to the list of formative influences upon her son. Like Dickens in similar circumstances (and there are more than a few resemblances between the two artists), Griffith was forced to quit public school and work to help support the family.

After a succession of menial jobs in Louisville, he became stage-struck and began to tour the Midwest with traveling stock companies. Griffith's acting career was probably less a matter of aptitude than of zeal and good looks (he was strikingly handsome and statuesque throughout his life), but between 1897 and 1905 he pursued this career from Minneapolis to New York to San Francisco by jumping freights, living in flophouses, and working his way to his next engagement at all manner of jobs, from shoveling ore to picking hops. From San Francisco, Griffith returned to the East in 1906 with a respectable part in the Nance O'Neill Company's production of *Elizabeth, the Queen of England,* after which he married the company's ingenue, Linda Arvidson (1884–1949), and began to write his own play, *A Fool and a Girl,* a serious melodrama derived from his recent experience of migratory workers in the California hop fields.

His acting career notwithstanding, Griffith's lifelong ambition had been to become a writer in the lofty and cultivated Victorian mode of his boyhood favorites. Unfortunately, he had little facility with language, and most of his literary productions were stilted and rhetorical. Miraculously, however, he sold his first play for one thousand dollars to the impresario James K. Hackett, who produced it in Washington, D.C., in the fall of 1907. *A Fool and a Girl* opened to hostile reviews and closed after two weeks, but Griffith was convinced of his talent and used his royalties to embark upon a new literary career. Within a year, he had managed to publish a handful of poems and short stories in mass-circulation middle-class magazines like *Collier's Weekly, Good Housekeeping,* and *Cosmopolitan,* and he had completed another play—a four-act epic drama of the American Revolution entitled *War,* based entirely on diaries and letters of the period which he found in the New York Public Library. Although much of its factual material was later incorporated

---

* Griffith always claimed that his father had died of complications from an improperly stitched Civil War wound; less romantic accounts suggest peritonitus.

into his film epic *America* (1924), *War* was never produced, and Griffith began to cast about again for steady employment.

It was under these circumstances in New York in late 1907 that he ran into Max Davidson, an old friend and acting colleague from Louisville, who advised him that a living might be made selling stories to the motion-picture companies which had suddenly sprung up in the city. Griffith was initially opposed to the idea, fearing that his literary reputation would be damaged by association with the vulgar new medium. He knew very little about the movies at this time, but he held them in utter contempt. Nevertheless, he had to eat, and screen stories were then selling for around five dollars apiece; so he tossed off an uncredited version of Victorien Sardou's play *La Tosca* under his stage name, Lawrence Griffith, and offered it to Edwin S. Porter at the Edison Company studios. Porter rejected the scenario on the grounds that it had too many scenes for a movie, but, impressed with the young man's looks, he offered Griffith the leading role in his current film, *Rescued from an Eagle's Nest,* at a salary of five dollars per day. Griffith ruefully accepted. When the film was completed, Porter had no further use for the actor-scenarist, so Griffith approached the American Mutoscope and Biograph Company, at 11 East Fourteenth Street, with some of his screen stories.

THE BEGINNING AT BIOGRAPH

The American Mutoscope and Biograph Company had been founded in 1895 as a partnership among E. B. Koopman, Henry Marvin, Herman Casler, and William Kennedy Laurie Dickson, the inventor of the Kinetograph and Kinetoscope, as the K.M.C.D. Syndicate. Alienated from the Edison Laboratory by a quarrel with the business manager, Dickson had combined with the others to perfect a motion-picture technology which would rival Edison's without infringing his patents. Dickson invented a portable peep-show device (the "Mutoscope"*) for the syndicate, and later a camera and projector (both called the "Biograph"), all of which legally circumvented Edison patents. Though American Biograph (the word "Mutoscope" was dropped shortly after Griffith was hired) joined the MPPC in 1909, the firm for years provided Edison with his only significant American competition and employed several of the most talented persons in the business—including the man who was to become Griffith's personal **cinematographer,** G. W. "Billy" Bitzer (1872–1944).

By late 1907, however, the company was in serious trouble: it was

---

* Rather than using a perforated film strip like the Kinetoscope, the Mutoscope mounted photographic impressions of individual film frames on cardboard cards and arranged them successively on a rotary wheel. When turned by a crank, the wheel would put the photographs in motion, flipping them rapidly one by one, to create "moving pictures" according to the same optical principles which govern the operation of camera and projector. Many Mutoscopes survive today in penny arcades and designated museums of Americana, official (the Smithsonian) and otherwise (Disneyland, Disney World). Due to the deterioration of so many early paper and nitrate prints, these Mutoscopes provide a rare opportunity to experience the images of primitive cinema at first hand.

3.2 K.M.C.D.'s Mutoscope, c. 1897.

$200,000 in debt to its bankers, and the public had begun to lose interest in its films. Furthermore, the health and energy of its director, Wallace McCutcheon, were flagging rapidly, and the company had fallen below its standard production rate of two one-reel films per week. The need to hire a new director was clear, but the handful of experienced motion-picture directors in the world at this time were all employed. Griffith, who was hired initially as an actor and story writer, was soon offered his first opportunity to direct by Biograph's general manager Henry Marvin on the basis of some perceptive remarks he had made to Marvin's brother Arthur, the studio's other cameraman.

Characteristically, Griffith chose as the subject of his first film a melodramatic (and racist) tale of a child kidnapped by Gypsies and improbably rescued after shooting the rapids in an empty water cask. Called *The Adventures of Dollie,* it was *Rescued from an Eagle's Nest* without the eagle and one of a number of films in the then-popular genre of chases involving a lost or kidnapped child. Griffith shot the film in two days on location at Sound Beach, Connecticut, in June 1908, with a great deal of advice and moral support from Bitzer and from Arthur Marvin, who was the cameraman. Though the film was scarcely innovative, it was respectable enough to garner Griffith a forty-five-dollar-a-week director's contract with Biograph and a royalty of one mil (the equivalent of one-tenth of one cent) per foot on every print sold.* By the time *The Adventures of Dollie* was given its first screening in July, Griffith had already directed five more films and completed one begun by another director.

INNOVATION, 1908–1909: INTER-FRAME NARRATIVE

In the five years that followed, Griffith directed over 450 one- and two-reelers for American Biograph, experimenting with every narrative technique which he would later employ in *The Birth of a Nation* (1915) and *Intolerance* (1916) and which would pass into the classical lexicon of the cinema. Yet Griffith seems to have been scarcely aware of his innovations, at least, in the process of making them. They were for him the unformulated results of practical problem-solving rather than of abstract theorizing, and his method of proceeding was always intuitive and empirical rather than formalistic. Unrestricted by narrative conventions, since there were very few at the time, Griffith simply adopted for his Biograph films what worked best in the particular circumstances, according to the dynamics of the tale. If he had any methodology at all, it consisted in creating analogies between the conventions of stage narrative, which he knew implicitly from his long experience as an actor, and certain uniquely

---

* William Johnson, however, correctly points out that *Dollie* contains an unusual high-angle shot of a field with action moving through it, as well as a shot in depth of a Gypsy wagon pulling away from the camera ("Early Griffith: A Wider View," *Film Quarterly* 29, 3 [Spring 1976]: 2–13). Neither of these would have been unprecedented in 1908, but they do suggest a more sophisticated concept of screen space than was common among film-makers at the time.

cinematic structural devices which he discovered as he went along. The narrative devices of the Victorian novels Griffith had loved in his youth also provided models for his innovations. Ultimately, Griffith combined his own analogies between dramatic/novelistic modes and cinematic modes with those of others, like Porter and Pastrone, and molded them into the visual narrative language which we call generically "film." In the course of his career, in fact, Griffith effected a nearly complete translation of nineteenth-century narrative modes into cinematic terms, insuring through the intensity, stature, and prestigiousness of his films that the cinema would remain a predominantly narrative form until some new technology or ideology was born to liberate it.

There is a prevailing sense among contemporary scholars that Griffith's role as an innovator has been overplayed and that in general "innovation was not simply a matter of a few daring filmmakers influencing each other," as Kristin Thompson has put it. Of the transition from **primitive** to **classical** cinema, 1907–17, she continues: "Individual innovations were certainly important, but people like Griffith and Maurice Tourneur changed production practices and filmic techniques in limited ways, governed by the overall production system." In light of the voluminous research assembled by Thompson and other contemporary film historians like Barry Salt, there can be no question that such a system was firmly in place by 1908, largely in response to the nickelodeon boom of 1906–8, and that film narrative had been systematically organized to accommodate the material conditions of production. My argument is simply that Griffith was prominent, if not preeminent, in the transformation of the production system from its primitive to its classical mode. The historical record is clear, for example, that Griffith's Biograph films were enormously popular with contemporary audiences and widely imitated by other filmmakers, as were his day-to-day production practices. Nor can there be any doubt that in terms of social history the fame and infamy of *The Birth of a Nation* (1915) changed forever the way that motion pictures were regarded by everyone from shoe clerks to national politicians to Wall Street financiers. On the other hand, Griffith did not operate in a vacuum; a case in point would be the evolution of the **180-degree system.**

The concept of screen direction originated in the films of the early primitive period, when the frame was basically a proscenium containing action which audiences viewed as if from a theater seat. The direction of movement was maintained naturally in such films, as it would be on the stage. But the rise of multi-shot films in the late primitive period, especially chase films, demanded that screen direction be maintained consistently from one shot to the next so that—as one cameraman put it—the characters wouldn't "bump into themselves." (In a chase sequence, if all the characters don't move across the frame in the same direction from shot to shot, they will seem to run toward one another, rather than vice versa.) The method that evolved for maintaining screen direction is known today as the 180-degree system of shooting, which assumes that a scene's action will always progress along a straight line from the right to left or left to right of the frame. In feature films of the classical era, the axis of action (or center line, as it is also called) becomes the imaginary vector of movements, character positions, and glances in a scene; shooting and cutting a film so that the camera never crosses the line insures that the spectator will always be on the same side of the story action and, metaphorically speaking, the screen. Obviously, this 180-degree rule wasn't "invented" by any one person, but developed out of the trial-and-error experience of countless directors (including Griffith, who was grappling with problems of screen direction as late as 1909–10), cameramen, and editors, as well as rising audience expectations of continuity on the screen.*

Griffith's first movement toward classical narrative form involved the use of a "cut-in" in *The Greaser's Gauntlet* (1908), made four months after *The Adventures of Dollie.*† As part of the new seriousness he brought to his craft, Griffith wanted to heighten the emotional intensity of a scene in which a young woman has just saved a man from a lynch mob. To effect this, he cut from a **medium long shot** of the hanging tree to a much closer **full shot** of the same space, showing the two actors from head to toe as they exchange a token of friendship. By changing the position of his camera in mid-scene, Griffith enabled the audience to read the actors' emotions in their faces rather than having to infer them from broad gestures. In so doing, Griffith had not only broken up his scene into a number of shots (which Porter and others seem to have done occasionally before him) but had broken down the standard distance between the audience and the action. The cut from medium long to full shot also worked effectively to solve a major narrative problem by emphasizing the exchange of a small gift, and Griffith used this type of cut again and again in the next few months, with very positive results.

Griffith's next narrative articulation was a logical extension of the first. In *After Many Years,* an October 1908 screen version of Tennyson's narrative poem *Enoch Arden,* Griffith resorted to parallel editing without benefit of a chase. Here, he interweaves the twin narratives of Annie Lee and her shipwrecked husband over a continuum of eleven shots, suggesting the psychological burden and uncertainty of their separation. This kind of editing prefigures not only the **subjective camera** of F. W. Murnau and Karl Freund but Eisenstein's "montage of attractions" (see pp. 129–30 and 150–53, respectively). Griffith would use it for the rest of his Biograph career in films like *A Corner in Wheat (1909),* where he cut from a shot of the wheat tycoon gorging himself at a sumptuous meal to a shot of poor sharecroppers standing in a breadline (an early form of associative montage as practiced later by the Soviets). He also employed the technique to create what he called "objects of attention" when he cut from a character looking at something offscreen to a shot of what the

---

* In these matters, however, I am inclined to agree with Edward Wagenknecht, who writes in *The Films of D. W. Griffith* (New York, 1975) that "absolute priority . . . is of very little interest; what counts in art is not who did it first but who does it best" (p. 17).

† Griffith's first "cut-in" was formerly ascribed to *For Love of Gold* (1908), adapted from Jack London's "Just Meat," on the basis of an anecdote told by Linda Arvidson Griffith in *When the Movies Were Young* (New York, 1927; 1969) and repeated by Lewis Jacobs and others.

character sees as he or she sees it. These have come to be known as "motivated point-of-view" shots, and, by placing the camera in the spatial position of the character, they induce a kind of optical subjectivity.* Griffith used a similar editing trope to effect the **flashback,** or "switchback," as he termed it—a shot or sequence of shots which interrupts the narrative present and returns us momentarily to the past.

In fact, what Griffith had begun to do in the Biograph films of 1908–9, and would continue to do more and more successfully throughout his career, was to *alternate shots of different spatial lengths* (i.e., of different camera-to-subject distance), none of which was dramatically complete in itself, to create cinematic "sentences" within scenes, cutting long shots, full shots, **medium shots,** close shots, and close-ups together in order to render a single dramatic scene from multiple points of view or angles of vision—i.e., from multiple camera set-ups. In the process, Griffith came especially to learn the immense symbolic and psychological value of the close-up, unexpectedly interpolated between shots of other spatial lengths. Phenomenologically, the close-up has the effect of isolating a detail from its background and giving it greater dramatic emphasis by making it fill the frame. In subsequent Biograph films like *Ramona* (1911) and *The Battle of Elderbush Gulch* (1913), Griffith would also learn the importance of the **extreme long shot** in rendering panoramic or epic action sequences of the type essential to *The Birth of a Nation* and *Intolerance.*

Now, however, the Biograph executives, who had opposed the production of *After Many Years* in the first place on the grounds that it had no action and no chase (and one of Griffith's many great achievements was to upgrade the intellectual content of contemporary films), were vocally shocked by this experiment, which violated every known canon of filmmaking in its disregard for the dramatic unities of time and space and for strict chronological sequence. Griffith's response to their criticism, as reported by Linda Arvidson Griffith, tells us a great deal about his attitude toward his new craft:

> When Mr. Griffith suggested a scene showing Annie Lee waiting for her husband's return to be followed by a scene of Enoch cast away on a desert island, it was altogether too distracting.
> "How can you tell a story jumping about like that? The people won't know what it's about."
> "Well," said Mr. Griffith, "doesn't Dickens write that way?"
> "Yes, but that's Dickens; that's novel writing; that's different."
> "Oh, not so much, these are picture stories; not so different."

As Griffith saw it, films were narratives, or stories, which were told through the arrangement not of words but of moving photographic images. Nevertheless, Biograph's managers felt Griffith had gone too far, and

---

* Motivated point-of-view cutting is similar to the so-called "eyeline match," which came into practice at approximately the same time: a shot of a character glancing offscreen is followed by a shot of the (obviously contiguous) space seen—not, however, from the character's point of view but from the perspective of the first shot, i.e., the "objective" perspective of the audience. (See p. 135).

3.3 Four shots of parallel action from the three-way rescue that concludes *The Lonely Villa* (1909): the besieged family and the husband rushing to the rescue. Missing are exterior shots of the robbers trying to break into the villa.

they closely watched the film's public reception. To their astonishment, *After Many Years* was hailed as a masterpiece, and, according to Lewis Jacobs, it was the first American film to be widely imported into foreign markets. In his first year as Biograph's director, in fact, Griffith's films had substantially, if anonymously, improved the company's fortunes, and the Biograph product was soon enjoying the kind of critical prestige normally reserved for successful stage plays.

Griffith's next step was even more radical, for it involved spatial and temporal fragmentation of the reality continuum to create the illusion of multiple parallel action, and achieve a new kind of dramatic suspense. He had attempted this as early as his eighth film, *The Fatal Hour* (August 1908), but it reached full development only in his June 1909 melodrama *The Lonely Villa*. Here Griffith wished to show three multiplane actions occurring simultaneously: a band of robbers attempting to break into a suburban villa from without, a frightened woman and her children desperately attempting to forestall the attack from within, and the husband rushing from town to rescue his family and drive away the robbers. In a logical extension of the technique he had employed in *After Many Years,* Griffith simply cut back and forth between one action and another, gradually increasing the tempo of alternation until all three actions converged in the dramatic climax of the tale. The effect of this **crosscutting** or **intercutting** among fifty-two separate shots was to transform the *dramatic* climax of his film into the *visual* or *cinematic* climax as well, so that the tale and the telling of the tale (i.e., the narrative technique) became the vehicles for one another—so that the medium, in effect, became the message. It was long thought that Porter had used a rudimentary form of intercutting in *The Life of an American Fireman* in 1903 (as discussed in Chapter 1), and it is clear that the filmmakers of the Brighton school and even Griffith himself (in films like *The Greaser's Gauntlet, The Fatal Hour,* and *After Many Years* [all 1908]) had experimented with the technique prior to 1909. But *The Lonely Villa* was probably the first dramatic film to employ the device as its basic structural principle across three separate spatial planes, and after its debut the practice of intercutting passed rapidly and permanently into the cinema's narrative lexicon.

So powerful was the impact of this film that its intercutting was widely imitated throughout the industry and came to be known generically as the "Griffith last-minute rescue." The term underscores an important element of this technique—its generation of suspense not simply through the rapid alternation of shots to portray simultaneous action but through the rapid alternation of shots of shorter and shorter duration. As Arthur Knight has noted, Griffith had discovered that the length of time a shot remained on the screen could create significant psychological tension in the audience—that the shorter the length of time a shot was held on the screen, the greater the tension it was capable of inducing. This is the chief principle of the intercut rescue sequences for which Griffith became world famous, though of course this kind of editing is not restricted to the chase. It became, in fact, the structural foundation of the narrative cinema from *The Birth of a Nation* to the present. In the intercut rescues of the type that conclude *The Birth of a Nation* and *Intolerance,* for example, the alternating shots of the simultaneous actions grow shorter and shorter as the dramatic climax mounts, until we end with the visual counterpart of a musical crescendo. In other words, the visual tempo of the cutting for simultaneous action parallels the dramatic tempo of the action photographed, so that content is perfectly embodied in form. Griffith's second major innovation, then, is the syntactical corollary of the first—to the alternation of shots of varying *spatial lengths,* he added the alternation of shots of varying *temporal lengths,* creating the basis for montage and the montage aesthetics which came to dominate the first fifty years of narrative cinema.

Once again, public approval of Griffith's innovations was resounding (although his name was still not associated with them because of Biograph's screen-credit policy and the industry's general tendency not to acknowledge directors), and he was offered his second contract with Biograph in August 1909. Though he still had misgivings about "working for the nickelodeons," as he called it, Griffith accepted the job and continued to pursue his vigorous experiments in film narrative.

INNOVATION, 1909–1911: INTRA-FRAME NARRATIVE

The discoveries of 1908–9 (the alternation of shots of varying spatial and varying temporal lengths) had all been functions of editing, of the dynamic relationship *between* the clusters of frames we call shots (*inter*-frame narrative), but Griffith soon showed himself equally concerned with what occurred *within* the frames and shots of his films (*intra*-frame narrative). For one thing, he began to insist upon stories of high quality for his films, many of them derived from literary sources. To be sure, Griffith directed a fair number of chase films, melodramas, and potboilers during his tenure at Biograph, but he also adapted dramatic films from Shakespeare, Poe, Tennyson, Browning, Dickens, and Tolstoi, and some of his films, such as *A Corner in Wheat* (1909, adapted from two muckraking novels by Frank Norris), even had serious if simplistically treated contemporary social themes. By making the content of his films more serious, Griffith was attempting to dignify the medium of motion pictures itself. Another aspect of this concern was the care he took in selecting and directing his actors.

Griffith was in fact the first great actor's director. Because he had been an actor himself and understood the psychology of the profession, he knew the value of careful rehearsals and rigidly imposed them upon his cast and crew, even though most other directors shot their films "cold." For their efforts, however, Griffith often paid his actors four times what they might receive at a rival studio, and by 1913 he had built his own stock company of ensemble players with such future luminaries as Mary Pickford and Lionel Barrymore (both soon to leave Griffith), Mae Marsh, Dorothy and Lillian Gish, Blanche Sweet, Henry B. Walthall, Bobbie

Harron, Donald Crisp, and Wallace Reid. Griffith also understood, as no director had before him, how immensely revealing the motion-picture camera is of exaggeration and artificiality in characterization, and he coached his performers for naturalness and subtlety of expression. Griffith's attention to detail extended even to his sets, whose design and construction he frequently supervised. To his employers, the care he lavished on his "nickelodeon" productions must at first have seemed a waste of time and money. Nevertheless, as early as 1909 audiences and critics alike were praising the "naturalness" and "authenticity" of films bearing the "AB" (American Biograph) trademark—as yet the only distinguishing mark of a Griffith production. Soon trade papers were writing enthusiastic articles on his motion pictures, and Biograph became the first studio to receive fan mail for individual films (Griffith's) rather than for individual stars.

Griffith's concern for the content of his films, however, went far beyond the care he bestowed upon his actors and sets. In late 1908, for example, in a film called *The Drunkard's Reformation,* he had begun to experiment with expressive lighting by illuminating a scene with firelight. At a time when electric mercury-vapor lamps had recently been introduced for indoor shooting, this was a radical step because convention then dictated the flat and uniform illumination of every portion of the set. (Mercury-vapors were also well-suited to the orthochromatic film stock used through most of the silent period, since they produced a light concentrated in the blue-green part of the spectrum to which orthochromatic was most sensitive. On the other hand, mercury-vapors were incapable of directional lighting of the sort just described precisely because of their uniform diffusion.)* But the results of the effort were impressive, and Griffith went on to experiment with lighting more elaborately in a 1909 film version of Browning's dramatic poem *Pippa Passes* (the first film, incidentally, to be reviewed by the *New York Times*). The events of this one-reeler take place in a single day, and the passage of time is effectively rendered by changes in directional lighting which simulate the movement of the sun across the sky. In Griffith's first all-California film, *The Thread of Destiny* (1910), interior scenes of an old Spanish mission were lit solely by the slanting rays of the sun as they came through a high window, illuminating some objects, like the pulpit, and leaving others in darkness. (This shaft of light later reappeared in *Intolerance* to illumine the "endlessly rocking" cradle of the transitional scenes.) Griffith went on to become a master of tonal or atmospheric illumination (dubbed "Rembrandt lighting" by Cecil B. DeMille's cameraman Alvin Wyckoff around 1915), which characterizes a given scene through patterns of highlight and shade. Moreover, although for financial reasons Griffith was forced to shoot most of his two great epics in direct sunlight, lighting for dramatic effect was soon established and elaborately refined by directors like Giovanni

3.4 **Lighting for dramatic effect in** *Pippa Passes* (1909).

---

* The Cooper-Hewitt mercury-vapor lamp was invented for industrial and commercial applications in 1901 and by 1907 was being used for interior lighting in film studios. Mercury-vapors were electrically efficient and provided a soft, evenly diffused light over an entire set. (See Chapter 9, p. 400.)

Pastrone in Italy, Ernst Lubitsch in Germany (and later the United States), and Cecil B. DeMille in the United States.

By far the most important of Griffith's contributions to intra-frame narrative, however, were made after he began to move his company to Southern California on a regular seasonal basis in early 1910. (Griffith was not the first filmmaker to locate in Hollywood: in the fall of 1907, the Selig Polyscope Company had built a small studio there.) Here, in films like *The Lonedale Operator* (1911) and *The Battle of Elderbush Gulch* (1913), he discovered the importance of camera movement and placement to the dramatic expressiveness of film. Before Griffith went to Hollywood, the camera had been largely static. There had been **panning** (horizontal) and **tilting** (vertical) movements in films like *The Great Train Robbery,* and Griffith had begun to experiment with narrative panning shots as early as 1908 (*The Call of the Wild*) and 1909 (*The Country Doctor*). But in 1910 most film narratives—even those of Griffith—were structured mainly through editing, whether the units edited together were scenes or shots. In California, Griffith became increasingly interested in structuring his films through intra-frame as well as inter-frame movement. In the horizontal sweep of the panning shot, Griffith was able not only to follow the movement of his principals through any given scene but to engage the audience in the total environment of his films. Moreover, in the tracking or traveling shot, in which the camera—and thus the audience—actively participates in the action by moving with it, Griffith brought a new kind of movement to the screen. In *The Lonedale Operator,* for example, in order to convey the breathless momentum of a locomotive speeding to the rescue of a young woman trapped by thieves, Griffith and Bitzer mounted their camera in the moving engine cab and crosscut between traveling shots of the engine plunging through the landscape and the desperate plight of the girl. In later years, Griffith and Bitzer would mount their camera in an automobile to follow moving action during the gathering of the Klan and the climactic riot sequence in *The Birth of a Nation,* and in the rescue sequence from the Modern story of *Intolerance.* (The Babylonian story of the latter film contains one of the longest and most elaborate tracking shots ever made. In order to move their camera from an extreme long shot of the mammoth set of Belshazzar's feast straight into a full shot of the action, Griffith and Bitzer built an elevator tower that rolled on rails and tracked it slowly forward in a single unbroken shot which lasts nearly sixty seconds onscreen.) With these additions to film language, the whole notion of the frame as a proscenium arch, pervasive since Méliès, began to break down, and by the time Griffith finished *The Birth of a Nation* in early 1915, it had nearly disappeared.

Griffith also discovered the dramatic expressiveness of camera placement during his early California years, becoming one of the first directors to compose his shots in depth, with simultaneous action in background, middleground, and foreground rather than on a single plane.* As early

3.5 Blanche Sweet in *The Lonedale Operator* (1911).

---

* Charles Musser points out that at this time the Vitagraph Company was much more oriented towards composing shots in depth than Griffith (Musser to author, 1/22/88).

as 1910, he found that the perspective from which a shot was taken could be used to comment upon its content or to create dramatic emphasis for certain of its elements. A great deal can be said about a person's character metaphorically, for example, when he or she is photographed from a very low **camera angle** in a back-lit shot instead of a naturally lit head-on medium shot. The actor in a shot like this would seem to tower over the audience, and the lighting would create seemingly sinister shadows on his face. The reverse angle might be used to characterize someone who is helpless or weak, like Mae Marsh in the courtroom scene from the Modern story of *Intolerance*. Thus Griffith, who had already learned to create visual metaphors through associative editing (*After Many Years; A Corner in Wheat*), was now learning to create visual metaphors *within* the frame through camera placement. The logical extension of Griffith's metaphoric or symbolic style, seen at its height in *Intolerance* (1916) and *Broken Blossoms* (1919), occurs in the angular perspectives of German Expressionism and the subjective camera technique of F. W. Murnau and Karl Freund as described in Chapter 4.

Griffith began other technical innovations at Biograph which seem decidedly minor by comparison with his breakthroughs in editing and in camera movement and placement, but which are important nonetheless. For one thing, he perfected the dissolve and the fade, both very crude transitional devices derived from Méliès before Griffith rendered them more fluid. Since the twenties, dissolves and fades have been synthetically processed in a machine called an **optical printer,** but in Griffith's time they were all accomplished in the camera. The scene which was to dissolve *out* was shot through a slowly closing lens diaphragm; then the film was stopped and rewound, and the scene which was to dissolve *in* was shot over the prior scene with the diaphragm slowly opening at the same speed. The **fade-in** and the **fade-out,** used by Griffith for the first time to begin and end film narratives, were accomplished by performing the same two processes separately. (Diaphragms, at this point, did not shut down completely and left a small open circle in the center of the frame which cameramen had to eliminate by cupping their hands over the lenses.)* Griffith perfected the dissolve and the fade, like so many other devices he brought to general recognition, simply by exercising more care in their achievement than earlier directors had done. Indeed, aside from his cinematic genius, Griffith's greatest attribute as a filmmaker was his compulsion to take everything about the cinema seriously once he had cast his lot with it. Many of his "discoveries" were not discoveries at all but

---

See Anthony Slide, *The Big V: A History of the Vitagraph Company,* rev. ed. (Metuchen, N.J.: Scarecrow, 1987).

* David Bordwell and Kristin Thompson point out that in 1918 an automatic shutter device was introduced that permitted cinematographers to fully close down their shutter apertures with the camera running and achieve nearly flawless fades ("Toward a Scientific Film History?" *Quarterly Review of Film Studies* 10, 3 [Summer 1985]: 234). By facilitating in-camera fades and dissolves, the automatic shutter virtually eliminated the iris as a transitional device after 1919, although Griffith continued to use it well into the twenties.

simply the result of bestowing a degree of care on operations which earlier directors had performed in a slapdash manner.

Several innovations do belong solely to Griffith or to the Griffith-Bitzer
collaboration. These include the flashback, the **iris shot,** the **mask,** the
systematic use of the **split screen** and the **soft-focus.** Like the dissolve and
the fade, these devices were all essentially *graphic* embellishments, and
today they are little used except by way of allusion to the Griffith era;
but we shall soon see how important they were in creating the rich visual
texture of *The Birth of a Nation* at a time when they were uncommon.

GRIFFITH'S DRIVE FOR INCREASED FILM LENGTH

Griffith's apprenticeship, as his Biograph period is often called, reached
its peak in 1911 when he was offered his third contract at the extravagant salary of seventy-five dollars a week plus royalties and when he
finally changed his working name back from Lawrence to David Wark
(D. W.) Griffith. The change signaled Griffith's increased pride in his
work and his new conviction that motion pictures were a significant art
form. The odd job he had taken three years earlier to keep from starving
had finally become a career. As Griffith saw his one-reelers grow increasingly popular between 1911 and 1912, he opted for narratives of greater
and greater complexity, like the tale of small-town hypocrisy, *The New
York Hat* (1912), written by Anita Loos (1893–1981), and the contemporary street drama *The Musketeers of Pig Alley* (1912), shot on location
in the streets of New York and often cited as a predecessor of Italian
neorealism. Yet, by late 1911 Griffith had begun to chafe under the constraints of the one-reel (ten- to sixteen-minute) limit. He felt that he had
exhausted the one-reel form and could continue his experiments in narrative only by increasing the length of his films. He also seems to have
understood that for the cinema to achieve the status of an art it would
have to evolve a form commensurate with that of other narrative arts,
and that such a form would have to be an expansive one which could
provide for the dynamic interplay of its own components. The idea of a
serious novel, opera, or play which takes only ten or fifteen minutes to
apprehend is ludicrous, and Griffith reasoned that the same was true of
cinema.

Accordingly, against the wishes of his employers, Griffith decided to
remake his successful one-reeler *After Many Years* (1908) as the two-reel
Enoch Arden in late 1911. Griffith had attempted a two-reeler in 1910
(*His Trust*), but Biograph had titled each reel separately and released
them both as separate films. After the completion of *Enoch Arden,* the
studio tried to do the same thing by releasing the film in two parts, but
the public, through the film's exhibitors, demanded the full version, and
Biograph ultimately yielded. In an ironic turnabout the following year,
Biograph actively encouraged Griffith to make two-reelers instead of the

3.6 An iris shot of Lillian Gish, from *The Birth of a Nation* (1915).

3.7 *The Musketeers of Pig Alley* (1912): Lillian and Dorothy Gish. Note the depth of the image.

standard product in order to compete with an increase in two-reel films from domestic and European producers. This pleased Griffith well enough for a time, and in 1912 he made three two-reel films in California (in addition to many others) which prepared both him and his audience for his 1913 feature *Judith of Bethulia*.

The first of these was *Man's Genesis* (remade the following year as *The Wars of the Primal Tribes*, or *Brute Force*), which the Biograph catalogue describes as "a psychological study founded upon the Darwinian theory of the Evolution of Man." While its allegorical account of intelligence triumphing over brute strength in prehistoric times is simplistic by contemporary standards, *Man's Genesis* was unique for its day.* In the same year, Griffith also made *The Massacre*, which Lewis Jacobs has called "America's first spectacle film." This two-reeler offered a historical reconstruction of a wagon-train massacre with overtones of Custer's Last Stand, and it presented Griffith with his greatest technical challenge to date. Nevertheless, its large-scale battle scenes look forward to those of *The Birth of a Nation* in their fluid editing continuity and their striking photographic composition, and Griffith had reason to expect that *The Massacre* would be hailed as a great achievement. Instead, it was barely noticed, for in the interim between the film's production and its release, *Queen Elizabeth* and other *films d'art* had come to America and touched off "feature fever" in a market once solely geared to shorts.

Except for its relative length, Griffith saw little to admire in *Queen Elizabeth*, a filmed play which contained only twenty-three separate shots in its entire fifty-three-minute running time. (Griffith's one-reel *The Sands*

---

* It later inspired Hal Roach's *One Million* B.C. (Hal Roach, Jr., 1940), for which Griffith served as technical advisor and probably directed some of the special effects. The Roach film was remade by Britain's Hammer Studios as *One Million Years* B.C. (Don Chaffey, 1966), with special effects by Ray Harryhausen.

of Dee, produced concurrently with *Queen Elizabeth,* used sixty-eight separate shots in less than ten minutes.) But he did not like being upstaged, and immediately began production of what he hoped would be a new masterpiece, *The Mothering Heart,* a contemporary melodrama whose extravagant budget was a source of deep concern to Biograph's president, J. J. Kennedy. Before the film was finished, however, Italy's spectacular *Quo vadis?* arrived in America, and *The Mothering Heart* fell into obscurity while audiences stood in line, naturally enough, to see the longest and most expensive motion picture ever made. Griffith was beside himself, for now he had been not only upstaged but outclassed. *Quo vadis?* was scarcely innovative in terms of its narrative technique and today looks archaic next to Griffith's more sophisticated two-reelers, but it was the elaborate, big-budget feature that he had longed to make for the past two years. Now he was determined to best his new European rivals; he set to work frenetically upon a lavish new production which he vowed would clinch his title as supreme master of the cinema.

JUDITH OF BETHULIA AND THE MOVE TO MUTUAL

It is uncertain whether or not Griffith had actually seen *Quo vadis?* when he began shooting *Judith of Bethulia* in the secrecy of Chatsworth Park, California, in June 1913, but he had read enough about the film in the trade press to know that its essence was epic spectacle. Griffith's own film was based on a story from the Apocrypha about the Bethulian widow Judith, who feigned love for the Assyrian conqueror Holofernes in order to assassinate him and save her besieged city. The film was budgeted at eighteen thousand dollars, a very large sum for its day, but Griffith ended up spending more than twice that amount in his compulsive quest for dramatic authenticity and grandeur of scale. A substantial portion of the film's budget was spent rehearsing elaborate battle sequences on the twelve-

3.8 *The Massacre* (1912).

3.9 *Judith of Bethulia* (1913).

mile-square set at Chatsworth, which housed, among other wonders, a full-scale reconstruction of Bethulia. Griffith's penchant for accuracy of detail in costuming and production design accounted for another large chunk of the budget. But the most expensive aspect of the film was its length: Griffith shot enough film to make *Judith of Bethulia* a feature-length epic, editing it later into four reels.

This film represents the summation of Griffith's Biograph career. Like that of *Intolerance,* its complex story is divided into four contrapuntal movements and employs nearly every narrative device Griffith had discovered or perfected in his five years with the studio. Nevertheless, the economy of the film's narrative development is often quite remarkable given the sophistication of its technique. As spectacle, *Judith of Bethulia* moved beyond anything seen on the screen to date, with its mass scenes of sieges, open-field battles, and chariot charges; and yet, as in Griffith's later masterpieces, the personal drama of the protagonists is never lost amid the epic scale of the action. Despite occasional lapses of taste (the pseudo-orgiastic dance of the Fish Maidens, for example), *Judith of Bethulia* is the most ambitious American film made before 1914. As Jacobs has remarked, "Even if Griffith had done nothing further than *Judith of Bethulia,* he would still be considered a sensitive and outstanding crafts-man."

Griffith's employers at Biograph, however, were stunned at their director's extravagance and audacity, and they resolved to take action against him. When Griffith returned to New York with a six-reel assembly print of *Judith of Bethulia,* Biograph vice-president and general manager Henry Marvin informed him that he had been "promoted" to production chief of the studio, from which position he would supervise the work of other directors but not direct films or handle budgets himself. Moreover, caught up in the *film d'art* craze produced by *Queen Elizabeth,* Biograph had signed an ill-fated contract with the theatrical producers Klaw and Erlanger to film their stage plays as five-reel features. The meaning of Griffith's new "promotion" was all too clear: he could stay at Biograph only if he would agree to supervise his former assistants in the mechanical reproduction of stage plays. This was impossible for him, and so he let it be known among the independent producers that he was looking for a new job.

Because his Biograph shorts had come to epitomize successful film craftsmanship in the American industry, Griffith was almost immediately offered fifty thousand dollars a year by Adolph Zukor, but he turned it down because he rightly saw that Zukor's company would offer him no more creative freedom than Biograph had. More to his liking was the proposition of Harry E. Aitken (1870–1956), the president of a new film distributing company called Mutual, to come to work for his subsidiary firm of Reliance-Majestic as an independent producer-director at a salary of fifty-two thousand dollars per year. Aitken promised to let Griffith make two independent feature films a year, in addition to the conventional program features he would be required to direct under his contract, and Griffith accepted the offer without hesitation. On December 3,

3.10 D. W. Griffith's advertisement for himself.

3.11 Bitzer and Girffith examining a shot on the set of Biograph's *The Avenging Conscience* (1913) shortly before their departure from the company.

1913, Griffith announced his departure from Biograph in an advertisement in the *New York Dramatic Mirror* which modestly proclaimed him to be "Producer of all great Biograph successes, revolutionizing Motion Picture drama and founding the modern technique of the art." The advertisement went on to enumerate, with some exaggeration, his specific technical contributions to the form ("the large or close-up figures, distant views, . . . the 'switch-back,' sustained suspense, the 'fade out,' and restraint in expression") and to list 151 of his most important and successful Biograph films from *The Adventures of Dollie* through the still unreleased *Judith of Bethulia*. In this manner, Griffith publicly and legitimately laid claim to the hundreds of films he had directed for Biograph in almost complete anonymity between 1908 and 1913; but more important was the fact that the man who had once been so ashamed of working for the "living pictures" now proclaimed himself to be the founding father of the narrative cinema and its first great personal artist or, to borrow a term from contemporary criticism, its first great *auteur*.

Griffith took with him to Mutual/Reliance-Majestic most of the stock company of ensemble players he had built up during the years at Biograph, but his brilliant and invaluable cameraman, Billy Bitzer, at first refused to follow him on the grounds that there was more security in working for a Patents Company member than for an independent. After several months, however, Bitzer was finally persuaded to join Griffith as his director of photography. He was to stay with Griffith throughout his career and to work on at least twenty-four of the thirty-five feature films he made between 1914 and 1931. With this, the Griffith company was once again complete and ready to embark upon the production of two of the most important and influential motion pictures ever made.*

THE BIRTH OF A NATION

Production

Before he turned to his first independent project in late 1914, Griffith took his company to Hollywood and hurried through four minor program features† for Reliance-Majestic, one of which, a potboiler entitled *The Battle of the Sexes,* was shot in four days. Griffith nevertheless insisted that Mutual's president, Harry Aitken, promote each film with expensive advance publicity and rent a Broadway legitimate theater for its opening. Griffith had become so committed to cinema that even the reception of his potboilers was of serious concern to him. But he was still haunted by

---

* After Griffith and his company left Biograph, the production company rapidly declined, and in 1915 it was liquidated.

† In recent years, one of these—*The Avenging Conscience* (1914), adapted from Poe's "The Tell-Tale Heart"—has been reappraised as an important avatar of surrealism. See, e.g., Vlada Petrić, "Griffith's *The Avenging Conscience:* An Early Dream Film," *Film Criticism* 6, 2 (Winter 1982): 5–27.

the success of the Italian superspectacles, and he sought everywhere for an epic subject that would enable him at last to rival them. He found it when one of his writers, Frank E. Woods, told him about a failed attempt to film a play entitled *The Clansman*. The play, adapted by southern-born clergyman Thomas E. Dixon, Jr., from his best-selling novel, was the story of a Confederate soldier's return to his ravaged home in South Carolina after the Civil War and his role there in organizing the Ku Klux Klan.* Both novel and play were decidedly mediocre as literature and openly racist in their depiction of the Reconstruction period as one in which renegade mulatto "carpetbaggers" and Negro thugs joined with unscrupulous white politicians to destroy the social fabric of the South. Yet this material had a natural fascination for Griffith, whose romantic image of the South and the Civil War had stayed with him since childhood. In fact, some of his most spectacular Biograph films had dealt with incidents from the Civil War, and now he seized the opportunity to do a feature-length epic on the subject.

Aitken was induced to buy the screen rights to the story from Dixon for $10,000,† and Griffith and Woods collaborated on a loose scenario, supplementing *The Clansman* with material from another Dixon book, *The Leopard's Spots,* and with Griffith's own idealized vision of the South. When they were done, the story covered not only the Reconstruction period but the years immediately preceding the Civil War and the war itself. The film was initially budgeted by Aitken at $40,000, or four times the usual rate for a conventional feature, but as Griffith became more and more obsessed with the project that figure grew until it nearly tripled. By the time the film was completed at a cost of $110,000, Griffith's entire personal fortune, including his weekly paychecks, had been pumped into the enterprise, along with the savings of many associates and friends.

Shooting began in total secrecy in late 1914, and, despite the rough scenario put together with Woods, Griffith worked wholly without a written script. Through six weeks of rehearsal and nine weeks of shooting—a remarkable schedule in an era when most features were cranked out in less than a month—Griffith carried around in his head every detail of the editing **continuity**, titles, settings, costumes, and props. So personal an undertaking was his Civil War epic that no one involved in the production but Griffith had any clear idea of what the film was about. The cast and crew were astonished at the number of camera set-ups he would demand for a single scene, and no one could imagine how the director intended to assemble into a single film the thousands of separate shots he

---

*Woods, who was also an editor of *Motion Picture News*, had worked briefly for the Kinemacolor Company (see Chapter 7), which in 1911 had commissioned William Haddock to shoot some experimental color footage of the play. According to Michael Pitts in *Hollywood and American History* (Jefferson, N.C.: McFarland & Co., 1984), Kinemacolor intended to use this footage to mount a feature-length adaptation of *The Clansman* that was subsequently abandoned but that became the source of Griffith's inspiration via Woods.

†Dixon accepted a $2,500 down payment and later opted for a percentage of the film's profits rather than the $7,500 balance, whereby he became very rich.

was taking. As Lillian Gish wrote of the filming: "We were rarely assigned parts, and the younger members of the company always rehearsed for the older members when the story was being developed, as all the 'writing' was done by Griffith as he moved groups of characters around. . . . When the story was ready to go before the camera, the older players . . . came forward and acted the parts they had been watching us rehearse for them. . . . Very often we would play episodes without knowing the complete story. . . . Only Griffith knew the continuity of *The Birth of a Nation* in its final form." Griffith did indeed have a grand design for his film, because he was quite consciously involved in creating "the greatest picture ever made," but this should not obscure the fact that he was a great *practical* genius whose finest effects were often improvised on the set to meet some specific requirement of the narrative or the shooting process.

Originally composed of over 1,544 separate shots—in an era in which the most sophisticated of foreign spectacles contained fewer than 100—*The Clansman* (as it was initially called) took Griffith some three months to edit and **score**. When the job was done, he had achieved on a vast scale the nearly total integration of every narrative technique he had ever used and, in collaboration with the composer Joseph Carl Breil* (1870–1926), had synthesized an orchestral score from the music of Grieg, Wagner, Tchaikovsky, Beethoven, Liszt, Rossini, Verdi, and American folk and period songs (e.g., "Dixie," "Marching Through Georgia"), which dramatically paralleled the editing continuity of the film. He had also produced the longest (twelve reels) and most expensive ($110,000) motion picture yet made in America, and because of its length the existing exchanges refused to distribute it. Griffith and Aitken were forced to form their own company, the Epoch Producing Corporation, to handle distribution of *The Clansman* amid widespread predictions that Griffith's "audacious monstrosity," as one MPPC member called it, would be a box-office disaster.† But within five years of its opening, Griffith's "monstrosity" would return more than fifteen million dollars.

The Clansman had its premiere on February 8, 1915, at Clune's audi-

---

*Breil had composed scores for the American versions of *Queen Elizabeth* (1912) and *Cabiria* (1914), and he later collaborated with Griffith to score *Intolerance* (1916), *The White Rose* (1923), and *America* (1924). In 1930, Griffith and Breil collaborated to produce a considerably shortened sonorized version of *The Birth of a Nation* with full orchestral accompaniment.

†The film was opened at first-class legitimate theaters in all of the major cities to garner publicity and two-dollar admissions (a marketing strategy later known as "road showing") and then distributed to small towns and cities on a "states' rights" basis. In this latter arrangement, regional distributors would buy the exclusive rights to control exhibition of the film in a given state or group of states, with Epoch receiving a percentage of the box-office grosses. In *D. W. Griffith: His Life and Work* (New York: Oxford University Press, 1972), Robert M. Henderson points out that Aitken's failure to set up an accurate accounting system for the states' rights returns (which he wrongly thought would be small) caused Mutual to lose millions of dollars in concealed profits to regional distributors (pp. 158–59). Operating as the states' rights distributor for Massachusetts, Louis B. Mayer alone made as much as one million dollars in rake-offs from *The Birth of a Nation* (a fortune which would later enable him to become the driving force behind Metro-Goldwyn-Mayer) before the film was legally banned.

torium in Los Angeles, and its first public opening on March 3, 1915, at the Liberty Theater in New York, where it was retitled *The Birth of a Nation* and ran for an unprecedented forty-eight consecutive weeks. At Aitken's insistence, it was the first film ever to command the two-dollar admission price of the legitimate theater, and its phenomenal popularity made it one of the top-grossing films of all time. By 1948, *The Birth of a Nation* had been seen in theaters by an estimated 150 million people all over the world and, according to trade legend, had grossed nearly forty-eight million dollars, or more than any film made anywhere in the world up to that time.* From its very first screening in Los Angeles, the critics were unanimous in their praise of the film's technical brilliance. As the trade paper *Variety* remarked on March 12, 1915, "Daily newspapers pronounced it the last word in picture-making," and for a while it seemed that no critical hyperbole was too strong to describe Griffith's achievement. "Epoch-making" and "prestigious" were the terms most frequently applied to his film, and after a special White House screening (the first of its kind), President Woodrow Wilson, who was himself a professional historian, is reputed to have said, "It is like writing history with lightning."

But the film's extraordinary success was marred by controversy and scandal. Several weeks after the New York opening, Griffith yielded to pressure from the National Association for the Advancement of Colored People (NAACP, founded in 1908) and city officials to cut the film's most blatantly racist sequences. He grudgingly removed some 558 feet, reducing the total number of shots from 1,544 to 1,375. This excised material has never been recovered, but it apparently included scenes of white women being sexually attacked by renegade blacks as well as an epilogue suggesting that the solution to America's racial problems was the deportation of the Negroes to Africa. No sooner had Griffith made this compromise than historians, President Wilson notwithstanding, began to assail his distorted view of Reconstruction; and prominent citizens and community leaders such as the president of Harvard University, Jane Addams of Hull House, and the editors of progressive urban weeklies started to attack *The Birth of a Nation* for its racial bigotry and to demand its suppression. Oswald Garrison Villard, the editor of the *Nation*, called the film "improper, immoral, and injurious—a deliberate attempt to humiliate ten million American citizens and portray them as nothing but beasts," and the governor of Massachusetts attempted to have the film banned throughout the state after a race riot at its Boston premiere. Riots also occurred when the film opened in Chicago and Atlanta, where it was directly instrumental in the birth of the modern Ku Klux Klan. So extreme was the antagonism created by Griffith's epic that it was ultimately refused licenses for exhibition in Connecticut, Illinois, Kansas, Massachusetts, Minnesota, New Jersey, Wisconsin, and Ohio; and President Wilson was

---

* According to *Variety*'s Seventy-fourth Anniversary edition for January 9, 1980, the true figure is closer to ten million dollars. But the business practices described in the preceding note suggest that the actual grosses far exceeded those reported by regional distributors.

forced to retract his praise publicly and to suggest that the film had used its brilliant technique in the service of specious ends.*

Griffith was shocked and deeply injured by the unexpectedly hostile reaction to *The Birth of a Nation*. From his point of view, he had struggled for a full year against nearly insurmountable odds to bring forth what he considered to be not only "the greatest picture ever made" but a great epic of the American nation. The widespread public attacks upon his film seemed to him like attacks upon American civilization itself, and he struck back by publishing a pamphlet, *The Rise and Fall of Free Speech in America*, which vigorously defended *The Birth of a Nation* against censorship by attacking the practice itself, but which offered no answers to the specific charges of racism. The charges were in fact unanswerable, for race was central to Griffith's interpretation of American history.

Epics are concerned with the origins of races, and the "nation" born out of Griffith's epic was quite clearly White America. It may be true, as a recent biographer has remarked, that Griffith's "racial bias was almost totally unconscious," but regional conditioning had so perverted his understanding of American history that his film became in many ways a pseudohistorical tract whose collective hero is the "Aryan" race (Griffith's term). In another sense, though, Griffith was simply confirming the stereotypes of his age, for *The Birth of a Nation* accurately incarnates the myth of Reconstruction propagated by politicians and historians alike in the late nineteenth and early twentieth centuries. The social economist and philosopher Thorstein Veblen remarked, after viewing the film in 1915, "Never before have I seen such concise misinformation"; but much of the misinformation contained in *The Birth of a Nation* belonged to an entire generation of Americans. If Griffith distorted history, then so did Woodrow Wilson in his five-volume *History of the American People* (1902), written while he was president of Princeton University, which in Volume V tells pretty much the same story as *The Birth of a Nation*, even to the point of spelling "negro" with a small "n"—a practice for which Griffith is still vilified.

In its monumental scale, in its concentration upon a crucial moment in American history, in its mixture of historical and invented characters, in its constant narrative movement between the epochal and the human, and, most significantly, in its chillingly accurate vision of an American society predicated on race, *The Birth of a Nation* is a profoundly *American* epic. We can fault Griffith for badly distorting the historical facts of Reconstruction, for unconscionably stereotyping the American Negro as

---

*The banning of *The Birth of a Nation* in Ohio led to the 1915 U.S. Supreme Court decision known as *Mutual Film Corporation v. Industrial Commission of Ohio*, or simply *Mutual v. Ohio*, which held that the exhibition of motion pictures was "a business pure and simple, originated and conducted for profit, like other spectacles, not to be regarded . . . as part of the press of the country or as organs [sic] of public opinion" (*Banned Films: Movies, Censors and the First Amendment*, ed. Edward de Grazia and Roger K. Newman [New York: Bowker, 1982], p. 5). This ruling effectively denied First Amendment protection to motion pictures as a form of expression and left them legally vunerable to censorship for the next thirty-seven years, until the Court reversed itself in *The Miracle* decision of 1952 (see "The Scrapping of the Production Code," pp. 535–37, in Chapter 12).

3.12 A classically structured Griffith battle sequence from *The Birth of a Nation*, moving from extreme long shot to long shot to medium shot to close shot: Henry B. Walthall as Ben Cameron.

either fool or brute, and for glorifying a terrorist organization like the Klan, but we cannot quarrel with his basic assumption that American society was, and is, profoundly racist.

Structure

The Birth of a Nation tells the story of the American Civil War and its aftermath from a southern point of view, treating, as an **intertitle** states, "the agony which the South endured that a nation might be born." It is well to remember that the events it depicts were recent history to the audiences of 1915, only fifty years distant. Like Griffith himself, many persons seeing the film in the year of its release knew intimate details of the war from parents who had survived it, and the political and social divisions produced by the conflict still ran very deep.

The film begins with a prologue explaining that the seeds of the tragedy were sown not by the South but by the seventeenth-century New England traders who first brought the slaves to America and who, ironically, Griffith claims, were the ancestors of the nineteenth-century abolitionists. There follows a brief prewar interlude in which two northern boys, both sons of the powerful abolitionist senator Austin Stoneman (modeled on Thaddeus Stevens, Republican congressman from Pennsylvania and leader of the radical Reconstructionists in the House of Representatives), visit their former boarding-school friends, the Cameron brothers, on the family's modest plantation in Piedmont, South Carolina. During this idyll, which is intended to show the grace and charm of southern culture as well as the general beneficence of plantation life, Phil Stoneman falls in love with the Cameron daughter, Margaret, while young Ben Cameron discovers his ideal of feminine beauty in a daguerreotype of Phil's sister, Elsie. Immediately following the visit, civil war breaks out, and both the northern and southern brothers heed the call to arms of their respective governments.

The next portion of *The Birth of a Nation* deals with the war itself and is very nearly self-contained. It is this part of the film which most truly merits the description "epic," for it combines a sophisticated narration of historical events with spectacle on a colossal scale. From the moment the Piedmont regiment marches off gaily and naïvely to its first battle, to the assassination of President Lincoln at Ford's Theater, we are swept along on a narrative current so forceful and hypnotic that it is impossible even today to escape its attraction. The siege of Petersburg, the burning of Atlanta, and Sherman's march to the sea are all recreated in battle scenes whose intensity is still compelling, despite seven decades of technological refinement. Griffith and Bitzer composed these scenes after Mathew Brady's Civil War photographs and shot them from many different perspectives, combining extreme long shots of the battlefields with medium and close shots of bloody hand-to-hand fighting to evoke the chaotic violence of combat itself. Griffith increased the tension of these sequences by radically varying the duration of each shot and by cutting on contrary movements: at one point in the Battle of Petersburg, Griffith cuts from a group of Confederate soldiers charging across the screen from the left side of the frame to a band of Union soldiers charging across from the right, while a third cut shows their ferocious head-on collision on the field. For the burning of Atlanta sequence, Griffith used a diagonally split screen containing blazing buildings in the upper half and Sherman's relentlessly marching troops in the lower half, all illuminated by bursting shells and flames (according to Bitzer, the only artificially lit sequence in the film).

Griffith continues the personal story of the Stonemans and the Camerons against this panoramic overview of the Civil War. The families' two youngest sons die in each other's arms on the battlefield; and Ben Cameron, the "little Colonel," is wounded and captured by federal troops after leading a daring charge against the Union lines at Petersburg. Meanwhile, in the South, a band of renegade Negro militiamen ransacks the Cameron homestead in Piedmont, leaving the family with little but their lives, and Atlanta is destroyed as Sherman marches to the sea. Griffith renders the devastating impact of this march in a striking iris shot. A small iris at the upper left-hand corner of the frame gradually opens to disclose a sorrowful mother with her children gathered about her on a hillside. As the iris opens further, the source of the woman's misery is revealed to be Sherman's troops marching like columns of black ants through the valley below: cause and effect are thus dramatically and visually linked.*

Concurrently, in a Union military hospital in Washington, D.C., Ben Cameron finally meets Elsie Stoneman, who nurses him back to health in her capacity as a volunteer. Mrs. Cameron soon joins her son in the hospital when she learns that he is under a death sentence for guerrilla activities, and she successfully intercedes for his life with a reverently portrayed President Lincoln. Despite their sentimentality, the detailed composition in depth of these hospital scenes, whose action in foreground, middleground, and background is autonomous, has long impressed critics with its verisimilitude. Equally authentic is the reconstruction of the Confederate surrender at Appomatox which follows—one of the several effective "historical facsimiles" that Griffith introduced from time to time into the narrative. As the war ends, the Camerons begin to rebuild their ravaged home, and Ben returns to Piedmont in a moving and understated homecoming scene.

In Washington, Phil and Elsie Stoneman attend a performance of *Our American Cousin* at Ford's Theater and witness the assassination of President Lincoln. Since the assassination sequence is one of Griffith's great

3.13   The wounded Ben Cameron is carried across the Union lines in Petersburg.

3.14   Sherman marches to the sea.

3.15   The surrender at Appomattox, an "historical facsimile" from *The Birth of a Nation:* Howard Gaye as Lee, Donald Crisp as Grant.

3.16   The homecoming.

---

* In his autobiography, *Billy Bitzer: His Story* (New York, 1973), Bitzer says that the mother and children were an actual family group which happened to stop along the hillside while the crew was setting up the Sherman's march sequence below. Griffith ordered him to sneak up the hill and shoot them unawares. This shot was later combined with the long shot of the marching troops through matting to create the single iris shot composition described above. As Bitzer comments, it was touches like this "that made *The Birth* so real and convincing to audiences accustomed to stilted acting and stock shots, especially in costume movies" (p. 108). It is worth noting here that the site of Griffith's famous battle scenes is now part of Forest Lawn Cemetery.

set pieces and provides an excellent example of his continuity editing, it is worth examining in some detail. The following excerpt from the script of the film prepared by Theodore Huff for MoMA illustrates Griffith's brilliant use of parallel editing to achieve tension in the scene:

TITLE
The gala performance to celebrate the surrender of Lee, attended by the President and staff.
THE YOUNG STONEMANS PRESENT.
An historical facsimile of Ford's Theater as on that night, exact in size and detail with the recorded incidents, after Nicolay and Hay in *Lincoln, a History*.   24 feet*

SCENE 444
Iris-in to circle bottom of screen
Elsie and her brother come to seats—speak to acquaintances—*Iris opens to full screen to long shot of theater (from above one side showing stage 1—orchestra, boxes, gallery, etc.)*   18 feet

SCENE 445
Semi-close-up of Phil and Elsie
She looks through her opera glasses.   3 feet

TITLE
"The play: *Our American Cousin*, starring Laura Keene."   4 feet

SCENE 446
As 444
The painted curtain rises—maid dusting table.   7 feet

SCENE 447
Medium-long shot of stage
Star enters grandly.   3 feet

SCENE 448
As 446
Star bows to audience's applause.   4½ feet

SCENE 449
As 445
Elsie with fan—applauds—smiles at brother.   6 feet

SCENE 450
As 447
Star blows kisses to audience—bows.   3½ feet.

SCENE 451
As 448
Star comes forward to footlights—receives flowers—applause— 9 feet

TITLE
"Time, 8:30
The arrival of the President, Mrs. Lincoln, and party."   4½ feet

---

* "The figure at the right of each scene is the footage; it also can be taken as the number of seconds the scene lasts. When scenes were under three feet, they were measured exactly—the figure in parentheses being the number of *frames*. Thus 2 (4) means two feet plus four frames, or a total of thirty-six frames (sixteen frames per foot-second)" [*Preface to the script*].

SCENE 452
Three-quarter shot of stairs back of box (sides rounded)
Stairs dark and shadowy—guard leads man, two women, and Lincoln
    up stairs. 8 feet

SCENE 453
Medium shot of theater box
First of party enter. 3 feet

SCENE 454
As 452
Lincoln hands hat and coat to man—enters box door right. 5 feet

SCENE 455
As 453
Lincoln comes forward in box. 4½ feet

SCENE 456
Semi-close-up of Phil and Elsie
They see Lincoln—applaud—rise. 6 feet

SCENE 457
Long shot of theater
Audience standing up, cheering. 2½ feet

SCENE 458
As 453
Lincoln bows. 2 (6)

SCENE 459
As 457
Audience cheering. 2½ feet

SCENE 460
As 458
Lincoln and party sit down. 6½ feet

TITLE
"Mr. Lincoln's personal bodyguard takes his post outside the presi-
    dential box." 6 feet

SCENE 461
Three-quarter shot of hall back of box (corners rounded)
Guard enters—sits in chair in front of box door. 10½ feet

SCENE 462
As 459
Audience still standing—play tries to go on— 4 feet

SCENE 463
As 460
The box—President and Mrs. Lincoln bowing. 8 feet

SCENE 464
Medium-long shot of audience and box (corners soft)
Cheers—waving handkerchiefs. 3 feet

SCENE 465
Medium shot of stage
Old-style footlights—painted scenery—people leave stage—couple
    alone, come forward—spotlight follows them. 9 feet

TITLE
"To get a view of the play, the bodyguard leaves his post." 2 (10)

SCENE 466
Medium shot of hall, rear of box (edges rounded)
Guard tries to see play. 3½ feet

SCENE 467
Medium shot of stage 3 feet

SCENE 468
As 466
Guard gets up—opens rear door to gallery. 6½ feet

SCENE 469
Long shot of theater   Iris-up toward boxes and gallery
Guard comes. 3 feet

SCENE 470
Medium shot of gallery (circle)
The guard seats himself at edge. 4 feet

TITLE
"Time, 10:13
Act III, scene 2" 2 feet

SCENE 471
Long shot of theater   Iris at upper right corner of screen
The gallery—man in shadows. 4 feet

SCENE 472
Semi-close-up of Phil and Elsie
Watching play—Elsie laughing behind fan—points with fan to man in
        balcony—asks who he is. 7 feet

TITLE
"John Wilkes Booth." (14)

SCENE 473
Semi-close-up of Booth (circle iris)
(Napoleon pose) in the shadows of gallery. 2 (2)

SCENE 474
As 472
Elsie is amused by his mysterious appearance—laughs behind fan—
        looks at him through opera glasses. 6 feet

SCENE 475
As 473
Booth waiting. 2 (3)

SCENE 476
Medium-long shot of gallery and audience (sides rounded)
Booth waiting 5½ feet

SCENE 477
As 475
Booth waiting. 4 feet

SCENE 478
Medium shot of stage play
Comedy line—man waves arms. 3½ feet

SCENE 479
Medium shot of Lincoln's box

They laugh—Lincoln feels draught—reaches for shawl.   6½ feet

SCENE 480
As 477
Booth watches.   3 feet

SCENE 481
As 479
The box—Lincoln drawing shawl around shoulders.   5½ feet

SCENE 482
Long shot of theater as 471   Iris opens
Booth goes to box door.   5 feet

SCENE 483
Medium shot (circle)
Guard in gallery—Booth opens door behind him.   1 (7)

SCENE 484
Medium shot of hall back of box (corners softened)
Heavy shadows—Booth enters softly—closes and locks door—peeks
    through keyhole at box door—stands up majestically—pulls out
    pistol—tosses head back—actor-like—   12½ feet

SCENE 485
Close-up of pistol (circle vignette)
He cocks it.   3 feet

SCENE 486
As 484
Booth comes forward—opens door to box—enters.   9 feet

SCENE 487
The box as 479
Booth creeps in behind Lincoln.   4½ feet

SCENE 488
The play as 478
The comic chases woman out—cheers.   4 feet

3.17   **The assassination of Lincoln: Raoul Walsh as
Booth, Joseph Henabery as Lincoln.**

SCENE 489
Medium shot of box
Lincoln is shot—Booth jumps from left side of box.   4½ feet

SCENE 490
Long shot of theater
Booth jumps on stage—shouts.   2½ feet

TITLE
"Sic semper tyrannis!"   2 feet

SCENE 491
Medium shot of Booth on stage
Holds arms out—limps back quickly.   3 feet

SCENE 492
Medium shot of box
Lincoln slumped down—Mrs. Lincoln calls for help.   2 (6)

SCENE 493
Semi-close-up of Phil and Elsie
They hardly realize what has happened—rise.   4½ feet

SCENE 494
Long shot of theater
Audience standing up in turmoil—Elsie in foreground faints—Phil
     supports her—   4 feet

SCENE 495
As 492
Man climbs up into box to Lincoln's aid.   5 feet

SCENE 496
Medium-long shot of theater and boxes
Audience agitated.   3½ feet

SCENE 497
Long shot of excited throng
Phil and Elsie leave.
Fade-out   11½ feet

SCENE 498
Medium shot of box
They carry Lincoln out.
Fade-out   10½ feet

3.18 In Piedmont, the Camerons learn of Lincoln's death: Ben, Flora (Mae Marsh), Dr. Cameron (Spottiswoode Aitken), Mrs. Cameron (Josephine Crowell), and Margaret (Miriam Cooper).

The sequence is composed of fifty-five shots, some held for only a few seconds; it establishes dynamic *visual* relationships among Lincoln, Booth, the bodyguard, the audience, and the play long before their *dramatic* relationship is energized by the assassination. One has only to imagine how a Porter or a Zecca might have handled this sequence in a single shot or perhaps several to understand the breadth of Griffith's achievement.

Lincoln's assassination, much lamented in the South, concludes the "War" section of *The Birth of a Nation* and inaugurates the most controversial part of the film—that dealing with Reconstruction. This section opens with the ascendancy of Senator Austin Stoneman to "the power behind the throne" after Lincoln's death. Determined, as a title informs us, to crush "the White South under the heel of the Black South" (a phrase from Wilson's *History of the American People,* incidentally, and not an invention of Griffith's), Stoneman leads the radical Reconstructionists to victory in Congress and sends his fawning but secretly ambitious mulatto protégé, Silas Lynch, to Piedmont to administer a program of universal Negro suffrage there. Lynch and his lieutenants, however, organize the recently freed slaves into a mob, and commit a series of outrages against the white community ranging from mere insult to bogus imprisonment and sexual assault.

3.19 Griffith's version of the South Carolina legislature.

Lynch subsequently becomes lieutenant governor of South Carolina and goes on to preside over a moronic all-Negro legislature which enacts statutes providing for the disenfranchisement of prominent whites and for interracial marriage. One of Griffith's most masterful uses of the dissolve appears in the state legislature scene. He opens it with a still photograph of the actual chambers and slowly dissolves to a replica of the hall swarming with raucous, gin-swilling Negro solons. The sequence concludes with a revoltingly effective iris-in. After the legislature has enacted its racial intermarriage bill, an iris begins to slowly close upon a group of Negroes on the assembly floor who are leering at something above them; then the iris moves like the lens of a telescope to reveal the object of this lustful attention: a group of frightened white women and children in the gallery.

While this travesty is enacted in the state capital, back in Piedmont Ben Cameron decides that the "Black Empire" of Lynch and his cronies must be combated by an "Invisible Empire" of white southern knights, organized, as a title tells us, "in defense of their Aryan birthright." This is Griffith's account of the birth of the Ku Klux Klan, and it must be said that the account is not much different from that offered by the historians of his era, including Woodrow Wilson, who wrote in the fifth volume of his *History of the American People:*

> The white men of the South were aroused by the mere instinct of self-preservation to rid themselves, by fair means or foul, of the intolerable burden of governments sustained by the votes of ignorant negroes and conducted in the interest of adventurers. . . . They could act only by private combination, by private means, as a force outside the government, hostile to it, proscribed by it, of whom opposition and bitter resistance was expected, and expected with defiance.

Meanwhile, Austin Stoneman has come to Piedmont with his family to oversee the implementation of his policies. The senator has fallen ill in the interim, however, and becomes an easy dupe of the vicious Lynch and of Stoneman's own mulatto mistress, Lydia Brown. The Elsie Stoneman–Ben Cameron and Phil Stoneman–Margaret Cameron romances start to blossom again in Piedmont but are cut short by the bitter residues of war. In one particularly striking scene, Phil proposes to Margaret, and Griffith intercuts the proposal with a flashback* to an earlier shot of her young brother lying dead on the field at Petersburg. Griffith once said,

---

* More accurately, in Bruce F. Kawin's term, a "mindscreen," or mental perspective (here, on the past) from the mind's eye of a character in the narrative—see his *Mindscreen: Bergman, Godard, and First-Person Film* (Princeton, N.J.: Princeton University Press, 1978).

"You can photograph thought," and in this flashback sequence, and many others like it sprinkled throughout *The Birth of a Nation*, he demonstrated his point remarkably well. Finally, after another wave of indignities committed by blacks against whites, the terrorist reprisals of the Klan begin in earnest, and Elsie rejects Ben when she learns of his involvement with the organization.

At this point, the film takes an extremely nasty turn as young Flora Cameron, the family's darling, is attacked (but not actually raped) and driven to take her life by Gus, a "renegade negro" who wants to marry her. Gus chases Flora through a forest and up a cliff from which she plummets to her death rather than submit to his embraces, even as brother Ben races desperately to the rescue. Filmed amid the beautiful pine forests and foothills of Big Bear Lake, California, this sequence is perhaps the most skillfully edited three-way chase Griffith ever conceived. But, like a similar sequence in Ingmar Bergman's *The Virgin Spring* (1962; see pp. 648–49), it is the most disturbing in the entire film, for there is no rational way for a viewer to defend against its wrenching images of racial violence and attempted violation. Here we see Griffith, like Eisenstein after him, a master of sensational manipulation, assaulting our sensibilities beyond the bounds of decency in order to drive home an ideological point. It is among the cinema's most compelling and horrifying sequences, as unforgettable—though by no means as forgivable—as the Odessa steps massacre in Eisenstein's *Potemkin* (1925; see pp. 162–76) and the bullet-riddled death agony of Arthur Penn's protagonists in *Bonnie and Clyde* (1967; see pp. 877–79).

After Flora's death, Gus is tracked down by the Klan and summarily executed in a scene which is dramatically apposite but morally loathsome for the legitimacy it accords the practice of lynching. The body is dumped on the lieutenant governor's doorstep as a warning, and Lynch's reply is to call out the Negro militia for a roundup of suspected Klansmen. Old Dr. Cameron, head of the family, is arrested in the process but is ultimately rescued by two "faithful" black "souls," his daughter Margaret, and Phil Stoneman (now turned against his father) and taken to the sanctuary of a small woodland cabin. Meanwhile, Elsie Stoneman attempts to intercede with Lynch on Cameron's behalf only to find herself being forced into an interracial marriage with the vicious mulatto, who has become "drunk with power and wine" (Griffith's phrase) as the troops of his "Black Empire" run amok in the streets of Piedmont, arbitrarily assaulting and killing whites.

Now the film starts to build to its climax as the Lynch-Elsie sequence is intercut with the "Summoning of the Clans" sequence in which two hooded Klansmen, or "Night Hawks," ride through the countryside far and wide, spreading news of the Piedmont rampage and sounding the call to arms. As their wild ride progresses, Klansmen are drawn to the Night Hawks like tributaries flowing into a central stream, until a vast army pours down the road to the rescue,* in the words of the poet and

3.20 Gus (Walter Long) about to be lynched by the "Invisible Empire."

3.21 The torrential ride of the Klan.

3.22 The arrival in Piedmont.

* As will be examined in Chapter 5, V. I. Pudovkin used a similar montage sequence for the climax of *Mother* (1926), in which individual workers flow together from the side streets

3.23 Ben Cameron leads a charge of liberators in a rapid backward tracking shot.

3.24 The triumphal march: Margaret Cameron, Elsie Stoneman (Lillian Gish), and friends.

critic Vachel Lindsay, like "an Anglo-Saxon Niagara." Meanwhile, Negro militiamen have discovered the cabin containing Dr. Cameron, Margaret, and Phil, and have besieged it with every intention of murdering its occupants. Shots of this action are now intercut with shots of the torrential ride of the Klan, Negroes rioting in the streets of Piedmont, and what has become by this time Lynch's impending rape of Elsie Stoneman; so that we have a suspense-filled, multi-pronged "last-minute rescue" elaborately wrought of four simultaneous actions converging toward a climax. Griffith heightens the tension of his montage by decreasing the temporal length of each shot and increasing the tempo of physical movement as the sequence races toward its crescendo. When at last the Klan arrives in town to clear the streets, there follows an action sequence that rivals the battle scenes of the war section. Its dynamic continuity cutting and breathlessly moving camera caused Vachel Lindsay to describe this episode as "tossing wildly and rhythmically like the sea."

After Piedmont is secured and Elsie Stoneman rescued from Lynch, the Klan learns of the besieged cabin in the woods and begins its second ride. Though anticlimactic, this second rescue is more urgent than the first since the band of Negroes has almost succeeded in breaking into the little stronghold when the ride begins, and danger to the principals is imminent. After a flurry of intercutting in which the Negroes finally enter the house and actually grasp Margaret Cameron by her long tresses, the Klan arrives to disperse them and save the whites from violation and / or murder. There follows a parade of the Klan and the rescued parties through the streets of Piedmont, and a new election, easily dominated by the whites. Clearly the "Black Empire" has collapsed in the face of the "Invisible Empire," as an intertitle had predicted earlier, uniting the white North

and byways of St. Petersburg into a mighty revolutionary stream heading toward the factories.

and white South "in defense of their Aryan birthright." The two Cameron-Stoneman marriages take place, and the film concludes with a symbolic epilogue in which the God of War dissolves into the Prince of Peace and the final title proclaims, somewhat prematurely: *"Liberty and union, / one and inseparable, / now and forever!"*

Impact

It should be obvious by this point that, whatever it represents ideologically, *The Birth of a Nation* is a technical marvel. Griffith created it in the absence not only of established narrative conventions but of modern cinematic technology—what he might have accomplished with **wide-screen** color cameras and **stereophonic sound** is beyond imagining.* And to have articulated these conventions and anticipated this technology in a film of epic proportions so early in the medium's history is a monumental achievement that no one can gainsay. Furthermore, in his symbolic use of objects in close-shot (inedible parched corn in the plate of a Confederate defender of Petersburg; a bird in the hands of the gentle "Little Colonel" during a rendezvous with Elsie Stoneman) and what might be called the "psychological" or "subjective" intercut (the image of Margaret Cameron's dead brother appearing during Phil Stoneman's proposal of marriage; flashbacks depicting recent Negro outrages in Piedmont as Ben Cameron narrates them to his family), Griffith moved the cinema in the direction of "symbolic realism," or the representation of reality which suggests a symbolic—i.e., a psychological or universal—meaning. Even without cutting, Griffith frequently manages to endow reality with symbolic significance. At the most rudimentary level, for example, Silas Lynch's cruelty to animals implies his capacity for evil, while Senator Stoneman's limp suggests his moral weakness and impotence. Griffith's approach to symbolic realism often degenerates into sentimentality, as when the "Little Colonel" and Elsie kiss the bird held in Ben's hand instead of each other, but his discovery and elaboration of the mode made possible the infinitely more sophisticated symbolic methods of Eisenstein and the school of Soviet montage as will be seen in Chapter 5.

The influence of *The Birth of a Nation* was not, of course, all benign. For one thing, it is a matter of historical record that the film's glowing portrait of the Ku Klux Klan was directly responsible for the modern revival and expansion of that organization, whose membership had reached five million by the time of World War II. Indeed, according to the Klan's current leaders, *The Birth of a Nation* was used as a key instrument of recruitment and indoctrination well into the 1960s. Less pernicious socially, but perhaps ultimately more destructive, was the enormous financial success of the film, which seemed to valorize Hollywood's taste for the emotional, sensational, and melodramatic as opposed to the rational, philosophical, and discursive at the very moment of its birth. As a supremely

---

*The film was in fact shot with a single camera—a three-hundred-dollar hand-cranked Pathé with two interchangeable lenses (a 2.52-inch and a wide-angle).

3.25 Sensationalistic posters, Peoria, Illinois, 1916.

manipulative film, *The Birth of a Nation* showed the American industry how effectively and lucratively the movies could pander to public frustration, anxiety, and prejudice—a lesson that Hollywood has hardly ever forgotten in its eighty-year history, as the recent crop of disaster-and-mayhem and grisly horror films demonstrates. Thus, "the man who invented Hollywood" gave that institution not only its initial direction and its emotional tenor but its first successful formula as well.

Yet, precisely because of its remarkable emotional power, its tendency to incite and inflame rather than to persuade, *The Birth of a Nation* marked the emergence of film as a potent social and political force in the modern world. As Harry M. Geduld writes:

> It was the first film to be taken seriously as a political statement and it has never failed to be regarded seriously as a "sociological document." . . . People who had previously dismissed the movies as nothing more than a crude entertainment suddenly realized that they had become the century's most potent and provocative medium of expression: the mechanized age had produced mass communications, mass entertainment, and also the possibility of mass indoctrination.

At the same time, *The Birth of a Nation* was so clearly a work of genius, however flawed, that it conferred great prestige upon the new medium of the feature film when it most needed it. The first film ever to be widely acclaimed as a great work of art and simultaneously reviled as a pernicious distortion of the truth, *The Birth of a Nation* is the cinema's seminal masterpiece, and its paradox is the paradox of cinematic narrative itself. Whereas literary narrative tells invented tales through the deliberate manipulation of verbal signs which exist at a third remove from reality, film constructs its fictions through the deliberate manipulation of photographed reality itself, so that in cinema artifice and reality become quite literally indistinguishable. Perhaps the final comment on *The Birth of a Nation* and the whole narrative tradition it founded belongs to Woodrow Wilson, despite his subsequent retraction. It was, he said, "like writing history with lightning," and lightning is powerful, illuminating, even magical. But it is also unpredictable, potentially destructive, and highly imprecise.

INTOLERANCE

Production

More persons saw *The Birth of a Nation* in the first year of its release than had seen any single film in history. Attendance in the Greater New York area alone was over 825,000, and nationally the figure was close to three million. Griffith had achieved his goal of outdoing the Italian superspectacles on their own terms, and he was universally acknowledged to be the supreme master of the screen. But his victory was mixed with bitterness. Attacks on *The Birth of a Nation*'s content continued (indeed, they have never stopped), and the accusation that he was a bigot disturbed Griffith deeply. In *The Rise and Fall of Free Speech in America* (1915), his counterblast to the film's detractors, he had declared:

> The integrity of free speech and publication was not . . . attacked seriously in this country until the arrival of the *motion picture,* when this new art was seized by the powers of intolerance as an excuse for an assault on our liberties. . . . Intolerance is the root of all censorship. Intolerance martyred Joan of Arc. Intolerance smashed the first printing press. Intolerance invented Salem witchcraft.

Early in 1916, still stinging from charges of racism, Griffith determined to produce a massive cinematic polemic against these "powers of intolerance" as they had endangered civilization throughout human history. The resulting film, *Intolerance,* was not—as is sometimes claimed—Griffith's "liberal" atonement for his "reactionary" Civil War epic but rather a spirited defense of his right to have made it. Both films are cut from the same cloth, and their liabilities and assets are quite similar.

Just after *The Birth of a Nation* was released, Griffith had gone to work on a modest contemporary melodrama entitled *The Mother and the Law.* A relatively low-budget feature by its predecessor's standards, more on the scale of *The Battle of the Sexes* (1914) than *The Birth of a Nation,* it was based upon a recent case in which Pinkerton guards had killed nineteen workers during a strike at a chemical plant. *The Mother and the Law* had already been completed when Griffith conceived the idea of combining it with three other tales into an epic exposé of intolerance through the ages. One tale would be set in ancient Babylon during the invasion and conquest of Cyrus the Persian (538 B.C.), another during the St. Bartholomew's Day Massacre in sixteenth-century France (1572), and another in Judea during the Crucifixion of Christ (we can guess which story Griffith saw as most closely paralleling his own recent martyrdom).

3.26 The Babylonian set of *Intolerance* (1916) prepared for the Belshazzar's feast sequence and the lengthy tracking shot.

This promised to be an expensive undertaking, but Griffith had been so elevated by the success of *The Birth of a Nation* that no project, however extravagant, could be denied him. He was now working for the Triangle Film Corporation, which his producer, Harry Aitken, had formed with Griffith, Mack Sennett, and Thomas H. Ince (see pp. 195–96) in late 1915, after he had been ousted from Mutual as the result of an internal power struggle. Triangle was not wealthy enough to produce Griffith's new epic, but Aitken incorporated the Wark Producing Corporation to finance the film, and investors fought one another for the privilege of betting on a second Griffith blockbuster.

It was well that they did, for with no standards left to exceed but his own, Griffith conceived of *Intolerance* on a scale so vast as to dwarf all of his previous work combined. Sparing no expense, financial or human, he threw up mammoth sets designed by the previously uncredited Walter W. Hall* for each of the four periods represented in the film, the most

---

* Hall surfaced as the production designer of *Intolerance,* apparently his only film, with the publication of Karl Brown's *Adventures with D. W. Griffith* (New York, 1973). Brown was Bitzer's assistant and provides a lively and detailed account of the making of *The Birth of a Nation, Intolerance,* and other Griffith features. Hall was responsible for creating the film's superb central perspective system, but the Babylonian sets themselves were conceived during a 1915 visit to San Francisco by Griffith, Bitzer, and Brown to research conditions in the city jail and San Quentin prison for the Modern story. On the way back to Los Angeles, the three passed by the San Francisco Exposition, whose Asiatic architectural theme so impressed the director that he had Bitzer take matte shots of the Tower of Jewels for future use. Griffith may also have visited the Italian Pavilion and been reminded of the opulent sets of *Cabiria* (pp. 59–60); such, at least, is the premise of Paolo and Vittorio Taviani's *Good Morning, Babylon* (1987; p. 640), which chronicles the fates of several

3.27 The Babylonian set under construction, seen from behind.

3.28 The walls of Babylon besieged.

elaborate of which was a full-scale model of ancient Babylon covering more than ten acres of land and standing some three hundred feet above the ground. He hired sixty principal players and thousands of extras to people the film, and at one point the production's payroll alone exceeded twenty thousand dollars a day. Among his eight assistant directors (*The Birth of a Nation* had none) were four who would later have significant Hollywood careers of their own—Allan Dwan, Christy Cabanne, Tod Browning, and Erich von Stroheim. When the project was finally completed, Griffith had spent fourteen months and, it was claimed, nearly two million dollars on it. *The Birth of a Nation,* by comparison, had been put together in seven months for one-twentieth the sum. Indeed, a single banquet scene in the Babylonian section of *Intolerance* was purported to have cost more than $250,000 to film, or well over twice the entire budget of its predecessor.* This unprecedented extravagance caused alarm among Griffith's backers, and he was forced to plow back a substantial portion of his profits from *The Birth of a Nation* (from which he ultimately earned about one million dollars) into *Intolerance* in order to keep the project afloat. If the film had been the popular success he expected, Griffith would have become one of the richest men in Hollywood. As it was, *Intolerance* produced heavy losses.

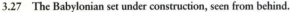

Italian immigrant masons brought down by Griffith from the Exposition to assist in the construction of the Babylonian sets. The sets also have sources, of course, in *Cabiria* itself and in several nineteenth-century religious paintings. (See e.g., Bernard Hanson, "D. W. Griffith: Some Sources," *The Art Bulletin* [December 1972]).

*In 1985, archivist/distributor Raymond Rohauer reconstructed *Intolerance* from Griffith's personal copy, complete with the original tinting and toning. To celebrate the film's seventieth anniversary, this print was shown on a 100-foot screen at the Avignon Film Festival in July 1986, accompanied by a new symphonic score composed by Antoine Duhamel and Pierre Jansen, and performed by the seventy-five-piece Orchestre de l'Île de France. This version, running 138 minutes at 20 fps, is currently available for rental in both 35 and 16 mm from The Rohauer Collection of Alan Twyman Presents.

The **rough cut** of *Intolerance* ran for eight hours, and Griffith toyed with the notion of distributing the film at this length in two separate parts. Practicality got the better of him, however, and he cut the negative from 200,000 to 13,500 feet, approximately three and one-half hours. After the box-office failure of *Intolerance* became apparent, Griffith rashly cut into the negative and re-edited *The Mother and the Law* and *The Fall of Babylon* for release as separate films to recoup his losses. Later, when he attempted to reconstruct the negative, nearly two thousand feet had been permanently lost, so that today we can never see *Intolerance* in its original form, which, according to the custom of the day, also included tinting in blue, red, green, and sepia to achieve atmospheric effects (blue for melancholy and night, red for war and passion, green for the pastoral and for calm, and sepia for interiors; see "The Introduction of Color," pp. 267–75). Nevertheless, the version which has come down to us closely resembles the original in terms of its formal structure, and this is the most important aspect of the film from our standpoint.*

Structure

For *Intolerance*, Griffith conceived the revolutionary notion of cross-cutting not only between parallel actions occurring simultaneously in separate spatial dimensions, as in his earlier films, but also between parallel actions occurring on separate temporal planes—those of the four stories. Thus, the plots of the four stories are interwoven like movements in a symphony until they converge in a crescendo at the film's climax. Before this quadruple climax, actions occurring in the separate historical periods are episodically self-contained and are drawn together by the recurrent transitional symbol of a mother rocking a cradle, emblematic of human continuity. This image is illuminated by a shaft of sacred light and accompanied by Walt Whitman's line "Out of the cradle endlessly rocking. . . ." As the separate stories move toward their conclusions, however, Griffith largely abandons this transitional device and cuts back and forth directly between incomplete climactic actions in the process of unfolding on all four temporal planes. He told a contemporary interviewer: "[The] stories will begin like four currents looked at from a hilltop. At first the four currents will flow apart, slowly and quietly. But as they flow, they grow nearer and nearer together, and faster and faster, until in the end, in the last act, they mingle in one mighty river of expres-

3.29 Transition: "Out of the cradle endlessly rocking . . ." Lillian Gish as The Woman Who Rocks the Cradle.

---

* The actual cost of *Intolerance* is still a matter of dispute. Griffith's own papers (*D. W. Griffith Papers*) contain a statement to the effect that the negative cost of the film was exactly $385,906.77, with the lion's share going to set construction and salaries. According to another source, a Price, Waterhouse audit in 1916 set the negative cost at $485,000, a figure still forty times the budget of a conventional feature in that year. In *D. W. Griffith: an American Life*, Richard Schickel attributes the myth of *Intolerance*'s vast production costs to Griffith's publicists and to a *Scientific American* article of September 2, 1916, whose authors were given inflated financial information by the film's accountants. Whatever the case, it is possible that the *total* cost incurred by Wark Producing Corporation for *Intolerance*, inclusive of promotion, print duplication, and distribution fees, doubled or even tripled the negative cost.

3.30 Christ on the road to Calvary: Howard Gaye.

3.31 The St. Bartholomew's Day Massacre begins.

3.32 Griffith and Bitzer shooting the climactic chase in the Modern story: Mae March (center) as The Dear One.

sion." Although the Biblical and St. Bartholomew's Day plots are resolved before the more complicated Babylonian and Modern stories, for the better part of the film's last two reels Griffith involves us in three separate three-way rescues and a dramatically excoriating Crucifixion. In these passages, Christ's progress toward Calvary, the desperate ride of the "Mountain girl" across the Euphrates plain to warn Babylon of its impending destruction, the massacre of the French Huguenots, and the modern wife's race against time to save her innocent husband from execution are all rapidly intercut in shots of shorter and shorter duration to create what is even today among the most exciting and unusual climactic sequences in motion-picture history. As Iris Barry said of it, "History itself seems to pour like a cataract across the screen." Like *The Birth of a Nation, Intolerance* concludes with a symbolic montage in which prison walls dissolve into flowered meadows and a grim battlesite becomes a field of frolicking children.

Contemporary audiences, who had only recently been exposed to the conventional if striking narrative intercutting of *The Birth of a Nation,* found this essentially metaphorical or symbolic intercutting difficult to understand—not surprisingly, for Griffith was cinematically years ahead of his time. He was already practicing in *Intolerance* the kind of abstract or "expressive" montage that Eisenstein and his Soviet colleagues would bring to perfection a decade later. Furthermore, the film contains the ultimate refinement of every narrative device Griffith had employed from *The Adventures of Dollie* through *The Birth of a Nation.* It uses revolutionary continuity editing, of course, but also huge close-ups, sweeping panoramas, assorted dissolves, irises, and masks (including a widescreen effect used for large battle sequences), dramatically expressive camera angles, and, finally, tracking movement that anticipates the elaborate maneuvers of F. W. Murnau and the German *Kammerspielfilm* (see Chapter 4, pp. 124–31) eight years later. For the climactic rescue in the Modern story, for example, Griffith mounted his camera in a moving automobile to follow a suspenseful chase between it and a train, just as he had done for the riot sequences in *The Birth of a Nation*. More important, Griffith built for *Intolerance* a huge elevator tower that rolled on rails to track the camera gradually from an extreme long shot of Babylon down into a full shot of actors on the set itself. The shot occurs several times in the film and is still one of the longest and most elaborate tracking shots in the American cinema.

Influence and Defects

For sheer technical virtuosity and inventiveness, then, *Intolerance* must rank as Griffith's greatest film. Moreover, Griffith's handling of massive crowd and battle scenes, as well as more intimate personal ones, surpassed anything he had ever done before or would attempt again. For the past decade, however, it has been customary to praise *Intolerance* far beyond its intrinsic worth because it had such a powerful influence upon the Soviet filmmakers who articulated and refined montage. It is also a relatively "safe" film to like compared to its volatile predecessor, and some critics have even tried (incorrectly) to make of it an apology for *The Birth of a Nation*. Yet, as an aesthetic experience rather than a narrative structure, *Intolerance* is something of a white elephant. Its spectacular proportions are unwieldy, and its elaborate intercutting apparatus does not always work. There are moments of incoherence: the St. Bartholomew's Day story sometimes gets lost in the shuffle, and the precise sequence of events in the Babylonian episode occasionally becomes unclear. Worse, Griffith's case-pleading in both his images and his titles becomes nearly hysterical at times, and his expressed intention to show "how hatred and intolerance, through the ages, have battled against love and charity" is scarcely germane to either the Babylonian or the Modern sequences. Indeed, Griffith hardly seems to have known what he meant by the term "intolerance," except that he associated it with the bitter outcry against *The Birth of a Nation*. In the context of the film itself, "intolerance" is simply an omnibus word encapsulating any form of human evil; and evil, of course, has never been a difficult or an unpopular subject to attack.

Intolerance is, in fact, the most Manichean of Griffith's feature films: in portraying the melodramatic struggle of Good against Evil through the ages, Griffith allowed his sentimentality to become distinctly overripe. Indeed, there are so many pious, pompous titles in *Intolerance* that Iris Barry was led to describe the film as "an epic sermon." Ultimately, *Intolerance* is an erratic but brilliant film of undeniable importance whose decisive influence upon figures as diverse as Cecil B. DeMille, Sergei Eisenstein, V. I. Pudovkin, Fritz Lang, and Abel Gance is a matter of historical record. As a self-contained work of art, it is by turns ponderous, awe-inspiring, obsessive, and thrilling. The film historian Jay Leyda, in an essay written on the occasion of Griffith's death in 1948, called *Intolerance* "a towering compound of greatness and cheapness," but the filmmaker John Dorr put it more precisely: "*Intolerance* succeeded as a film of spectacle and as a film of narrative action, but not as a film of ideas."

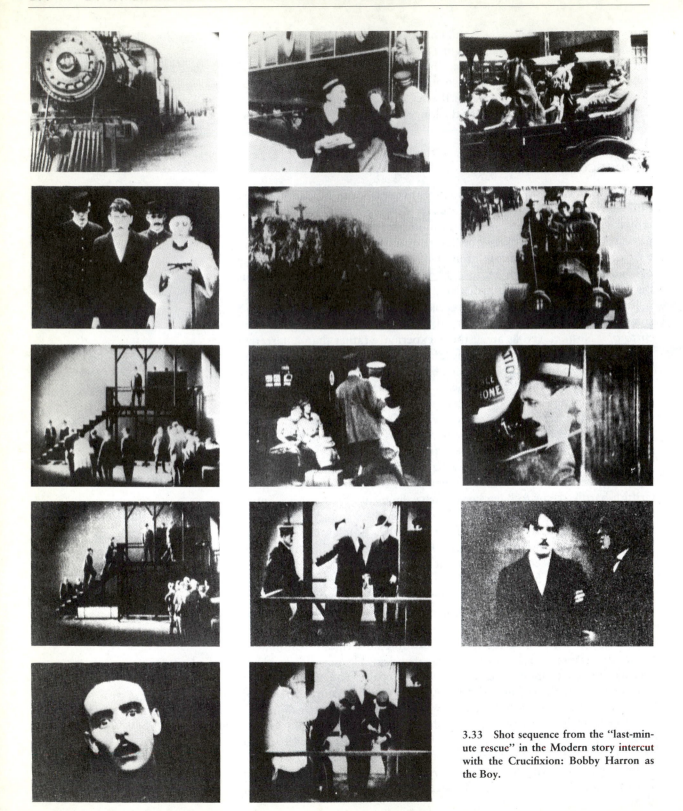

3.33 Shot sequence from the "last-minute rescue" in the Modern story intercut with the Crucifixion: Bobby Harron as the Boy.

For the audiences of 1916, which cared little for ideas in any event, *Intolerance* was simply too much—too big, too complicated, too serious, and too solemn. Ironically, the film's commercial failure was probably conditioned by its predecessor's enormous success. The millions who had been swept away by *The Birth of a Nation* expected Griffith's second epic to carry them off in the same tumultuous and inflammatory manner. Emotional appeal, however, was not one of *Intolerance*'s strong points, for Griffith had deliberately subordinated character development—hence, audience identification, to spectacle and historical process. Furthermore, the United States was preparing to enter the war in Europe when the film was released in September 1916, and a bellicose mood was sweeping the country. By a crushing historical irony, Griffith's rejoinder to the suppression of *The Birth of a Nation* was itself censured and suppressed in many American cities as a pacifist statement, despite the obvious enthusiasm of its battle scenes (many of them shot at night and illuminated by magnesium flares). Finally, after twenty-two weeks of distribution, the film was taken out of circulation, and in 1919 it was re-edited as two separate films, as previously described. This attempt by Griffith to salvage his enormous financial investment was only partially successful; he would continue to pay his debts on *Intolerance* until his death in 1948.*

GRIFFITH AFTER *INTOLERANCE*

The failure of *Intolerance* did not by any means end Griffith's career. It curtailed his independence as a producer and dampened his enthusiasm as a creator, but he went on to direct another twenty-six feature films between 1916 and 1931. Most critics see this period as one of marked decline in power. It is true that Griffith made no major narrative innovations after *Intolerance,* but it could reasonably be argued that there were very few left to make before the coming of sound. What seems to have happened is that Griffith lost touch with the prevailing tastes of the postwar era and, therefore, with the popular audience. Though the failure of *Intolerance* had convinced him of the necessity of catering to popular tastes, he experienced increasing difficulty in locating them after 1917. This was partially the result of rapid social change. Industrialization, modernization, and our involvement in World War I had caused an inversion of traditional American attitudes and values (see note, pp. 207–8). The nineteenth-century virtues of morality, idealism, and purity, incarnated by the Cameron family in *The Birth of a Nation,* had given way to the pursuit of sensation and material wealth in the disillusioned postwar era. The verities of rural romanticism, so crucial to Griffith's prewar epics, were replaced by the sophistication, urbanity, and wit of

---

* The crumbling Babylonian set stood for years at the intersection of Sunset and Hollywood Boulevards, becoming a familiar local landmark, because there was not enough money returned on *Intolerance* to have the structure torn down. It was finally removed by the WPA in the late thirties.

3.34 A "Hun" prepares to flog a French peasant girl (Lillian Gish) in *Hearts of the World* (1918). (Studio publicity still.)

filmmakers like Cecil B. DeMille and Ernst Lubitsch (see pp. 230–34), whose cynical amorality was all but incomprehensible to a director who had never permitted his lovers to so much as kiss on the screen. Griffith continued to make interesting films—he produced one masterpiece, *Broken Blossoms*—but most of his postwar features are either disappointingly conventional or hopelessly old-fashioned.* In effect, the movies had entered the Jazz Age, while Griffith still lived in the afterglow of the nineteenth century.

A great artist's failures, however, are as interesting as his successes, and Griffith's are worth recording briefly here. Before *Intolerance* had even started to sink at the box office, Griffith was invited to England by the British government to make a propaganda picture in support of the war effort against Germany and to convince America to join it (which occurred shortly after Griffith's arrival). Initially conceived as an extended newsreel on the Somme offensive of April 1917 to be financed by Lord Beaverbrook's powerful War Office Cinematograph Committee, *Hearts of the World* (1918) became instead a privately produced anti-German war epic shot on location in France and England which luridly depicted the effects of "Hunnish" occupation on a small French town. Recalling *The Birth of a Nation* in its battle scenes, *Hearts of the World* was enormously popular with domestic audiences during the war, although it lacked the focus and coherence of its predecessor. Griffith shot another film while he was in England—*The Great Love*, a morale-booster designed to show "the regeneration of British society through its war activities," according to advance publicity. This feature, which hasn't survived, was produced by Adolph Zukor's Paramount-Artcraft Company,† which had agreed to become the American distributor for *Hearts of the World*. Before leaving for England, Griffith had signed a contract with Zukor to direct six films for his company and to oversee the production of several others—a wise decision, since Triangle was about to be bankrupted through mismanagement and the depredations of rival production companies, Zukor's among them. Neither English film was a critical success; *Hearts of the World* seems especially crude today in its stereotyping of all German soliders as beasts, although that, of course, was its avowed intention in the year it was made. Returning to Hollywood, Griffith directed five feature films for Zukor in rapid succession between 1917 and 1919—*True-Heart Susie, The Romance of Happy Valley, The Greatest Thing in Life, The Girl Who Stayed at Home,* and *Scarlet Days* (his only feature-length Western, which also hasn't survived), all of them (except the last) dated, idyllic romances with little popular appeal. Next Griffith signed a contract to direct three quickie potboilers for First National in order to raise

---

* There has been a recent tendency to revaluate Griffith's later work (e.g., *True-Heart Susie* [1919]; *Sally of the Sawdust* [1925]) for the better. See William Cadbury, "Theme, Felt Life, and the Last-Minute Rescue in Griffith After *Intolerance*," *Film Quarterly* 28, 1 (Fall 1974): 39–48; Edward Wagenknecht and Anthony Slide, *The Films of D. W. Griffith* (New York, 1975); and John L. Fell, *A History of Films* (New York, 1978).

† Part of Zukor's Paramount Famous Players—Lasky empire, founded in 1916, originally to distribute Mary Pickford's films.

money for his newest project—the building of an independent studio on a large estate he had purchased near Mamaroneck, New York, where he hoped to become his own producer. According to one of Griffith's biographers, Robert Henderson, First National was interested only in the Griffith imprimatur and permitted him to leave the direction of these films to his assistants, which he apparently did. *The Greatest Question* (1919), a melodrama about spiritualism, and *The Idol Dancer* (1920; released 1922) and *The Love Flower* (1920), both exotic South Seas adventures, were of indifferent quality and did little to enhance the reputation of "the Master," as Griffith had recently been dubbed by the press. Between *The Greatest Question* and *The Idol Dancer,* however, Griffith independently produced *Broken Blossoms,* his last masterpiece and his first great commercial success since *The Birth of a Nation.*

Based on a story called "The Chink and the Child," from Thomas Burke's *Limehouse Nights, Broken Blossoms* concerns a young waif of the London slums, brutally mistreated by her father, who finds brief sanctuary in the chaste love of a gentle young Chinese man.* When her father learns of the relationship, he beats the child to death with a whiphandle; the boy then kills the father and commits suicide. Griffith shot this film entirely in the studio in eighteen days (with much prior rehearsal, however) on such a rigorously economical schedule that—according to Lillian Gish, who played the girl—there were no retakes and only two hundred feet of printed stock were left unused (the normal ratio of footage printed to footage used in a commercial film was about fifteen to one in 1919 and is ten to one today). Yet *Broken Blossoms* shows no evidence of its hasty construction and is simultaneously Griffith's most richly evocative and tightly controlled film. Despite some overly sentimental touches (such as the wretched young girl's attempts to counterfeit a smile by propping up the corners of her mouth with her fingers), *Broken Blossoms* succeeds admirably as pathos and is probably the closest Griffith ever came to incarnating his Victorian sensibilities in an appropriate dramatic form. But more important than its dramatic structure is the film's dreamlike atmospheric context—its mood-drenched *mise-en-scène.* Griffith derived the film's ambiance from a series of watercolors of London's Limehouse district, the city's Chinatown, by the English artist George Baker; but both photography and lighting in *Broken Blossoms* are distinctly Continental, probably because of the efforts of Billy Bitzer's recently acquired assistant, Hendrik Sartov,† a specialist in mood light-

---

* Griffith's sympathetic treatment of the Chinese boy in *Broken Blossoms,* during the height of anti-Oriental, "Yellow Peril" sensationalism in the United States, has troubled critics who prefer to see him as an unreconstructed and irredeemable racist. In fact, the historical record shows that Griffith took great pains in both the production and promotion of the film not to pander to the popular (and, by then, stereotypically Hollywood) image of the Oriental as inscrutable villain. Apparently, he was a man who at least could learn from his own mistakes. See Vance Keply, Jr., "Griffith's *Broken Blossoms* and the Problem of Historical Specificity," *Quarterly Review of Film Studies* 3, 1 (Winter 1978): 37–48.

† Sartov was Lillian Gish's personal photographer and cameraman, brought into the production at her insistence, and Griffith quickly came to admire his work. In additon to

3.35 A wharf scene from the studio-produced *Broken Blossoms* (1919): Lillian Gish at the right of the frame.

3.36 The climatic rescue in *Way Down East* (1920): Lillian Gish, Richard Barthelmess.

ing and soft focus, or "impressionistic," photography. Griffith, Bitzer, and Sartov together created out of brooding London fogs, smoke-filled opium dens, and the petal-like delicacy of the boy's rooms a *mise-en-scène* worthy of—and probably contributory to—the studio-produced *Kammerspielfilm* of the German cinema (as will be seen in Chapter 4).

For its release in May 1919 *Broken Blossoms* was tinted entirely in soft pastels, and, to further enhance its visual lushness, projected onto a screen washed from above and below by rich pastel lights. Unpredictably, the film was a smashing commercial and critical success. Produced for the now modest sum of ninety thousand dollars, it made nearly a million and was widely hailed as a masterpiece. One critic wrote that Griffith "had far exceeded the power of the written word," while others gave "the Master" a new title: "the Shakespeare of the screen." This praise was well deserved, for *Broken Blossoms* is Griffith's most highly integrated film, as well as his most personal and poetic. There are indications that the chief appeal of *Broken Blossoms* to contemporary audiences was nostalgic. Whether or not Griffith understood this is unclear, but it is certain that the resounding accolades for his film convinced him more than ever before that he was a natural genius who could do no wrong on the screen.

---

assisting Bitzer on *Broken Blossoms* (1919), *Way Down East* (1920), and, with Arthur H. C. ("Hal") Sintzenich, *The White Rose* (1923), Sartov was the principal cinematographer for *Dream Street* (1921), *Orphans of the Storm* (1922, with Paul Allen), *One Exciting Night* (1922), *America* (1924, with Bitzer, Marcel Le Picard, and Sintzenich), and *Isn't Life Wonderful?* (1924, with Sintzenich). In 1924 Sartov followed Gish to MGM (where, for example, he photographed her in Victor Seastrom's *The Scarlet Letter* [1926]), and Griffith continued to work with some combination of Sintzenich, Harry Fischbeck, and Karl Struss in consultation with Bitzer, whose alcoholism and domestic problems left him increasingly unreliable. See Erik Barnouw, "The Sintzenich Diaries," *The Quarterly Journal of the Library of Congress* 37, 3–4 (Summer–Fall 1980): 310–31.

Broken Blossoms was released through United Artists Corporation, the producing-distributing company that Griffith had formed with Charlie Chaplin, Mary Pickford, and Douglas Fairbanks in the spring of 1919, and the film's financial success made it possible for Griffith to equip his own studio at Mamaroneck as planned. His first project there was an adaptation of a creaky Victorian stage play of seduction and betrayal, *Way Down East,* for the rights to which he paid $175,000. Once again Griffith was emotionally in tune with his material, and he produced an exciting and credible melodrama. Shot on location in New York, Connecticut, and Vermont, *Way Down East* (1920) possesses an unexpectedly cinematic vitality and concludes with a skillfully edited last-minute rescue equal to Griffith's best montage work of the teens. After an elaborate chase through a real blizzard, the heroine collapses on an ice floe moving rapidly downriver toward a steep falls (actually Niagara, cut into the sequence from stock shots). The hero emerges from the storm, leaps downstream from one ice cake to another, and finally rescues her on the very brink of the plunging falls in a sequence which most certainly influenced Pudovkin's ice-floe montage at the conclusion of *Mother* (1926; see pp. 193–95). The audiences, if not the critics, were enthusiastic about *Way Down East* and made it Griffith's last great popular success. In fact, the film grossed four and one-half million dollars, returning the largest profit of any Griffith film after *The Birth of a Nation.**

DECLINE

Griffith took his share of the profits and plowed it back into his Mamaroneck studios. But he knew that the days of independent producing were rapidly drawing to a close, and there is evidence that with this knowledge he was driven to consider filmmaking more and more as a business activity and less and less as an art. His next several films confirmed this new preoccupation. *Dream Street* (1922) was a misbegotten effort to re-create the misty poetic ambiance which had proved so lucrative with *Broken Blossoms.*† *Orphans of the Storm* (1921) was a spectacular attempt to capitalize on the new vogue for historical costume films created by Ernst

---

* Stung by unfavorable reviews, Griffith re-edited *Way Down East* thoughout its life in distribution, which concluded in a 1931 rerelease with a musical soundtrack, eventually reducing its length by about 25 percent. In 1984, MoMA produced a 163-minute restored version with the original intertitles, based on Griffith's several extant versions, the original cued score, and Griffith's own copyrighted shot sequence in the Library of Congress. Though it lacks five or six minutes of the release print, narrative gaps are bridged by stills and intertitles, and the MoMA restoration comes as close to Griffith's original conception of the film as we shall probably ever get. See Tom Gunning, "Rebirth of a Movie," *American Film* 10, 1 (October 1984): 18–19, 93, and Steve Vineburg, "The Restored *Way Down East,*" *Film Quarterly* 39, 3 (Spring 1986): 54–57.

† Nevertheless, Griffith was still experimenting technically: *Dream Street* contained several songs recorded (not very successfully) with the early Photokinema sound-on-disk system (see pp. 253–54) and featured a prologue with Griffith himself speaking from the screen (not very audibly) on "the Evolution of the Motion Pictures."

3.37 Griffith directing the guillotine scene in *Orphans of the Storm* (1921).

Lubitsch's *Madame Du Barry* (*Passion*, 1919) by setting a dated Victorian melodrama against the background of the French Revolution. The film was expensively produced at Mamaroneck and well received by the critics, but it lost so much money that it nearly terminated Griffith's dream of independence. In an effort to recoup his losses, he made two more potboilers—a haunted-house mystery entitled *One Exciting Night* (1922) and an old-fashioned piece of Deep South exoticism called *The White Rose* (1923). Both films were failures that served only to deepen Griffith's financial crisis.

Now Griffith began to dream of saving his company by duplicating the phenomenal success of *The Birth of a Nation*. He remembered *War*, the drama of the American Revolution which he had written years before he had ever seen a movie, and decided to produce an epic film on the subject. This costly attempt to remake *The Birth of a Nation* in other terms was called *America* (1924), and it succeeded admirably as spectacle. Its enormous battle scenes easily rival anything Griffith ever produced, but its dull textbook account of the Revolution and its heavy-handed patriotism made it a museum piece even in its own time. Like every film he had made since *The Love Flower*, except *Way Down East*, *America* lost money, and the Mamaroneck studios were doomed. Griffith was now facing extinction as a producer and simultaneously being squeezed for more films by his United Artists partners. Accordingly, in the summer of 1924 he traveled to Germany to make *Isn't Life Wonderful?*, his last film as an independent producer for United Artists. Based on contemporary events with exteriors shot entirely on location, the film is a semidocumentary account of the ravages of postwar inflation upon the German middle class. It is thought to have influenced both G. W. Pabst's *Die freudlose*

Gasse (*The Joyless Street;* see p. 134), made in Germany the following year, and the neorealist cinema which sprang up in Italy after World War II (see pp. 380–93). Part of the film's uniqueness surely stemmed from the fact that before leaving America Griffith had secretly signed a contract to direct three fast films for Paramount Famous Players—Lasky in an attempt to stave off bankruptcy. He must have sensed that *Isn't Life Wonderful?* would be his last independent project.

Sadly, with the exception of his much maligned *The Struggle* (1931; q.v.), it was. Zukor had just lost Cecil B. DeMille as his premier director, and he promptly hired Griffith for the job, which meant that for the first time since his early Biograph days Griffith was unable to choose his own material. The apathy this produced in him was very nearly fatal. At Paramount's Astoria, New York, studios he made two limp W. C. Fields vehicles, *Sally of the Sawdust* (1925) and *That Royle Girl* (1926), and a studio-contrived fantasy-spectacle, *The Sorrows of Satan* (1926), which had originally been intended for DeMille; but his direction of these unappealing projects was so pedestrian that his Paramount contract was not renewed when it expired in late 1926. At this point, Joseph Schenck (1878–1961), now president of United Artists, offered Griffith a job directing films for his independently owned Art Cinema Corporation in exchange for the voting rights to Griffith's United Artists stock (a swindle nearly as flagrant as Edison's theft of Thomas Armat's Vitagraph projector), but Griffith was foundering rapidly and was forced to accept.

For Art Cinema, Griffith made three undistinguished films—*Drums of Love* (1928), a medieval Italian melodrama based on the Paolo and Francesca legend; *The Battle of the Sexes* (1928–29), a humorless remake of his old Reliance-Majestic farce with a synchronized sound-on-film score; and *Lady of the Pavements* (1929), a romantic "women's picture" released in both silent and sound versions which completely miscast the sexy Lupe Velez as an ingenue. Schenck was ready to fire Griffith (who, in addition to his other worries, had developed a drinking problem) when Griffith proposed that he direct a sound-film biography of Abraham Lincoln. The old *Birth of a Nation* mystique worked for Griffith one last time, and Schenck approved the project. The resulting film, *Abraham Lincoln* (1930), with a script by the American poet Stephen Vincent Benét, is a shadow of Griffith's great Civil War epic. The battle sequences and even the assassination look devitalized and grotesquely underbudgeted by comparison with analogous scenes in *The Birth of a Nation;* and, like most early sound films, *Abraham Lincoln* is visually wooden and static. But Griffith had turned in a respectable and intelligent performance in the most difficult years of the transition from silent pictures to sound, and he was rewarded for it. Several influential trade journals named him "Director of the Year," and the film itself was on most "Ten Best" lists for 1930.

Griffith now felt that he was one film away from complete rehabilitation, but he knew that he could never make that film for Schenck; so he quit Art Cinema and floated a bank loan of approximately $200,000 in order to produce what he hoped would be his first sound-era masterpiece—a version of Zola's *L'Assommoir* (*The Drunkard*) written by Anita

3.38 The last epic: *America* (1924).

3.39 Griffith directing his last film, *The Struggle* (1931), on location in New York City. The large disk is part of the sound-recording equipment.

Loos and entitled *The Struggle* (1931). It turned out, instead, to be his last film. Thinly capitalized and shot for reasons of economy in semi-documentary fashion in and around New York City, *The Struggle* was an abject failure with both contemporary critics and the public. Like all Griffith films, it was visually impressive and had a soundtrack far above average quality for its time, but in terms of drama *The Struggle* was as archaic as "The Face on the Bar-Room Floor." The film was released in January 1932 and permanently withdrawn after a week of exhibition: audiences had walked out on its opening night, and the critics were mocking it, although some today regard it as a much better film than *Abraham Lincoln*. Sixteen years after *The Birth of a Nation*, "the Shakespeare of the screen" had become a figure of ridicule, and Griffith was forced to retire in humiliation from the industry that he, more than any single figure in its brief history, had helped to create. He lived out the remainder of his life in modest comfort on an annuity he had purchased for himself in more prosperous times, overseeing retrospective exhibitions of his greatest films and attending testimonial banquets in his honor. He died in Los Angeles in 1948, only five months after Sergei Eisenstein in Moscow, and was eulogized around the world as "the man who invented cinema." None was more moving in their praise than those who had for the past sixteen years refused him employment.

THE IMPORTANCE OF GRIFFITH

Griffith remained until the end of his career the same paradoxical figure he had been at its beginning. To borrow Jay Leyda's terminology for *Intolerance*, the greatness and the cheapness of the man were inextricably mixed. By his own candid admission, Griffith derived most of his major narrative innovations from the techniques of nineteenth-century fiction and melodrama, but he also imbibed the simplistic world view of these two popular forms, to the everlasting detriment of his art. In his famous essay entitled "Dickens, Griffith, and the Film Today," Sergei Eisenstein pointed out that Griffith's constant resort to parallel editing was a function of his dualistic vision of human experience, in which an entire civil war or twenty centuries of human history were reducible to a melodramatic struggle between the forces of Good and Evil. As a dramatist, in fact, Griffith was less "the Shakespeare of the screen" than its Thomas Middleton. But Griffith was also perhaps the greatest cinematic genius in history—the man who discovered (sometimes, admittedly, in the work of others), synthesized, and articulated the narrative language of film as it is practiced even today. In effect, the way he structured the cinema is the way most of us still perceive it.

His genius, however, was fundamentally innovative and intuitive, rather than critical or analytic. When the days of innovation ceased and intuition was no longer essential to the filmmaking process, Griffith was thrown back upon a world view which was hopelessly inappropriate to the postwar era and which had never been intellectually respectable, even in its own century. To compound the misfortune, the lionization of Griffith which followed *The Birth of a Nation* and continued well into the twenties produced in him a kind of megalomania which permanently impaired his judgment. When Griffith began to think of himself as the prophet and philosopher of the film medium, he ceased to be its leading artist. And yet he achieved so much in so short a time with such limited means that to dwell upon the defects of his work or his character, however serious, is more than ungenerous. It is simply irrelevant, for the greatest of Griffith's achievements in a lifetime of achievement was that this fundamentally nineteenth-century man ultimately managed to transcend his defects of vision, judgment, and taste to become one of the great artists of the twentieth century.

German Cinema of the Weimar Period, 1919–1929

THE PREWAR PERIOD

Prior to the First World War, the German cinema had reached a less advanced state of development than the cinemas of France, Italy, England, and the United States. Although the Skladanowsky brothers had unveiled their "Bioskop" projector in the Berlin Wintergarten in November 1895, almost simultaneously with the first Lumière Cinématographe projection, an indigenous German film industry had somehow failed to evolve in the fifteen years that followed. One reason for this seems to have been that in Germany, more than in the other nations of the West, the cinema became a cultural refuge for the illiterate, disenfranchised, and unemployed. Consequently, very few educated Germans took films or filmmaking seriously during these years, and most of the films shown in the early tent shows (*Wanderkinos*) and nickelodeons (*Ladenkinos*) were either imported from other countries or produced in Germany by fly-by-night showmen. Many early native films were frankly pornographic; almost all were technically crude.

One notable exception to this general tendency was the work of Oskar Messter (1866–1943), an inventor who had been instrumental in perfecting the Maltese cross movement for projection systems (see pp. 9–10). In 1897, Messter established a small studio in the Berlin Friedrichstrasse and went on to produce hundreds of short entertainment films and *actualités* of a reasonably high caliber and some technical sophistication. He used close shots as early as 1903 and became one of the first directors anywhere in the world to light his sets artificially. Messter, who also experimented with synchronized sound using the phonograph, helped to upgrade the content of German films by featuring famous stars of cabaret and, ultimately, the legitimate stage in his productions between 1904 and 1908. In 1909 he ventured into the production of feature films (*Grossfilme*) with *Andreas Hofer,* directed by Carl Froelich, and devoted his energies to that form almost entirely until 1917, when his company and most others in Germany came under the control of the new government-subsidized conglomerate Universum Film Aktiengesellschaft (UFA). The main historical interest of Messter's features is that they provided the film debut of performers like Henny Porten, Emil Jannings, Lil Dagover, and Conrad Veidt, who became major stars in the twenties.

A more important development, however, began around 1910 when, in response to the great success of the French *film d'art* movement, directors, actors, and writers associated with the German theater began to take a serious interest in the cinema for the first time. In 1912 the first *Autorenfilm* ("famous author's film," and thus the German version of *film d'art*) was brought to the screen by the former stage director Max Mack (1884–?). This predictably static adaptation of Paul Lindau's highly successful stage play *Der Andere* (*The Other One*), about the split personality of a Berlin lawyer, starred the world famous German actor Albert Bassermann (1867–1952). The following year, the great stage director and producer Max Reinhardt (1873–1943) filmed versions of the plays *A Venetian Night* and *The Isle of the Dead,* and the poet-playwright Hugo von Hofmannsthal wrote the "dream-play" *Das fremde Mädchen* (*The Strange Girl*), the first serious German feature film to express a purely supernatural theme. The influx of literary and theatrical people into German film had the effect of radically elevating its social status, but, as in France, the movement also retarded the development of true cinematic narrative by binding it tightly to the narrative conventions of the stage.

The first prewar German film to break with stage conventions was the Danish director Stellan Rye's production of *Der Student von Prag* (*The Student of Prague*) in 1913, shot by the pioneering lighting cameraman Guido Seeber (1879–1940), and starring a former Reinhardt actor, Paul Wegener (1874–1948), in the title role. Based collectively on variants of the Faust legend in the work of E. T. A. Hoffmann, Edgar Allan Poe, and Oscar Wilde, the film concerns a young student who sells his mirror reflection, and thus his soul, to a sorcerer who in turn causes the image to become a murderous incarnation of the student's evil second self. Much of the film was shot on location in Prague, and it is distinguished by atmospheric lighting and many effective photographic illusions, as well as by Wegener's subtle performance in the double role of the student and the student's alter ego. The film's immediate impact, however, was felt more in terms of its content than of its technical virtuosity, for, as Siegfried Kracauer has noted, *Der Student von Prag* introduced the morbid theme of "deep and fearful concern with the foundations of the self," which was to obsess the German cinema from 1913 to 1933, at which point it was taken over and anesthetized by the Nazis.* Moreover, as a tale of psychological horror in a specifically supernatural setting, *Der Student von Prag* prefigures the German Expressionist cinema which began in earnest after the war; and, indeed, the film was itself remade in the Expressionist manner in 1926 by some of its original collaborators.

4.1 *Der Student von Prag* (Stellan Rye, 1913).

---

* It should be pointed out, however (as Kracauer does not), that German literature had been preoccupied with the notion of the Doppelgänger ("double") since the Middle Ages (witness the Faust legends); and *Der Andere,* the first German feature film of any merit, had, of course, provided a treatment of the theme. See Heide Schlüpmann, "The First German Art Film: Rye's *The Student of Prague* (1913)," in *German Film and Literature: Adaptations and Transformations,* ed. Eric Rentschler (New York and London: Methuen, 1986).

THE WAR YEARS

In 1915, after the outbreak of war, Wegener and the scriptwriter Henrik Galeen (1882–?; later to direct the 1926 version of *Der Student von Prag*) jointly directed another precursor of the Expressionist movement, *Der Golem* (*The Golem*), which was also set in Prague and photographed by Seeber. The film has not survived, but it too was remade after the war (by Wegener and Galeen in 1920), and we now know from the later version that it was based upon a Jewish legend in which a sixteenth-century rabbi brings to life a clay statue to guard his people against a pogrom. In the film, the giant statue is rediscovered in modern times, is infused with life, and becomes a raging monster who must be destroyed when his resuscitator's daughter rejects him (cf. *Frankenstein*, U.S.A. [1931]; *King Kong*, U.S.A. [1933]). The pre-Expressionist theme of soullessness embodied in *Der Golem* appears in another German film of the era, the six-part serial *Homunculus*, directed by Otto Rippert in 1916. The most popular film of the war years, *Homunculus* deals with an artificially created being of great intellect and will who has no soul. Like the Golem, he turns his energies to destruction when he discovers his synthetic origins, becoming a ruthless dictator who avenges himself upon the human race by means of war and mass murder.

The Scandinavian Influence

Taken together, *Der Student von Prague, Der Golem,* and *Homunculus* provide a clear indication of the direction the German cinema was to take after the war, but they also indicate the radically stepped-up pace of domestic production during the war itself. Between 1914 and 1919, Germany was cut off from its normally large supply of British, French, and American films. The only foreign productions it was able to import were those from neutral Sweden and Denmark, and consequently the Scandinavian and German industries grew very close during these years. Scandinavian films at this point were generally static and literary but often beautifully photographed by directors like Victor Sjöström and Mauritz Stiller; their visual clarity had a pronounced influence on postwar German cinema, which, with *film d'art* and the *Autorenfilm,* they helped to make intellectually respectable. Their popularity was also responsible for bringing a Danish production company (German Nordisk, a subsidiary of Nordisk Films Kompagni, until it was absorbed by UFA) and a whole colony of Scandinavian film artists, including the famous Danish actress Asta Nielsen and the great Danish director Carl Dreyer (see pp. 387–88), to Germany during World War I.

Sjöström (1879–1960), a Swede, and Stiller (1883–1928), born in Finland of Russian parents who moved to Sweden in 1904, were the founding fathers of the Scandinavian cinema. Both began directing in 1912 for Charles Magnusson's (1878–1948) newly formed Svenska Biografteatern company (later to become Svensk Filmindustri), and many of the films they made between 1914 and 1920 received international acclaim. A number of these films, like Sjöström's *The Girl from Marsh Croft* (*Tösen*

4.2 *The Phantom Chariot* (Victor Sjöström, 1920).

4.3 *Sir Arne's Treasure* (Mauritz Stiller, 1919).

från Stormytorpet, 1917) and *The Phantom Chariot* (*Körkarlen*, 1921), and Stiller's *Sir Arne's Treasure* (*Herr Arnes pengar*, 1919—influential of both Lang and Eisenstein) and *The Saga of Gösta Berling* (*Gösta Berlings saga*, 1924), were adapted from the work of the great Swedish novelist Selma Lagerlöf (1858–1940). The work of both directors has been described as stately, solemn, and static (terms which might be used to characterize the Scandinavian cinema generally until very recently), but Sjöström was the more ponderous of the two. Nevertheless, in his best dramas of pastoral life Sjöström managed to integrate the rugged Swedish landscape into the texture of his films with an almost mystical force— a feature noted and much admired by filmmakers in other countries. Stiller, who had a lighter touch, excelled at comedy, of which his *Erotikon* (1920), an acknowledged influence on Ernst Lubitsch, remains an impressive example. He must also be credited with introducing Greta Garbo (b. 1905) to the screen in *The Saga of Gösta Berling* and with helping to mold her early career. Both men went to Hollywood to work for MGM in the mid-1920s, where Sjöström (renamed Seastrom) made three neglected masterpieces—*He Who Gets Slapped* (1924), *The Scarlet Letter* (1926), and *The Wind* (1928)—and Stiller was reduced to directing star vehicles, only one of which (*Hotel Imperial* [1926]) remained completely his own work.

Sjöström returned to a life of semiretirement in Sweden in 1928, working occasionally as a director and an actor, and Stiller died in the same year, fatigued and disillusioned, some have said, by the Hollywood experience (see Chapter 6, p. 232). During the twenties, the Swedish film industry, virtually monopolized by Magnusson's Svensk Filmindustri after 1919, fell into a period of stagnation from which it was not to emerge until the outbreak of World War II. The slump, during which Sweden produced only a handful of films for export, has been blamed primarily on competition from Hollywood, which, as in the case of Sjöström, Stiller,

Garbo, and actors such as Lars Hanson and Nils Asther, siphoned off its major talent to work in the American film industry; there were minor exceptions in the work of Gustaf Molander (1888–1973—*One Night* [*En natt,* 1931]; *Intermezzo* [1936] and Alf Sjoberg (1903–80—*The Strongest* [*Den starkaste,* 1929]; *Life at Stake* [*Med livet som insats,* 1939]).

THE FOUNDING OF UFA

Nevertheless, there simply weren't enough Swedish and Danish motion pictures to fill the void created by the disappearance of other imported films from the German screen, and so the Germans renewed efforts to increase the quantity and quality of domestic production. The first major step was the establishment of the nationally subsidized film conglomerate Universum Film Aktiengesellschaft (UFA, commonly Ufa in German texts) by government decree in 1917. Aware of the depressed state of the domestic industry, and also of the growing number of effective anti-German propaganda films emanating from the Allied countries, General Erich Ludendorff, commander-in-chief of the German army, on December 18, 1917, ordered the merger of the main German production companies, as well as exhibitors and distributors, into a single unit for the making and marketing of high-quality nationalistic films to enhance Germany's image at home and abroad. Huge new studios were built at Neubabelsberg, near Berlin, and UFA immediately set about the task of upgrading production, distribution, and exhibition by assembling a team of first-rate producers, directors, writers, and technicians. Perhaps the best comment on the organization's effectiveness in this regard is that, by the end of the war, German production facilities were ten times what they had been at the outset, the feature had been institutionalized as the dominant form, and the German film industry was ready to compete commercially with that of any other nation in the world. For a brief time during the twenties, it became the only industry to successfully compete with Hollywood in foreign markets, including the American. When the war ended in a German defeat in November 1918, the government sold its shares in the company to the Deutsche Bank and to corporations like Krupp and I. G. Farben, and UFA was transformed into a private company. This caused little change in the studio's internal organization, which was fundamentally authoritarian, but its mission was altered slightly because of the compelling necessity of competing in a new international market.

It is often said that the German cinema as an art form was born with the founding of UFA, which was to become the greatest and largest single studio in Europe before World War II. The impression is often given that UFA monopolized German cinema during the twenties and thirties, or nearly so. But during the twenties, at least, it functioned more as a distributor for smaller companies (Terra Film A.G., National Film A.G., Deulig Film, to name a few) than as a producer in its own right. One reason for the confusion is that, of the few films UFA did produce during the twenties, nearly one and all became classics of the German cinema's so-called Golden Age.* As Kracauer points out, UFA was merely the instrument of the cinema's birth, which had its deeper causes in the *Aufbruch*—a wave of revolutionary intellectual excitement that swept over the whole of Germany in the wake of the war.

Germany's crushing defeat resulted in a complete rejection of the past by much of its intelligentsia and a new enthusiasm for the progressive, experimental, and avant-garde. A liberal democratic republic, culturally centered at Weimar, was established. Marxism became intellectually respectable for the first time in German history; **Expressionism**† became prominent in the arts; and in early 1919 the Council of People's Representatives abolished national censorship. In this creatively charged atmosphere, the last shreds of intellectual resistance to the cinema disappeared, and Germany's radical young artists were ready to accept it as a new means of communicating with the masses. The new freedom of expression manifested itself most immediately in a series of well-mounted, independently produced pornographic films (*Aufklärungsfilme*—"films of elucidation," or "films about the facts of life") with titles like *Prostitution, Vom Rande des Sumpfes* (*From the Verge of the Swamp*), *Verlorene Tochter* (*Lost Daughters*), *Hyänen der Lust* (*Hyenas of Lust*), *Aus Mannes Mädchjaren* (*A Man's Girlhood*), and *Fräulein Mutter* (*Maiden Mother*). Like the Scandinavian sex films which glutted the world market in the late 1960s, the postwar German productions masqueraded as vehicles of sex education and social reform. Their only significant effect, however, was to stir up anti-Semitic sentiments against their supposedly Jewish producers and to cause the National Assembly to reinstitute state censorship through the Reich Film Act in May 1920. Significantly, it was this act which would later enable the Nazis to assert ideological control over the German cinema.

UFA's first peacetime productions were lavish costume dramas (*Kostümfilme*), initially made to compete with Italian spectacles like *Quo vadis?* and *Cabiria* (see pp. 59–60). Joe May's *Veritas vincit* (1918), an ele-

4.4 *The Saga of Gösta Berling* (**Mauritz Stiller, 1924**): **Ellen Cederström, Greta Garbo.**

---

* According to Eric Rhode in *A History of the Cinema from Its Origins to 1970* (New York: Hill & Wang, 1976), UFA produced only 12 of the 185 German features for 1926, 15 of 222 for 1927 (while distributing 105 of these), 16 of 224 for 1928 (distributing 18), and 13 of 183 for 1929 (distributing 68). Furthermore, as Julian Petley points out in *Capital and Culture: German Cinema 1933–45* (London, 1979), although it was small by Hollywood standards, UFA was "extremely large, powerful, and highly capitalized" compared to other German film companies, and it held a commanding position in an exceptionally fragmented industry (p. 32). Finally, in addition to its studios and distribution interests, the combine controlled the German assets of Nordisk Film (Denmark) and Sascha-Film (Austria), 100 regional theaters, and the 10 finest first-run houses in Berlin.

† Expressionism, a movement that began in German painting, music, architecture, and theater before the war in reaction to the pervasive naturalism of late-nineteenth-century art, found a large public during the revolutionary *Aufbruch*. Unlike naturalism, which represented objective reality, Expressionism attempted to represent the artist's subjective feelings *in response* to objective reality. It employed a variety of non-naturalistic techniques, including symbolism, abstraction, and perceptual distortion, to achieve this end. In its rejection of bourgeois codes of representation, Expressionism was one of the first recognizably modernist movements in the arts.

phantine drama about the transmigration of souls through three different historical ages, probably established the conventions of the genre, but Ernst Lubitsch (1892–1947) was to become its master. Lubitsch had worked as an actor for Max Reinhardt and directed a popular series of short comedies before coming to UFA in 1918. In that year, he directed the Polish actress Pola Negri ((1894–1987) in two lush costume films, *Die Augen der Mumie Ma (The Eyes of the Mummy Ma)* and *Carmen* (English title: *Gypsy Blood*), both of which were successful enough for Lubitsch and his producer Paul Davidson to attempt a third in 1919. This was *Madame Du Barry* (English title: *Passion*), a story of the French Revolution, which became an international success and launched the famous series of historical pageants with which we associate the first part of Lubitsch's career. In rapid succession, Lubitsch directed *Anna Boleyn* (English title: *Deception*, 1920), *Das Weib des Pharao* (English title: *The Loves of Pharaoh*, 1921), and *Sumurum* (English title: *One Arabian Night*, 1921). These historical films—and Lubitsch directed many other types during his German period—were distinguished technically by his dynamic handling of crowd scenes and his brilliant use of artificial lighting, both of which he seems to have learned from Reinhardt. Furthermore, he made innovative use of camera angles and rapid cutting, which impressed American critics like Lewis Jacobs as "revolutionary," though in fact D. W. Griffith had already advanced the narrative syntax of film far beyond anything Lubitsch contributed. (Lubitsch emigrated to the United States in 1922, where he enriched the American cinema with his sophisticated comedies of wit, urbanity, and sexual innuendo; see p. 231.)

Nevertheless, Lubitsch's technical virtuosity was the first of its kind the German screen had witnessed, and this expertise, coupled with his painstakingly accurate rendition of period detail (called "historical realism" by contemporary critics) in film after film, made Lubitsch's spectacles among the most popular of the postwar years, not simply in Germany but all over the world. Other UFA directors successfully practiced the Lubitsch formula, among them Dmitri Buchowetski in *Danton* (1921), *Othello* (1922), and *Sappho* (1922), and Richard Oswald in *Lady Hamilton* (1922) and *Lucrezia Borgia* (1922), all of which exploited the postwar mania for craftsmanlike reconstructions of the past. Yet there was more to the popularity of the German historical spectacles than a simple fascination with the past, for, as Kracauer has suggested, they tended to present history as a slave to individual passions and psychoses rather than as a process dependent upon a wide range of social and economic variables. Thus, the films of German "historical realism" are antihistorical in an important sense and Romantic to the point of nihilism. Significantly, their popularity in Germany died out in 1924, the year which witnessed the rise of an undisguised and unabashed nihilistic **realism** in the triumph of the *Kammerspielfilm,* as will be discussed in a later section. Until this occurred, however, it was not the historical spectacle but another type of film entirely which was to dominate the German cinema.

DAS KABINETT DES DR. CALIGARI

In late 1918, a Czech poet, Hans Janowitz, and a young Austrian artist named Carl Mayer, who was later to become one of the most influential creative figures of the Weimar cinema, collaborated in writing a scenario based upon certain shared experiences of psychic phenomena and mysterious coincidence, as well as a bizarre sex-slaying in Hamburg known personally to Janowitz. In it, a strange mountebank named Dr. Caligari comes to the North German town of Holstenwall with a traveling fair. His "act" consists of interrogating an apparently hypnotized somnambulist named Cesare, who can forecast the future. Shortly after their arrival, a series of brutal, inexplicable murders is committed in Holstenwall, which the young student Francis later discovers to be the work of Cesare, done at the evil Caligari's bidding. Francis gives the alarm and pursues Caligari into the countryside and finally to his refuge in a state insane asylum, where, it turns out, the showman is not an inmate but the director. Papers found in his study indicate that the director had become obsessed with a homicidal eighteenth-century hypnotist named Caligari to the point of assuming his identity and causing one of his own patients (Cesare) to commit murders for him. Confronted with these proofs, the director goes mad and must be incarcerated in his own asylum. The script, entitled *Das Kabinett des Dr. Caligari** (*The Cabinet of Dr. Caligari*)—a reference to the coffin-like box in which Cesare is kept by his master—was clearly anti-authoritarian if not subversive in its equation of power and madness.

Nevertheless, when Janowitz and Mayer submitted the scenario to Erich Pommer (1889–1966), chief executive of Decla-Bioskop (an independent

4.5   The UFA studios at Neubabelsberg.

---

* Originally *Das Cabinet des Dr. Caligari*, the title was officially "Germanized" in the thirties to disguise its French derivation (a National Socialist policy). Many texts today prefer the original, but I have adopted the usage of Lotte Eisner from *The Haunted Screen* (Berkeley, 1969), *Murnau* (Berkeley, 1973), *Fritz Lang* (New York, 1977), and other of her works.

4.6 Pola Negri in *Madame Du Barry* (Ernst Lubitsch, 1919).

production company which was to merge with UFA in 1921), it was immediately accepted. Whether Pommer grasped the script's radical nature is unclear, but he certainly saw in it an opportunity for upgrading the artistic content of his studio's films. The young Austrian director Fritz Lang was initially assigned to the project but was replaced by Robert Wiene (1881–1938) so that Lang could direct the second part of Decla's successful adventure series *Die Spinnen* (*The Spiders*, 1919–20). However, it was Lang who, against the authors' violent objections, convinced Pommer to add a *Rahmenhandlung* (or framing story) to the film which inverted its meaning: Francis is made the narrator of the tale and introduced as a madman in an asylum which, we discover at the film's conclusion, is operated by the benevolent Dr. Caligari himself. Lang correctly thought that the reality frame would heighten the Expressionistic elements of the *mise-en-scène,* but it also transforms the body of the film from an anti-authoritarian fable into the recounting of a paranoid delusion, which ultimately justifies and glorifies the very authority it was intended to subvert. Still, in terms of its production design, *Das Kabinett des Dr. Caligari* became strikingly experimental under Wiene's direction.

Wiene hired three prominent Expressionist artists—Hermann Warm, Walter Röhrig, and Walter Reimann—to design and paint the sets for the film, which were to embody the tortured state of the narrator's psyche. Thus, the visual world of *Caligari* became a highly stylized one of exaggerated dimensions and deranged spatial relationships—an unnatural, sunless place in which buildings pile on top of one another at impossible angles, jagged chimneys reach insanely into the sky, and the very flesh of its inhabitants seems frozen under pounds of make-up. But the decision to use artificial backdrops was pragmatic as well as thematically appropriate, since in the economic recession which immediately followed the war, the film studios, like all other German industries, were allocated electric power on a quota basis. In a film like *Caligari* that required many dramatic lighting effects, it was cheaper and more convenient to simply

4.7 *Das Kabinett des Dr. Caligari* (Robert Wiene, 1919): Caligari (Werner Krauss), Cesare (Conrad Veidt), and prey (Lil Dagover).

4.8 *Caligari:* Cesare carries his victim over the rooftops of Holstenwall.

paint light and shadow onto the scenery itself than to produce the effect electrically (in fact, the Decla studio had nearly expended its power ration when *Caligari* was produced in late 1919—yet another instance of the way in which technological necessity can foster aesthetic innovation in the cinema).* On the other hand, there were several instances of stylized decor before *Caligari* that had nothing to do with technological imperatives. For example, *Thais* (1916, aka *Il perfido incanto* [*The Wicked Enchantment*]), directed by the Italian Futurist Anton Guilio Bragaglia, used a geometrically stylized set for its concluding scenes; Maurice Tourneur employed stylized scenery on painted backdrops in *The Blue Bird* (1918) and *Prunella* (1918); and Ernst Lubitsch used stylization to represent the world of dolls in a toy box in *Die Puppe* (*The Doll*, 1919). None of these films, however, was stylized in the truly Expressionist manner of *Caligari*, which probably derived more from the stagings of contemporary Expressionist theater than from any other source. Nevertheless, the angular distortion of the sets was clearly intended by Wiene to provide an objective correlative for the narrator's insanity, and for this reason *Caligari* became the progenitor and exemplar of the German Expressionist cinema.

4.9 *Caligari:* a villager falsely imprisoned for Cesare's crimes.

The classic study of this cinema, written by Lotte H. Eisner, is entitled *The Haunted Screen,* and the screen of German Expressionism was indeed a haunted one; but its terrors were those of morbid psychological states and troubled dreams rather than the more concrete horrors that Hollywood's Universal Studios was to offer us in the thirties (although Universal's horror films were the lineal descendants of Expressionism, created in many cases by the same artists, as will be seen in Chapter 8). The nightmarishly distorted decor of German Expressionist films and their creation of *stimmung* ("mood") through shifting **chiaroscuro** lighting were

4.10 *Caligari:* **in a forest of the mind.**

expressive of the disturbed mental and emotional states they sought to portray. The setting for *Caligari* is warped and out of joint because the film itself, we learn at its conclusion, occurs largely in the twisted mind of its narrator. Thus, the creators of *Caligari* and its successors made a deliberate effort to portray subjective realities in objective terms, to render not simply narratives but states of mind, moods, and atmosphere through the medium of the photographic image (a task more difficult than Expressionist representation in the other arts, since there is, seemingly, nothing more objective than a photographic image but the object itself). German Expressionism, then, attempted to express interior realities through the means of exterior realities, or to treat subjective states in what was widely regarded at the time as a purely objective medium of representation. This was perhaps as radical an innovation for the cinema as Porter's discovery of the shot, since it added a non-narrative and poetic dimension to what had been, even in the hands of Griffith, an almost wholly narrative medium.

In terms of narrative, however, *Caligari* was extremely conservative; its expressiveness was fundamentally a matter of decor and staging. We must remember that the years during which Germany was denied access to American films (1914–19) were precisely those in which Griffith made his most significant contributions to film langauge. Wiene practiced cinema in ignorance of the lessons of Griffith, and so the editing continuity of *Caligari* is essentially that of arranged scenes, though there is some rudimentary intercutting and some camera movement. In fact, the film is as stagy as any Méliès or Film d'Art production, despite its wildly avantgarde design. *Caligari* imported Expressionism into the cinema but did not exploit it in cinematic terms and, as a *narrative* structure, did nothing to advance the medium. Thus, despite international acclaim when it was released in February 1920 (Lewis Jacobs has called it "the most widely discussed film of the time"), *Caligari* had little direct impact on the course of other national cinemas. Yet in terms of its set design, its psychological probing and thematic ambiguity, its sinister and morbid subject matter, and, above all, its attempt to render the internal and subjective through the external and objective, *Calgari* had an immense influence upon the German films which followed it.

The production of *Caligari* marked the beginning of the German cinema's great decade. This era was to be characterized by films which, like *Caligari,* were completely studio-made, and by intense admiration for the German studio product all over the world. The emphasis on studio production seems to have stemmed less from economic considerations, as it did in Hollywood, than from aesthetic ones. German directors found that they could exercise complete authority over every aspect of the filmmaking process when they worked in the controlled environment of the studio, as they could not when they worked on location. As Arthur Knight has noted, these directors ultimately preferred to create their settings in the studio from the ground up rather than to discover them in reality at large; as a result, between 1919 and 1927 UFA became the largest and best equipped studio in the Western world. During this period, there was no set so extravagant that it could not be constructed on the vast backlots of the UFA studio at Neubabelsberg, which offered some forty thousand square meters for exteriors alone. Mountains, forests, cities, and entire ages were all recreated with such astonishing fidelity that the critic Paul Rotha coined the term "studio constructivism" to characterize "that curious air of completeness, of finality, that surrounds each product of the German studios." The "realistic" *Kammerspielfilm* (see the following section), no less than the aggressively artificial Expressionist film, profited aesthetically from the large measure of control that studio production permitted a director, and the great cinema of the Weimar Republic could almost certainly not have existed without it. And yet, as we shall see later, UFA's very organizational completeness ultimately led to its own destruction.

4.11 *Der Golem* (Paul Wegener, 1920): art direction by Hans Poelzig.

THE FLOWERING OF EXPRESSIONISM

In any case, between 1919 and 1924 many successors to *Caligari* appeared upon the German screen. Most of these *Schauerfilme* (films of fantasy and terror) used horrific plots and Expressionist decor to embody the theme of the human soul in search of itself. Some representative titles are: F. W. Murnau's *Der Januskopf* (*Janus-Faced*, 1920—adapted from Robert Louis Stevenson's *Dr. Jekyll and Mr. Hyde*), Paul Wegener's remake of *Der Golem* (1920), Arthur Robison's *Schatten* (*Warning Shadows*, 1922), Robert Wiene's *Raskolnikov* (1923—a bizarrely stylized but utterly convincing version of Dostoevsky's *Crime and Punishment*), Paul Leni's *Das Wachsfigurenkabinett* (*Waxworks*, 1924), and Henrik Galeen's remake of *Der Student von Prag* (1926). All of *Caligari*'s spiritual descendants were technically proficient and superbly designed, but two of them deserve special notice, both for their individual accomplishments and because their directors went on to become major figures in the cinema of the Western world. These are Fritz Lang's *Der müde Tod* (1921—literally, "The Weary Death," but usually entitled *Destiny* in English) and F. W. Murnau's *Nosferatu* (1922).

4.12 *Raskolnikov* (Robert Wiene, 1923): art direction by Andrei Andreiev.

Fritz Lang

Fritz Lang (1890–1976) had already directed several feature films and serials (such as the recently reconstructed *Die Spinnen**) when he and his wife, the scriptwriter Thea von Harbou (1888–1954), collaborated in the production of *Der müde Tod* for UFA. The film is a Romantic alle-

---

* Conceived by Lang as a Feuillade-like serial in four parts, only two were actually filmed— *Der goldene See* (*The Golden Lake*, 1919) and *Das Brillantenschiff* (*The Diamond Ship*, 1920), both photographed by Karl Freund. They have been restored by the film historian David Shepard as an adventure melodrama (*Abenteurerfilm*) in two parts, with an organ score composed and performed by Gaylord Carter.

4.13 *Der müde Tod* (Fritz Lang, 1921): the bereaved lover (Lil Dagover) in the cemetery garden. Art direction by Robert Herlth, Walter Röhrig, and Hermann Warm.

4.14 *Der müde Tod:* the Chinese episode.

4.15 *Siegfried* (Fritz Lang, 1923): geometrical stylization of space. Art direction by Otto Hunte, Erich Kellethut, and Karl Vollbrecht.

4.16 *Siegfried:* the forest.

gory, set in the Middle Ages, about a girl whose lover is snatched away by Death himself. She seeks out this figure and demands her lover's return, but Death refuses and instead offers her three fantastic narratives in which lovers attempt unsuccessfully to triumph over Death. These episodes are set in ninth-century Bagdad, in Renaissance Venice, and in a dreamlike, mystical China,* and in all of them the lovers are destroyed by cruel and insatiable tyrants. At the end of these exempla, Death tells the girl that only by offering her own life or that of another can she insure the return of her lover. Later, in saving a baby from a burning hospital, she is killed, but she is reunited with her dead lover by Death in fulfillment of his pledge. Kracauer sees *Der müde Tod* as a manifestation of Germany's postwar obsession with doom and *Götterdämmerung,* the logical culmination of the cultural pessimism of the late nineteenth century, as expressed in such works as Oswald Spengler's *The Decline of the West* (1918–22); and certainly the film's relationship to the major thematic concerns of Expressionism is clear. Lang added something new to the cinema, however, in his striking use of lighting to emphasize architectural line and space.

Lang had been trained as an architect, and he was to carry over his facility for stylized architectural composition as opposed to a purely graphic Expressionism into his other major films of the silent period. These were not intellectualized works in the manner of, say, *Caligari,* but they were all overwhelmingly impressive in terms of sheer plastic beauty and decorative design. *Dr. Mabuse, der Spieler (Dr. Mabuse, the Gambler,* 1922), for example, offers an Expressionistic treatment of a Caligariesque master criminal intent upon destroying the fabric of a postwar society whose

---

* Douglas Fairbanks claimed that the Chinese episode of *Der müde Tod* inspired him to make *The Thief of Bagdad* (1924), which features similar cinematic sleight-of-hand.

rottenness clearly deserves it. In *Siegfried* (1922–24) and *Kriemhilds Rache* (*Kriemhild's Revenge*, 1923–24), Lang again exercised his penchant for legendary romance and compositional majesty in a massive retelling of the Nordic Nibelungen saga,* complete with studio-constructed mountains, forests, and a full-scale fire-breathing dragon.

Finally, in his last major silent film, *Metropolis* (1926), Lang presented a terrifying if simplistic vision of a twenty-first-century totalitarian society whose futuristic architecture and technology were rendered brilliantly concrete through the process and model work of the special-effects photographer Eugen Schüfftan.† (Lang claimed that *Metropolis* was inspired by his first vision of the New York City skyline, from the deck of the SS *Deutschland* in October 1924, at night.) For *Metropolis* Schüfftan invented the trick-shot technique, still universally used and known today as the "Schüfftan process," which works as follows: miniatures are reflected onto a glass with a magnifying mirrored surface, which is placed at a forty-five-degree angle relative to the camera lens. This surface is scraped away from the areas in which live action is to take place, leaving holes behind which the actual sets are constructed and lit to correspond with the lighting of the model.

Lang made two other silent films (*Spione* [*The Spies*, 1928] and *Die Frau im Mond* [*The Woman in the Moon*, 1929]) before shooting his early sound masterpiece *M* (see Chapter 9).** Many of his silent films were made for UFA and written by Thea von Harbou, who later became an ardent Nazi, and Lang himself was offered the leadership of the German film industry by the Nazi propaganda minister, Josef Goebbels, in early 1933 (*Metropolis* was Hitler's favorite film—for all the wrong reasons, of course). Half-Jewish and a political liberal, Lang refused the

4.17 The forest in *Siegfried* under construction at UFA-Neubabelsberg.

---

* In Teutonic mythology, the Nibelungen are a race of dwarfs who possess a magic ring and a great hoard of gold. The *Nibelungenlied* ("song of the Nibelungen") is an anonymous thirteenth-century Middle High German epic in which Siegfried and Kriemhild, the archetypal Teutonic hero and heroine, become fatally involved with the Nibelungen and their treasure, bringing on cosmic chaos—the *Götterdämmerung,* or "Twilight of the Gods." The German classical composer Richard Wagner (1813–83) wrote a monumental tetralogy of music dramas based on the *Nibelungenlied,* but Lang's primary source was the original epic. (Lang had a particular dislike of Wagner's music, and he was outraged when UFA released shortened versions of *Siegfried* and *Kriemhilds Rache* abroad with Wagner scores.)

† Eugen Schüfftan (1883–1977) left Germany in 1932 after shooting only a few films and (as Eugene Schuftan) became a successful cinematographer, director, and technical advisor in England, France, and the United States.

** Many of Lang's films have not been seen in their original versions in the United States. *Metropolis,* for example, was cut from seventeen to ten reels for its 1927 American release, and a full hour is missing from *Kriemhilds Rache.* However, the Munich Film Museum is in the process of restoring Lang's German films, along with other classics of the Weimar period. See John Gillet, "Munich's Cleaned Pictures," *Sight and Sound* 47, 1 (Winter 1977–78), 37–39. In 1985, synth-rock composer Giorgio Moroder (*Midnight Express* [Alan Parker, 1978]; *Flashdance* [Adrian Lyne, 1984]; *Top Gun* [Tony Scott, 1986]) bought the rights to *Metropolis* from the West German government and offered American audiences a $2,000,000 color-tinted reconstruction, complete with lost footage, a contemporary "album-oriented" rock score, and subtitles based on a recently authenticated version of the Lang-von Harbou script.

4.18 An Expressionistic poster for Lang's *Metropolis* (1926).

offer and fled Germany for Hollywood, where he became an important director of American sound films.

F. W. Murnau and the *Kammerspielfilm*

The second major figure to emerge from the Expressionist movement was F. W. (Friedrich Wilhelm) Murnau (1888–1931), whose highly stylized vampire film *Nosferatu, eine Symphonie des Grauens* (*Nosferatu, a Symphony of Horrors*, 1922)* has become a classic of the **genre**. Trained as an art historian, Murnau became fascinated by the theater and began to write for films shortly after the war, collaborating with both Carl Mayer and Hans Janowitz. When he began to direct his own films, Murnau worked almost exclusively in the Expressionist vein, making films like *Der Bucklige und die Tänzerin* (*The Hunchback and the Dancer*, 1920—written by Mayer), *Der Januskopf* (*Janus-Faced*, 1920—written by Janowitz), and *Schloss Vogelöd* (*Castle Vogelod*, 1921—written by Mayer). It is *Nosferatu*, however, adapted loosely (and without credit) by Henrik Galeen from Bram Stoker's novel *Dracula* (1897), that represents the high point of Murnau's Expressionist period.

One of the remarkable things about *Nosferatu* is the apparent naturalness of its stylization, achieved, it should be noted, with a minimum of resources since the film was independently produced. Like the Scandinavian directors whose films flooded Germany during the war, Murnau had an affinity for landscapes, and he had most of *Nosferatu* shot on location in Central Europe by the great cinematographer Fritz Arno Wagner, whose specialty was a kind of low-contrast, realistic photography which exchanged stark black-and-white for a whole range of intermediate grays. While the film is essentially a thriller and is more than a bit creaky in terms of narrative structure, it nonetheless provides a succession of haunting visual images more authentically "expressive" of horror than those of *Caligari*. Whereas *Caligari*'s Expressionism was mainly graphic, *Nosferatu*'s is almost purely cinematic, relying upon camera angles, lighting, and editing rather than production design. Nosferatu, the vampire king, is frequently photographed from an extremely low angle which renders him gigantic and monstrously sinister on the screen (a device not lost upon Orson Welles, who would employ it obsessively throughout *Citizen Kane* eighteen years later; see Chapter 10). A number of these shots are lit so that the vampire's vast and angular shadow is cast across every object in the frame.† Many of the film's images are strikingly composed in depth, with action sharply in focus in the foreground, middleground, and background simultaneously. This mode of composing the frame has

---

* *Nosferatu* was remade under the same title by the brilliant German director Werner Herzog in 1978 (see Chapter 18). The original was recently reconstructed in its tinted version by the Munich Film Museum, for accompaniment by Hans Erdmann's 1922 score, newly arranged by Berndt Heller.

† A minor gaffe—a vampire casts no shadow, as all horror buffs are well aware.

4.19 *Metropolis:* the quarters of the ruling class. Art direction by Hunte, Kellethut, and Vollbrecht.

4.20 The subterranean city of the robotlike workers.

4.21 The electric Moloch which powers Metropolis and which the workers serve.

4.22 Lang shooting *Metropolis:* the mad scientist Rotwang creates "the False Maria."

4.23 Lang creating an "architecturalized" crowd. Lotte Eisner suggests that Lang's handling of crowd scenes was influenced by the practices of stage director Erwin Piscator (1893–1966).

4.24 Realization: the workers' revolt and flood near the end of *Metropolis.*

4.25 *Nosferatu* (F. W. Murnau, 1922): Max Schreck as the vampire. Art direction by Albin Grau.

the effect of integrating character and landscape, and much of *Nosferatu*'s "naturalness" derives from it. Composition in depth also produces some memorable expressive effects. Near the film's conclusion, its heroine, who is situated in the foreground of the frame, gazes through her window at a mass funeral procession for the vampire's victims, which is shot so that it seems to stretch away endlessly from the middleground to infinity, suggesting the enormity of Nosferatu's crimes. Less impressive today, perhaps, are the cinematic tricks that Murnau and Wagner used to create a supernatural atmosphere for the film. The forests surrounding Nosferatu's castle, for example, are made to seem ghostly through the use of **negative** footage, and the vampire's supernatural strength is rendered in terms of jerky accelerated action achieved through stop-motion photography, as discussed in Chapter 1. Nevertheless, *Nosferatu* as a whole remains one of the most ominous and expressive horror films ever made; as the Hungarian film critic Béla Balázs (see p. 699) wrote, "a chilly draft from doomsday" passes through its every scene.

Murnau's next important film was made in the genre which superseded Expressionism—that of the *Kammerspiel* (literally, "intimate theater"), or "instinct," film. The scriptwriter Carl Mayer, of *Caligari* fame, was the founder and chief practitioner of this genre, which dealt realistically with the oppressiveness of contemporary lower-middle-class life and, by extension, with the irresistibility of fate in a disintegrating society. All of Mayer's scripts for the "instinct" films showed great compression of form and were specifically tailored to the technical requirements of cinema. They generally avoided the use of intertitles altogether and contained only a few characters, each of whom represented a destructive and uncontrollable impulse. Mayer began writing *Kammerspiel* scripts in the heyday of Expressionism, and there is no question that they contain Expressionist elements. Indeed, the whole realistic cinema which grew out of the *Kammerspielfilm* can be seen as both an extension of and a reaction against the Expressionist cinema, in that it retained the morbid psychological themes of the earlier films but cast them in realistic form (and, furthermore, a realistic form which was the product of UFA studio shooting rather than documentary technique). The films made from Mayer's early *Kammerspiel* scripts are Leopold Jessner's *Hintertreppe* (*Backstairs*, 1921), and Lupu Pick's *Scherben* (*Shattered*, 1921) and *Sylvester* (1923); but it was *Der letzte Mann* (literally, "The Last Man," but usually entitled *The Last Laugh* in English), written by Mayer and directed by Murnau, which incarnated the type and inaugurated a new period of German realism in 1924.

Der letzte Mann, produced by Erich Pommer for UFA, is a distinguished film in every respect, and an extremely important one in terms of the enormous influence it exercised, especially upon German and American cinema. The script by Mayer, the acting by Emil Jannings (1884–1950), and the production design by Walter Röhrig and Robert Herlth are all impressive; but it is the innovative use of camera movement that makes *Der letzte Mann* so important to the history of film, and this was achieved largely by Murnau and his cinematographer, Karl Freund.* It was Mayer who suggested that the camera be put into nearly continuous motion (the "unchained camera," he called it), and he specified its involvement in the action in his script. Freund, however, was responsible for the brilliant tactical maneuvering that permitted this movement, and, Murnau, of course, directed it.

Like all *Kammerspielfilme, Der letzte Mann* has a fairly simple plot. It is also unrelievedly grim until the sudden appearance of a happy ending, which is emotionally satisfying in a primitive sort of way but wholly out of key with what has gone before. The film concerns an aging doorman (Jannings) in a fashionable Berlin hotel who loses his job and, more important, his resplendent uniform to a younger man. Within the lower-middle-class tenement where he lives with his daughter, the uniform has brought him prestige and dignity; its unexpected loss elicits a kind of furious ridicule from his neighbors that is chillingly sadistic. Demoted to the position of washroom attendant at the hotel and utterly humiliated in his own home, the old man begins to come apart. He becomes stoop-shouldered and slovenly overnight; he gets raging drunk at his daughter's wedding and experiences delusions of persecution; he even makes a desperate attempt to steal his uniform back out of a hotel locker. As the film nears its conclusion, we discover him crouched furtively against the wall of the hotel lavatory like a trapped beast, terrified of the entire world outside himself and apparently as mad as Caligari. But no: the film's single title flashes on the screen to explain that whereas in the real world things would end at this point, the filmmakers have decided to take pity on the ex-doorman. There follows a farcical conclusion in which he inherits a vast sum of money by an outlandish coincidence and shows up in the hotel dining room to flaunt his wealth before his former employers in a grandly vulgar but good-natured manner. It is thought that this contrived ending was tacked onto the film either to pander to the American audience's taste for such sentimental optimism or to parody it; no one is quite sure which. (The American cinema had finally begun to influence the German cinema by 1924 and was to have considerably more influence as the decade progressed.) But, whatever the case, the incongruity of the

4.26 *Der letzte Mann* (F. W. Murnau, 1924): Emil Jannings as the proud porter.

4.27 Expressionistic set design: the porter's tenement.

---

*Karl Freund (1890–1969) was director of photography for many of Germany's most distinguished silent films, including Murnau's *Januskopf* (1920), *Der letzte Mann* (1924), *Tartuffe* (1925), and *Faust* (1926); Lang's *Metropolis* (1926; with Günther Rittau); Walter Ruttmann's *Berlin, die Symphonie einer Grosßstadt* (*Berlin, Symphony of a Great City*, 1927; supervision only); and E. A. Dupont's *Varieté* (*Variety*, 1925). He also worked with Reinhardt, Lubitsch, Wegener (*Der Golem*, 1920), and Dreyer (see Chapter 9, p. 330). With Fritz Arno Wagner (1894–1958: Murnau's *Nosferatu* [1922]; Lang's *Der müde Tod* [1921], *Spione* [1928], *M* [1931], and *Das Testament des Dr. Mabuse* [1933]; and Pabst's *Die Liebe der Jeanne Ney* [1927; see below], *Westfront 1918* [1930], and *Kameradschaft* [1931]), Freund was one of the two great cinematographers of the Weimar period. After emigrating to Hollywood in 1930, he scored major successes both as a cinematographer (for Robert Florey's *Murders in the Rue Morgue* [1932], Tod Browning's *Dracula* [1931], George Cukor's *Camille* [1935], etc.) and as a director (*The Mummy* [1932], *Mad Love* [1935], etc.).

ending is the only notable flaw* in what is both cinematically and thematically a nearly perfect film.

Indeed, *Der letzte Mann* was the most technically innovative film to come out of Weimar cinema. Prior to it, most camera movement had been panning and tilting (see Chapter 1) wedded to a fixed tripod. With several significant exceptions (in the films of Griffith and the Italian film *Cabiria* [1914]), there had been little sustained *tracking* movement—i.e., movement in which the whole camera apparatus participates, either to follow another moving object or to isolate a static one by moving in close upon it. What is necessary to achieve this kind of fluidity is a *dolly*—a small wheeled cart on which to mount the camera during shooting, which may or may not use tracks (thus "tracking"). Today, the **boom** crane and a variety of sophisticated dollies (as well as Steadicams†) are available to permit such freedom, but these devices could only be improvised in 1924. (Murnau did, however, have access to motor-driven cameras, which allowed their operators to concentrate full attention on movement and focus.) Griffith, of course, had put his camera in the back of an automobile to follow the motion of the chase in *The Birth of a Nation* and *Intolerance*, and he had used an elevator tower that rolled on rails to track his machine into the gigantic set of Belshazzar's feast in *Intolerance;* other American directors had improvised dollies in order to follow the movement of actors within a scene without cutting; but *Der letzte Mann* was the first film in history to move its camera backward and forward, as well as up and down and from side to side, in scenes of substantial duration.**

These are scenes held for a single shot and kept alive almost solely through camera movement, rather than scenes built up out of a number of separate shots and kept alive through editing, as in the work of Griffith and Eisenstein. In the frequently cited opening sequence, for example, we ride via the camera down the hotel elevator, move through the bustling lobby, approach the revolving door (a major symbol of life's randomness in the film—a sort of existential roulette wheel), and come to focus on the doorman on the sidewalk in what appears to be a single unbroken shot (there is actually a discreet cut in the middle of the track through the lobby). The film is replete with shots like this, and their accomplishment was by no means simple in the absence of modern cranes and dollies. For the shot just described, Freund mounted his camera on a bicycle

4.28 Subjective camera: the porter imagines ridicule during his drunken dream.

4.29 *Der letzte Mann:* down and out.

---

* Or, perhaps not. Bruce Kawin has suggested to me that this incongruity is calculated and highly effective—"a perfect early working example of deconstruction (by Mayer)." The porter, like the film and the studio that produced it, is saved in the end by a bequest from the rich American "A.G. Monney," i.e. "Aktiengesellschaft [company] money" soon to flow into UFA's coffers as a result of the Parufamet deal.

† The trade name for a device which serves to stabilize the movement of hand-held cameras, introduced in 1976. See p. 904.

** Orson Welles would create a similar sequence in *Citizen Kane* (1940) when he had Gregg Toland track his camera straight through the El Rancho nightclub sign and through a rain-drenched skylight down into the club below. Welles was also clearly influenced by Murnau's American film *Sunrise* (1927), whose nocturnal moving camera shots anticipate the opening sequence of *Kane*.

in the descending elevator, rolled it out into the lobby, and tracked it several hundred feet to the revolving door. In other shots, the camera rode the ladder of a fire truck, anticipating the boom crane, and traveled on overhead cables. Indeed, Freund's camera seems to move almost continuously throughout *Der letzte Mann,* although there are actually many shots taken with the camera at full rest which provide an appropriate counterpoint for the others.

But of equal importance with the camera mobility achieved by Murnau and Freund was their use of the subjective camera—the technique whereby the camera lens becomes the eyes of a player in the film, usually the protagonist, so that the audience sees only what he or she sees and only from his or her angle of vision. Griffith's "objects of attention" intercut with facial close-ups are a rudimentary form of this technique: when he cuts from a character looking at something offscreen to a shot of what the character sees as he or she sees it, Griffith is practicing a kind of shorthand subjectivity. These "motivated point-of-view" shots, in combination with the eyeline match, were brought to a state of extreme refinement by the UFA director G. W. Pabst later in the twenties. No one before Murnau and Freund, however, had understood the full range of possibilities inherent in the subjective camera and the way in which it might be used to create multiple perspectives on a single narrative.*

The most famous subjective camera shot in *Der letzte Mann* occurs in the scene in which the doorman gets drunk in his apartment and sits down while the room seems to spin wildly about him. To render the character's point of view at this moment, Freund strapped a lightweight camera to his chest and stumbled drunkenly about the room. This is a fairly typical and straightforward use of the technique, but in *Der letzte Mann* the camera is subjective in another sense too, a sense which demonstrates the roots of German realism in Expressionism. Quite frequently, in addition to assuming the position of the doorman's *physical eye,* the camera assumes the position of his *mind's eye* as well. During the same drunken scene, he feels acutely humiliated at the loss of his job and his prestigious uniform, and he later dreams himself to be the object of ridicule and scorn which he will in fact become on the following day, when his misfortune becomes known to all. At the height of his despair in the dream sequence, we see on the screen not the doorman (as with the "objective camera"), but a visual embodiment of what he *feels*—a long lap-dissolved montage of malicious laughing faces in close-up. Earlier, after he steals his old uniform and runs out of the hotel into the street, the doorman looks back on the building, which seems to tremble and sway as if about to fall and crush him. There is also a dream sequence, shot with distorting mirrors (in the manner of the Gance film described

---

* An exception would be Abel Gance, whose Film d'Art short *La Folie du Docteur Tube* (1915) used distorting **mirror shots** throughout to suggest the hallucinatory effects of a drug; but the producers refused to distribute the film, so it cannot have influenced *Der letzte Mann.* Several similar shots occur in Germaine Dulac's *La Souriant Madame Beudet* (1922) and Jacques Feyder's *Crainquebille* (1923), where they are used to evoke a character's disturbed mental state. (On the work of all three, see Chapter 9.)

below), in which the porter imagines himself to be possessed of supernatural strength and bounces a large footlocker in the air like a balloon. We might say, then, that Murnau shows his Expressionist roots by using the subjective camera in a highly expressive way—to embody the morbid psychological state of his protagonist in terms of visual images. But there is more.

In scenes like these Murnau showed that he had grasped the concept that the camera was capable of first-person as well as third-person narration; that this first-person narration had both inner and outer modes; and, finally, that a director could alternate between these several modes of narration at will to create multiple perspectives on a given subject. Thus, while *Der letzte Mann* is simple in terms of plot, it has an extremely elaborate structure in which the narrative point of view is in constant rotation between the third-person objective camera and the two modes of first-person subjective camera. This was an innovation at least as significant for cinematic narrative as, say, Griffith's realization that a dramatic sequence could be built up from shots of varying temporal and spatial lengths. Like Griffith's innovations, both modes of subjective camera have now passed into the conventional lexicon of the cinema, but in 1924 they were virtually unprecedented, and the influence of *Der letzte Mann* upon contemporary cinema was immense. As *The Last Laugh*, it enjoyed worldwide success and had a greater effect upon Hollywood technique than any other single foreign film in history, in terms of both its fluidity and its titleless narration. As Murnau's biographer Lotte H. Eisner puts it, "It was the almost universal decision of Hollywood that this was the greatest picture ever made"; Murnau was to leave Germany for a Hollywood career after completing two final super-productions for UFA (*Tartuffe* [1925], and *Faust* [1926]).

Hollywood was to be almost equally impressed in the following year with *Der letzte Mann*'s immediate successor, E. A. (Ewald André) Dupont's (1891–1956) *Varieté* (1925), also produced by Erich Pommer for UFA and photographed by Karl Freund. The film deals with a love triangle among trapeze artists (Emil Jannings, Lya de Putti, Warwick Ward) at the Berlin Wintergarten which ends in murder, and it contains camera movement even more breathlessly dynamic than that of *Der letzte Mann*. In almost documentary fashion, Freund's camera penetrates everywhere the human eye can go. It darts frenetically from face to face in a crowded room; it flies through the air with the acrobats, focusing subjectively on the swaying audience below; and at one point it seems to plummet to the floor of the Wintergarten as a performer falls to his death. Much of this movement is less functional than that of *Der letzte Mann* and gives the impression of having been contrived for its own sake. Moreover, the film is highly derivative of *Der letzte Mann* in terms of atmosphere and theme as well as technique. Nevertheless, as Lewis Jacobs writes, "*Variety* put American movie-goers into a white heat of enthusiasm over film art," and it insured the permanence of German influence upon the Hollywood studios until the end of the silent era (which was soon matched by a tendency to "Americanize" the German film, as we shall see). For the German cinema, on the other hand, *Varieté* provided a bridge between

4.30 Decadence in *Varieté* (E. A. Dupont, 1925).

the introspective *Kammerspiel* genre and a more objective kind of realism which was to emerge after 1924.

THE PARUFAMET AGREEMENT AND THE MIGRATION TO HOLLYWOOD

In 1924 the German mark had been stabilized and the spiral of post-war inflation halted by Germany's acceptance of the Dawes Plan (named for the American banker Charles E. Dawes, who presided over an international committee set up to monitor Germany's war reparations payments). This provided for the long-term payment of reparations and admitted Germany back into the economic system of the Allies. The effect was to create in the German Republic a stabilized period of false confidence and even prosperity which lasted until the stock market crash of 1929. Ironically, however, the German film industry, which had survived rampant inflation, was seriously threatened by stabilization, because the Dawes Plan stipulated the curtailment of all exports. Thus, between 1924 and 1925 many independent production companies folded, and the surviving ones found it very difficult to borrow money from German banks. Sensing a chance to cripple its only European rival, Hollywood began to pour American films into Germany, founding its own distribution agencies and buying up theaters. By late 1925, UFA was on the brink of collapse due to external conditions and to the extravagance of its own recent productions, having lost over eight million dollars in the fiscal year just ended; at this point the American studios Paramount and MGM offered to subsidize UFA's huge debt to the Deutsche Bank by lending it four million dollars at 7.5 percent interest in exchange for collaborative rights to UFA studios, theaters, and personnel—an arrangement which clearly worked in the American companies' favor.* The result was the foundation of the "Parufamet" (Paramount-UFA-Metro) Distribution Company in early 1926. Within a year, however, UFA was showing losses of twelve million dollars and was forced to seek another loan, this time from the Prussian financier Dr. Alfred Hugenberg (1865–1951). Hugenberg, who had been a director of Krupp and was a leader of the right-wing German National Party (Deutschnationale Volkspartei, or DNVP), subsequently bought out the American companies and became chairman of the UFA board in March 1927.† Without fanfare, he established a nationalistic

---

* The loan was nearly made by Carl Laemmle's Universal in exchange for a mutual distribution contract and two of the five votes on the UFA board, but Paramount and MGM stepped in at the last minute with a better deal. See Kristin Thompson, *Exporting Entertainment: America in the World Film Market, 1907–1934* (London: BFI Publishing, 1985), pp. 106–11.

† Hugenberg exercised complete control over UFA by personally owning a majority share of its stock; the rest of the company's capital was held by DNVP associates. The board was chosen from the most conservative representatives of German heavy industry and finance, including Louis Hager, Emil Strauss, Fritz Thyssen, and Heinrich von Schrötter, who also controlled vast newspaper publishing, advertising, and telecommunications interests.

production policy which gave increasing prominence to Nazi Party rallies in UFA newsreels and which finally permitted the Nazis to subvert the German film industry in 1933. While the republic survived, however, Hugenberg was content to wait.

The most immediate effect of the Parufamet agreement was the migration of UFA film artists and technicians to Hollywood, where they worked for a variety of studios. Ernst Lubitsch had come to America in 1922 to direct *Rosita* for Mary Pickford, as had the world-famous UFA actress Pola Negri and her Russian-born director, Dmitri Buchowetski, shortly thereafter. They were joined in 1926–27 by the directors E. A. Dupont, Ludwig Berger, Lothar Mendes, Berthold Viertel, Paul Leni, F. W. Murnau, and Mihály Kertész (a Hungarian working for UFA, who became Michael Curtiz in America and went on to direct over one hundred films for Warner Brothers between 1927 and 1960, including the legendary *Casablanca* [1942]); the cinematographer Karl Freund; the performers Emil Jannings, Conrad Veidt (Cesare in *Caligari*), Greta Garbo (Swedish), and Lya de Putti (Hungarian); and the producer Erich Pommer and the scenarist Carl Mayer. This migration didn't decimate UFA, since it was random and temporary. Yet many German technicians, actors, and minor directors did settle in Hollywood and pursue modestly successful careers. Karl Freund, for example, not only became one of the most able Hollywood cinematographers of the thirties but also directed a handful of superbly atmospheric horror thrillers for Universal and MGM (see note, p. 127) which conferred a substantial legacy of German Expressionism upon the Hollywood horror film as a sound-film genre. But the fate of the major German directors in Hollywood was similar to that of the Scandinavians Sjöström and Stiller.

To put it simply, Hollywood didn't want them to film the kinds of subjects that had made them great directors in their native industries. In effect, the American studios had bought a boatload of foreign talent that they literally didn't know how to employ. The major artists rapidly became bored with their dull assignments and returned to Germany (some only to return to America later as refugees from the Nazis). Only Lubitsch was able to successfully adapt himself to the complexity and vapidity of the Hollywood production process, and his American career proved much more significant than his German one. Murnau stayed on too, and it is conceivable that he might have brought his American career to greatness had his life not been cut short by an automobile accident in 1931. As it was, after he made the visually exquisite if saccharine *Sunrise* in 1927 (produced by Fox, written by Mayer, and shot by Karl Struss and Charles Rosher, but devoid of the thematic power of *Der letzte Mann*), the quality of Murnau's work declined. His last film, the independently produced South Seas tragedy *Tabu* (1931), was an aesthetic success, but the director died one week before it reached the screen.

4.31 *Caligari's* American children: the Universal horror films of the thirties. Tod Browning's expressionistic *Dracula* (1931), photographed by Karl Freund.

G. W. PABST AND "STREET" REALISM

Another effect of the Dawes Plan on the German film industry was less direct than the Parufamet agreement but more important to the general

4.32 James Whale's *Frankenstein* (1931, Universal), photographed by Arthur Edeson.

trend of domestic production. The period after 1924 produced, superficially at least, a return to social normalcy in Germany. As a consequence, the German cinema began to turn away from the morbid and mannered psychological themes of Expressionism and *Kammerspiel* and toward the kind of literal (but still studio-produced) realism exemplified by the "street films" (*Strassenfilme*) of the second half of the decade—G. W. Pabst's *Die freudlose Gasse* (*The Joyless Street*, 1925), Bruno Rahn's *Dirnentragödie* (*Tragedy of the Street*, 1927), Joe May's *Asphalt* (1929), and Piel Jutzi's *Berlin Alexanderplatz* (1930). Named for their prototype, Karl Grune's *Der Strasse* (*The Street*, 1923), these films all dealt realistically with the plight of ordinary people in the postwar period of inflation and incarnated the spirit of *die neue Sachlichkeit* ("the new objectivity") which entered German society and art at every level during this time. Cynicism, resignation, disillusionment, and a desire to accept "life as it is" were the major characteristics of *die neue Sachlichkeit*, and these translated into a type of grim social realism in the street films.*

---

* While the shift to social realism of some sort was fairly general in the German cinema at this point, two other more popular genres deserve mention. The *Kulturfilme* were feature-length escapist documentaries on esoteric subjects, expensively produced by UFA. With titles like *Wege zu Kraft und Schönheit* (*Ways to Health and Beauty*, 1925), these films became a German specialty on the international market and were a vast financial success for the studio. The other popular genre was an exclusively national phenomenon—the mountain films of Dr. Arnold Fanck (1889–1974), which exploited the Germanic predilection for heroic scenery and winter sports in vehicles like *Berg des Schicksals* (*Peak of Destiny*, 1924), *Der heilige Berg* (*The Holy Mountain*, 1927), and *Die weisse Hölle von Piz Palü* (*The White Hell of Pitz Palu*, 1929; co-directed by Pabst). These were all fiction films, stunningly photographed on location by the best talent money could buy (the actress Leni

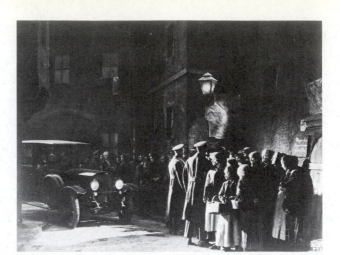

4.33 *Die neue Sachlichkeit: Die freudlose Gasse* (G. W. Pabst, 1925).

The undisputed master of the new realism was the Austrian-born director G. W. (Georg Wilhelm) Pabst (1886–1967). Trained in the theater, Pabst was a latecomer to the Weimar cinema who directed his first film, *Der Schatz* (*The Treasure*), rather perfunctorily in 1924. His next film, however, was *Die freudlose Gasse* (*The Joyless Street*, 1925), which achieved world recognition as a masterpiece of cinematic social realism. (In some countries recognition came in the form of censorship—England banned *Die freudlose Gasse,* and the prints seen in Italy, Austria, and France were substantially cut.) The film concerns the financial and spiritual ruin of the middle classes through inflation in postwar Vienna, focusing upon the lives of several destitute bourgeois families struggling to preserve their dignity and decency in the face of secret starvation. The misery of their existence is contrasted with the extravagant pleasure-seeking of the war profiteers. Daughters of the middle class—the most prominent played by the Swedish actresses Asta Nielsen and Greta Garbo (in her German screen debut)—sell themselves into prostitution to save their families, while the wealthy amuse themselves at opulent blackmarket nightclubs where these girls must eventually come to be "bought." Yet there is no sentimentality or symbolism in the presentation. Pabst captures "life as it is" with a kind of photographic realism that completely rejects the subjective camera of Murnau and Freund (his cinematographers were Guido Seeber, Robert Lach, and the prolific documentarist Curt Oertel [1890–1961]). Like theirs, of course, Pabst's camera does move, but the essential dynamism of his films is generated through cutting and, more specifically, cutting on a character's movement.

Pabst was the first German director to be substantially influenced by

Riefenstahl—see pp. 366–67—and the director G. W. Pabst were among Fanck's collaborators), which relied heavily upon spurious sentiment and inflated plots for their dramatic effect. Nevertheless, they enjoyed quite a cult among the German audience, and, according to Kracauer, their popularity was a harbinger of the heroic and irrational appeal of Nazism. See *New German Critique,* no. 40 (Winter 1987): Special Issue on Weimar Film Theory.

Eisenstein's theory and practice of montage, as will be discussed in Chapter 5. In fact, prior to Pabst, the German cinema had evolved through its various phases as essentially a cinema of *mise-en-scène* rather than of montage, since it had developed in isolation from the innovations of Griffith and his Russian successors. Pabst's own contribution to film technique was the discovery that the perceptual fragmentation created by editing within scenes could be effectively concealed for the purpose of narration by cutting a shot in the midst of a motion which is completed in the next shot.* The spectator's eye follows the character's movement and not the film's (not, that is, the cut itself), which renders the whole process of montage more fluid and comprehensible. Thus, a director who wished to cut smoothly from a full shot of an actor to a medium shot from the waist up might require the actor to begin some incidental movement or gesture in the full shot which could be completed in the medium shot after the cut—e.g., lighting a cigarette, answering a phone, or even rising from a chair. This kind of cutting (sometimes called "invisible editing" or **continuity editing** became fundamental to the classical sound film, where it is often necessary to create visual bridges between shots corresponding to aural bridges on the soundtrack (for instance, a character may move from one shot into several others while speaking continuous dialogue, so that the visual sequence must be made to seem continuous as well). Ironically, by neutralizing the perceptual fragmentation inherent in narrative montage, Pabst actually increased its potential for use in any given sequence, and one hallmark of his later films is the large number of barely perceptible cuts he uses per scene.

Another hallmark is Pabst's increasing use of motivated point-of-view through the eyeline match and the shot-reverse-shot figure. In an eyeline match, the first shot shows a character looking at something offscreen (i.e., beyond the borders of the frame), while the second shot shows the object of his or her gaze, creating an illusion of spatial contiguity. Shot-reverse-shot is cutting back and forth between eyelines as two characters look offscreen at each other, and it would become the most prevalent continuity figure in the classical Hollywood cinema of the thirties and forties.

Cutting on movement, in combination with motivated point-of-view in the eyeline match and the shot-reverse-shot figure, enabled Pabst to produce elaborate—but seemingly effortless—continuity structures. In *Die Liebe der Jeanne Ney* (*The Love of Jeanne Ney*, 1927), for example, one two-minute narrative sequence contains over forty fluid cuts representing—both subjectively and objectively—the perspectives of three separate characters as they move about a room during a heated argument. Pabst increasingly refined these techniques with each successive film, and it seems correct to say that, symbolically at least, he brought to its logical conclusion Edwin S. Porter's discovery that a scene may be broken down

---

*Barry Salt correctly points out that cutting on action was used by Ralph Ince (1887–1937) in films like *The Juggernaut* as early as 1915 (*Film Style and Technology: History and Analysis* (London: Starwood, 1983), p. 165. But Pabst was the first director to structure entire films around the practice.

4.34 *Geheimnisse einer Seele* (G. W. Pabst, 1926):
Freud on film.

into more than one shot and that the shot is the basic signifying unit of
the cinema.

Pabst's later films continue his involvement with social realism, although
they are sometimes diluted by melodrama and fantasy from the inescapable heritage of Expressionism. *Geheimnisse einer Seele* (*Secrets of a Soul*,
1926), for example, a cinematic case history of an anxiety neurosis (produced in collaboration with two disciples of Sigmund Freud [1856–1939],
the founder of psychoanalysis—Dr. Hans Sachs and Dr. Karl Abraham—
and shot by the brilliant team of Seeber, Lach, and Oertel) contains some
of the most vivid dream sequences ever recorded on film. In *Die Liebe
der Jeanne Ney* Pabst returned to the social arena to film the progress of
a love affair caught up in the turmoil of the Russian Revolution and its
aftermath. Photographed in semidocumentary fashion with natural lighting by Fritz Arno Wagner and Robert Lach, often using real locations,
the film portrays postwar European society in the process of rapid disintegration; in it Pabst carried his sophisticated cutting techniques to new
heights. Pabst's last two silent films,* *Die Büchse der Pandora* (*Pandora's Box*, 1929) and *Tagebuch einer Verlorenen* (*Diary of a Lost One*,
1929), both concern the lives of prostitutes (played in each case by the
striking American actress Louise Brooks [1906–85] and the way in which
their degraded roles relate to the general decadence of society. Pabst
adapted himself readily to sound and became one of the foremost masters
of the early sound film; his pacifist films *Westfront 1918* (1930) and
Kameradschaft (*Comradeship*, 1931) are both among the most important works of the period. Indeed Pabst's career extended well into the
fifties, but his greatest work was done between 1924 and 1931—a time,
ironically, when what has been called the Golden Age of German film
was drawing to a close and the German cinema was about to begin its
long decline.

---

*Excluding the melodramatic "mountain film" *Die weisse Hölle von Piz Palü* (1929), which
Pabst co-directed with Arnold Fanck.

DOWN AND OUT

In the past, it was fashionable to blame this decline upon the Nazis, who did indeed subvert UFA immediately after coming to power in 1933, turning the studio into a factory for the mass production of light entertainment and an instrument of propaganda for the state, under the direction of Josef Goebbels. Recently, however, it has come to be recognized that the German cinema was dying of internal disorders long before the Nazi takeover, long before even the coming of sound. This is not to suggest that it was completely moribund by the end of the silent era. Far from it; for Germany produced three of the most distinguished early sound films made anywhere in the world: Josef von Sternberg's *Der blaue Engel* (*The Blue Angel,* 1930; see Chapter 8), Fritz Lang's *M* (1931), and Pabst's *Westfront 1918* (1930). Yet there is no doubt that the general quality of production declined sharply after 1924 and that the causes were deep-seated and manifold.

For one thing, it seems certain that the emphasis on studio production, so important to the aesthetic quality of the German cinema between 1919 and 1924, had proved stifling by the end of the silent period. The UFA style of architectural composition and pictorial lighting was becoming an end in itself, and the sheer extravagance of its productions had substantially diminished the studio's economic stability (Murnau's *Faust,* for example, was rumored to have overrun its costs by four times the budgeted amount). It is significant in this regard that the last two important films of the Weimar cinema were "montage documentaries" shot on location in and around Berlin. Walter Ruttmann's *Berlin, die Symphonie einer Großstadt* (*Berlin, the Symphony of a Great City,* 1927), based on an idea by Carl Mayer, employed the candid camera and rhythmic montage techniques of Dziga Vertov's "kino-eye" group (see Chapter 5) to create an abstract portrait of the city and its teeming life from dawn to midnight on a late spring day.* *Menschen am Sonntag* (*People on Sunday,* 1929), a semidocumentary account of two young couples on a holiday at a lake outside Berlin, was the collaborative effort of several young men who would later become major directors of the sound era in America—Robert Siodmak, Fred Zinnemann, Edgar G. Ulmer, and Billy Wilder (Eugen Schüfftan, who would also emigrate to Hollywood, was the cinematographer). Like its wholly documentary predecessor, *Menschen am Sonntag* showed the marked influence of Vertov and Soviet montage.

---

* Karl Freund coauthored the script of *Berlin* with Ruttman and supervised the cinematography of Reimar Kuntze, Robert Baberske, and László Schäffer. Ruttman cut it himself to parallel the rhythms of a score by the German Marxist composer Edmund Meisel, whose stirring revolutionary music for Eisenstein's *Potemkin* had helped to get that film banned in Germany. (Mayer dissociated himself from *Berlin* at this point, claiming that it had become too "formalistic"; on this aspect of the film see Matthew Bernstein, "Visual Style and Spatial Articulations in *Berlin, Symphony of a City* (1927)," *Journal of Film and Video* 36, 4 [Fall 1984]: 5–12). Ironically, Ruttman (1897–1941) went on to become a leading documentarist of the Third Reich, assisting Leni Riefenstahl on *Olympiad* (1936) and directing the strident *Deutsche Panzer* (1940) to celebrate the victory over France.

4.35 *Berlin, die Symphonie einer Grosstadt* (Walter Ruttmann, 1927).

It was the American influence, however, which proved most powerful, and many film historians have blamed the decline of Weimar cinema on the intrusion of Hollywood money and manners into Germany after the Parufamet agreement was signed. It is well known, for example, that Pabst was ordered by UFA executives to direct *Die Liebe der Jeanne Ney* in the "American style" and that the film barely survived the attempt.* Indeed, the American style in Neubabelsberg proved even less successful than the UFA style in Hollywood. Other film scholars have argued that the German cinema was artistically impoverished by the talent raids which Hollywood made upon UFA in 1926; certainly the loss of Murnau and so many of his associates was significantly detrimental to the studio. Finally, UFA was literally impoverished by American competition, both international and domestic, in the wake of the Dawes Plan, so that it had to be bailed out by the political Right. It seems clear, however, that the most important reasons for Germany's decline as a major cinematic power run deeper than those put forth here already.

Lotte H. Eisner gets closer to the heart of the matter in the final chapter of *The Haunted Screen*, in which she suggests that the thematic legacy of Expressionism was tragedy and despair. Indeed, as Siegfried Kracauer shows time and time again in *From Caligari to Hitler*, the struggle for control of the self, which provided the great theme of the Weimar cinema, was always *lost* on the screen; and this had the effect of increasing the insecurity and thus the authoritarian tendencies of the masses, which in the postwar era included large segments of the middle class brought low by inflation. Since the German form of government was republican and Germany was a conquered nation, however, this authoritarian impulse had no means of expression, and the collective mind of the society was paralyzed by its inability to articulate itself. Thus, if Eisner and Kracauer are correct, and I believe that they are, the decline of the German cinema was due to multiple external factors underpinned by a nationwide inner paralysis which in some sense the German cinema, at least as an organ of German society, had helped to create. It was not the Nazis who destroyed the German cinema, then, but the cultural preconditions which permitted their rise to power; and though UFA managed to produce a handful of truly distinguished films between 1929 and 1933, the vital spark of the German screen had been extinguished. Thanks to the virulence of the Nazi plague and the partitioning of Germany which followed World War II, it could not be rekindled until the generation of Germans born after the war came to artistic and political consciousness in the late sixties. Since that time, the West German cinema has become one of the most exciting and influential in all of Europe, and, in the work of such brilliant filmmakers as Werner Herzog, Rainer Werner Fassbinder, Wim Wenders, and Jean-Marie Straub, it stands once again on the very cutting edge of the international avant-garde, as we shall see in Chapter 18.

---

*Ilya Ehrenburg, from whose novel the screenplay was adapted, provides an interesting account of the film's production in Volume III of *Men, Years—Life* (London: McGibbon & Kee, 1963), pp. 124–30.

Soviet Silent Cinema and the Theory of Montage, 1917–1931

THE PREREVOLUTIONARY CINEMA

Before the Bolshevik (Communist) Revolution of October 1917, the film industry in Russia was mainly European. Agents of Lumière Frères, Pathé, Gaumont, and Danish Nordisk had established large distribution branches in several cities at the turn of the century, and the first native Russian studio was not founded until 1908. About ninety percent of all films shown in Russia between 1898 and the outbreak of World War I were imported. Between 1914 and 1916, this figure declined to twenty percent as the number of domestic film-producing firms more than doubled, from eighteen to forty-seven, in the absence of foreign competition. But most of these operations were thinly capitalized, and by mid-1917 there were only three major production companies in the entire country (Ermoliev, Khanzhonkov, and Pathé). Ninety percent of all filmmaking activity was concentrated in the major cities of Moscow and Petrograd.* All technical equipment and film stock were imported from Germany or France.

The film industry in Russia was small because the cinema had not yet become a popular form, as it had in the West. Unlike their German counterparts, the Russian working classes were too impoverished to attend the movies, and the ultraconservative ruling classes simply didn't care to. Still, the prerevolutionary cinema produced several films of note. In 1913, the **Futurist** poet Vladimir Maiakovski (1893–1930) and his colleagues made a unique avant-garde manifesto in film entitled *Drama in Futurist Cabaret 13* (*Drama v futuristicheskom kabare 13*). Between 1915 and 1916, the great stage director Vsevolod Meyerhold (1874–1940) adapted two famous literary works for the screen—Oscar Wilde's novel *The Picture of Dorian Gray* (*Portret Doriana Greia*, 1915) and Stanislaw Przybyszewski's *The Strong Man* (*Silnyi chelovek*, 1917)—both of which show a uniquely cinematic conception of *mise-en-scène*. By far the most

5.1 *Father Sergius* (Yakov Protazanov, 1918).

---

* The city's more Germanic name, "St. Petersburg," had been changed to "Petrograd" when Russia entered the war against Germany in 1914. In 1924 it was renamed "Leningrad" by the Bolsheviks.

impressive film of the period, and the last important one made before the October Revolution, was Iakov Protazanov's production of Lev Tolstoi's *Father Sergius* (*Otets Sergii*, 1918), whose acting, photography, and narrative construction surpassed anything made to date. Most films of the period, however, were distinctly mediocre, consisting mainly of costume melodramas, horror thrillers, and an occasional farce.

When Russia entered the war in 1914, foreign films could no longer be imported, and the tsarist government attempted to stimulate domestic production, especially of documentary and educational films, by creating a Military Film Section within the Skobelev Committee (an organization named for its chairman, which had originally been founded to assist veterans of the Russo-Japanese War) and giving it exclusive rights to film at the battle front. The commercial film industry continued to make escapist entertainment, but the committee specifically encouraged the production of propaganda documentaries to stem growing discontent with the tsarist regime. This effort was not and could not have been successful, because social conditions in Russia had become so bad by the second year of the war that a revolution was imminent. The armed forces, underfed and underequipped, had suffered heavy losses. There were shortages of food and fuel everywhere, and the civilian population was completely demoralized.

THE ORIGINS OF THE SOVIET CINEMA

In March 1917, the tsarist regime was replaced by a provisional parliamentary government under Alexander Kerenski (1881–1970), who unwisely attempted to continue Russia's involvement in the war. Kerenski's government immediately abolished film censorship and reorganized the Skobelev Committee to produce anti-tsarist propaganda. But only two films (*Nicholas II* [*Tsar Nikolai II*] and *The Past Will Not Die* [*Proshloie ne umryot*]) were made under this new dispensation, because the provisional government was overthrown by the Bolsheviks, led by Vladimir Il'ich Lenin (1870–1924), in the October Revolution of 1917. There followed the establishment of the Soviet government at Petrograd; a bitter three-year civil war between the "Red" (pro-Communist) and "White" (anti-Communist) factions of the Russian army; an invasion by France, Britain, the U.S.A., Japan, and other World War I allies; a crippling foreign trade embargo; and, finally, economic collapse and famine.* In the midst of this chaos, the Bolshevik leaders looked to film as a

---

* Whatever its value as a film (which is not inconsiderable), Warren Beatty's *Reds* (1981) offers an impressive account of these events and of the revolutionary fervor that attended them. It is based on the life of the American radical journalist John Reed (1887–1920), who participated in the October Revolution and wrote of his experiences in *Ten Days That Shook the World* (1919), a source for Eisenstein's *October* (1928). (Reed's stirring reportage of the Mexican Revolution, *Insurgent Mexico* [1913], later influenced Eisenstein's choice of subject for *Qué Viva México!*, as will be seen in Chapter 9.) Reed is honored in the Soviet Union today as a founder of the Communist International, and his ashes are buried beneath the Kremlin Wall. Not to be outdone by Hollywood, the Soviets filmed their

means of reunifying their shattered nation. As a party of 200,000 which had assumed the leadership of 160 million people, most of them illiterate, scattered across the single largest contiguous land mass in the world* and speaking well over one hundred separate languages, the Bolsheviks' most immediate task was one of communication and consolidation, and they saw film as the perfect medium for this endeavor. Film, after all, speaks only one language—one that doesn't require literacy to comprehend—and, through mass distribution, can communicate the same ideas to millions of people at once. As Lenin himself declared of the situation, "The cinema is for us the most important of the arts."

Unfortunately, most producers and technicians of the prerevolutionary commercial cinema were capitalists openly hostile to the Bolshevik government (and vice versa). They emigrated to Europe, taking their equipment and film stock with them and, in the process, often wrecking the studios they left behind. No new equipment or film stock (i.e., celluloid) could be imported into Russia because of the foreign blockade, and massive power shortages severely restricted the use of what few resources remained. Nevertheless, in the face of these obstacles, the Soviet government scrapped the Skobelev Committee and set up a special subsection on cinema (ultimately, the "Cinema Committee") within the New People's Commissariat of Education (*Narodnyi kommissariat prosveshchen-iia*, abbreviated Narkompros), whose head was the playwright and literary critic Anatoli Lunacharski (1875–1933). In August 1919 the Soviet film industry was nationalized and placed under Narkompros. Headed by Lenin's wife, Nadezhda Krupskaya (1869–1939), the Cinema Committee founded a film school in Moscow to train actors and technicians for the cinema (another was established briefly at Petrograd): the VGIK (*Vsesoyuznyi gosudarstveni institut kinematografii*—"All-Union State Institute of Cinematography") or Moscow Film School. This school was the first of its kind in the world, and it remains today among the most widely imitated and respected. Its initial purpose was to train people in the production of *agitki*—newsreels edited for the purpose of agitation and propaganda, or "agitprop." Starting in 1918, these *agitki* toured Russia on specially equipped agit-trains and agit-steamers designed to export the Revolution from the urban centers to the provinces—an immense undertaking in a country containing one-sixth of the world's land mass and one-twelfth of its population.† Indeed, because of the severe shortage of film stock and the chaotic conditions of the new Soviet state, almost all films made during the years of the civil war (1918–21) were newsreels

---

own life of Reed in Sergei Bondarchuk's two-part epic *Red Bells* (*Red Bells: Mexico in Flames* [1982] and *Red Bells: I've Seen the Birth of the New World* [1983]), a coproduction with Mexico and Italy which has met with faint praise outside of the USSR.

* The USSR's area is 8,649,500 square miles, or 2.5 times that of the United States.

† Ironically, after 1922 much of this activity was financed by box-office receipts from American films imported for the purpose by the Soviet Commissariat of Foreign Trade on the orders of Lunacharski and Lenin. In fact, between 1918 and 1931, over seventeen hundred American, German, and French films were distributed in the Soviet Union, as opposed to less than seven hundred domestic features.

of this sort. Thus, at its birth, the Soviet cinema was a cinema of propaganda in documentary form. And its first major artist was, appropriately, the first great practitioner and theorist of the documentary form, Dziga Vertov.

DZIGA VERTOV AND THE KINO-EYE

Dziga Vertov (b. Denis Kaufman,* 1896–1954) was born in Bialystok, Poland, then part of the Russian Empire. In 1918 he became an **editor** of newsreels for the Cinema Committee. Cameramen traveling about the country to record the progress of the Red Army in the civil war and the activities of the new government would send their footage back to Moscow, where it was edited into newsreels by Vertov and others. At first, Vertov was content to assemble the footage in a purely functional manner, but he gradually began to experiment with more expressive kinds of editing. By 1921, Vertov had made three feature-length compilation documentaries from his weekly newsreel footage: *Anniversary of the Revolution* (*Godovshchina revoliutsii,* 1919—the first Soviet feature film), *The Battle at Tsaritsyn* (*Srazheniie v Tsaritsyne,* 1920), and a thirteen-part *History of the Civil War* (*Istoriya grazhdanskoi voiny,* 1921). In all of them he experimented with subliminal cuts of one to two frames each, color tinting by hand, expressive titles,† and the dramatic reconstruction of documentary events.

The period immediately following the revolution was one of extraordinary creative fervor in the arts. Since Vertov's early films were strongly pro-Soviet, and he was one of few pro-Soviets making films, his experiments were actively encouraged by the Cinema Committee, and he began to gather about him a small band of committed young documentarists who came to call themselves the *Kinoki* (from *kino-oki*—"cinema-eyes"). This group published a series of radical manifestoes in the early twenties denouncing conventional narrative cinema as "impotent" and demanding that it be replaced by a new cinema based on the "organization of camera-recorded documentary material" (Vertov). The key terms here are "camera-recorded" and "organization," for Vertov and his colleagues believed both in the absolute ability of the cinema apparatus to reproduce reality as it actually exists *and* in the necessity of editing to

---

* "Dziga" is a Ukrainian word meaning "spinning top" or "restless, fidgety, bustling person." "Vertov" is derived from the Russian word *vertet* meaning "to turn, spin, rotate or fidget." The pseudonym, adopted around 1915, suggests the sound of a hand-cranked movie camera; it is also, perhaps, Vertov's comment on the filmmaker's profession.

Vertov's brothers also earned places in film history. Boris Kaufman (1907–80) was acclaimed as one of the world's great black-and-white cinematographers. He worked with Jean Vigo in France and with Elia Kazan (winning an Academy Award for *On the Waterfront* [1954]), Sidney Lumet, and other American directors. Mikhail Kaufman (b. 1897) began as Vertov's cinematographer but later produced a number of distinguished documentaries of his own.

† Often, gigantic, abbreviated revolutionary slogans in capital letters that seemed to shout at the audience from the screen.

arrange this reality into an expressive and persuasive whole. This doctrine, called by Vertov **kino-glaz** ("cinema-eye"), contributed significantly to the montage aesthetics which, as we shall see, came to dominate the Soviet silent cinema after 1924. But it also produced a number of stunning documentary achievements in its own right.

In 1922, Lenin ordered that a fixed ratio (dubbed the "Leninist film proportion") be established between Soviet information and entertainment films. The exact ratio was unspecified, and in fact was never officially acknowledged, but Vertov militantly insisted that it should be four to one. Shortly thereafter, he launched a new series of consciously crafted newsreel-documentaries collectively entitled *Kino-pravda* ("film truth"), which were specifically designed to test his theories. The twenty-three *Kino-pravda* films Vertov made between 1922 and 1925 employed a wide variety of experimental techniques, but none was as startling as his first independently shot nonarchival feature, *Kino-glaz* (*The Movie-Eye* or *Cinema-Eye*, 1924), which used trick photography, animation, **microphotography,** multiple exposure, and "candid camera" techniques to create what one critic has called "an epic vision of actuality." Between 1925 and 1929 Vertov made three similar features—*Stride, Soviet!* (*Shagai, Soviet!*, 1926), *A Sixth of the World* (*Shestaia chast' mira*, 1926), and *Number Eleven* (*Odinnadtsatyi*, 1928)—but his most exhaustive essay in the "kino-eye" technique was his major work, *The Man with a Movie Camera* (*Chelovek s kinoapparatom*, 1929).

5.2 A poster by Alexander Rodchenko for *Kino-Glaz* (Dziga Vertov, 1924).

This film utilizes every resource of editing and camera manipulation known to silent cinema to create a portrait of "life as it is lived" on a typical day in Moscow from dawn to dusk. But *The Man with a Movie Camera* is less about Moscow than about cinema itself, for it constantly seeks to reveal the process of its own making. The film contains recurrent images of cameramen shooting it, Vertov's wife Elizaveta Svilova editing it, and people in a theater watching it. Point of view is manipulated to such an extent that it breaks down, and the camera's power to transform reality is flaunted in a continuous burst of cinematic pyrotechnics which include variable camera speeds, dissolves, split-screen effects, the use of prismatic lenses, multiple superimposition, animation, microphotography, and elaborately structured montage. In *The Man with a Movie Camera*, Vertov had progressed from documentarist to ciné-poet, creating a kind of meta-cinema, or self-reflexive cinema, which prefigures the work of the French New Wave (as will be explored in Chapter 13). To quote critic David Bordwell, "Long before the Marxist film theorists of *Cahiers du Cinéma* . . . called for a cinema which declares its sources in a context of production and consumption, Vertov was mounting a continuous *autocritique* of film-making."

5.3 *A Sixth of the World* (Dziga Vertov, 1926).

Unlike most other serious filmmakers of his day, Vertov welcomed the coming of sound, seeing it as a means of augmenting the "kino-eye" with the "radio-ear," and he continued to make films through the 1940s, including the experimental *Enthusiasm: Symphony of the Don Basin* (*Entuziazm: Simfoniia Donbassa*, 1931) and *Three Songs of Lenin* (*Tri pesni o Lenine*, 1934). Although his international influence throughout

5.4 & 5.5 Vertov's experimental sound film *Enthusiasm: Symphony of the Don Basin* (1931).

the thirties on both the avant-garde and the conventional documentary was strong, by the late 1920s Vertov's switch from short films (which, packaged with commercial entertainment features, were seen by huge audiences in the USSR) to documentary features (which were attended by almost no one) earned him the reputation of a sponsored filmmaker who could not cover his costs and was spending too much of the government's money. In the 1930s, Vertov fell into disfavor with Stalin and was accused of "formalist" error—the sometimes deadly sin of exalting the aesthetic form of a work above its ideological content. In the sixties and seventies, however, Vertov came to be regarded as a prophet of *cinéma vérité* (a term derived by translating *kino-pravda* into French) and the father of the new nonfiction film. Fittingly, the French New Wave director Jean-Luc Godard (b. 1930) and his political followers associated themselves with Vertov's work by naming their production cooperative after him: all of Godard's films between 1968 and 1973 were made collectively under the auspices of the Dziga-Vertov Group. More important, however, it is clear today that Vertov was a cofounder of the Soviet silent cinema, which gives him a major role in one of the greatest movements in the history of film.

LEV KULESHOV AND THE KULESHOV WORKSHOP

The other recognized cofounder was Lev Kuleshov (1899–1970), one of the few prerevolutionary filmmakers to remain in Russia after 1917. Kuleshov began his career as a set designer at the Khanzhonkov studios for the director Evgeni Bauer (1865–1917) in 1916, at the age of seventeen, and actually completed Bauer's last feature, *After Happiness* (*Za schast'en,* 1917) when the director was fatally injured while filming on location. During the civil war, he became a cameraman for the agit-trains and was active in establishing the VGIK in 1919. Like Vertov, Kuleshov was interested in the theory as well as the practice of cinema; he had published his first articles on the subject in the trade journal *Vestnik kinematografii* ("*Cinema Herald*") in 1917. But Kuleshov's superiors at the film school lacked confidence in the zealous twenty-year-old's ability to work within an orthodox curriculum, and they permitted him to conduct his own study group outside the formal structure of the institute. This "Kuleshov Workshop" drew the most radical and innovative young students at the film school, Sergei Eisenstein and V. I. Pudovkin among them, and concerned itself mainly with experiments in editing.

Because of the severe shortage of raw film stock and equipment which afflicted the Soviet Union in the immediate postrevolutionary period, the workshop's initial experiments involved the production of "films without celluloid." Kuleshov and his students would write scenarios, direct and act them out as if before cameras, and then—on paper—assemble the various "shots" into completed "films." Soon, however, Kuleshov had another subject and model for experimentation in the most sophisticatedly constructed film made to date—D. W. Griffith's *Intolerance* (1916).

Intolerance had been brought into Russia for commercial distribution in the year of its release,* but exhibitors had rejected it as incomprehensible. The film was shelved until after the Revolution, when the Bolshevik government arranged premiers in Petrograd (November 1918) and Moscow (May 1919) in recognition of its powerful "agitational" qualities. Lenin, impressed with what he took to be the proletarian sympathies of the Modern story, apparently ordered that it be shown throughout the Soviet Union—where, according to Iris Barry, it ran continuously for almost ten years. All available film stock was gathered up to be used in duplicating prints, and there are reports that Lenin actually cabled Griffith and offered him the directorship of the Soviet film industry, which Griffith supposedly declined only because of the opening of his new Mamaroneck studio. In any case, as the late Jay Leyda pointed out in his book *Kino,* a monumental history of the Russian and Soviet film, *Intolerance* went on to become the Soviet film industry's first great popular, political, and aesthetic success. To quote Leyda: "We know for certain of the popular success of *Intolerance,* and we know as certainly of the tremendous aesthetic and technical impetus given to *all* young Soviet filmmakers by this and subsequently shown Griffith films. No Soviet film of importance made within the following ten years was to be completely outside *Intolerance*'s sphere of influence."

5.6 *The Man with a Movie Camera* (Dziga Vertov, 1928).

That influence was imbibed, elaborated, and disseminated largely through the Kuleshov Workshop, where prints of *Intolerance* (and, after the lifting of the blockade in 1920, *The Birth of a Nation*) were screened continuously until, according to legend, they fell apart. Kuleshov and his students spent months studying the precise manner in which Griffith had built up his complicated multiple narrative out of thousands of separate shots, until they had mastered the principle themselves. Then, they reassembled his sequences in hundreds of different combinations to test the ways in which an arrangement of shots produces meaning. As raw film stock began to dribble back into the Soviet Union between 1922 and 1923 as a result of a Soviet-German trade agreement and the success of Lenin's New Economic Policy (NEP), Kuleshov struck out on his own and carried the analysis of film structure far beyond anything that had gone before.

Though the form of Kuleshov's initial experiments was dictated by the relative scarcity of raw stock, his ultimate goal was to discover the general laws by which film communicates meaning to an audience—to dis-

---

* According to Vance Kepley, Jr., it was imported by Jacques Robert Cibrario's film distribution firm, Transatlantic (*"Intolerance* and the Soviets: A Historical Investigation," *Wide Angle* 3, 1 [Spring 1979: 22–27]). After the Revolution, this same Cibrario offered himself to the Cinema Committee as an international purchasing agent for urgently needed film equipment and stock. Between 1918 and 1921, he was given access to one million dollars in prewar Russian bank deposits in New York City, where, by forging invoices and bills of lading, he embezzled most of it. In 1921, an indictment brought against him by the Soviets was dismissed because the United States did not recognize their government, and Cibrario fled to Europe where his "profits" had been deposited in British, Dutch, and Italian banks. (A comic dramatization of this affair by Jim Hawkins, entitled *Thank You, Comrades,* was produced for the BBC and broadcast in the United States on PBS in 1978.)

cover, that is, the way in which film *signifies*. In his most famous experiment, as recounted by V. I. Pudovkin in *Film Technique and Film Acting,* Kuleshov took unedited footage of a completely expressionless face (that of the prerevolutionary matinee idol Ivan Mozzhukhin, who had emigrated to Paris after the Revolution) and intercut it with shots of three highly motivated objects: a bowl of hot soup, a dead woman lying in a coffin, and a little girl playing with a teddy bear. When the film strips were shown to randomly selected audiences, they invariably responded as though the actor's face had accurately portrayed the emotion appropriate to the intercut object. As Pudovkin recalled: "The public raved about the acting of the artist. They pointed out the heavy pensiveness of his mood over the forgotten soup, were touched and moved by the deep sorrow with which he looked on the dead woman, and admired the light, happy smile with which he surveyed the girl at play. But we knew that in all three cases the face was exactly the same." Kuleshov concluded from these results, known today as the "Kuleshov effect,"* that the shot, or cinematic sign, has two distinct values: 1) that which it possesses in itself as a photographic image of reality, and 2) that which it acquires when placed in relationship to other shots. In another experiment, Kuleshov cut together a shot of a smiling actor with a close-up of a revolver and a second shot of the same actor looking frightened. Audiences naturally interpreted the sequence as portraying cowardice, but when Kuleshov reversed the position of the two shots of the actor within the sequence, the opposite interpretation was made. He reasoned from this that the second value of the shot implicit in the "Kuleshov effect," that which it acquires when juxtaposed with other shots, was infinitely more important in the generation of cinematic meaning than was the first. He concluded, that is, that meaning in cinema is a function of the celluloid strip, not of the *photographed reality,* and that it arises from the sequential arrangement of its parts. Griffith, of course, had practiced this principle instinctively in all of his major films, but Kuleshov was the first to give it a theoretical articulation and to suggest that it is the basis for the process of cinematic signification.

A further experiment involved the creation of "artificial landscapes" through "creative geography"—the juxtaposition of separate shots taken at separate places and times. In one of these, a shot of a man moving from right to left across the frame in one part of Moscow is cut together with a shot of a woman moving from left to right across the frame in another section of the city, while a third shot shows them suddenly meeting in yet another part of Moscow to shake hands. At the conclusion of this shot, the man points offscreen, and a fourth shot reveals the object of his attention to be the White House in Washington, D.C. The fifth and final shot of the sequence shows the two ascending the steps not of the White House, but of a well-known Moscow church. Kuleshov had thus created the cinematic illusion of spatial and temporal unity by cutting together five separate shots taken at five separate places and times. In yet

---

* Pudovkin later used this same effect in *Mother* (see p. 194, shots 5.43).

another experiment, he synthesized the body of a woman out of shots of the face, torso, hands, and legs of several separate women.

What Kuleshov demonstrated in these and similar experiments was that in cinema "real" time and space are absolutely subordinate to the process of editing, or *montage*, as the Soviets came to call it, after the French verb *monter*, "to assemble." Furthermore, as Ron Levaco points out, Kuleshov had shown that the associational power of montage was not inherent in the edited film strip itself but was the result of the viewer's *perception* of the edited film strip, which makes the montage process an act of consciousness for filmmaker and audience alike. Griffith, of course, had been the first to discover the profound psychological impact which editing could have upon an audience, and Soviet filmmakers had distilled many of their theoretical insights from his practice. But Kuleshov's theory of montage went beyond Griffith's editing in a manner described later by his former pupil Sergei Eisenstein: "Griffith's . . . close-ups create atmosphere, outline traits of character, alternate in dialogues of leading characters, and close-ups of the chaser and the chased speed up the tempo of the chase. But Griffith at all times remains on a level of representation and objectivity and nowhere does he try through the juxtaposition of shots to shape import and image." In other words, for Griffith, editing was primarily a narrative and representational mode. It generally served to advance a plot or tell a tale, and the "metaphorical" style of *Intolerance* was largely an aberration. As a result of their experiments, however—and, paradoxically, of their countless screenings of *Intolerance*—Kuleshov and his pupils conceived of montage as an expressive or symbolic process whereby logically or empirically dissimilar images could be linked together synthetically to produce metaphors (to produce, that is, nonliteral meaning). Building upon this fundamental notion, Eisenstein and Pudovkin, Kuleshov's two most brilliant students, went on to elaborate distinctly individual theories of montage in their own theoretical writings and films. But before this occurred, the Kuleshov Workshop had an opportunity to put its theories into practice.

By 1923, the workshop had secured enough equipment and film stock to begin work upon its first feature film—a parody of American detective thrillers entitled *The Extraordinary Adventures of Mr. West in the Land of the Bolsheviks* (*Neobychainye prikliucheniia Mistera Vesta v strane bolshevikov*, 1924), directed by Kuleshov. *Mr. West* was first and foremost a showcase for the workshop's newly acquired cinematic sophistication, but it was also a very intelligent and amusing satire on popular American misconceptions about the effects of the Bolshevik Revolution. The zany plot concerns an American YMCA president who journeys to Soviet Moscow on business, expecting it to be inhabited by brutes and criminals. Ironically, a street gang (composed of "counterrevolutionary degenerates") does latch on to him, and proceeds to act out the kind of horror show that Mr. West has expected to see all along. Just as he is about to pay a sum of money to these extortionists, he is rescued by the state police and shown the "real" Bolshevik Moscow. The film was an enormous success with Russian audiences, and it remains today a minor classic of silent comedy. The original Kuleshov group made one final

5.7 *The Extraordinary Adventures of Mr. West in the Land of the Bolsheviks* (Lev Kuleshov, 1924).

5.8 Kuleshov's *The Death Ray* (1925).

5.9 *Dura lex* (Lev Kuleshov, 1926).

5.10 **Kuleshov's sound film *The Great Consoler* (1933).**

feature together, a science-fiction mystery thriller called *The Death Ray* (*Luch smerti,* 1925), directed by Kuleshov and written by Pudovkin. *The Death Ray* was a technically dazzling but ultimately sterile attempt to synthesize material from several popular serials, including the American *Perils of Pauline* series and Feuillade's *Fantômas* and *Judex,* and it came under attack from the Communist Party leadership for not being sufficiently ideological.

His workshop broke up in 1925, apparently as a result of these attacks and because his leading actor-assistants got promoted to making their own films, but the following year Kuleshov went on to direct his most widely known film in the West. The feature, *By the Law* (*Dura lex*/*Po zakonu,* 1926), was sponsored by the newly centralized state cinema trust, Sovkino, which had been established in 1924 to control the film affairs of the entire Soviet Union through government financing.* Adapted from Jack London's short story "The Unexpected" with the collaboration of the Formalist critic Viktor Shklovsky (b. 1893), *By the Law* achieved an extraordinary blend of emotional intensity and geometrical stylization on the smallest budget ever allocated for a Soviet feature film. Set almost entirely in a one-room cabin in a desolate region of the Yukon during the winter, it tells the story of two people who are compelled by social conditioning to try, condemn, and execute a third person for the murder of two friends. There are no parallel lines of action and few changes of locale, but Kuleshov achieves an expansion of dramatic space through montage which is remarkable in a film of such narrowly defined scope and which probably influenced the style of Carl Dreyer's *La Passion de Jeanne d'Arc* (1928; see pp. 329–30) two years later. Indeed, the precision and economy of the film are such that one Soviet critic could write on its release, "*By the Law* was worked out in the spirit of an algebraic formula, seeking to obtain the maximum of effect with the minimum of effort." Unfortunately, the film was poorly received by most of the official critics, and Kuleshov's three subsequent silent features were unsuccessful. He made only one sound film of note, *The Great Consoler* (*Velikii uteshitel,* 1933), loosely based on some O. Henry short stories, which he may in fact have intended as an allegory of the plight of Soviet artists under Stalin. Like Vertov, Kuleshov was denounced for "formalist error" at the 1935 Congress of Film Workers and forced to recant much of his earlier work. He continued to make films until 1944, when he was rewarded for his Party loyalty by appointment to the position of head of the VGIK, where he taught and lectured until his death in 1970.

Though Kuleshov contributed a number of important films to his country's great cinema, it is as a theorist rather than a practitioner of

---

*With greater administrative power and a much firmer financial base, Sovkino replaced Goskino, the state distribution monopoly created in 1922 by the Council of People's Commissars. Though Goskino (an acronym for "Central State Photo-Cinema Enterprise") lost its distribution authority, it continued to function as a production company until 1930. Sovkino was itself replaced by Soiuzkino (an acronym for "All-Union Combine of Cinema-Photo Industries") at the beginning of the industrialization years in 1930, with Stalin's lieutenant Boris Shumiatski as its chairman (see pp. 205–6).

cinema that he will be most prominently remembered. He was in fact the first practical theorist of the cinema, as Pudovkin recognized when he wrote, in an introduction to Kuleshov's theoretical study *Art of Cinema* in 1929,* "We make films—Kuleshov made cinematography." Ron Levaco estimates that more than half of the major Soviet directors since 1920—including Eisenstein, Pudovkin, Boris Barnet, Mikhail Kalatozov, and Sergei Parajanov (see Chapter 16)—had been his students at the Film School at one time or another. His legacy to them and to us is again best articulated by Pudovkin:

> All he said was this: "In every art there must be first a material, and secondly, a method of composing this material specifically adapted to this art. . . ." Kuleshov maintained that the material in filmwork consists of pieces of film, and that the method of composing is their joining together in a particular creatively conceived order. He maintained that film-art does not begin when the artists act and the various scenes are shot—this is only the preparation of the material. Film-art begins from the moment when the director begins to combine and join together the various pieces of film. By joining them in various combinations, in different orders, he obtains differing results.

The discovery and articulation of this notion was the enabling act of the Soviet silent cinema and the montage aesthetics upon which it was founded. But it would be wrong to assume, as so many past accounts have done, that the montage idea came solely from the Kuleshov Workshop, or the influence of *Intolerance,* or the economies imposed upon Soviet filmmakers by the scarcity of celluloid. The idea had in fact been very much alive in avant-garde art between 1910 and 1918. As David Bordwell has pointed out, this was the great period of Futurist and Formalist experimentation, and the notion of fragmentation and reassembly as a means of artistic construction was distinctly in the air. Furthermore, the analogies between montage structure and the Marxist historical dialectic are impressive, as we shall see in the works of Sergei Eisenstein.

SERGEI EISENSTEIN

Sergei Mikhailovich Eisenstein (1898–1948) was, with D. W. Griffith, one of the two pioneering geniuses of the modern cinema. Yet, though their syntactical methods were similar and both worked on an epic historical scale, as artists the two men could hardly have been less alike. Griffith was a sentimentalist whose values were typically those of the Victorian middle class. His films were modernist in form, reactionary in feeling; they were seen by millions, and he made too many of them. Eisenstein, by contrast, was a contemporary Marxist intellectual whose vibrantly revolutionary films, while few in number and seen almost entirely

---

*Between 1917 and 1969, Kuleshov wrote eight books and over seventy essays on film theory and practice. Representative selections are contained in *Kuleshov on Film: Writings of Lev Kuleshov,* trans. and ed. Ronald Levaco (Berkeley: University of California Press, 1974). Technically, the first theorist of the cinema was the academic psychologist Hugo Münsterberg, who wrote *The Photoplay: A Psychological Study* in 1915 and published it in 1916.

5.11 Sergei Eisenstein seated on the tsar's throne in the Winter Palace during the shooting of *October* (1928).

by intellectuals, left an indelible mark on history and cinema alike. Where Griffith was unschooled and instinctive, Eisenstein was a modern Renaissance man whose exaggerated intellectualism and omnivorous knowledge astonished all who knew him. Though he completed only seven films in his twenty-three-year career, the impact of these films and of his theoretical writings on the film form itself has been greater than that of any other body of work in the history of the medium save Griffith's. Griffith had discovered, in editing, the fundamental narrative structure of the cinema, but he and his followers had used it conservatively to tell nineteenth-century tales. Eisenstein formulated a self-consciously modernist theory of editing, allegedly based on the psychology of perception and the Marxist historical dialectic, which made it possible for the cinema to communicate on its own terms for the first time, without borrowing either matter or form from other media. And, like Griffith, Eisenstein gave the world a handful of films which will always rank among the highest aesthetic achievements of the cinema.

The Formative Years

Eisenstein was born in Riga, Latvia, in 1898; his father was a well-to-do architect and city engineer. Despite early interests in art and the circus, Eisenstein was sent to the Institute of Civil Engineering in Petrograd, where he was a nineteen-year-old student when the tsarist regime began to crumble in February 1917. The institute immediately disbanded, Eisenstein's parents departed for Western Europe, and Eisenstein joined the Red Army as an engineer. After a year of building bridges and fortifications during the civil war, he drifted back toward his natural impulses, working in 1919 as a poster artist on an agit-train and helping to stage amateur theatricals for army troops. Then, through a chance meeting with an old friend, he became first a set designer and then a director for the Moscow Proletkult* Theater. The Proletkult concept, with more than two hundred local branches, had been established during the Revolution for the purpose of "replacing the bourgeois culture of tsarist times with a purely proletarian one." When Eisenstein joined Moscow's Proletkult Theater in 1920, it was a virtual clearinghouse for avant-garde experiment and modernist ideas. The world-famous stage director Konstantin Stanislavski (1863–1938) lectured daily on his naturalistic acting "method" here, while the equally prominent director Vsevolod Meyerhold railed against Stanislavski's **naturalism** and called for an antitraditional theater—a stylized, nonverbal, and popular theater which would use pantomime, acrobatics, Meyerhold's own system of "bio-mechanics," and all

---

* An acronym for "Proletarian Cultural and Educational Organizations." Founded in February 1917 as an independent organization for the production of proletarian culture (the necessary basis, in Bolshevik doctrine, for a socialist revolution), Proletkult became a Soviet government agency after October and was subordinated to the Commissariat of Education. Like many other revolutionary institutions, it was abolished during Stalin's consolidation of power in 1932.

the resources of circus spectacle and *commedia dell'arte** to create "a machine for acting." Here too the Futurist poet and playwright Vladimir Maiakovski expounded his radical aesthetic doctrines, the actor-director Mikhail Chekhov lectured on Hindu philosophy and yoga, and weekly seminars were held on Marxism, Freudian psychology, and Pavlovian reflexology.†

Eisenstein fell first under the influence of Meyerhold, who had not worked in the cinema again after his two prerevolutionary films; but Eisenstein spoke of him as his "artistic father," much later, after Meyerhold had been discredited and denounced during the Stalin-era purge trials.** Meyerhold, for his part, claimed that "all Eisenstein's work had its origins in the laboratory where we once worked together as teacher and pupil." What Eisenstein learned from Meyerhold was, essentially, the possibility of mixing two ostensibly contradictory artistic approaches— that of rigorous systematization and spontaneous improvisation. Under Meyerhold's method for acting, which he called bio-mechanics, spontaneity was systematically conditioned. According to Peter Wollen, the notion drew upon such varied sources as Pavlovian reflexology, Taylorism (the study of workers' physical movements, invented in America to increase production), the Italian *commedia dell'arte,* the philosophy of pragmatism articulated by William James, the acrobatic Douglas Fairbanks films, the German Romantic puppet theater, and the highly stylized Oriental theater. Eisenstein's encounter with bio-mechanics marks the beginning of his life-long theoretical concern with the psychological effects of the aesthetic experience: specifically, the question of what combination of aesthetic stimuli will produce what responses in the perceiver under what conditions.

Eisenstein's preoccupation with this phenomenon was encouraged by his friend and colleague at the Proletkult Theater, Sergei Iutkevich (1904– 85), who would become a prominent Soviet director during the sound era. It was Iutkevich who involved Eisenstein in designing sets for the Futurist Workshop Theater, run by an expatriate German baron named Foregger, where the use of parodic masks introduced him to the notion of **typage** so important to his early films, and it was he who later intro-

---

* A form of drama which originated in sixteenth-century Italy, *commedia dell'arte* employs standard characters (Pantaloon, Harlequin, Columbine), improvised dialogue, and clownish, often slapstick action based on a written script.

†The science founded by the Nobel Prize-winning physiologist Ivan Pavlov (1849–1936) which interprets all behavior as consisting of simple and complex physiological reflexes.

**In January 1938, the Meyerhold Theater in Moscow was liquidated for its director's refusal to follow the tenets of "socialist realism." After publicly denouncing that doctrine at the All-Union Conference of Stage Directors in June 1939, Meyerhold was arrested and his wife, the actress Zinaida Raikh, found murdered in their flat. Meyerhold himself was executed in a Moscow prison on February 2, 1940. In spite of the very real danger to himself, Eisenstein remained faithful to Meyerhold, visiting his home frequently during 1938 and 1939, and, according to Edward Braun (*The Theater of Meyerhold: Revolutions on the Modern Stage* [New York, 1979]), Eisenstein saved Meyerhold's papers and notes by secreting them in the walls of his dacha.

5.12   A scene from *The Wise Man* (1923).

duced Eisenstein to the FEX group in Petrograd. The Factory of the Eccentric Actor, or FEX, was a Futurist theatrical movement run by Grigori Kozintsev and Leonid Trauberg (later to collaborate as director and scenarist on many important Soviet films of the twenties and thirties) which combined elements of the circus, cabaret, and music hall, as well as of American adventure films and slapstick comedy films. Eisenstein's contact with the FEX group clearly influenced the form of his first stage production for the Proletkult in 1923, an adaptation of a work by the nineteenth-century dramatist Alexander Ostrovski (1823–86) entitled *Even a Wise Man Stumbles,* or simply *The Wise Man* (*Mudrets*). Eisenstein took the bare bones of the plot and organized them not into acts or scenes but into a series of "attractions," as in a circus or cabaret. The stage, in fact, was laid out like a circus arena, with trapezes, tightropes, and parallel bars, and the audience was treated to a long procession of acrobatic acts, satirical sketches, "noise bands" reproducing the sounds of the "new industrial age," and, finally, firecrackers exploding beneath every seat in the house. At one point in the performance, Eisenstein even projected a short film (his first) parodying Dziga Vertov's *Kino-pravda* newsreel. (Appropriately, this film, entitled *Glumov's Diary,* is preserved in Vertov's *Kinopravda* issue no. 16.)

Eisenstein called this assault on the audience's sensibility the "montage of attractions," and to elaborate the concept he published his first theoretical manifesto in Maiakovski's radical literary journal *Lef** in 1923 (the same issue contained Vertov's first manifesto on the "kino-eye"). Eisenstein wrote that he had long sought a scientific "unit of measurement" for gauging the emotional effects of art and had found it at last in the "attraction":

> [A] roll on the kettledrums as much as Romeo's soliliquy, the cricket on the hearth no less than the cannon fired over the heads of the audience. For all, in their individual ways, bring us to a single idea—from their individual laws to their common quality of *attraction. The attraction . . . is every element that can be verified and mathematically calculated to produce certain emotional shocks.*

Eisenstein said further that the montage of attractions ("units of impression combined into one whole") could be used to introduce "a new level of tension" into the aesthetic experience which would produce a theater "of such emotional saturation that the wrath of a man would be expressed by a backward somersault from a trapeze." Thus, before he ever attempted to make a serious film, Eisenstein had articulated a rudimentary theory of montage as a process whereby independent and arbitrary units of

---

* Published by a group calling itself LEF, an acronym for "Left Front [of the Arts]." The LEF group opposed idealist conceptions of art as the product of bourgeois culture. Specifically, it rejected passive realism, subjectivism, and "psychologism" in art in favor of what Maiakovski called "social command," or "straightforward agitation which molds life and custom according to a plan." (See Dave Laing, ed., *Marxist Theories of Art* [Harvester Press: Atlantic Highlands, N.J., 1978], pp. 30–34.) With Stalin's ascension in the late twenties, LEF was dissolved, and its ideas were offically censured for "formalist" deviation.

5.13 *Strike* (Sergei Eisenstein, 1924): the workers' leaders call a strike after a secret meeting in the factory scrap-iron heap.

"attraction" or "impression" were assembled to produce a total emotional effect different from the sum of its parts. As Eisenstein came more and more under the influence of Freud and of Ivan Pavlov, discoverer of the conditioned reflex, he replaced the notion of "attractions" with that of shocks or stimuli, and, as Peter Wollen notes, this dovetailed neatly with his Marxist concern for the agitational aspects of his work.

Eisenstein's next effort for the Proletkult was a production of *Do You Hear, Moscow! (Slyshis', Moskva!)*, Sergei Tretiakov's play about recent revolutionary events in Bavaria, which Eisenstein termed **"agit-Guignol."** Like *The Wise Man*, it had many cinematic elements, including a device for shifting the spectators' attention rapidly from one focal point on stage to another. As Yon Barna points out in his recent biography, *Eisenstein*, it was becoming apparent that Eisenstein had approached the limits of what he could achieve in the theater by cinematic means, and the cinema itself was exerting increasing appeal for him. In his last theatrical production for the Proletkult, however, Eisenstein went even farther afield in his effort to produce a chain of aesthetic shock effects by staging Tretiakov's agitational play *Gas Masks (Protivogazy)* in the Moscow gasworks. The audience sat on benches amidst the machinery and the grand finale was the arrival of the actual night-shift workers to light their gas jets as the actors departed. The play was not a success because the actors were dwarfed by the machinery, but the failure convinced Eisenstein that the theatrical form—however stylized, modernized, or revolutionized—could no longer contain his developing notions of montage. As he had written in *Lef* in 1923, with characteristic overstatement: "The theater as an independent unit within a revolutionary framework . . . is out of the question. It is absurd to perfect a wooden plough; you must order a tractor."

From Theater to Film

The "tractor" was ordered for Eisenstein by the Proletkult Theater when in early 1924 it decided to sponsor a series of eight films, to be

5.14 *Strike:* after a sumptuous meal, the owners resolve to act.

collectively entitled *Toward the Dictatorship of the Proletariat* (*K diktature proletariata*), which would trace the rise of the Communist Party from the late nineteenth century through 1917. One of the scripts was being written by Valeri Pletyov, director of the Proletkult, and he invited Eisenstein to collaborate with him on the project, which ultimately became the Proletkult-Goskino production *Strike* (*Stachka*, 1924; released 1925), Eisenstein's directorial debut. *Strike* was intended as the fifth film in the series, but it was the first and only one to be made since, according to Eisenstein, it contained "the most mass action" and was therefore "the most significant." Between 1920 and 1924, Eisenstein had seen countless German Expressionist and American films in Moscow, including the major works of Griffith,* and had apprenticed himself for several weeks in March 1923 to his friend Esther Shub (1894–1959), the skillful *agitki* editor and, later, director of Goskino documentaries, when she was re-editing a print of Fritz Lang's two-part *Dr. Mabuse, der Spieler* (pp. 122–23) for general release in Moscow as the single feature *Gilded Putrefaction* (*Pozolochennay gnil*)† He also attended the Kuleshov Workshop at the VGIK for three months in the winter of 1922–23. But, in fact, Eisenstein knew very little about the technical aspects of filmmaking when he began to work on *Strike*. Nevertheless, like Griffith, Eisenstein quickly apprenticed himself to the very best cinematographer at the Goskino studios, Eduard Tisse (1897–1961), and inaugurated a lifelong artistic collaboration whose importance is equaled only by the Griffith-Bitzer association. Yet even before he had learned how to use Goskino's technical equipment, Eisenstein undertook an exhaustive program of research into his subject from which he produced a minutely detailed scenario.

In it, Eisenstein conceived his film as a revolutionary assault upon the "bourgeois cinema," i.e., the narrative cinema as practiced in the West thus far. To this end, though all sequences were shot against natural backgrounds, the strike of the title was itself made typical and representative rather than historical. Furthermore, Eisenstein abandoned the traditional individual hero for a collective one—his film's aggregate protagonist was the striking workers in their struggle against the brutal and oppressive factory system, and no single one of them was shown to be more socially valuable or thematically significant than another. Finally, in an effort to forge an "unbreakable link" between the Marxist dialectic and cinematic form, Eisenstein planned the entire film as an extended montage of "attractions" or "shock stimuli" which would agitate the audience into identification with the striking workers. In the completed film, as in his theater productions, some of Eisenstein's "attractions" are

---

* Eisenstein later wrote that Griffith had played "a massive role in the development of montage in the Soviet film," concluding that "all that is best in the Soviet cinema has its origins in *Intolerance*" (quoted in Barna, *Eisenstein*, p. 74). Indeed, several scholars have recently argued that the Modern story of *Intolerance* provided the inspiration for Eisenstein's *Strike*.

† Shub transformed the concluding battle between Mabuse and the police into a class-inspired street rebellion.

5.15 *Strike:* local criminals hired as strikebreakers emerge from hiding to receive instructions from the police.

mere tricks designed to seize the audience's attention in the most direct and forceful manner, but much of the time he was engaged in creating uniquely cinematic metaphors through the juxtaposition of two (or more) images which suggest a meaning different from and greater than them both. He was engaged, that is, in practicing the first stage of the highly complex and sophisticated montage process on which his greatest films are built.

Although it contains many grotesque and circus like elements from Eisenstein's theater days, *Strike* evolves in a non-narrative chronicle form which was clearly influenced by Vertov's doctrine of the "kino-eye" (though, to underscore the agitational aspect of his work, Eisenstein would later say, "I don't believe in the kino-eye; I believe in the kino-fist") and the editing experiments of Kuleshov. The film opens with a montage of smokestacks, industrial machinery, evil factory owners, and noble but horribly oppressed workers. We soon discover that the workers are planning a strike and that the management has hired *agents provocateurs* and informers to infiltrate their ranks. After a worker's suicide triggers the strike, the factory is temporarily shut down and the strikers enjoy the first leisure they have known in their lives—but only briefly, for their grievances are ignored by the owners, who finally resolve to break the strike by violent means. The police are enlisted to "interrogate" strike leaders and to stage provocations with the help of local criminals, but the workers refuse to be intimidated despite counter-insurgency and a general famine among them. Frustrated with intrigue, the police chief orders an armed invasion of the workers' apartments and the massacre of all strikers and their families. The famous concluding montage intercuts graphic footage of this atrocity with shots of cattle being slaughtered in an abatoir, and the film ends with a long shot of the ground before the apartment block littered with the bodies of hundreds of adults and children.

Strike was the first revolutionary mass film of the new Soviet state,

5.16 *Strike:* the police chief (lap-dissolved with the workers' tenement) orders the final slaughter.

and, although some critics accused it of **formalism,*** its agitational impact upon the few who saw it was great (Eisenstein himself, with characteristic immodesty, proclaimed it "the October of the cinema").† More important, however, *Strike* inaugurated the classical period of Soviet silent cinema at a time when the silent cinemas of the West had very nearly reached their peaks. In America by 1924, D. W. Griffith had already produced his greatest work, and Griffith, Erich von Stroheim, Robert Flaherty, Charlie Chaplin, and Buster Keaton were all at work on major films (*America, Greed, Moana, The Gold Rush,* and *Sherlock Jr.,* respectively). The German cinema was passing from Expressionism to the "new realism" with F. W. Murnau's *Der letzte Mann* (1924), and the careers of Murnau, Ernst Lubitsch, and Fritz Lang were flourishing. In France, the avant-garde cinema had reached its height with the films of Germaine Dulac, Louis Delluc, Jean Epstein, Marcel L'Herbier, Jacques Feyder, and René Clair (Clair's influential *Entr'acte* and Fernand Léger's famous *Ballet mécanique* both appeared in 1924). The Italian silent cinema had peaked with its series of prewar superspectacles and had declined long before 1924, but in Sweden the silent film was still enjoying the twilight of its great masters, Victor Sjöström and Mauritz Stiller (*The Phantom Chariot* [1921]; *The Saga of Gösta Berling* [1924]). Thus, Soviet silent cinema was a latecomer compared to the silent cinemas of the West, in large part because of the socioeconomic chaos created by the 1917 Revolution and the civil war. But by 1924, though raw film stock and equipment were still in scant supply, the means of film distribution had once more been stabilized and all prerevolutionary cinema theaters (some twenty-five hundred of them) had been reopened: the Soviet film industry was at last prepared to embark upon a period of creative growth.

The Production of *Battleship Potemkin*

The year 1925 was the twentieth anniversary of the abortive 1905 Revolution against tsarism, and the Jubilee Committee decided to sponsor a series of films to commemorate it. On the basis of *Strike,* Eisenstein was selected to direct the keynote film, *Year 1905* (*1905 God*), which was to provide a historical panorama of the entire uprising from the Russo-Japanese War in January to the crushing of the armed rebellion in Moscow in December. Eisenstein and Nina Agajanova-Shutko (b. 1889), a professional agitator who had actively participated in the 1905 revolt, collaborated on a hundred-page scenario covering dozens of events that had taken place in at least thirty separate locations from Moscow to Siberia to the Caucasus. Shooting began in Leningrad in June 1925, and bad weather prevented completion of this "northern" episode. Sticking to the shooting schedule, however, Eisenstein's company moved south

---

* As distinct from "Formalism" a contemporaneous movement in literature which took the position that language had no inherent relationship with the reality it purported to signify.

†Though *Strike* was not exported for commercial distribution, the film's distinctiveness was recognized abroad when it won a major prize at the Exposition des Arts Decoratifs in Paris in 1925.

for sunnier (and therefore better lit) locations. Eisenstein took his crew first to Baku and then to the port of Odessa, on the Black Sea, where a short sequence of forty-two shots was to be made representing the mutiny of the tsarist battleship *Potemkin* and its bloody aftermath.* When Eisenstein arrived in Odessa, however, he became obsessed with the cinematic possibilities of the vast flight of marble steps leading down to the city's harbor, where Cossacks had massacred citizens supporting the mutineers. Having failed to finish the earlier "northern" episodes, and facing a mid-December deadline for a completed film, he made the fateful decision to limit his treatment of the Revolution to this single representative episode.

5.17 A revolutionary poster for *Battleship Potemkin* (Sergei Eisenstein, 1925), designed by Rodchenko.

Battleship Potemkin (*Bronenosets Potyomkin*, 1925), the film which emerged, has been called the most perfect and concise example of film structure in the history of the cinema. With *The Birth of a Nation* (1915) and *Citizen Kane* (1941), *Potemkin* is clearly one of the most important and influential films ever made, and its montage represents a quantum leap from the relatively simple juxtapositions of *Strike*. Indeed, Eisenstein created a completely new editing technique merely foreshadowed in his first film—one based upon psychological stimulation rather than narrative logic, which managed to communicate physical and emotional sensation directly to the audience. Furthermore, the film's revolutionary impact inaugurated a whole new school of filmmaking and caused the Soviet cinema to burst full-blown upon the international screen, where it has retained a powerful position ever since.

Potemkin took ten weeks to shoot (the Odessa steps sequence was finished in seven days) and two weeks to edit, and, contrary to the prevailing mythology, its montage was *not* constructed according to some carefully prearranged and systematic plan. Eisenstein himself lent credence to this notion through his intricate structural analyses of the film in his later theoretical writings, but the truth is that, like *The Birth of a Nation* and *Citizen Kane*, *Potemkin* was less a matter of careful planning than an intense release of creative energy. The completed version of the film ran 86 minutes at silent speed (16 fps) and contained 1,346 shots—a remarkably high number when we consider that the released version of *The Birth of a Nation,* with a running time of 195 minutes, contained only 1,375 shots, or that the average American film of 1925 ran 90 minutes and contained approximately 600 shots. Clearly, the most important aspect of *Potemkin* is its editing, but it would be wrong to assume that Eisenstein's interest in montage caused him to neglect the pictorial or compositional aspects of his film. In fact, Eisenstein composed every single frame of *Potemkin* with a painter's eye for the distribution of light, mass, and geometric design (the triangle, circle, and diagonal intersection were his basic visual motifs).

Nevertheless, the film Eisenstein created from these beautifully composed frames was first and foremost a political film intended to possess the broadest possible audience appeal. Though *Potemkin* is hardly the "efficiently engineered political cartoon" that one contemporary critic has called it, the film *is* intensely manipulative of audience response. Furthermore, though Eisenstein, like Griffith, was obsessed with the accuracy of historical detail in his work (to the extent of interviewing large numbers of survivors of the *Potemkin* mutiny and the Odessa massacre), he was also, like Griffith, wholly capable of distorting historical events to suit a specific set of ideological assumptions. This should serve to remind us that Soviet "realism" was at its root a popular ideological cinema whose announced purpose was primarily agitational and didactic. It was, in other words, a cinema of political propaganda and indoctrination. That Eisenstein so often yielded to this tendency should not surprise us, because he was at the time a committed Marxist whose filmmaking activity was completely subsidized by and dependent upon the state. Rather, it should surprise us that he so consistently and gloriously managed to transcend it.

The Structure of *Potemkin*

Like *Strike*, *Potemkin* is a drama of mass action with a collective hero, and it was shot entirely with non-actors against naturalistic backgrounds. (According to Eisenstein's theory of typage, actors were important not as individuals but as "types"—elements within the composition of the frame which acquire meaning only through montage. He also used typage to represent general characteristics or types of people; the types are like masks, since viewers will know what the actors are meant to embody when they see them.) Of its recognizably documentary surface Eisenstein would later write, "*Potemkin* looks like a chronicle or newsreel of an event, but it functions as a drama." Indeed, unlike its relatively formless predecessor, *Potemkin* is divided into five movements or acts whose structural symmetry is very nearly perfect.* The first act, entitled "Men and Maggots," begins with an image of natural turbulence as large waves break violently over an anonymous harbor jetty, creating a metaphor for the social tumult we are soon to witness aboard the battleship. A title quoting Lenin ("Revolution is the only lawful, equal, effectual war. It was in Russia that this war was declared and begun")† introduces us to a night of unrest aboard the *Potemkin* at sea, during which a petty

5.18 *Battleship Potemkin:* "Revolution is the only lawful, equal, effectual war."

---

* Tragically, *Potemkin* was Eisenstein's last silent film to be completed as he intended. He was forced to revise both *October* (*Ten Days That Shook the World,* 1928) and *Old and New* (original title: *The General Line,* 1929) as a result of political pressure.

† According to Steven P. Hill ("The Strange Case of the Vanishing Epigraphs," *The Battleship Potemkin: The Greatest Film Ever Made,*" ed. Herbert Marshall [New York, 1978], pp. 74–86), the film's original epigraph was derived from Leon Trotski's widely read, and contextually more appropriate, history of the 1905 revolution: "The spirit of insurrection hovered over the Russian land. Some enormous and mysterious process was taking place in countless hearts. The individual was dissolving in the mass, and the mass was dissolving in the outburst." These words were replaced by Lenin's in all circulating prints of *Potemkin* sometime after Trotski's fall from grace in 1927. Hill provides a detailed analysis of the various available prints of the film and concludes that, while none is entirely complete with regard to intertitles, the MoMA print used by David Mayer for his shot-by-shot presentation (*Eisenstein's "Potemkin"* [New York, 1972]) and for my discussion has the greatest visual and structural fidelity to the original negative.

officer beats a sleeping sailor in random anger, and Seaman Vakulinchuk (played by Alexander Antonov [1898–1962], one of the regular "types" from Eisenstein's stock company from the Proletkult Theater) urges his comrades to join their striking brothers on the shore and rise against tsarist oppression.

In the morning, the situation worsens as sailors on deck gather angrily around a maggot-ridden piece of meat intended for their consumption. Led by Vakulinchuk, they protest, "We have had enough of rotten meat," but the supercilious ship's surgeon, Dr. Smirnov, soon arrives to inspect the infested carrion through his pince-nez and, as the screen fills with a close-up of the swarming maggots, proclaims them to be "merely dead fly eggs that will wash off with salt water." Dispersed by senior officers, the outraged sailors go about their duties until the call for midday meal, which most refuse to eat. The ship's officers are furious, but their anger is purely institutional. The anger of the sailors, on the other hand, is deep and real, as we see from the scene which concludes this section of the film. A young sailor, washing dishes from the officers' mess, suddenly realizes that the plate in his hands bears the hypocritical inscription "Give us this day our daily bread." In a fit of rage which defies the laws of empirical time and space, he smashes this same plate against the table not once but *twice* in a four-second montage sequence which joins together nine separate but overlapping shots of the uncompleted action, ranging in length from one-quarter to three-quarters of a second, in order to emphasize the extreme violence of the sailor's response. By creating a cinematic metaphor for impotent fury erupting into violent action, this sequence leads us into *Potemkin*'s second movement, "Drama on the Quarterdeck."

This section opens with an assembly of officers and crew on the open quarterdeck of the battleship. Commander Golikov, the ship's captain, orders, "Those satisfied with the food . . . two paces forward," and only a handful of petty officers obey. Enraged, Golikov threatens the mass execution of all protesters and calls up the Marines to carry out punishment. Seaman Matiushenko breaks ranks and successfully rallies most of the men to the gun turret as the Marines arrive on deck, but several remain in the prow, where they are covered with a tarpaulin by officers in preparation for the firing squad. Group shots are juxtaposed with extreme close-ups as the situation becomes increasingly tense: the sailors massed around the gun turret are anxious about their comrades, the officers become nervous about their own safety, and the Marines show signs of reluctance to carry out their orders. The ship's priest, a white-bearded Russian Orthodox monk, appears from below, pompously praying for the condemned as the order is given to fire. The squad hesitates, and the priest begins to count off the seconds by tapping his palm with a crucifix. In a much-quoted sequence, Eisenstein intercuts a close shot of this action with another of a junior officer nervously stroking the hilt of his sword, suggesting the unholy alliance which existed between Church and State in tsarist Russia.

The sailors under the tarpaulin fall to their knees in terror, and a sec-

5.19   The rotting meat.

5.20   Tsarist might: the firing squad.

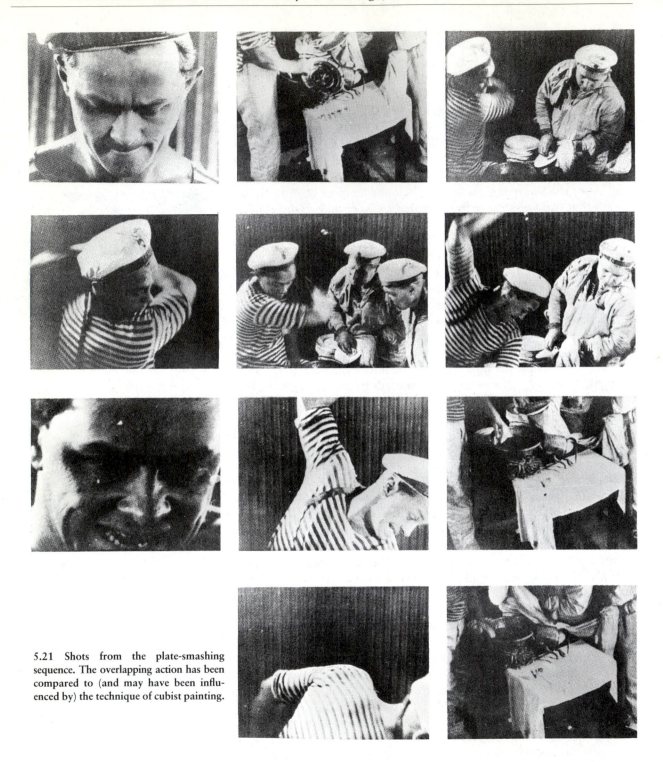

5.21 Shots from the plate-smashing sequence. The overlapping action has been compared to (and may have been influenced by) the technique of cubist painting.

ond order is given to fire. Suddenly Vakulinchuk cries out from the gun turret: "Brothers! Do you realize who you are shooting?" The rifles waver, and one after another the Marines lower their arms. It is important to note that although the incidents which occur between the mustering of the Marines and their refusal to fire on their shipmates would take only a few seconds in empirical reality, they last nearly three full minutes on the screen. Like Griffith and those who came after him, Eisenstein frequently used editing to compress time for the sake of narrative economy, but here and in the fourth section of *Potemkin*, "The Odessa Steps," he employs editing to *expand* time in order to create certain aesthetic and emotional effects. In "Drama on the Quarterdeck," by rendering the events just described into fifty-seven separate shots of varying temporal and spatial lengths, Eisenstein draws out the Marines' moment of decision for what seems an eternity, generating maximum psychological tension in the audience and achieving a highly expressive effect. After the firing squad has balked, the senior officer (played by Grigori Alexandrov) continues to scream the order to shoot, but it is too late: the mutiny has begun.

The quarterdeck is suddenly swarming with confusion. Sailors attack the officers and beat them to their knees. The melee spreads rapidly through the entire ship, as one by one the symbols of tsarist tyranny are chased down and killed by the crew. The old priest is knocked through a hatchway, and his fallen crucifix sticks upright in the wood of the deck like the instrument of oppression to which it has been recently compared. The ship's surgeon is dragged from his hiding-place and thrown overboard, raising an eddy of white foam on the dark surface of the ocean. Eisenstein cuts abruptly to a close-up of white maggots swarming on a dark field of meat and follows it with another of the surgeon's pince-nez dangling pathetically from the riggings where he has gone over, reminding us of the gross moral indifference which produced the mutiny. The bloodshed on deck continues until finally the cry goes up: "Comrades! The ship is in our hands!" But in another part of the ship a brutal senior officer has cornered Vakulinchuk, leader of the rebellion, and shot him in the head. As the sailor topples from the yardarm, he is caught in a cradle of ropes and hangs suspended above the water as though crucified. Vakulinchuk's body is carefully recovered and given a martyr's funeral by his comrades.

5.22 Mutiny: **crushing the symbols of oppression.**

5.23 Vakulinchuk's martyrdom and canonization.

That evening a launch bearing the dead hero's corpse and attended by an honor guard of seamen steams slowly toward the port of Odessa. There, in a tent at the end of the quay, Vakulinchuk's remains come to lie in state, an inspirational symbol of the revolution for which he perished. A mood of somber calm prevails as night descends on both the harbor and the bier.

This mood is sustained through the famous "fog montage" which opens the third section of the film, "An Appeal from the Dead." In it, Eisenstein joins together a sequence of shots depicting various aspects of the harbor just before daybreak—sailing vessels and steamships at anchor, a gull-covered buoy, dockside cranes, Vakulinchuk's tent outlined against the sky—each of which grows progressively lighter as the sun rises and gradually disperses the thick Odessa fog. By the end of this lyrical sequence, dawn has fully broken, and the harbor resumes its normal waking activity. Now the tent begins to attract attention. At first only a handful of Odessa's citizens come to pay homage to the fallen hero, but as the day grows lighter a large procession of mourners starts to descend the steps to the quay and file past the bier. Soon the crowd has grown into a vast, classless multitude which surges excitedly toward the quay from all quarters of the city.

At this point, Eisenstein begins to intercut extreme close-ups of individual mourners with long shots of the masses as they stream endlessly across the breakwater and swarm about the tent, the tempo of the cutting increasing with the anger of the crowd as agitators begin to harangue it. Suddenly, to a student's cry of "Down with the executioners!" a supercilious bourgeois responds, "Down with the Jews!" Heads turn in unison; a paroxysm of violent emotion grips the crowd, and the bourgeois is beaten to the ground. In Odessa, the masses continue to surge convulsively across and under a huge stone viaduct toward the quay, where raised fists now bristle into the sky in a show of solidarity. A delegation of workers from the shore arrives on the quarterdeck of the battleship to assure the mutineers of their support. As one of the delegates proclaims his mission from the bridge of the ship, a large red flag is raised on the mainmast, to the jubilant cheers of both the sailors and the masses assembled on the quay. (In the original release prints of *Potemkin*, this revolutionary flag was actually hand-tinted bright red.)

The fourth section of *Potemkin*, "The Odessa Steps," is constructed around what is probably the single greatest and most influential montage

5.24 Shots from the fog montage.

sequence in the history of the cinema—that depicting the massacre of the Odessa citizens by tsarist troops on the stone steps leading down to the harbor. This was the incident which had gripped Eisenstein's imagination from the outset of the production, for he saw it as a virtual paradigm of tsarist treachery, brutality, and oppression. Part Four begins on the same joyful note of solidarity with which Part Three concluded, as dozens of yawls sail out to the battleship from Odessa, laden with food and supplies for the mutineers. Townspeople are massed along the quay, shouting encouragement to the men on the ship and cheering on the yawls. Close-ups reveal individuals in the crowd who will later figure prominently in the mass action of the massacre—a white-bloused woman with dark bobbed hair, accompanied by a bearded man in black; a well-dressed elderly woman wearing pince-nez, with her arm about a schoolgirl; an ardent young student in wire-rimmed glasses.

5.25 Vakulinchuk on his bier. The hand-lettered sign reads: "For a spoonful of soup."

As they approach the *Potemkin* at anchor, the yawls are seen as photographed from a launch moving with them across the bay. One by one, the sailboats overtake the camera and glide past it toward the battleship, where cheering sailors greet the boatmen and help the gift-bearing civilians on board. On shore, the inhabitants of Odessa watch this fraternal encounter from the harbor steps and signal their enthusiastic support by waving. On the deck of the battleship, civilians and sailors embrace. The townspeople on the steps continue to wave and cheer en masse, and Eisenstein again cuts to close shots of individual members of the crowd. We see the old woman in pince-nez once more, an elegantly attired lady with an open white parasol, a legless child—premonitory of the horror soon to come—who scoots along the steps with one hand and hails the ship with the other, a young mother directing her son's attention toward the anchored ship and urging him to wave, two children held up above the crowd by adult hands to get a better view.

Then, a single, sinister title—"Suddenly"—and a chilling close shot of a row of jackbooted feet stepping in perfect unison onto the first flight of stone stairs. The dark bobbed hair of the woman in white (played by Alexandrov's wife, Olga Ivanova) fills the screen from one edge of the frame to the other and jerks backward so violently that the image is blurred by the motion. Through a series of **jump cuts** which abruptly eliminates the forward return, she yanks her head back again and again in utter horror at what she sees—which, however, Eisenstein doesn't permit the audience to see yet. The cripple leaps wildly on his hands down the steep balustrades which flank the steps, and the lady with the open parasol dashes madly into the camera, filling the entire screen with its white, beribboned fabric. Eisenstein pulls back to a long shot from below of townspeople scrambling pell-mell down the vast sweep of the stairs, and then reverses the angle to show the object of their terror from above: at the top of the stairs, a line of white-jacketed troops carrying rifles with fixed bayonets has started its murderous descent. Another long shot from below of townspeople pouring down the stairs, and the slaughter begins.

Eisenstein cuts to close shots of knees buckling, of bodies falling through the air and sprawling across the steps in heaps. Now a second line of troops has appeared and begun its descent, and the camera starts to track

5.26 The gathering on the quay. Accelerated intercutting of long shots and close-ups produces agitational frenzy on the screen, but compositional continuity is preserved in the geometrical motifs which dominate the individual shots—here, as throughout the film, the circle, the triangle, and the diagonal intersection.

laterally down the side of the steps with the escaping civilians. When the militiamen fire downward into the fleeing mass, the small boy we have seen earlier on the quay falls wounded. His mother screams in horror as he is trampled by the stampeding crowd: her face and then her eyes in extreme close-up fill the screen. She gathers his body into her arms to march up the corpse-littered steps against both the downward flight of the masses and the inexorable advance of the troops. Meanwhile, the woman in pince-nez, who has sought refuge with several others behind a parapet, decides to appeal to the troops. Now two groups are moving up the death-strewn stairs in opposition to the troops—the enraged mother with her dead son, screaming at the troops in anguish, and the woman in pince-nez and her followers, who attempt to supplicate them. The camera moves up the steps with both groups, and the troops move rhythmically and irresistibly down. The mother with the child stops on a landing so close to the bristling rifles of the troops that their shadows fall upon her. There is a pause as she madly entreats the soldiers to help her son. Instead they fire, she falls with her son, and the troops sweep calmly over their bodies. At the bottom of the steps, more horror: saber-slashing Cossack horsemen appear from nowhere and charge into the crowd as it reaches the quay, cutting off the only line of escape. On the steps, volley after volley is fired into the crowd, and the long line of troops continues its implacable, orderly descent, in complete contrast to the chaotic flight of the masses below.

Now Eisenstein begins the tour de force of his sequence, cutting to yet another young mother as she pushes her baby's carriage hurriedly across a landing in advance of the firing troops. Fleeing civilians rush past her, jolting the carriage, which she is clearly afraid to push down the next steep flight of steps. Above her, the troops march relentlessly on. Trapped between them and the steps, she hesitates and screams. We see a line of jackboots in close shot slowly descend the stairs and then a line of rifles against the sky erupting into smoke. The mother's head sways back in close-up; another close shot shows the wheels of the baby carriage teetering on the edge of the steps. The mother's white-gloved hands clutch the silver buckle of her belt, while on the quay below we see people being trampled, slashed, and beaten indiscriminately by Cossacks. Now a close-up returns us to the mother as blood begins to drip over her gloves and belt. Her body starts to sway forward and sink slowly off-screen. Behind her, the baby in the carriage reaches into the air; before her, the troops continue their measured cadence down the stairs. Slowly, the mother sways back against the carriage and pushes it off-screen. From a lower level of the steps, the woman in pince-nez screams in horror as the rear wheels of the carriage roll over the edge of the landing and the steps. Now, through a series of quick cuts, we see the carriage bounce its way unevenly down the stairs past the dead and wounded, slowly at first, then with gathering speed. The camera moves with it from the side, as Eisenstein intercuts its fatal progress with medium shots from above of the baby jostling violently inside and with close reaction shots of the horror-stricken woman in pince-nez and the student with wire-rimmed glasses. On the

5.27 **Shot sequence from the Odessa steps massacre (continues through page 175).**

steps above the carriage, we see a line of soldiers from the waist down firing their bayoneted rifles into a heap of supplicating wounded. Below, the student screams as the carriage fairly leaps across the steps, then suddenly tilts and flips end over end.*

The wrenching "agit-Guignol" of the massacre ends as it began, with a series of violent jump cuts. On the quay below, we see a ferocious young Cossack slash his saber down again and again in a series of four discontinuous close shots—some no longer than a few frames apiece—which eliminate his backward strokes and intensify the shocking violence of his action. Then Eisenstein cuts to the object of this murderous assault in the final shot of the massacre sequence—a close-up of the elderly woman in pince-nez beneath whose shattered glasses blood spurts from a slashed and blinded eye.

In the harbor, the muzzles of the *Potemkin*'s two huge turret guns swing slowly into the camera. A title informs us: "The brutal military power answered by the guns of the battleship. . . ." Onshore, the decorative stone sculpture of the Odessa Theater, headquarters of the tsarist generals, stands silhouetted against the sky. White smoke erupts from the *Potemkin*'s battle cannon, and Eisenstein cuts again to the sculptured parapet of the theater. Then, from several angles, we see the ornamental iron gate and heavy stone columns of the theater burst asunder and topple in a billowing cloud of debris and smoke. Finally, in a brief but justly famous three-shot montage sequence, a sculptured stone lion rises from

---

* This part of the Odessa steps sequence is clumsily recreated in Brian De Palma's American gangster film *The Untouchables* (1987), in the context of a shoot-out on the steps of a train station; in this case, the baby—but not the film—survives.

his sleep and roars, symbolizing the outrage of the Russian people at the atrocity just committed on the steps and their awakening anger against the regime which perpetrated it. The shots, of course, are of three separate stone lions posed in three separate positions and actually located near Yalta, far from Odessa, but by joining them together in the manner of Kuleshov's "creative geography" to create the illusion of a continuous action impossible in empirical reality, Eisenstein generates a cinematic metaphor for rage much more forcefully and economically than he could have done in a straightforward narrative sequence.

Eisenstein created another cinematic metaphor in the timing of the massacre sequence itself. Even though the rate of the cutting in this sequence is terrifically accelerated (the average shot length is fifty-two frames, or just over two seconds, as opposed to eighty-eight frames, or nearly four seconds, for the rest of the film), it takes much longer for the massacre to occur on the screen than it would take in actuality. This is because Eisenstein wished to suggest a *psychological* duration for the horrible event that far exceeded its precise chronological duration. As Arthur Knight writes, "Eisenstein realized that for the people trapped on the steps these would be the most terrifying (and, for many, the final) moments of their lives." By drawing out, through the montage process, the time it would normally take for the militiamen and their victims to reach the bottom of the stairs, Eisenstein manages to suggest destruction of a much greater magnitude than we actually witness on the screen, just as at the end of Part One he had suggested the black rage of the oppressed seamen by drawing out the time it takes the sailor to smash the officer's plate.

Part Five of *Potemkin,* "Meeting the Squadron," is both literally and aesthetically anticlimactic after the dynamic, emotionally draining Odessa steps sequence. It begins with a contentious shipboard meeting in which the citizens of Odessa urge the sailors to land and join forces with the army in rebellion against the tsar. But it is learned that the Admiralty squadron has been sent out against the *Potemkin,* and the sailors vote unanimously to face it at sea. Here Eisenstein cuts to the empty deck of the battleship some time later, and a title tells us: "A night of anxiety begins." Now a montage of sixty-eight shots evokes the calm which precedes the storm. From a variety of camera angles we see the ship at anchor in the moonlight, the watch moving slowly about the deck, a searchlight directed on the water, the motionless needles of the pressure gauges in the engine room, and sailors sleeping fitfully below deck. Meanwhile, the squadron creeps up stealthily in the darkness. At last, a seaman with a telescope spots the squadron on the horizon and sounds the alarm. Agitated sailors leap from their berths and assume their battle stations. The cannons are loaded with heavy shells. A title appears—"Full speed ahead"—and yet another breathless montage sequence begins.

At an ever-increasing tempo Eisenstein intercuts close shots of the churning pistons, rotating cam shafts, and plunging piston heads of the powerful ship's engines with Matiushenko giving orders from the bridge, the ship's funnels belching smoke, the *Potemkin* itself cutting rapidly through the waves, and the port cannons seeking the range of the squad-

ron, which has begun to mass on the horizon. As the *Potemkin* draws closer and closer to the squadron, Eisenstein increases the tension by accelerating the cutting rate to fever pitch. Suddenly the sequence is augmented by shots of two large battleships bearing down on the *Potemkin*. The *Potemkin*'s cannon swing slowly toward them as they steam into firing range. From the bridge, Matiushenko orders the semaphorist to run up the signal "Don't fight—join us." Billowing signal flags are now injected into the sequence, as the fleet remains mute, drawing ever nearer. The *Potemkin*'s gigantic cannon stretch diagonally across the screen, outlined against the sky; the gunners await their signal.

Now the *Potemkin* swings the muzzles of its huge cannon directly into the camera, filling the entire screen. The cannon of the fleet ships are raised menacingly toward those of the *Potemkin*. On the mast, the mutineers' red flag is whipped by the wind. Cannon confront each other across a brief expanse of sea, and the intent faces of sailors peer forth from the gun turrets in a painfully drawn-out agony of suspense. Suddenly, one of them smiles, and a title exclaims, "Brothers!" The faces of elated seamen crowd the screen. The *Potemkin*'s deserted quarterdeck begins to swarm with cheering, laughing sailors. The ship's cannons are lowered as the tsarist ships, their decks packed with friendly, cap-waving sailors, steam past within a thousand yards. A title reads: "Over the heads of the tsarist admirals roared a brotherly cheer. . . ." Without a shot being fired, the *Potemkin* is allowed to pass unmolested through the ranks of the fleet. Caps fly in the air, and shots from all angles show the jubilant mutineers crowding the decks of their ship. The red flag flutters victoriously above them, and from the waterline we see the *Potemkin*'s giant prow steam straight into the camera and seemingly break through the frame in enormous close-up as it carries its crew to safety and freedom.

Potemkin was given a gala public opening in Moscow on January 18, 1926, but its run on the screen lasted only a few weeks, and it was replaced by more commercially ·slanted entertainment films. Rival filmmakers claimed that *Potemkin* was a glorified documentary, inaccessible to the average audience. But when Soviet embassies in Paris and Berlin showed the film to left-wing opinion makers at invitational screenings, its word-of-mouth reputation soared. In the spring of 1926, the German Marxist composer Edmund Meisel worked closely with Eisenstein to prepare a stirring revolutionary score for *Potemkin* (a collaboration which Eisenstein later described as his "first work in the sound film," which made the film's agitational appeal very nearly irresistible. *Potemkin* was shown commercially in Germany for several weeks, but was officially banned in many other European countries where it was nevertheless shown underground to small audiences of leftists and intellectuals, and its fame spread rapidly throughout the Western world. The film's triumphs abroad (at its Berlin screening the great stage director Max Reinhardt, whose styles of lighting had so influenced German Expressionism, observed, "After viewing *Potemkin,* I am willing to admit that the stage will have to give way to the cinema") earned Eisenstein the temporary favor of Soviet officials. Critical attacks on *Potemkin* ceased, and the film was revived for second-run showings in the Soviet Union, where it became quite popular.* As Eisenstein later wrote, "I awoke one morning and found myself famous."

Eisenstein's Theory of Dialectical Montage

Part of Eisenstein's growing fame was as a theorist of film as well as a practitioner. The body of his writings on the medium—later collected into two volumes, *The Film Sense* (1942) and *The Film Form* (1948)—had been steadily accumulating since 1923, and after the resounding international success of *Potemkin,* he began to articulate his most important contribution to film theory—his notion of dialectical montage. To summarize briefly, Eisenstein saw film editing, or montage, as a process which operated according to the Marxist dialectic. This dialectic is a way of looking at human history and experience as a perpetual conflict in which a force (*thesis*) collides with a counterforce (*antithesis*) to produce from their collision a wholly new phenomenon (*synthesis*) which is not the sum of the two forces but something greater than and different from them both. The process may be diagrammed thus:

---

* The official attendance figures indicate this, at least. But they may have been exaggerated by the authorities, who had a stake in demonstrating to the rest of the world that there was a large Soviet audience for Soviet films. See the casebook of contemporary reviews and documents, *The Battleship Potemkin: The Greatest Film Ever Made,* ed. Herbert Marshall (New York, 1978), which reminds us, among other things, that Eisenstein's film inspired a Soviet opera (1937), a Polish ballet (1967), a poem by Brecht, and otherwise influenced numerous novels, plays, and paintings of its day (not to mention a whole generation of American wartime musicals with production numbers staged on the quarterdecks of battleships). In 1986, *Potemkin* was revived for a multi-city European tour with the original Edmund Meisel score performed by the Netherlands' Brabants Orchestra.

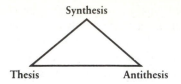

The synthesis emerging from the thesis-antithesis conflict will ultimately become the thesis of a new dialectic, which will in turn generate a new synthesis, and so on until the end of historical time. Eisenstein maintained that in film editing the shot, or "montage cell," is a thesis which when placed into juxtaposition with another shot of opposing visual content—its antithesis—produces a synthesis (a synthetic idea or impression) which in turn becomes the thesis of a new dialectic as the montage sequence continues.* This visual opposition between shots may be a conflict of linear directions, planes, volumes, lighting, etc., and need not extend to the dramatic content of the shot. Thus, Eisenstein defined montage as a series of ideas or impressions which arise from "the collision of independent shots," and in a characteristically industrial metaphor he compared its process to "the series of explosions of an internal combustion engine, driving forward its automobile or tractor." Similarly, he wrote, "the dynamics of montage serve as impulses driving forward the total film." Another of Eisenstein's favorite analogies was linguistic: just as the individual words in a sentence depend for their meaning upon the words which surround them, so the individual shots in a montage sequence acquire meaning from their interaction with the other shots in the sequence.

The underlying cognitive assumption of this theory is that the viewers of a film perceive the shots in a montage sequence not *sequentially,* or one at a time, but rather *simultaneously,* as if one were continuously superimposed upon another. That is, they respond not to an incremental or additive process in which each shot is modified by the ones which precede it (ABC≠A + B + C) but to a *gestalt*—a totality or a whole which is different from and greater than the sum of its parts (ABC = x). This is so because shots A, B, and C can be strictly said to follow one another only on the film strip; when the film strip is projected, however, the viewer's mind puts the shots together in a manner analogous to photographic superimposition. Thus, at the end of the Odessa steps section of *Potemkin,* when we are shown three consecutive shots of a stone lion sleeping, a stone lion awakening, and a stone lion rising, we see the sequence not as a combination of its parts but as something quite different—a single unbroken movement with a specifically ideological signification.

Although Griffith's two great epics and Kuleshov's experiments in edit-

---

* In a very important sense, as Eisenstein realized, the dialectic can also be used to describe the psycho-perceptual process of cinema itself: in projection, two (or more) independent still photographs on a film strip collide to produce something different from and greater than them both—the illusion of continuous motion.

ing clearly stand behind these notions, Eisenstein developed many of them from his study of the psychology of perception; and to illustrate the process of dialectical montage, he would frequently use the example of the Japanese pictograph or ideogram. In Japanese character-writing, completely new concepts are formed by combining the symbols for two separate older ones. Moreover, the new concept is never merely the sum of its parts and is invariably an abstraction which could not be represented graphically on its own terms. For example, the symbol for "dog" plus the symbol for "mouth" create an ideogram meaning not "dog's mouth," as one might expect, but "bark." Similarly,

child + mouth = scream
bird + mouth = sing
knife + heart = sorrow
water + eye = weep
door + ear = listen

Thus, in every case the combination of two distinct signs for concrete objects produces a single sign for some intangible or abstraction. What Eisenstein was attempting to suggest by these examples was the way in which film, whose signs are moving photographic images and therefore *wholly* tangible, can communicate conceptual abstractions on a par with other art forms. Griffith had intimated as much when he said, "You can photograph thought," but he was referring specifically to the narrative use of close-ups and flashbacks. Eisenstein characteristically went far beyond Griffith, to suggest that the cinema contains within its most essential structuring process (editing) a mechanism for creating conceptual abstractions (dialectical montage) which need only be exercised to be perceived.

Eisenstein conceived that whole films, as well as autonomous sequences within them, could be constructed according to the dialectic. In theoretical essays like "A Dialectical Approach to Film Form" (1929) and "The Structure of the Film" (1939), he wrote lengthy post-factum analyses of the dialectical structure of *Potemkin*. Eisenstein claimed that each part or act of *Potemkin* was broken into two equal halves by a "caesura," a term (borrowed from poetry and music) denoting a strong medial pause in the action, and that the film as a whole was similarly divided by the harbor mist sequence which begins the third act. The dialectical pattern of each act (and of the film itself) was one of mounting tension followed by a resolution or exploding of tension, which together produced a synthesis that became the thesis of the next act. Eisenstein diagrammed the structure of Acts II through V as follows:

II. Scene with the tarpaulin ⟶ mutiny
III. Mourning for Vakulinchuk ⟶ angry demonstration
IV. Lyrical fraternization ⟶ shooting
V. Anxiously awaiting the fleet ⟶ triumph

He also described the transition point or caesura peculiar to each act:

In one part (III), this is a few shots of clenched fists, through which the theme of mourning the dead leaps into the theme of fury.

In another part (IV), this is a subtitle—"SUDDENLY"—cutting off the scene of fraternization, and projecting it into the scene of the shooting.

The motionless muzzles of the rifles (in Part II). The gaping mouths of the guns (in Part V). And the cry of "Brothers," upsetting the awful pause of waiting, in an explosion of brotherly feeling—in both moments.

Finally, Eisenstein outlined the ideological dialectic of sequences within acts. At the outset of the Odessa steps massacre, for example, he perceives the following dialectical structure:

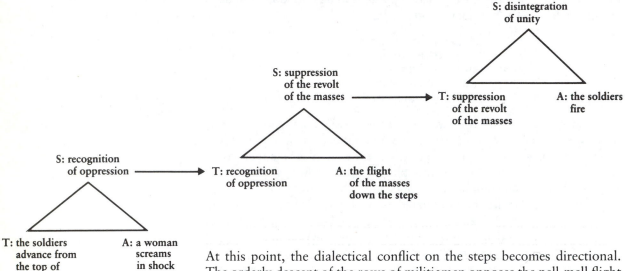

At this point, the dialectical conflict on the steps becomes directional. The orderly descent of the rows of militiamen opposes the pell-mell flight of the disordered masses in terms of tempo and volume, but both together oppose the movement of the individual supplicants and the lone mother and child who are simultaneously ascending. The young mother stopped still on the landing with her baby opposes the movement of all four groups, and later her rapidly descending baby carriage adds a new dimension of motion to the sequence, which might be diagrammed as follows:

As the sequence ends at the bottom of the steps, the young Cossack savagely swinging his saber collides with the bloodied face of the woman in pince-nez to produce the synthesis: rage. Then, the guns of the *Potemkin* collide with the generals' headquarters to produce the ultimate synthesis: collective action.

In other articles Eisenstein attempted to distinguish five separate types or "methods" of montage, all of which may be used simultaneously within any given sequence: 1) the metric, 2) the rhythmic, 3) the tonal, 4) the overtonal, and 5) the intellectual or ideological. "Metric montage" is concerned solely with the tempo of the cutting, regardless of the content of the shots. The basis for editing is thus the temporal length or duration of each shot, and these lengths are determined by the imposition of a regular metrical pattern upon the cutting rate. In this method, shots of one length may alternate regularly with shots of another, or the shots may progressively increase or decrease in length as the sequence moves forward, but the proportional relationship of one shot to another must remain constant throughout the sequence. A good example of accelerating metric montage would be the Griffith intercut chase sequence, in which the climax is reached by alternating shots of progressively shorter duration.* Eisenstein felt that metric montage was both mechanical and primitive, and he identified it (in the main, unfairly) with his major Soviet rival, V. I. Pudovkin.

"Rhythmic montage" Eisenstein described as an elaboration of metric montage in which the cutting rate is based upon the rhythm of movement *within* the shots as well as upon predetermined metrical demands. This rhythm may be used either to reinforce the metric tempo of the sequence or to counterpoint it. As an example of the latter, Eisenstein cites the Odessa steps sequence from *Potemkin*, in which the steady rhythm of the soldiers' feet as they descend the stairs within the frame is made to regularly violate the metric tempo of the cutting. This type of editing sets up a counterpoint between rhythmic and metric movement which sustains the high tension of the sequence.

"Tonal montage," Eisenstein claimed, represents a stage beyond the rhythmic in which the dominant emotional *tone* of the shots becomes the basis for editing. Eisenstein makes the following distinction between the two modes:

> In rhythmic montage it is movement within the frame that impels the montage movement from frame to frame. Such movements within the frame may be of objects in motion, or of the spectator's eye directed along the lines of some immobile object.

> In tonal montage, movement is perceived in a wider sense. The concept of movement embraces *all affects* of the montage piece. Here montage is based on the characteristic *emotional sound* of the piece—of its dominant. The general *tone* of the piece.

---

* As Griffith wrote of his own method in 1925: "The action must quicken to a height in a minor climax, then slow down and build again to the next climax, which should be faster than the second and on to the major climax, where the pace should be fastest. Through the big moments of the story, the pace should be like the beat of an excited pulse." ("Pace in the Movies," *Liberty,* April 18, 1925.)

As an example of tonal montage, Eisenstein cites the fog sequence at the beginning of the third act of *Potemkin*. Here, the basic tonal dominant of the shots is the quality of their light ("haze" and "luminosity"), which all the other plastic elements of the shots subserve. Tonal montage, then, has to do with neither the cutting rate nor the content of the shots, but rather with their texture, and it predicates a tenuous psychological or associative relationship between emotional and visual tones.

"Overtonal montage," according to Eisenstein, is basically a synthesis of metric, rhythmic, and tonal montage which emerges in projection rather than in the editing process (where only the "undertones" are visible). This is not really a distinct category but another way of looking at montage based upon the tonality of stimuli. Eisenstein writes of it: "The visual *overtone* cannot be traced in the static frame, just as it cannot be traced in the musical score. Overtonal conflicts, foreseen but unwritten in the score, cannot emerge without the dialectical process of the passage of the film through the projection apparatus, or that of the performance by a symphonic orchestra."

"Intellectual or ideological montage" was the type that most fascinated Eisenstein in both his theory and his practice. All of the preceding montage methods are concerned with inducing emotional and/or physiological reactions in the audience through a sophisticated form of behavioristic stimulation. But Eisenstein also conceived that montage was capable of expressing abstract ideas and making direct intellectual statements. Thus, in intellectual montage, cutting is based primarily upon neither tempo, rhythm, nor tone (although all of these components may be present in a given sequence) but upon the *conceptual* relationship between shots of opposing visual content, i.e., upon their ability to create metaphors for ideas and abstractions. The intercutting of the massacre of the workers with the slaughter of an ox at the end of *Strike* and the intercutting of the priest tapping his crucifix with the ship's officer tapping his sword in the second act of *Potemkin* are simple manifestations of intellectual montage. But the most sophisticated use of this metaphorical technique occurs in Eisenstein's third film, *October* (*Oktiabr;* alternatively titled *Ten Days That Shook the World*, 1928), a magnificent failed attempt to recount the events of the Bolshevik Revolution in terms of pure intellectual cinema. Eisenstein himself cited the "gods" sequence of this film, omitted from most American prints, as a prime example of the method. In it, he offers a montage of various religious icons, beginning with a baroque statue of Christ and concluding with a hideous primitive idol, to debunk the traditional concept of God. As Eisenstein pointed out later: "These pieces were assembled in accordance with a descending intellectual scale—pulling back the concept of God to its origins, forcing the spectator to perceive this 'progress' intellectually." A more complex example of intellectual montage in *October* is the famous sequence depicting the rise to power of Alexander Kerenski, head of the Coalition or Provisional Government which preceded the Bolshevik Revolution. Eisenstein presents successive shots of Kerenski solemnly climbing the baroque marble staircase of the Winter Palace and intercuts them with

5.28 **Final frames from the "gods" sequence in *October*** (Sergei Eisenstein, 1928).

grandiose titles announcing his ascent through the ranks of the government ("Minister of the Army," "And the Navy," "Generalissimo," "Dictator") and with shots of military flunkies bowing and scraping before him on the landings. At one point, Kerenski passes beneath a statue of Victory that seems about to place a crown of laurels on his head. Then, as he reaches the top of the stairs and stands before the doorway to his office, Eisenstein cuts from his highly polished military boots to his gloved hands, and finally to a mechanical peacock spreading its tail in prideful splendor. The whole sequence is meant to suggest the inflated vanity, monumental pride, and dictatorial ambition of Kerenski and his government.

5.29 Intellectual montage: Kerenski and the peacock in *October*.

All of Eisenstein's thinking on montage worked toward the establishment of a uniquely cinematic language based upon psychological association and stimulation which had little or nothing to do with narrative logic. Deriving from his lifelong study of the dynamics of aesthetic perception, this language, which Eisenstein chose to call "dialectical montage," operated according to a precise manipulation of audience psychology on both the emotional and cerebral levels of experience. Some recent critics, notably followers of the French film theorist André Bazin, have claimed that dialectical montage is *too* manipulative, even "totalitarian," in its selective ordering of the viewer's response. Their objection is largely philosophical, for they believe that the analytical fragmentation of a filmed event through montage, as in the Odessa steps sequence, destroys "the

5.30 Heroic metaphor and documentary realism in *October*.

reality of space" (Bazin) which provides the necessary relationship between the cinematic image and the real world. They believe, in other words, that dialectical montage substitutes artificial and contrived spatial relationships for natural ones. And yet it is precisely its lack of dependence upon "real" or "natural" spatial relationships which renders dialectical montage a symbolic and metaphoric—and, therefore, a *poetic*—language rather than a narrative one. As Paul Seydor points out in an essay intended to be highly critical of Eisenstein: "Eisenstein's early cinema is quintessentially a cinema of (though not necessarily for) the mind. Space and movement are not literally seen, that is, are not on the screen; they exist only in the viewer's imagination, his eye serving to register the details with which his mind will make the 'proper' points." And as Eisenstein himself wrote in *The Film Sense:* "The strength of montage is this, that it includes in the creative process the emotions and mind of the spectator. The spectator is compelled to proceed along the selfsame creative road that the artist travelled in creating the image." Whether or not such a process is ideologically appropriate is a moot point when it works as well aesthetically as it does, say, in *Potemkin.* But, for Eisenstein and for others, it didn't always work, and his third film provides a measure of its limitations.

October (Ten Days That Shook the World, 1928): A Laboratory for Intellectual Montage

In the spring of 1927, Eisenstein was commissioned by the Central Committee of the Communist Party and Sovkino to make a film commemorating the tenth anniversary of the Bolshevik Revolution. Using hundreds of personal memoirs and interviews, newsreel and newspaper accounts, and John Reed's book *Ten Days That Shook the World* (the title by which a heavily edited version of the film was known in America and Great Britain), Eisenstein and his co-scenarist, Grigori Alexandrov (1903–84),* wrote a meticulously detailed shooting script, entitled *October,* which initially covered the history of the entire revolution. But, as with *Potemkin,* Eisenstein ultimately narrowed his scope to focus on a few representative episodes—the events in Petrograd (now Leningrad) from February to October 1917. Vast resources, including the Soviet army and navy, were placed at Eisenstein's disposal, and life in Leningrad was completely disrupted during the six months of shooting as mass battles like the storming and bombardment of the Winter Palace were restaged with casts of tens of thousands. When editing was completed in November 1927, the film ran approximately thirteen thousand feet, or just under three hours, with a carefully integrated score composed by Edmund Meisel. But during its production Leon Trotski (1879–1940), who as commissar of war had played an enormously important role in the Revolution and civil war, was expelled from the Politburo (executive committee) of

---

* For an account of Alexandrov's own career as a director in the thirties and forties, see Norman Swallow, "Alexandrov," *Sight and Sound,* 48, 4 (Autumn 1979): 246–49.

the Communist Party and forced into exile by Iosif Stalin (1879–1953),*
and Eisenstein was compelled to cut *October* by several thousand feet†
in order to eliminate all references to the ousted leader. (For the same
reason, Reed's book was banned in the Soviet Union from late 1927 until
after Stalin's death in 1953.) When this truncated version** was finally
released to the public in March 1928, it was poorly received. Audiences
could not understand its abstract intellectual montage, and Party critics
attacked it bitterly for "formalist excess"—a charge which publicly
announced the widening rift between Eisenstein's aesthetics and the new
Stalinist establishment. (Eisenstein was hardly alone in this: during the
key years of Stalin's rise, 1927 and 1928, half of the 135 films produced
by the Soviet industry were suppressed—thirteen permanently so—and
over one-third restricted to limited audiences.)

Yon Barna has called *October* "an experimental film of immense proportions," and indeed it was, for Eisenstein used it as a laboratory in
which to test his theories of intellectual montage upon an actual audience. In *October*, Eisenstein employed intellectual montage on the order
of the stone lion sequence in *Potemkin* to comment upon each and every
aspect of the Revolution depicted in the narrative portion of the film.
Thus, Kerenski is compared to a peacock and his militia to tin soldiers
and empty wineglasses through the insertion of shots from outside the
dramatic context of the film. Similarly, the treacherous pleading of the
Mensheviks at the Second Congress of Soviets is intercut with shots of
soft female hands stroking harps, and the union of the Motorcycle Bat-
talion with the Congress is juxtaposed with shots of abstractly spinning
bicycle wheels, in association with the entrance of the new delegates.
(Eisenstein wrote of this sequence in *Film Form*, "In this way the large-
scale emotional content of the event was transformed into actual dynam-

5.31 *October:* Kerenski hiding in the
Winter Palace.

---

* Born Iosif Vissarionovich Jugashvili in Gori, Georgia, Stalin was one of Lenin's several
lieutenants before, during, and after 1917. He adopted his pseudonym—Russian for "man
of steel"—shortly after being named by Lenin to the Bolshevik Central Committee in 1912.
He played an important, if not crucial, role in the October Revolution, and afterwards
became secretary-general of the Central Committee of the Communist Party. Lenin was
preparing to remove Stalin from this post for abuse of power when he suffered the series of
strokes that led to his death in 1924. Thereafter, Stalin outmaneuvered his opponents (chiefly
Trotski, Grigory E. Zinoviev [1883–1936], and Nikolai I. Bukharin [1888–1938]—all of
whom he later had executed) to become virtual dictator of the Soviet Union from 1928 to
1953. See Alex de Jonge, *Stalin: and the Shaping of the Soviet Union* (New York: Morrow,
1986). (See also pp. 313–22 and pp. 567–68.)

† Estimates range from 1,000 feet or about eleven minutes (Ephraim Katz, *The Film Encyclopedia* [New York: Crowell, 1979], p. 381) to 4,000 feet (Barna, *Eisenstein*, p. 123).
Eisenstein himself was vague, but remarks he made while editing the film indicate that
about one-third of what he shot is missing.

** The version released as *Ten Days That Shook the World* in Britain and North America
was even further shortened through the elimination or abridgement of key montage sequences.
For the Fiftieth Anniversary celebration of the Revolution in 1967, Grigori Alexandrov
reconstructed the original version of *October* on the basis of Eisenstein's notes, with a new
score by Dmitri Shostakovich. The reconstruction contains over 3,200 shots, counting the
intertitles; see *Octobre: continuité photogrammatique intégrale* (Paris, 1980), a published
shot-by-shot continuity.

5.32 Synecdoche and symbol in *October:* wheels spinning, a broken statue.

5.33 The faces of the Soviet people: typage in *October*.

ics.") At one point, Eisenstein suggests the stolid emptiness of the tsarist regime through a series of still shots of elaborate ornamental façades and heavily beribboned military tunics. Synecdoche—the use of a part to symbolize the whole—is everywhere apparent: rifles waving in the air tell us that the army has joined the Bolshevik cause; the hands of bureaucrats frantically clicking their telephone receivers indicate that the Kerenski government has lost control.

Countless other rhetorical devices are used by Eisenstein to maximize the film's ideological effect, from complicated inter-frame symbolism (as when the history of religion is condensed into a series of shots proceeding from the most "civilized" of icons to the most primitive and barbarous) to simple cinematic trickery (as when a statue of Tsar Alexander III, demolished earlier in the film to represent the success of the Revolution, is magically reassembled through reverse projection to represent the monarchists' vain hopes of returning to power). In a much-discussed sequence, Eisenstein uses the agonizingly slow raising of a drawbridge to suggest that the city of Petrograd has been split asunder by the revolution. From one side of the rising bridge dangles a live horse still harnessed to a cart, from the other the flaxen hair of a dead girl, shot during a demonstration, and this hair for a long time spans the crevice between the two halves before falling into the breach. In narrative terms, the drawbridge has been raised by the police in order to cut off retreating workers from their quarters, but Eisenstein turns the event into a poetic metaphor by lingering on the slowly widening gulf between the two sides and by drawing out the moment of their separation far beyond the time it would naturally take in reality. As in the plate-smashing sequence and the Odessa steps massacre of *Potemkin,* Eisenstein here expands time to represent the psychological duration of an event as opposed to its chronological duration.

In its publicly released form *October* does appear to be, as its critics charged, excessively formalistic—concerned more with the intricacies of its own cinematic mechanisms than with its revolutionary content. Furthermore—and, by Eisenstein's own standards, most damning of all—the film's intellectual montage does not always work. There is sometimes a disturbing disparity between the idea Eisenstein seeks to communicate and its technical expression. Eisenstein wrote in 1929: "The hieroglyphic language of the cinema is capable of expressing any concept, any idea of class, any political or tactical slogan, without recourse to the help of a rather suspect dramatic or psychological past."* And yet a cinema of pure intellectual abstraction, excepting certain specialized forms of animation, can never really exist, since cinematic statements can be made only through the juxtaposition of concrete images. Eisenstein's notion, of course, was that concrete images properly arranged can *suggest* abstract ones, and this is true. But all available evidence indicates that the technique of intellectual montage will work only when it is firmly grounded in some specific narrative or dramatic context. When intellectual montage usurps its narrative context, as it often does in *October,* it tends to create a class of nonreferential symbols which have meaning neither as abstractions nor as objects.

5.34 *October:* shots from the draw-bridge sequence.

Eisenstein after *October*

Eisenstein's next film was a continuation of a project begun just prior to the commissioning of *October.* Initially entitled *The General Line* (*General'naya liniia*)—i.e., the "general line" or policy of the Communist Party—and renamed *Old and New* (*Staroe i novoie,* 1929) when Stalinist bureaucrats disavowed it, and the film was conceived by Eisenstein as a lyrical hymn of praise, in semidocumentary form, to the collectivization of Soviet agriculture. It tells the didactic tale of the evolution of a typical Russian peasant village from backwardness and poverty to prosperity through the establishment of a collective farm. For the first time, Eisenstein told his story through a central character, Marfa Lapkina, a simple peasant woman (played in the film, according to Eisenstein's theory of typage, by a real peasant) who becomes a devoted supporter of the cooperative effort and is instrumental in its ultimate success. Like all Eisenstein films, *Old and New* was carefully researched and shot mainly on location, and, as with *October,* Eisenstein used it as a laboratory for experiment—this time not with "intellectual" but with "overtonal" montage, and much more successfully than before. According to this technique, which Eisenstein also called "polyphonic montage" and "the filmic fourth dimension," a film is assembled through the harmonic orchestration of tonal dominants—i.e., through what André Bazin would later term *mise-en-scène* as opposed to wholly analytic editing, as we will see in Chapter 13. Unlike the intellectual montage of *October,* all the shots

---

* An index of how firmly Eisenstein believed this statement is that between 1927 and 1928 he seriously considered making a film of Marx's massive socio-economic dissection of capitalism, *Das Kapital* (1867), which he hoped would raise intellectual montage "into the realm of philosophy." (Quoted in Yon Barna, *Eisenstein* [Boston, 1973], p. 126.) After reading James Joyce's *Ulysses* (which he called "the Bible of the new cinema") in February 1928, Eisenstein also came to believe that intellectual montage could be practiced in literature: "Indeed," he wrote, "in the linguistic kitchen of literature Joyce occupies himself with the same thing that I rave about in relation to laboratory researches on cinema language." (Eisenstein, *Immoral Memories,* trans. Herbert Marshall [Boston, 1983], p. 213.) The following year in Paris, Eisenstein would spend hours talking with Joyce about adapting *Ulysses* to the screen—a hopeful but unlikely prospect, since the writer by this time was nearly blind.

5.35 *October:* fraternization between Russian and German soldiers at the front.

5.36 Lenin addresses his supporters at various points in *October*.

5.37 The ultimate typage: Marfa Lapkina as Marfa Lapkina in Eisenstein's *Old and New* (1929).

in this method arise naturally out of the dramatic context of the film, and they are carefully composed in depth within the frame to orchestrate the "thematic major" and "thematic minor" keys.

Eisenstein's analogy, of course, was with the composition of symphonic music. As he wrote of *Old and New* in *The Film Form*, "The whole intricate, rhythmic and *sensual* nuance scheme of the combined pieces (of certain sequences) is conducted almost exclusively according to a line of work on the 'psychophysiological' vibrations of each piece." Famous sequences include Marfa's first encounter with a mechanized cream separator, the arrival and mating of the village bull, and the final "dance" of the tractors; but Eisenstein's cutting throughout the film is the most sophisticated and subtle he was ever to achieve. In fact, many critics have come to regard it as his most beautiful silent film. Sounding like one of his Italian neorealist successors, Eisenstein wrote that his purpose in *Old and New* was "to exalt the pathos of everyday existence." And indeed the film's extraordinary lyrical quality—its feeling for sky, sun, and soil, and for humanity itself—works in tandem with its superb visual form to create a kind of "total cinema" that Eisenstein was never to attain again. However, when the film was completed in the spring of 1929, Soviet officials were dissatisfied, and Eisenstein was forced to shoot another ending at Stalin's command. Despite this adjustment and much popular acclaim, *Old and New* was bitterly denounced by Party critics, who dissociated themselves from its politics and again raised the old charge of formalism. This reaction portended serious trouble for Eisenstein, but in 1929 he stood at the height of his international fame, and the Party could not afford to overlook the prestige he was bringing to the Soviet Union from all parts of the globe.

With *Old and New,* Eisenstein had taken the silent film form about as far as it would go, just as six years earlier he had reached the outer limits of the legitimate stage and "fallen into the cinema." Now, at the peak of his artistic powers, he stood on the very brink of the sound film, in whose aesthetic prospect he had become almost insatiably interested. Sadly, for the next decade Eisenstein's contributions to the art of the sound film were to be almost solely theoretical, for this great architect of the Soviet silent cinema was not permitted to complete another motion picture until *Alexander Nevski* in 1938. A political tragicomedy was about to be enacted in the Soviet Union which would make it impossible for Eisenstein to practice cinema in his own country for nearly nine years. For the moment, however, Eisenstein was an internationally acclaimed master with several huge successes to his credit, and many persons throughout the West looked to him as the supreme arbiter of cinematic form. Accordingly, in August 1929, at the age of thirty-one, Eisenstein was sent by Soiuzkino together with scenarist Alexandrov and cinematographer Tisse to study the cinemas of Western Europe and especially the United States, where for much of 1930 he was to work on several abortive projects for Paramount*

5.38 Overtonal montage: old and new.

5.39 Hostile kulaks, superstitious peasants.

* Notably, *Sutter's Gold,* based on Blaise Cendrars' Futurist novel *L'Or* (1925) about John Augustus Sutter, the German immigrant who started the California gold rush and built an empire on this wealth, but who ultimately became a Communist, for which Eisenstein

5.40 Marfa transformed by the operation of the cream separator.

5.41 Marfa's vision of fertility: a cow decked with bridal flowers on her way to mate with a bull.

5.42 The dream parade of the tractors which concludes *Old and New*.

before journeying to Mexico to shoot his remarkable unfinished epic *Que viva México!* (1931–32). Eisenstein's American sojourn marked his first practical encounter with the new technology of sound recording and the beginning of a series of tragic complications which would plague him until his early death in 1948; these will be examined in Chapter 9.

VSEVOLOD PUDOVKIN

Vsevolod I. Pudovkin (1893–1953), the second great director of the Soviet silent cinema, had been trained as a chemist, but he decided to renounce his profession and become a filmmaker after seeing D. W. Griffith's *Intolerance* in Moscow in 1920. He joined the Moscow Film School and spent two years as a member of the Kuleshov Workshop, where he participated in the famous editing experiments described earlier in this chapter and was directly involved in the production of *The Extraordinary Adventures of Mr. West in the Land of the Bolsheviks* (1924) and *The Death Ray* (1925). Pudovkin's first full-length film was a documentary on Pavlovian reflexology entitled *The Mechanics of the Brain* (*Mekhanika golovnova mozga*, 1926), in which he successfully used editing principles discovered by Kuleshov as a pedagogical device to explain con-

wrote a script showing "the paradise of primitive, patriarchal California, destroyed by the lust for gold," and a Marxist treatment of Theodore Dreiser's *An American Tragedy* (1926), both of which were rejected as being too critical of American society. *An American Tragedy* was finally made at Paramount by Josef von Sternberg in 1931 with a new script (as we will see in Chapter 8) and made again by the same studio twenty years later as *A Place in the Sun* (George Stevens, 1951—see Chapter 12) from yet a third script. Eisenstein's *Sutter's Gold* treatment was revised by William Faulkner for Howard Hawks in 1934; both Faulkner and Hawks then abandoned the project, which was ultimately produced by Universal in 1936, with James Cruze directing. Ironically, the same year saw a Nazi version of Sutter, *Der Kaiser von Kalifornien* (*The Kaiser of California*, Tobis, 1936), directed by and starring the Austian filmmaker Luis Trenker, which portrayed Sutter as a visionary German nationalist who heroically rejects "degenerate" American capitalism.

ditioning theory to an unsophisticated audience. At about the same time, Pudovkin shot *Chess Fever* (*Shakhmatnaia goriachka*, 1925; co-directed with Nikolai Shpikovski), a two-reel comedy in the manner of Mack Sennett's Keystone films (see pp. 209–10), but constructed according to Kuleshovian principles (woven into the plot is footage of the chess champion José Capablanca obtained by one of Pudovkin's cameramen posing as a newsreel photographer). Both films were photographed by Anatoli Golovnia (1900–82), who was to become Pudovkin's constant collaborator from 1925 to 1950, and both were popular with domestic audiences, but it was Pudovkin's first dramatic feature film, *Mother* (*Mat*, 1926), that thrust him into the international limelight as Eisenstein's closest Soviet rival.

Loosely adapted by Pudovkin and the scenarist Nathan Zarkhi (another frequent collaborator) from Maxim Gorki's novel of the same title,* and photographed by Golovnia, *Mother* is set during the time of the 1905 Revolution. It tells the story of a politically naïve woman married to a brutal (and brutalized) drunkard who works with their son, Pavel, in a factory. The family leads a life of abject poverty, and to finance his drinking the father joins the ranks of the Black Hundreds, a counterrevolutionary goon-squad in the pay of the tsarist government. During a violent confrontation between striking workers and the Black Hundreds in the factory yard, the father discovers that Pavel is one of the strikers. They fight, and the father is accidentally killed by one of Pavel's friends. Later, the police come to Pavel's home searching for weapons, and the mother, in her naïveté, betrays her son, believing that he will be exonerated. Instead, Pavel is arrested and sentenced to prison in a rigged trial; the mother is first anguished and then radically politicized by this experience of tsarist tyranny. She maintains close contact with Pavel's friends and later helps him to escape from jail. At the conclusion of the film, they meet again, on May Day, at the head of a workers' demonstration. A regiment of Cossacks attacks the demonstrators, and mother and son die heroically confronting tsarist tyranny.

Mother enjoyed an immediate international success similar to that of *Potemkin*, and for some of the same reasons.† It is a beautifully proportioned film, carefully photographed by Golovnia and brilliantly edited by Pudovkin. Its action proceeds rhythmically through four symmetrical parts, and its montage effects are masterfully controlled. Yet *Mother* is in many ways a quieter, less spectacular film than its predecessor. Though it is essentially a political parable dealing with violent action, it eschews the epic proportions of *Potemkin* to concentrate on the human drama played out against the backdrop of a great historical moment. Eisenstein's film was about that moment itself, Pudovkin's about the people caught up in

---

* The German playwright Bertolt Brecht (1898–1956) dramatized the novel for the stage in 1932; his highly stylized adaptation (which includes songs) provides an interesting contrast to Pudovkin's film.

† In a poll of 117 film critics from twenty-six countries to choose the twelve best films of all time at the 1958 Brussels World's Fair, *Potemkin* ranked first and *Mother* eighth.

5.43 Shots from the mourning sequence in *Mother* (Vsevolod Pudovkin, 1926).

it. This is the pattern which appeared throughout Pudovkin's silent films and which above all others made them more popular with the Soviet masses than Eisenstein's. Whereas Eisenstein was the grand master of the mass epic, Pudovkin's approach to filmmaking was more personal. As the French critic Léon Moussinac would later write, "A film of Eisenstein's resembles a scream, one of Pudovkin a song." Pudovkin had learned from Griffith to contrast scenes of mass action with the more intimate drama of the "little people" whose lives are transfigured by it. Though he subscribed in part to current theories of typage, Pudovkin had also learned from Griffith the importance of emotionally credible film acting, and he coaxed magnificent performances from his two leading players, Vera Baranovskaia (1880–1935) as the mother and Nikolai Batalov (1898–1937) as the son. Their presence alone imbues the film with a kind of emotional lyricism completely alien to Eisenstein's work, with the sole exception of parts of *Old and New*.

But despite the more direct emotional appeal of his film, Pudovkin's montage was every bit as sophisticated as that of Eisenstein, from whom of course, he and all Soviet filmmakers had learned a great deal (Pudovkin always said that the second major film experience of his life, after *Intolerance,* was *Potemkin*). Some of the great montage sequences from *Mother* include that in which the mourning mother keeps vigil over her husband's corpse while water drips slowly into a bucket beside her; Pavel's lyrical fantasy of escape from prison, in which images of spring coming to the land are intercut with his smiling face; and Pavel's actual escape from prison over the ice floes, which eventually modulates into the concluding massacre. The sequence on the ice derives from Griffith's *Way Down East* (1920) rather than from Gorki's novel, but Pudovkin reveals the heritage of the Kuleshov Workshop by making the montage metaphorically as well as narratively functional. As the sequence begins, ice cakes floating downriver are intercut with workers marching toward the factory and their heroic confrontation with the troops. As the river becomes more and more clogged with ice, the ranks of the workers swell, until they overflow the curbs of the street. The narrative function of the ice floes becomes apparent when we see that the river runs past the prison and will provide Pavel with the medium for his escape. He joins the marchers on the opposite bank by leaping across the floes like the hero at the climax of *Way Down East,* but the metaphorical function of the sequence reasserts itself as the floes smash suddenly and violently into the piers of a stone bridge—the very bridge upon which moments later the workers will clash head-on with the troops. The complex montage of the massacre itself, second only to the Odessa steps sequence of *Potemkin* in conveying the plight of individuals caught up in violent action, provides an emotionally gripping, revolutionary climax to an intensely affecting film.

From the foregoing account it should be clear that Pudovkin's montage, even at its most symbolic, usually serves some narrative purpose. Unlike Eisenstein, Pudovkin rarely engaged in intellectual abstraction. He had good theoretical reasons for this, believing that the process of

5.44 Shots from the concluding massacre in *Mother*.

montage operated differently from the way Eisenstein conceived it. For Pudovkin, the key process of montage was not collision but *linkage*. As he wrote in the introduction to the German edition of his book *Film Technique and Film Acting* (1926; trans. Ivor Montagu, London, 1950): "The expression that the film is 'shot' is entirely false, and should disappear from the language. The film is not *shot*, but *built*, built up from the separate strips of celluloid that are its raw material." Thus, Pudovkin chose an architectonic model for film structure and Eisenstein a dialectical one, though in practice both frequently mixed effects.* Ultimately, however, the argument between Eisenstein and Pudovkin was less about the formal aspects of montage than about the psychology of the viewer, with Eisenstein believing that cinematic meaning is generated through the cognitive collision of frames within the viewer's mind and Pudovkin that it is generated through the cognitive linkage of frames. The opposition between these two points of view has never been resolved, and it will not be until we know a good deal more about the processes of perception involved in watching films. By August 1928, however, confronted with the imminent introduction of sound, Eisenstein and Pudovkin had managed to resolve their aesthetic differences sufficiently to issue a joint manifesto (with Grigori Alexandrov) endorsing the use of asynchronous, or contrapuntal, sound as opposed to lip-synchronized dialogue, or synchronous sound, which they correctly saw as a threat to the art of montage as practiced in the silent film.

Pudovkin's next film, like Eisenstein's *October,* was commissioned by the Central Committee to commemorate the tenth anniversary of the Bolshevik Revolution. It was entitled *The End of St. Petersburgh* (*Koniets Sankt-Peterburga,* 1927), and, as he had done in *Mother,* Pudovkin once again chose to focus upon the personal drama of individuals caught up in the Revolution. The first half of the film tells the story of a peasant boy who comes to the tsarist capital, St. Petersburg, on the eve of World War I to find employment. Because he is politically unenlightened, the boy takes work as a strikebreaker and informer. When he later comes to understand the plight of the workers under capitalism, however, he attacks his employer in a frenzy and is tossed into jail, from which he is conscripted into the army when war is declared. Then the focus of the film shifts to the war itself and to the Revolution as experienced by the young soldier. The second part of *The End of St. Petersburg,* covering the years 1915 to 1917, often resembles Eisenstein's work in its use of expressive montage to communicate the historic impact of great events. But in Pudovkin's films the human element is always intertwined with the epic and symbolic. He uses montage brilliantly throughout this section to contrast the profiteering of the capitalists with the human misery caused by war. As he had done in *Mother,* Pudovkin also makes use of expressive

5.45 A bombastic tsarist orator addressing a mindless crowd in *The End of St. Petersburg* (Vsevolod Pudovkin, 1927).

---

* For a sustained analysis of the influence of the classical Hollywood style ("maintaining narrative linearity . . . [and] . . . establishing a scenographic space that assures spectator orientation from one shot to the next") on Pudovkin's theory and practice, see Vance Kepley, Jr., "Pudovkin and the Classical Hollywood Tradition," *Wide Angle* 7, 3 (Fall 1985): 53–61.

camera angles in the manner of Griffith. When the boy comes to St. Petersburg for the first time, the camera observes him from an extremely high angle, so that he seems dwarfed by the great buildings and monuments of the city. But when he returns as a Bolshevik soldier at the conclusion of the film to storm the Winter Palace, the angles are effectively reversed. *The End of St. Petersburg,* which unlike Eisenstein's film, was completed and released on schedule, was very successful in the Soviet Union and was hailed as a masterpiece abroad. Many critics today consider it superior to Eisenstein's film as an analysis of the Revolution, although *October* is such a singular and eccentric work that it is difficult to compare them.

Pudovkin's last great silent film, *Heir to Genghis Khan* (*Potomok Chingis-Khana,* 1928; English title: *Storm over Asia*), continued the narrative pattern, begun in *Mother,* in which a politically naïve person is galvanized into radical action by tsarist tyranny. But *Heir to Genghis Khan* is set in Soviet Central Asia in 1920, and its protagonist is a Mongol trapper who is exploited not by Russians but by the foreign armies of intervention which fought against the Red Army in Asia during the civil war.* As this most exciting of Pudovkin film opens, the young Mongol Bair attacks an English fur trader who has badly cheated him and flees to join the Soviet partisans in the north. The British army of intervention eventually tracks him down, shoots him, and leaves him gravely wounded; but a colonel finds an amulet among Bair's belongings which declares him to be a direct descendant of Genghis Khan. The British nurse Bair back to health and set him up as a puppet ruler over Buryat Mongolia. The Mongol accepts his role at first but ultimately realizes that he is being used to oppress his own people, and he turns against the British with a fury that assumes nearly cosmic proportions as the film concludes: like Samson, Bair literally pulls the British headquarters down upon the heads of his captors; then he leaps on a pony and gathers an impossibly vast horde of Mongol horsemen, who ride in wave after wave after wave against the British oppressors, becoming finally an apocalyptic windstorm that hurls the interventionists helplessly about and literally blows them from the face of the land.

This magnificent symbolic conclusion initially contained hundreds of shots (some prints derived from the German version shorten it to twenty-seven) and was roundly attacked by literal-minded critics who considered it unrealistic—which, of course, it was meant to be—and insufficiently ideological. Critics also found fault with the luxuriant pictorial beauty of the film, shot on location by Golovnia, which they thought indulgently formalistic. *Heir to Genghis Khan* was a great popular success, and foreign audiences were much taken with its technical virtuosity; but Pudovkin had been shaken by the bitterness of official Soviet criticism, and his next film, an attempt to put his theory of contrapuntal sound into practice, was a failure. Entitled *A Simple Case* (*Prostoi sluchai,* 1932), it was

5.46 *Heir to Genghis Khan* (Vsevolod Pudovkin, 1928).

---

* Political pressure from foreign ministries made it necessary to label the British "White Russians" in many exported versions of the film, but they remain unmistakably British.

a very subjective love story told in impressionistic bits and pieces that seems much closer to Eisenstein's theories than to Pudovkin's own earlier films. *A Simple Case* was released briefly, after much reworking, in a silent print only, and Pudovkin was publicly charged with formalism, signaling again that the great experimental period of Soviet art was drawing to a close. Though Pudovkin managed to weather the storm of criticism that was about to engulf the great montage artists of the Soviet cinema—he went on to make several respected sound films (*Deserter* [*Dezertir*, 1933]; *Suvorov* [codirected with Mikhail Doller, 1941])—he would never again achieve the stature of his three silent masterpieces, owing to the constant interference of Party bureaucrats.*

ALEXANDER DOVZHENKO

The third major artist of the Soviet silent film, and perhaps the most unconventional, was Alexander Dovzhenko (1894–1956). The son of Ukrainian peasants, Dovzhenko had been a teacher, a diplomat, a political cartoonist, and a painter before joining the Odessa Studios in 1926 at the age of thirty-two. Like Griffith, he knew little about cinema when he began his career in it ("I very rarely saw films," Dovzhenko wrote of his former life), and his first three productions for Odessa were highly derivative of the American slapstick comedies then popular with Soviet audiences. But in 1928 he made a film which revealed a remarkable depth of poetic feeling and which was so technically unconventional that officials of the Ukrainian Film Trust asked Eisenstein and Pudovkin to preview it in order to certify its coherence. The film was *Zvenigora*, a boldly stylized series of tales about a hunt for an ancient Scythian treasure. The tales are set at four different stages of Ukrainian history, enabling Dovzhenko to contrast the region's past and present and to formulate a contemporary political allegory; Eisenstein and Pudovkin immediately recognized its importance. Eisenstein wrote later that its striking blend of fantasy, reality, and "profoundly national poetic invention" was reminiscent of the work of the Russian writer Nikolai Gogol (1809–52). Dovzhenko himself called the film "a catalogue of my creative possibilities," and indeed it was, for in its bold stylization of narrative form, its emotional lyricism, and its passionate sensitivity to Ukrainian life, *Zvenigora* prefigured *Arsenal* (1929) and *Earth* (*Zemlia*, 1930), the two great silent masterpieces to come.

Arsenal is an epic film poem about the effects of revolution and civil war upon the Ukraine. Beginning with the world war and ending in a violent strike by workers at a munitions factory in Kiev, the film does not

5.47 & 5.48 Pudovkin's experimental sound film *A Simple Case* (1932); released silent.

* The Party loyalist Doller, for example—who had assisted him brilliantly on *Mother*—was assigned by Mosfilm to collaborate with Pudovkin on several occasions (*Victory* [*Pobeda*, 1938], *Minin and Pozharsky* [*Minin i Pozharski*, 1939], *Suvorov*) to insure his adherence to "socialist realism," as were Sergei Iutkevich and Alexander Ptushko (*Three Encounters* [*Tri vstrechi*, 1948]) and Dmitri Vasiliev (*Zhukovski*, 1951) in later films. According to Yon Barna, Herbert Marshall, and others, Pyotr Pavlenko and Dmitri Vasiliev were appointed to "assist" Eisenstein on *Alexander Nevsky* (1938) for similar reasons.

5.49   The absurd horror of war in *Arsenal* (Alexander Dovzhenko, 1929).

so much tell a story as create an extended visual metaphor for revolution
encompassing the nightmarish horrors of war, the miseries of economic
oppression, and, finally, the ineradicable spirit of freedom in the hearts
of the Ukrainian people. Structurally, *Arsenal* provides a synoptic view
of the Ukrainian revolution through a series of imagistic vignettes in which
history, caricature, folklore, allegory, and myth are combined. In the
beautifully composed frames of cameraman Danylo Demutsky (1893–
1954), people not only live and die, but horses talk, portraits come to
life, and, at the end of the film, the protagonist himself bares his breast
to volley after volley of reactionary bullets and miraculously continues
to stand, a symbol of the irrepressible revolutionary spirit. Of the film's
highly symbolic, non-narrative organization, Eisenstein remarked that it
was the prime example in cinema of a "liberation of the whole action
from the definition of time and space." Indeed, the official critics experienced some difficulty with *Arsenal,* and yet, according to Jay Leyda, the
public seemed to accept the film almost intuitively upon its own terms.

Dovzhenko's next film, *Earth* (*Zemlia,* 1930), is universally acknowledged to be his masterpiece. Though its scant plot concerns a commonplace manifestation of the class struggle, the film is essentially a non-
narrative hymn to the continuity of life and death in Dovzhenko's beloved
Ukraine. Unfolding with a slow, natural rhythm, like the processes of life
itself, *Earth* tells the simple story of the tension between a family of well-
to-do landowning peasants (kulaks) and the young peasants of a collective farm in a small Ukrainian village.* When the kulaks refuse to sell

---

* Kulaks were identified as class enemies by Stalin in 1928, and "dekulakization" became
part of his brutal collectivization campaign begun the following year, in which millions of

5.50   *Earth* (Alexander Dovzhenko, 1930): visual poetry.

their vast land holdings to the collective, Vasyl, the village chairman, commandeers the property, buys a new tractor, and turns the collective into a thriving enterprise. One evening, after making love to his betrothed, Vasyl is shot dead on the way home by the kulaks' deranged son. In his grief, Vasyl's father sends away the village priest and demands a "modern" funeral for his son "with new songs about new life," and the film concludes with an ecstatic funeral celebration for the young man, after which rain begins to descend upon the crops. Lewis Jacobs has accurately described *Earth* as "a luminous contribution to the realm of lyric cinema." It is a rare film of mysterious beauty that perpetually transcends its contemporary political context to exalt the everlasting fecundity of the soil and the inevitable cyclic recurrence of birth, life, love, and death. The film begins with an old man joyfully biting into an apple as he dies and concludes with the mystically sensuous funeral procession, during which Vasyl's fiancée rips her clothes from her body in grief, his mother goes into labor with her last child, and warm rain falls to replenish the earth.

The central sequence of *Earth* follows the plenteous harvest and is dominated by what Dovzhenko called a "biological, pantheistic conception." Young couples lie in ecstasy under the moonlit summer's night, the hands of the boys on the girls' breasts. Vasyl and his fiancée are among them. They part, and, alone on the dusty road, Vasyl breaks spontaneously into a dance celebrating his deep spiritual joy in life and love.

land-owning peasants were arrested, deported, and / or executed, and their property expropriated by the state. The remaining peasants were then forced onto collective farms or left to starve to death in the artificially created famine of 1932–33. Starvation was particularly brutal in the Ukraine, where some historians believe it was used to eradicate local nationalism. In *The Harvest of Sorrow* (Oxford: Oxford UP, 1986), Robert Conquest estimates that 14.5 million Ukrainians citizens died in the process of collectivization and the subsequent famine.

5.51 *Earth:* **Vasyl dances by moonlight.**

Suddenly, in the middle of a slow-motion pirouette, he falls dead, pierced by the bullet of his hidden assassin. But what would be tragedy in the work of other directors becomes jubilant affirmation in Dovzhenko, for Vasyl has died at the moment of his young life's most perfect self-expression, and life will continue to renew itself as ever before. Ivor Montagu has written: "Dovzhenko's films are crammed with deaths. . . . But no death in Dovzhenko was ever futile. . . . The sum of his films instead is beauty and glory. He is saying to the widow: 'Glory in your children,' and to the childless widow: 'Glory in all the children of man.' "

Though it was later twice voted among the twelve greatest films of all time by panels of international film experts, when first released *Earth* was poorly received by the Soviet critics, who denounced it as "defeatist," "counterrevolutionary," and, in one case, "fascistic." Dovzhenko's domestic reputation, like those of Eisenstein and Pudovkin, was about to enter a period of political eclipse. After a self-imposed hiatus of nearly

5.52 & 5.53 Dovzhenko's sound film *Aerograd* (1935).

two years, Dovzhenko readily adapted his talents to the new demands of the sound film (*Ivan* [1932]; *Aerograd* [1935]; *Shchors* [1939]), but increasing pressure to conform to the Party line made it impossible for him to ever again reach the lyric heights of *Arsenal* and *Earth*, even though for the rest of his life he courageously continued to try.

OTHER SOVIET FILMMAKERS

5.54 *New Babylon* (Grigory Kozintsev and Leonid Trauberg, 1929).

Before examining the reasons for the dramatic decline of the Soviet cinema in the 1930s and the selective suppression of some of its major artists, it is necessary to mention several other filmmakers who played an important role in the great decade of experiment that followed the Revolution. Most notable, perhaps, was the team of Grigori Kozintsev, director (1905–73) and Leonid Trauberg, scenarist (b. 1902), who had founded FEX, the Factory of the Eccentric Actor, in 1921. Kozintsev and Trauberg together produced a number of ebullient, wildly experimental shorts like *The Adventures of Oktiabrina (Pokhozhdeniia Oktiabrini*, 1924) before turning to an extremely successful expressionistic adaptation of Gogol's *The Overcoat* (*Shinel*) in 1926. Their masterpiece, however, magnificently scored by the great modernist composer Dmitri Shostakovich, was *New Babylon* (*Novyi Vavilon*, 1929), a highly stylized drama of the rise and fall of the Paris Commune,* set in a luxurious Parisian department store. (The Kozintsev-Trauberg collaboration would continue through the celebrated "Maxim Trilogy" of 1935–39 [see pp. 369–70] and end with *Simple People* [*Prostye Liudi*, 1946], which was banned for a decade by the Central Committee of the Communist Party as a "false and mistaken" film; Kozintsev subsequently produced several important literary adaptations and Trauberg turned to screen-writing.) Trauberg's younger brother, Ilia (1905–48), after working as an assistant to Eisenstein on *October*, made a remarkable feature debut with *The Blue Express* (*Goluboi ekspress*, 1929), an exciting adventure film set in the Far East which also functions as a political allegory of China's movement toward Communism.

Boris Barnet (1902–65), a pupil of Kuleshov, directed several impressive comedies of contemporary manners in the late silent era, among them *Girl with the Hatbox* (*Devuska s korobkoi*, 1927), a gently satiric tale of everyday life in Moscow under the New Economic Policy. Two prerevo-

---

* After the siege of Paris which ended the Franco-Prussian war of 1870–71, many of the inhabitants of the city rebelled against the government of the Third Republic and established their own council of municipal self-government, called the Commune of Paris. Ostensibly socialist, the Commune governed for two months, until it was brutally suppressed by the French army. Karl Marx hailed the Paris Commune as the first great revolt of the proletariat against the bourgeoisie, and in Marxist-Leninist dogma the Commune is thought to have prefigured the Bolshevik Revolution of 1917. *New Babylon* was revived with its original score at the 1976 Paris Film Festival, performed by Marius Constant's Ars Nova ensemble. Subsequent performances took place in London, New York, and San Francisco in 1982 and 1983.

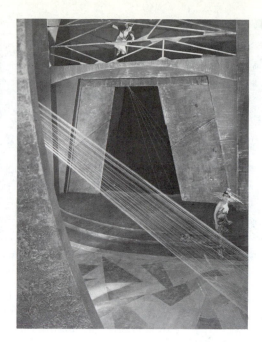

5.55 & 5.56 Iakov Protazanov's *Aelita* (1924).

lutionary directors reemerged to make significant films during this period: Iakov Protazanov (1881–1945) created a science-fiction fantasy entitled *Aelita* (1924), which is notable as the only Soviet film ever designed completely in the **Constructivist** style. Its sets notwithstanding, *Aelita* was basically an exotic and expensively produced entertainment, and the film was attacked for "commercialism" by many Party critics. Protazanov went on to regain his position as the country's top box-office director with a series of comedies starring Igor Ilinski. The former Protazanov actress Olga Preobrazhenskaia (1884–1966) directed a somber and poetic evocation of traditional Russian peasant life, *Women of Riazan* (*Baby Riazanski*, 1927). *Bed and Sofa* (*Tretia meshchanskaia*, 1927), directed by Abram Room (1894–1976) and designed by Eisenstein's friend Sergei Iutkevich, was a realistic love story about a ménage à trois caused by the housing shortage. Iutkevich himself, who had helped to form the FEX and was to become an important figure in the sound film, produced two lively features at the end of the silent era, *Lace* (*Kruzheva*, 1928) and *The Black Sail* (*Chernyi parus*, 1929). Three other directors who were to become major figures in the Soviet sound film began their careers during this period: Friedrich Ermler (1898–1967) of Leningrad, with socially critical realistic dramas like *Fragment of an Empire* (*Oblomok imperii*, 1929); Mikhail Kalatozov (1903–73) of Georgia, with *Salt for Svanetia* (*Sol Svanetii*, 1930), and Mark Donskoi (1901–81) of Moscow, with *In the Big City* (*V bol'shom gorode*, 1928).

Finally, some mention must be made of the documentaries of the Ukrainian director Viktor Turin (1895–1945) and those of Eisenstein's friend and teacher Esther Shub. Turin's *Turksib* (1929), a dynamic fea-

5.57 *Women of Riazan* (Olga Preobrazhenskia, 1927).

5.58   *Bed and Sofa* (Abram Room, 1927).

5.60   *Salt for Svanetia* (Mikhail Kalatozov, 1930.

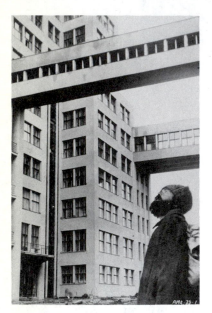

5.59   *Fragment of an Empire* (Friedrich Ermler, 1929).

ture-length account of the building of the Turkistan-Siberian Railway, won international acclaim and influenced the development of the British documentary tradition, but his other films are uneven. The work of Shub is broader, more substantial, and more consistent. From her early experience as a Goskino editor she perfected the **compilation film,** a documentary form which mixes together existing newsreel footage from other films, and her remarkable sense of rhythm and tempo in cutting allowed her to create several brilliant feature-length chronicles of Russia's revolutionary past. Her greatest achievements are *The Fall of the Romanov Dynasty* (*Padenie dinastii Romanovyh,* 1927) and *The Great Road* (*Velikii put,* 1927), made to commemorate the tenth anniversary of the February and October Revolutions. Together with her next film, *The Russia of Nicholas II and Lev Tolstoi* (*Rossiya Nikolaia II i Lev Tolstoi,* 1928), these compilations form an epic trilogy of three decades of Russian and Soviet history, 1897–1927.

SOCIALIST REALISM AND THE DECLINE OF SOVIET CINEMA

The fate of the Revolution was also the fate of the Soviet cinema, whose decline coincided with the coming of sound but was not directly attributable to it. Some Soviet directors, of course, had difficulty adjusting to the new technology of sound, but on the whole its arrival was greeted enthusiastically as a means of expanding the medium's artistic potential. Dziga Vertov had eagerly anticipated the introduction of sound since the mid-twenties; in August 1928 Eisenstein, Pudovkin, and Alexandrov published a manifesto collectively endorsing the creative use of sound in motion pictures; and Eisenstein, Alexandrov, and Tisse journeyed to Western Europe and America in 1929 and 1930, where they were able to investigate developments in the sound film at first hand. The truth seems to be that the Golden Age of Soviet cinema, like that of German

5.61 *The Fall of the Romanov Dynasty* (Esther Shub, 1929).

cinema, came to an end as much for political reasons as for technological ones.

At the Fifteenth Communist Party Congress in 1927, Iosif Stalin, who had been the general secretary of the Central Committee since 1922, succeeded in outmaneuvering his opponents to become dictator of the Soviet Union for the next twenty-six years. Unlike his predecessors, Lenin (died 1924) and Trotski (exiled 1928), Stalin and many of the men who surrounded him were insular, provincial, and highly intolerant of the arts—especially of the avant-garde experiments of the past decade. As a ruthlessly practical politician, Stalin recognized the enormous importance of film as a means of mass communication, but whereas Lenin had said, "The cinema is for us the most important of the arts," Stalin was more blunt: "The cinema," he wrote, "is the greatest medium of mass agitation. The task is to take it into our hands." And this is precisely what happened.

At the Sixteenth Party Congress in 1928, Stalin demanded greater state control of the arts in order to make them both more accessible and more relevant to the masses. In 1929, Stalin removed Sovkino from Anatoly Lunacharski's authority in the Commissariat of Education (Lunacharski resigning as commissar shortly thereafter) and placed it under the direct control of the Supreme Council of the National Economy. Reorganized as "Soiuzkino" (an acronym for All-Union Combine of Cinema-Photo Industries), the film trust was turned over to the doctrinaire bureaucrat Boris V. Shumiatski, who openly discouraged all manner of "formalism," symbolism, and montage experiment in favor of didactic plots and, ultimately, blatant propaganda. In 1933, Soiuzkino was itself reorganized as the main Administration of the Cinema-Photo Industry with Shumiatski as central manager. In 1936, Shumiatski was also made head of the Motion-Picture Section of the Committee on Art Affairs, which gave him near-dictatorial control of the Soviet film industry until he was purged in 1938.

(On his sworn enmity with Eisenstein, see Chapter 9, p. 372.) Where Lunacharski had suggested, Shumiatski decreed, and as the Soviet leadership grew more and more authoritarian, the arts were pushed increasingly toward the narrow ideological perspective known as **socialist realism.**

This was a prosaic and heavy-handed brand of didacticism which idealized the Soviet experience in order to inspire the masses with the glories of life under Lenin and, especially, Stalin. The guiding principle was that individual creativity should be subordinated to the political aims of the state and that the present should be interpreted in the light of the future predicted by the current Party line. Socialist realism was officially defined as the "artistic method whose basic principle is the truthful, historically concrete depiction of reality in its revolutionary development, and whose most important task is the Communist education of the masses." It was, in other words, an artistic method which demanded the "socialization" of Soviet art as a propaganda medium for Communist Party policy. Since that policy has shifted with expediency, the doctrine can only be contextually defined. In general, however, socialist realism involves an extreme literal-mindedness which eschews the "symbolic" and "psychological" for simple narratives centering on representative Soviet heroes (and, rarely, heroines). (During the thirties and forties, it was obligatory that these heroes resemble Stalin, which obviously is not the case today, although many of the original strictures of socialist realism still apply.) When socialist realism was declared the official style of all Soviet art at the first Congress of the Soviet Writers Union in 1934, the genius of the Soviet cinema was devastated, since anything unique, personal, or formally experimental was explicitly forbidden to appear upon the screen.

In 1933, immediately following the imposition of socialist realism, Soviet film production fell to its lowest level in a decade; only fifty-three features were completed, as compared with 119 the year before. Shumiatski blamed the transition to sound, but confusion and fear in the studios were equally responsible. Tragically, if characteristically, it was the founders of Soviet cinema who were most injured by this reactionary decree. Eisenstein, Pudovkin, Dovzhenko, Kuleshov, and Vertov were all variously denounced and, in some cases, publicly humiliated for their past "formalist aberrations." They continued to work under the burden of official disfavor for the rest of their lives, their visions and their methods strait-jacketed by Stalinist paranoia from that time forth. With the sole exception of Eisenstein, none of them produced work in the sound era equal to their greatest silent films because (as the Nazis would discover almost simultaneously with the Stalinists) art shackled by ideology ceases to be art and becomes something else. Great art may sometimes be ideological, as *Potemkin,* *Mother,* and *Arsenal* clearly illustrate, but ideology in the service of itself alone can never be great art. The film in the Soviet Union has only recently begun to recover from the creative sterility induced by Stalinism, and so long as totalitarian attitudes prevail over the arts, it will be some time before we witness a recurrence of the Soviet cinema's Golden Age.

Hollywood in the Twenties

By the end of World War I, the American film industry had assumed the structure it would retain for the next forty years. The independent producers, led by Adolph Zukor, William Fox, and Carl Laemmle, had triumphed over the monopolistic Motion Picture Patents Company to become vertically integrated monopolies themselves, controlling their own theater chains and distributorships. With the refinement of the feature film, motion picture audiences became increasingly middle-class, and exotic "atmospheric" theaters which could seat up to three thousand patrons spread to cities small and large across the country. Thanks to increased film length, monetary inflation, and the monumental salaries newly commanded by stars, production budgets rose by as much as ten times their prewar level, and the movies became a major national industry in the span of several years. Filmmaking practices and narrative formulas were standardized to facilitate mass production, and Wall Street began to invest heavily in the industry for both economic and political gain (i.e., it was in the material interest of the wealthy and the powerful to have the new mass medium of the movies—and later of radio—under their control). New money, new power, and the "new morality"* of the postwar Jazz Age all combined to make Hollywood in the twenties the modern Babylon of popular lore.

The industry giants at the beginning of the twenties, known collectively as the "Big Three," were Zukor's Famous Players—Lasky Corporation, which had acquired Paramount Pictures as its distribution and exhibition wing in 1916 and was commonly known as "Paramount"; Loew's, Incorporated, the national theater chain owned by Marcus Loew which had moved into production with the acquisition of Metro Pictures in 1920; and First National (after 1921, Associated First National)—the

6.1 A typical "atmospheric" theater interior of the twenties, with Moorish decor and cloud machine.

6.2 A drawing of the auditorium of the Roxy Theater—"the Cathedral of the Motion Picture"—in New York City, c. 1927.

---

* The mood of postwar America was one of bitterness, disillusionment, and cynicism not unlike that of the post-Watergate era, but intensified by the deaths of 500,000 Americans during the "Spanish flu" epidemic of 1918–19. The "new morality" was an adjunct of this mood. It rejected the "old morality" of Victorian idealism for a fashionable materialism which emphasized wealth, sensation, and sexual freedom. The "new morality" encouraged the widespread use of drugs (mainly nicotine and alcohol; in Hollywood, cocaine), female liberation (women won the vote in 1920), and sexual promiscuity. Its spread was facilitated by the decade's relative economic prosperity and by simultaneous revolutions in communications (mass distribution of films; the booming of network radio) and transportation (mass marketing of the private automobile; the beginnings of commercial aviation). Politically, however, the period was characterized by violent strike-breaking, anti-Bolshevism, and right-wing reaction.

6.3 The formation of United Artists, 1919: Fairbanks, Griffith, Pickford, and Chaplin.

company founded in 1917 by twenty-six of the nation's largest exhibitors to combat the practice of block booking by financing its own productions (see pp. 46–47). United Artists was formed in 1919 by the era's four most prominent film artists—D. W. Griffith, Charlie Chaplin, Mary Pickford, and Douglas Fairbanks—in order to produce and distribute their own films, and it was a major force in the industry until the advent of sound (and became so again, in the seventies). Metro-Goldwyn-Mayer emerged as a powerful new studio combine in 1924 through the merger of Metro Pictures, Goldwyn Pictures, and Louis B. Mayer Productions under the auspices of Loew's, Incorporated. Hollywood's second string in the twenties, the "Little Five," consisted of the Fox Film Corporation; Producers Distributing Corporation (PDC); Film Booking Office (FBO); Carl Laemmle's Universal Pictures; and Warner Bros. Pictures, which would force the industry to convert to sound by introducing the Vitaphone process in 1926 and would absorb First National in the process. Below these were about thirty thinly capitalized minor studios, of which only Columbia, Republic, and Monogram survived the coming of sound.*

THOMAS INCE, MACK SENNETT, AND THE STUDIO SYSTEM OF PRODUCTION

It was in the twenties that the studios became great factories for the large-scale production of mass commercial entertainment, and this was mainly due to the example of Thomas Harper Ince (1882–1924) in the previous decade. Like Griffith, Ince had begun his career as an actor-director at American Biograph in 1910 and ultimately established his own studio, "Inceville," in the Santa Ynez Canyon near Hollywood in 1912. Here Ince directed over a hundred films, ranging in length from two to five reels, before turning exclusively to production in late 1913. Between 1914 and 1918, he built Inceville into the first recognizably modern Hollywood studio, complete with five self-contained shooting stages; his mode of production became the prototype for the highly orga-

6.4 The original Inceville at Santa Ynez, with the Pacific Ocean in the background, c. 1912.

* Some sense of the studios' economic strength during the decade is provided by the following figures. In 1923, Famous Players–Lasky, First National, Loew's, Fox, and Universal each released between forty-six and sixty-three features apiece; Warner Bros. and United Artists released eleven each; and all of the other companies combined released 123 (including twenty-six by the American branch of the Pathé exchange, mainly Hal Roach and Mack Sennett comedies). Simultaneously, the "Big Three" were moving to eliminate competition by extending distribution internationally and purchasing first-run theaters in major urban markets, foreign and domestic. Famous Players–Lasky arrived on the top of the heap in 1926 when it acquired First National's most profitable theater chains, notably the Balaban & Katz circuit in Chicago. The coming of sound, of course, would change all of these relationships radically. See Simon N. Whitney, "Anti-Trust Policies and the Motion Picture Industry," *The American Movies Industry*, ed. Gorham Kindem (Carbondale, Ill.: University of Southern Illinois Press, 1982), pp. 161–201; and Tino Balio, "Stars in Business: The Founding of United Artists," *The American Film Industry*, rev. ed., ed. Tino Balio (Madison: The University of Wisconsin Press, 1985), pp. 153–72.

nized studio system that was to dominate the American film industry for the next forty years. Ince's practice was to set up a number of production units on his lot, each headed by a director. Writers, working in close collaboration with both Ince and the directors, would prepare detailed shooting scripts (also known as continuities or scenarios) in which the entire production was laid out shot by shot. Ince would then approve the script, and the film would go into production according to a strict time-table. When the shooting was finished, Ince would supervise the editing and retain authority over the final cut.* This kind of filmmaking was very much the opposite of Griffith's mode of improvisation, but it represented the wave of the American cinema's heavily capitalized future, and it helps to explain why Griffith was not to be a part of that future for very long. Still, Ince was like Griffith in his genius for visualizing narrative, and most of his productions—the vast majority of them action-packed West-erns—tended to be well-paced, tightly constructed features which bore the strong stamp of his personality.

Ince and Griffith actually became business partners for several years with Mack Sennett in the ill-fated Triangle Film Corporation, founded by Harry Aitken after he left Mutual in 1915. In conception, this orga-nization was sound: each of the three directors was to supervise the pro-duction of films of the type that had made him popular and famous— action films and Westerns for Ince, two-reel slapstick comedies for Sen-nett, melodrama and spectacle for Griffith. In practice Triangle failed after three years due to miscalculation of the public's taste and misguided attempts to bring stars of the legitimate stage to the screen. When the failure occurred, Ince built himself a large new studio at Culver City (which would become the physical plant of MGM some ten years later) and continued to produce features there until his death in 1924. In the course of his career, Ince had introduced the detailed scenario, or conti-nuity script, to the filmmaking process and pioneered the studio system of production. He had also given many talented actors and directors their first important opportunities to work in film: William S. Hart, Sessue Hayakawa, Billie Burke, Frank Borzage, Henry King, Lloyd Ingraham, Fred Niblo, Rowland V. Lee, Lambert Hillyer, and Francis Ford all trained at Inceville. Finally, Ince had contributed to the cinema a number of tautly constructed feature films, such as *The Battle of Gettysburg* (1913), *The Typhoon* (1914), *The Coward* (1915), *Hell's Hinges* (1916), *The Aryan* (1916), *Civilization* (1916), *The Patriot* (1916), *The Beggar of Cawn-pore* (1917), *Human Wreckage* (1923), and *Anna Christie* (1923), which are for the most part models of fast-paced and economical narrative form.

6.5 Part of the Ince studio at Culver City (later MGM).

---

* For an economic analysis of the Ince system and the central role of the continuity script as a blueprint for shot assembly and quality/cost-control, see Janet Staiger, "Dividing Labor for Production Control: Thomas Ince and the Rise of the Studio System," *Cinema Journal* 28, (Spring 1979): 16–25. See also Staiger, "Mass-Produced Photoplays: Economic and Signifying Practices in the First Years of Hollywood," *Wide Angle* 4, 3 (Fall 1982): 12–27; and ch. 12, "The Central Producer System: Centralized Management After 1914," Bord-well, Staiger, and Thompson, *The Classical Hollywood Cinema* (New York: Columbia University Press, 1985), pp. 128–41.

As John Ford remarked, "Ince had a great influence on films, for he tried to make them move."

Another architect of the American studio system, and the founder of silent screen comedy, was Ince's and Griffith's partner in the Triangle Films Corporation, Mack Sennett (1880–1960). Sennett had worked as an actor in many of Griffith's Biograph films and set himself consciously to study the director's methods. He too began to direct films for Biograph in 1910, but was given very little creative freedom. So in September 1912 Sennett founded the Keystone Film Company in Fort Lee, New Jersey, with the financial backing of Adam Kessel, Jr., and Charles O. Bauman, the owners of the New York Motion Picture Company, and within the month he had moved his company to the old Bison studios in Hollywood. Here, between 1913 and 1935, he produced thousands of one- and two-reel films and hundreds of features which created a new screen genre—the silent slapstick comedy—that was to become the single most vital American mode of the twenties. Influenced by circus, vaudeville, burlesque, pantomime, the comic strip, and the chase films of the French actor Max Linder, Sennett's Keystone comedies posited a surreal and anarchic universe where the logic of narrative and character was subordinated to purely visual humor of a violent but fantastically harmless nature. It is a world of inspired mayhem—of pie-throwing, cliff-hanging, auto-chasing, and, preeminently, of blowing things up. The slam-bang comic effect of these films depended upon rapid-fire editing and the "last-minute rescue" as learned from Griffith, and also upon Sennett's own incredibly accurate sense of pace. He had a genius for timing movement, both the frenetic physical activity which filled the frames of his films and the breathless editing rhythms which propelled them forward at breakneck speed. Sennett's films often parodied the conventions of other films, especially those of Griffith (e.g., *Teddy at the Throttle,* 1916), or satirized contemporary America's worship of the machine (*Wife and Auto Trouble,* 1916). Just as often, they would develop a single improvised sight gag involving the Keystone Kops or the Sennett Bathing Beauties into a riotous series of visual puns whose only logic was associative editing (*The Masquerader,* 1914; *The Surf Girl,* 1916).

In the first two years at Keystone, Sennett directed most of his films himself, but after 1914 he adopted the Inceville model and began to function exclusively as a production chief in close association with his directors, actors, and writers. Unlike Ince, however, Sennett preferred simple story ideas to detailed shooting scripts, and he always left room in his films for madcap improvisation. The number of great comedians and directors who began their careers at Keystone is quite amazing. Sennett discovered and produced the first films of Charlie Chaplin, Harry Langdon, Fatty Arbuckle, Mabel Normand, Ben Turpin, Gloria Swanson, Carole Lombard, Wallace Beery, Marie Dressler, and W. C. Fields. He also provided the training ground for some of the most distinguished directors of comedy in the American cinema: Chaplin and Keaton, of course, but also Malcolm St. Clair, George Stevens, Roy Del Ruth, and Frank Capra. Furthermore, the enormous international popularity of

6.6   Keystone mayhem in an unidentified Sennett film.

Sennett's Keystone comedies contributed substantially to America's commercial dominance of world cinema in the years following World War I. Sennett's realization that the cinema was uniquely suited to acrobatic visual humor established a genre which in the twenties would become perhaps the most widely admired and vital in the history of American film. Many serious critics, at least, regard it as such. And yet Sennett's conception of comedy was wed to the *silent* screen. Purely visual humor loses a great deal to the logic of language and naturalistic sound; and when silence ceased to be an essential component of the cinema experience, the genre that Sennett had founded vanished from the screen. Sennett himself continued to make films after the conversion to sound, but by 1935 Keystone was bankrupt, and its founder did not produce another film before his death in 1960.

CHARLIE CHAPLIN

Sennett's most important and influential protégé was Charlie Chaplin (1889–1977). Chaplin, the son of impoverished British music hall entertainers, had spent his childhood on stage. Like Charles Dickens and D. W. Griffith, both of whom he greatly resembles, Chaplin's vision of the world was colored by a youth of economic deprivation, and he felt deeply sympathetic toward the underprivileged all of his life. Chaplin was already a performer on an American vaudeville tour when he was engaged by Keystone Film in 1913 for $150 a week. In his first film for Sennett, *Making a Living* (1914), he played a typical English dandy, but by his second, *Kid Auto Races at Venice* (1914), he had already begun to develop the character and costume of "the little tramp" which would make him world-famous and become a kind of universal cinematic symbol for our common humanity. Chaplin made thirty-four shorts and the six-reel feature *Tillie's Punctured Romance* (Mack Sennett, 1914) at Keystone, progressively refining the character of the sad little clown in oversized shoes, baggy pants, and an undersized coat and derby.

But Chaplin's gifts were meant for a more subtle style of comedy than the frenetic rhythms of the Keystone films allowed, so in 1915 he signed a contract with Essanay to make fourteen two-reel shorts for the then-enormous sum of $1,250 a week. He directed these and all of his subsequent films himself, based on his experiences at Keystone. In fact, in terms of narrative technique, Chaplin scarcely ever advanced *beyond* what he had learned from Sennett. With the possible exception of *A Woman of Paris* (1923), which was unavailable in the West until 1978, his films are interesting not for their form but for their content—specifically, for his brilliant characterization of the little tramp, totally at odds with the world about him, through the exquisite art of mime. Chaplin's best Essanay films were *The Tramp, Work, The Bank,* and *A Night at the Show* (all 1915), and they made him so popular that in the following year he was able to command a star salary of $10,000 a week plus a signatory bonus of $150,000 in a contract for twelve films with Mutual, of which the greatest are *The Floorwalker* (1916), *The Fireman* (1916), *One A.M.*

6.7 **The final shot of Chaplin in *The Tramp*** (Charles Chaplin, 1915).

6.8 *The Immigrant* (Charles Chaplin, 1917): arriving at Ellis Island.

(1916), *The Pawnshop* (1916), *The Rink* (1916), *Easy Street* (1917), *The Immigrant* (1917), and *The Adventurer* (1917). These two reelers were produced with infinite care and constitute twelve nearly perfect masterpieces of mime. They also made Chaplin internationally famous and first showed his great gift for social satire—a satire of the very poor against the very rich, of the weak against the powerful, which endeared him to the former but not to the latter, especially during the Depression. In *The Immigrant,* for example, one of the most memorable sequences is predicated upon the hypocrisy of American attitudes toward immigration and upon the brutality of the immigration authorities themselves. As Charlie's ship arrives at Ellis Island, he looks up with hope and pride at the Statue of Liberty. Then a title announcing "The Land of Liberty" is followed by a shot of the New York port police forcibly herding together a large number of immigrant families for processing like so many cattle. In the next shot, Charlie casts another glance at the Statue of Liberty—this one suspicious, even disdainful.

By June 1917 Chaplin had gained such star power that he was offered a one-million-dollar contract with First National to produce eight films for the company, regardless of length. This deal enabled him to establish his own studios, where he made all of his films from 1918 until he left the country in 1952. His cameraman for all of these productions was Rollie Totheroh (1891–1967), whom he had first met in 1915 at Essanay. Most of Chaplin's First National films were painstakingly crafted two-reelers, like *A Dog's Life* (1918), *Shoulder Arms* (1918), *The Idle Class* (1921), and *Pay Day* (1922), which continued the vein of social criticism begun at Mutual. But Chaplin's most successful effort for First National was the first feature-length film he directed, *The Kid* (1921). This was an autobiographical comedy/drama about the tramp's commitment to an impoverished little boy of the slums which combined pathos with tender humor and became an international hit, earning over 2.5 million dollars for its producers in the year of its release and making its child lead, the five-year-old Jackie Coogan, a star. Chaplin's last film under the First National contract was the four-reel feature *The Pilgrim* (1923), a social satire in which an escaped prisoner (Chaplin) is mistaken for a minister by the venal parishioners of a small Texas town, with hilarious results. The film is a brilliant comic assault on religious hypocrisy, and it may well have contributed to the venomous personal attacks launched against Chaplin by religious groups a few years later.

After he had fulfilled his obligation to First National, Chaplin was free to release his films through United Artists. His first United Artists film was the much-admired *A Woman of Paris* (1923), a sophisticated "drama of fate" whose subtle suggestiveness influenced filmmakers as diverse as Ernst Lubitsch and René Clair (see p. 231; pp. 388–90). Chaplin appeared only briefly as a porter in *A Woman of Paris,* which like all of his films after 1923 was a full-length feature, but in his comic epic *The Gold Rush* (1925) he returned to the central figure of the little tramp. Set against the Klondike gold rush of 1898, this film manages to make high comedy out of hardship, starvation, and greed as three prospectors fight it out for the rights to a claim. In the subtlety of its characterization, the brilliance of its mime, and its blending of comic and tragic themes, *The Gold Rush* is Chaplin's most characteristic work. It is as popular today as it was in 1925, and it remained his personal favorite. *The Circus* (1928), in which the tramp attempts to become a professional clown, is a beautifully constructed silent film released during the conversion to sound. In honor of it, Chaplin was given a special award at the first Academy Awards ceremony in 1929 for "versatility and genius in writing, acting, directing, and producing." During the filming of *The Circus,* however, Chaplin was involved in a divorce suit brought by his second wife, and he became the target of a vicious campaign of personal abuse on the part of religious and "moralist" groups which nearly drove him to suicide. It was the first of many clashes between Chaplin and the established order in America.

Characteristically, Chaplin's first two sound films were produced with musical scores (written by Chaplin) and sound effects but little spoken dialogue: it was his way of extending the great art of silent mime into the era of sound.* *City Lights* (1931) is a sentimental but effective film in which the unemployed tramp falls in love with a blind flower girl and goes through a series of misadventures, including robbery and a jail term,

6.9 Chaplin with Jackie Coogan in *The Kid* (Charles Chaplin, 1921).

6.10 *A Woman of Paris* (Charles Chaplin, 1923): Edna Purviance, Adolphe Menjou.

* Since *A Woman of Paris,* Chaplin had taken active interest in the musical accompaniment for his silent films, and he went on to compose the scores for all seven of his sound features, plus the silent compilation film *The Chaplin Revue* (1959). The legend of Chaplin's "heroic" resistance to sound seems to have been largely self-propagated. *City Lights,* e.g., meticulously shot over a three-year period (December 1927–January 1931), contains numerous visual cues for sound effects, and *Modern Times,* in production even longer (September 1933–January 1936), mounts a sophisticated critique of the dialogue film by having all of its audible speech issue from machines (phonographs, P.A. systems, etc.).

6.11   Chaplin makes a meal of a boot in *The Gold Rush* (Charles Chaplin, 1925).

in order to raise money for the operation which can restore her sight. Chaplin called the film "a comedy romance in pantomime," and it is, but *City Lights* is also a muted piece of social criticism in which the cause of the poor is defended against that of the rich. If there were any remaining doubts about the nature of Chaplin's social attitudes, they were dispelled by *Modern Times* (1936), a film about the dehumanization of the common working man in a world run for the wealthy by machines. In it, Chaplin plays a factory worker who is fired when he suffers a nervous (but hilarious) breakdown on the assembly line, moves through a variety of other jobs, and ends up unemployed but undefeated.* The film's satire on industrialization and inequity in the "modern times" of the Great Depression earned it little popularity among the powerful in the United States, where in some quarters it was called "Red propaganda," or in Germany and Italy, where it was banned. But *Modern Times* was enormously successful in the rest of Europe, and it remains today one of Chaplin's funniest, best structured, and most socially committed works.

In *The Great Dictator* (1940) Chaplin produced his first full talkie and one of the first anti-Nazi films to come out of Hollywood. A satire on European dictatorships, the film chronicles the rule of Adenoid Hynkel, dictator of Tomania, as he persecutes the Jews and plunges Europe into yet another war. Chaplin played the dual role of Hynkel and an amnesiac Jewish barber who is Hynkel's double. Released some eighteen months before Pearl Harbor, the film was not well received by the critics: many thought its politics too serious, others found them not serious enough. Still, *The Great Dictator* was a commercial hit owing to its maker's continuing popularity as a star. During the war, however, Chaplin gave a series of openly political speeches in support of the Soviet Union which made him a prime candidate for the postwar blacklist (which will be

---

* According to David A. Hounshell in *From the American System to Mass Production* (Baltimore: Johns Hopkins University Press, 1984), the assembly line in *Modern Times* was based on Henry Ford's Model T "factory belt" system—the result of a VIP tour Chaplin had been given by Ford of his Highland Park plant in 1923 (Chapter 8, "The Ethos of Mass Production and Its Critics," pp. 19–20). The film itself, however, which Chaplin had originally wanted to call *The Masses,* was inspired by René Clair's 1931 feature *A nous la liberté* (see pp. 389–90)

6.12 *Modern Times* (Charles Chaplin, 1936).

6.13 Chaplin in *The Great Dictator* (Charles Chaplin, 1940).

discussed in Chapter 11). Worse, he became ensnared in a notorious paternity suit by a former "protégée" (Joan Barry) and was put on federal trial in 1944 for violating the Mann Act.* Not unreasonably, Chaplin's next film was the dark and cynical *Monsieur Verdoux* (1947), "a comedy of murder" based upon the exploits of the infamous French mass-murderer Landru, originally suggested to him by Orson Welles. In it, a Parisian bank clerk (Chaplin) loses his job and takes up the practice of marrying and then murdering rich, middle-aged women in order to support his invalid wife and small son. He is caught, and while awaiting execution Verdoux states the film's theme concisely in an argument with a fellow prisoner: "Wars, conflict, it's all business. One murder makes a villain; millions a hero. Numbers sanctify." The film was bitterly attacked in the United States, where it was released on the eve of the hysterical anti-Communist witch-hunts of the Cold War era; it was withdrawn from circulation after six weeks but had great success in France. The relationship between Chaplin and his American audiences had grown increasingly strained since the disappearance of the little tramp and the emergence of the liberal social critic, but resentment of Chaplin went back at least as far as the moralistic campaigns of the twenties. Some of this animosity was generated by Chaplin's retention of British citizenship since coming to the United States and his inconsistency in paying his federal income tax.

In his last American film, *Limelight* (1952), Chaplin returned to the London music halls of his childhood to tell the bittersweet tale of an aging performer who triumphs over his own declining power and imminent death by curing a young ballet dancer of paralysis and starting her on her career. The film is long (two and a half hours), slow, and cine-

---

* Chaplin was ultimately acquitted of these charges, which had been clandestinely encouraged by the FBI, which had kept the filmmaker under continuous surveillance since 1922.

matically archaic, but it is one of Chaplin's finest testaments to that dignity and decency of human nature which he felt the twentieth century had done so much to destroy. In September 1952, Chaplin and his family were granted six-month exit visas to attend a royal premiere of *Limelight* in London. On the first day at sea, Chaplin received news by radio that the U.S. Attorney General had rescinded his re-entry permit, subject to his appearance before an Immigration and Naturalization Service board of inquiry to answer charges of political and moral turpitude. In this manner, the highest-paid and most popular star in the history of American film was forcibly ushered from his adopted country. Chaplin chose to take up residence in his homeland and later, in Switzerland.

Five years later he responded to the U.S. Justice Department with *A King in New York* (1957). This strained political parable, independently produced in England, is about a European head of state who, while visiting the United States, is ruined by the malicious charges of the House Un-American Activities Committee, as Chaplin himself had been. *Limelight* had been subjected to an American Legion picketing campaign that forced the major theater chains to withdraw it after several weeks of distribution, and, given the prevailing climate, *A King in New York* could not be distributed in the United States at all. The former was re-released in this country in 1972 and promptly won an Academy Award for the year's Best Original Score. (In that same year, Chaplin received an Honorary Academy Award "for the incalculable effect he has had on making motion pictures, the art form of this century.") *A King in New York* had its first American release in 1976, to generally unenthusiastic reviews. The film is understandably bitter and indifferently directed, but it does contain some fine satire on life in America during the fifties.

Chaplin's last film was a limp bedroom farce, *The Countess from Hong Kong* (1966), starring Marlon Brando and Sophia Loren. The film is misconceived in terms of both script and direction, and it underscores the conventionality of Chaplin's cinematic intelligence as distinguished from his great intelligence as a performer. His genius was as an actor and a mime. So long as his little tramp character stood at the center of his films, they were masterworks of comedy and pathos. When the tramp disappeared, the limitations of Chaplin's directorial ability became increasingly apparent. With few exceptions, it was Chaplin's *presence* in his films, rather than anything in their formal structure, that made them interesting, important, and distinguished. During the twenties, the image of the little tramp became a worldwide symbol for the general excellence of the American cinema. When Chaplin the man began to replace Chaplin the persona in the late thirties and forties, Chaplin the filmmaker became what he had always been—a competent, conventional director with some unconventional ideas.*

---

* Chaplin's status as a director is likely to be more positively reassessed in light of the materials assembled by film historians Kevin Brownlow and David Gill for their three-hour Thames Television series *The Unknown Chaplin* (1985). Working with Chaplin's widow

BUSTER KEATON

It's useful to compare Chaplin's essentially theatrical cinema with that of his fellow filmmaker and comic genius Buster Keaton (1895–1966). Like Chaplin, Keaton had been raised in vaudeville by his parents; he made his first stage appearance with them at the age of three. From earliest youth, he was involved in solving complicated problems of *mise-en-scène* for the family act, and his later skill in direction may be traced to this experience. Though his reputation was eclipsed by Chaplin's throughout the twenties, it seems clear today that Keaton was Chaplin's equal as an actor and his superior as a director. When the family act broke up in 1917, the twenty-one-year-old Keaton was already a star. He was offered a contract to appear in the Shuberts' popular *Passing Show of 1917;* but he decided to enter the movies instead by going to work as a supporting player at Joseph M. Schenck's Comique Film Corporation, formed in the spring of 1917 to produce the films of Roscoe "Fatty" Arbuckle for release through Paramount. Here Keaton made fifteen two-reel shorts with Arbuckle—from *The Butcher Boy* in 1917 to *The Garage* in 1919—in which the quality and sophistication of the studio's product increased notably in both form and substance.

In late 1919, Schenck formed Buster Keaton Productions to produce two-reel comedy shorts starring Keaton and acquired the former Chaplin studios for the purpose. Schenck handled all of the financing but gave Keaton complete creative freedom in writing and directing at a salary of one thousand dollars per week plus 25 percent of the profits. The resulting nineteen shorts, made between 1920 and 1923 and released through Metro and First National, represent, with Chaplin's Mutual films, the high point of American slapstick comedy.* The best of them are films like *One Week* (1920), *The Goat* (1921), *Playhouse* (1921), *The Boat* (1921), *Cops* (1922), and *The Balloonatic* (1923), whose complexity of structure and fine visual sense make them unique among slapstick shorts. Keaton always maintained that comedy must be funny without being ridiculous, and for this reason he took great pains to make his films credible in dramatic as well as comic terms. Unlike Sennett and his many imitators, much of Keaton's excellence as a filmmaker stemmed from a strict adherence to the dramatic logic of his narratives and the use of gags which progress in a geometrical pattern grounded in character and plot. Kea-

6.14 *One Week* (Buster Keaton, 1920): a hand blocks the lens for privacy.

Oona and silent film collector Raymond Rohauer, Brownlow and Gill recovered from Chaplin's private archive and other sources some 300,000 feet of film never before seen by the public, including rushes and out-takes from the Mutual two-reelers *The Circus, City Lights* and *Modern Times,* plus home movies, camera tests, and two complete shorts, *How To Make Movies* (1918) and *The Professor* (1922). The footage reveals Chaplin to have been a fanatical perfectionist who "rehearsed" on film, shooting and printing literally hundreds of takes until he got a particular sequence right or rejected it. He never intended the public to see these "rough drafts" of his work, but they document a hitherto unsuspected concern for technical precision.

* Sixteen of these were nominally co-directed by Sennett veteran Eddie Cline and two by Malcolm St. Clair (1897–1952).

6.15 Keaton bumbles into a police parade in *Cops* (Buster Keaton, 1922).

6.16 Perfect timing: part of a trajectory gag from *Cops*.

ton's first feature was the seven-reel *The Saphead*, directed by Herbert Blaché (1882–1953) for Metro late in 1920. This rather limp adaptation of an 1887 comedy about a family of Wall Street brokers was important to Keaton's development since it gave him his first opportunity to create a continuous dramatic characterization in film. By 1923, two-reelers were becoming increasingly unprofitable to produce due to the public's mania for features, and Schenck* changed the Keaton studio's production output from eight shorts to two independent features per year, to be distributed by Metro/MGM, but over which the filmmaker was to retain complete artistic control. Keaton's salary was raised to star level (twenty-five hundred dollars per week plus 25 percent of the profits), and he entered the period of his greatest creativity.

It has been said that after 1923 Keaton was as important as any director practicing in Hollywood, and so strong was his creative personality that this is true even of the films which do not bear his name on the direction credits. His first independent feature for Keaton Productions, *The Three Ages* (1923), was a sparkling parody of Griffith's *Intolerance* directed by Keaton in collaboration with Eddie Cline (1892–1961) which depicted the trials of courtship through the ages by intercutting stories from three separate historical periods: the Stone Age, ancient Rome, and contemporary America. Though its *mise-en-scène* is not as elaborate nor its narrative as tightly integrated as those of his subsequent films, *The Three Ages* is a successful comedy whose hilarious conclusion introduced

---

* By this time, Schenck and Keaton were brothers-in-law, the latter having married Natalie Talmadge (1898–1969) in 1921. Schenck had married the actress Norma Talmadge (1897–1957) in 1917 and promoted both her and her sister Constance (1900–73) to stardom by the mid-twenties. Natalie seems to have been the least talented of the three Talmadge sisters, although she costarred admirably with Keaton in three of his silent features. They were divorced in 1932.

a classical Keaton device—the "trajectory" gag, in which the perfect timing of acting, directing, and editing propels the Keaton character through an extended series of dramatically connected sight gags ending in the denouement of a sequence or of an entire film. At the conclusion of the modern sequence of *The Three Ages*, for example, Keaton in long shot leaps from the fire escape of a six-story building toward an adjacent building, misses the ledge, and falls. A second long shot shows him falling through two canvas window awnings and catching hold of a third. In the next shot, Keaton uses the awning for ballast as he grabs hold of a drainpipe which comes loose in his arms. Another long shot shows him, still holding the pipe, pivoting into an open window two stories down. We cut here to a medium shot of the interior of a firehouse dormitory, with Keaton hurtling through the window, catching hold of the firemen's pole, and sliding down it. In the next shot, he arrives at the ground floor below and leaps onto the back of a fire engine about to answer an alarm. The final shot of the sequence shows Keaton arriving at a burning building and recognizing it as the police station from which he has just escaped as a wanted man. He slips quietly away, thus completing the trajectory.

Keaton's second independent feature, *Our Hospitality* (1923), represents a tremendous advance over *The Three Ages* and is one of his greatest films. Directed by Keaton in collaboration with Jack Blystone (1892–1938), it concerns a young man's involvement in a bloody family feud in the American South in the early days of the railroad. The film is a nearly perfect example of Keaton's ability to create serious narrative situations and then cause the gags to grow naturally out of them. It is also a film of great pictorial beauty which makes significant use of the **long take,** or **sequence shot,** composed in depth with dramatic action in the foreground, middleground, and background of the frame. As always, Keaton's editing is fluid and perfectly timed, but unlike Griffith and his followers (Henry King, King Vidor, Rowland V. Lee, Frank Borzage), he does not exploit the montage effect for its own sake. And, as in many of Keaton's later films, **location shooting** (on Lake Tahoe) and close attention to the details of period costume and setting give *Our Hospitality* a realistic surface which both involves us in the narrative and lends credibility to the action.

Sherlock Jr. (1924), directed and edited solely by Keaton, is perhaps his most extraordinary feature-length work. In it, Keaton plays a projectionist in a neighborhood theater who is accused of theft by his girlfriend's father. Later, he falls asleep at work, while a ghostly image of himself leaves the projection booth, walks through the auditorium below, and enters the screen to become a part of the action, which has been transformed into the real-life drama of the framing story. At first, Keaton is thrown out of the frame by the villain. As he scrambles back into it, the scene changes through a cut and he is suddenly standing in front of a door. As he reaches to open it, the scene changes again and he finds himself in a garden. As he tries to sit down on a garden bench, there is a cut to a crowded street scene and Keaton tumbles into a stream of rushing traffic. This routine goes on for nearly three minutes before leading

6.17 **Keaton projects himself onto the screen within the screen in *Sherlock Jr.* (Buster Keaton, 1924).**

us into a more continuous dream narrative in which Keaton becomes "Sherlock Jr." and clears himself of all false charges, finally waking to his girlfriend's embrace in the projection room. The film is full of breathtakingly complicated (and dangerous) trajectory gags, but the sequence which depicts a real person trapped inside a movie is in many ways a comment on the process of film editing itself; the French avant-garde director René Clair called attention to its surrealistic aspects as early as 1925, when he compared *Sherlock Jr.* to Luigi Pirandello's play *Six Characters in Search of an Author* (1921),* and Woody Allen (see pp. 510–11) has demonstrated the continuity of its influence as recently as *The Purple Rose of Cairo* (1985).

Keaton's next film, *The Navigator* (1924), directed in collaboration with Donald Crisp (1880–1974), was another virtuoso piece of sustained comic narrative. In it, Rollo Treadway (Keaton), a useless millionaire who can't even shave himself, and his scatterbrained fiancée are set adrift on an ocean liner by foreign spies. Alone, "these beautiful spoiled brats—the most helpless people in the world," as Keaton called them in a contemporary newspaper interview, must chart their survival through some hilarious adventures at sea. Unlike Chaplin, Keaton did not play the same character over and over again, but the narrative situation in which his characters find themselves was always pretty much the same: a vulnerable but plucky human hero, as in *The Navigator,* is confronted with some vast and seemingly insurmountable problem, usually involving objects and machines rather than other humans. It is a classical absurdist situation, and the comic effect arises from the hero's spirited but futile attempts to surmount the insurmountable, at which he ultimately—and for totally arbitrary reasons—somehow succeeds. Remarkably, Keaton never once repeated a narrative formula in his entire career.

Seven Chances (1925), directed by Keaton and adapted from an old David Belasco† farce, concerns a young man who stands to inherit a fortune if he can marry within twenty-four hours. The news is made public, and Keaton soon finds himself being pursued through the Southern California hills by hundreds of rampaging prospective brides. The chase ends in one of Keaton's most striking and dangerous trajectories, as he is forced to run down the sheer face of a hill dodging a landside of

---

* In fact, Keaton's films were widely admired among European avant-gardists of the era, dadaists, surrealists, and absurdists alike. His work was known not only to Pirandello (1867–1936) but to Eugène Ionesco (b. 1912), Federico García Lorca (1899–1936—who wrote the short surrealist farce *El paseo de Buster Keaton* [*Buster Keaton Takes a Walk*] in 1930), and Samuel Beckett, who is said to have written *Waiting for Godot* (1952) with Keaton in mind and who later cast him in the leading role of his original screenplay *Film* (directed by Alan Schneider, 1965). Keaton's films also seem to have inspired both of the Luis Buñuel—Salvador Dali collaborations, *Un Chien andalou* (1928) and *L'age d'or* (1930).

† David Belasco (1854–1931) was an extremely successful writer, director, and producer of spectacular stage melodrama at the turn of the century. Griffith may have borrowed certain styles of lighting and decor from Belasco's *mise-en-scène* since he was well aware of them from his own career in the theater.

fifteen hundred papier-mâché boulders which range in diameter from one to eight feet. Once the sequence was set up, the rest was left to chance and to Keaton's great improvisatory talent as both director and performer: the conclusion of *Seven Chances* remains one of the most stunning of any slapstick comedy, and it clearly provided the inspiration for the opening of Steven Spielberg's *Raiders of the Lost Ark* (1981). Keaton's next two films were somewhat gag-impoverished, perhaps because he had lost the team of writers who had been collaborating with him since the days of the shorts—Clyde Bruckman, Jean Havez, and Joseph Mitchell. *Go West* (1925), a parody of the popular Western genre, misfires through uncharacteristic sentimentality and disunity, while *The Battling Butler* (1926) is a tale of a spoiled rich boy who pretends to be a boxing champion in order to impress his girlfriend. The latter film concludes with an unaccountably brutal fight sequence which reminds us that Keaton's comedy, like Chaplin's, could occasionally turn bitter, melancholy, and surprisingly unpleasant.

In 1927, Keaton returned to the top of his form with *The General,* which he directed in collaboration with his former scriptwriter Clyde Bruckman for release by United Artists, of which Joseph Schenck had become president in 1926. Although it was poorly received by Keaton's contemporaries, many critics today regard this film as his masterpiece, and Walter Kerr has linked it with Chaplin's *The Gold Rush* (1925) as one of the two great comic epics of the cinema. Based on a real incident from the American Civil War in which Union undercover agents hijacked a Southern locomotive,* *The General* achieved a nearly perfect integration of dramatic action and comedy. Keaton plays Johnny Gray, a civilian railroad engineer during the war who has been unjustly accused of cowardice. His locomotive, "The General," and his fiancée are seized by Union spies and driven northward. Johnny singlehandedly pursues the train into the heart of enemy territory, recaptures it along with his fiancée, and speeds back to the South with what seems to be the entire Union army in hot pursuit. At Rock River, he burns a railroad bridge behind him and precipitates a spectacular comic catastrophe, as a Union locomotive hurtles onto the bridge, causing its collapse, and plunges thirty feet into the river, creating a huge geyser of smoke and steam. In sheer pictorial beauty *The General* surpasses even *Our Hospitality* (1923). Shot on location in the forests of Oregon, its battle scenes are lit and composed, like those of *The Birth of a Nation,* to resemble the Civil War photographs of Mathew Brady. But Keaton achieves a more authentic recreation of the era than either Griffith or John Huston twenty-five years later in *The Red Badge of Courage* (1951) through the impeccable veri-

6.18 Keaton examines a mortar in *The General* (Buster Keaton, 1927).

6.19 The collapse of the railroad bridge in *The General.*

---

* Walt Disney Productions made an adventure film based on the same incident, entitled *The Great Locomotive Chase* (Francis D. Lyon, 1956). The Keaton film was remade once, by MGM, as *A Southern Yankee* (Edward Sedgwick, 1948), with Red Skelton in the Keaton role. Ironically, both later films were commercial hits, while *The General* was a dismal box-office failure, actually losing money for Schenck and UA. It was apparently too complicated for contemporary audiences to follow.

similitude of his costumes and sets. As for comedy, the timing and structure of *The General*'s trajectories have never been equaled. The film seems to validate the statement by his biographer that Keaton "could perform miracles as easily as he breathed."

Keaton made only two more independent features—both distributed at a loss by United Artists—before his studio was acquired by the MGM conglomerate. *College,* co-directed with James W. Horne (1880–1942), has Keaton as a contemporary college student, a bookworm who aspires to the hand of the most popular girl in school by constantly attempting to prove his nonexistent athletic prowess. The film is conventionally structured and photographed (perhaps because of the interference of the studio's new business manager), but it is as crammed full of energetic gags and trajectories as any Keaton short. *Steamboat Bill Jr.* (1928), the last film Keaton produced himself, was one of his finest. The plot is classical Keaton: an effeminate youth returns from college to his burly father's Mississippi riverboat and falls in love with the daughter of his father's rival, wreaking havoc on both families. The film concludes with a spectacularly realized cyclone that blows away the whole town, a sequence that contains Keaton's most dangerous stunt: in the midst of the storm, an entire house front collapses on him, but he is saved by virtue of standing precisely at the point of a window opening in the façade, the frame clearing his head and body by inches on either side. As Keaton remarked to an interviewer, "It's a one-take scene. . . . You don't do those things twice." Co-directed with Charles F. Reisner (1887–1962), *Steamboat Bill Jr.* is one of Keaton's most technically polished films, full of fluid camera movement and striking composition in depth, as well as the perfectly edited cyclone sequence. Once again, however, the public failed to respond, and the picture lost money.

In 1928, Keaton allowed his company to be absorbed by MGM with the promise that Joseph Schenck's brother Nicholas, the newly installed president of Loew's, Incorporated, would allow him to continue his creative mode of production. There was little hope that the promise would or could be kept within the factory-like system of the world's largest studio, and Keaton soon found his team of directors, writers, and technicians dispersed to work on other MGM projects. Keaton himself was cast in a film about a bumbling Hearst newsreel cameraman trying to win the hand of another Hearst employee (Hearst owned large shares of MGM stock, and his papers could be counted on for good reviews). The improbable result was *The Cameraman* (1928), Keaton's last great film, co-directed with Edward Sedgwick (1892–1953), which has been described as "a newsreel by Buster Keaton of a newsreel by Buster Keaton." In many ways, *The Cameraman* is as self-reflexive as *Sherlock Jr.,* mixing documentary footage of real events with footage of dramatically staged events and at some points integrating the two completely—as when Keaton and his sweetheart are showered with confetti in a New York tickertape parade and the camera pulls back to reveal the world-famous aviator Charles Lindberg, who had made the first transatlantic flight the year before, seated in the car behind them. Keaton's last silent feature, *Spite*

6.20 Two shots from the cyclone sequence in *Steamboat Bill Jr.* (Charles F. Reisner, 1928).

Marriage (Edward Sedgwick, 1929), was a great popular success, even though it was released at the height of the public's new mania for sound. It contained a great many subtle gag routines growing out of the situation in which a lowly pants-presser marries a beautiful actress, but the film was not the equal of its predecessors and showed signs of interference by MGM executives.*

There is no question that Keaton's talent could have survived and even profited from the conversion to sound, but in 1933, after appearing in seven witless talking features for MGM, he was fired from the studio by vice president and general manager Louis B. Mayer. Keaton always insisted that he had been dismissed because of a personal insult to Mayer; but, according to his most recent biographer, Tom Dardis, the situation was more complex. The evidence shows that Keaton's sound films (e.g., *Doughboys* [Edward Sedgwick, 1930]; *Sidewalks of New York* [Jules White, 1931]; *The Passionate Plumber* [Edward Sedgwick, 1932]; *What! No Beer?* [Edward Sedgwick, 1933]), however bad, were quite successful at the box office, and no one at MGM, from Schenck through Thalberg through Mayer, *wanted* to fire him. But Keaton could simply not adapt himself to working within the restrictive environment of the studio system, and his unhappiness manifested itself in heavy drinking. His increasingly erratic behavior and long absences from the set caused costly production slowdowns, and Mayer finally decided to fire him on February 2, 1933, less for personal reasons (although he loathed Keaton as he loathed all artists) than for corporate ones.† Simultaneously, his personal life fell apart, and though he played small parts in numerous talkies (most prominently, Billy Wilder's *Sunset Boulevard* [1950] and Chaplin's *Limelight* [1952]) and appeared occasionally on television, his career as a filmmaker effectively ended in 1929. It seems clear today that of the two great silent clowns, Chaplin and Keaton, Keaton was the superior director. Like Chaplin, he had a great gift for timing, but he had an even stronger sense of narrative structure and *mise-en-scène*. Keaton's films are often formally beautiful where Chaplin's are not, and one has only to compare Chaplin's epic masterpiece *The Gold Rush* (1925) in purely visual terms with any of Keaton's features after *The Three Ages* (1923) to discover why. Furthermore, Keaton's technical genius for setting up and filming his strenuously elaborate gags, and the reckless physical courage with which he performed them, were extraordinary. (Keaton never used a stunt man once in all of his films, although he did employ an Olympic

---

* Like *The General,* Keaton's last two silent features were remade by MGM as Red Skelton vehicles—*Spite Marriage* as *I Dood it* (Vincente Minnelli, 1943) and *The Cameraman* as *Watch the Birdie* (Jack Donohue, 1950). Keaton was an uncredited gag writer on all three.

† After 1937, MGM employed Keaton sporadically as an uncredited gag-writer for Red Skelton and the Marx Brothers for $200–$300 a week. He also served as technical advisor for Paramount's specious and unfunny "biopic," *The Buster Keaton Story* (Sidney Sheldon, 1957), which cast Donald O'Connor in the title role. See Tom Dardis, *Keaton: The Man Who Wouldn't Lie Down* (New York: Charles Scribner's Sons, 1979), pp. 158–227. See also Robert Benayoun, *The Look of Buster Keaton,* ed. and trans. Randall Conrad (New York: St. Martin's Press, 1983).

6.21 *The Cameraman* (Buster Keaton and Edward Sedgwick, 1928): a riot in Chinatown.

champion to run the decathlon for him in *College*.) Yet, like Chaplin, Keaton was a magnificently subtle actor. His "great stone face" was actually capable of suggesting a vast range of emotion, and there was very little that he could not express with his body. Like Chaplin, Keaton knew that great comedy always exists close to the brink of tragedy, but sentimentality does not play an important part in Keaton's work, as it does in Chaplin's. For both artists, comedy was a strange blend of logic and fantasy in which the impossible was made to seem real. But Keaton alone seems to have understood how dreamlike and surreal is the process of film itself.

HAROLD LLOYD AND OTHERS

6.22 Harold Lloyd in *Safety Last* (Fred Newmeyer and Sam Taylor, 1923).

Another important architect of silent comedy was Harold Lloyd (1893–1971). Lloyd was working as an extra for Universal Pictures in 1914 when he met Hal Roach, Sr. (b. 1892), who was to become Sennett's only major rival in the production of comic shorts in the twenties. Roach had just established his own production company on the basis of a three-thousand-dollar inheritance, and he hired Lloyd as a comic at three dollars per week. Between 1915 and 1917 Lloyd played tramp figures called "Lonesome Luke" and "Willie Work" that were highly imitative of Chaplin's tramp. But in a 1917 two-reeler entitled *Over the Fence* he discovered for the first time his very own comic persona—the earnest, mild-mannered boy-next-door with his horn-rimmed glasses. Over the next decade Lloyd developed this character into an archetype of American "normalcy" and niceness. Like all Americans, "Harold" was eager to succeed and could become quite aggressive in competition, but beneath it all there was a sound core of decency and innocence.

6.23 Laurel and Hardy in *Leave 'Em Laughing* (Clyde Bruckman, 1928).

When he began to do feature work in the twenties, Lloyd specialized in the "comedy of thrills"—a bizarre variant of Keystone mayhem in which the protagonist placed himself in real physical danger to elicit shocks of laughter from the audience. Lloyd's most famous film of this sort was

Safety Last (directed by Fred Newmeyer and Sam Taylor, 1923), in which he scales the sheer face of a twelve-story building, apparently without safety devices, and ends up hanging above the rushing traffic thousands of feet below, suspended from the hands of a large clock. Other important Lloyd features were *Grandma's Boy* (Fred Newmeyer, 1922), *Dr. Jack* (Fred Newmeyer, 1922), *Why Worry?* (Fred Newmeyer and Sam Taylor, 1923), *Girl Shy* (Newmeyer and Taylor, 1924), and *The Freshman* (Newmeyer and Taylor, 1925). By the mid-twenties, Lloyd had become more popular with American audiences in box office terms alone than either Chaplin or Keaton. But, as with so many of the great silent clowns, his highly kinetic brand of humor did not survive the coming of sound, although he managed to make four sound films (including Preston Sturges' *The Sin of Harold Diddlebock* [1947])* before retiring in 1952. Lloyd's comic genius had neither the intellectual depth of Keaton's nor the emotional depth of Chaplin's. But as a slam-bang, razzle-dazzle acrobat Lloyd had no peers, and, as Walter Kerr has put it, his comedy of pure sensation made a whole generation of Americans fell good about themselves.

Two other popular Hal Roach comedians were Stan Laurel (1890–1965) and Oliver Hardy (1892–1957). Laurel was an Englishman who had first come to America in the same vaudeville troupe as Chaplin and had become a minor comic star for a variety of studios in the teens. Hardy was a native of Georgia who made his living as a singer and bit player until he was signed to a long-term acting contract by Roach in 1926. Laurel was signed shortly afterwards, and in 1927 the two were teamed together in a two-reeler called *Putting the Pants on Philip* (Clyde Bruckman, 1927), initiating a comic partnership which lasted another twenty-five years. Between 1927 and 1929, Laurel and Hardy made twenty-seven silent shorts for Roach, including the minor classics *You're Darn Tootin'* (Edgar Kennedy, 1928), *Two Tars* (James Parrot, 1928), *Liberty* (Leo McCarey, 1929), *Wrong Again* (Leo McCarey, 1929), *Big Business* (James Horne, 1929), *Men of War* (Lewis Foster, 1929), *Bacon Grabbers* (Lewis Foster, 1929), and *The Hoosegow* (James Parrott, 1929); and they became the first important comic team in the history of film.

Since Laurel and Hardy had both been trained for the stage, they made an easy transition to sound, and as a consequence of two-reel talkies like *Hog Wild* (Parrott, 1930), *Another Fine Mess* (Parrott, 1930), *Laughing Gravy* (Horne, 1931), *Helpmates* (Parrott, 1931), *The Music Box* (Parrott, 1932), *Scram* (Raymond McCarey, 1932), *Busy Bodies* (Lloyd French, 1933), and *Them Thar Hills* (Charles Rogers, 1934), the team became extremely popular in the thirties. They also survived the inevitable conversion from shorts to features in *Pardon Us* (Parrott, 1931), *Pack Up Your Troubles* (George Marshall and Raymond McCarey, 1932), *Fra Diavolo* (Hal Roach and Charles Rogers, 1933), *Sons of the Desert* (Wil-

---

* Released by United Artists at 89 minutes; recut and reissued by RKO in 1950 as *Mad Wednesday* at 77 minutes. See Tom Dardis, *Harold Lloyd: The Man on the Clock* (New York: Viking, 1983), pp. 263–84.

6.24 Harry Langdon in *The Strong Man* (Frank Capra, 1926).

liam A. Seiter, 1933), *Babes in Toyland* (Gus Meins and Charles Rogers, 1934), *Our Relations* (Harry Lachman, 1936), *Way Out West* (Horne, 1937), *Blockheads* (John G. Blystone, 1938), and *A Chump at Oxford* (Alfred Goulding, 1940). Though they frequently worked with such fine directors as George Stevens and Leo McCarey, Laurel was the guiding genius of the team. He wrote many of their scripts and produced some of their major films of the thirties. The careers of Laurel and Hardy effectively ended after 1940, when they stopped working for Roach and were absorbed into the megalithic studio system. At Fox and MGM they were unable to shape their own material, and the features which they made after 1940 were weak attempts to recycle the great humor of their heyday.

Like Harold Lloyd's comedy, that of Laurel and Hardy was in the visually violent tradition of Keystone and usually ended in some form of anarchic destruction. Unlike the randomly organized Sennett shorts, however, Laurel and Hardy films always had a kind of structural logic whereby a single misbegotten incident would be progressively multiplied toward some catastrophic infinity. As characters, both comedians were simply overgrown children whose naked aggression and vengefulness was mirrored in the middle-class world about them. And the physical contrast they presented on the screen was undeniably funny. Laurel, the weak, whimpering, and barely coordinated little fool, and Hardy, the inept, self-important, and grossly inflated bully, offered a comic version of bourgeois stupidity which Flaubert might have admired.

Two other silent comics deserve mention here, although, like Laurel and Hardy, both are decidedly minor by comparison with Chaplin, Keaton, and Lloyd. Harry Langdon (1884–1944) came to work for Mack Sennett from vaudeville in 1924. In numerous shorts at Keystone between 1924 and 1926 he developed the haunting character of a middle-aged, baby-faced innocent whose pathetic naïveté was somewhat reminiscent of Chaplin without Chaplin's dignity. Langdon rose briefly to stardom in a series of three popular features made between 1926 and 1928—*Tramp, Tramp, Tramp* (Harry Edwards, 1926), *The Strong Man* (Frank Capra, 1926), and *Long Pants* (Frank Capra, 1927). Since the first of these films was written and the latter two were directed by Frank Capra, it has been suggested that he alone was responsible for the appeal of Langdon's whimsical comic presence. But Langdon was a brilliant pantomimist in his own right, and there was something uncanny in his infantile foolishness that belonged exclusively to the character he first created at Keystone. Nevertheless, Langdon's own features as a director, *Three's a Crowd* (1927), *The Chaser* (1928), and *Heart Trouble* (1928), were not as successful as the Capra films, and his stardom did not survive the coming of sound, although he continued to work as a character actor until his death.

Roscoe "Fatty" Arbuckle (1881–1933), tipping the scales at 270 pounds, also began at Keystone, where he worked successfully with Chaplin from 1914 to 1916 and became Sennett's principal star after Chaplin's departure for Essanay. Arbuckle's comic appeal rested almost solely upon the broad base of his fatness, his childishness, and a certain Sennettesque flair

6.25 Fatty Arbuckle in a Sennett short.

for mayhem. But his popularity was second only to Chaplin's during the brief course of his career. In 1917, Joseph M. Schenck founded the Comique Film Corporation to produce Arbuckle's work, and Arbuckle gave his friend Buster Keaton his first job in films there as a supporting player. In the earliest Arbuckle-Keaton collaborations, the latter was clearly the foil, but by 1919 Keaton had totally usurped Arbuckle as a comic talent. Arbuckle was still extremely popular and made eight successful features for Paramount between 1919 and 1921, when his career ended in a catastrophic scandal that rocked the movie industry and changed the course of Hollywood history.

HOLLYWOOD SCANDALS AND THE CREATION OF THE MPPDA

Since the earliest days of the nickelodeon, moralists and reformers had agitated against the corrupting nature of the movies and their effects upon American youth, much as similar groups are concerned about the effects of television in our own era. Powerful pressure groups, often working through religious organizations, had been formed to protect American audiences from the display of morally pernicious materials on the screen. Though differently motivated, the storm of well-organized protest which greeted *The Birth of a Nation* in 1915 and caused its suppression in twelve states is a good example of how effective such pressure groups could be. (And Griffith's response to the protest—outrage followed by an attempted vindication in the shape of *Intolerance*—is a good example of how American filmmakers have characteristically reacted to such pressure.) All of this is to say that the American film industry has been threatened by the specter of external censorship since its very beginnings; and to describe the attitude of Hollywood towards its audiences as one of paranoia would not be at all extreme, especially considering that those audiences were overwhelmingly Christian and that the moguls of Hollywood were virtually all immigrant Jews. But World War I, the coming of Prohibition, and increasing middle-class patronage of the movies had alleviated some of this tension; and after the war, the content of American films became increasingly sophisticated and risqué, reflecting the "new morality" of the Jazz Era—a compound of materialism, cynicism, and sexual license. The sentimental conventions of Griffithian melodrama were abandoned by all but a few, as films suddenly began to depict and even glorify adultery, divorce, drinking, and drug-taking. Simultaneously, the Hollywood of Babylonian legend was born of the impossibly extravagant production budgets and star salaries which mushroomed in the late teens— the Hollywood of baronial mansions, orgiastic parties, sexual promiscuity, and multiple divorce which has fascinated the American tabloid press from that day to our own. For a while, the stars were worshiped by the public from afar as a kind of new American royalty, a race of beautiful demigods basking in the sun-drenched splendors of Beverly Hills. But it transpired that many of the stars were human after all, some quite scandalously so, and producers soon sought to play down the publicity given to their private lives, properly fearing a moralistic backlash against the amorality of their life-styles, which frequently involved the abuse of drugs, alcohol, and sex.

These fears were realized with a vengeance in September 1921, when Fatty Arbuckle was charged with the rape and murder of a young starlet named Virginia Rappe in the aftermath of a Labor Day weekend drinking party at a hotel suite in San Francisco. Arbuckle was indicted for manslaughter and stood trial three times before he was finally acquitted for lack of evidence in 1923. Miss Rappe had a history of peritonitis and had apparently died of a ruptured bladder aggravated by alcohol, but there were widespread allegations in the press that Arbuckle had raped her with a champagne bottle and crushed her beneath his great weight. Tabloids across the country portrayed him as a perverted beast, and the public outcry became so violent during this period that his pictures had to be withdrawn from circulation. To appease the moralists, Paramount fired Arbuckle, who was permanently barred from working in the industry again, even after he was exonerated by the courts. But Hollywood had more to account for than Fatty's indiscretions. During Arbuckle's second trial in February 1922, the chief director of Famous Players–Lasky and current president of the Screen Directors Guild, William Desmond Taylor (1877–1922), was found murdered in his Beverly Hills apartment. It seems that he had been conducting simultaneous affairs with the actress Mary Miles Minter (1902–83) and the popular Keystone comedienne Mabel Normand (1894–1930), who had been the last person to see him alive. Hungry for more scandal, the tabloid press implicated both women in the murder, though they were manifestly innocent, and destroyed their careers in the process. Within a year, Wallace Reid (1891–1923), a handsome actor who was a prototype of the clean-living American male, died of a drug overdose and was revealed to have been a long-term narcotics addict. These three scandals, as well as many smaller ones which were unearthed by the sensational press, produced a storm of public outrage against the depravity of Hollywood which was unprecedented in the film industry's brief history. Editorial denunciations by respectable publications like *Good Housekeeping* became commonplace; ministers and priests across the nation forbade their parishioners to go to the movies; women's clubs and reform groups demanded a mass boycott; and, by early 1922, thirty-six states and the federal government were considering the enactment of censorship laws. (The 1915 U.S. Supreme Court decision *Mutual* v. *Ohio* had placed motion pictures in a class with circuses "and all other shows and spectacles"; they were not protected against censorship by the First Amendment until the Court's *Miracle* decision of 1952—see Chapters 3, p. 81*n*, and 12, p. 535.) The threat was rendered even more serious by a steep decline in film attendance in 1922, a result less of the scandals than of two new sources of competition for Americans' leisure time—the radio, which began commercial broadcasting in 1922, and the family automobile, which became available through installment credit loans at about the same time. In brief, 1922 was the dawning of the age of mass communications and mass consumption in America, and Hollywood, whose chief business was both, found itself in the embarrassing position of having deeply offended its audience.

Following the example of major-league baseball, which had recently whitewashed a national bribery scandal (See John Sayles' *Eight Men Out* [1988]) by appointing a conservative federal judge to oversee its operations, the frightened Hollywood producers formed a self-regulatory trade organization, the Motion Picture Producers and Distributors of America (MPPDA) in March 1922, amid much publicity, and hired President Warren G. Harding's postmaster general, Will Hays (1879–1954), for $150,000 a year to head it. Hays was an ultraconservative Republican, Mason, Kiwanian, Rotarian, and Presbyterian elder from Indiana, and his presence made the film industry's gesture of self-censorship convincing to the public and the government alike. Initially, the Hays Office, as the MPPDA* came to be called for the next twenty-three years, was a public relations and lobbying organization which engaged in little real censorship, although it did help producers to compile a blacklist of 117 stars who were banned from the industry because of unfavorable publicity about their personal lives. There was a gently chiding "Purity Code" known facetiously as the "Don'ts and Be Carefuls," and producers were required to submit summaries of their screenplays to the Hays Office for approval. But the only "censorship" consisted of informal advising according to the principle of "compensating values" whereby, to paraphrase Arthur Knight, vice could be flaunted for six reels so long as virtue triumphed in the seventh. The main task of the Hays Office in the twenties was to stave off the threat of government censorship by mollifying pressure groups, managing news, deflecting scandal, and generally discouraging close scrutiny of the industry. In the early thirties, when sound helped to produce a new wave of excess in American films and touched off another round of national protest concerning the way in which the sounds of violence and vulgar language were exploited by early sound producers, the Hays Office became the medium for a very rigid form of censorship indeed, as administrator of the Draconian "Production Code." But in the twenties it merely provided whitewash for overly enthusiastic manifestations of the "new morality" and helped producers subvert the careers of stars whose personal lives might make them too controversial. Today, it is clear that Hays himself was one of the more crooked members of the corrupt Harding administration, but he was an undeniably effective figurehead for the MPPDA who lent Hollywood a much-needed

---

*Hays was succeeded as "movie tsar" by U.S. Chamber of Commerce president Eric A. Johnston (1896–1962) in 1945, when the organization's name was changed to the Motion Picture Association of America (MPAA). Johnston was ultimately replaced by Jack Valenti (b. 1921) in 1966, and the Production Code was scrapped in favor of a ratings system instituted in 1968 (see pp. 535–37); like Hays, both successors have had close ties with the White House. Hays' crucial role in the creation and administration of the MPPDA during the twenties is chronicled in *The Will Hays Papers, Part I: December 1921–March 1929*, ed. Douglas Gomery, a 43-reel microfilm publication with printed guide (Frederick, Md.: University Publications of America, 1987).

aura of respectability, sobriety, and moral rectitude at a time when its "sinfulness" had become a major national issue. (Hays was also an effective lobbyist for the industry in Washington, where he helped to minimize federal taxes and forestall antitrust litigation.)

CECIL B. DEMILLE

6.26 "Rembrandt" or "Lasky" lighting in Cecil B. DeMille's *The Woman God Forgot* (1917).

6.27 *The Ten Commandments* (Cecil B. DeMille, 1923).

The most successful and flamboyant representative of the "new morality" in all of its manifestations was Cecil B. DeMille (1881–1959). A virtual incarnation of the values of Hollywood in the twenties, DeMille had an uncanny ability to anticipate the tastes of his audiences and give them what they wanted before they knew they wanted it. He began his career by directing *The Squaw Man* (1914), the first feature-length Western ever made in Hollywood, for Jesse Lasky's Feature Play Company. The film was a great popular and critical success, and DeMille followed it with a series of Western features (*The Virginian,* 1914; *Call of the North,* 1914) and stage adaptations (*Carmen,* 1915) that made him famous. Like Griffith, DeMille had apprenticed in the melodramatic theatrical tradition of David Belasco, and these early films were striking for their expressive "Rembrandt" or "Lasky" lighting and vivid *mise-en-scène.* During the war, DeMille made a group of stirringly patriotic films—*Joan the Woman* (1917); *The Little American* (1917); *Till I Come Back to You* (1918)—and then shifted gears to pursue the postwar obsession with extramarital sex among the leisure class. In a series of sophisticated comedies of manners aimed directly at Hollywood's new middle-class audience—*Old Wives for New* (1918), *Don't Change Your Husband* (1919), *Male and Female* (1919), *Why Change Your Wife?* (1920), *Forbidden Fruit* (1921), *The Affairs of Anatol* (1921), *Fool's Paradise* (1921), *Adam's Rib* (1922), and *Saturday Night* (1922)—DeMille made the bathtub a mystic shrine of beauty and the act of disrobing a fine art, as "modern" marriages collapsed under the pressure of luxuriant hedonism. These films did not simply embody the values of the "new morality"; they also legitimized them and made them fashionable.

When the Hays Office was established, DeMille embraced the "compensating values" formula and made it uniquely his own in *The Ten Commandments* (1924), a sex- and violence-drenched religious spectacle that made him internationally famous. Costing over 1.5 million dollars to produce, with Biblical sequences in two-color Technicolor (generally lost today—see p. 270), this film became one of the most profitable motion pictures of the era, and it offers a good example of the way in which the Hays Office worked to permit the lurid depiction of "sin" so long as it was shown to be ultimately punished. This successful formula for religious spectacle became a DeMille trademark, and he used it time and again throughout his career—in *King of Kings* (1927), *The Sign of the Cross* (1932), *Samson and Delilah* (1949), and finally in his last film, *The Ten Commandments* (1956), a full-color widescreen remake of the prototype. But DeMille excelled at other forms of spectacle as well: historical (*Cleopatra,* 1934; *The Crusades,* 1935; *The Buccaneer,* 1938), Western

(*The Plainsman,* 1938; *Union Pacific,* 1939), and circus (*The Greatest Show on Earth,* 1952). With the exception of a brief venture into independent production between 1925 and 1929, DeMille worked all of his life for some incarnation of Paramount—first the Lasky Feature Play Company, then Famous Players—Lasky, and finally Paramount itself after 1930. A frequent collaborator was the scenarist Jesse Lasky, Jr. (1908–58—*Union Pacific, Samson and Delilah*), son of the studio's cofounder, and in the sound era DeMille became closely identified with the Paramount "style" as described in the next chapter. A few of his films, such as *Male and Female* (1919) and *Union Pacific* (1939), are classics of their genres, but on the whole DeMille was a great showman, rather than a great director, who incarnated the values of Hollywood in the twenties throughout his career. He was extravagant, flamboyant, and vulgar, but he possessed a remarkable instinct for the dualistic sensibilities (some would simply say "hypocrisy") of his middle-class American audiences, who paid by the millions for over fifty years to sit through his kinetic spectacles of sex, torture, murder, and violence so long as some pious moral could be drawn from them at the end.

THE "CONTINENTAL TOUCH": LUBITSCH AND OTHERS

Another director of sophisticated erotica during the twenties, but a filmmaker of much greater taste and refinement than DeMille, was Ernst Lubitsch. Lubitsch, a German Jew, was the originator of the lavish postwar *Kostümfilm* at UFA (see pp. 115–16) and had come to Hollywood in late 1922 with the scenarist Hans Krähly (1885–1950) to direct Mary Pickford in *Rosita* (1923). Once there, he embarked upon a series of stylish sex comedies which made him famous for his subtle visual wit. In films like *The Marriage Circle* (1924), *Three Women* (1924), *Forbidden Paradise* (1924), *Kiss Me Again* (1925), *Lady Windermere's Fan* (1925), *So This Is Paris* (1926), and *The Student Prince* (1927), Lubitsch pioneered the functional use of decor to avoid titles and became a master of sexual innuendo. Soon all Hollywood spoke of the "Lubitsch touch"—the use of symbolic detail, such as a meaningful glance or gesture, or the closing of a bedroom door, to suggest sexual activity which could not have been depicted with impunity upon the screen. In sum, Lubitsch brought a touch of Continental elegance and irony to Hollywood in the twenties which was widely imitated by other directors. He went on to become an important innovator of the early sound film with *The Love Parade* (1929), *Monte Carlo* (1930), and *The Smiling Lieutenant* (1931), and by 1935 he had become production chief of Paramount. As a French critic of the day wrote of Lubitsch, "He set about bringing to the Americans the European comedy in all its charm, decadence, and frivolity."

There were other Europeans in Hollywood during the twenties, most of them Germans who had come to work for the American film industry as a result of the Parufamet Agreement of 1926. Between 1926 and 1927,

6.28 Ernst Lubitsch directing Marie Prevost and Charlotte Vidor in *The Marriage Circle* (1924).

6.29 *Sunrise* (F. W. Murnau, 1927).

Hollywood saw the arrival of the UFA directors F. W. Murnau (*Sunrise*, 1927;* *4 Devils*, 1928; *Tabu*, 1931), Paul Leni (*The Cat and the Canary*, 1927, which pioneered the popular "comedy-mystery" genre; *The Last Warning*, 1929), Lothar Mendes (*A Night of Mystery*, 1927), Ludwig Berger (*The Sins of the Fathers*, 1928), Dmitri Buchowetski (*Crown of Lies*, 1926), Mihály Kertész (*Noah's Ark*, 1928), and Alexander Korda (*The Private Life of Helen of Troy*, 1927); the UFA cinematographer Karl Freund; the UFA performers Emil Jannings, Conrad Veidt, Werner Krauss, Pola Negri, Greta Garbo, and Lya de Putti; and the UFA producer Erich Pommer and scenarist Carl Mayer. The Hungarian director Paul Fejos (b. Pál Fejös, 1898–1963) made *The Last Moment* (1927) and the experimentally naturalistic *Lonesome* (1928) for Universal before returning to Europe in 1930; the Frenchman Jacques Feyder (1885–1948) directed some mediocre melodramas for MGM (*The Kiss* [1928]; *Daybreak* [1931]; *Song of India* [1931]); and the Dane Benjamin Christensen (1879–1959), famous for his Swedish film *Heksen* (1921—shown in a heavily edited English-language version as *Witchcraft Through the Ages*);† directed a fine series of melodramas for MGM (*The Devil's Circus* [1926]; *Mockery* [1927]) and comedy-mysteries for First National (*The Haunted House* [1928]; *Seven Footprints of Satan* [1929]). The great Swedish directors Victor Sjöström and Mauritz Stiller (see note, pp. 112–13) were both imported in the mid-twenties by MGM, where Sjöström—renamed Seastrom—produced three neglected masterpieces—*He Who Gets Slapped* (1924), *The Scarlet Letter* (1926), and *The Wind* (1928)—and Stiller was reduced to directing star vehicles, although his atmospheric *Hotel Imperial* (1926) remained a distinguished film. Sjöström returned to a life of semi-retirement in Sweden in 1928, and Stiller died in the same year, fatigued and disappointed by the Hollywood experience.

The fate of most foreign directors in Hollywood during the twenties was similar to that of the Swedes. The American industry had imported them to lend Continental elegance and class to the standard studio product, but it had in fact refused to let them tamper with the nature of the product itself; and so, bitterly disillusioned, most went home. Of the directors, only Lubitsch and the Hungarian-born Mihály Kertész (Michael Curtiz) stayed on to adapt themselves to the Hollywood production sys-

---

* *Sunrise* was an extraordinary film produced by William Fox but made almost entirely by UFA personnel. It featured a scenario by Carl Mayer from Hermann Sudermann's novella *Journey to Tilset,* photography by Charles Rosher and Karl Struss, production design by Rochus Gliese, Edgar G. Ulmer, and Alfred Metscher, and, of course, direction by Murnau. In its balletically moving camera shots and complex lighting effects—techniques first learned by Rosher at UFA as a consultant on Murnau's *Faust* (1926)—*Sunrise* influenced Hollywood production techniques even more than *Der letzte Mann* (Murnau, 1924); and it won 1927–28 Academy Awards for Best Actress (to Janet Gaynor), Cinematography, and Artistic Quality of Production.

† Usually spelled *Häxan* in American texts and not shown in the United States until 1929, the film is a unique blend of historical documentary and fiction—alternately macabre, erotic, and realistic—which deeply influenced Continental surrealists such as Luis Bunuel. *Heksen* was the most expensive film produced in Scandinavia to date, and a restored and tinted print of the original exists today in the Royal Danish Film Museum.

6.30 *Heksen (Witchcraft Through the Ages* [Benjamin Christensen, 1921]).

6.31 The enormous crane constructed by Universal for Paul Fejos' art-deco musical *Broadway* (1929), shot in both silent and sound versions.

6.32 *The Scarlet Letter* (Mauritz Stiller, 1926): Lillian Gish as Hester Prynn.

tem. Murnau stayed too but was killed in an auto accident in 1930, before he had achieved his promise. Yet the European, and especially the Germanic, presence in Hollywood during the twenties influenced the American cinema far more deeply than a purely descriptive account might suggest. The Germans taught American filmmakers at first hand the Expressionistic use of lighting and camera that had helped to produce their native cinema's greatest works. Some, like Freund, made long, successful careers in Hollywood, and soon, in the early years of sound, were joined by their distinguished countrymen Max Reinhardt, Fritz Lang, Max Ophüls, Detlef Sierck (Douglas Sirk), Curt and Robert Siodmak, William Dieterle, Billy Wilder, Edgar G. Ulmer, Eugen Schüfftan (Eugene Schuftan), Theodor Sparkuhl, Hans (John) Brahm, Otto Preminger, and Fred Zinnemann, after the collapse of the Weimar Republic. All told, the Germanic influence upon Hollywood camera style, lighting, and decor was a permanent, if understated, one, and it contributed substantially to the visual texture of American cinema in the sound era before the advent of widescreen.

IN THE AMERICAN GRAIN

Despite the sophisticated cinema of the "new morality" and all of the European incursions just discussed, there was still a homegrown American tradition of sentimental melodrama and rural romance based upon the uncomplicated narrative montage of Griffith's prewar films. Griffith had established this tradition in his Biograph shorts and continued it well into the twenties in features like *True Heart Susie* (1919), *A Romance of Happy Valley* (1919), *The Love Flower* (1920), *Way Down East* (1920), *The White Rose* (1923), and *Sally of the Sawdust* (1925). Other practitioners were Henry King ([1888–1982] *The White Sister*, 1923; *Stella Dallas*, 1925; *The Winning of Barbara Worth*, 1926), whose narrative montage in *Tol'able David* (1921) was much admired and analyzed by V. I. Pudovkin; King Vidor ([1894–1982] *The Jack-Knife Man*, 1919; *Happiness*, 1923; *The Big Parade*, 1925); William Wellman ([1896–1975] *The Vagabond Trail*, 1923; *Beggars of Life*, 1927); Clarence Brown ([1890–1987] *Smouldering Fires*, 1924; *The Goose Woman*, 1925); Rowland V. Lee ([1891–1975] *Alice Adams*, 1923; *Doomsday*, 1925); Allan Dwan ([1885–1981] *Robin Hood*, 1922; *The Iron Mask*, 1927); and Frank Borzage ([1893–1962] *Humoresque*, 1920; *Seventh Heaven*, 1927).

Side by side with the Griffith tradition, which was extinguished by the coming of sound, there grew up two native genres—the Western and the action spectacle. The Western had been a major component of the American cinema since Edwin S. Porter's *The Great Train Robbery* in 1903, and Thomas Ince had become a master of the tough, realistic Western as exemplified in the films of William S. Hart in the teens (*Hell's Hinges* [Ince, 1916]; *The Aryan* [Ince, 1916]; *The Narrow Trail* [Lambert Hillyer, 1917]). But it wasn't until the twenties that the Western came into its own as a unique feature genre; as David Robinson suggests, this may well have been a function of collective public nostalgia for the lost frontier. When Porter made the first Western in 1903, the American West was still an authentic borderland between civilization and the wilderness. By the mid-twenties, America had become an urbanized, industrialized mass society predicated upon mass consumption, mass communications, and rapid transit; and the Edenic potential of the frontier had been permanently circumscribed by a mushrooming corporate economy. So it was during the twenties that the classical form of the Western genre was codified and given its first epic expression in films like King Baggott's *Tumbleweeds* (1925), James Cruze's *The Covered Wagon* and *The Pony Express* (1925), and John Ford's *The Iron Horse* (1924).

The adventure spectacle was largely the province of a single performer, Douglas Fairbanks (1883–1939), whose star personality so influenced the character of his films that he deserves to be called an *auteur*. Fairbanks began his career at Griffith's Triangle Company where he starred in comedies like *Manhattan Madness* (Allan Dwan, 1916), *Reaching for the Moon* (John Emerson, 1917), and *The Mollycoddle* (Victor Fleming, 1920), which debunked contemporary manners and parodied current film genres and fads. In these films, most of them written by Anita Loos, Fairbanks played an all-American boy—boisterous, optimistic, and athletic—who detested weakness, insincerity, and social regimentation in any form. After Fairbanks became a superstar and helped form United Artists, he cast himself as the protagonist in a series of lavish costume-adventure spectacles, including *The Mark of Zorro* (Fred Niblo, 1920), *The Three Musketeers* (Fred Niblo, 1921), *Robin Hood* (Allan Dwan, 1922), *The Thief of Bagdad* (Raoul Walsh, 1924), *Don Q, Son of Zorro* (Donald Crisp, 1925), *The Black Pirate* (Albert Parker, 1926), *The Gaucho* (F. Richard Jones, 1927), and *The Iron Mask* (Allan Dwan, 1929). In these extravagant seriocomic "swashbucklers," the very first of their kind, Fairbanks displayed the full gamut of his energetic athleticism to contemporary audiences, thrilling them with a nearly continuous succession of breathtaking stunts. Fairbanks' physical agility was his major virtue as a performer, and he was forced into retirement in 1934 under the twin pressures of sound and advancing age. But during his meteoric ascent to stardom he had initiated a perennially popular genre (witness the success of Richard Lester's *The Three Musketeers*, 1974; *The Four Musketeers*, 1975; *Royal Flash*, 1975; and *Robin and Marion*, 1976; John Milius' *The Wind and the Lion*, 1975; and John Huston's *The Man Who Would Be King*, 1976), and he incarnated for millions of Americans Hollywood's obsession with physical culture and glamor.

A third genre, which might be called the "narrative documentary," was founded in the twenties by the American explorer and amateur cameraman Robert Flaherty (1884–1951). Flaherty was originally a mineralogist in the Canadian Arctic who had surveyed the Belcher Islands in 1917 and became interested in the harsh lives of the Eskimos who populated them. In 1920, sponsored by the fur company Revillon Frères, Flaherty returned to the islands to live with an Eskimo family and make a film about the daily lives of its members. After sixteen months he returned to the United States with the footage and edited it into the seventy-five-minute feature documentary *Nanook of the North* (1922), which was distributed internationally by Pathé with great commercial and critical success. One source of *Nanook*'s popularity was its exoticism: it represented the first sustained encounter between the civilized world and the Eskimo, outside of professional ethnographic circles. But *Nanook* was also unique in using the editing syntax of narrative film to portray a documentary reality. Flaherty had shot close-ups, **reverse angles,** tilts, and pans on location to be intercut later with the rest of his footage, and he had assumed a third-person point of view toward his subject throughout the film. He had also directed the Eskimos in enacting or reenacting certain scenes before the camera to accord with a loosely constructed story line which was true to the spirit if not the letter of their lives.

The American industry was so impressed with *Nanook*'s high audience appeal and low cost (about $55,000) that Jesse L. Lasky of Paramount commissioned Flaherty to make another such film anywhere in the world

6.33 *The Iron Horse* (John Ford, 1924).

6.34 *The Thief of Bagdad* (Raoul Walsh, 1924), produced and written by Douglas Fairbanks for United Artists.

6.35 *Nanook of the North* (Robert Flaherty, 1922).

6.36 *Moana* (Robert Flaherty, 1925).

on a subject of his choice.* The result was *Moana* (1926), an idyllic documentary of life on the South Seas island of Samoa photographed over a period of twenty months, which Herman G. Weinberg described in a contemporary review as an "intensely lyrical poem on the theme of the last paradise." Its beauty was enhanced by the recently introduced Eastman **panchromatic stock,** which was sensitive to the entire visible spectrum, as opposed to the then-standard **orthochromatic stock** (on which *Nanook* had been shot), which was relatively insensitive to yellows and reds (see pp. 340–41). Flaherty also used a high percentage of telephoto-lens shots in *Moana,* which became a hallmark of his later camera style. Once again, Flaherty had edited his film as a narrative and had reconstructed reality instead of simply recording it. The film was attacked by anthropologists as poetic fantasy (which it was) rather than an accurate representation of Samoan life, and it was acclaimed by critics on precisely the same grounds. But audiences stayed away this time, despite Paramount's crude attempt to bill the film as "The Love Life of a South Sea Siren."

Flaherty was next commissioned by MGM to collaborate with W. S. Van Dyke (1889–1943) on the production of *White Shadows in the South Seas* (1929), a dramatic feature based on a popular book by Flaherty's friend Frederick O'Brien to be shot on location in Tahiti, but he quit the project in revulsion at its commercialism. A subsequent collaboration

---

* The popular interest in primitive peoples stimulated by *Nanook* led Paramount to commission two other important films, Merian C. Cooper and Ernest B. Schoedsack's *Grass* (1925) and *Chang* (1927). The former was a documentary about the arduous seasonal migration of some 50,000 Bakhtiari tribesmen over the Zardeh Kuh mountains from Persia (now Iran) into Turkey in search of grasslands for their herds; the latter, a dramatized documentary about villagers struggling to survive in the jungles of Siam (now Thailand). Both films exhibit a taste for exotic fiction epitomized in Cooper and Schoedsack's classical thriller *King Kong* (1933).

with F. W. Murnau on the independently produced *Tabu* (1931), a narrative about the lives of Tahitian pearl divers, proved more successful, but Flaherty became disillusioned with Murnau's melodramatic approach to the material and withdrew from the film after supervising its photography.* At this point in his career, thoroughly disgusted with the Hollywood studio system, Flaherty emigrated to England, where he exercised a decisive influence upon John Grierson and the British social documentary movement of the thirties, contributing both *Industrial Britain* (1932, edited by Grierson) and the lyrical *Man of Aran* (1934),† which continued his experiments with long-focus lenses. He also directed the Indian location scenes for Zoltan Korda's *The Elephant Boy* (1937), based on Kipling's famous *Jungle Book* story, "Toomai of the Elephants." Flaherty was far too personal and individual an artist to ever work again in Hollywood, but he did return to the United States in later life to make two more powerful films for nontheatrical release—*The Land* (1942), produced for the U.S. Department of Agriculture under the auspices of another documentarist, Pare Lorentz (b. 1905), and *Louisiana Story* (1948), produced for Standard Oil of New Jersey—both among the finest achievements in documentary narrative.

Despite the presence of so much individual talent in Hollywood in the twenties, most American films were produced according to formula. Soaring production costs throughout the decade forced the studios toward a rigid standardization of product. Whereas Griffith had spent just over $100,000 to produce *The Birth of a Nation* in 1914, MGM spent more than $4.5 million to produce *Ben Hur* (Fred Niblo, 1925) only ten years later. In fact, Benjamin Hampton estimates that there was a 1,500 percent across-the-board increase in the cost of feature production during this period, which meant that the pressure to make films according to tried-and-true formulas was extreme. Experimenting with public taste

6.37 The Hollywood boom: the castle set for Douglas Fairbanks' extravagant 1922 production of *Robin Hood* (directed by Allan Dwan), made six years after Griffith's *Intolerance*, at twice the cost.

6.38 The interior of the castle set.

---

* Originally to have been a Technicolor silent, *Tabu* was released in black and white with a post-synchronized score owing to the financial collapse of its original backer, Colorart Studio, and the industry's conversion to sound during its production. Flaherty shared script and production credits with Murnau and the photography credit with Floyd Crosby (b. 1899), who won an Academy Award for his debut effort and went on to collaborate on important documentaries with Pare Lorentz and Joris Ivens. On Flaherty's specific contributions to the film, see Mark J. Langer, *"Tabu: The Making of a Film," Cinema Journal* 24, 3 (Spring 1985): 43–64. See also *Studies in Visual Communication* 6, 2 (Summer 1980): "A Reevaluation of Robert J. Flaherty, Photographer and Filmmaker," ed. Jay Ruby and Larry Gross; and Richard Barsam, *The Vision of Robert Flaherty: The Artist as Myth and Filmmaker* (Bloomington: Indiana University Press, 1988).

† The subject of *Aran* (1979), a documentary about *Man of Aran* by the French filmmaker George Combe. Flaherty's film, edited to 76 minutes from thirty-seven hours of original negative, provoked a storm of ideological controversy about the nature and function of documentary cinema when it was attacked by leftist critics for romanticizing the harsh lives of the Aran islanders. Socially committed writers charged it with perpetuating the fascist paradigm of the "noble savage," a misreading encouraged by Mussolini's awarding *Man of Aran* the Gold Cup at the 1934 Venice Film Festival. See William T. Murphy, *Robert Flaherty: A Guide to References and Resources* (Boston, 1978), pp. 70–75, and Paul Rotha *Robert Flaherty: A Biography*, ed. Jay Ruby (Philadelphia, 1983), pp. 139–60.

(never very advanced) for the sake of art could result in a crippling capital loss, and it was during the twenties that "Play It Safe" became the enduring First Commandment and Golden Rule of the American film industry. Consequently, of the more than five thousand American features produced between 1920 and 1929, only a handful made contributions either to the "literature" of world cinema or to the evolution of narrative form; and most of these, as we have seen, were in the realm of slapstick comedy. But there was a towering exception to this general law in the work of a single man—the enigmatic, distasteful, and finally tragic figure of Erich von Stroheim (1885–1957).

ERICH VON STROHEIM

6.39   Erich von Stroheim as "The Man You Love to Hate" in Griffith's *Hearts of the World* (1918).

Von Stroheim was born Erich Oswald Stroheim in Vienna, the son of a Jewish merchant from Silesia, and emigrated to the United States at some time between 1906 and 1909. Little is known of his early life here, but he eventually came to Hollywood, where he affixed the "von" to his surname and propagated the myth that he was descended from the Austrian aristocracy and had been a cavalry officer in his youth. As Erich von Stroheim, he first went to work as an extra and developed a great admiration for Griffith after a brief appearance in *The Birth of a Nation* (1915).* He subsequently became an assistant to Griffith on *Intolerance* (1916) and, between 1915 and 1917, to Triangle Company directors John Emerson (1878–1946), Allan Dwan, and George Fitzmaurice (1885–1941). In 1918, von Stroheim served as assistant director and military advisor on Griffith's World War I epic, *Hearts of the World,* in which he also played his first feature role as a brutal Prussian officer—the kind of role that later made him famous to American audiences as "The Man You Love to Hate."†

Von Stroheim was given his first chance to direct by Carl Laemmle of Universal Pictures, who permitted him to adapt his original screenplay, *The Pinnacle,* as *Blind Husbands* in 1918. The film concerns the seduction of a naïve American wife by a cynical Prussian officer (played by von Stroheim) at a resort in the Austrian Alps, and it was among the very first American postwar films to deal with sex in a sophisticated way. Despite its rather conventional plot, *Blind Husbands* is full of subtle psychological insights and visual wit, and it was a tremendous popular suc-

---

* Von Stroheim often claimed to have appeared in blackface in the film, but he is only identifiable as the white man who falls off the roof during the guerrilla raid on Piedmont.

† The title of a feature-length documentary on von Stroheim's life and work, directed by Patrick Montgomery and written by Richard Koszarski, is *The Man You Loved to Hate* (1979). Koszarski's critical biography of the same title (*The Man You Loved to Hate: Erich von Stroheim and Hollywood* [New York: Oxford University Press, 1983]) points out that while von Stroheim was never one of Griffith's closest assistants, he grasped the significance of Griffith's achievement better than any of his contemporaries and modeled his own career on it. Von Stroheim later wrote of his mentor, "He was the man who had put beauty and poetry into a cheap and tawdry form of amusement."

cess.* Von Stroheim's next two films repeated the pattern of *Blind Husbands* with something like obsessiveness: each concerns a sexual triangle in which an American wife in Europe is seduced by an army officer, and each is rendered with unsparing documentary and psychological realism. Moreover, the three films among them brought together the production team with which von Stroheim was to work for most of his career—the cameramen Ben Reynolds and William Daniels, and the performers Gibson Gowland, Sam de Grasse, May Busch, and Maude George. There are no surviving prints of *The Devil's Passkey,* which was made for Universal in 1919, but it ran to the amazing length of twelve full reels (well over two hours) and forecast von Stroheim's desire to expand the narrative cinema to a form commensurate with that of the great realistic novels of the nineteenth century. Based on the evidence of contemporary reviews, it contained some spectacular tinting and toning effects, including a rhythmic montage sequence involving alternating colors. *The Devil's Passkey* was also the last film that the director was ever permitted to finish as he had planned.

To complete his trilogy of adultery (although, according to the formula of the day, the act of adultery itself was never shown to be consummated), von Stroheim made *Foolish Wives* (1922), which most critics consider to be his first great film. This sordid and satiric tale of a lecherous Russian "count" (von Stroheim), who makes his living on the Riviera by bilking rich American tourists, was initially conceived by Laemmle as the perfect von Stroheim vehicle and shooting began in July 1920. To augment its realism, von Stroheim constructed an elaborate full-scale reproduction of the main square of Monte Carlo on the Universal backlot, with hotels, cafés, and casinos represented in minute detail. Furthermore, von Stroheim insisted that the exteriors for these sets be constructed at an isolated location on the Monterey Peninsula, three hundred miles from the studio, where the California coast most resembles the Mediterranean. Originally budgeted at $250,000, the costs of *Foolish Wives* began to soar toward $750,000, and the Universal publicity department seized upon the opportunity to promote it as the most expensive motion picture ever made. (E.g., a Universal advertisement in *Moving Picture Weekly* in October 1920 showed von Stroheim's Russian count wielding a whip above the logo, "He's going to make you hate him! Even if it takes a million dollars of our money to do it!") Finally completed in June 1921 at $1,124,500, the film ran twenty-four† reels (approximately 315 minutes, or five and one-quarter hours), much of it hand-colored by Gustav Brock, and von Stroheim planned to release it in two parts, as Lang's *Dr.*

---

* *Blind Husbands,* which Richard Koszarski calls "the most impressive and significant debut in Hollywood history" before *Citizen Kane* (1941), no longer exists in its original form. Universal cut into the negative in 1924 to eliminate nineteen minutes of running time for a streamlined reissue, and all surviving prints derive from this or subsequently scaled-down versions (*Man You Loved to Hate,* p. 45).

† Von Stroheim alternately claimed thirty and thirty-two, but the running time of 315 minutes agrees with all sources.

6.40 The casino, the hotel, and the Café de Paris in Monte Carlo reconstructed to scale on the Universal backlot in the San Fernando Valley for *Foolish Wives* (Erich von Stroheim, 1922).

Mabuse, der Spieler had been released that year in Europe. But the Universal production manager, Irving Thalberg (1899–1936), ordered it cut to fourteen reels (210 minutes) by studio editor Arthur Ripley (1865–1961) for its New York premiere in January 1922 and changed many of its titles to read less candidly than its director intended—this, partially in response to the Hollywood scandals of late 1921. *Foolish Wives* was cut still further for general release to ten reels, but even in its mutilated version* it remains a brilliant, brutal film, full of studied vignettes of postwar European decadence and rich psychological characterization. Thanks to Universal's publicity campaign, *Foolish Wives* was a *succés de scandal,* but thanks to its huge budget, the film produced a loss of $255,200. Nevertheless, its reception had established von Stroheim as an industry giant, very nearly on a par with Griffith, and his next film for Universal was *Merry-Go-Round* (1922), the beginning of another erotic trilogy, set

---

* The negative of the ten-reel version, which von Stroheim described widely in the press as "only the skeleton of my dead child," was recut by Universal to eight reels in 1928 for a general reissue with music and sound effects. The narrative was completely restructured and most of the titles rewritten to change the names and identities of the characters. This is the version distributed by MoMA and most other archives today. The only other surviving version is an eleven-reel composite prepared by Arthur Lennig for the American Film Institute from the 1928 reissue and several European versions derived from 1922 export prints. This latter is probably as close as we shall ever come to the original *Foolish Wives.*

On the reception of *Foolish Wives*—which *Variety* called a "leering insult to Americans in general, and American womanhood in particular" and *Moving Picture World* a "Darwinian Phantasy of Bad Manners and Sneers"—see Janet Staiger, "The Handmaiden of Villainy": Methods and Problems in Studying the Historical Reception of a Film, *Wide Angle* 8, 1 (Winter 1986): 19–27.

this time in prewar Austria during the decline of the Hapsburg Empire. Midway through the shooting, in October, Thalberg removed the director from the film because of his lavish and expensive attention to detail (including the construction of a full-scale model of the Prater, Vienna's mammoth amusement park) and replaced him with Rupert Julian (1889–1943), terminating von Stroheim's association with Universal. But his celebrity as both an actor and a director was such that within a month he had negotiated a three-film contract with Goldwyn Pictures, the first

6.41   Von Stroheim and crew shooting *Greed* (1924) on location in the streets of San Francisco, 1923.

6.42   *Greed:* Prologue, 1908. McTeague (Gibson Gowland) as a car-boy in the Big Dipper gold mine in the northern California hills. Note the composition-in-depth.

6.43   Ten years later: McTeague with a patient in his "dental parlours" on Polk Street, San Francisco (seen through the bay windows, below).

6.44   Von Stroheim directing Cesare Gravina and Dale Fuller as Zerkow the junkman and Maria Macapa the scrubwoman in a bizarre sub-plot cut entirely from the released version of *Greed*. Their story echoed that of McTeague's degenerate parents (also cut) and foreshadowed McTeague and Triana's decline.

of which was to be the realization of a long-cherished project—an adaptation of Frank Norris' naturalistic American novel *McTeague* (1899).*

Norris's novel, like Zola's *L'assommoir* (1877), was a model of the nineteenth-century naturalist convention by which some hereditary flaw or character trait brings its protagonists to ruin through a steady process of degeneration. The title character of *McTeague* is a young man with a family heritage of brutality who sets up as a dentist in San Francisco and eventually marries Trina Sieppe, the daughter of lower-middle-class German immigrants. Trina wins five thousand dollars in a lottery and becomes a monster of avarice in her attempts to retain the entire sum without spending a penny. McTeague loses his job through trusting a rival, and the couple sinks lower and lower in the socioeconomic scale until they are reduced to a state of total degradation. McTeague begins to drink; finally, his hereditary brutishness asserts itself and he murders Trina for her gold. The novel ends in Death Valley, where the fugitive McTeague encounters his rival Marcus and beats him to death with a pistol butt. But McTeague too is doomed, for in the process of his struggle with Marcus he has become handcuffed to the corpse. This grim tale was unlikely raw material for Hollywood commercial entertainment, but it was von Stroheim's intention to translate the novel, as a totality, into cinematic terms and to render its naturalism photographically meaningful.†

The film was shot by Ben Reynolds and William Daniels entirely on location in the streets and roominghouses of San Francisco,** in Death Valley, and in the northern California hills, on the basis of von Stroheim's own script. The process took nine months and cost over half a million dollars—three times the amount originally budgeted but all of it approved in stages by Goldwyn executives. After von Stroheim had personally edited the film in early 1924, he presented Goldwyn with a forty-two-reel work print running over nine hours (an alternative account has forty-five reels at nine-and-one-half hours). He was asked to reduce it to a reasonable length for commercial distribution in two parts. This twenty-

---

* *McTeague* had been adapted once before as the five-reel *Life's Whirlpool* (1916) by the director Barry O'Neil. The film has not survived, but on the basis of contemporary reviews and production stills, Richard Koszarski suggests that von Stroheim may have been influenced by its stark visual quality (*Man You Loved to Hate*, p. 117).

† In fact, von Stroheim undertook several significant adaptations of the text and added a thirty-page prologue to his script showing the environmental and hereditary origins of McTeague's degeneration in his harsh youth in a gold-mining camp, his father's death through alcoholism, and his mercenary apprenticeship to a traveling dentist. These scenes, occupying close to an hour of screen time, were shot on location in and around the Big Dipper Mine in northern California—the actual site of the character's youth in the novel—which von Stroheim had specially restored for the purpose. (Von Stroheim's script for *Greed* was published by Simon and Schuster in 1972.)

** Since the novel was set in the 1890s, von Stroheim went to great lengths to recreate the look of the city before it was destroyed by the 1906 earthquake and fire. But as Richard Koszarski points out, the costumes, street traffic, and calendar events were all deliberately updated to coincide with the period 1908–22, making the film "a bizarre amalgam of Norris's events jammed into the chronology of von Stroheim's life in America" (*Man You Love to Hate*, p. 129).

6.45 Zerkow and Maria set out in the junk-wagon to bury their dead child. Like the deranged McTeague, Zerkow will later murder his wife because of his lust for gold. Note the density and depth of the frame.

6.46 Saturday dinner at the Sieppes' (cut from the released version). Far right: McTeague's friend Marcus Schouler (Jean Hersholt) and Marcus' cousin, Trina Sieppe (Zasu Pitts), with whom McTeague will soon become infatuated.

6.47 After he has repaired her broken tooth in his "parlours," McTeague pays court to Triana and visits the Sieppe house with Marcus.

two reel, five-hour version was completed in March but was still too long for Goldwyn, so von Stroheim shipped the film to his friend, the Metro director Rex Ingram (1892–1950), for further reduction. Collaborating with the editor Grant Whytock, who had worked with von Stroheim on *The Devil's Passkey,* Ingram broke the film into two halves, eliminating some of the subplots. This eighteen-reel print, which Ingram and von Stroheim considered the absolute minimum to which the film could be cut without destroying its continuity, ran approximately four hours and was intended for release in two parts. In the meantime, however, Goldwyn Pictures had merged with Metro Pictures and Louis B. Mayer Productions to become MGM, and Mayer replaced Goldwyn as executive in charge of production. Among Mayer's first acts as studio chief was to

6.48 McTeague contemplates a gigantic golden molar, a birthday gift from Trina, meant to hang in his window to advertise his trade. Like other objects and / or symbols of gold in the film, it was tinted gold-yellow by the Handschiegl stencil process in the original release print to emphasize the obsessive nature of greed.

6.49 Meticulous *mise-en-scène:* McTeague and Triana's wedding feast, an orgy of feeding.

6.50 A sequence cut from the released version: Triana madly worshipping her lottery winnings, converted now to gold coin.

turn von Stroheim's epic over to his new assistant and the director's old adversary, Irving Thalberg, for further editing. The film was eventually cut to ten reels by an MGM title writer, Joseph Farnham, who had read neither the novel nor the shooting script, and the excised footage was destroyed. Retitled *Greed* (1924), this mutilated version of the film was the only one ever publicly seen, and it opened to modest critical acclaim, despite its incoherence, and actually made a profit of a quarter million dollars.*

* In 1971, von Stroheim's close friend, the film critic Herman G. Weinberg, published *"Greed": A Reconstruction of the Complete Erich von Stroheim Film from Stills*, using 348

6.51 Von Stroheim, with the cinematographer Ben Reynolds, directing the final scenes of *Greed* in Death Valley during the summer of 1923. The other cameramen on the film were William H. Daniels and Ernest B. Schoedsack.

6.52 Marcus alone in the desert, in desperate pursuit of McTeague.

6.53 From the final frames of *Greed:* McTeague bludgeons Marcus with his revolver, sealing his destiny—to die like a beast in the wild.

At one-fourth of its original length, *Greed* is a fragmentary masterpiece with vast gaps in continuity bridged by lengthy and often ludicrous titles, but it is a masterpiece nonetheless. Because von Stroheim was an original master of the long take and built up his most powerful effects *within* shots rather than editing between them, many of the film's greatest sequences have survived intact. Even as it stands, *Greed* is overwhelming in its psychological intensity, for von Stroheim used strikingly clear deep-focus photography and a documentary-like *mise-en-scène* to

still photographs left to him by the director, together with 52 production stills. Weinberg has performed the same valuable service for *The Wedding March* (1974) and the other films in the von Stroheim canon (1975).

totally immerse us in the reality of the film. His camera moves very little, and, in a manner forecasting the work of Michelangelo Antonioni (whose films will be studied in Chapter 15), the narrative proceeds through a gradual accretion of detail in which the time and space of the characters in the film become our own. Palpably real photographic objects—a caged canary, a funeral cortège, a huge gold tooth, cuts of meat—acquire symbolic value through composition-in-depth rather than expressive montage or the Griffithian intercut close-up. Finally, despite *Greed*'s structural disunity and its unpleasant subject matter, the atmospheric density of the film holds us from beginning to end. *Greed* is not a "realistic" film, as, for example, G. W. Pabst's *Die freudlose gasse* strives to be, but rather a "naturalistic" one in the literary sense of the term. In its uncompromising depiction of degradation and despair, it raises reality to the level of symbol and asks profound questions about the nature of human experience.

Von Stroheim, who had mortgaged his home and his car to support himself during the editing of *Greed* (he was paid only for direction), disowned the film and refused to see it after it was released.* Incredibly, he was hired back by MGM in 1925 and given a free hand in adapting the Franz Lehar operetta *The Merry Widow* (1925), although he was forced to use the stars John Gilbert and Mae Murray against his will. By reducing the operetta to less than one-half of the film's running time and adding his own material, von Stroheim was able to turn this purely commercial venture into the second film in his darkly satiric trilogy on the corruption of the Viennese aristocracy. Although technically set in an imaginary Ruritanian kingdom named Monteblanco, *The Merry Widow* clearly reflects the decadence of the Hapsburg Empire at the turn of the century and reveals the rottenness and perversion concealed beneath its elegant façade. The studio deleted a few scenes from the release print due to their explicit sexual content, but *The Merry Widow* came closer to realizing its director's intentions than any film he had made since *The Devil's Passkey* in 1919. Stencil-colored by the Handschiegl process, with a concluding two-minute Technicolor sequence shot by Ray Rennahan, it was an international success, both critically and commercially, and it made a fortune for MGM.

At this point in his career, von Stroheim left MGM for good in a bitter dispute over financial and creative differences to make a film of his choice for Pat Powers' independent Celebrity Pictures. The result was *The Wedding March* (1928), von Stroheim's last great film and the concluding section of his trilogy on the decadence of Imperial Austria. It tells the bitterly sardonic tale of a forced marriage between an impoverished Viennese nobleman (von Stroheim) and the crippled daughter of a wealthy industrialist; and it is among the most visually extravagant films ever

---

* Von Stroheim finally saw what was left of his epic in 1950, at the instigation of Henri Langlois of the Cinémathèque Française. Immediately afterwards he commented: "This was like an exhumation for me. In a tiny coffin I found a lot of dust, a terrible smell, a little backbone and shoulder-bone."

6.54 Ruritanian decadence: Crown Prince Mirko of Monteblanco (John Gilbert) and his party prepare for an evening of mirth in *The Merry Widow* (Erich von Stroheim, 1925).

6.55 The wedding in *The Wedding March* (1928): Erich von Stroheim, Zasu Pitts.

made. *The Wedding March* was also to have finally realized von Stroheim's perennial desire to make a long film in two parts, whose form would approximate that of the great nineteenth-century novels. Shooting began in June 1926, and *Part I* was completed as von Stroheim had intended (except that he had replaced cinematographers Henry Thorpe and Bill McGann with Hal Mohr, who would himself resign and be replaced by Roy Klaffki). But midway through the filming of *Part II,* in January 1927, he was removed from the project by Paramount, to whom Powers had been forced to sell his option when von Stroheim overran his original budget of $750,000 by $400,000. Paramount turned the footage over to Josef von Sternberg (see pp. 319–24) to edit into a single film. Between them, von Stroheim and von Sternberg were able to put together a version of *The Wedding March* which corresponded roughly to the original *Part I* and concluded with the wedding of the protagonists in St. Stephen's Cathedral (shot in Technicolor by Ray Rennahan). But Vice President for Production Jesse Lasky rejected this version and had it recut by studio editor Julian Johnston into what eventually became a twelve-reel release print. The film was scheduled for a January 1928 premiere but was temporarily shelved due to the advent of sound while studio executives decided to add a synchronized score by J. S. Zamecnik and Louis Francesco. This version was finally released in October 1928 to dismal reviews and box-office failure. Paramount editors then combined footage from *Parts I* and *II* into a hodgepodge entitled *The Honeymoon,* which was released in Europe in 1929 and subsequently disowned by von Stroheim. Just before his death in 1957, the director recut the first part of the film to conform more closely to his original intention, and there is now preserved in the archives of the Cinémathèque Française von Stroheim's own 16 mm sound-on-film reconstruction of this most lavish and erotic masterpiece of *mise-en-scène.*

6.56 "Queen Kelly" imprisoned in an African brothel.

After the *Wedding March* debacle, as after *Greed,* von Stroheim's reputation among Hollywood producers was not good, but his singular talent was indisputable. In 1928, he was commissioned by Joseph Kennedy (then an independent producer) to write and direct a star vehicle for Gloria Swanson (1897–1983), who had quit Paramount in 1926 to produce her own films for release through United Artists. The two-part script, which was approved by the Hays Office and originally called *The Swamp,* can only be described as bizarre. In the European episode, Prince Wolfram, betrothed to the queen of the small Bavarian state of Cobourg-Nassau, falls in love with a young convent girl named Kitty Kelly (Swanson) and later abducts her to his apartments in the royal palace. They are caught by his fiancée, Queen Regina, who whips Kelly from the palace with a riding crop and has Wolfram imprisoned. Meanwhile, after an abortive suicide attempt, Kelly finds she has been summoned to German East Africa, where her guardian aunt lies dying in Dar-es-Salaam. *Part II* begins when Kelly arrives in Africa to discover that her aunt is the owner of a run-down brothel. Penniless, the old woman has arranged for her niece to marry "the richest guy in Africa," an aged, degenerate planter named Jan, which in a delirium of disgust Kelly does. Eight months later, Kelly has transformed the seedy whorehouse into the classy "Poto-Poto" bordello and installed herself as its reigning queen. Subsequently, Jan dies of syphilis; and Prince Wolfram arrives by steamer from Germany, where Queen Regina has also expired. He ultimately convinces Kelly to return with him to Cobourg-Nassau, where they are married and she is coronated "Queen Kelly," institutionalizing the regal spirit she has carried within her all along—but also suggesting the continuity of depravity between "civilized" Europe and "barbaric" Africa.

Working with cinematographers Gordon Pollack and Paul Ivano, von Stroheim had shot more than half of this fantastic film, including some harrowing African sequences, when he was removed from the project at Swanson's insistence in January 1929. Increasingly fearful of censorship of the African scenes and morally outraged at what she later called "Mr. von Stroheim's apocalyptic vision of hell on earth," Swanson authorized Kennedy to find another director to salvage the project, but this ultimately proved impossible owing to the industry's wholesale conversion to "talkies" and other factors. (Among those who tried and failed in this salvage operation over the next few years were Paul Stein, Edmund Goulding, Richard Boleslavski, Sam Wood, and Delmer Daves.) Finally, in November 1931, Swanson—who had invested about $800,000 in the production so far—tacked an abrupt conclusion onto the European episode showing Kelly's suicide attempt (shot by Gregg Toland) to have been successful, added an orchestral score by Adolf Tandler, and released the film in Europe the following year as "an original von Stroheim," where it was widely hailed but little seen. Like the mutilated *Greed* and *The Honeymoon,* this remnant was disowned by von Stroheim, but a recent reconstruction has restored *Queen Kelly* as the director originally shot it, although it remains of course, incomplete.

Von Stroheim had shot ten reels of a projected thirty in precise dramatic sequence when the film was canceled. Eight reels constituted the European episode; the other two contained scenes set in Dar-es-Salaam. Miss Swanson used only the European footage in her "released version," whose most famous apparition is in Billy Wilder's self-reflexive black comedy *Sunset Boulevard* (1950) where a clip of it is projected for the faded silent star Norma Desmond (Swanson) by her has-been director / husband Max von Mayerling (von Stroheim). But two edited reels containing nearly all of the African footage were discovered in 1965, and in 1978 Donald Krim of Kino International began negotiating for the rights to the entire film. Finally, in collaboration with Dennis Doros, Krim put together a 96-minute restoration print of *Queen Kelly* which was premiered at the Los Angeles Country Museum of Art in February 1985. Working from detailed production notes and von Stroheim's final shooting script, Doros assembled this version from sixty-six minutes of the Swanson 1932 European release (eliminating the tacked-on ending), twenty-two minutes of the African reels, and an additional ten minutes of out-takes and stills from archives all over the world to bridge continuity gaps. The 1985 reconstruction also includes new titles by Doros and remixes Adolf Tandler's original score. All told, it suggests that, if completed as planned, *Queen Kelly* might well have been von Stroheim's greatest film.

The cancellation of *Queen Kelly* was a professional disaster for von Stroheim. It seemed to confirm his vastly inflated reputation for excess and perversity in the eyes of all Hollywood, and the conversion to sound became a pretext on the part of his many enemies for squeezing him out of the industry. He was reduced to writing screenplays (*Tempest*, 1927; *East of the Setting Sun*, 1929) and acting in other people's films (*The Great Gabbo* [James Cruze, 1929]; *Three Faces East* [Roy Del Ruth, 1930]; *As You Desire Me* [George Fitzmaurice, 1932]) to make a living. Yet, after an abortive attempt to remake *Blind Husbands* for Universal in sound and (two-color) Technicolor between 1930 and 1931, von Stroheim was given his last chance to direct by Winfield Sheehan, an executive for the Fox Film Corporation, who signed him to adapt an unproduced Dawn Powell play, *Walking Down Broadway*, in late 1931. Though this story of two small-town girls rooming together in contemporary New York City was conceived as a modest program picture* by Fox, von Stroheim lavished infinite care upon its visual texture, working in close collaboration with the cinematographer James Wong Howe (1899–1976). After several delays, shooting started on September 2, 1932, and *Walking Down Broadway* was completed in an exemplary manner forty-eight days later for the budgeted amount of $300,000, but in the process it seems to have become a study of morbid psychology with crypto-lesbian undertones. When Fox vice president Sol Wurtzel saw the film, he was outraged and halted its release. Von Stroheim was fired, the script rewritten, and the film turned over to several directors, including Alan Cros-

---

* A cheaply produced second feature—the bottom half of a double bill (also called a "B-film"), although the budget of $300,000 was very generous for this type of film.

land, Raoul Walsh, Sidney Lanfield, Edwin Burke, and Alfred Werker, to be reshot. The revised version, containing about one-half of the original, was released in March 1933 as *Hello, Sister!* without von Stroheim's name appearing on the credits. Fired by Universal, MGM, Paramount, United Artists, and Fox in turn, von Stroheim's reputation as a filmmaker was completely destroyed, and he was never permitted to direct again. He worked for a while as a dialogue writer at MGM, much as Keaton was forced to do, before turning his career completely to acting. Between 1934 and 1955, von Stroheim appeared in some fifty-two films for other directors and gave many distinguished performances (for instance, in Jean Renoir's *La grande illusion* [1937] and Billy Wilder's *Sunset Boulevard* [1950]). He made a fair living at this profession, wrote several novels, and was still a celebrity when he died in France in 1957.

Simultaneously a romanticist, a determinist, and a cynic, Erich von Stroheim was Hollywood's last great independent director and its last great personal *auteur*. For most of his films he was his own scenarist, art director, costume designer, editor, assistant cameraman, and star. His obsessive realism became a Hollywood legend, and yet realism for von Stroheim was always a means toward the end of symbolic naturalism— a mode practiced by late-nineteenth-century novelists like Zola, Maupassant, Crane, and Norris, in which the accumulation of surface detail ultimately leads us beneath the surface of things to some deeper human meaning. To this end as well, von Stroheim rejected Griffithian montage in favor of the long take, or sequence shot, composed in depth from a relatively static camera—shots which have the naturalistic effect of linking characters with their environment. In his classic essay "The Evolution of the Language of the Cinema," André Bazin has described von Stroheim as "the creator of the virtually continuous cinematic story, tending to the permanent integration of the whole space. . . . He has one simple rule for direction. Take a close look at the world, keep doing so, and in the end it will lay bare for you all its cruelty and its ugliness." But if von Stroheim was a naturalist, he was also, often simultaneously, an ironic fantasist. His fascination with sexual perversion is a case in point. He did not use it to titillate, as DeMille might have done, or even to display his worldliness, as might have been expected of Lubitsch. Like Luis Buñuel after him (as we will see in Chapter 15), von Stroheim used sexual pathology as a metaphor for a more pervasive cultural decadence which was his major philosophical concern. The corruption of the European aristocracy, the corruptibility of the American bourgeoisie, and the degradation of the masses are the recurrent themes of von Stroheim's major work. They bespeak a profound cultural pessimism born of late-nineteenth-century Europe—the bitter dregs of a failed idealism—which is balanced in the films themselves by an obvious sympathy for the individual humans caught up in the self-destructive impulses of the race.

"Self-destructive" is an adjective which many persons have applied to von Stroheim himself, and it is true that he was in some sense a victim of his own temperament and his own myth. But he was also a casualty of Hollywood's transformation from a speculative entrepreneurial enterprise into a vertically and horizontally integrated big business, and his beleaguered career as a director from 1918 to 1932 is a virtual paradigm of that transformation. What happened to von Stroheim in Hollywood during the twenties was the same thing that happened to Griffith, Chaplin, and Keaton, those three other great independent producer-directors of the American silent film. When von Stroheim and Griffith first began to make feature films in Southern California in the teens, there was no established procedure for producing them since they were an unprecedented commodity. As things evolved at the time, some individual or group of individuals with investment capital—a Harry Aitken or a Carl Laemmle, for example—would provide the financial backing, and Griffith and von Stroheim would "produce" their own films in the most literal sense of the term. Script writing, casting, locations, set design, art direction, and the general logistics of shooting the film, in addition to the shooting and editing itself, were all directorial responsibilities; and this assured a high degree of personal artistic freedom for the individual director. As American film production grew into what its promoters claimed to be the nation's fourth largest industry* between 1919 and 1927, this system of independent production yielded first to the privately owned studio (Triangle Films, Keaton Productions, Chaplin Productions) and finally to the monopolistic industrial combines of Paramount, Fox, Associated-First National, and MGM. By 1927, the studio filmmaking process had been standardized under the supervisory production system pioneered by Thomas Ince and Mack Sennett a decade before, and there was little place within the system for such an individual and eccentric talent as a von Stroheim or a Keaton or a Griffith.

The coming of sound was to clinch the matter. The studios had to borrow huge sums of money to pay for the conversion on the very eve of the Great Depression, which spurred them to increase the efficiency of their production process by totally effacing the concept of the personal director and replacing it with the concept of the executive producer, modeled on MGM's Irving Thalberg, the man who had done such injury

---

* This "fourth largest industry" claim, long accepted as gospel by film historians (and, apparently, for at least a decade by the U.S. Chamber of Commerce), has recently been challenged by J. Douglas Gomery. In "Hollywood, the National Recovery Administration, and the Question of Monopoly Power" (*Journal of the University Film Association* 31, 2 [Spring 1979], 49; rpt., with commentary, *The American Movie Industry: The Business of Motion Pictures,* ed. Gorham Kindem (Carbondale, Ill: Southern Illinois University Press, 1982), pp. 205–14), he maintains that on the basis of total sales for 1933, the industry ranked somewhere between the thirty-seventh and forty-fifth, so that it could hardly have been the fourth largest a decade before. Gomery believes that the industry began circulating this specious claim to power during the twenties as a form of self-advertisement and, perhaps, intimidation of government regulatory agencies. (See also his "Rethinking American Film History: The Depression Decade and Monopoly Control," *Film and History* 10, 2 [May 1980]: 32–38.) This may be so, but in terms of its *social* as opposed to its economic influence—in terms of the sheer number of persons deeply and permanently affected by its values—the American film industry was surely among the most powerful since the Industrial Revolution. Only radio and television would exceed its power as a medium of mass persuasion and social control.

to *Foolish Wives* and *Greed*. Thus, the coming of sound meant a great deal more for the American cinema than the transformation of those dreamlike, hallucinatory demigods of the silent screen into mere mortals with accents, drawls, and lisps—more even than the regressive inertia temporarily caused by the early technology of recording sound. It meant the transformation of a wildcat business run largely by filmmakers fascinated with the process of film itself into a large-scale technological industry controlled by corporate managers who exercised supreme authority over all artistic variables in order to maximize profits. Like so many other aspects of modern American life—including mass communications, mass consumption, and rapid transit—gigantic corporate capitalism was born of the twenties. That decade was the only time in the history of American film that so much talent has ever been allowed to display itself so extravagantly and magnificently, and then has been so ruthlessly destroyed.

The Coming of Sound, 1926–1932

SOUND-ON-DISK

After the invention of the cinema itself, the most important event in film history was the introduction of sound. In fact, the idea of combining motion pictures with some type of synchronized sound had been present since their inception. Thomas Edison originally commissioned the invention of the Kinetograph with the notion of providing a visual accompaniment for his phonograph, and W. K. L. Dickson had actually achieved a rough synchronization of the two machines as early as 1889. Many other inventors, such as Georges Demeny and Auguste Baron in France, and William Friese-Greene in England, experimented with devices for coupling sound and image before the turn of the century. At the Paris World Exposition of 1900 three separate systems which synchronized phonograph recordings with projected film strips were exhibited: the Phonorama of L. A. Berthon, C. F. Dussaud, and G. F. Jaubert; Léon Gaumont's Chronophone; and the Phono-Cinéma-Théâtre of Clément-Maurice Gratioulet and Henri Lioret, which offered minute-long performances by great stars of the theater, opera, and ballet. In Germany, Oskar Messter began to produce short synchronized sound films as novelty items in 1903, and by 1908 he was supplying exhibitors with recorded musical scores for nearly all of his productions. In Britain, Gaumont's Chronophone proved popular, as did Cecil Hepworth's system, Vivaphone; and in the United States the Edison Corporation achieved some popular success with two phonofilm systems—Cinephonograph and **Kinetophone.**

All of these early systems relied on the phonograph to reproduce the sound component of the filmed performance. The earliest ones used wax cylinders and the later ones disks, but all had three difficulties in common: the problem of synchronizing the sound recording with the filmed event, of amplifying the sound for presentation to a large audience, and of the brevity of the cylinder and disk formats in relation to the standard length of motion pictures. The first problem was partially solved by a number of regulatory devices which were intended to insure an exact correspondence of sound and image but were usually imperfect in operation. If the phonograph stylus skipped a groove in performance, for example, or if the film strip broke in the projector, regaining synchronization was nearly impossible. The problem of amplification was generally dealt with by concealing a battery of single-horn speakers behind the screen, although experiments with compressed-air speakers of the sort used today began around 1910. The third problem was the most difficult. By 1905, the length of the standard narrative film had far exceeded the four-minute playing time of the phonograph cylinder and the five-minute time of the twelve-inch disk. The introduction of automatic changers and multiple phonographs did not resolve the difficulty, since changing records frequently caused a loss of synchronization, and the use of oversized disks only resulted in poor sound quality. In the years before the First World War, as the standard length of films grew even longer and their inter-frame structure more complex, experimental interest in the imperfect phono-film sound systems died out. They remained extant through the war mainly as a means of making short novelty films in single takes.

But the imperfection of the phono-film systems did not leave the motion pictures soundless. In fact, the "silent" cinema was rarely that. Sound effects provided by individual performers or by sound-effect machines like the Allefex and Kinematophone were a standard feature of films after 1908, and live music had been a part of the cinema since its beginnings. A pianist had accompanied the first commercial motion picture exhibition, the Lumière Cinématographe program at the Grand Café, Paris, December 28, 1895, and Méliès personally provided piano accompaniment for the Paris debut of *Le Voyage dans la lune* in 1902. Pianists were employed in most storefront theaters and nickelodeons in the first decade of this century to improvise music to fit the scenes. As the standard film length increased from one reel (about one thousand feet, or sixteen minutes at the average silent speed of 16 fps) to six-to-ten reels (ninety to 160 minutes) between 1905 and 1914, film narratives grew increasingly sophisticated; and, according to Harry M. Geduld, the practice of musicians playing intermittently during film programs gave way to continuous musical accompaniment in which the nature of each scene determined the kind of music played with it.

During this period, the nickelodeons and storefronts began to be replaced by "dream palaces" that could seat thousands of movie-goers and accommodate hundred-piece orchestras, or, at the very least, a mighty Wurlitzer organ that could produce a wide range of orchestral effects. By the time the feature film had become the dominant cinematic form in the West, many producers were commissioning original scores for their class-A productions; and during the twenties all features, regardless of quality, were accompanied by cue sheets suggesting appropriate musical selections to be played at designated points in the film. The first original piece of film music was composed in 1907 by Camille Saint-Saëns for the Film d'Art Company's *L'Assassinat du Duc de Guise* (1908). Other memorable and distinguished scores of the "silent" era were Joseph Carl Breil's scores for Griffith's *The Birth of a Nation* (1915) and *Intolerance* (1916), Victor Schertzinger's score for Thomas H. Ince's *Civilization* (1916), Hugo Riesenfeld's score for James Cruze's *The Covered Wagon* (1925) and

7.1 A Kimball organ at the Roxy Theater, New York City, with the theater's manager, S. L. "Roxy" Rothapfel. (Kimball was one of Wurlitzer's many competitors in the theatrical market.) Publicity still, c. 1926.

F. W. Murnau's *Sunrise* (1927), Louis F. Gottschalk's scores for Griffith's *Broken Blossoms* (1919) and *Orphans of the Storm* (1921), Mortimer Wilson's score for Douglas Fairbanks' *The Thief of Bagdad* (1923), William Frederick Peters' score for Griffith's *Way Down East* (1920), Erno Rapee's score for John Ford's *The Iron Horse* (1924), and Leo Kempinski's score for Erich von Stroheim's *Greed* (1924). In Europe, Edmund Meisel wrote brilliant revolutionary scores for Eisenstein's *Potemkin* (1925) and *October* (1928), and Gottfried Huppertz composed for Fritz Lang's *Siegfried* (1923) and *Metropolis* (1926). Other European composers who scored films during the twenties include George Antheil, Erik Satie, Darius Milhaud, Arthur Honegger, Jacques Ibert, Jean Sibelius, Roger Desormière, Paul Hindemith, and Dmitri Shostakovich.

SOUND-ON-FILM

The notion that sound could complement and vivify the experience of cinema, then, came of age with the cinema itself. But since only a handful of exhibitors in major cities could afford full-scale orchestras or even Wurlitzer organs, the search for an inexpensive and effective means of recording sound for films continued during and after the war, when experimental emphasis shifted from sound-on-disk to sound-on-film systems. It was reasoned at this point that the massive problems of synchronization encountered in the disk systems could be solved by recording the sound on the same strip of film as the images. The potential for recording sound photographically, or optically, by converting sound waves into patterns of light and shade, had been understood a decade before the invention of the Kinetograph, but the first successful attempt to record sound directly on a film strip, side-by-side with the image track, was made by Eugene Augustin Lauste, a former mechanical assistant to W. K. L. Dickson, in 1910, on the basis of a 1907 British patent for converting sound-modulated light beams into electrical impulses by means of a photoconductive selenium cell. Though he could find no significant financial backing for his system, which he called "Photocinematophone," Lauste's experiments were to become the basis for RCA Photophone, one of the two major sound-on-film systems adopted by Hollywood in the early sound era. Another pioneer of sound-on-film technology was the Polish-American inventor Joseph T. Tykociner, who had experimented with a sound-modulated gas flame as a light source as early as 1896, but the first workable sound-on-film, or optical sound, systems were not perfected until after the war.

In 1919, three German inventors—Josef Engl, Joseph Massole, and Hans Vogt—patented the "Tri-Ergon" (literally, "the work of three") process, a sound-on-film system which used a photoelectric cell to convert sound waves into electric impulses and electric impulses into light waves which were then recorded photographically on the edge of the film strip. Built onto their projector was a "reader," composed of an incandescent light and another photoelectric cell, which retranslated the patterns of light and shade back into sound waves as the film strip passed through the projector, insuring perfect synchronization of sound and image. The Tri-Ergon process also incorporated a flywheel mechanism on a sprocket which prevented variations in film speed as the strip passed through the projector—a device necessary to maintain the continuous reproduction of sound without distortion. This flywheel was heavily protected by international patents, so that between 1920 and 1927 all other manufacturers of optical sound equipment had to either pay royalties to Tri-Ergon, infringe the patent, or market an inferior product. Tri-Ergon, whose technology was later employed throughout Germany, eventually sold its American rights to William Fox of Fox Film Company in 1927 (a sale ruled illegal by the U.S. Supreme Court in 1935) and its Continental rights to UFA, which in 1928 sold them to Tonbild Syndicate A.G., merged as Tobis-Klangfilm in 1929.

In 1923 an American inventor who had been active in the development of radio broadcasting, Dr. Lee De Forest (1873–1961), patented (independently of the German inventers) a sound-on-film system, very similar to the Tri-Ergon process, which also decisively solved the problem of amplification. In 1907, to improve radio reception, De Forest had patented the Audion 3-Electrode Amplifier Tube, or triode, a vacuum tube which amplified the sound it received electronically and drove it into a speaker. The audion tube became essential to the technology of all sound systems requiring amplification—radio, public address, sound film, and, ultimately, high-fidelity recording and television—because it is to sound reproduction what the lens is to projection; that is, it enables its message or signal to reach large numbers of people simultaneously.* De Forest became preoccupied with the development of "talking pictures" in 1919, when he realized that incorporating his audion tube into an optical sound-on-film process would provide more amplification than was possible with any other system of the period. By 1922, De Forest had worked enough of the bugs out of his system to test it commercially, and in November of that year he founded the De Forest Phonofilm Company to produce a series of short sound films in cooperation with Dr. Hugo Riesenfeld, a composer of silent film scores.

Working at the Norma Talmadge Studios in New York City, De Forest made several one- and two-reel Phonofilms each week, and their success was such that by the middle of 1924 some thirty-four theaters in the East had been wired to show them and another fifty were in the process of being wired elsewhere in the United States, in Britain, and in Canada. The content of De Forest's films was varied, but they all somehow exploited sound. They included set pieces from grand opera, instrumental performances by famous musicians, popular vaudeville acts, scenes from current plays, speeches by prominent persons such as President Calvin Coolidge, Senator Robert La Follette, and George Bernard Shaw, and even an original narrative from time to time. (It is also possible that De

---

* De Forest sold the telephone rights to his audion patents to AT&T in 1913, enabling it to open the first coast-to-coast long-distance circuits in 1915, using vacuum tube reamplifiers, or repeaters. He sold the radio rights to the same company in 1914.

Forest used the Phonofilm process to provide full-length recordings of Riesenfeld's scores for James Cruze's *The Covered Wagon* in 1924 and Fritz Lang's *Siegfried* in 1925, but the historical record on this point is unclear.) Although De Forest experienced some popular success with the more than one thousand short sound films he made in New York between 1923 and 1927, his attempts to interest Hollywood producers in the Phonofilm process proved fruitless, because they did not want to spend the money required to convert their entire system of production and exhibition. As early as 1923, he had offered it to moguls like Carl Laemmle of Universal and Adolph Zukor of Paramount, only to be ignored. The studio chiefs tended to regard "talking pictures" as an expensive novelty that had no future beyond causing financial ruin for its backers, and not a single Hollywood executive showed the slightest interest in Phonofilm until the phenomenal success of a rival sound-on-disk system called Vitaphone forced them to reassess their options in 1926.

VITAPHONE

Vitaphone was a sophisticated sound-on-disk system developed at great expense by Western Electric and Bell Telephone Laboratories, a subsidiary firm of American Telephone and Telegraph Corporation (AT&T), in blithe ignorance of (or at least indifference to) Hollywood's antipathy toward sound. When representatives of Western Electric attempted to market the system to the major studios in 1925, they were politely refused. But the financially venturesome and, at the time, emphatically minor Warner Bros. Pictures decided to take a chance on sound. Warner Bros. was not on the verge of bankruptcy, as is frequently claimed. In fact, it had embarked upon an aggressively expansionist campaign against its larger competitors and was having temporary cash-flow problems. The studio's executives conceived the acquisition of sound as an offensive rather than a defensive maneuver. So, in April 1926, Warner Bros., with the financial assistance of the Wall Street banking group Goldman Sachs,* established the Vitaphone Corporation, formally leased the sound-system from Western Electric, and for $800,000 secured the exclusive right to sublease it to other studios. There was at first no question of making "talking pictures." Warner Bros.' notion was that Vitaphone could be used to provide synchronized musical accompaniment for all Warner Bros. films, enhancing their appeal to the second- and third-run theaters that had no orchestras. An official statement prepared for Vitaphone underscored the Warners' appeal to smaller exhibitors: "The invention will make it possible for every performance in a motion picture theater to have a full orchestral accompaniment to the picture regardless of the size of the house." Having cast its lot with Vitaphone, Warner Bros. decided

7.2 **The Western Electric Vitaphone projection system.**

7.3 **An actual Vitaphone projection in progress.**

---

* Waddill Catchings, head of the Goldman Sachs investment division, arranged for the studio to underwrite a $4,200,000 note issue to finance Vitaphone. Catchings subsequently became a Warner board member and facilitated the acquisition of the Stanley theater chain and the First National studio and exchanges in late 1928.

to promote it on a spectacular scale at a total cost of over three million dollars. For its world premier at the "Refrigerated* Warner Theater" at Broadway and Fifty-second Street in New York City on August 6, 1926, Warners presented *Don Juan* (Alan Crosland, 1926), the latest and most lavish John Barrymore costume drama, with an elaborate recorded orchestral score performed by the New York Philharmonic. The feature was preceded by a one-hour, one-million-dollar program of sound shorts, featuring the stars of the Metropolitan Opera and the New York Philharmonic Orchestra, which was itself preceded by a brief filmed speech by Will Hays, president of the MPPDA, announcing "the beginning of a new era in music and motion pictures."

Again, it was as a revolutionary way of providing synchronized musical accompaniment for "silent" films that Vitaphone was initially promoted, and its debut as such was enormously successful. The first Vitaphone program ran eight weeks in New York, where it was seen by more than 500,000 people who paid nearly $800,000. It went on to have record-breaking runs in Chicago, Los Angeles, Boston, Detroit, St. Louis, and many European cities. The critics were unanimous in their praise of the Vitaphone system, describing it as "uncanny in its excellence," "impossible to imagine," and "the eighth wonder of the world." Of Hays' filmed speech before the program, Professor of Physics Michael Pupin of Columbia University remarked, "No closer approach to resurrection has ever been made by science." Nevertheless, the future of Vitaphone was still uncertain in late 1926. No one could determine at this point whether its warm public and critical reception was the result of a passing fancy or a legitimate interest in sound films. But, as Harry M. Geduld writes, "Warners had too much at stake to accept the idea that Vitaphone might be an ephemeral novelty—while the rest of the film industry had too much at stake to entertain the notion that it might not."

The rest of the film industry had a very good reason for hoping that the enthusiasm for Vitaphone would pass. It was understood among studio chiefs that a full-scale conversion to sound would cost an incalculable amount of money and perhaps even bring the industry to financial collapse. New sound studios would have to be built and costly recording equipment installed.† Thousands of cinema theaters across the country, many of them now owned by the studios, would have to be wired for sound and perhaps wired twice due to the incompatibility of competing

7.4 A billboard in New York City, 1926.

---

* Although it could be enormously expensive, costing up to $40,000 per theater, air conditioning of some sort had become a standard feature of most American picture palaces during the twenties, and installations proceeded (with a brief pause for World War II) until by 1950 three-quarters of all domestic theaters were cooled. Initiated by the Chicago chain of Balaban & Katz in a borrowing from the meat-packing industry c. 1917, fan-coiled air-cooling systems provided a major attraction for large first-run theaters during the summer months and ultimately transformed summer into the film industry's major season. As Douglas Gomery points out, "few Americans ever experienced air-conditioning during the 1930s and 1940s outside a movie house" ("Movie-Going During Hollywood's Golden Age," *North Dakota Quarterly* 51, 3 [Summer 1983]: 40).

† Alexander Walker: "For most studios sound did not mean adaptation but wholesale replacement. Glass and plywood came down and the California sunshine that had been one

7.5 *Variety* proclaims the arrival of a new era in film.

systems. (In 1927 the installation of Vitaphone equipment alone could cost as much as twenty-five thousand dollars per theater.) Each studio would suddenly have a huge backlog of silent films representing millions of dollars in capital investment, and the industry's vast overseas market would be decimated if easily translated intertitles gave way to spoken dialogue. The star system which sustained the American studios and helped to sell their product all over the world would also be thrown into disarray when actors and actresses trained solely in the art of mime suddenly had to start speaking dialogue. Finally, as *Variety,* the industry trade paper asked, "What would happen to the class theatres with expensive orchestras and stage shows, if any jerk-water movie joint was able to give its patrons gorgeous feasts of music via the screen?" In short, conversion to sound threatened the entire economic structure of the American (and, therefore, the Western) film industry, and the industry had every reason to resist it. But by the beginning of 1927, Vitaphone's popular success

of the lures for the early pioneers was shut out by thick walls of brick and concrete. All wood used had to be kiln-dried, to get rid of resin which generated electric static. Doors were of intimidating thickness and rubber-sealed. In the very early days the main stages on some lots were surrounded by a twenty-foot moat to eliminate vibrations." (*The Shattered Silents: How the Talkies Came to Stay* [London, 1978], p. 74.)

could not be ignored, and in February of that year executives of the "Big Three"—Loew's (MGM); Famous Players–Lasky, soon to become Paramount; and First National—and the largest of the "Little Five"—Universal and Producers Distributing Corporation (PDC)—signed an accord (known somewhat confusingly as the "Big Five Agreement") to adopt a uniform sound system if and when conversion became necessary; it was this agreement that ultimately led to the promotion of rival systems and the eventual triumph of sound-on-film over sound-on-disk.

For the time being, however, Vitaphone was still the best system on the market, and, buoyed by the success of the *Don Juan* program, Warners announced that all of its silent films for 1927 would be produced with synchronized musical accompaniment. It also announced plans to buy one major theater in every large American city and wire it for sound. By April 1927, the Vitaphone Corporation had completed 150 installations, an average of twelve per week. In the same month, Warners completed construction of the first sound studio in the world, where, a month later, production began on the picture that would insure the triumph of the sound film and determine its future direction: Alan Crosland's *The Jazz Singer* (1927). Although Warners had been recording synchronized scores for its pictures and providing with them programs of sound shorts since August 1926, *The Jazz Singer* was to be the start of the studio's regular production of Vitaphone features for distribution to Vitaphone theaters. It was planned as a prestigious production ("Warner Brothers' Supreme Triumph," said the publicity posters), and the popular vaudeville star Al Jolson (1886–1950) was hired for twenty thousand dollars to play the lead.

The Jazz Singer, adapted from a successful Broadway play which had originally starred George Jessel (1898–1981), told the sentimental story of the son of a Jewish cantor who undergoes an anguished conflict between his religion, his family, and his career as a music-hall singer.* Like previous Vitaphone productions, it was conceived as a silent picture with a synchronized orchestral score, some Jewish cantorial music, and seven popular songs performed by Jolson. It was conceived, that is, as a "singing" rather than a "talking" picture, and all dialogue was to be provided by interpolated titles (intertitles). But, during the shooting of two musical sequences, Jolson ad-libbed some dialogue on the set which Warners shrewdly permitted to remain in the finished film. At one point near the beginning of the picture, Jolson speaks to his audience in the middle of a nightclub act and delivers his famous "Wait-a-minute. . . . Wait-a-minute. . . . You ain't heard nothin' yet!" Later in the film, as he sits at a piano in his mother's parlor, he has a sentimental exchange with her that lasts several minutes, between verses of "Blue Skies." This was the only spoken dialogue in the film, yet its impact was sensational. Audiences had heard synchronized speech before, but only on formally contrived and easily anticipated occasions, such as the speech which preceded *Don*

7.6 A contemporary poster for *The Jazz Singer* (Alan Crosland, 1927).

7.7 Al Jolson in *The Jazz Singer*.

---

* *The Jazz Singer* has been twice remade as a theatrical film—once in 1952, with Michael Curtiz directing Danny Thomas in the Jolson role, and again in 1980, with Richard Fleischer directing Neil Diamond. There have also been several television versions.

Juan. Suddenly, though, here was Jolson not only singing and dancing but speaking informally and spontaneously to other persons in the film as someone might do in reality. The effect was not so much of *hearing* Jolson speak as of *overhearing* him speak, and it thrilled audiences bored with the conventions of silent cinema and increasingly indifferent to the canned performances of the Vitaphone shorts. Thus, we say that the "talkies" were born with *The Jazz Singer* not because it was the first feature-length film to employ synchronized dialogue but because it was the first to employ it in a realistic and seemingly undeliberate way.

The combination of Jolson, Vitaphone, and synchronized dialogue made *The Jazz Singer* an international success, eventually earning over three million dollars. By the end of 1927, it was playing to huge crowds in cities all over the world, and Warner Bros. was already starting to recoup its massive investment in the Vitaphone system. Most important, the film's success had convinced the other Hollywood studios that sound was here to stay in the form of "talking" pictures, and in accordance with the "Big Five Agreement" they began a series of maneuvers to acquire sound-recording equipment of their own.

FOX MOVIETONE

Another organization which hastened the conversion to sound was the Fox Film Corporation, like Warner Bros. a minor studio at the time. In 1927 its president, William Fox, secretly acquired the American rights to the Tri-Ergon sound-on-film process, including the flywheel mechanism, for fifty thousand dollars. A year earlier he had bought the rights to an American sound-on-film system from Theodore W. Case and Earl I. Sponable; this system was similar in many respects to De Forest's Phonofilm and had, in fact, been based on it as the unintended result of a De Forest-Case collaboration between 1922 and 1925. Neither knowing nor caring about the latter,* Fox formed the Fox-Case Corporation in July 1926 to make short sound films with the system and exhibit them in his theaters under the name of Fox Movietone. Fox-Case experimented with Movietone for nearly a year before presenting its first program in New York City on January 21, 1927 (some six months after the premier of Vitaphone), a short series of canned performances by a Spanish cabaret singer, followed by the silent feature *What Price Glory?* (Raoul Walsh, 1926). Several newsreels followed (of marching West Point cadets [April 30]; of Charles A. Lindbergh's fabled takeoff for Paris [May 20]), as well as an ambitious program on May 25, 1927 of three short performance films, including a brief dialogue sketch by comedian Chic Sale entitled "They're Coming to Get Me," followed by the feature film *Seventh Heaven* (Frank Borzage, 1927), with a synchronized orchestral score by Erno Rapee.

---

*He should have done both, since De Forest's suit against Fox for patent infringement helped to cause the mogul's downfall a decade later. *De Forest sold the telephone rights to his audion patents to AT&T in 1913, enabling it to open the first coast-to-coast long-distance circuits in 1915, using vacuum tube reamplifiers, or repeaters. He sold the radio rights to the same company in 1914.

But it was the fifth Movietone program, offered on June 14, 1927, some four months before the opening of *The Jazz Singer,* that received international acclaim and convinced Fox of the value of the "talkies." On a bill with a conventional silent feature, Fox presented Movietone shorts of Lindbergh's reception at the White House by President Coolidge and of a speech by Italian dictator Benito Mussolini. These shorts of famous personalities speaking directly and clearly from the screen electrified the audience, and popular reaction to them was so favorable that Fox and his newsreel producer Courtland Smith established the Fox Movietone News that autumn in response to it. This was the first regular sound newsreel series, and its success was phenomenal. Within the year, Fox Movietone was sending camera crews around the world to interview everyone from George Bernard Shaw to the Pope, and delivering three to four newsreels to Fox theaters per week.

When he inaugurated the Movietone News, Fox was certain that sound was on its way in, so he negotiated a reciprocal contract between Fox-Case and Vitaphone in which each corporation licensed the other to use its sound systems, studios, technicians, and theaters. This had the effect of covering both Fox and Warners if one sound system won out over the other, and of combining their resources to insure survival in the face of any rival system which might be promoted by their competitors. As it turned out, though, most of the competition came over to their side. Financially, 1927 had been a very bad year for every Hollywood studio but Warners, and 1928 was already looking worse. Movie audiences had been dwindling since 1926, when the public apparently began to tire of Hollywood's retrograde production formulas and its heavily promoted stars. In addition, the ready availability of the automobile and the radio to the average American family since the early twenties had created considerable competition for the silent cinema, much as television would challenge the sound film in the late forties and fifties. In 1927, only sound films had been able to regularly attract large audiences, and, according to the film historian Richard Griffith, by the spring of the next year the worst sound film would outdraw the best silent picture in any given community in the country.

THE PROCESS OF CONVERSION

By 1928, then, the American public had clearly chosen sound, and the studios could only acquiesce or be damned. The signatories of the "Big Five Agreement" and their peers were at this point able to choose among several competing optical systems. While still marketing Vitaphone, Western Electric had developed a sophisticated sound-on-film process similar to that of Pedersen and Poulsen* which was ready for diffusion

---

*A rival optical process developed by the Danish engineers P. O. Pederson and Valdemar Poulsen in 1923 used an oscillograph to modulate light in recording and a selenium cell in reproduction, apparently to obviate the Tri-Ergon patents. This process was marketed as Tonfilm in Germany and was licensed by Gaumont in France and British Acoustic, Ltd., in England.

through its nontelephone subsidiary Electrical Research Products, Incorporated (ERPI); Fox stood ready to market Movietone (though he currently lacked the financial muscle to back it up); and Radio Corporation of America (RCA) was offering a newly perfected General Electric system called Photophone. RCA general manager David Sarnoff came very close to winning over Paramount and Loew's, but in the end ERPI's John Otterson was able to offer the studios a better deal, and on May 11, 1928, Paramount, Loew's, First National, and United Artists all signed licensing agreements with Western Electric; Universal, Columbia, Tiffany-Stahl, Hal Roach Comedies, and Christie Comedies soon followed. Sarnoff's reaction was to create his own vertically integrated major to exploit the Photophone process, acquiring Joseph P. Kennedy's production-distribution syndicate Film Booking Office (FBO), Pathé (which had itself just taken over PDC), and the Keith-Albee-Orpheum chain of two hundred downtown vaudeville theaters. This combine was merged as Radio-Keith-Orpheum (RKO), and by the summer of 1928 every studio in Hollywood, willingly or not, had somehow prepared itself for the conversion to sound.

Warner Bros., however, continued to lead the way. Having produced the first "part-talkie"—*The Jazz Singer*—it went on to produce the first "100 percent all-talkie"—*Lights of New York* (Brian Foy, 1928), a clumsily plotted tale of two small-town barbers who come to the city to seek their fortunes and become dangerously involved with a gang of bootleggers. *Lights of New York* ran only fifty-seven minutes and was awkwardly directed, but twenty-two of its twenty-four sequences contained recorded dialogue, making it the first film in history to rely entirely upon the spoken word to sustain its narrative. The enormous popular success of *Lights of New York* demonstrated to Hollywood that all-dialogue films not only could be made but could draw huge audiences as well. In fact, the talkies (or "audible photo-plays," as the trade press called them) were drawing so well by the end of 1928 that it was clear to all that the silent cinema was dead. This was an unexpected blow to the film industry, since it had been assumed by nearly everyone in Hollywood that sound and silent pictures would be able to coexist, for a while at least. Now, suddenly, Hollywood became aware that the public would no longer pay to see silent films.

The upshot was a nearly total conversion to sound by the end of 1929 which radically changed the structure of the film industry and revolutionized the practice of cinema all over the world. In that year, fully three-fourths of all films made in Hollywood were released with some kind of prerecorded sound. *Film Daily Yearbook* for 1929 lists the production of 335 all-dialogue features, ninety-five features with a mixture of dialogue and subtitles, and seventy-five features with musical scores and sound effects. The films in the last two categories were silent pictures to which some sound had hastily been added to satisfy public demand, a common way of salvaging expensively produced silent features during the year of transition. Hollywood also released 175 straight silent features in 1929 for exhibition in those provincial theaters which had not yet been wired for sound (an operation costing between eighty-five hundred

7.8 The first all-dialogue film: Warner Bros.' *Lights of New York* (Brian Foy, 1928). Enormously popular, it returned its producers' $75,000 investment more than fourteen times.

7.9 MGM's *Our Dancing Daughters* (Harry Beaumont, 1928), a silent film hastily salvaged by the addition of Movietone sound effects and a musical score. Joan Crawford is the actress in the center.

and twenty thousand dollars, depending on the seating capacity and the sound process); but by the end of the year, almost every American theater of any size had installed sound equipment. In fact, the number of theaters wired for sound increased more than fifty times between December 31, 1927, and December 31, 1929. As Alexander Walker writes, "There has never been such a lightning retooling of an entire industry—even wartime emergencies were slower. . . ." Yet, the transition was orderly and well-planned, with the Academy of Motion Picture Arts and Sciences functioning as a clearinghouse for information and a general industry resource. Starting in May 1928, it organized intensive educational seminars for studio personnel and set up special committees to help the studios solve technical problems and handle contractual disputes with equipment manufacturers.

The cost of the conversion, however, was staggering, requiring that the studios borrow huge sums of money from Wall Street. In July 1929, Fox's general manager, Winfield Sheehan, estimated that Hollywood had invested more than fifty million dollars in the changeover. The final figure would be in excess of three hundred million—nearly four times the market valuation of the entire industry for fiscal year 1928.* Much of this capital was lent to the studios by the two corporate giants of the era, the Morgan and the Rockefeller groups, which also controlled Western Electric and RCA, thus strengthening the alliance between Hollywood and Wall Street which had begun in the early twenties and which exists ever more visibly today. As Arthur Knight remarks, representatives of the financiers were soon sitting on the boards of the motion picture companies, making policy decisions and giving power to sound engineers imported from the broadcasting and telephone industries who knew nothing about film.

Nevertheless, the prodigious borrowing of 1928–29 was offset by the prodigious profits of the same year. Weekly attendance shot up from sixty million in 1927 to ninety million in 1930, with an increase in box office receipts of 50 percent. After a deficit of over one million dollars in 1927 owing to its heavy investment in Vitaphone, Warner Bros. reported profits of over two million dollars for 1928 and over seventeen million for 1929, when the production company was able to gain control of five hundred exhibition outlets by buying the Stanley theater chain and First National (one of the "Big Three" with which, two years earlier, Warners had been in such unequal competition) to become for over a decade one of the most powerful studios in Hollywood. By 1929, Fox's profits had soared high enough for the company to build itself a new ten million-dollar all-sound studio (Movietone City, in the Los Angeles suburb of Westwood) and for Fox himself to pay fifty million dollars for a controlling interest in Loew's, Inc., which owned MGM, and another twenty

---

*This estimate is from Alexander Walker's well-researched *The Shattered Silents*, and it includes the costs of wiring theaters as well as converting production. Other estimates vary, and the true figure will probably never be known owing to the untrustworthy, if creative, accounting procedures of the day.

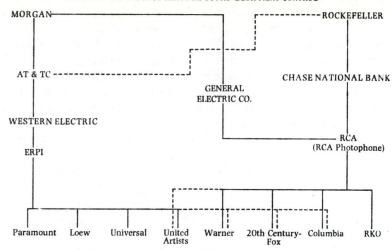

INDIRECT DEPENDENCE THROUGH SOUND EQUIPMENT CONTROL

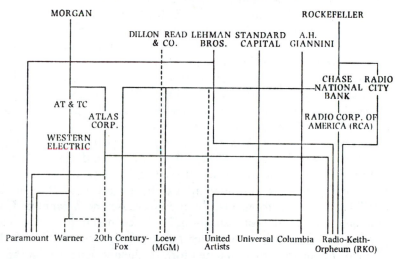

DIRECT FINANCIAL CONTROL OR BACKING, 1936

7.10 Charts showing direct and indirect financial control of the American sound film (and thus of the American film industry) during the thirties. (From F. D. Klingender and Stuart Legg, *Money Behind the Screen* [London, 1937]). Reprinted by permission of Lawrence & Wishart Ltd.) A critique of Klingender and Legg's analysis is contained in Janet Wasko, *Movies and Money* (Norwood, N.J.: Ablex, 1982), Chapter 3, "The Introduction of Sound and Financial Control (1927–1939), pp. 47–102.

million dollars for a 45-percent share of Gaumont-British, England's largest producer/distributor/exhibitor.* In the same year, Paramount, with its

---

* This bid on Fox's part to control the largest production companies and major theater chains in the United States and England respectively, as well as to control all of the West's sound-on-film patents through Movietone, was nothing less than an attempt to consolidate the film industries of both countries under his personal command; and for several months, the "Fox-Loew's Corporation" became the largest motion picture company on earth. This extraordinarily ambitious and avaricious plan collapsed about Fox's ears within a year of its implementation, when the Justice Department of the newly elected Hoover administration (notoriously chummy with Louis B. Mayer, who stood to lose a fortune in the Fox-Loew's deal) ordered Fox to divest himself of the Loew's stock. The stock market crashed simultaneously, killing the Gaumont-British deal and forcing Fox to sell his shares in Loew's

international distribution network and vast Publix theater chain, acquired one-half of the newly formed Columbia Broadcasting System (CBS) and proposed a merger with Warner Bros. If things had continued on course, "Paramount-Vitaphone" and "Fox-Loew's" would have divided the entertainment industries of the entire English-speaking world between them, but the Justice Department of the Hoover administration intervened to prevent these combinations. Most of the other studios' profits doubled between 1928 and 1930 due to the public's mania for the talkies, and it is probably true that the introduction of sound, more than any other single factor, enabled Hollywood to survive the Great Depression, which began with the stock market crash of October 1929.* As Kenneth Macgowan aptly comments: "If the producers had waited till late October 1929—as they might well have done except for the daring of Warner Brothers and Fox—sound would have been impossible for ten more years, and receiverships [bankruptcy] would have come quite some time before 1932."

When the Depression finally did hit Hollywood in 1932, the silent cinema was a distant memory. All sound equipment had been standardized by international agreement in 1930. Sound-on-film—Fox Movietone and RCA Photophone in the United States, Tobis-Klangfilm's Tri-Ergon process on the Continent—had won out over sound-on-disk because of the superior quality of reproduction in the former and the massive problems of synchronization posed by the latter. Sound-on-film had also proved the most flexible system for recording on location, as the naturalistic soundtrack of Fox's *In Old Arizona* (Raoul Walsh, 1928), the first all-talkie shot outdoors, had demonstrated. The immense profits Warners had reaped from Vitaphone enabled it to switch systems in its studios and theaters without risk. And in 1935, after nine years of litigation, Dr. Lee De Forest, who had spent $200,000 of his own funds developing the sound-on-film system that Hollywood eventually adopted, but who had lacked the resources to promote it, was finally awarded the sum of $100,000 for patent infringement by the Fox-Case and Vitaphone Corporations. Even with the compensation, De Forest had to borrow money to pay his legal fees, but he had at least won the right to call himself the inventor of the process that changed forever the aesthetic configuration of the cinema.

---

at a thirty-million-dollar loss. In 1931, Fox was ousted from his company by a coalition of executives and stockholders, and he finally declared bankruptcy in 1936. His legal entanglements continued until 1941, when he was sentenced to a year in prison for attempting to bribe a federal judge at his bankruptcy hearing. After serving six months of the term in 1943, he retired to live reasonably well on the several sound film patents he had managed to retain through the court battles of the thirties. Fox's apologia for this incredible career is contained in *Upton Sinclair Presents William Fox* (Los Angeles, 1933).

* Some characteristic studio profits for fiscal year 1929 were: Warner Brothers $17,271,805; Fox $9,469,050; Paramount $15,544,544; and MGM $11,756,956.

THE INTRODUCTION OF COLOR

The so-called "natural" or photographic color processes became institutionalized at approximately the same time as sound, although, like sound,
color had been a component of the film experience for a long time. Hand-
tinting had been widely practiced during the primitive period when films
were short enough to make it commercially viable. Méliès, for example,
employed twenty-one women at Montreuil to hand-tint his most spectacular films frame by frame, and Edison regularly tinted portions of his
films (e.g., the bursts of gunsmoke in Porter's *The Great Train Robbery*
[1903]). In 1905, as the length of films and the number of prints required
by exhibitors increased, Charles Pathé invented the Pathécolor stencil
process (renamed Pathéchrome in 1929) to mechanize the application of
color. Frame-by-frame stencils were cut by pantograph to correspond to
those areas to be tinted in any one of six standard colors. After a stencil
had been made for the whole length of film, it was placed into contact
with the print to be colored and run at high speed (60 feet per minute)
through a staining machine, a process repeated for each set of stencils
and dyes to be applied. By 1910, Pathé Frères employed over four hundred
women in its stencilling operation at the Vincennes factory (Gaumont
had adopted a similar system in 1905), and the process was used in Europe
well into the thirties. In the United States, another form of stencilling was
patented in 1916 by the St. Louis engraver Max Handschiegl and cinematographer Alvin Wyckoff of the Famous Players–Lasky Corporation
laboratory. Popularly known as the Handschiegl process, it employed the

7.11 *The Phantom of the Opera* (Rupert Julian,
1925): Lon Chaney, Mary Philbin. This sequence
was originally shot in Technicolor's two-color
"cemented-positive" process.

principles of three-color lithography to machine-tint such big-budget studio productions as Cecil B. DeMille's *Joan, the Woman* (1917), Erich von Stroheim's *Greed* (1924) and *The Merry Widow* (1925), Rupert Julian's *Phantom of the Opera* (1925), and King Vidor's *The Big Parade* (1925).

As film became a major international industry during the twenties, however, the need to mass-produce prints led to the development of tinting and toning, both mechanized nonphotographic color processes. Tinting, the most commonly used, involved immersing black-and-white positive stock in a bath of dye, whose color was varied according to the mood and / or setting of a given scene. (Theoretically, at least—in practice, the colors were often chosen arbitrarily from a range of exotically trade-named dyes, including Verdante, Azure, Nocturne, Purplehaze, Fleur de lis, Amaranth, Inferno, Argent, Rose doree, Firelight, Peachblow, and Sunshine.) Toning affected only the black-silver portion of the image, leaving the rest of the film translucent; it was accomplished by chemically treating the silver to convert it into colored silver salts. Whereas tinting produced a uniform color throughout, toning colored only the half-tones and shadows. The two processes could also be used in combination to produce more elaborate effects, such as an orange-tinted sunset in a blue-toned sky; and by the early twenties 80–90 percent of all American films used some form of tinting or toning for at least some scenes. But the colors provided by both were notably artificial, and the coming of sound presented new problems because the dyes used in tinting and toning interfered with the soundtrack by absorbing too much light. Eastman Kodak responded quickly in 1929 by introducing Sonochrome, a black-and-white positive stock available on a range of sixteen tinted bases corresponding to the standard dyes used in tinting. But by this time developments in the field of color cinematography had overtaken the quest for color.*

The principles on which color photography is based were first proposed by the Scottish physicist James Clerk Maxwell (1831–79) in 1855 and demonstrated by him at the Royal Institution in London in 1861. At this time, it was known that light is comprised of a spectrum of different

---

* Tinting and toning continued to be used for expressive effect well into the sound era and are occasionally used for the same end today. In the thirties and forties Westerns were often filmed on sepia-tinted stock to evoke old photographs, and several important films of the period—e.g., *The Rains Came* (Clarence Brown, 1939), *Of Mice and Men* (Lewis Milestone, 1939), *Ziegfield Girl* (Robert Z. Leonard, 1941), *Tortilla Flat* (Victor Fleming, 1942)—employed sepia toning for the same purpose. David O. Selznick used green tinting for the storm sequence of *Portrait of Jennie* (William Dieterle, 1948), and RKO's *Mighty Joe Young* (Ernest B. Schoedsack, 1949) was tinted red for a fire sequence and amber for the sentimental conclusion. Postwar science fiction films had occasional recourse to tinting (e.g., bluish pink for the Mars sequence of *Rocketship XM* [Kurt Neumann, 1950], green for the lost world in *The Lost Continent* [Samuel Newfield, 1951]), as have such major directors as Alfred Hitchcock (the orange-red gunblast into the audience in *Spellbound* [1945]; the red suffusions indicating psychological disorder in *Marnie* [1965]) and Sergei Parajanov (*Shadows of Forgotten Ancestors* [1964] makes extensive use of both tinting and toning).

wavelengths which are perceived as different colors as they are absorbed and reflected by natural objects. What Maxwell discovered was that all natural colors in this spectrum are composed of different combinations of three primary colors—red, green, and blue—which, when mixed together equally, produce white. Color, it followed, could be produced either by adding together various measures of the primary colors or by subtracting various measures from white light. These two methods, the additive and the subtractive, are the ones that have been used to produce color photographically in film.

The first process to successfully employ these principles in motion-picture photography was Charles Urban's two-color sequential additive system Kinemacolor. It was based on the work of Brighton filmmaker G. A. Smith, who in 1906 had discovered that by fusing two primary colors, red and green, through persistence of vision, he could obtain a range of colors nearly equivalent to those produced by three.* The American entrepreneur Charles Urban (1871–1942) bought the patent rights and demonstrated the system publicly as Kinemacolor before the Royal Society of Arts on December 9, 1908. Urban and Smith began commercial operations shortly thereafter, forming the Natural Color Kinematograph Company to produce and distribute Kinemacolor films. At first, these were shown on an occasional basis in London, Nottingham, and Blackpool, but by April 1911 Urban had begun showing complete programs of Kinemacolor actualitiés, such as the coronation of George V, at the Scala in London. Kinemacolor's most spectacular production and greatest commercial succcess was the two-and-one-half hour *Durbar at Delhi* (1912), shot on location in India by Urban and a crew of twenty-three cameramen. By 1913, Kinemacolor films were being shown regularly in thirteen countries, including the United States, where Kinemacolor of America was incorporated in 1910; and Urban had camera crews all over the world shooting and releasing new films at the rate of two to three per week.

Yet by 1915, Kinemacolor was all but defunct, a victim of patent litigation brought on by the rival Bioschemes, Ltd.; as a result, Smith's patent was revoked in April 1914. Other difficulties affecting Kinemacolor were the rising popularity of dramatic features at a time when the company was militantly committed to the factual film, and technological problems inherent in the system itself, among which were color fringing in moving objects and the poor registration of blues. But Urban had demonstrated that a lucrative market existed world-wide for color films and, as Gorham Kindem points out, no color process seems to have rivaled the early commercial success of Kinemacolor until Technicolor began to market its two-color subtractive process in the 1920s.

Still, other systems were constantly being developed and tested, including such three-color additive systems as Gaumont's Chronochrome (pat-

---

* The claim that two colors could transmit the full spectrum contradicts classical color theory. Nevertheless, the CBS field-sequential color television system first broadcast in 1951 operated on the same principle.

ented 1912), which used a three-lens camera and projector, and such two-color non-sequential additive systems as Cinechrome (1914) and British Raycol (1929). In the two-color non-sequential additive systems, a single camera lens was fitted with a system of prisms which split the light beam in two, creating two pairs of red and green exposures simultaneously, which would be superimposed in projection. Ultimately, however, additive systems proved too complicated, costly, and imprecise* to bring color wholesale into the cinema. The first entirely successful motion-picture color system was two-strip subtractive Technicolor.

The Technicolor Corporation was formed in 1915 in Boston by Dr. Herbert T. Kalmus (1881–1963), Dr. Daniel F. Comstock, and W. Burton Wescott† as an offshoot of their successful industrial consulting firm, to exploit a two-color additive process in which a prismatic beam-splitter produced separate red and green exposures in-camera and superimposed them in projection. The company produced only one film in this process, *The Gulf Between* (Irvin Willat, 1917); its failure led Kalmus to abandon the additive system for a subtractive one. His goal was to have both color components printed in register on positive film stock and eliminate the superimposition of images in projection (and thus special projectors). The new system, patented in 1922, used a beam-splitting camera to produce two separate negatives which were printed separately as positives on specially thin-based Kodak stock. These were then chemically treated to remove the silver and form transparent "relief images" of exposed gelatin, dyed red-orange on one print and green on the other. Finally, the two relief prints were cemented base-to-base for projection through an ordinary projector.

The industry was so excited by this innovation that Loew's, Inc., offered to produce Technicolor's first film in the process, *The Toll of the Sea* (Chester Franklin, 1922), which was supervised by Joseph M. Schenck and released through Metro Film Company by Nicholas Schenck. The film was a great success, grossing more than $250,000 (of which Technicolor received approximately $165,000), and it demonstrated the commercial viability of subtractive Technicolor in no uncertain terms. Although its cost was inordinately high (Technicolor had to charge twenty cents per foot for release prints), this "cemented positive" process worked well enough to be used for color sequences in several major productions of 1923–24, including Paramount's *The Ten Commandments* (Cecil B.

---

* All additive systems suffered from a loss of illumination in projection, with as much as 70 percent of the light being absorbed by the color filters, causing registration difficulties. In additions, systems like Kinemacolor and Chronochrome, which involve high-speed shooting and projection, used more film stock and required more rapid print replacement than black-and-white. Finally, the special projection equipment required by additive systems at a time when the exhibition sector was becoming increasingly powerful and conservative militated against their use.

†Kalmus and Comstock were alumni of the Massachusetts Institute of Technology who had returned to teach there after earning Ph.D.s abroad, and many of the company's early employees were MIT students. As Kalmus was later to acknowledge, MIT is the "Tech" in Technicolor.

DeMille, 1923) First National's *Cytherea* (George Fitzmaurice, 1924), and MGM's *The Merry Widow* (von Stroheim, 1925), and for such complete features as Jesse L. Lasky's *Wanderer of the Wasteland* (Irvin Willat, 1924) and Douglas Fairbanks' *The Black Pirate* (Albert Parker, 1926).

In 1928, however, Technicolor introduced an improved two-color process in which the two relief prints became *matrices* for the transfer of dyes to a third and final print. Specifically, when the matrix prints were brought into contact with a blank, gelatin-coated film, the dyes were transferred in exact registration through a process known as *imbibition,* which became the basis for the Technicolor process from 1928 through the seventies. Imbibition dye-transfer eliminated the use of a "cemented positive" and made it possible to mass produce release prints from the matrices, which could simply be re-dyed between successive transfers.

The innovation of Technicolor's second subtractive system, of course, coincided with the coming of sound, and this circumstance helped to create a boomlet for the process. For one thing, as noted earlier, dyes used in the nonphotographic tinting and toning processes so popular during the twenties were rendered obsolete by sound because they interfered with the optical soundtrack. Although this problem was addressed by Eastman Kodak's introduction of Sonochrome in 1929, it gave Technicolor an open field during the most crucial year of the conversion. For another thing, many early sound films were musicals, a genre whose fantastic, spectacular nature was particularly suited to color representation.* In fact, Technicolor's new process was first used for sequences in *Broadway Melody* (Harry Beaumont, 1929) and *The Desert Song* (Roy Del Ruth, 1929), and the first all-Technicolor sound films were Warner Bros.' *On with the Show* (Alan Crosland, 1929) and *Gold Diggers of Broadway* (Roy Del Ruth, 1929)—both smashing box-office hits, the latter grossing over $3,500,000.

In 1930, Technicolor was under contract for thirty-six features, some of the most lavishly produced in that year, including *Whoopee!* (Thorton C. Freeland), *The Vagabond King* (Ludwig Berger), *No, No, Nanette* (Clarence Badger), *Rio Rita* (Luther Reed), *Paramount on Parade* (Dorothy Arzner and Otto Brower), and *Rogue Song* (Lionel Barrymore). Yet by 1932 the production of Technicolor films had nearly ceased. The sudden rush to color failed because audiences grew increasingly dissatisfied with the poor registration of the two-color process, in which flesh tones could vary from pink to orange (according to Technicolor, a phenomenon resulting from misuse of the process by untrained studio cameramen), and also because the process itself was expensive, adding as much as 30 percent (or $100,000 to $300,000 in Depression currency) to the production costs of the average feature and raising distribution costs from three to five cents a foot over black-and-white. By contrast, recent

---

* According to Gorham Kindem in "Hollywood's Conversion to Color," fourteen of seventeen full-color features and twenty-three of thirty-four black-and-white features with color sequences released in 1929 and 1930 were musicals (*American Movie Industry,* p. 156).

improvements (c. 1925) in Eastman's panchromatic stock had made it sensitive to a wider range of tones than ever before and lowered its price; and in 1928 incandescent, or tungsten, lighting had been established as the relatively inexpensive norm (as opposed to the arc lighting required by Technicolor) for use with it. Thus, black-and-white became the standard medium for the sound film through the early fifties, when less expensive color and lighting systems were devised.

In 1932, however, Technicolor perfected the three-color system whose predictability and accuracy was to give it a virtual monopoly over the production of color in motion pictures for the next twenty years. The camera employed a prismatic beam-splitter behind the lens to expose three separate black-and-white negatives running through two gates at right angles to one another (see diagram). The gate on the left contained a "bipack" of two negatives, the one in front dyed red-orange so that it absorbed the blue light and filtered the red light through to the one behind it. The gate on the right contained a single negative sensitive to green. Each of these "color separation" negatives would be developed as matrices for the same imbibition dye-transfer process used previously by Technicolor's two-color systems, resulting in a single three-color release print. (A blank silver negative containing the optical soundtrack was combined with the matrices during the imbibition stage, and Technicolor sometimes used a black fourth matrix to achieve a subtler range of colors, as was the case with *Gone with the Wind* [Victor Fleming, 1939].)

Bipack Film: *(emulsion surfaces in contact), front sensitive to BLUE; rear sensitive to RED*

Film: *receiving GREEN image; emulsion facing prism.*

LIGHT: *enters camera through lens*

Magenta Filter: *transmitting red and blue light*

Aperture II

Aperture I

Filter. *transmitting green light only*

Aperture plates

Gold-flecked Mirror: *(between prisms) which allows some light to pass straight through Aperture I; the rest being deflected at right angles through Aperture II*

Richard Harrison

The three-color system was technically superior to any yet produced, but still it had its drawbacks. The "three-strip" cameras, which cost $30,000 apiece to manufacture, were large and heavy, complicating location shooting, and the process of exposing three black-and-white negatives simultaneously required a great deal of light, which further increased production costs. Furthermore, as David Bordwell has pointed out, because the 1929–31 two-strip boom had resulted in so many unqualified cinematographers using the process, Technicolor standardized three-strip filming procedures and exerted a large measure of control over production:

> To make a Technicolor film, a producer had to rent the cameras, hire a Technicolor cameraman (eventually to be called a "camera optical engineer"), use Technicolor make-up, and have the film processed and printed by Technicolor. The producer would also have to accept a "color consultant" who would advise what color schemes to use on sets, costumes, and make up. . . . Only trained crews could operate the camera, and the production's cinematographer had to work closely with the Technicolor cameraman. (*The Classical Hollywood Cinema*, p. 354.)[14]

For all of these reasons, plus the general decline in film attendance caused by the Depression, producers were a good deal more conservative about adopting three-color Technicolor than its predecessors. Technicolor, for similar reasons, did not want to venture into production on its own, so it offered the process initially to the small independents Walt Disney and Pioneer Films (operated by Merian C. Cooper and John Whitney); and Disney became the first to use it in his "Silly Symphony" cartoon *Flowers and Trees* (1932) and *The Three Little Pigs* (1933), which were so successful—both winning Oscars and *Pigs* grossing over $750,000—that Disney contracted with Technicolor for a whole series of films and ultimately adopted the process for all of his studio's productions. (Disney actually negotiated a three-year exclusive contract for use of Technicolor in the field of animation in 1933, but it was subsequently revised to one year in order to accommodate demand from the majors.)*

The first live-action film in three-color Technicolor was Pioneer Films' *La Cucaracha* (1934), a thinly plotted two-reel short focusing on the romantic passions of two cantina dancers. The film was basically an extended test of the process under conditions of live production, and it impressed the industry so favorably that it won the 1934 Academy Award for the best Comedy Short Subject. Buoyed by this success, Pioneer ventured the first three-color feature, an 83-minute version of Thackeray's classic Victorian novel *Vanity Fair* (1847–48), entitled *Becky Sharp* (Rouben Mamoulian, 1935).† At first, audiences rushed to see the one-

---

* Disney retained exclusive rights to three-color Technicolor until the spring of 1935, while the other animators were allowed to use only the two-color process. See Richard Neupert, "A Studio Built of Bricks: Disney and Technicolor," *Film Reader 6: Investigations in Film History and Technology* (1985): 33–40.

† Technicolor produced a total of 448 prints of the film, of which none has survived. Ironically, until it was restored by the UCLA Film Archives in 1984, *Becky Sharp* could only be seen in an inferior two-color Cinecolor version and in an edited-for-television black-and-

million-dollar costume film, but after a few weeks interest peaked, and the release ended in commercial failure. Undaunted, Kalmus organized a British subsidiary, Technicolor, Ltd., which in 1936 produced England's first Technicolor feature, the race-track melodrama *Wings of the Morning* (Harold Schuster). In Hollywood, the majors began to cautiously test the waters—20th Century-Fox with a rendition of the classic Indian saga *Ramona* (Henry King, 1936) and Paramount with *Trail of the Lonesome Pine* (Henry Hathaway, 1936), the first Technicolor film shot entirely on location. But it was David O. Selznick's newly formed independent company Selznick International that proved the commercial viability of Technicolor feature production once and for all with the star-studded hits *The Garden of Allah* (Richard Boleslawski, 1936; with Charles Boyer and Marlene Dietrich), *Nothing Sacred* (William Wellman, 1937; with Fredric March and Carole Lombard), and *A Star Is Born* (William Wellman, 1937; Fredric March and Janet Gaynor), the first and last of which were honored with Special Academy Awards for their color cinematography (to the team of W. Howard Greene and Harold Rossen). Selznick scored again in 1938 with *The Adventures of Tom Sawyer* (Norman Taurog), and by this time nearly the whole industry had climbed on the bandwagon—MGM with *Sweethearts* (W. S. Van Dyke, 1938; first Academy Award in newly created Color Cinematography classification to Oliver Marsh); Paramount with *Ebb Tide* (James Hogan, 1937), *Vogues of 1938* (Irving Cummings, 1938), *Men with Wings* (William Wellman, 1938), and *Her Jungle Love* (George Archainbaud, 1938); 20th Century-Fox with *Kentucky* (David Butler, 1938); Sam Goldwyn Productions with the lavish musical review *The Goldwyn Follies* (George Marshall, 1938); London Films (Alexander Korda) with *Drums* (Zoltan Korda, 1938) and *The Divorce of Lady X* (Tim Whelan, 1938), and, most prominently, Walt Disney with *Snow White and the Seven Dwarfs* (1937), the first full-length animated feature, and Warner Bros. with *Robin Hood* (Michael Curtiz, 1938), a film whose aesthetic use of the Technicolor system earned it three Academy Awards.

By the end of the year, Technicolor had twenty-five features in production, and on the books for the banner year of 1939–40 were Fox's *The Little Princess* (Walter Lang, 1939) and *Drums Along the Mohawk* (John Ford, 1939), Warner Bros.' *Dodge City* (Michael Curtiz, 1939) and *The Privates Lives of Elizabeth and Essex* (Michael Curtiz, 1939), two Disney features—*Fantasia* (1940) and *Pinocchio* (1940)—and the era's quintessential blockbusters, MGM's *The Wizard of Oz* (Victor Fleming, 1939) and David O. Selznick's *Gone with the Wind* (Victor Fleming, 1939). Though not technically a full-length color film since it began and ended in sepia, *The Wizard of Oz* sustained its illusion of fantasy through the most imaginative and sophisticated use of Technicolor yet (amply assisted by the stunning art direction of Cedric Gibbons and William A. Horn-

---

white print. The Archive next plans to restore *Toll of the Sea*, the first two-color subtractive feature, from the original negative. For details, see Robert Gitt and Richard Dayton, "Restoring *Becky Sharp*," *American Cinematographer* 65, 10 (November 1984): 99–106.

ing). *Gone with the Wind,* on the other hand, was the first film to be shot using Technicolor's new, faster, fine-grained stock—a major technical breakthrough in that it cut lighting levels by 50 percent, bringing them closer to those used for monochrome. This in turn provided for the use of smaller, directional units for facial lighting, improved color rendition (especially in the green part of the spectrum), and increased depth of field. Appropriately, when *Gone with the Wind* swept the Academy Awards for 1939, Ray Rennahan and Ernest Haller shared the Oscar for its cinematography and William Cameron Menzies received a special plaque for his "outstanding achievement in the use of color for the enhancement of dramatic mood" in the film.

During the forties, the improved three-color system received greater use in such major productions as *Blood and Sand* (Rouben Mamoulian, 1941), *The Black Swan* (Henry King, 1942), *Henry V* (Lawrence Olivier, 1944), *Leave Her to Heaven* (John M. Stahl, 1945), *The Yearling* (Clarence Brown, 1946), *Forever Amber* (Otto Preminger, 1947), and *Black Narcissus* (Michael Powell, 1947), but it was still limited by its expense and the Technicolor Corporation's virtual monopoly of the field. The former was improved somewhat in 1941 by the introduction of Technicolor Monopack, a multilayered film stock based on Eastman Kodachrome. Monopack produced a direct color positive from exposure in a conventional camera, which was then printed through red, green, and blue filters as separate matrices for the Technicolor dye-transfer process. The new stock proved valuable for location shooting, since it eliminated the bulky three-strip camera, and it was first used for aerial sequences (*Dive Bomber* [1941] and *Captain of the Clouds* [1942, both Michael Curtiz]) and exteriors (*The Forest Rangers* [George Marshall, 1942]; *Lassie Come Home* [Fred M. Wilcox, 1943]). By 1944, Monopack had been improved to the point that it could be used to shoot entire features (e.g., *Thunderhead—Son of Flicka* [Louis King, 1945]), and Kalmus seriously considered abandoning the three-strip process in favor of it. But the postwar film attendance boom escalated the demand for Technicolor services and prevented any wholesale conversion until the fifties, when the rival Eastmancolor system—cheaper, faster, but less stable—rendered the three-strip Technicolor camera obsolete, as we will see in Chapter 12.

PROBLEMS OF EARLY SOUND RECORDING

It is important to note that the introduction of sound is analogous in almost every respect to the invention of the cinema itself. In each case, the technological principles upon which the invention was based had been known for decades prior to their combination into a workable apparatus. In each case, the apparatus was developed and exploited for the purposes of novelty and commerce without a thought to aesthetic ends (early "movies" are comparable to early "talkies" in that both initially exploited their most novel feature at the expense of proportion and common sense).

Finally, there was a long delay between the introduction of the sophisticated machine and the sophisticated artistic use of it.

The aesthetic and technical problems caused by the introduction of sound to the cinema were immense, and, if the transition was orderly from a corporate perspective, inside the studio sound stages there was confusion often bordering on chaos. For one thing, there were initially three competing systems (Western Electric Vitaphone, Fox Movietone, and RCA Photophone), none of which was compatible with the others, and equipment for all three was being so constantly modified and redesigned that it was sometimes obsolete before being uncrated.

The most serious problems involved sound recording in production (there was no postrecording yet), but there were also less spectacular difficulties at the exhibition sites. The initial deployment in 1928 of RCA Photophone, the optical sound system which was to become the industry standard, provides a good example of these. For one thing, RCA's original theater speakers were of the twelve-inch cone type, nondirectional and barely adequate for speech reproduction. By early 1929 RCA was forced to add five-foot horns to its speakers to improve their directional quality. These "directional baffles" were used with modest success in Photophone-wired theaters until a cross-licensing agreement in 1930 permitted RCA to install the superior horn-type speakers originally patented by Western Electric for its Vitaphone system. These speakers were highly directional and concentrated sound energy on the audience rather than diffusing it throughout the auditorium, and they eventually were adopted industry-wide.

Another immediate problem lay in projection. Before 1928, projection depended on the regular but intermittent motion of the film strip as it passed frame by frame between the lamp and shutter and the lens. To insure fidelity of reproduction, however, the optically recorded soundtrack had to move with constant linear velocity across the photoelectric sound head. And, since in all optical systems the image track and the soundtrack were separated by only twenty frames, intermittent motion would be transferred to the sound head, causing audio distortion. RCA met the problems first with a mechanical "compensator" and then with a series of filters, which were not perfected and adopted as the industry standard until 1930. A further difficulty for exhibitors during the early transitional period was the necessity of maintaining both sound-on-disk and sound-on-film reproduction equipment until a uniform industry standard was chosen. As late as 1931, studios were still releasing films in both formats to accommodate theaters owned by sound-on-disk interests.

More important, as it has become almost axiomatic to say, the movies ceased to move when they began to talk, because between 1928 and 1931 they virtually regressed to their infancy in terms of editing and camera movement. In large part this was because the early microphones that were used to record sound had two substantial defects. First, they had a very limited range, so that to be heard on the soundtrack at all actors were forced to speak directly into them. This had the regressive effect of

7.12 On an unidentified Vitaphone set, 1927. Note the camera booth and microphone.

7.13 A Vitaphone camera in its soundproof booth.

rendering actors motionless within the frame while they delivered their lines, and led to some remarkable exercises in concealing microphones on the set in flowerpots, ship's lanterns, and clumps of sagebrush. The second major defect of the microphones was, paradoxically, that within their limited range they were highly sensitive and omnidirectional—they picked up and recorded *every sound* made within their range on the set. This characteristic not only created problems in sound engineering but rendered the camera almost totally inert: in order to avoid distortion in the synchronized soundtrack, all cameras were motorized to run at a standard speed (24 fps) in 1929. This meant, for one thing, that cameras could no longer be undercranked or overcranked by their operators to achieve expressive effects. But motorization also caused cameras to make a noisy, whirring clatter which would inevitably be picked up by the microphones. To prevent this, early sound cameras and their operators were at first enclosed in soundproof glass-paneled booths, six feet on a side, ironically dubbed "iceboxes" because they were so hot and stuffy. This practice literally imprisoned the camera, since it could neither tilt nor track (although it could pan as much as 30 degrees on its tripod), which helps to account for the static nature of so many early sound films. At their worst, these resembled the "filmed theater" of Méliès and *film d'art* far more than they resembled their immediate silent predecessors.

In fact, sound recording briefly rendered the cinema even *more* static than the filmed plays of its first decade because actors had to keep within range of both a static microphone *and* a static camera. Not only was the frame or camera itself rendered motionless, but the actors had to remain motionless *within* the frame (that is, within a given camera set-up) if they were to have their voices picked up by the crude recording equipment. In filmed plays like *Queen Elizabeth* (1912) the actors, at least, could move around on the set, even though the cameras didn't move at all, but now they too were rendered immobile.

Another production problem was studio lighting. The carbon arc lamps which had provided principle lighting during the twenties produced a

7.14 Sound men inside a studio monitor booth.

7.15 An early recording room.

humming noise and could not be used when recording synchronized dialogue. In 1930, muting circuits were selectively introduced in the arcs, but most studios had by then converted to incandescent tungsten lamps. These were less intense than arcs and had their own liabilities—as, for example, the sheer numbers required to light for two or three cameras at once, as was often the case in the early sound period when multiple shots would be made of the same scene to avoid editing the soundtrack in postproduction.

The impact of sound recording on film editing was probably the single most important factor in causing the regression of the transitional era. In the silent film, editing was unrestricted by content: dialogue was scarcely ever spoken word by word and intertitles could either encapsulate it or eliminate it altogether to facilitate the montage structure of a given sequence. In the early sound film, editing—like camera movement, placement, and lighting—was subordinated absolutely to the technology of recording dialogue and became purely functional rather than expressive. In sound-on-disk films, scenes were initially made to play for nearly ten minutes in order for dialogue to be recorded continuously on sixteen-inch disks. Editing these scenes was out of the question, of course, until the technology of rerecording was perfected in the early thirties, although if multiple cameras were used to shoot the same scene some variety could be added to the image track.* (It was also possible, if not very practical, to vary "shots" by alternating lenses of different focal length within the same camera set-up.) Sound-on-film systems also militated against editing at first because of the necessary displacement between image and soundtrack in optical systems, in which the sound runs twenty frames in advance of its corresponding image.† This initially made it impossible to edit a composite optical print without eliminating portions of the relevant sound. In both sound-on-disk and sound-on-film systems, therefore, most early editing was largely *transitional*—a device for changing lin-

---

* David Bordwell points out that multiple-camera shooting became the dominant studio practice from 1929 to 1931, as filmmakers strove to retain the option of cutting. The resultant editing structures, however, were "repetitive, even routine" (Bordwell, Thompson, and Staiger, *The Classical Hollywood Cinema* [New York: Columbia University Press, 1985], Ch. 23, "The Introduction of Sound," p. 305). See also Ron Mottram, "American Sound Films, 1926–1930," Elizabeth Weis and John Belton, eds., *Film Sound: Theory and Practice* (New York: Columbia University Press, 1985), pp. 221–31.

† Since it is mechanically impossible for the lens and the sound head of a projector to be located in the same place, there must be a displacement between image and soundtrack on composite sound-on-film exhibition prints. In 35mm filming, the soundtrack runs twenty frames in advance of the corresponding image track, making it impossible to edit a composite print without eliminating portions of the relevant sound. (In many of today's magnetic recording systems the sound runs *behind* the image, and the separation varies a great deal from one format to the other.) From a production standpoint, this problem was resolved by the introduction and refinement of postsynchronization, or dubbing, between 1929 and 1932. But to keep very early dialogue scenes from lapsing into inertia, the same sequence was frequently filmed simultaneously by as many as four cameras and later intercut. In this way, the images could be varied while the soundtrack remained constant, but the method was prohibitively expensive.

7.16 On the set of *Lummox* (Herbert Brenon, 1930). Before the advent of post-synchronization, any sounds to be heard simultaneously in the finished film had to be recorded simultaneously on the set. Here, a mother (right) listens to her daughter (left) singing in the room next door, which required that the two scenes be photographed and recorded at the same time.

early from one scene to the next, rather than a mode for expressing multiple points of view—since, in general, cuts could only be made (as the camera could only be moved) when no sound was being recorded synchronously on the set. Crosscutting between actors speaking to one another, close-ups intercut with shots of other spatial lengths, all the editing syntax of Griffith, the montage structure of Eisenstein, and the fluid, expressive camera movement introduced by Murnau and Freund—all were effectively, if temporarily, eliminated by the clumsy technology of early sound recording. They were replaced by a series of talking photographs taken from the same angle at medium range and varied only when the talking stopped. Ironically, Edison's original conception of the film as a sequence of moving pictures to accompany and illustrate sound recordings was fully realized in the first few years of the sound era.

To make matters worse, the studio were so anxious to exploit the novelty of sound and amortize their borrowings that they turned to scripts (called "properties") which emphasized and even exaggerated the cinema's new inertia. Many producers assumed that the sound film would provide a perfect medium for photographing stage hits with their original casts and bringing them to a mass audience; between 1929 and 1931 much of the American cinema became "canned theater" in which Broadway plays and musicals were transferred from stage to screen verbatim with little or no adaptation. The impulse to record stage performances live on film at the beginning of the sound era was the same as that which had motivated the *film d'art* craze of 1908–12, and its failure was no less emphatic. The public rapidly tired of these "100 percent all-talking" productions (or "teacup dramas," as they were sometimes called), but they had the lasting effect of bringing Broadway players and directors to Hol-

7.17 "Canned theater": Warner Bros.' *Disreali* (Alfred E. Green, 1929). George Arliss, Anthony Bushell.

lywood on a more or less permanent basis.* Similarly, the urgent necessity for dialogue scripts revolutionized the profession of screenwriting and caused the studios to import literary talent from the East in the form of editors and critics, playwrights and novelists, many of whom stayed on to make lasting contributions to the quality and sophistication of American sound films.†

Actors with stage experience were especially valuable during the early sound era, because directors could no longer shout out instructions on the set as they had done before and therefore needed players who could work on their own through long dialogue takes. They also needed players with good voices and clear articulation, which meant that stage actors, and film actors with stage experience,** rapidly replaced many silent stars who spoke with heavy foreign accents (like Emil Jannings, Pola Negri, Vilma Banky, and Lya de Putti) or whose voices somehow did not match their screen images (like Norma Talmadge, Colleen Moore, Corinne Griffith, and John Gilbert††). Other silent stars, such as Greta Garbo, Gary Cooper, and Janet Gaynor, were able to make the transition with the aid of voice specialists and diction coaches from the theater world. The advent of sound caused other new arrivals in Hollywood. Sound technicians from the broadcasting and telephone industries who had no understanding of filmmaking suddenly appeared on the studio sets endowed

---

* Among the Broadway players who came to stay were George Arliss, Helen Hayes, Humphrey Bogart, Fredric March, Leslie Howard, Clark Gable, Sylvia Sidney, Fred Astaire, Paul Muni, Spencer Tracy, and Katharine Hepburn. The directors included Richard Boleslawski, George Cukor, and Rouben Mamoulian. For a brief period in 1928, it even seemed as though the migration might be reversed and that the film industry might shift its production base back to New York City in order to be close to Broadway talent (it took nearly four days to cross the country by train in this era; only the super-rich could afford to fly) and to the sophisticated audio technology of the recording and broadcasting industries. By midsummer of that year, Paramount, MGM, First National, and Warners had all set up soundstages in New York, but after a brief flurry of filmmaking activity there, economies of scale brought the conversion back home to Hollywood. See Alexander Walker, *The Shattered Silents,* pp. 90–106.

† (Among the more prominent—Herman Mankiewicz, Robert Benchley, P. G. Wodehouse, Donald Ogden Steward, Dorothy Parker, Samson Raphaelson, S. J. Perelman, S. N. Behrman, Charles Lederer, Ben Hecht, Charles MacArthur, George S. Kaufman, Maxwell Anderson, James M. Cain, Dashiell Hammett, F. Scott Fitzgerald, William Faulkner, and Nathanael West.

** These included Ronald Colman; Claudette Colbert; William Powell; Ethel, John, and Lionel Barrymore; George Bancroft; Herbert Marshall; Marie Dressler; Clive Brook; Boris Karloff; and Charles Laughton. British actors like Colman, Brook, Marshall, and Laughton were particularly valued in Hollywood for their low-pitched, well-modulated voices which registered with near perfection on the soundtrack.

†† A recent biography by Gilbert's daughter, Leatrice Gilbert Fountain, maintains that her father's early sound-film appearances were mechanically sabotaged during the recording process by MGM executive Louis B. Mayer, who apparently hated every artist in his employ (*Dark Star,* with John R. Maxim [New York: St. Martin's Press, 1985]). This may indeed be true, but there is significant evidence to suggest that audiences conditioned by the silents did not *want* their favorite screen idols to talk at all and were inevitably disappointed when voices made them merely human.

with tremendous authority to determine camera and microphone placement. Arthur Knight writes of their brief but dictatorial rule: "[The] experts, concerned with nothing beyond the sound quality of the pictures they worked on, continually simplified their problems by insisting that scenes be played in corners, minimizing long-shots for the more readily controllable close-up. In no time at all the techniques, the artistry that directors had acquired through years of silent films were cast aside and forgotten in the shadow of the microphone."

THE THEORETICAL DEBATE OVER SOUND

Indeed, so great a threat to the cinema as a creative form did sound recording seem at the outset that many directors and theorists of film violently opposed its arrival. They were appalled that the cinema, which was currently in its most advanced state of articulation, might be permanently retarded by the public's passing fancy for a crude novelty. Paul Rotha spoke for this group in 1930:

> No power of speech is comparable to the descriptive value of photographs. The attempted combination of speech and pictures is the direct opposition of two separate mediums, which appeal in two utterly different ways. . . . [A] silent visual film is capable of achieving a more dramatic, lasting, and powerful effect on an audience by its singleness of appeal than a dialogue film. . . . Immediately a voice begins to speak in a cinema, the sound apparatus takes precedence over the camera, thereby doing violence to natural instincts.

Others, like Eisenstein and Pudovkin, perceived the threat posed by sound but also recognized its potential for adding a new dimension to the medium. In "Sound and Image," a manifesto published on August 5, 1928, Eisenstein, Pudovkin, and Alexandrov correctly predicted:

> The sound film is a two-edged sword, and it is very probable that its users will follow the path of least resistance, that is, they will attempt simply to satisfy the public's curiosity. First we shall see commercial exploitation of the merchandise which is easiest to manufacture and sell: the talkie, the film in which the recorded word coincides most exactly and realistically with the movement of lips on the screen, in which the public enjoys the illusion that it is really listening to an actor, an automobile horn, a musical instrument, etc.
>
> This first period of sensationalism will not prejudice the new art's development, but there will be a second period—a terrible period. With the decline of the first exploration of practical possibilities, people will try to substitute dramas taken from "good literature" and will make other attempts to have theater invade the screen.
>
> Used in this way, sound will destroy the art of montage.

Then, they offered an antidote to the situation:

> Only the use of sound as counterpoint to visual montage offers new possibilities of developing and perfecting montage. The first experiments with sound must be directed toward its "noncoincidence" with visual images. Only this method can produce the feeling we seek, the

feeling which, with time, will lead to creation of a new orchestral counterpoint of image-vision and image-sound.

Finally, they pointed out that the sound film provided one distinct technical advantage over the silent cinema:

> The new technical discovery is not a chance factor in the history of cinema but is a natural way out for the cinema's avant-garde, thanks to which filmmakers can escape from a large number of dead ends which probably had no exit.
> The title, despite innumerable attempts to incorporate it into the movement or images of a film, is the first such dead end.
> The second is the explanatory hodgepodge which overloads the composition of scenes and slows the film's rhythm. . . .
> Sound, treated as a new element of montage (and as an element independent of the visual image), will inevitably introduce a new, extremely effective means of expressing and resolving the complex problems which we have not been able to solve so far. It is impossible to find the necessary solutions if we have only visual elements with which to work.

Eisenstein, especially, spoke from a long and generally negative experience of trying to integrate his titles with his images. Titles were a definite liability to the silent cinema, since they interfered with the flow of its narratives and the rhythms of its montage. It is often pointed out, for example, that one of the last great films of the silent era, Carl Theodor Dreyer's *La passion de Jeanne d'Arc* (1928), was seriously flawed by the insertion of dialogue titles at crucial positions within the narrative and would have profited immensely from a recorded soundtrack. By eliminating the necessity for titles, the sound film had liberated the cinema from its thirty-year bondage to the printed word and provided it with a narrative dimension that need not interefere with the visual dynamics of montage. The task now was not to reshackle the medium to the spoken word of the talkie.

Another European cinematic formalist had similar feelings about sound. The young French director René Clair (born René-Lucien Chomette, 1898–1981) wrote in 1929 that he was opposed to the "100 percent talkie" but could see distinct possibilities for the creative use of sound in films (a potential which he would later realize in 1931 with his own films *Le million* and *A nous la liberté*): "The film is not everything. There is also the sound film—on which the last hopes of the advocates of the silent film are pinned. They count on the sound film to ward off the danger represented by the advent of talkies. . . . [If] *imitation* of real noises seems limited and disappointing, it is possible that an *interpretation* of noises may have more of a future in it." Clair reserved special praise for the early American musical, MGM's *Broadway Melody* (Harry Beaumont, 1929), as a film which used its soundtrack with great intelligence. He particularly admired a sequence in which the noise of a door being slammed and a car driving off are heard on the soundtrack but not illustrated on the image track, which contains only a close-up of the heroine's anguished face witnessing the departure. In another sequence the heroine is on the verge of tears, and as her face disappears in a fade-out we hear a single sob from the blackened screen. Clair concludes from this: "In these two instances the sound, at an opportune moment, has replaced the shot. It is by this economy of means that the sound film will most probably secure original effects."

What the three Soviet filmmakers and Clair had all realized was that sound recording posed a threat to the cinema *only* if the microphone became as slavishly subservient to the spoken word, or to "naturalistic" sound, as the early camera had been to empirical reality in its unwillingness to disrupt the natural continuity of time and space. So they denounced **synchronous** or "*naturalistic*" sound, whereby the audience *hears* exactly what it sees on the screen as it sees it and *sees* exactly what it hears on the soundtrack as it hears it, as a noncreative form of recording which threatened the formal achievement of the silent cinema. And they advocated instead the use of **asynchronous** or **contrapuntal** sound—sound which would counterpoint the images that accompanied it for expressive effect, in the same way that conflicting shots in a silent montage sequence counterpointed one another. That is, they endorsed sound recording as an extension and expansion of montage, in which noise, dialogue, and music were all to be used in counterpoint to visual images like individual shots in a montage sequence. As Pudovkin wrote, "Sound and human speech should be used by the director not as literal accompaniment, but to amplify and enrich the visual image on the screen."

The controversy between the advocates of synchronous versus asynchronous sound became the great theoretical debate of the early sound era, and it was precisely analogous to that which we may imagine to have occurred in the first decade of film itself. The question became whether the soundtrack, like the early camera, should simply record reality "naturalistically" or whether it should create a synthetic reality of its own. Practically speaking, the question was whether sound should be synchronized with the images to produce "naturalistic" or *literal* sound, or whether it should be placed in creative conflict with the image track. Because of the large middleground between these two positions, there was clearly an either/or fallacy involved in the debate: in fact, the best cinema mixes both practices, as all the pioneers of creative sound recording were to discover. But for the first several years, at least, it seemed that the future of the sound film lay in one direction or the other.

From 1928 to 1931, the main emphasis had been on obtaining high quality sound in production, with little thought given to the possibility of modifying the soundtrack after it had been recorded. The idea that sound as originally produced on the set was the necessary end product of the recording process had several sources. One was that the model for early sound recording was live radio broadcasting, where sound was produced for spontaneous transmission. Since many of the audio technicians who flooded the gates of Hollywood in the early years of the transition came directly from the broadcast industry, they brought their practices and preconceptions with them intact. A deeper reason lay in the conservatism of the American producers, who believed that an absolute pairing of sound and image was necessary to avoid confusing their literal-minded audiences. They felt that to separate sound and image—even to the small extent of recording naturalistic sound but not visualizing it (for

7.18   MGM's *Broadway Melody* (Harry Beaumont, 1929): innovative use of sound. The film won the Academy Award for Best Picture of 1929, certifying the new medium's ascendancy.

example, having a door slam offscreen, as in *Broadway Melody*)—would disorient audience perception, just as their predecessors had thirty years earlier been loath to fragment the visual reality continuum. So for several years both practice and ideology in the American studios dictated that sound and image be recorded simultaneously, with the result that everything heard on the soundtrack would be seen on the screen and vice versa. Thus the huge number of "100 percent talkies" (films like *Lights of New York*) which were little more than illustrated radio plays. On the other side of the issue were the cinematic formalists, like Eisenstein, Pudovkin, and Clair, who saw contrapuntal sound as the only way to use the new technique—sound in which music, choruses, sound effects, and perhaps a bare minimum of dialogue would be used to counterpoint and comment upon the visuals. The controversy was ultimately resolved through the discovery of a process known as **postsynchronization,** or **dubbing,** which permitted synchronous and asynchronous sound to be used together consistently and simultaneously within the same film.

THE ADJUSTMENT TO SOUND

Postsynchronization was first used by the American director King Vidor (1894–1982) for his first talking picture, *Hallelujah!* (1929), which is also generally regarded as the first major film of the sound era. *Hallelujah!* was shot on location in and around Memphis, Tennessee, with an all-black cast, and its final sequence depicts a wild chase through an Arkansas swamp. Vidor shot the entire sequence silent with a continuously moving camera, and then later in the studio he added to it a soundtrack containing naturalistic noises of the pursuit—breaking branches, screeching birds, heavy breathing, etc.—all of which had been separately recorded.* Given the crudity of early sound-recording equipment, this was a technically brilliant achievement. But since the soundtrack was physically separate from the image track, though printed beside it on the same strip of film,† the potential for postdubbing sound had existed in the sound-on-film systems from the time of their invention. Lewis Jacobs explains: "The detachment of sound and its reproduction in a film are made possible by the mechanical nature of the recording apparatus and the editing process. Microphone and camera are independent instruments, recording what is seen and heard either together simultaneously or separately at different times." Vidor, however, was the first to realize this and to realize simultaneously that sound could create a psychological impact quite independent of the images. Another American director, Lewis

---

* This was in part the result of a happy accident: Vidor's sound truck failed to show up when the crew arrived in Memphis, so he started to shoot the movie silent out of necessity and simply continued the practice when he realized how liberating it was. The post-dubbing process itself was extremely difficult, and Vidor's editor is said to have suffered a nervous breakdown in the midst of it.

† But see note on displacement, p. 359.

7.19 MGM's *Hallelujah!* (King Vidor, 1929).

7.20 Universal's ***All Quiet on the Western Front*** (Lewis Milestone, 1930): Lew Ayres and comrade.

7.21 On the set of Paramount's *The Love Parade* (Ernst Lubitsch, 1929).

Milestone (1895–1980), used postdubbing for the battlefield sequences of his great pacifist film in *All Quiet on the Western Front* in 1930, shooting them with a mobile silent camera on location and dubbing in the battle sounds later.* In 1931, Milestone was able to keep his camera

---

* Winner of the 1929/30 Academy Awards for Best Picture and Director, this classic anti-war film was cut by twenty-five minutes for general release but archivally restored to its original 130-minute running time in the 1980s and is available in this form today on videocassette.

constantly in motion during the fast-talking dialogue comedy *The Front Page,* adapted from the stage play by Ben Hecht and Charles MacArthur. Ernst Lubitsch also used dubbing in his first sound films, the dynamic musicals *The Love Parade* (1929) and *Monte Carlo* (1930), as did René Clair in *Sous les toits du Paris* (1930). These films and others like them (for example, Edward Sutherland's *The Saturday Night Kid* [1929], Victor Fleming's *The Virginian* [1929], Paul Sloane's *Hearts of Dixie* [1929], and William Wellman's *Chinatown Nights* [1929]) demonstrate a gradual shift in emphasis from production recording to rerecording during the period 1929–31, with increased importance finally being given to the latter.

In all of the cases just cited, sound was recorded and manipulated on a single track, but Rouben Mamoulian (1897–1987), a Broadway stage director, introduced a new element into sound recording when he used two separate microphones to record overlapping dialogue in a single scene of *Applause* (1929) and mixed them together on the soundtrack. Earlier soundtracks had consisted of a single channel, which meant that there was no way to isolate one type of sound from another. Everybody on the set spoke into the same microphone, and there could be no background music or sound effects while dialogue was being delivered unless these were provided off-camera simultaneously as the lines were spoken. By introducing two microphones and mixing the sound from each, Mamoulian opened up the possibility of multiple-channel recording and postrecording which would permit the precise manipulation of all sounds on the track—a possibility realized for four-channel recording as early as 1932. Two years later, in *City Streets* (1931), Mamoulian introduced the first sound "flashback," as snatches of dialogue spoken earlier in the film recur on the soundtrack accompanied by a close-up of the heroine, suggesting the process of memory.

In general practice, however, one type of sound or the other dominated the soundtrack through 1932—i.e., there was either dialogue or music on the track, but rarely both together unless they had been recorded simultaneously on the set, as in fact they sometimes were (e.g., Josef von Sternberg's *Der blaue Engel* [1930]). By 1933, however, technology had been introduced to mix separately recorded tracks for background music, sound effects, and synchronized dialogue without audible distortion at the dubbing stage, and by the late thirties it was possible in the RCA system to record music on multiple channels. By 1935, according to veteran sound editor James G. Stewart, the supervising dubbing mixer on a production often occupied a position equal to that of the film editor. The subsequent introduction of elaborate dialogue equalizers to alter level and frequency, and of compression and noise-suppression technology, further refined the dubbing process. By the late thirties, postsynchronization, or rerecording, originated as a means of adding sound effects to moving camera sequences, had become a process for the production of the entire release track. Today, the practice is nearly universal for theatrically released features, and it is not uncommon for as much as 90 percent of the dialogue in these films to be rerecorded in postproduction.

7.22 Paramount's *Applause* (Rouben Mamoulian, 1929), the first film to use a double-channel soundtrack. Helen Morgan.

7.23 On the set of Warner Bros.' *Mammy* (Michael Curtiz, 1930). The camera is still enclosed, but the microphone is suspended from an improvised boom.

Since the introduction of magnetic sound in the late fifties, any number of separate channels can be rerecorded onto a single track or stereophonically rerecorded onto as many as six tracks, and it was not uncommon for widescreen epics in the fifties and sixties to use as many as fifty channels for mass scenes. In the seventies, sound quality was further enhanced through the adoption of a wireless eight-track recording system which uses radio microphones and, increasingly, the nonmagnetic stereo-optical Dolby noise-reduction system for playback in exhibition.

The practice of postsynchronization was a prime force in liberating the sound film camera from its glass-paneled booth and the sound film generally from the single-minded notion that everything seen on the screen must be heard on the soundtrack, and vice versa. In its infancy, sound recording had bound film of the laws of empirical reality more securely than ever before, but postsynchronization reintroduced the plastic, manipulative element. From the experience of dubbing, directors gradually came to understand that the most "cinematic" soundtrack was neither wholly synchronous nor asynchronous but a composite of many different types of sound, all of which were under their control—perhaps even more so than the visuals, since sound could be synthetically produced.* Arthur Knight writes: "Each sound could be independently distorted, muffled, exaggerated or eliminated at will. The director could shoot his scene with a silent camera and dub in the sound later. He could reinforce dialogue passages with music, combine them with noises or bury them under other, post-synchronized sounds. . . . Post-synchronization became the first point of departure in the development of a new art."

---

* In certain sound-on-film processes employed today, a special stylus can be used to scrape light patterns directly onto the surface of the soundtrack, creating synthetic sound effects and music.

Other developments which helped to liberate the sound film from its initial stasis were more purely technological. Most such problems had been resolved by 1933 through various combinations of practical necessity, ingenuity, and technological refinement. By 1931, for example, both sound-on-disk and multiple-camera filming had been abandoned, and all studios had removed their cameras from the "iceboxes" and converted to the use of **blimps.** These were lightweight, soundproof housings which encased the cameras to muffle the clatter of their motors and enabled them to record synchronous sound outside of the booth. Within several years, smaller, quieter, self-insulating cameras were produced, eliminating the need for external soundproofing altogether. Blimping permitted studios to return to the free use of arc lamps, although most continued to employ tungsten units throughout the thirties for "soft light" effects. Tracking was again made possible by the introduction of a wide range of boom cranes, camera supports, and steerable dollies between 1931 and 1933 (forecast as early as 1929 when directors like Alfred Hitchcock [*Blackmail*] and Rouben Mamoulian [*Applause*] had moved their cameras by putting their booths on wheels). Microphones too became increasingly mobile as a variety of microphone booms were developed from 1930 onward. These long radial arms suspended the mike just above the set and out of the frame, allowing it to follow the movements of the actors and rendering the stationary, clumsily concealed microphones of the early years obsolete. Microphones also became more directional throughout the decade—better able to "hear" at one frequency or in one direction only—and track noise suppression techniques came into use as early as 1931.

During the same years, technology was introduced that greatly facilitated the editing process. The sound Moviola first became available in 1930 and went through several stages of evolution during the decade. Adapted from the silent film-editing machine of the same name, the sound Moviola consisted of contiguous picture and sound heads that could be operated separately or locked together to run in synchronization. Optical sound film was pulled through the machine by a continuously moving sprocket drive, as in a projector, but could be stopped and moved across either head by hand. In 1932, the system known as "rubber numbering" or "edge numbering" was introduced to insure the precise synchronization of sound and image track in the cutting process itself. Machine-coded footage numbers were stamped on the outer edges of the image and soundtrack for each shot, so that both tracks could be edited autonomously and resynchronized as empirically measured units. (With modifications for wide-gauge film and multitrack stereo sound, both the Moviola and coded numbering system are still used in studio editing today.)

As Barry Salt points out, it was only in the middle thirties that the technical innovations of 1929–32 began to have their full effect. Even then, some aspects of the recording process were not fully understood, and optical systems were still of two separate types: variable density and variable area. In the former, the density of the soundtrack varies longitudinally from opaque to transparent along the length of the film strip; in the latter there is no gradation of variants but a binary modulation of

7.24 A "blimped" camera shooting a dialogue scene whose sound is recorded by an off-frame boom microphone. (The film is Warner Bros. First National's *Lilies of the Field* [Alexander Korda, 1930], with Corinne Griffith and Ralph Forbes; behind the camera are Lee Garmes, the cinematographer [left], and William Goetz, the producer [right].)

two densities, complete opacity and complete transparency, over the width (or area) of the track. The variable density format, first used by Fox Movietone in 1927, was superior in dialogue reproduction, while variable area, introduced by RCA Photophone in 1928, was superior in musical reproduction, owing to its higher output and greater frequency range. From 1928 to 1935, variable area suffered from volumetric distortion at the high and low extremes of voice frequency, and it was assumed by RCA engineers to be a nonlinear system, since variable density was presumably linear. Not until these technicians experimented with transferring the variable area soundtrack for Rouben Mamoulian's *Becky Sharp* (1935) to variable density did they discover that the opposite was true. Thus, optical sound had been in use in the industry for over eight years before its fundamental nature was understood. When this finally occurred, RCA engineers were able to design a compressor for variable area recording that eliminated distortion in dialogue, and this was put into use in the dubbing stage in 1936. In 1937 RCA began to manufacture compressors to be used in original recording equipment on the set, and after 1938 compressors were used in all variable area recording. The format's superior volume and frequency range then made it preferable to variable density for all types of sound, and by 1945 the latter format had been gradually phased out. Although most motion-picture and television sound today is *recorded* magnetically (a technology introduced in 1958–59), the soundtracks for composite release prints in both media are always optical variable area.

The Sound Film and the American Studio System

NEW GENRES AND OLD

Sound radically changed the configuration of the Western cinema. In the United States, it gave rise to important new genres and a system of production which determined the character of American films for more than twenty years. The most significant of the new genres was the musical film, whose development parallels that of the sound film. Photographed versions of Broadway musicals were among the first sound films ever made, and *The Jazz Singer* (1927), of course, was one of them. At first, these movie musicals were little more than filmed theater, but within a few years the form had grown enough in cinematic sophistication to become the major genre of thirties cinema. This was largely the work of two men—Busby Berkeley (1895–1975) and Fred Astaire (1899–1987).

A dance director from the New York stage, Berkeley came to Hollywood to work for Samuel Goldwyn in 1930, but his genius was not revealed until he moved to Warner Bros. in 1933. There, as dance director for musicals like *42nd Street* (Lloyd Bacon, 1933), *Gold Diggers of 1933* (Mervyn LeRoy, 1933), *Footlight Parade* (Lloyd Bacon, 1933), *Dames* (Roy Enright, 1934), *Gold Diggers of 1935* (Busby Berkeley, 1935), *In Caliente* (Busby Berkeley, 1935), and *Gold Diggers of 1937* (Lloyd Bacon, 1937), most of which starred some combination of Dick Powell, Joan Blondell, and Ruby Keeler, he developed a flamboyant visual style which turned the production numbers of pedestrian backstage romances into surreal fantasias for the eye. Based upon the use of swooping aerial photography (or "crane choreography"*), kaleidoscopic lenses, highly expressive camera movement, and sophisticated montage techniques, Berkeley's production numbers come closer to an experimental cinema of abstract impressionism than to anything in the traditional narrative film.

Fred Astaire, by contrast, achieved a much greater integration of music and dance with narrative in the series of RKO musicals in which he played

---

* Aerial photography accomplished by means of a large boom crane.

8.1   Busby Berkeley's choreography: *Gold Diggers of 1933* (Mervyn LeRoy, 1933). Warner Bros.

8.2   Berkeley choreography: *Dames* (Ray Enright, 1934).

8.3   *Gold Diggers of 1935* (Busby Berkeley, 1935). Warner Bros.

opposite Ginger Rogers between 1933 (*Flying Down to Rio*, Thornton Freeland) and 1939 (*The Story of Vernon and Irene Castle*, H. C. Potter). Beginning as a performer, Astaire left an extremely successful stage career to work in films, and he went on to direct and choreograph his dance sequences in *The Gay Divorcee* (Mark Sandrich, 1934), *Roberta* (William Seiter, 1935), *Top Hat* (Mark Sandrich, 1935), *Swing Time* (George Stevens, 1936), *Follow the Fleet* (Mark Sandrich, 1936), *A Damsel in Distress* (George Stevens, 1937), *Shall We Dance?* (Mark Sandrich, 1937), and *Carefree* (Mark Sandrich, 1938), developing a sophisticated but highly functional camera style in which the camera itself became a partner in the dance through cutting and movement designed to preserve its physical integrity. Furthermore, Astaire's RKO musicals contributed signifi-

8.4 *Gold Diggers of 1937* (Lloyd Bacon, 1937): Joan Blondell heads the Berkeley formation. Warner Bros.

cantly to the development of creative recording techniques through their rhythmic pairing of sound and image.*

Another contribution to sound film genres was made by Walt Disney (1901–66), whose "Silly Symphony" series, begun in 1929 with *The Skeleton Dance,* pioneered what might be called the "animated musical," or the musical cartoon. Unhampered by the restrictions of early sound filming procedures, Disney could combine sound and image in an expressive manner impossible for his peers in the live-action narrative cinema and nevertheless achieve perfect frame-by-frame synchronization (today, the precise coordination of sound and image in animation is still called "Mickey Mousing"). The success of his first musical cartoon, *Steamboat Willie* (1928), which introduced Mickey Mouse to the world, and his "Silly Symphony" shorts, in which all of the action is set to music and which culminated in 1933 with the immensely popular all-color hit *The Three Little Pigs,* led Disney to produce three extraordinary animated color features before World War II—*Snow White and the Seven Dwarfs*

8.5 Fred Astaire and Ginger Rogers in a dance sequence from *Top Hat* (Mark Sandrich, 1935). RKO.

* Although he was the chief creative force behind all of his dance sequences, Astaire often worked with a "dance director" or "choreographer" who received official billing in the credits. His closest collaborator in this regard was Hermés Pan (b. 1910), the choreographer for seventeen of Astaire's thirty-one musicals, including all of his RKO films.

(1937), *Pinocchio* (1940), and the experimental *Fantasia* (1940), which attempted a total fusion of animated visuals and classical orchestral scores.

At the other end of the spectrum, the new realism permitted by sound bred a cycle of tersely directed urban gangster films which exploited armed violence* and tough vernacular speech in a context of social alienation. There were a handful of silent antecedents in the work of Lewis Milestone (*The Racket,* 1928) and Josef von Sternberg (*Underworld,* 1927), but sound films like Mervyn LeRoy's *Little Caesar* (1930), William Wellman's *The Public Enemy* (1931), and Howard Hawks' *Scarface* (1932) forged a new generic tradition extending through Arthur Penn's *Bonnie and Clyde* (1967), Francis Ford Coppola's *The Godfather* (1972) and *The Godfather, Part II* (1974), and Brian De Palma's *The Untouchables* (1987). In 1933–34, however, the brutal violence of these films provoked a public outcry which caused producers to shift emphasis from the gangster as "tragic hero," to borrow Robert Warshow's phrase, to the gangster as social victim.† This produced a cycle of prison films (such as Lloyd Bacon's *San Quentin,* 1937) and socially oriented crime films (among them William Wyler's *Dead End,* 1937; Fritz Lang's *You Only Live Once,* 1937; Lloyd Bacon's *Marked Woman,* 1937; and Michael Curtiz' *Angels with Dirty Faces,* 1938) later in the decade.

Another tough-talking, realistic film cycle which emerged from the early sound years was that of the newspaper picture. Comprised of films like *The Front Page* (Lewis Milestone, 1931), *Five Star Final* (Mervyn Le Roy, 1931), *Scandal Sheet* (John Cromwell, 1931), and *Platinum Blonde* (Frank Capra, 1931), the cycle was immensely popular during the thirties and important for helping to refine the technique of the dialogue film. While many newspaper films were made according to formula (*Front*

8.6 Mickey Mouse in *Steamboat Willie* (Walt Disney, 1928).

8.7 *Pinocchio* (Walt Disney Productions, 1940).

---

* A recurrent motif in the Depression-era gangster film was the sound of the recently invented Thompson submachine gun.

† A similar sort of critical outrage was vented against the violence of *Bonnie and Clyde* in 1967 (as we will see in Chapter 18), but that may have been because its protagonists represented social revolutionaries, rather than gangsters, to its audience. In any case, one reason for Hollywood's obsession with gangsters during the Depression may well have been organized crime's entry into the film industry in the early thirties. According to Eugene Rosow in *Born to Lose: The Gangster Film in America* (New York: Oxford, 1978) and other sources, gangsters began loan-sharking to the studios following the Wall Street crash. Harry Cohn, e.g., wrested control of Columbia Pictures from his brother Jack in 1932 with mob money borrowed through Johnny Roselli, and William Fox turned to similar sources in his unsuccessful bid to regain control of his own company in 1933. At the same time, the MPPDA was hiring gangsters as strike breakers against the Hollywood unions, and the Chicago mob was infiltrating the International Alliance of Theatrical Stage Employees and Moving Picture Operators (IATSE), which represented both stagehands and projectionists. By 1935, the racketeers George Browne and Willy Bioff had taken control of IATSE and begun to extort protection money from the Big Five in the sum of $50,000 per studio per year. In exchange, IATSE kept the wage demands of its members low and provided "safety" in the majors' theaters. In *The Hollywood Studio System* (p. 88), Douglas Gomery estimates that over $1 million changed hands this way before the racket was exposed at the decade's end. Bioff, Browne, and five of their associates were convicted of racketeering and went to jail, as did 20th Century–Fox board chairman Joseph Schenck (briefly—for tax evasion in the transfer of payoff funds), who was the Big Five's corporate bagman.

8.8 Edward G. Robinson in *Little Caesar* (Mervyn LeRoy, 1930). Warner Bros.

8.9 *The Public Enemy* (William Wellman, 1931): Mae Clark, James Cagney. Warner Bros.

8.10 The "biopic": Paul Muni in *Juarez* (William Dieterle, 1939). Warner Bros.

Page Woman [Michael Curtiz, 1935]; *Libeled Lady* [Jack Conway, 1936]), the cycle produced several comic masterpieces (such as Howard Hawks' *His Girl Friday,* 1940—a remake of *The Front Page* with the gender roles switched) and influenced the content of many more, including Orson Welles' *Citizen Kane* (1941), whose central figure is a newspaper magnate. (In the seventies, the genre resurfaced in such films as Alan J. Pakula's *The Parallax View* [1974] and *All the President's Men* [1975], and, in the eighties, James L. Brooks's *Broadcast News* [1987] and Ted Kotcheff's *Switching Channels* [1988—a remake of *His Girl Friday*], which latter use TV news reporting as a central element of plot.)

The historical biography, or **biopic,** was another important sound genre. The vogue began in 1933 with the international triumph of Alexander Korda's *The Private Life of Henry VIII,* the first British film to achieve success in the United States. *Henry VIII* had its origins in the lavish *Kostümfilme* pioneered by Ernst Lubitsch in postwar Germany, but there can be no question that the addition of sound enhanced the historical verisimilitude of the genre so enormously as to transform it. Perhaps the popularity in the thirties of films about the private lives of famous persons stems from the impact of the first Fox Movietone newsreels (c. 1927), in which audiences heard the actual voices of prominent celebrities. In any case, between 1934 and 1940, historical biographies became staple products of every major American and British studio; and films like *Voltaire* (John Adolfi, 1933), *Queen Christina* (Rouben Mamoulian, 1933), *Viva Villa!* (Howard Hawks* and Jack Conway, 1934), *House of Rothschild* (Alfred Werker, 1934), *Catherine the Great* (Paul Czinner, 1934), *Cardinal Richelieu* (Rowland V. Lee, 1935), *Rembrandt* (Alexander Korda, 1936), *Lloyd's of London* (Henry King, 1936), *Marie Antoinette* (W. S. Van Dyke, 1938), *The Private Lives of Elizabeth and Essex* (Michael Curtiz, 1939), and William Dieterle's *The Story of Louis Pasteur* (1936), *The Life of Émile Zola* (1937), *Juarez* (1939), and *Dr. Ehrlich's Magic Bullet* (1940) were very successful on the international market.

In addition to creating new genres, sound permanently changed some older ones. Perhaps the most vital of silent genres, slapstick comedy, was replaced in the thirties by the anarchic dialogue comedies of the Marx Brothers (*The Cocoanuts* [Robert Florey and Joseph Santley, 1929]; *Animal Crackers* [Victor Heerman, 1930]; *Monkey Business* [Norman Z. McLeod, 1931]; *Horse Feathers* [Norman Z. McLeod, 1932]; *Duck Soup* [Leo McCarey, 1933]; *A Night at the Opera* [Sam Wood, 1935]; *A Day at the Races* [Sam Wood, 1937]) and W. C. Fields (*The Golf Specialist* [Monte Brice, 1930]; *The Dentist* [Leslie Pierce, 1932]; *Million Dollar Legs* [Eddie Cline, 1932]; *The Fatal Glass of Beer* [Arthur Ripley, 1933]; *Six of a Kind* [Leo McCarey, 1934]; *The Man on the Flying Trapeze* [Clyde Bruckman, 1935]; *You Can't Cheat an Honest Man* [George Marshall, 1939]; *The Bank Dick* [Eddie Cline, 1940]), and the **screwball comedies** of such directors as Frank Capra (*Platinum Blonde,* 1931; *Lady for a Day,* 1933; *It Happened One Night,* 1934; *Mr. Deeds Goes to*

* Uncredited.

8.11 Dialogue comedy: the Marx Brothers in *Horse Feathers* (Norman Z. McLeod, 1932). Paramount.

8.12 W. C. Fields and Mae West in *My Little Chickadee* (Eddie Cline, 1940). Universal.

Town, 1936; *You Can't Take It with You,* 1938) and Howard Hawks (*Twentieth Century,* 1934; *Bringing Up Baby,* 1938; *His Girl Friday,* 1940). The screwball comedy was a film type characterized by wisecracking dialogue, furious pacing, and a certain element of visual burlesque carried over from the silent slapstick days. The focus of the action was usually a couple in a bizarre predicament. Some other memorable screwball comedies of the decade were: *Private Lives* (Sidney Franklin, 1931) and *Design for Living* (Ernst Lubitsch, 1933), both adapted from plays by Noël Coward; *The Good Fairy* (William Wyler, 1935); *My Man Godfrey* (Gregory La Cava, 1936); *Theodora Goes Wild* (Richard Boleslawski, 1936); *Nothing Sacred* (William Wellman, 1937); *Easy Living* (Mitchell Leisen, 1937); *The Awful Truth* (Leo McCarey, 1937); and *Midnight* (Mitchell Leisen, 1939).

In the forties, screwball comedy provided a precedent for the darker social satire of the writer-director Preston Sturges (1898–1959), who between 1940 and 1944 produced eight films, mainly for Paramount, that are recognized today as important and highly original contributions to the American comic tradition. The objects of Sturges' satire, however, were much more serious than the frivolous rich of the screwball comedy: American politics (*The Great McGinty,* 1940), American materialism and avarice (*Christmas in July,* 1941; *The Palm Beach Story,* 1942), American sexual attitudes (*The Lady Eve,* 1940), American small-town life (*The Miracle of Morgan's Creek,* 1944; *Hail the Conquering Hero* 1944), and American cinema (*Sullivan's Travels,* 1941). At a time when Hollywood was unabashedly extolling the virtues of American society for the purposes of war propaganda (see Chapter 11), Sturges' films offered audiences a vision of a corrupt, ridiculous, but often vital people whose chief flaw was a profound lack of self-knowledge.

The careers of Mack Sennett, Harold Lloyd, Harry Langdon, and Buster Keaton all declined rapidly with the coming of sound, and even Chaplin's two features of the thirties, *City Lights* (1931) and *Modern Times* (1936),

8.13 The screwball comedy as satire: Veronica Lake and Joel McCrea in *Sullivan's Travels* (Preston Sturges, 1941). Paramount.

were basically silent films with synchronized soundtracks. Some silent comedians, such as Laurel and Hardy, survived by creating a unique blend of slapstick and dialogue, but purely visual comedy was necessarily destroyed by sound, except insofar as it found a new home in the animated sound cartoon. Another important silent genre, the Western, went underground in the early years of sound, when it existed largely as a "B" form, only to emerge at the end of the thirties with renewed vitality and realism in John Ford's *Stagecoach* (1939). From 1939 to 1950, however, the Western would experience a renaissance. Finally, sound provided a new impetus for films of mystery and detection like *The Thin Man* (W. S. Van Dyke, 1934) and its sequels, and for the horror-fantasy genre. Traditionally rooted in the silent cinema of German Expressionism, this latter genre was greatly enhanced by sound, which not only permitted the addition of eerie effects but restored the dimension of literary dialogue present in so many of the original sources. In fact, Hollywood's three great horror classics—*Dracula* (Tod Browning, 1931), *Frankenstein* (James Whale, 1931), and *The Mummy* (Karl Freund, 1932)—were all early sound films.

STUDIO POLITICS AND THE PRODUCTION CODE

It is impossible to comprehend the American film during the thirties without understanding the mechanisms of the Hollywood studio system. The great studios were founded in the era before World War I when the Motion Picture Patents Company was destroyed and the independents moved to assume monopolistic control over film production, distribution, and exhibition. Through a series of complicated business maneuvers, both legal and illegal, they succeeded, and by the end of the war the studios were on the brink of becoming the vast industrial empires of popular mythology. In the period of economic growth that followed the war, Wall Street began to invest heavily in the studios for both financial and political reasons. It was clear, in the first place, that motion pictures were on their way to becoming a major industry; it was equally clear during these years of the "Red Scare" that the movies were a medium of mass persuasion and propaganda par excellence. For Hollywood films to extol the virtues of corporate capitalism and "the American way of life" was to erect an impenetrable barrier against Bolshevism.* This percep-

---

* On the whole, the decade from the end of World War I in 1919 to the stock market crash of 1929, which began the Great Depression, was one of the least liberal in America history. In the early twenties, America's business leaders were panicked by the success of the Bolshevik Revolution in Russia and by the attempted organization of labor at home. Woodrow Wilson's attorney general, A. Mitchell Palmer (1872–1936), played upon these fears by declaring the country to be in the grip of a Communist conspiracy, much as Senator Joseph McCarthy would do thirty years later. In January 1920 he authorized the infamous "Palmer Raids," in which over five thousand persons—most of them labor organizers—in thirty-three different American cities were rounded up and held without trial for alleged "revo-

tion encouraged Wall Street to invest massive sums in the Hollywood studios immediately following the war. The capital of Adolph Zukor's Famous Players–Lasky (soon to become Paramount) alone rose from ten to twenty million dollars in two years, and every important studio received large corporate loans from American big business.

Lewis Jacobs describes the inevitable results: "New men from Wall Street, educated in finance, became the overseers of the motion picture business. Characteristic of the new managerial figures were two directors of a new and powerful company, Loew's: W. C. Durant, at that time also head of General Motors Corporation, and Harvey Gibson, president of the Liberty National Bank." Naturally enough, the leadership of these men left its permanent imprint upon the process of production. As David Robinson puts it, "The bureaucrats and accountants, eager to overcome the unpredictable and intractable element in the creation of films, began to codify certain principles of commercial production that still prevail in the industry: the attempt to exploit proven success with formula pictures and cycles of any particular genre which temporarily sells, at the expense of other and perhaps unorthodox product; the quest for predictable sales values—star names, best-selling success titles, costly and showy production values—which have little to do with art." Films came to be made according to the most efficient production method American industry had ever devised—the standardized assembly-line technique. The producer's role as supervisor became enormously important in this process, while the director's role declined, and by the time sound was introduced filmmaking in America had become a fairly conventionalized and predictable operation.

It was to become even more so through the intervention of the Hays Office and the Catholic Church in 1934. The Hollywood scandals of 1921–22 had alerted many civic-minded persons to the power of the movies to influence social attitudes and behavior; and, when the first data on movie attendance in the United States was systematically gathered in 1922, it was discovered that some 40 million tickets were sold every

lutionary activities." (J. Edgar Hoover [1895–1972] was Palmer's chief organizer for these raids, out of which the FBI was born several years later, with Hoover as director.) Many were imprisoned for long periods of time; great numbers of those who were not native-born were deported; Palmer became a national hero and a serious contender for the 1920 Democratic presidential nomination (he lost to James M. Cox). This latter fact provides some indication of the temper of the times: the country was in a nasty, insular mood, and aliens of all sorts were regarded with hostility. Patriotism became a façade for racism of murderous intensity. Immigrants, blacks, and Jews were openly persecuted for not being "100 percent American," and the Ku Klux Klan's membership grew so rapidly that by 1925 the organization had nearly attained the status of a third political party. Organized crime also grew, thanks to the Eighteenth Amendment (1918) and the Volstead Act (1921), providing for federal enforcement of Prohibition. During the same period the average weekly film attendance was fifty million Americans per week, making the cinema a mass medium on a par with network radio and the tabloid press (or with television today). It was therefore essential to the maintenance of the status quo that the ideological content of films be as carefully controlled as the ideological content of other mass media.

week. By the end of the decade, the figure had more than doubled to 90 million, among whom there were an estimated 40 million minors, including 17 million children under the age of fourteen. As with television during the sixties, the rapid spread of the medium and its easy accessibility to children was cause for national alarm, and—just as with television—there was a widespread public demand for research. In 1928, William H. Short, executive director of a newly formed "procensorship" body called the Motion Picture Research Council, solicited a large grant ($200,000, or about $1 million in current value) from the Payne Fund, a private philanthropic foundation, to conduct a nationwide study of the influence of motion pictures on children by a group of university psychologists, sociologists, and education specialists. The result was a series of twelve specific investigations, known as the Payne Fund Studies, undertaken by nationally known researchers over the period 1929–32. The project's conclusions, published in eleven volumes between 1933 and 1935, were popularly summarized by the journalist Henry James Forman in his 1933 volume *Our Movie Made Children*—a title which came to characterize the whole generation of Americans who grew up during the Depression, came of age in World War II, and became the first national audience for network television in their middle years. The Payne Fund findings confirmed the worst—the movies did seem to bring new ideas to children; did influence interpretations of the world and day-to-day conduct; did present moral standards, particularly with regard to sexual behavior, different from those of many adults. The media effects that researchers today take for granted, in fact, were shocking new knowledge to an America that had just begun to enter the media age.

Concurrent with these studies, the coming of sound had produced a wave of grim, often violent, screen realism and yet another public outcry against the "immorality" of Hollywood films. This time the reaction was organized by the American bishops of the Roman Catholic Church, who—armed with the Payne Fund volumes, Forman's *Our Movie Made Children,* and, apparently, a mandate from the Vatican itself—set up the "Legion of Decency" to fight for better and more "moral" motion pictures. In April of 1934, with the support of both Protestant and Jewish organizations, the Legion called for a nationwide boycott of movies considered indecent by the Catholic church. The studios, having lost millions of dollars in 1933 as the delayed effects of the Depression finally caught up with the box office, were intimidated into imposing self-censorship before it was too late. In 1927, a Motion Picture Production Code had been drafted by the MPPDA based on the "Don'ts and Be Carefuls" formula of the immediate post-scandal years (see pp. 227–30), and in 1930 the Hays Office had adopted a more formal but still voluntary "Code to Maintain Social and Community Values." Now Hays was authorized to create the Production Code Administration (PCA) and to appoint a prominent Catholic layman, Joseph I. Breen, to head it. Under Breen's auspices, Father Daniel A. Lord, a Jesuit priest, and Martin Quigley, a Catholic publisher, coauthored the Draconian "Production Code" whose provisions would dictate the content of American motion pictures, without exception, for the next twenty years.*

In a pendulum swing away from the excesses of the "new morality" of the Jazz Era, the Production Code was awesomely repressive, and it prohibited the showing or mentioning of almost everything germane to the situation of normal human adults. It forbade depicting "scenes of passion" in all but the most puerile terms, and it required that the sanctity of the institution of marriage and the home be upheld at all times (married couples, however, were never to be shown sharing a bed). Adultery, illicit sex, seduction, or rape could never be more than suggested, and then only if they were absolutely essential to the plot and were severely punished at the end (a favorite means was death from accident or disease). Also prohibited were the use of profanity (a term extended to include "vulgar" expressions like "cripes," "guts," and "nuts") and racial epithets; any implication of prostitution, miscegenation, sexual aberration, or drug addiction; nudity of all sorts; sexually suggestive dances or costumes; "excessive and lustful kissing"; and excessive drinking. It was forbidden to ridicule or criticize any aspect of any religious faith, to show cruelty to animals or children, or to represent surgical operations, especially childbirth, "in fact or in silhouette."

But the Code's most labyrinthine strictures were reserved for the depiction of crime. It was forbidden to show the details of a crime, or to display machine guns, submachine guns, or other illegal weapons, or to discuss weapons at all in dialogue scenes. It was further required that law enforcement officers never be shown dying at the hands of criminals, and that all criminal activities within a given film were shown to be punished. Under no circumstances could a crime be shown to be justified. Suicide and murder were to be avoided unless absolutely necessary to the plot, and the suggestion of excessive brutality or wholesale slaughter of any kind was absolutely prohibited. The antiviolence strictures of the Code seem positively civil in this age of the cinema of cruelty, but the Code as a whole was obviously restrictive and repressive. From 1934 until the mid-fifties it rigidly dictated the content of American films, and in a very real sense kept them from becoming as serious as they might have, and, perhaps, should have, been.

Under the administrative provisions, no studio belonging to the MPPDA was to distribute or release any film without a certificate of approval signed by Breen, as director of the PCA, and bearing the PCA's seal. Failure to comply would cause a fine of twenty-five thousand dollars to be levied by the MPPDA against the offending company (the fine was never imposed, but it proved an effective sanction for over twenty years). The process whereby this certification was obtained was a long and

---

* The code was completely revised to eliminate its censorship provisions in 1966, but it had become basically unenforceable by the mid-fifties (see pp. 535–37).

sometimes humiliating one for filmmakers. Raymond Moley has outlined its major stages:

1. A preliminary conference between Breen or other members of the staff of the PCA and the producer, to consider the basic story before the screen adaptation is written or purchased; at this point the plot as a whole is discussed in its relation to the Code.
2. Careful scrutiny of the script submitted by the producing company.
3. Scenario conference with writers and others to effect necessary changes in the script.
4. Approval in writing by Breen of the script for production.
5. Continued conferences during production, so that any change made in the script as well as all lyrics, costumes and sets may be observed and passed upon.
6. Preview of separate sequences during the course of production, whenever the producer is in doubt about their conformity with the Code; this is done upon the request of the producer.
7. Preview of the completed picture in the PCA viewing theatre by the same two staff members who worked on the script and by a third staff member who comes to the picture with a fresh mind.
8. After deletion of scenes, dialogue, etc., which violate the Code, issue of its certificate of approval by the Production Code Administration.

The reasons that the moguls were willing not merely to accept but to institutionalize what was clearly a system of de facto censorship and prior restraint were several—all of them ultimately related to staying in business. For one thing, obviously, the economic threat of a boycott during the worst years of the Depression was real, and an industry dependent upon pleasing a mass audience several times a week must deliver to that audience what it thinks, at least, the audience wants. For another thing, producers found that they could turn the Code to work decisively in favor of more efficient production. By rigidly prescribing and proscribing the kinds of behavior that could be shown or described on the screen, the Code could be used as a kind of scriptwriter's blueprint. A love story, for example, could only move in one direction (toward marriage), adultery and crime could only have one conclusion (disease and / or horrible death), dialogue in all situations had well-defined parameters, and so forth. The Code, in other words, provided a framework for the construction of screenplays and enabled studios to streamline what had always been (and still is) the thorniest and yet most formative task in the production process—the creation of filmable continuity scripts. Finally, we should remember that the Depression was a time of open political anti-Semitism in the United States, with Henry Ford's *Dearborn Independent* editorials, Father Coughlin's network radio show, and lesser demogogues inveighing against the economic treachery of the Jews every week. If Will Hays alone couldn't reassure the moguls' Christian audience of their decency, perhaps a code of ethics dictated by the Catholic bishops could.

THE STRUCTURE OF THE STUDIO SYSTEM

The most significant force shaping the American sound film, however, was economic. In 1928, the studios had greatly increased their debt to Wall Street by borrowing vast sums of capital for the conversion to sound (see business chart, p. 265). Wall Street was happy to oblige, since the novelty of sound had nearly doubled weekly admission figures over the previous year. By 1930, a series of mergers and realignments had concentrated 95 percent of all American film production in the hands of eight studios, five "majors" and three "minors." The major studios were organized as vertically integrated corporations, controlling the means not only of production but of distribution and exhibition (or consumption) as well, through their ownership of film exchanges and theater chains. Distribution was conducted at a national and international level: since about 1925, foreign rentals had accounted for half of all American feature revenues and would continue to do so for the next two decades. Exhibition was controlled through the majors' ownership of 2,600 first-run theaters, that 16 percent of the national total which generated 75 percent of the revenue. Despite the national mania—actively stimulated by studio publicity and marketing departments—for the "Hollywood of the Stars," production throughout the thirties and forties consumed only 5 percent of total corporate assets, with another 1 percent accounted for distribution. With 94 percent of total investment going to the exhibition sector, as Douglas Gomery has pointed out, the five majors during the studio era can best be characterized as "diversified theater chains, producing features, shorts, cartoons, and newsreels to fill their houses."

These studios were, in order of relative economic importance, Metro-Goldwyn-Mayer, Paramount, Warner Bros., 20th Century–Fox, and RKO. The minor studios—which owned no theaters* and were dependent upon the majors for first-run exhibition outlets—were Universal, Columbia, and United Artists.

As David Robinson points out, the nearly total domination of the studios by Wall Street had far-reaching consequences for the organization of the American film industry and for the character of the American film in the period between the introduction of sound and the Second World War, especially when the Depression finally took effect in Hollywood:

---

* United Artists had initiated its own theater circuit in 1926 but sought participation with the majors (mainly Loew's and Paramount) to minimize its risk. The company owned first-run houses outright only in Detroit, Chicago, and Los Angeles, and it agreed to halt theater expansion during the thirties in exchange for distribution agreements with the Big Five. In 1936, UA severed corporate ties with its theater operations; today, however, United Artist Communications, Inc., is the country's largest theater circuit, with 1,093 screens reported as of 1987.

Depression in the industry, which reached its peak in 1933, when a third of the nation's cinemas were closed down, only served to tighten the financiers' control over the organisation of film production. There was even less place for imponderables. Emphasis was laid upon achieving the highest possible standards in those aspects of film-making which could be controlled: quality of equipment, techniques, photography, staging and costuming. Every step was taken to eliminate those unpredictable elements which are of the nature of art.*

Charles Higham describes how these results were achieved at Warner Bros., perhaps the most typical American studio of the era:

The writers [of whom as many as twenty would frequently work on a single script] . . . unquestionably occupied first place: they set the entire tone of the pictures of the time. The scripts were prepared in detail, even down to specific compositions of the shots, and the writers were almost invariably present on the sets during the shooting. Once a producer had approved a finished screenplay, he cast the stars of the picture. The director was called in, and in rare instances helped with casting of minor roles or changes in the writing. For economic reasons, he had orders to rehearse his players, then only use one take for a scene. The producer or studio manager selected the art directors, the composers, the cameramen, the cutters. These were seldom the choice of the directors, and all conformed to studio style.

Between 1930 and 1945, the Hollywood studios mass-produced some seventy-five hundred feature films in which every stage of production from conception to exhibition was carefully controlled. These films took their styles and values as much from the studios that made them as from the individual artists involved in their production, and so it is important to understand how these studios were composed.

MGM

MGM was the biggest, most prosperous, and most prolific of American studios in the thirties. At mid-decade, it was producing an average of one feature per week, which, as John Baxter notes, was the largest output of any studio in the history of the cinema. Its parent firm, Loew's, Incorporated, ruled from New York by Nicholas Schenck (1881–1969), pro-

---

* The source of this information is F. D. Klingender and Stuart Legg, *Money Behind the Screen* (London, 1937). Discussing the impact of Wall Street control in *Movie-Made America: A Cultural History of the American Movies* (New York, 1976), Robert Sklar suggests that it makes much less difference who *owns* a movie company (or eight of them) than who operates it. He argues that although four of the eight Hollywood studios (Paramount, Twentieth Century–Fox, RKO, and Universal) experienced major changes in management during the thirties, the character of American filmmaking did not significantly change, since all of the studio managers, old and new—if not the studio owners—were entertainment industry veterans intimately familiar with their product and its consumers. But it also seems likely, as David Robinson implies (in *The History of World Cinema* [New York: Stein and Day, 1973; 2nd ed, 1981]), that financial concentration brought with it a much more relentless emphasis on economies of scale than the industry had experienced in its first three decades, resulting in an unprecedented standardization of production and a high-quality product.

vided MGM with a large national exhibition outlet,* and its close affiliation with the Chase National Bank gave the studio access to nearly unlimited capital. There was no film so big that MGM couldn't produce it, no talent so large that MGM couldn't buy it. The studio had under contract some of the greatest film talent of the thirties—the directors Frank Borzage, Clarence Brown, King Vidor, George Cukor, Sidney Franklin, W. S. Van Dyke, Jack Conway, Sam Wood, and Victor Fleming; the cinematographers Karl Freund, William Daniels, George Folsey, and Harold Rosson; the design director Cedric Gibbons; and, finally, a cast of stars unparalleled in Hollywood history ("More stars than there are in Heaven," as the MGM publicity slogan had it)—Greta Garbo, Jean Harlow, Norma Shearer, Joan Crawford, Margaret Sullavan, Myrna Loy, Clark Gable, Spencer Tracy, Robert Montgomery, the Barrymores, Marie Dressler, Wallace Beery, William Powell, James Stewart, Robert Taylor, Nelson Eddy, Jeanette MacDonald, Judy Garland, and Mickey Rooney. MGM was run during this period (and until his ouster in 1951) by its vice president in charge of production, Louis B. Mayer (1885–1957), a ruthless businessman with little concern for art, or even entertainment, except insofar as it could be merchandised; but the studio's canny young production manager, Irving Thalberg, was able to maintain a consistently high level of achievement in MGM films until his early death. Mayer's son-in-law, David O. Selznick (1902–65), who was hired from RKO to assist Thalberg in 1933, also acquired the reputation of an artistic producer, and between them the two men produced some of the most prestigious MGM films of the decade.

8.14 An aerial view of the MGM studio complex, Culver City, c. 1935.

8.15 A ballroom scene from *Marie Antoinette* (W. S. Van Dyke, 1937), illustrating the MGM style of high-key lighting and elaborate production design.

---

* Actually, MGM's theater chain was the smallest of the Big Five, a circumstance which helped it to maintain profits when attendance dropped off during the worst years of the Depression. See Douglas Gomery, *The Hollywood Studio System* (New York: St. Martin's, 1986), pp. 6–23.

The predominant visual style of these films was characterized by **high-key lighting** and opulent production design (the one employed to reveal the other), and their cultural values were the typically American middle-class ones of optimism, materialism, and romantic escapism. MGM's major genres in the thirties were the melodrama, the musical, and the prestigious literary or theatrical adaptation; some of its most characteristic films were *Anna Christie* (Clarence Brown, 1930); *Grand Hotel* (Edmund Goulding, 1932); *Dinner at Eight* (George Cukor, 1933); *Queen Christina* (Rouben Mamoulian, 1933); *Viva Villa!* (Jack Conway, 1934); *Mutiny on the Bounty* (Frank Lloyd, 1935); the Marx Brothers' *A Night at the Opera* (1935) and *A Day at the Races* (1937), both directed by Sam Wood; *David Copperfield* (George Cukor, 1935); *Anna Karenina* (Clarence Brown, 1935); *Romeo and Juliet* (George Cukor, 1936); *San Francisco* (W. S. Van Dyke, 1936); *Libeled Lady* (Jack Conway, 1936); *Rose Marie* (W. S. Van Dyke, 1936); *The Great Ziegfeld* (Robert Z. Leonard, 1936); *Camille* (George Cukor, 1937); *The Good Earth* (Sidney Franklin, 1937); *Captains Courageous* (Victor Fleming, 1937); *Boys Town* (Norman Taurog, 1938); *Too Hot to Handle* (Jack Conway, 1938); *The Citadel* (King Vidor, 1938); *Marie Antoinette* (W. S. Van Dyke, 1938); *Goodbye, Mr. Chips* (Sam Wood, 1939); and *Broadway Melody of 1940* (Norman Taurog, 1940).

MGM also produced some of the most popular low-budget cycles of the decade, including the Andy Hardy, Tarzan, Dr. Kildare, and "Thin Man" series, as well as a few controversial and / or technically innovative productions like King Vidor's *Hallelujah!* (1929) and Fritz Lang's *Fury* (1936). Yet the studios' ambience and attitudes during the thirties are best summed up by its two super-productions of 1939, *The Wizard of Oz* and *Gone with the Wind* (actually a Selznick International production released and partially financed by MGM; see p. 346B), both nominally directed by Victor Fleming. Neither film has the depth or force of personal artistic vision, but both are opulent, epic, and spectacularly entertaining products of the studio system at its most efficient, spinning out beautifully crafted fairy tales for children and adults like. (In 1973 MGM ceased to exist as a studio, although it remained marginally involved in the production of theatrical films through investment and resumed distribution in 1979; it acquired United Artists to become MGM / UA Entertainment Company in 1981 and was itself absorbed by Turner Broadcasting in 1985, which sold it in 1986 to Las Vegas financier Kirk Kerkorian who reorganized the corporation as MGM / UA Communications, selling off UA to Qintex Entertainment Group of Australia in 1990.

Paramount

If MGM was the most "American" of the American studios, Paramount was the most "European." Many of Paramount's directors, craftsmen, and technicians had come to it directly from Germany via the Parufamet agreement of 1926, and the UFA influence on the Paramount style was substantial. For this reason, Paramount made the most sophisticated and visually ornate films of the thirties. The studio's German art

director, Hans Dreier, and its German cinematographer, Theodor Sparkuhl (1894–1945), as well as his American colleagues Victor Milner (b.
1893) and Karl Struss (1891–1981), created for its films a baroque pictorial style which was counterpointed by their subtle content. As John
Baxter remarks, "Paramount's was the cinema of half-light and suggestion; witty, intelligent, faintly corrupt." The studio was controlled
throughout the thirties (and some twenty years after) by its founder, Adolph
Zukor and, after 1936, its president, Barney Balaban (1887–1971).
Through its acquisition of the 1,200-house Publix theater chain in 1925,
Paramount owned the largest motion-picture circuit in the world; this
forced the company into receivership during the worst years of the
Depression but brought it record profits in the forties when World War
II drove public demand for movie entertainment to an all-time high (see
pp. 461–64). Lacking MGM's Depression-era financial stability, Paramount nevertheless made almost as many films. And, because it was less
tightly organized at the level of production than its rivals, these films
often bore the personal imprint of their directors more than the standard
thirties studio product.*

8.16 The Paramount studios, Hollywood, c. 1935.

Cecil B. DeMille (see pp. 230–31) continued to turn out the lavish sex-
and-violence-soaked spectacles that had made him the star talent of Famous
Players–Lasky in the silent era. His most profitable films for Paramount
in the thirties were *The Sign of the Cross* (1932), *Cleopatra* (1934), *The
Crusades* (1935), *The Plainsman* (1937), *The Buccaneer* (1938), and *Union
Pacific* (1939). At the other extreme were the films of the urbane Ernst
Lubitsch (see pp. 116; 231), innovator of the UFA *Kostümfilm* and the
silent comedy of manners, who had come to America in 1922 and stayed
on to become Paramount's most prestigious director of the thirties. (He
was also in charge of production from 1935 to 1936—the only director
ever to be given complete creative authority over the output of a major
studio.)

In the sound era, Lubitsch specialized in musical comedy, light opera,
and, once again, the comedy of manners. His major films of the decade
were *The Love Parade* (1930), *Monte Carlo* (1930), *The Smiling Lieutenant* (1931), *One Hour with You* (1932), *Trouble in Paradise* (1932),
Design for Living (1933), *The Merry Widow* (1934), *Angel* (1937), *Bluebeard's Eighth Wife* (1938) and *Ninotchka* (1939), to all of which he lent
a distinctly European lightness of touch and a vaguely decadent charm.†

---

* Unlike the other majors, Paramount did not have an executive continuously in charge of
production until 1936, when William LeBaron (1883–1958) assumed the role.

† The last two were produced for MGM; Lubitsch's Paramount contract permitted him to
direct one outside film per year, but he left the studio after eleven years in 1938 and began
to free-lance, producing *The Shop Around the Corner* (1940) for MGM, *That Uncertain
Feeling* (1941, a remake of his 1925 *Kiss Me Again*) for UA, and *To Be or Not to Be*
(1942—a sophisticated and, at the time, controversial black comedy focussed on the Nazi
invasion of Poland, starring Carole Lombard and Jack Benny, and remade in 1983 as a
vehicle for Anne Bancroft and Mel Brooks, Alan Johnson directing) for Alexander Korda–
UA. Lubitsch finally signed a three-year producer-director contract with 20th Century-Fox,
where he made *Heaven Can Wait* (1943, his first film in color), *Cluny Brown* (1946), and

8.17 "Erotic-historical baroque": Cecil B. DeMille's *The Sign of the Cross* (1932). Claudette Colbert, Fredric March. Paramount.

8.18 Paramount's Continental touch: Ernst Lubitsch's *Design for Living* (1933). Miriam Hopkins, Fredric March, Gary Cooper.

Equally decadent but far more bizarre were the Paramount films of Josef von Sternberg, all of which cast his protégée Marlene Dietrich (b. 1901) as the archetypal *femme fatale* in some impossibly exotic setting: *Morocco* (1930), *Dishonored* (1931), *Shanghai Express* (1932), *Blond Venus* (1932), *The Scarlet Empress* (1934), and *The Devil Is a Woman* (1935). In these virtually (and deliberately) content-less films, von Sternberg achieved a degree of visual elegance which has led one critic to describe them as "poems in fur and smoke." Paramount was also the producer of the mannered, technically innovative films of the Armenian-born director Rouben Mamoulian, including *Applause* (1929), *City Streets* (1931), *Dr. Jekyll and Mr. Hyde* (1932), *Love Me Tonight* (1932), *Song of Songs* (1933), and *High, Wide, and Handsome* (1937).

Other notable Paramount directors of the thirties were Mitchell Leisen (1898–1972), whose stylish films *Death Takes a Holiday* (1934), *Hands Across the Table* (1935), *Easy Living* (1937), and *Midnight* (1939) are much admired today for their sense of visual design; Henry Hathaway (1898–1985), who demonstrated a high degree of technical polish in such handsome productions as *Lives of a Bengal Lancer* and *Peter Ibbetson* (both 1935); and Dorothy Arzner (1900–1979), one of the industry's few women directors (*Working Girls*, 1931; *Christopher Strong*, 1933; *Nana*, 1934; *Craig's Wife*, 1936; *The Bride Wore Red*, 1937; *Dance, Girl, Dance*, 1946), who was famous for her editing skills. Finally, the best and most anarchic of the Marx Brothers' comedies, *The Cocoanuts* (Robert Florey and Joseph Santley, 1929), *Animal Crackers* (Victor Heerman, 1930), *Monkey Business* (Norman Z. McLeod, 1931), *Horsefeathers* (Norman

---

two films completed by Otto Preminger, owing to his failing health, *A Royal Scandal* (1945) and *That Lady in Ermine* (1948). Lubitsch died of a heart attack at the age of fifty-five during production of the latter on November 30, 1947.

Z. McLeod, 1932), and *Duck Soup* (Leo McCarey, 1933) were made for Paramount, as were the thirties films of W. C. Fields (1879–1946) and Mae West (1892–1980). Major Paramount stars of the decade were George Raft, Ray Milland, Fredric March, Claudette Colbert, Miriam Hopkins, Herbert Marshall, Sylvia Sidney, Gary Cooper, Cary Grant, Kay Francis, Bing Crosby, Dorothy Lamour, Fred MacMurray, and Carol Lombard. In the early forties, the Bing Crosby–Bob Hope "Road" pictures (*Road to Singapore* [Victor Schertzinger, 1940], *Road to Zanzibar* [Victor Schertzinger, 1941], *Road to Morocco* [David Butler, 1942], etc.) brought Paramount the highest grosses of any series of the studio era. (As a subsidiary of Gulf and Western Industries from 1966–1988 and of Paramount Communication, Inc. (PCI) thereafter, Paramount remains today a major producer of theatrical films [*The Godfather*, 1972; *Saturday Night Fever*, 1977; *Star Trek*, 1979, and sequels; *Raiders of the Lost Ark*, 1981, and sequels; *Terms of Endearment*, 1983; *Beverly Hills Cop*, 1984, and sequel; *Witness*, 1985; *Top Gun*, 1986; *The Untouchables* and *Fatal Attraction*, 1987] and television series; see pp. 889–90.)

Warner Bros.

In the cultural hierarchy of American studios in the thirties, Warner Bros. fell below the sophisticated Paramount and the respectably middle-class MGM. It was in fact the studio of the working class, specializing in low-life melodramas and musicals with a Depression setting throughout the decade. Conditioned by its origins as a minor studio, Warner Bros. imposed a strict code of production efficiency on its directors, technicians, and stars alike. Directors were expected to produce at least five features a year. Actors and actresses were hired at low salaries and held to them long after they had become stars. Sometimes, when a film was being prepared for distribution, Warners' editors were required to cut single frames from every shot simply to tighten the film's structure and increase its speed. (The process was salutary: Warners' editor-in-chief, Ralph Dawson, won three Academy Awards for the studio during the thirties.) Finally, the Warners cinematographers, Hal Mohr, Ernest Haller, Tony Gaudio, and Sol Polito, were required to adopt a style of flat, low-key lighting in order to obscure the spareness of the studio's economical sets.

This emphasis on maximum economy of means, enforced by executives like Hal B. Wallis (b. 1899), Henry Blanke (1901–81), and the ruthlessly pragmatic Jack L. Warner* produced a group of films which were models of fast-paced, disciplined narrative construction. Warners in the thirties was preeminently the home of the gangster cycle (*Little Caesar* [Mervyn LeRoy, 1930]; *Public Enemy* [William Wellman, 1931]) and the Busby Berkeley backstage musical (*42nd Street* [1933]; the *Gold Dig-*

8.19 The Warner Bros. First National studios, Hollywood, c. 1935. Warners purchased First National in 1929 with the windfall profits from its early Vitaphone films.

---

* Of all the majors, only Warners was family-run: Jack (1892–1981) was in charge of production; Albert ("Abe"—1884–1967) supervised distribution; and Harry (1881–1958), as president, managed the entire system. Samuel Warner (1888–1927), who reputedly had convinced his brothers to convert to sound, died of a cerebral hemorrhage one day before the premiere of *The Jazz Singer*.

8.20 Warner Bros. realism: Paul Muni in *I Am a Fugitive from a Chain Gang* (Mervyn LeRoy, 1932).

8.21 Warner Bros. fantasy: *A Midsummer Night's Dream* (Max Reinhardt and William Dieterle, 1935). Titania (Anita Louise) and the Indian Prince (Kenneth Anger).

gers series); but it also undertook some major works of social realism like William Wellman's *Wild Boys of the Road* (1933), Mervyn LeRoy's *I Am a Fugitive from a Chain Gang* (1932), and Michael Curtiz's *Black Fury* (1935). Warners was also responsible (and rather courageously so) for the first American anti-Nazi film, Anatole Litvak's *Confessions of a Nazi Spy* (1939), as well as for a series of prestigious biographical films directed by the former UFA actor William Dieterle (b. 1893) which included *The Story of Louis Pasteur* (1936), *White Angel* (1936—a biography of Florence Nightingale), *The Life of Émile Zola* (1937), *Juarez* (1939), and *Dr. Erhlich's Magic Bullet* (1940). Dieterle also directed a marvelously expressionistic and, for Warners, utterly uncharacteristic version of *A Midsummer Night's Dream* in collaboration with the great German stage director Max Reinhardt in 1935. Other top directors at Warners in the thirties were Michael Curtiz, the Hungarian filmmaker who had worked for UFA in the twenties, and Mervyn LeRoy (1900–1987). Given the studio's rigid organization and tight production schedule, neither Dieterle, Curtiz, nor LeRoy was able to pursue a personal vision in their Warners films, but all three proved themselves to be remarkably versatile professional filmmakers who could function as master craftsmen within a system which militated strongly against creative freedom. Warners was also distinguished in the thirties for its art directors, Anton Grot and Robert Haas, and its two great composers, Erich Wolfgang Korngold and Max Steiner, both of whom joined the studio in 1935. Among the major Warners stars of the period were Bette Davis, Barbara Stanwyck, Paul Muni, James Cagney, Humphrey Bogart, Pat O'Brien, Edward G. Robinson, and Errol Flynn—players who seemed to embody the tough vernacular pragmatism of the studio's films themselves. (Warner Bros. prospers today as the film [*The Exorcist,* 1973; *All the President's Men,* 1976; *Superman,* 1978, and its sequels; *The Shining,* 1980; *Blade Runner* 1982; *Risky Business,* 1983; *Pale Rider,* 1985; *Full Metal Jacket,* 1987; *Batman,* 1989] and television production division of Warner

Communications, Inc. (WCI); it also has close ties to Orion Pictures and The Ladd Company; in 1989 WCI merged with Time, Inc. to become Time Warner; see pp. 889–90.)

20th Century–Fox

20th Century–Fox was born of financial difficulties, and yet it would become, after MGM and Paramount, the most profitable studio of its era. In March 1935, the U.S. Supreme Court ruled against William Fox in his all-or-nothing attempt to retain complete control of the U.S. patent rights to the Tri-Ergon sound-on-film process which was the basis for the Fox Movietone system. Had Fox won, he would have been due incalculable sums in damages from every producer of sound films in the country and would have come very close to his dream of monopolizing the entire American film industry. As it was, he lost his personal fortune of one hundred million dollars in bankruptcy proceedings and was ousted as president of Fox Film Corporation by Sidney Kent, who arranged a merger with Joseph M. Schenck's Twentieth Century Pictures in late 1935, forming 20th Century–Fox and securing Twentieth Century executive producer, Darryl F. Zanuck (1902–79), as the new company's vice president in charge of production.* (Fox was forced out of his company in 1931; he didn't declare bankruptcy until 1936.) Zanuck, who reigned as production chief through 1956, replaced Fox's lieutenant Winfield Sheehan (1883–1945). Despite William Fox's depredations, 20th Century–Fox was heir to the Movietone City complex in Los Angeles and newsreel studios in New York; extensive theater chains in the United States (National Theater), England (Gaumont British Pictures), Australia (the Hoyts Circuit),

8.22 The Fox Movietone studios, built in 1928–29 to produce sound films; from 1935 through the present, the home of 20th Century-Fox.

8.23 The gloss of Fox: Lionel Barrymore and Shirley Temple in *The Little Colonel* (David Butler, 1935).

* Kent died of a heart attack in 1941, and Schenck, who was board chairman, went to jail for tax evasion in the same year (after serving four months, he returned to the Fox board but remained in the background of the industry until forming the Magna Corporation with Michael Todd in 1953). As its new president in 1942, 20th Century-Fox selected Spyros Skouras (1883–1971), then head of Fox Metropolitan Theaters, who served until he was ousted by Zanuck following the *Cleopatra* debacle of 1963 (see Chapter 12).

New Zealand, and South Africa; and 147 film exchanges serving every country on earth but the Soviet Union.

The studio's films of the thirties acquired a reputation for hard, glossy surfaces produced through careful budgeting and production control. Fox's major director at this time was John Ford, although he also worked sporadically for other studios. Ford's most important films for Fox during the period were *Dr. Bull* (1933), *Judge Priest* (1934), and *Steamboat Round the Bend* (1935)—all three starring the popular vaudeville wit Will Rogers; *The Prisoner of Shark Island* (1935), *Young Mr. Lincoln* (1939), *Drums Along the Mohawk* (1939), *The Grapes of Wrath* (1940), and *How Green Was My Valley* (1941). Fox also specialized in musicals like Henry King's *Alexander's Ragtime Band* (1938), American period nostalgia like the same director's *State Fair* (1933) and *In Old Chicago* (1938), and such popular B-film series as the Charlie Chan mysteries, starring Warner Oland and then Sidney Toler in the title role, but its fortunes in the thirties were also built in large part upon the films of its popular child star Shirley Temple,* which included *Stand Up and Cheer* (Hamilton McFadden, 1934), *Curly Top* (Irving Cummings, 1935), *Captain January* (David Butler, 1935), *The Littlest Rebel* (David Butler, 1935), *The Little Colonel* (David Butler, 1935), *Wee Willie Winkie* (John Ford, 1937), *Heidi* (Allen Dwan, 1937), *Rebecca of Sunnybrook Farm* (Allen Dwan, 1938), and *The Blue Bird* (Walter Lang, 1940). Other Fox stars of the thirties were Tyrone Power, Charles Boyer, Alice Faye, Don Ameche, Warner Baxter, Henry Fonda, Loretta Young, and Janet Gaynor. The studio's major cinematographers were Bert Glennon and Arthur Miller, and its music director was the brilliant arranger Alfred Newman. Finally, Fox was noted for having the best special effects department of all the major studios—a reputation borne out by the disaster sequences of *Dante's Inferno* (Harry Lachman, 1935) and *The Rains Came* (Clarence Brown, 1939)—as well as producing the most Technicolor features through 1949. (20th Century–Fox remains today an important producer of film [*Star Wars,* 1977, and sequels; *Alien,* 1979, and sequel; *All That Jazz,* 1980; *Quest for Fire,* 1982; *Romancing the Stone,* 1984, and sequel; *Prizzi's Honor,* 1985; *The Fly,* 1986; *Wall Street,* 1987] and television [*M.A.S.H.*]; with Walt Disney Productions, it is the only major Hollywood studio not under the control of a corporate conglomerate, although it was acquired by Texas oilman Marvin Davis in 1981, who sold half of it to media baron Rupert Murdoch in 1985. see p. 890).

RKO

The smallest of the majors was RKO, which remained financially unstable through the thirties and forties and finally ceased production in 1953, when it sold its entire twenty-four-year output of features to television. (Two years later, RKO was sold to the General Tire and Rubber

---

* She had so endeared herself to the American public by 1937 that Louis B. Mayer offered Clark Gable and Jean Harlow to 20th Century-Fox in exchange for the child star, whom he wanted to play the lead in *The Wizard of Oz.* Negotiations were terminated by Miss Harlow's sudden death in 1937, and Judy Garland was cast in the role.

Company, which in turn sold the studio facilities to Desilu Television Productions in 1957; today, as RKO General, it holds broadcasting and cable television franchises for its parent firm, GTR, and produces an occasional feature.) RKO was ruled by eight successive regimes from 1929 to 1952 (the last being that of millionaire Howard Hughes [1905–76], who is credited with wrecking it), and it was the most volatile and risk-taking of all studios of the era; the decade of the thirties, however, was its most stable period—probably because the corporation was in receivership from 1933 to 1939 and placed under the administration of a federal district court.* In 1934, RKO became the home of the Fred Astaire–Ginger Rogers musical with the success of their first film together, *Flying Down to Rio* (Thornton C. Freeland, 1933), in which they had second billing. From 1934 to 1939, the studio made eight Astaire–Rogers vehicles under the auspices of its innovative young producer Pandro S. Berman (b. 1905) and star directors like Mark Sandrich (1900–1945) and George Stevens (1904–75). Films like *The Gay Divorcee* (Sandrich, 1934), *Top Hat* (Sandrich, 1935), and *Swing Time* (Stevens, 1936) made the Astaire-Rogers team one of the most popular box-office attractions in America and gave RKO a reputation for stylishness and sophistication throughout the decade, although it produced its share of B-films for the second half of double bills.

8.24 The RKO studios, Los Angeles, c. 1935.

The studio also had a penchant for literary adaptations like *Little Women* (George Cukor, 1933), *Of Human Bondage* (John Cromwell, 1934), and *The Hunchback of Notre Dame* (William Dieterle, 1938). John Ford directed three such films for RKO in the thirties: adaptations of two plays—Maxwell Anderson's *Mary of Scotland* (1936) and Sean O'Casey's *The Plough and the Stars* (1936)—and a masterly, expressive rendition of Liam O'Flaherty's novel *The Informer* (1935), which some historians regard as the first recognizably modern sound film in its symbolic, nonliteral use of the medium. RKO's most extraordinary production of the decade and one of its most successful was the monster thriller *King Kong* (Merian C. Cooper and Ernest B. Schoedsack, 1933), whose brilliant stop-motion photography and special effects by Willis O'Brien (1886–1962) are still a marvel of technical achievement. The studio's major star during this period was Katharine Hepburn (b. 1907), who made fourteen films for RKO between 1932 and 1938, including *A Bill of Divorcement* (George Cukor, 1932), *Little Women* (Cukor, 1933), *Mary of Scotland* (John Ford, 1936), *A Woman Rebels* (Mark Sandrich, 1936), *Stage Door* (Gregory La Cava, 1937), and the classic screwball comedy *Bringing Up Baby* (Howard Hawks, 1938). RKO's art director from 1930 to 1943 was the

---

* In 1931, RKO had embarked upon an expansionary campaign by acquiring Pathé Exchange, Inc. This gave it new studio space in Culver City, a newsreel service (Pathé News), and an international distribution network, but left it badly overextended. Then, in 1932, it opened the 6,200-seat Radio City Music Hall, part of whose lease required RKO to move its corporate headquarters to Rockefeller Center, the most expensive piece of real estate in the country. By January 1933, the company had defaulted on more than $3.5 million in loans and was placed under the authority of the court. (The distinct styles of RKO's eight successive management teams are recounted in Betty Lasky's closely researched *RKO: The Biggest Little Major of Them All* [New York: Prentice Hall, 1984].)

8.25 RKO's spectacular *King Kong* (Merian C. Cooper and Ernest B. Schoedsack, 1933).

distinguished Van Nest Polglase (b. 1898), whose genius was equally responsible for the stylish elegance of the Astaire-Rogers musicals and the murky expressiveness of Ford's *The Informer* and *Mary of Scotland*. In addition to its own films, RKO also released independent productions for Samuel Goldwyn and David O. Selznick, and it became the distributor for Walt Disney's animated features and shorts with the release of *Snow White and the Seven Dwarfs* in Christmas week, 1937.* The studio ended the decade with bravado by signing the *enfant terrible* of broadcasting, Orson Welles, to a highly publicized six-film contract in 1939, the first product of which was *Citizen Kane* (1941; see pp. 408–27).

The Minors

Universal Pictures, which remained under the control of its founder, Carl Laemmle, until 1936, had been a leading studio in the twenties, producing for such talents as Erich von Stroheim, Lon Chaney, and Rudolph Valentino, but by the thirties the company had slipped into a minor position. Unlike the Big Five, it had failed to acquire a chain of downtown first-run theaters and was forced to concentrate its production and distribution efforts on subsequent-run houses in suburban and rural areas.† It produced a number of prestigious films during the decade,

---

* Rereleased for the seventh time in 1987 to commemorate its fiftieth anniversary, *Snow White* was a phenomenon in its own day and has become one of the most profitable films in history, earning the equivalent of $325 million worldwide. Its original release was accompanied by multiple marketing tie-ins with sheet music, toys, and books, plus an original soundtrack recorded on RCA Victor 10-inch 78s. As the first American animated feature, *Snow White* represented an enormous risk for Disney, who had spent the equivalent of $32 million ($1,488,000 in 1937 currency) and three years to produce it. Nearly 750 artists were employed to draw the two million drawings that comprise the film—which was known in the industry as "Disney's Folly" until it returned its investment five times over in 1938.

† Universal did, however, maintain an international distribution network and had considerable success releasing its Westerns in Europe.

8.26   Universal horrors: *Dracula* (Tod Browning, 1931): Bela Lugosi, Dwight Frye. *Frankenstein* (James Whale, 1931): Boris Karloff.

including Lewis Milestone's *All Quiet on the Western Front* (1930), James Whale's *Showboat* (1936), and George Marshall's *Destry Rides Again* (1939), and it achieved some commercial success with the popular melodramas of John M. Stahl (1886–1950—*Back Street,* 1932; *Imitation of Life,* 1934; and *Magnificent Obsession,* 1935), but its standard product was the low-budget feature designed for double bills. Nevertheless, Universal did manage to distinguish itself in the horror-fantasy genre during the thirties, drawing upon the UFA tradition of Expressionism and the talents of the directors James Whale (1889–1957) and Tod Browning (1882–1962), and the former UFA cameraman Karl Freund.

Tod Browning's *Dracula,* broodingly photographed by Freund, began the Universal horror cycle in 1931, and it was continued by James Whale's powerful and chilling version of *Frankenstein* in the same year. Whale, an Englishman of great sophistication with a fine feeling for Gothic atmosphere, became Universal's star director of the thirties on the basis of his elegantly mounted horror films. He went on to direct *The Old Dark House* (1932), *The Invisible Man* (1935), and the oddly baroque *The Bride of Frankenstein* (1935) for the studio before turning to other genres. Other important Universal horror films of the thirties were Robert Florey's Caligariesque *Murders in the Rue Morgue* (1932), photographed by Freund; Edgar G. Ulmer's bizarre essay in Expressionist mayhem, *The Black Cat* (1934); Karl Freund's evocative thriller *The Mummy* (1932); Stuart Walker's *Werewolf of London* (1935); and Lambert Hillyer's *The Invisible Ray* (1935) and *Dracula's Daughter* (1936). The latter concluded the cycle of serious horror films begun with *Dracula* in 1931. A second cycle was begun at Universal in 1939 with *Son of Frankenstein,* stylishly directed by Rowland V. Lee, and George Waggoner's atmospheric *The Wolfman* (1941). These were worthy successors to the Whale series, but the films of the second cycle quickly lapsed into imitation and self-parody with titles like *The Invisible Man Returns* (1940),

8.27   *The Bride of Frankenstein* (James Whale, 1935): Elsa Lanchester, Colin Clive.

8.28 *The Mummy* (Karl Freund, 1932): Boris Karloff in the title role.

The Mummy's Hand (1940), *The Ghost of Frankenstein* (1942), and *Frankenstein Meets the Wolfman* (1943). When the first horror cycle ended, Universal discovered the teenage singing star Deanna Durbin and featured her in a series of musical comedies made by the producer-director team of Joe Pasternak and Henry Koster (*Three Smart Girls*, 1936; *Mad About Music*, 1938; *Three Smart Girls Grow Up*, 1939; *Spring Parade*, 1940) which kept the studio from bankruptcy until the second horror cycle began to pay off. Other stars under contract to Universal during the thirties included, appropriately, Boris Karloff, Bela Lugosi, and Lon Chaney, Jr.; and, in the early forties, W. C. Fields (*The Bank Dick*, 1940; *My Little Chickadee*, 1940; *Never Give a Sucker an Even Break*, 1941—all directed by Edward Cline), Abbot and Costello (*Buck Privates*, 1941; *In the Navy*, 1941; *Hold that Ghost*, 1941; *Keep 'Em Flying*, 1941; *Ride 'Em Cowboy*, 1942—all directed by Arthur Lubin), and Basil Rathbone and Nigel Bruce, stars of the twelve-film "modern" Sherlock Holmes cycle* (e.g., *Sherlock Holmes Faces Death*, 1943; *The Scarlet Claw*, 1944), most of them produced and directed by Roy William Neill. (As a subsidiary of the entertainment conglomerate MCA, Universal is today Hollywood's leading studio, producing more theatrical films [*Jaws*, 1975, and sequels; *The Deer Hunter*, 1978; *1941*, 1979; *E.T. The Extra-Terrestrial*, 1982; *Conan the Barbarian*, 1982; *The Dark Crystal*, 1982; *Scarface*, 1983; *Back to the Future*, 1985; *Out of Africa*, 1985; *Twins*, 1988] and prime-time television series than anyone else in industry; see pp. 889–90.)

Columbia Pictures was the brainchild of a single man, Harry Cohn (1891–1958), who founded the corporation in 1924 and ruled over it absolutely until his death in 1958. Columbia owned no theater circuits but maintained a successful international distribution network under the management of Harry's brother Jack (1889–1956), which enabled it to sustain continuous profits during the Depression and finally to double its assets during the postwar boom. Columbia's staple product during the studio era was the low-budget cofeature, mainly Westerns and long-run series films adapted from other media (e.g., the twenty-eight-film "Blondie" series, 1938–51, based on the Chic Young comic strip), but Cohn had a policy of hiring, for single pictures, stars who were temporarily disaffected from their regular studios, and he managed to produce a number of first-class films at low overhead in this manner, including George Cukor's *Holiday* (1938); Rouben Mamoulian's *Golden Boy* (1939); and Howard Hawks's *Twentieth Century* (1934), *Only Angels Have Wings* (1939), and *His Girl Friday* (1940). The studio's star director was Frank Capra (b. 1897), whose New Deal and screwball comedies written by Robert Riskin (1897–1955) were largely responsible for keeping Columbia solvent during the thirties. The prototype of the form was the enormously

---

* As opposed to the two Fox big-budget period films, *The Hound of the Baskervilles* (Sidney Lanfield, 1939) and *The Adventures of Sherlock Holmes* (Alfred Werker, 1939), both produced by Darryl F. Zanuck and starring Rathbone and Bruce, which initiated American sound film adaptations of the Conan Doyle stories. There were, of course, countless silent versions on both sides of the Atlantic and numerous sound films from England, Germany, and Czechoslovakia.

8.29 Columbia's "sleeper" *It Happened One Night* (Frank Capra, 1934): Claudette Colbert, Clark Gable.

8.30 *Mr. Deeds Goes to Town* (Frank Capra, 1936): Gary Cooper on the tuba. Columbia.

successful *It Happened One Night* (1934), written by Riskin and starring Clark Gable (on loan from MGM) and Claudette Colbert (on loan from Paramount). This romantic comedy concerns the adventures of a runaway heiress and a newspaperman who discovers her identity and ends by marrying her. The film is full of witty, fast-talking dialogue, ingenious gags, and incredible twists of plot that established a new style in Hollywood comedy for the rest of the decade. Other Capra-Riskin films—the social comedies *Mr. Deeds Goes to Town* (1936) and *You Can't Take It with You* (1938), the more serious *Mr. Smith Goes to Washington* (1939), and the utopian fantasy *Lost Horizon* (1937)—possess the same qualities of refreshing informality mixed with New Deal optimism and populism, constituting what one critic has called "fantasies of good will." Other Columbia assets were the gifted comedienne Jean Arthur and the opera star Grace Moore, whose popular series of musicals—*One Night of Love* (Victor Schertzinger, 1934), *Love Me Forever* (Schertzinger, 1935), and *I'll Take Romance* (Edward H. Griffith, 1937)—put it well on its way to becoming a major studio in the forties and fifties, when, through its Screen Gems division (established 1952), Columbia became the first Hollywood studio to produce programming for the new medium of television. (As a subsidiary of the Coca-Cola Company 1982–89, Columbia Pictures Industries, Inc., was a financially powerful producer of theatrical films [*Close Encounters of the Third Kind*, 1977; *Kramer vs. Kramer*, 1979; *Tootsie*, 1982; *The Big Chill*, 1983; *Ghostbusters*, 1984, and its sequel; *Jagged Edge*, 1985; *Stand By Me*, 1986] and television; in 1989, it merged with Tri-Star to become Colombia Pictures Entertainment and was acquired by Sony Corp., see Chapter 18.)

United Artists was not, strictly speaking, a studio at all but a distributor for the films of independent producers. It had been founded by Charlie Chaplin, Mary Pickford, Douglas Fairbanks, and D. W. Griffith in 1919 to distribute their own films, and in the thirties it handled the independent productions of Samuel Goldwyn, David O. Selznick, Walter

Wanger, Hal Roach, and the Hungarian-born British producer-director Alexander Korda, among others. United Artists was unique in that it owned no production facilities and no exhibition chains, so production and distribution of its films were negotiated on an individual basis. Because United Artists had no studio and no stars, it did not fare well financially during this period of Hollywood's massive corporate growth, but by the same token the absence of a huge overhead enabled it to survive, if not always to prosper, during hard times. Its most important releases of the thirties were Chaplin's *City Lights* (1931) and *Modern Times* (1936), King Vidor's *Street Scene* (1931) and *Our Daily Bread* (1934), Lewis Milestone's *The Front Page* (1931), Howard Hawks' *Scarface* (1932), René Clair's *The Ghost Goes West* (1936), William Cameron Menzies' *Things to Come* (1936), and Alexander Korda's *The Private Life of Henry VIII* (1933), *Rembrandt* (1936), and *Elephant Boy* (1937)*—the last five all products of a long-term contract with Korda's London Films production company. United Artists also had a distribution contract with Samuel Goldwyn, who released through the company, as an independent producer, *Stella Dallas* (King Vidor, 1937), *Dead End* (William Wyler, 1937), and *Wuthering Heights* (William Wyler, 1939), among other films.

Throughout the studio era, UA relied upon the Big Five for access to first-run theaters; this was generally not a problem during the reign (1924–35) of board chairman—and from 1927, president—Joseph M. Schenck, since his brother Nicholas was concurrently president of Loew's, Inc., and helped him to negotiate bookings with the majors, including, of course, MGM. But when Joseph left to head up the newly formed 20th Century–Fox in 1935, UA was left without an ally among the Big Five, and its fortunes declined rapidly as producers turned away from it one by one (Goldwyn and Wagner in 1941, Korda in 1942, Selznick in 1945). For these reasons, UA became the only Hollywood studio that did not profit from the postwar boom. (After it was acquired by the entertainment lawyers Arthur B. Krim and Robert S. Benjamin in 1951, the company absorbed the B-film studio Eagle-Lion and was revitalized by the production of several major hits [*The African Queen*, 1951, *High Noon*, 1952]. During the fifties, UA supported a large roster of independent producers and began television distribution operations in 1957; it subsequently acquired long-term distribution contracts with the Mirisch Corporation and Eon Productions, the Albert R. Broccoli-Harry Saltzman partnership that produced the James Bond series of the sixties and seventies [Harry Saltzman sold his share in Eon to UA in 1974; see 517–18n]. As a subsidiary of the Transamerica Corporation from 1967 to 1981, UA produced the commercial hits *Rocky* [1976] and *Rocky II* [1979] and such critically esteemed films as *One Flew Over the Cukoo's Nest* [1975], *Annie Hall* [1977], and *The French Lieutenant's Woman* [1981] but was brought to its knees through the financial debacle of *Heaven's Gate* [1980; see p. 889]. In 1981 it was merged with MGM to form MGM/UA Entertainment Company and went on to produce the popular *Rocky III* [1982]

---

* Co-directed by Zoltan Korda and Robert Flaherty.

and *IV* [1985] and *Poltergeist* [1982] and *Poltergeist II* [1985], as well as such recent hits as *Rain Man* [1988]; in 1985, MGM/UA was acquired by Turner Broadcasting, which sold the company in 1986 to Kirk Kerkorian who restructed it as MGM/UA Communications and eventually sold the UA component to Australia's Qintex Entertainment in 1990.)

There were a handful of independent producers in Hollywood during the heyday of the studio system, most of whom released their films through United Artists or RKO. The two most influential were Samuel Goldwyn of Samuel Goldwyn Productions and David O. Selznick of Selznick International Pictures. As Samuel Goldfish, Goldwyn had founded the Goldwyn Pictures Corporation with the brothers Edgar and Archibald Selwyn in December 1916, combining the first and last syllables of their respective names into the famous surname that Goldfish legally took as his own in 1918. In 1923, shortly before the merger which created Metro-Goldwyn-Mayer (and which simultaneously dealt him out of the new corporation), Goldwyn formed Samuel Goldwyn Productions, a completely independent company, and he went on to become one of the most prestigious producers of the thirties and forties. The logo "Samuel Goldwyn Presents" became synonymous with high-quality family entertainment during these years and served to introduce much new talent to the industry. Although he produced the films of many important directors (e.g., King Vidor, John Ford), Goldwyn's most fruitful association was with William Wyler, who provided him with some of his biggest hits (*Dodsworth*, 1936; *Dead End*, 1937; *Wuthering Heights*, 1939; *The Little Foxes*, 1941; *The Best Years of Our Lives*, 1946). David O. Selznick left MGM to found Selznick International Pictures in 1936 and became the very type of creative independent producer that so many filmmakers enmeshed in the cogs and gears of the studio system longed to be. His motto "In a tradition of quality," Selznick produced a series of lavish but tasteful films whose meticulous attention to detail borders on the obsessive: William Wellman's *A Star Is Born* (1937) and *Nothing Sacred* (1937); Alfred Hitchcock's *Rebecca* (1940), *Spellbound* (1945), and *The Paradine Case* (1948); John Cromwell's *Since You Went Away* (1944); King Vidor's *Duel in the Sun* (1946); William Dieterle's *Portrait of Jenny* (1948); and, as coproducer with Alexander Korda, Carol Reed's *The Third Man* (1949). Although like Goldwyn he released mainly through UA and RKO, Selznick's most famous film, *Gone with the Wind* (1939), was produced for MGM so that he could cast MGM contract star Clark Gable in the role of Rhett Butler.

"Poverty Row"

Below even the minor studios were the "B" studios. These came into existence in the thirties as the result of a uniquely American movie phenomenon: the double bill. When the novelty of sound had worn off and the Depression had set in, audiences began to stay away from the movies. From ninety million admissions a week in 1930, the figure dropped to sixty million by 1932. By midsummer of 1935, five thousand of the sixteen thousand movie theaters in the United States were closed. To combat this situation Hollywood invented the double bill, which offered two features, a cartoon, and a newsreel for the price of a single admission. By 1935, 85 percent of all American theaters were offering double bills, and from 1935 to around 1950 American audiences expected three-hours-plus worth of entertainment every time they went to the movies. The B-studios were created by the rental system which the major studios devised for double features. Whereas the producer / distributor and the exhibitor would split the box-office receipts for the main feature, or the A-film (usually sixty / forty or eighty / twenty), the B-film was rented to the exhibitor at a flat rate. This meant that there was very little financial risk involved in producing B-films (since distribution was guaranteed), but that there was also very little profit in it since the film would never make more money than the fixed rate allowed. For this reason the major studios initially had scant interest in producing B-features (although the minors produced them in quantity, and the Big Five started operating B-units around 1935, and so in the early thirties about a dozen small companies sprang up in Hollywood for the specific purpose of producing cheap, hour-long genre films for the bottom half of double bills.

Collectively known as "The B-Hive," or "Poverty Row," these studios operated on an extremely thin profit margin with very little capital. A B-feature might cost seventy-five thousand to eighty thousand dollars to produce and make a profit of ten thousand to fifteen thousand dollars nationwide; but the average budget and profit figures were $20,000 and $3–$4,000, respectively. Shooting schedules ranged from seven to fourteen days, depending on the material, and were rigidly followed: to keep a cast and crew on tap for a single day beyond the scheduled completion date would often destroy the small profit margin. The most important B-studios were Republic Pictures, Monogram Productions, Grand National Films, and—in the forties—Producers Releasing Corporation (PRC) and Eagle-Lion Films. At their peak, each studio produced forty to fifty films per year, much of which was trash. But the B-studios also provided the training ground for many a director who went on to better things (in the thirties, for example, Christy Cabanne, Richard Thorpe, and Charles Vidor; in the forties, Edward Dmytryk, Laslo Benedek, Anthony Mann, Budd Boetticher, Ida Lupino, Jacques Tourneur, and Phil Karlson), and they produced a number of extraordinary films in their own right (for example, Edgar G. Ulmer's *Detour,* 1946; Ben Hecht's *The Spectre of the Rose,* 1946; Orson Welles' *Macbeth,* 1948; Allan Dwan's *The Sands of Iwo Jima,* 1949; and Joseph H. Lewis's *Gun Crazy,* 1949). In the wake of the postwar boom, Herbert J. Yates' Republic even became successful enough to produce such A-films as Frank Borzage's *Moonrise* (1948), Lewis Milestone's *The Red Pony* (1949), Fritz Lang's *House by the River* (1950), and Nicholas Ray's *Johnny Guitar* (1954), and to distribute John Ford's Argosy productions, *Rio Grande* (1950), *The Quiet Man* (1952), and *The Sun Shines Bright* (1953), although this extravagance eventually contributed to its bankruptcy in 1958.

When the major studios were divested of their theater chains between 1948 and 1953, the double bill was no longer profitable. The B-studios folded, and the B-film found a new home in the form of the television series. Only Monogram survived: in the form of Allied Artists (incorporated 1952), it went on to produce such successful features as *Friendly Persuasion* (William Wyler, 1956) and *Love in the Afternoon* (Billy Wilder, 1957). Allied continued to produce films occasionally during the sixties and seventies (*Cabaret*, 1972; *Papillon*, 1973; *The Man Who Would Be King*, 1975), until it was sold to the television company Lorimar Productions in 1980.

The studio system of production could exist only so long as the majors maintained their monopolistic control of the means of exhibition.* Without a guaranteed weekly audience, films would have to be made and sold on terms other than the system allowed. In July 1938, in *The United States v. Paramount Pictures*, the federal government began litigation against the five major studios for combining and conspiring to restrain trade unreasonably and to monopolize the production, distribution, and exhibition of motion pictures. The three minors were charged with combining and conspiring with the majors for the same purpose. When war seemed imminent in 1940, a consent decree was issued permitting the studios to retain their exhibition chains, with minor restrictions, but the case was reactivated in 1945 and concluded in May 1948, when the U.S. Supreme Court ruled that the vertical integration of the majors violated federal antitrust laws and ordered the five companies to divest themselves of their theaters over a five-year period (see pp. 461–64). The divestiture order, known as the "Paramount decrees" or "consent decrees," destroyed the studio system by eliminating the guaranteed distribution and guaranteed weekly audience which were its mainstay.

MAJOR FIGURES OF THE STUDIO ERA

The period 1930 to 1939 saw the production of some five thousand feature films in the United States and was, in many ways, a Golden Age for the American cinema. Despite the rigors and impersonality of the Hollywood production system, at least four directors working in America in the thirties emerged as major figures of the sound film. They were Josef von Sternberg, John Ford, Howard Hawks, and Alfred Hitchcock.

Josef von Sternberg

Born Jonas Stern in Vienna, Josef von Sternberg (1894–1969) began his career in the United States during World War I as a maker of training and indoctrination films for the Army Signal Corps. He spent his appren-

---

* As previously stated, the Big Five actually owned only 16 percent of the nation's theaters, but that 16 percent comprised more than 70 percent of the first-run houses in the ninety-two largest cities. This de facto monopoly on first-run theaters guaranteed the majors bookings for all new productions and ensured that their features would capture 75 percent of all box-office revenues during the studio era, with another 20 percent going to the minors. Today, without that guarantee, filmmaking in America has become a much greater speculative risk than it was during the years of the studio system.

ticeship as a technical assistant, scenarist, and cameraman for a variety of filmmakers in America and England before directing his first film, the independently produced *The Salvation Hunters,* in 1925. Constructed according to the principles of the German *Kammerspielfilm* and strongly influenced by the psychological naturalism of von Stroheim, whose *The Wedding March* (1928) he would later re-edit for Paramount, this highly symbolic tale of low life on the San Pedro mud flats was shot on location in three weeks for the extremely small sum of forty-five hundred dollars. Distributed by UA, *The Salvation Hunters* established von Sternberg as an important new director in Hollywood.

In 1927, after several failed attempts at films for Charlie Chaplin (*The Sea Gull* [1926]) and MGM (*The Exquisite Sinner* [1926]), von Sternberg went to work for Paramount, where he made *Underworld* (1927), generally considered to be the first modern gangster film, although its realism was tempered by the lush visual poetry which would soon become a von Sternberg trademark. Based on a contemporary story idea by Ben Hecht,* this sumptuously photographed film was an immediate international success and had a great influence on European directors, especially Jacques Prévert, Marcel Carné, and Julien Duvivier (whose work will be explored in Chapter 9) in its treatment of the gangster as modern anti-hero. *Underworld* was so popular that it made von Sternberg and everyone connected with it world-famous. In 1928, after directing Emil Jannings in an immensely successful melodrama of the Russian Revolution entitled *The Last Command,* von Sternberg returned to *Kammerspielfilm* with *The Docks of New York.* This brooding tale of an encounter between a ship's stoker and a prostitute along the New York waterfront is renowned as a masterpiece of pictorial composition. The film was produced entirely in the studio, and its visually complex *mise-en-scène* creates a dreamlike atmosphere, reminiscent of Griffith's *Broken Blossoms* (1919), which was resurrected a decade later in Carné and Prévert's *Quai des brûmes* (*Port of Shadows,* 1938).

Von Sternberg made the transition to sound with the realistic gangster / prison drama *Thunderbolt* in 1929, and in that year he was summoned to Germany by Erich Pommer to direct, for UFA, Emil Jannings' first talking picture, a version of Heinrich Mann's novel *Professor Unrat* (1905); it became the first real classic of the sound film, *Der blaue Engel* (*The Blue Angel,* 1930). Adapted from the novel by von Sternberg, *Der blaue Engel* is a powerful film on the theme of sexual domination in which a middle-aged bourgeois teacher, played by Jannings, becomes

---

* Ben Hecht (1894–1964) was a journalist and playwright who collaborated with Charles MacArthur (1895–1956) on some of the best Hollywood screenplays of the thirties, including an adaptation of their own popular stage play *The Front Page* (1931); *Scarface* (1932, Hecht solo); *Twentieth Century* (1934); *Soak and Rich* (1936); *Nothing Sacred* (1937); and *Wuthering Heights* (1939). In the forties, Hecht worked on his own for Hitchcock (*Spellbound,* 1945; *Notorious,* 1946) and numerous other directors into the fifties and sixties. (Howard Hawks collaborated on the *Underworld* script with Hecht, but did not receive screen credit.)

8.31 Marlene Dietrich as Lola-Lola in Josef von Sternberg's *Der blaue Engel* (1930).

8.32 "High cinema-baroque": Anna May Wong and Dietrich in von Sternberg's *Shanghai Express* (1932).

enslaved to a sensual cabaret singer named Lola-Lola. The singer was played by Marlene Dietrich, a stage and film actress under contract to UFA whom von Sternberg chose for the part and subsequently brought to stardom in America. *Der blaue Engel* is striking for its creative use of sound and its impressive recreation of the sleazy atmosphere of cabaret life; it owed a great deal in this regard to the *Kammerspiel* tradition. But it is also the film in which von Sternberg first began his career-long struggle with the problem of "dead space," that is, the space that separates the camera from its subject and the subject from its background. (Initially, as in *Der blaue Engel*, he attempted to occupy this space with a variety of streamers, nets, posters, veils, and even cardboard cutouts hanging from the ceiling above the stage,* but in his later films he realized that only by thickening the air with camera filters, diffusers, and gauzes could he achieve the gradations of light necessary to fill the screen as he wished.) Though Dr. Alfred Hugenberg, the right-wing head of UFA, denounced the film as an attack on the German bourgeoisie (which it was), *Der blaue Engel* was an instant international success.

In 1930, von Sternberg returned with Dietrich to the United States to begin the series of six films for Paramount that were to make her one of Hollywood's most glamorous and sought-after stars and simultaneously to wreck his career. The first of these was the successful *Morocco* (1930), the story of a romance between a European cabaret singer and a Foreign Legionnaire in Mogador, North Africa, written by Jules Furthman (1880–1960). Photographed by Lee Garmes and designed by Hans Dreier, *Morocco* presents Dietrich in all of her seductive, androgynous charm,

8.33 Dietrich in von Sternberg's *Blonde Venus* (1932).

* Cinematographer Günther Rittau (1893–1971) was able to give these images (as well as those of Dietrich's face) a diffusely luminous quality without sacrificing depth of field through the use of a "Rosher bullseye"—a customized soft-focus lens given to him by the American cinematographer Charles Rosher (1885–1974) during the latter's term as consultant on UFA's *Faust* (Murnau, 1926).

and was one of the most innovative of early American sound films. Upon its release, Sergei Eisenstein, then visiting Hollywood, sent von Sternberg a telegram stating: "Of all your great works, *Morocco* is the most beautiful." After making a sardonic and not particularly inspired spy thriller, *Dishonored* (1931), set in prewar Vienna, von Sternberg directed a low-budget version of Theodore Dreiser's novel *An American Tragedy* (1931), a project originally meant for Eisenstein but abandoned when studio executives found his treatment too "political." Characteristically, von Sternberg turned Dreiser's great work of social criticism into a tale of erotic obsession, much to the disgust of the author.* By this time, von Sternberg's reputation had grown so large that his name was appearing on theater marquees with the titles of his films—a rare practice in America at that time—and he was frequently ranked with Eisenstein as one of the foremost directors of the era.

With *Shanghai Express* (1932), written by Furthman, von Sternberg entered his richest period of creativity. Herman G. Weinberg has called this film "high cinema-baroque," and it is certainly one of the most visually evocative that the director ever made. It concerns the interactions of a group of passengers on an express train running from Peking to Shanghai which is hijacked by a rebellious warlord, and it focuses on a glamorous prostitute, "Shanghai Lily" (Dietrich), and her former lover, a glacial British army officer played by Clive Brook. Essentially a melodrama of deception and desire, *Shanghai Express* is a film in which decor becomes a theme in itself. From the hypnotic chiaroscuro photography of Lee Garmes, the incredibly exotic costumes of Travis Banton, and the lavish production design of Hans Dreier, von Sternberg created a mythological China where "dead space" is virtually absent. The tour-de-force opening sequence in which the train leaves the chaotic, flag-draped Peking station, the poetic encounters between Dietrich and Brook on the observation deck of the express, and the long lateral tracking shots down the latticed corridors of the cars themselves—all constructed in the studio—achieve a visual saturation rare outside of German Expressionism and the later work of Eisenstein.

Von Sternberg's next Dietrich vehicle was the bizarre *Blonde Venus* (1932), another stylistically striking film with a weak narrative concerning the broken life of yet another beautiful cabaret singer. (Dietrich's "Hot Voodoo" production number in this film may well contain the most outrageous variation upon the "beauty and the beast" metaphor in the history of modern culture: she comes onstage as a snarling gorilla and strips off the costume slowly, piece by piece, to reveal her own blonde loveliness and another costume of feathers and sequins beneath.) Then followed a fantastic and beautiful film "based on episodes from the private diaries of Catherine the Great," *The Scarlet Empress* (1934). This

---

*Paramount produced yet another version in 1951 as *A Place in the Sun*, with George Stevens directing. Though this film is closer to the tragedy of entrapment contained in the novel, its lush romanticism (for which it won six Academy Awards) would probably have pleased Dreiser (1871–1945) even less than von Sternberg's eroticism.

film re-created eighteenth-century Russia with as much poetic license as *Shanghai Express* had re-created contemporary China, and yet was visually more sumptuous than the original could have ever been. With grotesque statues and gargoyles by the Swiss sculptor Peter Balbusch, Byzantinesque icons and portraits by the German painter Richard Kollorsz, impossibly magnificent costumes by Travis Banton, and perhaps the most lavish production design ever undertaken by Hans Dreier, *The Scarlet Empress* apotheosized Dietrich as the ultimate symbol of sexual domination and degradation. The operatic grandeur and massive scale of the film are thought to have influenced Eisenstein's stylized design for *Ivan the Terrible, Parts I* (1945) and *II* (1946). Enormously expensive to produce, *The Scarlet Empress* failed at the box office (predictably so in a year whose smash hit was Frank Capra's populist fantasy *It Happened One Night*), and its director's favored status at Paramount was abruptly ended. Von Sternberg's final film with Dietrich for the studio and the one which virtually ended his career was *The Devil Is a Woman* (1935), based on the novel *La Femme et le pantin* (*Woman and Puppet*, 1898) by the decadent French romanticist Pierre Louys.* It tells the now familiar Sternbergian tale of a middle-aged man—this time an aristocratic member of the Spanish Civil Guard at the turn of the century—who is dominated and humiliated by a temptress. Thought by many critics to be among the most beautiful films ever made, *The Devil Is a Woman* is the only film for which von Sternberg took credit for cinematography (with Lucien Ballard), although he had supervised the photography and lighting of all his other films. In it, he achieved the ultimate in his attempt to make the two-dimensional cinema frame three-dimensional by filling dead space with decor and subtle gradations of light.

Sadly, *The Devil Is a Woman* was suppressed by Paramount shortly after its release due to protests by the Spanish government that it insulted the Spanish armed forces; it was not resurrected until after World War II. Simultaneously, the sympathetic B. P. Schulberg (1892–1957) left his post as production manager of Paramount to go to work for Columbia and was replaced by Ernst Lubitsch, who had a deep personal and cultural antipathy toward von Sternberg. This was the end for the director. Destroyed by his refusal to compromise with the studio system and by his own profligate style, his contract was canceled, and von Sternberg and Dietrich went their separate ways. Following a wretched term at Columbia during which he directed a limp modern version of Dostoevsky's *Crime and Punishment* (1935) and a silly Grace Moore vehicle entitled *The King Steps Out* (1936), von Sternberg went to London to direct an epic version of Robert Graves' novel *I, Claudius* for Alexander Korda. This star-crossed production failed financially and aesthetically at midpoint and was never completed, though the surviving footage, preserved in the BBC television documentary *The Epic That Never Was* (1966),

8.34 *Shanghai Express:* Dietrich, Warner Oland, Clive Brook.

8.35 Von Sternberg's *The Scarlet Empress* (1934): Dietrich as Catherine the Great, with John Lodge.

* Also the source for the opera *Conchita* (1911) by Riccardo Zandonai, the operetta *Frasquita* (1922) by Franz Lehar, and two other films—Julien Duvivier's *La femme et le pantin* (English title: *A Woman Like Satan*, 1958) and Luis Buñuel's *Cet obscur objet du désir* (*That Obscure Object of Desire*, 1977); see p. 692.

confirms von Sternberg's photographic genius. Returning to America, von Sternberg directed a low-grade police thriller for MGM entitled *Sergeant Madden* (1939) and the independently produced *Shanghai Gesture* (1941), a baroque attempt to evoke the stylish eroticism of the Paramount-Dietrich cycle in forties terms. After a graceful documentary short on American cultural values for the Office of War Information (see pp. 456–57) called *The Town* (1944), several abortive projects in the late forties, and an unhappy two-picture contract with RKO which produced *Jet Pilot* (1951; released 1957, with sequences reshot by Jules Furthman and Howard Hughes) and *Macao* (1952, with retakes directed by Nicholas Ray), von Sternberg ended his career with the Japanese-American coproduction *The Saga of Anatahan* (1953). This unusual film, the only one over which the director had total artistic control, tells the story of the tensions between twelve Japanese sailors shipwrecked on an isolated Pacific jungle island and a man and his mistress—an Asian variant of the typical Sternbergian seductress—who already inhabit the atoll. Produced, directed, photographed, designed, written, and narrated by von Sternberg alone, *The Saga of Anatahan* was shot in black-and-white, in a lush artificial jungle constructed on a soundstage in Kyoto. It is utterly appropriate that the last film by this master of cinematic artifice should have been made in a studio, when real jungles were available not far away.

The British documentarist John Grierson objected to one of von Sternberg's more visually extravagant productions by remarking, in a contemporary review, "When a director dies, he becomes a photographer." (Von Sternberg *was,* in fact, a photographer, having begun as a cameraman and having maintained his membership in the prestigious American Society of Cinematographers throughout his career.) Von Sternberg would have considered this a compliment because, for him, the image was the only true medium of cinematic art. Strongly influenced by graphic art, his greatest films constituted a kind of painting with light. It is fruitless to maintain that his plots are trivial or frivolous, because von Sternberg was not attempting to create a narrative cinema. In fact, he had little but contempt for the American tradition of narrative film as exemplified by the work of Griffith, Ince, and DeMille. On the contrary, von Sternberg's great achievement was to create *within* the American narrative cinema a cinema of mood and atmosphere based upon European styles of camera composition and lighting and his own eccentric vision of human passion and desire. It was a cinema of exoticism, eroticism, and, ultimately, cultural decadence, but one of astounding sensuous beauty which is unique in the history of film and modern art.

John Ford

Like von Sternberg, John Ford (b. Sean Aloysius O'Feeney, 1895–1973) began his career in the silent film, but beyond that similarity it would be difficult to imagine two more different directors. Whereas von Sternberg had contempt for American narrative cinema and for American values, Ford was a staunch proponent of both. Whereas von Sternberg contributed to the cinema a handful of exotic and eccentric masterworks between 1927 and 1935, Ford directed over 125 films, most of them popular and commercial products of the studio system, in a career that extended from 1917 to 1970.

John Ford first came to Hollywood in 1914 to work as a prop man for his older brother, Francis (1881–1953), a **contract director** at Universal. From 1917 to 1921, as Jack Ford, he was employed by Universal as a director of low-budget Westerns and adventure dramas, including twenty-five films with the former silent star Harry Carey (1878–1947), only one of which—*Straight Shooting* (1917)—survives. In 1922 he went to work for Fox, winning fame as a stylist with *The Iron Horse* (1924), a feature-length epic on the building of the first transcontinental railroad which became a smash hit, and a sweeping drama of the Dakota land-rush entitled *Three Bad Men* (1926), which did not. In 1927, deeply impressed by the Fox-produced *Sunrise*, Ford fell under the influence of F. W. Murnau and made a series of films—*Mother Machree, Four Sons, Hangman's House*, all 1928—replete with expressive decor, stylized lighting effects, and elaborate moving camera shots in imitation of the German director. Murnau's realist-Expressionist influence is also evident in Ford's first talking features, *The Black Watch* (1929),* which has been described by one critic as a "neo-Wagnerian music-drama," but Ford's first major sound film was the lost *Men Without Women* (1930), a submarine drama in which one man must die to save the rest of the crew. For this film, Ford used a real submarine and submerged his camera underwater in a glass box, among other innovative techniques. It also marked the beginning of Ford's long and fruitful collaboration with the scenarist Dudley Nichols† and the cameraman Joseph August (1890–1947) on many a successful project. Other notable Ford films of the early sound era were his version of Sinclair Lewis' novel *Arrowsmith* (1931), a critical and commercial hit produced by Samuel Goldwyn for UA; the Murnau-esque *Air Mail* (1932), made for Universal and photographed by the frequent Murnau collaborator Karl Freund; his Fox "Americana" trilogy starring the famous humorist Will Rogers (1879–1935); *Dr. Bull* (1933), *Judge Priest* (1934), and *Steamboat Round the Bend* (1935); and an RKO desert adventure called *The Lost Patrol* (1934). But he was not regarded as a major figure until *The Informer*, his first great critical success, cheaply and quickly produced for RKO in 1935. Adapted by Nichols from the 1925 novel by

---

* Fox, of course, was instrumental in the innovation of sound, and Ford directed both the studio's first dramatic talkie (*Napoleon's Barber* [1928], a three-reeler which has been lost) and its first on-screen song (in *Mother Machree*). *Mother Machree* and *Four Sons* both were released with music and synchronized sound effects. *The Black Watch*, which was Fox's top-grossing film of 1929, was remade by the studio in 1954 in CinemaScope as *King of the Khyber Rifles* (Henry King).

† Dudley Nichols (1895–1960) was another important scriptwriter of the thirties and forties, working not only with Ford but also with Howard Hawks (*Bringing Up Baby* [1938]; *Air Force* [1943]); Fritz Lang (*Man Hunt* [1941]; *Scarlet Street* [1945]); and Jean Renoir (*Swamp Water* [1941]; *This Land Is Mine* [1943]).

Liam O'Flaherty and ingeniously, if frugally, designed by Van Nest Polglase, it tells the symbol-laden story of an ignorant hulk of a man who betrays a fellow member of the Irish Republican Army to the British for money during the Irish Rebellion of 1922 and is psychologically tormented by his act until the IRA finally kills him in retribution. The film was photographed by Joseph August in a brooding manner reminiscent of classical German Expressionism and the *Kammerspielfilm,* and much use was made of subjective camera techniques to portray the informer's tortured state of mind, as when a crumpled "wanted" poster for the friend he has betrayed appears to pursue him down a foggy Dublin street like his own guilty conscience. Though it looks somewhat less impressive today, *The Informer* became one of the most highly regarded films of the decade, winning unanimously the New York Critics' Award for Best Film of the Year and four awards from the Academy of Motion Picture Arts and Sciences—Best Direction, Ford; Best Actor, Victor McLaglen in the title role; Best Writing (i.e., Screenplay), Dudley Nichols; Best Score, Max Steiner. (Nichols refused his Oscar, becoming the first person ever to do so, and both Nichols and Ford boycotted the Awards cermony of 1936 to show their solidarity with the various Screen Guilds then involved in labor disputes with Academy producers.)*

---

* The Academy of Motion Picture Arts and Sciences (AMPAS) was founded in 1927 by Louis B. Mayer and other film industry leaders—including Cecil B. DeMille, Douglas Fairbanks, and Mary Pickford, in their roles as producers—with the expressed purpose of advancing the educational, cultural, and technical standards of American movies. Its real, and, ultimately, unsuccessful, purpose was to combat trade-unionism among the growing ranks of directors, technicians, and performers who were pressing for higher wages and better working conditions as filmmaking became one of the nation's largest industries. In 1937, in the wake of considerable negative publicity, the Academy officially removed itself from the arena of labor relations and concentrated in earnest on its annual awards for professional achievement and on technical research, helping to achieve within a decade the industry-wide standardization of everything from script format, to back projection, to the official shade of white in black-and-white panchromatic film (see Bordwell, Staiger, and Thompson, *The Classical Hollywood Cinema,* pp. 258–61). The Academy's membership (originally 36, now 4,120) is drawn from prominent individuals in every branch of the industry, and its chief function is, and always has been, the annual presentation of "Oscars" (Academy Awards) for distinguished film achievement in the previous year. In actual practice, the correlation between Academy Awards and cinematic excellence is not at all precise. For one thing, the winning of Oscars involves a great deal more than prestige, since they inevitably increase the earning power of the films and performers that receive them. Each year, expensive campaigns are mounted by studios and other financial backers to "lobby" Academy members for votes which can be translated into profit in the marketplace. (For a detailed account of Universal Pictures' $300,000 promotion to impress Academy members with the merits of *The Deer Hunter* [Michael Cimino, 1978], see *Advertising Age,* April 16, 1979, pp. 1, 80.) Furthermore, Hollywood is a closed and really rather small community, many of whose members have known one another for a long time. The Academy's judgment is often colored by personal sentiment, both positive and negative, and there is always the implicit bias that what is good for the community in material terms (financially successful films and film careers) is good in critical terms as well. In short, it would be a mistake to assume that Academy Awards invariably signal excellence in films or performances. In fact, the Awards are probably best regarded as a company town's certification

After this success, Ford was given projects with a more social and historical orientation than his action films had possessed. Fox's *The Prisoner of Shark Island* (1936) told the true story of the fate of Dr. Samuel Mudd, who was imprisoned for unwittingly treating Lincoln's assassin. RKO's *Mary of Scotland* (1936) was an intelligent political tragedy adapted by Nichols from the Maxwell Anderson play, but the same studio's *The Plough and the Stars* (1936) was an awkward version of the Sean O'Casey play about the Easter Rising of 1916, when a small group of IRA troops seized control of Dublin and held off the huge British garrison for twenty-four hours. Ford's most unusual film of the period, and certainly his most commercially successful, was *The Hurricane* (1937),* a Samuel Goldwyn-UA production which concerned the sadistic imprisonment of a South Seas islander by a brutal European governor and concluded with a spectacularly realized tropical storm.†

The year 1939, however, witnessed the release of three of Ford's finest films. In *Stagecoach,* produced by Walter Wanger for UA, Ford returned to the Western for the first time in thirteen years and produced a film that was to revitalize the genre, largely in his own hands, for another twenty. Written by Dudley Nichols and photographed by Bert Glennon, this tale of a dangerous coach ride through hostile Indian territory by a group of misfits from every level of frontier society embodies what was to become a classical Fordian theme—the convolutions of human character under the pressure of extreme stress. Its stark and awesome setting in Monument Valley, Arizona—a location to which Ford would return time and time again—creates a symbolic landscape of the individual alone in an alien environment. The film was a great popular and critical success, receiving awards from both the New York Film Critics and the Academy of Motion Picture Arts and Sciences (it also made John Wayne [1907–79] a star). At Fox again, Ford made *Young Mr. Lincoln,* whose formal qualities have been much admired in recent years; the film provided a dignified and somber treatment of the Maxwell Anderson play and succeeded in raising the story of Lincoln's early career as a small-town lawyer to the level of national myth. Ford's final film of 1939, *Drums Along the Mohawk,* dealt with yet another aspect of the American past. His first work in color, the film is a visually striking re-creation

8.36 Henry Fonda in *Young Mr. Lincoln* (John Ford, 1939).

of the company product, and in this regard they do at least provide some indication of Hollywood's ever-changing image of itself as fabricator of American dreams. (For more, see Andrew Sarris, "The Importance of Winning Oscar," *Film Comment,* 15, 2 [March–April, 1979], 53–56; and Emanuel Levy, *And the Winner Is . . . The History and Politics of the Oscar ® Awards* (New York: Ungar, 1987). In addition to giving its annual Awards, the Academy also maintains a large collection of printed matter relating to film, and an extensive film archive with screening facilities open to the public in Hollywood; retrospectives are common.

* Remade, disastrously, under the same title by Jan Troell in 1979.

† This sequence was created by the special effects expert James Basevi (b. 1890?), with the assistance of Stuart Heisler. Basevi, who worked with Ford as art director on seven subsequent films, was renowned for his disaster sequences during the thirties, including (in collaboration with Arnold Gillespie) the famous earthquake in MGM's *San Francisco* (W. S. Van Dyke, 1936).

8.37 *Stagecoach* (John Ford, 1939).

8.38 The Welsh mining village in *How Green Was My Valley* (John Ford, 1941).

8.39 *The Grapes of Wrath* (John Ford, 1940): Henry Fonda as Tom Joad.

of the American Revolutionary era in New York State which was shot on location in the forests of Utah's Wasatch Mountains.*

Ford's new burst of creative energy continued into the forties with *The Grapes of Wrath* (1940), perhaps the most important Hollywood film of the Depression era. Adapted by Nunnally Johnson (1897–1977) from the John Steinbeck novel, it concerns a family of dispossessed farmers migrating to California across the Dust Bowl of the Southwest during the Depression. Although the film sentimentalizes the suffering of the Joad family, it is notable for the stark documentary texture of its exteriors, achieved through the beautifully restrained camerawork of the cinematographer Gregg Toland. Like *The Informer* and *Stagecoach*, *The Grapes of Wrath* was recognized as a distinguished film by both the New York Critics and the American Academy (although Ford himself never particularly liked it). After lukewarm adaptations of Eugene O'Neill's play *The Long Voyage Home* (1940, Walter Wanger-UA—Ford's only non-Fox film until the postwar period)† and Erskine Caldwell's novel *Tobacco Road* (1940), Ford directed his last commercial film before World War II, *How Green Was My Valley* (1941), adapted from the novel by Richard Llewellyn. This romantic and nostalgic film, for which an elaborate Welsh village was constructed on the 20th Century-Fox backlot, deals with the disintegration of a Welsh mining family and the communal soci-

---

* Original plans to shoot on location in the Mohawk Valley had to be scrapped when it was learned that industrialization had completely destroyed the landscape. See John E. O'Connor, "A Reaffirmation of American Ideas: *Drums Along the Mohawk* (1939)," *American History/American Film*, ed. John E. O'Connor and Martin A. Jackson (New York, 1979), pp. 97–120.

† *The Long Voyage Home*, was, however, distinguished by Toland's deep-focus cinematography and was the first film before *Citizen Kane* (1941—also shot by Toland) in which composition in depth appears as a consistent visual style (see pp. 399–400).

ety in which it lives at the turn of the century; in the year of *Citizen Kane*, it won five Academy Awards.*

During the war, Ford joined the navy and made documentaries for the Office of Strategic Services (OSS), including the famous *Battle of Midway* (1942, theatrically released by Fox), which he photographed himself from a water tower during the Japanese air attack, winning the Purple Heart (he was wounded in his left arm) and an Academy Award for Best Documentary in the process. Ford became chief of the Field Photographic Services of the OSS (which later became the CIA), supervising the production of such restricted and/or classified films as *How to Operate Behind Enemy Lines, How to Interrogate Enemy Prisoners, Living Off the Land, Nazi Industrial Manpower, Inside Tibet*, etc., as well as filmed reports on battle conditions, Allied defenses, bombing raids, and landings. In addition to *Battle of Midway*, Ford personally co-directed *December 7th* (1943) with cinematographer Gregg Toland, which went unreleased in its original 85-minute version, but whose 35-minute recut won the 1943 Academy Award—Ford's fourth Oscar—for Best Documentary.†

Ford's first postwar film, *They Were Expendable* (1945, MGM), was a moving tribute to the unstinting courage and discipline of the men with whom he had served. Exquisitely photographed by Joseph August, it tells the story of the sailors who pioneered the use of the PT boat during the American evacuation of the Philippines, and it is one of Ford's most intensely personal films. His next film, *My Darling Clementine* (1946, Fox), is among the most classically beautiful Westerns ever made. It concerns the events leading up to the legendary gunfight between the Earp brothers, here assisted by Doc Holliday, and the Clanton family at the OK Corral in Tombstone, Arizona; and it contains scenes of frontier communal life (like the lyrical dedication ceremony of Tombstone's first church) which are among Ford's most visually poetic creations.

In March 1946, like several other major Hollywood directors, Ford formed his own production company, Argossy Pictures Corporation, with the producer Merian C. Cooper (1894–1973: *Grass*, 1925; *Chang*, 1927; *King Kong*, 1933; *The Last Days of Pompeii*, 1935; etc.).** Its first film

8.40 A communal celebration in *My Darling Clementine* (John Ford, 1946): Cathy Downs, Henry Fonda.

---

* Best Picture, Best Director, Best Supporting Actor (Donald Crisp, as the father), Best Cinematography—Black-and-White (Arthur Miller), Best Art Direction—Black-and-White (Richard Day, Nathan Juran, and Thomas Little).

† For a detailed account of Ford's obsession with the military and his own military career, see Andrew Sinclair's biography *John Ford* (New York, 1979). For a more intimate portrait, see his grandson Dan Ford's *Pappy: The Life of John Ford* (New York, 1979); and on the OSS films themselves, see Tag Gallagher, *John Ford: The Man and His Films* (Berkeley: University of California Press, 1986).

** In the euphoric atmosphere of the postwar boom, amid speculation that the federal courts were going to break up the studio system's monopoly, a number of important filmmakers attempted to achieve independence (and, less nobly, to exploit capital gains loopholes in the Revenue Act of 1945) by forming their own companies—among them Frank Capra, William Wyler, and George Stevens (Liberty Films, 1945–47); Fritz Lang (Diana Productions, 1945–47); Alfred Hitchcock (Transatlantic Pictures, 1946–48); and Howard Hawks (Monterey Productions, 1946–47; Winchester Pictures Corporation, 1950–52).

was the final Ford-Nichols collaboration—a version of Graham Greene's 1940 novel *The Power and the Glory* entitled *The Fugitive* (1947), co-produced by the distinguished Mexican director Emilio Fernández (1904–86) and photographed by his cameraman Gabriel Figueroa (b. 1907), which in both theme and technique was reminiscent of *The Informer*. Like its predecessor, *The Fugitive* lost money and Ford shot a series of brilliantly mythic Westerns on location in Monument Valley to recoup his losses, including the so-called Cavalry trilogy—*Fort Apache* (1948), which inaugurated Ford's long association with the screenwriter Frank S. Nugent,* *She Wore a Yellow Ribbon* (1949), and *Rio Grande* (1950)—and *Wagon Master* (1950). These, together with his final Argossy films—*The Quiet Man* (1952), a nostalgic paean to Irish village life shot on location at the Feeney family homestead in Connemara, and *The Sun Shines Bright* (1953), a picaresque remake of *Judge Priest,* which was the director's favorite film—stand today among Ford's finest achievements.†

After Argossy was dissolved, Ford returned to working for the studios and produced some extraordinary films—the African adventure *Mogambo* (1953, MGM), a remake of Victor Fleming's *Red Dust* (1932); *The Long Gray Line* (1955, Columbia), a biography of West Point athletic trainer Marty Maher and Ford's first film in CinemaScope; and, preeminently, the epic questing / captivity narrative *The Searchers* (1956, Warners), widely regarded today as one of the greatest Westerns ever made. There were other interesting, if increasingly uneven, films—*The Wings of Eagles* (1957, MGM), an oddly incohesive biography of Ford's friend Spig Wead, a World War I flying ace who became a Hollywood screenwriter after being paralyzed by an accident; *The Rising of the Moon* (1957, Warners), a trilogy of Irish tales shot on location and performed by the Abbey Theater Players; the London police procedural *Gideon's Day* (1958, Columbia British);** *The Last Hurrah* (1958, Columbia), a film of Boston politics

---

Like Argossy, they proved no match for the majors, even after the divestiture ordered by the Paramount decrees of 1948, although by the late fifties independent production had come into its own (see pp. 531–34).

* Frank S. Nugent (1908–65), a former newspaper critic and Ford's son-in-law, collaborated with him on ten subsequent films, including *Three Godfathers* (1949), *She Wore a Yellow Ribbon* (1949), *Wagonmaster* (1950), *The Quiet Man* (1952), *Mister Roberts* (1955—a troubled production only nominally directed by Ford), *The Searchers* (1956), *The Rising of the Moon* (1957), *The Last Hurrah* (1958), *Two Rode Together* (1961), and *Donovan's Reef* (1963). Nugent also worked occasionally for other directors—never with the same degree of success—on films with Fordian themes, e.g., Stuart Heisler (*Tulsa,* 1948), Otto Preminger (*Angel Face,* 1953), Raoul Walsh (*The Tall Men,* 1955), and Phil Karlson (*They Rode West,* 1954; *Gunman's Walk,* 1958).

† Although *The Quiet Man* was Ford's biggest box-office hit to date, grossing nearly $4 million on an investment less than half the size, and won Oscars both for direction and color cinematography (to Winton C. Hoch), its success was not enough to prevent Argossy's dissolution in 1953. In its seven-year existence, it had produced eight Ford films (the seven noted, plus the Western comedy-drama *Three Godfathers* (1949), which is dedicated to Harry Carey and stars his son), and *Mighty Joe Young* (Ernest B. Schoedsack, 1949), a revamping of *King Kong* with Academy Award-winning special effects by Willis O'Brien and Ray Harryhausen.

** A film whose expressive use of color we have been denied by Columbia's decision to

8.41 *The Horse Soldiers* (John Ford, 1959): John Wayne compositions like this one influenced Japanese director Akira Kurosaw (see pp. 786–91).

8.42 *Cheyenne Autumn* (John Ford, 1964).

adapted from the best-selling novel by Edwin O'Conner; a disjointed Civil War epic called *The Horse Soldiers* (1959, the Mirisch Coporation-UA), based on an actual Union cavalry raid into the deep South in 1863; *Sergeant Rutledge* (1960, Warners) a courtroom drama about a black cavalryman on trial for the rape and murder of a white woman, narrated in flashback and shot in expressionistic color by Bert Glennon; *Two Rode Together* (1961, Columbia), a sort of pessimistic inversion of *The Searchers* about the ransoming of some white captives from the Commanches. In his later life, Ford had clearly lost interest in certain formal aspects of his art, and, until recently, the period 1962–65 was viewed as one of continuing decline. A critical consensus seems to be emerging, however, that Ford's last work was his greatest and approaches the sublime. This could certainly be argued of the elegaic, meditative Westerns *The Man Who Shot Liberty Valence* (1962) and *Cheyenne Autumn* (1964), although the apparent excesses of *Donovan's Reef* (1963) and *Seven Women* (1965) make them more difficult to see in this light.

Sometimes racist (the Indians in his Westerns are either bloodthirsty devils or noble savages—but always, with the notable exception of *Cheyenne Autumn*, formidable opponents), frequently sentimental, and always culturally conservative, John Ford was nevertheless a great American director. His accommodation with the studio system did not prevent him from making films of great technical virtuosity and strong personal vision that are admired for their classicism all over the world.* In his Westerns,

release the film (retitled *Gideon of Scotland Yard*) in black-and-white rather than go to the expense of striking color prints. See Tag Gallager, *John Ford: The Man and His Films* (Berkeley: University of California Press, 1986), pp. 358–63, on the Technicolor version.

* Among the filmmakers who have acknowledged Ford's influence are Sergei Eisenstein, V. I. Pudovkin, Orson Welles, Frank Capra, Howard Hawks, Ingmar Bergman, Mark Don-

he created a coherent mythology of the American past which brings him close to Griffith—for both men, in fact, history was the embodiment of moral rather than empirical truth, and their visions of the past do not often conform to fact. Historical inaccuracy notwithstanding, all of Ford's major films sustain a world view based upon his admiration for the traditional values of community life—for honor, loyalty, discipline, and, finally, courage—and it is a world view as consistent and compelling as any the cinema has to offer.

Howard Hawks

Another important director who dealt with typically American themes was Howard Hawks (1896–1979). Less a stylist than either von Sternberg or Ford, Hawks characteristically concerned himself with the construction of tough, functional narratives that embodied his personal ethic of professionalism, quiet courage, and self-respect. He directed forty-three features,* contributing major films to every popular American genre, during a career that spanned nearly half a century.

Hawks had been an aviator in World War I before entering the cinema in 1919 as a prop man for the Mary Pickford Company. Between 1920 and 1925, he rose to editor, scriptwriter, and, finally, assistant director, before leaving to work as a contract director for the Fox Film Corporation. He made seven silent films at Fox, one of which, *A Girl in Every Port* (1928), was modestly successful in France, but Hawks' career did not begin in earnest until the arrival of sound, when he began to work independently of long-term studio contracts. His first all-talking picture was First National's *The Dawn Patrol* (1930), a grim World War I drama about the awesome death toll among air force flyers, which featured some splendid aerial photography. After a fine prison picture for Columbia, *The Criminal Code* (1931), and a motor racing drama for Warners, *The Crowd Roars* (1932), Hawks directed his most important work of the early thirties—the classical gangster film *Scarface,* produced by Howard Hughes for UA. Loosely based by screenwriter Ben Hecht upon the career of Al Capone and superbly photographed by Lee Garmes (1898–1978), this violent, cynical film portrays the rise and fall of a Chicago mobster named Tony Camonte whose gang is like a dynasty of murderous Renaissance princes.† *Scarface,* the greatest of the thirties gangster films, marked

---

skoi, Akira Kurosawa, Elia Kazan, Douglas Sirk, Samuel Fuller, Budd Boetticher, Lindsay Anderson, Jean-Marie Straub, Peter Bogdanovich, John Milius, Bertrand Tavernier, and Peter Weir.

* Forty-six and one-fifth, if we count Hawks' three uncredited features—*The Prize Fighter and the Lady* (W.S. Van Dyke, 1933), *The Outlaw* (Howard Hughes, 1941), and *The Thing* (Christian Nyby, 1951)—plus "The Ransom of Red Chief," contribution to the five-part *O. Henry's Full House* (1952).

† Hughes, who was very proud of the film, withdrew it from circulation several years later; it did not become available again until three years after his death, in 1979, when his Summa Corporation sold the rights to Universal (before that date, *Scarface* could be seen only in bootleg prints). Four years later, the studio produced an ultraviolent remake, directed by Brian De Palma, which set the story among Cuban drug smugglers in contemporary Miami.

the beginning of the brilliant Hecht-Hawks collaboration that was to continue throughout the decade. (They had, of course, worked earlier together on the script of von Sternberg's 1927 gangster film *Underworld*, which Garmes also photographed and whose visual texture is very similar to that of *Scarface*.)

The title card of *Scarface* claims that it is based on a novel by Armitage Trail, but there is little resemblance between the book and the film beyond their titles and their source of inspiration: Capone. The film, Hawks' favorite, was shot in 1930 but not released for two years, while Hughes fought with the Hays Office (MPPDA) over cuts. The film was finally released in 1932, but only after some scenes were expurgated, a moralistic conclusion and several inserts added, and the title changed to *Scarface, Shame of a Nation*. Nevertheless, *Scarface* became a cause célèbre among those forces agitating for the imposition of the Production Code because of its violence and supposed amorality.

Hawks' next important project was *Viva Villa!* (1934), a distinguished MGM biopic written by Hecht and Hawks but completed by Jack Conway owing to the interference of Louis B. Mayer. But the subsequent Hecht-Hawks collaboration for Columbia, *Twentieth Century* (1934), was a smashing success. It tells the story of a tyrannical Broadway producer (John Barrymore) who spends the entire film, much of which takes place aboard the Twentieth Century Limited Express from Chicago to New York, attempting to cajole his estranged actress-wife (Carole Lombard) into appearing in his next show. With its rapid-fire dialogue and fast-paced editing, *Twentieth Century* became the prototype of the screwball comedies of the later thirties and forties. Perhaps Hawks' most distinguished film of the thirties was *The Road to Glory* (1936),* which ranks with Lewis Milestone's *All Quiet on the Western Front* (1930) and Stanley Kubrick's *Paths of Glory* (1957) and *Full Metal Jacket* (1987) as one of the American cinema's strongest antiwar statements. The film, produced by Darryl F. Zanuck for Fox, was the product of an unusual combination of talents. Directed by Hawks, written by William Faulkner and Joel Sayre (with the uncredited assistance of Hawks and Nunally Johnson), photographed by Gregg Toland, and superbly acted by Fredric March and Warner Baxter, it tells a searing tale of the horrors of trench warfare during World War I and ultimately suggests that professionalism, comradeship, and devotion to duty are the only forces that will sustain men in such a brutally hostile environment.

A similar theme pervades *Only Angels Have Wings* (1939, Columbia),

8.43   *Only Angels Have Wings* (Howard Hawks, 1939): Rita Hayworth, Cary Grant, Jean Arthur. Note the framing and eye-level composition.

---

* Not to be confused with his 1926 directorial debut, which has the same title but a completely different subject. *The Road to Glory* (1936) was closely modeled on the French antiwar film *Les Croix de bois* (*Wooden Crosses* [Raymond Bernard, 1932]), which Fox had bought for its battle footage. Bruce Kawin informs me that there is a great deal of Bernard footage in the Hawks film, and that there are many sequences for which Hawks shot new material to match something in Bernard. Kawin also says that in matters of characterization and plot the original script of *The Road to Glory* was much closer to *Wooden Crosses* than the final film. For more, see Bruce F. Kawin, *Faulkner and Film* (New York: Ungar, 1977), pp. 88–95.

which Hawks wrote with Jules Furthman on the basis of his own experience as a flyer during World War I. Thought to be his most beautiful aviation film, this tale of a small commercial airline pioneering the delivery of airmail in Latin America is a classical Hawksian parable of the necessity of professionalism and esprit de corps in the face of daily peril and death. Hawks enlarged his contribution to the screwball comedy with the anarchic *Bringing Up Baby* (1938, RKO), which provided the model for Peter Bogdanovich's rather pallid *What's Up, Doc?* (1972, Warners), and *Ball of Fire* (1941, RKO).* He also successfully remade Lewis Milestone's *The Front Page* (1931) as *His Girl Friday* (1940, Columbia), replete with fast-paced overlapping dialogue, before returning to more serious themes in the quietly patriotic biography of America's greatest World War I hero, *Sergeant York* (1941), which, like his next three films, was produced for Warners.

During World War II, Hawks made the tough combat drama *Air Force* (1943), photographed with documentary-like realism by James Wong Howe, and the hard-boiled romantic melodrama *To Have and Have Not* (1944), adapted from an Ernest Hemingway novel by William Faulkner and Jules Furthman and teaming Humphrey Bogart for the first time with Lauren Bacall (in her screen debut). The couple also starred in Hawks' bizarre and atmospheric **film noir**, *The Big Sleep* (1946), whose plot is so convoluted that even the director and his screenwriters (Faulkner, Furthman, and Leigh Brackett, working from the Raymond Chandler novel) claimed that they didn't understand it. Hawks' last serious film of the forties was the epic Western *Red River* (1948), which sets the psychological duel between a man (John Wayne) and his adopted son (Montgomery Clift) against the sweeping backdrop of the first cattle drive from Texas to Kansas in 1865.† Hawks returned to comedy with three films for Fox, *I Was a Male War Bride* (1948) and *Monkey Business* (1952),

8.44 *Bringing Up Baby* (Howard Hawks, 1938): Cary Grant, Katharine Hepburn.

---

* Remade by Hawks, not very happily, as the Danny Kaye-Virginia Mayo musical comedy *A Song Is Born* (1948, Goldwyn-RKO). Other remakes from Hawks include Lloyd Bacon's *Indianapolis Speedway*, (1939, from *The Crowd Roars*, with footage from same) and Michael Winner's soporific *The Big Sleep* (1975). On Hawks' unrealized film projects, see Todd McCarthy, "Phantom Hawks," *Film Comment* 18, 5 (September–October 1982): 63–76.

† *Red River* was Hawks' first and only film for his independent company Monterey Productions. Budgeted at $2 million, it was shot on location in 1947 and bankrupted Monterey by running $800,000 over cost. The film could not be released until 1948 because of injunctions threatened by the Teamster's Union, which represented Arizona cowhands owed $20,000 in back pay by Monterey when it went broke; by Pathé Film Laboratory, which had not been paid for processing; and by Howard Hughes, who claimed that Hawks had plagiarized the ending from his 1941 film, *The Outlaw*. When *Red River* was finally distributed in 1949, the ending had been re-edited (by Hughes! in order to placate him) and a voice-over narration added to shorten the running time by seven and one-half minutes to just under two hours. When United Artists rereleased the film several years later, it struck new prints from Hawks' original negative, which contained the unedited version of the ending and handwritten narration (from the pages of the book, *Early Tales of Texas*). When UA realized its error, Hawks advised them for legal reasons to reissue not his original but the Hughes-authorized release print, which was the only version available to the public until UA released the 125-minute Hawks version on video in 1987 through CBS / Fox. See Gerald Mast, *Howard Hawks: Storyteller* (New York: Oxford, 1982), pp 337–46 for details.

which endeavored to resurrect the screwball genre, and the robust CinemaScope musical *Gentlemen Prefer Blondes* (1953). In *Big Sky* (1953), he produced a modestly successful Western from a Dudley Nichols script,* and he continued to make films sporadically throughout the fifties and sixties. Most of these were disappointing in the light of his achievements of the thirties and forties (for example, *Land of the Pharoahs* [1955]; *Man's Favorite Sport* [1964]; *Red Line 7000* [1965]; *Rio Lobo* [1970—his last film]), but several, such as the African adventure-comedy *Hatari!* (1962) and the Westerns *Rio Bravo* (1959) and *El Dorado* (1967), still contain the vital spark of hard-hitting, fast-paced Hawksian narrative.

Like one of his own heroes, Howard Hawks was a versatile professional who distinguished himself in every major American film genre and virtually inaugurated several of them. Having begun his career as a screenwriter, he worked on the script of almost every film he ever made. Hawks was not primarily a visual stylist—he generally composed his scenes into the eye-level medium shots† favored by the studios and worked within the frame as much as possible, avoiding both spectacular montage effects and self-conscious camera movement. As for lighting, he left it to his cameramen, who were among the most distinguished Hollywood has ever known: Gregg Toland, Lee Garmes, James Wong Howe, Tony Gaudio, Ernest Haller, Russell Harlan, and Sid Hickox. But Hawks was a great visual storyteller with an urbane wit and a nearly existential concern with the condition of men in extreme situations. His films are frequently characterized as "masculine," and there is no question that his heroes prize the company only of women who, like the characters played by Lauren Bacall, seem to share the code by which these men live. But it is probably more accurate to call his films simply "American," in the sense expressed by the French film archivist Henri Langlois: "He [Hawks] is the embodiment of modern man. It is striking how his cinema anticipates his time. An American he certainly is, no less than a Griffith or a Vidor, but the spirit and physical structure of his work is born from contemporary America and enables us to better and more fully identify with it, both in admiration and criticism."

8.45 *To Have and Have Not* (Howard Hawks, 1944): Lauren Bacall, Humphrey Bogart.

---

* One of two films produced by Hawks' second independent company, Winchester Pictures Corporation, for distribution by RKO. The other was the paradigmatic science fiction film, *The Thing* (1951), nominally directed by Christian Nyby (b. 1919—Hawks's brilliant editor on *To Have and Have Not, The Big Sleep, Red River,* and *The Big Sky*), but clearly bearing the stylistic influence of Hawks. (*The Thing* was remade—horribly—by John Carpenter in 1982.) Hawks was also the uncredited director of Howard Hughes' production of *The Outlaw* (1941; release 1943). Though tame by contemporary standards, this notorious "sex-Western" challenged the MPPDA by including a rape scene and prominent footage of star Jane Russell's cleavage. After minor cuts and a protracted legal battle, *The Outlaw* was granted the PCA Seal of Approval but was withheld by Hughes for two years while he mounted a salacious, not to say sexist, advertising campaign for it fetishizing Ms. Russell's breasts. See Tony Thomas *Howard Hughes in Hollywood* (Secaucus, N.J.: Citadel Press, 1985).

† As Gerald Mast points out, this would be at the eye-level of a sitting on-looker, which is not so conventional after all since such shots establish a casual intimacy between characters and audience by aligning the camera's perspective with that of the spectator.

Alfred Hitchcock

The fourth major figure of the American sound film in this period was an Englishman trained within the British studio system, Alfred Hitchcock (1899–1980). Like Ford and Hawks, he was a brilliant craftsman; like von Sternberg, a subtle stylist. He spent most of his career working in a single genre—the suspense thriller—but his mastery of film form transformed and finally transcended it. Indeed, Andrew Sarris has called him the only contemporary director whose style unites the divergent classical traditions of Murnau (camera movement and *mise-en-scène*) and Eisenstein (montage). In the past two decades, moreover, Hitchcock has arrested the attention of critics and theorists of every imaginable hue, from conservative Roman Catholicism to radical poststructuralist feminism.

After receiving his formal education from the Jesuits at St. Ignatius College and working as a draftsman in the advertising department of a telegraph company, Hitchcock joined the London branch of Famous Players–Lasky at Islington as a title writer in 1921. He became a script writer, set designer, and finally, assistant director; and when producer Michael Balcon bought the Islington studio to form Gainsborough Pictures in 1924, Hitchcock joined the company as a contract director. Because of a reciprocal agreement between Balcon and Erich Pommer of UFA, Hitchcock's first two features were made in German studios,* where he fell under the spell of Expressionism and *Kammerspielfilme;* this influence was to last throughout his silent period and linger on considerably beyond it. Appropriately, his first major success, *The Lodger* (subtitled *A Story of the London Fog,* 1926; released 1927),† was in the genre that he was to make so uniquely his own. This Expressionistic suspense thriller, based on Marie Belloc-Lowndes' sensational Jack-the-Ripper novel of the same title, earned Hitchcock a high reputation at the age of twenty-seven; and it already contained one of his most memorable effects: the pacing feet of a suspected murderer on the floor above shot through a one-inch-thick plate-glass ceiling from the perspective of a family group seated below. The young director made six more silent films (two for Gainsborough—*Downhill,* 1927, and *Easy Virtue,* 1927; four for British International Pictures—*The Ring,* 1927; *The Farmer's Wife,* 1927; released

---

* The melodramas *The Pleasure Garden* (1925) and *The Mountain Eagle* (1925; lost film), both made for Emelka Studios–Munich and released in 1927. Shortly before producing these, Hitchcock had worked at UFA as art director on Gainsborough's *The Blackguard* (Graham Cutts, 1925). Here, Murnau was simultaneously shooting *The Last Laugh,* and the German director gave Hitchcock some pointers on the use of forced perspective which he immediately applied to his own work. See Donald Spoto, *The Dark Side of Genius; The Life of Alfred Hitchcock* (Boston: Little, Brown, 1983), pp. 77–104.

† *The Lodger* was the first film in which Hitchcock made a brief walk-on appearance, an in-joke and, later, publicity ploy which would characterize all of his subsequent features, except *The Wrong Man* (1957), which he personally introduces in a brief prologue. In addition to being trademarks, however, these appearances offered a legimate way for him to "sign" his work.

1928; *Champagne*, 1928; *The Manxman*, 1928; released 1929) before returning to the genre again in his—and Britain's—first talkie.

Blackmail (1929) was initially made as a silent film but reshot and partially dubbed as a sound film (the voice of the heroine, played by a Polish actress, had to be dubbed by the English actress Joan Barry) with some RCA Photophone equipment hastily imported from America by British International Pictures (BIP) president John Maxwell. It is one of the best films of its era, notable for its fluid camera style and its expressive use of both naturalistic and nonnaturalistic sound. Adapted from a popular play by Charles Bennett, the plot concerns a woman who is being blackmailed for the murder of an attempted rapist, and Hitchcock used the new medium of sound to inaugurate his characteristic theme of the nightmarish amidst the commonplace. At one point, for example, the heroine's subjective feelings of guilt are conveyed by the seemingly endless clanging of a shop bell; later the word "knife," recalling the murder weapon, emerges from a harmless conversation to haunt her long after the conversation itself has become an indistinct murmur on the soundtrack. Hitchcock's freedom to achieve such creative effects arose from the necessity of postsynchronizing scenes which had already been shot silent. For the same reason, the action sequences of *Blackmail*, especially those of the first and last reels, manifest a fluidity quite remarkable for an early sound film. And *Blackmail* concludes with what would become a characteristic Hitchcock motif: a spectacularly realized chase through famous settings—in this case, the pursuit of the blackmailer by police across the dome of the British Museum.

After directing portions of a BIP musical review entitled *Elstree Calling* (1930) and an uninspired version of Sean O'Casey's *Juno and the Paycock* (1930), Hitchcock returned to the thriller form with *Murder* (1930; adapted by Alma Reville* from a play by Helen Simpson and Clemence Dane) and again proved himself an innovator in the creative use of sound. This story of a famous actor who, convinced of a condemned girl's innocence, solves a murder to prove it, contains the first improvised dialogue sequence, the first use of the soundtrack to convey a character's stream of consciousness (while a thirty-piece orchestra plays the Prelude to Wagner's *Tristan und Isolde*, supposedly issuing from the radio, offscreen), and many other experiments with nonnaturalistic sound, including a 360-degree pan while dialogue is spoken. Hitchcock was by now regarded as Britain's most important director. After three more BIP films of varying quality—an adaptation of John Galsworthy's talky social melodrama *The Skin Game* (1931); the parodic thriller *Number Seventeen* (1931; released 1932), which concludes with an ingenious train chase-collision sequence

8.46 Hitchcock on the set of *Blackmail* (1929), attempting to record Anny Ondra's voice. Note the camera enclosed in the soundproof booth.

8.47 The British Museum chase from the conclusion of *Blackmail*.

8.48 *The Man Who Knew Too Much* (Alfred Hitchcock, 1934): the scream that prevents a murder in the Royal Albert Hall.

---

* Hitchcock's wife, Alma Reville (1900–1982), provided screenplays, adaptations, or continuities for many of his films from 1927 to 1950. She began her career as an editor at Famous Players–Lasky, Islington, where she met Hitchcock in 1923. They were married in 1926, and she became his lifetime collaborator, adviser, and companion. Their only child, Patricia (b. 1928), was an occasional actress who appeared in small roles in two of her father's films, *Strangers on a Train* (1951) and *Psycho* (1960).

assembled from stock footage and model shots; *Rich and Strange* (1932), an episodic romantic comedy structured around a recently married couple's world cruise—and the independently produced *Waltzes from Vienna* (1933), a quite good musical about the Strauss family, he signed a five-film contract with Gaumont-British, where Michael Balcon had become production chief in 1931, and launched the series of thrillers which was to make him internationally famous; the first was *The Man Who Knew Too Much* (1934). This complicated and darkly Expressionistic film, the only one that Hitchcock ever remade, concerns a couple on holiday in St. Moritz who learn of a plot to assassinate a visiting statesman in London. Their daughter is kidnapped by the assassins (led by Peter Lorre, who had become internationally famous as the child-murderer in Fritz Lang's *M* [1931, q.v.], in his first English-speaking role), and the couple must simultaneously recover their child and foil the murder plot without telling the police. The film is a classical Hitchcockian parable of horror asserting itself in the midst of the ordinary and innocent. Its famous set pieces include the concert in the Royal Albert Hall (shot by using the Schüfftan process), where the assassination is aborted by the mother's scream, and the gun battle in the East End, with which the film concludes.

8.49   The famous sound match from *The 39 Steps* (1935).

Hitchcock's next film, *The 39 Steps* (1935), freely adapted from the John Buchan novel, is among his finest achievements. Suspenseful but light of touch, it deals with yet another classical Hitchcock situation—that of an innocent man who must prove his innocence while being simultaneously pursued by both villains and police. In *The 39 Steps,* a female secret service agent is mysteriously murdered in the apartment of Richard Hannay (Robert Donat), who flees London to the north by train and arrives in Scotland. There, he inadvertently walks into the hands of the villain himself, escapes, and then walks into the hands of the police. After a series of further misadventures, he finds himself being pursued across the Scottish moors by both groups while handcuffed to a pretty young teacher (Madeleine Carroll) who believes him a murderer. This exciting chase, with its superb ensemble playing by Donat and Carroll, eventually ends in London, where all secrets are revealed and all problems resolved. Witty, fast-paced, and technically brilliant, *The 39 Steps* is narrative filmmaking at its very best.* It also contains some classic examples of audiovisual montage, as when the scream of Hannay's cleaning lady on discovering the secret agent's corpse becomes the shriek of the whistle on the locomotive of the train carrying Hannay to Scotland.

8.50   *The Lady Vanishes* (Alfred Hitchcock, 1938): Linden Travers, Naunton Wayne, Basil Radford.

Hitchcock's next film was a curious version of a play by Campbell Dixon, based on Somerset Maugham's "Ashenden" adventure stories, entitled *Secret Agent* (1936). It concerns a famous writer (John Gielgud) who works as a British agent to track down and kill a German spy in Switzerland during World War I, and its calculated moral ambiguity left

---

* *The 39 Steps* has been remade twice—first by Ralph Thomas in 1959, then by Don Sharp in 1978. Neither production (both are British) even approaches the stature of the original.

many viewers confused, as did its remarkable successor, *Sabotage* (1936). This film, Hitchcock's grimest prior to *Psycho* (1960), was, confusingly enough, a contemporary version of Joseph Conrad's novel *The Secret Agent* (1907), in which Verloc, the owner of a small London cinema, works secretly for a group of anarchists bent on destroying the city. *Sabotage* contains some of Hitchcock's most masterful sequences. The film's high point occurs when Verloc sends his wife's young brother out to plant a time bomb, without the boy's knowledge. The child is waylaid through circumstance at almost every point in his journey—here a crowd, there a puppet show. As the time for detonation grows closer and closer, he boards an omnibus, and Hitchcock's montage becomes increasingly complex until at last the tension is released in a spectacular audience-alienation effect: the bomb explodes, and the boy and his fellow passengers are blown to bits. Later, Mrs. Verloc learns of the death and her husband's responsibility for it, and she murders him at the dinner table with a carving knife. The editing of the dinner scene which immediately precedes this act is among the most powerful and restrained in all of Hitchcock's work: Mrs. Verloc's mounting determination to kill her husband is gradually shown to coincide with his own desire to die for his crime.* In addition to such sophisticated montage effects, *Sabatoge* is full of references to the cinema and cinematic spectating owing to Verloc's role as theater manager (in the novel, he is a dealer in pornographic literature!): for example, Verloc himself loathes murder films but books them anyway to pander to his audience; Mrs. Verloc's decision to kill her husband is catalyzed by the apparition of a Disney cartoon in which a robin is shot though the breast with an arrow by another bird while the sound track intones "Who Killed Cock Robin?"; and so forth.

After a light double-chase film entitled *Young and Innocent* (1937), which contained a 145-foot tracking movement from a long shot into a close-up of a character's eye, Hitchcock made *The Lady Vanishes* (1938), the last of his British thrillers.† This was a stylish film of espionage and intrigue in Central Europe, set largely aboard a train. It revealed the same deftness as *The 39 Steps* and was a clear parable of England's blindness to the Nazi threat.

At this point in his career, having brought international prestige to the British film industry, Hitchcock decided to come to Hollywood. Certainly, America's economic bounty and Europe's uncertain political future were factors in this move, but it was unquestionably motivated by aesthetic considerations as well.The British economy and the domestic film industry were shrinking (see pp. 361–62) while Hitchcock's artistic ambitions were soaring; and by the end of the Depression, the Hollywood studios had become what UFA had been during the twenties (almost literally, since they were employing small armies of former UFA per-

---

* See the shot sequence on pages 343–44.
† Remade in 1978, with a script by George Axelrod and direction by Anthony Page.

sonnel [see p. 132]—the center of big-budget film art in the West. He made one more British film, a melodramatic adaptation of Daphne du Maurier's gothic thriller *Jamaica Inn* (1939) for Erich Pommer and Charles Laughton's Mayfair Productions, and began a seven-year contract with David O. Selznick by adapting another du Maurier novel for the film *Rebecca* (1940).* The stately rhythms of this highly polished film marked a change of pace for Hitchcock, who now had the vast technical resources of the American studios at his disposal. Despite (or perhaps, *because* of) Selznick's now notorious interference with the project, *Rebecca* was recognized by Academy Award nominations in every major category of achievement, winning two—Best Picture and Best Black-and-White Cinematography (to George Barnes). Hitchcock's second American film was a tour de force of anti-isolationist propaganda (the war had been going on in Europe for several months when production began) cast in the mold of his very best British thrillers, *Foreign Correspondent* (1940), which was also nominated for several major Oscars. Produced by Walter Wanger for UA, it was loosely based on the memoirs of Vincent Sheehan and contained several elaborate effects, including a spectacular seaplane crash, created by production designer William Cameron Menzies (1896–1957) and cinematographer Joseph Valentine (1900–49).

His next two films were for RKO—a fine, if uncharacteristic, screwball comedy entitled *Mr. and Mrs. Smith* (1941), commissioned for the talented comedienne Carole Lombard (1908–42), who died in a plane crash shortly thereafter, and the tense psychological thriller *Suspicion* (1941), a film of considerable intelligence and his first with Cary Grant (1904–86). In *Suspicion,* Grant plays a ne'er-do-well fortune hunter who marries a wealthy—and, clearly, sexually repressed—Joan Fontaine (in her first appearance since *Rebecca*); and she gradually comes to suspect him of plotting to murder her for her money. Though set convincingly in the English countryside, the film was shot entirely on a soundstage by Harry Stradling (1902–70); and it is both sinister and psychologically subtle—qualities not significantly damaged by the studio-mandated ending in which Fontaine's fears are shown to be the product of neurotic delusion (which, in a way, is more sinister yet.) In a perfect example of Hollywood's institutional / ideological sexism,† RKO ordered this ending so as not to blemish Grant's image as a star persona.

Hitchcock then returned to the subject of espionage with *Saboteur* (1942), a spectacular double-chase film which includes newsreel footage

---

* Disliked by Hitchcock, du Maurier, and most critics to this day, *Jamaica Inn* was nevertheless extremely popular with British audiences and rereleased twice, in 1944 and 1948. Only three films were for Selznick International under Hitchcock's contract (*Rebecca*, 1940; *Spellbound*, 1945; and *The Paradine Case*, 1947), but Selznick himself profited handsomely by hiring Hitchcock out to other producers and studios (Walter Wanger, RKO, Universal, and 20th Century–Fox) between 1940 and 1944—a period during which Selznick International was in liquidation for tax purposes.

† The 1987 television remake of *Suspicion,* directed by the British filmmaker Andrew Grieve and starring Jane Curtin in the Joan Fontaine role, rectifies the sexism but keeps the equivocal ending.

of an actual act of sabotage (the burning of the S.S. *Normandie*) and concludes with a mad pursuit at the top of the Statue of Liberty. In 1943 Hitchcock made what he considered his best American film, *Shadow of a Doubt,* a restrained tale of a psychotic murderer's visit to relatives in the small California town of Santa Rosa, where he is perceived to be normal. Produced by Jack H. Skirball for Universal, the film is distinguished by Joseph Valentine's subtle camera work, superb performances by the entire cast—especially Teresa Wright as the devoted niece and Joseph Cotten as the charming, menacing, and finally lethal "Uncle Charlie"—and Thorton Wilder's intelligent screenplay, resonating perversely of *Our Town,* written five years before. The soundtrack employs overlapping dialogue mixes of the type used by Orson Welles in *Citizen Kane* (1941) and *The Magnificent Ambersons* (1942; see pp. 427–29), but it is ultimately the visual texture of the film, with its intricate psychological doublings, that makes *Shadow of a Doubt* one of Hitchcock's three or four undisputed masterworks. Hitchcock turned to the war itself with *Lifeboat* (1944), an allegory of the world conflict in which a group of people representing a wide cultural and political spectrum are trapped together in a lifeboat after a Nazi U-boat attack. Based on a story by John Steinbeck, the film was shot in a studio tank at 20th Century–Fox and is constructed mainly of close shots.

Hitchcock's first postwar film was the psychological thriller *Spellbound* (1945), in which the head psychiatrist of an asylum comes to believe that he is in reality a murderous amnesiac. Expensively produced by Selznick International, this movie was cluttered with Freudian symbols and contained many spectacular technical effects, including a dream sequence designed by the artist Salvador Dalí and the American cinema's first partially electronic score (for which composer Miklos Rozsa won an Academy Award). *Notorious* (1946), a tale of atomic espionage by Nazis set in Rio de Janeiro, was equally well-produced and directed by Hitchcock at RKO. Its elegant black-and-white photography by Ted Tetzlaff (b. 1903) was an aesthetic triumph. There are several splendid sequences in the film, but the most stunning involves a swooping crane shot that begins at the top of a ballroom staircase and proceeds through a whole series of chambers before finally coming to rest in close-up on a key held in the heroine's hand. *Notorious* was an enormous popular success, not least because of the erotic frisson generated between stars Cary Grant and Ingrid Bergman during a prolonged kissing sequence.

8.51 *Lifeboat* (Alfred Hitchcock, 1944).

After directing a technically dazzling but ponderous courtroom melodrama called *The Paradine Case* (1947), from a disjointed screenplay by Selznick, Hitchcock made two films for his own production company, Transatlantic Pictures. He had formed this company in 1946 with the British theater-chain owner Sidney Bernstein (b. 1899), a friend and adviser who had long admired the director's work.* Hitchcock's first Transat-

---

* A life-long film enthusiast, Bernstein began his career as a small distributor and went on to become a leading figure in British film culture. He founded the London Film Society (where he first met Hitchcock) in 1924, the Granada theater chain in 1930, and the Gran-

lantic film was also his first film in color—the boldly experimental *Rope* (1948). It was adapted from a play by Patrick Hamilton (based upon the infamous Leopold-Loeb case of 1924) in which two young intellectuals murder a friend in order to prove their Nietzschean superiority to conventional morality,* conceal his corpse in a living room chest, and then stage a dinner party around it for his relatives. The film was shot by Joseph Valentine (in facilities rented from Warner Bros.) within the confines of a single large penthouse set in ten-minute takes with a continuously moving camera, for which Hitchcock developed tracking shots of extraordinary complexity.† The few cuts were concealed by invisible editing and confined to reel changes, and there were no time lapses in the narrative, so the running time of the film and dramatic time of the action coincide, and the film appears to have been shot as a single continuous take. The camera's costar in *Rope* was the set's arduously constructed background—an exact miniature replica of some thirty-five miles of New York skyline lighted by eight thousand tiny incandescent bulbs and two hundred neon signs, each wired separately, which marked time by gradually representing the coming of twilight and nightfall to a vault of spun glass clouds. Yet *Rope* was a critical and popular failure because the ten-minute take didn't work to sustain dramatic tension as Hitchcock had intended and because of its unpleasant subject matter.

The second and last Transatlantic production, *Under Capricorn* (1949), was also shot in color, by Jack Cardiff (b. 1914), at Elstree Studios, London. This costume film set in nineteenth-century Australia continued Hitchcock's experiments with the long take in several sequences of extraordinary beauty, but it ultimately failed to cohere as a narrative and was poorly received. Similar difficulties afflicted *Stage Fright* (1950), a

---

ada television group in 1954. During World War II, Bernstein served as film adviser to the British Ministry of Information and was chief of the Film Section of Supreme Headquarters, Allied Expeditionary Forces. It was in this latter capacity that he commissioned Hitchcock to make a compilation film on the Nazi concentration camps at the end of the war, with the purpose of showing the German people the specific nature of their leaders' crimes. This uncompromising hour-long documentary was suppressed by the military command as too volatile, but a copy was discovered in the Imperial War Museum in 1983, where it is preserved today as Film F3080—see Elizabeth Sussex, "The Fate of F3080," *Sight and Sound* 53, 2 (Spring 1984): 92–97. (In 1944, Hitchcock had made two short films celebrating the French Resistance—*Bon Voyage* and *Aventure Malgache*—at Bernstein's behest; both were shelved, but copies exist today at the British Film Institute.) Bernstein was made a baron in 1969. For more, see Caroline Moorhead, *Sidney Bernstein: A Biography* (London: Cape, 1984).

* Friedrich Wilhelm Nietzsche (1844–1900) was a German philosopher who emphasized the will to power as the driving force of all organisms, individual and social. The posthumous debasement of his thought by right-wing German ideologues created the myth of the superman—the notion that certain people could *will* themselves out of normal moral categories and commit with impunity acts that would ordinarily be regarded as crimes (mass murder, say, or other forms of barbarism). The first articulation of this ideology in Hitchcock is offered quite explicitly by the Nazi U-boat commander in *Lifeboat,* so much so that some critics wrongly accused Hitchcock of embracing it.

†The piano music Hitchcock chose for *Rope*'s credit sequence, later played by one of the murderers during the dinner party, is Francis Poulenc's *"Mouvement perpétuel n. 1."*

8.52   The master shot for the dinnertable scene in Hitchcock's *Sabotage* (1936), followed by the shot sequence of the murder. Sylvia Sidney, Oscar Homolka.

Warner Bros. production shot in London, much admired today for its subtle interplay of cinematic and theatrical illusion and the fluid camera-work of Wilkie Cooper (b. 1911). Actively seeking now to produce a commercial hit, Hitchcock entered his second major period with *Strangers on a Train* (1951, Warners), based on a Patricia Highsmith novel with a screenplay by Raymond Chandler and Czenzi Ormonde. This psychological thriller concerns a murder pact jokingly made between two young men, Bruno and Guy, who meet on a train, each agreeing to kill someone who stands in the other's way. Bruno, a psychotic, unexpectedly fulfills the pact by murdering Guy's troublesome wife, and then expects Guy to murder his (Bruno's) father. Horrified and consumed with guilt, Guy refuses to carry out his end of the deal, and Bruno attempts to frame him for the murder already committed. Photographed on location by Robert Burks (b. 1910), who with a single exception became Hitchcock's constant collaborator from 1951 until his death in 1968, this film contains some of Hitchcock's most psychologically subtle characterizations (especially in Robert Walker's Bruno) and concludes with a spectacular fight between Bruno and Guy on a merry-go-round that careens out of control and collapses. As Hitchcock had anticipated, *Strangers on a Train* was an enormous popular success, and he made two more films for Warners. *I Confess* (1952), shot on location in the city of Quebec, concerns a priest who hears the confession of a murderer and is then accused of committing the murder himself. *Dial M For Murder* (1953) was an ingenious adaptation of a stage play filmed in color and 3-D* but released "flat" when the vogue for the process had died away (see pp. 484–86). In addition to eliciting a superb performance from Grace Kelly (1929–82), Hitchcock made the film a model of narrative economy and staging in depth.

Hitchcock's next four films were made in color for Paramount. In *Rear Window* (1954) he restricted his scope of action even more rigidly than he had done in either *Lifeboat* or *Rope*. The entire film is shot from a camera confined within the apartment of a professional photographer, L. B. Jeffries, who is recovering from a broken leg, and during most of the film the camera records what he sees through his rear window. To pass the time, the photographer begins to spy on his neighbors through his telescopic lenses and gradually forms the conviction that one of them has murdered his wife, dismembered the corpse, and buried it in the courtyard garden. Jeffries subsequent attempts to prove the murder endanger his fiancée's life (and, finally, his own), while—like the audience itself—he can only sit and watch from a perspective limited by the sequencing of his neighbors' windows and the power of his lens. *Rear Window* is a disturbing and profoundly modern film: its theme of the moral complicity of the voyeur (and, by extension, the film spectator) in

8.53 The murders confronted in Hitchcock's *Rope* (1948): James Stewart, Farley Granger, John Dall; the miniature skyline.

8.54 The collapse of the merry-go-round in *Strangers on a Train* (Alfred Hitchcock, 1951).

---

* A desperate attempt to compete with the burgeoning popularity of television, 3-D, or "Natural Vision," was a cumbersome stereoscopic process for producing three-dimensional moving pictures which enjoyed a brief vogue between 1953 and 1954. Only sixty-nine films were made in 3-D, and some, like *Dial M for Murder,* had to be released "flat" because of audience disenchantment with the process.

8.55 The photographer as voyeur: Hitchcock's *Rear Window* (1954).

8.56 *Rear Window:* "We've become a race of peeping Toms . . ." James Stewart, Grace Kelly, Thelma Ritter.

what he watches anticipates both Antonioni's *Blow-Up* (1966; see p. 629) and Francis Ford Coppola's *The Conversation* (1973; see p. 891), to say nothing of Hitchcock's own *Psycho* (1960).

In 1955 (the year he became a naturalized American citizen), Hitchcock directed *To Catch a Thief,* a stylish comedy thriller about a cat burglar, shot on location on the French Riviera in Paramount's new widescreen process, VistaVision. As we might expect, he became one of the first directors to use the wide screen effectively for pictorial and dramatic composition, and all of his subsequent films, with the exception of *The Wrong Man,* were shot in widescreen ratios. *The Trouble with Harry* (1955), which inaugurated his brilliant nine-year collaboration with composer Bernard Herrmann (1911–75), used VistaVision to capture the autumn splendor of the Vermont woods as a background to a sophisticated* and witty black comedy about a corpse which refuses to stay buried because someone keeps digging it up. In the same year, Hitchcock remade *The Man Who Knew Too Much* as a big-budget commercial entertainment, featuring a lush Bernard Herrmann score and sequences shot on location in Morocco and London. Though updated and modernized, the second version reprises the Albert Hall sequence of the original on a vast scale, with Herrmann conducting the one hundred-piece London Symphony Orchestra in Arthur Benjamin's "Storm Cloud Cantata" in six-track stereophonic sound. One of its director's favorites and a great box-office success, the film is gorgeously photographed in VistaVision; even today we scarcely notice Hitchcock's experiments with the oblique 360-degree editing continuities he would later use so stunningly in *Vertigo.* As if to expiate his extravagance, Hitchcock next made a stark semidocumentary of false arrest and imprisonment, *The Wrong Man* (1957),

---

*Too much so for the mass audience, apparently—*The Trouble with Harry* became the only Hitchcock film of the decade to actually *lose* money at the box office. On Herrmann's collaboration, see Royal S. Brown, "Herrmann, Hitchcock, and the Music of the Irrational," *Cinema Journal* 21, 2 (Spring 1982): 14–49.

his last Warners film, shot on location in black-and-white in New York City.

In 1958 Hitchcock directed *Vertigo,* shot on location in San Francisco in VistaVision, which many critics consider his greatest and most visually poetic film. Cast in the form of a detective thriller, *Vertigo* is actually a tale of romantic obsession brilliantly adapted by Alex Coppel and Samuel Taylor from the novel *D'entre des Morts* (*From Amongst the Dead*), by Pierre Boileau and Thomas Narcejac, the authors of *Les Diaboliques.* Scottie (James Stewart), a former police detective, has acquired a pathological fear of heights (acrophobia, or vertigo) by accidentally causing a fellow officer to fall to his death from a rooftop—facts conveyed by an extraordinary twenty-five-shot montage sequence in the film's first ninety seconds. He quits the force because of this debility but reluctantly accepts a job from a wealthy acquaintance named Gavin Elster to follow his wife, Madeleine (Kim Novak), who believes herself to be a reincarnation of her Spanish great grandmother, Carlotta Valdez—a much-abused woman who died insane, by her own hand. In the process of trailing Madeleine through the precipitous streets of San Francisco and saving her from an apparent suicide attempt near the Golden Gate Bridge, Scottie falls in love with her. She dies—or seems to—by throwing herself off the bell tower of an old Spanish mission, in part because Scottie's vertigo prevents him from stopping her. After an inquest ascribing her death to his negligence, Scottie plunges into madness, but is subsequently cured.

Later, still deeply bereaved, he discovers a shopgirl, named Judy, who bears a striking physical resemblance to Madeleine, although she is coarse and common whereas Madeleine was a romantic idol—and he spends the rest of the film obssesively trying to re-create the image of the dead woman in the living one. The two women are actually the same woman who has acted as a foil in an audacious murder plot of Elster's—a fact which Hitchcock reveals to the audience (but not to Scottie) two-thirds of the way through the film, destroying suspense in order to concentrate our attention on mood and ambience. The poignancy of Scottie's situation (and also of Judy's, since she has fallen in love with him during her masquerade) is that the closer he comes to making Judy over as Madeleine, the farther he moves from both, since Madeleine wasn't real in the

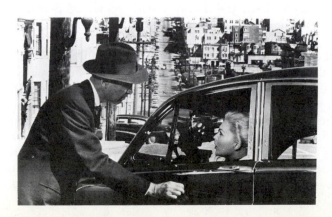

8.57 *Vertigo* (Alfred Hitchcock, 1958): James Stewart, Kim Novak.

first place but rather—like an actress in a film—someone playing a made-up part. The logic of this awful double bind produces *Vertigo*'s harrowing, inevitable conclusion in which Scottie, having at last re-created Madeleine perfectly in Judy, realizes that they have been the same person all along. Then, his vertigo finally cured, he literally drags her to the top of the bell tower where Madeleine "died," and Judy-Madeleine falls accidentally to her—this time, very real—death. No brief description can really do justice to the intricate structure of this remarkable film, whose theme of love transcending death resonates through such mainstays of Western narrative art as Shakespeare's *Romeo and Juliet,* Emily Brontë's *Wuthering Heights,* and Richard Wagner's *Tristan und Isolde.* Bernard Herrmann's haunting score sustains this resonance, alternating passages of discordant contrary movement with lush orchestral leitmotifs based on Wagner's opera, especially the *Liebestod* ("love-death") aria of its conclusion.

Visually and aurally, *Vertigo* is constructed as a series of descending spirals, as Scottie is drawn irrevocably deeper into the spiritual vortex created by his romantic longing for Madeleine, whose very inaccessiblity is her most fatal attraction. His vertigo—the image and emblem of this longing—is transferred to the audience at various points through dizzying reverse-tracking/forward-zoom shots, elaborately executed by Hitchcock's special effects team, as Scottie peers into chasms from precarious heights (a city street from a rooftop, the bottom of the bell tower from its staircase, etc.). Madeleine's unattainability is conveyed—as when Scottie first glimpses her at Ernie's Restaurant—through oblique 360-degree cutting which, by violating the rules of classical Hollywood editing, creates for her a narrative space that doesn't (or, at least, shouldn't) exist. Such "vortical" editing, combined with Burks' subtly tracking subjective camera and the film's highly stylized use of color, are strategies whereby we become so completely identified with Scottie's perspective that his vision of Madeleine—i.e., his psychological entrapment by a manufactured romantic goddess—becomes our own.

But after Judy's revelation of the murder plot, our perceptual path diverges from Scottie's, and his delusion, which we can no longer share, appears to us increasingly pathetic, hopeless, and doomed. The critic Robin Wood, who wrote the first serious English-language study of Hitchcock's art (*Hitchcock's Films,* 1965), has recently remarked that the last third of *Vertigo* is "among the most disturbing and painful experiences the cinema has to offer," and this is unquestionably true. Because we have shared the failure of Scottie's romantic aspirations so thoroughly in the body of the film, its horrible recurrence at *Vertigo*'s conclusion defies all of our narrative expectations. We are robbed not merely of a Hollywood-style happy ending but also of the cathartic satisfaction of classical tragedy. When *Vertigo* ends, all the pain and death has meant nothing: in ending, the film suggests that its whole torturous process is about to start again. By consistently revealing the vulnerability of its male protagonist and the spurious nature of its heroine, and in refusing (emotionally, at any rate—like the closed circle of a descending spiral) to end, *Vertigo* suggests not only the fraudulence of romantic love but of the whole Hollywood narrative tradition that underwrites it. At a deeper level, however, it suggests a more difficult truth: that the ultimate consequence of romantic idealism—of aspiring beyond the possible—is, successively, neurosis, psychosis, and perversion, or, more specifically, necrophilia.

Vertigo* was not successful with either the critics or the public, and it is not difficult to see why in a year in which Josh Logan's *Sayonara* and *South Pacific* were among the country's top-grossing films. Hitchcock always claimed dismay at this negative response, and blamed it privately on Stewart's age and Novak's inexperience (both crucial attributes of their characters in the film, of course). This was not only mean-spirited but dishonest: Hitchcock surely understood the risk he took in making such a nihilistic and radically experimental film for the American mass market. (Scriptwriter Samuel Taylor: "Hitchcock knew exactly what he wanted to do in this film, exactly what he wanted to say, and how it should be seen and told. I gave him the characters and the dialogue he needed and developed the story, but it was from first frame to last his film. There was no moment when he wasn't there. And anyone who saw him during the making of the film could see, as I did, that he felt it very deeply indeed.")

8.58 Cary Grant pursued by a crop-duster in Hitchcock's *North-by-Northwest* (1959).

Whatever the case, Hitchcock was determined that his next film should be a great popular success, and he produced exactly that in *North by Northwest* (1959), a return to the witty double-chase mode of *The 39 Steps* (1935), which at times it seems intended to parody. Stylishly scripted by Ernest Lehman (b. 1920) and shot by Burks in VistaVision for MGM, this film of a New York advertising man pursued across America by both government authorities and nuclear spies contains some classic Hitchcock sequences, most notably the (literally) cliff-hanging conclusion on Mount Rushmore and the superbly constructed machine-gun attack on the hero by a crop-duster in the middle of an Indiana cornfield. It also employs a sophisticated manipulation of Freudian symbols, especially those of the Oedipal fantasy, and a stunning Bernard Herrmann score to create a totality of effect wholly satisfying to the senses, emotions, and intellect. Or, as Hitchcock confessed to Lehman at one point during the shooting: "Ernie, do you realize what we're doing in this picture? The audience is like a giant organ that you and I are playing. At one moment we play *this* note on them and get *this* reaction, and then we play *that* chord and they react *that* way. And someday we won't even have to make a movie—there'll be electrodes implanted in their brains, and we'll just press differ-

8.59 Archetypal horror: Norman Bates (Anthony Perkins) stands before his mother's house in *Psycho* (Alfred Hitchcock, 1960).

---

* Until recently, *Vertigo* was a "lost" film, in that it was part of a group including *Rope, Rear Window, The Trouble with Harry,* and *The Man Who Knew Too Much* (1956) to which Hitchcock owned the rights and which, for financial reasons, he kept out of circulation during the last years of his life. In 1983, all five were rereleased theatrically in their original ratios (thought not, of course, in the case of *Harry* and *Vertigo,* in the now obsolete VistaVision process) by Universal Classics, which proved a great intellectual boon for Hitchcock scholarship and an economic one for MCA, since all did handsomely at the box office.

ent buttons and they'll go 'ooooh' and 'aaaah' and we'll frighten them, and make them laugh. Won't that be wonderful?"

That was to be *Psycho,* adapted by Joseph Stephano from the novel by Robert Bloch,* Hitchcock's coldest, blackest, and most brilliant Hollywood film. Hitchcock produced *Psycho* for $800,000, using his own television crew at Revue Studios, the television branch of Universal Pictures. Shot for Paramount in black-and-white by John L. Russell, *Psycho* is at once the fulfillment of *Vertigo*'s necrophilic longing and a savage revenge on that film's critics. Before one-third of the film is over, the beautiful and sexually provocative heroine (Janet Leigh), who is on the run from the police for having stolen $40,000 from her boss, is slashed to death in a motel shower in a harrowing forty-five-second montage sequence which many critics think rivals the Odessa Steps sequence of Eisenstein's *Potemkin.*

Psycho is an outrageously manipulative film and is thus, like *Potemkin,* a stunningly successful experiment in audience stimulation and response. Hitchcock's precisely planned knife murder sequence is in fact a masterful vindication of the Kuleshov-Eisenstein school of montage: in a series of eighty-seven rapidly alternating fragmentary shots, we seem to witness a horribly violent and brutal murder on the screen, and yet only once do we see an image of the knife penetrating flesh, and that image is completely bloodless.† A second murder is so perfectly and unpredictably timed that it delivers a large perceptual shock, even after many viewings. Time and again, Hitchcock uses his camera and his montage to deceive the audience by leading it up cinematic blind alleys and strewing the screen with visual red herrings. He also offers the most morbid narrative of his career—the knife murderer is Norman Bates (Anthony Perkins), a psychotic momma's boy who lives in a gothic house with the rotting corpse of his mother, some twelve years dead by his own hand (or so we are told at the end, by the police psychiatrist). Many critics in 1960 were revolted by *Psycho* and appalled at its cynicism, but today its technical brilliance places it among the most important of postwar American films, and its blackness and bleakness look decidedly modern.** (Probably

---

* Bloch's novel was based on the real-life case of Ed Gein, a Wisconsin mass murderer whose killing spree also inspired Tobe Hooper's *The Texas Chainsaw Massacre* (1974).

† The sequence is perfectly complemented by the shrieking staccato violins of Bernard Herrmann's edgy score. Hitchcock had wanted to use only naturalistic sound effects for the murder, but Herrmann, felicitously, talked him out of it—an impressive example of artistic collaboration in a professional relationship that lasted from *The Trouble with Harry* (1956) through *Marnie* (1964). Two other Hitchcock collaborators of the late period deserve special mention here: Henry Bumstead, art director for *The Man Who Knew Too Much* (shared credit with Hal Pereira), *Vertigo* (shared credit with Pereira), *Topaz,* and *Family Plot;* and the graphic designer Saul Bass (b. 1920), who did the striking title designs for *Vertigo,* *North by Northwest,* and *Psycho,* as well as the storyboard for *Psycho*'s shower sequence.

** There have, of course, been several sequels, and, for better or worse, the Norman Bates character has become something of a cult figure. *Psycho II* (Richard Franklin, 1983) has Norman released from a mental asylum some twenty years after his crimes to become a

8.60 *Psycho:* shots from the shower sequence. Anthony Perkins, Janet Leigh.

because it was the second highest-grossing film of 1960—after William Wyler's lumbering religious epic *Ben Hur*—*Psycho* did win Academy Award nominations for direction and black-and-white cinematography; it received neither [*Ben Hur* did] but went on to earn over $11 million in its initial run.)

By the late forties, Hitchcock had become one of the major clients of the talent agency MCA (formerly Music Corporation of America) and formed a close relationship with its president, Lew Wasserman, that would influence much of his later career. In 1955, Wasserman packaged a deal for Hitchcock to produce and lend his name to a program of weekly half-hour telefilms for CBS, which from 1955 to 1960 became one of the highest-rated shows in television history. Hitchcock personally directed only twenty episodes, but the programs, and especially his droll introductions to them, made Hitchcock a national figure. They also made him rich: by exchanging his rights to the series, plus *Psycho,* in 1962 for 150,000 shares of MCA stock, he became the third largest shareholder in the conglomerate, which gave him considerable freedom to produce his own films. *No other director in America* could have produced *Vertigo* as a big-budget feature with major stars in 1958, or, conversely, have received an Academy Award nomination for a film as dark and cheaply made as *Psycho* in 1960. As with virtually every other aspect of his life, Hitchcock used his television career to further his all-consuming, solitary passion to make films.*

After becoming one of the three largest shareholders in MCA, Hitchcock produced all of his films for Universal. The first of these, *The Birds* (1963), was nearly three years in preparation and at the time of its release seemed to many an exercise in pure technique. Adapted by Evan Hunter from a Daphne du Maurier short story, it concerns a savage assault by the millions of birds in the vicinity of Bodega Bay, California, upon the human population of the area. The special effects (consisting of 371 trick shots) by Hitchcock and Ub Iwerks (1901–71), one of Disney's greatest animators, are remarkable, as is the menacing electronic soundtrack produced and recorded by Reni Gossman and Oskar Sala. But the film is slowly paced until the bird attacks begin en masse, and it has an oddly formal quality. Today, critics are inclined to see *The Birds* as forming the third part of a trilogy with *Vertigo* and *Psycho,* which posits a world gone speechless and numb through the dislocation of human feeling. Although the bird attacks on the town are spectacularly rendered through classically structured montage, the overall mood of the film is no less stark than that of *The Wrong Man.* (Its art director Robert Boyle has said that the film's overall design was inspired by Edvard Munch's *The*

8.61 A shot from the second murder sequence in *Psycho:* Martin Balsam, Anthony Perkins.

8.62 *The Birds* (Alfred Hitchcock, 1963).

victim himself. *Psycho III* (Anthony Perkins, 1986) is an eighties-style gore-fest which nevertheless demonstrates an intelligent grasp of Hitchcockean mood and theme, as well as reprising some set pieces from his other films. Perkins plays Bates in both sequels.

* See John McCarty and Brian Kelleher, *Alfred Hitchcock Presents: An Illustrated Guide to the Ten-Year Television Career of the Master of Suspense* (New York: St. Martins, 1985).

Scream—"the sense of bleakness and madness in a kind of wilderness expressing an inner state.")

The Birds, Hitchcock's most expensive film, was also one of his most successful, and he went on to cast its star Tippi Hedren (b. 1935) in his last important work, *Marnie* (1964), based by Jay Presson Allen on the novel by Winston Graham. Like *Vertigo,* it is a film of obsession in which a man falls in love with a severely neurotic woman (here, an incorrigible kleptomaniac) and attempts to cure her. While it was much maligned for the visible artificiality of the process photography and painted backdrops of some of its scenes (whose stylization may, in fact, have been intentional), *Marnie* contains sequences of hallucinatory beauty worthy of Hitchcock's finest work, and it belongs, at the very least, to that category designated by François Truffaut as "greatest flawed films." *Marnie,* however, failed miserably at the box office, and it became Hitchcock's last film with the three most important collaborators of his late period—cinematographer Robert Burks and editor George Tomasini, both of whom died shortly after *Marnie* was completed, and composer Bernard Herrmann, whose score was blamed by Universal for *Marnie*'s unpopularity and whom Hitchcock stupidly fired.

8.63 *Marnie* (Alfred Hitchcock, 1964): the last obsession. Tippi Hendren, Sean Connery.

He next made two cold war espionage films—*Torn Curtain* (1966), based on an original screenplay by Brian Moore, and *Topaz* (1969), adapted by Samuel Taylor from Leon Uris' best-selling novel—which showed progressive indifference, if not decline. *Frenzy* (1971), however, deftly scripted by Anthony Shaffer from Arthur Labern's novel *Goodbye Piccadilly, Farewell Leicester Square,* marked a strong comeback by combining the excitement of the British double-chase films with the psychological introspection, kinetic violence, and technical virtuosity of *Psycho.* Shot on location in London by Gil Taylor, this film concerns a sexual psychopath who strangles women with neckties; although it is profoundly misogynistic and contains a strangulation scene that borders on the pornographic (and for which it was duly rated "R"), *Frenzy* became one of the most popular films of 1972.

With *Family Plot* (1976), adapted by Ernest Lehman from a Victor Canning novel, Hitchcock returned to black humor in a bizarre tale of kidnapping, phony spiritualism, and murder which contained distinct overtones of *The Man Who Knew Too Much* (1956 version) and *North by Northwest.* He was working on the screenplay of *The Short Night,* an espionage thriller based on the real-life case of the British double agent George Blake, when he died at his home in Beverly Hills on April 29, 1980.

Owing to his rigorous preproduction practices, in which each film was conceptualized, story-boarded, and planned logistically from beginning to end in advance of shooting, Hitchcock exercised an unusual degree of control over the fifty-three features he made between 1925 and 1976, even when he was working for such a megalomaniac as David Selznick. (After leaving Selznick International in 1947, he functioned as his own producer no matter who was financing and releasing his films.) Yet the tendency to see him as merely a brilliant technician, long the prevailing critical trend, gave way in the seventies to a more judicious assessment of him as both a formalist and moralist, a status acknowledged by the American Film Institute's presentation to him of its Life Achievement Award in 1979. Today, Hitchcock is understood to be one of the leading figures in film history, the peer of Griffith, Eisenstein, Renoir, and Welles.

About his commitment to style there can be no question—during the thirties, he was one of the few directors to use Eisensteinian montage in an era of primarily functional editing; his mastery of the long take and the moving camera have been apparent since the forties; and his achievements in widescreen composition in the fifties are of major historical importance for the contemporary film. Beyond form, however, there is Hitchcock the moralist and fatalist who created an image of the modern world in which the perilous and the monstrous lurk within the most ordinary circumstances of everyday life. It is a world that shares much with the work of Franz Kafka and comprehends what Hannah Arendt termed "the banality of evil." It is also a world in which, as Robin Wood has noted, there erupts from time to time "an animus against women and specifically against the female body," every bit as real as Griffith's racism. Hitchcock's designation as "the master of suspense" was a public relations gambit based on the popular misperception of his work. His greatest films—*Sabotage, Shadow of a Doubt, Vertigo, Psycho, The Birds*—have little or none of that quality. Hitchcock did not so much work in a genre as create one—the "Hitchcock film"—which has been endlessly imitated but never surpassed.* He was an authentic original whose life was his art and who succeeded, perhaps more than any other artist of the century, in making his own fears, obsessions, and fantasies part of our collective psyche.

George Cukor, William Wyler, and Frank Capra

Three other directors of historical importance emerged from Hollywood in the thirties, although their work was less substantial and cohesive than that of the four major figures discussed in this chapter.

George Cukor (1899–1983) originally came to Hollywood from Broadway as a dialogue director, working with both Lewis Milestone and Ernst Lubitsch before directing his first important film, *A Bill of Divorcement*, starring Katharine Hepburn and John Barrymore, in 1932. With a series of stylish comedies and sophisticated literary adaptations, he established himself as one of the foremost craftsmen of the American cinema. Cukor had a flair for elegant decor and witty dialogue, and a facility for directing female stars which has typed him as a "women's director," but his talent was really more versatile than the term implies. Cukor worked exclusively under contract to MGM in the thirties and forties but began to freelance in the postwar era.

---

* For the record, *North by Northwest* inspired the James Bond cycle, *Psycho* the slasher cycle, *The Birds* the disaster film, all of which are still very much with us; *Vertigo* has been remade time and time again (and not just by Brian De Palma); *Shadow of a Doubt* stands firmly behind *Blue Velvet* (David Lynch, 1986); and so on.

8.64 *Camille* (George Cukor, 1936): Greta Garbo, Robert Taylor.

8.65 Cukor's *Philadelphia Story* (1940): Cary Grant, Katharine Hepburn, James Stewart.

Among his most important films are *Dinner at Eight* (1933), *Little Women* (1933), *David Copperfield* (1935), *Camille* (1936), *Holiday* (1938), *The Women* (1939), *The Philadelphia Story* (1940), *Gaslight* (1944),* *Adam's Rib* (1949), *Born Yesterday* (1950), *The Marrying Kind* (1951), *Pat and Mike* (1952), *It Should Happen to You* (1954), *A Star Is Born* (1954),† *Bhowani Junction* (1956), *Les Girls* (1957), and *My Fair Lady* (1964), which earned him a long-deserved Oscar for direction. These are all handsome, graceful productions which feature brilliant performances by some of the most talented actors and actresses in the American cinema, many of whom he guided to awards: John Barrymore, Jean Harlow, Marie Dressler, Greta Garbo, Katharine Hepburn, Cary Grant, Norma Shearer, Joan Crawford, Rosalind Russell, James Stewart, Ingrid Bergman, Charles Boyer, Judy Holliday, Spencer Tracy, Judy Garland, Jack Lemmon, James Mason, and Audrey Hepburn. Cukor's work reveals no strong personal vision, but it is remarkably consistent in its intelligence, sensitivity, and taste. In 1981, he received the prestigious D. W. Griffith Award from the Directors Guild of America and, with *Rich and Famous*, became the oldest director ever to make a major studio film; in 1982, the film won the Golden Lion at Venice.

---

*A remake of the 1940 British version of Patrick Hamilton's play directed by Thorold Dickinson. MGM purchased the rights to the play and withdrew the British film from circulation in the United States.

†*A Star Is Born*, Cukor's first film in Technicolor, CinemaScope, and stereophonic sound, was made for Warner Bros. at a cost of $5 million; it originally ran 181 minutes, but was cut to 140 for distribution, against Cukor's wishes. In 1983, it was restored to its original form by Ronald Haver, head of the Film Department of the Los Angeles County Museum. (See R. Haver, "A Star Is Born Again," *American Film* 8, 9 (July–August 1983):28–33; 59.) Cukor's film was a remake of an earlier version directed by William Wellman for David O. Selznick in 1937, which was itself inspired by Cukor's *What Price Hollywood?* (1932). There was another remake in 1976, directed by Frank Pierson, set in the context of high-rolling rock music, rather than motion-picture stardom.

William Wyler (1902–81) was another fine American filmmaker. He began his career by directing B-Westerns and shorts for his uncle, Carl Laemmle, at Universal Pictures. In 1935 he went to work for Samuel Goldwyn and earned a reputation as an accomplished adaptor of other people's work—most notably Lillian Hellman's play *The Children's Hour,* which Wyler filmed as *These Three* in 1936 and remade under its original title in 1962; Sidney Kingsley's play *Dead End,* with a screenplay by Hellman (1937); and Hellman's play *The Little Foxes* (1941). He also directed adaptations of novels—*Dodsworth* (1936), *Wuthering Heights* (1939), *Mrs. Miniver* (1942, MGM), and *The Heiress* (1949, Paramount—from Henry James' *Washington Square*)—and other plays (*Jezebel,* 1938; *The Letter,* 1940, both for Warners). His collaborator for much of this period was the brilliant cinematographer Gregg Toland, who experimented with deep-focus photography in Wyler films like *Wuthering Heights* and *The Little Foxes* before he used the process so magnificently in Orson Welles' *Citizen Kane* (1941; see pp. 408–27). Wyler's *The Best Years of Our Lives* (1946), his last film for Goldwyn, was hailed as a masterpiece in the year of its release and swept the Academy Awards (as *Mrs. Miniver* had done four years before), although it is really a rather conventional, if intensely felt, drama of the problems of servicemen attempting to adjust to postwar American life. The inflated reputation brought him by his wartime films led Wyler to pursue ever more inflated projects in the fifties, culminating in the widescreen blockbusters *The Big Country* (1958, UA) and *Ben Hur* (1959, MGM) which set an all-time record by receiving eleven major Oscars. Nevertheless, he continued to produce interesting work during this period, much of it for Paramount, including his tough, cynical action film *Detective Story* (1951), his adaptations of Dreiser's turn-of-the-century novel *Sister Carrie* (*Carrie,* 1952), and Joseph Hayes' tense contemporary drama *The Desperate Hours*

8.66 William Wyler's version of *Wuthering Heights* (1939), shot by Gregg Toland on the moors of the San Fernando Valley: Merle Oberon and Laurence Olivier as Cathy and Heathcliff.

8.67 Wyler's adaptation of *The Little Foxes* (1941), photographed by Toland. Note the depth of the image and how the action occurs on several planes at once. Herbert Marshall, Bette Davis.

8.68 *Lost Horizon* (Frank Capra, 1937): Ronald Coleman, John Howard, Edward Everett Horton, Thomas Mitchell, *et al.*

(1955), the delightful romantic comedy *Roman Holiday* (1953), and the unconventional (for the fifties) *Friendly Persuasion* (1956, Allied Artists), the story of an Indiana Quaker family trying to maintain its pacifism in the midst of the Civil War. In the sixties, Wyler staged something of a critical comeback with a powerful adaptation of John Fowles' novel *The Collector* (1965), but *Funny Girl* (1968) and *The Liberation of L. B. Jones* (1969) did little to confirm his renewed reputation. Nevertheless, in 1975 Wyler was selected for the American Film Institute's Life Achievement Award, in recognition of his past contributions.

Frank Capra (b. 1897) is a Sicilian who emigrated with his family to Los Angeles in 1903, where he ultimately earned a degree in chemical engineering from the California Institute of Technology. Unable to find employment in that field, he went to work as a gag writer for Hal Roach, Mack Sennett, and finally Harry Langdon, for whom he wrote the hit *Tramp, Tramp, Tramp* (1926) and directed *The Strong Man* (1926) and *Long Pants* (1927). When this collaboration ended in creative differences, Capra went to work for Harry Cohn at Columbia Pictures, where he made the studio's first talking feature (*The Donovan Affair*, 1929) and a popular series of armed forces adventure films with the team of Jack Holt and Ralph Graves (*Submarine*, 1928; *Flight*, 1930; *Dirigible*, 1931). In 1931, Capra made his first film with screenwriter Robert Riskin (the Jean Harlow vehicle *Platinum Blonde*) and began the collaboration which would produce the great Columbia screwball comedies *Lady for a Day* (1933), *It Happened One Night* (1934), *Mr. Deeds Goes to Town* (1936), *You Can't Take It with You* (1938), and *Mr. Smith Goes to Washington* (1939), as well as the sumptuous utopian fantasy *Lost Horizon* (1937).* Capra won the Academy Award for direction three

---

* Originally 132 minutes but later cut to 108, *Lost Horizon* was recently restored as a joint venture of the American Film Institute and the UCLA Pacific Archives, with permanently

times with this series, and he ended the decade as one of the most sought-after filmmakers in Hollywood. Such was his clout that he and Riskin were able to form an independent company (Frank Capra Productions) to produce and distribute their next film, the antifascist parable *Meet John Doe* (1941), which was a failure and ended their relationship.

During World War II, Capra was inducted into the army and quickly became head of the Morale Branch's newly formed film unit. Here, with the backing of Army Chief of Staff General George C. Marshall, Capra became producer-director of the extraordinary documentary series *Why We Fight* (see p. 394). Originally commissioned to indoctrinate servicemen, this seven-film series was ultimately shown to general audiences in theaters around the country at President Roosevelt's behest, so powerful was it as an instrument of mass persuasion (Capra won his fourth Oscar for *Prelude to War*, 1942, the series' first installment). Only months after the war, Capra attempted independence again by forming Liberty Films with George Stevens and William Wyler. Capra made only two Liberty films before the company was sold to Paramount in 1947, *It's a Wonderful Life* (1946)* and *State of the Union* (1948), both of which failed at the box office. After two Bing Crosby films (*Riding High,* 1950, and *Here Comes the Groom,* 1951) made to fulfill his part of the Liberty deal with Paramount, Capra went into semiretirement, emerging to direct the Frank Sinatra vehicle *A Hole in the Head* (1959) and *Pocket Full of Miracles* (1961), a remake of *Lady for a Day.* After he published his best-selling autobiography, *The Name Above the Title,* in 1971, Capra became something of a cult figure but made no more films. His influence, however, has been acknowledged across so wide a range of directors as John Ford, Ermanno Olmi, Milos Forman, Satyajit Ray, and Yasujiro Ozu, and he received the American Film Institute's Life Achievement Award in 1982. During the thirties, Capra had achieved a degree of autonomy and recognition unprecedented within the American studio system, and it may be that the failure of his own company after the war embittered him to the filmmaking establishment. Whatever the case, he made only one great film after his triumphs of the Depression years, *It's a Wonderful Life,* and that is a work which, for all of its apparent buoyancy, suggests some extremely dark possibilities for postwar American life.

The coming of sound threatened to destroy the international market that film had enjoyed since Méliès by introducing the language barrier between national industries. During the first few years of sound, Frenchmen would hiss and boo the dialogue in German films, and vice versa; the British and Americans found each other's accents incomprehensible; and there was the problem of regional dialects within a single nation. To

8.69 *It's a Wonderful Life* (Frank Capra, 1946): Jimmy Stewart, H. B. Warner.

---

lost footage replaced by voice-over dialogue and stills. The film was remade (ill-advisedly) as a musical, with direction by Charles Jarrott and songs by Burt Bacharach, in 1973.

* Remade as the telefilm *It Happened One Christmas* (Donald Wrye, 1977), with a gender change (Marlo Thomas for Jimmy Stewart) and considerably less darkness.

overcome this barrier, films were for several years shot in different language versions at the time of production. This expensive practice was soon abandoned when a whole new branch of the industry was evolved for the dubbing and subtitling of films for foreign markets. The American industry, long accustomed to international dominion, was able to maintain its control of the world market by virtue of its vast capital and, for a while at least, its wholesale ownership of the major patents for sound equipment.* But because of the economic domination of the American studios themselves by the country's largest corporate interests, the American cinema of the thirties had a specifically ideological orientation, which the Production Code incarnated.

The central tenets of the Code were that the Depression, if it existed at all, had little impact on most people's lives; that there was no crime in the streets or corruption in government; that the authority of the police and the military were absolute; that religion and the nuclear family were sacred, coextensive institutions; and, finally, that most Americans in the thirties lived in bungalows behind white picket fences on peaceful streets in Anytown, U.S.A. By regulating the "moral" content of American films, the Breen Code was regulating their social content as well, so that what purported to be a blueprint for "cleaning up the movies" was actually an instrument of social control in a period of economic chaos. Thus, however great its aesthetic achievements—and they are clearly manifold—the American cinema of the thirties consistently concealed the *reality* of the Depression and, later, of the war in Europe from the American people. This is a matter not of opinion but of historical record: with several notable exceptions (e.g., Warner Bros.' *I Am a Fugitive from a Chain Gang*, Mervyn LeRoy, 1932; United Artists' *Our Daily Bread*, King Vidor, 1934), Hollywood did not seriously confront the social misery caused by the Depression until the release of Fox's *The Grapes of Wrath* (John Ford) in 1940; the first Hollywood film to acknowledge the Nazi threat in Europe, Warner Bros.' *Confessions of a Nazi Spy* (Anatole Litvak), did not appear until 1939.† So perhaps the final comment on Hollywood

---

* In Hollywood, foreign-language versions of English-language features could be made for under 30 percent of the original budget, and in early 1930, Paramount built a vast studio at Joinville in the suburbs of Paris to mass-produce films in five separate languages. Within months the other Hollywood majors had joined Paramount, and Joinville—already christened "Babel-sur-Seine"—became a movie factory which operated twenty-four hours a day to produce films in as many as fifteen languages (including Romanian, Lithuanian, Egyptian, and Greek), often in less than two weeks per feature. The quality of the Joinville product was predictably low, although many promising young directors like Marc Allégret and Claude Autant-Lara (see Chapter 13) were trained there. By the end of 1931, the technique of dubbing had been sufficiently improved to provide an inexpensive alternative to multilingual production, the latter practice was abandoned, and Paramount converted the Joinville studios into a dubbing center for all of Europe. Dubbing (and, less frequently, subtitling) is still practiced for foreign release versions throughout the world today (see Chapter 9).

†One reason for the latter was that studio executives did not wish to antagonize Axis or neutral countries where their corporations had major markets and / or holdings. As incredible as it must seem today, a faction within the Hays Office in 1939 demanded that the___

in the thirties should be this: Sound had been added to the cinema as the result of a bitter economic struggle between competing American production companies; the technology of sound recording had first been perfected by American engineers; and the creative use of sound had been pioneered almost exclusively by American filmmakers. Yet, with regard to the social, sexual, and political dimensions of human experience, the American sound film throughout the thirties remained quite effectively "silent."

script of *Confessions of a Nazi Spy* acknowledge Hitler's "unchallenged political and social achievements" and eliminate its "unfair" references to the recent dismemberment of Czechoslovakia (see Clayton R. Koppes and Gregory D. Black, *Hollywood Goes to War* [New York: The Free Press, 1987], pp. 28–30). The Warners forged ahead, less for political reasons than for personal ones: their chief salesman in Germany, Joe Kaufman, had been beaten to death by Nazi thugs in a Berlin alleyway in 1936, and Jack Warner would never forget it. (See Colin Shindler, *Hollywood Goes to War: Films and American Society, 1939–1952* [London: Routledge & Keegan Paul, 1979], pp. 8–9.)

THE INTERNATIONAL DIFFUSION OF SOUND

Having successfully created large new markets for their sound recording technologies at home, Western Electric and RCA were anxious to do the same abroad, and this motive went hand in glove with the desire of American studios to extend their control of the international film industry into the sound era. Accordingly, the Big Five began to export sound films in late 1928, and ERPI (Electrical Research Products, Inc.—Western Electric's aggressive marketing agent) and RCA began installing their equipment in first-run European theaters at the same time. British exhibitors converted most rapidly, with 22 percent wired in 1929 and 63 percent by the end of 1932.

German and French exhibitors converted more slowly, largely because in 1928 a German cartel had been formed to stem the invasion of American sound equipment. Backed by German, Dutch, and Swiss capital, Tobis (the Tonbild Syndicate, A.G.) had acquired the European rights to the Tri-Ergon sound-on-film system and begun to wire German theaters for its use. At the same time, Germany's two largest electrical manufacturers, Siemens and Halske, A.G., and Allgemeine Elektrizitätsgesellschaft (AEG), formed the Klangfilm Syndicate to exploit a competing system mutually developed by the corporations on the basis of Kuchenmeister, Pederson-Poulsen, and Messter patents. After several months of feuding with each other over European markets, Tobis and Klangfilm merged in March 1929 to combat the threat of American domination of the sound film. With capital assets of over $100 million and venture capital provided by the Dutch bank Oyens and Sons, Tobis-Klangfilm quickly concluded cross-licensing agreements with the British and French Photophone Company and British Talking Pictures, Ltd., giving it production, distribution, and manufacturing branches in every country in Europe.

Almost immediately, Tobis-Klangfilm began to enter suits against Western Electric and ERPI, and their licensees, for patent infringement in all of its territories, and won final injunctions in Germany, Holland, Czechoslovakia, Hungary, Switzerland, and Austria. As American foreign grosses plummeted by 75 percent, the Hollywood monopolists agreed to boycott the markets in dispute. Simultaneously, in July 1929, the General Electric Corporation (which held a controlling interest in RCA) acquired part interest in AEG and nudged Tobis-Klangfilm into a cooperative releasing agreement with RKO. To avoid a self-destructive patent war, ERPI (i.e., Western Electric), RCA, and Tobis-Klangfilm convened the German-American Film Conference in Paris on June 19, 1930. Their purpose was to carve up among themselves a world market for sound film equipment conservatively valued at $250 million. A final agreement signed on July 22, 1930, divided the world into four territories: Tobis-Klangfilm was given exclusive rights to central Europe and Scandinavia; ERPI and RCA got the United States, Canada, Australia, New Zealand, India, and the Soviet Union; the United Kingdom was split between them, 25 percent going to Tobis-Klangfilm and 75 percent to ERPI and RCA; and the rest of the world was open territory. The three giants also agreed to pool all of their patents, exchange technical information, and drop all pending litigation. This informal cartel never really held together very well, and its terms were renegotiated several times before it collapsed in 1939 in the face of war in Europe. Nevertheless, Tobis-Klangfilm had succeeded in fending off the American bid for world domination and had produced, in conjunction with other factors, a marked decline in Hollywood's influence in Europe.

BRITAIN

Due to the rapidity with which its theaters were wired and the (relative) lack of a language barrier, however, the United Kingdom became Hollywood's first major foreign market for sound films. The British cinema had always been a stepchild of the American industry, and during the twenties it had almost ceased to exist. But in 1927 Parliament passed the Cinematograph Film Act, setting strict quotas on the number of foreign films that could be shown in the country; this had the effect of stimulating domestic production and investment. The British film industry doubled in size from 1927 to 1928, and the number of features it produced rose from 20 to 128. The expansion continued well into the thirties, enabling the British to compete with Hollywood not merely nationally but—for the first time in its history—internationally. Many of the films produced by the new boom were "quota quickies"—the British equivalent of the low-budget American B-film—but many more were distinguished undertakings by serious producers such as Alexander Korda (b. Sándor Kellner, 1893–1956) and Michael Balcon (1896–1977).

The producer-director Korda and his two younger brothers, the director Zoltán (1895–1961) and the art director Vincent (1897–1979), were Hungarians who settled in England and founded London Film Productions there in the early thirties. They collaborated on many outstanding costume spectacles, including *The Private Life of Henry VIII* (Alexander Korda, 1933), *Rembrandt* (Alexander Korda, 1936), *Elephant Boy* (Robert Flaherty and Zoltán Korda, 1937), *The Four Feathers* (Zoltán Korda, 1939), *The Thief of Bagdad* (Ludwig Berger, Michael Powell, Tim Whe-

9.1 The original "biopic". Alexander Korda's *The Private Life of Henry VIII* (1933): Charles Laughton's performance as the gluttonous monarch made him internationally famous.

9.2 London Films' spectacular *The Thief of Bagdad* (Ludwig Berger, Michael Powell, and Tim Whelan, 1940): Sabu and the genie's foot. The film won American Academy Awards for art direction, color cinematography, and special effects.

lan, 1940), and *The Jungle Book* (Zoltán Korda, 1942), which did much to establish Great Britain's position in the international market.

Michael Balcon was successively director of production for the most important and discriminating British studios of the era: Gainsborough (which he founded in 1924), Gaumont-British (where he produced for Hitchcock), Ealing Studios, and the Rank Organization. This was the era in British cinema which witnessed the flowering of Hitchcock's thrillers, the literate period films of Anthony Asquith (1902–68—*A Cottage on Dartmoor*, 1930; *Tell England*, 1931; the Jessie Matthews musicals of Victor Saville (1897–1979—*Evergreen*, 1934; *First a Girl*, 1935; *It's Love Again*, 1936), and the excellent documentaries produced by John Grierson (1898–1972) and his socially "committed" British Documentary Movement (see p. 589) for the Empire Marketing Board (EMB—e.g., *Drifters* [Grierson, 1929]; *Upstream* [Arthur Elton, 1931]; *Industrial Britain* [Robert Flaherty, 1933]) and the General Post Office (GPO—e.g., *Coalface* [Alberto Cavalcanti, 1935]; *Song of Ceylon* [Basil Wright, 1935]; *Night Mail* [Wright, 1936]). By 1937, the British industry had the second largest annual output in the world (225 features), and British films were competing strongly with American films on an international scale. Yet British producers were also deeply in debt, and the following year witnessed many bankruptcies and studio closings. In 1938, less than one hundred features were made and fewer released, a reflection of Europe's uncertain political future and the troubled world economy.

GERMANY

The German industry entered the sound era from a position of relative strength due to its ownership of the Tobis-Klangfilm recording patents, although the Weimar Republic was already on the brink of collapse. As in the United States, the first German sound films were unremarkable popular musicals, and the trend toward escapist entertainment grew as the nation sank ever more deeply into economic and political trouble. Yet some very important and distinguished films came out of the early sound period in Germany.

Perhaps the most significant and influential work of Germany's early sound period was Fritz Lang's *M* in 1930, with a script by Thea von Harbou (Lang's wife) based on the famous Dusseldorf child-murders. In *M*, Peter Lorre (1904–64) plays a psychotic murderer of little girls in a large German city who is ultimately tracked down not by the police but by members of the local underworld. Through cutting, Lang establishes a clear parallel between the two groups. Lorre is brilliant as the tortured psychopath who wants desperately to stop killing but is constantly overpowered by his uncontrollable compulsion, and *M* is very much in the gloomy tradition of *Kammerspiel*. Studio-produced and highly stylized in its realism, the film contains no musical score but is distinguished by its expressive use of nonnaturalistic sound, as in the recurring theme from Grieg's *Peer Gynt* Suite, which the murderer whistles offscreen before committing his crimes. Not the least amazing thing about *M* is the way in which it deals with a revolting subject in a subtle and tasteful manner. Lang achieves this primarily through editing and the fluid camera style of Fritz Arno Wagner. Near the beginning of the film, for example, Lorre entices a little girl with a balloon; Lang cuts to shots of the girl's worried mother waiting for her return in an apartment; then he cuts to a shot of the balloon floating out and away from a small forest thicket to become entangled in some utility wires, and we know that the child has been murdered. At another point, to establish the identity between the bosses of the local underworld and the police, Lang contrives to have the chief of police complete a gesture begun by the chief of thieves in the previous shot. This persistent equation of authority with criminality, and a brooding sense of destiny, make *M* as much about the crisis of German society at the time it was made as about child-murder. One has the constant sense in watching *M* that one is in the presence of a culture on the brink of utter collapse. (Indeed, there is grim irony in the fact that the state which so diligently pursues the child-murderer in Lang's film would itself become responsible for the murder of millions of children in death camps little more than a decade later.)

Lang's next film was a sequel to his popular silent thriller about the master criminal Dr. Mabuse, *Dr. Mabuse, der Spieler* (*Dr. Mabuse, the Gambler*, 1922). In *Das Testament des Dr. Mabuse* (*The Last Will of Dr. Mabuse*, 1932), also sumptuously photographed by Wagner, the arch-tyrant directs his league of world crime from a lunatic asylum. Lang later claimed to have modeled Mabuse on Hitler and put Nazi slogans into the mouths of his criminal minions. This claim may be the result of hindsight, but the Nazis apparently recognized something of themselves in the film and banned it when they came to power in 1933. After bluntly refusing Goebbel's offer of an important post with UFA, Lang escaped to France on the next train (leaving behind his wife, a devout Nazi),

9.3   Peter Lorre in *M* (Fritz Lang, 1930).

where in 1934 he adapted Ferenc Molnár's play *Liliom* to the screen for Fox-Europa.

He later emigrated to America, where he made two brilliant films before the war. *Fury* (1936), shot at MGM, is a compelling indictment of mob violence that probes as deeply into the complex relationship between will and fate as had Lang's German films. *You Only Live Once* (1937), produced by Walter Wanger for UA, is another powerful tale of injustice and destiny: a young ex-convict is falsely accused of murder and sentenced to death; with his wife's help he escapes from prison hours before his execution, and together the two flee across America until they are hunted down and killed at a roadblock on the Canadian border. Expressionist in atmosphere, composition, and lighting, *You Only Live Once* became the model for Joseph Lewis' *Gun Crazy* (1950) and Arthur Penn's *Bonnie and Clyde* (1967; see pp. 877–80). The couple's desperate flight through nocturnal America has a tragic, brooding character that both later films preserve. Lang directed another twenty-one films in the United States for a variety of studios between 1938 and 1956, but only his **film noir** masterpiece, *The Big Heat* (1953, Columbia), achieved the quality and depth of his greatest work.

The German film industry which Lang had left was controlled from 1933 to 1945 by Goebbels, who spent considerable energy banning undesirable and "unhealthy" films like *Kameradschaft* and *M* as the work of *entarte Künstler,* or "degenerate artists." Working through the Reich Film Chamber (*Reichsfilmkammer,* established July 1933), under the authority of the Reich Cinema Law (*Reichslichtspielgesetz,* enacted February, 1934), he mounted a rigorous campaign to rid the industry of its many Jews, but he saw no reason to nationalize the German cinema until well into the war, in 1942. Like the Soviet leaders, Goebbels regarded film as the century's most important communications medium, but unlike them he was not much concerned with agit-prop. Under his regime, Goebbels encouraged German films to remain well-made but primarily trivial and escapist, since he wished the populace entertained rather than enlightened. The Nazis were in fact quite skilled at manipulating the symbols of popular culture to objectify their ideals—see, for example, the musical comedies *Viktor und Viktoria* (Reinhold Schnüzel, 1933) and *Amphytrion* (Schnüzel, 1935). Of the eleven to thirteen hundred features produced under Nazi rule, perhaps less than 25 percent contained overt propaganda. Propaganda as such was confined to newsreels and *Stattsauftragsfilme*—films conceived and financed by the state. These included biographical and historical films of the heroic national past like *Bismarck* (Wolfgang Liebeneiner, 1940), *Der grosse König* (*Frederick the Great,* Veit Harlan, 1942), and *Kolberg* (Harlan, 1945)—both of the latter in Agfacolor; dramatic films directly adulatory of the Nazi Party, like *S. A. Mann Brandt* (Franz Seitz, 1933), *Hitlerjunge Quex* (Hans Steinhoff, 1933), and *Hans Westmar* (Franz Wenzler, 1933); and, finally, scurrilous racial propaganda films like the infamous *Jud Süss* (*Jew Süss,* Veit Harlan, 1940) and *Der ewige Jude* (*The Eternal Jew,* Fritz Hippler, 1940), as well as such anti-Semitic, anti-British hybrids as *Die Rothschilds Aktien*

9.4 Nazi cinema: Werner Krauss in *Jud Süss* (Veit Harlan, 1940).

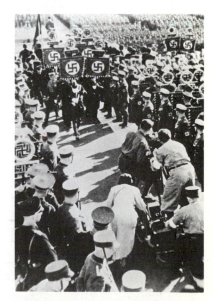

9.5 A camera crew shooting *Triumph des Willens* (Leni Riefenstahl, 1935) at the 1934 Nazi Party Rally in Nuremberg.

von Waterloo (The Rothschilds' Share in Waterloo, Erich Waschweck, 1940; 1941).

The only great films to emerge from Nazi Germany were two propaganda "documentaries," both personally commissioned by Hitler for the Nazi Party. The first, *Triumph des Willens (Triumph of the Will,* 1935), is a film of nearly mythic dimensions. Assigned to the direction of Leni Riefenstahl (b. 1902) at Hitler's insistence, *Triumph* portrays the 1934 Nazi Party Rally at Nuremberg as a quasireligious, mystical experience. Working with virtually limitless financial resources, thirty cameras and a crew of 120 persons, and her own utter ideological commitment, Riefenstahl shot the film in six days with the active cooperation of party leaders. She later wrote, "The preparations for the party congress were made in concert with the preparations for the camera work," but recent studies document that the entire congress was *staged* for her cameras by Hitler's architect Albert Speer and that nothing was left to chance.

It took her eight months to edit the footage, some of it shot after the fact to cover mistakes and continuity gaps, into a powerfully persuasive and visually beautiful piece of propaganda. Hitler is depicted as the new messiah descending from the clouds in his airplane to succor his people (the titles for this sequence were written and designed by Walter Ruttmann, who had been given the original commission on the film). Once on earth, he is greeted by the awakening city of Nuremberg and begins a god-like procession to the *Kongresshalle* (Congress Hall), where the impassioned rhetoric of his followers rings through the chamber. The rest is all pseudo-Wagnerian music composed by her career-long collaborator Herbert Windt, monumental Nazi architecture, mass rallies, and torchlight parades choreographed for Riefenstahl's camera. The Führer himself speaks at several points in the pageant but never more forcefully than at its emotional conclusion, where the Nazi ideal of *Blut und Boden* ("blood and soil") is invoked against the backdrop of a gigantic swastika, while S.A. men in a superimposed low-angle shot seem to march into distant clouds.

9.6 Leni Riefenstahl's (and Adolf Hitler's) *Triumph des Willens.*

9.7 *Olympiad* (Leni Riefenstahl, 1936).

Triumph of the Will was effective enough to be banned in Britain, the United States, and Canada, and to become a model for film propaganda among the Allies during the coming war. Hitler was so impressed that he commissioned Riefenstahl to make a spectacular film of the 1936 Berlin Olympics.* Again, unlimited resources were placed at her disposal, and her team of cameramen shot 1.5 million feet of film, which took her eighteen months to edit. The completed motion picture was released in two parts as *Olympische Spiele 1936 (Olympiad / Olympia)* in 1938 with a dynamic score by Windt, and it stands even today as a great testament to athletic achievement, a forerunner of Kon Ichikawa's *Tokyo Olympiad* (1965) and the omnibus film of the 1972 Munich Olympics, *Visions*

---

* Goebbels, in a speech of February 9, 1934: "We are convinced that in general film is one of the most modern and far-reaching methods of influencing the masses. A regime thus must not allow film to go its own way." (Quoted in David Weinberg, "Approaches to the Study of Film in the Third Reich: A Critical Appraisal," *Journal of Contemporary History,* vol. 19 [1984], p. 105.)

of Eight (Juri Ozerov, Mai Zetterling, Arthur Penn, Michael Phleghar, Kon Ichikawa, Miloš Forman, Claude Lelouch, and John Schlesinger, 1973). Riefenstahl's innovative use of slow-motion photography and telephoto lenses created images of compelling kinetic beauty, but, like *Triumph of the Will,* the film is steeped in the Nazi mystique which makes a cult of sheer physical prowess. Beyond these two powerful and disturbing films, the Nazi cinema produced few films of note, probably because most of the major filmmakers of the Weimar period had been either deported to prison camps or forced into exile.

One exception among the exiles was G. W. Pabst. Like so many of his colleagues, Pabst emigrated to Hollywood when the Nazis came to power in 1933, and he made one film, *A Modern Hero* (1934), for Warner Bros. This mildly anticapitalist melodrama was a commercial failure, effectively ending Pabst's American career, and he moved with his family to Paris where he made a series of indifferent films for the French industry (e.g., *Mademoiselle Docteur,* 1937). Just before Germany invaded Poland in September 1939, Pabst announced his intention to re-emigrate to the United States and become a citizen, but he then crossed the Swiss border into Austria where he spent the rest of his life. Pabst would always claim that he was trapped inside the Reich by the war, yet he made three features for the Nazis, two of which, *Komödianten* (*Comedians,* 1941) and *Paracelsus* (1943), survive. These are not propaganda films as such (although Pabst may have contributed to such propaganda "documentaries" as *Feldzug em Polen* [*Campaign in Poland,* 1939] but ideological epics of "German genius." After the war, Pabst made the anti-Nazi films *Der Prozess* (*The Trial,* 1949), a study of pograms in nineteenth-century Hungary which won the Golden Lion at Venice; *Der letzte Akt* (*The Last Act / The Last Ten Days,* 1955—Hitler in the bunker); and *Es geschah am 20 Juli* (*The Jackboot Mutiny,* 1955), on the 1944 generals' plot to assassinate Hitler. None of this, however, could remove the moral stain of Pabst's return to the Greater German Reich to make films for Goebbels, and he did not work for the last ten years of his life.

ITALY

Sound came slowly to the Italian cinema because competition from the American and German industries during the twenties had already pushed it to the brink of collapse. By 1925, from a peak of 150 features in 1919, annual production had fallen to fifteen films, most of which were coproductions with other nations. In an effort to combat the "foreign invasion" and revive the failing domestic industry, the entrepreneur Stefano Pittaluga (1887–1931), founded the Società Anonima Stefano Pittaluga (S.A.S.P.) in 1926. S.A.S.P. absorbed the major Italian studios (Cines, Italia, Palatina) into a private monopoly with government sanction. (An earlier attempt at private combination, L'Unione Cinematografica Italiana, [UCI, founded 1919] had recently gone bankrupt and provided the core for Pittaluga's company.) In 1927, Fascist dictator Benito Mussolini (1883–1945) granted the S.A.S.P. exclusive distribution rights to the documentaries and newsreels produced by L'Unione Cinematografica Educativa (whose acronym, LUCE, is Italian for "light"), representing the first major collaboration between the commercial film industry and the Fascist state. It was an S.A.S.P. subsidiary, Cines-Pittaluga, that produced Italy's first talkie—Gennaro Righelli's *La canzone dell'amore* (*The Song of Love*, 1930); it ultimately provided the basis for the Ente Nazionale Industrie Cinematografiche (ENIC), the distribution and exhibition agency through which the Fascists controlled the Italian industry after 1935.

The earliest Italian sound films were notably undistinguished, with the exception of Alessandro Blasetti's *Terre madre* (*Mother Earth*, 1931) and *Resurrectio* (*Resurrection*, 1931) and Mario Camerini's *Figaro e la sua gran giornata* (*Figaro and His Big Day*, 1931) and *Gli uomini, che mascalzoni!* (*What Rascals Men Are!*, 1932), the latter starring the future neorealist director Vittorio De Sica. (Ironically, Camerini's *Rotaie* [*Rails*], shot and edited as a silent film in 1929 but released in 1931 with music and sound effects, was the Italian sound film's first great popular and critical success.) The introduction of sound, however, did draw Mussolini's attention to the enormous propaganda value of film, and his regime successfully manipulated the Italian industry through the decade by encouraging its expansion and controlling film content. The specific tactics will be discussed in Chapter 11, but, in general, economic incentives and subsidies caused production to rise annually until it reached eighty-seven features by 1939. As in Nazi Germany, strict Fascist censorship dictated the production of escapist fare—mainly frothy romantic comedies (known as "*telephono bianco*" or "white telephone" films, owing to their glamorous studio sets) and a modicum of nationalist propaganda centered on "heroic" themes from the past (for example, Blasetti's *1860*, 1934; Luis Trenker's German-Italian coproduction *Condottieri*, 1937; Carmine Gallone's *Scipione l'Africano* [*Scipio Africanus*, 1937]), and the Fascist movement itself (Giovacchino Forzano's *Camicia nera* [*Black Shirt*, 1933]; Blasetti's *Vecchia guardia* [*The Old Guard*, 1934]).

THE SOVIET UNION

Sound was also slow in coming to the Soviet Union. Although the Soviet engineers P. G. Tager and A. F. Shorin had designed optical systems (variable density and variable area respectively) as early as 1926–27, neither was workable until 1929, and only Tager's was adopted by the industry. (The first Soviet sound films, such as Iuli Raizman's [b. 1903] *The Earth Thirsts* [*Zemlia zhazhde*, 1930], were recorded with German equipment.) It is often argued that the Soviets' late start enabled them to profit from the mistakes of their Western counterparts, and it is true, for example, that the Soviet studios never had to struggle with sound-on-disk, which was already obsolete by the time they started sound production. But it is also true that the earliest Soviet transitional films were technically inferior to those of the West and clearly suffered from their makers' lack of instruction and experience.

Furthermore, after the transition began, sound and silent cinema con-

9.8, 9.9, 9.10 Vertov's experimental sound film *Three Songs About Lenin* (1934).

tinued to coexist for nearly six years, the last Soviet silent production being released in 1936, the same year as the first Soviet color film. (Indeed, the majority of Soviet theaters were not wired for sound until 1938.) There were exceptions, of course—Kuleshov's *The Great Consoler* (*Velikii uteshitel,* 1933), Vertov's *Enthusiasm* (*Entuziazm,* 1931, suppressed) and *Three Songs of Lenin* (*Tri pesni o Leninye,* 1934), Pudovkin's *A Simple Case* (*Prostoi sluchai,* 1932—released silent due to Party intervention) and *Deserter* (*Dezertir,* 1933), and Dovzhenko's *Ivan* (1932). Moreover, it was Soviet directors like Vertov who pioneered the sound documentary and sound montage.

Sound arrived in the Soviet Union, as it had in Germany, during a period of political reaction. The first of the great purges in which millions of Soviet citizens, as well as government functionaries, were imprisoned or executed during the decade, began in 1934. Fear and xenophobia were rife, and, again as in Germany, the Soviet cinema became increasingly escapist as the government became increasingly repressive. The bold revolutionary experiments of the past decade were dead. They were replaced by Hollywood-influenced musicals like Grigori Alexandrov's *The Jolly Fellows* / *Jazz Comedy* (*Veselye rebiata,* 1934); historical spectacles like Valdimir Petrov's *Peter the Great, Parts I* and *II* (*Petr Pervyi,* 1937–38); and biographies of revolutionary heroes, like the Vasilievs' *Chapaev* (1934)* and Dovzhenko's *Shchors* (1939), putatively evocative of Stalin. Related to the latter genre were dramatic reconstructions of revolutionary events in the stolid style of socialist realism, such as Mikhail Romm's *Lenin in October* (*Lenin v oktiabre,* 1937) and *Lenin in 1918* (*Lenin v 1918 godu,* 1939).

Perhaps the most vital Soviet films of this period were two trilogies. The first, directed by Grigori Kozintsev and Leonid Trauberg, created a

---

* Sergei (1900–1959) and Georgi (1899–1946) Vasiliev were unrelated filmmakers who met as students of Eisenstein at the VGIK. As "the Vasiliev brothers," they collaborated closely on the direction of six features between 1930 and 1943.

9.11 *Chapayev* (Sergei and Georgi Vasiliev, 1934): Boris Babochkin as the famous Red Army commander.

9.12 *The Youth of Maxim* (Grigori Kozintsev and Leonid Trauberg, 1935): Boris Chirkov.

9.13 *The Childhood of Maxim Gorki* (Mark Donskoi, 1938): Alexei Lyarski.

"synthetic biography" of a typical young Party worker during the revolutionary period in *The Youth of Maxim* (*Yunost Maksima*, 1935), *The Return of Maxim* (*Vozvrashchenie Maksima*, 1937), and *The Vyborg Side* (*Vyborgskaia storona*, 1939). All three films were shot by the brilliant cinematographer Andrei Moskvin (1901–61), who would later work closely with Eisenstein. Mark Donskoi contributed a robust adaptation of the three-volume autobiography of the Soviet writer Maxim Gorki (1868–1936)—*The Childhood of Maxim Gorki* (*Detstvo Gorkogo*, 1938), *My Apprenticeship* (*V Liudiakh*, 1939), and *My Universities* (*Moi universitety*, 1940).

During most of this period, the man who might have returned the Soviet cinema to its former glory remained inactive. Sergei Eisenstein had returned to Moscow from his American sojourn badly discouraged. All of his Paramount projects had been abortive, so in late 1930 he had signed a contract with the Mexican Film Trust, a corporation formed by the American novelist Upton Sinclair (1878–1968)* and other investors to produce an Eisenstein film in Mexico. Eisenstein had long been interested in Mexico as both a cultural and a revolutionary phenomenon, and he later wrote that the film he had envisioned would have been "four novels framed by prologue and epilogue, unified in conception and spirit, creating its entity." Provisionally entitled *Que viva México!*, the film would have been an attempt to encapsulate revolutionary Mexican history and evoke the spirit of the culture and the land. Eisenstein (working with Alexandrov and Tisse) had shot all of the film's sections except the last by 1932, when, as the climax of a series of misunderstandings, Sinclair abruptly ordered him to abandon the project, claiming correctly that Eisenstein had far exceeded his budget. All of the footage was in Hollywood for processing, and it was never sent back to Eisenstein. Although Sinclair had promised to ship the negative to Moscow for Eisenstein to edit into a feature film, he eventually turned it over to the independent producer Sol Lesser (1890–1980). Lesser cut parts of one episode into a silent melodrama of revenge entitled *Thunder Over Mexico* (1933), with a recorded orchestral score by Hugo Riesenfeld. Parts of the epilogue, also edited by Lesser, were released in 1934 as *Death Day*. Both films were critical and commercial failures, and there was a heated controversy among American artists and intellectuals over the question of who was to blame. The rest of the footage ultimately found its way into various documentaries about the making of the film, and into the archives of MoMa in New York. From what is left of it, we can surmise that *Que viva México!* might have been Eisenstein's greatest film and the ultimate vindication of his theories of montage. Its dismemberment disturbed Eisenstein deeply, and it remains, with von Stroheim's *Greed* (1924; see Chapter 6) and Welles's *The Magnificent Ambersons* (1942; see chapter 10), one of the great lost master-

---

* Sinclair was an internationally prominent socialist writer and a friend of the Bolshevik Revolution. Like Lenin, he believed that film was the most powerful medium of ideological persuasion in modern times, and he saw in the Eisenstein venture a chance to produce a sort of Latin American *Potemkin*.

9.14 Stills from Eisenstein's aborted epic *Que viva México!* (1930–32, uncompleted and unreleased).

works of the cinema.*

In Moscow again, Eisenstein conceived a number of projects, but they were systematically thwarted by Boris Shumiatski, the head of the Soviet film industry, who with full official sanction began a campaign to dis-

---

* In 1973 the Soviet state film archive Gosfilmofond negotiated a deal with MoMA and the Sinclair estate to secure copies of all extant footage of Eisenstein's Mexican film. In August 1979, Sovexport released an "official" restoration of *Que viva México!* by Grigori Alexandrov, Eisenstein's assistant on the production, who claims to possess Eisenstein's original cutting schedule. Reviews were unenthusiastic, but the Alexandrov reconstruction is as close as we are ever likely to come to the film Eisenstein intended.

9.15 Stills from Eisenstein's suppressed *Bezhin Meadow* (1935, uncompleted and unreleased).

9.16 Nikolai Cherkassov in *Alexander Nevski* (Sergei Eisenstein, 1938).

credit Eisenstein and reduce his influence within the Soviet cinema. The Stalin government believed that Eisenstein had grown too independent during his American tour and that he set a dangerous example for other Soviet artists. Also, Shumiatski hated Eisenstein personally, not an uncommon response to the director's eccentric personality and irreverent sense of humor. In 1935 Eisenstein was publicly insulted at the Congress of Party Film Workers and attacked in the official press. He was also offered projects by Shumiatski which he seemed likely to reject, but the most flagrant abuse committed against him was the suppression of what would have been his first sound film, *Bezhin Meadow* (*Bezhin lug*), which had been approved for production in 1935.

Starting from a short story by the nineteenth-century writer Ivan Turgenev, Eisenstein planned to dramatize the real-life tragedy of a contemporary kulak who killed his son (Pavlik Morozov) for turning informer and for supporting collectivization. Shooting began in the spring of 1935 but was interrupted in September when Eisenstein fell ill with smallpox. Upon Eisenstein's return to the set, Shumiatski demanded major revisions in the script to force it in the direction of socialist realism. Eisenstein undertook these, in collaboration with Isaac Babel, and he had nearly completed the film before he fell ill again. This time, Shumiatski halted production and published a harsh attack on Eisenstein in *Pravda;* the director himself was forced to publicly recant the film and confess to ideological errors which, in fact, had little to do with its content. This act of self-abasement apparently satisfied the Party bureaucrats: a year later, after Shumiatski was deposed, Eisenstein was entrusted with the production of a big-budget historical film of major political importance, *Alexander Nevski* (1938).

On what many observers felt was the eve of a Nazi invasion, Eisenstein was chosen to make a film about how the great Slavic hero Prince Alexander Nevski of Novgorod had rallied the Russian people to repel an invading force of Teutonic Knights in the thirteenth century. It was Eisenstein's first sound film and the consummate realization of his theories of contrapuntal sound. According to Georges Sadoul, Eisenstein conceived the entire film as an opera in which Sergei Prokofiev's brilliant score would alternately complement and conflict with the film's visual rhythms. And these rhythms are among the most beautiful the director ever achieved. Every shot in *Alexander Nevski* is painstakingly composed in terms of the plastic arrangement of space, mass, and light within the frame. The Teutonic Knights, for example, always appear in strictly geometrical formations, while the Russian ranks are asymmetrical, suggesting the monolithic rigidity of the Germans as contrasted with the vital but disorganized Russians. Eisenstein closely supervised the details of the production, including costume design and makeup,* and one of his most striking conceptions was the battle dress of the German invaders. Prob-

---

* According to Jay Leyda and Zina Voynow in *Eisenstein at Work* (New York, 1982), this careful planning permitted much of the actual shooting to be done by Eisenstein's assistant director, Dmitri Vasiliev (unrelated to "the Vasiliev brothers"); they also maintain that *Nevsky* was released with a reel missing, which has never been recovered.

9.17   *Alexander Nevski:* **Teutonic barbarism in the captured city of Pskov.**

ably influenced by the sinister headgear of the Ku Klux Klansmen in *The Birth of a Nation,* Eisenstein costumed his Teutonic Knights throughout the film in menacing steel helmets with tiny slits for eye-holes, so that their faces were not visible, unlike those of the Russians. The barbaric military regalia which adorned these helmets, the symbol of the red cross on the Knights' white tunics and capes (cleverly positioned to resemble armbands with swastikas), and the atrocities which they commit upon the people of Pskov in the second reel all serve to clearly identify the Teutons with the Nazis.

The film's most impressive sequence is the famous Battle on the Ice on frozen Lake Peipus in northwest Russia, actually shot in the outskirts of Moscow in midsummer with artificial snow and ice. Here the decisive battle between the Teutons and the Russian defenders is rendered in a spectacular audiovisual montage complete with **swish pans** and a jolting, rough-and-tumble camera style that would not be seen again until the early days of the French New Wave. (The Battle on the Ice in *Nevski* greatly influenced the staging of the Battle of Agincourt in Laurence Olivier's *Henry V* [1944], a film with similar nationalistic / patriotic motives.) Eisenstein appropriately called *Alexander Nevski* "a fugue on the theme of patriotism." Despite the objections of some foreign critics to its operatic structure, the film was an enormous critical and popular success in many Western countries as well as in the Soviet Union, where it temporarily restored Eisenstein to his position of esteem within the Soviet cinema. (He received both the Order of Lenin and the Stalin Prize for it in 1939 and 1941, respectively.)

Alexander Nevski was discretely withdrawn from domestic distribution in the wake of the Nazi-Soviet Nonaggression Pact of 1939, but it was revived with a great display of patriotism after Hitler's treacherous invasion of Russia in 1941. In the meantime, Eisenstein wrote the scenario for *The Great Ferghana Canal* (with Petr Pavlenko, his coscenarist on *Nevski*), which he envisioned as "a triptych about the struggle for water" in the central Asian desert spanning three stages of history from antiquity to the present. The project was approved, and Eisenstein had begun location shooting in Uzbekistan when—for reasons still unknown— it was abruptly cancelled. Shortly thereafter, however, he was invited to

9.18 *Alexander Nevski:* the Battle on the Ice is joined.

stage Wagner's opera *Die Walküre* at the Bolshoi Theater to commemorate a state visit by the Nazi propaganda minister, Goebbels, "in the mutual interests of German and Russian culture." Eisenstein accepted and produced a remarkable version of the massive Teutonic music-drama in which he attempted, as he later wrote, to achieve "a fusion between the elements of Wagner's score and the wash of colors on the stage" through lighting. The psychologist of perception was still very much alive in Eisenstein, but he had advanced from reflexology to synesthesia.* And just as he had used the Proletkult Theater as a testing ground for his developing theories of montage, he used his 1940 production of Wagner's opera as a laboratory for his new ideas on the dramatic interplay of sound, space, and color, so important to his last two films.

9.19 *Alexander Nevski:* the Russians celebrate their victory.

Sometime in 1940, Eisenstein conceived the notion of making an epic film trilogy about the life of Tsar Ivan IV, known in Russian as *grozny* ("awesome," "terrible"), the Nevski-like figure who had first unified much of Russia in the sixteenth century. This project was to be the consummation of all his theory and practice, and Eisenstein spent two full years studying his subject. Production began simultaneously on all three films at the Alma-Ata studios in central Asia in 1943.† Instead of a shooting script, Eisenstein used a series of his own sketches as his scenario. *Ivan the Terrible (Ivan Grozny)*, *Part I* was completed and released in early 1945, and it immediately won the Stalin Prize for artistic achievement. *Part II, The Boyars' Plot (Boyarskii zagovor)*, completed in Moscow between 1945 and 1946, was previewed in August 1946 and promptly banned by the Party Central Committee for "ignorance in the presentation of historical fact." (Eisenstein had apparently been too critical of the *oprichniki,* Ivan's political police, for Stalin's paranoid taste.) When this happened, Eisenstein was in the hospital recovering from a heart attack, and the four completed reels of *Part III* were surreptitiously confiscated and destroyed. In February 1947, Eisenstein bargained personally with Stalin for alterations that would permit *Part II*'s distribution, but he never regained his health sufficiently to make them. (The film was suppressed until 1958, five years after Stalin's death.) Eisenstein wrote his memoirs, dreamed of adapting *War and Peace,* and died at the age of fifty, on February 11, 1948, only a few months before D. W. Griffith.

His last bequest to the cinema was a two-part film of incomparable formal beauty of which he wrote, "The grandeur of our theme necessitated a grandiose design." *Ivan the Terrible, Parts I and II,* is quintessentially a film whose meaning is its design. The montage aesthetics of the great silent films are subordinated here, like all other plastic elements, to elaborate compositions within the frame photographed by Tisse (exteriors) and Moskvin (interiors) in which even the actors become part of the decor (much as they were part of the montage patterns of the silent

---

* The use of one mode of sensory stimulation to produce responses in other senses.

† Soviet motion-picture studios and equipment factories near the invasion front were evacuated eastward with their personnel after June 1941. Mosfilm, Lenfilm, and the VGIK were relocated to Alma-Ata in the Kazakh Republic, whose modest facilities (actually, the former Palace of Culture) could accommodate only one set at a time. The interiors for *Ivan's* three parts were shot there in 1943 and 1944 from dusk to dawn, when electricity could be safely diverted from war-time industries. Exteriors for *Part I* and some of *Part II* were also shot at Alma-Ata; but the Soviet production system resumed its normal configuration after the Allied victory in May 1945.

9.20 Eisenstein's *Ivan the Terrible, Part I* (1945): the coronation of Ivan Vasilievich as tsar of Moscow, autocrat of all the Russias, in the Ouspensky Cathedral, January 16, 1547. Nikolai Cherkasov as Ivan.

9.21 The wedding feast of Ivan and the Tsarina Anastasia.

9.22 Ivan in his study with an ambassador to England.

9.23 Ivan and his subjects at Anastasia's bier in the cathedral; she has been poisoned by the tsar's scheming aunt, Euphrosinia.

9.24 Retired to a provincial palace, the grief-stricken Ivan is petitioned to return to Moscow by his people.

films). Eisenstein demanded highly expressive and even contorted performances from his actors—especially from Nikolai Cherkasov (1903–66), in the role of Ivan (he had also played Nevsky)—and achieved a *mise-en-scène* whose hieratic stylization is deliberately reminiscent of the work of the sixteenth-century painter El Greco. Like *Alexander Nevski, Ivan the Terrible* is an operatic film with a magnificent Prokofiev score employed contrapuntally throughout. Furthermore, in his quest for synesthesia and total sensory saturation, Eisenstein even used a color sequence (his first—made with Agfacolor stock captured from the Germans) in *Part II* to create a certain emotional tonality for the wild dance of the *oprichniki*.

Ivan the Terrible may seem a strange ending to a career that began with *Strike* and *Potemkin*. It is heavy, ornate, and static where they are light and fast. But, ultimately, all of Eisenstein's films are cut from the same cloth. His devotion to pictorial beauty, his fascination with the psychology of perception, and his epic aspirations pervade everything he undertook. If Eisenstein turned from agit-prop to grand opera in his later years, it was perhaps because, after nearly two decades of bitter experi-

9.25 *Ivan the Terrible, Part II* (1946): in the pompous throne-room of King Sigismond of Poland, the conspirators against the tsar learn of his return to Moscow.

9.26 In Moscow, Pimen, archbishop of Novgorod, plots with Euphrosinia to murder Ivan and place her weak-minded son Vladimir on the throne.

9.27 The tsar is informed.

9.28 Having plied Vladimir with drink, Ivan convinces the simpleton to wear his robes and regalia in a religious procession.

ence under the Stalin regime, he no longer believed in any cause beyond the nobility and the necessity of art.

FRANCE

Avant-Garde Impressionism, 1921–1929

Next to America's, the film industry with the most prominent national image in the thirties was that of France. After World War I, Paris had become the center of an international avant-garde encompassing cubism, surrealism, Dadaism, and Futurism, and many intellectuals involved with these movements had become intensely interested in the possibilities of film to embody dream states and to express modernist conceptions of

9.29 Vladimir is murdered in the tsar's stead, the plotters are arrested, and Ivan ascends his throne as absolute monarch of all Russia.

9.30 *Le Femme de nulle part* (Louis Delluc, 1922).

9.31 *La Souriante Madame Beudet* (Germaine Dulac, 1922).

time and space. The most prominent among them was the young author and editor Louis Delluc (1890–1924), who founded the journal *Cinéma* and became, long before Eisenstein, the first aesthetic theorist of the film. Delluc's practical mission was the founding of a truly French national cinema which would be authentically cinematic. To this end, he rejected much of French cinema as it had evolved before the war—especially the theatrical abuses of *film d'art*—and turned instead to the models of Sweden (Sjöstrom and Stiller), America (Chaplin, Ince, and Griffith), and Germany (Expressionism and *Kammerspiel*). Delluc began to write original scenarios and gathered about him a group of young filmmakers which became known as the French "impressionist" school,* or the "first avant-garde"—Germaine Dulac, Jean Epstein, Marcel L'Herbier, and Abel Gance—although, as Richard Abel points out, "narrative avant-garde" would be a better term, since all of them worked at the periphery of the French commercial industry making feature films.

Delluc himself directed a handful of important films, including *Fièvre* (*Fever*, 1921) and *La Femme de nulle part* (*The Woman from Nowhere*, 1922), both of which are reminiscent of *Kammerspiel* in their concern with creating atmosphere and preserving the unities of time and place. Germaine Dulac (1882–1942), one of cinema's first female artists, directed Delluc's first scenario *La Fête espagnole* (*The Spanish Festival*, 1920) and went on to become an important figure in the avant-garde and documentary cinema. Her most significant impressionist films were *La Souriante Madame Beudet* (*The Smiling Madame Beudet*, 1923), an intimate psychological portrait of middle-class marriage in a drab provincial setting adapted from the play by avant-gardists André Obey and Denys Amiel, and *La Coquille et le clergyman* (*The Seashell and the Clergyman*, 1928), a surrealist exposition of sexual repression from a scenario by Antonin Artaud. Jean Epstein (1897–1953), like Delluc, began his career in film as a theorist but contributed a major work to the impressionist cinema in 1923 with *Coeur fidèle* (*Faithful Heart*), the story of a working-class love triangle in Marseille with a fine feeling for landscape and atmosphere which is nevertheless boldly experimental in form. Yet according to the film historian Georges Sadoul, this film, for all its sophisticated use of the moving camera and rapid cutting, incarnates the quality of *populisme* which may be seen in French films as early as the Lumière shorts† and which was the major legacy of impressionism to the French cinema—a fascination with ordinary people and settings, with dramas of the working class, and with outdoor shooting in natural settings such as seaports,

---

* Unrelated to the late-nineteenth-century movement in painting known as French Impressionism. See Eugene C. McCreary, "Louis Delluc, Film Theorist, Critic, and Prophet," *Cinema Journal* 16, 1 (Fall 1976): 14–35.

† Later (and, predominantly, Marxist) French critics, however, have found little *populisme* in the Lumière films. Vincent Pinel writes of them, for example: "The image which these 'views' give of appearances (by the choice of subjects more than by a bias caused by any deliberate rhetoric or deformation) is the image that the dominant class at the end of the century seeks to give of the world and itself. An image of self-satisfaction, a clear conscience, a quiet certainty, and values posited (or imposed) as universal and eternal. Lumière's

fairgrounds, and bistros. Epstein's later *La Chute de la maison Usher* (*The Fall of the House of Usher*, 1928) used a variety of brilliant technical effects to create for this Edgar Allan Poe tale what Henri Langlois called "the cinematic equivalent of Debussy," while his *Finis Terrae* (1929), shot on location at Land's End in Brittany, was an avant-garde forecast of neorealism.

9.32 *El Dorado* (Marcel L'Herbier, 1921).

The most faithful follower of Delluc's theories was Marcel L'Herbier (1890–1979), who had been a prominent symbolist poet before turning to filmmaking in 1917. The most cerebral member of the impressionist group, L'Herbier was concerned largely with abstract form, and with the use of visual effects to express inner states. His *L'Homme du large* (*The Big Man*, 1920) was an adaptation of a short story by the nineteenth-century realist Honoré de Balzac shot on location on the southern coast of Brittany, whose frames were composed to resemble Impressionist paintings. The visual texture of *El Dorado* (1921), a melodrama of Spanish lowlife set in a cabaret, recalls the paintings of Claude Monet and virtually synthesizes early avant-garde technique, while *Don Juan et Faust* (*Don Juan and Faust*, 1923) used cubism to the same end. L'Herbier's most extravagant impressionist film, *L'Inhumaine* (*The Inhuman*, 1924), with a score by Darius Milhaud and sets by the cubist painter Fernand Léger and Robert Mallet-Stevens, was an essay in visual abstraction thinly disguised as science fiction; it ends with an apocalyptic montage sequence designed to synthesize movement, music, sound, and color.* But *L'Argent* (1929)—a spectacular updating of Zola's 1891 novel about stock-market manipulation during the Second Empire (c. 1868)—is widely regarded today as L'Herbier's greatest film. In it, he employed antitraditional camera and editing strategies to create a destabilized narrative space within a series of immense, streamlined studio sets designed by André Barsacq and Lazare Meerson, providing both an image and a critique of unbridled capitalism on the brink of the Great Depression.

Abel Gance (1889–1981), like Erich von Stroheim, was one of the great maverick talents of the cinema, and his affiliation with the impressionists was fleeting at best. Born into a bourgeois family, Gance had been a poet, an actor, and a scriptwriter before forming his own production company in 1911. Despite some impressive experimental work, including the Caligariesque *La Folie du Docteur Tube* (*Dr. Tube's Mania*,

films praise in their way—and admirably—the virtues of Work, Family, and Fatherland. Which after all is surely a normal effect of the historical situation. . . ." ("Louis Lumière," *Anthologies du cinema*, No. 78 [Paris, 1974], p. 447).

* Like American films of the era, most French films were tinted and/or toned in a variety of colors during the twenties, often with spectacular psychological effect (see Chapter 7, on tinting and toning). Most of the color in these films, like their original musical arrangements and special scores, has been lost, as has the singular impact of those few films which were exhibited exclusively in black and white (e.g., Dreyer's *La Passion de Jeanne d'Arc*, [1928]; Epstein's *La Chute de la maison Usher*, [1928]). See Kevin Brownlow, "The Glory That Was France," *Sight and Sound* 56, 3 (Summer 1987): 204–9, on the two-part British National Film Theater season celebrating French cinema of the twenties (January–April 1987). See also Maureen Turim, "French Melodrama: Theory of a Specific History," *Theater Journal* 39, 307–27.

9.33 Sisif (Séverin-Mars) blinded by a steam valve in *La Roue* (Abel Gance, 1922).

1915), Gance did not achieve fame until the success of his beautifully photographed* melodramas, *Mater Dolorosa* (1917) and *La Dixième symphonie* (*The Tenth Symphony,* 1918; restored from an original tinted print in 1986 by the Cinémathèque Française). Then he struck out on his own to pursue a dual obsession with technical innovation and epic form. Deeply influenced by *Intolerance,* Gance practiced complex metaphorical intercutting in his symbolic antiwar narrative *J'accuse* (*I Accuse,* 1919),† and then contributed the extraordinary modern epic *La Roue* (*The Wheel,* 1922–23) to the impressionist movement.

Written, directed, and edited by Gance, *La Roue* was shot almost entirely on location, from the railway yards at Nice to the Alps at St. Gervaise, and took nearly three years to complete. It tells the tragic story of an engine driver and his son who are both in love with the same woman—their adopted daughter and sister, respectively—and deliberately resonates with the myths of Oedipus, Sisyphus, Prometheus, and Christ. Like von Stroheim's *Greed* (1924), the film was intended for release in a nine-hour version but was cut by Gance at the request of its producer (Charles Pathé) to two and a half hours. *La Roue* also attracted the intense admiration of Griffith, to whom Gance had shown *J'accuse* during a visit to the United States in 1921. *La Roue,* whose editing clearly owes much to the contact with Griffith, was originally thirty-two reels long and divided into a prologue and three parts; Gance cut the general release version to fourteen, and re-releases have reduced it even further. Even in the shortened version, Gance's intercutting approaches Eisenstein's in its sophistication and metaphorical power, and its atmospheric evocation of life in the railway yards is close to the spirit of the nineteenth-century epic naturalist Émile Zola. Monumental, technically dazzling, hyper-romantic, and frequently tasteless, *La Roue* influenced a whole generation of French avant-garde filmmakers, including Fernand Léger and Jean Cocteau, and its editing was widely studied in the Soviet film schools during the twenties.

Gance's next film, *Napoléon vu par Abel Gance: première époque: Bonaparte* (*Napoleon as Seen by Abel Gance: First Part: Bonaparte,* 1927) was produced by the Société Génerale des Films and financed largely by Russian emigré funds. It stands today with *Intolerance* (1916) and *Greed* (1924), as one of the great eccentric masterpieces of the silent cinema. Twenty-eight reels in its original version but reduced to eight by subsequent distributors, *Napoléon* required four years to produce and was only the first part of a projected six-part film of the life of Bonaparte (strikingly played by Albert Dieudonné) which was never completed. As it stands, it covers his youth, the revolution, and the opening of the Italian campaign, and there is scarcely a passage in the film which does not make use of some innovative and original device. From beginning to end,

---

*The cinematographer for most of Gance's silent features was Léonce-Henri Burel (b. 1892), a pioneering genius of a cameraman who also did distinguished work for Jacques Feyder and Jean Renoir, and ended his career by collaborating with Robert Bresson on his greatest films from 1951 to 1963.

†Remade by Gance as a sound film in 1937.

9.34 Polyvision triptych from *Napoléon vu par Abel Gance* (1927).

Gance assaulted his audience with the entire arsenal of silent-screen techniques, and the effect is impressive. As in *La Roue*, he used sophisticated metaphorical intercutting to inundate the viewer with significant images, many of them lasting only a few frames; and at times he superimposed as many as sixteen simultaneous images on the screen. At several points in *Napoléon*, Gance also used a widescreen process called Polyvision,* which expanded the frame to three times its normal width, but the most original achievement of *Napoléon* was the astonishing fluidity of its camera work.

The recent manufacture in France of light, portable cameras (specifi-

---

* Gance used the term "Polyvision" to refer to both the optical system itself and to the possibilities for multiple imaging created by it.

cally, the Debrie Photociné Sept) made possible many extraordinary subjective camera shots and traveling shots which went far beyond the pioneering work of Murnau and Freund in *Der letzte Mann* (1924) and which would not be seen again until the advent of the hand-held 35mm sound camera some twenty-five years later. In the Corsican sequence, for example, the camera was strapped to the back of a galloping horse to shoot the landscape as it would have been seen by the rider. Later, encased in a waterproof box, the camera was hurled from a steep cliff into the Mediterranean to approximate the impressions of Napoléon as he dived. To film the tumultuous Paris Convention, Gance mounted the camera on a huge pendulum to convey the radical swaying back and forth between Girondist and Jacobin factions, and he intercut this shot with one of Napoléon's boat on its way to France pitching to and fro in a storm at sea. Finally, in scenes from the siege of Toulon, a small camera was even mounted in a football and tossed into the air to simulate the perspective of a cannonball.

The Polyvision process, conceived by Gance specifically for *Napoléon* and designed by camera pioneer André Debrie, anticipated the modern Cinerama process in that it employed a triptych, or three-panel screen, to show three standard 35mm images side by side. Gance used the process in two distinct ways. Often he would supplement the primary image on the middle screen with complementary and / or contrapuntal images on either side to achieve a kind of lateral montage within the frame. At several points during the Italian campaign, for instance, huge close-ups of Bonaparte's head or of a symbolic eagle dominate the middle screen while marching troops of the Grand Armée stream across the side panels. (This widescreen triptych effect was not again used successfully until Michael Wadleigh's documentary *Woodstock* in 1969; see p. 886.) At other times, Gance used Polyvision more naturalistically to explode the screen into a single vast panoramic image for mass scenes, as during the Italian campaign and the Convention. This image was photographed by three identical Parvo-Debrie cameras mounted one on top of the other in an arc and synchronized to run concurrently by means of a flexible motor shaft. Like so many other elements of *Napoléon,* Polyvision was twenty-five years ahead of its time (and, by his own admission, it gave Professor Henri Chrétien, the father of modern widescreen processes, the idea for inventing the **anamorphic lens** in 1941).

Gance made nothing comparable to *Napoléon* for the rest of his career,* although he constantly returned to it, adding stereophonic sound for Arthur Honegger's original score, some dialogue scenes, and, as late as 1971, re-editing it in a four-hour version with new footage as *Bonaparte et la révolution.* Yet audiences in only eight European cities saw *Napoléon* in its original form, which, of course, included a full range of tints and tones, with the triptych screen becoming an enormous blue, white, and red tricolor at the film's stirring conclusion. It was cut to less than one

---

* Some critics would argue that Gance's *Un Grand amour de Beethoven* (1936), recently restored by Images Archives, represents a contribution to the aesthetics of the sound film comparable *in kind,* if not degree, to that of *Napoléon* to silent cinema.

third of its length for overseas distribution, and there was no definitive print of the original silent film until a Herculean task of restoration was performed by the British filmmaker and film historian Kevin Brownlow (b. 1938) in 1979. A seventeen-reel reconstruction by the Cinémathèque Française excited the passionate admiration of the young **cinéastes** of the French **New Wave** when it was shown in Paris in the late fifties and contributed substantially to a resurrection of Gance's critical reputation. But Brownlow's full-triptych reconstruction runs twenty-eight reels, or six hours at 20 fps, although approximately one half-hour of the original footage is still missing. It was premiered at the Telluride (Colorado) Film Festival in September 1979—with Gance present, in honor of his nine-tieth birthday*—demonstrating with finality what Brownlow has main-tained all along: "The visual resources of the cinema have never been stretched further than in *Napoléon vu par Abel Gance*. The picture is an encyclopedia of cinematic effects—a pyrotechnical display of what the silent film was capable of in the hands of a genius."

The "Second" Avant-Garde

Louis Delluc died of tuberculosis in 1924, and the French impressionist film entered a period of decadent formalism shortly thereafter; but Del-luc's influence survived him and the school he had founded, in the rise of serious French film criticism and the *ciné-club* (film society) movement. By the mid-twenties, film reviews had become a standard feature of almost every newspaper published in France. Professional film writers like Léon Moussinac (1890–1964) were establishing a tradition of cinema studies in France which was to make that country the home of the most advanced and subtle thinking on film from 1925 through the present. As Georges

*In Telluride, Gance announced plans for another film epic, to be entitled *Christopher Columbus*. "Right now the cinema is dead," he said; "*Columbus* will bring it back to life." (*Variety*, September 18, 1979, p. 28.) On the general difficulty of seeing Gance films in the United States, see William M. Drew, "Abel Gance: Prometheus Bound," *Take One* 6, 8 (July 1978): 30–32, 45. Brownlow's reconstruction, produced by the British Film Institute and Images Archives in association with Thames Television, was distributed theatrically in the United States by Francis Ford Coppola's Zoetrope Studios with an orchestral score by Carmine Coppola and tinted triptych sequences for projection at 24 fps. In the summer of 1983, an even more complete version was shown by Brownlow in Paris and deposited with the Cinémathèque Française as the definitive print (to date). A full account of Brownlow's twenty-year struggle to restore *Napoléon* is contained in Kevin Brownlow, "Abel Gance's Epic *Napoleon* Returns from Exile," *American Film* 6, 1 (January–February 1981): 28–31, 68–72; and *Napoleon: Abel Gance's Classic Films* (New York: Knopf, 1983). See also James Welsh and Steven Kramer, *Abel Gance* (Boston: Twayne, 1978), which contains previously unpublished material from the *Columbus* script; William K. Everson, "The Many Lives of 'Napoleon'," *Film Comment* 17, 1 (January–February, 1981): 21–23; Peter Pap-pas, "The Superimposition of Vision: Napoleon and the Meaning of Fascist Art," *Cinéaste* 11, 2: 4–13; Sean French, "The *Napoleon* Phenomenon," *Sight and Sound* 51, 2 (Spring 1982): 93–96; Richard Abel, "Charge and Counter-Charge: Coherence and Incoherence in Gance's *Napoléon*," *Film Quarterly* 35, 3 (Spring 1982): 2–14; and Norman King, *Abel Gance: A Politics of Spectacle* (London: BFI Publishing, 1984). Films on Gance include Nelly Kaplan's *Abel Gance: hier et demain* (*Abel Gance: Today and Yesterday*, [1963, 28m.]); Kevin Brownlow's *Abel Gance: The Charm of Dynamite*, (1968, 56m.); and Kaplan's *Abel Gance et son Napoléon* (*Abel Gance and His Napoléon*, 1984).

9.35 Part of a film loop from *Ballet mécanique* (Fernand Léger, 1924) in which a woman seems to endlessly climb a flight of stairs.

9.36 *Entr'acte* (René Clair, 1924): a ballet dancer shot from a subterranean perspective.

Sadoul has written: "This group of men was the first in Europe to assert the stature of the film as an art—the equal (or even the superior) of music, literature and the theatre—and to obtain recognition for it as such. With the creation of independent film criticism they gave body and substance to their claim. . . . Henceforward the cinema became a subject of dinner-table conversation like the novel or the play, and there emerged a group among the intellectual elite for whom it was a major artistic preoccupation." The *ciné-club* movement was founded by Delluc, Moussinac, and Ricciotto Canudo (1879–1923) in Paris, where it achieved great success and spread rapidly to the provinces. Some *ciné-clubs* ultimately became specialized film theaters where a knowledgeable public could see serious films unavailable to it in conventional cinemas. Since French commercial film production reached a new low point during the twenties, both financially and aesthetically, it was largely these specialized theaters and *ciné-clubs* that kept the creative tradition of French cinema alive and that transmitted it into the sound era by enabling a second wave of French avant-garde filmmakers to find an audience.

The "second" avant-garde had its roots in the literary and artistic movements of Dadaism and surrealism. Like the impressionists, the members of this later group represented the first generation to "think spontaneously in animated images," as Émile Vuillermoz put it in a contemporary review of Gance's *La Roue*. Unlike them, however, they wished to create a pure cinema of visual sensation completely divorced from conventional narrative—or, as they put it in their manifestoes, to make films without subjects. The first to attempt this was an American photographer living in Paris, Man Ray (1890–1976), whose brief *Le Rétour à la raison* (*Return to Reason*, 1923) offered its audience a kaliedoscopic succession of barely discernible images. A year later the cubist painter Fernand Léger and his American technical collaborator Dudley Murphy produced *Ballet mécanique*, in which isolated objects, pieces of machinery, posters, and newspaper headlines were animated into a rhythmic ballet of plastic forms. The most famous of the early avant-garde films was indisputedly René Clair's *Entr'acte* (1924), made to be shown at the intermission of Francis Picabia's dadaist ballet *Relâche* (*Performance Suspended*). With a score by Erik Satie, who also wrote the music for the ballet, *Entr'acte* was a logically meaningless succession of outrageous images, many derived from the tradition of the Pathé/Gaumont *course comique* and the serials of Feuillade (see pp. 49–53). Clair's *Paris qui dort* (English title: *The Crazy Ray*, 1924) was an irreverent but lyrical non-story of a mad scientist who invents an invisible ray to immobilize all of Paris except for six persons who eventually take up residence in the Eiffel Tower. Clair went on to become a major figure in the sound film, as did the Spanish-born director Luis Buñuel (1900–1983), whose *Un Chien andalou* (*An Andalusian Dog*, 1929) represents the avant-garde at its most mature, most surreal, and most Freudian.

Written in collaboration with the surrealist painter Salvador Dali (1904–89), *Un Chien andalou* provides a seemingly incoherent stream of brutal, erotic images from the unconscious which Buñuel called "a despairing, passionate call to murder." In the course of the film, we witness in close-up a woman's eyeball being slashed in two with a razor, a man in full harness pulling two grand pianos upon which are draped the rotting carcasses of two donkeys, swarms of ants crawling from a hole in a man's palm, and a whole succession of gratuitous murders, severed limbs, and symbolic sexual transformations. Designed to create a series of violent antagonisms within the viewer through shock, titillation, and repulsion, *Un Chien andalou* is the prototype of film surrealism. Yet Buñuel later added a recorded score comprised of popular contemporary tangoes and the *Liebestod* from Wagner's opera *Tristan und Isolde,* as if to suggest that *Un Chien andalou* was as much about the collapse of European culture between the wars as a subterranean voyage through the recesses of the unconscious mind. A subsequent Buñuel-Dali collaboration in the early sound period produced *L'Âge d'or* (*The Golden Age,* 1930), a film no less surreal than its predecessor but one whose attacks upon religion and the established social order were so violent as to excite the wrath of the French Fascists, who ultimately succeeded in having it banned. Buñuel made no more overtly surrealist films after *L'Âge d'or,* but the surrealistic strain remained strong in his films throughout his career (see pp. 655–65).

9.37 *Un Chien andalou* (Luis Buñuel, 1929).

One of the most remarkable works of the new avant-garde was Dmitri Kirsanoff's *Ménilmontant* (1924), which employed elaborate montage effects nearly a year before the release of Eisenstein's *Strike* and *Potemkin.* Kirsanoff (1899–1957), a Russian émigré who apparently knew nothing of the montage experiments of Kuleshov, Pudovkin, and Eisenstein, was deeply influenced by Gance's cutting of *La Roue* (the Soviets also later acknowledged a debt to Gance, as did Akira Kurosawa). *Ménilmontant* clearly anticipates the rapid metaphorical cutting of Kirsanoff's Soviet counterparts in many ways. The film itself tells the story of two young women from the country whose lives are ruined by the brutal murder of their parents. The women come to the Parisian suburb of Ménilmontant, where one drifts into prostitution, and the remainder of the film recounts their sordid existence there. Some scholars see Kirsanoff's film as a precursor of Italian neorealism (which will be discussed in Chapter 11) in its sensitive use of on-location photography and natural settings.

The poet and playwright Jean Cocteau (1889–1963) turned to the avant-garde cinema for the first time as the director of *Le Sang d'un poète* (*Blood of a Poet,* 1930), a collage of intensely personal poetic symbols which attempts to evoke the sacrificial nature of art. By the end of the decade, however, the avant-garde had taken an abrupt turn away from introspection toward social commitment. Abstract films continued to be made by artists such as Man Ray (*Les Mystères du château du Dé* [*The Mysteries of the Chateau of the Dice,* 1929]) and Jean Grémillon (*Tour au large,* [1927]), but the main tendency after 1927 was toward documentary cinema.

Influenced by the screening of the officially banned films of Vertov, Eisenstein, and Pudovkin in the *ciné-clubs,* French avant-garde *cinéastes* turned from abstractionism to the poetry of everyday life in a group of

9.38 *À propos de Nice* (Jean Vigo, 1929).

9.39 *Les Nouveaux messieurs* (Jacques Feyder, 1929).

9.40 Renée Falconetti in *La Passion de Jeanne d'Arc* (Carl-Theodor Dreyer, 1928).

films that anticipated both the British documentary school of John Grierson and Italian neorealism. As early as 1926, the Brazilian-born filmmaker Alberto Cavalcanti (1897–1982), later to become a major figure in the British documentary and narrative cinemas (*Coal Face*, 1936; *Dead of Night*, 1945), directed *Rien que les heures,* a composite chronicle of a day in the life of a modern city (which happens, in this case, to be Paris) which may well have influenced Ruttmann's *Berlin, die Symphonie einer GroBstadt* (1927; see p. 137). Georges Lacombe (b. 1902), in *La Zone* (1928), offered a moving account of the lives of ragpickers in the shanty-towns of Paris, while the first film of Marcel Carné (b. 1909), *Nogent, Eldorado du dimanche* (*Nogent, Sunday's Eldorado*, 1929), was a short documentary about Sundays at a popular working-class resort on the Marne.

During this same period, Jean Painlevé (1902-89) began to produce the series of beautiful nature films which culminated in *L'Hippocampe* (1934), a poetic documentary on the life cycle of the seahorse. A bit later, Luis Buñuel combined surrealism with social commitment in the powerful and subversive *Las Hurdes* (English title: *Land without Bread*, 1932), which depicts the degradation, misery, and ignorance of the denizens of Spain's poorest district in the coolly ironic tones of a conventional travelogue. But the indisputable masterpiece of the French avant-garde documentary movement was the first film of Jean Vigo, *À propos de Nice* (1929). Vigo used the "kino-eye" techniques of Dziga Vertov—whose brother Boris Kaufman was Vigo's cameraman—to create a lyrical but angry polemic against bourgeois decadence in a fashionable resort town. Vigo and Kaufman followed with *Taris* (1931), a formally subversive sound short on the championhip swimmer Jean Taris that begins as an instructional documentary and ends as a dreamlike fantasy on weightlessness and water.

The general bleakness of the French commercial cinema during this period of widespread independent experimentation was illuminated here and there by the films of Jacques Feyder, René Clair, and Carl-Theodor Dreyer. Feyder (born Jacques Frédérix, in Brussels, 1885–1948) was a Belgian who made dozens of French commercial films before establishing his reputation with *L'Atlantide* (1921), an opulent tale of the lost continent of Atlantis with exteriors shot in the Sahara desert. His critical and popular success continued through *Crainquebille* (1922), a semi-impressionistic version of the novel by Anatole France, which was much admired by Griffith, and a highly praised adaptation of Zola's *Thérèse Raquin* (1929), which has not survived. But when his gently satiric sound film *Les Nouveaux messieurs* (*The New Gentlemen*, 1929) was unfairly banned for impugning "the dignity of Parliament and its ministers," Feyder left France temporarily for Hollywood, where he spent four years working on melodramas (among them two Garbo films: *The Kiss*, 1930; and the German-language version of Clarence Brown's *Anna Christie*, 1932).

René Clair had turned from the avant-garde to the commercial cinema in 1925 but did not achieve artistic success until he made the delightful *Un Chapeau de paille d'Italie* (*The Italian Straw Hat*, 1927), and *Les Deux timides* (*Two Timid Souls*, 1928), which transformed popular nineteenth-century farces by Eugène Labiche into highly cinematic comic chase films in the manner of Mack Sennett and Jean Durand.

Clair's art director for the remarkable series of films from *Un Chapeau de paille d'Italie* (1927) through *Quatorze juillet* (1932) was the brilliant Lazare Meerson (1900–1938), who more than any other single individual helped to create the style of "poetic realism." In his studio-built street scenes for Clair and, later, for Feyder (*Le Grand jeu,* [1934]; *Pensions Mimosas,* [1935]; *La Kermesse héroique,* [1935]), Meerson turned away from Expressionism, impressionism, and naturalism to create an ambiance described by Georges Sadoul as "simultaneously realistic and poetic." In addition to being one of the greatest designers in the history of European cinema, Meerson also trained a group of young assistants who became important figures in their own right (most notably, Alexandre Trauner, [b. 1906—*Quai des brumes,* 1938; *Hôtel du Nord,* 1938; *Le Jour se lève,* 1939; *Les Visiteurs de soir,* 1942; *Les Enfants du paradis,* 1945; *Othello,* 1952]), and his influence was felt well into the sixties.

Carl-Theodor Dreyer (1889–1968) is an important director, the major body of whose work lies outside the mainstream of film history. Like that of Robert Bresson (see pp. 542–43) and Yasujiro Ozu (see pp. 794–99), Dreyer's art has been called religious and his style "transcendental" because of its simplicity and austerity (see Paul Schrader, *Transcendental Style in Film* [Berkeley, 1972]). Originally a journalist and a scriptwriter for Danish Nordisk, Dreyer began by making films in direct imitation of Griffith (such as *Blade af Satans bog* [*Leaves from Satan's Book,* 1921]). But by the late twenties he was making films (like *La Passion de Jeanne d'Arc*) of such an extraordinary character as to defy classification.

The Danish director made his late silent masterpiece *La Passion de Jeanne d'Arc* (*The Passion of Joan of Arc,* 1928) for the Société Génerale des Films (S.G.F.) in Paris between 1927 and 1928. This austere and anguished film, which condenses the trial, torture, and execution of St. Joan (Renée Falconetti, 1892–1946) into a single tension-charged twenty-four-hour period, was based on actual trial records and shot in sequence, largely in extreme close-ups against stark white backgrounds, to enhance its psychological realism. To the same end, Dreyer and his chief cameraman, Rudolph Maté (1889–1964), chose to photograph the film on newly available low-contrast panchromatic stock, and the actors and actresses were forbidden to wear make-up. Dreyer had intended to make *La Passion de Jeanne d'Arc* a sound film, but he abandoned the notion for lack of equipment, so the film remains the last great classic of the international silent screen. Jean Cocteau wrote of it: "*Potemkin* imitated a documentary and threw us into confusion. *La Passion de Jeanne d'Arc* seems like an historical document from an era in which the cinema didn't exist" and yet the film is also a radical formal experiment whose strategy, as David Bordwell points out, is to subvert the classical stylistic relationships between narrative logic and cinematic space.

Dreyer also made his first sound film in France, the hauntingly atmospheric *Vampyr* (1932), shot on location in the village of Courtempierre by Maté. Designed, like *La Passion,* by Hermann Warm (who had also designed the sets for *Caligari, Der müde Tod,* and other Expressionist

9.41 Dreyer's *Vampyr* (1932): **Julian West.**

works), *Vampyr* seems less distinctly Gallic than *La Passion*, perhaps because its soundtrack was postrecorded in Berlin.

Because of the physical confinement he imposed on his dramas, Dreyer has sometimes been accused of theatricality (*Du skal aere din hustru* [*Master of the House*, 1925], for example, was shot entirely in a small four-room house). But, typically, Dreyer's subject is deep human emotion, frequently suffering, and his ability to evoke spiritual intensity through concentration and confinement was perhaps his greatest gift as a film artist. Dreyer's work is characterized by extraordinarily complex camera movement and luminous photography (often by great cinematograhers like Rudolph Maté, Karl Freund, and Gunnar Fischer), expressive decor, antitraditional edition, and a totally radical construction of narrative space. His painstaking production procedures and his fierce artistic integrity led him to make only fourteen films in a career that spanned forty-five years. The most significant are *Michaël* (1924), *Du skal aere din hustru* (1925), *La Passion de Jeanne d'Arc* (1928), *Vampyr* (1932), *Vredens dag* (*Day of Wrath*, 1943), *Ordet* (*The Word*, 1954), and his last film, *Gertrud* (1964). When he died in 1968, Dreyer was preparing to make a historical film on the life of Jesus from his own original screenplay.*

Sound, 1929–1934

The coming of sound spelled the end for the French experimental avant-garde cinema. Production costs soared with the introduction of sound because France, unlike the United States and Germany, possessed no patents for the new process. Thus, the French studios were at the mercy of Western Electric and Tobis-Klangfilm, both of which exacted crippling sums for the rights to use their sound equipment. But the success of American and German sound films in France was such that financiers were eager to invest in the foreign patent rights. Hollywood and Tobis attempted to further plunder the French industry by establishing huge production facilities in the suburbs of Paris. Paramount built a vast plant at Joinville, but the quality of its mass-produced multilingual films fell to such a low level that the facility eventually became a dubbing studio for American-made films. The Tobis operation in Epinay was a much more respectable affair; its very first production was a motion picture praised around the world as the first artistic triumph of the sound film: René Clair's *Sous les toits de Paris* (*Under the Roofs of Paris*, 1930).

As with several other French directors making the transition to sound, Clair's involvement with the avant-garde of the twenties had predisposed him to experiment with the new process. *Sous les toits de Paris* was a brisk musical comedy about ordinary people set in a delightfully designed Parisian *faubourg* (residential district); it used a bare minimum of dialogue and vindicated Clair's own theoretical defense of asynchronous or contrapuntal sound. Advertised as "the most beautiful film ever made,"

---

* The definitive work on Dreyer in English is David Bordwell's superbly crafted *The Films of Carl-Theodor Dreyer* (Berkeley: University of California Press, 1981).

9.42 *Vredens dag* (Carl-Theodor Dreyer, 1943).

9.43 *Ordet* (Carl-Theodor Dreyer, 1954).

9.44 Clair's *Sous les toits de Paris* (1930).

Sous les toits de Paris was an international triumph, and its stunning integration of sound with sophisticated visuals earned Clair a somewhat inflated reputation as a master of the sound film. His next Tobis film was another ebullient musical comedy, *Le Million* (*The Million*, 1931), which employed a whole range of non-naturalistic effects on the soundtrack and a wild chase through an opera house to create what many historians feel is the best European musical comedy of the period between the wars.

With *A nous la liberté* (*Liberty Is Ours*, 1931), Clair turned to the more serious themes of industrialization and economic depression, still, however, using the musical-comedy form. Based loosely on the life of Charles Pathé (see pp. 49–50), the film tells the story of an escaped convict who becomes a fabulously wealthy industrialist. He is subsequently discovered and blackmailed by a prison buddy, but in the utopian conclusion he gives up his role as a captain of industry to become a happy vagabond. The buoyant wit of this film, its great visual precision, and its

9.45 The bleakly futuristic assembly-line in *A nous la liberté* (René Clair, 1931), and the open road of possibility with which the film concludes.

brilliant use of asynchronous sound have made it a classic. But it is also notable for its humanistic indictment of mechanized modern industry, which Clair, through parallel editing, consistently equates with the experience of imprisonment. *A nous la liberté* has many similarities with Chaplin's *Modern Times* (1935; see p. 214)—so many, in fact, that Tobis pressed Clair to sue Chaplin for copyright infringement after the latter film's release. Clair declined, saying that he could only be honored to have inspired so great a filmmaker as Chaplin.

Clair's next film for Tobis, another Parisian musical entitled *Quatorze juillet* (*The Fourteenth of July*, 1932), was less successful aesthetically than his earlier films; the old formula was beginning to wear thin. Clair changed modes with *Le Dernier milliardaire* (*The Last Multimillionaire*, 1934), a satire on dictatorship which was begun for Tobis but completed for Pathé when Goebbels, head of the German film industry since 1933, terminated the project.* The film was not up to Clair's best work, but it was maliciously defamed by France's increasingly powerful right-wing press upon its release. Deeply disturbed by this reaction, Clair accepted a contract to direct *The Ghost Goes West* (1935), a fantasy-satire about an American millionaire who buys a haunted Scottish castle and takes it home with him, for Alexander Korda in London. After this project and the independently produced musical comedy, *Break the News* (1937), Clair returned briefly to France where he began shooting *Air Pur*, a film about the urban poor, in Nice. Production was halted in 1939 by the outbreak of war, and Clair went west, to Hollywood, where he worked on a series of fantasy-comedies (*I Married a Witch*, 1942; *It Happened Tomorrow*, 1943) until the end of World War II, when he returned to France.†

---

* All films made for Tobis at Epinay were shot in French and German versions, which gave a dual nationalistic edge to the studio's productions as France and Germany, for the second time in a generation, veered toward war.

† Clair's later films—*Le Silence est d'or* (English-language title: *Man About Town*, 1947); *La Beauté du diable* (*Beauty and the Devil*, 1950); *Les Belles-de-nuit* (*Beauties of the Night*,

9.46 The pillow fight in *Zéro de conduite* (Jean Vigo, 1933).   **9.47** The newlyweds in Vigo's *L'Atalante* (1934).

Another important figure of the early sound film in France, although his total output amounts to little over three hours of viewing time, was Jean Vigo (1905–34). The son of a famous anarchist who was jailed and probably murdered by the French government during World War I, Vigo spent his youth as an orphan in a series of wretched boarding schools. He later became an assistant cameraman and met one of Dziga Vertov's brothers, the cameraman Boris Kaufman, with whom he made his first feature: the forty-five-minute masterpiece *Zéro de conduite* (*Zero for Conduct*, 1933). This much-admired film concerns the revolt of the boys of a rundown provincial boarding school against their petty, mean-spirited teachers; it is autobiographical in its anarchic spirit and many of its specific details. The film is simultaneously lyrical, surrealistic, comical, and profoundly serious. Important sequences include the balletic, slow-motion pillow fight during the dormitory rebellion in which feathers swirl about the room like snowflakes in a blizzard; the official visit of the schools-inspector—a dwarf wearing a top hat; and the final assault on the court-yard, in which the boys stand on the school roof and bombard dignitaries at a pompous assembly with rubbish. *Zéro de Conduite* was remarkably scored by Maurice Jaubert (1900–1940). A symphonic composer who began writing film music in 1929 (for *Le Petit Chaperon rouge* [Alberto Cavalcanti]), Jaubert created a musical analogue for *Zéro*'s visual fantasy by having his score for it played and recorded backwards. In rerecording, he invented a process whereby the notes were in the right order but their emission reversed—an effect at once eerie and playful.

1952); *Les Grandes Manoeuvres* (English-language title: *Summer Maneuvers*, 1955—his first color film); *Porte des Lilas* (*Gates of Paris*, 1957); *Tout l'Or du monde* (1961); *Les Fêtes galantes* (1965)—rarely approach the brilliance of his early work, and their prevailing mood is melancholy. In the late fifties, Clair was attacked by the young critics of *Cahiers du cinéma*—unfairly it would now seem—as a paragon of the studio-based "scenarist" tradition against which they were in revolt (see Chapter 13). This circumstance, combined with the poor reception of his last two features, led Clair to retire from directing and devote himself to creative writing (three novels, several short stories) and criticism (*Cinéma d'Hier, Cinéma d'Aujourd'hui*, 1970). During his active career, 1923–65, Clair either wrote or collaborated in writing the screenplay of every film he made.

By pitting the free and rebellious spirit of the children against the bourgeois repressiveness of the adults, Vigo was sounding a classical anarchist theme, and French authorities acknowledged this by banning *Zéro de conduite* from public viewing until the Liberation in 1944. This intensely personal film, with its subtle blend of poetry, fantasy, and realism, has had a great impact upon succeeding generations of directors, especially that of French New Wave filmmakers such as François Truffaut. Truffaut's *Les Quatre-cents coups* (*The Four Hundred Blows,* 1959), and the British director Lindsay Anderson's *If . . .* (1968), for example, both owe a great deal to it in terms of structure, style, and theme.

Vigo's next film, and his last, *L'Atalante* (1934), was another unique masterpiece sensuously photographed by Kaufman. Based upon a commissioned script about the life of two young newlyweds aboard a river barge, it was planned as an eighty-nine-minute commercial feature; Vigo turned it into a powerful lyric poem about life and love. By blending realistic details of life on the barge, and of the bleak industrial landscape through which it passes, with surreal fantasy and bizarre exaggeration of character, Vigo created a film which both revived the tradition of *populisme* from the twenties and announced the "poetic realism" of the brief but glorious era of French cinema that was about to begin. Georges Sadoul speaks correctly of "the astonishing quality of poetry [*L'Atalante*] engenders from a world superficially ordinary and drab." Poetry meant little to the film's distributors, however, who cut and re-edited *L'Atalante* as *Le Chaland qui passe* (*The Passing Barge*) in order to exploit a popular song by that title which was added to the soundtrack as its theme, mutilating Maurice Jaubert's vibrant score in the process. Vigo died of tuberculosis complicated by heart disease on the day of the film's premiere in Paris; he was twenty-nine. In a tragically brief career he had made two great films whose influence on future generations would be immense, and there can be no question that the French cinema lost one of its geniuses when he died.

Poetic Realism, 1934–1940

The character of French production during the twenties had been artisanal and craftlike—a large number of small studios leased their facilities to independent companies, often formed to produce single films—while the French exhibition system was, on the whole, familial and independent. This arrangement had lent itself readily to experimentation, encouraging the great work of the narrative avant-garde previously discussed; but it left producers and exhibitors alike vulnerable to the highly organized distribution networks of the Americans and the Germans. In the face of this threat, the French industry regrouped itself into two mammoth consortia formed around the former giants of the teens, Pathé and Gaumont. In February 1929, producer Bernard Natan (born Natan Taneuzapf) bought a controlling interest in Pathé-Cinema, Pathé-Consortium, and the Lutetia cinema chain to form a huge production / distribution / exhibition conglomerate called Pathé-Natan. The same summer, Franco-Film consortium bought the Aubert cinema chain and was itself absorbed a year later by Gaumont, with the backing of the Swiss electrical industry, to form Gaumont-Franco-Film-Aubert (G.F.F.A.). It seemed briefly that the French industry had reconstituted its pre-World War I glory and approached the condition of the American industry circa 1921. The appearance was false; within five years both companies were bankrupted through mismanagement and fraud.

Except for the work of Clair and Vigo, the French cinema of the early sound era had not been in good health either aesthetically or financially, and in 1934—the year of Clair's departure for England and Vigo's death— the industry experienced a major economic crisis. In that year, because of worldwide depression and internal mismanagement, domestic production fell off significantly, Gaumont and Pathé collapsed, and the end of French cinema was widely prophesied. Instead, the French cinema entered its period of greatest creative growth. The fall of the studio combines necessitated a return to the system of independent production that had prevailed before the coming of sound, at a time when sound itself had stimulated an unprecedented demand for French-language films on French themes. The figures tell the tale: between 1928 and 1938, French production nearly doubled, from 66 to 122 features annually; box-office receipts increased to the point that the French audience was considered second in strength only to the American, and far ahead of those of the USSR, the United Kingdom, and Germany; by 1937–38 the French cinema had become the most critically acclaimed in the world, winning prizes and leading export markets in every industrial country, including the United States.

The predominant style of this period (1934–40) has been characterized by Georges Sadoul as "poetic realism"—a blend of lyricism and realism which derives from "the influence of literary naturalism and Zola, certain traditions of Zecca, Feuillade, and Delluc, certain lessons also from René Clair and Jean Vigo." Poetic realism seems to have had two phases—one born of the optimism created by the Popular Front movement* of 1935–37, the other a product of the despair created by the movement's failure and the realization that Fascism in some form was at hand. The same directors and scriptwriters contributed films to both phases.

Among the first practitioners of poetic realism was Jacques Feyder, who had returned to France from self-imposed exile in the United States in 1934, as if to compensate for the loss of Vigo and Clair. Feyder made his most important films of the period in collaboration with the art director Lazare Meerson and Charles Spaak (1903–75), the screenwriter who,

---

* In 1934, the coalition of Radicals and Socialists which had taken control of the Chamber of Deputies in 1932 was in serious jeopardy. By that year, right-wing agitation, much of it overtly Fascist, had become so violent that there was a threat of civil war. As an emergency measure, all of the parties of the Left, including the Communists, banded together into a "Popular Front" in 1935 and reasserted their control of the country and the government by delivering the premiership to the Socialist leader Léon Blum early in 1936. This alliance was never very sound, but it was effective until 1937, when the Blum government was overthrown by a coalition of rightist and centrist parties. With Hitler arming his legions just across the Rhine, many Frenchmen saw the collapse of the Popular Front as a sign that Fascism was inevitable.

9.48 *La Kermesse héroique* (Jacques Feyder, 1935).

9.49 Jean Gabin in *Pépé le Moko* (Julien Duvivier, 1937).

with Jacques Prévert (1900–1977), contributed most to the development of poetic realism. Together, Feyder and Spaak produced *Le Grand jeu* (*The Great Game*, 1934), a brooding melodrama of life in the Foreign Legion; *Pension Mimosas* (1935), a grim, naturalistic drama of gambling in high society and low, which provided the foundation for poetic realism as practiced later by Feyder's assistant Marcel Carné; and the beautiful costume film *La Kermesse héroique* (English title: *Carnival in Flanders*, 1935) set in sixteenth-century Flanders, with a *mise-en-scène* based on the paintings of the great Flemish masters. This elaborate period farce won numerous international awards but was banned by Goebbels after the Nazi invasion because it dealt humorously with the subject of collaboration.

During this same period, Spaak also collaborated successfully with Julien Duvivier (1896–1967), a prolific director of commercial films who did his best work under the influence of poetic realism. Together, Duvivier and Spaak produced *La Bandera* (English title: *Escape from Yesterday*, 1935), the story of a criminal seeking refuge in the Foreign Legion, and *La Belle équipe* (English title: *They Were Five*, 1936), which tells how five unemployed Parisian workers make a cooperative effort to open a restaurant on the banks of the Marne. Both films starred Jean Gabin (1904–76), who later became the archetype of the doomed modern hero in Duvivier's internationally successful *Pépé le Moko* (1937). Written by Henri Jeanson (and influenced by Howard Hawks' 1932 film *Scarface* and other American gangster films), *Pépé le Moko* is about a Parisian gangster (Gabin) hiding out with his gang in the Casbah in Algiers while the police wait outside for the move that will betray him. The love of a woman draws Pépé out of his sanctuary, and he is gunned down by the police. As a genre film, *Pépé le Moko* can compete with the very best of the Hollywood gangster cycle,* but in its muted violence and fatalism it is highly representative of the pessimistic side of poetic realism.

The greatest exponent of this darker aspect of poetic realism was the young Marcel Carné, who had made the avant-garde documentary *Nogent, Eldorado du dimanche* in 1930 and had begun his career in the sound film as an assistant to Feyder. Carné's great collaborator was the surrealist poet Jacques Prévert, with whom he produced a series of films in the late thirties which incarnate the romantic pessimism of the French cinema in the latter part of its great creative decade. Influenced by the films of von Sternberg and the German tradition of *Kammerspiel*, *Quai des brumes* (*Port of Shadows*, 1938) deals with a deserter from the colonial army (Jean Gabin) who finds himself trapped in the port of Le Havre. Like Pépé le Moko, he becomes involved with the underworld and is doomed to die through his love for a woman. Photographed entirely in the studio by Eugen Schüfftan, with art direction by Alexandre Trauner and music by Maurice Jaubert, *Quai des brumes* is an ominously gloomy film. It exudes such a pervasive sense of fatality that a spokesman for the

---

* *Pépé le Moko* was remade twice in Hollywood—first as the romantic thriller *Algiers* (John Cromwell, 1938), then as the musical *Casbah* (John Berry, 1948).

collaborationist Vichy government later declared, "If we have lost the war, it is because of *Quai des brumes*...." (Carné replied that the barometer shouldn't be blamed for the storm.) In the Carné-Prévert film *Le Jour se lève* (*Daybreak*, 1939), released just before the war, a man (Gabin) commits murder and locks himself in an attic room to await the inevitable police assault at dawn. Through the night (in what is perhaps the most structurally perfect flashback ever filmed) he remembers the love affair which led to his crime, and at daybreak he commits suicide. Simultaneously metaphysical and realistic, *Le Jour se lève* exploits the metaphor of a decent man irreversibly trapped by fate more persuasively and powerfully than any other French film of the period, and it had enormous influence abroad during the war, even though it was banned in Nazi-occupied Europe.

During the Occupation, the Carné-Prévert association produced two of the most spectacular films ever made in France. *Les Visiteurs du soir* (English title: *The Devil's Envoy*, 1942), an adaptation of a medieval legend about a failed attempt by the Devil to intervene in a human love affair, provided a stunning re-creation of fifteenth-century France. (Carné and Prévert intended the Devil in the film to represent Hitler, but the allusions were necessarily so indirect as to be unrecognizable.) *Les Enfants du paradis* (*The Children of Paradise*,* 1945), more than three hours long, evoked the world of the nineteenth-century theater. Inspired by the great French novelists of that era, the film explores the classic theme of the relationship between life and art, and, more specifically, between reality, cinema, and theater, in the context of a complicated love affair between a beautiful woman and a famous professional mime. Elaborate, intelligent, superbly acted, and beautifully mounted, *Les Enfants du paradis* has become a classic of the French cinema. It is clearly Carné and Prév-

9.50 *Quai des brumes* (Marcel Carné, 1938): Jean Gabin, Michele Morgan.

9.51 Carné's *Les Enfants du paradis* (1945): Jean-Louis Barrault.

* A reference to theatergoers who can afford only the cheapest seats in the theater, those at the very top, known in theatrical slang as "Paradise," or "the gods."

ert's masterpiece, and though they collaborated several times more after the war, they never again produced a work equal to this one.

Some mention must also be made of the films of Marcel Pagnol (1895–1974), the famous playwright who built his own studio in the south of France in order to transfer his stage plays to film. An outspoken advocate of "canned theater" who saw film primarily as an actor's medium, Pagnol produced a series of robust and vigorous comedies that probably did much to establish the reputation of French cinema in English-speaking countries. His trilogy of life among the ordinary people of Marseilles—*Marius* (directed by Alexander Korda, 1931), *Fanny* (directed by Marc Allégret, 1932), and *César* (directed by Pagnol, 1936)—and the delightful farce *La Femme du boulanger* (*The Baker's Wife*, directed by Pagnol, 1938), also set in Marseilles, are flavored by a kind of populist realism (or *populisme*) which brings them very close to the mainstream of poetic realism in its more optimistic days. Another French filmmaker with roots firmly in the theater was the actor and playwright Sacha Guitry (1885–1957), who, even more than Pagnol, saw film as essentially a means of preserving his own stage plays and performances. Guitry's most important cinematic achievement was the feature *Le Roman d'un tricheur* (*The Story of a Cheat*, 1936), in which he used a voice-over commentary by the protagonist (Guitry himself) to describe the action on the screen, which occurred wholly in pantomime.

Jean Renoir

By far the greatest and most influential director to emerge from French poetic realism was Jean Renoir (1894–1979). Son of the Impressionist painter Pierre-Auguste Renoir (1841–1915),* he began his career in cinema with an uneven series of eight silent films, including a brilliant adaptation of Zola's novel *Nana* (1926) inspired by von Stroheim's *Foolish Wives* (1922)†; *La Petite marchande d'allumettes* (1927), a modern-dress version of Hans Christian Andersen's fairy tale *The Little Match Girl;* and *Tire-au-flanc* (1928), a farce that compares well with Clair's *Un Chapeau de paille d'Italie,* combining slapstick, satire, and poetic fantasy. Renoir's other silent films were strictly commercial vehicles, and it was not until the coming of sound that he began to distinguish himself as an artist. His first sound film was *On purge bébé* (*Purging the Baby,* 1931), adapted from a play by Georges Feydeau and starring Renoir's frequent collaborator during this period, Michel Simon (1895–1975). This relatively trivial domestic comedy was nevertheless a great commercial success and permitted Renoir to make his first important sound film,

9.52 *Nana* (Jean Renoir, 1926): Catherine Hessling, Valeska Gert.

9.53 A shot in depth from Renoir's *La Nuit de carrefour* (1932).

---

* Renoir is also the uncle of the cinematographer Claude Renoir (b. 1914) and the brother of the actor Pierre Renoir (1885–1952), with both of whom he worked frequently in the thirties.

† In *The Man You Loved to Hate* (New York, 1983), Richard Kozarski maintains that the rabbit-hunting sequence in *La Règle du jeu* (1939) is an homage to the pigeon-shooting episode of *Foolish Wives.*

La Chienne (*The Bitch*, 1932), a year later. This melodrama of a middle-class bank clerk and Sunday painter (Simon) who has an affair with a prostitute and later kills her for deceiving him owed much to the example of von Sternberg's *Der blaue Engel* (1929; see pp. 320–321), and it achieved a degree of social realism in evoking its milieu which exceeded even that of its German predecessor.

After the suspenseful detective film *La Nuit de carrefour* (*Night at the Crossroads*, 1932), adapted from a work by Georges Simenon, and the lightweight comedy *Chotard et cie* (*Chotard and Company*, 1932), Renoir once again returned to the theme of *La Chienne*, pitting the bourgeois life against the anarchic values of a tramp in *Boudu sauvé des eaux* (*Boudu Saved from Drowning*, 1932.)* In this film, a respectable Parisian book-dealer saves a seedy vagabond, Boudu (Michel Simon), from drowning in the Seine and insists that he move in with him. After seducing both the wife and mistress of his benefactor, and generally wreaking havoc on the household, Boudu leaves happily to resume his wanderings. Produced independently with complete creative freedom, *Boudu*, like *La Chienne*, was a commercial failure. Renoir's next film was a fine adaptation of Flaubert's *Madame Bovary* (1934) in which he attempted to translate the novel's symbolic substructure into cinematic terms. Originally more than three and a half hours long, but cut to two hours by its distributors, *Madame Bovary* was another commercial failure; fortunately, Renoir was given a chance in the following year to undertake a much-cherished project by producer Marcel Pagnol. This was *Toni* (1935), a story of Italian immigrant workers in the quarries of southern France. Shot entirely on location and making extensive use of nonactors, *Toni* harks back to Soviet realism and is a forerunner of Italian neorealism (see Chapters 5 and 11).

After this attempt to make a film, in Renoir's words, "as close as possible to a documentary," Renoir entered into his only collaboration with the scriptwriter Jacques Prévert; the resulting film marks a major turning point in his work. Shot during the great electoral triumphs of the Popular Front in 1935, *Le Crime de Monsieur Lange* (*The Crime of Monsieur Lange*, 1935) is in many ways a political parable of the need for collective action in the face of capitalist corruption. The employees of a publishing house form a cooperative to run the business when they learn of the accidental death of their lecherous and exploitative boss. The co-op experiences great success until the boss unexpectedly returns to claim his business. One of the workers, a writer of Wild West serials named M. Lange (his name is a pun on the French *l'ange*, "angel"), shoots him and flees the country for freedom. Shot largely on a single set representing the courtyard of a Parisian working-class tenement, *Le Crime de Monsieur Lange* announced the new spirit of social commitment which would pervade Renoir's work through his last prewar films. The strength of this commitment was demonstrated in *La Vie est à nous*, (*Life Is Ours / People of France*, 1936), an election propaganda film for the French Com-

9.54 Renoir's *Boudu sauvé des eaux* (1932): Marclele Hainia, Charles Granval, Michel Simon, Séverine Lerczinska.

9.55 Depth perspective in *Madame Bovary* (1934): Valentine Tessier.

9.56 Experimenting with depth in *Toni* (Jean Renoir, 1935).

---

* *La Chienne* was remade in the United States by Fritz Lang as *Scarlet Street* (1945); *Boudu* was remade by Paul Mazursky as *Down and Out in Beverly Hills* (1985).

9.57 Two shots from *Le Crime de Monsieur Lange* (Jean Renoir, 1935) emphasizing depth.

9.58 *La Grande illusion* (Jean Renoir, 1937): von Rauffenstein welcomes Boieldieu, Maréchal, and the other French prisoners-of-war to Wintersboro.

munist Party which mixes newsreel footage with dramatic episodes to show the necessity of presenting a united front against Fascism. Financed solely by public subscription, the film was banned from French commercial theaters but enjoyed a lively underground reputation in the *ciné-clubs* and specialist theaters. It was thought to have been destroyed during the war, but a copy came to light in 1969, and *La Vie est à nous,* appropriately, had its first commercial success in France during the height of the student-worker rebellion of the late sixties.

Renoir's next two films were literary adaptations. *Une Partie de campagne* (*A Day in the Country*) was a version of a brief Maupassant story shot in 1936 but not edited and released until 1946. Just forty minutes long, *Une Partie* is the bittersweet tale of an 1880 Parisian bourgeois who takes his wife, his daughter, and her fiancé to the country for a Sunday outing. At a restaurant on the banks of the Marne they meet two men who take the women for a short boat ride up the river. In the process, the daughter falls in love with one of them. They embrace briefly but realize that they must return to their separate worlds. The pictorial quality of the film—its unique feeling for landscape and nature—is reminiscent of the paintings of Renoir's father and of his fellow Impressionists Manet, Monet, and Degas. Renoir's other adaptation of 1936 was a somewhat inconclusive version of Maxim Gorki's play *The Lower Depths* (*Les Bas-fonds,* 1936), written by Renoir and Charles Spaak, set not in late-nineteenth-century Russia but in some unidentified time and place.

Renoir's next film, *La Grande illusion* (*Grand Illusion,* 1937), also written in collaboration with Spaak, has proved to be an enduring masterpiece. It portrays European civilization on the brink of cultural collapse and pleads for the primacy of human relationships over national and class antagonisms, simultaneously asserting the utter futility of war and the necessity of international solidarity to combat this most destructive and degrading "grand illusion" of the human race. One winter during World War I, three downed French pilots—an aristocrat (Pierre Fresnay), a mechanic (Jean Gabin), and a Jewish banker (Marcel Dalio)—are captured by the Germans and ceremoniously welcomed into the enemy officers' mess. They are subsequently transferred to a series of prison camps—each one a microcosm of European society—and finally to the impregnable fortress of Wintersborn, commanded by the sympathetic Prussian aristocrat von Rauffenstein (Erich von Stroheim). Boieldieu, the French aristocrat, and von Rauffenstein become close friends because they are of the same caste, and they pursue a long intellectual dialogue on the role of their dwindling class in European society. Despite the cultural barrier between Boieldieu and his two compatriots, he has earlier assisted them in digging a tunnel under a prison wall in the dead of winter—the whole film takes place in this season—because it is his duty as an officer to help them escape. Equally trapped by his officer's code, von Rauffenstein must later shoot Boieldieu during an escape attempt at Wintersborn in which he willingly plays the decoy. Boieldieu dies painfully in von Rauffenstein's quarters, and the German commander, in a gesture of remorse, snips the flower from his much-cherished geranium plant. Both

9.59 Brother aristocrats: Boieldieu (Pierre Fresnay) and von Rauffenstein (Erich von Stroheim). Note the potted geranium between them, a small symbol of hope in the arid environment of the prison camp.

9.60 An alliance of the working class and the bourgeoisie: Maréchal (Jean Gabin) and Rosenthal (Marcel Dalio) plan their escape.

men have been victims of a rigid code of behavior which has left them no option but mutual destruction despite their friendship; Renoir suggests that the old ruling class of Europe is doomed for precisely the same reasons (which are also the same reasons for the "grand illusion" of war). The future of Europe seems to lie with the Jew, Rosenthal, and the mechanic, Maréchal—representatives of the bourgeoisie and working class, respectively—who have escaped together over the castle wall. After a grueling trek across Germany during which they argue continuously and nearly desert one another, Rosenthal and Maréchal finally cross the border to Switzerland, and freedom, as a result of their cooperation.

This extraordinarily rich and humane film contains magnificent ensemble playing by all of its leading actors, as well as the best performance of von Stroheim's career, perhaps because he played a character whose demeanor and doomed idealism so closely resembled his own. But the most striking aspect of *La Grand illusion* is Renoir's use of the **long take**, or **sequence shot**—unedited shots made from a single camera set-up which generally (but not always) constitute entire dramatic sequences within a film. Dramatic tension in such shots is created through *composition in depth*, or the simultaneous arrangement of dramatically significant action and objects on several spatial planes within the frame. Composition in depth is essentially an attempt to make the two-dimensional space of the cinema screen three-dimensional, and it can be achieved only through what is known as **deep-focus** photography—a mode of filming in which the foreground, middleground, and background of a shot are simultaneously in sharp focus. Technically, deep-focus photography is the achievement of a nearly perfect **depth of field** (the range of distances within which objects will be in sharp focus) within the frame; it should

9.61 Stills from the sequence shots of Boieldieu's death.

not be confused with depth of focus, a term used in describing the relationship between the lens and the surface of the film. Aesthetically, deep-focus photography provides a way of incorporating a close shot, medium shot, and long shot within a single frame, and of linking character with background. It also *appears* to reproduce the field of vision of the human eye, although the eye does not possess extreme depth of field but, rather, is able to so rapidly alter focus within a depth perspective that we are never aware of the discontinuity.

The earliest film stock—and that used by nearly all commercial film-makers until 1927—was *orthochromatic*. It possessed an extraordinary capacity for deep focus, or depth of field, in that it was relatively "fast," or sensitive to light, enabling cameramen to use small lens apertures which kept both the foreground and background of their shots in focus (see, for example, the still from Griffith's *Musketeers of Pig Alley,* 1912, on p. 74). To attain its full depth of field, orthochromatic stock requires a strong, penetrating source of light to strike the negative through the narrow aperture of the lens—the sun during the cinema's first decade, mercury vapor lamps during its second, and finally carbon arc lamps during its third. But orthochromatic was limited by its insensitivity to the red and yellow areas of the spectrum and required special filters to register them. In 1927, concurrent with the arrival of sound, orthochromatic was replaced as the industry standard by *panchromatic* stock, a film sensitive to all parts of the spectrum from blue to red but initially "slower" than the earlier film.[*] Simultaneously, the carbon arc lamps, which sputtered and popped noisily in operation, were replaced by incandescent, or tungsten, lighting, which was soundless. The new incandescent light, however, was softer and less penetrating than the light provided by the arc lamps, so cameramen were forced to widen their lens apertures and decrease the depth of field of the image. Thus, early panchromatic focus was relatively shallow; the backgrounds of close shots were diffused and a face in close-up would tend to become detached from its environment. With a few notable exceptions (such as James Wong Howe's photography for *Trans-atlantic* and *Viva Villa!* in 1933, and Hal Mohr's for *Tess of the Storm Country* in 1932),[†] this "soft" style of photography characterized the sound film until 1940, when technical innovations in lenses, film stock, and lighting, and the creative genius of Orson Welles and Gregg Toland,

---

[*] Eastman Kodak had introduced panchromatic stock in 1913 for use in such experimental color processes as Charles Urban's Kinemacolor and Léon Gaumont's Chronochrome (both q.v.), but the company's marketing campaign didn't begin until 1925, when the film's price was lowered and its speed increased. By 1928, panchromatic had been adopted as the standard stock of the sound era, just as the dominant stock of the silent period had been orthochromatic.

[†] In Charles Higham's *Hollywood Cameramen* (Bloomington, Ind.: Indiana University Press, 1970), Howe claims that for William K. Howard's *Transatlantic,* "I used wide angles, deep focus throughout, long before *Kane.* Eighty percent of the picture was shot with a twenty-five millimeter lens. . . . I carried focus from five feet back to twenty, thirty feet" (p. 84). Other uses of wide-angle lenses in early sound films are discussed in David Bordwell, "Deep-focus Cinematography," Chapter 27 of Bordwell, Staiger, and Thompson, *The Classical Hollywood Cinema* (New York: Columbia University Press, 1985), pp. 341–52.

restored the cinema's physical capacity for deep focus, as we will see in Chapter 10.

Despite underdeveloped technology, however, Renoir was the first major director of the sound film to compose his shots in depth, even though the depth was achieved artificially by constantly adjusting the focus of his camera to follow dramatic action within a given take. He had experimented with this technique in many of his early sound films, most successfully in *Toni* (1934), but *La Grande illusion* was his first film based consistently on the principle of the long take, or sequence shot. Generally, Renoir's films include realistic and dramatically significant background and middleground activity in every sequence shot. Actors range about the set transacting their business while the camera shifts its focus from one plane of depth to another and back again. Significant off-frame action is often followed with a moving camera, characteristically through a series of pans within a single continuous shot. The scene of Boieldieu's death in *La Grande illusion,* for example, is rendered through three evocative panning shots. Von Rauffenstein has just finished a bedside conversation with the dying Frenchman in which both have agreed that their caste is doomed to extinction. In a single shot, the camera follows von Rauffenstein as he rises from his chair, walks some distance to his liquor cabinet, takes a drink, and returns to the bedside when a nurse calls from off-frame. In the next shot, the camera moves with von Rauffenstein's hand in close-up as it reaches toward Boieldieu's eyes to close them. Finally, the camera observes von Rauffenstein at some distance as he walks from the bedside to the window, gazes at the falling snow, and, at last, cuts the flower from his prized geranium with a pair of scissors. Renoir makes the transition to his next scene with yet another pan: his camera moves slowly over the snowy German countryside in long shot to discover Rosenthal and Maréchal, dressed in dirty civilian clothes, hiding in a ditch at the end of the pan. *La Grande illusion* is composed almost completely of such moving sequence shots, but Renoir and his cinematographer, Christian Matras (b. 1903) never permit them to become flashy or self-conscious.

In the year of its release, *La Grande illusion* won both the New York Critics Award for the Best Foreign Language Film and a special prize at the prestigious Venice Film Festival, even though it was banned from commercial exhibition in both Italy and Germany. In 1957, together with *Potemkin* and *Mother,* *La Grande illusion* was voted one of the twelve greatest films of all time at the Brussels World's Fair.

Renoir's next project was *La Marseillaise* (1937), a semidocumentary reconstruction of some major episodes from the French Revolution, financed by the trade unions and flavored with the politics of the Popular Front. Next came *La Bête humaine* (*The Human Beast,* 1938), an adaptation of Zola's naturalistic novel about an alcoholic railroad engineer (played by Jean Gabin) cast in modern terms.* Renoir's final French film

9.62 Depth: Renoir's *La Marseillaise* (1937).

---

* Fritz Lang directed another adaptation of Zola's novel in 1954, under the title *Human Desire.*

of the period was his greatest masterpiece and one of the great works of the cinema, *La Régle du jeu* (*The Rules of the Game*, 1939). Like *La Grande illusion*, it is about a culture teetering on the brink of collapse, but it is a much more complicated film in both attitude and technique.

Informed by the gracious rhythms of Mozart, Johann Strauss, and Chopin, and patterned on the classical French theater of Marivaux and Beaumarchais,* *La Règle du jeu* is an elegant tragicomedy of manners whose intricate plot defies easy summarization. Briefly, the young aviator André Jurieu, who has just completed a daring transatlantic flight, is in love with Christine, the wife of a wealthy Jewish landowner, the Marquis Robert de la Chesnaye (Marcel Dalio). La Chesnaye organizes a large weekend hunting party at his country estate, La Colinière, to which he invites Jurieu, Octave (a mutual friend of Jurieu and Christine, played by Renoir), and his own mistress. After a day of hunting in which hundreds of rabbits and birds are slaughtered and maimed, we are treated to a series of love intrigues among the *haute bourgeoisie* abovestairs and among the servants belowstairs—who, in their snobbery, insincerity, and pride, are the precise mirror images of their masters. The major characteristic of these intrigues is that not a single one is serious, and Jurieu has broken an important "rule of the game" by sincerely declaring his love for Christine in the most public way imaginable—in a radio broadcast from Orly Airport just after his transatlantic flight. Later, during an evening fête featuring extravagant theatrical entertainment and a fancy-dress ball, a jealous gamekeeper attempts to shoot his wife's suspected lover (a local poacher) in a comic chase through the ballroom reminiscent of a Marx Brothers film. Finally, the gamekeeper decides that Octave, not the poacher, is the lover, and he shoots Jurieu to death on the veranda, mistaking him for Octave and Christine for his wife. A model of civilized restraint, the marquis takes immediate command of the situation, apologizes to his guests for the "regrettable accident," and takes all appropriate steps to restore equilibrium to the world of La Colinière.

Witty, elegant, and profoundly pessimistic, *La Règle du jeu* is ultimately concerned with social breakdown and cultural decadence at a particularly critical moment in European history. Renoir presents us with a world in which feeling has been replaced by manners and all that remains of civilized values is their external form—a form which will itself soon crumble. Society has become a vast collective lie, and those, like Jurieu, who break its "rules" by telling the truth, come to no good. *La Règle du jeu* has the moral and intellectual depth of a great novel, but it is also a brilliant piece of filmmaking. Renoir had never used the long take and deep focus to such striking dramatic effect. Sequence shots dominate nearly every major scene, and the camera moves continuously to follow significant action within the frame. Fluid, graceful, and exquisitely precise are terms which describe Renoir's camera style in *La Règle du jeu*. He resorts

---

* Renoir, in fact, conceived of the film as an updated version of the comedy *Les Caprices de Marianne* by the Romantic poet and playwright Alfred de Musset (1810–57).

9.63 *La Règle du jeu* (Jean Renoir, 1939): Christine de la Chesnaye (Nora Grégor) questions her maid, Lisette (Pauline Dubost) about her own marriage.

9.64 Christine (Nora Grégor) and Octave (Jean Renoir) by moonlight at La Colinière.

to expressive montage only once in the entire film—appropriately, to render the mindless organized violence of the hunt.

Renoir expected *La Règle du jeu* to be controversial, but he could hardly have anticipated the extremity of the reaction. The film provoked a political riot at its Paris premiere, was cut and re-edited by its distributor from 113 to 80 minutes, and was finally banned in late 1939 by French military censors as "demoralizing." The Nazis banned it during the Occupation, and Allied bombing destroyed the original negative in 1942. Happily, the integral version of *La Règle du jeu,* minus one short scene, was reconstructed under Renoir's supervision by two French film producers in 1956 and has enjoyed a prestigious international reputation ever since. In 1962 and 1972 an international poll of film critics ranked it among the ten greatest films ever made.

In the summer of 1939, Renoir accepted an invitation to teach at the Centro Sperimentale in Rome (Italy's national film school) and to direct there a version of Puccini's opera *La Tosca,* with a screenplay by Luchino Visconti (see pp. 441–42).* The film was begun by Renoir's crew but completed by others, notably the director and coscenarist Carl Koch, because Italy joined Hitler's war against France on June 10, 1940, and Renoir, who was on the Nazis' extermination list because of his leftist

---

* The invitation, sent through diplomatic channels, came from Mussolini himself, who greatly admired Renoir as a filmmaker despite his politics (Il Duce was said to own a private copy of *La Grande illusion,* although it was officially banned by his Fascist government). Renoir accepted the invitation at the behest of the French government, which was anxious to preserve Italy's neutrality in the "phony war" with Germany, which began on September 3, 1939, and ended on May 10, 1940, when SS Panzer divisions smashed through the Maginot Line. On Renoir's reception in the United States, see Alexander Sesonske, "Discovering America: Jean Renoir: 1941," *Sight and Sound* 50, 4 (Autumn 1981): 256–61.

9.65   Guests at La Colinière on their way to the hunt.

9.66   Shots from the hunting sequence in *La Règle du jeu*.

9.67   The marquis (Marcel Dalio) and his gamekeeper (Gaston Modot) encounter a poacher (Julien Carette).

politics, was forced to emigrate to the United States. Here he went to work for a variety of studios, filming in rapid succession *Swamp Water* (1941)—a sort of commercial, American *Toni* shot on location in the swamps of Georgia—and two war propaganda films—*This Land is Mine* (1943) and *Salute to France* (1944). Renoir's most distinguished American film was The *Southerner,* made in 1945 for United Artists. This austere, semidocumentary account of the lives of poor white farmers in the deep South was shot on location with complete creative freedom; more than any other of Renoir's American films, it harks back to the poetic realism of the thirties. With *The Diary of a Chambermaid* (1946), Renoir returned to French sources (Octave Mirbeau's novel, which Luis Buñuel would also film, in 1964), but moved away from the realism of his greatest period. Independently produced and shot entirely in the studio, this film about the decadence of French bourgeois society in the late nineteenth century resembled *La Règle du jeu* in theme, but lacked the great depth of the earlier work, and it was universally condemned in Europe, where Renoir's prewar reputation had declined. His last American film was *The Woman on the Beach* (1947), a tale of romantic obsession in a wild coastal setting. The film failed commercially and aesthetically, in large part because RKO re-edited it no fewer than three times.

At this point Renoir became increasingly interested in theater and spectacle, as they contrasted with his earlier "realistic" style. He left Hollywood to make *The River* (1951), a British coproduction, on the banks of the Ganges River. This beautiful film—Renoir's first in color—was strikingly photographed by the director's nephew, Claude Renoir, and is about the response of a fourteen-year-old British girl to India. Renoir next went to Italy to make *Le Carrosse d'or* (*The Golden Coach,* 1952), a color film about a *commedia dell'arte* theater troupe in eighteenth-century Peru which attempted to explore the relationships among film, theater, and reality. Renoir appropriately abandoned composition in depth and the moving camera for *La Carrosse d'or* in favor of a more theatrical *mise-en-scène* using long takes from a relatively stationary camera.

In 1954 Renoir returned to his native land for the first time since the war and began his last important series of French films. *French CanCan* (1954) is set in Montmartre in the late 1890s of Renoir's childhood and tells the story of the impresario who founded the famous Moulin Rouge theater. Its brilliant use of color in motion evokes the paintings of the Impressionists but goes beyond them, reaching its height in the spectacular twenty-minute cancan dance with which the film concludes. *Eléna et les hommes* (English-language title: *Paris Does Strange Things,* 1957),* a romantic costume drama set during the Franco-Prussian War, showed signs that Renoir's creative power was waning; his next two films seemed to many to confirm this. *Le Testament du Dr. Cordelier* (1959) is a mod-

9.68 *The River* (Jean Renoir, 1951).

---

* Distributed by Warner Bros., this Americanized version was dubbed, cut from 98 to 86 minutes, and given a different beginning and ending than Renoir intended to romanticize the persona of Ingrid Bergman in its title role. Critically attacked for incoherence, the film was disowned by Renoir, but a restored version is currently available in the United States from Interama, Inc., in New York City.

ern adaptation of Robert Louis Stevenson's *Dr. Jekyll and Mr. Hyde* shot in black-and-white for French television. *Le Déjeuner sur l'herbe* (*Picnic on the Grass,* 1959) is a rather silly futuristic fantasy whose visual texture is nevertheless closer to that of French Impressionist painting than anything Renoir had ever filmed. In his final feature film, *Le Caporal epinglé* (*The Elusive Corporal,* 1962), Renoir returned to the subject of prisoners of war with a lightweight comedy about the multiple escape attempts of a French corporal from a German prison camp during World War II. Renoir's filmmaking career ended in 1969 with a series of short plays for French television entitled *Le Petit théâtre de Jean Renoir* (*The Little Theater of Jean Renoir,* 1969). Later, Renoir retired to southern California, where he wrote plays, a biography of his father, seven novels, and, finally, his own memoirs.

Jean Renoir, indisputably one of the great masters of world cinema, resolutely refused to be compromised by his own success. In a career that spanned forty-six years of cinema, he never ceased to experiment and explore, to consistently renew his creative vitality by striking out in new directions. *La Règle du jeu* (1939) is as different from *La Carrosse d'or* (1954) as both are from *Toni* (1934) and *The Southerner* (1945), and yet all four of these films are masterworks on their own terms. Renoir was also the pioneer of composition in depth in the sound film, and, according to André Bazin, he became the father of a new aesthetic: "He alone in his searchings as director prior to *La Règle du jeu* . . . forced himself to look back beyond the resources provided by montage and so uncovered the secret of film form that would permit everything to be said without chopping the world up into little fragments, that would reveal the hidden meanings in people and things without disturbing the unity natural to them." Renoir's influence on Orson Welles, who brought the technique of composition in depth to its ultimate perfection in *Citizen Kane,* is well known,* and his impact on Italian neorealism was strong. His technical genius notwithstanding, Renoir was perhaps the most humanistic of all the Western cinema's major figures. He wrote: "I'm not a director—I'm a story-teller. . . . The only thing I bring to this illogical, irresponsible, and cruel universe is my love." An artist of strong and uniquely personal vision, Jean Renoir also represents the flowering of the period of poetic realism (1934–1940), when French films were generally regarded as the most important and sophisticated in the world.

---

* Welles wrote a moving eulogy when Renoir died on February 12, 1979, at his home in Beverly Hills, after a long illness. It appeared in the *Los Angeles Times* on February 18, 1979.

Orson Welles and the Modern Sound Film

At the very moment that France was being occupied by the Nazis and the rest of Europe was engulfed in war, a young American director made a film which was to substantially transform the cinema. In 1939 Orson Welles (1915–85) was brought to Hollywood by the financially troubled RKO Pictures under an unprecedented six-film contract which gave him complete control over every aspect of production. At twenty-four, Welles' experience in radio and theater was vast. From 1933 to 1937 he directed and acted in numerous Broadway and off-Broadway plays, including a production of *Macbeth* with a voodoo setting and an anti-Fascist *Julius Caesar* set in contemporary Italy; in 1937, with John Houseman (1902–88), he founded the famous Mercury Theatre company; and between 1938 and 1940 he wrote, directed, and starred in the weekly radio series *Mercury Theatre on the Air,* whose pseudo-documentary broadcast based on H. G. Wells' *War of the Worlds* caused a nationwide panic on Halloween night in 1938.

Welles had made several short films in connection with his theatrical productions (such as *Too Much Johnson,* 1938),* but he had never been on a **soundstage** in his life. His first feature film was to be an adaptation of Joseph Conrad's *Heart of Darkness,* filmed with a subjective camera from the point of view of the narrator (who is also a participant in the action), but this project was abandoned indefinitely due to technical problems, cost overruns, and other difficulties, including the outbreak of war in Europe and the internment of its female lead, the German actress Dita Parlo.† Next, Welles undertook to film a script written by himself and Herman J. Mankiewicz (1898–1953) about the life and personality of a great American entrepreneur. Originally entitled simply *American,* the Welles-Mankiewicz scenario ultimately became the shooting script for *Citizen Kane* (1941), the now-legendary crypto-biography of America's most powerful press lord, William Randolph Hearst (1863–1951).

---

* See Frank Brady, "The Lost Film of Orson Welles," *American Film* 4, 2 (November 1978): 63–69, and the recent biographies by Charles Higham (*Orson Welles: The Rise and Fall of an American Genius* [New York: St. Martin's, 1985]) and Barbara Leaming (*Orson Welles: A Biography* [New York: Viking, 1985]).

†Dita Parlo (1906–71) was working in the French film industry when the war began (she had played featured roles in Vigo's *L'Atalante* [1934] and Renoir's *La Grande illusion* [1937], among other films); military officials had her arrested as an alien and, ultimately, deported to Germany. For a full account of the *Heart of Darkness* project and its termination, see Robert L. Carringer's *The Making of Citizen Kane* (Berkeley: University of California Press, 1985), Ch. 1.

CITIZEN KANE

Production

Welles claimed that his only preparation for directing *Citizen Kane* was to watch John Ford's *Stagecoach* (1939) forty times. Ford's influence on the film is pronounced, but it is equally clear that Welles was steeped in the major European traditions, especially those of German Expressionism and the *Kammerspielfilm,** and French poetic realism. If *Kane*'s narrative economy owes much to the example of Ford, its visual texture is heavily indebted to the chiaroscuro lighting of Lang, the fluid camera of Murnau, the baroque *mise-en-scène* of von Sternberg, and the deep-focus realism of Renoir. Credit is also due Welles' remarkably talented collaborators—Mankiewicz; the Mercury Theatre players; the composer Bernard Herrmann; the editor Robert Wise; and the unit art director, Perry Ferguson.†

But Welles' greatest single technical asset in the filming of *Kane* was his brilliant director of photography, Gregg Toland (1904–48). Toland had earned a distinguished reputation as a cinematographer in Hollywood in the thirties and had experimented with deep-focus photography and ceilinged sets in his three most recent films, *Wuthering Heights* (William Wyler, 1939), for which he had won an Academy Award, *The Grapes of Wrath* (John Ford, 1940), and *The Long Voyage Home* (John Ford, 1940). Welles (or Mankiewicz) had conceived *Kane* as a film which occurs largely in flashback as characters recall their acquaintance with the great man (played by Welles himself) after his death, and he wanted the narrative to flow poetically from image to image in a manner analogous to the process of human memory. Thus, Welles used straight cuts largely for shock effect and made the most of his narrative transitions through lingering, in-camera lap dissolves. More important, Welles planned to construct the film as a series of long takes, or sequence shots, scrupulously composed in-depth to eliminate the necessity for narrative cutting within major dramatic scenes.

To accomplish this, Toland perfected for Welles a method of deep-focus photography capable of achieving an unprecedented depth of field. As explained in Chapter 9, the "soft" style of photography favored by

---

* As John Russell Taylor has observed, "*Citizen Kane* may be the best American film ever made; but it just might be also the best German film ever made." (Quoted in *German Film Directors in Hollywood: Catalogue of an Exhibit of the Goethe Institutes of North America* [San Francisco, 1978], p. 5.) To make the question of influence even richer, Howard Hawks claimed in a 1976 interview that Welles modeled *Kane* on his own *His Girl Friday* (1940) and had told him so in 1941 (Bruce F. Kawin, "Introduction: *No Man Alone*," p. 41, *To Have and Have Not*, ed. Bruce F. Kawin (Madison: University of Wisconsin Press, 1980).

† As administrative head of the RKO art department, Van Nest Polglase received official screen credit for this function, with Ferguson listed as "Associate," but the latter was art director in fact. This practice reflected the bureaucratic hierarchy of the studio system, whereby department heads were contractually entitled to screen credits (and, therefore, to awards) for work performed by their subordinates.

10.1 Gregg Toland and Orson Welles shooting *Citizen Kane* (Orson Welles, 1941): the *Inquirer* set.

10.2 Welles directing Toland and Dorothy Comingore in an opera sequence near the end of the principal photography. (Welles had broken his ankle running down the stairs in pursuit of "Boss" Jim Gettys in the scene depicted in 10.29.)

the studios during the thirties was characterized by diffused lighting and relatively shallow focus—a product of the wider lens apertures required for filming in incandescent light. By the end of the decade, technical improvements in film stocks and lighting permitted greater depth of field, but most studio cinematographers were conservative and continued to practice the "soft" style. Toland, however, was a bold experimenter whose work in-depth—especially in *The Long Voyage Home*—had earned him a reputation for the kind of flamboyant originality prized by Welles in his Mercury Theatre productions. Toland's self-styled "pan focus" photography for *Kane* was a synthesis of many techniques he had used before. It employed the newly available Eastman Super XX film stock (an ultra-fast film with a very high sensitivity to light—four times faster, in fact, than its standard Super X, without a notable increase in grain) in combination with a 24mm **wide-angle lens** whose aperture was stopped down to f-8 or less—a radical reduction in its size (see Chapter 9, note). The scenes were lit by the high-intensity arc lamps recently introduced for Technicolor production and the lenses were coated with a clear plastic substance (magnesium fluoride) to reduce glare. Finally, Toland used the Mitchell Camera Corporation's self-blimped BNC, a relatively small and portable camera first used professionally in *Wuthering Heights*, which greatly increased the operator's freedom and range of movement.* With these tools, Toland was able to achieve something very close to "universal" focus within the frames of *Citizen Kane*, and Welles was able to distribute dramatic action across a depth perspective unlike anything ever used in a sound film. Since the early 1960s, improvements in lenses, light-

---

* Additionally, a new fine-grain stock for producing release prints had been introduced in 1939. It virtually eliminated graininess in print generation and preserved image depth in films like *The Long Voyage Home* and *Kane*.

ing, and film emulsions have greatly simplified deep-focus photography, but the technical principles remain much the same. Welles' use of the deep-focus sequence shot in *Kane* demonstrated an absolute mastery of composition in depth. Like Renoir, he used the deep-focus format functionally, to develop scenes without resorting to montage, but he also used it expressively—as Eisenstein had used montage—to create metaphors for things that the cinema cannot represent directly on the screen.

At the height of his arrogance and power, for example, Kane often looms like a giant in the foreground of the frame, dwarfing other characters in the middleground and background, and towering over the audience, often from a low camera angle. Later, Kane's self-absorbed alienation from the world and everyone in it is conveyed by the growing distance which separates him from all other characters within the frame. In these instances, Welles' use of depth perspective involves an expressive distortion of space which creates a metaphor for something in Kane's psychology. At other times, Welles uses deep focus both to achieve narrative economy and to echelon characters dramatically within the frame. Early in the film, a brilliant deep-focus sequence shot encapsulates the story of Kane's lost childhood. We see the front room of a boardinghouse in which Charlie Kane's mother signs the agreement that will permit her son to be taken to the East and later inherit a fortune. In exchanging her son's childhood for an adult life of fantastic wealth, she is selling him, and she knows it. Welles set the shot up like this: In the foreground of the frame, Mrs. Kane and Mr. Thatcher, whose bank is the executor of the estate, sign the agreement. The middleground is occupied by Charlie's weak-willed father, whose vacillation about the agreement is rendered visible as he paces back and forth between foreground and background. In the

10.3 Charles Foster Kane (Orson Welles) and his first wife, Emily Norton (Ruth Warrick), at breakfast: the growing distance. (From Leland's narrative.)

10.4 The aging Kane with his second wife, Susan Alexander (Dorothy Comingore), at Xanadu. The depth perspective which separates them suggests an unbreachable gap. (From Susan's narrative.)

back of the room is a window through which, in the extreme background of the frame, we see Charlie playing unsuspectingly in the snow with his sled and shouting, "The Union forever!," while in the foreground of the same shot, he is being indentured to his own future. Thus, in a single shot, Welles is able to communicate a large amount of narrative and thematic information which would require many shots in a conventionally edited scene.

Kane is a film of much fluid intra-frame movement. The sequence just described, for instance, actually begins with a medium long shot of Charlie at play in the snow through the open window of the boardinghouse; then the camera pulls back rapidly to reveal the other characters and elements in the composition. But there are three virtuoso moving camera shots in the film, each of which is a tour de force of fluidity and continuity. In the first, from a shot of a poster announcing the appearance of Kane's second wife, Susan, at the El Rancho nightclub, the camera cranes up vertically to the club's flashing neon sign, then tracks horizontally *through* it and down onto the rain-spattered glass of a skylight. The movement continues after a quick dissolve (made invisible by flashing lightning and distracting thunder), as the camera descends to a medium shot of Susan Alexander Kane and a newsman talking together at a table in the club's interior. In another shot, midway through the film, the camera cranes up vertically from a long shot of Susan singing on the stage of the Chicago Municipal Opera House to a catwalk some four stories above it, where a stagehand makes a vulgar but richly deserved gesture of contempt for her performance. Finally, there is the long swooping **crane shot** with which the film concludes, as the camera tracks slowly across the vast collection of artifacts that Kane has amassed in a lifetime of collecting, coming to rest on the object of the search for "Rosebud" that gives the film its narrative impulse or motive.

Other remarkable aspects of this wholly remarkable film are its expressive chiaroscuro lighting* and frequent use of extreme low-angle photography in connection with the figure of Kane. The latter necessitated many muslin ceilinged sets, which had been used in Hollywood before, especially in the work of Toland, but never so consistently and effectively to suggest a sense of claustration and enclosure. (Filmmakers have conventionally left their interior sets roofless, first to admit the sunlight and later to facilitate artificial lighting and the free movement of the boom crane and microphone.) Finally, and most significantly, attention must be called to *Kane*'s innovative use of sound.

Welles' experience in radio served him well in recording the soundtrack for *Kane*. He invented for his few montage sequences a technique he called the "lightning mix," in which shots were rapidly linked together not by the narrative logic of their images but by the continuity of the soundtrack. Kane's growth from child to adult is conveyed in a matter of

10.5 Depth as fate: Mrs. Kane (Agnes Moorehead) and Thatcher (George Coulouris); Mr. Kane (Harry Shannon); Charlie (Buddy Swan) outside, framed by the window. (From Thatcher's narrative.)

---

* There are two major lighting styles in *Kane*—the sharp, high-contrast "daylight" style associated with Kane's youth and rise to power, and the dark, expressionistic "low-light" style which characterizes his corruption and decline.

10.6 Jed Leland (Joseph Cotton) confronts Kane after the lost election. The low camera angle and expressive lighting create a sense of menace and tension. Note that the camera shoots into the ceiling. (From Leland's narrative).

10.7 Kane alone, after wrecking Susan's bedroom. The extreme low camera angle and sinister backlighting characterize an alienated, destructive (and, finally, self-destructive) personality. Again, note the ceiling. (From Raymond's narrative.)

10.8 Kane finishing Leland's review: visual and aural depth combined. (From Leland's narrative.)

seconds: a shot of his guardian giving him a sled and wishing him "a Merry Christmas" is cut together with a shot of the same man some fifteen years later, as he completes the sentence—"and a Happy New Year"—again addressing Kane, but in a different dramatic context. Another lightning mix conveys the entire progress of Kane's campaign for governor of New York State in four brief shots. First we see Kane listening to Susan Alexander sing (wretchedly) at the piano in the parlor of her boardinghouse. This dissolves into another shot of the two in the same relative positions in a much more elegantly appointed parlor, that of an apartment in which Kane has obviously set her up. At the end of Susan's performance, Kane claps, and the shot is dovetailed with another of a friend addressing a small street rally in Kane's behalf. The applause, which has been continuous on the soundtrack since the parlor shot, grows louder and multiplies in response to the speaker's words: "I am speaking for Charles Foster Kane, the fighting liberal . . . who entered upon this campaign with one purpose only—". We cut finally to a long shot of Kane himself addressing a huge political rally at Madison Square Garden and completing the sentence as the camera begins to track toward the speaker's platform: "—to point out and make public the dishonesty, the downright villainy of Boss Jim Gettys' political machine." The address continues, and the narrative resumes a more conventional form.

Another device introduced by Welles in *Kane* was the overlapping sound montage in which—as in reality—people speak not one after another (as they do on the stage) but virtually all at once, so that part of what is said is lost. Overlapping dialogue between major players in a film had been used as early as 1931 by Lewis Milestone in *The Front Page,* but it had not been used to produce a sense of realistic collective conversation as in *Kane.* A good example in the film (and there is an example in almost every major sequence) occurs in the screening room after the projection of the "News on the March" newsreel. So many persons are speaking on the track simultaneously that one has the distinct sense of having accidentally stumbled into the aftermath of a board meeting. Welles continued to use this technique in his later films, and it has influenced many other filmmakers—both his contemporaries, like Carol Reed, and more recent directors, like Robert Altman, who has been so firmly committed to overlapping sound montage that unknowledgeable critics complain about the "poor quality" of his soundtracks.

A final example of Welles' subtle refinement of sound occurs in one of his best deep-focus set-ups. Kane, in a newsroom, is seated at a typewriter in the extreme foreground of the frame finishing a bad review of Susan Alexander Kane's Chicago opera debut which his ex-friend Jed Leland has written. Correspondingly, we hear the tapping of the typewriter keys on the "foreground" of the soundtrack. From a door in the background of the frame, Leland emerges—barely recognizable, so great is the distance—and begins to walk slowly towards Kane. As he moves from the background to the foreground of the frame, Leland's footsteps move from the "background" to the "foreground" of the soundtrack—from being initially inaudible to having nearly an equal volume with the keys. Similarly, in the Chicago Opera House shot, as the camera dollies up from the stage to the catwalk, Susan's voice grows ever more distant on the track, creating once more a precise correspondence of visual and aural "space."

Structure

The formal organization of *Citizen Kane* is extraordinary. Like a Jorge Luis Borges story, it begins with the death of its subject. Through an elaborate series of lap-dissolved stills, we are led from a "No Trespassing" sign on a chain link fence farther and farther into the forbidding Kane estate of Xanadu, as if by the tracking movement of a camera, until at last we approach a lighted window high in a Gothic tower. The light is suddenly extinguished, and Welles dissolves to the interior of the room, where Charles Foster Kane dies in state, clutching a small glass globe which contains a swirling snow scene and whispering "Rosebud"—the word that motivates the film and echoes through it until the final frames. Kane drops the globe in dying; it rolls down the steps and breaks in close-up. Through the distorting lens of the convex broken glass (actually, a wide-angle lens focused through a diminishing glass), we watch a nurse enter the room from a door in the background in long shot; she walks to the foreground in close shot, folds Kane's arms, and pulls the covers up to his chest. After a fade to a medium shot of Kane's body silhouetted against the window, we suddenly cut to a logo projected obliquely on a screen, and the soundtrack booms the title "News on the March!"—

10.9 Reality frame: the opening shots of *Citizen Kane*. The camera pans up from the fence from the "No Trespassing" sign and slowly dissolves to the crested gate and then into Xanadu.

10.10 Reality frame: as Kane dies, the glass globe drops from his hand and shatters.

10.11 Reality frame: the nurse, shot as through broken glass.

10.12 "News on the March": logo.

10.13 "News on the March": Teddy Roosevelt and Charles Foster Kane.

10.14 "News on the March": Kane in exile at Xanadu, shot candidly by a hidden cameraman.

10.15 Reality frame: a startling change of camera angle at the newsreel's conclusion takes us out of the film within the film and places us unexpectedly in a projection room.

10.16 Reality frame: Thompson (William Alland) is dispatched to find "Rosebud—dead or alive . . . ."

introducing a sophisticated parody of a "March of Time" newsreel* on Kane's life and death. Welles is thus able to give a brief and coherent, if unsequential, overview of the major events in Kane's life before they become jumbled like the pieces of a jigsaw puzzle in the succeeding narratives.

In a sense, the newsreel is *Citizen Kane* itself in miniature. Like the larger film, it begins with Kane's death (or his funeral), covers the same events in a similar overlapping, chronological manner, and ends with the mystery of Kane's character unresolved. We learn from the newsreel that Kane was an enormously controversial figure, hated and loved by millions of Americans, whose vast wealth was inherited by fluke: a supposedly worthless deed left to his mother in payment for a boardinghouse room gave him sole ownership of the priceless Colorado Lode. We learn that in an earlier period of American history, near the turn of the century, Kane's wealth and the influence of his newspapers were incalculable. We learn that he was married twice—first to a president's niece, then to Susan Alexander, "singer," for whom he built the Chicago Municipal Opera House and Xanadu. We learn that Kane's promising and apparently nonstop political career was destroyed during a campaign for the governorship of the State of New York by a "love-nest" scandal involving Susan Alexander. We learn finally that Kane's newspaper empire was crippled by the Depression and that he subsequently exiled himself to the solitude of Xanadu, where, after many years of seclusion, he died in 1941. The newsreel ends, and the camera discovers a dimly and expressionistically lit projection room, where the contemporary media journalists (succes-

---

* "The March of Time" was a popular series of skillfully (some would say slickly) produced film news journals released monthly in the the United States between 1935 and 1951. Each issue was twenty minutes long, and, generally, focused on a single subject. These films were usually shown as preludes to features, so that *Citizen Kane*'s original audiences might well have watched an authentic "March of Time" newsreel just before seeing the parodic "News on the March" in *Kane*. "The March of Time" series was politically conservative, reflecting the editorial policies of its financial backer, Time-Life, Inc., and of Time-Life's director, Henry R. Luce (1898–1967). Time-Life succeeded the Hearst empire, which was badly crippled by the Depression, to become a major shaper of public opinion during the thirties, forties, and fifties. The identification in *Citizen Kane* of Rawlston's news organization with the Luce press is entirely deliberate, since it extends the Kane / Hearst analogy.

sors of the Kane/Hearst empire and identified with the Luce press) who produced the film, discuss it. Rawlston, the executive in charge, thinks it needs an "angle" that will somehow explain the paradoxical figure of Kane. Someone seizes upon the man's dying words, the film's release is postponed, and a journalist named Thompson (played by William Alland) is sent out to interview all of Kane's intimate acquaintances to discover the meaning of "Rosebud" and, it is hoped, of Kane himself.

The rest of the film is contained in a series of five narratives—told in flashback by each of the people Thompson talks to—and a balancing epilogue of sorts. The narratives overlap with each other and with the "News on the March" newsreel at certain points, so that some of the events in Kane's life are presented from several different points of view within the total film. From the screening room, a shock cut takes us to a poster on a brick wall, suddenly illuminated by lightning, which announces the El Rancho nightclub appearance of the second Mrs. Kane. Through the elaborate craning movement previously described, we are brought into the interior of the club, where a drunk and hostile Susan Alexander Kane (Dorothy Comingore) refuses to talk to Thompson. He can get no information from the headwaiter either, and the screen then fades out and into a daytime sequence at the Walter P. Thatcher Memorial Library. (Thatcher, we come to understand later in the sequence, was Kane's guardian and executor of the Colorado Lode estate.) Here, Thompson is grudgingly given access to Thatcher's memoirs, and, as he reads the words "I first encountered Mr. Kane in 1871...," the screen dissolves from a close-up of Thatcher's longhand to a lyrical shot of a boy playing with a sled in front of Mrs. Kane's boardinghouse, somewhere in Colorado, during a snowstorm.

In the long deep-focus shot described above, Mrs. Kane (Agnes Moorehead) signs the papers that make Thatcher's bank the boy's guardian and certify his inheritance. Outside, young Kane is told of his imminent departure for the East; he pushes Thatcher (George Coulouris) into the snow with his sled. We dissolve to a medium shot of the sled, some time later, covered with drifting snow, and then into the "Merry Christmas— Happy New Year" lightning mix, which places us in New York City many years later on the occasion of Kane's twenty-first birthday.* We learn that of all the holdings in "the world's sixth largest private fortune," which Kane is about to inherit, only the financially failing daily newspaper, the *New York Inquirer,* interests him, because he thinks "it would be fun to run a newspaper." Next, in a brief but potent montage sequence, we see Thatcher increasingly outraged by the *Inquirer*'s populist, muckraking (and anti-Republican) headlines, until he finally confronts Kane in the *Inquirer* office. Their apparent antipathy for one another—both ideological and personal—is apparent, and Thatcher warns Kane of financial disaster. As if to confirm this prophecy, the following sequence, composed in depth, shows Kane, much older, signing his now

10.17 Thatcher's narrative: Thatcher meets young Charles for the first time outside his mother's boardinghouse.

10.18 Thatcher's narrative: the Kane-Thatcher confrontation in the *Inquirer* office.

10.19 Thatcher's narrative: some twenty years later, Thatcher takes the Kane papers into receivership. Bernstein (Everett Sloane) is in the foreground of the frame.

---

* An apparent inconsistency in the continuity script, since seconds earlier in Colorado we have heard Thatcher tell Mrs. Kane that the fortune is "to be administered by the bank in trust for your son ... until he reaches his twenty-fifth birthday."

vast but bankrupt newspaper chain over to Thatcher in the midst of the Depression, and here Thatcher's narrative ends.

Thompson next visits Mr. Bernstein (Everett Sloane), once Kane's general manager and right-hand man, now the aging chairman of the board of the Kane Corporation. Bernstein's narrative begins by recalling in flashback the first day at the *Inquirer* office, when he, Kane, and Kane's old college buddy Jedediah Leland (Joseph Cotten) arrived to claim the paper, in what was clearly to be a lark for all three young men. But the playfulness is mitigated a few scenes later when, in the presence of Bernstein and Leland, Kane composes a "Declaration of Principles" for his first front page.* Leland asks to keep the manuscript, comparing it facetiously to the Declaration of Independence. In this sequence, the twenty-one-year-old Kane is revealed to be the romantic idealist of the crusading populist headlines so repugnant to Thatcher, and Leland's admiration for him is unqualified. In the next sequence, Kane, Leland, and Bernstein are seen reflected in the window of the *New York Chronicle* Building, gazing at a photograph of the *Chronicle*'s top-flight staff, which, they admit, has made it the most successful newspaper in the city. The camera moves in close upon the picture and then back out to reveal the group, suddenly animated and sitting for another photograph six years later—this time to commemorate their joining the staff of the *Inquirer* en masse. A raucous banquet sequence follows, in which the dining table is photographed in extreme depth, with ice sculptures of Leland and Bernstein in the foreground at one end, Kane in the background at the other, and the new staff members occupying the space in between. During the revelry, Leland expresses to Bernstein his concern that these new men, so fresh from the *Chronicle* and its policies, will change Kane, and the scene dissolves into another one of Bernstein and Leland uncrating boxes of sculpture that Kane has been collecting on a European tour. It is revealed by Bernstein that Kane may also be "collecting" something (or someone) else. A dissolve brings us to the interior of the *Inquirer* office some time later, on the day of Kane's return from Europe. The staff attempts to present him with an engraved loving cup, and he awkwardly leaves them a notice announcing his engagement to Miss Emily Monroe Norton, the niece of the President of the United States. The staff watches from the windows of the *Inquirer* Building as Kane and his fiancée drive off in a carriage; and the second narrative draws to a close with Bernstein speculating to Thompson that maybe "Rosebud" was "something he lost."

Thompson next pays a visit to Leland, who has become a somewhat senile (but still intelligent) old man confined to a nursing home. Indeed, the dissolves into the Leland narrative flashback are among the most

---

*Both an allusion to a 1935 incident in which Hearst, threatened with a boycott of his newspapers, bought advertising space in rival papers to publish a statement of principles ("The Hearst Papers Stand for Americanism and Genuine Democracy," etc.) and an *hommage* to the Mercury Theatre's "declaration of principles" published on the front page of the *New York Times* Sunday drama section on August 29, 1937, thanks to Welles' friendship with *Times* theater critic Brooks Atkinson.

10.20 Bernstein's narrative: youthful exuberance. Leland, Kane, and Bernstein on their first day at the *Inquirer*. (Production still from a scene which doesn't appear in the finished film.)

10.21 Bernstein's narrative: youthful idealism. Kane proposes his "Declaration of Principles."

10.23 Bernstein's narrative: chorus girls enliven the celebration as Leland worries about the future.

10.22 Bernstein's narrative: depth as character. The banquet for the former *Chronicle* staff. Twin ice sculptures of Bernstein and Leland in the extreme foreground frame the real Bernstein and Leland in the middle foreground; the former *Chronicle* men stretch away from them toward the extreme background; Kane stands in the middle distance bantering with Bernstein. The shot renders in compositional terms what Leland will moments later suggest to Bernstein verbally—that Kane will become increasingly distanced from his old friends and his liberal ideals by the intervention of all the new men from the *Chronicle*.

10.24 Bernstein's narrative: Leland uncrates statues while Bernstein reads a cable from Kane hinting at a romantic involvement.

10.25 Leland's narrative: the breakfast-table sequence. (How Leland could recount these intimate details without having been present at the table is never made clear, and his ability to do so verbatim constitutes one of several violations of dramatic point of view in the film. The cinematic logic of the narratives is so perfect, however, that we scarcely notice.) Like so many others, this sequence begins and ends with the four-part in-camera dissolves used throughout the film to evoke the process of memory: first the background of a scene fades out while that of a new scene fades in, then the foreground figures fade out and the new ones fade in. This is accomplished by dimming the light banks in sections on the first set, and bringing them up in the same sequence on the second, then superimposing them photographically.

10.26 Leland's narrative: Shortly after Kane's first meeting with Susan Alexander, she sings for him in the parlor of her apartment at 185 West 74th Street, where he has set her up.

10.27 Leland's narrative: candidate Kane addresses a huge rally in Madison Square Garden on the eve of what should be a smashing victory over his opponent, Jim Gettys.

lingering in the whole film, as if to suggest the sluggishness of his memory; and not a little of the film's impact derives from this flashback technique of narration, which permits us to see all of the major characters in youth and age almost simultaneously. Like those of the other characters, Leland's narrative is chronological but not continuous. Initially, he relates the story of Kane's first marriage in a sequence which convincingly compresses the relationship's slow decline into a series of brief breakfast-table conversations linked by swish pans and overlapping sound—that is, a lightning mix. Next, in a much longer flashback, Leland describes Kane's first meeting with Susan Alexander and Kane's subsequent political ruin at the hands of his opponent, "Boss" Jim Gettys (and as a result of his own stubborn, egomaniacal refusal to withdraw from the race.) Of particular note is the scene in which Leland confronts Kane after he has lost the election. The entire sequence is shot in depth from an extremely low angle (the camera was actually placed in a hole in the floor to make the shot), so that Kane looms above both Leland and the audience, a grotesque, inflated parody of the politically powerful figure he has so desperately tried (and failed) to become. Drunk, and disillusioned with his idol, Leland insists that he be transferred to the Chicago office, and Kane reluctantly consents. The final section of Leland's narrative concerns Kane's marriage to Susan Alexander and her singing debut at the opera house he has built for her. The lengthy vertical craning shot from Susan performing abjectly on the stage to the stagehand holding his nose occurs here, as does Leland's long, deep-focus walk from the back of the *Chicago Inquirer* newsroom to the extreme foreground of the frame, where an embittered Kane finishes Leland's bad review of the performance, and summarily fires him.

Here Leland's narrative ends, and Thompson returns once more to the El Rancho nightclub. Again the camera travels up from the poster of

10.28 Leland's narrative: Kane betrayed. After the rally, Kane accompanies his wife to Susan's apartment, where she discloses the contents of a blackmail note dictated to Susan by Gettys.

10.29 Leland's narrative: from the staircase of the apartment, Kane rains empty threats on Gettys (Ray Collins) in a low-angle, deep-focus shot.

10.30 Leland's narrative: after his election defeat Kane still looms large, in a low-angle, deep-focus shot.

10.31 Leland's narrative: Susan Alexander's debut as a singer, from Leland's optical perspective.

10.32 Leland's narrative: roused from a drunken stupor, Leland is informed by Bernstein that Kane is in the next room finishing Leland's review of Susan's debut "just the way you started it."

10.33 Susan's narrative: the debut from her own optical point of view.

Susan Alexander, cranes through the sign, and dissolves through the skylight to a medium close shot of Thompson and Susan sitting at a table. Susan, who has finally agreed to talk, begins her story with a flashback to a session with her voice coach, Signor Matisti, which occurred shortly after her marriage to Kane. Susan, Matisti, and a pianist occupy the foreground of a deep-focus shot of a large, expensively decorated room. Susan's voice is so bad that Matisti refuses to continue the lesson, but at this point Kane emerges from a door in the back of the room and walks toward the group, becoming larger and larger as he moves toward the lens. When he reaches the foreground, he browbeats both Matisti and Susan into continuing the humiliating session, until a dissolve brings us to the second version of Susan's singing debut at the Chicago Municipal Opera House. We have already seen her performance from Leland's point of view in his narrative, and now we see virtually the same events from Susan's perspective as she looks out into the vast and terrifying void of the audience, invisible beyond the footlights. Her aria begins, and as she attempts to fill the huge theater with her frail voice,* Welles intercuts subjective shots of Matisti frantically coaching her with audience reaction shots (contempt, boredom, disbelief) and close-ups of an aging Kane peering grimly toward the stage. When the performance ends with very

---

* In 1973, at a symposium at the George Eastman House in Rochester, New York, Bernard Herrmann pointed out that Susan (or, rather, the singer dubbing her voice) actually *can* sing, but only modestly. The high tessitura overture to *Salammbô*, the fake opera Herrmann composed for her debut, was purposely designed to exceed the capacity of her voice and create "that terror-in-the-quicksand feeling" of a singer hopelessly out of her depth at the very outset of a long performance. (Quoted in *Sound and the Cinema*, ed. Evan William Cameron [Pleasantville, N.Y., 1980], p. 128).

10.34 Susan's narrative: shots from the montage showing her rapid rise to stardom through media hype, her collapse, and the half-empty glass of poison after her suicide attempt.

light applause, Kane claps loudly, as if to fill the hall with his solitary accolade. A dissolve brings us to Kane and Susan the morning after in a Chicago apartment, where Susan shrilly denounces Leland for his bad review—actually completed by Kane. We learn that Kane has fired Leland and sent him a check for twenty-five thousand dollars, which Leland has returned along with the pompously idealist "Declaration of Principles" that Kane had printed in his first issue of the *New York Inquirer* years before. We also learn that Susan's singing career has been imposed upon her by Kane, who insists that it continue.

There follows a rapid montage of dissolves, overlaid on the soundtrack by Susan's voice, in which *Inquirer* headlines from cities around the country acclaiming Susan Alexander's meteoric rise to stardom are lap-dissolved alternately with shots of flashing call lights, Susan onstage, Matisti in the prompter's box, and Susan receiving flowers at an ever-increasing rate until a klieg light suddenly fizzles and goes out, cutting off Susan's voice and leaving us in total darkness. Moments later, we slowly fade in on a deep-focus shot of a darkened room: in the extreme foreground is a near-empty glass of liquid and a spoon (this particular foreground object is reproduced not through deep focus but an in-camera matte shot); in the middleground Susan tosses in bed, breathing heavily; in the background a door flies open and Kane bursts into the room, barely foiling her suicide attempt. Susan is treated by a discreet doctor, and Kane promises that she needn't sing again.

Now we fade to Xanadu, some time later, where the final portion of Susan's narrative takes place. Here, in deep-focus shots that grotesquely distance them from one another across the breadth of a palatial chamber, Kane and Susan pursue a series of conversations that show them to be utterly at odds. Kane has become a cynical domestic tyrant and Susan a virtual prisoner of the estate; she passes the time endlessly working and

10.35 Susan's narrative: working puzzles interminably at Xanadu, increasingly estranged from Kane.

10.36 Susan's narrative: in the Everglades, a bloated, domineering Kane as he appears to Susan after slapping her.

10.37 Susan's narrative, conclusion: in her bedroom at Xanadu, Kane pleads with Susan to stay, but she refuses.

reworking jigsaw puzzles—a metaphor for the mystery of identity in the film. Against Susan's will, Kane arranges a spectacularly extravagant weekend "picnic" in the Everglades, where the two break openly and he slaps her. The next day at Xanadu, Susan announces to Kane that she is leaving him for good; he begs her to stay, but, realizing Kane's nearly constitutional inability to return love, she refuses and walks out the door. Susan concludes her narrative by advising Thompson to talk to Raymond the butler, who "knows where all the bodies are buried," when he visits Xanadu. The camera moves back and up, dissolves through the skylight, and pulls back through the El Rancho sign, reversing the movement of its entry.

Dissolves bring us to the gate of Xanadu and then to the interior for Raymond's brief narrative, which begins where Susan's ended. It opens

10.38 Raymond's narrative: Raymond (Paul Stewart) watches a now totally isolated Kane vanish as he stands in the doorway to Susan's room just after she has left him.

10.39 Raymond's narrative: Kane, berserk, destroying Susan's room.

10.40 Reality frame: Thompson and Raymond in the great hall.

10.41 Reality frame: a high-angle shot of the newspeople preparing to leave Xanadu; Thompson (slightly right of center) admits that his quest has failed.

10.42 Reality frame: an extreme high-angle shot of the hall, replicating a news photographer's point of view.

10.43 Reality frame: a still from the long, slow track of Kane's vast collection of "things."

not with a dissolve but with a shocking straight cut from Raymond (Paul Stewart) and Thompson on the stairs to a close shot of a shrieking cockatoo, behind which we see Susan in the middleground emerging from the same door she has begun to walk through (from the other side) at the end of her own narrative as she leaves Kane and Xanadu. Raymond's flashback then depicts the violent tantrum Kane throws as she departs: he staggers about Susan's bedroom like some mechanized madman, smashing furniture, mirrors, cosmetic jars, and all manner of trinkets and bric-a-brac until his hand finally comes to rest on the glass globe with the snow scene that we first saw at his death in the beginning of the film and later saw in Susan's apartment when they met. We hear Kane whisper "Rosebud!" and watch him shuffle slowly out of Susan's demolished room, past a gauntlet of staring servants and guests, and down a huge hall of mirrors as Raymond's narrative concludes.

Now Thompson and Raymond move down the central staircase into the great hall of Xanadu, where we see in long shot that a multitude of reporters, photographers, and workmen have assembled in a mass effort to catalog and liquidate Kane's huge collection of objects. The camera pulls back to follow the two men as they pass through the hall, discovering as it does so newspeople photographing both the treasures and trash of the Kane collection—Renaissance sculpture, Kane's mother's pot-bellied stove, Oriental statuary, the loving cup presented to Kane by the *Inquirer* staff on his return from Europe, priceless paintings, a myriad of jigsaw puzzles. Thompson's colleagues ask him whether he has discovered the meaning of "Rosebud." He replies that he hasn't and that, in any case, he no longer believes in the quest: "I don't think any word can explain a man's life. No, I guess 'Rosebud' is just a piece in a jigsaw puzzle, a missing piece."

Thompson and the others leave to catch the train back to New York, and a lap dissolve brings us to an aerial view of the hall, with the camera shooting down over the vast collection that stretches away into the distance. Another lap dissolve brings the camera a little closer to the collection as it begins to track slowly over the entire mass of crates, statues, boxes, and belongings—the ruins and relics of Kane's loveless life—which, from our aerial perspective, resemble nothing so much as the pieces of a jigsaw puzzle. The shot continues for some time until the camera reaches the humble possessions of Mrs. Kane and dollies down gracefully into an eye-level shot of her things. We see a man grab a sled and, in the next shot, throw it into a furnace at Raymond's command. We dissolve to a close-up of the burning sled and can read on it the word "Rosebud" just before the letters melt away in flames. A dissolve brings us to an exterior long shot of Xanadu at night, as we first encountered it, with smoke billowing from its chimneys. The camera tilts up to follow the smoke, dissolves to the chain link fence surrounding the estate, and pans down slowly to the "No Trespassing" sign with which the film began.

Thus, *Citizen Kane* concludes with the mystery of its central figure unresolved. The identity of "Rosebud" is clearly inadequate to account for the terrible emptiness at the heart of Kane, and of America, and is

10.44 Reality frame: the burning sled in Xanadu's incinerator.

10.45 reality frame: "Rosebud."

meant to be. Its power as a symbol of lost love and innocence lies in its very insufficiency, for the "missing piece" of the jigsaw puzzle of Kane's life, the "something he lost," turns out to be an inanimate object, and a regressive one at that. In its barrenness, "Rosebud" becomes a perfect symbol of Kane's inability to relate to people in human terms, or to love, and the ultimate emblem of his futile attempt to fill the void in himself with objects. In the film's two-hour running time we have seen Kane from seven separate perspectives—those of the newsreel, the five narrators, and the concluding reprise—and we probably have come to know more about the circumstances of his life than the man would have known himself. We know what he did and how he lived and died, but we can never know what he *meant*—perhaps, Welles seems to suggest, because, like "Rosebud," he was ultimately meaningless, or perhaps because reality itself is ambiguous and unreliable. In any case, it is the quest for meaning rather than its ultimate conclusion that makes *Citizen Kane* such a rich and important film.

Influence

In the year of its release, *Citizen Kane* was a radically experimental film—fully twenty years ahead of its time—and was widely recognized as such by American critics. But it failed at the box office less because of its experimental nature than because of an aura of fear in Hollywood created by attacks on Welles and RKO in the Hearst press. Hearst was still living, and his vassals attempted to suppress what they correctly took to be an unflattering portrait of their master. Though they were unsuccessful in preventing the film's release, the adverse publicity made it difficult for *Kane* to get bookings and advertising.* As a result, the film did poorly outside of New York City and was withdrawn from circulation until the mid-fifties, when it played the **art house** circuit and began to acquire a more sophisticated audience. Since then, *Kane* has been voted the "Best Film of All Time" in four successive international polls (Brussels, 1958; *Sight and Sound,* 1962, 1972, 1982), and there is every indication that its critical reputation continues to grow.

The influence of *Citizen Kane* upon the cinema has been enormous and nearly universal. The film's impact did not begin to be felt until after the war, when its use of low-key lighting and wide-angle lenses to achieve greater depth of field influenced the visual style of American *film noir* and its flashback narrative technique began to be imitated in more conventional films like Robert Siodmak's *The Killers* (1946). There were also imitations of Kane's structure and / or theme: George Cukor's *Keeper of the Flame* (1942), Max Ophüls' *Caught* (1949), and, after the revival, José Ferrer's *The Great Man* (1957). Directors like Britain's Carol Reed (*Odd Man Out* [1947]; *The Third Man* [1949]; *An Outcast of the Islands* [1952]—all highly Wellesian films) absorbed much of the film's visual

10.46 Reality frame: Xanadu, scattering the ashes.

---

* For the fullest account of *Kane*'s post-production and release, see Carringer, *The Making of Citizen Kane,* Chapter 5.

10.47 Welles in the studio publicity still for *Citizen Kane*.

10.48 Economy of means: the matte used for the exterior of Xanadu, painted for RKO by Mario Larinaga.

and aural texture; and, according to François Truffaut, the young French *cinéastes* who would later form the New Wave found in *Kane*'s 1946 Paris premiere the ultimate justification of their reverence for American cinema.

Kane's most important and pervasive influence, however, did not begin to be felt until the mid-fifties, after the advent of the widescreen processes, when European critics—notably Bazin—discovered in it (and, less emphatically, in Renoir's films) the model for a new film aesthetic based not upon montage but upon the "long take," or sequence shot. The primary concern of the long take aesthetic is not the *sequencing of images,* as in montage, but the *disposition of space within the frame,* or *mise-en-scène.* Welles is today regarded for all practical purposes as the founder and master of this aesthetic (in the same way that Eisenstein is regarded as the founder and master of montage), though its lineage can be traced as far back as Louis Feuillade. Finally, *Kane* was the first recognizably modern sound film; and it stood in the same relationsihp to its medium in 1941 as did *The Birth of a Nation* in 1914 and *Potemkin* in 1925—that is, it was an achievement in the development of narrative form, years in advance of its time, which significantly influenced most of the important films that followed it. *La Règle du jeu* (1939), the only close competitor for this honor, not only lacked the technology available to Welles but was deliberately conservative, or classical, in narrative form, while *Citizen Kane* is very much our contemporary in both regards. Through deep-focus photography, *Kane* attempts to technically reproduce the actual field of vision of the human eye in order to structure our visual perception of screen space by means of composition in depth. Through its innovative use of sound, it attempts to reproduce the actual aural experience of the human ear and then to manipulate our aural perception of screen space by distorting and qualifying this experience. And in both respects, though the technology is not the same, *Kane* brilliantly anticipates the contemporary cinema of widescreen photography and stereophonic sound.

Contrary to popular belief, *Kane* was anything but a financially extravagant production. The entire film—cavernous ceilinged sets and all—was made for $839,727,* with a remarkable economy of means: for many scenes Welles and Ferguson converted standing sets from other RKO pictures, and, in the Everglades sequence, they actually used jungle footage from *Son of Kong* (1933), complete with animated bats. Nevertheless, the financial failure of the film stigmatized Welles as a loser in Hollywood, and he was never again permitted to have total control of an industry production.†

WELLES AFTER *KANE*

Welles' second film, *The Magnificent Ambersons* (1942), is one of the great lost masterworks of the cinema. Like von Stroheim's *Greed* (1924) and Eisenstein's *Que viva México!* (1929–31), *The Magnificent Ambersons* was taken out of its director's hands and radically recut to satisfy perceived commercial demands. While Welles was in Brazil shooting footage for a semidocumentary entitled *It's All True*, cosponsored by RKO and the State Department, RKO cut *The Magnificent Ambersons* from 132 to 88 minutes and provided it with a totally incongruous happy ending shot by the film's production manager, Freddie Fleck.**

10.49 *The Magnificent Ambersons* (Orson Welles, 1942): the Amberson family circle in the 1890's, with the mansion in the background and the pampered young George Amberson Minafer in the foreground center.

10.50 Eugene Morgan (Joseph Cotton), inventor of horseless carriages, who knows implicitly that automobiles will "change men's minds."

* This figure includes postproduction costs. Only about 7 percent of it, or $59,207, went to the construction of *Kane*'s record number of 116 sets. By contrast, the many fewer sets of *The Magnificent Ambersons* cost $137,265, or about 13.5 percent of that film's total budget of $1,013,760.

† Welles' notoriously difficult personality also figured in his alienation from (and of) the American film industry.

** In addition, one scene was reshot by the editor, Robert Wise, and another by Mercury Theatre business manager Jack Moss. The forty-five minutes of footage cut from *The Mag-*

Flawed though it is, *The Magnificent Ambersons* remains a great and powerful film. Adapted by Welles from Booth Tarkington's novel, it parallels the turn-of-the-century decline of a proud and wealthy provincial family with the rise of the modern industrial city of Indianapolis. It is an unabashedly nostalgic film whose *mise-en-scène* is carefully calculated to create a sense of longing for the past. Although he was no Gregg Toland, cinematographer Stanley Cortez's high-contrast lighting and deep-focus photography of the interior of the Amberson mansion produced some of the most beautiful sequence shots ever to appear on the American screen. Like *Citizen Kane*, the film is constructed largely of long takes, with much spectacular tracking movement of the camera, and Welles' revolutionary use of the lightning mix and sound montage exceeds even his own earlier work. Though the 88-minute version which has survived can only hint at the epic sweep of the original, *The Magnificent Ambersons* as it stands today is a masterpiece of mood, decor, and composition in depth. It is also a remarkably intelligent and prophetic film which suggests (in 1942, and in a story set in 1905) that the quality of American life will ultimately be destroyed by the automobile and urbanization.

The Magnificent Ambersons, distributed on a double bill with a Lupe Velez comedy, was a commercial disaster. So was *Journey into Fear* (1942; released 1943), a stylish adaptation of an Eric Ambler espionage novel set in the Middle East, starring Welles and the Mercury Players, and co-directed by Welles (uncredited) and Norman Foster (1900–76). With his third box-office failure behind him, Welles was recalled from Brazil and removed from *It's All True*, which was never completed; the Mercury Players were given forty-eight hours to clear off the RKO lot. Originally entitled *Pan-American, It's All True* was to have been a four-part anthology feature shot on location in the United States, Mexico, and Brazil, with the purpose of promoting hemispheric cooperation as part of FDR's anti-Nazi "Good Neighbor Policy." (Behind the venture was Nelson Rockefeller, then Coordinator of Inter-American Affairs and a major RKO stockholder.) The project was terminated for various financial and political reasons, and the film's negative, including a Technicolor carnival sequence shot in Rio, dumped into Santa Monica Bay. This was the beginning of a long-standing antagonism between Welles and those who run the American film industry, an antagonism which was never fully resolved. Welles returned to broadcasting and the theater for the remainder of the war, though his striking performance as Rochester in *Jane Eyre* (Robert Stevenson, 1943), whose direction he seems to have influenced, did much to establish him as a popular film actor (a circumstance which would later permit him to finance his own productions when times got hard, as they frequently did).

---

nificent Ambersons is said to exist intact in the film vaults of Paramount Pictures, which bought portions of the RKO feature library in 1958. These cuts have all been documented by Charles Higham in *The Films of Orson Welles* (Berkeley, 1970), so there is at least a *possibility* of the restoration of *The Magnificent Ambersons*.

10.51   The Amberson ball, "the last of the great, long-remembered dances that everybody talked about": Eugene Morgan and Isabel Amberson (Dolores Costello).

10.52   A grown George Amberson Minafer (Tim Holt) confronts his spinster aunt (Agnes Moorehead) on the main staircase of the Amberson mansion, an emblem of splendor and the central dramatic locus of the film.

10.53   A Morgan Motors "Invincible" rides into a Currier and Ives landscape self-consciously framed by a Griffith-like iris.

10.54 In a classical Wellesian dissolve, Fanny grieves for her brother's death as townspeople comment on its significance.

10.55 George is enjoined by his bachelor Uncle Jack (Ray Collins) in deep focus.

10.56 Shortly before his death, old Major Amberson stares into the fire and remembers things past: "The sun. It must be the sun."

10.57 A Wellesian low-angle shot from *Journey into Fear* (Orson Welles and Norman Foster, 1943): Joseph Cotton.

10.58 Welles as the Nazi war criminal Franz Kindler in *The Stranger* (Orson Welles, 1945).

In 1945, Welles returned to Hollywood to direct and star in *The Stranger* (1946) for RKO on the condition that he use an existing script and a prearranged editing schedule, following both of them precisely. Welles submitted to the condition, and the resulting film is an intentional if preposterous self-parody about the tracking down of a Nazi war criminal (Welles) who is, somehow, posing as a master at a New England prep school and is married to the headmaster's daughter (Loretta Young). Technically, the film is fairly conventional, and Welles regarded it as his worst. Nevertheless, its commercial success helped him to land a job at Columbia directing his brilliant and exotic essay in *film noir, The Lady from Shanghai* (1947; released 1948), which starred Welles and his second wife, Rita Hayworth (1918–87). This bizarre film of corruption, murder, and betrayal is cast in the form of a thriller, but its theme is the moral anarchy of the postwar world. Though its intricate, rambling plot is almost impossible to follow,* cinematically the film is one of Welles' finest achievements: the haunting sequence shots of the assignation between Welles and Hayworth in the San Francisco Aquarium, the perfectly cut chase in the Chinese theater, and, most of all, the montage of the two-way shootout in the hall of mirrors which concludes the film have become textbook examples of Welles' genius. Because of the obscurity of its narrative, *The Lady from Shanghai* was a financial failure, and Welles became persona non grata in Hollywood for nearly a decade.

In order to continue making films, he was forced to exile himself to Europe, but before he left, he turned out a final Mercury Theatre production—a nightmarishly expressionistic version of *Macbeth* (1948) shot in twenty-three days on papier-mâché and cardboard sets for the B-studio, Republic Pictures. More Welles than Shakespeare, with Welles playing Macbeth, the film still manages to convey an atmosphere of brooding evil and to create a convincing portrait of a man driven by ambition beyond the bounds of the moral universe (a characteristic theme of both

* A fact abetted by Harry Cohn, president of Columbia Pictures, who held up the film's release by a year (it was originally completed in 1946) while it was re-edited, redubbed, and rescored under Welles' supervision.

10.59   *The Lady from Shanghai* (Orson Welles, 1947; released 1948): the fantastic love scene before the aquarium tanks. Welles ' as Michael O'Hara, Rita Hayworth as Elsa Bannister.

10.60   *The Lady from Shanghai:* Elsa in Chinatown.

10.61   Lost in the fun house: O'Hara plunges toward the hall of mirrors.

Shakespeare and Welles) in a culture which has only just emerged from barbarism. Originally 112 minutes long, *Macbeth* was cut to 86 minutes by its producers after Welles had left for Europe, and the soundtrack—in which the actors spoke with Scottish burrs for verisimilitude—was rerecorded to "Americanize" the accents. This recut, redubbed version was the only one known in the United States until 1979, when a UCLA archivist discovered the original among the university's collection of NTA Film Services (Republic's distributor) nitrate prints. In 1980, *Macbeth* was restored to its original form through a joint endeavor of UCLA and the Folger Shakespeare Library, complete with the Scottish-accented soundtrack and an 8-minute overture by the film's composer, Jacques Ibert. Among the most startling discoveries within the missing footage was a 10-minute-long take of continuous dramatic action, probably the first ever attempted in a theatrical film (Hitchcock's *Rope* went into production a few months after Welles' film was completed).

10.62 A studio publicity still, followed by frames from the final shoot-out in *The Lady from Shanghai:* O'Hara; Elsa; and her husband, Arthur Bannister (Everett Sloane).

10.63 *Macbeth* (Orson Welles, 1948): "The Three"—Druidic sorceresses who control Macbeth's destiny.

In moving to Europe, Welles lost the great technical and financial resources of the Hollywood studios, but he gained much in creative freedom. As a result, his European films tend to be technically imperfect and imaginatively unrestrained. The first of these was another Shakespeare adaptation, *Othello* (1952), with Welles in the title role; the film was made over a period of four years from 1948 to 1952, while Welles financed the production by acting in other people's films. With interiors shot all over Europe and exteriors shot in the ancient citadel at Mogador, Morocco, *Othello* is a film of light and openness—of wind, sun, and sea—as opposed to the brooding darkness of *Macbeth* and *The Lady from Shanghai*. Continuously recast, reshot, recut, and redubbed, *Othello* nevertheless won the Grand Prix at the Cannes Film Festival when it was finally completed in 1952.

Welles' next film, *Mr. Arkadin* (British title: *Confidential Report,* 1955), a failed attempt to remake *Citizen Kane* in European terms, was shot on an extremely low budget during an eight-month period in Spain, Germany, and France. On the French Riviera, a down-at-the-heels adventurer named Van Stratten is hired by the mysterious European business tycoon Gregory Arkadin (based on the real-life war profiteer Miles Krueger, and played by Welles) to piece together the details of his buried past. Van Stratten's Kafkaesque quest takes him all over Europe as he interviews the people who possess the secrets of Arkadin's past life, only to discover at the end of the film that he is the finger-man in a murder plot

10.64 Macbeth (Welles) confronts the murdered Banquo's ghost.

10.65 Iconographic violence: Lady Macbeth (Jeanette Nolan) tormented by blood-guilt.

10.66 Macbeth prepares for his climatic battle with Macduff.

10.68 Othello (Welles) and Desdemona (Suzanne Cloutier) on the castle ramparts.

10.69 The Moor prepares to murder his bride.

10.67 *Othello* (Orson Welles, 1952): Othello's ship arrives in Cyrus (Mogador) after an engagement with the Turks.

whereby the tycoon is systematically destroying all who can reveal his criminal past as soon as they are identified. Poorly acted, written, and recorded, with Welles himself dubbing in the voices of most of the other characters, *Mr. Arkadin* is an ambitious and intermittently brilliant failure.

No such difficulties attend *Touch of Evil* (1957), for which Welles returned to Hollywood for the first time in ten years. Universal, still a minor studio, had signed Welles and Charlton Heston to play the leads in what was to be a conventional police melodrama, and Heston insisted that Welles also direct. Welles accepted the job and was permitted to rewrite the script, turning it into a nightmarish parable of the abuse of power in a dark and sinister world. Shot against the garish background of Venice, California, *Touch of Evil* is another study of a man like Kane, Macbeth, and Arkadin, whose obsession with control causes him to transgress the laws of the moral universe. Hank Quinlan (Welles), a police captain in a seamy Mexican-American border town, has spent thirty years framing murder suspects about whose guilt he had "a hunch" in order to insure their conviction. He ultimately runs afoul of an honest Mexican narcotics agent (Heston) who exposes his practices and indirectly causes his death. The grotesque, inflated, and yet somehow sympathetic Quinlan is superbly played by Welles as a man whose once strong character has been utterly corrupted by an obsession.

As a director, Welles demanded the impossible from the cinematographer Russell Metty (*The Stranger,* 1946) and got it. The film opens with

10.70 Welles in *Mr. Arkadin* (Orson Welles, 1955).

10.71 From the conclusion of the lengthy tracking shot which opens *Touch of Evil* (Orson Welles, 1957): Charlton Heston, Janet Leigh.

10.72 Welles as Hank Quinlan in *Touch of Evil*.

10.73 Quinlan with his once-devoted henchman, Lieutenant Menzies (Joseph Calleia).

a continuous moving crane shot (unfortunately obscured in the release print by the credits), which begins with a close-up of a time bomb and ends with the explosion of the device in a car nearly two and a half minutes later, making it one of the longest unbroken tracking shots attempted to date. Later, Metty was required to track his camera from the exterior of a building through a lobby and into a crowded elevator, and then ride up five floors to shoot Heston greeting the occupants as the doors slide open from within. There is also significant use of deep-focus photography and sound montage for the first time since *The Lady from Shanghai* (1947). Like Welles' previous films, *Touch of Evil* was shot in high-contrast black and white. Ignored in every country but France (where it won the Cannes Grand Prix) in the year of its release, *Touch of Evil* is today considered a Welles masterpiece whose technical brilliance and thematic depth bring it close to the stature of *Kane*. When it was released, the film was cut from 108 to 95 minutes under the supervision of Universal postproduction head Ernest Nims to make its editing continuity easier for contemporary audiences to follow.* In 1976, the deleted footage was restored by Universal, and Welles' original version was released for distribution in 16mm and, subsequently, on video cassette. The restoration resolves certain obscurities of dialogue in the 1957 version and provides for a fuller characterization of the film's protagonists.

But the film's financial failure in 1958 confirmed Welles' status as a pariah in Hollywood; he returned to Europe, where French producers offered him an opportunity to direct a film based on a major literary work of his choice. He selected Kafka's novel *The Trial*, published in 1925. Despite budgeting problems, *The Trial* (1962) became the only one

---

* As Nims would later remark: "He [Welles] was ahead of his time. He was making those *quick* cuts—in the middle of a scene you cut to another scene and then come back and finish the scene and then cut to the last half of the other scene" (quoted in Barbara Leaming, *Orson Welles*, p. 428). Specifically, Nims recut the film's first five reels to conform to conventional continuity practice, deleted certain auditory shock effects Welles had devised for the sound track, and added several inserts shot by a Universal contract director—apparently either Harry Keller (b. 1915) or Jack Arnold. See John Belton, "A New Map of the Labyrinth: The Unretouched *Touch of Evil*," *Movietone News*, no. 47 (January 21, 1976): 1–9, and no. 48 (February 29, 1976): 23.

of his films since *Kane* over which Welles exercised total control. His customary visual complexity notwithstanding, the results are disappointing. Shot in black-and-white in the streets of Zagreb, Yugoslavia, and in the fantastic Gare d'Orsay in Paris, the film finally fails to evoke the antiseptic modern hell of Kafka's novel, perhaps because of some disparity between the world views of the two artists.

Welles' next European film and his last completed feature, *Chimes at Midnight* (British title: *Falstaff,* 1966), is widely regarded as a masterpiece. Returning to an idea that he had first tried in his 1938 Theater Guild production *Five Kings,* Welles assembled all the Falstaff parts from *Henry IV, Parts I* and *II, The Merry Wives of Windsor,* and *Henry V,* and linked them together with a narration from Holinshed's *Chronicles* (the medieval source of Shakespeare's history plays) to create a portrait of the character as his privileged friendship with Prince Hal passes gradually from affection to bitterness, disillusionment, and decay. Like *Citizen Kane,* it is film about decline and loss, and like *The Magnificent Ambersons,* it is full of nostalgia for a vanished past; but it is as much the work of an older man as *Kane* and *The Magnificent Ambersons* are the work of a younger one. Shot in Spain (for financial reasons) over a period of several years, *Chimes at Midnight* is superbly photographed and acted, with Welles at his best in the title role. Its moving crane shots have been widely praised, and the lengthy montage sequence depicting the Battle of Shrewsbury has been favorably compared to Eisenstein's Odessa Steps sequence in *Potemkin* (1925) and the Battle on the Ice in *Alexander Nevski* (1938). Yet *Chimes at Midnight* is anything but technically extravagant. It is rather a quiet, elegiac, and dignified film whose restrained style and austere black-and-white photography correspond perfectly with its sober themes of human frailty, mortality, and decay.

It is no longer possible—as it was, perhaps, even several years ago—to speak of Orson Welles as a director important for a single, if monumental and awe-inspiring, film. Welles produced five masterpieces—*Citizen Kane, The Magnificent Ambersons, The Lady from Shanghai, Touch of Evil,* and *Chimes at Midnight*—and his Shakespearean films, extravagant and eccentric as they sometimes are, represent major contributions to the genre. In *Citizen Kane* he gave us the first modern sound film and effectively pioneered the aesthetic of the long take, or composition in depth. All of his films of the forties significantly anticipated the contemporary cinema of widescreen photography and stereophonic sound. But technological wizardry notwithstanding, Welles produced a body of work which deserves to be ranked with the great narrative art of our century. Welles was a traditional moralist whose major themes were characteristically those of classical Western literature: the corrupting nature of ambition; the disparity between social and psychological reality; the destructive power of self-delusion, appetite, and obsession; and the importance of a sense of the past. Confirming these thematic concerns was his intermittent work from 1955 until his death in 1985 on a version of *Don Quixote* set in modern times (a more or less complete work print of which is currently being restored by Welles' companion and collaborator Oja Kodar). Stylistically, however, Welles was always an innovator and a radical exper-

10.74 *The Trial* (Orson Welles, 1962): Anthony Perkins as "K."

10.75 Welles as Falstaff in *Chimes at Midnight* (Orson Welles, 1966).

10.76 *Chimes at Midnight:* Prince Hal (Keith Baxter) with Falstaff before his father's castle.

10.77 *Chimes at Midnight:* from the Battle of Shrewsbury sequence.

10.78 *The Immortal Story* (Orson Welles, 1968): Jeanne Moreau as Virginie.

10.79 Orson Welles playing himself in *F for Fake* (1976).

imenter—an authentic American expressionist with a decidedly baroque sense of form which has profoundly influenced the course of Western cinema.

In his latter years, he made several attempts to become an active part of that cinema again, in collaboration with Kodar, as his principal script-writer and actress, and the cinematographer Gary Graver, most notably in the still unreleased *The Other Side of the Wind*. This three-hour color film, which Welles described as "ninety-six-percent finished" in 1979, stars John Huston as a Welles-like director contemplating his career in flashback at the end of his life. In a tribute presented to him by the American Film Institute in 1975, Welles showed some provocative footage from it in an unsuccessful attempt to raise money for its completion. Between 1978 and 1985, he worked on *The Dreamers*, a romantic adventure story based upon two of Isak Dinesen's *Gothic Tales,* but only a few scenes of it were actually shot.

When he died, Welles was working on a long-cherished project—his own adaptation of *King Lear* in video, with himself in the title role and Kodar as Cordelia—which also remained unfinished. Welles' death on October 10, l985, was mourned around the world, appropriately, as the passing of a twentieth-century American genius. It is difficult to know who or what to blame for the wasteful attenuation of his later career, and it is probably better not to try. But surely Welles would have appreciated the irony in the fact that only his death would make a whole generation of Americans aware that its favorite public fat man and talk-show raconteur was the single most important architect of the modern film. As Jean-Luc Godard observed of him at the height of the French New Wave, "Everyone will always owe him everything."*

---

* Quoted in Michel Ciment, "Les Enfants terrible," *American Film* (December 1984): 42.

Wartime and Postwar Cinema: Italy and America, 1940–1951

THE EFFECTS OF WAR

World War II left the national cinemas of Western Europe in a state of economic, physical, and psychological paralysis. Cinema is an industry, and industries are dependent for their survival upon the stability of the economic systems in which they function. The Nazis had destroyed the shaky prewar economy of Europe and set up another in its place. That in turn had been destroyed by the Allied victory in the spring of 1945. Until the Marshall Plan for the economic rehabilitation of Europe began to take effect in 1948–49, national industries of all types found it impossible to resume production on a large scale. Furthermore, the physical devastation wreaked upon the European film industries by the war was immense. In England, air raids destroyed 330 film theaters, or close to 25 percent of the total number. Germany lost nearly 60 percent of its film-production facilities in the firebombing of Berlin. And in France, which had managed to maintain fairly high standards of film production during the German Occupation, the industry was reduced to a state of chaos by Allied bombardment of Paris and street fighting during the liberation of the city in August 1944. In all of Europe, only the Italian film industry was left with its production facilities reasonably intact, a result of Italy's early surrender and the unique circumstances of its liberation.

More devastating to the cinema than either economic instability or physical destruction of facilities, however, was the state of psychological and moral collapse in which Europe found itself immediately following the Nazi surrender. It is estimated that World War II killed over 48 million people in Europe and created more than 21 million refugees. Whole urban districts, with nearly their entire civilian populations, had been wiped out in minutes by firebombing, and the artifacts of centuries-old civilizations reduced to rubble. Indeed, at least 35 percent of all permanent dwellings in Western Europe were destroyed by the war. Liberation was joyful when it came, but the experience of Nazi barbarism left a dark imprint on the European consciousness; and the revelation of the true extent of Nazi atrocities in the occupied territories was nothing less than shattering. In one large province of the Soviet Union, for example, 40 percent of the inhabitants had been deported to death camps, and Poland had lost 25 percent of its entire population to the camps. The German-born sociologist and philosopher Theodor Adorno, himself a refugee from Hitler, was moved to state that there could be "no poetry after Auschwitz,"* and indeed, for a while there could not. The human spirit rekindles quickly, however—too quickly, some have felt, given the magnitude of this particular horror. Economies, on the other hand, most frequently do not, and until the benefits of the Marshall Plan began to be felt, the European national cinemas, except for that of Italy, were unable to approach anything like their prewar levels of production.† In Italy, the revitalization of the national cinema was set in motion even before the war had ended.

ITALY

The Italian Cinema Before Neorealism

When the Fascists, under Benito Mussolini, seized power in 1922, Italian cinema had already fallen far from the position of international leadership it held during the early silent period (see Chapter 2). Epic spectacles like Enrico Guazzoni's world-famous *Quo vadis?* (1913) and Giovanni Pastrone's *Cabiria* (1914) were a thing of the past; and by the time sound arrived in 1930, Italian studios were producing only a handful of features per year, the majority of which were either stagily photographed operas or *"telefono bianco"* ("white telephone") films—trivial romantic comedies set in blatantly artificial studio surroundings (see Chapter 9). But the Fascists, aware of cinema's immense potential for propaganda, were committed to reviving the Italian industry and putting it in the service of the state.

A former Marxist, Mussolini was particularly impressed by the Soviet achievement in blending film and politics (he even paraphrased Lenin in calling cinema *"l'arma più forte"*—"the strongest weapon" of the age), and he sought to reorganize the Italian industry along Soviet lines (see Chapter 5). In 1924 Mussolini founded L'Unione Cinematografica Edu-

---

* The streamlined mass-extermination complex built by the Nazis in eastern Poland, where over 1 million people died in two years.

† In the United States, by contrast, 1946 was the most profitable year in the history of Hollywood before 1973. Box office receipts exceeded 1.7 billion dollars, no small part of which derived from the exhibition of American films in Europe (people *will* have movies—in the worst of times probably more than in the best). In fact, it is arguable that the regeneration of the European national cinemas was substantially and deliberately retarded by a massive influx of American films in the immediate postwar period. However, the superior craftsmanship of Hollywood productions may have inspired the European cinemas to new levels of technical competence when their renewal finally began.

cativa (LUCE), a state film service to produce documentaries and newsreels about his regime for the purpose of "civil and national education." Then, gradually but deliberately, he cultivated financial relations with the private sector, culminating in the creation of the Ente Nazionale Industrie Cinematografiche (ENIC) in 1934 as a centralized bureaucracy to control the distribution and exhibition of all films within the Fascist state. The following year, Mussolini ordered the establishment of a national film school (unprecedented outside of the Soviet Union), the Centro Sperimentale della Cinematografia, and authorized the construction of the vast **Cinecittà** studios in Rome, whose size and technical facilities rivaled those of UFA-Neubabelsberg, with sixteen soundstages, 600,000 square meters for exteriors, and corridor upon corridor of dressing rooms.* To emphasize the importance of film to his regime, Mussolini personally inaugurated the facility in 1937—on April 21, the mythical date of the founding of Rome—and within a year Cinecittà had released more than eighty films, doubling the rate of Italian film production.

Meanwhile, the Centro Sperimentale, under the direction of the filmmaker Luigi Chiarini (1900–75), a covert Marxist, had attracted such promising students as Roberto Rossellini, Luigi Zampa, Pietro Germi, Giuseppe De Santis, and Michelangelo Antonioni—all to become major directors of the postwar cinema—and had begun to publish its own theoretical journal, *Bianco e nero (Black and White),* which remains Italy's premier academic film journal to this day. A rival periodical called *Cinema* was soon founded under the editorship of Vittorio Mussolini, son of *Il Duce. Cinema* published translations of the major theoretical writings of Eisenstein, Pudovkin, and Béla Balázs (see Chapters 5 and 16), as well as contributions from native talents like the young Luchino Visconti. Finally, to further upgrade and increase production Mussolini attempted to establish a wholly protected industry by imposing strict import quotas on foreign films; and when Italy entered the war in 1940, he banned American films altogether. (Previously, he had contented himself with rather childishly maligning American films through "imperial edict." In 1933, for example, Italian audiences had been forbidden to laugh at the Marx Brothers in *Duck Soup,* but the film itself was not banned.) During the first year of the war Italian production reached the all-time high of eighty-six films per annum.

The cinema subsidized by Mussolini and his Fascist state was an enormous popular success. As Ted Perry has written, "the fifteen years from the coming of sound to the end of Mussolini's reign provided . . . an entertainment industry that rivaled Hollywood in the charm and sophistication of its narratives, its acting and direction." According to James Hay, moreover, the films produced by this industry helped form Italy's first truly national *cultura popolare* (see *Popular Film Culture in Fascist Italy: The Passing of the Rex* [Bloomington: Indiana University Press,

---

*Both the Centro Sperimentale and Cinecittà are in operation today. After the VGIK in Moscow (founded 1919), the Centro is the oldest state film school in the world; and Cinecittà, its wartime bombing damage repaired, is still the largest studio in Europe.

11.1 Calligraphism: Renato Castellani's *Un colpo di pistola* (1941). Fosco Giachetti, Massimo Serato.

1987]). This cinema's most salient artistic feature was the style neorealist film critic and director Giuseppe De Santis (b. 1917) designated as calligraphism—a sort of decorative formalism which manifested itself in meticulously photographed adaptations of late-nineteenth-century and early-twentieth-century fiction. Among the more prominent works of calligraphism were Luigi Chiarini's adaptation of *Via delle Cinque Lune* (*Five Moons Street*, 1941), a story by the Neapolitan realist Matilde Serao; Mario Soldati's (b. 1906) *Piccolo mondo antico* (*Little Old-Fashioned World*, 1941), a nineteenth-century tale of passion adapted from the novel by Antonio Fogazzaro; Renato Castellani's *Un colpo di pistola* (*A Pistol Shot*, 1942), a version of Pushkin's 1831 short story *The Shot*; and Alberto Lattuada's *Giacomo l'idealista* (*Jacob, the Idealist*, 1943), based on a turn-of-the-century melodrama by the Lombard novelist Emilio De Marchi. In many ways the antithesis of neorealism, calligraphism nevertheless provided a training ground for the scriptwriters, technicians, performers, and other creative personnel associated with it. So, too—ironically—did the Fascist propaganda documentary of the period.

Francesco De Robertis (1902–59), as head of the film section of the naval ministry, was responsible for several semidocumentary feature films which anticipated neorealism in their use of nonprofessional actors, on-location shooting, and a photographic style similar to that of contemporary newsreels. In *Uomini sul fondo* (*Men on the Bottom*; English title: *S.O.S. Submarine*), which he directed as his first feature in 1941, De Robertis recreated the undersea rescue of a disabled Italian submarine so authentically that critics all over the country took note. In the same year, he supervised the production of *La nave bianca* (*The White Ship*), which realistically reconstructed life aboard an Italian hospital ship by combining staged scenes with actual footage and gave Roberto Rossellini (1906–77) his first job directing a feature film. The influence of De Robertis was mainly technical, however, for he was a devout Fascist whose world view was in no way compatible with the liberal humanism which neorealism came to espouse. (Yet Rossellini went on to make two more films under his tutelage—*Un pilota ritorna* [*A Pilot Returns*, 1942; scripted in part by Antonioni and Vittorio Mussolini] and *L'uomo dalla croce* [*The Man of the Cross*, 1943]—which, together with *La nave bianca*, form a sort of Fascist trilogy.)

More attuned to neorealism conceptually was the middle-class comedy of manners as practiced by Alessandro Blasetti (b. 1900) in *Quattro passi fra le nuvole* (*Four Steps in the Clouds*, 1942) and Vittorio De Sica in *I bambini ci guardano* (*The Children Are Watching Us*, 1942). Although both films are elaborations of an older genre perfected by Mario Camerini (1895–1981) in the thirties, and are slightly flawed by sentimentality, they are notable for their studied social observation and their realistic scripts by the Marxist screenwriter Cesare Zavattini (1902–89), who was shortly to become to neorealism what Carl Mayer had been to the *Kammerspielfilm*—its chief ideological spokesman and major scenarist.*

DE ROBERTIS

---

* Zavattini continued to write screenplays long after neorealism's decline (for example, *Un cuore semplice* [*A Simple Heart*—from Flaubert, directed by Giorgio Ferrara, 1978]; *Liga-*

The Foundations of Neorealism

Zavattini was the theoretical founder of neorealism. In 1942 he called for a new kind of Italian film—one that would abolish contrived plots, do away with professional actors, and take to the streets for its material in order to establish direct contact with contemporary social reality. Plot was inauthentic, according to Zavattini, because it imposed an artificial structure on "everyday life," and professional actors simply compounded the falsehood since "to want one person to play another implies the calculated plot." It was precisely the dignity and sacredness of the everyday life of ordinary people, so alien to the heroic ideal of Fascism, which Zavattini demanded that the new realism capture. As he was to write later of the emergence of neorealism: "The reality buried under the myths slowly reflowered. The cinema began its creation of the world. Here was a tree; here, an old man; here, a house; here, a man eating, a man sleeping, a man crying. . . . The cinema . . . should accept, unconditionally, what is contemporary. *Today, today, today.*"

In early 1943, Umberto Barbaro (1902–59), an influential critic and lecturer at the Centro Sperimentale, published an article that attacked the reactionary conventions of the Italian film and invoked the term "neorealism" to refer to what was lacking. Barbaro's specific allusion was to French poetic realism—the thirties cinema of Renoir, Carné, Duvivier, and Clair—but the term was soon picked up by Giuseppe De Santis and other progressive critics at *Bianco e nero* and *Cinema* to designate the revolutionary agitation for a popular and realistic national cinema which was soon to sweep the Italian film schools, cinema clubs, and critical journals. The influences on the young men demanding a "new realism" were many and varied. For one thing, most of them were clandestine Marxists in addition to being professionally trained film critics, and the "realism" they wished to renew was quite specifically the Soviet expressive realism of Eisenstein, Pudovkin, and Dovzhenko. This influence was less technical than ideological, however, and the stylistic resemblances between Italian neorealism and Soviet expressive realism, although they do exist, are slight.

A more direct and practical influence on the neorealist movement was French poetic realism, which had achieved international preeminence by 1939. In addition to being technically brilliant, the films of poetic realism espoused a kind of socialist humanism which Italians found at least as appealing as the strident Soviet Marxism. *Toni* (1934), Jean Renoir's drama of immigrant Italian laborers shot on location in the south of France with nonprofessional actors, provided an important structural model. Furthermore, several major directors of the neorealist cinema actually served their apprenticeships under French filmmakers. Luchino Visconti (1906–76), for example, had been an assistant on Renoir's *Une Partie de campagne* (1936; released 1946), as well as a scriptwriter for the version of *La Tosca* (1940) begun by Renoir and completed by Carl

bue [directed by Salvatore Nocita, 1978]; and *La veritaaa'* [*The Truuuth*, 1982–directed by Zavattini at age 80]).

Koch (see Chapter 9); and Michelangelo Antonioni (see p. 627) had worked as an assistant to Marcel Carné on *Les visiteurs du soir* (1942). Most significant of all, perhaps, is the fact that the cinema of poetic realism represented aesthetic and intellectual freedom to young Italian artists trapped in the hothouse atmosphere of the Fascist studios. Many, like Rossellini, had begun their careers as government loyalists but turned bitterly against the regime as they were forced to make compromise after compromise to Fascist policy and public taste. In fact, as Roy Armes has suggested, by straitjacketing Italy's film artists Fascism probably contributed to the rise of neorealism more than did any other single historical force.

Indeed, Italian Fascism had always contained the seeds of its own destruction, and in 1943 political and historical events conspired to liberate the forces of neorealism from the journal pages. The Allies invaded Sicily in July, and Mussolini was turned out of office by his own party. An armistice was then signed with the Allies, whose forces landed on the mainland and began their sweep up the peninsula. To add to the confusion, the new Italian government, under Marshal Badoglio, declared war on Germany, while in the north of Italy Mussolini was installed as the head of a Nazi puppet state called the Salò Republic. Partisan fighting erupted everywhere, the Nazis occupied Rome, and the Allied movement northward was slowed. Rome did not fall until June 1944, and even then it took another year of heavy fighting to effect the Germans' unconditional surrender. But in the midst of this chaos, Fascist control of the Italian film studios relaxed somewhat, and the armistice of 1943 had no sooner been signed than neorealism was heralded by the release of Luchino Visconti's grim tale of passion and murder in modern Italy, *Ossessione* (*Obsession*).

Ossessione was based (without permission) on the luridly poetic thriller *The Postman Always Rings Twice* by the American novelist James M. Cain; it could not be shown outside of Italy until 1976 because it infringed the author's copyright.* The novel is a violent tale of sexual obsession and corruption in which a young drifter contracts an affair with the sensual wife of the owner of a roadside cafe. Together they murder the husband for his insurance money, but they are later trapped in their own deceptions. Visconti retained the melodramatic plot and brutal characters but transferred the setting to the contemporary Italian countryside near Ferrara, whose bleakness, provinciality, and poverty he captured with great fidelity. In 1948, the coscenarist (with Giuseppe De Santis) of *Ossessione*, Angelo Pietrangeli, offered this description of the film's visual texture: "Ferrara, its squares, its gray and deserted streets; Ancona and

---

* It was Renoir who brought *The Postman Always Rings Twice* to Visconti's attention and gave him a French typescript of the book during the shooting of *Une partie de campagne* in 1936. Appropriately, the American version of Cain's novel, directed by Tay Garnett in 1946, is one of the great classics of *film noir*, a type of film discussed later in this chapter. There is also a 1937 French version directed by Pierre Chenal, entitled *Le Dernier tournant*, but Visconti had not seen it at the time he directed *Ossessione*. A second American version of the novel was directed by Bob Rafelson in 1980.

its San Ciriaco Fair; the Po and its sandy banks; a landscape streaked with a rubble of cars and men along the network of highways. Against this backdrop are silhouetted the wandering merchants, mechanics, prostitutes and inn boys . . . beset by violent proletarian love affairs, primitive anger, and the sins that the flesh is heir to."

Clearly, the technical virtuosity of *Ossessione* would have made it an important film under any circumstances, but coming as it did upon the heels of the neorealist manifestoes of Zavattini and Barbaro, it seemed to validate their notion that a new Italian cinema was about to be born—one which would take its cameras out of the studios and into the streets and countryside to probe the lives of ordinary men and women in relation to their environment. Thus, *Ossessione* can be said to have provided the blueprint for neorealism. It anticipated some of the movement's themes and styles (popular setting, realistic treatment, social content), though lacking the neorealist political commitment and historical perspective. But, unfortunately, political and economic circumstances intervened to make the film less immediately influential than it might have been. The Fascist censors still controlled the industry, and though they had originally approved the project, they were shocked at the harsh portrait of Italian provincial life Visconti had painted. Their response was to ban the film and subsequently release it in a version cut to less than half its original length. Visconti reconstructed *Ossessione* after the war, but even then the film could not be shown abroad due to its copyright violation; for this reason, the first Italian neorealist film to reach the other countries of the West was Roberto Rossellini's *Roma, città aperta* (*Rome, Open City*, 1945).

11.2 *Ossessione* (Luchino Visconti, 1943): Giovanna (Clara Calamai) in her kitchen.

11.3 *Ossessione:* character as fate.

Neorealism: Major Figures and Films

A remarkable film of Italian resistance and Nazi reprisal, *Roma, città aperta*, was based upon events that had occurred in Rome in the winter of 1943–44, when the Germans declared that the city was "open."* It tells the story of a Communist underground leader who brings death to himself and his friends in a vain but heroic attempt to outlast a Gestapo manhunt. The film was planned in the midst of the Nazi occupation by Rossellini and his associates (Sergio Amidei, Anna Magnani, Aldo Fabrizi, and Federico Fellini—several of whom were actively involved in the Resistance at the time). Shooting began only weeks after Rome's liberation. Because Cinecittà had been damaged by Allied bombing, only two studio sets were used in the entire film, and the rest was shot on location in the streets of Rome, where the events it dramatized had actually taken place. In the interest of speed, Rossellini shot *Roma, città aperta* silent and dubbed in the actors' voices after it was edited. Moreover, because his film stock was of relatively low quality (Rossellini having bought it

---

* An "open city" is one that is not to be fought through or bombed, according to international rules of war, but in this case, the Nazis declaration was grimly ironic, since they themselves had imposed brutal martial law on Rome during their occupation of the city.

11.4 *Roma, città aperta* (Roberto Rossellini, 1945): Pina (Anna Magnani) murdered by the S.S.

11.5 *Roma, città aperta:* the tortured Communist (Marcello Pagliero).

piecemeal from street photographers and spliced it onto motion picture reels), the finished film had the look of a contemporary newsreel. Indeed, many who saw *Roma, città aperta* when it was first released in 1945 thought that they were watching a record of actual events unfolding before the cameras and were astonished that Rossellini could have been permitted to reveal so much of Nazi brutality with the Germans still in Rome. They were equally amazed at the intelligence, integrity, and technical ingenuity of the film because, as far as international audiences were aware, these qualities had been absent from the Italian cinema since 1922, when the Fascists came to power.

For all of these reasons, and because it has an appealing melodramatic plot line, *Roma, città aperta* enjoyed immense success in almost every country in the Western world. In the United States alone its distributors grossed over half a million dollars, and in Italy it was the most profitable film since the outbreak of the war. Furthermore, *Roma, città aperta* won major prizes in a number of international film festivals, including the Grand Prix at Cannes in 1946, and critical acclaim for it was very nearly universal. The American critic James Agee, for example, was so awed by the film that he publicly refused to review it. Only in Italy was *Roma, città aperta* coldly received by the established critics, and this was less for aesthetic reasons than for ideological and political ones. It is true, of course, that the film has a number of structural flaws and that these relate at least as much to Rossellini's limitations as a director as to the difficult conditions under which it was made; but in spite of these defects, *Roma, città aperta* is one of those watershed films, like *The Birth of a Nation, Das Kabinett des Dr. Caligari, Potemkin,* and *Citizen Kane,* that changed the entire course of Western cinema. Rossellini's film became the paradigm for Italian neorealism and set the standard for everything that succeeded it—in its achievement of a documentary surface through on-location shooting and post-synchronization of sound,* its mixture of professional performers (Magnani and Fabrizi) and nonprofessionals, its references to contemporary national experience (or at least very recent national history), its social commitment and humanistic point of view, and, above all, what Penelope Houston has called its "driving urge" to rehabilitate the national reputation. It could be argued that its primacy is the result of a historical accident, given the suppression of *Ossessione,* but that primacy itself is indisputable.

Rossellini's next two films confirmed his mastery of the neorealist mode and extended his commitment to his country's recent past. *Paisà* (*Paisan,* 1946), like its predecessor, was written by Rossellini, Amidei, and Fellini. It recounts six unrelated episodes in the liberation of Italy, from the American landing in Sicily in 1943 to the Nazi evacuation of the Po Valley in 1945, and was shot on location all over the country: in Sicily, Naples, Rome, Florence, and the Po delta. Unlike *Roma, città aperta, Paisà* was a rather costly venture (in fact, the most expensive Italian film of 1946). Nevertheless, Rossellini once again combined professional and nonprofessional actors—using an American black man who was not an

---

* Postsynchronization, or postdubbing, has been standard Italian practice since the war.

11.6 Three episodes from Rossellini's *Paisà* (1946): Sicily, Naples, the Po Valley.

actor to play a GI along with people from the district in which the director happened to be shooting—and he improvised part of his script to create what James Agee called in a contemporary review of *Paisà* "the illusion of the present tense." Like *Roma, città aperta*, the film contains flaws of structure (which Agee, incidentally, had recovered sufficiently from the first film to point out), but in its authentic representation of common people caught up in the madness and horror of war, *Paisà* validates the broadly humanistic world view of neorealism and confirms the effectiveness of its improvisatory techniques.*

---

*Seeing *Paisà* for the first time had a formative influence on numerous future directors, including Ermanno Olmi, Paolo and Vittorio Taviani, and Gillo Pontecorvo, by their own accounts (see Chapter 15). It was also the experience which convinced Ingrid Bergman (1915–81), then at the height of her popularity in Hollywood, to make a film with Rossellini—an impulse that resulted in an international scandal when she left her husband and infant daughter to marry the director and bear him three children. The couple was subjected to a well-coordinated hate campaign in the United States, and Bergman was blacklisted by Hollywood until the late fifties. Bergman starred in five much-maligned features for the Italian director, from *Stromboli* (1949) through *La Paura* (*Fear*, 1954–55).

11.7 Rossellini's *Germania, anno zero* (1947): Edmund Moeschke as the boy.

Rossellini's next film, the final one in what is often called his "war trilogy," was *Germania, anno zero* (*Germany, Year Zero,* 1947). Shot on location in bombed-out Berlin and acted entirely by nonprofessionals, the film is an attempt to probe the social roots of Fascism through the rather contrived story of a young German boy corrupted by Nazism who murders his bedridden father and commits suicide in the wake of the German defeat. It is generally agreed that *Germania, anno zero* represents a personal failure for Rossellini (who, in addition to directing, wrote the script), but its specifically neorealistic elements have been widely praised. For example, the long, nearly wordless concluding sequence in which the boy wanders through a gutted Berlin toward his personal *Götterdämmerung* is frequently cited as one of the glories of Italian neorealist cinema. In the end, however, that cinema proved nontransplantable in alien soil, and the relative failure of *Germania, anno zero*—both commercially and critically—foreshadowed the larger failure of the neorealist movement to transcend its specific social and historical contexts. Rossellini did not attempt another film in the neorealist vein, but he outlasted the movement to become a major figure in world cinema.*

The second major director of the Italian neorealist movement, and one who worked within it until its demise in the fifties, was Vittorio De Sica

11.8 Rossellini's documentary-like *La prise de pouvoir par Louis XIV* (1966).

* Rossellini's major films after 1947 were *Il miracolo* (*The Miracle,* 1948; released in the United States in 1950 and banned in New York State for "sacrilege," the film was exonerated in a landmark U.S. Supreme Court decision in 1952 that extended First Amendment protection to motion pictures as a form of expression, for the first time in history); *Stromboli, terra di Dio* (*Stromboli, Land of God;* released in the United States as *Stromboli,* with twenty minutes cut by the distributor, RKO); *Francesco, giullare di Dio* (*Francis, God's Jester;* released in America as *The Flowers of St. Francis,* 1950); *Europa '51* (1952); *Viaggio in Italia* (*Voyage to Italy;* released in the United States as *Strangers,* 1953); the influential semidocumentary *India* (1958); *Il generale Della Rovere* (*General Della Rovere,* 1959; starring Vittorio De Sica); *Viva Italia!* (1960, an epic of the Risorgimento); *Vanina Vanini* (*The Betrayer,* 1961); *La prise de pouvoir par Louis XIV* (*The Rise of Louis XIV,* 1966; made for French television, ORTF, but theatrically distributed abroad); *Atti degli apostoli* (*Acts of the Apostles,* 1969; made for Italian television, RAI, ORTF, and TVE, Madrid); *Socrate* (*Socrates,* 1970, made for RAI, ORTF, and TVE); *Augustino d'Ippona* (*St. Augustine of Hippo,* 1972; made for RAI); *Blaise Pascal* (1972; made for RAI); *L'Età di Cosimo de'Medici* (*The Age of the Medici,* 1972; RAI); *Cartesius* (*Descartes,* 1974; RAI, ORTF); and *Il Messia* (*The Messiah,* 1975; independently produced for television). When he died on June 3, 1977, Rossellini was planning a biography of Karl Marx, for which he had just completed the script. In his films of the fifties, Rossellini had become a master of the long take and the Pancinor zoom lens (which he invented and operated himself), and he exercised an enormous influence on the young directors of the French New Wave and *cinéma vérité* movements (see Chapter 13), which was appropriate, given his own reverence for the French masters of the thirties. His later docudramas for RAI and ORTF helped to break down the barriers between cinema and television—he was, in fact, the first major film director to take the new medium seriously. Furthermore, as Andrew Sarris has remarked, Rossellini's biographical films are the most impressive in the history of the cinema. But despite the director's claim of neutrality, his vision of history was highly deterministic, because he always believed in a given human nature which did not change according to historical era. For this reason, his historical films are still the subject of intense critical and ideological controversy. The definitive study of Rossellini's work—a staggering eighty-four hours of screen time in a forty-year career—is Peter Brunette's exhaustively researched *Roberto Rossellini* (New York: Oxford University Press, 1987).

(1901–74). A matinee idol during the "white telephone" era of the thirties, De Sica began his directing career near the end of that decade with a number of conventional middle-class comedies, at least one of which (*I bambini ci guardano*, 1942), anticipates the neorealist concern with social problems. This film began De Sica's collaboration and lifelong friendship with the scriptwriter and theoretician of neorealism, Cesare Zavattini. Though De Sica's sensibility was essentially comic, he apparently fell under the influence of Zavattini's ideas sometime during the war, for in 1946 the two men began a series of films concentrating on the urban problems of postwar Italy.

Sciuscià (*Shoeshine*, 1946), shot in three months under primitive conditions, is a bleak tale of the corruption of innocence in Nazi-occupied Rome. Two young shoeshine boys who are best friends become involved in a black-market deal, in an effort to buy a horse. They are caught and sent to prison, where one inadvertently betrays the other and is later killed by him in revenge. Like *Roma, città aperta*, *Sciuscià* was not well received in Italy but proved highly successful in the United States, where it won a special Academy Award in 1947.* De Sica's next film with Zavattini, *Ladri di biciclette* (*Bicycle Thieves* / *The Bicycle Thief*, 1948), received even greater international acclaim and is thought by some critics to be the most important film of the postwar era. In it, a family man who has been out of work for almost two years (unemployment in postwar Italy had reached 22 percent by 1948) finds a job as a municipal bill poster, for which he must provide his own transportation. He pawns the family's sheets in order to buy a bicycle, which is stolen his first day out. For the rest of the film he and his little boy search in vain for the thief;

11.9 Vittorio De Sica's *Sciuscià* (1946): Rinaldo Smordoni and Franco Interlenghi.

11.10 De Sica's *Ladri di biciclette* (1948): Antonio (Lamberto Maggiorani) with his son (Enzo Staiola).

---

*The award was for "an Italian production of superlative quality made under adverse circumstances," which the next year the Academy Board of Governors turned into an award for Best Foreign Language Film, a category that still exists.

near the conclusion the man is driven to steal a bicycle himself but is caught in the act. Shot on location in Rome with nonactors in the leading roles (the protagonist was played by a factory worker brilliantly coached by De Sica), *Ladri di biciclette* was an international success, winning among other honors the 1949 Academy Award for Best Foreign Language Film, and its rambling narrative form was widely imitated by other directors. As was recognized at the time, the film actually has meaning on several different planes: it is a powerful social document firmly committed to the reality it portrays, a poignant story of the relationship between a father and his son, and a modern parable of alienated man in a hostile and dehumanized environment. De Sica and Zavattini were to collaborate on two more neorealist endeavors, mixing social protest with fantasy in *Miràcolo a Milano* (*Miracle in Milan*, 1951) in the manner of Clair's *Le million* and *À nous la liberté* (both 1931), and giving neorealism its final masterpiece in *Umberto D.* (1952). But before we examine the decline of the movement, it is necessary to mention a film which will probably prove to be the single most enduring legacy of neorealism to world cinema, though its own neorealist traits are of a paradoxical nature: Luchino Visconti's *La terra trema* (*The Earth Trembles*, 1948).

La terra trema was the first part (*L'episòdio del mare* [*The Sea Episode*]) of a never-completed trilogy Visconti had planned on the economic problems of fishing, mining, and agriculture in postwar Sicily. It was the first film he had directed since the Fascist assault on *Ossessione* (in the interim, he had worked for the Resistance and directed theater in Rome), and it was shot entirely on location in the Sicilian fishing village of Aci Trezza without a script and with a cast of nonprofessionals recruited from the local populace. Initially financed by the Italian Communist Party but modestly subsidized later by a commercial company, *La terra trema*

11.11 *La terra trema* (Luchino Visconti, 1948).

was adapted by Visconti from a novel by the nineteenth-century realist Giovanni Verga (*I malavoglia* [*The House by the Medlar Tree,* 1881]) which relates the story of the downfall of a proud family of peasant fishermen through economic exploitation by wholesalers and market men. By transferring the tale from 1881 to 1947 and giving it a Marxist interpretation, and by shooting the film on location with nonactors, Visconti was clearly working within the neorealist conventions he had helped to establish in *Ossessione.*

But despite its neorealist attributes, *La terra trema* is not a purely neorealist film, because Visconti was a paradoxical artist whose work always hovers somewhere between realism and aestheticism—some would say between realism and decadence. For one thing, though much of the Sicilian dialogue was improvised on the spot, every other aspect of the film was elaborately planned in advance and carefully controlled in the production process itself. *La terra trema*'s formal structure is masterful, and most of its shots are so sumptuously composed and photographed by the veteran cinematographer G. R. Aldo (1902–53) that Orson Welles (perhaps in a fit of professional jealousy) once remarked that Visconti was the only director in the history of the cinema to photograph starving peasants like fashion models in *Vogue.* But realism in cinema (and in any art form) is a style, not an ideology, and it is an error to equate it with ugliness or desolation. Rather, in his sweeping, stately camera movements, his rhythmic editing, and above all the beautiful and elaborate composition of his shots, Visconti achieves for his peasant tragedy a visual grandeur which is not at all at odds with its social polemic but which lends it an almost mythic resonance. One critic has called the style of *La terra trema* "a kind of operatic **cinéma vérité**," and the tension between visual lushness and social realism which this term suggests characterizes all of Visconti's work from *Ossessione* (1943) to the posthumously released *L'innocente* (*The Innocent,* 1979). It has frequently been remarked that this tension was the product of ambiguities within the artist himself—an aristocrat by birth, a Marxist by philosophy, and a director of grand opera and theater several months out of each year by choice. Nonetheless, it is important to recognize that in the course of his career Visconti proved himself to be one of the world's greatest film directors, and that *La terra trema* is one of his most significant works.

Like *Ossessione,* *La terra trema* unfortunately had little immediate impact upon contemporary cinema. Running over two and a half hours and spoken in a dialect all but incomprehensible to mainland Italians, the film was a commercial disaster on the domestic market and suffered the same fate as its predecessor under Fascism: it was drastically cut and dubbed into Italian for rerelease. *La terra trema* was exported only to France, where a voice-over narration completely destroyed its ideological content but where the film critic and theorist André Bazin saw it and communicated its importance to the generation of young film enthusiasts from whose ranks would soon be drawn the directors of the French New Wave. Visconti himself temporarily abandoned the cinema once more for the theater, returning in 1951 to direct Anna Magnani in *Bellissima,* a melodrama with few roots in neorealism, and to begin thereby a new phase of his career.*

If the relationship of *La terra trema* to neorealism is problematic, it is because Visconti as an artist was never comfortable working within the confines of a single perspective or cinematic mode, and informed all of his work with a uniquely personal vision, whether he was adapting American pulp fiction, Giovanni Verga, or Thomas Mann. But other Italian directors of the postwar period identified more closely with the new movement, and the years 1946 to 1949 witnessed a number of neorealist films by relatively minor figures who nevertheless deserve mention. Inspired by the successes of Rossellini and De Sica, the Italian partisan organization (ANPI) produced two films between 1946 and 1947, both collectively written,† which examined the war and its aftermath from the point of view of the partisan Left. Aldo Vergano's *Il sole sorge ancora* (*The Sun Rises Again,* 1946) tells of the formation of the Resistance in Lombardy through the adventures of a young Italian soldier who has deserted in order to join it; Giuseppe De Santis' *Caccia tragica* (*The Tragic Hunt / Pursuit,* 1947) shows the continuation of the partisan spirit after the

---

* Visconti continued to produce eccentric, operatic masterpieces after his neorealist phase. The most significant of these are elaborate historical dramas—*Senso* (1954), set among the Venetian aristocracy during the Risorgimento; *Il caduta degli dei* (*Götterdämmerung;* English title: *The Damned,* 1969), a lurid, epic parable of the Nazis' corruption of the German bourgeoisie; *Ludwig* (1973), a fantastic biography of Ludwig II [1845–86], the mad king of Bavaria, which was released, badly cut from 257 to 189 minutes, then restored to its original length at Venice in 1980; and literary adaptations—*Le notti bianche* (*White Nights,* 1957; from the novella by Dostoevsky); *Il gattopardo* (*The Leopard,* 1962; from the novel by Giuseppe Tomasi di Lampedusa; released dubbed and horribly cut from 205 to 160 minutes, then restored to its original length in 1983); *Lo straniero* (*The Stranger,* 1969; from the novel by Albert Camus); and *Morte a Venezia* (*Death in Venice,* 1971; from the novella by Thomas Mann). *Rocco e i suoi fratelli* (*Rocco and His Brothers,* 1960) was conceived by Visconti as a sequel to *La terra trema;* it is a loosely structured epic about the migration of a peasant family from southern Italy to the industrial north. *Vaghe stelle dell'Orsa . . .* (*Beautiful Stars of the Ursa . . .* [English title: *Sandra,* 1965]) is a Sartrean drama, loosely based on the Electra myth, of a contemporary Italian family's decline. Most of these films were shot in color by Giuseppe Rotunno (b. 1923), Visconti's close collaborator and one of the world's great cinematographers, or, after 1969, by Pasqualino De Santis. Other important Visconti collaborators were the editors Mario Serandrai and Ruggero Mastroianni, the scriptwriters Enrico Medioli and Suso Cecchi d'Amico, and the composer Nino Rota (b. 1911). In the last twenty years of his career, Visconti became increasingly famous for his expressive use of color and decor. His final films—*Gruppo di famiglia in un interno* (*Conversation Piece,* 1975; from the novel by Mario Praz) and *L'innocente* (1979; from the novel by Gabriele D'Annunzio) were released posthumously. See Donald Lyons, "Visconti's Magnificent Obsession," *Film Comment* 15, 2 (March-April 1979): 9–13; and James McCourt, "*The Innocent*: Visconti's Last Fresco," same issue: 14–16. See also Monica Stirling's critical biography, *A Screen of Time: A Study of Luchino Visconti* (New York: Harcourt Brace Jovanovich, 1979); Gaia Servadio's *Luchino Visconti: A Biography* (New York: Watts, 1983); Luciano de Giusti's *I Film di Luchino Visconti* (Rome: Gremese Editore, 1985); and Elaine Mancini's *Luchino Visconti: A Guide to References and Resources* (Boston: G. K. Hall, 1986).

† Although Giuseppe De Santis, Michelangelo Antonioni, Umberto Barbaro, Cesare Zavattini, and others contributed, the principal author of both film scripts was the Marxist intellectual Carlo Lizzani (b. 1922).

liberation, as the members of a collective farm pursue and capture a gang of thieves which has robbed them. Alberto Lattuada (b. 1914), a practitioner of calligraphism in the early forties, made three films between 1946 and 1949 which, while unmistakably commercial, are essentially neorealist in method and theme. His *Il bandito* (*The Bandit*, 1946) is the story of a former Italian prisoner of war who cannot find a place for himself in the corrupt society of postwar Turin and turns in desperation to a life of crime. In *Senza pietà* (*Without Pity*, 1948), written by Federico Fellini and Tullio Pinelli, with Luigi Comencini (b. 1916),* two lovers, both displaced persons, are corrupted by their involvement in black-market activities in Livorno. Lattuada's final film with neorealist affinities was *Il mulino del Po* (*The Mill on the Po,* 1948), also written by Fellini and Pinelli, which uses the events of a farm-workers' strike in the Po Valley in 1876 to depict the plight of contemporary agricultural workers.

11.12 Alberto Lattuada's *Senza pietà* (1948): John Kitzmiller and Carla del Poggio.

At the other end of the country, Pietro Germi (b. 1914) traveled to Sicily to direct the neorealist *In nome della legge* (*In the Name of the Law,* 1948), which explores the pervasive influence of the Mafia upon contemporary Sicilian life, and *Il cammino della speranza* (*The Road to Hope,* 1950), which dramatizes the hardships of postwar emigrants from the poverty-stricken island as they struggled across the length of Italy on their way to France. In the same period, the former critic Giuseppe De Santis directed two noteworthy neorealist films on agrarian themes. His *Riso amaro* (*Bitter Rice,* 1948) initially concerns the economic exploitation of itinerant female rice workers in the Po Valley but degenerates rapidly into the sensational melodrama and eroticism which brought international fame to its two leading performers, Silvana Mangano and Vittorio Gassman, and which some believe marked the beginning of neorealism's ultimate decline into commercialism.† De Santis' *Non c'e pace tra gli ulivi* (*No Peace Among the Olives,* 1949) is less ideologically equivocal in its tale of a young soldier who returns from the war to find both his girlfriend and his farm stolen by a powerful provincial bourgeois and who must take the law into his own hands to regain them. Finally, a list of minor neorealist works should not omit the comedies of Luigi Zampa (b.1905—*Vivere in pace* [*Living in Peace,* 1947]), Renato Castellani (1914–86—*Sotto il sole di Roma* [*Under the Roman Sun,* 1947]), and Luciano Emmer (b.1914—*Domenica d'agosto* [*Sunday in August,* 1949]), all of which borrowed the production techniques of the movement without adopting its themes. Like *Riso amaro,* these works in their lack of serious social commitment foreshadowed the collapse of neoreal-

11.13 Giuseppe De Santis' *Riso amaro* (1948): Silvana Mangano (center).

---

* Comencini is now a highly respected director within the Italian commercial cinema (e.g., *L'ingorgo* [*Bottleneck,* 1979]; *Cuore* [*Heart,* 1985]; *La storia* [*History,* 1986]; *Un ragazzo di Calabria* [*A Boy from Calabria,* 1987]).

† *Riso amaro,* described by one Italian critic as a "neorealist colossal," employed a huge cast and crew and took seventy-five days to shoot on location and another two months to edit. A potent brew of sex, violence, and anti-Americanism—and the only neorealist film to succeed commercially in the domestic market—it was meticulously choreographed by De Santis, who used elaborate dolly and crane mechanisms to move his cameras flamboyantly over the rice fields.

11.14 *Umberto D.* (Vittorio De Sica, 1952): Carlo Battisti.

ism into the slick sensationalism of the fifties. But before that collapse occurred, neorealism produced its last masterpiece through the next collaboration of Vittorio De Sica and Cesare Zavattini in *Umberto D.* (1952).

Umberto D. probably comes as close to realizing Zavattini's ideal of a pure cinema of everyday life as any film the neorealist movement produced. It has no plot but is structured around a series of loosely connected incidents in the title character's life. Although most of these incidents are generated by a single circumstance (Umberto D. is poor and can't pay his rent), the film begins and ends *in medias res* because it is about a condition rather than about a series of events. Filmed on location in Rome with an entirely nonprofessional cast, *Umberto D.* offers a portrait of an old-age pensioner attempting to eke out a meager existence for himself and his dog in a furnished room, while retaining a modicum of personal dignity. The fragile equilibrium Umberto has managed to maintain between mere want and degrading poverty is destroyed when his callous landlady, in an effort to drive him out, demands that he pay his back rent in a lump sum. Umberto sells what few possessions he has, attempts to borrow money from ex-colleagues (he is apparently a retired civil servant), and even tries to beg, but he finds it impossible to raise the amount he needs. Finally, after the landlady has publicly humiliated him by letting his room to prostitutes and has all but thrown him out into the street, Umberto resolves to commit suicide. He ultimately fails, however, because he can't bring himself to abandon his dog. The conclusion leaves the two alive together, but with no place to go and no prospects for the future.

Obviously, a film about a downtrodden old man and his dog is prone to be sentimental by its very nature, and *Umberto D.* does not avoid this pitfall (no neorealist film about victimized people ever did). But most of the emotion the film contains is honest enough, because De Sica and Zavattini do not attempt to make their protagonist seem better or nobler than he is. Umberto can be thoroughly disagreeable, and he is in most respects an average person. Roy Armes suggests that as a character he is Chaplinesque (and De Sica admired Chaplin extravagantly)—a little man adrift in an alien environment that continually threatens him. It is true, of course, that *Umberto D.* is a closely observed social document which comments on the hypocrisy, cruelty, and indifference of bourgeois society toward its own aged members, but as in the earlier De Sica-Zavattini collaborations, an examination of emotional relationships lies at the center of the film. In *Sciuscià* the crucial relationship was that between the two young shoeshine boys; in *Ladri di biciclette,* between the father and son. In *Umberto D.,* however, the only significant relationship is that of the protagonist and his dog, as if to imply that relationships between human beings have become increasingly difficult or even impossible in our emotionally attenuated modern society. Others have found *Umberto D.* less pessimistic than this comment suggests, but it seems clear that its commercial failure was a direct result of the grim view it took of contemporary life.* In the year of its release, in fact, some Italian politicians,

---

* As if to validate his own pessimistic premise, De Sica's career declined after this film, although he continued to work closely with Zavattini until almost the end. With *Stazione*

notably the Hon. Giulio Andreotti (see p. 461), attempted to prohibit the film's exportation on the grounds that it presented a falsely gloomy picture of Italian society.

The Decline of Neorealism

Neorealism in Zavattini's ideal sense ("the ideal film would be ninety minutes of the life of a man to whom nothing happens") probably never existed. In practice, it was a cinema of poverty and pessimism firmly rooted in the immediate postwar period. When times changed and economic conditions began to improve, neorealism lost first its ideological basis, then it subject matter. As Penelope Houston puts it, neorealism was a revolutionary cinema in a nonrevolutionary society, and certainly the movement could never have outlasted the prosperity and affluence of the fifties. But even if Italy had remained unchanged from *Roma, città aperta* to *Umberto D.*, the neorealist cinema would have failed for other reasons. In the first place, for all of its collectivist aspirations, neorealism had never been a popular cinema in Italy and was dependent for its survival upon foreign markets—especially the United States. The Italian film industry experienced a major crisis in 1949 due to the wholesale importation of American films (the sociologist George Huaco has found that only 10 percent of the feature films exhibited in Italy in December of that year were Italian, while 71 percent were American). The government then passed the protective Andreotti Law, named for Giulio Andreotti, the Undersecretary of Public Entertainment. *La legge Andreotti* taxed imported films and required theaters to show Italian films for eighty days out of the year, thus tripling domestic distribution. It also established the *Direzione Generale del Spectacolo,* which was empowered to grant government-subsidized production loans to scripts submitted for prior approval that were found "suitable" and to ban from both domestic screening and exportation films deemed inimical to the "best interests of Italy." The Andreotti Law, then, placed the Italian film industry under state control, and when the government became openly hostile to neorealism in the early fifties, backing for projects dried up altogether. Since Italy joined

---

Termini (*Station Terminus,* 1953), produced for David O. Selznick and released cut and re-edited in the United States as *Indiscretion of an American Wife* (1954), De Sica entered a long period of commercial compromise dominated by romantic melodrama (*L'oro di Napoli* [*The Gold of Naples,* 1954]; *Amanti* [*A Place for Lovers,* 1968]) and slick sex comedies (*Ieri, oggi, domani* [*Yesterday, Today, and Tomorrow,* 1963]; *Matrimonio all'Italiana* [*Marriage Italian Style,* 1964]; *Caccia alla volpe* [*After the Fox,* 1966]; *Sette volte donna* [*Woman Times Seven,* 1967]), with an occasional recurrence to neorealist modes and themes (*Il tetto* [*The Roof,* 1956]—regarded by many critics as "the last neorealist film"; *La ciociaria* [*Two Women,* 1960], adapted from the novel by Alberto Moravia; *Uno mondo nuovo* [*A New World,* 1966], an essay in *nouvelle vague* styles and social concerns shot on location in Paris). The beautiful and poignant *Il giardino dei Finzi-Contini* (*The Garden of the Finzi-Continis,* 1971) helped to reestablish his critical reputation and reaffirm his essentially tragic vision of human experience, as did the posthumously released *Una breva vacanza* (*A Brief Vacation,* 1974), his last collaboration with Zavattini, and *Il viaggio* (*The Voyage*), adapted from the Luigi Pirandello novel, but De Sica was clearly an artist in eclipse before his death in 1974.

the North Atlantic Treaty Organization (NATO) in March 1949, some have speculated that the Andreotti Law was enacted with the implicit purpose of slowly strangling neorealism, whose ideological orientation was Marxist. This is quite possible, given the general stupidity of governments in their relations with the arts, but it also seems clear that neorealism had burned itself out internally before the Andreotti Law had any significant effect on production.

In their desire to achieve "the illusion of the present tense" which James Agee had noted in Rossellini's *Paisà*, the neorealist directors frequently ignored the narrative elements of their films or treated them as irrelevant, causing the plots to degenerate into stereotypes. The same concentration on methodology also resulted in the lapses into sentimentality which led the British critic Raymond Durgnat to label neorealist films the "male weepies," as opposed to the "female weepies" of Hollywood melodramatists like Vincent Sherman, Irving Rapper, and Daniel Mann. To all of this it might first be replied that the neorealists were interested not so much in constructing narratives as in reconstructing the atmosphere and ambiance of a contemporary reality, something they achieved admirably. And, as André Bazin suggests in his essay on neorealism called "An Aesthetic of Reality," it is not at all unrespectable or even unusual for an innovative movement in cinema to dissipate its creative energies in a brief span of time. Innovation in an art form whose medium is photographic reproduction and whose influence literally travels with the speed of light is bound to be short-lived (as innovation, that is) and to produce its own reaction rapidly. But the real vindication of the neorealist movement has been its influence on the international cinema, which has been enormous.

The Impact of Neorealism

Neorealism completely revitalized Italian film so that today it has become one of the major creative forces in world cinema. Not only did neorealism itself produce masterpieces and become the temporary medium for great directors like Rossellini and Visconti, but it provided training for two men currently thought to be among the international cinema's greatest artists—Federico Fellini (b.1920), who worked extensively as a scriptwriter on neorealist films (*Roma, città aperta; Paisà; Senza pietà; Il mulino del Po; In nome della legge; Il cammino della speranza*), and Michelangelo Antonioni (b. 1912), who was writing criticism for *Cinema* and directing documentaries during the same period (e.g., *Gente del Po* [*People of the Po*, 1943; 1947], *N.U. / Nettezza urbana* [*Dustmen*, 1948], *La villa dei mostri* [*The House of Monsters*, 1950]). In their films of the fifties, especially Fellini's *I vitelloni* (1953) and Antonioni's *Le amiche* (1955), both directors may be said to have continued the neorealist mode by turning it inward, so that the object of attention becomes not society but the human self. This element of what might be called introspective neorealism largely disappeared from their work in the sixties, but it is not farfetched to see in their mature images of modern alienation and disorder vestiges of the bombed-out, fragmented neorealist landscapes of the late forties. Indeed, Penelope Houston suggests that the strength of the Italian cinema lies precisely in its *in*ability to escape the neorealist heritage, so that even the generation of filmmakers which succeeded that of Fellini and Antonioni has felt compelled to confront and come to terms with the neorealist tradition (see Chapter 15). Gillo Pontecorvo (b. 1919), Francesco Rosi (b. 1922), Pier Paolo Pasolini (1922–75), Vittorio De Seta (b. 1923), Elio Petri (1929–82), the Taviani brothers—Vittorio (b. 1929) and Paolo (b. 1931)—Lina Wertmuller (b. 1930), Ermanno Olmi (b. 1939), Marco Bellocchio (b. 1939), and Bernardo Bertolucci (b. 1940) have responded variously to that tradition by adopting its techniques while modifying or rejecting its vision (see Rosi's *Salvatore Giuliano* [1961], Pasolini's *Accattone* [1961], Olmi's *Il posto* [1961], De Seta's *Banditi a Orgosolo* [1961], Wertmuller's *I basilischi* [1963], Bertolucci's *Prima della rivoluzione* [1964], Pontecorvo's *La battaglia di Algeri* [1965], Belloc-chio's *I pugni in tasca* [1966], and the Tavianis' *Padre padrone* [1977]).

Neorealism was the first postwar cinema to liberate filmmaking from the artificial confines of the studio and, by extension, from the Holly-wood-originated studio system. On-location shooting, the use of non-professional actors, and improvisation of script, which have all become a part (though not always a large part) of conventional filmmaking today, were techniques almost unknown to the narrative sound film before neo-realism. The movement's influence on the French New Wave directors in this regard is a matter of record, but its impact on the American cinema has been generally ignored: in the postwar work of American directors as diverse as Nicholas Ray (*They Live by Night,* 1948), Elia Kazan (*Boomerang!,* 1947), Jules Dassin (*The Naked City,* 1948), Joseph Losey (*The Lawless,* 1950), Robert Rossen (*Body and Soul,* 1947), and Edward Dmytryk (*Crossfire,* 1947), substantial elements of neorealism can be found, including a political commitment to the left.* Finally, several scholars have pointed out the profound influence of neorealism on film-makers in countries that lacked strong national cinemas of their own. Michael Cacoyannis (b. 1922—*Zorba the Greek,* 1964) in Greece; Luis Garcia Berlanga (b. 1921—*Las pirañas,* 1967) and Juan Antonio Bardem (b. 1922—*Muerte de un ciclista,* 1955) in Spain; and Satyajit Ray (b. 1921—the Apu trilogy: *Pather Panchali,* 1955; *Aparajito,* 1956; *Apur sansar,* 1957) in India have all testified to the enormous influence of neo-realism upon their work (see Chapters 16 and 18). Indeed, Ray has claimed that a single viewing of De Sica's *Ladri di biciclette* in London in 1950 led him to film his trilogy according to neorealist methods. It is clear that neorealism was a great deal more than a localized national phenomenon; its formative influence extended well beyond the Italian cinema. There

---

* It is no coincidence that all of these American directors except Ray were targeted in the anticommunist witch-hunt of the late forties and fifties (described in the second part of this chapter). Other American filmmakers influenced by neorealism include the director Henry Hathaway (*13 Rue Madeleine,* 1946; *Kiss of Death,* 1947; *Call Northside 777,* 1948), the producer-director Stanley Kramer (b. 1913—*Home of the Brave* [Mark Robson, 1949]; *The Men* [Fred Zinnemann, 1950]), and screenwriter Paddy Chayefsky (1923–82—*Marty* [1955]; *The Bachelor Party* [1957]; *In the Middle of the Night* [1959]—all directed by Delbert Mann); see Chapter 12.

can be no question today that, whatever its limitations of vision and form, Italian neorealism was one of the great innovative movements in the history of the cinema, whose importance and impact are comparable in degree to that of Soviet silent realism or the French New Wave, between which it most appropriately mediates.

AMERICA

Hollywood at War

Like Italian cinema, American film had been moving toward a heightened kind of realism in the early forties when the war interrupted and Hollywood was pressed into the service of the federal government. On December 18, 1941, immediately following the attack on Pearl Harbor and our declaration of war upon Japan, President Franklin D. Roosevelt established a Bureau of Motion Picture Affairs within the Office of War Information to mobilize the studios for the national defense effort. Hollywood responded by creating the War Activities Committee, comprised of studio executives, distributors, exhibitors, actors, and labor union officials, to coordinate American filmmaking activity with the propaganda and morale-boosting programs of the government.* The government suggested six thematic categories for Hollywood films which would be consonant with its war-aims information campaign but which would not preclude conventional entertainment values. As listed by Lewis Jacobs, these were: (1) The Issues of the War: what we are fighting for, the American way of life; (2) The Nature of the Enemy: his ideology, his objectives, his methods; (3) The "United Nations": i.e., our allies in arms; (4) The Production Front: supplying the materials for victory; (5) The Homefront: civilian responsibility; and 6) The Fighting Forces: our armed services, our allies and our associates. Hollywood complied at first by producing a raft of fatuous, superpatriotic melodramas of the battlefield and homefront which glorified a kind of warfare that had never existed in the history of the human race, much less in the current upheaval. With titles like *Salute to Courage, Dangerously We Live, Captain of the Clouds, To the Shores of Tripoli, United We Stand, The Devil with Hitler,* and *Blondie for Victory,* these unsophisticated films disappeared rapidly from the American screen when Hollywood and the general public were con-

---

* Hollywood's cooperation with the war effort was encouraged considerably by the Selective Service System's 1942 ruling that the movies were an "essential industry" whose equipment and materials were subject to price controls and whose personnel could not be drafted. In addition, the Justice Department temporarily backed off of its antitrust suit against the studios and did not resume the case until August 1944, with the war in Europe very nearly won. A final reason that Hollywood was only too glad to cooperate with the government was that it lost 33–50 percent of its traditional revenues as markets in Europe and the Far East closed one by one due to the war. Through the Office of the Coordinator of Inter-American Affairs, however, the State Department proposed to help the industry exploit the South and Central American markets to offset losses (see note, p. 428).

fronted with an infinitely more authentic version of the war, contained in newsreels from the battlefronts and government-produced information films.

From 1941 to 1945, the War Department, the Army Pictorial Services, the Army Educational Program, the American Armed Forces (AAF) First Motion Picture Unit, the Signal Corps of the combined services, the U.S. Navy, the U.S. Marine Corps, and the Overseas Branch of the Office of War Information (OWI) were involved in the production of documentary films designed to explain and justify the war to the servicemen fighting it and the civilian populace actively supporting it. Major Hollywood directors like Frank Capra, John Huston, John Ford, George Stevens, and William Wyler had been recruited into the armed forces, together with professional documentarists like Willard Van Dyke (1906–86) and Irving Lerner (1909–76), to operate these programs, and the films they produced collectively are among the most outstanding documentaries in the history of the form. The seven films of the *Why We Fight* series produced by Frank Capra, for example—*Prelude to War* (Frank Capra, 1942), *The Nazis Strike* (Frank Capra and Anatole Litvak, 1942), *Divide and Conquer* (Capra and Litvak, 1943), *The Battle of Britain* (Capra and Litvak, 1943), *The Battle of Russia* (Litvak, 1943), *The Battle of China* (Capra and Litvak, 1943), *War Comes to America* (Litvak, 1944)—were documentaries edited from stock footage which persuasively and unromantically explained the necessity of America's involvement in the war. Other information films, like Wyler's *Memphis Belle* (1944) and *Thunderbolt* (1945), Ford's *December 7th* (1943; co-directed and photographed by Gregg Toland) and *The Battle of Midway* (1944), and Huston's *Report from the Aleutians* (1943) and *The Battle of San Pietro* (1944),* were shot on location in every theater of operations in the war and constitute masterly pieces of reporting. The characteristic feature of these films was their sobriety. War was shown to be a brutal, unglamorous, and murderous business which was pursued out of utter necessity and which had nothing to do with the Yankee-Doodle-Dandy heroics of Hollywood. Vast numbers of Americans saw these documentaries at home and overseas, and there can be little doubt that they did much to upgrade the realism and honesty with which Hollywood approached the war.

The years 1943 and 1944 witnessed many films whose presentation of the war and attendant themes was much more convincing than that of their predecessors. Whereas earlier films had caricatured Fascists as either cowardly buffoons or stock villains, Frank Capra's *Meet John Doe* (1943), Herman Shumlin's *Watch on the Rhine* (1943; adapted by Lillian Hell-

11.15 *The Nazis Strike* (Frank Capra and Anatole Litvak, 1942) and *Divide and Conquer* (Capra and Litvak, 1943).

11.16 *The Battle of San Pietro* (John Huston, 1944).

---

*The third film in Huston's war trilogy, *Let There Be Light* (1946), was shelved by the U.S. War Department as "unsuitable" for public viewing. Finally released in 1980, the fifty-eight-minute documentary is in fact an intensely moving account of the recuperation of shell-shocked soldiers in an Army psychiatric hospital. It was apparently suppressed to maintain the heroic "warrior" mythology of the nation's World War II experience. See Scott Hammen, "At War with the Army," *Film Comment* 16, 2 (March-April 1980): 19–23.

11.17 *The Hitler Gang* (John Farrow, 1944): Robert Watson as the *Führer*.

11.18 Fredric March plays a German who rejects Nazism and must flee his country in *So Ends Our Night* (John Cromwell, 1941).

11.19 Stalin (Mannart Kippen) and Churchill (Dudley Field Malone) in the film version of Ambassador Joseph E. Davies' memoir, *Mission to Moscow* (Michael Curtiz, 1943).

man from her own play), George Cukor's *Keeper of the Flame* (1943), Edward Dmytryk's *Hitler's Children* (1943) and *Behind the Rising Sun* (1943), Fritz Lang's *Ministry of Fear* (1944), Leslie Fenton's *Tomorrow the World* (1944), John Farrow's *The Hitler Gang* (1944), Herbert Biberman's *The Master Race* (1944), William Cameron Menzies' *Address Unknown* (1944), and Alfred Hitchcock's semiallegorical *Lifeboat* (1944) all portrayed the dangers of Fascism abroad and on the homefront with a sophisticated understanding of the ruthlessness, intelligence, and actual power of the enemy.* Another group of films provided a more realistic treatment than heretofore of "our allies in arms." Abjuring the formulaic platitudes of Henry King's *A Yank in the R.A.F.* (1941) and the saccharine stereotypes of William Wyler's *Mrs. Miniver* (1942), these films attempted with varying degrees of success to show what life was like inside the occupied countries and to promote a bond of sympathy with them. Though a far cry from Rossellini's *Roma, città aperta,* Frank Tuttle's *Hostages* (1943), Irving Pichel's *The Moon Is Down* (1943), Jean Renoir's *This Land Is Mine* (1943), Fritz Lang's *Hangmen Also Die* (1943), Lewis Milestone's *Edge of Darkness* (1943), and Tay Garnett's *The Cross of Lorraine* (1943) offered fairly convincing representations of oppression and resistance in Nazi-occupied Europe (specifically in Norway, Czechoslovakia, Hungary, and France). Other films, like Lewis Milestone's *North Star* (1943), Gregory Ratoff's *Song of Russia* (1943), Jacques Tourneur's *Days of Glory* (1944), and Michael Curtiz's *Mission to Moscow* (1943), attempted to promote goodwill between America and its incongruous new ally, the Soviet Union—in the case of *Mission to Moscow,* by trying to rationalize Stalin's purge trials of the thirties. (It is one of the bitterest ironies of recent American history that many of the people who worked on these *government-authorized* propaganda films were subjected to vicious accusations of disloyalty and treason during the late forties and early fifties; see pp. 471–77.)

Perhaps the most telling index of the documentary influence on American cinema during the war years was the increasing number of serious-minded and realistic combat films which portrayed the war very much as it must have seemed to the men who were fighting it. Indeed, one of the reasons that Hollywood outgrew its post–Pearl Harbor romanticism so quickly was a massive GI reaction against the patent phoniness of the early war films, but by 1944 the true horror and anguish of warfare devoid of flag-waving jingoism was being brought home to Americans in films like Tay Garnett's *Bataan* (1943) and Lewis Seiler's *Guadalcanal Diary* (1944). Lewis Jacobs notes another significant category of late combat films, such as Lloyd Bacon's *Action in the North Atlantic* (1943), Delmer Daves' *Destination Tokyo* (1943) and *Pride of the Marines* (1945), Zoltán Korda's *Sahara* (1944), Lewis Milestone's *The Purple Heart* (1944) and *A Walk in the Sun* (1945), Raoul Walsh's *Objective, Burma!* (1945),

* A handful of intelligent anti-Fascist films were made between 1940 and Pearl Harbor: for instance, Alfred Hitchcock's *Foreign Correspondent* (1940), Frank Borzage's *The Mortal Storm* (1940), and John Cromwell's *So Ends Our Night* (1941).

11.20   The crew of a downed bomber are tried for war crimes against the Japanese in *The Purple Heart* (Lewis Milestone, 1944): Dana Andrews, Farley Granger, Sam Jaffe.

11.21   The realities of war: Lewis Milestone's *A Walk in the Sun* (1945): Dana Andrews.

John Ford's *They Were Expendable* (1945), Henry King's *A Bell for Adano* (1945), and William Wellman's *The Story of GI Joe* (1945), in which the battle action becomes a vehicle for a more personal kind of cinema—one concerned with "the deep emotional crisis and individual agony of the average Joe, anxiously examining his own conscience." In their focus on the individual American in conflict with himself, these productions anticipate the searching, introspective, and ultimately disillusioned films of the immediate postwar period, in which the democratic ideals for which so many Americans fought and died are brought into serious question.*

In 1945, however, with the end of the war clearly in sight, Hollywood was more concerned with empirical victory than metaphysical defeat, and had already begun its search for buoyant postwar subject matter. War themes were jettisoned for lighter material which would coincide with the momentary mood of public euphoria, and for a brief season on the American screen, following August 14, 1945, it was as if the war had never taken place at all.† But the war had not been unkind to Hollywood, even though it had lost its foreign markets and had devoted nearly

---

* Two other categories of American wartime cinema were films of women coping on the home front, such as *Tender Comrade* (Edward Dmytryk, 1943) and *Since You Went Away* (John Cromwell, 1944), and also morale-boosting "service musicals," which featured radio and film celebrities and "bevies of beautiful girls" in service settings epitomized by *Hollywood Canteen* (Delmer Daves, 1944).

† Box office figures tell the tale. In fiscal year 1941–42, six out of twenty-one top-grossing films had had some connection with the war. In 1942–43, 1943–44, 1944–45, 1945–46, and 1946–47, the ratio rose and fell as follows: thirteen out of twenty-four, twelve out of twenty-five, six out of thirty-four, two out of thirty-six, and one (*The Best Years of Our Lives*) out of twenty-six. So strong, in fact, was the national revulsion against the war and all things military that the AAF film unit suppressed many of its own late productions, of which *Let There Be Light* (see note, p. 457) is the classic case.

one-third of its production between 1941 and 1945 to the war effort (according to Lewis Jacobs, more than five hundred out of the seventeen hundred films made during this period were directly concerned with Fascism and war). Hollywood had even complied with the government's discomfiting request to reduce the length of A-films on double bills to economize on theater lighting—a measure which caused at least one catastrophe for the international cinema when RKO cut Orson Welles' second masterpiece, *The Magnificent Ambersons* (1942), by forty-three minutes and made it the first half of a double bill with the comedy *Mexican Spitfire Sees a Ghost* (see Chapter 10). Nevertheless, Hollywood enjoyed the most profitable four-year period in its history during the war, with weekly attendance estimated at 85 million persons (four times the current figure), despite the restrictions imposed upon it by the government and its own errors of judgment about what the public wanted to see. For one thing, all of its combat films were (and, with few exceptions, still are) produced with the "technical assistance" of the armed forces, which can be worth up to 50 percent of a motion picture's budget in free production values.* For another, the government had cleverly levied a special war tax on theater tickets in 1942, so that going to the movies during the war years took on the character of a patriotic act. Full employment and unprecedented prosperity after a decade of economic depression also helped to keep attendance high. (In most industrial centers the theaters stayed open twenty-four hours a day to accommodate shift workers.) But most important of all in determining Hollywood's high wartime profits was the perennial therapeutic function that films assume in periods of social stress. It is almost literally true that, since the inception of the medium, the worst of times for human history have been the

---

* For the purpose of public relations, the American military establishment has traditionally cooperated in helping Hollywood to produce films that glorify the armed forces. The military can help production companies by providing them with free historical and technical research and, at cost, heavy equipment and armaments, large casts of uniformed extras, and authentic locations for shooting. (It is rumored, for example, that the maneuvers required of the combined services in restaging the 1944 Allied invasion of Normandy for 20th Century-Fox's *The Longest Day* [Ken Annakin and Bernhard Wicki, 1962] were more complicated than those of the actual event and were worth well over one million dollars to the studio.) That this relationship, probably a necessity in wartime, can become corrupt was demonstrated by the 1972 CBS television documentary "The Selling of the Pentagon." Today, the office of the Assistant Secretary of Defense for Public Affairs receives approximately two hundred requests for production assistance a year. After reviewing a film's script for "authenticity"—which to the Pentagon means portraying the services in a favorable light—the office decides whether military help should be offered. In general, films like *The Right Stuff* (Philip Kaufman, 1983) and *Top Gun* (Tony Scott, 1986) receive it, while films like *Platoon* (Oliver Stone, 1986) and *Full Metal Jacket* (Stanley Kubrick, 1987) do not. It should be noted, though, that an equally close relationship exists between the military establishments and national cinemas of certain communist countries, where the relationship is mediated by the state rather than by mutual self-interest. Sergei Bondarchuk's eight-hour adaptation of Tolstoi's *War and Peace* (1965–67), e.g., involved the entire Red Army in re-staging the Battle of Borodino, as Eisenstein and Pudovkin had used the Soviet armed forces in their epics of the Revolution, and as World War II is frequently refought in grand scale on Soviet soil—most recently in Elem Klimov's award-winning *Go and See* (1985)—with the Red Army taking both sides.

best of times for the cinema, even bad cinema, because there is no fantasy realm within our waking experience which renders its make-believe so inescapably and ineluctably real.

The Postwar Boom

For all of these reasons, Hollywood came through the war years with its powerful studio production system and time-tested film genres pretty much intact, making the American the only major national cinema in the West to preserve a direct continuity of tradition with its past after 1945. In Europe—even in Italy—national cinemas had to be entirely rebuilt, which in most cases involved a beneficial process of rejuvenation, and a subsequent influx of new talent and ideas. But Hollywood had experienced the war as the most stable and lucrative four years in its history with a mere change of pace, and the industry gave every indication that it intended to march into the postwar period in the same way that it had marched out of the Depression—by avoiding the depiction of any of the unpleasant realities of American life. In 1946 there was much cause for confidence. Victory had opened vast, unchallenged markets in the war-torn countries of Western Europe and Southeast Asia, and Hollywood had already resumed its economic domination of international cinema because only America was in a material position to provide high-quality films to a world hungry for diversion. Moreover, the domestic audience had reached its highest peak ever, at an estimated 100 million per week (two-thirds of the population), and the yearly box office receipts of 1.75 billion dollars broke all previous records.* Thus, by the end of 1946 it seemed that Hollywood's most lucrative path lay in maintaining the prewar status quo; but no sooner had the industry charted this course than serious obstacles began to appear.

An eight-month studio union strike in 1945 combined with spiraling postwar inflation led to a 25 percent pay increase for studio personnel in the following year.† Moreover, Hollywood's chief overseas market, Great Britain, from which it drew one-quarter to one-third of its net income, levied a 75 percent protective tax on all foreign film profits, and this reduced the American industry's annual British revenue from 68 million dollars in 1946 to under 17 million dollars in 1947. Other Commonwealth countries and European nations followed suit (Italy, for example, with the Andreotti Law), and though in some cases Hollywood was able to retaliate successfully with boycotts, the damage was significant. With the end of the War Production Board's price controls in August 1946, the industry's major suppliers of raw film stock, Eastman and Dupont, raised their prices, by 18 and 13 percent, respectively, adding over 2.5

---

* The 1946 profits of the majors—39 million dollars at Paramount; 25 million dollars at Fox; 22 million dollars at Warner's; 18 million dollars at Loew's; and 12 million dollars at RKO—were not approached again in real dollars until the seventies.

† Many of those active in the strike fell victim to the witch-hunt of the late forties and early fifties (see pp. 471–77).

million dollars in annual costs for the studios. Most disastrous of all from a financial standpoint, however, was the adjudication of the antitrust suit begun by the federal government against the five major and three minor studios in 1938, resulting in the "Paramount decrees" or "consent decrees" of May 1948. These were court orders which forced the companies to divest themselves of their lucrative exhibition circuits according to a mutually agreed-upon schedule over the next five years.* Most immediately, divestiture meant the end of block booking and of the automatic box office receipts which this practice had created; ultimately, it meant the end of the powerful studio system which had been the shaping force of the American film industry for thirty years. Hollywood was faced with the task of restructuring its entire production and delivery system in the midst of the most severe financial crisis it had experienced since the coming of sound. Even worse was to follow, but at the beginning of 1948 things were bad enough: in the major studios unemployment had risen by 25 percent; the independent companies Rainbow, Liberty, and Eagle-Lion† had failed completely; and Warner Bros. was preparing for a temporary shutdown. As early as 1947, radical economizing had begun. Production budgets were cut by as much as 50 percent, and expensive projects like costume films, extravagant spectacles, and grade-A musicals were abandoned altogether. Only months after the American film industry's banner year of 1946, Hollywood people were starting to ask themselves how the bubble had burst, unaware that their bad luck had only just begun.

But for a while, at least, the urgent necessity to cut back on production costs had a vitalizing and invigorating effect upon the American cinema. As Charles Higham and Joel Greenberg point out, efficiency became the order of the day. The industry's perpetual obsession with lavish production values temporarily gave way to a new concern for high-quality scripts and preplanning at every stage of the shooting process to avoid expensive retakes. For the first time in Hollywood's history, studios gave high priority to projects that could be shot on location with small casts and crews, and the content of films thus took on a greater social and psychological realism than ever before. The influence of the wartime documentary tradition and of Italian neorealism, which had earned a high reputation among American filmmakers by 1947, had a great deal to do with this sudden rejection of escapist subject matter, but much of the credit must go to the cultural impact of the war itself upon the American people.

---

* The Supreme Court found that the majors, with the collusion of the minors, had exercised a clear monopoly over motion picture production, distribution, and exhibition from 1934 through 1947, and in 1948 it forced the Big Five to spin off either their distribution or exhibition channels. They naturally chose to retain the distribution function, where control over product resides, enabling them to set clearance and minimum admission prices and to limit the supply of features at the exhibitors' expense.

† Eagle-Lion's product was distributed by United Artists from 1949–51, when its studio space (formerly PRC's) was auctioned off and its film rights acquired by United Artists. During that period, it produced the influential *films noir* of Anthony Mann (e.g., *T-Men* and *Raw Deal*, 1948; *The Black Book*, 1949).

After the elation of victory had passed, a mood of disillusionment and cynicism came over America which had at least as much to do with the nation's image of itself as with the distant horror of the war. The federal government's wartime propaganda machine, of which Hollywood was the most essential component, had created an image of an ideal America of white picket fences, cozy bungalows, and patiently loyal families and sweethearts*—a pure, democratic society in which Jews, blacks, Italians, Irish, Poles, and WASP farm boys could all live and work together, just as they had done in the ethnically balanced patrol squads of so many wartime combat films. This America, of course, had never existed, but a nation engaged in a global war of survival had an overwhelming need to believe that it did. When the war ended and the troops returned home, however, people began to discover that the basic goodness and decency of American society was more difficult to find than, for example, John Cromwell's slickly directed domestic fantasy *Since You Went Away* (1944) had made it appear—more difficult even than William Wyler's relatively sophisticated *The Best Years of Our Lives* (1946), which dealt with the successful attempts of three returned combat veterans to reintegrate themselves into civilian life, made it seem. Less difficult to locate in postwar America were social inequities and racial prejudices in every part of the country, profiteering in big business, and corruption in state and local government. What is more, many of our "boys"—especially those who had been maimed in defense of their country—came home to discover that they couldn't get jobs, obtain loans, or even resume their educations. The film critic and director Paul Schrader has suggested that postwar

11.22 Coming home: William Wyler's *The Best Years of Our Lives* (1946). Dana Andrews.

---

* In fact, according to John Costello in *Virtue Under Fire: How World War II Changed Our Social and Sexual Attitudes* (Boston: Little, Brown, 1986), by the third year of our involvement in the war, the juvenile crime rate in the United States had doubled, the divorce rate had soared, and infidelity was the order of the day. Since 1941, teenage prostitution had risen 70 percent, and major cities like New York had to set up special Wayward Minors courts to process the arrests.

disillusionment was in many ways a delayed reaction to the thirties and to the socioeconomic imbalances that had helped to cause the Depression. Whatever the reasons, when the euphoria of victory had passed, America suddenly found itself in worse shape internally than Hollywood or any other element of American society would have dared to suggest during the war. The war was over now, however, and as a result of its self-imposed economies Hollywood had become increasingly dependent upon the talents of individual writers and directors—people whose vision of things was frequently less sanguine than what the studio system, under normal circumstances, would permit them to express. But circumstances were not normal for either the industry or the nation, and soon manifestations of America's social malaise began to appear on screens all over the country.

POSTWAR GENRES IN AMERICA

"Social-Consciousness" Films and Semidocumentary Melodramas

The Hollywood films generated by postwar disenchantment with American life were of several basic types.* The least complex were those that dealt melioristically with contemporary social problems and their resolution. Often called "social-consciousness," or "problem," pictures, these films enjoyed a tremendous vogue in the late forties (in 1947, for example, nearly one-third of the films produced in Hollywood had a "problem" content of some sort) and concerned themselves with such subjects as racism, political corruption, and other inequities within our social institutions. In this category, Edward Dmytryk's *Crossfire* (1947), a tersely directed melodrama of murderous anti-Semitism in postwar America, is outstanding for both its thematic candor and its cinematic excellence. Elia Kazan's *Gentleman's Agreement* (1947) provides a much

---

* Traditional genres of film did not fare at all poorly in postwar Hollywood. On the contrary, the late forties produced major films in every genre except comedy (assuming Chaplin's *Monsieur Verdoux,* 1947, and the films of Preston Sturges to be in a class by themselves), including conventional melodrama (Max Ophüls' *The Reckless Moment* [1949]); fantasy (Frank Capra's *It's a Wonderful Life* [1946] and William Dieterle's *Portrait of Jennie* [1949]); horror (Val Lewton's RKO cycle [1942–46, see p. 470]; Robert Florey's *The Beast with Five Fingers* [1946]); suspense (Hitchcock's *Notorious* [1946]); adventure (Vincent Sherman's *The Adventures of Don Juan* [1948] and Henry King's *Captain from Castile* [1947]); the Western (John Ford's *My Darling Clementine* [1946], King Vidor's *Duel in the Sun* [1946], Howard Hawks' *Red River* [1948], William Wellman's *Yellow Sky* [1948]); the musical (Vincente Minnelli's *The Pirate* [1948]; Gene Kelly's *On the Town* [1949]); and what were known in studio parlance as "women's pictures" (see note, p. 470)—romantic melodramas designed to appeal to female audiences and constructed around a popular female star (Edmund Goulding's *The Razor's Edge* [1946, Gene Tierney], Curtis Bernhardt's *A Stolen Life* [1946, Bette Davis], Jean Negulesco's *Humoresque* [1946, Joan Crawford], Max Ophüls' *Letter from an Unknown Woman* [1948, Joan Fontaine], and *Caught* [1949, Barbara Bel Geddes]).

11.23 Juano Hernandez in *Intruder in the Dust* (Clarence Brown, 1949).

11.24 Broderick Crawford as Willie Stark in *All the King's Men* (Robert Rossen, 1949).

less honest treatment of the same theme, and his *Pinky* (1949), the sentimental tale of a young black woman who tries to pass for white, is even less credible. Nevertheless, 1949 was a good year for films on racial intolerance. Mark Robson's *Home of the Brave* (1949; produced by Stanley Kramer), sympathetically portraying the psychiatric odyssey of a black veteran, initiated what has come to be known as the "Negro cycle" of that year, which included Clarence Brown's restrained and dignified version of William Faulkner's *Intruder in the Dust,* shot on location in Oxford, Mississippi, as well as Alfred Werker's *Lost Boundaries* (produced by the documentarist Louis de Rochemont), which was based on the true story of an ostensibly "white" man's shattering discovery of his black parentage. The latter was also shot on location (in Maine and New Hampshire) with a largely nonprofessional cast. This same technique was practiced in the "problem" cycle's most elaborate exposé of political corruption, Robert Rossen's adaptation of Robert Penn Warren's novel *All the King's Men* (1949), a portrait of an authentic American demagogue based upon the career of Louisiana governor Huey Long. Other social-consciousness films dealt realistically for the first time in Hollywood history with the problems of alcoholism (Billy Wilder's *The Lost Weekend* [1945]; Stuart Heisler's *Smash-Up* [1947]), mental illness (Anatole Litvak's *The Snake Pit* [1948]), juvenile delinquency (Nicholas Ray's *Knock on Any Door* [1949]), prison injustice (Jules Dassin's *Brute Force* [1947; produced by Mark Hellinger [1903–47]; Crane Wilber's *Cañon City* [1948]), war profiteering (Irving Reis' *All My Sons* [1948]; from the play by Arthur Miller), and the rehabilitation of paraplegic veterans (Fred Zinnemann's *The Men* [1950; also produced by Kramer]). Moreover, though they can scarcely be described as problem pictures, there were several other films of the postwar era which employed various forms of social corruption as metaphors for more serious disorders in the cosmos and in the human soul. Robert Rossen's *Body and Soul* (1947; written

11.25 *The Lost Weekend* (Billy Wilder, 1945): Ray Milland.

11.26 *The Set-Up* (Robert Wise, 1949): Robert Ryan, down for the count.

by Abraham Polonsky [b. 1910])* and Robert Wise's *The Set-Up* (1949), for example, both used corruption in the prize-fighting business and the brutality of the "sport" itself to suggest something about the nature of human evil; while Abraham Polonsky's own poetically directed *Force of Evil* (1948) used the numbers racket in New York City to create a paradigm of capitalism collapsing internally from its own rottenness.

Closely related to the problem pictures was a series of semidocumentary crime melodramas which frequently had social overtones. These films were usually based on true criminal cases and shot on location with as many of the original participants in the cast as it was feasible to assemble. The first was Henry Hathaway's *The House on 92nd Street* (1945), a dramatic re-enactment of an authentic case of domestic espionage based entirely on FBI files and produced for 20th Century–Fox by Louis de Rochemont (1899–1978), creator of *The March of Time* newsreels (1935–43). De Rochemont followed this film with three other semidocumentary productions which gave Fox clear leadership in the field: Hathaway's *13 Rue Madeleine* (1946), a re-creation of OSS† activity in Montreal during the war; Elia Kazan's critically acclaimed *Boomerang!* (1947), based on the true story of a state's attorney who faced the wrath of an entire Connecticut town to clear an accused man of murder; and Hathaway's *Kiss of Death* (1947), an unglamorized account of criminals and cops in New York City's underworld. The outstanding commercial success of these films produced many others using the same formula of a fictionalized story based on fact and shot on location with nonprofessional actors; Jules Dassin's *The Naked City* (1948) is among the best of these (but see also Dassin's *Brute Force* [1947], William Keighley's *The Street with No Name* [1948], Robert Siodmak's *The Killers* [1946], and Anthony Mann's *T-Men* [1948]). In *The Naked City,* conceived and produced by Mark Hellinger, Dassin used a conventional crime melodrama as the vehicle for an uncompromisingly naturalistic portrait of the brutal and impersonal modern city; much of this film was shot by cinematographer William Daniels (1895–1970) in *cinéma vérité* fashion with hidden cameras. After 1948, the semidocumentary melodrama largely degenerated into stereotype, and most critics consider that the final collaboration of Hathaway and de Rochemont, *Call Northside 777* (1948), based on the true case of a Chicago reporter (played by James Stewart) who attempted to clear a Polish-American of a murder charge, was the last important film of its type. Nevertheless, the influence of these motion pictures continued well into the fifties, as the documentary surfaces of fiction films like John

11.27 *Call Northside 777* (Henry Hathaway, 1948): James Stewart.

---

* Remade, badly, in 1981, with an all-black cast under the direction of George Bower.

† The abbreviation for Office of Strategic Services, the American intelligence operation during World War II. The OSS provided the model and much of the personnel for the Central Intelligence Agency (CIA), which was established in 1947. *13 Rue Madeleine* was a paragon of cost-cutting semidocumentary technique, taking a total of seventy-five days on location, and not one day in the studio, to complete. Like other films of the type, its story material was drawn from contemporary documents and newspaper accounts, which were virtually costfree.

Huston's *The Asphalt Jungle* (1950), Elia Kazan's *On the Waterfront* (1954), and Alfred Hitchcock's *The Wrong Man* (1957) attest.

Film Noir

For a while, both the problem pictures and the semidocumentary crime thrillers made it seem that Italian neorealism had found a home in an uneasy, if affluent, America. The critic James Agee wrote in 1947, "One of the best things that is happening in Hollywood is the tendency to move out of the place—to base fictional pictures on fact and, more importantly, to shoot them not in painted studio sets but in actual places." But another variety of postwar American film, one which depended on the controlled environment of the studio as well as upon real locations for its depiction of the seamy underside of American life, soon appeared. This was *film noir* (literally, "black film"), discovered and named by French critics in 1946 when, seeing American motion pictures for the first time since 1940, they perceived a strange new mood of cynicism, darkness, and despair in certain crime films and melodramas. They derived the term from the "Serie Noire" detective novels then popular in France, many of which were translations of works by members of the "hard-boiled" school of American crime writers—Dashiell Hammett, Raymond Chandler, and James M. Cain (later joined by Horace McCoy, Mickey Spillane, and Jim Thompson)—whose books were also frequently adapted in *films noir.* Like the novels, these films were characterized by a down-beat atmosphere and graphic violence, and they carried postwar American pessimism to the point of nihilism by assuming the absolute and irredeemable corruption of society and of everyone in it. Billy Wilder's corrosive *Double Indemnity* (1944), which startled Hollywood in the year of its release and was almost banned by the Hays Office, may be regarded as the prototype for *film noir,* although some critics trace the origins back to such tough but considerably less cynical films as *This Gun for Hire* (Frank Tuttle, 1942), *The Maltese Falcon* (John Huston, 1941; adapted from Hammett), and *Stranger on the Third Floor* (Boris Ingster, 1940).* Adapted by Wilder and Raymond Chandler from a James M. Cain novel, *Double Indemnity* is the sordid story of a Los Angeles insurance agent (Fred MacMurray) seduced by a client's wife (Barbara Stanwyck) into murdering her husband for his death benefits; it has been called "a film without a single trace of pity or love."

Indeed, these are qualities notably absent from all *films noir,* as perhaps they seemed absent from the postwar America which produced them. Like *Double Indemnity,* these films thrived upon the unvarnished depiction of greed, lust, and cruelty because their basic theme was the depth

---

* It is possible, as Paul Schrader has argued ("Notes on *Film Noir,*" *Film Comment* 8, 1, Spring 1972), that *film noir* would have evolved naturally out of the late thirties and early forties had the war not intervened. But it also seems likely that the antiheroic vision of *film noir* was generated specifically in response to the actual horrors of the war and the multiple hypocrisies of postwar American society.

11.28 The prototypical *film noir: Double Indemnity* (Billy Wilder, 1944). Barbara Stanwyck, Fred MacMurray, Edward G. Robinson.

11.29 *Detour* (Edgar G. Ulmer, 1945): Ann Savage, Tom Neal.

of human depravity and the utterly unheroic nature of human beings—lessons that were hardly taught but certainly re-emphasized by the unique horrors of World War II. Most of the dark films of the late forties take the form of crime melodramas because (as Dostoevsky and Dickens knew) the mechanisms of crime and criminal detection provide a perfect metaphor for corruption that cuts across conventional moral categories. These films are often set in southern California—the topographical paradigm for a society in which the gap between expectation and reality is resolved through mass delusion. The protagonists are frequently unsympathetic antiheroes who pursue their base designs or simply drift aimlessly through sinister night worlds of the urban American jungle,* but they are just as

11.30 *The Blue Dahlia* (George Marshall, 1946): Alan Ladd, Veronica Lake.

* And they are antiheroes in the most extreme sense of the term: murderous *femmes fatales* (*Double Indemnity;* Edgar G. Ulmer's perverse "quickie" classic *Detour* [1945]; Tay Garnett's *The Postman Always Rings Twice* [1946]; John Cromwell's *Dead Reckoning* [1947]; Orson Welles' darkly brilliant *The Lady from Shanghai* [1948]); down-at-the-heels and / or paranoid private eyes (Edward Dmytryk's *Murder, My Sweet* [1945]; George Marshall's *The Blue Dahlia* [1946]; Jacques Tourneur's *Out of the Past* [1947]); fugitive criminals (Robert Siodmak's *The Killers* [1946], *Cry of the City* [1948], and *Criss Cross* [1949]; Delmer Daves' *Dark Passage* [1947]; Nicholas Ray's *They Live by Night* [1949]; Joseph H. Lewis' quintessential fugitive couple film *Gun Crazy* [also known as *Deadly Is the Female,* 1950]); ruthless con-men, blackmailers, and racketeers (Anthony Mann's *Desperate* [1947], *Railroaded* [1947], and *Raw Deal* [1948]; John Farrow's *The Big Clock* [1948]; Jules Dassin's *Night and the City* [1950]); psychopathic killers and / or mental patients (John Brahm's *The Locket* [1947]; Rudolph Maté's *The Dark Past* [1948]; Raoul Walsh's apocalyptic *White Heat* [1949]); corrupt, victimized, or simply neurotic cops (Otto Preminger's *Laura* [1944] and *Where the Sidewalk Ends* [1950]; Rudolph Maté's *D.O.A.* [1949]; Fritz Lang's *The Big Heat* [1953]); and, into the fifties, assorted punks, madmen, mobsters, and degenerates (John Huston's *The Asphalt Jungle* [1950]; Nicholas Ray's *In a Lonely Place* [1950] and *On Dangerous Ground* [1952]; Samuel Fuller's *Pickup on South Street* [1953]; Joseph H. Lewis' *The Big Combo* [1955]; Robert Aldrich's *noir* masterpiece *Kiss Me Deadly* [1955]). Significantly, many of *film noir*'s male protagonists are cynical, war-weary combat veterans—sometimes afflicted with amnesia or other psychological disabilities—and many

often decent people caught in traps laid for them by a corrupt social order. In this latter sense, *film noir* was very much a "cinema of moral anxiety" of the sort practiced at various times in postwar Eastern Europe, most recently in Poland at the height of the Solidarity movement—i.e., a cinema about the conditions of life forced upon honest people in a mendacious, self-deluding society.

The moral instability of this world was translated into a visual style by the great *noir* cinematographers John Alton, Nicholas Musuraca, John F. Seitz, Lee Garmes, Tony Gaudio, Sol Polito, Ernest Haller, Lucien Ballard, and James Wong Howe. These technicians rendered moral ambiguity palpably real through what has been called antitraditional cinematography. The style included the pervasive use of wide-angle lenses, permitting greater depth of field but causing expressive distortion in close-ups; low-key lighting and night-for-night shooting (that is, actually shooting night scenes at night rather than in bright daylight with dark filters), both of which create harsh contrasts between the light and dark areas of the frame, with dark predominating, to parallel the moral chaos of the world; and angular, unnatural compositions. If all of this seems reminiscent of the artificial studio technique of German Expressionism, it should, because—like the Universal horror cycle of the thirties—*film noir* was created to a large extent by German and Eastern European expatriates, many of whom had received their basic training at UFA in the twenties and early thirties. The *noir* directors Fritz Lang, Robert Siodmak, Billy Wilder, Otto Preminger, John Brahm, Anatole Litvak, Max Ophüls, William Dieterle, Douglas Sirk, Edgar G. Ulmer, and Curtis Bernhardt; the director-cinematographer Rudolph Maté; the cinematographers Karl Freund and John Alton; and the composers Franz Waxman and Max Steiner had all been associated with or influenced by the UFA studio style.

Nevertheless, given its subject matter, *film noir* could scarcely escape the general realistic tendency of the postwar cinema, and *noir* directors frequently shot exteriors on location. Such wartime innovations as smaller camera dollies and portable power packs, higher speed lenses and more sensitive, fine-grain film stocks simplified the logistics of location shooting and helped to create for *film noir* a nearly homogeneous visual style.* For this reason, it has become fashionable to speak of *film noir* as a type

11.31 *D.O.A.* (Rudolph Maté, 1949): Edmond O'Brien.

11.32 Female gothic: *Dragonwyck* (Joseph L. Mankiewicz, 1946): Gene Tierney, Vincent Price in the foreground; Anne Revere, Spring Byington, Jessica Tandy behind them.

11.33 *The Big Heat* (Fritz Lang, 1953): Glenn Ford.

---

of the women are wives, fiancées, and sweethearts who have betrayed their men with other lovers during the war. Furthermore, many stars of *film noir* (such as Dick Powell, Barbara Stanwyck, Fred MacMurray, John Garfield, Lana Turner, Alan Ladd, Joan Bennett, Deanna Durbin, Robert Cummings, Van Johnson, Robert Young, and Tyrone Power) were playing totally unsympathetic characters for the first time in their careers—playing, that is, against their established box office images, which added yet another touch of eeriness to the form.

* As Alain Silver and Elizabeth Ward point out in *Film Noir* (London: Secker & Warburg, 1979), in a random selection of productions—*The Big Clock* (Paramount), *Cry of the City* (RKO), *Strangers on a Train* (Warner's), *People Against O'Hara* (MGM), *Out of the Past* (RKO), *Criss Cross* (Universal), and *Dead Reckoning* (Columbia)—seven different directors and cinematographers, of great and small technical reputations, working at seven different studios, completed seven ostensibly unrelated motion pictures with one cohesive visual style.

11.34 The image of post-war *angst: In a Lonely Place* (Nicholas Ray, 1950). Humphrey Bogart, Gloria Grahame.

11.35 *The Big Combo* (Joseph H. Lewis, 1955).

11.36 *Kiss Me Deadly* (Robert Aldrich, 1955): Ralph Meeker.

(some believe it is a genre) of "romantic" or "expressive" realism; but its heritage includes such a wide range of cultural forces—German Expressionism and horror, American gangster films of the thirties, Sternbergian exoticism and decadence, the poetic realism of Carné and Duvivier, the hard-boiled tradition of American fiction, the forties popularization of Freud, postwar American disillusionment (especially a sense of sexual betrayal among returning GIs) and the wave of cinematic realism it engendered, cold war paranoia, and of course, *Citizen Kane*—that it seems better to characterize it as a cycle rather than to delimit its boundaries too rigidly.

Furthermore, as several critics have recently suggested, *film noir* describes a period as well as a style or a genre, for darkness and cynicism invaded *all* genres in the late-forties cinema, not simply that of the crime thriller and melodrama. Raymond Durgnat points out that films as disparate as John M. Stahl's bizarre romance *Leave Her to Heaven* (1945), King Vidor's epic western *Duel in the Sun* (1946), and Frank Capra's *It's a Wonderful Life* (1947) have distinctly *noir* elements, and there was a whole series of late-forties melodramas which may be said to range from off-black to gray, the models for which were Hitchcock's *Rebecca* (1940) and George Cukor's *Gaslight* (1944),* not to mention the atmospheric low-budget horror cycle of RKO producer Val Lewton (1904–51)—*Cat People, I Walked with a Zombie,* and *The Leopard Man* (Jacques Tourneur, 1942, 1943, and 1943); *The Seventh Victim* and *The Ghost Ship* (both Mark Robson, 1943); *The Curse of the Cat People* (Gunther Von Fritsch; Robert Wise, 1944); *Isle of the Dead* (Mark Robson, 1945); *The Body Snatcher* (Robert Wise, 1945); *Bedlam* (Mark Robson, 1946). In the end, perhaps the most categorical thing we can say about *film noir* is that both thematically and stylistically it represents a unique and highly creative countertradition in the American cinema, derived from eclectic sources and motivated by the pervasive existential cynicism of the postwar era. With several significant exceptions (*very* significant—for example, Mervyn LeRoy's *I Am a Fugitive from a Chain Gang* [1932], Fritz Lang's *Fury* [1936] and *You Only Live Once* [1937], Orson Welles' *Citizen Kane* [1941], John Huston's *The Maltese Falcon* [1941]), most American films of the prewar period—and most American films, for that matter—had

---

* Closely related to the *noir* cycle and concurrent with it, these gothic romances frequently had period settings and were produced by almost every studio in Hollywood between 1940 and 1952. Like the contemporary melodramas known as "women's pictures" (see note, p. 464), they were intended primarily for female audiences, and their appearance during the forties was the result of a widespread impression among studio executives that women comprised a majority of the film-going public. This may have been true for a short time during World War II, but, as Leo A. Handel pointed out in *Hollywood Looks at Its Audience: A Report of Film Audience Research* (Urbana: The University of Illinois Press, 1950), it was not at all the case before and after, when the sexes were almost evenly distributed in the national market. Representative gothic titles are *Rebecca* (1940), *Gaslight* (1944), *Experiment Perilous* (André De Toth, 1944), *Hangover Square* (John Brahm, 1945), *Dragonwyck* (Joseph L. Mankiewicz, 1946), *So Evil My Love* (Lewis Allen, 1948), *Sleep, My Love* (Douglas Sirk, 1948), and *My Cousin Rachel* (Henry Koster, 1952).

been optimistic, affirmative, and generally supportive of the status quo. We have seen, however, that postwar America produced, with the problem picture and the semidocumentary melodrama, a cinema of disillusionment and searching which rejected the epic heroics and callow idealism of World War II films—but always suggested that the inequities of American society could be resolved through good faith and work. Yet *film noir* showed all human values to be seriously embattled, if not ultimately corrupt, and sneered at the prospects for change (perhaps, as some suggest, because the atomic future was too frightening to contemplate). Never before had the American cinema handed down such extreme indictments of American society or any other, and it would not do so again until the late sixties, when the indictments would be mitigated by libertarian idealism. However briefly, then, *film noir* held up a dark mirror to postwar America and reflected its moral anarchy.* Not surprisingly, a number of important and powerful Americans did not like what they saw.

The Witch-Hunt and the Blacklist

Our cold war with the Soviet Union began officially in July 1947 when Stalin refused to accept the Marshall Plan for the Soviet Union or any of its satellites; but, of course, Soviet-American tensions, although briefly relaxed during the alliance to defeat Hitler, had been mounting ever since the Bolshevik Revolution. Among other things, this meant that in the public mind the menace of Nazi agents and fifth columnists was replaced by the menace of communist spies and "fellow travelers," doubly sinister since they looked just like everyone else and didn't speak with an accent.

---

* The revival of the genre in the Watergate era (*The Long Goodbye* [Robert Altman, 1973]; *The Outfit* [John Flynn, 1974]; *Chinatown* [Roman Polański, 1974]; *Farewell, My Lovely* [Dick Richards, 1975; a remake of Dmytryk's 1945 *Murder, My Sweet*]; *Night Moves* [Arthur Penn, 1975]; *The Nickel Ride* [Robert Mulligan, 1975]; *Hustle* [Robert Aldrich, 1975]; *Taxi Driver* [Martin Scorsese, 1976]) and during the morally bankrupt presidency of Ronald Reagan (*Body Heat* [Lawrence Kasdan, 1981]; Bob Rafelson's remake of *The Postman Always Rings Twice* [1981]; *Blade Runner* [Ridley Scott, 1982]; *Breathless* [Jim McBride, 1983]; *Against All Odds* [Taylor Hackford, 1984; a remake of Tourneur's *Out of the Past*]; *Blood Simple* [Joel and Ethan Coen, 1984]; *Body Double* [Brian De Palma, 1984]; *Jagged Edge* [Richard Manquard, 1985]; *Angel Heart* [Alan Parker, 1986]; *Blue Velvet* [David Lynch, l986]; *No Mercy* [Richard Pearce, 1987]; *Black Widow* [Bob Rafelson, 1987]; *Tough Guys Don't Dance* [Norman Mailer, 1987]; *Manhunter* [Michael Mann, 1987]; *No Way Out* [Roger Donaldson, 1987; a remake of *The Big Clock*]; *The Big Easy* [Jim McBride, 1987]; *Fatal Attraction* [Adrian Lyne, 1987]; *Best Seller* [John Flynn, 1987]; *Deadly Illusion* [William Tannen, 1987]; *House of Games* [David Mamet, 1987]; *Someone to Watch Over Me* [Ridley Scott, 1987]; *Slow Burn* [Matthew Chapman, 1987; Showtime]; *Lady Beware* [Karen Arthur, 1987]; *Suspect* [Peter Yates, 1987]; *The Stepfather* [Joseph Rubin, 1987]; *Positive ID* [Andy Anderson, 1987]; *Laguna Heat* [Simon Langton, 1987; HBO]; *Julia and Julia* [Peter Del Monte, 1987]; *Slamdance* [Wayne Wang, 1987]; *The Killing Time* [Rick King, 1987]; *Dead of Winter* [Arthur Penn, 1987]; *Masquerade* [Bob Swaim, 1988]; *The House on Carroll Street* [Peter Yates, 1988]; *D.O.A.* [Rocky Morton, 1988; a remake of the Rudolph Maté original, also remade in Australia as *Color Me Dead*, 1969]) suggests a continuing relationship between *film noir*, political malaise, and social disintegration.

Furthermore, what David Caute has called "the myth of the Vital Secret"—the half-baked notion that members of the American Communist Party were feverishly conducting atomic espionage on behalf of the Soviet Union—was widespread during this era and would result in the conviction of Alger Hiss (1948), the rise and fall of Senator Joseph R. McCarthy (1950–54), and the executions of Julius and Ethel Rosenberg (1953). Politically, the country was in the throes of an anti–New Deal backlash which had been building since the tumultuous thirties, and Hollywood, as a signal beneficiary of FDR's economic and social policies,* became the target for a squalid inquisition that brought shame and / or ruin to hundreds of key industry personnel.

In the spring of 1947 the House Committee on Un-American Activities (commonly—and pejoratively—known as HUAC), which had been inactive since the hot war ended, decided to undertake a full-scale investigation of what its chairman, J. Parnell Thomas (R-N.J.), called "communism in motion pictures." As John Howard Lawson, one of the victims of this investigation, later wrote, the charge that American films contained "communist propaganda" in the late forties or at any other time was wholly laughable, because the American film industry was one of the most conservative elements in the country. There were, however, recent films of predominantly liberal sentiment, such as the problem pictures and the semidocumentary melodramas, and there were the apolitical *films noir,* which did not take a very sanguine view of life under any system of government. There were also all of those pro-Russian films made at the OWI's behest during the war, when the Soviet Union had been our ally (a HUAC subcommittee report would later claim that "some of the most flagrant Communist propaganda films were produced as a result of White House pressure" during the war and that Roosevelt's National Labor Relations Board had infiltrated communists into the industry). But most damaging of all, because there was at least factual substance to the charge, a number of famous Hollywood directors, screenwriters, and actors had joined the Communist Party or contributed funds to its activities during the Depression, when it had seemed to offer a viable alternative to starving under capitalism. Some had merely supported causes, such as relief for refugees from Franco's Spain, that also were supported by communists. It was among these people, most of whom had dropped their Communist Party affiliation years before, that HUAC was able to do the most damage.

In September 1947 the tragicomedy began as the Committee subpoe-

---

* In addition to the perks mentioned in the note on p. 456, Roosevelt had exempted motion pictures from war censorship in 1941 and, together with other information media, from licensing as a condition of sale or distribution in 1942—effectively, if temporarily, granting films First Amendment protection under the Constitution. Furthermore, as Richard Maltby points out in "Made for Each Other: The Melodrama of Hollywood and the House Committee on Un-American Activities, 1947," by doing so, FDR's administration had provided the film industry with an unprecedented degree of social and political status. (See, *Cinema, Politics and Society in America,* ed. Philip Davies and Brian Neve [New York: St. Martin's, 1981], pp. 76–96.)

11.37 Subpoenaed filmmakers leaving the HUAC hearing-room in October 1947; ten would soon go to jail for contempt of Congress. Left to right: (front row) Lewis Milestone, Dalton Trumbo, John Howard Lawson, and attorney Bartley Crum; (center row) Gordon Kahn, Irving Pichel, Edward Dmytryk, and Robert Rossen; (back row) Waldo Salt, Richard Collins, Howard Koch, Albert Maltz, Herbert Biberman, Lester Cole, Ring Lardner, Jr., and attorney Martin Popper.

naed forty-one witnesses, nineteen of whom declared their intention to be "unfriendly"—i.e., to refuse to answer questions about their political beliefs. When the hearings began on October 20, the so-called friendly witnesses—among them the producers Jack L. Warner and Louis B. Mayer; the writers Ayn Rand and Morrie Ryskind; the actors Adolph Menjou, Robert Taylor, Robert Montgomery, George Murphy, Ronald Reagan, and Gary Cooper; the directors Leo McCarey and Sam Wood; and producer-director Walt Disney—were called first. They proved their patriotism by naming people whom they identified as leftists, and generally telling the congressmen what they wanted to hear ("Hollywood," claimed the right-winger Menjou, "is one of the main centers of Communist activity in America"; Disney testified that the Screen Cartoonists Guild was Communist-dominated and had tried to take over his studio). Of the nineteen unfriendly witnesses, eleven were summoned to the witness stand the following week for questioning about their alleged Communist Party membership*—the German émigré playwright Bertolt Brecht; the screenwriters Alvah Bessie, Lester Cole, Ring Lardner, Jr., John Howard Lawson, Albert Maltz, Samuel Ornitz, Adrian Scott, and Dalton Trumbo; and the directors Herbert Biberman and Edward Dmytryk. Hollywood liberals, including John Huston, William Wyler, Gene Kelly, Danny Kaye, Humphrey Bogart, and Lauren Bacall, responded by forming the Committee for the First Amendment (CFA) to fight for the constitutional rights of the "accused witnesses"—a contradiction in the terms of jurisprudence, if there ever was one—but opposition faltered when the now-famous "Hollywood Ten" listed above (less Brecht, who temporized before the

---

* There was about this more than a whiff of anti-Semitism, as thirteen of the nineteen were Jewish and a number of Congressmen were on record as believing that America had been duped into supporting the wrong side in World War II by a "Jewish-Bolshevist" (read "anti-Nazi") conspiracy in Hollywood—a ridiculous, not to say criminally stupid, attitude given the moguls' unwillingness to offend even Hitler himself before our entry into the war (see note, pp. 359–60).

Committee and fled the country several days later) defied HUAC by refusing to testify and were subsequently given prison sentences of six months to a year for contempt of Congress.* The Committee's action was scandalous, but its meaning was crystal clear: HUAC wished to purge Hollywood and, if possible, the entire country of any and all liberal tendencies by creating and then exploiting anticommunist hysteria. The threat of state censorship loomed, and panic broke out in the nation's most image-conscious industry, which was already plagued by antitrust actions, unemployment, and rapidly declining profits.

On November 24, 1947, the same day that the House of Representatives by a nearly unanimous vote approved HUAC's contempt citations for the Ten, Hollywood closed ranks against some of the most talented artists it had ever known. The fifty members of the Motion Picture Association of America (MPAA; MPPDA before 1945) and the Association of Motion Picture Producers† (representing the industry's most powerful executives, including Eric Johnston, Nicholas M. Schenck, Harry Cohn, Joseph M. Schenck, Walter Wanger, Samuel Goldwyn, Henry Ginsberg, Albert Warner, Louis B. Mayer, Dore Schary, Spyros Skouras, and William Goetz) produced the "Waldorf Statement" censuring the behavior of the Ten, firing them, and refusing to reemploy any one of them "until such time as he is acquitted or has purged himself of contempt and declares under oath that he is not a Communist." The statement continued by spelling out future industry policy: "We will not knowingly employ a Communist or member of any party or group which advocates the overthrow of the government of the United States by force or by illegal or unconstitutional methods." This was the beginning of the infamous practice of blacklisting, which brought to an end one of the most creative

---

* Since the hearings were not a court of law, "unfriendly" witnesses were not allowed to be accompanied by their lawyers or to cross-examine other witnesses, nor was documented evidence required of their accusers. The Ten tried to read prepared statements but only Maltz was permitted to do so. When questioned about their own political activities and beliefs—and those of their friends and casual acquaintances—they refused to answer (Ring Lardner, Jr., quipped: "I could answer that question, but I would hate myself in the morning"), invoking their rights under the First and Fifth Amendments to the U.S. Constitution. The Ten were cited for contempt by the House in November and indicted by a federal grand jury the following month. Blacklisted and unemployed, they spent the next few years raising funds for their appeals and other costs (this included lecture tours and the production of a polemical twenty–minute short called *The Hollywood Ten,* 1948). The appellate process was exhausted in April 1950, when the Supreme Court denied *certiorari,* and in June all ten went to federal prison—two of them for six months and eight for a year— along with the chairman of the Committee, who had, in the interim, been convicted of mishandling public funds. See Larry Ceplair and Steven Englund, *The Inquisition in Hollywood: Politics in the Film Community, 1930–1960* (Garden City, N.Y.: Doubleday, 1980; repr. Berkeley: University of California Press, 1983); Victor S. Navasky, *Naming Names* (New York: Simon and Schuster, 1980); also *Hollywood on Trial* (Tristam Powell, 1973), a feature-length documentary on the hearings produced by the BBC.

† The business and public relations component of the MPAA, now the Association of Motion Picture and Television Producers (AMPTP). Among other functions the AMPTP negotiates labor contracts for its members and maintains Central Casting Corporation as a means of supplying extras.

periods in the history of American film and made Hollywood a wasteland of vapidity, complacency, and cowardice for well over a decade. From 1948 to 1951, there was a lull of sorts as the production community drew a cautionary lesson from the fate of the Ten and allowed the Committee for the First Amendment to disintegrate, with Bogart and Bacall, for example, publicly calling their participation a "mistake."* The once-liberal Screen Actors Guild (SAG), under the new leadership of Ronald Reagan, required that its members take a loyalty oath, and in the following year openly condoned the blacklist. But in March 1951 HUAC, now chaired by John S. Wood (D-Ga.), began a new onslaught by subpoenaing forty-five unfriendly witnesses who were called upon very specifically to name names and inform on former colleagues. By the end of the second round of hearings—which were televised, adding to their *frisson*—110 men and women had testified, fifty-eight of them confessing past Party membership and collectively providing the Committee with the names of 212 alleged fellow travelers. Those who refused to inform were put under tremendous pressure to "come clean"—a process of self-abasement which involved denouncing one's friends (especially if they had already been denounced by previous witnesses), confessing one's own guilt by association, and groveling not only before HUAC but before a host of self-appointed Grand Inquisitors and "clearance" agencies in the private sector, such as the American Legion and American Business Consultants, editors of the scurrilous public blacklists *Counterattack* and *Red Channels*.

Some refused to cringe, and at the end of the process in 1951 (which was resumed when Senator Pat McCarran's Internal Security Subcommittee reopened the hearings in 1952, subpoenaing Judy Holiday, Burl Ives, and others), 324 persons had been fired by the studios and were no longer permitted to work in the American film industry.† Among them were some of the most talented directors, writers, and actors of the postwar cinema: Joseph Losey (*The Lawless*, 1950), Michael Gordon (*Another Part of the Forest*, 1947), Jules Dassin (*The Naked City*, 1948), Abraham

---

* The format for Bogart's recantation was an article he wrote for the March 1948 issue of *Photoplay* magazine entitled "I'm No Communist," in which he admitted being a "dope." The title is resonant of many such public confessions of the era, for example, John Garfield's self-abasing "I Was a Sucker for a Left Hook," which was to have appeared in a fall 1951 issue of *Look* magazine shortly before his death, and Edward G. Robinson's wretched "How the Reds Made a Sucker Out of Me," ghost-written for him by the professional Red-hunter and Hearst columnist George Sokolsky, which was published in the *American Legion Magazine* in October 1952.

† The Waldorf Statement also admitted the risk of "creating an atmosphere of fear" and "hurting innocent people," but the hard-line implications of the policy were clear, and many observers felt that the film executives had been pressured into adopting it by their conservative Wall Street financiers, who had approximately 60 million dollars invested in the industry at the time. Ed Sullivan, for example, remarked of the Waldorf Statement, "Wall Street jiggled the strings, that's all" (quoted in Andrew Dowdy, *The Films of the Fifties: The American State of Mind* [New York: William Morrow, 1973], p. 20). The blacklist extended also to radio, television, Broadway, and even folksinging and provincial theater.

Polonsky (*Force of Evil,* 1948), and Herbert Biberman (*The Master Race,* 1944); also Carl Foreman, Donald Ogden Stewart, Albert Maltz, Guy Endore, Dorothy Parker, Lillian Hellman, Gordon Kahn, Howard Koch, Sidney Buchman, Ring Lardner, Jr., John Howard Lawson, Dalton Trumbo, Lester Cole, Samuel Ornitz, Adrian Scott, and Waldo Salt; Gale Sondergaard, Karen Morley, Dorothy Comingore, Lee Grant, Sam Jaffe, Lionel Stander, Zero Mostel, Anne Revere, Larry Parks, Paul Muni, John Garfield, Jeff Corey, Will Geer, Howard Da Silva, and many others.

Some of the writers were able to make a living by selling their scripts on the black market under the names of real people, or "fronts."* (The 1956 Academy Award for the Best Original Screenplay, for example, went to a mysterious "Mr. Robert Rich" for Irving Rapper's *The Brave One*—the Oscar could not be picked up at the time because Rich was actually Dalton Trumbo; four years later, tensions had relaxed to the point that Trumbo could receive screen credit in his own name—for Otto Preminger's *Exodus* and Stanley Kubrick's *Spartacus,* both 1960.) But the highly visible actors and directors were doomed to unemployment (Muni) or exile (Losey and Dassin went to Europe). Some lost their lives: Philip Loeb, one of the stars of the popular television series *The Goldbergs,* committed suicide; the screen actors John Garfield, Canada Lee, J. Edward Bromberg, and Mady Christians died as a result of the stress they were subjected to. Hundreds of other film people were maligned by HUAC but managed to survive under the cloud of either marginal blacklisting (e.g., Lewis Milestone, Fredric March, Jose Ferrer, Edward G. Robinson) or their own collaboration with the investigating body (e.g., Elia Kazan, Richard Collins, Harold Hecht, Clifford Odets, Isobel Lennart, Bernard Schoenfeld, Lee J. Cobb, Lucille Ball, Sterling Hayden, Lloyd Bridges, Frank Tuttle, Budd Schulberg, and ultimately, Edward Dmytryk and Robert Rossen). Several commentators have suggested that for members of the latter group the moral catastrophe of informing proved as destructive as the practical effects of being blacklisted, but materially, at least, quite the reverse was true. While the victims of the blacklist lost their jobs, families, and even their lives, most of the informers prospered. Ball, Cobb, Schulberg, and Kazan, for example, were all rewarded with stunning career success in the fifties, Kazan winning an Academy Award for directing a paean to informing in *On the Waterfront* (1954)—which, not coincidentally, was written by Schulberg, starred Cobb, and was also named Best Film of the Year by the Academy, the New York Critics Society, and the National Board of Review. At the same time, Lester Cole was working in a warehouse, Sidney Buchman operated a parking garage, and Alvah Bessie was a stagehand at a nightclub; others struggled to support their families as maître d's, appliance repairmen, and outside salesmen.

---

* As in *The Front* (Martin Ritt, 1976), a film about television blacklisting made by a formerly blacklisted writer, director, and producer, with Woody Allen in the title role. The first Hollywood film to deal openly with the blacklist was Sidney Pollack's *The Way We Were* (1973), which was nevertheless heavily cut for general release.

The practice of blacklisting in the American film industry continued well into the fifties, and its impact was felt throughout the sixties.* Abraham Polonsky, for example, was not able to direct again in Hollywood until 1968, when his *Tell Them Willie Boy Is Here* appeared—twenty-one years after *Force of Evil*. But as damaging to the American cinema as the loss of individual talent, was the pervasive mood of fear, distrust, and self-loathing that settled over Hollywood in the wake of the hearings. Everyone was scared of the government and of everyone else, and the industry tacitly imposed a form of self-censorship more repressive and sterile than anything HUAC could have devised. As early as 1948, William Wyler speculated that a modestly progressive film like his own *The Best Years of Our Lives* (1946) could not be made in America again, adding, "In a few months we won't be able to have a heavy who is an American." Wyler was right. No one in Hollywood was willing to take the slightest chance on anybody or anything; the industry had had its fill of trouble and wanted no more of it. Safety, caution, and respectability were the watchwords of the studio chiefs, and controversial or even serious subject matter was avoided at all costs. Thus, vitiated, frightened, and drained of creative vitality, Hollywood experienced in miniature what the whole of American society was to experience during the McCarthy-era witch-hunts—intellectual stagnation and moral paralysis.

The Arrival of Television

Finally, as if the devastating impact of the hearings were not enough to sink Hollywood's already foundering ship, a new entertainment medium suddenly emerged which threatened to do the job all by itself. This, of course, was **television**—a system for transmitting moving images based on the process of electronic image analysis and synthesis† patented by the independent inventor Philo T. Farnsworth in 1930. RCA, which had been moving toward the development of just such a system for several years through the work of the Russian scientist Vladimir K. Zworkin, attempted first to buy and then to preempt Farnsworth's patents through litigation. But in 1939 the courts gave legal priority to Farnsworth, and in September RCA licensed his patents for a period of ten years for a

---

*In the American theater, blacklisting continued until the late fifties. In radio and television, it did not end until the mid-sixties. The effect of blacklisting on the content of American motion pictures, as charted by Dorothy B. Jones, shows the following shift: 28 percent of all Hollywood films dealt with "social themes or psychological problems" in 1947; the percentage declined to only 9.2 in 1954. See Jones, "Communism and the Movies: A Study of Film Content," in John Cogley, *Report on Blacklisting* (New York: Fund for the Republic, 1956), Volume I, pp. 196–233.

†In this process, simply put, the image to be transmitted is broken down into 100,000 to 200,000 "bits" of discrete audiovisual information, or "picture elements," by a camera tube; these are broadcast as FM electronic signals to video receivers where they are resynthesized as images by picture tubes (see note, p. 898). William Lafferty points out, however, that in very broad terms, "the technical development of television paralleled that of motion pictures, although displaced by almost fifty years." See Lafferty, "Chapter II: Film and Television," in *Film and the Arts: A Research Guide*. ed. Gary Edgerton (forthcoming).

million dollars—the first and only time in its history that the corporation was forced to pay royalties rather than collect them. Formally introduced to the public at the 1939 New York World's Fair, television was a smashing success, and RCA began marketing receivers in the same year for regularly scheduled daily broadcasts (about fifteen hours per week) via its NBC subsidiary. CBS began telecasting in the following year, and in July 1941 the FCC set format standards for black-and-white transmission and authorized the full operation of commercial television. Wartime restrictions soon put a halt to the manufacture of television transmission equipment and receivers, and the networks were forced to sharply curtail their telecasts. When the war ended, however, they resumed regular daily telecasting, and the production of transmitters and receivers burgeoned. By 1949 there were 1 million TV sets in use in the United States, and the television broadcasting industry had begun in earnest. Only two years later, there were ten times that many sets in use, and by 1959 the number had risen to 50 million. In 1946, when two-thirds of the total population of the country went to the movies weekly, attendance had been guaranteed by the nearly complete lack of alternate sources of audiovisual entertainment. Now that lack was met with a vengeance.

At first, Hollywood attempted to enter the television business by applying for station licenses in major markets and by innovating large-screen television in its theater circuits (HBO-like subscription programming for in-house viewing was also tested). But the studios were out-maneuvered politically by the dominant radio networks, and NBC, CBS, and ABC moved directly into television broadcasting with the blessing of an FCC which looked askance at the movie monopolists' recent conviction in the Paramount case; in this context, moreover, theater / subscription television simply could not compete with the "free" programming provided by the networks.* When it became clear that film and television were in direct competition for the same audience, the members of the MPAA adopted a bunker mentality and until 1956 refused to sell or lease their product for broadcast—a strategy that in the long run may have hurt the industry financially more than either direct competition from television itself or the Paramount decrees. Furthermore, many studios contractually restrained their stars from appearing on television, which simply stimulated the new medium to develop star personalities on its own, and by 1949 the American film industry was seriously threatened by television. In that year, attendance dropped to 70 million, from 90 million in 1948, and it continued to decline in direct proportion to the number of television sets in use. In the first quarter of 1949, only twenty-two features, or half the normal number, were in production in Hollywood, and by the end of the year the major studios were ordering large layoffs and salary reductions, star contracts were being permitted to lapse, and all over the country the great movie palaces had begun to close their doors.

11.38 As the fifties begin, America's dream palaces succumb to television.

---

* Paramount did, however, acquire a controlling share of the short-lived Dumont network (1945–55); and United Paramount Theaters, the 1,424–screen exhibition chain Paramount was forced to spin off in 1949 by the consent decrees, was merged with ABC from 1952 until 1978, when the broadcaster sold it to Plitt Theaters, Inc.

In the wake of three years of unprecedented bad luck, a spiritual torpor descended upon Hollywood (some critics have speculated that the most manic of the late *films noir* are unconscious reflections of this malaise). From the pinnacle of its creative and commercial power in 1946–47, the American cinema, assisted by labor disputes, antitrust actions, political investigations, and television, had been brought very low indeed, and in 1949 many people took it for granted that Hollywood could never recover its losses. But those who predicted the demise of Hollywood overlooked the American film industry's quintessential feature: its nearly protean capacity for adaptation. Though Hollywood was never to recover its immediate postwar status or to recapture its once vast audiences from television, in the decade of the fifties it adapted, counterattacked, and—as always (to date, at least)—survived.

Hollywood, 1952–1965

Everything that characterized Hollywood between 1952 and 1965 can be understood as a response to anticommunist hysteria and the blacklist on the one hand and to the advent of television and economic divestiture on the other. In the name of combatting communism, films of serious social comment, such as the "problem pictures" and semidocumentary melodramas so popular in the immediate postwar years, could no longer be made. Instead, Westerns, musical comedies, lengthy costume epics, and other traditional genre fare—sanitized and shorn of political and social referents—became the order of the day. Such films dominated the domestic market of the era both because their subject matter was uncontroversial and because their spectacular nature was suited to the new screen formats, which the studios had embraced to combat television and, simultaneously, to make their product more attractive to their former subsidiaries, the newly independent first-run exhibitors.

THE CONVERSION TO COLOR

Television threatened Hollywood with a new technology, and Hollywood fought back in kind by isolating and exploiting the technological advantages that film possessed over television. The cinema had two such advantages in the early fifties, both of them associated with spectacle—the vast size of its images, and the capacity to produce them in color. (Soon, the capacity for stereophonic sound would be added to the list.) It was the competition with television that resulted in Hollywood's rapid conversion from black-and-white to color production between 1952 and 1955. In 1947 only 12 percent of American feature films were made in color; by 1954 the figure had risen to over 50 percent.*

The changeover was made possible by the breakup of Technicolor's *de facto* monopoly over color technology and aesthetics. The Justice Department had filed an antitrust suit against Technicolor and its supplier Eastman Kodak in 1947 for monopolization of color cinematogra-

---

* Ironically, color production declined to about 25 percent of the total between 1955 and 1958, when Hollywood began to sell recent features to television and created an important second market for its theatrical films. At this point, using black-and-white film became an effective way to cut production costs (at least for the television market), since almost all television broadcasts of the day were in black and white. But as American television converted to full-color broadcasting between 1965 and 1970, color films became an attraction for both the theatrical *and* the television market, causing Hollywood color production to increase dramatically until it reached 94 percent of the total by 1970.

phy. Even though yearly Technicolor production did not increase dramatically—from under twenty films in the early forties to over fifty in 1948—and rival processes such as Cinecolor and Trucolor were in general use, the company was judged to exercise a monopoly by virtue of its authoritarian control of the three-color process. In 1950, a federal consent decree ordered the corporation to set aside a certain number of its three-strip cameras for use by independent producers and minor studios on a first-come, first-served basis. But it was another event of that year, commercial introduction of a viable single-strip color process in Eastmancolor, that finally brought Technicolor's effective monopoly to an end.

First used experimentally in 1949, Eastmancolor was based on the German Agfacolor process invented for 16mm use by the Agfa Corporation in 1936. Like Technicolor monopack, Agfacolor used a multilayered film stock, but the layers were composed of photographic emulsions sensitive to red, green, and blue bonded together in a single roll. This "integral tripack" negative formed three color images simultaneously and, after development through a process known as "dye-coupling,"* was printed onto a multilayered positive film for release. First used commercially in 1940, the process briefly became a jewel in the crown of Nazi cinema when it was used in such spectacular productions as *Die goldene Stadt* (*The Golden City,* Viet Harlan, 1942), *Immensee* (*Immense,* Veit Harlan, 1943), *Baron Münchausen* (Josef von Baky, 1945), and *Kolberg* (Veit Harlan, 1945; rereleased 1966). Eisenstein used Agfacolor stock captured from the studios of liberated Prague to film the color sequences of *Ivan the Terrible, Part II* (1945–46), and it became the technical basis for the Sovcolor system officially adopted by the Soviet industry during the fifties (Sergei Yutkevich's *Othello,* 1956, was the first major Sovcolor feature). After the war and the release of Agfa's patents, Agfacolor principles were also used in a number of Western systems, most notably Anscocolor, which had wide currency in Hollywood from 1953 to 1955 and appeared in such popular productions as *The Wild North* (Andrew Marton, 1953), *Kiss Me Kate* (George Sidney, 1953), *Seven Brides for Seven Brothers* (Stanley Donen, 1954), *The Student Prince* (Richard Thorpe, 1954), and *Brigadoon* (Vincente Minnelli, 1954). But it was Kodak's subtle refinement of integral tripack that permitted Eastmancolor to replace Technicolor as the dominant color system of the West (just as Fujicolor, another Agfa-based system introduced in 1955 in Japan, would replace it in the East).

Unlike Agfacolor, Sovcolor, or Anscocolor, Eastmancolor incorporated "automatic color masking," a principle already used successfully in Kodacolor still photography to enhance the clarity and brilliance of the final print. Eastmancolor was thus able to offer the industry a low-cost negative tripack stock capable of excellent color contrast, which could be shot through a conventional single-lens camera and processed in a

---

* The globules of dye in the different emulsion layers are coupled to silver grains and their dyes are released during development of those grains.

conventional laboratory, just like black and white. When it was discovered simultaneously that imbibition printing did not yield enough resolution for the new anamorphic widescreen processes (see pp. 488–90), Technicolor's fate was sealed. In 1952, Kodak received an Academy Award for Eastmancolor (Scientific or Technical Award, Class I), and within two years the Technicolor three-strip camera and special processing service was rendered obsolete. (Technicolor cameras were used for the last time in the production of *Foxfire* [Joseph Pevney, 1955], but Technicolor continued its imbibition printing activities—subsequently improved for use with widescreen—until 1975, using Eastmancolor negatives to produce its matrices.) Though the system has since come to be known by the trade names of the studios who pay to use it (Warnercolor, Metrocolor, Pathecolor) or the labs that do the processing (Movielab, Technicolor, Deluxe), it was Kodak Eastmancolor which inaugurated and sustained the full-color age with integral tripack and dye-coupler printing, and by 1975 even the Technicolor Corporation had converted to a printing process similar to Eastman's.* Since the fifties, color has become an infinitely more subtle medium than black-and-white (which does *not* mean that black-and-white originals have anything to gain aesthetically from computerized colorization), and color cinematography has today reached an unparalleled degree of sophistication. By 1979, 96 percent of all American feature films were being made in color.

WIDESCREEN† AND 3-D

Multiple-Camera / Projector Widescreen: Cinerama

In a simultaneous attempt to exploit the *size* of the screen image, Hollywood began to experiment with new optical systems that lent greater width and depth to the image. The earliest of the new formats was a multiple-camera / projector widescreen process called **Cinerama,** introduced in September 1952, that was similar to the Polyvision process Abel Gance had used in *Napoléon* (1927) some twenty-five years before (see

---

* The problem with the Eastman-based systems, unforeseen at the time of their introduction and not manifest until a decade afterward, is that dye-coupling produces color much less stable (i.e., more subject to fading) than Technicolor's older imbibition process. (Ironically, the only Technicolor imbibition printing plant in operation in the world today is in the People's Republic of China.) While all color prints are subject to fading, most color films and negatives made in dye-coupler processes—that is, most American films made between 1955 and the present—are in imminent danger of extinction, and preserving them is the number-one problem facing film archivists today.

† Several scholars (e.g., Bruce F. Kawin in *How Movies Work* [New York: Macmillan, 1987]) use the term "widescreen" to refer specifically to flat (i.e., nonprocessed) film formats with aspect ratios of 1.66:1 (European standard) or 1.85:1 (American standard), which are achieved by either masking 35mm film or using one of several wide-film systems. Here and throughout the book, I use the term more broadly to denote *all* formats that give a screen image wider than the Academy ratio of 1.33:1, whether processed or not. (See p. 488.)

12.1 A schematic diagram of the multiple-camera Cinerama photography and projection process. Reprinted by permission of the University of California Press from *The Quarterly of Film, Radio, and Television*, XI, 2 (Winter 1956); 126.

Chapter 9) and that was originally devised as a battle simulator for gunnery training during World War II by the inventor Fred Waller (1886–1954). In Cinerama, three synchronized 35mm cameras linked together in an arc would simultaneously record a wide-field image, which three similarly linked projectors would later cast upon a vast wraparound screen (actually a three-screen triptych). The projected image was thus three times as wide as the standard 35mm image; it was also nearly twice as tall because of two extra sprocket holes (six instead of four) per frame on the film strip.* The seams between the three images were concealed by a slight overlapping of the camera lenses and by floating metal combs in the projectors, a technique that never proved wholly satisfactory. Nevertheless, the Cinerama image was six times the standard size, and its curvilinear shape added the phenomenon of peripheral vision to the screen. Cinerama also surrounded its audience with seven-track stereophonic sound, recorded magnetically rather than optically on a separate strip of 35mm film, which permitted a directional use of sound appro-

---

* The Cinerama aspect ratio varied from 3:1 to 2.6:1; it covered a visual field which extended 146 degrees horizontally and 55 degrees vertically, approximating the cone of human sight (180 degrees horizontally and 90 degrees vertically). Furthermore, Cinerama was originally shot and projected at twenty-six frames per second to achieve crisper resolution and heighten the illusion of actuality.

priate to its sprawling image. All of these factors combined to create an illusion of depth and spectator involvement which was quite thrilling to audiences accustomed to the flat rectilinear screen of decades past, and for a time Cinerama became immensely popular.

But the process was cumbersome and very expensive for both film-maker and exhibitor, and therefore for the paying public. Only theaters in large cities could afford to install the complicated projection equipment and the huge three-panel screens (the installation cost seventy-five thousand dollars), and so it was as a costly urban novelty that Cinerama enjoyed its initial success. Accordingly, it offered its audiences circuses rather than narrative. Films like *This Is Cinerama* (1952),* *Cinerama Holiday* (1955), *The Seven Wonders of the World* (1956), *Search for Paradise* (1957), *Cinerama South Seas Adventure* (1958), and *Windjammer* (1958—shot in a rival process called Cinemiracle, which had been bought out by the Cinerama Corporation) featured a succession of wild rides, extravagant spectacles, and exotic travelogues, but no stories. The first story films made in Cinerama, *How the West Was Won* (1962) and *The Wonderful World of the Brothers Grimm* (1962), proved that the multiple-camera process was simply too clumsy and costly for the production of conventional narratives.† *How the West Was Won,* for example, required the services of three directors (John Ford, Henry Hathaway, and George Marshall) and four cinematographers; it cost the then staggering sum of 14 million dollars to shoot.

In 1963, driven by economic necessity, Cinerama appropriated a wide-film widescreen system (Ultra Panavision) for its next film, *It's a Mad, Mad, Mad, Mad World* (1963), and finally adopted its own wide-film system, Ultra Cinerama, which combined with a special elliptical projection lens, allowed it to keep and fill its deeply curved screen. Given its great expense and peculiar technology, multiple-camera Cinerama never really had a chance of becoming a widely used process. At the height of its popularity, only a hundred cities all over the world were equipped to show Cinerama films. But the astounding success of Cinerama in the early fifties was the catalyst that started the widescreen revolution and brought audiences back into the theaters again in large numbers for the first time since 1946. For this reason alone, Cinerama holds a special place in the history of film.

Depth: Stereoscopic 3-D

Hollywood's next experiment with new optical formats was considerably less successful, although like Cinerama, it was initially quite popular. Stereoscopic 3-D had precedents in the cinema's earliest days, when such pioneers as William Friese-Greene and the Lumières experimented

---

* Coproduced by Merian C. Cooper, with a prologue directed by Ernest B. Schoedsack— the creators of *King Kong* twenty years before.

† In fact, to simplify logistics, portions of both films were shot with a single-camera 65mm system whose negative was optically divided into three 35mm positive prints for Cinerama projection.

12.2   A contemporary advertisement for *Kiss Me Kate* (George Sidney, 1953), giving a fanciful impression of 3-D illusion: Howard Keel, Ann Miller, Kathryn Grayson. MGM.

12.3   A 1953 audience wearing 3-D glasses.

with anaglyphic systems. In these, two strips of film, one tinted red and the other blue-green, were projected simultaneously for an audience wearing glasses with red and blue-green filtered lenses. The effect was stereoscopic synthesis in monochrome,* and experiments with anaglyphic 3-D continued into the twenties when Harry K. Fairall produced the first feature film, *The Power of Love* (1922), in the process. In the late thirties, MGM released a series of anaglyphic shorts produced by Pete Smith under the title of "Audioscopiks," but in the meantime Edwin Land had developed polarized filters which permitted the production of full-color 3-D images. Polarized features using lenses developed concurrently by Zeiss-Ikon, A.G., were produced in Italy in 1936 (*Nozze vagabone* [*Beggar's Wedding*]) and in Germany in 1937 (*Zum Greifen Nah* [*You Can Nearly Touch It*]) and in 1939 (*Sech Madel Rollen in Wochenend* [*Six Girls Drive into the Weekend*]), and the Chrysler Corporation presented a polarized 3-D short in Technicolor at the New York World's Fair in 1939 (also the site of the "the Perisphere," Fred Waller's first multiple camera / projector demonstration), but the war postponed further exploitation of the process.

In November 1952, however, the independent producer Arch Oboler (b. 1909) introduced a polarized 3-D process called Natural Vision that had been invented by a team of opticians and camera engineers, in the

---

* In stereoscopy, as in reality, depth perception is a function of binocular vision: because our eyes function separately and are spaced apart, each has a slightly different perspective on the same image; the brain resolves the two images into a single one with a depth dimension. Stereoscopy depends upon photographic mimicry of this process: The viewer is presented with a set of paired images, each of which represents the angle of vision of the left or the right eye, and is accessible to that eye only (e.g., through anaglyphasis, or polarization), so that the brain is forced to process the two images as a single three-dimensional one, even though both are flat.

12.4 Warner Bros.' *House of Wax* (André de Toth, 1953; re-released, 1971), originally filmed in Natural Vision and Warnercolor.

Anscocolor feature *Bwana Devil*. In Natural Vision, two interlocked cameras whose lenses were positioned to approximate the distance between the human eyes recorded a scene on two separate negatives. In the theater, when the two positive prints were projected simultaneously onto the screen from the same angles as the camera lenses, spectators wearing disposable glasses with polarized lenses perceived them as a single three-dimensional image. Roundly trashed by reviewers, *Bwana Devil* nevertheless became a phenomenal box-office hit, and the studios were so impressed that most of them rushed into 3-D production, using either Natural Vision or some other stereoscopic process. As Arthur Knight points out, the great appeal of Natural Vision for Hollywood was that it required no large-scale conversion of existing equipment, as did Cinerama, but only the addition of a twin-lens Natural Vision camera. Similarly, the cost of projector installation to exhibitors was less than two thousand dollars, a bargain compared with Cinerama's seventy-five thousand dollars. The second Natural Vision feature, Warner Bros.' *House of Wax* (André de Toth, 1953; re-released in 1971), featuring six-track stereophonic sound, was a critical as well as a popular success, returning 5.5 million dollars on an investment of 680,000 dollars, and the race to produce "depthies," as the trade press was now calling them, became a stampede.

Between 1953 and 1954 Hollywood produced sixty-nine features in 3-D, mostly action films that could exploit the depth illusion—Westerns like *Charge at Feather River* (Gordon Douglas, 1953) and *Taza, Son of Cochise* (Douglas Sirk, 1954), science-fiction films like *It Came from Outer Space* (Jack Arnold, 1953) and *Creature from the Black Lagoon* (Jack Arnold, 1954),* and horror films like *The Maze* (William Cameron Menzies, 1953) and *Phantom of the Rue Morgue* (Roy Del Ruth, 1954). The craze for stereoscopic 3-D reached its peak in June 1953, when Warners announced that two of its upcoming super-productions, *A Star Is Born* and *East of Eden,* would be shot in Natural Vision. In fact, the only (relatively) big-budget films made in 3-D turned out to be the independently produced *Hondo* (John Farrow, 1953; distributed by Warners'), Columbia's *Miss Sadie Thompson* (Curtis Bernhardt, 1953), MGM's *Kiss Me Kate* (George Sidney, 1953), and Warners' *Dial M for Murder* (Hitchcock, 1954), the latter two nationally released flat in 1954 because the popularity of the process had taken a nosedive and Natural Vision suddenly had become, in the Hollywood phrase, box-office poison.

---

* *Creature from the Black Lagoon* was the first 3-D feature exhibited in a single-strip process with the two stereoscopic layers stacked one above the other in alternating frames. Such systems vastly simplified the projection of stereoscopic films and received considerable attention in the waning days of the 3-D craze. Today, all commercially viable systems rely on stacked imagery and single-projector polarization, whether they employ one or two cameras in the production process. Some mention should be made here of the Soviet lenticular stereoscopic system, known as Stereokino, perfected by S. P. Ivanov during the forties. This system, introduced to the public in the feature *Robinson Crusoe* (1946) and still used today, employs an intricately ribbed glass screen to reflect the left and right stereoscopic images into the corresponding eye of the viewer, and it requires no glasses.

Top left: *The Adventures of Robin Hood* (Michael Curtiz, 1938). Cinematography: Tony Gaudio, Sol Politio, W. Howard Greene. Three-strip Technicolor; 35mm.

Top right: *Gone with the Wind* (Victor Fleming, 1939). Cinematography: Ernest Haller and Ray Rennahan, assisted by Lee Garmes, Joseph Ruttenberg, and Wilfred Cline. Technicolor; 35mm. Academy Award for Color Cinematography.

Bottom left: *The Wizard of Oz* (Victor Fleming, 1939). Cinematography: Harold Rosson. Technicolor; 35mm.

Center right: *Fantasia* (Disney, 1940). Directors of Animation: Samuel Armstrong, Bill Roberts, Jems Algar, Wildred Jackson, *et al.* Technicolor; 35mm.

Bottom right: *Meet Me in St. Louis* (Vincente Minnelli, 1944). Cinematography: George J. Folsey. Technicolor; 35mm.

Top left: *Henry V* (Laurence Olivier, 1945). Cinematography: Robert Krasker. Technicolor; 35mm.

Top right: *Black Narcissus* (Michael Powell, 1946). Cinematography: Jack Cardiff. Technicolor; 35mm. Academy Award for Color Cinematography.

Center left: *She Wore a Yellow Ribbon* (John Ford, 1949). Cinematography: Winton C. Hoch. Technicolor; 35mm. Academy Award for Color Cinematography.

Bottom right: *The African Queen* (John Huston, 1951). Cinematography: Jack Cardiff. Technicolor; 35mm.

Bottom left: *Kismet* (Vincente Minnelli, 1955). Cinematography: Joseph Ruttenberg. Eastmancolor; CinemaScope.

Top left: *The Ten Commandments* (Cecil B. DeMille, 1956). Cinematography: Loyal Griggs, assisted by John Warren, Wallace Kelly, and Peverel Marly. Technicolor; VistaVision.

Center left: *South Pacific* (Joshua Logan, 1958). Cinematography: Leon Shamroy. Technicolor; Todd-AO.

Top right: *Vertigo* (Alfred Hitchcock, 1958). Cinematography: Robert Burkes. Technicolor; VistaVision.

Bottom left: *Il gattopardo* (*The Leopard* [Luchino Visconti, 1963]). Cinematography: Giuseppi Rotunno. Technicolor; Technirama (Europe); DeLuxe Color; CinemaScope (Britain, USA, and Canada).

Bottom right: *Kwaidan* (Masaki Kobayashi, 1964). Cinematography: Yoshio Miyajima. Eastmancolor; Tohoscope.

Top left: *Dr. Zhivago* (David Lean, 1965). Cinematography: Freddie Young. Metrocolor; Panavision. Academy Award for Color Cinematography.

Top right: *Fahrenheit 451* (François Truffaut, 1966). Cinematography: Nicholas Roeg. Technicolor; 35mm (projected 1:1.66).

Bottom right: *Belle de jour* (Luis Buñuel, 1967). Cinematography: Sacha Vierny. Eastmancolor; 35mm (projected 1:1.66).

Center left: *2001: A Space Odyssey* (Stanley Kubrick, 1968). Cinematography: Geoffrey Unsworth, with additional photography by John Alcott. Technicolor and Metrocolor; 35mm and Super Panavision, presented in Cinerama. British Academy Award for Cinematography.

Bottom left: *The Wild Bunch* (Sam Peckinpah, 1969). Cinematography: Lucien Ballard. Technicolor; 35mm and Panavision 70 (USA); 70mm and CinemaScope (Europe).

Top left: *Fellini Satyricon* (Frederico Fellini, 1969). Cinematography: Giuseppe Rotunno. DeLuxe Color; Panavision.

Top right, center right, and center left: *Il conformista* (*The Conformist* [Bernardo Bertolucci, 1970]). Cinematography: Vittorio Storaro. Technicolor; 35mm (projected 1:1.66).

Bottom right: *Morte a Venezia* (*Death in Venice* [Luchino Visconti, 1970]). Cinematography: Pasquale De Santis. Technicolor; 35mm and Panavision.

Top left: *McCabe and Mrs. Miller* (Robert Altman, 1971). Cinematography: Vilmos Zsigmond. Technicolor; Panavision.

Top right: *Ludwig* (Luchino Visconti, 1973). Cinematography: Armando Nannuzzi. Technicolor; Panavision.

Bottom right: *The Godfather* (Francis Ford Coppola, 1972). Cinematography: Gordon Willis. Technicolor; 35mm.

Center left: *The Godfather, Part II* (Francis Ford Coppola, 1974). Cinematography: Gordon Willis. Technicolor; 35mm.

Bottom left: *The Passenger* (Michaelangelo Antonioni, 1975). Cinematography: Luciano Tovoli. Metrocolor; 35mm (projected 1:1.66).

Top left: *Picnic at Hanging Rock* (Peter Weir, 1975). Cinematography: Russell Boyd. Eastmancolor; 35mm.

Top right: *Days of Heaven* (Terrence Malick, 1978). Cinematography: Nestor Almendros. Metrocolor; 35mm. Academy Award for Cinematography.

Bottom right: *Heaven's Gate* (Michael Cimino, 1980). Cinematography: Vilmos Zsigmond. Technicolor; Panavision.

Center left: *The Shining* (Stanley Kubrick, 1980). Cinematography: John Alcott. Color process uncredited.

Bottom left: *Poltergeist* (Tobe Hooper, 1982). Cinematography: Matthew F. Leonetti. Metrocolor; Panavision.

Top left: *The Year of Living Dangerously* (Peter Weir, 1982). Cinematography: Russell Boyd. Metrocolor, Panavision.

Top right: *Indiana Jones and the Temple of Doom* (Steven Spielberg, 1984). Cinematography: Douglas Slocombe. DeLuxe Color; Panavision.

Center left: *Legend* (Ridley Scott, 1985). Cinematography: Alex Thompson. Technicolor; 35mm (projected 1:1.66).

Bottom right: *My Life as a Dog* (Lasse Hallstrom, 1985). Cinematography: Jorgen Persson and Rolf Lindstrom. Fugicolor; 35mm.

Bottom left: *Manhunter* (Michael Mann, 1986). Cinematography: Dante Spinotti. Technicolor; 35mm.

12.5 Universal's *Creature from the Black Lagoon* (Jack Arnold, 1954), the first 3-D film projected in a single-strip system.

Stereoscopic 3-D died in that year for a number of reasons. One was that producers found it difficult to make serious narrative films in such a gimmicky process, although Hitchcock's work, as usual, was an exception. Most of the 3-D films of 1953–54 were blatant attempts to exploit the illusion of stereoscopic depth by having animals leap and people hurl objects into the Natural Vision camera lens. Another problem was that the illusion of depth created by 3-D was not particularly authentic or satisfying because the planes of depth within the image were highly stratified. Things appeared not in the round, as they do in a hologram,* but as a series of stratified two-dimensional planes. In fact, deep-focus widescreen photography is actually capable of producing a greater illusion of depth than stereoscopic 3-D. Also, people disliked wearing the polarized glasses necessary to achieve the 3-D effect; many complained of eyestrain and headaches. But the biggest single factor in 3-D's demise was probably the sweeping nationwide success in the fall of 1953 of a self-proclaimed rival, the anamorphic widescreen process patented by 20th Century–Fox as CinemaScope (see pp. 488–89). Though nonstereoscopic, this process exploited depth through peripheral vision, and advertised itself to 3-D's disadvantage as "The Modern Miracle You See Without Glasses."

Attempts to revive 3-D in the last three decades have met with varying degrees of success. Arch Oboler's *The Bubble* (1966; rereleased as *Fantastic Invasion of Planet Earth,* 1976) was a commercial failure, but the 1969 soft-core pornographic feature *The Stewardesses* (Alf Silliman) grossed 26 million dollars and sparked an X-rated 3-D miniboom, culminating in *Andy Warhol's Frankenstein* (1974). Then, in the summer of 1981, the unexpected success of the independently produced Western *Comin' at Ya* (Fernando Baldi) demonstrated the continuing popularity of 3-D with general audiences and led to the production of several mainstream Hollywood features in the process (*Friday the Thirteenth, Part III,* Steve Miner; *Jaws 3-D,* Joe Alves—both 1983), whose commercial success proved that stereoscopic 3-D could once again sustain a pattern

---

* An image produced through holography—a new process of photography which uses lasers to create perfect three-dimensional facsimiles of objects photographed.

of wide general release. At about the same time, vintage 3-D films from the fifties began to be broadcast over the air on commercial television. Today, the notion of an authentically three-dimensional cinema continues to fascinate filmmakers and audiences alike, as Hollywood's recent experiments with holographic photography and such nonstereoscopic 3-D processes as Showscan and Omnimax (see Chapter 18) make clear.

The Anamorphic Widescreen Processes

The new optical format that came to stay during the war with television was **CinemaScope,** which arrived in September 1953 with 20th Century–Fox's biblical epic *The Robe* (Henry Koster). This system was based on the "Hypergonar" anamorphic distorting lens invented by Dr. Henri Chrétien (1879–1956) for tank periscopes during World War I and first used in film as early as 1928 (in Claude Autant-Lara's *Pour construire un feu* [*Origins of Fire*]). In it, a wide-field image is "squeezed" laterally by a cylindrical lens with a compression ratio of 2:1 onto conventional 35mm film stock and redeemed as a widescreen image by a compensating lens in projection. The conventional **aspect ratio** of the cinema screen (the ratio of width to height), known as the **Academy aperture,** had been standardized at 4:3, or 1.33:1, in 1932 by the Academy of Motion Picture Arts and Sciences.* CinemaScope offered a radically new ratio of 2.55:1 (approximately 8:3), subsequently reduced to 2.35:1, which gave the screen image a broadly oblong shape like that of Cinerama, and similarly enhanced peripheral vision when used in combination with a curved screen. The process also featured four-track stereophonic sound recorded magnetically on the film strip, and it was aggressively marketed by Fox as a cost-effective alternative to both 3-D and Cinerama. CinemaScope had the distinct advantage that it required no special cameras, film stock, or projectors, only special lenses, a metallicized wide screen, and a four-track magnetic stereophonic sound system available in a package costing between fifteen and twenty-five thousand dollars, depending on the size of the theater (the price dropped considerably in July 1954 when Fox made the stereo equipment optional). Its initial disadvantages were a loss of picture brightness, since standard projectors were designed to illuminate less than half the screen area required for widescreen (Fox's reflective Miracle Mirror screen helped to compensate for this loss by directing light into the useful seating area of the theater), and problems of geometrical distortion inherent in the early lenses manufactured by Bausch and Lomb. Because these were curved outward to extend their peripheries, objects in close-up appeared disproportionately large and horizontal lines seemed to run the wrong

12.6 CinemaScope: *The Robe* (Henry Koster, 1953): Richard Burton and foe.

12.7 When "unsqueezed" in projection, this close shot of Marilyn Monroe in Fox's CinemaScope production of *How to Marry a Millionaire* (Jean Negulesco, 1953) reveals distortion and lots of wasted space.

---

* This was done to achieve a uniform international standard for the gauge of sound film, although in practice most films had conformed to the 4:3 ratio since the early 1890s, when Edison standardized the width of theatrical film at 35mm. The "Academy aperture" is the aperture plate dimension 0.864 inches by 0.63 inches in printer and projector that produces the Academy ratio on screen. The camera uses a full-screen aperture of 0.98 inches by 0.735 inches, in order to create the largest possible negative for printing.

way at the edges of the frame; distortion was also common in lateral movement across the frame and in tracking shots. Finally, textures could become grainy and colors indistinct through the blowing-up process: the early **Scope** image was often described as fuzzy. Nevertheless, Cinema-Scope brought the widescreen revolution to the everyday world of functional filmmaking because, unlike Cinerama and 3-D, it was cheap, flexible, and simple enough to be used on a regular basis in the commercial cinema.

Most important, the public adored it. *The Robe* was an indifferent DeMille-like spectacle, but its box-office receipts of over 17 million dollars in the year of its release made it the third most lucrative production in the history of American film, after *The Birth of a Nation* (1915) and *Gone With the Wind* (1939). Within the next few months, the anamorphic process took Hollywood by storm as Fox agreed to sell its CinemaScope lenses and conversion kits to rival production companies.

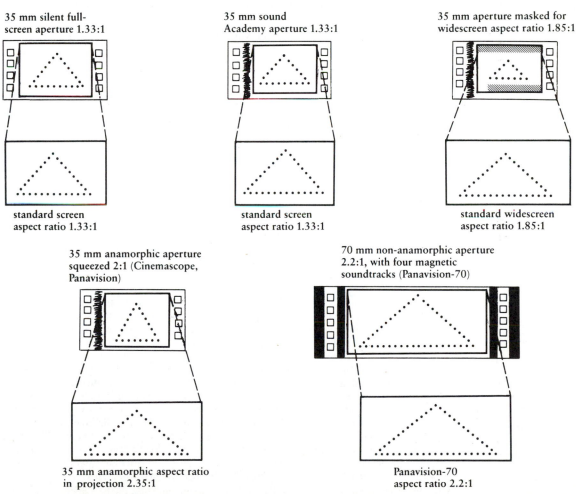

35 mm silent full-screen aperture 1.33:1

standard screen aspect ratio 1.33:1

35 mm sound Academy aperture 1.33:1

standard screen aspect ratio 1.33:1

35 mm aperture masked for widescreen aspect ratio 1.85:1

standard widescreen aspect ratio 1.85:1

35 mm anamorphic aperture squeezed 2:1 (Cinemascope, Panavision)

35 mm anamorphic aspect ratio in projection 2.35:1

70 mm non-anamorphic aperture 2.2:1, with four magnetic soundtracks (Panavision-70)

Panavision-70 aspect ratio 2.2:1

12.8 A schematic diagram of standard film gauges and screen aspect ratios for silent, sound, and sidescreen cinema. Please note that, with the exception of 12.7, all of the widescreen stills in this chapter have been cropped for publication. This practice will be duly noted in subsequent chapters, where it occurs.

At first, Fox president Spyros Skouras insisted that all CinemaScope productions be shot in full color and with four-track stereo, but he soon relaxed these conditions in order to accommodate smaller producers and exhibitors who could not afford to convert their sound systems.

By the end of 1953, every major studio in Hollywood except Paramount had been licensed to make CinemaScope films, seventy-five full-color anamorphic features were in production, and five thousand theater installations had been performed. A year later, the latter figure had tripled, and by 1957, CinemaScope had virtually saturated the market, with 84.5 percent of all U.S. and Canadian theaters (17,644 of 20,971) converted to the process. Indeed, the widescreen look had become so popular that films still shot in the old ratio of 1.33:1 were cropped for exhibition—that is, their tops and bottoms were masked in projection and the image was cast over a wider area of the screen, which was ultimately standardized at 1.85:1 in the United States and 1.66:1 in Europe. (This unfortunate practice forced directors working in the old format, or later, in VistaVision to compose shots "loose," so that action would be kept away from the top and bottom of the frame. Many directors today, acutely aware that their widescreen films will eventually appear on television screens whose shape was modeled on the Academy frame, attempt to keep significant action in the midframe, "TV-safe," or "safe-action," area, which imposes similar artistic constraints.)* In the next few years, a great many problems with the CinemaScope system were solved. The aspect ratio was reduced from 2.55:1 to 2.35:1, which gave the image more visual density in projection,† and the anamorphic lenses were consistently improved to give a sharper and clearer screen image.

---

* The shape of the American television screen, standardized by the FCC in 1939, was and is modeled on the Academy frame, so that all widescreen films lose image space when shown on TV or released on videotape or videodisc, often as much as 50 percent. To restore lost visual information, video technicians commonly employ a process known as "panning and scanning" which follows significant dramatic action back and forth across the width of the frame, in effect redirecting the film and creating camera movement that wasn't originally there. (At first, scanning was performed optically with a telecine converter; today, it is done electronically by a flying-spot scanner which scans each frame line by line for translation as a video image.) Worse, in scenes where side-to-side action or dialogue occurs too rapidly for scanning to follow, technicians resort to cutting from one side of the frame to the other as if they were separate shots. In either case, the original composition and structure of the image is badly compromised. Furthermore, title and credit sequences of anamorphic films are usually shown squeezed on television, so that their printed matter will remain within the border of the screen. Add to this the fact that a film's light levels, color balance, and sound values all must be adjusted for the conditions of electronic transmission and in-home viewing, and you will have a good sense of how different the experience of watching a film in video format can be from a theatrical screening. In this light, in fact, the threat of colorization becomes one more step in the long-term process of the degrading of the filmic image in the name of "enhancing" it for television. See John Belton, "Pan and Scan Scandals," *The Perfect Vision* 1, 3 (Indian Summer 1987): 40–49.

† The immediate reason for the change was to provide space on the filmstrip for a combined magnetic and optical soundtrack in response to exhibitor demand. In the original CinemaScope system, stereophonic sound was recorded on four magnetic tracks running on either side of the perforations, which were reduced in size to accommodate them. In July 1954, under

In 1960, Robert E. Gottschalk invented the variable prismatic **Panavision** lens, which offered a nearly distortion-free definition of image to anamorphic films, and Panavision gradually replaced CinemaScope as the leading anamorphic system. Today it is practically the only process used in 35mm widescreen cinematography.* By the mid-fifties, the conversion to anamorphic widescreen films in America was nearly total, and the process spread rapidly to other parts of the world as foreign audiences found themselves suddenly confronted by a bewildering array of "scopes." In 1956 alone, France introduced Franscope and Dyaliscope, Italy contributed Ultrascope and Colorscope, Sweden Agascope, the USSR Sovscope, and Japan Tohoscope, Daieiscope, and Nikkatususcope; all were variations of the CinemaScope system.

There was a single holdout in Hollywood, however. Paramount had refused to adopt an anamorphic process on the advice of its technicians, who said that the squeezing and blowing-up process would debase the visual quality of the image. They also thought that the ribbonlike CinemaScope image was too long and narrow to permit good composition. Accordingly, in April 1954 in *White Christmas* (Michael Curtiz), Paramount introduced its own widescreen system called **VistaVision**. This was a unique nonanamorphic process in which 35mm film stock was run through the camera *horizontally* rather than vertically to produce a double-frame negative (eight sprocket holes per frame) twice as wide as the conventional 35mm frame, and slightly taller. The negative was then optically rotated 90 degrees in the printing process, so that the positive prints could run vertically on any projector. (VistaVision films were occasionally shown full-frame on horizontal transport projectors—as, for example, at the system's premiere at Radio City Music Hall, where *White Christmas* appeared on a giant 55- by 30-foot screen—but the normal practice was to reduce the image in printing to standard 35mm stock, increasing not its size but its density.) The VistaVision aspect ratio was variable from 1.33:1 to 1.96:1 and could therefore accommodate any theater, but Paramount recommended projection in the "golden ratio" of 1.85:1 to achieve a modified widescreen effect. The enhanced picture resolution and clarity produced by VistaVision's larger negative was immediately apparent to audiences, and exhibitors liked the system because it required no modification of existing equipment. VistaVision films were released in Perspecta sound, an audio process which used a single optical

12.9 Though cropped by the studio for publicity distribution, this still from the VistaVision production *To Catch a Thief* (Alfred Hitchcock, 1955) illustrates the crisp resolution which the paramount process was capable of achieving on nearly every plane of depth: Cary Grant, Grace Kelly.

pressure to lower installation costs, Fox agreed to make its features available in a choice of four-track magnetic, single-track magnetic, or single-track optical sound, which, of course, meant striking three separate prints per film. By 1956, however, only 4,609 of the 17,591 CinemaScope theaters in America had converted to magnetic sound. So in June of that year, Fox announced that it would release all future product with both magnetic *and* optical tracks, requiring a 10 percent reduction in picture area per print.

* Panavision's success stemmed from its resolving many of CinemaScope's optical problems. For one thing, its images are better illuminated because the system uses a smaller picture area (the Academy aperture) for its squeeze and reduces its aspect ratio to 2.25:1. Furthermore, Panavision eliminated CinemaScope's wide-angle distortion almost entirely through the use of highly curved spherical lenses.

track for playback through a conventional single speaker but which could be combined with a Perspecta Sound Integrator to produce a simulated stereo effect through three horns. The Perspecta Sound Integrator and speakers cost less than half the price of Fox's four-track stereo, and the process was a highly effective marketing tool for Paramount among exhibitors. (In fact, it was competition from VistaVision and Perspecta sound that initially caused Fox to make CinemaScope prints available in both magnetic and optical versions.) Pararmount continued to use the VistaVision process throughout the decade. In 1961, following the release of *One-Eyed Jacks* (Marlon Brando), the studio converted to the perfected Panavision anamorphic process for financial reasons, but VistaVision is still used extensively today in optical special-effects work.

The Nonanamorphic, or Wide-Film, Widescreen Processes

As theater screens grew increasingly large in response to public demand (many measuring three to four times their original size), one of the reasons for Paramount's dissatisfaction with CinemaScope became apparent. The anamorphic image cast on a 60- by 30-foot screen lost clarity and brightness because its visual information was distributed across too large a field through the magnification process. The only technical answer to this problem was to increase the actual width of the film stock itself so that it would correspond to the wide field of the camera lens. Then the visual information from the photographic field and the visual information recorded on the negative film stock would be approximately proportional in scale, and the positive print would reproduce the density of the photographic field in projection. But the introduction of wide-gauge film would require special wide-gauge projectors, and the studios were loath to force another expensive conversion upon the exhibitors, with whom relations had become increasingly strained since the Paramount decrees of 1948 (see Chapter 11). One way to meet the problem was to shoot a wide-film negative and reduce it photographically to 35mm for projection, which would increase the visual density of the image without altering its shape. This was the method used most often by VistaVision and Fox's experimental wide-film process, CinemaScope-55.*

Nevertheless, in 1955 a 70mm wide-film process was introduced to selected American theaters in a film version of the Rodgers and Hammerstein stage hit *Oklahoma!* (Fred Zinnemann), independently produced by Michael Todd (1907–58). The process, called Todd-AO, was developed by the American Optical Company and designed to compete not only with CinemaScope but with Cinerama as well, since its wide-

12.10 Tofdd-AO: *Oklahoma!* (Fred Zinneman, 1955). Gordon MacRae.

---

* Introduced in 1955 and used in only two productions (*Carousel* [Henry King, 1956] and *The King and I* [Walter Lang, 1956]), CinemaScope-55 was an anamorphic system that used a 55mm negative for striking 35mm prints. The squeeze ratio was the same as for standard CinemaScope, 2:1, but reducing the image size increased grain and definition, rendering a vastly improved pricture in projection.

gauge film and wide-angle lenses offered the wraparound visual coverage of that process without resorting to its multiple cameras and projectors. Designed for running at 30 frames per second to enhance its resolution, Todd-AO proved to be a beautifully precise optical system, and *Oklahoma!*, which also featured seven-track stereophonic sound, was a huge financial success. Todd produced two more blockbusters using the process—the elephantine *Around the World in Eighty Days* (Michael Anderson, 1956) and the spectacularly garish *South Pacific* (Joshua Logan, 1958)—then died in a plane crash in 1958. Fox purchased the rights to the system at that time and has produced eight films in Todd-AO since, including the multimillion-dollar *Cleopatra* (1963) and *The Sound of Music* (1965).

Other wide-film systems developed simultaneously with Todd-AO were Super-Panavision, or Panavision-70, which used an unsqueezed 65mm negative, and Ultra-Panavision (originally called MGM Camera 65 when introduced in 1956), which combined anamorphic and wide-gauge principles to squeeze a wide-field image onto 65mm stock (the squeeze ratio was only 1.25:1, but since the picture area was already 2.25:1, the 70mm anamorphic positive projected an image with the enormous aspect ratio of 2.75:1, which was perfect for epic spectacle but probably not much else—David Lean's gargantuan *Lawrence of Arabia,* 1962, e.g., used this process). All of these other wide-film systems, however, were subject to the same limitations as Todd's process. Wide-film cameras are bulky (at least twice the normal size) and difficult to move, especially since wide-angle lenses are subject to distortion in panning. And, like Cinerama, the wide-film processes are very expensive to use; film stock, shooting, processing, exhibition (often at a higher than normal frames-per-second rate)—everything—costs about twice as much as it would in a conventional 35mm film. For these reasons, the wide-film systems and Cinerama in the past few decades have been used almost solely for spectacular productions like *Spartacus* (Stanley Kubrick, 1960), *El Cid* (Anthony Mann, 1961), *Lawrence of Arabia* and *Doctor Zhivago* (David Lean, 1965), *Grand Prix* (John Frankenheimer, 1966), and *2001: A Space Odyssey* (Stanley Kubrick, 1968), which can be "road-shown"—toured from city to city for exclusive engagements at inflated admission prices to recoup high production costs. For general release, such films were usually reduced to 35mm prints for anamorphic projection. Wide-film systems continue to provide the most optically flawless widescreen image, but today it is rare for films to be shot in a 65mm negative because of the expense. Instead, the vast majority of widescreen films—which is to say the vast majority of films—are either made in an anamorphic process or shot in 35mm and blown up to 70mm prints for special showing through such processes as Super-Technirama-70.

An important footnote to the coming of the widescreen processes is that it produced a nearly total conversion from optical to magnetic sound recording (though sound was still played back optically in exhibition). As already noted, most early widescreen films—whatever their process— were accompanied by multiple-track stereophonic sound recorded magnetically either on a separate strip (Cinerama) or on the filmstrip itself

(CinemaScope, Todd-AO, etc.). Multiple-track stereo not only inundated the audience with realistic sound and enhanced the illusion of depth but allowed early widescreen filmmakers to use sound *directionally* by having dialogue and naturalistic effects emanate from that portion of the huge screen appropriate to the image at a given moment. Thus, stereophonic sound permitted a director to differentiate aurally what was often undifferentiated visually within the vast space of the early widescreen frame. As we have seen, most theaters outside of large cities could not afford the conversion to stereophonic speaker systems in the fifties, and even today many still use optical playback equipment only. But after the widescreen revolution, magnetic sound became the preferred means of recording and mixing in all segments of the industry because of its flexibility, its accuracy, and the compactness of its equipment. By the late seventies, the use of a wireless eight-track recording system which employs miniature radio microphones and the **Dolby** noise reduction system (see Chapter 18) for playback in exhibition was increasingly common.

Adjusting to Widescreen

The advent of the widescreen processes in many ways parallels the introduction of sound. Once again, a financially troubled industry gambled on a novelty long implicit in the medium, and once again the novelty produced a technological and aesthetic revolution that changed the narrative form of the cinema. Like sound, widescreen photography presented many difficulties to filmmakers used to an older mode of production. Close-ups were suddenly problematic, given the vast size of widescreen images and the tendency of early anamorphic lenses to distort them. Even undistorted, on a 60-foot screen close-ups frequently appeared ludicrous, menacing, or both, which made critics wonder whether intimate scenes would be possible in the widescreen medium at all. Montage became problematic for the same reason: the perceptual disorientation produced by the rapid intercutting of widescreen images was less exciting than simply confusing. Focal shifts and tracking shots were similarly subject to distortion. Finally, composition and lighting for the widescreen image was difficult for directors and camera operators accustomed to the 4:3 rectangle of the Academy frame. Because early anamorphic lenses had short focal lengths (and, therefore, shallow depth of field), for example, deep focus composition was initially out of the question. There was, moreover, the purely practical problem of how to fill and balance all that newly available space. For these reasons, many felt that the widescreen processes would destroy the cinema as an art form, and it is true that, like the first sound films, the first widescreen films were static and theatrical, with a heavy-handed emphasis on spectacle.

But as widescreen filmmaking practices and optics were refined throughout the fifties and into the sixties, it became apparent that many of the initial assumptions about the limitations of widescreen were false. With certain stylistic modifications, close-ups and montage were not only possible but more effective in widescreen than in the old format; intimate scenes *could* be played with total authenticity in widescreen; and the cinema did *not* ultimately succumb to circus spectacle as a result of its new shape and size. For one thing, a director using widescreen could bring his characters into a tight close-up without eliminating the background and middleground of the shot, as often happened in Academy ratio close-ups of the thirties and forties. He could also have two or even three speaking characters in close-up, with ample space between their faces, instead of having to cut back and forth from one to the other or to squeeze them together artificially within the narrow borders of the Academy frame. Furthermore, with the introduction of distortion-free variable-focus Panavision lenses in the early sixties, it became clear that widescreen could greatly enhance the image's capacity for depth (and thus for spectator involvement) as well as width, due to increased peripheral vision. Whereas early widescreen pioneers like Otto Preminger (*River of No Return*, 1954), Elia Kazan (*East of Eden*, 1955), and Nicholas Ray (*Rebel Without a Cause*, 1955), had been able to exploit compositional depth only by pushing against the limits of their technology (by using big, brightly lit sets or by shooting out-of-doors in direct sunlight, for example, which enabled them to stop down their lens apertures), by the mid-sixties, for all practical purposes, the deep-focus capacity Welles and Toland had labored so hard to attain in *Citizen Kane* (1941) had suddenly become available to any director who possessed the imagination to use it. Finally, for a variety of reasons, widescreen encouraged the use of longer-than-average takes, and it seems clear today that the widescreen processes created the functional grounds for a new film aesthetic based upon composition in width and depth, or *mise-en-scène*, rather than upon montage.

In this new aesthetic, which might be called the long take, or *mise-en-scène*, aesthetic, the major emphasis would shift from editing to shooting, since a long take composed in width and depth is capable of containing a long shot, medium shot, and close-up, action and reaction, within a single frame without resorting to fragmentation of the image. At least one veteran Hollywood director recognized this as early as 1955. In an interview with the British film journal *Sight and Sound*, Henry King said: "This lens [the anamorphic] enables the director . . . for the first time to show on the screen cause and effect in the same shot, whereas before we used to have to *cut* from cause to effect in a story" [my italics]. Obviously, film narratives would continue to be assembled through the editing process, but the primary unit of narration would no longer be the dialectical shot (or "montage cell," in Einsenstein's phrase) but the long take or sequence shot composed in width and depth and/or constantly moving to reframe significant dramatic action. Theorists of the long-take aesthetic like André Bazin and his follower Charles Barr would later maintain (in *Cahiers du cinéma* and the British journal *Movie*, respectively) that the long take preserves the integrity of time and space by linking foreground, middleground, and background within the same shot, whereas montage destroys it. The close-up is a case in point (ironically, since early critics thought widescreen incapable of close-ups). In montage, the figure in close-up is divorced from its background by virtue of both focal limitations and the rapidity with which images flash upon the screen. In the

12.11 Widescreen potential: dialogue in close-up without cutting in *The Wild Bunch* (Sam Peckinpah, 1969, Panavision-70). William Holden, Ernest Borgnine.

12.12 Using widescreen to link character and environment: *Rebel Without A Cause* (Nicholas Ray, 1955) and *Wild River* (Elia Kazan, 1960). James Dean; Jo Van Fleet. CinemaScope.

12.13 The "democratic" perspective of widescreen, preserving the integrity of real time and space: *Bad Day at Black Rock* (John Sturges, 1955, CinemaScope). Spencer Tracy.

long-take close-up, the figure in close-up is temporally and spatially linked with its environment by virtue of the shot's *mise-en-scène,* and for Bazin and Barr, at least, this constitutes a more authentic mode of representation than the dissociated close-up of montage.

According to the long-take theorists, montage evolved historically because it was the first technologically feasible way to structure film, or to give it "speech." But in the fifties and sixties, they argued, the technology of cutting was usurped by the technology of shooting, so that the radical fragmentation of montage could be replaced by the organization of complex images within the frame. This is certainly true to the extent that the widescreen image, composed in depth, is capable of containing much more visual information than the old Academy frame, and its greater visual density makes it the perfect medium for rendering detail, texture, and atmosphere in relation to character. Finally, both Bazin and Barr insisted that the width and depth perspective created by the widescreen long take offer the viewer a "democratic" and "creative" alternative to the manipulative process of montage. Though shot composition can guide his or her seeing to some extent, they reasoned, the viewer of a long take can choose which details or actions to concentrate upon within a given shot,* rather than have them pointed out to him by close-ups or be drawn to some inexorable conclusion through a montage sequence like Eisenstein's massacre on the Odessa steps. Although montage was the traditional aesthetic of the cinema, extending from Griffith through Eisenstein to the classical Hollywood paradigm of the studio years, Bazin and his followers were able to construct a historical countertradition for the long-take aesthetic stretching back to Feuillade and including the "integral style" of von Stroheim and Murnau, the deep-focus "realism" of Renoir and Welles, and the postwar neorealism of Rossellini and De Sica. According to this version of film history, Welles began the revolution in favor of the long take with *Citizen Kane* in 1941, and the arrival of widescreen technology in the early fifties assured its permanent success. As a corrective to the influence of Soviet-style montage and three decades of classical Hollywood continuity editing, the Bazinian view was healthy, if impressionistic (overlooking, e.g., the integration of montage and *mise-en-scène* in *both* Griffith and Welles). But in any case, it took the widescreen aesthetic yet another decade to evolve, and the years 1953–60, like the years 1928–35, witnessed much experimental blundering before the major artists of the new form of cinema could emerge.

---

* The classical example of this *laissez-faire* composition for the long-take theorists was the raft sequence in Preminger's *River of No Return* (1954), described here by V. F. Perkins: "As Harry . . . lifts Kay from the raft, she drops the bundle which contains most of her 'things' into the water. Kay's gradual loss of the physical tokens of her way of life has great symbolic significance. But Preminger is not overimpressed. The bundle simply floats away offscreen while Harry brings Kay ashore. It would be wrong to describe this as understatement. The symbolism is in the event, not in the visual pattern, so the director presents the action clearly and leaves the interpretation to the spectator." (*Film as Film* [Baltimore: Penguin, 1972], p. 80.)

The Widescreen "Blockbuster"

In Hollywood, the emergence of a widescreen aesthetic was delayed by the sudden proliferation of a venerable film type known as the "block-buster,"* newly renovated to exploit the physical novelty of the big screen. These inflated multimillion-dollar productions were the widescreen counterparts of the "100 percent all-talking, all-singing, all-dancing" films of the early sound period—lavish and excessively lengthy superspectacles in the DeMille tradition, every element of which was made to subserve sheer visual magnitude. The blockbuster craze started in 1956 when King Vidor's *War and Peace* (VistaVision; 3 hours, 28 minutes), Michael Anderson's *Around the World in 80 Days* (Todd-AO; 3 hours, 30 minutes), and C. B. DeMille's remake of his own *The Ten Commandments* (VistaVision; 3 hours, 39 minutes) were all released simultaneously in wide-film widescreen processes and full stereophonic sound. Because the production costs for blockbusters were abnormally high, the films had to have a correspondingly high box-office gross simply to break even, and this factor, combined with their artistic unwieldiness, would ultimately destroy them. But for a while they reigned supreme. *Around the World in 80 Days,* for example, which cost 6 million dollars to produce, grossed over 22 million in the year of its release, and *The Ten Commandments,* which cost 13.5 million dollars, grossed nearly 43 million.

Other major blockbusters of the era were Joshua Logan's *South Pacific* (1958—Todd-AO; 3 hours), William Wyler's *Ben-Hur* (1959—MGM Camera-65; 3 hours, 37 minutes), Stanley Kubrick's *Spartacus* (1960—Super Technirama-70; 3 hours, 16 minutes), Otto Preminger's *Exodus* (1960—Panavision-70; 3 hours, 33 minutes), Anthony Mann's *El Cid*

12.14   A shot from the chariot race in the blockbuster *Ben-Hur* (William Wyler, 1959, MGM Camera-65): Charlton Heston.

12.15   *Lawrence of Arabia* (David Lean, 1962, Ultra-Panavision; restored and re-released, 1988): exploiting the new width and depth for spectacle. Peter O'Toole.

---

* A term traditionally used in Hollywood to designate any large-scale, big-budget production. *Intolerance* (1916) and *Gone with the Wind* (1939) were both called "blockbusters" in their day. The term now means a film that earns more than 100 million dollars.

12.16 A scene from *Cleopatra* (Joseph L. Mankiewicz, 1963, Todd-AO), the blockbuster that nearly sank 20th Century-Fox.

(1961—Super Technirama-70; 3 hours, 6 minutes), Lewis Milestone's *Mutiny on the Bounty* (1962—Ultra-Panavision; 3 hours, 5 minutes), and David Lean's *Lawrence of Arabia* (1962—Ultra-Panavision; 3 hours, 42 minutes—rereleased in 1989 in its original 70mm format, restored and recut by Lean, at 3 hours, 36 minutes). By the early sixties, production budgets for blockbusters had grown so large through inflation that most were produced abroad in Italy (by Dino De Laurentiis at Rome's Cinecittà studios), Spain (at Samuel Bronston's vast studio complex on the outskirts of Madrid), and Yugoslavia (at the Zagreb studios) to cut costs. Even so, many—such as *El Cid, Mutiny on the Bounty,* and Nicholas Ray's *55 Days at Peking* (1963—Super Technirama-70)—went down to ruin at the box office, alerting producers to the fact that the blockbuster trend had exhausted itself with the public. But the film that demonstrated this most graphically was Joseph L. Mankiewicz's disastrous *Cleopatra* (1963—Todd-AO; 4 hours, 3 minutes), which took four years and 40 million dollars to produce, nearly destroying 20th Century–Fox. This film still has not returned its negative cost, despite several revivals and sale to network television. Other blockbusters have been made since, including the fantastically successful *The Sound of Music* (Robert Wise, 1965) and *Dr. Zhivago* (David Lean, 1965), but few were able to recover their production costs before sale to television, and producers turned away from the blockbuster policy until it was revived, with substantial modifications, in the mid-seventies.

American Directors in the Early Widescreen Age

Some American films that are notable for their early innovative use of widescreen are Otto Preminger's *River of No Return* (1954), *Carmen Jones* (1954), *Bonjour Tristesse* (1958), and *Exodus* (1960; Panavision-70); George Cukor's *A Star Is Born* (1954) and *Bhowani Junction* (1956); William Wellman's *Track of the Cat* (1954); John Sturges' *Bad Day at Black Rock* (1955); Elia Kazan's *East of Eden* (1955) and *Wild River* (1960); Nicholas Ray's *Rebel Without a Cause* (1955), *The True Story*

12.17 Composition for widescreen: *Wild River* (Elia Kazan, 1960, CinemaScope) and *Exodus* (Otto Preminger, 1960, Panavision-70). Both films were conventional narratives distinguished by their creative use of the widescreen frame.

of Jesse James (1957), *Bitter Victory* (1958), and *Party Girl* (1958); Douglas Sirk's *Battle Hymn* (1956) and *The Tarnished Angels* (1958); Robert Aldrich's *Vera Cruz* (1954) and *The Angry Hills* (1959); John Huston's *Heaven Knows, Mr. Allison* (1957), *The Barbarian and the Geisha* (1958), and *The Roots of Heaven* (1958); Bud Boetticher's *Ride Lonesome* (1959) and *Commanche Station* (1960); Anthony Mann's *The Man from Laramie* (1955), *The Last Frontier* (1955), *Man of the West* (1958), and *El Cid* (1961; Super Technirama-70); Stanley Donen's *Seven Brides for Seven Brothers* (1954) and *It's Always Fair Weather* (1955); Vincente Minnelli's *Brigadoon* (1954), *Kismet* (1955), *The Cobweb* (1955), *Lust for Life* (1956), *Some Came Running* (1959), and *Home from the Hill* (1960); Samuel Fuller's *Hell and High Water* (1954) and *China Gate* (1957); Richard Quine's *My Sister Eileen* (1955) and *Strangers When We Meet* (1960); Richard Fleischer's *20,000 Leagues Under the Sea* (1954), *The Girl on the Red Velvet Swing* (1955), *Violent Saturday* (1955), *Bandido* (1956), *The Vikings* (1958), and *Barrabas* (1962; Technirama-70); and Sam Peckinpah's *Ride the High Country* (1962). Nearly all of these films were shot in CinemaScope or Panavision, and some are obviously less important in themselves than for their purely formal achievements, but most of their directors were major talents who made other significant films during the fifties and early sixties. As usual, Hitchcock was different: his work in VistaVision—*To Catch a Thief* (1955), *The Trouble with Harry* (1955), *The Man Who Knew Too Much* (1956), *Vertigo* (1958), and *North-by-Northwest* (1959)—formed a category unto itself, with *Vertigo* standing as the single greatest film of the fifties and perhaps of the entire postwar American cinema.

In addition to pioneering widescreen composition, Otto Preminger (1906–86), who had made his first film in Vienna in 1932 and emigrated to Hollywood in 1936, made major contributions to the social history of American film by breaking both the Production Code (with *The Moon Is Blue* [1953], a sex farce; *The Man with the Golden Arm* [1955], a film about narcotics addiction; and *Anatomy of a Murder* [1959], a court-room drama about rape) and the blacklist (by giving Dalton Trumbo screen credit for writing the script for *Exodus, 1960*). Moreover, his haunting *film noir* of 1945, *Laura,* and semidocumentary *Where the Sidewalk Ends* (1950) are minor classics of their respective genres. Preminger continued his contributions to widescreen in the political thriller *Advise and Consent* (1962), which also contains one of Hollywood's first treatments of a homosexual theme; *The Cardinal* (1963); *In Harm's Way* (1965); and *Bunny Lake is Missing* (1965); but much of his later work (e.g., *Hurry Sundown,* 1967; *Tell Me That You Love Me, Junie Moon,* 1970; and *Rosebud,* 1975) was disappointing.

Stage director Elia Kazan gave the decade of the fifties three of its most persuasive and characteristic films: *A Streetcar Named Desire* (1951; adapted by Tennessee Williams from his own play), *Viva Zapata!* (1952; from an original story and screenplay by John Steinbeck), and *On the Waterfront* (1954; from an original story and screenplay by Budd Schulberg), all starring Marlon Brando (b. 1924). Much of Kazan's work of the era was shaped in one form or another by his friendly testimony before HUAC in 1952, in the course of which he denounced former colleagues at New York's radical Group Theater as communists. *Viva Zapata!* he described to the Committee as an "anticommunist picture," despite its focus on a revolutionary hero; his next film, *Man on a Tightrope* (1953), was in fact a trenchantly anticommunist thriller set in postwar Czechoslovakia; and *On the Waterfront* used labor racketeering as a metaphor for communist espionage to build an unequivocal case for the morality of informing. The enormous critical and commercial success of the latter enabled Kazan to form his own company, Newtown Productions, for which he made his next three films. *Baby Doll* (1956) was a potboiler based on two of Tennessee Williams' one-act plays, but *A Face in the Crowd* (1957, also scripted by Schulberg from his own story) proved to be a prescient indictment of the abuses of celebrity power within the television industry, and *Splendor in the Grass* (1961) was a well-received version of William Inge's play about the traumas of adolescent sexuality. In addition to his motion picture career, Kazan was also a successful Broadway theater director from the late forties through 1964, when he turned his attention to novel-writing, interrupted occasionally by personal films such as *America America* (1963) and *The Arrangement* (1969), both adapted from his own writings. Kazan's last film was an unsatisfying verison of F. Scott Fitzgerald's *The Last Tycoon* (1976), scripted by Harold Pinter.

In his films of the fifties, especially *Rebel Without a Cause* (1955), Nicholas Ray (born Raymond Nicholas Kienzle, 1911–79) provided a definitive statement of the spiritual and emotional ills that beset America during the period. Initially identified with *films gris* (*They Live by Night,* 1947, released 1949; *Knock on Any Door,* 1949) and *noir* (*In a Lonely Place,* 1950; *On Dangerous Ground,* 1951), Ray simultaneously became a cult figure in Europe and one of the highest paid directors in Hollywood, until his career collapsed beneath the weight of two commercially unsuccessful blockbusters, *King of Kings* (1961) and *55 Days at Peking*

12.18 Alienated youth: *Rebel Without a Cause* (Nicholas Ray, 1955, Cinema-Scope). Jim Backus, James Dean, Ann Doran.

(1963). In later life, he taught filmmaking at Harpur College and collaborated with his students on a number of experimental projects combining film and video; Ray is also the focus of the one-hour documentary *I'm a Stranger Here Myself* (David Helpren, Jr., 1975) and the feature-length *Lightning Over Water* (1980), a painfully personal film which he made in collaboration with the brilliant German director Wim Wenders on the subject of his own lingering death from cancer.

Douglas Sirk (b. Detlef Sierck, Denmark, 1900–87) proved himself a master stylist of color in *Magnificent Obsession* (1954), *All That Heaven Allows* (1956), *Interlude* (1957), *Written on the Wind* (1957), and *Imitation of Life* (1959)—a series of visually stunning motion pictures whose content bordered on soap opera. Before retiring in 1959 from filmmaking, Sirk also contributed several impressive widescreen action films (*Sign of the Pagan,* 1954; *Captain Lightfoot,* 1955; *Battle Hymn,* 1957), as well as the moving antiwar film *A Time to Love and a Time to Die* (1958), adapted from the novel by Erich Maria Remarque. He spent the remainder of his life in Germany, directing stage plays and teaching at the Munich Academy of Film and Television.

Robert Aldrich (1918–83) emerged at this time as America's most powerful practitioner of post-forties *film noir* in *Kiss Me Deadly* (1955; adapted from Mickey Spillane), a masterpiece of the form whose commercial success led Aldrich to establish his own production company, Associates and Aldrich, for which he directed twelve films in the next seventeen years. Aldrich had begun his directing career in television, and his first big-budget film had been the boisterous widescreen Western *Vera Cruz* (1954), shot on location in Mexico and a clear antecedent of Sam Peckinpah's *The Wild Bunch* (1969). During the fifties, he earned a distinguished reputation for such award-winning films as *The Big Knife* (1955; adapted from Clifford Odets; Silver Prize, Venice), *Autumn Leaves* (1956; Silver Bear, Berlin), and *Attack* (1956; Italian Critics Award, Venice), although he also directed a number of indifferent features under contract to various studios (e.g., *The Angry Hills,* 1959; *The Last Sunset,* 1961;

12.19   *The Big Knife* (Robert Aldrich, 1955): a cynical portrait of Hollywood from the play by Clifford Odets. Ida Lupino, Ilka Chase, Jack Palance.

Sodom and Gomorrah, 1963). During the sixties, however, Aldrich became a major figure with the sardonic *noir* hits *What Ever Happened to Baby Jane?* (1962) and *Hush, Hush, Sweet Charlotte* (1964) and the violent World War II commando epic *The Dirty Dozen* (1967), which became the year's highest-grossing film (18.2 million dollars) and enabled him to purchase his own studio. Always a maverick, he produced three controversial and unpopular films at Aldrich Studios—*The Killing of Sister George* (1968), *Too Late the Hero* (1970), and *The Grissom Gang* (1971)— before its failure forced him to return to contract directing. In his later years, Aldrich made such intelligent films as *Ulzana's Raid* (1972), *The Emperor of the North* (1973), *The Longest Yard* (1974), *Hustle* (1975), and *Twilight's Last Gleaming* (1977); he served two distinguished terms as president of the Directors Guild of America between 1975 and 1979 and directed several unsuccessful comedies (*The Frisco Kid,* 1979; . . . *All the Marbles,* 1981) before his death in 1983.

Other filmmakers associated with adult themes during the fities were John Huston (1906–87), Budd Boetticher (b. 1916), and Anthony Mann (1906–67). Originally an actor and a screenwriter, Huston had become famous as a director during the forties through his classic detective film *The Maltese Falcon* (1941) and his classic adventure film *The Treasure of the Sierra Madre* (1948), both of which have proved highly influential (*Falcon* e.g., of *film noir* and *Sierra Madre,* of such important later works as Peckinpah's *The Wild Bunch*). After directing *Key Largo* (1948), a moody adaptation of Maxwell Anderson's play, and *We Were Strangers* (1949), a controversial drama about revolutionary activity in 1930's Cuba starring the soon-to-be-blacklisted John Garfield, Huston began the fifties with a surge of creative energy in the naturalistic *film noir The Asphalt Jungle* (1950), a documentary-like adaptation of Stephen Crane's *The Red Badge of Courage* (1951), and the award-winning *The African Queen* (1952), his first theatrical film in color. For the rest of the decade, Huston displayed his talents for both parody (*Beat the Devil,* 1954) and imaginative literary adaptation (*Moulin Rouge,* 1953; *Moby Dick,* 1956; *Heaven*

12.20 John Huston's final film, *The Dead* (1987): Angelica Huston in the middleground.

12.21 Epic scale in Anthony Mann's *El Cid* (1961).

Knows, Mr. Allison, 1957; *The Roots of Heaven,* 1958). In the sixties, he turned increasingly to original material in such films as *The Misfits* (1961; screenplay by Arthur Miller) and *Freud* (1962; screenplay by Wolfgang Reinhardt and Charles Kaufman). Nevertheless, the written word remained a major source of Huston's inspiration in his later career, whether it derived from popular fiction (*The List of Adrian Messenger,* 1963; *Casino Royale,* 1967; *The Kremlin Letter,* 1970; *The Mackintosh Man,* 1973; *Phobia,* 1980), literature (*The Bible,* 1966; *Reflections in a Golden Eye,* 1967; *The Man Who Would Be King,* 1975; *Wise Blood,* 1980; *Under the Volcano,* 1984), or something in between (*The Night of the Iguana,* 1964; *A Walk with Love and Death,* 1969; *Fat City,* 1972; *Victory,* 1981; *Annie,* 1982; *Prizzi's Honor,* 1985). When he died of emphysema in December 1987, Huston had become a prominent spokesman for the Directors Guild of America against the practice of "colorization" (of which *The Maltese Falcon* was an early victim) and had just completed a sublime adaptation of James Joyce's short story *The Dead* (1987), scripted by his son, Tony, and starring his daughter, Angelica.

Boetticher and Mann were the architects of the modern adult Western during the fifties, but both were also notable for other kinds of films. Boetticher, for example, was a professional bullfighter, whose films on the subject—*The Bullfighter and the Lady* (1951; produced by John Wayne for Republic Pictures; released at 87 minutes in a version edited by John Ford, and restored to its original 124–minute running time by UCLA archivist Bob Gitt in 1987), *The Magnificent Matador* (1965), and *Arruza* (1971; an epic documentary on the great Mexican matador Carlos Arruza, which took Boetticher a decade to complete)—are much admired. Mann, on the other hand, began his career as a specialist in such gritty, low-budget *films noir* as *Desperate* (1947), *Railroaded* (1947), *Raw Deal* (1948), and *T-Men* (1948) for B-studios like Eagle-Lion, but by the early sixties had become an acknowledged master of the widescreen epic in *El Cid* (1961) and *The Fall of the Roman Empire* (1964). Stanley Donen (b. 1924) and Vincente Minnelli (1903–86) were also closely associated with a single genre during the fifties (the musical), but Donen later dealt successfully in suspense (*Charade*, 1963; *Arabesque*, 1966) and romantic comedy (*Two for the Road*, 1967; *Bedazzled*, 1967), and Minnelli was able to turn a number of literary potboilers into the gorgeously stylized widescreen melodramas *The Cobweb* (1955), *Lust for Life* (1956), *Some Came Running* (1959), *Home from the Hill* (1960), *Two Weeks in Another Town* (1962), and *The Sandpiper* (1965).

Other American directors whose work is associated mainly with the decade of the fifties but extended beyond it are the Austrian-born Fred Zinnemann (b. 1907—*The Men*, 1950; *High Noon*, 1952; *A Member of the Wedding*, 1953; *From Here to Eternity*, 1953; *Oklahoma!*, 1955; *A Hatful of Rain*, 1957; *The Nun's Story*, 1959; *The Sundowners*, 1960; *Behold a Pale Horse*, 1964; *A Man for All Seasons*, 1966; *Julia*, 1977; *Five Days One Summer*, 1982); Robert Rossen (1908–66—*Body and Soul*, 1947; *All the King's Men*, 1949; *The Brave Bulls*, 1951; *Alexander the Great*, 1956; *Island in the Sun*, 1957; *They Came to Cordura*, 1959; *The Hustler*, 1961; *Lillith*, 1964); and the important action directors Don Siegel (b. 1912—*Riot in Cell Block 11*, 1954; *Invasion of the Body Snatchers*, 1956; *Baby Face Nelson*, 1957; *The Line-Up*, 1958; *The Killers*, 1964; *Madigan*, 1968; *The Beguiled*, 1970; *Dirty Harry*, 1972; *Charley Varrick*, 1973; *The Shootist*, 1976; *Escape from Alcatraz*, 1979); and the more primitive Samuel Fuller (b. 1911). Both have become cult figures in the past several decades, but Fuller has contributed more to the American cinema in terms of his vital creative energy and unique personal style. *The Steel Helmet* (1950), for example, is simply the best domestic feature about the Korean War, while *Pickup on South Street*

12.22 *Pickup on South Street* (Samuel Fuller, 1953): Jean Peters, Thelma Ritter.

(1953; winner of a Bronze medal at that year's Venice Festival), contains the fullest exposition of fifties-style anticommunist paranoia of any American film. *Shock Corridor* (1963) and *The Naked Kiss* (1965) are forceful treatments of contemporary social pathology and corrupted human nature. Working throughout the fifties, sixties, and seventies in such action genres as war film (*Fixed Bayonets,* 1951; *Hell and High Water,* 1954; *China Gate,* 1957; *Verboten!,* 1959; *The Big Red One,* 1979), crime films (*House of Bamboo,* 1955; *The Crimson Kimono,* 1959; *Underworld U.S.A.,* 1961; *Dead Pigeon on Beethoven Street,* 1972; *Les voleurs de la nuit* [*Thieves After Dark*], 1984); and Westerns (*I Shot Jesse James,* 1949; *The Baron of Arizona,* 1950; *Run of the Arrow,* 1957; *Forty Guns,* 1957; *Merrill's Marauders,* 1962), Fuller has produced a major body of work characterized by violent metaphor and raw emotional power.

The seasoned action director Raoul Walsh (1892–1981; an *original* widescreen pioneer, having directed *The Big Trail* in Fox's 70mm Grandeur process in 1930) did his last major work during the fifties (*Battle Cry,* 1955; *The Tall Men,* 1955; *Band of Angels,* 1957), as did George Stevens (1905–75), a veteran studio director who had made some fine genre films in the thirties and forties (*Swing Time,* 1936; *Gunga Din,* 1939; *Woman of the Year,* 1942; *The More the Merrier,* 1943), though sententiousness sometimes got the better of his scripts. *Shane* (1953), *Giant* (1956), and *A Place in the Sun* (1951), his melodramatic rendition of Theodore Dreiser's novel *An American Tragedy* (1925), are all films that American cinema would be the poorer without. Sententiousness was also a problem in the films directed during this period by Stanely Kramer (b. 1913), which tended to be visually limp and heavily laden with social commentary. Still, a few Kramer films, like *The Defiant Ones* (1958), *Inherit the Wind* (1960), *Judgment at Nuremberg* (1961), and the later *Ship of Fools* (1969) and *Oklahoma Crude* (1973), are notable despite their flaws. A similarly erratic producer-director is Richard Brooks (b. 1912), who specializes in literary adaptations for which he writes the scripts himself. His successes (*The Blackboard Jungle,* 1954; *Cat on a Hot Tin Roof,* 1959; *Elmer Gantry,* 1961; *Sweet Bird of Youth,* 1962; *The Professionals,* 1966; *In Cold Blood,* 1967) balance his failures (*Something of Value,* 1957; *The Brothers Karamazov,* 1958; *Lord Jim,* 1964; *Looking for Mr. Goodbar,* 1977) pretty evenly.

Finally, after the Hollywood witch-hunts had destroyed their American careers, Jules Dassin (b. 1911—*Brute Force,* 1947; *The Naked City,* 1948; *Thieves Highway,* 1949) and Joseph Losey (b. 1909—*The Boy with the Green Hair,* 1948; *The Lawless,* 1950; *The Prowler,* 1951) become important figures abroad. Dassin, influenced by Lang, originally specialized in *film noir,* and his last American production was the urban *noir* classic *Night and the City* (1950) shot on location in London for Fox. In France during the fifties and sixties, he turned increasingly to popular "caper" films and comedies like *Rififi* (*Du Rififi chez les hommes,* 1955), *Never on Sunday* (1960), and *Topkapi* (1964); but he has also produced such serious films as *He Who Must Die* (*Celui qui doit mourir,* 1956), based on *The Greek Passion* by Nikos Kazantzakis, a modern

12.23 Interracial fraternity: *The Defiant Ones* (Stanley Kramer, 1958). Sidney Poitier, Tony Curtis.

12.24 Sex: *Cat on a Hot Tin Roof* (Richard Brooks, 1959). Paul Newman, Elizabeth Taylor.

version of *Phaedra* (1961), an all-black version of John Ford's *The Informer* entitled *Up Tight* (1969), and *A Dream of Passion* (1978), a contemporary meditation on the Medea legend shot in Greece. Like Dassin, Losey had been associated with the socially committed *film noir,* but in exile in England he tended to become a stylish and somewhat strained student of contemporary alienation, often collaborating with British playwright Harold Pinter on his screenplays (e.g., *The Servant,* 1964; *Accident,* 1967; *The Go-Between,* 1971). (Losey's more recent work is discussed in Chapter 14.)

FIFTIES GENRES

Despite the balanced work of many fine craftsmen, Hollywood's mania for producing films on a vast scale in the fifties affected even the conventional dramatic feature. For one thing, the standard feature length rose from ninety minutes to an average of three hours before stabilizing at a more manageable two hours in the mid-sixties. Moreover, there was a tendency on the part of the studios to package every class-A production as a splashy big-budget spectacle whether or not this format suited the material. Thus, from 1955 to 1965 most traditional American genres experienced an inflation of production values that destroyed their original forms and caused them to be re-created in new ones.

The Musical

The Hollywood musical had reached an exquisitely high point of sophistication and color at the turn of the decade under the auspices of the MGM producer Arthur Freed (1894–1973), who in the mid- to late-forties assembled a stellar production unit featuring the talented directors Vincente Minnelli (*Meet Me in St. Louis,* 1944; *Yolanda and the Thief,* 1945) and Stanley Donen; the choreographer-directors Charles Walters (b. 1911) and Gene Kelly (b. 1912); and such gifted performers as Kelly himself, Fred Astaire, Judy Garland, June Allyson, and Cyd Charisse. Over the next decade, this team produced some thirty medium-budget musicals, among them the extraordinary *The Pirate* (Minnelli, 1948), *Easter Parade* (Walters, 1948), *On the Town* (Kelly / Donen, 1949), *An American in Paris* (Minnelli, 1951), *Singin' in the Rain* (Kelly / Donen, 1952), *Brigadoon* (Minnelli, 1954), *It's Always Fair Weather* (Kelly / Donen, 1955), and *Invitation to the Dance* (Kelly, 1956), as well as more lavish efforts like *The Band Wagon* (Minnelli, 1953), *Kismet* (Minnelli, 1955), *Silk Stockings* (Rouben Mamoulian, 1957), and *Gigi* (Minnelli, 1958). As a professional lyricist himself, Freed believed that musical production numbers should be integrated with a film's dialogue and plot, rather than stand alone as intermezzos. In theory, this meant that the songs and dances should serve to advance the narrative, but in practice it produced the unrealistic convention of a character's bursting into song at the slightest dramatic provocation. The first such "integrated" musical

12.25 *Singin' in the Rain* (Gene Kelly and Stanley Donen, 1952): Gene Kelly.

was probably *The Wizard of Oz* (1939), for which Freed was the associate producer, but by the time of *On the Town* integration had become the state of the art, and the practice was continued throughout the fifties and sixties. By 1955, however, the musical genre contracted a fifteen-year case of elephantiasis, as well as a compulsion to abandon original scripts in favor of adapting successful stage plays, often concurrently running hits. Such Broadway vehicles as *Oklahoma!* (Fred Zinnemann, 1955), *Guys and Dolls* (Joseph L. Mankiewicz, 1955), *The King and I* (Walter Lang, 1956), *South Pacific* (Joshua Logan, 1958), *West Side Story* (Robert Wise, 1962), *The Music Man* (Morton da Costa, 1962), *Gypsy* (Mervyn LeRoy, 1963), and *My Fair Lady* (George Cukor, 1964) proved successful with the public, although many of them employed stars who could neither sing nor dance (the voices of professional singers were frequently dubbed in and professional dancers stood in for the production numbers), and many were directed by men who had never filmed a musical before. This tendency peaked with the release of 20th Century-Fox's astoundingly popular film *The Sound of Music* (Robert Wise, 1965), the ultimate big-budget super-musical, which grossed more money (79 million dollars in domestic rentals) than any American film produced before the era of *The Godfather* (Francis Ford Coppola, 1972), *Jaws* (Steven Spielberg, 1975), and *Star Wars* (George Lucas, 1977). *The Sound of Music* (subsequently known in the industry as *"The Sound of Money"* and to the readers of critic Pauline Kael as *"The Sound of Mucus"*) was a glossily professional adaptation of a Rodgers and Hammerstein stage musical based on the true story of the Trapp family singers and their heroic escape from Nazi-occupied Austria. The production, shot on location in Salzburg, was one of Hollywood's last great escapist confections—a sort of conflation of *The Bells of St. Mary's*, *The Wizard of Oz*, and *Gone with the Wind*. The great success of this film gave rise to a host of multimillion-dollar descendants—*Camelot* (Joshua Logan, 1967), *Star* (Robert Wise, 1968), *Dr. Doolittle* (Richard Fleischer, 1968), *Funny Girl* (William Wyler, 1968), *Good-bye Mr. Chips* (Herbert Ross, 1969), *Oliver* (Carol Reed, 1969), *Hello Dolly* (Gene Kelly, 1969)—which nearly destroyed the fortunes of their respective studios, glutted the public on musicals, and virtually killed the form of the genre as it had evolved since the thirties by blowing it out of all proportion. Bob Fosse's (1927–87) intelligent, socially conscious, and masterfully crafted film version of the stage success *Cabaret* (1972) signaled a resurrection of the genre in a form more appropriate to the seventies—one which featured increased realism, serious subject matter, a re-segregation of musical numbers and plot, and renewed emphasis on the authentic musical talent of its stars. Fosse's *All That Jazz* (1979), Milos Forman's *Hair* (1979), Luis Valdez's *Zoot Suit* (1981), and Herbert Ross's *Pennies from Heaven* (1981) seemed to confirm that resurrection at the decade's turn, although such MTV-inspired musicals of the mid-eighties as *Flashdance* (Adrian Lyne, 1983) and *Footloose* (Herbert Ross, 1984) raised some doubts about its longevity (see Chapter 18).

12.26 *West Side Story* (Robert Wise, 1962): George Chakiris as the leader of the "Sharks."

12.27 *The Sound of Music* (Robert Wise, 1965): Julie Andrews.

12.28 *Cabaret* (Bob Fosse, 1972): Joel Grey as the master of ceremonies.

Comedy

Comedy was another genre that suffered seriously from widescreen inflation and the generally depressed social ambiance of the McCarthy-Cold War era, although there were clear exceptions in such small gems as Vincente Minnelli's *Father of the Bride* (1950) and *Father's Little Dividend* (1951). The big-budget widescreen comedy was represented by films like *How to Marry a Millionaire* (Jean Negulesco, 1953), *The Long Long Trailer* (Vincente Minnelli, 1954), *High Society* (Charles Walters, 1956—a widescreen color remake, with music by Cole Porter, of George Cukor's 1940 *Philadelphia Story*), and *A Hole in the Head* (Frank Capra, 1959). The strong point of film comedies like these was less verbal or visual wit than excellent production values. This was, after all, the major strategic element in Hollywood's war on television, and for a while the strategy worked, although the new medium continued to woo both audiences and comedians away from the cinema as the decade progressed. Bob Hope (b. 1903—*Son of Paleface,* Frank Tashlin, 1952; *Casanova's Big Night,* Norman Z. McLeod, 1954) and Danny Kaye (b. 1913—*The Court Jester,* Norman Panama, 1956; *Merry Andrew,* Michael Kidd, 1958), whose film careers had begun in the decade past, were both popular in class-A productions throughout the fifties,* as was the slapstick team of Dean Martin and Jerry Lewis (b. 1917 and 1926, respectively), who had succeeded that of Abbott and Costello. Martin and Lewis made seventeen films together between 1949 and 1956, the best among them *At War with the Army* (Hal Walker, 1951), *Sailor Beware* (Walker, 1952), *Jumping Jacks* (Norman Taurog, 1952), *The Stooge* (Taurog, 1953), *Scared Stiff* (George Marshall, 1953), *Living It Up* (Taurog, 1954), *You're Never Too Young* (Taurog, 1955), *Artists and Models* (Frank Tashlin, 1955), and *Pardners* (Taurog, 1956). When the team split up after *Hollywood or Bust* (Tashlin, 1956), Martin began a successful career as an actor and television entertainer, while Lewis went on to become a major comic star by himself in such films as *The Delicate Delinquent* (Don McQuire, 1957), *Rock-a-Bye Baby* (Tashlin, 1958), and *The Geisha Boy* (Tashlin, 1958), ultimately directing (and often writing and producing) his own films in the sixties—e.g., *The Bellboy* (1960), *The Errand Boy* (1961), *The Nutty Professor* (1963), *The Patsy* (1964), and *The Family Jewels* (1965). Today he still directs an occasional film (*Hardly Working,* 1981; *Cracking-Up,* also known as *Smorgasbord,* 1983) and is regarded by the French as a major *auteur,* but his idiotic comic persona has not found much favor with American critics.

Much more sophisticated than Lewis, and certainly as brilliant as Hope and Kaye, were the era's two major comediennes: Judy Holliday (1922–

12.29 *Scared Stiff* (George Marshall, 1953): Jerry Lewis, Lizabeth Scott, Dean Martin.

---

*Between 1941 and 1953, Hope ranked consistently among Hollywood's top ten box-office attractions; during the eighties, he continued to occupy superstar status, ranking in popularity with the likes of Clint Eastwood and Barbara Streisand. In fact, Hope may well be the longest continuously popular entertainer in the history of mass communications, and, with an estate valued at nearly one billion dollars, he is certainly the richest.

65—*Born Yesterday,* George Cukor, 1950; *It Should Happen to You,* George Cukor, 1954; *Phffft,* Mark Robson, 1954; *The Solid Gold Cadillac,* Richard Quine, 1956; *Full of Life,* Richard Quine, 1957; *Bells Are Ringing,* Vincente Minnelli, 1960) and Marilyn Monroe (1926–62—*Gentlemen Prefer Blondes,* Howard Hawks, 1953; *How to Marry a Millionaire,* 1953; *The Seven Year Itch,* Billy Wilder, 1955; *Some Like It Hot,* Billy Wilder, 1959). Both of them appeared in a number of witty, adult comedies before early deaths (Monroe was an apparent suicide; Holliday died of cancer) cut short their careers. These films were succeeded by the sanitized sexiness of the expensively produced Rock Hudson / Doris Day battle-of-the-sexes cycle, beginning in 1958 with *Pillow Talk* (Michael Gordon), and continuing to *Lover Come Back* (Delbert Mann, 1961) and *Send Me No Flowers* (Norman Jewison, 1964). These films and others that imitated them* were in turn succeeded by a cycle of cynical big-budget sex comedies concerned with the strategies of seduction (David Swift's *Under the Yum-Yum Tree,* 1963; Richard Quine's *Sex and the Single Girl,* 1965 and *How to Murder Your Wife,* 1965; Gene Kelly's *A Guide for the Married Man,* 1967; Fielder Cook's *How to Save a Marriage* [*And Ruin Your Life*], 1968) which reflected, sometimes rather perversely, the "sexual revolution" of the late sixties.† Related to the amoral cynicism of this cycle was what might best be called the "corporate comedy" of films like *Cash McCall* (Joseph Pevney, 1960) and the *Wheeler Dealers* (Arthur Hiller, 1963), which dealt openly and humorously with business fraud and prefigured the morass of corporate and governmental deceit underlying the Watergate and "Koreagate" scandals of the seventies. The elegant big-budget comedies of Blake Edwards (*The Pink Panther,* 1964; *A Shot in the Dark,* 1964; *The Great Race,* 1965; *The Party,* 1968) relied on sight gags to provide a lighter kind of humor, as did his later films in the Pink Panther series (*The Return of the Pink Panther,* 1975; *The Pink Panther Strikes Again,* 1976; *The Revenge of the Pink Panther,* 1978; *The Trail of the Pink Panther,* 1982, etc.); but by the eighties, with such films as *"10"* (1979), *S.O.B.* (1981), *Victor/Victoria* (1982), *The Man Who Loved Women* (1983), *Micki & Maude* (1984), and *That's Life!* (1986), Edwards had indisputably become a major practitioner of social satire.

The dark genius of American comedy during this period was the Ger-

12.30 *Born Yesterday* (George Cukor, 1950): Judy Holliday, Broderick Crawford.

12.31 *The Seven Year Itch* (Billy Wilder, 1955): Tom Ewell, Marilyn Monroe.

---

* The formula was to cast the stubbornly virginal Day against a rapacious and sexy leading man—Hudson in the originals, Cary Grant in *That Touch of Mink* (Delbert Mann, 1962), James Garner in *Move Over, Darling* (Michael Douglas, 1963) and *The Thrill of It All* (Norman Jewison, 1963), and Rod Taylor in *Do Not Distrub* (Ralph Levy, 1965); Tony Randall or Gig Young were frequently involved as an alternative love interest (for Day). Although *Pillow Talk* catalyzed this astonishingly dishonest cycle, its progenitor was probably the more intelligent and urbane *Teacher's Pet* (George Seaton, 1958), written by Fay and Michael Kanin, where Day is pitted against no less a power than Clark Gable in one of his last major roles.

† The attitudes underlying these later films were marvelously satirized at the decade's conclusion in Paul Mazursky's *Bob & Carol & Ted & Alice* (1969) and earnestly, if joylessly, dissected in Mike Nichols' *Carnal Knowledge* (1970). See Chapter 18.

12.32 *Sunset Boulevard* (Billy Wilder, 1950): Gloria Swanson.

man emigre director Billy Wilder, whose *Double Indemnity* (1944) had been one of the prototypes for *film noir*. Wilder carried this strain into the fifties with the relentlessly cynical *Ace in the Hole* (also known as *The Big Carnival*, 1951), which portrayed the media circus created by a corrupt reporter around a New Mexico mining disaster and won an international prize at Venice, but he began increasingly to specialize in *comédie noir*. In *Sunset Boulevard* (1950) he served up the decadence of Hollywood, old and new, in a tale of a bitterly symbiotic relationship between an aging silent-film star and a fortune-hunting young writer. *Stalag 17* (1953) was a perverse satire on heroism set in a German POW camp during World War II; *The Seven Year Itch* (1955) was a send-up of American sexual mores and advertising practices; *Witness for the Prosecution* (1958) was a sardonic courtroom thriller derived from a play by Agatha Christie; and *Some Like It Hot* (1959) was a torrid, fast-paced sex farce set amidst gangster wars and an "all-girl" band during Prohibition. Wilder also enriched the decade with a pair of sparkling romantic comedies, *Sabrina* (1954) and *Love in the Afternoon* (1957), as well as his inventive, underrated account of Charles Lindberg's transatlantic crossing, *The Spirit of St. Louis* (1957). He entered the sixties with *The Apartment* (1960), a film about the battle of the sexes made in dark parody of the Hudson / Day cycle, which won numerous critical accolades and awards, including Oscars for Best Film and Best Direction. *One, Two, Three* (1961) satirized the Cold War and American corporate imperialism, and in *Irma La Douce* (1963) and *Kiss Me, Stupid* (1964) Wilder brought the cynical sex comedy *à la* Lubitsch into contemporary American film. In *The Fortune Cookie* (1966), he did a comic turn on *Ace in the Hole*, as an ambulance-chasing lawyer presses a phony damage claim against a professional football team and the city of Cleveland and nearly wins; and by the end of the decade he was spoofing the most revered of Victorian detectives in *The Private Life of Sherlock Holmes* (1969). In the seventies, Wilder directed, among other films, a contemporary version of Lewis Milestone's *The Front Page* (1974) and an elegant reworking of the *Sunset Boulevard* theme in *Fedora* (1979). He also produced the farces *Avanti!* (1972) and *Buddy, Buddy* (1982), about which there are considerably mixed opinions. Wilder has always coauthored his own screenplays, in close collaboration with such professional scriptwriters as Charles Brackett, Raymond Chandler, George Axelrod, and since 1959, I. A. L. Diamond (Wilder began his film career as a scriptwriter for UFA).

Through the influence of Wilder and others (for instance, Stanley Kubrick in *Dr. Strangelove*, 1963, a radical masterpiece far in advance of its time), American comedy became increasingly sophisticated through the fifties and sixties, until it emerged in the seventies as a wholly adult genre. Films like *M.A.S.H.* (Robert Altman, 1970), and the work of comic *auteurs* like Woody Allen (b. Allen Konigsberg, 1935—*Take the Money and Run*, 1969; *Bananas*, 1971; *Play It Again Sam*, 1972; *Everything You Always Wanted to Know About Sex, but Were Afraid to Ask*, 1972; *Sleeper*, 1973; *Love and Death*, 1975); and Mel Brooks (b. Melvin Kaminsky, 1927—*The Producers*, 1968; *Blazing Saddles*, 1973; *Young Franken-*

stein, 1974; *Silent Movie*, 1976; *High Anxiety*, 1977; *History of the World Part I*, 1981; *Space Balls*, 1987) all bear testimony to the increasing maturity of American film comedy—much of it undertaken in parody of other traditional genres. Allen, especially, has emerged as an important and extremely intelligent filmmaker, moving from the broad social satire of his earlier works to the pointed social commentary of *Annie Hall* (1977), *Manhattan* (1979), and the remarkable psuedodocumentary *Zelig* (1983), whose special photographic effects were brilliantly rendered by Gordon Willis, Allen's regular cinematographer from 1977 through 1985. All of Allen's work is filmically literate, and he has produced self-reflexive meditations on the film experience ranging from the narcissistic *Stardust Memories* (1980) to the ingenious *The Purple Rose of Cairo* (1985), which deconstructs the psychology of spectatorship in the manner of Keaton's *Sherlock Jr.* (1924). *A Midsummer Night's Sex Comedy* (1982) has its roots in Shakespeare's *A Midsummer Night's Dream* and Max Reinhardt's 1935 Warner Bros. film of it, but also, less obviously, in Bergman (*Smiles of a Summer Night,* 1955), and Renoir (*Une Partie de campagne,* 1936; *La Régle du jeu,* 1939), while *Broadway Danny Rose* (1984) has been seen by some critics as a recapitulation and inversion of Francis Ford Coppola's *The Godfather* (1972). Allen's most mature films to date are *Hannah and Her Sisters* (1986), a serio-comic narrative of adult relationships set among Manhattan's upper-middle class, and *Radio Days* 1987) a personal memoir structured around a nostalgic history of America's first broadcast medium. Although it is generally agreed that he has been less successful with straight dramatic material, notably in *Interiors* (1978), *September* (1987), and *Another Woman* (1988), there can be no question of Allen's seriousness of purpose and genuine cinematic talent.

12.33 *Love and Death* (Woody Allen, 1975): Woody Allen with the Grim Reaper.

The Western

The genre that seems to have best survived the widescreen inflation of the fifties and sixties is the Western, where the landscape provides a naturally important element, although Westerns, too, experienced some major changes in attitude and theme corresponding to changes in American society. The heroic, idealized, epic Western of John Ford and his imitators remained popular in the fifites but was gradually replaced by what was called the "adult Western." This genre, whose prototypes were *The Gunfighter* (Henry King, 1950) and *High Noon* (Fred Zinnemann, 1952), concentrated on the psychological or moral conflicts of the individual protagonist in relation to his society, rather than creating the poetic archetypes of order characteristic of Ford. The directors Delmer Daves (*Jubal,* 1956; *3:10 to Yuma,* 1957; *Cowboy,* 1958) and John Sturges (*Gunfight at the O.K. Corral,* 1957; *Last Train from Gun Hill,* 1958) both contributed to the new psychological style during this period, but the foremost director of adult Westerns in the fifties was Anthony Mann, who made eleven such films between 1950 and 1960, five of them in close collaboration with the actor James Stewart (for example, *Winchester '73,*

12.34 The "adult Western": *High Noon* (Fred Zinneman, 1952). Gary Cooper.

12.35 *Gunfight at the O.K. Corral* (John Sturges, 1957).

12.36 *Ride Lonesome* (Budd Boetticher, 1959): Randolph Scott.

12.37 *Ride the High Country* (Sam Peckinpah, 1962): (above) Randolph Scott, Mariette Hartley, Joel McCrea; (below, clockwise) L. Q. Jones, John Anderson, Warren Oates, John Davis Chandler.

12.38 Eastern Western: from the showdown which concludes *Yojimbo* (Akira Kurosawa, 1961). Toshiro Mifune.

1950). Mann's Westerns tended to be more intensely psychological and violent than those of his peers, and he was among the first to discover that the topography of the genre was uniquely suited to the widescreen format. In films like *Bend of the River* (1952), *The Naked Spur* (1953), *The Far Country* (1955), *The Man from Laramie* (1955), *The Last Frontier* (1955), *The Tin Star* (1957), and *Man of the West* (1958), Mann carried the genre permanently into the realm of adult entertainment and created an austere visual style which, according to Andrew Sarris, closely resembles that of Michelangelo Antonioni.

Mann's successor was Budd Boetticher, who directed a series of adult Westerns in collaboration with producer Harry Joe Brown and actor Randolph Scott for Ranown Productions in the late fifties. In such films as *Seven Men from Now* (1956), *Decision at Sundown* (1957), *The Tall T* (1957), *Buchanan Rides Alone* (1958), *Ride Lonesome* (1959), and *Comanche Station* (1960), Boetticher forged elemental and even allegorical dramas of ethical heroism in which men alone are forced to make moral choices in a moral vacuum. The Fordian tradition of the epic romance was carried on, of course, by Ford himself in *Wagonmaster* (1950), *Rio Grande* (1950), and preeminently, *The Searchers* (1956—see Chapter 8), and by the makers of such "big" widescreen Westerns as *Shane* (George Stevens, 1953)—a film shot in the old ratio and disastrously blown up for widescreen exhibition; *The Big Country* (William Wyler, 1958); *The Alamo* (John Wayne, 1960); *How the West Was Won* (John Ford, Henry Hathaway, George Marshall, 1962—Cinerama); and the inflated big-budget Westerns of Andrew V. McLaglen (*McClintock*, 1963; *Shenandoah*, 1965; *The Rare Breed*, 1966). It was the Mann-Boetticher tradition that won out in the sixties, as the early films of Sam Peckinpah (*The Deadly Companions*, 1961; *Ride the High Country*, 1962) clearly demonstrate. But the new-style Westerns were soon deeply influenced by another tradition, the Japanese *samurai* film, with its heavy emphasis on honor, fatality, and violence (see Chapter 17).

This influence was first demonstrated in John Sturges' violent and popular *The Magnificent Seven* (1960), a version of Akira Kurosawa's *The Seven Samurai* (1954) set in the American West. In both films, seven hardened warriors (gunmen in Sturges) are inexplicably driven to risk their lives to defend the inhabitants of a small rural village from bandits. *The Magnificent Seven* was a popular success and sparked an international trend toward *samurai* imitations which ultimately produced the "spaghetti Western"—violent films of the American West starring American actors that were shot in Italy or Yugoslavia by Italian filmmakers. The master craftsman of the spaghetti Western was Sergio Leone (1921–89), whose *A Fistful of Dollars*—a direct, almost shot-for-shot copy of Kurosawa's *Yojimbo* (1961), itself reputedly a version of Boetticher's *Buchanan Rides Alone*—started the cycle in 1964. Leone, who turned out to have talent of his own, followed up with *For a Few Dollars More* (1965), *The Good, the Bad, and the Ugly* (1966), and finally, *Once Upon a Time in the West* (1967)—a bold, brilliant parody of all the mythic/

romantic themes of the traditional American Western.* The films of Leone and his many imitators tended to be stylish, colorful, and excessively bloody—the latter achieved through the practice of graphically depicting, for the first time on the screen, impact and exit wounds produced by bullets. For this reason mainly, one fears, the spaghetti Westerns were enormously successful in the United States and produced a number of American-made imitations (e.g., Ted Post's gratuitously brutal *Hang 'Em High*, 1968). They also played a major role in conditioning American audiences to the new levels of violence that were to emerge at the end of the decade in the non-Western gangster film *Bonnie and Clyde* (Arthur Penn, 1967) and in Sam Peckinpah's apocalyptic *The Wild Bunch* (1969; see Chapter 18). The latter work probably did more to demythologize the American West than any single film of its era, but the process had been going on since Anthony Mann's *The Naked Spur* (1953).

Mann, Boetticher, Sturges (in *The Magnificent Seven*), the Italians, and Peckinpah evolved a Western tradition counter to that of Ford—one that was antiheroic and realistic. One important index of this change was a complete reversal of the genre's attitude toward Indians. The hostile savages of the thirties, forties, and most of the fifties were suddenly presented as a race of gentle, intelligent people upon whom the U.S. military establishment had committed genocide. Two films of the period, Ralph Nelson's *Soldier Blue* (1970) and Arthur Penn's *Little Big Man* (1971), graphically depicted the massacre of defenseless Indians by U.S. Cavalry troops (the analogy with the My Lai massacre in both films was inescapable and deliberate). Good "classical" Westerns continued to be made in the sixties by such Fordian craftsmen as Henry Hathaway (*The Sons of Katie Elder*, 1965; *True Grit*, 1969) and by maverick individualists like Howard Hawks (*Rio Bravo*, 1959; *El Dorado*, 1967), but the prevailing trend was toward graphic realism (*Will Penny* [Tom Gries, 1967]; *Monte Walsh* [William Fraker, 1970]) or parody (*Cat Ballou* [Eliot Silverstein, 1965]; *Waterhole No. 3* [William Graham, 1967]; *Butch Cassidy and the Sundance Kid* [George Roy Hill, 1969]). From *Fort Apache* (John Ford, 1948) and *Red River* (Howard Hawks, 1948) to *Soldier Blue* (Ralph Nelson, 1970) and *The Wild Bunch* (Sam Peckinpah, 1969), the external form of the American Western did not significantly change. The Ford and Nelson films, for example, have precisely the same subject, the same landscape, and very nearly the same plot; and *The Wild Bunch* duplicates many of the mythic elements of *Red River* without parody. It is the way in which these elements are viewed by American filmmakers and their

---

* *The Good, the Bad, and the Ugly* and *Once Upon a Time in the West* were both shortened by their American distributors—the first from 180 to 148 minutes, the second from 168 to 144 minutes—to allow for more screenings per day, causing obvious damage to them. The initial appeal of the spaghetti Westerns involved a combination of Clint Eastwood's persona as "The Man with No Name," Leone's dynamic montage, and the innovative musical scores of Ennio Morcone (b. 1928—also the composer for Gillo Pontecorvo's *Battle of Algiers* [1965] and *Queimada* [1968], and, more recently, Bernardo Bertolucci's *1900* [1976], Terrence Malik's *Days of Heaven* [1978], and all of Leone's films).

audiences which has changed. That change is profound, but it has more to do with alterations in the way America perceives itself and its past than with the evolution of a film genre.

The Gangster Film and the Anticommunist Film

The gangster film, which had been replaced by the domestic espionage film during the war, re-emerged in the late forties in shades of black. At that time, "dark" crime films like *The Killers* (Robert Siodmak, 1946), *Kiss of Death* (Henry Hathaway, 1947), *I Walk Alone* (Byron Haskin, 1947), *The Naked City* (Jules Dassin, 1948), *Force of Evil* (Abraham Polonsky, 1948), *They Live by Night* (Nicholas Ray, 1949), *White Heat* (Raoul Walsh, 1949), *Gun Crazy* (Joseph H. Lewis, 1950), *Kiss Tomorrow Goodbye* (Gordon Douglas, 1950), and *Where the Sidewalk Ends* (Otto Preminger, 1950) tended to concentrate on the individual criminal in his relationship to the underworld. In the paranoid fifties, the emphasis shifted from the individual wrongdoer to the existence of a nationwide criminal conspiracy, commonly known as "the syndicate," which was responsible for many of America's social ills—murder, gambling, prostitution, narcotics, and labor racketeering. Since Prohibition, American gangster films have been firmly rooted in the reality of American crime, and—paranoia notwithstanding—that such a criminal conspiracy did exist and that it was closely connected with the Sicilian secret society known as the Mafia was demonstrated by the findings of the Senate Special Committee to Investigate Organized Crime, headed by Senator Estes Kefauver, in 1951. Based on the revelations of the Kefauver Committee, *The Enforcer* (also called *Murder, Inc.;* Bretaigne Windust, 1951) was the first film to posit such an organization on the screen, but it became the major component in *The Big Heat* (Fritz Lang, 1953), *On the Waterfront* (Elia Kazan, 1954), *New York Confidential* (Russell Rouse, 1954), *The Big Combo* (Joseph Lewis, 1955), *The Phenix City Story* (Phil Karlson, 1955), *The Brothers Rico* (Phil Karlson, 1957), *The Garment Jungle* (Vincent Sherman, 1957), *Murder, Inc.* (Stuart Rosenberg, 1960), *Underworld USA* (Samuel Fuller, 1960), and many other gangster films of the decade. The syndicate cycle experienced a decade-long hiatus in the sixties—except for Martin Ritt's *The Brotherhood* (1968)—only to re-emerge with unprecedentedly graphic violence in the blood-soaked seventies with *The Godfather,* and *The Godfather, Part II* (Francis Ford Coppola, 1972 and 1974), *The Valachi Papers* (Terence Young, 1972), *The French Connection* (William Friedkin, 1971) and *The French Connection, II* (John Frankenheimer, 1975), and *Honor Thy Father* (Paul Wendkos, 1971; released 1973).

Another type of gangster film, the biography of the Prohibition and / or Depression criminal, was initiated by Don Siegel's *Baby Face Nelson* (1957). Films in this cycle—*The Bonnie Parker Story* (William Witney, 1958), *Machine Gun Kelly* (Roger Corman, 1958), *Al Capone* (Richard Wilson, 1959), *The Rise and Fall of Legs Diamond* (Budd Boetticher, 1960), *Mad Dog Coll* (Burt Balaban, 1961), *Portrait of a Mobster* (about Dutch Schultz; Joseph Pevney, 1961)—tend to rely on period reconstruc-

12.39 *On the Waterfront* (Elia Kazan, 1954): Marlon Brando.

tion, and their apotheosis came in the late sixties with Arthur Penn's *Bonnie and Clyde* (1967), Roger Corman's *The St. Valentine's Day Massacre* (1967) and *Bloody Mama* (1969), and John Milius' *Dillinger* (1973).

Two interesting subtypes of the gangster film which appeared in the fifties were the "caper" film and the "anti-Red" action thriller. The caper film, which began with John Huston's *The Asphalt Jungle* (1950), concentrates on the mechanics of pulling off a big heist and is still a very popular type. It is sometimes deadly serious, sometimes light and witty. Subsequent manifestations both in America and abroad include *Rififi* (Jules Dassin, 1955), *The Killing* (Stanley Kubrick, 1956), *Odds Against Tomorrow* (Robert Wise, 1959), *Seven Thieves* (Henry Hathaway, 1960), *Big Deal on Madonna Street* (Mario Monicelli, 1960), *The League of Gentlemen* (Basil Dearden, 1960), *Topkapi* (Jules Dassin, 1964), *Grand Slam* (Giuliano Montaldo, 1967), and *They Came to Rob Las Vegas* (Antonio Isasi, 1968). The anti-Red action film was a localized, primitive type endemic to the early fifties and exemplified by Robert Stevenson's *I Married a Communist* (also known as *The Woman on Pier 13*, 1950), Gordon Douglas' *I Was a Communist for the FBI* (1951),* Edward Ludwig's *Big Jim McLain* (1953), and Samuel Fuller's more morally ambiguous *Pickup on South Street* (1953). In this type, the criminal figure is a communist spy and the syndicate is the "international communist conspiracy," but the traditional iconography of the gangster film is maintained.

The communist-as-gangster film was part of a larger cycle of more than fifty anticommunist films produced by nearly every studio in Hollywood between 1948 and 1955 (the exceptions were Disney and Universal-International) in ritual self-abasement before HUAC and the minions of Senator Joseph McCarthy.† Many of these, such as *The Iron Curtain*

12.40 *The Asphalt Jungle* (John Huston, 1950); Louis Calhern, Sam Jaffe.

---

* *I Was a Communist for the FBI* was adapted for television by producer Frederick W. Ziv and syndicated as *I Led Three Lives* in 1953; it was enormously popular, running 117 half-hour episodes, and was still being shown on local stations as late as 1980.

† Joseph McCarthy (1908–57), junior Republican senator from Wisconsin from 1948 through 1956, was the most successful and infamous exploiter of the anticommunist hysteria churned up by HUAC and the atomic spy syndrome (see Chapter 11). On February 9, 1950, in Wheeling, West Virginia, McCarthy began a political reign of terror that would last more than four years by accusing the State Department of selling out China to the communists and harboring 205 known Communist Party members among its senior staff. He went on to accuse countless U.S. civil servants and private citizens of treason on the basis of half-truths and innuendo, mobilizing a rising tide of anti-intellectualism and class suspicion that focused on WASPish establishment figures (like Secretary of State Dean Acheson) and their educated urban Jewish counterparts. As chairman of the Senate Subcommittee on Investigations from 1953 to 1955, McCarthy conducted sensational public witch-hunts and proved himself to be a skilled manipulator of mass opinion, especially through the new medium of television. Appropriately, it was television that brought him down, first through a negative profile on Edward R. Murrow's *See It Now* in March 1954 and then, in April and May, through the televised Army-McCarthy hearings, where McCarthy's mendacity and fraudulence were revealed at last to the nation. On December 2, 1954, his conduct was officially censured by an overwhelming majority of his fellow senators, and though he served out his term, McCarthy's political career was over from that point on. McCarthyism itself, however, lived on, and in its paranoid style and bullying tactics gave the fifties and part of the next decade their dominant mood. See Emile de Antonio's film on the McCarthy hearings, *Point of Order* (1971).

12.41 Brutally un-American: *Pickup on South Street* (Samuel Fuller, 1953). Jean Peters, Richard Widmark.

(William Wellman, 1948), *Walk a Crooked Mile* (Gordon Douglas, 1948), *The Red Menace* (R. G. Springsteen, 1949), *The Whip Hand* (William Cameron Menzies, 1951), *Diplomatic Courier* (Henry Hathaway, 1952), *The Thief* (Russell Rouse, 1952), *The Atomic City* (Jerry Hopper, 1952), *Walk East on Beacon* (Alfred L. Werker, 1952), and *A Bullet for Joey* (Lewis Allen, 1955), had their roots in the World War II espionage film (see Chapter 11) and simply substituted villainous Reds for villainous Nazis. Others were set inside the Iron Curtain and focused on innocent individuals attempting to get out (*The Red Danube* [George Sidney, 1949], *The Steel Fist* [Wesley Barry, 1952], *Assignment—Paris* [Robert Parrish, 1952], *Man on a Tightrope* [Elia Kazan, 1953]), *Never Let Me Go* [Delmer Daves, 1953], while still others posed as domestic melodramas (*Shack Out on 101* [Edward Dein, 1955]), semidocumentaries (*Red Snow* [Boris L. Petroff and Harry S. Franklin, 1952]; *Invasion U.S.A.* [Alfred E. Green, 1952]), science fiction (*Red Planet Mars* [Henry Horner, 1952]; *Project Moonbase* [Richard Talmadge, 1953]), combat films (*Prisoner of War* [Andrew Morton, 1954]), Westerns (*California Conquest* [Lew Landers, 1952]), or even South Seas adventures (*Savage Drums* [William Berke, 1951]). But the ultimate anticommunist film was indisputably *My Son John* (1952), written, produced, and directed for Paramount by the talented Leo McCarey (1898–1969), one of the great comic filmmakers of the thirties (*Duck Soup*, 1933; *Ruggles of Red Gap*, 1935; *The Awful Truth*, 1937), who had apparently lost his sense of humor. A feverish blend of anti-intellectualism, oedipal obsession, and pseudo-Christian piety, *My Son John* stars the brilliant young actor Robert Walker (1918–1951) in his last role* as a State Department Red whose treachery stops just

---

* Walker, who had recently suffered a series of nervous breakdowns, died on the set of *My Son John* following the administration of sedative by a doctor. Since the conclusion had not yet been shot, McCarey was forced to piece one together from out-takes from Walker's previous film, Hitchcock's *Stranger on a Train* (1951).

short of parricide. So impassioned and viscerally engaging is this film that it deserves to be ranked with *The Birth of a Nation* and *Triumph of the Will* among the cinema's definitive works of authoritarian propaganda, and like them, it has remained controversial since the day of its release.

The anticommunist cycle coincided almost precisely with the period between the first HUAC Hollywood hearings and the U.S. Senate's censure of Joseph McCarthy, but a trickle of films continued—*The River Changes* (Owen Crump, 1956), *The Girl in the Kremlin* (Russell Birdwell, 1957), *The Fearmakers* (Jacques Tourneur, 1958)—through the end of the decade when the last communist-as-gangster film appeared in *The FBI Story* (Mervyn LeRoy, 1959), which also dealt with Prohibition / Depression gangsters and Nazi spies. The central impulse of the anticommunist film was preserved in the James Bond espionage thrillers of the sixties, which were adapted from the novels of British writer Ian Fleming and produced by Albert R. Broccoli and Harry Saltzman's London-based Eon Productions for distribution by United Artists. These immensely popular films and their imitators in effect usurped the gangster genre between 1962 and 1969 by positing criminal conspiracy on a worldwide scale and offering violent gangsterism on the part of both the conspirators and the superhero ("licensed to kill") sent to stop them. Fleming's work was probably brought to the attention of Broccoli and Saltzman by an article that appeared in *Life* magazine on March 17, 1961, naming *From Russia with Love* as one of President Kennedy's ten favorite books (the ninth, in fact—just ahead of Stendhal's *The Red and the Black*). The President didn't live to see the movie, whose American premier was in April 1964, but Eon's sexy, gadget-ridden James Bond series became the most successful in motion picture history, earning nine Academy Award nominations and over half a billion dollars in rentals from 1962 through 1985. The sixties Bond films—*Dr. No, From Russia with Love,* and *Thunderball* (Terence Young; 1962, 1963, 1965), *Goldfinger* (Guy Hamilton, 1964), *You Only Live Twice* (Lewis Gilbert, 1967), and *On Her Majesty's Secret Service* (Peter Hunt, 1969)—greatly influenced the decade's popular culture, spawning imitative television series like *The Man from U.N.C.L.E.* (1964–68), *Secret Agent* (1965–66), *I Spy* (1965–68), and *Mission Impossible* (1966–71), and such theatrical clones as the two Charles Vine films (*Second Best Secret Agent in the Whole, Wide World* [also known as *Licensed to Kill,* Lindsay Shonteff, 1965] and *Where Bullets Fly* [John Gilling, 1966]), the two Derek Flint films (*Our Man Flint* [Daniel Mann, 1966] and *In Like Flint* [Gordon Douglas, 1967]), and the Matt Helm series (*The Silencers* [Phil Karlson, 1966]; *Murderer's Row* [Henry Levin, 1966]; *The Ambushers* [Henry Levin, 1967]; and *The Wrecking Crew* [Phil Karlson, 1968]), whose formula of gangster-as-international-conspirator versus gangster-as-government-agent, however playful, sank the espionage thriller into a state of moral confusion from which it never emerged.*

12.42 Oedipal anti-Communism: Leo McCarey's *My Son John* (1952). Robert Walker, Helen Hayes, Dean Jagger.

---

*The first five James Bond films starred the Scottish-born actor Sean Connery, and he became closely identified in the public mind with the series. But he grew tired of the role and refused it for *On Her Majesty's Secret Service,* which offered the Australian actor

12.43 Part of a theater lobby display for *Destination Moon* (Irving Pichel, 1950).

12.44 *Rocketship XM* (Kurt Neumann, 1950): an accidental landing on Mars.

12.45 *The Thing* (Christian Nyby, 1951): earthlings measure an alien craft embedded in ice at a remote Artic air base.

12.46 *The Day the Earth Stood Still* (Robert Wise, 1951): a flying saucer lands in Washington, D.C.

In the late fifties and early sixties, the young directors of the French New Wave borrowed heavily from the conventions of the American gangster film in works like *Breathless* (Jean-Luc Godard, 1960) and *Shoot the Piano Player* (François Truffaut, 1960), but the genre remained dormant in America itself until 1967, when Arthur Penn's *Bonnie and Clyde* revitalized it for the seventies. Penn's film, very much a product of the rebellious spirit of the late sixties, owed a great deal stylistically to the example of the French New Wave, but *Bonnie and Clyde* also restored the gangster to his traditional position as tragic hero and unified the genre by borrowing motifs from three great crime films of the past—Fritz Lang's *You Only Live Once* (1937), Nicholas Ray's *They Live by Night* (1949), and Joseph Lewis' *Gun Crazy* (1950). Since *Bonnie and Clyde,* the gangster film, like the Western has re-entered the mainstream of American cinema as the vehicle for serious artistic and social expression (e.g., *The Godfather* and *The Godfather, Part II*) that it was during the thirties.

Science Fiction

Another interesting development of the fifties was the emergence of the science fiction film as a distinct genre. There had been films of science fantasy long before World War II. One of the first important narrative films, Georges Méliès' *Le Voyage dans la lune* (1902), fits the description, as do Fritz Lang's *Metropolis* (1926) and *Die Frau im Mond* (*The Woman in the Moon,* 1929). But with the exception of William Cameron Menzies' futuristic fantasy *Things to Come* (1936) and Lothar Mendes' *The Man Who Could Work Miracles* (1937)—both based on works by H. G. Wells—science fiction before World War II concentrated on individual conflicts rather than global ones. With the war and the threat of nuclear holocaust came a widespread recognition that science and technology were in a position to affect the destiny of the entire human race, and shortly after, the modern science fiction film, with its emphasis on global catastrophe and space travel, began to take shape. The first important example of the form was *Destination Moon* (Irving Pichel, 1950), which was followed rapidly by *Rocketship XM* (Kurt Neumann, 1950), *Five* (Arch Oboler, 1951), *The Thing* (also known as *The Thing from Another World;* Christian Nyby, 1951), *The Day the Earth Stood Still* (Robert

George Lazenby in the part with scant popular success. The first Eon production of the seventies, *Diamonds Are Forever* (Guy Hamilton, 1971), brought Connery back, but no one was really happy with the arrangement. After *Live and Let Die* (Hamilton, 1973), Saltzman sold his share in Eon to UA; from then until 1985—in *The Man with the Golden Gun* (Hamilton, 1975); *The Spy Who Loved Me* (Lewis Gilbert, 1977); *Moonraker* (Gilbert, 1979); *For Your Eyes Only* (John Glen, 1981); *Octopussy* (Glen, 1983); and *A View To Kill* (Glen, 1985)—Bond was played by the urbane Roger Moore, who had achieved fame as Simon Templar in the Bondlike British TV series *The Saint.* In 1987, the fifteenth Eon production, *The Living Daylights* (Glen), introduced a new Bond in the person of Timothy Dalton. Two Bond films have been made outside of the Eon-UA umbrella—*Casino Royale* (John Huston, 1967), adapted from the only Fleming novel (his first) not originally optioned by Broccoli and Saltzman, and *Never Say Never Again* (Irvin Kershner, 1983), a virtual remake of *Thunderball,* produced by Jack Schwartzman for Warner Bros., which brought Connery back as an older, heavier, but still effective James Bond.

12.47 Visions of a catastrophic future: *When Worlds Collide* (Rudolph Maté, 1951).

Wise, 1951), *When Worlds Collide* (Rudolph Maté, 1951), *The Man from Planet X* (Edgar G. Ulmer, 1951), *Flight to Mars* (Lesley Selander, 1951), *Invaders from Mars* (William Cameron Menzies, 1953), *War of the Worlds* (Byron Haskin, 1954), *This Island Earth* (Joseph Newman, 1955), *Forbidden Planet* (Herbert Wilcox, 1956), and *Invasion of the Body Snatchers* (Don Siegel, 1956).* All of these films were well-produced on budgets of widely varying scale, and the element common to most was some form of world-threatening crisis produced by nuclear war or alien invasion (and, in the Siegel film, an invasion which threatens not destruction but conversion)—with obvious political implications.

In fact, with their constant warnings against infiltration and invasion, the paranoid politics of the Cold War permeated the fifties science fiction boom almost as thoroughly as state-of-the-art special effects, which reached a new plateau in the early years of the decade with the films of producer George Pal (1908–80) and special effects director Ray Harryhausen (b. 1920). Pal, a native-born Hungarian whose brilliant matte work won Special Effects Oscars for *Destination Moon, When Worlds Collide,* and *War of the Worlds,* had begun his career as a UFA set-designer and become a puppet animator in Hollywood during the war (e.g., Paramount's *Puppetoons* series, 1943–44); after his successes of the early fifties, Pal went on to produce and direct such fantasy films as *Tom Thumb* (1958; Academy Award for Special Effects), *The Time Machine* (1960; Academy Award for Special Effects), *Atlantis, the Lost Continent* (1961), *The Wonderful World of the Brothers Grimm* (codirected with Henry Levin, 1962;

---

* *Rocketship XM* was rushed into production several months after *Destination Moon* but was actually released two months before it, having many fewer special effects. *Invasion of the Body Snatchers* was remade by Philip Kaufman in 1978, with appearances by its original director, Don Siegel, and star, Kevin McCarthy. *The Thing* was remade by John Carpenter as a high-tech eighties-style gore fest in 1982; *Strange Invaders* (Michael Laughlin, 1983) contains significant elements of *The Day the Earth Stood Still;* and *Invaders from Mars* was remade by Tobe Hooper in 1986.

Cinerama), and *The Seven Faces of Dr. Lao* (1964). Harryhausen was a protégé of special effects pioneer Willis O'Brien (1886–1962; *The Lost World,* 1925; *King Kong* and *Son of Kong,* 1933; *The Last Days of Pompeii,* 1935; *Mighty Joe Young,* 1949; etc.),* who specialized in a three-dimensional, stop-motion process that enabled him to combine animated models with live action. Patented in 1957 as Dynamation, versions of the technique were used in some of the best of the monster films (see pp. 521–23), as well as in the more elaborate Sinbad series (*The Seventh Voyage of Sinbad* [Nathan Juran, 1958]; *The Golden Voyage of Sinbad* [Gordon Hessler, 1974]; *Sinbad and the Eye of the Tiger* [Sam Wanamaker, 1977]); adaptations from Swift (*The Three Worlds of Gulliver* [Jack Sher, 1960]), Verne (*Mysterious Island* [Cy Enfield, 1961]), and Wells (*First Men in the Moon,* [Nathan Juran, 1964]); the prehistoric adventure epic *One Million Years, B.C.* (Don Chaffey, 1967), and the mythological fantasies *Jason and the Argonauts* (Don Chaffey, 1963) and *Clash of the Titans* (Desmond David, 1981).

All of the decade's science fiction films contained an element of dread, but *The Thing,* which concerned the coming to Earth of a dangerous creature from another galaxy, started a phenomenally popular cycle of films about monsters and mutations produced by nuclear radiation or materialized from outer space which dominated the genre for the next ten years. Science fiction purists argue that the monster films of the fifties were less science fiction than horror, but the line between the two categories is sometimes quite difficult to draw. The films of the Universal horror cycle of the thirties (*Dracula, Frankenstein,* etc.—see Chapter 8) and the imaginative widescreen color remakes of them produced by England's Hammer films in the late fifties and the sixties, for example, are clearly distinguishable in iconography and theme from science fiction classics like *Invasion of the Body Snatchers* and *Forbidden Planet.* Here science fiction seems to be concerned with the catastrophic impact of technology on civilization—an impact which means the end of evolution—while horror focuses upon the potential evil within the human heart. But monster films pose the specifically modern (that is, postwar) problem of how human evil and technology *combine* to threaten the existence of the race, and therefore they seem to straddle the generic fence between science fiction and horror.†

Some of the early monster films were carefully produced by the majors, like R.K.O.'s *The Thing,* Warner Bros.' *The Beast from 20,000 Fathoms* (Eugene Lourie, 1953; effects by Harryhausen), and the same studio's

12.48 *Invasion of the Body Snatchers* (Don Siegel, 1956): Dana Wyler and Kevin McCarthy pursued by pod-people.

12.49 *It Came from Outer Space* (Jack Arnold, 3-D, 1953)—and Steven Spielberg must have watched it over and over again.

---

* O'Brien worked into the fifties and early sixties, contributing special effects to the monster films *The Black Scorpion,* 1957 and *The Giant Behemoth,* 1959, a remake of *The Lost World* (Irwin Allen, 1960), and *It's a Mad Mad Mad Mad World* (Stanley Kramer, 1963; Cinerama). He also wrote the story for *The Beast of Hollow Mountain* (Edward Nassour, 1956), a combination Western–science-fiction thriller shot on location in Mexico.

† Of course, works of fiction as far back as Mary Shelley's novel *Frankenstein* (1819) have contemplated this problem, but it was not until the discovery of nuclear fission and its "practical" applications that technology and malevolence could *literally* combine to destroy the species.

12.50 *Them!* (Gordon Douglas, 1954): an avatar of *Aliens* (James Cameron, 1986)—see still 18.84.

Them! (Gordon Douglas, 1954). Other monster films of the fifties—Columbia's *It Came from Beneath the Sea* (Richard Gordon, 1955) and *Twenty Million Miles to Earth* (Nathan Juran, 1957), both with effects by Harryhausen; Fox's *Kronos* and *The Fly* (both Kurt Neumann; 1957, 1958); and Paramount's *The Colossus of New York* (Eugene Lourie, 1958) and *The Blob* (Irvin S. Yeaworth, 1958)*—relied heavily on their special effects. By mid-decade, monster films had largely become the province of exploitation producers, but there were clear exceptions in the inventive work of Jack Arnold (b. 1916), most of it for Universal-International, who directed *It Came from Outer Space* (1953; 3-D), a major source for Steven Spielberg's *E.T. The Extra-Terrestrial* (1982); *Creature from the Black Lagoon* (1954; 3-D) and its sequel, *Revenge of the Creature* (1955; 3-D), the last film released in the fifties version of 3-D (the final entry in the "Gill Man" cycle was *The Creature Walks Among Us*, 1956, directed by Arnold's protege John Sherwood); *Tarantula* (1955), one of the best of the insect mutation thrillers; *The Incredible Shrinking Man* (1957), a film that cleverly inverts the premise of the monster / mutant cycle (ineptly parodied by Joel Schumacher in *The Incredible Shrinking Woman* twenty-four years later); *Monster on the Campus* (1958); and *The Space Children* (1958), one of the era's first antinuclear science fiction films.†

---

* *The Fly* was strikingly remade for Fox by the Canadian director David Cronenberg in 1987. The original version had generated two sequels, both Fox productions: *Return of the Fly* (Edward Bernds, 1959) and *Curse of the Fly* (Don Sharp, 1963). *The Blob* was remade for Tri-Star in 1988, with high-tech special effects and direction by Chuck Russell.

† Arnold, who began his career as a documentarist for the U.S. State Department, directed successful films in other genres during this period, including *film gris* (*The Tattered Dress, Man in the Shadow*, both 1957) and comedy (*The Lady Takes a Flyer*, 1958; *The Mouse That Roared*, 1959; *Bachelor in Paradise*, 1961). He occasionally coproduced and coscripted his own work (e.g., *Tarantula*) as well as that of colleagues (e.g., *The Monolith Monsters*, John Sherwood, 1957), and he directed additional scenes (uncredited) for Universal's re-edited version of Welles' *Touch of Evil* (1957). See Dana M. Reeves, *Directed by Jack Arnold* (Jefferson, N.C.: McFarland & Company, 1988).

12.51 *The Beast from 20,000 Fathoms* (Eugene Lourie, 1953).

12.52 Making a lot with a little: Jack Arnold's *The Incredible Shrinking Man* (1957). Grant Williams.

The Japanese, recent witnesses to nuclear horror themselves, entered the atomic monster field with a well-crafted series of films directed by Inoshiro Honda (b. 1911) for Toho studios with effects by Eiji Tsuburaya (1901–70), beginning with *Godzilla, King of Monsters* (*Gojira*, 1954; English-language version, Terry Morse) and continuing through such widescreen color epics as *Rodan* (1957), *Varan the Unbelievable* (1958; rereleased 1962), *The Mysterians* (1959), *Battle in Outer Space* (1960), *Mothra* (1962), *Gorath* (1962), *Atragon* (1964), and, with increasing silliness, *King Kong vs. Godzilla* (1963), *Godzilla vs. the Thing* (1964), *Ghidra, the Three-Headed Monster* (1965), *Frankenstein Conquers the World* (1966), *Monster Zero* (also known as *Invasion of the Astro-Monster*, 1966), *War of the Gargantuas* (1967), *King Kong Escapes* (1968), and the cycle's *Götterdämmerung, Destroy All Monsters* (1969). Typically, American distributors enhanced the box-office appeal of these imports by peppering them with extraneous footage of American actors like Raymond Burr, Russ Tamblyn, or Nick Adams, with the result that their plots, never a strong point, became virtually incoherent. But during the fifties, at least, their imaginative special effects and model work made the Japanese monster films very popular with audiences all over the world.

Most of the American low-budget science fiction quickies of the fifties were made by Allied Artists (AA) or American International Pictures (AIP), the successors to the B-film studios of the thirties and forties.* AA was

---

* The popularity of the form was such, however, that virtually every film-releasing organization in the country, from the largest studio to the sleaziest distributor, was involved. Fox contributed several interesting CinemaScope entries shot in black-and-white by Karl Struss (*She Devil* [Kurt Neumann, 1957]; *The Alligator People* [Roy Del Ruth, 1959]); Paramount offered the exploitationally titled but intriguing *I Married a Monster from Outer Space* (Gene Fowler, Jr., 1958); MGM handled *Fiend Without a Face* (Arthur Crabtree, 1958) and *The First Man into Space* (also known as *Satellite of Blood* [Robert Day, 1959]); Columbia contributed *The Creature with the Atom Brain* (Edward L. Cahn, 1955), *The Gamma People* (John Gilling, 1956), *The Mole People* (Virgil Vogel, 1956), and *The Deadly*

in fact a reincarnation of Monogram Productions, which had changed its corporate name in 1952. The studio struggled through much of the fifties and sixties, producing a handful of good science fiction entries—notably, *Invasion of the Body Snatchers, The Giant Behemoth* (Eugene Lourie, 1959; effects by Willis O'Brien), and Britain's *Day of the Triffids* (Steve Sekely, 1963)—but surviving mainly on such cheapies as *Target Earth* (Sherman A. Rose, 1954), *The Indestructible Man* (Jack Pollexfen, 1956), *The Attack of the Crab Monsters* and *Not of This Earth** (both Roger Corman, 1956), *From Hell It Came* (Dan Milner, 1957), *Attack of the 50 Foot Woman* (Nathan Hertz [Juran], 1958), *The Cosmic Man* (Herbert Greene, 1958), *Frankenstein 1970* (Howard W. Koch, 1958), *The Atomic Submarine* (Spencer G. Bennet, 1959), and *The Wasp Woman* (Roger Corman, 1959), plus an occasional essay in widescreen and color (*World Without End* [Edward Bernds, 1956]; *The Queen of Outer Space* [Ben Schwab, 1958]).†

The ultimate exploitation producer of the era, however, was American International Pictures (AIP), founded as American Releasing Corporation (ARC) in 1954 with working capital of three thousand dollars by

---

Mantis (Nathan Juran, 1957)—written and produced by the former Mercury Theater actor William Alland (who played the reporter Thompson in *Kane* and was also the producer of Universal-International's popular Creature series), *The Giant Claw* (Fred F. Sears, 1957), *The Night the World Exploded* (Sears, 1957), *The Twenty-seventh Day* (William Asher, 1957), and *The Electronic Monster* (Montgomery Tully, 1960); Universal-International was responsible for *The 4-D Man* (Irvin S. Yeaworth) and *The Leech Woman* (Edward Dein, 1960); United Artists fronted *The Magnetic Monster* (Curt Siodmak, 1953), *Gog* (Herbert L. Strock, 1954; 3-D), *The Monster that Challenged the World* (Arnold Laven, 1957), *It! The Terror from Beyond Space* (Edward L. Cahn, 1958), *(It Fell from) the Flame Barrier* (Paul Landers, 1958), and *Invisible Invaders* (Edward L. Cahn, 1959); the minuscule Astor Films inflicted *Robot Monster* (Phil Tucker, 1953; 3-D—allegedly made for $502.25), *Cat Woman of the Moon* (Arthur Hilton, 1953), its remake, *Missile to the Moon* (Richard Cunha, 1959), and *She Demons* (Cunha, 1958); Distributor's Corporation of America (DCA) had the fortune to distribute the works of Edward D. Woods (1922–78), widely considered to have been the worst director of all time (*Glen or Glenda?*, 1953; *Jail Bait*, 1954; *Bride of the Monster*, 1956; *Plan Nine from Outer Space*, 1959; *Night of the Ghouls*, unreleased), as well as *Monster from Green Hell* (Kenneth Crane, 1958), the British imports *The Cosmic Monster* (Gilbert Gunn, 1958) and *The Crawling Eye* (Quentin Lawrence, 1958); finally, regional pickup distribution accounted for the release of such films as *Fire Maidens from Outer Space* (Cy Roth, 1956), *Giant from the Unknown* (Richard Cunha, 1958), *The Brain from Planet Arous* (Nathan Hertz [Juran], 1958), *The Hideous Sun Demon* (Robert Clarke and Thomas Cassarino, 1959), *The Giant Gila Monster* (Ray Kellogg, 1959), *The Killer Shrews* (Ray Kellogg, 1959), *The Beast of Yucca Flat* (Coleman Francis, 1961), and *The Slime People* (Robert Hutton, 1963).

* *Not of This Earth* was remade in 1988 by Corman's Concorde Pictures, with direction by Jim Wynorski.

†The fortunes of Allied Artists turned up in 1965 with its release of the popular Elvis Presley vehicle *Tickle Me* (Norman Taurog, 1965), but in 1967 it sold its studio and under the leadership of Emanuel L. Wolf briefly became a releasing company for foreign films— notably *A Man and a Woman* (Claude Lelouch, 1966), *Belle de jour* (Luis Buñuel, 1968), and *The Story of O* (Juste Jaeckin, 1975)—before returning to production in the seventies, financing such successful films as *Cabaret* (Bob Fosse, 1972), *Papillon* (Franklin J. Schaffner, 1973), The *Man Who Would Be King* (John Huston, 1975), and *Conduct Unbecoming* (Michael Anderson, 1975). An attempt at diversification failed in 1979, and AA and its library of 450 films were sold to Lorimar Productions the following year (see Chapter 18).

James H. Nicholson and Samuel Z. Arkoff. Nicholson and Arkoff were able to build an empire from these humble beginnings by tapping into a market that mainstream producers were ignoring—the children of the baby boom and their teenaged precursors. With the exception of late afternoons and Saturday mornings, fifties television programming was targeted at adults, and so was Hollywood's widescreen Eastmancolor counterprogramming. The majors welcomed box-office spillover from the kids and were always happy to have produced a family hit, but only Disney among them was actually producing films *for* children, and for younger ones, parents in tow, at that.* But AIP discovered a market of kids alone, kids who were ready to pay good money for the cheapest kind of audiovisual thrills, so long as their cultural values weren't offended.

During the fifties AIP produced its share of bargain-basement Westerns, crime thrillers, and teenage exposés, but its real profit center was the monster film, the more sensational and lurid the better. Like its B-studio predecessors, AIP initially rented its features to exhibitors at a flat rate, which meant that they usually wound up at the bottom half of double bills, but by 1956 Nicholson and Arkoff had arrived at the successful formula of packaging their films as already-paired double bills, which enabled them to both better control the market and to double their rentals. The idea was so successful that other exploitation producers copied it, with the result that nearly all of the low-budget films described in this section were seen by their original audiences as parts of a two-film program, yoked with their mates through dual promotion and publicity. AIP was set up as a constellation of five independent producers, among whom were the producer-directors Bert I. Gordon (b. 1922) and Roger Corman (b. 1926). Gordon, who sometimes wrote his own scripts, specialized in low-budget special effects which he produced himself through extensive use of rear-screen projection and mattes, often quite successfully. His insect mutation film (giant grasshoppers) *Begining of the End* (1957) was distributed by Republic, but his next five films—*The Cyclops* (1957); *The Amazing Colossal Man* (1957); its sequel, *The War of the Colossal Beast* (1958); *Attack of the Puppet People* (1958); and *The Spider* (1958)—were all big money-makers for AIP.†

Corman, a much more important figure, initially specialized in monster / horror quickies, some of which—*Monster from the Ocean Floor* (1954), *The Day the World Ended* (1956), *It Conquered the World* (1956),

---

* The Disney studios actually produced one of the science fiction classics of the decade, albeit a specialized one: *20,000 Leagues Under the Sea* (Richard Fleischer, 1954), with elaborate special effects by Ralph Hammeras. This 4-million-dollar CinemaScope version of Jules Verne's 1870 novel, first adapted by Méliès in 1907, was a remake of Universal's 1916 silent spectacular (directed by Stuart Paton, with effects by the father of underwater photography, John Ernest Williamson), and its popular success led to a cycle of Verne adaptations over the next decade, including *From the Earth to the Moon* (Byron Haskin, 1958), *Journey to the Center of the Earth* (Henry Levin, 1959), *Master of the World* (William Witney, 1961), *Mysterious Island* (Cy Enfield, 1961; effects by Harryhausen), and *Around the World Under the Sea* (Andrew Marton, 1966).

† AIP continued to grind out fifties-style monster fare until 1963, when it struck a new vein with *Beach Party* (William Asher, 1963), which established a successful formula that was reworked in such near-clones as *Bikini Beach* (William Asher, 1964), *Muscle Beach Party*

12.53   AIP's *I Was a Teenage Werewolf* (Gene Fowler, Jr., 1957): Whit Bissell, Vladimir Sokoloff, Michael Landon (as the werewolf). Earlier in the decade, Fowler had been an editor for Fritz Lang.

12.54   Bargain-basement spectacle: Bert I. Gordon's *The Amazing Colossal Man* (1957).

The Undead (1957), *The Viking Women and the Sea Serpent* (1957), *The She Gods of Shark Reef* (1959), and *The Wasp Woman* (1959)—were reputedly produced in less than three days. But he also produced the much-admired black-humor trilogy *A Bucket of Blood* (1959), *Little Shop of Horrors* (1960),* and *Creature from the Haunted Sea* (1960)—the latter two for his own company, Filmgroup—and when AIP decided to make its films in CinemaScope and color, Corman was given the first such assignment, *House of Usher* (1960), adapted from Edgar Allan Poe by the novelist Richard Matheson and budgeted at a princely 350,000 dollars. This film was both a critical and commercial success, becoming the first AIP release since 1956 to play by itself (in most theaters) and the first ever to rent on a percentage basis in the manner of a standard mainstream feature. It was followed by a series of increasingly successful Poe

(Asher, 1964), *Pajama Party* (Don Weis, 1964), *Beach Blanket Bingo* (Asher, 1965), *Dr. Goldfoot and the Bikini Machine* (Norman Taurog, 1965), *How to Stuff a Wild Bikini* (Asher, 1965), and *Ski Party* (Alan Rifkin, 1965). Teenage exploitation films, or "teenpics," had been launched by Columbia's *Rock Around the Clock* (Fred F. Sears), starring Bill Haley and the Comets, in 1956 and immediately cloned at AIP by Edward L. Cahn (*Shake, Rattle, and Roll*, 1957) and Roger Corman (*Rock All Night*, 1957); these were followed by a host of other rock 'n roll-themed cheapies like *Rock, Pretty Baby* (Richard Barlett, 1957), *Rock, Rock, Rock* (Will Price, 1957), and *Don't Knock the Rock* (Fred F. Sears, 1957). In the same year, AIP gene-spliced the teenpic with the monster film in a remarkably successful cycle produced by Herman Cohen—*I Was a Teenage Werewolf* (Gene Fowler, Jr.), *I Was a Teenage Frankenstein* (Herbert L. Strock), *Blood of Dracula* (Strock), and in later years *How to Make a Monster* (Strock, 1958) and *Konga* (aka *I was a Teenage Gorilla* (John Lemont, 1961). (Other contributions came from James Marquette [*Teenage Monster*, aka *Meteor Monster*, 1957], Roger Corman [*Teenage Caveman*, 1958], Tom Graeff [*Teenagers from Outer Space*, 1959], and Jerry Warren [*Teenage Zombies*, 1960].)

* Adapted as a successful Broadway musical and a film in 1987.

12.55 Production values: Roger Corman's *The Raven* (1963). AIP.

films, scripted by some combination of Matheson, Charles Beaumont, and Robert Towne, and produced and directed by Corman: *The Pit and the Pendulum* (1961), *The Premature Burial* (1962), *Tales of Terror* (1962; an anthology of three Poe stories woven together in the manner of the British classic *Dead of Night,* 1945), *The Raven* (1963), *The Haunted Palace* (1963; "inspired" by Poe's poem but actually adapted from an H. P. Lovecraft story), *The Masque of the Red Death* (1964; cinematography by Nicholas Roeg; see Chapter 14), and *The Tomb of Ligea* (1965).* In between, Corman was churning out box-office fodder like *The Last Woman on Earth* (1960), *Ski Troop Attack* (1960), *The Tower of London* (1962), *The Young Racers* (1963), and *The Secret Invasion* (1964), in addition to a chilling portrayal of lynch-mob violence in *The Intruder* (1962), the now-legendary *The Terror* (1963—a film shot in two days on the dismantled sets of *The Raven,* which combined the acting talents of Boris Karloff and Jack Nicholson with the directorial skills of Corman, Francis Coppola, and Monte Hellman),† and *X—The Man with X-Ray Eyes* (1963), an intelligent moral allegory of *seeing* in the form of medical science fiction. Corman demonstrated his continued prescience by producing two visually imaginative films that helped to shape the "youth cult" boom of the late sixties, *The Wild Angels* (1966), a graphically violent, *cinéma verité*-style biker epic which became the American entry in the Venice Film Festival for that year, and *The Trip* (1967), a guided tour through an LSD experience, both starring Peter Fonda. Corman also made two excellent medium-budget gangster films (having already pro-

---

* To the AIP Poe cycle should be added *War Gods of the Deep* (Jacques Tourneur, 1965), because it was technically based on the poem "The Doomed City" and the short story "A Descent into the Maelstrom." Produced by Daniel Haller, the film owed nothing to Corman except that it was inspired by the success of his Poe films.

† Old habits die hard—in 1987, Corman produced two films, *Big, Bad Mama II* and *Daddy's Boys* (Joe Minion, 1988) simultaneously in twenty-two days, and on the same set.

duced two striking low-budget ones in *Machine Gun Kelly* and *I Mobster,* both 1958)—*The St. Valentine's Day Massacre* (1967, Fox), whose ballistic *grand guignol* forecasts that of *Bonnie and Clyde* (Arthur Penn, 1967) later in the year, and *Bloody Momma* (1969), an account of the brutal Ma Barker family made to cash in on *Bonnie and Clyde*'s phenomenal popularity. In 1970, Corman left AIP to form New World Pictures, which over the next decade was to become the largest independent producer / distributor in the United States.

Here, as at AIP, Corman was able to back a number of talented but unknown young directors in their first features. In fact, Francis Ford Coppola (*Dementia 13,* 1963), Peter Bogdanovich (*Targets,* 1968),* Martin Scorsese (*Boxcar Bertha,* 1972), Jonathan Demme (*Caged Heat,* 1974; *Crazy Mama,* 1975), Joe Dante (*Hollywood Boulevard,* with Allan Arkush, 1976; *Piranha,* 1978), and Ron Howard (*Grand Theft Auto,* 1977) all debuted in Corman productions. Furthermore, during the seventies New World Pictures became the American distributor for some of the decade's most important foreign films, including *Cries and Whispers* (Ingmar Bergman, 1972), *The Harder They Come* (Perry Henzell, 1973), *Fantastic Planet* (Rene Laloux, 1974), *Amarcord* (Federico Fellini, 1974), *The Story of Adèle H.* (François Truffaut, 1975), *The Lost Honor of Katharina Blum* (Volker Schlöndorff and Margarethe von Trotta, 1975), *Lumière* (Jeanne Moreau, 1977), *Small Change* (Truffaut, 1977), *Derzu Uzala* (Akira Kurosawa, 1978), *Autumn Sonata* (Bergman, 1980), *The Tin Drum* (Schlöndorff, 1980), *Mon Oncle d'Amerique* (Alain Resnais, 1980), and *Breaker Morant* (Bruce Beresford, 1980). Although he has not personally directed a film since 1971 (*Von Richtofen and Brown,* UA), Corman continues to exert an important influence on the American cinema as a producer (*Death Race 2000* [Paul Bartel, 1975]; *Saint Jack* [Peter Bogdanovich, 1979]; *Humanoids from the Deep* [Barbara Peeters, 1980]; *Battle Beyond the Stars* [Jimmy T. Murakami, 1980]; *Love Letters* [Amy Jones, 1981]; *Android* [Aaron Lipstadt, 1982]; etc.), and, although he sold it in 1983 to form Concorde Pictures with his wife Julie (first productions: *Streetwalkin'* [Joan Freeman, 1985]; *Big Bad Mama II* [Jim Wynorski, 1987]), New World continues to produce such Cormanesque films as *Children of the Corn* (Fritz Kiersch, 1984), *The Philadelphia Experiment* (Steward Raffill, 1984), and *Reform School Girls* (Tom DeSimone, 1986).

In the sixties and early seventies, science fiction too became more

---

* *Targets* is an excellent example of the kind of synergy Corman could create among his young collaborators at AIP. The film began when Corman approached Bogdanovich with the proposition that he make a Boris Karloff film by combining new footage of the actor (who still owed Corman two days under contract from *The Terror*) with footage from *The Terror.* Bogdanovich quickly produced a remarkable script which told concurrent stories of an aging horror star and a young Charles Whitman–style mass murderer whose fates converge in a drive-in theater at the film's conclusion. *Targets* was produced for $130,000 and sold to Paramount, which released it with a brief prologue entitled "Why Gun Control?" in the wake of the Robert Kennedy assassination in June 1968. It has deservedly become a cult classic and remains, with *The Last Picture Show* (1972), Bogdanovich's best film.

mainstream, if frequently less exciting. In the United States* a series of medium-to-high budget films replaced the exploitation quickies in productions like *The Time Machine* (George Pal, 1960), *The Day Mars Invaded the Earth* (Maury Dexter, 1963), *Robinson Crusoe on Mars* (Byron Haskin, 1964; effects by Pal), *The Day the Earth Cracked* (Andrew Marton, 1965), *Fantastic Voyage* (Richard Fleischer, 1966), *Planet of the Apes* (Franklin Schaffner, 1968),† *The Omega Man* (Boris Sagal, 1971—a remake of the Corman-produced *The Last Man on Earth* [Sidney Salkow and Ubaldo Ragona, 1964], itself a version of Richard Matheson's postnuclear vampire novel, *I Am Legend*), and *The Andromeda Strain* (Robert Wise, 1971). From England came a number of inventive, well-crafted features, including *Gorgo* (Eugene Lourie, 1961), *The Day the Earth Caught Fire* (Val Guest, 1961), *The Day of the Triffids* (Steve Sekely, 1963; adapted from the novel by John Wyndham), and *The Earth Dies Screaming* (Terence Fisher, 1964). England was also the setting for Wolf Rilla's eerie *Village of the Damned* (1960), adapted from John Wyndham's novel about alien children, *The Midwich Cukoos,* and it begat sequels in *Children of the Damned* (Anton M. Leader, 1965) and the more portentous *The Damned* (also known as *These Are the Damned* [Joseph Losey, 1961]; released in the United Kingdom, 1963; in the United States, 1965]). Finally, Britain produced *Five Million Miles to Earth* (also known as *Quatermass and the Pit* [Roy Ward Baker, 1968]), the third film in Hammer's Quatermass series based on the popular BBC-TV serial written by Nigel Kneale, the first two having been *The Creeping Unknown* (also known as *The Quatermass Experiment* [Val Guest, 1956]) and *Enemy from Space* (also known as *Quatermass II* [Val Guest, 1957]).

In fact, that science fiction had become a fully respectable genre by the mid-sixties was demonstrated by the number of serious filmmakers who had begun to work in it. These included Joseph Losey, Jean Luc-Godard (*Alphaville,* 1965), François Truffaut (*Fahrenheit 451,* 1966), Elio Petri (*The Tenth Victim,* 1965), Alain Resnais (*Je t'aime, je t'aime,* 1968), and, of course, Stanley Kubrick, who apotheosized the science fiction film in *2001: A Space Odyssey,* with its multimillion-dollar special effects by

---

*Although most of the science fiction films of the era came from American and British producers, a strong and serious tradition for it was evolving in the countries of Eastern Europe, including Czechoslovakia (*Krakatit* [Otakar Vávra, 1951; adapted from Karel Capek]; *The Fabulous World of Jules Verne* [also known as *The Invention of Destruction,* Karel Zeman; animated]; *Man of the First Century* [Oldrich Lipsky, 1962], *Ikarie XB1* [Jindrich Polak, 1963]; *The Lost Face* [Pavel Hobi, 1965]; *The End of August at the Hotel Ozone* [Jan Schmidt, 1965; 1967]; *I, Justice.* [Zbynek Brynych, 1968]); Poland (*The First Spaceship on Venus* [Kurt Matzig, 1959; 1963); Yugoslavia (*War* [Veijko Bulajíc, 1960]); and the Soviet Union (*Planet of Storms* [Pavel Klushantsev, 1962; adapted from Stanislaw Lem's *Planet of Death*] and *The Amphibious Man* [Y. Kasancki, 1963]). See Chapter 16, pp. 667–99; 724–38; 759–77.

†Loosely adapted from Pierre Boulle's novel, this popular blend of science fiction and satire inspired four sequels—*Beneath the Planet of the Apes* (Ted Post, 1970), *Escape from the Planet of the Apes* (Don Taylor, 1971), *Conquest of the Planet of the Apes* (J. Lee Thompson, 1972), and *Battle for the Planet of the Apes* (J. Lee Thomopson, 1973), as well as a short-lived television series.

Douglas Trumbull and its deeply metaphysical theme (see Chapter 18). In the seventies, American science fiction proved to be a rather dreary affair (e.g., the four *Planet of the Apes* sequels; *Westworld* [Michael Crichton, 1973]; *Soylent Green* [Richard Fleischer, 1973]; *Rollerball* [Norman Jewison, 1975]; *Logan's Run* [Michael Anderson, 1976]). However, there were notable exceptions, such as Joseph Sargent's *Colossus: The Forbin Project* (also known as *The Forbin Project, Colossus 1980,* 1970), George Lucas' *THX-1138* (1971), Douglas Trumbull's *Silent Running* (1972), John Boorman's *Zardoz* (1974), and Nicholas Roeg's *The Man Who Fell to Earth* (1976), and finally the phenomenal success of George Lucas' *Star Wars* in 1977. This film combined sophisticated computerized effects (created by John Dykstra), Dolby stereo sound, and a fantasy-adventure plot containing folkloric elements to create a new breed of American science fiction, perpetuated in the sequels *The Empire Strikes Back* (Irvin Kershner, 1980) and *The Return of the Jedi* (Richard Marquand, 1983), as well as in Steven Spielberg's *Close Encounters of the Third Kind* (1977; effects by Dykstra and Trumbull) and *E.T. The Extraterrestrial* (1982), and the *Star Trek* series (*Star Trek: The Motion Picture* [Robert Wise, 1979; effects by Trumbull]; *Star Trek II: The Wrath of Kahn* [Nicholas Meyer, 1982]; *Star Trek III: The Search for Spock* [Leonard Nimoy, 1984]; *Star Trek IV: The Voyage Home* [Nimoy, 1986]). Among the many, many imitators of the *Star Wars* formula, *The Last Starfighter* (Nick Castle, 1984) stands out for its imaginative integration of live action with special effects generated entirely by computer.* During the eighties, this emphasis on high-tech special effects and sound continued in science fiction films which, successful or not, often had a more serious edge, including Peter Hyams' *Outland* (1981) and *2010* (1984—the inevitably doomed sequel to *2001*), Ridley Scott's *Alien* (1979) and *Blade Runner* (1982; effects by Trumbull), Douglas Trumbull's *Brainstorm* (1983), John Carpenter's *Starman* (1984), David Lynch's *Dune* (1984), Wolfgang Petersen's *Enemy Mine* (1985), Tobe Hooper's *Lifeforce* (1985; effects by Dykstra), Ron Howard's *Cocoon* (1985), Terry Gilliam's *Brazil* (1985), James Cameron's *The Terminator* (1984) and *Aliens* (1986), Rene Laloux's *Light Years* (1987), John McTiernan's *Predator* (1987), and Paul Verhoeven's *Robocop* (1987).

Distinct subgenres of science fiction that emerged during the decade were the pornographic (*Flesh Gordon* [Michael Beveniste and Howard Zeihm, 1973], *Cafe Flesh* [Dream Rinse, 1982]); the parodic/satiric (*Time After Time* [Nicholas Meyers, 1979], *Flash Gordon* [Mike Hodges, 1980], *Time Bandits* [Terry Gilliam, 1981], *The Adventures of Buckaroo Banzai Across the Eighth Dimension* [W. D. Richter, 1983], *Space Balls* [Mel Brooks, 1987]); and the punk (*Liquid Sky* [Slava Tsukerman, 1982], *Vortex* [Scott B and Beth B, 1982], *Repo Man* [Alex Cox, 1984], *The Brother from Another Planet* [John Sayles, 1984], *Day of the Comet* [Thom Eberhardt, 1984]), *Uforia* [John Binder, 1986]). In the years surrounding the

---

* Whereas the effects for *Star Wars* were computer-assisted, those for *The Last Starfighter* were entirely digitalized, an important distinction.

Reagan administration's deployment of intermediate-range missiles in Western Europe, there was a rash of films dealing with the *immediate* effects of a nuclear war—rather than life in some postnuclear future, whose treatment extends from Arch Oboler's *Five* (1951) through George Miller's *Mad Max* series, 1978–85 (see Chapter 14). These films, all originally made for television, were *The Day After* (Nicholas Meyer, 1983), *Testament* (Lynn Littman, 1983), *Threads* (Mick Jackson, 1984), *Special Bulletin* (Edward Wick, 1983), and *Countdown to Looking Glass* (Fred Barzyk, 1984). Other science fiction subtypes include the witty if sometimes juvenile Superman cycle—*Superman: The Movie* (Richard Donner, 1978); *Superman II* (Richard Lester, 1980; 1981) *Superman III* (Lester, 1983); and *Superman IV: The Quest for Peace* (Sidney J. Furie, 1987), as well as the unique and occasionally loathsome science fiction/horror films of the Canadian director David Cronenberg—*They Came from Within* (1975); *Rabid* (1976); *The Brood* (1978); *Scanners* (1979); *Videodrome* (1982); *The Dead Zone* (1983); *The Fly* (1986); *Dead Ringers* (1988); and the recent wave of films involving gene-splicing and genetic mutation—*Coma* (Michael Crichton, 1978); *Parts: The Clonus Horror* (Robert Fiveson, 1979); *Re-Animator* (Stuart Gordon, 1985); *The Kindred* (Stephen Carpenter and Jeffrey Obrow, 1987).

The "Small Film": American *Kammerspiel*

The final generic development of the American fifties was the brief appearance of the "small film," a low-budget black-and-white film shot in the Academy frame format with television techniques and concerned with the everyday lives of ordinary people. Clearly influenced by Italian neorealism, these films were independently produced, shot largely on location, and usually adapted from original teleplays for live drama by writers like Rod Serling, Paddy Chayefsky, and Reginald Rose. The first small film was *Marty* (Delbert Mann, 1955), based on a downbeat Chayefsky teleplay about the life of a shy, unattractive butcher in New York City. It was produced by the independent Hecht-Lancaster organization (see p. 531) and was an unprecedented critical success, winning both the Grand Prix at Cannes and the American Academy Award for Best Actor (to Ernest Borgnine) in the year of its release. *Marty* was also a great commercial success, and this encouraged the production of other small films adapted from teleplays. Rod Serling's tense drama about the viciousness of corporate power struggles, *Patterns of Power,* was adapted by Fielder Cook as *Patterns* (1956), while Hecht-Lancaster attempted to repeat the success of *Marty* in *The Bachelor Party* (1957), written by Chayefsky and directed by Delbert Mann. Reginald Rose's *12 Angry Men* (Sidney Lumet, 1957), Serling's *Requiem for a Heavyweight* (Ralph Nelson, 1962), and Chayefsky's *The Catered Affair* (Richard Brooks, 1956) and *Middle of the Night* (Delbert Mann, 1959), were all adapted for the screen as "small films," but as live drama began to disappear from television in the late fifties, to be replaced by weekly filmed series, the small-film movement vanished too. The barrier between cinema and television had been broken by the small film, however, and the relationship was to

12.56   The "small film". *Marty* (Delbert Mann, 1955). Ernest Borgnine.

remain an open one, so that ultimately the two media learned to co-exist and even to subsist upon one another. By the late fifties, for instance, the major studios were devoting a substantial percentage of their production facilities to the filming of weekly television series modeled on the B-pictures of the thirties and forties. And by the mid-sixties some of the American cinema's most important new directors—John Frankenheimer, Irvin Kershner, Sidney Lumet, and Sam Peckinpah, to name a few—had begun their careers in studio television production.

12.57 The "small film": *Middle of the Night* (Delbert Mann, 1959). Fredric March.

INDEPENDENT PRODUCTION AND THE DECLINE OF THE STUDIO SYSTEM

As this account of the small film suggests, independent production outside of the studio was on the rise in the fifties. Four of the decade's most brilliant American films—*Kiss Me Deadly* (Robert Aldrich, 1955; Parklane Productions), *The Night of the Hunter* (Charles Laughton, 1955; Paul Gregory Productions—the actor's only film as a director), *The Sweet Smell of Success* (Alexander Mackendrick, 1957; Hecht-Hill-Lancaster), and *Paths of Glory* (Stanley Kubrick, 1957; Harris-Kubrick Productions)—were independently produced, all of them for United Artists release, as were seven of the films given the Academy Award for Best Picture between 1954 and 1962. Stanley Kramer started his independent production activities as early as 1948, producing *Home of the Brave* (Mark Robson, 1949), *Champion* (Mark Robson, 1949), *The Men* (Fred Zinnemann, 1950), and *High Noon* (Fred Zinnemann, 1952) on modest budgets in rapid succession. While Kramer's status as a director is equivocal, his production record is distinguished; it also includes the film version of Arthur Miller's play *Death of a Salesman* (Laslo Benedek, 1952), *The Member of the Wedding* (Fred Zinnemann, 1953), and *The Wild One* (Laslo Benedek, 1954). United Artists, which distributed most of Kramer's films, found that its liabilities of the thirties and forties became assets during the fifties and sixties. Having no expensive production facilities to maintain in an era of ever-increasing location shooting, and no theater circuits to lose to the consent decrees, United Artists had become the most important independent producer in Hollywood by 1956. In this capacity, it distributed some of the era's landmark films, including Fred Zinnemann's anti-McCarthy Western *High Noon* (1952), Chaplin's controversial *Limelight* (1952), the first film in Natural Vision (Oboler's *Bwana Devil,* 1953), Otto Preminger's code-breaking *The Moon Is Blue* (1953) and *The Man with the Golden Arm* (1955), most of the "small films" mentioned above, and such road-shown widescreen blockbusters as *Around the World in Eighty Days* (Michael Anderson, 1956) and *Exodus* (Preminger, 1960). United Artists also produced much of John Huston's major work during the period—*The African Queen* (1952), *Moulin Rouge* (1953), *Beat the Devil* (1954), and *The Misfits* (1961), as well as the early films of Stanley Kubrick (*Killer's Kiss,* 1955; *The Killing,* 1956; *Paths of Glory,*

1957). The Hecht-Lancaster Company (Hecht-Hill-Lancaster after 1956), organized in 1947 by producer Harold Hecht and actor Burt Lancaster, was another successful independent. From the early fifties, it specialized in sophisticated action films starring Lancaster, such as *The Crimson Pirate* (Robert Siodmak, 1952), *Apache* (Robert Aldrich, 1954), *Vera Cruz* (Robert Aldrich, 1954), *The Kentuckian* (Burt Lancaster, 1955), and *Trapeze* (Carol Reed, 1956), although it also produced a number of important "small films." Other notable independent production companies born in the fifties, all of which released through United Artists, were the Walter Mirisch Corporation, Seven-Arts, and actor Kirk Douglas' Bryna Productions. By 1958, in fact, 65 percent of Hollywood's motion pictures were made by independents, as the focus of production shifted away from the studios to the production unit itself.

No account of independent production in the fifties would be complete without mentioning two distinct phenomena at the high and low ends of the exploitation scale. As the search for new formats in the war with television intensified in 1959–60, several filmmakers introduced Aromarama and Smell-o-Vision, systems designed to let theater audiences smell what they saw on screen. Aromarama pumped its scents through a theater's existing air-conditioning system and removed them (not entirely successfully) with electronic air filters. Smell-o-Vision (also known as Scentovision) used individual atomizers strategically positioned between the rows of seats. Only one feature was made with each process—Aromarama's *Behind the Great Wall,* a documentary on China which premiered at the Mayfair Theater in New York City on December 2, 1959, and Smell-o-Vision's *Scent of Mystery,* produced by Mike Todd, Jr., and premiered at the Cinestage Theater in Chicago on January 12, 1960 (the latter was rereleased, odorless, the same year as *Holiday in Spain*). Like 3-D earlier in the decade, neither system survived its novelty period, although, when working properly, both could create an impressive olfactory illusion. (The Baltimore-based producer-director John Waters revived the idea for *Polyester* [1981], providing theater patrons with "Odorama" scratch-and-sniff cards keyed to numbers flashed on-screen.)

Closer to Waters' own sensibility in the late fifties was the independent producer-director William Castle (see Waters' "Whatever Happened to Showmanship?" *American Film* 9, 3 [December 1983]: 55–58). Castle (1914–77) evinced a genius for cheap but effective exploitation gimmicks that were often more engaging than the films they were employed to market. For *Macabre* (1958), for example, a ninety-thousand-dollar uncredited remake of Clouzot's *Diabolique* (1955), he insured the life of every theater patron for one thousand dollars with Lloyd's of London against death from fright; *The House on Haunted Hill* (1959) boasted a "process" called "Emergo," which was actually a twelve-foot plastic skeleton that would zoom over the audience on a wire at a certain point in the film; *The Tingler* (1959) was "shot" in "Percepto," which meant that a seat in each theater row was wired with an electric buzzer that would causes the spectator to "tingle" when the monster supposedly got loose in the theater—an unconsciously Brechtian moment, when the pro-

jector "breaks" and a character, Vincent Price, speaks directly to the
audience from the dark screen of its peril; *Thirteen Ghosts* (1960) offered
"Illusion-O," which permitted audiences to see infrared superimpositions of ghostly images by using special glasses; *Homocidal* (1961), a
shameless rip-off of *Psycho* (1960), had a "Fright Break" of two minutes
before its horrific conclusion during which patrons could have their
admissions refunded if they were willing to stand in "Coward's Corner"
first; finally, Castle shot two separate endings for *Mr. Sardonicus* (1961),
so that viewers could vote on the fate of the villainous title character in
a "Punishment Poll" near the film's conclusion. Castle went on to produce and direct such gimmick-free shockers as *Strait-Jacket* (1964), which
handily cast Joan Crawford in the role of an ax-murderess, *I Saw What
You Did* (1965), *Let's Kill Uncle* (1966), and *Project X* (1968), and to
produce the almost entirely respectable *Rosemary's Baby* (Roman Polanski, 1968); but he is best remembered for his successful practice of par-
ticipatory cinema, albeit of the dime-store variety, long before the advent
of *The Rocky Horror Picture Show* (Jim Sharman, 1975) and its breth-
ren.

The old studio production system remained in operation throughout
the fifties, but continued to crumble under the combined threats of political pressure, television, rising independent production, and perhaps most
serious, loss of the exhibition chains. By mid-decade, steadily increasing
monetary inflation could be added to this catalogue of woes, and all of
these forces spelled the beginning of the end for Hollywood as it had
been structured since the twenties. From the peak year of 1946, when
American theaters had averaged nearly 100 million admissions per week,
film attendance dropped to 46 million in 1955. Production fell from nearly
500 features per year throughout the thirties, to 383 in 1950, to 254 in
1955. Decca Records absorbed Universal Pictures in 1952, and was
absorbed in turn by the huge entertainment conglomerate MCA between
1959 and 1962.* RKO ceased production entirely in 1957 (although the
famous name survives in RKO General, the broadcast ownership division
of the General Tire and Rubber Corporation). American film production
and audience attendance both continued to decline, while production costs
soared, until, by 1966, 30 percent of all films made in the United States

---

* Music Corporation of America (MCA) was founded in 1924 by Dr. Jules Stein (1896–
1981) as a booking agency for dance bands in Chicago. MCA moved to Hollywood in
1936 and became a major talent-broker there under the aggressive leadership of Stein's
protégé Lew Wasserman (b. 1913), who became corporate president in 1946 and still serves
as chairman of the board. Wasserman's genius lay in engineering deals for his clients. By
the early fifties MCA had become one of the most powerful forces in the industry, controlling 1,400 top entertainers and moving into the new field of television production through
its Revue subsidiary. In July 1952, Ronald Reagan, then president of the Screen Actors
Guild, granted MCA a seven-year waiver of the guild's prohibition against agents acting
simultaneously as producers, giving the company an enormous competitive edge over its
rivals and creating a clear conflict of interest for the duration. Meanwhile, MCA continued
to grow, acquiring Decca Records and Universal Pictures between 1959 and 1962, when
the Justice Department finally forced the divestiture of its agency business. Called the "star-
spangled octopus," or simply the Octopus, by its critics, MCA remains one of Hollywood's
most powerful conglomerates.

were independently produced, and 50 percent of all American films were "runaway" productions—that is, films shot on location in foreign countries (usually Italy, Yugoslavia, or Spain) to economize on sets and labor (nonunion, and therefore cheaper). In other words, by the mid-sixties, 80 percent of all American films were made outside the once ironclad studio system. Moreover, as discussed in the next chapter, the foreign industries had recovered from the war by the late fifties and for the first time were offering Hollywood vigorous commercial competition. Stiff postwar import duties on nondomestic productions had severely restricted Hollywood's most profitable European markets—especially England, Italy, and France—while American demand for foreign films had been growing steadily since the divestiture order of 1948 first permitted U.S. exhibitors to show what they chose rather than what the studios had chosen for them. In fact, between 1958 and 1968, the number of foreign films in distribution in the United States would actually exceed the number of domestic productions, often by a ratio of two (and sometimes, three) to one.

As the studio system declined throughout the fifties, so too did the star system with which it had been intimately linked for over thirty years. As studios were forced to cut back on production due to the inroads of television, inflation, and other blights, expensive promotional campaigns were abandoned and star contracts went from long-term to short-term, and finally to simple profit-sharing options on individual films. This practice began as early as 1949, when *Variety* reported that Warner Bros. and Paramount had negotiated profit-sharing deals for as high as 33 percent with John Garfield, Danny Kaye, Milton Berle, Bob Hope, and Bing Crosby. But the historic catalyst for the shift occurred in 1950, when Lew Wasserman of MCA negotiated a 50 percent share of Universal's *Winchester '73* for Jimmy Stewart, earning him six hundred thousand dollars when the film became a popular success. Obviously, deals like these made the stars increasingly independent of the studios, and some, like Burt Lancaster and Kirk Douglas, even formed their own production companies. There were American stars in the fifties, to be sure, and many whose careers had begun under the studio system—among them, Lancaster, Douglas, James Stewart, Cary Grant, Henry Fonda, John Wayne, Rock Hudson, Tony Curtis, Charlton Heston, Montgomery Clift, Robert Mitchum, William Holden, Frank Sinatra, Yul Brynner, Glenn Ford, Gregory Peck, Gary Cooper, Ava Gardner, Jean Simmons, Grace Kelly, Audrey Hepburn, Susan Hayward, Gina Lollobrigida, Sophia Loren, Deborah Kerr, Debbie Reynolds, Elizabeth Taylor, Kim Novak, Doris Day, and—quintessentially—Marilyn Monroe, Marlon Brando, and James Dean. But they worked more independently of the system than had earlier stars, and to quote Alexander Walker, the fifties in general were the transitional period "from studios who owned stars to stars who owned pictures."

THE SCRAPPING OF THE PRODUCTION CODE

A final important development of the fifties in America was the breaking of the Production Code and the achievement of an unprecedented freedom of expression for the cinema. Ever since a U.S. Supreme Court decision of 1915 involving D. W. Griffith's *The Birth of a Nation* (*Mutual v. Ohio*), the movies had not been considered a part of the press, whose freedom is guaranteed by the First Amendment to the Constitution. For this reason, six states and hundreds of local communities had film censorship boards, and of course, through the Production Code, Hollywood had imposed an extreme form of censorship upon itself. But this situation changed in 1952, after the State of New York attempted to prevent the exhibition of the Italian film *Il miracolo* (*The Miracle* [Roberto Rossellini, 1948; written by Federico Fellini, Tullio Pinelli, and Rossellini himself]) on the grounds that it committed "sacrilege." Producer-distributor Joseph Burstyn took the case to the U.S. Supreme Court, which ruled in May 1952 that movies were "a significant medium for communication of ideas" and were, therefore, protected against the charge of sacrilege by both the First and Fourteenth Amendments. Subsequent court rulings between 1952 and 1958 clarified the *Miracle* decision, and by the early sixties films were guaranteed full freedom of expression.*

While these legal battles were in progress, the Production Code was being challenged from within by the influx of "unapproved" foreign films and, especially, by the rise of independent production. Since the studios no longer owned America's theaters, they could no longer force them to accept their product exclusively. Shrewdly realizing this, director Otto Preminger openly challenged the Code by producing two films for United Artists with sensational (for that era) content—*The Moon Is Blue* (1953), which used the forbidden word *virgin,* and *The Man with the Golden Arm* (1955), in which Frank Sinatra portrayed a heroin addict. As Preminger had anticipated, both films were denied the Production Code's Seal of Approval, and both were released independently to great commercial success. It didn't take long for the studios to find out which way the wind was blowing: Elia Kazan's *Baby Doll,* released by Warner Bros. in 1956 to a storm of protest, was the first motion picture of a major American studio ever to be publicly condemned by the Legion of Decency, the Catholic organization responsible for instituting the Production Code in the first place. The financial success of these three films sounded the death

12.58 Breaking the Code: Frank Sinatra shooting dope in *The Man with the Golden Arm* (Otto Preminger, 1955).

---

* This trend is currently being reversed in federal and state court cases dealing with obscenity. The U.S. Supreme Court ruling of 1973, which left the definition of obscenity to elusive "community standards," confused the whole issue of film and freedom of speech, since the Court did not specify what it meant by "community." Thus, films like Juste Jaeckin's *Histoire d'O* (*The Story of O,* 1976)—the softest of soft-core erotica—have been successfully prosecuted in cities like Detroit on the grounds that they are offensive to the "community."

knell for the Legion's influence in Hollywood, and the Production Code was scrapped altogether in the sixties in favor of a ratings system administered by the Motion Picture Association of America (MPAA), which does not proscribe the content of films but rather classifies them as appropriate for certain segments of the public, according to age.

Instituted in 1968 and revised in 1972 and 1984, the MPAA ratings system uses the following five classifications for films: G (general audience); PG (parental guidance suggested for children under seventeen); PG-13 (parental guidance suggested for children under thirteen); R (restricted to persons seventeen or older unless accompanied by an adult); and X (prohibited to persons under seventeen). Many people believe that the ratings system has contributed significantly to the decline of high-quality films in the G and PG range and to the sharp increase in exploitative sex and violence in the R and X classifications. Like the concept of "Family Viewing Time" on network television, it would seem that a system designed to protect children from debasing entertainment has served to debase the entertainment of both children and adults.

In about 1955, human sexuality began to be overtly depicted on the American screen for the first time since the Code's imposition some twenty years before, and more generally, a fascination with veiled (and increasingly unveiled) eroticism came to pervade American films in the late fifties and early sixties. This, more than any other single factor, accounts for the vast popularity of the *Pillow Talk* cycle, the seven adaptations from the exotic plays of Tennessee Williams, and such sexy imports as *And God Created Woman* (*Et Dieu créa la femme* [Roger Vadim, 1956]; 1957), *The Lovers* (*Les amants* [Louis Malle, 1958; 1959]), and *La dolce vita* (Federico Fellini, 1960) during this period.

Other taboos were broken too, as a new realism of content entered the American cinema after a long period of repression. Social problems like juvenile delinquency (*Rebel Without a Cause*, 1955; *Blackboard Jungle*, 1955), alcoholism, drug addiction, and even race were suddenly fair game for filmmakers working both inside and outside the studios.* Crime began to be treated less moralistically and melodramatically, so that it became possible by the end of the decade to sympathize with criminals as human beings, though they did not become wholly admirable ones until Arthur Penn's *Bonnie and Clyde* (1967). The next cultural taboo the American cinema was to overcome (simultaneously with Italy and preceded slightly

---

* Important films on these themes made outside of the system during the sixties include the *cinéma-vérité* work of Shirley Clarke (b. 1925)—*The Connection* (1961), which deals with drug addiction; *The Cool World* (1964), focusing on the lives of young blacks in the ghetto; and *Portrait of Jason* (1967), an extended monologue by a black homosexual prostitute—and the improvisational dramas of John Cassavetes (1929–89) on race (*Shadows*, 1961) and middle-class malaise (*Faces*, 1968; *Husbands*, 1970). Clarke moved on to video, but Cassavetes continued to make films (*Minnie and Moskowitz*, 1971; *A Woman Under the Influence*, 1974; *The Killing of a Chinese Bookie*, 1976, 1978; *Opening Night*, 1978; *Gloria*, 1980; *Love Streams*, 1983; *Big Trouble*, 1984) in collaboration with his wife, the brilliant actress Gena Rowlands (b. 1934). See Raymond Carney, *American Dreaming: The Films of John Cassavetes and the American Experience* (Berkeley: University of California Press, 1985).

by Japan) was the convention against the graphic, excessive, and / or poetic depiction of brutality and violence. This, however, could not occur until President Kennedy and his alleged assassin had been gunned down before running movie cameras in Dallas in 1963, and the war in Vietnam had been brought nightly for much of the decade that followed into American living rooms.

The French New Wave and Its Native Context

THE OCCUPATION AND POSTWAR CINEMA

During the German Occupation of 1940–45—when Feyder, Renoir, Duvivier, and Clair were all in exile—a new generation of French directors emerged, most of whom had worked as scriptwriters or assistants under the major figures of poetic realism in the thirties.* Claude Autant-Lara (b. 1903), who had worked as a designer for L'Herbier and as an assistant to Clair, directed a number of sophisticated period films during the Occupation, including *Le Mariage de Chiffon* (1942), *Lettres d'amour* (1942), and the satirical *Douce* (1943). Autant-Lara's critical reputation rests most firmly, however, upon a series of stylish literary adaptations written by Jean Aurenche (b. 1904) and Pierre Bost (b. 1901) that he made in the postwar era—especially *Le Diable au corps* (*The Devil in the Flesh*, 1947; from the Raymond Radiguet novel),† *L'Auberge rouge* (*The Red Inn*, 1951; from Aurenche), *Le Blé en herbe* (*The Ripening Seed*, 1954; from Colette), *Le Rouge et le noir* (*The Red and the Black*, 1954; from Stendhal), and *Le Joueur* (*The Gambler*, 1958; from Dostoevsky). Writing as a team, Aurenche and Bost became specialists in tightly scripted films; they also worked closely with the director René Clément (b. 1913), whose first film had been a neorealistic account

---

* Perhaps the most important film event of the Occupation was the foundation of the Institut des Hautes Études Cinématographiques (IDHEC) by Marcel L'Herbier in 1943. This government-subsidized film school today offers professional training in every aspect of film production as well as in history and aesthetics. It provides certification for persons wishing to enter the French film industry, and its high standards have attracted students from all over the world. See André Bazin, *French Cinema of the Occupation and Resistance*, trans. Stanley Hochman (New York: Ungar, 1981); see also, Evelyn Ehrlich, *Cinema of Paradox: French Filmmaking Under the German Occupation* (New York: Columbia University Press, 1985); and Edward Lowry, *The Filmology Movement and Film Study in France* (Ann Arbor, Mich.: UMI Research Press, 1985).

† Remade in separate versions by the Australian director Scott Murray in 1985 and the Italian director Marco Bellocchio in 1986.

13.1 *Jeux interdits* (René Clément, 1952): Brigitte Fossey, Georges Poujouly.

13.2 *La Belle et la bête* (Jean Cocteau and Renée Clément, 1946): Josette Day, Jean Marais.

of the activities of the French Resistance, *La Bataille du rail* (*The Battle of the Rails,* 1946).

Clément also co-directed *La Belle et la bête* (*Beauty and the Beast,* 1946) with playwright Jean Cocteau and made the suspenseful anti-Nazi thriller *Les Maudits* (*The Damned,* 1947). But his two greatest films of the postwar era, both written by Aurenche and Bost, were the poetic antiwar drama *Jeux interdits* (*Forbidden Games,* 1952) and a strikingly evocative adaptation of Zola's *L'Assommoir* entitled *Gervaise* (1956). These films won multiple international awards, as did his comic master-piece *Monsieur Ripois* (*The Knave of Hearts*), shot in England in 1954. Afterward Clément turned to big-budget international coproductions like *Is Paris Burning?* (1966) and *Rider on the Rain* (1969), most of them distinctly mediocre.*

Jean Grémillon (1902–59), who had made important films in the silent era (*Un Tour au large,* 1927; *Maldone,* 1928), produced his greatest work during the Occupation—*Lumière d'été* (1943), a Renoiresque portrait of the decadent French ruling classes written by Jacques Prévert, and *Le Ciel est à vous* (English title: *The Woman Who Dared,* 1944), a beautiful film about a provincial woman who breaks the world record for long-distance flying with the help of her husband and the people of her town. After the war, Grémillon turned to the documentary but continued to exercise great influence upon French cinema as president of the Cinémathèque Française (see p. 551).

Jean Cocteau (1889–1963), who had confined himself to writing scripts during the Occupation (for Jean Delannoy's modernized version of the Tristan and Isolde legend, *L'Éternel retour* [*The Eternal Return,* 1943]; for Robert Bresson's *Les Dames du Bois de Boulogne* [*The Ladies of the*

---

* Like Autant-Lara, Clément continued to contribute traditional narrative films to the French cinema well into the eighties. So, too, did Jean Delannoy (e.g., *Bernadette,* 1988), see above.

Bois de Boulogne, 1945]; see pp. 542–43), returned to filmmaking in the postwar years. Perhaps more than any other figure he incarnated the literary tendency of French cinema during this period. In 1946 he wrote and co-directed (with Clément) an enchantingly beautiful version of the Flemish fairy tale *La Belle et la bête* (*Beauty and the Beast*) in a visual style based upon the paintings of Vermeer; it stands today as perhaps the greatest example of the cinema of the fantastic in the history of film.* Next, Cocteau directed two film versions of his own plays, the satirical *Ruy Blas* (1947) and *Les Parents terribles* (English title: *The Storm Within,* 1948), a domestic tragicomedy set within the confines of a single room. With *Orphée* (1950), a modern version of the Orpheus legend, Cocteau returned to the surreal, psycho-mythic regions of *Le Sang d'un poète* (*Blood of a Poet,* 1930) to create his most brilliant film. He adapted his play *Les Enfants terribles* (*The Terrible Children,* directed by Jean-Pierre Melville) for the screen in 1950 and gave the cinema his final artistic testament in *Le Testament d'Orphée* (*The Testament of Orpheus,* 1959), a surrealistic fable that is replete with personal symbols and that attempts to suggest the relationships among poetry, myth, death, and the unconscious.

Jacques Becker (1906–60) is another figure who emerged during the Occupation and came to prominence in the postwar years. As assistant to Renoir from 1931 to 1939, Becker tended to direct films that cut across the traditional class barriers of French society. *Goupi Mains-Rouge* (English title: *It Happened at the Inn,* 1943) is a realistic portrait of peasant life; *Falbalas* (English title: *Paris Frills,* 1945) is a drama set in the Parisian fashion houses; *Antoine et Antoinette* (1947) is a tale of young love in a working-class milieu; *Rendez-vous de juillet* (1949) offers a sympathetic study of the attitudes and ambitions of postwar youth; and *Edouard et Caroline* (1951) examines young married life in high society. But Becker's masterpiece is unquestionably *Casque d'or* (*Golden Helmet / Golden Marie,* 1952), a visually sumptuous tale of doomed love set in turn-of-the-century Paris and written by Becker himself. Cast in the form of a period gangster film and based upon historical fact, *Casque d'or* is a work of great formal beauty whose visual texture evokes the films of Feuillade and engravings from *la belle époque. Touchez pas au grisbi* (English title: *Honor Among Thieves,* 1954), adapted from an Albert Simonin novel, was a sophisticated tale of rivalry between contemporary Montmartre gangs; it started the vogue for gangster films and thrillers that typified French cinema in the late fifties (for instance, the American émigré Jules Dassin's *Rififi,* 1955). After making three commissioned films of uneven quality, Becker directed his final masterpiece, *Le Trou* (*The Hole / The Night Watch*), shortly before his death in 1960. Like Bresson's *Un Condamné à mort s'est échappé* (*A Man Escaped,* 1956; see p.

13.3 *Le Trou* (Jacques Becker, 1960): Jean Keraudy.

---

* *Beauty and the Beast* was remade in 1979 by the Slovak surrealist Juraj Herz (b. 1934), mixing French and Middle European folk traditions (see Chapter 16). On Cocteau himself, see Edgardo Cozarinsky's film *Jean Cocteau—Autoportrait d'un inconnu* (*Jean Cocteau—Portrait of an Unknown Man,* 1984).

542), this film, set entirely in a prison cell where five men plot an ill-fated escape, is a restrained exploration of loyalty, freedom, and human dignity.*

Another important director whose career began during the Occupation was Henri-Georges Clouzot (1907–77), a former scriptwriter for E. A. Dupont and Anatole Litvak at UFA. Clouzot's first feature was unremarkable, but his second, *Le Corbeau* (*The Raven,* 1943), established him as the chief progenitor of French *film noir.* This darkly pessimistic tale of a town destroyed by poison-pen letters is a masterpiece of psychological suspense, but because it was produced by the Nazi-owned Continental Corporation and seemed to be anti-French (although it was actually misanthropic), both Clouzot and his coscenarist, Louis Chavance (b. 1907), were accused of collaboration and briefly suspended from the French film industry after the Liberation. Clouzot, in fact, was apolitical, but his films typically dealt with the brutal, the sordid, and the neurotic, and his entire career was marked by an aura of scandal. His first postwar film, *Quai des orfèvres* (English title: *Jenny Lamour,* 1947) was a violent thriller that transcended its genre by creating Hitchcockian suspense. In *Manon* (1949), Clouzot modernized the Abbé Prévost's eighteenth-century classic, *Manon Lescaut,* setting it in the post-Liberation context of the Paris black market and the illegal emigration of Jews to Palestine. And with *Le Salaire de la peur* (*The Wages of Fear,* 1953),† Clouzot achieved a masterpiece of unrelenting horror and alienation in a film about a group of down-and-out European expatriates trapped in a miserable South American town who are driven by despair and greed to undertake the suicidal mission of hauling nitroglycerine for an American oil firm.

Always a meticulous and professional craftsman in the French studio tradition, Clouzot became increasingly erratic as the fifties progressed. The film that confirmed his international reputation, *Les Diaboliques* (*Diabolique,* 1955), is a brilliantly manipulative exercise in horrific suspense involving a complicated murder plot in a boarding school. Like Hitchcock's *Vertigo,* it was adapted from a novel by Pierre Boileau and Thomas Narcejac. Similarly, *Le Mystère Picasso* (*The Picasso Mystery,* 1956) is an ingenious seventy-five-minute study of Picasso at work shot in desaturated color and CinemaScope. But *Les Espions* (*The Spies,* 1957), set in a psychiatric clinic, is a failed attempt to combine the bitter naturalism of his earlier films with surrealistic fantasy. *La Vérité* (*The Truth,* 1960) is a professional but glib film cast in the form of a murder trial and narrated in flashbacks. A projected film on the destructive effects of jealousy, *L'Enfer* (1964), was scrapped because of Clouzot's ill health, and he was able to complete only a single feature before his death in 1977— the controversial and somewhat experimental *La Prisonnière* (*The Pris-*

13.4 *Le Salaire de la peur* (Henri-Georges Clouzot, 1953): Charles Vanel.

---

* Becker's son Jean emerged as an important figure in the eighties with *L'Eté meurtrier* (*One Deadly Summer,* 1983), a superior adaptation of Sebastien Japrisot's suspense thriller, scripted by the author.

† Remade by the American director William Friedkin in 1977 as *Sorcerer.*

13.5 *Justice est faite* (André Cayatte, 1950): Valentine Tessier.

oner, 1968), which returns to the perverse and pathological mode of *Le Corbeau* to examine the dynamics of sexual degradation.

Mining the same dark vein as Clouzot in the postwar period was Yves Allégret (b. 1907), who became something of a specialist in *film noir* with *Dédée d'Anvers* (*Dedee*, 1947), *Une Si jolie petite plage* (*Riptide / Such a Pretty Little Beach*, 1948), and *Manèges* (English title: *The Cheats*, 1950), all written by Jacques Sigurd (b. 1920). The former lawyer André Cayatte (b. 1909) was another popular director of dark films in the late forties. But his major claim to significance rests upon his four "judicial" films scripted by Charles Spaak—*Justice est faite* (*Justice Is Done*, 1950), *Nous sommes tous des assassins* (*We Are All Murderers*, 1952), *Avant le déluge* (*Before the Deluge*, 1953), and *Le Dossier noir* (*The Black File*, 1955)—a series of scathing attacks upon the French legal system.* The same period witnessed the best work of Jacqueline Audry (1908–77), who collaborated closely with her husband, the scriptwriter Pierre Laroche (1902–62), to produce tasteful adaptations of work by Sartre (*Huis clos* [*No Exit*, 1954]) and Colette (*Mitsou*, 1956).

Robert Bresson and Jacques Tati

Clearly, except for *film noir*, the prevailing mode of postwar French cinema was literary adaptation, which caused French films to become increasingly verbal and theatrical. It was against this tendency—identified as "the tradition of quality" ("*la tradition de la qualité*") by François Truffaut and the *Cahiers* critics—that the New Wave reacted in the late fifties and sixties. In fact, the war had not produced a break with cinematic traditions in France as it had in Italy and other European nations, except for the innovative work of Robert Bresson and Jacques Tati.

Robert Bresson (1907–82), a former scriptwriter, was the more important of the two. His two Occupation films—*Les Anges du péché* (*The Angels of Sin*, 1943), written with the playwright Jean Giraudoux, and *Les Dames du Bois de Boulogne* (*The Ladies of the Bois de Boulogne*, 1945), freely adapted by Bresson and Jean Cocteau from a story by the eighteenth-century writer Jacques Diderot—established Bresson as a serious and disciplined artist within the "scenarist," or literary, tradition of French cinema. But in *Le Journal d'un curé de campagne* (*The Diary of a Country Priest*, 1950), adapted from the novel by Georges Bernanos, Bresson displayed a highly personalized style whose psychological realism is predicated upon an absolute austerity of acting, dialogue, and *mise-en-scène*. All of Bresson's later films display this austerity and precision of style, which has led some critics to call him a classicist, although he preferred to be thought of as a realist practicing close to the borderline of abstraction. His masterpiece, *Un Condamné à mort s'est échappé* (*A Man Escaped*, 1956), concerns the arrest, escape, and recapture of a young Resistance fighter during the Occupation, and it takes place almost entirely

13.6 *Le Journal d'un curé de campagne* (Robert Bresson, 1950): Claude Laydu, Nicole Maurey.

---

* Cayatte made *La Raison d'état* (*Reasons of State*) in 1978, a polemical film on the corrupt practices of the French government in its arms sales to terrorists.

in the condemned man's cell. Most of Bresson's subsequent films—*Pick-pocket* (1959), *Le Procés de Jeanne d'Arc* (*The Trial of Joan of Arc,* 1961, which, like Dreyer's film, is based upon the actual trial records), *Au hasard, Balthasar* (1966), *Mouchette* (1967), *Un Femme douce* (*A Gentle Creature,* 1969), and *Quatre nuits d'un rêveur* (*Four Nights of a Dreamer,* 1971, an adaptation of Dostoevsky's novella *White Nights*)—were derived from literary sources and dealt with humanist themes. Others are more pessimistic. *Lancelot du lac* (*Lancelot of the Lake,* 1976) offers a dark, ascetic vision of a Camelot that has outlived its own ideals. In *Le Diable probablement* (*The Devil Probably,* 1977), it is our own society which has outlived its ideals and its promise. *L'Argent* (1983), based on a short story by Tolstoi, is a film devoid of all psychology; it is about a man's irreversible descent into crime and degradation and shared the Cannes Grand Prix for Best Direction with Andrei Tarkovsky's *Nostalghia* in the year of its release. All of Bresson's films are painstakingly crafted attempts to bring to life the spiritual dilemmas of the race through the moral struggles of individuals, which makes Bresson a kind of contemporary Carl Dreyer. And, indeed, André Bazin often suggested that Bresson, more than any practicing director, had succeeded in fusing the values of the silent cinema with those of sound.

Jacques Tati (b. Jacques Tatischeff, 1908–82), a former music-hall entertainer and pantomimist, became one of the international cinema's great comic talents in the postwar era, rivaling such masters of the silent film as Max Linder, Charlie Chaplin, and Buster Keaton. In his first feature, *Jour de fete* (*Big Day / The Village Fair,* 1949), which took him several years to complete, Tati plays a French postman who is seduced by a documentary into employing sophisticated American Postal Service technology in his small village, with disastrous results. As in all of Tati's films, the humor, which is largely visual, is achieved through scrupulous planning and brilliant mime.* In *Les Vacances de M. Hulot* (*Mr. Hulot's Holiday,* 1953), Tati created a new comic character, M. Hulot, a vague, wacky, middle-class Frenchman who goes to spend his holiday at a seaside resort in Brittany. Hulot's misadventures there are represented to us as a series of meticulously worked-out sight gags, in which things simply "happen" to the character with no particular logic or cause. With *Mon oncle* (*My Uncle,* 1958), his first film in color, Tati turned to the more serious vein of satire. Here, Hulot's traditional and somewhat archaic lifestyle in an old quarter of Paris is contrasted to the antiseptic and mechanistic environment of his brother-in-law, Arpel, who lives in an

13.7 Jacques Tati as M. Hulot in *Mon oncle* (Jacques Tati, 1958).

---

* *Jour de fête,* which took prizes at both Venice and Cannes, was originally shot in a three-color additive lenticular process patented as Thomsoncolor that proved to be undevelopable in postproduction. Fortunately, Tati had simultaneously shot a black-and-white backup version of the film, and this was ultimately cut together as the release print. In 1987, it was discovered that the original 15,000–foot color negative had been preserved by Tati's daughter, the film editor Sophie Tatischeff (whose credits include her father's *Trafic* and *Parade*), and efforts were mounted at the Eurocitel labs in Joinville to restore it. Had it been released as intended, *Jour de fête* would have been one of the first French features in color. (Interestingly, it is estimated that the restoration will cost approximately $517,000, whereas the original was produced for $36,000.)

ultramodern house in the city's new suburban wasteland and works as an executive in a plastics factory. The humanistic impact of the satire is not unlike that of Clair's *A nous la liberté* (1931) or Chaplin's *Modern Times* (1936), although its appeal is totally unsentimental.

Tati's next film, *Playtime* (1967), took him three years to complete and was shot in color and 70mm Panavision with five-track stereophonic sound. Using the full resources of the widescreen format to create spectator involvement, Tati offers in *Playtime* a series of quietly humorous vignettes about a group of American tourists who come to see the "real" Paris and end up experiencing a space-age city of steel, glass, chrome, and plastic. Widely regarded today as a modernist masterpiece, it is not a film of belly laughs but of sustained, intelligent humor, and it clearly represents Tati's finest achievement. But *Playtime* was a multimillion-dollar commercial failure,* and since he had financed it himself, the director was nearly bankrupted. To recoup his losses, Tati made *Trafic* (*Traffic*, 1971), a minor Hulot film that comments upon the auto mania of modern industrial society. His last work was *Parade* (1974), a children's film made for Swedish television that featured Tati performing pantomimes at a circus show. After this, he developed the scenario for another Hulot film to be called *Confusion* but was unable to find backing for it. When he died at the age of seventy-four, Tati had made only five features in his entire career because he was a painstaking craftsman who planned every detail of his films far in advance of production. He was a master cinematic humorist whose concept of comedy was almost purely visual, and he deserves to be ranked with the greatest of the silent comedians for the breadth of his humanity and the restrained brilliance of his comic achievement.

Max Ophüls

Another major figure working in French cinema in the fifties, and one who had a profound influence on the New Wave generation that succeeded him, was Max Ophüls (b. Max Oppenheimer, 1902–57). Ophüls was a German Jew who had directed films for UFA between 1930 and Hitler's rise to power in 1933 (*Die verkaufte Braut* [*The Bartered Bride*, 1932]; *Liebelei* [1933]). For the next seven years he made films in Italy, the Netherlands, and France, where he ultimately became a citizen in 1938. Ophüls was forced to flee to Hollywood when France fell to the Nazis in 1940, and after four years of anonymity, he was finally able to make a series of stylish melodramas for Paramount: *The Exile* (1947), *Letter from an Unknown Woman* (1948), *Caught* (1949), and *The Reckless Moment* (1949), which are among his very best films. Returning to France in 1949, Ophüls entered the period of his greatest creativity, making four elegant, masterful films in succession between 1950 and 1955;

---

* In an effort to salvage the film, Tati reduced it from 155 to 108 minutes for European distribution; for distribution in the United States in 1972, *Playtime* was further reduced to 93 minutes and released in a 35mm monaural format.

he died in 1957. Ophüls had always worked within the studio system, so that the subject matter of his films—often light and operettalike—was never as important to him as visual style. And it is for their dazzling *mise-en-scène* that Ophüls' last four films, all photographed by the great French cameraman Christian Matras (b. 1903), are most remarkable.

La Ronde (1950) is an adaptation of an Arthur Schnitzler play set in turn-of-the-century Vienna. Its ten separate episodes posit that love is a perpetual roundabout in which one partner is regularly exchanged for another until the pattern comes full circle, like the movements of a waltz, only to begin again. This unbroken circle of affairs is presided over by a master of ceremonies who manipulates and comments on the behavior of the characters, becoming a surrogate for Ophüls himself. *Le Plaisir* (English title: *House of Pleasure*, 1952) is derived from three Maupassant stories, linked by a narrator; they illustrate the theme that pleasure may be easy to come by but happiness is not. Like all of Ophüls' work, the film is marked by meticulous attention to period detail and by an incessantly moving camera. In one famous sequence, the camera circles the exterior of a brothel time and time again, never entering the set but peering voyeuristically through windows at significant dramatic action taking place within. In *Madame de . . .* (English title: *The Earrings of Madame de . . .*, 1953), also set at the turn of the century, Ophüls constructs yet another circular narrative that rotates around a central axis of vanity, frivolity, and lust. Here, the passage of a pair of earrings from a husband to his wife to the husband's mistress to the wife's lover and finally back to the husband again constitutes a single perfect revolution in the roundabout of infidelity. The characters are ultimately shallow, because everything in *Madame de . . .* is subordinate to its aesthetic design. As if to mirror the movement of the waltzes on the soundtrack, the camera whirls and pirouettes continuously to follow the film's principals through its glittering period decor, suggesting that life is itself a kind of waltz in which all of us are caught up while the music plays.

Lola Montès (1955) is generally considered to be Ophüls' masterpiece, the consummation of his entire life's work. Conceived by its producers as a big-budget superspectacle in Eastmancolor and CinemaScope with an international cast of stars, it was based on the scandalous life of a mediocre nineteenth-century dancer who became the mistress of the composer Franz Liszt and, during the revolutions of 1848, of Ludwig I, deposed king of Bavaria. She finally ended as a circus performer selling kisses to earn her keep. Ophüls cared nothing for the subject, remarking of Lola herself, "Her role is roughly the same as that of our pair of earrings in *Madame de . . . .*" That is, he merely used her story to create a dazzling exercise in visual style, and *Lola Montès* became one of the most intricate, opulent, and elaborate films to appear on the French screen since Abel Gance's *Napoléon* (1927). Ironically, Ophüls was initially opposed to the use of CinemaScope, but his sense of visual patterning was such that he turned *Lola Montès* into a stunning exhibition of composition for the widescreen frame. He frequently broke the horizontal space of the screen with vertical dominants and framed shots through arches, col-

13.8 *Le Plaisir* (Max Ophüls, 1952): Simone Simon.

13.9 *Madame de . . .* (Max Ophüls, 1953): Danielle Darrieux.

13.10 *Lola Montès* (Max Ophüls, 1955): Martine Carol.

umns, and drapery. He learned to compose close-ups by balancing both sides of the frame, and at other times—as during the circus scenes—he would fill the entire CinemaScope frame with significant dramatic action. The film begins and ends within the circus tent, where the ringmaster introduces Lola's act by recalling the circumstances of her past life, which is then represented on the screen in a series of achronological flashbacks. Ophüls uses color nonnaturalistically throughout the film, especially in these flashback sequences, where each is tinted according to its prevailing emotional tone. Finally, the camera seems never to stop its circular tracking around some invisible axis, in or out of the tent, making the circularity of things seen on the screen a metaphor for life itself. As Andrew Sarris has remarked, "With Ophüls it is movement itself that is emphasized rather than its terminal points of rest."

As with *Intolerance* (1916) and *Citizen Kane* (1941), the narrative technique of *Lola Montès* was so unconventional that audiences stayed away from it. In response, its producers, the Gamma Company, first cut the film from 140 to 110 minutes, and finally re-edited the story in chronological sequence for release in a ninety-minute version. Still, the film's commercial failure was so complete that Gamma was eventually bankrupted by it, and it seems likely that Ophüls' death from a rheumatic heart condition in 1957 was hastened by the mutilation of his masterpiece. In 1969, however, the original version was reconstructed and re-released, to great critical acclaim.

The key to Ophüls' style is his mastery of the long take and, especially, of the continuously moving camera. Ophüls was also a genius at composition within the frame, and the influence upon him of both German Expressionism and French pictorial Impressionism was profound. In his passion for decor and his obsession with the sensuous surfaces of reality, Ophüls most closely resembles von Sternberg. In his cynicism and worldly wit, he is close to Ernst Lubitsch. That his films are devoid of content—a charge frequently leveled against both von Sternberg and Lubitsch—is the New Wave generation was to argue and to demonstrate time and again, the substance of cinema is *audiovisual,* not verbal, and it exists on a level of discourse—like that of the circular tracking shots in *Lola Montès*—where perception and conceptualization become one.

INFLUENCE OF THE FIFTIES DOCUMENTARY MOVEMENT AND INDEPENDENT PRODUCITON

By 1955, French commercial cinema had reached a dangerous point of stagnation. The new generation of directors that had emerged during the Occupation for the most part had simply continued prewar trends. By the mid-fifties, many young filmmakers were firmly ensconced within the studio system or working on big-budget spectacles and international coproductions. The cinematic individualism of Bresson and Tati, and also of Cocteau, offered a succeeding generation of French directors examples of how film could be used as a medium of personal expression; and Ophüls had forecast the possibility of a purely audiovisual language for the screen. But the major stylistic influences upon this younger generation of film-makers came from the French documentary movement of the fifties, which was their training ground, and from the films of independent directors working outside the studio system of production.

13.11 *Farrebique* (Georges Rouquier, 1946).

The documentary movement can be said to have begun in 1946 with Georges Rouquier's *Farrebique,* a lyrical feature-length documentary about peasant life on a farm through the four seasons.* Jean Grémillon (*Le Six juin à l'aube* [*The Sixth of June at Dawn,* 1945]) and Roger Leenhardt (*Les Dernières vacances* [*The Last Holiday,* 1947]) both made countless short documentaries throughout the fifties on art and on the lives of great men. But the master of French documentary cinema during this period was Georges Franju (1912–87), a totally original filmmaker who was deeply influenced by German Expressionism and has often been called a surrealist.

Franju had been working in cinema since 1937, when he made a 16mm amateur film with Henri Langlois. However, his first major film was *Le Sang des bêtes* (*The Blood of the Beasts,* 1949), a brutally graphic documentary short about the daily activity of a slaughterhouse in a quiet Parisian suburb, whose butchery was made deliberately resonant of the horrors of the Nazi death camps. *En Passant par la Lorraine* (*Passing by Lorraine,* 1950) depicted the steel mills of that peaceful region as furnaces consuming the lives of the men who work them. In *Hôtel des invalides,* possibly his finest film, Franju turned an ostensibly objective account of the French War Museum into a devastating antiwar statement by exposing the human suffering that underlies the myths of heroism and glory enshrined by that institution. Other important Franju shorts were *Le Grand*

13.12 *Le Sang des bêtes* (Georges Franju, 1949).

---

* Thirty-five years later Rouquier produced, with funds from the U.S. National Endowment for the Humanities, a sequel, *Biquefarre* (1983), which focuses on the new generation of the same farming community.

13.13 *Les Veux sans visage* (Georges Franju, 1959): Edith Scob.

Méliès (1952) and *Monsieur et Madame Curie* (1953), documentary tributes to the great pioneers of modern cinema and modern science, respectively. In 1958 Franju directed his first feature, *La Tête contre les murs* (English title: *The Keepers*), a half-documentary, half-surrealistic account of a sane man who is committed to a French lunatic asylum; the film is often cited as a forerunner of the New Wave. The grisly horror film *Les Yeux sans visage* (*Eyes Without a Face*, 1959; released—cut and dubbed— in the United States as *The Horror Chamber of Dr. Faustus*) concerns a mad doctor who kidnaps young girls in a futile effort to transplant their faces onto the head of his own disfigured daughter. His *Pleins feux sur l'assassin* (*Spotlight on the Murderer*, 1961) is an atmospheric thriller adapted from a novel by Boileau and Narcejac. Franju's next two films were adaptations from François Mauriac: *Thérèse Desqueroux* (1962) and *Judex* (1963), an *hommage* to Louis Feuillade's twelve-part serial of 1916. Franju made only five other features—*Thomas l'imposteur* (*Thomas the Imposter*, 1965), *Les Rideaux blancs* (*The White Curtains*, 1966), *Marcel Allain* (1966), *La Faute de l'Abbe Mouret* (*The Sin of Abbé Mouret*, 1970), and *L'Homme sans visage* (*Man Without a Face*, 1974)—all but one of them intensely poetic visualizations of literary works, which have little in common with the style of the New Wave that his own documentaries helped to create.

Alain Resnais (b. 1922), whose first feature, *Hiroshima, mon amour* (1959), became the clarion call of the New Wave, was another important figure in the French documentary movement. He made documentary shorts for the first eleven years of his career, beginning with a series of art films— *Van Gogh* (1948), *Gauguin* (1950), *Guernica* (1950)—and progressing to *Nuit et brouillard* (*Night and Fog*, 1955), a profoundly disturbing meditation upon the horrors of the death camps ten years after and upon the effects of time and memory on the way we perceive them, written and narrated by Jean Cayrol* with an original score by Hans Eisler. *Toute la memoire du monde* (*The Memory of the World*, 1956), a study of the books "imprisoned" in the French National Library, has a similar temporal theme, as do most of Resnais' features.

Other figures associated with the documentary short in the fifties were Chris Marker (see p. 586), an original and highly personal filmmaker who would later organize the radical cooperative, la Société pour le Lancement des Oeuvres Nouvelles (SLON), for the production of *Loin du Vietnam* (1967) and similar polemical work; the ethnographic filmmaker Jean Rouch (b. 1917), who became the apostle of *cinéma-vérité* in the sixties (he invented the term by translating Dziga Vertov's *kino-pravda* into French for his coproduction, with the sociologist Edgar Morin, *Chronique d'un été* [*Chronicle of a Summer*, 1961]); Frédéric Rossif (b. 1922), who specialized in compilation films (*Mourir à Madrid* [*To Die*

---

* Cayrol (b. 1911) is a French novelist and scriptwriter who was himself deported to the camps. The title and controlling metaphor of Resnais' film was borrowed from *Poèms de la nuit et du brouillard,* a volume of poetry Cayrol published on the experience in 1945. He later wrote the script of Resnais' masterpiece *Muriel* (1963).

13.14   *Nuit et brouillard* (Alain Resnais, 1955).

in Madrid, 1962]); and Agnès Varda (b. 1928), a former photographer whose first feature, the influential *La Pointe-Courte* (1955), is discussed below.

The example of independent production outside of the traditional studio system was another important influence upon the emergent New Wave generation. Jean-Pierre Melville (b. Jean-Pierre Grumbach, 1917–73) was a vastly significant figure in this regard. A lover of cinema from an early age, Melville founded his own production company in 1945. His first feature, *Le Silence de la mer* (*The Silence of the Sea,* 1947), earned him the admiration of Cocteau, who commissioned him to direct *Les Enfants terribles* in 1949. The commercial success of *Quand tu liras cette lettre* (*When You Read This Letter,* 1952) allowed Melville to purchase his own studio and move into totally independent production. The result was the much-admired gangster film *Bob le flambeur* (1955), a highly personalized work whose production methods—location shooting, small crew, use of unknown actors (all borrowed, of course, from neorealism)—became the model for New Wave filmmakers. Melville's work itself became increasingly commercial after he directed *Léon Morin, prêtre* (*Léon Morin, Priest,* 1961), a star vehicle for Jean-Paul Belmondo, but his fascination with the iconography of the American gangster film and the underworld of urban crime caused him to produce a trilogy of popular gangster films in the sixties that are among the most admired in the genre— *Le Doulos* (*The Fingerman,* 1962), *Le deuxième souffle* (*Second Breath,* 1965), and *Le Samouraï* (*The Samurai,* 1967).

Another independent production that foretold the New Wave—and that some critics have called its first manifestation—is Agnès Varda's *La Pointe-Courte* (1955). This film about the dissolution and reconstruction of a marriage set against the backdrop of a small fishing village was produced by a collective of crew and actors. It was edited by Alain Resnais

13.15   *Le Doulos* (Jean-Pierre Melville, 1962): Jean-Paul Belmondo.

13.16 *Et Dieu créa la femme* (Roger Vadim, 1956): Jean-Louis Trintignant, Brigitte Bardot.

and is considered to be a direct antecedent of his own *Hiroshima, mon amour* (1959). The drama of the husband and wife is highly stylized and "literary," but the day-to-day life of the village is presented in semidocumentary form. (Varda apparently got the idea of using two counterposed structures from reading the first French translation of Faulkner's *The Wild Palms* in 1953.)

It was the early films of Roger Vadim (b. 1928), however, that contributed most to the economic development of the New Wave. The spectacular commercial success of his independently produced first feature, *Et Dieu créa la femme* (*And God Created Woman*, 1956), demonstrated to the stagnant French film industry that young directors and new themes could attract large audiences. A visually sumptuous production in widescreen and color, *Et Dieu créa la femme* was a sensitive examination of the vagaries of amoral youth set against the luxurious background of St. Tropez. It starred Vadim's wife, Brigitte Bardot, and featured a number of explicit love scenes, which made it an international hit. In subsequent films, such as *Les Liaisons dangereuses* (*Dangerous Liaisons*, 1959), *Et Mourir de plaisir* (English title: *Blood and Roses*, 1960), *La Ronde* (English title: *Circle of Love*, 1964—a remake of the Ophüls film), *Barbarella* (1968), and *Pretty Maids All in a Row* (United States, 1971), Vadim's commercialism and exploitativeness increased, but he remained an impeccable craftsman and elegant stylist of the widescreen color film.* Moreover, it was Vadim, more than any other single figure in the French cinema, who opened the doors of the industry to his generation of filmmakers and provided the economic justification for the New Wave.

THEORY: ASTRUC, BAZIN, AND *CAHIERS DU CINÉMA*

The theoretical justification for the New Wave cinema came from another source: the film critic Alexandre Astruc (b. 1923), who published a highly influential article in *L'Ecran française* (no. 144) in March 1948 on the concept of the **caméra-stylo,** which would permit the cinema "to become a means of expression as supple and subtle as that of written language" and would therefore accord filmmakers the status of authors, or *auteurs*. Astruc's notion was to break away from the tyranny of narrative in order to evolve a new form of audiovisual language. He wrote: "The fundamental problem of the cinema is how to express thought. The

---

* Vadim's adaptation of *Les Liaisons dangereuses* modernized Choderlos de Laclos' controversial 1786 novel, setting it in contemporary Paris and Deauville. In 1988, a period version was filmed in France by the British director Stephen Frears; and in the same year Vadim himself remade *And God Created Woman* in the United States with Rebecca De Mornay in the Bardot role.

creation of this language has preoccupied all the theoreticians and writers in the history of cinema, from Eisenstein down to the scriptwriters and adaptors of the sound cinema." Like Bazin, Astruc questioned the values of classical montage and was an apostle of the long take, as exemplified in the work of Murnau. Astruc later became a professional director after apprenticing himself to Marc Allégret (1900–73), but his own films (*Le Rideau cramoisi* [*The Crimson Curtain;* English title: *End of Desire*, 1952] and *Une vie* [*A Life*, 1958]) do not attempt to realize the ideal of the *caméra-stylo*. Following the example of German Expressionism, Astruc's films tend to be highly stylized elaborations of visual imagery that make excessive use of mannered compositions and camera angles.

Astruc was succeeded as a theorist by the vastly influential journal *Cahiers du cinéma* (literally, "cinema notebooks"), founded in 1951 by André Bazin (1918–58) and Jacques Doniol-Valcroze (b. 1920), which gathered about it a group of young critics—François Truffaut, Jean-Luc Godard, Claude Chabrol, Jacques Rivette, and Eric Rohmer—who were to become the major directors of the New Wave. These young men were **cinéphiles,** or "film-lovers." They had grown up in the postwar years watching great American films of the past and present decades (many available for the first time only when the German Occupation ended) as well as classical French films at the amazing **Cinémathèque Française** in Paris, the magnificent film archive and public theater founded in 1936 by Georges Franju and Henri Langlois to promote cinema study and cinema culture in France and throughout the world. During the Occupation, Langlois kept the enterprise in operation secretly at great personal risk, and afterward, through André Malraux, minister of culture, he obtained a large government subsidy for it. Today the Cinémathèque is the largest public film archive in the world, housing over fifty thousand films, three theaters, and a museum in the Palais de Chaillot devoted entirely to film history.* It was Langlois who preserved the works of Griffith, Keaton, Gance, Vigo, and Renoir for the postwar generation of *cinéphiles* and introduced them to the then-unrecognized genius of directors like Ingmar Bergman and the great Japanese masters Akira Kurosawa and Yasujiro Ozu (see Chapters 15 and 17). Under Langlois' tutelage, these young men came to love film and desperately wanted to become filmmakers themselves, but they found the French commercial cinema inaccessible to them because of the powerful influence exerted by the trade unions. So, since they knew more about film than any other generation in history, based on the experience of actual viewing, they became critics and theorists instead.

13.17 *Le Rideau cramoisi* (Alexandre Astruc, 1952): Anouk Aimée.

---

* Although a warehouse fire in 1980 destroyed some seven thousand of its French titles, the Cinémathèque today has access to the State Film Archive (les Archives du Film, Centre national de la Cinématographie) at Bois-d'Arcy where, since 1977, the government has mandated the deposit of one print of every new French release. See Richard Roud, *A Passion for Films: Henri Langlois and the Cinémathèque Française* (New York: Viking, 1983), and Michel Ciment, "The Legacy of Langlois," *American Film* 12, 3 (December 1988): 17–19.

The *Cahiers* critics had two basic principles. The first, deriving from Bazin, was a rejection of montage aesthetics in favor of *mise-en-scène,* the long take, and composition in depth. *Mise-en-scène,* the "placing-in-the-scene," is probably best defined as the creation of mood and ambience, though it more literally means the structuring of the film through camera placement and movement, blocking of action, direction of actors, etc.—in other words, everything that takes place on the set prior to the editing process. Integral to the concept of *mise-en-scène* is the notion that film should be not merely an intellectual or rational experience but an emotional and psychological one as well. The second tenet of the *Cahiers* critics, derived from Astruc, was the idea of personal authorship which François Truffaut expressed in a 1954 essay entitled *"Une certaine tendance du cinéma français"* ("A Certain Tendency in French Cinema", as *la politique des auteurs.* This "policy of authors," christened "the *auteur* theory" by the American critic Andrew Sarris, states that film should ideally be a medium of personal artistic expression and that the best films are therefore those that most clearly bear their maker's "signature"—the stamp of his or her individual personality, controlling obsessions, and cardinal themes. The implicit assumption was that with each successive film an *auteur* grows increasingly proficient and mature of vision, an assumption that is not always borne out by fact.

Truffaut's essay, which appeared in *Cahiers du cinéma* (no. 31) for January 1954, began by attacking the postwar "tradition of quality," that is, the commercial scenarist tradition of Aurenche and Bost, Spaak, and directors such as Clair, Clément, Clouzot, Autant-Lara, Cayatte, and Allégret, with its heavy emphasis on plot and dialogue. The key figure in this literary / theatrical cinema was the scriptwriter, the director being merely "the gentleman who added the pictures." To these *"littérateurs"* and their *"cinéma de papa,"* Truffaut counterposed *"un cinéma d'auteurs"* in the work of such French writer-directors as Gance, Vigo, Renoir, Cocteau, Becker, Bresson, and Ophüls, and of numerous American directors—both major and minor—who had somehow managed to make personal statements despite the restrictions imposed upon them by the studio system. Some of the American choices—Welles, Hitchcock, Hawks, Lang, Ford, Nicholas Ray, and Anthony Mann, all masters of *mise-en-scène*—made perfect sense. Others—Jerry Lewis, Otto Preminger, Roger Corman—were based less on the quality of their films than on evidence of their personal directorial control. And the unquestioning allegiance which the *Cahiers* group gave to the figures in its pantheon made many skeptics wonder whether one form of iron-clad dogmatism had not simply been exchanged for another. But for all its deficiences (and a proneness to fanaticism and cultism seems to be a major one), the *auteur* theory does offer a valuable schematic model for interpreting the filmmaking process and goes some way toward solving a very basic methodological problem of film criticism: that is, to whom or what does one attribute cinematic creation? Furthermore, the *Cahiers* critics were able to partially vindicate the *auteur* theory by becoming filmmakers themselves and practicing it.

THE NEW WAVE: FIRST FILMS

The first films of this "new wave" (*nouvelle vague*)* of French directors were independently produced dramatic shorts, many of them shot in 16mm and subsequently blown up for 35mm exhibition. Jacques Rivette's *Le Coup du berger* (*Fool's Mate*, 1956), François Truffaut's *Le Mistons* (*The Mischief-Makers*, 1957), and Jean-Luc Godard's *Tous les garçons s'appellent Patrick* (*All Boys Are Named Patrick*, 1957) all fall into this category. But the first feature-length success of the New Wave is generally acknowledged to have been Claude Chabrol's first film, *Le Beau Serge* (*The Handsome Serge / Bitter Reunion*, 1958), though Varda's *La Pointe-Courte* preceded it by three years. While still a *Cahiers* critic, Chabrol (b. 1930) shot *Le Beau Serge,* about the rehabilitation of a village drunkard, on location with funds provided by a small inheritance. The success of *Le Beau Serge* enabled Chabrol to follow it with *Les Cousins* (*The Cousins*, 1959), an ironic study of sexual intrigue and murder set against the backdrop of Parisian student life. The influence of Hitchcock became increasingly apparent in *A Double tour* (English title: *Leda / Web of Passion*, 1959), a highly stylized tale of pathological murder, and the darkly satiric *Les Bonnes femmes* (*The Good Women*, 1960), a film about the lives (and, in one case, the death) of Parisian shopgirls; its huge commercial failure caused Chabrol to turn for a while from the New Wave mode to more conventional thrillers like *Landru* (English title: *Bluebeard*, 1962) and *Le scandale* (English title: *The Champagne Murders,* 1966).

Nevertheless, 1959 was the *annus mirabilis* for the New Wave because in that year three of the major figures of the movement released their first features. François Truffaut's *Les Quatre-cents coups* (*The 400 Blows*), made for 75 thousand dollars with a loan from his father-in-law when the director was twenty-seven years old, is a lyrical but wholly unsentimental account of an adolescent delinquent, shot on location in Paris. Dedicated to the memory of André Bazin (who died on the second day of shooting) and photographed in Dyaliscope (a French version of CinemaScope) by the talented New Wave cinematographer Henri Decaë (b. 1915), the film is consciously evocative of Vigo's *Zéro de conduite* (1933). It won the prize for Best Direction at Cannes in the year of its release, as well as the New York Critics award for Best Foreign Language Film in 1959.† (In the same year, the highly coveted Cannes Golden Palm

---

*The term was apparently first applied to the phenomenon by critic François Giroud of *L'Express* and traveled almost immediately to the United States, where the movement was sometimes facetiously referred to as the "new vague," owing to the perceived difficulty of its films.

†The title derives from the French expression "*Il a fait les quatre-cents coups,*" meaning that a youth has gotten himself into a lot of trouble "raising hell," so to speak. Originally ninety-four minutes, *Les Quatre-cents coups* was re-edited by Truffaut to one hundred and one minutes for the Annency Film Festival tribute to him in 1967; for the same event, he reduced *Les Mistons* from twenty-six to seventeen minutes.

13.18 Jean-Pierre Léaud in *Les Quatres-cents coups* (François Truffaut, 1959), the first Antoine Doinel film.

13.19 *Hiroshima, mon amour* (Alain Resnais, 1959): Emmanuele Riva, Eiji Okada.

award went to the work of another unpracticed, unconventional French director, Marcel Camus' *Orphée noir* [*Black Orpheus*, 1958]). It was also the first film in Truffaut's Antoine Doinel series, a kind of continuing cinematic autobiography starring Jean-Pierre Léaud (b. 1944), an actor who physically resembles Truffaut. The series includes *Antoine et Colette* (a contribution to an international compilation film entitled *L'Amour à vingt ans* [*Love at Twenty*, 1962]), *Baisers volés* (*Stolen Kisses*, 1968), *Domicile conjugal* (*Bed and Board*, 1970), and *L'Amour en fuite* (*Love on the Run*, 1979).

More remarkable in structure and theme was Alain Resnais' first feature, *Hiroshima, mon amour* (1959), which, like *Nuit et brouillard,* examines the relationship between time and memory in the context of a terrible atrocity. With a brilliant script by the novelist Marguerite Duras (who was to become an important director herself in the seventies) and cinematography by Sacha Vierny (b. 1919), the film concerns a love affair between a French actress working in Hiroshima and a Japanese architect, in the course of which both recall their memories of the past war in Asia and Europe. Resnais maintains the counterpoint between present and past by continuously shifting narrative modes from objective to subjective and, in several extraordinary sequences, by combining dramatic footage of the couple making love with documentary footage of the aftermath of the Hiroshima blast. *Hiroshima, mon amour*, like *Les Quatre-cents coups,* was a great commercial success and conferred further prestige upon the New Wave by winning the New York Critics award for Best Foreign Language Film in 1960.

The third important New Wave film of 1959, Jean-Luc Godard's *A bout de souffle* (*Breathless*), was in many ways the most characteristic and influential film of the movement. *Breathless*, which was written by Godard after a story by Truffaut and shot by cinematographer Raoul

13.20 *À bout de souffle* (Jean-Luc Godard, 1959):
Jean-Paul Belmondo, Jean Seberg.

Coutard (b. 1924) in four weeks for less than ninety thousand dollars,*
is dedicated to Monogram Pictures, one of the larger American B-film
studios of the thirties and forties, which were famous for their ability to
turn out tightly paced films on short shooting schedules and poverty-line
budgets. This was precisely the ideal of the New Wave (or, at least, of its
dominant *Cahiers* branch), but instead of making cheap films in order to
make a quick profit, the New Wave directors made cheap films in order
to be able to make films at all, since their productions were necessarily
independent of the industry. (Happily, many of the first New Wave films,
including *Breathless,* made a great deal of money, which temporarily
insured the future of the movement.) Modeled on the American gangster
film in a simultaneous spirit of parody and *hommage, Breathless* is about
an amoral young thug on the run who is finally betrayed to the police by
his American girlfriend (deliberate shades of *Pépé le Moko,* 1936, and
Quai des brumes, 1938), and it contains virtually every major technical
characteristic of the New Wave film. These include use of shaky **hand-
held** 35mm camera shots,† **location shooting,** natural lighting, improvised plot and dialogue, and **direct sound** recording on location with
portable tape machines that were electronically synchronized with the
camera.

But the most important technical characteristic of the New Wave film
was its jagged, elliptical style of editing, which employed a high percentage of **jump cuts** within and between scenes to destroy the spatial and
temporal continuity of the viewing experience. As *Breathless* begins, for

---

* *Breathless* was filmed on location in Paris and Marseilles from August 17 to September
15, 1959, and released on March 16, 1960. Truffaut wrote the original story in 1955–56,
and his name also appears as scriptwriter in the credits. This was a ploy to gain financial
backing for *Breathless,* since *Les Quatre-cents coups* had just won the *Grand prix de la
mise-en-scène* at Cannes (the scenario was actually writtten by Godard alone). *Breathless*
was remade in 1983 by independent director Jim McBride, with a new script by McBride
and L. M. Kit Carson set in contemporary Los Angeles.

† For the tracking shots of *Breathless,* e.g., Godard pushed Coutard around in a wheelchair.

13.21 Belmondo in *À bout de souffle.*

example, we witness the following sequence of events: Michel, the young hood, steals a car in Paris with the help of his French mistress and speeds out into the countryside alone; he passes several other vehicles on his side of the road at high speed; he briefly contemplates picking up two female hitchhikers; and he talks to himself and to the audience about a variety of subjects, to occupy the time. Next, he passes a large truck at a road construction site and suddenly finds himself pursued by two motorcycle cops; he pulls off the road into a small wooded area and pretends to be having car trouble. One cop passes him by, the second spots him and pulls into the wood. At this point, Michel reaches into the car, removes a revolver, and guns down the cop. He then flees across an open field and hitchhikes back to Paris. In a conventional commercial film of the day— French, American, British, or Italian—this sequence would have been rendered in many separate shots fully depicting each of the actions. In *Breathless,* the whole sequence is conveyed in only several brief shots: alternating close-ups of Michel and his mistress on a Paris street; a quick take of the car theft at eye level; medium-close shots of Michel driving the car, taken from the passenger's seat; medium-long shots of the road and later the hitchhikers passing away rapidly through the windshield; a shot of the motorcycle cops appearing in the rearview mirror, followed by one of Michel pulling off the road and opening the hood of his car as the cop discovers him; an extreme close-up of the revolver, followed by a medium-long shot of the murder; a long shot of Michel running across a field, and a medium shot of him arriving in Paris as a passenger in the backseat of an unidentified car. Later in the film, Godard begins many scenes with a huge disorienting close-up and only later cuts, or pulls his camera back, to reveal the context of the action—which completely reversed conventional practice of the day.

Most radical of all, however, was Godard's use of the jump cut, in which a section of a single continuous shot is eliminated and then what remains is spliced together, creating a completely nonnaturalistic ellipsis in the action and calling attention to the director's power to manipulate all aspects of his medium. This radical elimination of transitional scenes (of what Hollywood calls **establishing shots**—medium or long shots of exteriors that indicate changes in dramatic space), and even of continuity *within* the shot itself, was thought extremely confusing when Godard and his peers first practiced it on a large scale, and yet it is no more than a logical extension of the discoveries of Méliès, Porter, and Griffith that cinematic narrative is by its nature *dis*continuous, or, as Eisenstein discovered, that spatial and temporal continuity in the cinema resides not on the screen but in the viewer's mind as it makes the connections that the images on the screen, by their arrangement, suggest. In the conventional continuity, or "invisible," editing style of classical Hollywood cinema, orderly narrative transitions were felt to be crucial. As late as 1957, Orson Welles was forced by Universal to shoot additional establishing scenes for his *Touch of Evil,* so that his fast-paced editing would not confuse contemporary audiences. Today, elliptical editing and the jump cut have passed into our conventional cinematic lexicon so pervasively that it is not unusual to find them in abundance in any television series. But in 1959 elliptical editing was thought radically innovative, and it became paramount among the stylistic conventions associated with the New Wave.

THE NEW WAVE: ORIGINS OF STYLE

These conventions, like all film conventions, sprang from two sources— theoretical conviction and material circumstances (not necessarily in that order). The material circumstances were these: the young directors of the New Wave were the first *film*-educated generation of filmmakers in history. They approached the cinema from the experience of having viewed almost the whole of its history at Langlois' Cinémathèque Française and from having written about it theoretically and critically in *Cahiers du cinéma* for nearly a decade. When they finally came to practice cinema, they knew more about the medium as an art form and less about the practical aspects of production than anyone who had ever made films before them. Consequently, they made many mistakes which their low budgets and tight shooting schedules would not permit them to correct. Like the Soviet filmmakers during the film-stock shortage that followed the 1917 Revolution, the New Wave directors could not afford to retake shots, so they relied on elliptical editing to conceal technical defects on the screen. Jump cuts, for example, were a means not only of creating perceptual dislocation in the audience but also of restoring botched scenes by excising some actor's or cameraman's blunder from the middle of a take. But there were sound theoretical reasons for the stylistic conventions of the New Wave as well as budgetary ones. If location shooting with hand-held cameras was inexpensive, it was also totally at odds with the fluid, studio-bound cinematography of the contemporary commercial film. If jagged editing and jump-cutting were useful in concealing defective footage, they also eliminated the smooth transitions that permit an audience to forget that it is watching a film—that is, a consciously crafted product of human imagination rather than some "found" reality.

The psychological effect of these conventions—and they must be considered calculated effects by the directors as well as functions of economic necessity—is to establish aesthetic distance between the audience and the film. New Wave films constantly remind us that we are watching a film, and *not* the reality that a film inevitably resembles, by calling attention to their "filmicness," that is, to their artificially created nature. The abrupt and, above all, obvious manipulation of our perception in these films, through the use of the jump cut, hand-held cameras, and so forth, jolts us out of our conventional involvement with the narrative and our traditional identification with the characters, who are often less recognizable as characters than as actors playing characters. This is because New Wave cinema is, in a sense, *self-reflexive cinema,* or *metacinema*— film about the process and nature of film itself. According to the New Wave *cinéastes* (loosely, film artists), the conventional cinema had too faithfully and for too long reproduced our normal way of seeing things through its studiously unobtrusive techniques. The invisible editing and imperturbably smooth camera styles of the commercial cinema of the thirties, forties, fifties, and much of the sixties were designed to draw the spectator's attention away from the fact that he or she was watching a consciously crafted artifact. But the disruptive editing and camera styles of the New Wave say to us constantly, "Look, there's a film being made right before your eyes," and to emphasize the point a director or his technical crew will sometimes appear just inside the frame of a narrative sequence, as if by accident, to remind us that whenever we watch a film a handful of artists are controlling the process immediately beyond the borders of the frame.

The theoretical position of the New Wave filmmakers is therefore that film must constantly call attention to the process of its own making and to the medium's own unique language—thus, the unparalleled cinematic *éclat,* or explosiveness, of the New Wave, its emphasis upon "magical" cinematic tricks like the jump cut, the iris-in and iris-out, decelerated and accelerated motion, and optically violent camera movement—all devices of which film and no other medium is capable. In this sense, the New Wave represents a return to Méliès and his conspicuously cinematic brand of conjuring. It envisions film as a special kind of magic that requires of its viewers a uniquely cinematic way of seeing in order to comprehend. On the other hand, the New Wave reaches back equally to Lumière because its most characteristic techniques are essentially documentary in practice. In fact, *cinéma-vérité,* the chief documentary mode of the sixties and seventies, constitutes an application of New Wave shooting and recording practices to real events rather than staged ones. Furthermore, Jean-Luc Godard, the most innovative and radical director to emerge from the New Wave, has virtually rejected narrative cinema in favor of cinematic "essays" on ideology and social praxis. New Wave cinema is aware of this paradox because it is aware of its history and conscious of the mediating position it holds between the narrative and documentary traditions of Western film. The allusions to and "quotations" from films of the past (sometimes called *hommages*) with which New Wave films are replete are no mere mannerisms but rather testaments to the critical-historical cinematic consciousness out of which the movement grew.

MAJOR NEW WAVE FIGURES

The critical and commercial success of the New Wave in 1959 was so great that between 1960 and 1962 over one hundred new French directors were able to find funding for their first features—an extraordinary thing in an industry formerly so conservative. In some cases, the director of a commercial hit, like Godard or Truffaut, would produce for a less fortunate friend. In many others, a French commercial studio would produce, hoping to come up with a smash hit like *Breathless* on a B-film budget. In fact, the climate of creative and commercial enthusiasm during could obtain financial backing to make a low-budget film, though many who turned to directing lacked either the talent or the discipline to bring their projects to a successful conclusion. The commercial failures of the less talented began en masse in 1962, and by 1964 the studios had been so badly disappointed by well-intentioned amateurs that production money for first features was more difficult to raise than it had been in the fifties. By this time, the New Wave as a collective phenomenon was over, and the French film industry had resumed its conventionally rigid contours. But French cinema continued to be dominated creatively by the handful of young *cinéastes* who had initiated the movement and who emerged from it as distinctly major figures—François Truffaut, Jean-Luc Godard, Alain Resnais, Claude Chabrol—and by a small group of sophisticated but less spectacular talents, such as Louis Malle, Eric Rohmer, Jacques Demy, Jacques Rivette, and Agnès Varda.

François Truffaut

François Truffaut (1932–84), the most commercially successful of the post-New Wave group, was able to maintain his independence by forming his own production company, Les Films du Carrosse (1961), named in *hommage* to Renoir's *Le Carrosse d'or* (1952). His major cinematic influences were the American B-film, *film noir,* and the work of Alfred Hitchcock and Jean Renoir. He followed *Les Quatre-cents coups* (1959) with what he called "a respectful tribute to the Hollywood B-film," *Tirez sur le pianiste* (*Shoot the Piano Player,* 1960) based on an American gangster thriller (*Down There*) by David Goodis. The film concerns Charlie, a timid honky-tonk piano player in a sleazy Parisian bar who, we learn in a series of extended flashbacks, was once the great concert pianist Edouard Saroyan. He and his girlfriend, Lena, become involved with two gangsters who are after his younger brother, and the couple is forced to flee the city when Charlie accidentally kills his employer in self-defense. The film ends with a shoot-out between the three brothers and the gang-

13.22 *Tirez sur le pianiste* (François Truffaut, 1960): Charles Aznavour as Charlie/Edouard, Marie Dubois as Lena.

13.23   The triad in Tuffaut's *Jules et Jim* (1961): Jeanne Moreau, Henri Serre, Oscar Werner.

sters at a farmhouse in the snow, in which Lena is killed. Criticized on its relaease for its radical shifts in mood from comedy to melodrama to tragedy, and for the manipulativeness of its disjointed narrative style, *Shoot the Piano Player* was nevertheless Truffaut's *Breathless*—a quintessentially New Wave film replete with bizarre visual puns, allusions to other films, a mixture or "explosion" of genres, and all the self-reflexive anti-conventions of the movement. Like *Les Quatre-cent coups,* it was stunningly photographed by the innovative New Wave cinematographer Raoul Coutard in Dyaliscope.

Truffaut's third feature, *Jules et Jim* (1961), stands as a tribute to the influence of Renoir and the French lyrical tradition.* As in Renoir's work, the basic themes of *Jules et Jim* are friendship and the impossibility of achieving true freedom in love (or, as Truffaut himself put it, "monogamy is impossible, but anything else is worse"). Adapted from a novel by Henri-Pierre Roché, this beautiful and sensitive film concerns two close friends—one French, the other Austrian—who fall in love with the same woman (Catherine), are separated by World War I, and afterward attempt to live together in a *ménage à trois*. Intellectually sound, the situation proves emotionally impossible for all three, and at the end of the film Catherine drowns herself with Jim, leaving Jules to cremate and bury them. The film is striking in its re-creation of the period through natural settings and in the remarkable performances of its principals—especially Jeanne Moreau† as the manic, enigmatic Catherine. While it appro-

---

* Truffaut has said that *Jules et Jim* was also influenced by Edgar G. Ulmer's B-Western *The Naked Dawn* (1956); it, too, concerns the psychological and emotional vagaries of a sexual triangle.

† Moreau (b. 1928) became a director in her own right, making an impressive debut with the semiautobiographical *Lumière* (1977), a film about four independent and interdependent women and the dynamics of stardom. It was followed by *L'Adolescente* (*The Adolescent,* 1979), which deals with a young girl's passage from childhood to adolescence. Her *Lillian Gish* (1984) is an affectionate documentary portrait of the venerable actress.

priately avoids the self-conscious pyrotechnics of *Shoot the Piano Player*, *Jules et Jim* is gorgeously composed and photographed in Franscope, yet another version of CinemaScope, by Raoul Coutard and sustains its emotional lyricism through the unconventional use of telephoto zooms, slow motion, freeze frames, anamorphic distortion (of World War I combat footage), and even a helicopter shot. After directing *Antoine et Colette*, also shot by Coutard in Franscope, for the anthology film *L'Amour à vingt ans* (1962), Truffaut produced in collaboration with this inventive cinematographer a restrained and sympathetic study of middle-aged adultery, *Le Peau douce* (*The Soft Skin*, 1964), which was marred by an overly melodramatic ending. His erratic adaptation of Ray Bradbury's *Fahrenheit 451* (1966), Truffaut's first film in color and English, is generally regarded as a failure because it played down traditional science fiction themes. But its portrait of a near-future society of emotionless, hedonistic people mindlessly tripped out on big-screen color television seems more than prophetic today, and Nicholas Roeg's cinematography is first-rate.

13.24 Jeanne Moreau and her dead bridegroom in *La Mariée était en noir* (François Truffaut, 1967).

In 1967, Truffaut published a book-length interview with Alfred Hitchcock in which he demonstrated his reverence for the American director by comparing him not only to Griffith, Hawks, and Ford, but to Kafka, Dostoevsky, and Poe. Appropriately enough, Truffaut's next two features were conceived as direct tributes to the Hitchcock thriller. *La Mariée était en noir* (*The Bride Wore Black*, 1967), photographed by Coutard, is a suspenseful tale of vengeance in which a woman (Jeanne Moreau) relentlessly tracks down and kills the five men responsible for the accidental shooting of her husband on their wedding day. Adapted from a novel by William Irish—the author of the novel on which the film *Rear Window* (Hitchcock, 1954) is based—and with a musical score by a frequent Hitchcock collaborator, Bernard Herrmann, Truffaut's film contains a dense pattern of allusions to specific Hitchcock films, uses Hitchcockian plot construction, and is intensely manipulative of audience expectations in order to generate suspense. *La Sirène du Mississippi* (*Mississippi Mermaid*, 1969), also adapted from a William Irish novel and shot in Dyaliscope by Denys Cherval, is dedicated to Jean Renoir and contains many allusions to his films (especially in its "open" ending, which is a visual *hommage* to the conclusion of *La Grande illusion*, 1937). But in terms of style and construction, this minor thriller about the degradation of an honest man by a *femme fatale* is pure Hitchcock.

Between *La Mariée était en noir* and *La Siréne du Mississippi*, Truffaut made his second Antoine Doinel feature, *Baisers volés* (*Stolen Kisses*, 1968), handsomely photographed by Cherval, a tender and affectionate portrait of Antoine's coming to adult consciousness through a series of affairs and, finally, his engagement to Christine (Claude Jade). *Domicile conjugal* (*Bed and Board*, 1970), the third feature in the Doinel series, examines the first few years of Antoine and Christine's marriage, its deterioration under the pressure of an affair, and its ultimate, uneasy reconstitution. The film is light and humorous, and its comedy is quite successful, but like *Jules et Jim* it also raises some serious questions about the institution of marriage and its alternatives. Truffaut concluded the Doinel

13.25 Truffaut's *Baisers volés* (1968), the second Antoine Doinel film: Jean-Pierre Léaud, Claude Jade.

13.26 *L'Enfant sauvage* (François Truffaut, 1969): Jean-Pierre Cargol.

series, begun with *Les Quatre-cents coups* twenty years before, with *L'Amour en fuite* (*Love on the Run*, 1979), which begins with Antoine's uncontested divorce from Christine and proceeds through his chance encounters with figures from his past.

For *L'Enfant sauvage* (*The Wild Child*, 1969), based upon the true account of a "wolf-boy" captured in the forests of central France in 1806, Truffaut both directed and played the part of Dr. Itard, the eighteenth-century rationalist who undertakes the painstakingly slow education of the wild child. Set in its period and shot in quasidocumentary style by the award-winning cinematographer Nestor Almendros,* *The Wild Child* allowed Truffaut to explore more intensively those themes of confinement versus freedom, and social conditioning versus nature, which he had first broached in *Les Quatre-cents coups*. *Les Deux Anglaises et le continent* (*Two English Girls*, 1971), adapted from another novel by Henri-Pierre Roché and set at the turn of the century, inevitably evokes comparison with *Jules et Jim*, of which it contains many deliberate echoes. The story of a young Frenchman's love for two English sisters, it was Truffaut's most visually sensuous work to date. Its sumptuous recreation of *la belle époque* is conveyed in shots composed after Impressionist paintings of the period, and its use of color was the most subtle Truffaut had achieved so far.

Une Belle fille comme moi (*Such a Gorgeous Kid Like Me*, 1972) is a sardonic portrayal of a murderous nymphomaniac which failed, on the whole, to break new ground. But *La Nuit américaine* (*Day for Night*, 1973) provided the ultimate in self-reflexive cinema: a film starring Jean-Pierre Léaud (the Truffaut figure in the Antoine Doinel series) and directed by Truffaut, about the making of a film starring Leaud and directed by Truffaut. **Day for night** (or *la nuit américaine*) is the technical term for shooting night scenes in daylight through a filter; by choosing it as his title Truffaut intended to evoke the entire arsenal of cinematic tricks of which it is merely typical. Dedicated to Dorothy and Lillian Gish, the great Griffith actresses, the whole film is predicated upon cinematic illusion, and in this respect it recalls Fellini's *8 1/2* (1963) and Bergman's *Persona* (1966). It is difficult from the outset to tell whether a scene is occurring in the film or in the film *within* the film because the cast and crew live so closely together that there is little distinction between their work and their personal lives. The film is funny, affectionate, and strangely disquieting in its gradual revelation that the same people making the film within the film are simultaneously making *Day for Night* and that confusion between illusion and reality is the very essence of the cinema.

Day for Night was in many ways a consummation for Truffaut. It

---

* Almendros, a native of Cuba, won the American Academy Award for Cinematography in 1978 for *Days of Heaven* (Terrence Malick, 1978). He worked closely with Truffaut on all the director's subsequent films except *Une Belle fille comme moi* (1972), *La Nuit américaine* (1973), and *L'Argent de poche* (1976)—all shot by Pierre William Glenn—and *La Femme d'à côté* (1981), which was shot by William Lubchantsky. Almendros also collaborates regularly with Eric Rohmer and Barbet Schroeder (see pp. 576–77).

13.27 The set within the set of Truffaut's *La Nuit américaine* (1973).

13.28 *L'Histoire d'Adèle H.* (François Truffaut, 1975): Isabelle Adjani.

combined the stylistic influence of American realism with that of French lyricism and drew together his dual thematic obsessions with autobiography and psychology in a hymn of praise to the cinema—an art form to which he was passionately devoted for his entire life. It answered the question posed by its own director-character—"Are films more important than life?"—with an emphatic "Yes!"

Truffaut's next project was *L'Histoire d'Adèle H.* (*The Story of Adèle H.*, 1975).* Based upon the diary of Victor Hugo's youngest daughter, this subtle and powerful film is about the psychology of a woman in the grip of a romantic obsession. Adèle's romantic fascination with a young English lieutenant leads her to follow him all over the world until she finally goes mad in Barbados and must spend the last forty years of her life in an asylum. The film begins like a conventional romantic melodrama, but as it progresses we are drawn into the increasingly demented world of the heroine with an impact that is both shocking and hauntingly beautiful. In *The Story of Adèle H.,* Truffaut demonstrates a total mastery of the new cinematic language that he helped to create and triumphantly confirms his status as one of the most important film artists of our time. His films of the late seventies include the comedies *L'Argent de poche* (*Small Change,* 1976) and *L'Homme qui amait les femmes* (*The Man Who Loved Women,* 1977); *La Chambre verte* (*The Green Room,* 1978), based on several short stories by Henry James; and *Le Dernier métro* (*The Last Metro,* 1980), a fascinating account of life in a small Paris theater under the Nazi Occupation—inspired by the autobiography of the stage and film actor Jean Marais (b. 1913)—which became his biggest box-office success. In 1979, Truffaut was honored with an

---

* For the scores of this film and his next three, Truffaut used the music of the great French film composer Maurice Jaubert (1900–40), who had contributed so much to the success of poetic realism (see Chapter 9).

extraordinary twenty-year retrospective by the American Film Institute and the Los Angeles County Museum of Art; but many critics feared he was becoming the kind of mainstream establishment director he had begun his career by attacking. His last two films, however, marked a modest return to the familiar terrain of obsessive romance (*La Femme d'à côté* [*The Woman Next Door,* 1981]) and the Hitchcockian comic thriller *Vivement dimanche* (*Finally Sunday,* 1983; American release title *Confidentially Yours*).* On October 21, 1984, François Truffaut died of a brain tumor; he was fifty-two years old.

Jean-Luc Godard

Jean-Luc Godard (b. 1930) is the most prolific and stylistically radical of all the directors who came to prominence during the New Wave. He has made some twenty-eight feature films since *Breathless* (1960), working closely with Raoul Coutard as his director of photography on most of them, and he is among the most influential figures in world cinema today. Unlike Truffaut, Godard is a militantly intellectual and ideologically committed filmmaker whose films almost always involve some form of *autocritique* or interrogation of cinema itself. In a certain sense, they collectively constitute a *theory* of cinema because, better than any of his peers, Godard understood the essential impulse of the New Wave: "The whole New Wave," he wrote in *Cahiers,* "can be defined, in part, by its new relationship to fiction and reality." Godard's films have consistently tested this relationship by rejecting narrative in favor of *praxis,* the working out of social or political theory within the cinematic process. Since the early sixties, his films have become increasingly dialectical and rhetorical in structure, and Godard himself calls them "critical essays." Most of these "essays" are personal to the point of being idiosyncratic, and Godard has maintained his independence by producing them quickly and cheaply. His films are therefore not as carefully crafted as those of Truffaut and his other peers, and they frequently appear to be less finished films than unvarnished journals about the making of a film, full of technical blunders and undigested facts. And, unlike his peers, Godard is still in the business of breaking every known cinematic convention—even the more recent conventions established by the New Wave itself—in a ceaseless attempt to expand the medium's form and pursue its potential for artistic, intellectual, and political self-expression.

Several of Godard's early films were characteristic New Wave tributes to the American cinema. *A bout de souffle* (*Breathless,* 1960) was modeled on the B-film gangster thriller. *Une Femme est une femme* (*A Woman Is a Woman,* 1961), described by Godard as "a neorealist musical—that is, a contradiction in terms," was a studio-produced tribute to the American musical comedy, made in Franscope and color. *Le Petit soldat* (*The*

13.29 *Une Femme est une femme* (Jean-Luc Godard, 1961): Anna Karina, Jean-Paul Belmondo.

13.30 An *hommage* to Lumière in Godard's *Les Carabiniers* (1963).

---

* *Vivement Truffaut* is the title of a documentary tribute to Truffaut assembled by Claude de Givray for the 1985 Cannes Film Festival; *Finally Truffaut* is a film-by-film guide to the director's work by his friend Don Allen (New York: Beaufort Books, 1985).

Little Soldier, 1960), made between these two films, was banned by the French government for three years because it commented on the Algerian War. Like *Breathless,* it has the form of a gangster film and turns on the theme of betrayal; but its protagonist belongs to a fascist terrorist organization fighting the Algerian liberation front in Geneva, and the film graphically depicts the use of torture by both sides. Both *Le Petit soldat* and *Une Femme est une femme* starred Godard's sensuously beautiful first wife, Anna Karina, and his fourth film seemed intended as a kind of portrait of her. *Vivre sa vie (My Life to Live,* 1962), a study of a woman who chooses to be a prostitute, is constructed in the form of a twelve-part sociological tract on the problem of prostitution, complete with statistics and pseudo-clinical jargon.

With *Les Carabiniers (The Soldiers / The Riflemen,* 1963), an adaptation of Beniamino Joppolo's play *I carabinieri,* cowritten by Roberto Rossellini, Godard created a fable about the nature of war in a style that is both a parody of and an *hommage* to the early documentary style of Lumière. The film, whose narrative line is often fragmented to the point of breaking down, achieves an almost Brechtian detachment from its subject and is clearly among Godard's most important works. It is the first of his "critical essays," for, as one critic has said, *Les Carabiniers* is less a war movie than "a series of propositions about war." *Le Mépris (Contempt,* 1963), based upon Alberto Moravia's novel *A Ghost at Noon,* was Godard's sixth feature. It was an international coproduction starring Jack Palance and Brigitte Bardot shot in widescreen and color, and like Truffaut's *Day for Night* it concerns the making of a movie. This film within the film is a version of Homer's *Odyssey* being shot in Rome by Fritz Lang, who plays himself. The narrative portion of *Le Mépris,* which concerns the dissolution of the scriptwriter's marriage, is less important than Godard's use of the self-reflexive conceit.

13.31 **Image and reality merge in *Les Carabiniers*.**

Godard had disputes with the producers of *Le Mépris* over the editing and scoring of the film, and for his seventh feature he formed his own production company, Anouchka Films. *Bande à part (Band of Outsiders,* 1964) is based upon an American pulp thriller and constitutes Godard's first return to the gangster genre since *Breathless.* It deals with a burglary attempt on the part of three Parisian students—two men and a woman—that ends in tragic farce when one of the would-be criminals is killed. The

13.32 *Le Mépris* (Jean-Luc Godard, 1963): images of image-making Jack Palance, Brigitte Bardot, Michel Piccoli.

13.33 Allusion (to *Jules et Jim*) and pulp violence in Godard's *Bande à part* (1964)—a film, the credits tell us, by "Jean-Luc/Cinema/ Godard": Sami Frey, Anna Karina, Claude Brasseur.

13.34 *Une Femme mariée* (Jean-Luc Godard, 1964): Macha Meril.

13.35 Godard's *Alphaville* (1965): Eddie Constantine as Lemmy Caution, with Anna Karina.

narrative is filmed straightforwardly, but our experience of it is strangely distanced through a running commentary spoken by Godard in which he summarizes the plot for latecomers, tells us what the characters are thinking, makes observations upon the drab suburban setting, or simply reads newspaper headlines. In *Une Femme mariée* (*A Married Woman*, 1964), ironically subtitled "Fragments of a Film Shot in 1964," Godard mixed a wide range of narrative and documentary styles to create a sociological study of woman's role in modern culture. The film portrays twenty-four hours in the life of a married woman who is having an affair, and its visual texture is quite complex: straightforward narration is broken up by three highly stylized scenes of lovemaking, seven *cinéma-vérité*-type interviews with the people around the protagonist, a typically Godardian dissertation on advertising for women's underwear, and a clip from Resnais' *Nuit et brouillard* (1955), which two of the characters watch in a theater.

In *Alphaville* (1965) Godard used the form of the science fiction thriller to create a parable about the alienating effects of technology. At some time in the future, secret agent Lemmy Caution (played by the pop thriller star Eddie Constantine) travels through intergalactic space from the Outer Countries to the City of Alphaville, where his mission is to destroy Dr. von Braun. Von Braun is the inventor and operator of Alpha-60, the computer that runs the desensitized, lobotomized society of Alphaville. Caution succeeds in destroying both the doctor and his invention, and he escapes the crumbling Alphaville with von Braun's daughter. Originally entitled *Tarzan vs. IBM*, *Alphaville* is one of Godard's most sustained and disciplined performances. He makes brilliant use of contemporary Paris to evoke the future, which serves to remind us that the world of Alphaville is already upon us.

In *Pierrot le fou* (*Crazy Pete*, 1965), Godard returned to the disjointed and self-reflexive narrative style of *Les Carabiniers* and to the generic model of the gangster film: a man (Jean-Paul Belmondo) and a woman (Anna Karina) run away from a Parisian gang to live an idyllic, desert-islandlike existence in the south of France, until a series of betrayals causes their horribly violent, if apparently accidental, deaths.* Scriptless and virtually plotless, the film comes close to realizing the Godardian ideal of "a film where there has been no writing, no editing, and no sound mixing." *Masculin / féminin* (1965) marks a definitive turning away from narrative. Like *Vivre sa vie* and *Une Femme mariée*, it is a film of sociological inquiry hung upon a slender plot, but here the plot is almost irrelevant to the inquiry. The film is concerned with illustrating fifteen distinct problems of the younger generation, the "children of Marx and Coca-Cola," members of which are interviewed and interview one another in

---

* The idea for *Pierrot le fou* was almost certainly implanted by David Newman and Robert Benton's screenplay for *Bonnie and Clyde* (Arthur Penn, 1967), which had been submitted for consideration to Truffaut and then passed on to Godard in mid-1965. Godard actually wanted to direct the American script, but only if he could begin shooting immediately—a condition unacceptable to the producers.

cinéma-vérité fashion. Godard shows that their idealism is belied by the world of cynical sex and violence that surrounds them. Since *Masculin / féminin*, Godard's films have become increasingly ideological and, in some cases, structurally random. As he wrote in 1966: "Cinema is capitalism in its purest form. . . . There is only one solution, and that is to turn one's back on the American cinema." The ironic result of this logic was *Made in U.S.A.* (1966).

Though it is loosely based on a detective thriller, *Made in U.S.A.* has no narrative thread at all and is a film intent upon destroying virtually every illusion of which cinema—especially traditional American cinema—is capable. Ostensibly a remake of Hawks' *The Big Sleep* (1946) with Karina in the Bogart role, the film is so self-reflexive as to have no content: characters speak to the audience, explaining their behavior and commenting on the triviality of the plot, the dialogue is nonsensical and sometimes deliberately rendered inaudible on the soundtrack. The film's meaning lies at its periphery, in its comment upon political violence, the viciousness and stupidity of the right, the sentimentality and fecklessness of the left. *Deux ou trois choses que je sais d'elle* (*Two or Three Things I Know About Her*, 1966) is a collage of images and interviews centering around a Parisian housewife who has turned to casual prostitution in order to keep herself in middle-class luxury. The film is a radical indictment of capitalist technocracy in the West, which, Godard holds, makes prostitutes of us all through its system of economic constraints. So too is *La Chinoise* (1967), subtitled *A Film in the Making*, which depicts five students who set up a Maoist cell and fail, each in his or her separate way, to achieve cultural revolution. Godard also contributed a long, single-take monologue to the collective polemic *Loin de Vietnam* (*Far from Vietnam*) produced by SLON in 1967.

But Godard's most savage attack upon the values of Western capitalist

13.36 Lyricism in *pierrot le fou* (Jean-Luc Godard, 1965): Anna Karina.

13.37 Godard's *La Chinoise* (1967): Anne Wiazemsky about to be napalmed by the Esso (now Exxon) tiger.

13.38 Capitalist apocalypse: Godard's *Weekend* (1967), alternately subtitled "A Film Lost in the Cosmos" and "A Film Found on the Scrap Heap." Jean Yanne, Mireille Darc.

society is *Weekend* (1967), a film that begins as a recognizable, if violent, narrative and ends as an apocalyptic vision of the collapse of civilization in the West. A young bourgeois couple set out to visit the woman's mother in Normandy in order to borrow some money from her. They become trapped in a monumental weekend traffic jam, which Godard renders in a single slow lateral tracking shot lasting fully four minutes on the screen. Gradually, we pass from a real landscape into a symbolic one in which the highway is littered with burning automobiles and the bloodied, mutilated bodies of crash victims. From this point on, the film is dominated by images of mindless slaughter and mayhem from which the thin veneer of civilization has been stripped away. When the couple reach the mother's house and are refused the money, they hack her to pieces and steal it.* As they return to Paris, they are overtaken by a band of Maoist renegades armed with submachine guns, who have turned to cannibalism—the mirror image of capitalism, for Godard—to survive. The husband is killed, and his wife joins the group in eating him. *Weekend* is a harsh and brutal film which uses vivid color photography and tight dramatic construction to drive home the point that Western civilization is merely a facade elaborated by technology concealing a hard core of bestiality.

After *Weekend* and the political "events of May" 1968,† Godard attempted to abandon narrative altogether, considering it a bourgeois form. *Le Gai savoir* (1968) is a ramblng cinematic essay on language as an instrument of social conditioning and control, based on the philosophical assumptions of structural linguistics. All of Godard's films between 1968 and 1973 were produced by the Dziga-Vertov Group (actually an uneasy creative partnership between Godard and the ideologist Jean-Pierre Gorin), and Godard came to make increasing use of the arsenal of agitational techniques employed by the Soviet revolutionary cinema of 1924–28. *Un Film comme les autres* (*A Film Like Any Other*, 1968), for example,

---

* Godard remarked to interviewers that his films after *Pierrot* might seem to have a lot of blood in them, but it was really a lot of "red." During this period, *Cahier du cinéma* became politicized along Marxist-Leninist lines—alienating all members of its founding group but Godard, who was militantly committed to this political position. The journal also fell deeply under the influence of Bertolt Brecht's radical theories of theater.

† French society was thrown into an unexpected political crisis in May 1968. Early in the month a series of rallies by student radicals on university campuses in Paris mushroomed into civil disorder. The immediate catalyst for the demonstrations was the firing of Henri Langlois as director of the Cinémathèque Française by the Gaullist minister of culture André Malraux, but the rallies were also related to the recent success of the North Vietnamese Tet offensive in Vietnam and the political upheavals it had produced in the United States and all over the world. By the middle of May, the disturbance had spread beyond Paris to universities in other cities and to unionized workers, some ten million of whom participated in a series of strikes that paralyzed the country. On May 30, however, President Charles de Gaulle (1890–1970) managed to turn the workers against the students by appealing for law and order on national television and calling for new national elections to be held on June twenty-third. On that day, faced with a choice between what the president called "de Gaulle and anarchy," the French people chose the former; but the "events of May" 1968 left many thoughtful Frenchmen in doubt about the legitimacy of their government and continue to haunt those who lived through them.

is a 16mm record of an elementary political discussion that takes place among several people lying in tall grass, none of whom is clearly distinguishable. Godard makes a point of its randomness by suggesting that a coin be tossed to determine which of its two hour-long reels is screened first. *One Plus One* (*Sympathy for the Devil*, 1968) is a film of seemingly unrelated fragments: a Bolivian revolutionary hiding out in a London men's room, the Rolling Stones rehearsing the song "Sympathy for the Devil," black power militants plotting revolution in a junkyard, a television interview with a lobotomized fairy godmother called Eve Democracy, a man reading *Mein Kampf* in a Soho porno shop, etc.

At one point in *One Plus One* a character remarks: "There is only one way to be an intellectual revolutionary, and that is to give up being an intellectual." Some critics believe that Godard followed the logic of this statement to the point of nihilism. All of his films for the now defunct Dziga-Vertov Group—*British Sounds* (*See You at Mao*, 1969), *Pravda*(1969), *Le Vent d'est* (*Wind from the East*, 1969), *Luttes en Italie* (*Struggles in Italy*, 1969), *Vladimir et Rosa* (1970), *Tout va bien* (1972),* and *Letter to Jane* (1972)—show Godard concerned with the nature and function of ideology, regardless of its medium. Although his later work demonstrates a renewed interest in narrative, it has been suggested that Godard's cinematic "essays" are not films in the conventional sense at all but a form of narrative embattled with discourse. Nevertheless, Godard's impact on contemporary cinema generally, as distinct from his importance to the French New Wave, has been immense. As Roy Armes puts it: "He has made a whole generation question the accepted conventions of filmmaking, and his spontaneous, semi-improvised methods of direction have been widely imitated. But he himself remains a solitary, independent figure, pursuing the logic of his own development, totally indifferent to fashion."

Since the end of his assocation with Gorin in 1973, Godard has been experimenting with a combination of film and **videotape** that permits him to superimpose two or more images on the screen simultaneously. In film / tapes like *Numéro deux* (*Number Two*, 1975), *Comment ça va?* (*How Goes It?*, 1975), *La Communication* (1976), *Ici et ailleurs* (*Here and There*, 1970; 1976), and *Six fois deux* (*Six Times Two*, 1976),† he has pioneered a new means of interrogating the cinematic image by offering us two contradictory perspectives on "reailty" at once. In 1980, Godard produced his first theatrical feature in nearly eight years. Technically evocative of his late-sixties films, *Sauve qui peut la vie* (*Every Man*

13.39 Combining video and film in *Numéro deux* (Jean-Luc Godard, 1975).

* The uncharacteristic two-year hiatus in Godard's normally breakneck production schedule was occasioned by a nearly fatal motorcycle accident in June 1971. Although Godard intended the title *Tout va bien* (*All's Well*) as an ironic comment on bourgeois complacency, it also signified his literal well-being in having fully recovered from his injuries. See James Roy MacBean, "Godard and the Dziga-Vertov Group: Film and Dialectics," *Film Quarterly* 26, 1 (Fall 1972): 30–43.

† The last two were made in collaboration with Anne-Marie Miéville. Of *Numéro deux*, Godard said he was remaking *Breathless*, so the title has the ironic force in French of "*Breathless II*."

for Himself / Slow Motion) is an essay on the metaphysics of survival shot on location in Switzerland, that paradigm of Western capitalist survivorship, which characteristically constructs a sustained analogy between sexual degradation and economic exploitation. Godard, who now lives in Switzerland himself, has continued to make features, renewing his extraordinary collaboration with Raoul Coutard in *Passion* (1982), *Prénom Carmen* (*First Name: Carmen*, 1983), and the controversial *Je vous salue Marie* (*Hail, Mary*, 1984), a modern retelling of the immaculate conception that affronted much of the Catholic world. In 1987, Godard—who once said that "one could make a good film in twenty seconds"—began directing jeans commercials for the designers Marithé and François Girbaud (M.F.G.) in exchange for the foreign distribution of his French telefilm *Grandeur et decádence d'un petit commerce de cinéma*—confirming for himself, no doubt, his 1967 declaration that "cinema is capitalism in its purest form." Godard's most recent features are *Detective* (1985), *King Lear* (1986)—a remarkable contemporary "approach" to the play with Burgess Meredith in the title role and Molly Ringwald as Cordelia (and Peter Sellars as Shakespeare), and *Soigne ta droite* (*Keep Up Your Right*, 1987).

Alain Resnais

Alain Resnais is identified with the New Wave because his first major successes, *Hiroshima, mon amour* (1959) and *L'Année dernière à Marienbad* (*Last Year at Marienbad*, 1961), both appeared during its height. But Resnais is a generation older than the *Cahiers* group, and he began his film career not as a critic but as an editor and director of short films in the scenarist tradition. Unlike several of his New Wave counterparts, he prefers to work from an original script, usually one written especially for the screen by a major novelist like Jean Cayrol, Marguerite Duras, Alain Robbe-Grillet, or Jorge Semprun. He also works slowly and plans his films meticulously in advance of production, in close collaboration with his writers and technicians, believing that film is basically a collective art. Yet Resnais is an avant-garde intellectual who has been strongly influenced by the philosophy of Henri Bergson.* And because his major theme is the effect of time on human memory and the relationship between memory and politics, he communicates by exploding the conventional boundaries of narrative form. His almost Proustian fascination with time and memory leads Resnais to create remarkable structures for his films, in which past, present, and future are perceived upon the same spatial and temporal plane, and in which objectivity and subjectivity are never clearly distinguishable.

In *L'Année dernière à Marienbad* (1961), written by French experimental novelist Alain Robbe-Grillet, a man, X, meets a woman, A, at a baroque chateau that seems to be a resort for the very rich and that may

13.40 *L'Année dernière à Marienbad* (Alain Resnais, 1961): **human geometry.**

* Bergson (1859–1941) was a French philosopher whose theories of time and "creative evolution" have had considerable impact upon twentieth-century thought.

or may not be Marienbad (a spa in Czechoslovakia). He claims to have met her, or a woman like her, with a man, M, who was perhaps her husband, "last year at Marienbad." She denies this, and their debate, which is a debate about the nature of reality itself, recurs endlessly through the film as labyrinthine images of past, present, and future framed in Dyaliscope by cinematographer Sacha Vierny seem to merge in the same visual continuum of highly stylized tracking shots (a Resnais trademark) and frozen geometric compositions. X and A seem to have had or to be having or to desire to have an affair; the end is A's death at the hands of her husband. Whether the film represents an attempt to re-create the process of memory in the mind of X, a long interior monologue on the part of A, or an exercise in sheer visual abstractionism, is impossible to say. But, like Bergson's philosophy, the film is clearly concerned with mental process rather than narrative—or perhaps with redefining mental process *as* narrative. As Resnais remarked, *Marienbad* represents "an attempt, still crude and primitive, to approach the complexity of thought and its mechanisms." The film won the prestigious Golden Lion at the Venice Film Festival in 1961 and is one of *the* authentically modernist works in cinema.

In *Muriel, ou le temps d'un retour* (English title: *Muriel,* 1963), written by Jean Cayrol, author of the commentary for *Nuit et brouillard* (1955), Resnais returned to the material world for a film about a mother and her stepson haunted by the past. The mother must confront her lover of twenty-two years past who arrives for a visit accompanied by his most recent mistress, and the stepson is tormented by the memory of Muriel, a young Algerian girl whom he and a friend tortured and killed during the recently concluded French-Algerian War. In terms of content, *Muriel* is a brilliant political film and, although government censors did not recognize it at the time, perhaps the most damning of all films about the Algerian situation as it affected France. But in its remarkably complex montage of nearly a thousand shots, Sacha Vierny's luminous color cinematography, the innovative sound recording of Antoine Bonfanti, and a score featuring the music of avant-garde composer Hans Werner Henze, *Muriel* approaches "the cinema of pure association" and is clearly Resnais' greatest work.

13.41 *Muriel, on le temps d'un retour* (Alain Resnais, 1963): Delphine Seyrig.

With *La Guerre est finie* (*The War Is Over,* 1966), written by the Spanish novelist Jorge Semprun, Resnais entered the arena of political commitment. More conventional in narrative structure and more realistic than his other features, this film still manages to suggest the overlapping of memory and imagination and the relationship that necessarily exists between an individual's past and present and his or her identity. *La Guerre est finie* concerns three days in the life of a middle-aged revolutionary named Diego (Yves Montand) who, some thirty years after the Spanish Civil War, still works for the overthrow of the Franco regime. Diego has come to Paris to plan strategy and see his mistress, but he also has a chance affair there with a radical young student. His sense of identity is called into question by her revolutionary friends, who challenge Diego's methods and his commitment to the struggles of the past. As he re-crosses the border into Spain at the end of the film, he imagines his arrest by

13.42 Resnais' *La Guerre est finie* (1966): Yves Montand.

13.43 *Stavisky* (Alain Resnais, 1975): Jean-Paul Belmondo as Stavisky, Charles Boyer as Baron Raoul.

13.44 John Gielgud as the novelist Clive Langham in Resnais' *Providence* (1977).

Spanish secret police, but through a slow dissolve we see that his mistress is on her way to save him, suggesting the possibility of a new beginning.

After contributing to the 1967 anthology *Loin de Vietnam,* Resnais produced *Je t'aime, je t'aime* (*I Love You, I Love You,* 1968), a science fiction film written by Jacques Sternberg with a score by Krzysztof Penderecki about a man, projected into the past after an unsuccessful suicide attempt, who becomes lost within the structure of time itself. With Chris Marker's short *La Jetée* (1962) and Stanley Kubrick's *2001: A Space Odyssey* (1968)—which also had a score by Penderecki—*Je t'aime, je t'aime* was one of the most provocative science fiction films of the decade. However, its elliptical narrative structure and densely poetic dialogue prevented it from reaching a large audience, and its commercial failure was at least partially responsible for a five-year hiatus in Resnais' career.

During the sixties, Resnais' films, like Godard's, became increasingly unfashionable and unconventional as he pursued the logic of his own artistic development at the cost of financial gain. If Godard's films became critical essays on ideological praxis, Resnais' had always been philosophical investigations into the workings of the human mind, and this meant the loss of popular audiences after his initial success with *Hiroshima, mon amour.* As a result, Resnais was unable to make a film between 1968 and 1974 for lack of financial backing. But in 1975 his *Stavisky* was released to both critical acclaim and commercial success. Written by Jorge Semprun and starring Jean-Paul Belmondo in the paradoxical title role, *Stavisky* is a political period film about a colossal financial scandal which toppled the French government in 1934. With a melodic score by Stephen Sondheim, it was shot by Sacha Vierny to evoke the two-color Technicolor process of the early thirties, and it became Resnais' most popular film to date. *Providence* (1977), scripted by David Mercer, which takes place entirely within the mind of a dying novelist, won an American Academy Award for John Gielgud as Best Actor. Resnais himself won a unanimous Special Jury Prize at Cannes in 1980 for *Mon oncle d'Amérique* (*My Uncle in America*), a narrative of interpersonal relationships poisoned by ambition, based upon the behaviorist theories of the French biologist Henri Laborit, who appears in his laboratory at several points during the film to offer short discourses on the science of "aggressiology." In the eighties, Resnais sustained this metaphor of sociological observation in *La Vie est un roman* (*Life Is a Novel;* British title: *Life Is a Bed of Roses,* 1983), which superimposes three historically distinct stories—each narrated according to contemporaneous cinematic styles—on the quotidian proceedings of an educational conference; *L'Amour à mort* (1984), a film about the archaeology of knowledge set in the southern French Protestant town of Uzés and structured around the avant-garde compositions of Hans Werner Henze; and *Mélo,* an extraordinary real-time adaptation of a 1929 boulevard melodrama by the forgotten playwright Henry Berstein, which had already been filmed five times before. Like *Mon oncle d'Amérique,* all of these last three films were scripted by Jean Gruault, who had worked extensively with Truffaut; none has yet been distributed in the United States.

Frequently accused of coldness and abstractionism, Resnais is a serious, committed filmmaker whose technical mastery of his medium has enabled him to create a handful of films of great visual beauty and intellectual depth that rank among the masterworks of French cinema. When asked, in a recent interview, about the filmmakers who had most influenced him, Resnais mentioned Griffith, Pudovkin, and Eisenstein. He also spoke of the Czech-born British director Karel Reisz (see Chapter 14) as his "real teacher" through Reisz's book *The Technique of Film Editing.** In other words, Resnais clearly sees his work as growing out of the tradition of classical montage. And in his fascination with the manipulation of the space-time continuum, Resnais serves to remind us that montage aesthetics are still alive and well in a film culture that looks to *mise-en-scène* as a kind of cinematic god.

Claude Chabrol

Claude Chabrol (b. 1930), who had been forced to make a series of commercial thrillers after the financial failure of *Les Bonnes femmes* in 1960, returned to the top of his form with *Les Biches* (*The Does*, 1968), a subtle, visually exquisite study of lesbian sexual obsession and domination set in St. Tropez in winter. *Les Biches* marked the beginning of his long collaboration with the cinematographer Jean Rabier (b. 1927), formerly the camera operator for Henri Decaë, who had shot Chabrol's earliest films. Like Resnais, Chabrol believes that filmmaking is a collective enterprise, and since *Les Biches* he has had a team of collaborators who work with him on every film. These include, in addition to Rabier, his coscenarist, Paul Gégauff; his art director, Guy Littaye; his editor, Jacques Gaillard; and his leading actress (and wife), Stéphane Audran.

Chabrol achieved absolute mastery of his medium with *La Femme infidele* (*The Unfaithful Wife,* 1968)—an investigation into the violent consequences of adultery in a typical French bourgeois family—which owes much technically to Hitchcock. Like Truffaut, Chabrol (with Eric Rohmer) wrote a book on Hitchcock; in fact, Chabrol was stylistically influenced by the American director more than was any other figure of the New Wave generation. One critic sees the whole body of Chabrol's work as an extended *hommage* to Hitchcock. But while Chabrol frequently employs Hitchcockian structures and metaphors (such as the simultaneous tracking out and zooming in that occurs near the end of *Vertigo* [1958], and in the final shot of *La Femme infidèle*), he has a theme that is very much his own—the impact of a crime of passion on a small but intimate network of human relationships, such as those that exist within a middle-class family, a love triangle, or even a small community. Chabrol dissects the psychological complexities of these relationships with clinical precision; yet in his mature films this ironic detachment from his material never seems indifferent or cold, and at its best can evoke feelings

13.45 *Les Biches* (Claude Chabrol, 1968): Stéphane Audran, Jacqueline Sassard.

---

* Appropriately, the second edition of Reisz's authoritative manual, cowritten with Gavin Millar (London: The Focal Press, 1968) includes a lengthy analysis of *L'Année dernière à Marienbad*.

13.46 Chabrol's *Le Boucher* (1969): Stéphane Audran, Jean Yanne.

of compassion devoid of sentimentality. Perhaps it is Fritz Lang and his deterministically plotted cinema of destiny (*M*, 1931; *Fury*, 1936; *The Big Heat*, 1953), rather than Hitchcock, whom Chabrol most resembles in this respect.

Que la bête meure (*Killer* / *The Beast Must Die*, 1969) is an ironic revenge tragedy about a man who relentlessly tracks down the driver of an automobile that has killed his young son in a hit-and-run accident and comes to love the murderer's son in the process. Chabrol continued to probe the violence and bestiality that lie just beneath the surface of everyday life in *Le Boucher* (*The Butcher*, 1969), which one Parisian critic hailed as the best French film since the Liberation and which is clearly among the best two or three works to emerge from the immediate post–New Wave period. Told with a remarkable economy and purity of cinematic style, *Le Boucher* is essentially a love story set in a small French village in which one of the lovers is a sexual psychopath given to murdering young women and mutilating their bodies. This "butcher," however, is made the most sympathetic character in the entire film, and the compassionate psychological study of his relationship with a young schoolteacher, who loves him even as she becomes increasingly convinced of his guilt, represents a high point in contemporary French cinema.

Since *Le Boucher*, Chabrol has directed approximately one film a year. *La Rupture* (*The Break-Up*, 1970); *Juste avant la nuit* (*Just Before Nightfall*, 1971); *Le Decade prodigieuse* (*Ten Days' Wonder*, 1972); *Les Noces rouges* (*Blood Wedding*, 1973); *La Banc de desolation* / *De Grey*, two hour-long telefilms based on Henry James stories (1973); *Nada* (English title: *The Nada Gang*, 1974); *La Parti de plaisir* (*A Piece of Pleasure*, 1974) and *Les Innocents aux mains sales* (English title: *Dirty Hands*, 1974); *Les Magiciens* (*The Magicians*) and *Folies bourgeoises* (*Bourgeois Madness*), both 1975; *Alice, ou la derniere fugue* (*Alice, or the Last Escapade*) and *Les Liens de sang* (*Blood Relatives*), both 1977; and *Violette Noziere* (English title: *Violette*, 1978), a macabre film of patricide based on the true story of an eighteen-year-old girl who poisoned her parents in 1933, e.g., were his contributions of the seventies.

Like Truffaut, Godard, and Resnais, Chabrol is a major figure in contemporary French cinema, although his films of the eighties have been uneven. *Le Cheval d'orgueil* (*Horse of Pride*, 1980), for example, was a successful exposition of pre–World War I French country life, but *Les Fantômes du Chapelier* (*The Hatter's Ghosts*, 1982) was a clumsy version of a Georges Simenon novel. *Le Sang des autres* (*The Blood of Others*, 1984), a Simone de Beauvoir adaptation set in occupied Paris, was well received but two subsequent *films noir*—*Poulet au vinaigre* (1985), and its sequel, *Inspector Lavardin* (1986)—were not. In 1987, however, Chabrol returned to form by all measures with the psychological thrillers *Masques* (*Masks*) and *Le Cri du hibou* (*The Cry of the Owl*), while *Une Affaire de femmes* (*Women's Affair*, 1988) won international acclaim for its serious treatment of the last woman to receive capital punishment in France—a provincial housewife tried as an abortionist and sent to the guillotine by the Vichy government in 1943.

Louis Malle

Louis Malle (b. 1932), a former assistant to Bresson and the celebrated underwater filmmaker Jacques-Yves Cousteau (with whom he codirected *Le Monde du silence* [*The Silent World*, 1955]), began his career as a director two years before the debuts of Godard and Truffaut, with the taut suspense thriller *L'Ascenseur pour l'echafaud* (*Frantic* / *Elevator to the Gallows*, 1957) and earned an international reputation the following year with *Les Amants* (*The Lovers*, 1958). This lyrical film about a brief love affair between a bored socialite and a young student for whom she leaves her husband was beautifully photographed by Henri Decaë and produced with Malle's own funds. *Zazie dans le métro* (1960) was an anarchic adaptation of Raymond Queneau's novel about a foulmouthed ten-year-old girl who comes to visit her uncle in Paris and wreaks havoc everywhere she goes. The film is a technically exciting attempt to find visual equivalents for Queneau's neo-Joycean puns through the use of trick shots, superimposition, variable camera speeds, jump cuts, and multiple allusions to other books and films (especially Resnais' *Hiroshima, mon amour*, Fellini's *La dolce vita*, and Malle's own *Les Amants*). Malle continued his experiments in narrative form in *Vie privee* (*Private Life*, 1961), a film about a young provincial girl's rise to stardom based loosely on the experience of its own star, Brigitte Bardot.

But *Le Feu follet* (*The Fire Within* / *Will o'the Wisp*, 1963), adapted by the director from a novel by Drieu La Rochelle, with a piano score by Erik Satie, is regarded as Malle's masterpierce of the sixties. It depicts the last forty-eight hours in the life of an alcoholic playboy who is relentlessly driven to suicide by his disgust at the world around him. Many critics feel that the film's mood of psychological intensity and Malle's sureness of touch in sustaining it bring *Le Feu follet* close to the best work of Bresson. As a change of pace from the brooding atmosphere of *Le Feu follet*, Malle attempted a romantic spectacle in *Viva Maria* (1965), set at the turn of the century, in which Jeanne Moreau and Brigitte Bardot, as traveling entertainers, invent the striptease and foment a revolution in the imaginary South American republic of San Miguel. In *Le Voleur* (*The Thief*, 1967), Malle used a period setting to create a portrait of a wealthy young bourgeois driven to burglary by his hatred of society. His "William Wilson" episode (based on a Poe story) in the anthology film *Histoires extraordinaires* (*Spirits of the Dead*, 1968) hauntingly examines the phenomenon of the *döppelganger*, or "double."

After contributing to the 1967 collective film *Loin de Vietnam*, Malle journeyed to the East to film the feature-length *Calcutta* (1969), part of his brilliant six-hour documentary essay *Phantom India* (1970), for French television. This film, which has also been shown theatrically, offers a marvelously complex vision of the paradoxical subcontinent which has always so fascinated and puzzled the West. Using his own consciousness as a sounding board, Malle ultimately fails to penetrate the Indian mystery, ostensibly by refusing to interpret it through Western eyes. In 1971, Malle produced a masterpiece equal to *Le Feu follet* in the remarkable *Le Souffle au coeur* (*Murmur of the Heart*), a delicate and irresistibly

13.47 *Le Feu follet* (Louis Malle, 1963): Maurice Ronet.

13.48 Mother and son in Malle's *La Souffle au coeur* (1971): Lea Massari, Benoît Ferreux.

funny tale of casual incest among the bourgeoisie of Dijon in 1954—the time of the fall of Dien Bien Phu, Vietnam. Scripted by Malle and sumptuously photographed by Decaë, this film offers an amiable, intelligent, and perversely humorous portrait of middle-class French family life in the postwar era, as well as a sensitive study of the sexual and social agonies of adolescence. Malle's next film, *Lacombe Lucien* (1974), received international acclaim for its subtle portrayal of a seventeen-year-old peasant boy who joins the French Gestapo during the Occupation for no particular reason and is subsequently torn between destroying and protecting a Jewish family with whose daughter he has fallen in love. With *Black Moon* (1975), photographed by the Swedish cinematographer Sven Nykvist (a frequent collaborator of Ingmar Bergman; see Chapter 15), Malle moved from realism to symbolism in a film that the Paris newspaper *L'Express* described as existing "at the crossroads of fantasy and science fiction." In 1978, Malle directed *Pretty Baby* in the United States. Shot entirely on location in New Orleans by Nykvist, this controversial film deals with a love affair between an eccentric photographer and a child prostitute in a turn-of-the-century Storyville brothel. In 1980 Malle turned northward to direct *Atlantic City,* an ironic drama of small-time hoods that shared the Venice Golden Lion that year with John Cassavetes' *Gloria*. Malle's subsequent American films include the brilliant tour-de-force conversation piece *My Dinner with Andre* (1981) and the documentary panorama of recent immigrant experience *And the Pursuit of Happiness* (1986), as well as the less successful *Crackers* (1984), a remake of Mario Monicelli's 1956 caper classic *Big Deal on Madonna Street,* and *Alamo Bay* (1985), a fictionalized account of conflict between Vietnamese immigrants and American fishermen on the Gulf coast of Texas. In 1987, Malle returned triumphantly to France to make the quasi-autobiographical *Au revoir, les enfants (Good-bye, Children)*, a chronicle of a friendship between a Catholic and a Jewish boy set in a provincial boarding school during the last months of World War II.

Malle, unquestionably an important filmmaker, is frequently accused of eclecticism because of his wide range of subjects and styles. Pauline Kael has pointed out that had he chosen a single theme and stuck with it—as Chabrol has done, say, since 1968—Malle would have been acclaimed as a major figure long ago. But Malle's intellectual restlessness and his remarkable ability to present material from simultaneously opposing points of view have led some critics to dismiss him as an elegant stylist with little substance at the core. *Le Feu follet, Phantom India, Le Souffle au coeur, Lacombe Lucien, Atlantic City, My Dinner with André,* and *Au revoir, les enfants* offer ample proof that only the first part of this proposition is true.

Eric Rohmer and Jacques Rivette

The former *Cahiers* critic Eric Rohmer (b. Jean-Marie Maurice Schérer, 1920) began to blossom as a director in the late sixties. His first feature, *Le Signe du lion (The Sign of Leo,* 1959), received virtually no notice in the year of its release, but between 1962 and 1963 Rohmer made the first two of his six "Moral Tales," or *"Contes moraux,"* whose basic theme is the antagonism that exists between personal identity and sexual temptation, or between the spiritual and passional sides of human nature.*

Le Boulanger de Monceau (*The Baker of Monceau,* 1962) and *La Carriere de Suzanne* (*Suzanne's Vocation,* 1963) were both shorts shot in 16mm and produced by Barbet Schroeder, who produced the entire series. Schroeder (b. 1941) became an important director himself in the seventies with *More* (1969); *La Valée* (*The Valley, Obscured by Clouds,* 1972); *Maitresse* (*Mistress,* 1976); *Idi Amin Dada* (1976); *Koko, le gorilla qui parle* (*Koko, the Talking Gorilla,* 1978)—all photographed by Nestor Almendros—and *Les Tricheurs* (*The Cheaters,* 1984) and *Barfly* (1987), both photographed by Robby Muller. *Ma Nuit chez Maud* (*My Night at Maud's,* 1967), *La Collectionneuse* (*The Collector,* 1968), *Le Genou de Claire* (*Claire's Knee,* 1969), and *L'Amour, l'apres midi* (English title: *Chloe in the Afternoon,* 1972) are the 35mm features that complete the *Contes moraux,* providing four more variations on Rohmer's single theme and inaugurating his long-term collaboration with the cinematographer Nestor Almendros. Abstract, intellectual, supremely ironic, these inquiries into the nature of human passion are constructed with all the precision of Cartesian logic, and they have been hailed internationally as components of a philosophical masterpiece. Subsequently, Rohmer made a beautiful, ambiguous version of Heinrich von Kleist's *Die Marquis von O.* (*The Marquise of O.,* 1975) which continues his metaphysical probing of human sexuality in the story of a young noblewoman who awakes one day to find herself inexplicably pregnant. With *Perceval le Gallois* (English title: *Perceval,* 1978), he successfully attempted to evoke the consciousness of the Middle Ages in his own adaptation of a twelfth-century poem by Chrétien de Troyes set in the time of King Arthur. In its stylized sets, artificial scenery, and deliberately foreshortened perspective, *Perceval* captures the mimetic sensibility of both medieval literature and painting; it demands of its viewers a quite extraordinary revision of narrative expectations.

Perhaps because of his late start, Rohmer is one of the few original New Wave figures still consistently producing major work. During the eighties he contributed yet another extraordinary contemporary cycle entitled "Comedies and Proverbs," achieving in *La Femme de l'aviateur* (*The Aviator's Wife,* 1981), *Le Beau marriage* (*The Perfect Marriage,* 1982), *Pauline à la plage* (*Pauline at the Beach,* 1983), *Les Nuits de la pleine lune* (*Full Moon in Paris,* 1984), *Le Rayon vert* (*Summer,* 1986), and *L'Ami de mon amie* (*My Girl Friend's Boy Friend,* 1987) a formal beauty and classical precision unequaled even in his previous work. Like his *Quatre aventures de Reinette et Mirabelle* (*Four Adventures of Reinette and Mirabelle,* 1987), several of these were shot in 16mm and blown up for 35mm theatrical exhibition, as in the earliest days of the New Wave.

13.49 Jean-Louis Trintignant as the protagonist and narrator of *Ma Nuit chez Maud* (Eric Rohmer, 1967).

---

* Rohmer wrote the *"Contes moraux"* as short stories in the late fifties before filming them. They have been published in English as *Six Moral Tales,* trans. Sabine d'Estrée (New York: 1979).

13.50 *Le Religieuse* (Jacques Rivette, 1965): Anna Karina as the novice Suzanne Simonin.

Jacques Rivette (b. 1928), another *Cahiers* critic, and former assistant to both Renoir and Becker, also directed a handful of important films in the sixties that show a marked predilection for literature and the theater. *Paris nous appartient* (*Paris Belongs to Us*, 1960) concerns the members of a Parisian acting troupe who are rehearsing a version of Shakespeare's *Pericles,* and who, through a series of coincidences and insinuations, come to believe themselves enmeshed in a Fascist conspiracy to destroy the world. At the end of the film, this "conspiracy" turns out to be the invention of a paranoid American novelist, but the confusion has caused two deaths and wrecked the lives of everyone involved. Rivette shot *Paris nous appartient* on a day-to-day basis between 1957 and 1959 with money for film stock borrowed from Truffaut and a camera borrowed from Chabrol. (Appropriately, the "film" that the Doinel family goes to see at the Gaumont-Palace in *Les Quatre-cents coups* is *Paris nous appartient,* although it was in fact still in the proccess of production.) None of the cast or crew was paid until after the film's release, at which time the *Cahiers* group issued a joint statement concerning its crucial importance to *la politique des auteurs.* Rivette's film, they wrote, was "primarily the fruit of an astonishing persistence over several years to bring to the screen a personal vision of the world as rich and diverse *as if expressed by any other means*" [italics added].

Rivette's second feature, *La Religieuse* (*The Nun,* 1965), was based upon Denis Diderot's eighteenth-century novel about a woman driven to prostitution and suicide through the hypocrisy of religious orders. This bleak film acquired something of a sensational reputation due to its suppression in France, but its sober camera style and rather conventional narrative structure lend it a seriousness that no amount of scandal can belie. Rivette's third film is his greatest to date, and it too reveals his literary tastes. *L'Amour fou* (*Crazy Love,* 1968) is a four-hour study of the slow disintegration of a marriage set against the filming of a television production of Racine's tragedy *Andromaque,* in which the protagonist of the film plays the lead. Cold, austere, and agonizingly slow, *L'Amour fou* provides Rivette with a laboratory in which to explore questions about the nature of film and stage illusion, as Renoir did in *Le Carrosse d'or* (1952). During the seventies, Rivette made six features—*Out One* (1971), which exists only as a thirteen-hour workprint; *Out One: Spectre* (1972), a four-and-one-half-hour abridgment, or "spectre," of *Out One; Celine et Julie vont en bateau* (*Celine and Julie Go Boating,* 1974); *Duelle* (1976); *Noroit* (1977); and *Merry Go Round* (1978)—but only *Celine et Julie* and *Duelle* have been distributed outside of France.* The eighties saw Rivette continuing to elaborate the mysteries of identity in such vaguely surrealistic films as *Le Pont du nord* (*North Bridge,* 1981) and *L'Amour par terre* (*Love on Earth,* 1984), culminating, oddly, in his most accessi-

---

* *Duelle* and its companion piece, *Sérial* (1976), a deliberate exercise in mystification directed by Rivette's scenarist Eduardo de Gregorio, were featured together at the 1976 New York Film Festival and later released commercially on the east and west coasts. De Gregorio went on to better things in *La Memoire courte* (*Short Memory,* 1979) and *Céline et Julie,* which was released in the United States in 1982.

ble film so far, *Hurlevent* (*Wuthering Heights*, 1985), a straightforward adaptation of the Emily Brontë novel that shifts the setting from nineteenth-century England to the early 1930s in France. Because of his obscurity and artistic integrity, Rivette has had little commercial success with his films, but as to the seriousness of his intent to become a great "novelist" in film there can be no question.

Agnès Varda, Jacques Demy, and Others

Agnès Varda, whose *La Pointe-Courte* (1955) had been something of a New Wave landmark, continued to write and direct fine films in the sixties. Her second feature, *Cléo de cinq à sept* (*Cléo from Five to Seven*, 1962), photographed by Jean Rabier, depicts exactly ninety minutes (the running time of the film) in the life of a young pop singer who is waiting for a lab report that will tell her whether or not she has cancer. *Le Bonheur* (*Happiness*, 1965) is a strangely detached film about a happily married family man whose affair with another woman causes his wife to commit suicide and who proceeds to lead a happy existence with his mistress after his wife's death. The film is highly decorative but ambiguous in terms of psychological and moral considerations. In *Les Créatures* (*The Animals*, 1966), Varda examined the relationship between fantasy and reality in the mind of a writer who talks to animals and cannot distinguish real people from the characters in his novels. Varda also contributed to the collective *Loin de Vietnam* (1967), and in 1969 she came to America to make the improvisational feature *Lion's Love*.

13.51 *Cléo de cinq à sept* (Agnès Varda, 1962): Corinne Marchand.

During the seventies Varda directed the semidocumentary *Daguerréotypes* (1976; French release, 1979), a feature-length study of the rue Daguerre in Paris where she had lived for many years, and *L'Une chante, l'autre pas* (*One Sings, the Other Doesn't*, 1977), a fifteen-year chronicle of two women friends pursuing totally different lifestyles. In the United States once more, Varda made a pair of films that commented on each other—*Murs murs* (*Walls Walls*, 1981), a documentary study of Los Angeles wall murals, and *Documenteur: An Emotion Picture* (1981), a 16mm mood piece about a secretary working on the production of *Murs murs* while taking care of her young son (Varda's own). In *Sans toit ni loi* (*Without a Roof and Beyond the Law;* English title: *Vagabond*, 1985), Varda produced a Bressonian film about an aimlessly drifting teenage girl and the people she meets before her wretched death from exposure. More recently, Varda made a diptych of features on the British actress Jane Birkin, who, since marrying the director Jacques Doillon, has become a French movie star—*Jane B. par Agnès V.* and *Kung Fu Master* (the title of a particularly obsessive video game), both in 1987.

13.52 Varda's *Le Bonheur* (1965): François (Jean-Claude Drouot) and his mistress Emilie (Marie-France Boyer).

Varda's husband, Jacques Demy (b. 1931), became a specialist during the sixties in colorful, bittersweet melodramas reminiscent of poetic realism and the work of Max Ophüls. His *Lola* (1961), which is dedicated to Ophüls and owes much to the fluid camera work of Raoul Coutard, is a gay, lighthearted film about love, set in Nantes and similar in style to *La Ronde*. It has been called "a musical without songs or dances," and it earned Demy an international reputation. *Les Parapluies de Cherbourg*

13.53 *Les Demoiselles de Rochefort* (Jacques Demy, 1966): Catherine Deneuve, Gene Kelly, Françoise Dorleac.

(*The Umbrellas of Cherbourg,* 1964) is an actual musical about a romance between a shop girl and a service station attendant in which the dialogue is sung, as in an opera; it is also notable for the vivid decor of designer Bernard Evein (b. 1929) and the riotous color cinematography of Jean Rabier. *Les Demoiselles de Rochefort* (*The Young Girls of Rochefort,* 1966) is a lively *hommage* to the Hollywood musical directed in collaboration with Gene Kelly. After the American-made *Model Shop* (1968), Demy's work declined into such frivolity as *L'Événement le plus important depuis que l'homme a marché sur la lune* (*The Most Important Event Since Man Walked on the Moon,* 1973)—a film about a pregnant man—and the Japanese-French coproduction *Lady Oscar* (1979), a period romance set during the French Revolution and based on a popular comic strip. In 1982, Demy returned successfully to his all-singing formula with *Une Chambre en ville* (*A Room in Town*), his first French-language film in over eight years, but *Parking* (1985), a pop-musical remake of Cocteau's 1950 *Orphée,* was generally thought to be a failure.

Other noteworthy French filmmakers since the New Wave who have distinct ties with it are Phillipe de Broca (b. 1933), a former assistant to Chabrol and Truffaut, who has become a skilled director of sophisticated comedy and satire (*Cartouche,* 1961; *L'Homme de Rio* [*That Man from Rio,* 1964]; *Le Roi de coeur* [*The King of Hearts,* 1966]; *Tendre poulet* (*Dear Detective,* 1977); *On a volé la cuisse de Jupiter* [*Someone Has Stolen Jupiter's Thigh,* 1980]; *L'Africain* [*The African,* 1983]; *La Gitane* [*The Gypsy,* 1986]; and *Chouans,* 1988).* Also Pierre Étaix (b. 1928), a former circus clown and gag-writer for Jacques Tati, directed a number of excellent comic films (*Le Soupirant* [*The Suitor,* 1962] and *Yoyo* [1965]) in the tradition of Max Linder and Buster Keaton before abandoning the cinema altogether in 1971. The former actor Jean-Pierre Mocky (b. 1929) became a fine and prolific director of iconoclastic comedy in films like *Les Snobs* (1961), *Les Vierges* (*The Virgins,* 1963), and, more recently, *Litan* (1982), *À mort l'arbitre* (*Kill the Referee,* 1984), *Le Pactole* (*The Boodle,* 1985), *La Machine à découdre* (*The Unsewing Machine,* 1986), *Agent Trouble* (*Trouble Agent,* 1987), and *Les Saisons du plaisir* (*The Seasons of Pleasure,* 1988). Alain Robbe-Grillet (b. 1922), the major practitioner of the French *nouveau roman,*† and the scriptwriter for Resnais' *L'Année dernière a Marienbad,* turned to directing in the sixties and seventies with *L'Homme qui ment* (*He Who Lies,* 1968), followed by *Le Jeu avec le feu* (*Playing with Fire,* 1975) and *La Belle captive* (*The Beautiful Prisoner,* 1983). His films are all narratives about the mental process

---

* In 1984, de Broca directed the dual cinema / television superproduction *Louisiane* (*Louisiana*), distributed as both a three-hour theatrical feature and a six-hour video miniseries.

†Literally, the "new novel"—an influential form of avant-garde fiction practiced in France in the fifties and sixties by such writers as Robbe-Grillet, Marguerite Duras (now a filmmaker herself), Nathalie Sarraute, and Michel Butor. Formally influenced by the cinema, the *nouveau roman* was antihumanist in its concentration on the objective, even clinical, description of material phenomena at the expense of character, motivation, and plot. The *nouveau roman* was often "meta-fictional," in that it created narrative metaphors for the process of its own writing (see Robbe-Grillet's *Dans la labyrinth* [*In the Labyrinth,* 1959]).

of constructing narratives, and he makes no distinction between them and his novels, calling both *cine romans* (film novels). In 1973, Jean Eustache (1938–81) contributed perhaps the last authentically New Wave film in *La Maman et la putain* (*The Mother and the Whore*). This provocative 220–minute assault on the intellect and senses focuses on the disillusionment of the generation that produced "the events of May," and it won the Special Jury Prize at Cannes in the year of its release. Unfortunately, Eustache was unable to sustain his success through *Mes petites amoureuses* (*My Little Sweethearts*, 1976) and several later works, and he comitted suicide in the wake of a disabling accident in 1981.

Alain Jessua (b. 1932) produced several important films during the sixties, including the remarkable *La Vie à l'envers* (*Live Upside Down*, 1963), a subjective portrait of the inception of madness, and *Jeu de massacre* (*The Killing Game*, 1967), in which the protagonist becomes so obsessed with the heroes of his favorite comic strip that he can no longer distinguish fantasy from reality. Later, Jessua directed *Traitement de choc* (*Shock Treatment*, 1974), a horror film by genre but thematically a parable of capitalist exploitation of the underdeveloped nations (Portuguese workers are murdered so that their blood may be given to a rich Frenchman undergoing an exotic medical treatment). *Les Chiens* (*The Dogs*, 1979) is a parable of the violence of modern life focusing on the increased use of guard dogs for self-protection by citizens of contemporary France. Jessua continued in this vein with the medical science-fiction film *Paradis pour tous* (*Paradise for All*, 1982); *Frankenstein 90* (1984), a comic version of the classic with a cybernetics genius replacing the doctor; and the *noir* thriller *En toute innocence* (*No Harm Intended*, 1988). The single New Wave feature by Jacques Rozier (b. 1926), *Adieu Philippine* (1962), has acquired the reputation of a minor masterpiece, although it is really something less than that: an engagingly improvised narrative about a Parisian youth in the sixties filmed in *cinéma-vérite* fashion, which contains a hilarious parody of French television. Rozier's only other significant feature, *Du Côté d'Oroüet* (1973), is a hyper-realistic film about the experience of three girls on holiday in Brittany; but his confusing comeback film, *Maine-Océan* (*Maine-Ocean Express*, 1986), seemed to confirm the decadence of New Wave-style auteurism. The Greek-born director Constantin Costa-Gavras (b. 1933), formerly associated with conventional thrillers, developed into a masterful director of political films in the seventies with *Z* (1969) and *L'Aveu* (*The Confession*, 1971)—both shot by Raoul Coutard; *L'État de siège* (*State of Siege*, 1973), *Section spéciale* (*Special Section*, 1975), *Clair de femme* (*Womanlight*, 1979), all starring Yves Montand; and for the American producers Edward and Mildred Lewis (Universal) *Missing* (1981). Costa-Gavras' move recent films, such as *Hannah K* (1983) and *Conseil de famille* (*Family Council*, 1986), suffer from weak scripts or, like *Betrayed* (1988), from excessive polemics.

Much interesting work whose origins are traceable to the New Wave appeared during the seventies in the French-speaking Swiss cinema. The director Alain Tanner's first feature, *Charles mort ou vif* (*Charles Dead or Alive*, 1969), was a characteristic product of the sixties in which a

13.54 *La Salamandre* (Alain Tanner, 1971): Jacques Denis, Bulle Ogier.

middle-aged businessman drops out of bourgeois society, goes to live with some young intellectuals, and is subsequently committed to an asylum by his family. Tanner (b. 1929) had worked at the British Film Institute and for BBC television in London from 1955 to 1958, and he was deeply influenced by the British Free Cinema movement (see Chapter 14) and its New Left ideology. His *La Salamandre* (*The Salamander*, 1971) and *La Milieu du monde* (*The Middle of the World*, 1974), both concerned with day-to-day existence in modern industrial society, have been compared to the best work of Rohmer, while his *Retour d'Afrique* (*Return to Africa*, 1974) is as experimental and politically committed as anything attempted by Godard. With the critical success of *Jonah qui serais 25 dans l'année 2000* (*Jonah Who Will Be 25 in the Year 2000*, 1976), Tanner was proclaimed a major European filmmaker—a status confirmed by his harrowing dissection of Swiss society in *Messidor* (1979) and his wry portrait of Ireland in *Light Years Away* (1981), which won the prize for Best Direction at Cannes. In the eighties Tanner continued his exploration of people living on the social and psychological periphery of the modern urban wasteland with *Dans la ville blanche* (*In the White City*, 1983), set in Lisbon; *No Man's Land* (1985), set on the Franco-Swiss border; and *La Vallée fantome* (*The Ghost Valley*, 1987), set in an Italo-American neighborhood in Brooklyn.

Other Swiss directors with a marked personal style are Jean-Louis Roy—*Black-Out*, 1970; Claude Goretta—*L'Invitation* (*The Invitation*, 1972), *Pas si méchant que ça* (*Not as Wicked as That / The Wonderful Crook*, 1975), *La Dentellière* (*The Lacemaker*, 1977), *Les Chemins de l'exil* (*The Roads of Exile*, 1978), *La Provinciale* (*The Girl from Lorraine*, 1980), *La Mort de Mario Ricci* (*The Death of Mario Ricci*, 1983), *Si le soleil ne revenait pas* (*If the Sun Never Returns*, 1987); Michel Soutter—*L'Escapade* (*The Escapade*, 1973), *Repérages* (English title: *Location Hunting*, 1978), *L'Amour des femme* (*Women's Love*, 1981), *Signé Renaut* (*Signed Renart*, 1987); and Yves Yersin—*Les Petites fuges* (*The Little Escapes*, 1979). Like Tanner, these four French-speaking directors were part of Groupe Cinq (Group Five), a band of young *cinéastes* who came together in 1968 in Geneva to make films in coproduction with Swiss television. At the same time, the country's leading Swiss-German director emerged in Daniel Schmid (*Nacht oder Nie* [*Tonight or Never*, 1972]; *La Paloma* [1974]; *Violanta* [1978]; *Hecate* [1982]; *Il Bacio di Tosca* [*Tosca's Kiss*, 1984]; *Jenatsch* [1987]). By the late eighties, Switzerland was producing more than twenty features a year, most with some form of government subsidy.

The work of Claude Lelouch (b. 1937) is more controversial than that of the filmmakers discussed above because of its blatant appeal to a mass audience. Lelouch uses all the modern narrative techniques of his New Wave counterparts, and he is an *auteur* in the most comprehensive sense of the term in that he produces, directs, writes, photographs, and edits all of his own films (such as *Un Homme et une femme* [*A Man and a Woman*, 1966]; *Vivre pour vie* [*Live for Life*, 1967]). But while these films are visually engaging, they lack emotional depth and have the quality of extended television commercials. There are exceptions in the ingenious comedy-thriller *Cat and Mouse* (1978), and the picaresque *À nous deux* (*Us Two / An Adventure for Two*, 1979), but the work of Lelouch during the eighties (*Les Uns et les autres* [*The Ins and the Outs*, 1981]; *Edith et Marcel* [1983]; *Vive la vie!* [*Long Live Life!*, 1984]; *Partir revenir* [*Departure, Return*, 1985]; *Un Homme et une femme vingt ans déja* [*A Man and a Woman 20 Years Later*, 1986]; *Attention bandits* [*Warning, Bandits*, 1987]) confirms his essential vacuity.

Another French director whose films were largely unaffected by the New Wave but whose recent work has become quite prominent is Claude Sautet (b. 1924). After graduating from IDHEC in 1950 and working as an assistant to both Georges Franju and Jacques Becker, Sautet began his career as a director with a series of *Rififi*-style thrillers (*Classe tous risques* [English title: *The Big Risk*, 1960]; *L'Arme à gauche* [English title: *Guns for the Dictator*, 1965]). During the seventies, he began to collaborate with the scriptwriter Jean-Loup Dabadie and became an astute observer of French bourgeois society, famous for his direction of ensemble playing. Sautet's *Les Choses de la vie* (*The Things of Life*, 1970), *Max et les ferrailleurs* (*Max and the Junkmen*, 1971), *César et Rosalie* (*Cesar and Rosalie*, 1972), *Vincent, François, Paul, et les autres* (*Vincent, François, Paul, and the Others*, 1974), *Mado* (1976), *Une Histoire simple* (*A Simple Story*, 1978), *Un Mauvais fils* (*A Bad Son*, 1980), *Garçon!* (1983), and *Quelques jours avec moi* (*A Few Days with Me*, 1988), all deal with middle-class people trapped at mid-life by the patterns of their own routines, and the films have been much admired for their sympathetic understanding of a class that it has become almost obligatory for contemporary European directors to malign.

Another important French filmmaker not *of* the New Wave but decisively influenced by it is Bertrand Tavernier (b. 1941). Originally a film critic and learned cinéphile, Tavernier in many ways represents a reconciliation between the post-New Wave generation of directors and the "tradition of quality" so roundly attacked by the *Cahiers* school. His

13.55 *Coup de torchon* (Bertrand Tavernier, 1981): Phillipe Noiret, Stephane Audran.

favorite screenplay collaborator, for example, is Jean Aurenche who, with Pierre Bost, had been the prime target of Truffaut's vilification in "A Certain Tendency in French Cinema" in 1954. In fact, Tavernier chose Aurenche and Bost as the scriptwriters for his first feature, *L'Horloger de Saint Paul* (*The Clockmaker*, 1974), an adaptation of a Simenon murder mystery with a metaphysical twist, which is dedicated to another great screenwriter of "quality," Jacques Prévert. Since that time, Tavernier has produced films covering an extraordinary range of material, all of them characterized by a combination of New Wave-style cinematic *éclat* and classically tight narrative construction. *Que la fête commence* (*Let Joy Reign Supreme*, 1975) is an ironic tale of palace intrigue set in the court of Louis XVI; *Le Juge et l'assassin* (*The Judge and the Assassin*, 1976) coolly dissects the symbiotic relationship between a nineteenth-century judge and a serial killer; *Des enfants gâtes* (*Spoiled Children*, 1977) chronicles a filmmaker's May-September romance, as well as his various aesthetic and political commitments; *Le Mort en direct / Death-watch* (1979), Tavernier's first film in English, presents an Orwellian vision of a future world in which the pornography of sex has been replaced by that of death; and *Une Semaine de vacances* (*A Week's Vacation*, 1980) is about a young French schoolmistress' search for identity; like *L'Horloger de Saint Paul*, it is set in his native city of Lyons. Tavernier's two most important films to date are clearly *Coup de torchon* (*Clean Slate / Pop. 1280*, 1981) and *Un Dimanche à la campagne* (*A Sunday in the Country*, 1984), the former a delicious black comedy of adultery and murder adapted from a Jim Thompson novel and set in a French colonial town in West Africa in 1938, and the latter, based on a novella by Pierre Bost, a lyrical account of a day in the life of an aging Impressionist painter, who receives a visit from his grown-up children at his country home in the late summer of 1912. Sublimely photographed by his new collaborator Bruno de Keyzer, *Un Dimanche à la campagne* won Tavernier the Best Director prize at Cannes in the year of its release. These films—together with his documentary on the American South, *Mississippi Blues*

13.56 Tavernier's *Un Dimanche à la campagne* (1984): Sabine Azema, Louis Ducreux.

(codirected with Robert Parrish); *Round Midnight* (1986), a superbly crafted feature about the roots of American jazz; and *La Passion Beatrice* (*The Passion of Beatrice*, 1987), a dark and violent period piece set in the fourteenth century during the Hundred Years War—have insured Tavernier's position as the most respected French filmmaker of his generation. As a producer, he has also given many younger *cinéastes* their first opportunities to direct, and as president of the French directors guild, La Société des Realisateurs de Films, Tavernier has become a major force within the leadership of the domestic industry.

Other prominent post–New Wave directors are Maurice Pialat (b. 1925), Bertrand Blier (b. 1939), Alain Corneau (b. 1943), Claude Miller (b. 1942), and Diane Kurys (b. 1949). Pialat was a much acclaimed television director when he started making a series of powerful, emotionally confrontational features with *L'Enfance nue* in 1969, which concerned the problems of an unwanted child; then came *Nous ne viellirons pas ensemble* (*We Won't Grow Old Together*, 1972), which dealt with the breaking up of a love affair, and *La Gueule ouverte* (*The Mouth Agape*, 1974), which many consider to be his masterpiece, about a woman's losing battle with cancer. The uncompromising nature of Pialat's material and his contentious methods of working with actors have kept the quantity of his output relatively low, but in films like *Passe ton bac d'abord* (1979), a chronicle of teenage life in a provincial town, *Loulou* (1980), a violent tale of working-class sexual passions, and *A nous amours* (1983), a disturbing film on the dissolution of bourgeois family life, Pialat achieved an intensity of vision unrivaled in the French cinema. Recently he has made a metaphysical detective thriller, *Police* (1985), and an extraordinary adaptation of Georges Bernanos' 1926 novel *Sous le soleil de Satan* (*Under the Sun of Satan*, 1987).

After several false starts in the sixties (e.g., *Hitler, connais pas*, 1963), Bertrand Blier found his metier in anarchic sexual comedy, often featuring the seduction of adults by children (*Les Valseuses* [English title: *Going Places*, 1974] and *Preparez vos mouchoirs* [*Get Out Your Handkerchiefs*, 1977]); incest (*Beau-pere*, 1981); and, of course, the classical ménage à trois (*La Femme de mon pôte* [*My Best Friend's Girl*, 1983] and *Tenue de soirée* [*Evening Dress*, 1986]). Blier's other vein is the Buñuelian allegory of *Buffet froid* (*Cold Cuts*, 1979) and *Notre histoire* (*Our Story / Separate Rooms*, 1984). Blier's most recent film is the intricately structured comedy of adultery *Trop belle pour toi* (*Too Beautiful for You*, 1989). Deeply influenced by American cinema,* especially the crime thriller, Alain Corneau appropriated the ever popular *"policier"* genre as a vehicle for social criticism in such sober and deliberately paced films as *France société anonyme* (*France, S.A.*, 1974), *Police Python 357* (1976), *La Menace* (1977), *Série noire* (1979), and *Les Choix des armes* (*Choice of Weapons*, 1981), turning briefly to the colonial epic *Fort Saganne* (1984— reputedly the most expensive film made in France to date), before resum-

---

* Always popular with French audiences and filmmakers alike, American movies climbed from 27 to 37 percent of total box-office returns between 1976 and 1986, making France the largest export market for the U.S. film industry after Canada and Japan.

ing his engagement with the urban underworld in *Le Môme* (*The Kid*, 1986). Claude Miller, a former assistant to both Truffaut and Godard, has produced a small body of high quality films that have won him an international critical following; Miller's best works—*La Meilleur façon de marcher* (*A Better Way of Walking*, 1975), *Dites-lui que je l'aime* (*Tell Her That I Love Her*, 1977), *Garde à vue* (English title: *The Grilling*, 1981), *Mortelle randonée* (*Deadly Circuit*, 1983), and *L'Effrontée* (*The Hussy*, 1985)—deal persuasively with the theme of obsession and are clearly influenced by the style of American *film noir*. In 1989, Miller directed *La Petite Voleuse (The Little Thief)*, a lively homage to Truffaut based on a script by him and longtime collaborator Claude de Givray. The films of Diane Kurys, on the other hand, have all been vaguely autobiographical and yet charmingly eclectic—*Diable menthe* [*Peppermint Soda*, 1979] is about the quotidian lives of teenage sisters, 1963–64; *Cocktail Molotov* (1980) concerns her own participation in "the events of May" 1968, *Coup de foudre* (also known as *Entre nous,* 1983) deals with the friendship of two young women in the period 1952–53, and is modeled on the experience of her parents, and so on, leading finally to her much accclaimed English-language film *Un Homme amoureux* (*A Man in Love*, 1987).

In the field of documentary cinema, Chris Marker (b. Christian Francois Bouche-Villeneuve, 1921) has produced a number of brilliant film essays (*Cuba sí*, 1961; *Le Joli mai*, 1963; *Le Mystere Koumiko*, 1965), as well as the Bergsonian science fiction short *La Jetée* (1962), composed almost entirely of still photographs. Marker is a close associate of Resnais' and the chief organizer of SLON, the film cooperative that produced *Loin de Vietnam* (1967) and several other political documentaries of the era. In 1977, Marker made the striking four-hour compilation film *Le Fond de l'air est rouge* (literally, *The Essence of the Air Is Red*), a documentary on the state of radical politics in France in the mid-seventies. More recently, he has produced *Sans soleil* (*Sunless,* 1983), a remarkable meditation on obsession and repetition that won the British Film Institute award and *A.K.* (1985), a documentary portrait of Akira Kurosawa at work on *Ran* (see Chapter 17). The work of the *cinéma-vérité* documentarist Jean Rouch (b. 1917—*Chronique d'un été* [*Chronicle of a Summer*, 1961] and *La Punition* [*Punishment*, 1963], and that of Mario Ruspoli (b. 1925—*Les Inconnus de la terre* [*The Unknown of the Earth*, 1961]) had wide influence during the sixties on both the documentary (in the films of the Americans D. A. Pennebaker, Albert and David Maysles, and Frederick Wiseman) and the narrative cinema (in the work of Rozier, Godard, and Tanner, and in countless individual French, Swiss, Italian, West German, British, and American films). In the seventies, Rouch continued to produce distinguished ethnographic films, focusing mainly on black African culture (*Funérailles à Bongo: le vieux Anai, 1849–1971* [*Funeral in Bongo: Old Anai, 1849–1971*, 1979]), but in the eighties he turned to such unusual features as *Brise-glace* (*Icebreaker,* codirected with Titte Törnroth and Raúl Ruiz, 1988) and *Enigma* (1988).

The most prominent French documentarist, however, is Marcel Ophüls (b. 1927), the son of the great postwar director Max Ophüls. Marcel

13.57 Citizens of Paris in *Le Joli mai* (Chris Marker, 1963).

13.58 *Le Chagrin et la pitié* (Marcel Ophüls, 1971): Hitler admiring the Eiffel Tower after his troops have occupied Paris.

Ophüls' masterpiece is the four-and-a-half-hour *Le Chagrin et la pitié* (*The Sorrow and the Pity*, 1971), a shattering documentary that mixes newsreel footage with contemporary interviews in an attempt to assess the impact of the Nazi Occupation on the provincial city of Clermont-Ferrand and, by extension, on the whole of France. The verdict is that, except for the systematic murder of Jews and of those non-Jews who openly opposed the Nazis, business went on very much as usual during the Occupation, largely because the Nazis obtained the cooperation of most of the French bourgeoisie and because the existence of a large, efficiently coordinated Resistance movement was a myth propagated after the war. Originally made for Swiss and West German television companies, *Le Chagrin et la pitié* was not shown on French television (ORTF), a state monopoly, until 1981, but as a theatrical release in France and abroad it received much attention. Ophüls' more recent films are *A Sense of Loss* (1974), which chronicles the plight of Northern Ireland, and *A Memory of Justice* (1976), a remarkable documentary meditation on collective guilt that counterposes the question of the Nazi death camps and the Nuremberg war crimes trials with that of French atrocities in Algeria and American atrocities in Vietnam. The difficulties of trying to get the latter distributed against the wishes of myriad political censors and special interest groups led Ophüls to give up filmmaking for over a decade, and to turn to writing instead. In 1987, however, he renewed his filmic confrontation with history in *Hotel Terminus: Klaus Barbie, His Life and Times*. Released at 267 minutes in 1988, this film was shot on three continents and concluded with the unrepentant Nazi's widely publicized trial. Ophüls' documentary influence can be seen most clearly in the work of his friend Claude Lanzman, whose astonishing nine-and-a-half-hour meditation on the Holocaust, *Shoah* (1985—from the Hebrew word for annihilation), was assembled from 350 hours of interviews and took ten years to produce.

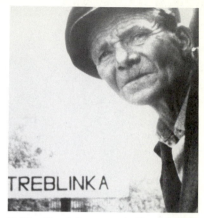

13.59 Claude Lanzmann's *Shoah* (1985): a Polish railroad engineer who worked the tracks running into the death camp Treblinka.

13.60 *L'homme à crane rasé* (André Delvaux, 1966).

THE SIGNIFICANCE OF THE NEW WAVE

The impact of the French New Wave upon world cinema would be difficult to overestimate. The movement can be credited with almost singlehandedly revitalizing the stagnant British and American cinemas during the sixties, and it produced similar chain reactions in Italy, West Germany, Eastern Europe, and indeed around the world. To suggest that the New Wave was a monolithic phenomenon is simplistic. Varda, Resnais, Marker, and Malle, for example, evolved from a completely different context than did Truffaut, Godard, Chabrol, Rivette, and Rohmer. The former had begun their filmmaking careers as assistants and editors within the established industry; the latter had begun theirs as theorists and critics in total revolt against the industrial system.* And all of them, of course, went their separate artistic ways in the later sixties and seven-

13.61 *La rouge aux Levres (Daughters of Darkness* [Harry Kumel, 1971]: Delphine Seyrig, Daniele Ouimet, John Karlen.

---

* Rivette alone among the *Cahiers* group had received some practical training as an assistant director to Renoir and Becker in the early fifties.

ties. But two common notions bound them together and made their films vastly important to the evolution of narrative cinema. First, they believed that film was an art form that could provide an artist with a medium of personal expression as rich, as varied, and as sensitive as any other. This assumption is implicit in the concept of personal authorship, or *la politique des auteurs,* according to which film directors are not simply analogous to writers of novels but are literally capable of "writing novels" in the audiovisual language of film. Second, they shared the belief that the narrative conventions they had inherited from the thirties and forties were insufficient to achieve these ends, that in fact many of these conventions prevented the audiovisual language of film from approaching its full range of expression. So they broke the old conventions and established new ones in the process, elaborating an audiovisual language that could express a whole gamut of internal and external states. This is implicit in the notion of *mise-en-scène,* according to which a film should not be simply a succession of meaningful images telling a story but an all-engrossing, mind- and sense-engaging experience. The number of major filmmakers who emerged from the New Wave and who are still in the process of making ever greater and more influential features is astounding. But even more astounding is the impact that these new ideas about audiovisual language and its operations have had and continue to have upon the international cinema at large. By calling into question the very form and process of narrative cinema, the filmmakers of the New Wave insured that the cinema could never again rely upon the easy narrative assumptions of its first fifty years.

New Cinemas in Britain and the English-Speaking Commonwealth

GREAT BRITAIN

Postwar British Cinema and Its Context

While the French were experiencing the New Wave, the British were enjoying a film renaissance of their own. Before World War II, Britain had produced a vastly important contribution to documentary cinema in the government-funded work of John Grierson (see Chapter 9) and his protégés Alberto Cavalcanti (1897–1982)—*Coalface*, 1935; Paul Rotha (b. 1907)—*Shipyard*, 1935, and *The Face of Britain*, 1935; Basil Wright (1907–87)—the four-part *Song of Ceylon*, 1934, and *Children at School*, 1937); Arthur Elton (b. 1906) and Edgar Anstey (b. 1907)—*Housing Problems*, 1937; Stuart Legg (b. 1910)—BBC—*The Voice of Britain*, 1935; Harry Watt (b. 1906)—*Night Mail*, co-directed with Wright, 1936 and *The North Sea*, 1938; and Humphrey Jennings (1907–50)—*Spring Offensive*, 1939. All of these directors had trained under Grierson in 1933 at the General Post Office (GPO) Film Unit, which had succeeded the Empire Marketing Board (EMB) Film Unit. It was renamed the Crown Film Unit in 1940 and became part of the Ministry of Information (MOI).

During the war, the Crown Film Unit moved toward a blending of narrative and documentary form in such films as Watt's *London Can Take It* (1940) and *Target for Tonight* (1941); Jenning's *Heart of Britain* (1941), *Words for Battle* (1941), *Listen to Britain* (1941), and *Fires Were Started* (1943); and Pat Jackson's *Western Approaches* (1944; Technicolor). Meanwhile the commercial industry produced quasidocumentary features praising the armed forces—the navy, in *In Which We Serve* (Noel Coward, 1942); the army, in *The Way Ahead* (Carol Reed, 1944); the air force, in *The Way to the Stars* (Anthony Asquith, 1945); and the home front, in *Next of Kin* (Thorold Dickinson, 1942), *Went the Day Well?* (Alberto Cavalcanti, 1942), and *Millions Like Us* (Frank Launder and Sidney Gilliat, 1943). Since the innovations of the Brighton school at the turn of the century, however, Britain had produced little significant narrative cinema, outside of the work of Alfred Hitchcock; the films directed or produced by Alexander Korda (1893–1956)—*The Private*

14.1 Part of the futuristic "Everytown" set in *Things to Come* (William Cameron Menzies, 1936).

14.2 Anthony Asquith's adaptation of Shaw's *Pygmalion* (1938): Leslie Howard and Wendy Hiller as Henry Higgins and Eliza Dolittle.

14.3 Laurence Olivier in his production of *Hamlet* (1948).

14.4 Pip confronts Magwitch in David Lean's adaptation of Dickens' *Great Expectations* (1946): John Mills, Finlay Currie.

Life of Henry VIII, 1933; *Rembrandt*, 1936; *Things to Come*, directed by William Cameron Menzies, 1936; *The Thief of Bagdad*, codirected by Tim Whelan, Ludwig Berger, and Michael Powell, 1940; and such stage adaptations of Anthony Asquith (1902–68) as *Pygmalion*, co-directed with Leslie Howard, 1938. This paucity of important British narrative film resulted from the long domination of the industry by Hollywood. Most British commercial production was geared toward making second features to accompany American films on double bills.

During and after World War II, however, a traditional staple of native British cinema—literary adaptation—experienced a sharp upswing. Two lavish Technicolor productions—Gabriel Pascal's version of George Bernard Shaw's *Caesar and Cleopatra* (1945) and Korda's translation of Oscar Wilde's *An Ideal Husband* (1947)—proved to be expensive failures. But the actor-director Laurence Olivier (1907–89) offered distinguished adaptations of three plays by Shakespeare—*Henry V* (1944; Technicolor); *Hamlet* (1948), the first British production ever to receive an American Academy Award as Best Film; and *Richard III* (1955; Technicolor and VistaVision). And David Lean (b. 1908), after adapting several plays of Noel Coward's (*Blithe Spirit*, [1945], and *Brief Encounter*, [1945], among them), produced two carefully crafted, atmospheric adaptations of Charles Dickens' works, *Great Expectations* (1946) and *Oliver Twist* (1947), both models of their form. Anthony Asquith's stylish adaptations of Terence Rattigan's plays *While the Sun Shines* (1947), *The Winslow Boy* (1948), and *The Browning Version* (1951), and of Oscar Wilde's play *The Importance of Being Earnest* (1952; Technicolor), were matched by a brilliant expressionistic version of Alexander Pushkin's story *The Queen of Spades* (1949), directed by Thorold Dickinson (b. 1903). Carol Reed (b. 1906) directed *Odd Man Out* (1946), *The Fallen Idol* (1948), and *The Third Man* (1949), the latter two adapted from stories by Graham Greene), and *Outcast of the Islands* (1951; adapted from Joseph Conrad's novel). These finely wrought dramatic narratives were resonant at their best of French poetic realism and the films of Orson Welles. *The Red Shoes* (1948) and *Tales of Hoffman* (1951), the extravagant ballet spectaculars made by Michael Powell (b. 1905) and Emeric Pressburger (1903–88) also appeared during this period. So, too, did the best work of the twin Boulting brothers, John (1913–85) and Roy (b. 1913), who alternated as producer and director on such fine postwar films as *Brighton Rock* (1947; adapted from the Graham Greene novel), *The Magic Box* (1951; the story of William Friese-Greene, the putative inventor of the first British cinema machines), *Lucky Jim* (1957; adapted from the Kingsley Amis novel), and *I'm All Right, Jack* (1959).

Among the most important British films of the postwar era was a series of intelligent and witty comedies made for Michael Balcon's family-run Ealing Studios. These films were directed by Charles Crichton (b. 1910)—*Hue and Cry*, 1947; *The Lavender Hill Mob*, 1951; *The Titfield Thunderbolt*, 1953; by Alexander Mackendrick (b. 1912)—*Whisky Galore / Tight Little Island*, 1949; *The Man in the White Suit*, 1951; *The Ladykillers*, 1955; by Henry Cornelius (1913–58)—*Passport to Pimlico*, 1948;

14.5 Maligned masterpiece: Michael Powell's *Peeping Tom* (1959). Anna Massey, Carl Boehm.

14.6 *The Red Shoes* (Michael Powell and Emeric Pressburger, 1948): Moira Shearer, Robert Helpmann, Leonide Massine.

14.7 *Kind Hearts and Coronets* (Robert Hamer, 1949): Alec Guinness surrounds Valerie Hobson with six of his eight incarnations in Ealing Studios' most famous comedy.

Genvieve, 1953; and by Robert Hamer (1911–63)—*Kind Hearts and Coronets*, 1949; *Father Brown*, 1954. The splendid work of the actor Alec Guinness (b. 1914) in a number of these films made him an international star. The omnibus film *Dead of Night* (1945), codirected by Alberto Cavalcanti, Robert Hamer, Charles Crichton, and Basil Dearden, is also a landmark of British postwar cinema because of its convincing *mise-en-scène* and circular narrative structure.

By the mid-fifties British cinema had begun to decline into cliché, and Britain was once again in danger of becoming a Hollywood colony. As early as 1947, the Oxford University film journal *Sequence* (1947–52), edited by the future directors Lindsay Anderson (b. 1923) and Karel Reisz (b. Czechoslovakia, 1926), had attacked the controlling assumption of British cinema: "The British commercial cinema has been a bourgeois rather than a revolutionary growth; and it is not a middle-class trait to

14.8 Alberto Cavalcanti's "The Ventriloquist's Dummy" episode in *Dead of Night* (Cavalcanti, Hamer, Crichton, and Dearden, 1945): Michael Redgrave, with John Maguire as Hugo the dummy.

examine oneself with the strictest objectivity, or to be able to represent higher or lower levels of society with sympathy and respect."

Anderson and Reisz went on to act upon their beliefs in 1954 and 1955 by organizing the **Free Cinema** movement, which, like Italian neorealism, celebrated, as a manifesto put it, "the importance of the individual and . . . the significance of the everyday." Like the French New Wave, the Free Cinema movement was dedicated to the belief that film should be a medium of personal expression for the filmmaker, who should be socially committed to illuminating the problems of contemporary life.

The Free Cinema Movement

In practice, Free Cinema meant the production of short, low-budget documentaries like Anderson's *O Dreamland* (1954), a satirical assault on the spiritual emptiness of working-class life, set in an amusement park, and Reisz's and Tony Richardson's *Momma Don't Allow* (1956), a study of postwar youth in the environment of a London jazz club. Between February 1956 and March 1959, the Free Cinema movement presented a series of six programs at the National Film Theater that featured most prominently *O Dreamland; Momma Don't Allow; Every Day Except Christmas* (1959), Anderson's study of Covent Garden flower and vegetable vendors; *We Are the Lambeth Boys* (1958), Reisz's portrait of a South London youth club; and a number of recent Continental films: Georges Franju's *Le Sang des bêtes* (1949); Alain Tanner and Claude Goretta's *Nice Time* (1957, shot in Piccadilly Circus; see Chapter 13); François Truffaut's *Les Mistons* (1957); Roman Polánski's *Two Men and a Wardrobe* (*Dwaj ludzie z szafa*, 1958; see Chapter 16); and Claude Chabrol's *Le Beau Serge* (1958).

At the time that the Free Cinema movement emerged, a revolution was under way in British theater and literature in which liberal working-class values emanating from the East End of London and the provinces were overturning the established bourgeois tradition of the preceding decades. John Osborne's anti-establishment diatribe *Look Back in Anger* rocked the world of traditional culture when it was staged at the Royal Court Theatre in May 1956 by calling into question the whole class structure of British society and assailing the moral bankruptcy of the welfare state.* The following years witnessed the appearance of a new group of young, anti-establishment, working-class novelists, such as David Storey, John Braine, Alan Sillitoe, and Shelagh Delaney, who treated similar themes in a style that can be accurately characterized as "social realism." By 1959— significantly, the year that the French New Wave won a great number of the prizes at Cannes—the time was ripe for the overthrow of the class-bound British feature cinema in favor of working-class social realism.

In that year, the industry itself produced two films that announced the revolution: Jack Clayton's (b. 1921) adaptation of John Braine's novel

---

* Since World War II, Britain has had one of the highest degrees of state ownership and one of the most comprehensive welfare systems in Western Europe.

Room at the Top and Tony Richardson's adaptation of *Look Back in Anger,* scripted by the author. Both films were big-budget commercial productions with well-known stars that nevertheless dealt seriously with the disillusionment and frustration of the British working classes, and both were international hits. *Look Back in Anger* was so successful, in fact, that Richardson (b. 1928) and Osborne (b. 1929) were able to form, with the financial backing of producer Harry Saltzman (later responsible for the slick James Bond series), their own production company, the short-lived but influential Woodfall Films (1959–63). In Woodfall's first feature, coproduced with Holly Films, Richardson collaborated with Osborne again to adapt his second play, *The Entertainer* (1960). It starred Laurence Olivier as the seedy music-hall comedian Archie Rice and was partially shot on location in Blackpool. Woodfall's first completely independent production, Karel Reisz's *Saturday Night and Sunday Morning* (1960), a version of the Alan Sillitoe novel, was shot on location in Nottingham with unknown actors for a budget of under three hundred thousand dollars, or less than one-third of the standard feature allocation. But it recovered this figure in the first two weeks of its London run alone and went on to become the biggest international success the British film industry had known since the thirties.

14.9 *Look Back in Anger* (Tony Richardson, 1959): Richard Burton, Mary Ure.

British "New Cinema," or Social Realism

Saturday Night and Sunday Morning became the prototype for what may be fairly labeled British "New Cinema," a social-realist film movement whose themes were borrowed from Italian neorealism and whose techniques were modeled upon the Free Cinema documentary of the late fifties and the films of the French New Wave.* The New Cinema movement's films were generally set in the industrial Midlands and shot on location in black and white against the gloomiest backgrounds their makers could find. The films featured unknown young actors, and their protagonists were typically rebellious working-class youths like Richardson / Osborne's Jimmy Porter or Reisz / Sillitoe's Arthur Seaton—youths who were contemptuous of the spiritual torpor that had been induced in their parents and friends by the welfare state and by mass communications, as exemplified by the BBC. The films' heroes spend a good deal of their time in pubs, drinking and brawling, and use a tough vernacular speech until then unheard in British cinema. Major New Cinema productions include Tony Richardson's *A Taste of Honey* (Woodfall, 1961; script by Shelagh Delaney) and *The Loneliness of the Long Distance Runner* (Woodfall, 1962; adapted from a Sillitoe novel); John Schlesinger's *A King of Loving* (1962) and *Billy Liar* (1963); Lindsay Anderson's *This Sporting Life*

14.10 *Saturday Night and Sunday Morning* (Karel Reisz, 1960): Shirley Anne Field, Albert Finney, Norman Rossington.

---

* Another film of 1960 that forecast social realism was *The Angry Silence,* coproduced by Bryan Forbes and Richard Attenborough and directed by Guy Green. Shot on location in the Midlands, the film deals with the manipulation of an industrial strike by communist agitators, and though it shares many formal characteristics with *Saturday Night and Sunday Morning, The Angry Silence* is as politically equivocal as was Elia Kazan's *On the Waterfront,* which probably inspired it.

14.11 *A Taste of Honey* (Tony Richardson, 1961): Rita Tushingham, Robert Sevens.

14.12 Richardson's *The Loneliness of the Long Distance Runner* (1962): Tom Courtenay (no. 14) in the lead.

14.13 *A Kind of Loving* (John Schlesinger, 1962): Alan Bates, June Ritchie.

14.14 Schlesinger's *Billy Liar* (1963): Billy (Tom Courtenay) daydreams of military glory.

14.15 *This Sporting Life* (Lindsay Anderson, 1963): Richard Harris as a second-rate Yorkshire rugby player.

(produced by Reisz, 1963); Canadian-born Sidney J. Furie's *The Leather Boys* (1963); and Karel Reisz's *Morgan: A Suitable Case for Treatment* (1966).

14.16 Anarchic violence at the conclusion of *If* . . . (Lindsay Anderson, 1968).

Like the French New Wave, British New Cinema reached its peak around 1963 and then rapidly declined as a movement while its directors went their separate ways. During the mid-sixties, in fact, a reaction to the bleakness of social realism set in, and the depressing images of the industrial Midlands were replaced by those of "swinging London" in big-budget widescreen color productions like *Alfie* (Lewis Gilbert, 1966), *Smashing Time* (Desmond Davis, 1967), and *Joanna* (Michael Sarne, 1968), all of which, however, did have working-class protagonists. Nevertheless, Lindsay Anderson continued to pursue anti-establishment themes in *If* . . . (1968), a brilliant film about the nature of individualism and authority cast in the form of a surrealist satire on the British public school system. One of the sixties' most important films, *If* . . . can be favorably compared with Vigo's *Zéro de conduite* (1933), to which it contains several explicit allusions; it established Anderson as the most influential figure to emerge from the New Cinema movement. In Anderson's powerful *O Lucky Man!* (1973), whose mock-poetic title refers back to his first film, *O Dreamland*, the protagonist of *If* . . . continues his education through the various levels of corruption in London society, only to be totally corrupted himself at the end of the process—by being "discovered" by the director Lindsay Anderson to star in a motion picture entitled *O Lucky Man*. *Britannia Hospital* (1982) continued Anderson's dissection of the contemporary British psyche in an unsparing absurdist satire on labor strikes, racial tensions, and the misuse of the National Health Service by doctors and patients alike. More recently, he directed *The Whales of August* (1987), a delicate mood piece adapted by David Berry from his own 1981 play, about two elderly sisters (played in the film by Bette Davis and Lillian Gish) living out their last years in a family home on the coast of Maine.

After an impressive start in *Saturday Night and Sunday Morning*, the work of Karel Reisz generally declined during the sixties (e.g., *Isadora*, 1968), with the exception of *Morgan* (1966; also known as *Morgan: A Suitable Case for Treatment*), a subtle and painfully funny film about mental breakdown. But Reisz's intelligent, American-made *The Gambler* (1975) signaled renewed vigor. His second American feature, *Who'll Stop the Rain?* (1978), a corrosive adaptation of Robert Stone's best-selling allegorical thriller *Dog Soldiers*, about heroin smuggling during the Vietnam war, marked his return to prominence His version of John Fowles' complex "Victorian" novel *The French Lieutenant's Woman* (1981), scripted by Harold Pinter and strikingly photographed by Freddie Francis, was a triumph of the filmmaker's art. More recently, Reisz has directed *Sweet Dreams* (1985), an intelligent biography of country singer Patsy Cline, who was killed in a plane crash at the height of her success. Wherever Reisz's far-ranging aesthetic sensibilities lead him next, it should be noted that his important book, *The Technique of Film Editing*, has greatly influenced such major film artists as Alain Resnais.

14.17 *The Charge of the Light Brigade* (Tony Richardson, 1968): Ben Aris, Corin Redgrave.

14.18 *Sunday, Bloody Sunday* (John Schlesinger, 1971): Glenda Jackson, Murray Head.

The same general falling-off was seen in the work of Tony Richardson, who, after a series of three excellent working-class films and the flamboyant period comedy *Tom Jones* (1963; adapted from Henry Fielding's novel), abandoned social commitment for big-time commercial cinema. Since then, most of his films, like the American-made *The Loved One* (1965), have been failures. But a filmmaker of substantial verve is still perceptible in *The Charge of the Light Brigade* (1968), *Ned Kelly* (1970), and *Joseph Andrews* (1977), another Fielding adaptation. More recently, Richardson has been working in the United States to produce *The Border* (1981), a tale of passion and intrigue on the Mexican-American border, and *The Hotel New Hampshire* (1984), an adaptation of John Irving's rambling chronicle of an eccentric American family.

John Schlesinger (b. 1926), who began his career as a BBC documentarist, has been much more successful artistically than either Reisz or Richardson. He made his first feature, *A Kind of Loving,* in 1962. After *Billy Liar* (1963), he achieved great commercial success with *Darling* (1965), a modish examination of upper-class decadence filmed *à la nouvelle vague,* which brought Julie Christie to stardom. During the seventies, Schlesinger specialized in stylish and cinematically intelligent films such as *Far from the Madding Crowd* (1967; from the Thomas Hardy novel), *Midnight Cowboy* (1969), *Sunday, Bloody Sunday* (1971), *The Day of the Locust* (1975; from the novel by Nathanael West), *Marathon Man* (1976), and *Yanks* (1979). After a failed attempt at social satire in *Honky-Tonk Freeway* (1980), he redeemed himself with the BBC telefilm *An Englishman Abroad* (1983), based on an incident from the life of Cold War defector and spy Guy Burgess, and the American-produced real-life espionage film *The Falcon and the Snowman* (1984), both of which ponder the moral implications of treason. Many critics felt that Schlesinger's violent voodoo-cult thriller *The Believers* (1986) was an exercise in needless mystification, but *Madame Sousatzka* (1988), a leisurely narrative focused on a middle-aged piano teacher and her circle, was much admired.

Jack Clayton, whose *Room at the Top* (1959) is often credited with having begun British social realism, turned away from the movement in his second feature, *The Innocents* (1961), a beautiful, terrifying, and appropriately ambiguous visualization of Henry James' novel *The Turn of the Screw.* But Clayton continued to make distinctly individual films such as *The Pumpkin Eater* (1964; script by Harold Pinter) and *Our Mother's House* (1967). Clayton's career as a director was nearly ended by the commercial and critical failure of his opulent, Hollywood-produced version of F. Scott Fitzgerald's *The Great Gatsby* (1974) but resumed with his skillful adaptations of Ray Bradbury's horror novel *Something Wicked This Way Comes* (1982) and Brian Moore's *The Lonely Passion of Judith Hearne* (1987).

Other important British filmmakers of the sixties were Bryan Forbes (b. 1926)—whose *Whistle Down the Wind* (1961), *The L-Shaped Room* (1963), *Seance on a Wet Afternoon* (1964), *King Rat* (1965), *The Wrong Box* (1966), *The Whisperers* (1967), *Deadfall* (1967), and *The Raging*

Moon (1970) demonstrate a remarkably subtle sense of atmosphere and *mise-en-scène*—and the more traditional Basil Dearden (1911–71)*— whose archetypal British police thriller *The Blue Lamp* (1949) won numerous awards and made Dirk Bogarde a star and who also directed *Sapphire* (1959), *The League of Gentlemen* (1960), *The Mind Benders* (1963), and *Khartoum* (1966). Also of interest is the work of Ronald Neame (b. 1911)—*The Horse's Mouth* (1958), *Tunes of Glory* (1960), *The Prime of Miss Jean Brodie* (1969).† During the same years, the television director Peter Watkins (b. 1935) made two brilliant pseudodocumentary films for the BBC—*Culloden* (1964), a historical re-creation of the bloody suppression of the 1746 Jacobite rebellion, and *The War Game* (1965), a projection of what would happen to Britain in the aftermath of a nuclear attack. The BBC refused to broadcast *The War Game,* and it was banned from television internationally for the next twenty years.** Watkins's first theatrical feature, *Privilege* (1967), offered a strikingly original vision of England as a totalitarian state but could not be compared with his television work. His more sophisticated *Punishment Park* (1971) depicted a fascist America in the wake of the Vietnam War. And his *Edvard Munch* (1974; 1976) used documentary techniques to dramatize the life, milieu, and creative agonies of the Norwegian Expressionist painter.‡ After a decade of making docudramas in Sweden and Denmark (e.g., *Fallan* [*The Trap,* 1975]; *Aftenlandet* [*Evening Land,* 1977]), Watkins produced his fourteen-and-one-half-hour "Film for Peace," *The Journey* (1987), an epic documentary on the arms race and the threat of nuclear holocaust. Shot between 1984 and 1986 in sixteen countries on five continents and in eight separate languages, *The Journey* was the result of an extraordinary international fund-raising effort begun in 1981. The British stage director Peter Brook (b. 1925) made several fine films during the sixties, including versions of William Golding's novel *The Lord of the Flies* (1962), of Peter Weiss's drama *Marat / Sade* (1966), and of Shakespeare's *King Lear* (1969; released 1971), as well as *Tell Me Lies* (1967), a bitter and incisive polemic against American involvement in

14.19 *Privilege* (Peter Watkins, 1967): Paul Jones as the messianic rock star Steve Shorter.

---

*Dearden's son, James, also directs. His first feature was the psychological thriller *The Cold Room* (1984), telecast in the United States by HBO.

†The films made in the seventies and eighties by both Forbes and Neame, the majority for American studios, were uneven but demonstrated skilled craftsmanship. Forbes made *The Stepford Wives* (1975), *The Slipper and the Rose—Story of Cinderella* (1976), *International Velvet* (1978), *Sunday Lovers* (1980), *Better Late Than Never* (1983), and *The Naked Face* (1984); Neame directed *Scrooge* (1970; a musical based on Dickens' *A Christmas Carol*), *The Poseidon Adventure* (1972), *The Odessa File* (1974), *Meteor* (1978), *Hopscotch* (1980), *First Monday in October* (1981), and *Foreign Body* (1986).

**After months of debate, the BBC did permit the film to be released theatrically in 1966; it won the American Academy Award for Best Documentary Feature. The BBC finally televised *The War Game* on July 31, 1985, as part of a week's programs commemorating the fortieth anniversary of the destruction of Hiroshima (the film had originally been scheduled to commemorate the twentieth).

‡Originally produced for Norwegian television, *Edvard Munch* was first telecast in Sweden and Norway in November 1974 with a running time of 210 minutes; the theatrical version distributed in the United States in 1976 was cut to 167 minutes.

14.20 *The Servant* (Joseph Losey, 1963):
Dirk Bogarde, James Fox.

Vietnam. Brook subsequently has produced *Meetings with Remarkable Men* (1979) and an odd three-cast version of Bizet's *Carmen* (*La Trage-die de Carmen*, 1983), adapted from his own Paris stage hit. Also notable was a film directed by Kevin Brownlow (b. 1938) and Andrew Mollo (b. 1941), the independently produced *It Happened Here* (1964; released 1966), a "documentary" reconstruction of an imagined German occupation of England during World War II.*

British cinema was further enhanced in the sixties and seventies by the presence of two American expatriates, Joseph Losey (1909–84) and Richard Lester (b. 1932). Losey, who became a British citizen after being hounded out of Hollywood during the McCarthy era, produced some of the most significant British films of the decade in collaboration with absurdist playwright Harold Pinter (b. 1930). These included *The Servant* (1963); *Accident* (1967); and *The Go-Between* (1971), adapted from the novel by L. P. Hartley. A subtle stylist whose major themes are the destructiveness of the erotic impulse and the corrupting nature of technocracy, Losey has also produced important films from his own scripts, notably *Eve* (1962), totally mutilated in its commercial version, and the remarkable antiwar drama *King and Country* (1964). Losey's films of the seventies were *The Assassination of Trotsky* (1972); a version of Henrik Ibsen's *A Doll's House* (1973); *The Romantic Englishwoman* (1975), an elegant and witty film about modern marriage scripted by the playwright Tom Stoppard; *M. Klein* (1976), a study of anti-Semitism in occupied France; a version of Mozart's opera *Don Giovanni* (1979), shot on location in northern Italy; and *Les Routes du sud* (*Roads of the South*, 1979), an intimate portrait of a father-son relationship set in rural France that

---

* Since that time, Brownlow and Mollo have made only one other film together, *Winstanley* (1975), another "imaginary documentary" based on David Caute's novel about the seventeenth-century English Digger movement. Brownlow, of course, is also a prominent film historian whose numerous books (e.g., *The Parade's Gone By*, 1967), reconstructions (e.g., Abel Gance's 1927 epic *Napoléon*—see Chapter 9), and compilation films (e.g., *The Unknown Chaplin*, 1985—see Chapter 6) have greatly enhanced our understanding of the silent era. But unlike *It Happened Here*, which was personally financed by the filmmakers and took seven years to complete, *Winstanley* was subsidized by the British Film Institute (BFI) Production Board. Since the mid-sixties, this institution has made limited funds available to independent filmmakers such as Don Levy (b. 1932—*Herostratus*, 1967); American-born Steve Dwoskin (b. 1939—*Central Bazaar*, 1976); David Gladwell (*Requiem for a Village*, 1974); Peter Smith (*A Private Enterprise*, 1974); and Nick Broomfield and Joan Churchill (*Juvenile Liaison*, 1975). The first truly impressive work made with BFI support was Bill Douglas' autobiographical trilogy *My Childhood* (1972), *My Ain Folk* (1974), and *My Way Home* (1978). This series of bleakly beautiful films tells the story of a poor and unwanted boy coming of age in a Scottish mining town; some critics feel that it was the greatest achievement of British cinema in the seventies, although Douglas' first full-length feature, *Comrades* (1986)—a film about the "Tolpuddle martyrs" presented in the style of 1830s dioramas and magic lantern shows—disappointed some critics. The first feature-length BFI production was Richard Woolley's metaphysical murder mystery *Brothers and Sisters* (1980); but the most ambitious BFI project by far (also funded in part by the private national broadcasting network Channel Four) was Peter Greenaway's strikingly original *The Draughtsman's Contract* (1982). Other recent productions funded in whole or part by the BFI include *Doll's Eve* (Jan Worth, 1983), *Ascendancy* (Edward Bennet, 1983), *1919* (Hugh Brody, 1984), and *The Terence Davies Trilogy* (Terence Davies, 1984).

contains autobiographical elements. The director's final work was the visually riveting *La Truite* (*The Trout*, 1982), based on an existential novel by Roger Vailland, and *Steaming* (1985), an adaptation of Nell Dunn's ebulliently feminist stage play.

Richard Lester directed several award-winning shorts, notably *The Running, Jumping, and Standing Still Film* (1960)* and *The Mouse on the Moon* (1963; a sequel to Jack Arnold's *The Mouse That Roared*, 1959), before he came to fame and fortune through his two Beatles films, *A Hard Day's Night* (1964) and *Help!* (1965), which employ the full cinematic arsenal of the New Wave—telephoto zooms and swoops, flash-backs, jump cuts, and every conceivable device of narrative displace-ment—to create a dazzling new kind of audiovisual comedy. His subsequent films—*The Knack* (1965), *How I Won the War* (1967), *Petulia* (1968), and *The Bed-Sitting Room* (1969)—use the same techniques to more serious dramatic purpose, often with less success, though *Petulia*'s dis-jointed narrative style works perfectly to embody the psychological dis-integration of its principal characters. During the seventies, Lester directed the highly successful swashbucklers *The Three Musketeers* (1973), *The Four Musketeers* (1975), and *Royal Flash* (1975); the historical romance *Robin and Marian* (1976); an adaptation of the Broadway comedy *The Ritz* (1977); the comic Western "prequel" *Butch and Sundance: The Early Days* (1979); and *Cuba* (1979), a political thriller set in the last days of the Batista regime. His films in the eighties included two entries in the *Superman* cycle, *Superman II* (1980) and *Superman III* (1983), the caper farce *Finders Keepers* (1984), and the final installment of his Musketeers trilogy, *The Return of the Musketeers* (1989), which combines the casts of the two earlier films.

14.21 An archetypal image of the six-ties: the Beatles in *A Hard Day's Night* (Richard Lester, 1964).

The End of Social Realism and Beyond

In the late sixties, with the decline of social realism and the increasing influence of American investment in the now lucrative British cinema (90 percent by 1968), the distinctly national flavor of British films was lost. Many American directors (such as Billy Wilder, Richard Fleischer, Sidney Lumet, Delbert Mann, Stanley Donen, George Stevens, Otto Preminger, Anthony Mann, Richard Brooks, William Wyler, Fred Zinnemann, John Huston, and Stanley Kubrick) came to work in British studios during these years, as did such major Continental figures as Roman Polánski (*Repulsion*, 1965; *Cul-de-sac*, 1966); François Truffaut (*Fahrenheit 451*, 1966); and Michelangelo Antonioni (*Blow-Up*, 1966). Furthermore, the British-based directors Richardson, Lester, and Schlesinger—not to men-

---

* Featured in this Lester short were the Goons—Peter Sellers, Spike Milligan, and Harry Secombe—stars of the long-running BBC radio hit "The Goon Show," which paved the way for the upsurge of brilliant British comedies in the fifties and sixties. Some examples are Frank Launder's "St. Trinian's" series, with Alastair Sim (*The Belles of St. Trinian's*, 1954; *Blue Murder at St. Trinian's*, 1957; *The Pure Hell of St. Trinian's*, 1960); *The Wrong Arm of the Law*, (Cliff Owen, 1962), and *Heavens Above!*, (Roy Boulting, 1963), both starring Sellers; *Bedazzled*, (Stanley Donen, 1967), featuring Peter Cook and Dudley Moore, etc., right up through Monty Python, who very clearly inherited the Goons' mantle.

tion David Lean (*The Bridge on the River Kwai*, 1957; *Lawrence of Arabia*, 1962; *Dr. Zhivago*, 1965; *Ryan's Daughter*, 1970) * and Carol Reed (*The Agony and the Ecstasy*, 1965; *Oliver*, 1968; *Flap*, 1970)—all began to make films within the American industry. And Reisz (*Isadora*, 1968) and Forbes (*The Madwoman of Chaillot*, 1969) both became involved in big-budget international co-productions.

Nevertheless, in the late sixties a new, more visually oriented generation of British directors began to appear. Some, like Clive Donner (b. 1926)—*The Caretaker* (1974), *Here We Go Round the Mulberry Bush* (1967), *Rogue Male* (1976), *To Catch a King* (1984), *Stealing Heaven* (1988)—and Hungarian-born Peter Medak—*Negatives* (1968), *A Day in the Death of Joe Egg* (1970), *The Ruling Class* (1972), *The Changeling* (1980), *The Men's Club* (1986)—produced a handful of interesting films before going heavily commercial. Others, such as the former television directors Alan Bridges (b. 1927)—*The Hireling* (1973), *Return of the Soldier* (1982), *The Shooting Party* (1984)—and Ken Loach (b. 1936)—*Poor Cow* (1967), *Kes* (1969), *Family Life* (1972), *Black Jack* (1979), *The Gamekeeper* (1980), *Looks and Smiles* (1982), *Fatherland* (1986)—sacrificed popularity to integrity, with the austerely analytical work of Loach proving especially influential.

Perhaps the most significant directors of this generation, however, managed to combine both impulses in films that were commercially viable and at the same time formally significant. Peter Yates (b. 1929), a director known for his ability to combine action with an intelligent exploration of character, has worked in America since the success of *Bullitt* in 1968 (producing, e.g., such fine films as *The Friends of Eddie Coyle* [1973], and *Breaking Away* [1979], and such uneven ones as *The Deep* [1977]; *Eyewitness* [1981]; and *Krull* [1983]), but he returned to British themes with *The Dresser* (1984), a film about the last performance of an aging provincial actor, and to international ones in the politically controversial *Eleni* (1985), based on Nicholas Gage's true account of his search for the men who killed his mother during the Greek civil war.

John Boorman (b. 1933) also scored his first successes in the United States with *Point Blank* (1967), *Hell in the Pacific* (1969), and *Deliverance* (1972), returning briefly to England to make *Leo the Last* (1970), a contemporary revolutionary allegory for which he won the Director's Prize at Cannes. Shooting on location in Ireland, he confirmed his taste for esoteric subjects in the mythical science fiction epic *Zardoz* (1974), which he also wrote and produced, and, in the United States once more, the disappointing *Exorcist II—The Heretic* (1977). Next, however, Boorman produced an authentically British masterpiece, *Excalibur* (1981), also shot in Ireland, an intellectually and visually powerful retelling of the Arthurian legend from the mystical perspective of Merlin. This ambitious project was followed by his most exotic work, *The Emerald Forest*

---

* Lean returned to directing after an absence of fourteen years with his beautifully restrained adaptation of E. M. Forster's *A Passsage to India* (1984), which he wrote and edited himself.

14.22 *The Emerald Forest* (John Boorman, 1985): Charley Boorman as Tomme.

14.23 Ken Russell's ultra-violent *The Devils* (1971): Oliver Reed.

(1985), which concerns the young son of an American engineer (played by Boorman's own son, Charley) raised by a primitive Amazonian tribe and the murderous clash of cultures that ensues when his father attempts to "rescue" him. In an unpredictable change of pace, Boorman delighted 1987 audiences with *Hope and Glory,* a richly detailed account of English middle-class family life during World War II that was derived from his own childhood experience.

The two most original British directors of the seventies were undeniably Ken Russell and Nicolas Roeg. Russell (b. 1927) first attracted attention in the mid-sixties with a series of fictionalized biographies of composers, dancers, and poets flamboyantly directed for BBC-TV. International recognition came with his lavish theatrical adaptation of D. H. Lawrence's *Women in Love* (1969). This was followed by a series of controversial features—*The Music Lovers* (1971); *The Devils* (1971; adapted from Aldous Huxley's *The Devils of Loudun*); *The Boy Friend* (1972); *Savage Messiah* (1972); *Mahler* (1974); *Tommy* (1975, a version of the popular rock opera by The Who); *Lisztomania* (1975); *Valentino* (1977); and *Altered States* (1981), which oscillated between the outrageously vulgar and the outrageously brilliant. Russell directed opera exclusively from 1982 through 1984 (including a spectacular updated version of Puccini's *Madame Butterfly* at the Spoleto Festival in Charleston, S.C., in 1983), before returning to features with *Gothic* (1987), an account of the stormy June night in 1816 at Lord Byron's villa in Switzerland which inspired both Dr. Polidori's *The Vampyre* and Mary Shelley's *Frankenstein*. Russell portrays the evening as a descent into orgiastic, drug-induced horror in which—as in all of his best work—the line between

14.24 Nicholas Roeg's *Performance* (1968; released 1970), co-directed with Donald Cammell. Mick Jagger, James Fox.

14.25 Ridley Scott's futuristic *film noir* *Blade Runner* (1982), an American release. Rutger Hauer as a rebellious replicant.

reality and fantasy is not simply blurred but destroyed. The same atmosphere characterizes his rigorous adaptation of Oscar Wilde's banned *symboliste* drama, *Salome* (1892), titled *Salome's Last Dance* (1988). The film was brilliantly conceived by Russell in the form of a private, homoerotic performance staged for the author in a London brothel on the eve of his fateful arrest for sodomy. Equally inspired are *The Lair of the White Worm* (1988), a hilarious send-up of British class values, kinky sex, and sixties Hammer horror films, freely adapted by Russell from Bram Stoker's last novel (1905), and a lushly romantic adaptation of *The Rainbow* (1989), Lawrence's novelistic "prequel" to *Women in Love*.

Less flamboyant than Russell, but quite as unique, Nicolas Roeg (b. 1928) began his career as a cinematographer for Lester, Schlesinger, Truffaut, and others before co-directing *Performance* (1968; released 1970) with Donald Cammell.* Like his other films of the decade—*Walkabout* (1971); *Don't Look Now* (1973); *The Man Who Fell to Earth* (1976); and *Bad Timing* (1979)—it was cut by distributors to make it more accessible to the public and exists in several versions. Often experimental in form, Roeg's beautiful and enigmatic films go far beyond narrative to immerse the viewer in a fluent stream of audiovisual images whose most legitimate meaning is its psychological affect. His films of the eighties, however—*Eureka* (1983), *Insignificance* (1985), *Castaway* (1986), and *Track 29* (1988)—have taken somewhat more conventional narrative forms.

After Russell and Roeg, the most influential British director of the past decade has probably been Ridley Scott (b. 1939), a former set designer and television-commercial director, whose first feature, *The Duellists* (1977), adapted from a short story by Joseph Conrad, won high praise at Cannes in the year of its release. Scott's next film was the smash hit *Alien* (1979), made for 20th Century-Fox in the United States and hailed as a minor masterpiece of science fiction and visceral horror. He mixed science fiction and *film noir* with the same effectiveness in the technically dazzling *Blade Runner* (1982), based on Phillip K. Dick's 1968 genre classic *Do Androids Dream of Electric Sheep?*, but his British-produced fantasy *Legend* (1985) was a critical failure and for its 1986 release in the United States was cut by twenty minutes.† Nevertheless, Scott's stylish thriller *Someone to Watch Over Me* (1987) was among the most successful entries in the *film noir* cycle of the late eighties.

Scott is one of several directors who came to work in the American industry at the turn of the decade from British "new wave" advertising. The most consistently successful has been Alan Parker (b. 1944), whose first feature, *Bugsy Malone* (1976), a musical spoof of gangster films using an all-child cast, was followed by the harrowing *Midnight Express* (1978),

---

* Cammell has directed only two other features—*The Demon Seed* (1977) and *White of the Eye* (1987)—both thrillers of unusual interest.

† The European version of *Legend* runs 109 minutes and has music by Jerry Goldsmith; the 89–minute American version has an electronic score by Tangerine Dream.

which won Academy Awards for its screenplay and score. Parker's other work has been equally original—*Fame* (1980), *Shoot the Moon* (1982), *Pink Floyd—The Wall* (1982), *Birdy* (1984), the controversial *noir* shocker *Angel Heart* (1987), which he also scripted, and the equally controversial *Mississippi Burning* (1988), based on a 1964 FBI investigation into the murders of three civil rights workers in the deep South. Michael Apted (b. 1943) scored his first American success with *Coal Miner's Daughter* (1980), a strikingly intelligent biography of country singer Loretta Lynn, and continued in this vein with his adaptation of Martin Cruz Smith's *Gorky Park* (1983), *Firstborn* (1984), the British documentaries *28 Up* (1985) and *Bring on the Night* (1985), and *Gorillas in the Mist* (1988), the life story of the murdered anthropologist Dian Fossey. Less consistent has been the work of Adrian Lyne, whose films seem to vacillate between music video (*Foxes* [1980] and *Flashdance* [1982]) and sexually provocative *film noir* (*9½ Weeks,* 1986, and *Fatal Attraction,* 1987). Tony Scott, Ridley's brother, demonstrated a similar preference for style over substance in his pretentious vampire thriller *The Hunger* (1983), but he enjoyed enormous popular success with the slickly calculated blockbusters *Top Gun* (1986) and *Beverly Hills Cop II* (1988).

Another recent source of vitality in British cinema has been the work of the multitalented comedy team Monty Python (essentially, the performers John Cleese, Michael Palin, Eric Idle, and Graham Chapman; writer-director Terry Jones; and American-born animator-director Terry Gilliam). Their first film, *And Now for Something Completely Different* (Ian McNaughton, 1973) was merely a collection of sketches derived from their popular BBC-TV series "Monty Python's Flying Circus," but *Monty Python and the Holy Grail* (Jones and Gilliam, 1975) was a wholly original parody of the Arthurian romance which also managed to convey the look and feel of the Middle Ages in a quite convincing way. The same was true of Gilliam's version of Lewis Carroll's *Jabberwocky* (1977) and, in biblical terms, of Jones' irreverent and controversial *Monty Python's Life of Brian* (1979), which was the first production of the independent company Handmade Films. Handmade, whose chairman is ex-Beatle George Harrison, has since been responsible for Gilliam's *Time Bandits* (1981), a bizarre fantasy in which six dwarfs romp through history, and such other comic work as *The Missionary* (Richard Loncraine, 1982), *Bullshot* (Dick Clement, 1983), and *A Private Function* (Malcolm Mowbray, 1984), as well as more serious films like John Mackenzie's *The Long Good Friday* (1980; distribution only), Mai Zetterling's *Scrubbers* (1984), and Neil Jordan's *Mona Lisa* (1986). The Python group itself was featured in the omnibus *Monty Python's Meaning of Life* (Terry Jones, 1983), and Terry Gilliam went on to produce for Handmade the darkly brilliant *Brazil* (1985), which posits an alternately absurd and terrifying distopia in Britain's near future, and for Columbia the phantasmagorical *The Adventures of Baron Munchausen* (1989), a dazzling if somewhat empty display of pyrotechnics rumored to have cost over 50 million dollars.

In the realm of the narrative avant-garde, several British filmmakers became prominent during the eighties, most notably Peter Greenaway (b.

14.26 *Monty Python's Life of Brian* (Terry Jones, 1979). Graham Chapman as Brian, fleeing the Romans and about to land on the head of Michael Palin in a Judean marketplace.

14.27 Britain as nightmare state: Terry Gilliam's *Brazil* (1985). Jonathan Price.

14.28 *The Draughtsman Contract* (1982), Peter Greenaway's Chinese puzzle about the nature of art. Anthony Higgins, Janet Suzman.

14.29 Wacky Shakespeare: Derek Jarman's *The Tempest* (1979).

1943), whose early structural films (*A Walk Through H*, 1978; *Vertical Features Remake*, 1978) and the three-hour absurdist fantasia *The Falls* (1981) won the support of the British Film Institute (BFI) and Channel 4 for his enigmatic medium-budget feature *The Draughtsman's Contract* (1982). Set in an English country house in 1694, this is a densely allusive work about the relationships among artists, patrons, and spectators cast in the form of a metaphysical murder mystery. In 1984, Greenaway, whose regular cinematographer is Sacha Vierny, directed a pair of documentaries profiling American avant-garde composers (*Modern American Composers I* and *II*). He recently returned to feature work with the uncompromisingly intellectual *A Zed and Two Noughts* (1985) and the more mainstream *The Belly of an Architect* (1987).

The former painter and set designer for Ken Russell (*Savage Messiah; The Devils*), Derek Jarman (b. 1942) burst upon the avant-garde scene with *Sebastiane*, a profane, homoerotic account of the famous saint and martyr that was performed in Latin, with English subtitles and a Brian Eno score. *Jubilee* (1977) offered a vision of anarchic social breakdown to mark both the royal Jubilee and Britain's "Summer of Punk." Jarman's version of Shakespeare's *The Tempest* (1979), shot in the fire-gutted ruins of a Warwickshire estate, was an overwhelming critical success. The same was true of Jarman's richly imagined biography *Caravaggio* (1986), which re-created Renaissance Italy on the London docks to project the life of the influential painter (1571–1610) who, among his other achievements, is said to have invented chiaroscuro lighting. *The Last of England* (1987) is a bleak comedy about life in the ruins of empire inventively shot in Super 8mm. But Jarman's *War Requiem* (1988) is a stunning visualization of Benjamin Britten's oratorio made for the BBC on the (relatively) enormous budget of 1.2 million dollars.

14.30 David Puttnam's Oscar-winning hit *Chariots of Fire* (Hugh Hudson, 1981). Ian Charleson, Ben Cross.

14.31 A Scottish cinema, of sorts: Bill Forsyth's *Local Hero* (1982). Peter Capaldi, Peter Riegert.

14.32 Goldcrest's *Absolute Beginners* (Julien Temple, 1986). Eddie O'Connell, Patsy Kensit.

14.33 *My Beautiful Laundrette* (Stephen Frears, 1985), produced by Channel Four. Saeed Jaffrey, Daniel Day Lewis.

Much of the work discussed above was financed, in various combinations, by the producer David Puttnam, the British film and television investment company Goldcrest, and the independent television network Channel 4. Puttnam produced early films by Ken Russell, Alan Parker, Michael Apted, Ridley Scott, and Adrian Lyne, before producing an international hit, the Oscar-winning *Chariots of Fire* (Hugh Hudson, 1981). Subsequently, he produced Bill Forsyth's Scottish-American comedy *Local Hero* (1982), the Irish-based *Cal* (Pat O'Connor, 1984), and, for his Enigma

Company, *The Killing Fields* (Roland Joffe, 1984) and *The Mission* (Roland Joffe, 1986). Both of the latter films received American Academy Awards for Chris Menges' cinematography and *The Mission* also won the Golden Palm at Cannes; they brought Puttnam to the attention of Columbia Pictures Industries, Inc., where he served a brief term as chairman from 1986 to 1987, before returning to England. Most of these films also were backed by Goldcrest, as were the films in Puttnam's *First Love* series, e.g., Gavin Millar's *Secrets* (1984), which premiered on Channel 4. In addition, Goldcrest funded in whole or part such notable non-Puttnam productions as Richard Attenborough's *Ghandi* (1982), which swept the Oscars for the year of its release; Marek Kanievska's *Another Country* (1984); Julien Temple's *Absolute Beginners* (1986); and Attenborough's *Cry Freedom* (1987).*

Launched in 1980 to provide alternative programming, Channel 4 has become the fourth largest national television network in Britain, after the two BBC services and the advertiser-supported Independent Television (ITV). Unlike the other networks, however, Channel 4 produces no programs of its own but commissions production companies for original work. In this way, it provided funding for such important low- and medium-budget features as Jerzy Skolimowski's *Moonlighting* (1981; see Chapter 16); Peter Greenaway's *The Draughtsman's Contract* (1982); Neil Jordan's *Angel* (1982; Irish); Richard Eyre's *The Ploughman's Lunch* (1983); Michael Radford's *Another Time, Another Place* (1983); David Hare's *Wetherby* (1985); Chris Bernard's *Letter to Brezhnev* (1985); Stephen Frears *My Beautiful Laundrette* (1985); Mike Newell's *Dance with a Stranger* (1985); James Ivory and Ishmail Merchant's *Heat and Dust* (1983), *Room with a View* (1986), and *Maurice* (1987); and Peter Ormrod's *Eat the Peach* (1987; Irish). Channel 4 coproduced as well some non-British films like Gregory Nava's *El Norte* (1983), Wim Wenders's *Paris, Texas* (1984), Andrei Tarkovski's *The Sacrifice* (1986), and Mrinal Sen's *Genesis* (1986). In the late eighties, Channel 4 was the single largest producer of independent features in England and a major force in the cultural life of the nation, functioning on a par with West Germany's ZDF and Italy's RAI.

Like the French New Wave, from which it partially sprang, the British social realist cinema disappeared along with the social context that had motivated it. But its formal and thematic legacy to British national cinema was great. It bequeathed the then radical stylistic conventions of the New Wave to a cinema stagnant with armchair narrative traditions carried over from the prewar era. And in its new concern for the aesthetics

14.34 Neil Jordan's Freudian fairytale *The Company of Wolves* (1984).

---

* The commercial failure of several recent Goldcrest-financed films—Puttnam's *The Mission, Absolute Beginners,* and *Revolution* (Hugh Hudson, 1986)—has forced the company to concentrate mainly on distribution and sales. Hemdale Films, a tiny firm when it was founded in 1967, has moved to fill the vacuum in creative production by buying the American rights to major British independent films like *Defense of the Realm* (David Drury, 1985) and *In the Belly of an Architect* (Greenaway, 1987), and financing such unconventional American work as *The Terminator* (James Cameron, 1984), *At Close Range* (James Foley, 1986), and *Salvador* (Oliver Stone, 1986). Hemdale also provided one-third of the financing (7 million dollars) for Bernardo Bertolucci's *The Last Emperor* (1987).

of everyday life and outspokenness about the dynamics of sex, class, and power in the postindustrial world, it gave the class-ridden, hidebound British film a vastly wider range of themes than it had ever known before. Social realism also produced a handful of important directors, like Lindsay Anderson, John Schlesinger, Tony Richardson, and Karel Reisz, and a new pool of international acting talent in the person of young and previously unknown stars such as Albert Finney, Rita Tushingham, Rachel Roberts, Alan Bates, Tom Courtenay, Susannah York, Richard Harris, Oliver Reed, Michael Caine, David Warner, Julie Christie, Glenda Jackson, James Fox, Terence Stamp, David Hemmings, Michael York, Vanessa Redgrave, and Lynn Redgrave.

14.35   Alec Cox's *Sid and Nancy* (1986): Gary Oldham, Chloe Webb.

The fact that British film has rarely been a major force in world cinema is partially explained by America's domination of the English-language film market, and partially by the innate conservatism of British visual and aural culture. Satyajit Ray once said that the British are "temperamentally unsuited" to cinema, and François Truffaut claimed that the terms "cinema" and "Britain" were incompatible. Yet the work of the British directors discussed above offers ample proof to the contrary, and so does that of such relative newcomers as Christopher Petit (*Radio On* [1980]; *An Unsuitable Job for a Woman* [1982]; *Flight to Berlin* [1984]; *Chinese Boxes* [1984]), Julien Temple (*The Great Rock and Roll Swindle* [1979]; *The Secret Policeman's Other Ball* [1982]; *Running Out of Luck* [1985]; *Absolute Beginners* [1986]; *Earth Girls Are Easy* [1988]), Gavin Millar (*The Weather in the Streets* [1983]; *Unfair Exchanges* [1984]; *Dreamchild* [1985]), Stephen Frears (*Gumshoe* [1971]; *Bloody Kids* [1980]; *Saigon—Year of the Cat* [1983]; *The Hit* [1984]; *My Beautiful Laundrette* [1985]; *Loving Walter* [1986]; *Prick Up Your Ears* [1987]; *Sammy and Rosie Get Laid* [1987]; *Dangerous Liaisons* [1988]), Neil Jordan (*Angel* [1982]; *The Company of Wolves* [1984]; *Mona Lisa* [1986]), Michael Radford (*Another Time, Another Place* [1983]; *1984* [1984]; *White Mischief* [1987]), Chris Bernard (*Letter to Brezhnev* [1985]), Mike Newell (*Dance with a Stranger* [1985]; *The Good Father* [1986]; *Soursweet* [1988]), Alex Cox (*Repo Man* [1984]; *Sid and Nancy* [1986]; *Straight to Hell* [1987]), Andrew Grieve (*On the Black Hill* [1988]), and the former cinematographer Chris Menges (*A World Apart* [1988]). Taken as a group, the works of these and other British filmmakers* range across a broad spectrum of styles and themes, from the minimalist aspirations

---

* Other British directors of note are Franc Roddam (*Quadrophenia*, 1979; *Lords of Discipline*, 1983, USA; *The Bride*, 1985, USA; *War Party*, 1988, USA); Franco Rosso (*Babylon*, 1980; *Sixty-four Day Hero*, 1986); Brian Gibson (*Breaking Glass*, 1980; *Poltergeist II: The Other Side*, 1986); Derek Burbidge (*Urgh! A Music War*, 1981); Tom Clegg (*MacVicar*, 1980; *G'Ole!*, 1983; *The Inside Man*, 1984); John Mackenzie (*The Long Good Friday*, 1980; *Beyond the Limit*, 1983; *The Innocent*, 1984; *The Fourth Protocol*, 1987); Lewis Gilbert (*The Spy Who Loved Me*, 1977; *Moonraker*, 1979; *Educating Rita*, 1983; *Not Quite Jerusalem*, 1984); John Irvin (*The Dogs of War*, 1980; *Ghost Story*, 1981, USA; *Champions*, 1984; *Turtle Diary*, 1985); Mike Hodges (*Get Carter*, 1971; *Flash Gordon*, 1980; *A Prayer Before Dying*, 1987); Jack Gold (*The Naked Civil Servant*, 1975; *Praying Mantis*, 1982; *Who?*, 1982; *Red Monarch*, 1982; *Good and Bad at Games*, 1983; *Sakharov*, 1984; *The Chain*, 1985); Richard Loncraine (*Brimstone and Treacle*, 1982; *The Missionary*, 1982); Joseph Despins (*The Disappearance of Harry*, 1983); Sally Potter (*Thriller*,

of the contemporary European avant-garde through that absurdist tradition of British art, associated in literature with Laurence Sterne, Lewis Carroll, Virginia Woolf, and James Joyce.

AUSTRALIA AND NEW ZEALAND

A recent and most unexpected development in English-language cinema has been the emergence of Australian film from nearly total obscurity into international prominence. Maintained by the British as a penal colony from 1788 to 1840, Australia (from the Latin *australis*, meaning *southern*) existed as a British protectorate until 1901, when it became a self-governing commonwealth of six federated states. It had a small film industry during the silent era and produced a handful of features after World War I that were successful with both domestic and British audiences (e.g., Raymond Longford's *The Sentimental Bloke*, 1919, and Norman Dawn's *For the Term of His Natural Life*, 1927), but the coming of sound left the country with only one major production facility (Cinesound, formerly Australasian Films) from 1932 to 1956. During World War II, Australia produced only ten features, although the numerous documentaries of the Commonwealth Film Unit claimed international attention. In the postwar period, Australia virtually ceased to have a film industry of its own but became instead a location for such British productions as *The Overlanders* (Harry Watt, 1946), *Bush Christmas* (Ralph Smart, 1947; remade as an all-Australian production by Henri Safran in 1983), and *Robbery Under Arms* (Jack Lee, 1957; remade as an all-Australian production by Donald Crombie and Ken Hannam in 1985). American productions shot in Australia included *Kangaroo* (Lewis Milestone, 1952—not to be confused with Tim Burstall's adaptation of the D. H. Lawrence novel of the same title in 1986), *On the Beach* (Stanley Kramer, 1959), and *The Sundowners* (Fred Zinnemann, 1960). As late as 1970, Australia was known to the world mainly as the exotic site of such foreign-backed features as Tony Richardson's *Ned Kelly*, Nicolas Roeg's *Walkabout*, and Ted Kotcheff's *Wake in Fear*.

14.36 *The Chant of Jimmy Blacksmith* (Fred Schepsi, 1978).

1979; *The Gold Diggers*, 1983); Richard Eyre (*The Ploughman's Lunch*, 1983; *Loose Connections*, 1983; *The Insurance Man*, 1985; *Past Caring*, 1985); Mike Leigh (*Meantime*, 1983; *Four Days in July*, 1984; *We Think the World of You*, 1988); John Goldschmidt (*She'll Be Wearing Pink Pajamas*, 1985; *The Song for Europe*, 1985; *Maschenka*, 1987); Pat O'Connor (*Cal*, 1984; *A Month in the Country*, 1987); David Drury (*Defense of the Realm*, 1985); Ken McMullen (*Ghost Dance*, 1983; *Zina*, 1985); Peter Richardson (*The Supergrass*, 1985; *Eat the Rich*, 1987); David Wheatley (*The Magic Toyshop*, 1986); Paul Mayersberg (*Captive*, 1986); Ann Guedes (*Rocinante*, 1986); Maureen Blackwood and Isaac Julien (*The Passion of Remembrance*, 1986); David Leland (*Wish You Were Here*, 1987); Harry Hook (*The Kitchen Toto*, 1987); Roger Graef (*Closing Ranks*, 1987); Alfio Bernabei (*Dangerous Characters*, 1987); Tony Palmer (*Testimony*, 1987); Christopher Rawlence (*The Man Who Mistook His Wife for a Hat*, 1988); and Martin Stellman (*For Queen and Country*, 1988). A recent British-American coproduction of note is *Aria* (1987), a feature-length anthology of excerpts from ten separate operas visualized by ten highly original directors—Nicolas Roeg, Charles Sturridge, Jean-Luc Godard, Julien Temple, Bruce Beresford, Robert Altman, Franc Roddam, Ken Russell, Derek Jarman, and Bill Bryden—and produced by Don Boyd (*Scum, The Tempest, Captive*, etc.).

But Australia underwent a profound socioeconomic transformation in the late sixties and early seventies, and in 1970 the federal government established the Australian Film Development Corporation (the Australian Film Commission, or AFC, after 1975) to subsidize the growth of an authentic national cinema. In 1973, the government set up the Australian Film and Television School (AFTS)—with Jerzy Toeplitz, formerly of the Polish State Film School at Lodz, as director—to train filmmakers to work in a new domestic feature industry. The government simultaneously enacted a system of lucrative tax incentives to attract foreign investment capital to Australian film production. The result was a creative explosion unprecedented in the English-language cinema. Australia produced nearly four hundred films between 1970 and 1985—more than were made in all of its prior history—with financing from the AFC and such semiofficial bodies as the New South Wales Film Corporation (by the end of the decade each of the federal states had its own funding agency).

The first films, appearing in the early seventies, were *The Adventures of Barry Mackenzie* (Bruce Beresford, 1972) and *Alvin Purple* (Tim Burstall, 1973). Within the next few years some extraordinary work emerged in the films of Peter Weir (b. 1944)—*Picnic at Hanging Rock*, 1975, and *The Last Wave*, 1977; Beresford (b. 1940)—*Don's Party*, 1976, and *The Getting of Wisdom*, 1977; Fred Schepisi—*The Devil's Playground*, 1976, and *The Chant of Jimmy Blacksmith*, 1978; George Miller—*Mad Max*, 1979; and the feature debuts of the first AFTS graduates: Phillip Noyce (b. 1950)—*Newsfront*, 1978—and Gillian Armstrong (b. 1950)—*My Brilliant Career*, 1979. Unlike the productions financed with foreign capital through the Canadian Film Development Corporation during the same period (see p. 617), these new Australian films were mandated to have indigenous casts and crews and to treat distinctly national themes, often by adapting novels and stories from the turn-of-the-century literary revival that accompanied federation. By the end of the seventies, Australian films were being prominently featured at the Cannes International Film Festival and were competing strongly at European box offices. What made these films so appealing to non-Australian audiences was a combination of their cinematic vitality as the latest international new wave; their remarkable diversity of locations on the world's only island continent; and the clear, lambent quality of natural southern light, an asset that filmmakers exploited to capture the bright colors of the Australian land and its people, and also to compensate for a shortage of studio facilities. (On the other hand, Australian light is so pure that leading cinematographers, such as Russell Boyd, Don McAlpine, and Brian Probyn, must often use diffusion filters to reduce its harshness, giving their outdoor shots a subdued, "romantic" look.)

In 1981, Australia penetrated the American market with two critical hits. The first was *Breaker Morant* (Beresford, 1980), an adaptation of a play about the actual court-martial of three Australian irregulars by the British on trumped-up atrocity charges during the Boer War. The second, *Gallipoli* (Peter Weir, 1981), was based upon another episode of British treachery in which the World War I Allied command under Winston Churchill sent some 35,000 Anzac (Australian-New Zealand Army Corps)

14.37   *Mad Max* (George Miller, 1979).

14.38   *My Brilliant Career* (Gillian Armstrong, 1979): Judy Davis, Sam Neill.

14.39 *Breaker Morant* (Bruce Beresford, 1980).

troops to be slaughtered in a suicidal attempt to invade Turkey across the Dardanelles. The following year, the Australian industry achieved a smashing commercial success in the United States with George Miller's *Mad Max II* (1981; retitled *The Road Warrior* for distribution by Warner Bros.). But Australia's banner year was 1986, when Peter Raiman's tongue-in-cheek *Crocodile Dundee*, starring the popular television comic Paul Hogan, became the highest grossing Australian film *both* at home and in the United States, reversing a consistent postwar trend and earning a total of 120 million dollars. In that same year, in order to generate more internal revenue, the federal government was able to lower the ceiling on its tax incentives for film investment by 13 percent without causing a negative impact on production, and it seemed as if Australia's experiment in creating a thriving and prestigious national cinema out of nothing had become a resounding, certifiable, and permanent success.

Historically, however, such success has always had its price—the migration of the very best native talent to Hollywood—and the Australian experience proved no exception. By the early eighties, many Australian directors had come to work for the American industry. Gillian Armstrong, for example, followed her Australian punk-rock musical *Starstruck* (1982) with an American-produced film, *Mrs. Soffle* (1984), based on the turn-of-the-century case of the Biddle brothers. Its commercial failure returned her to regional Australian themes, in *High Tide* (1987) and *Bingo, Bridesmaids, and Braces* (1988). Bruce Beresford, who came to Hollywood after *Puberty Blues* (1981) and *The Club* (1981), both adapted from Australian authors, scored a critical hit with *Tender Mercies* (1982). But his filming of the biblical tale of *King David* (1985) was a commercial disaster, and his version of Beth Henley's play *Crimes of the Heart* (1986) was only a limited success, as was the offbeat mystery-comedy *Her Alibi* (1989). Beresford has returned occasionally to Australia to direct such culturally indigenous material as *The Fringe-Dwellers* (1986), concerned with the plight of unassimilable aborigines in Queensland. Fred Schepisi has experienced similar ups and downs with his American productions *Iceman* (1981); *Barbarosa* (1982); *Plenty* (1985; adapted from the David Hare play); *Roxanne* (1987), a contemporary reworking of Edmond Rostand's *Cyrano de Bergerac;* and the highly acclaimed *A Cry in the Dark* (1988), based on Australia's infamous "Dingo dog" murder case against Lindy Chamberlain for infanticide in 1980. Even George Miller, whose lively if overblown *Mad Max: Beyond Thunderdome* (1985) was one of the year's top-grossing films, performed equivocally in his adaptation of John Updike's *The Witches of Eastwick* (1987).

The most consistent Australian director working in America today is Peter Weir, who is also the most internationally prominent figure to emerge from his nation's new wave. Weir's first two films were the quirky black comedies *Homedale* (1971) and *The Cars That Ate Paris* (1974), both made and distributed domestically on an *ad hoc* basis. But his first serious feature, *Picnic at Hanging Rock* (1975), was a haunting adaptation of Joan Lindsay's novel about the mysterious disappearance of the three

14.40 Gillian Armstrong's *Mrs. Soffle* (1984): Matthew Modine, Mel Gibson, Diane Keaton.

girls and a mistress from a country boarding school during a holiday outing in the bush on St. Valentine's Day 1900. While this visually and aurally arresting film contains elements of Antonioni's *L'avventura, Picnic* is finally about the dangerous energy released in the clash of alien cultures and environments—here, the disciplined bourgeois repressiveness of Appleyard College and the seductive but menacing physicality of the strange volcanic formation known as Hanging Rock. No less spiritually harrowing is *The Last Wave* (1977), based on an original idea by Weir, in which a cataclysmic deluge is announced to a resolutely conventional Sydney corporate lawyer (Richard Chamberlain) in a series of strange premonitory dreams; as the mystery unravels we learn that the attorney has entered the mythic "dream time" of tribal aborigines where he is the messianic avatar of a primal apocalypse which does, in fact, occur at the film's conclusion. In 1978 Weir wrote and directed a 16mm feature for Australian television entitled *The Plumber,* which explored the limits of rationality on a more human scale than his previous films. In it, an enigmatic handyman disrupts the lives of two repressive, hidebound academics (anthropologists, no less). *Gallipoli* (1981) was Weir's last completely Australian-funded feature. His fourth, *The Year of Living Dangerously* (1982), was the first to be fully financed by an American major (MGM). This film adapts Christopher Koch's novel about the experiences of a young Australian journalist stationed in Jakarta, Indonesia, during the fall of the Sukarno government in 1965. With its 6 million-dollar budget and star performances by Sigourney Weaver and Mel Gibson, it is somewhat glossier than Weir's earlier work. But *The Year of Living Dangerously* probably renders more vividly than any non-Marxist film of its era the appalling degradation of Third World poverty and its symbiotic relationship with political violence. *Witness* (1984), shot in the United States by the Australian cinematographer John Seale (Weir's previous films had employed the Australian Russell Boyd), pits the pacifist subculture of the Amish, who maintain a seventeenth-century agrarian lifestyle, against the violent world of urban American cops. In *The Mosquito Coast* (1986), shot by Seale on location in Belize from a screenplay by Paul Schrader, Weir adapted Paul Theroux's novel of a contemporary Swiss Family Robinson as yet another fateful impingement of worlds, in which a man destroys his family and himself by attempting to live in harmony with nature on a remote Caribbean island. In 1989, Weir and Seale collaborated on *Dead Poets Society,* a lyrical evocation of youth in a New England prep school that resonates with Vigo's *Zéro de conduite* and its heirs (see p. 595).

Of the large number of excellent directors who have chosen to remain in Australia, the most prominent are Phillip Noyce, John Duigan, Tim Burstall, Donald Crombie, Carl Schultz, Simon Wincer, and the Dutch expatriate Paul Cox.* Noyce's (b. 1950) major films are the socially inci-

14.41 *Picnic at Hanging Rock* (Peter Weir, 1975): Anne Lambert.

14.42 *The Last Wave* (Peter Weir, 1977): Richard Chamberlain.

*A significant minority of Australian filmmakers are émigrés. This is because Australia, with its total population of 16 million, contains over 3 million immigrants, including 1 million British, 300,000 Italians, 178,000 Yugoslavs, 154,000 Greeks, and 80,000 Viet-

14.43 Weir's *The Year of Living Dangerously* (1982): Mel Gibson, Bembol Roco.

14.44 *Newsfront* (Phillip Noyce, 1978): Gerard Kennedy.

sive thriller *Backroads* (1977), shot in four weeks for 25,000 dollars; *Newsfront* (1978), focusing on the competition between rival Australian and American newsreel companies in the early years of television; *Heatwave* (1982), a visually opulent *film noir* set among the power elite of Sydney; *Shadow of the Peacock* (1987), a stylish melodrama about an interracial love affair; and the inventive suspense thriller *Dead Calm* (1989), based on the Charles Williams novel partially filmed by Orson Welles between 1967 and 1969 as *The Deep* (see p. 536). The British-born John Duigan (1949) is known for such intelligent, well-acted human dramas as *Mouth to Mouth* (1978), *Winter of Our Dreams* (1981), *One Night Stand* (1984), and *The Year My Voice Broke* (1987), as well as the failed musical *Dimboola* (1979), and also *Far East* (1982), an inventive reworking of *Casablanca*. Involved in filmmaking since the early sixties, Tim Burstall (b. 1929) was a pioneer director of the new Australian cinema. His sex comedy *Alvin Purple* (1973) did much to establish the commercial viability of the industry, as did *Petersen* (1974), *End Play* (1975), and the period piece *Eliza Fraser* (1976). His adaptation of the John Powers play *The Last of the Knucklemen* (1979) and his World War II commando film, *Attack Force Z* (1981), were also commendable. Although his marital melodrama, *Duet for Four* (1982), misfired, Burstall's survival epic, *The Naked Country* (1986), and his D. H. Lawrence adaptation, *Kangaroo* (1986), were solid critical hits. Donald Crombie (b. 1942) is considered a sensitive chronicler of underdogs. His dramatized documentaries *Caddie,* (1976), about the life and death of a Sydney barmaid

namese. All are apparently treated with great tolerance. By contrast, the country's 160,000 aborigines, an authentic Stone Age people, are widely regarded in Australia as barely human. It may also be worth noting here that two-thirds of all Australian children end their formal education at age sixteen; and that welfare accounts for more than one-fourth of the entire federal budget.

during the Depression, and *Cathy's Child,* (1979), based on an actual case of child abduction, both were critical and commercial successes. His Ford-like saga *The Irishman* (1978) and the comic *Kitty and the Bagman* (1982) were notable for their historical reconstruction of Australian life in the 1920s. Crombie's *The Killing of Angel Street* (1981) is a telling exposé of rampant corruption in the contemporary urban redevelopment enterprise, and his *Robbery Under Arms* (co-directed with Ken Hannam, 1985) is a handsome remake of a 1957 British film. *Playing Beatie Bow* (1986) is a time-travel fantasy in the mold of Robert Zemeckis' *Back to the Future.* Hungarian-born Carl Schultz debuted with the scenic family film *Blue Fin* (1978) and continued with the stylish comedy-drama *Goodbye Paradise.* But he produced a truly complex major work in *Careful, He Might Hear You* (1983), a marvelously ornate drama of a child custody battle fought between two sisters in Depression-era Sydney. Recently, Schultz directed the outdoor adventure film *Bullseye* (1986), a pungent adaptation of *Traveling North* (1986), David Williamson's popular stage play about retirement and old age. Schultz's first Hollywood venture (for Tri-Star) was *The Seventh Sign* (1988), a dramatization of the coming of the Judeo-Christian apocalypse. Simon Wincer, who got off to a rocky start with *Snapshot* (1979) and the intriguing but manipulative *Harlequin* (1980), produced in *Phar Lap* (1983) a superb biography of the champion Australian racehorse that died under mysterious circumstances in California in 1932. Also outstanding was his rousing cavalry adventure epic, *The Lighthorsemen* (1987), about the victorious charge of an Australian Light Horse regiment on Turkish-held Beersheba in 1917.*

14.45 *Careful, He Might Hear You* (Carl Schultz, 1983): Wendy Hughes, Nicholas Gledhill.

---

* A second echelon of Australian directors is important mainly for a single film or genre. George Miller, for example, who also works in television and is not to be confused with the creator of "Mad Max" (who, not incidentally, was trained as a medical doctor), was responsible for *The Man from Snowy River* (1982), which became Australia's first international blockbuster, its highest-grossing film before *Crocodile Dundee.* Stage director Jim Sharman (b. 1945) is best known for the cult classic *Rocky Horror Picture Show* (1975), shot in England, and his rendering of Patrick White's psychodrama *The Night the Prowler* (1978). Tom Jeffrey (b. 1938), who works today largely as a producer, directed a very successful adaptation of William Magle's tragicomic Vietnam War novel, *The Odd Angry Shot* (1979). Ken Hamman turned in *Dawn!* (1979), an inventive biography of Australia's most famous swimming champion. John Honey's *Manganinnie* (1980) was the first feature produced by the Tasmanian Film Corporation and concerns the fate of a lone aboriginal woman separated from her tribe during the notorious "black drive" in that island during the 1830s, an attempt by white settlers to exterminate the native people. Albie Thoms (*Sunshine City,* 1974; *Palm Beach,* 1979); Linda Blagg (*Just Out of Reach,* 1979); and Ebsen Storm (b. 1950—*27A,* 1974; *In Search of Anna,* 1979; *With Prejudice,* 1982; *Stanley,* 1983), have worked mainly in the low-budget narrative avant-garde. Richard Franklin (*Patrick,* 1978; *Roadgames,* 1981; *Psycho II,* 1983, USA), Brian Trenchard-Smith (*Turkey Shoot,* 1983; *Frog Dreaming,* 1985; *Dead-End Drive In,* 1986; *Out of the Body,* 1988), and French-born Phillipe Mora (b. 1949—*The Howling III,* 1987), all specialize in horror. Igor Auzins is a former television director who has made two visually stylish period films, *We of the Never Never* (1982) and *The Coolangatta Gold* (1984). Another television director, French-born Henri Safran, has enjoyed success with such literary adaptations as *Storm Boy* (1976, from the novel by Sonia Borg) and *The Wild Duck* (1983, from Ibsen), as well as with his remake of *Bush Christmas* (1983). In the documentary field, recognized figures are Leigh Tilson and Rob Scott (*Street Kids,* 1983); Megan McMurchy, Margot Oliver,

14.46 Paul Cox's *Cactus* (1986): Isabelle Huppert, Robert Menzies.

14.47 *Razorback* (Russell Mulcahy, 1984).

Paul Cox (b. 1940), however, is unquestionably the most important director working in Australia today. Born in the Netherlands, Cox emigrated to Melbourne and began to make low-budget experimental films in 1965. His first features—*Illuminations* (1976) and *Inside Looking Out* (1977)—were autobiographical mood pieces with shoestring budgets, but *Kostas* (1979), about a Greek journalist in exile working as a Melbourne taxi driver, was solidly funded by the Victorian Film Corporation and proved to be Cox's breakthrough film. His next feature, *Lonely Hearts* (1982), won several international awards for its sensitive depiction of the slowly developing romance of a shy, middle-aged couple; and his visually and aurally striking *Man of Flowers* (1983) impressed many critics with its tense, Hitchcock-like rendition of an emotionally isolated eccentric. *My First Wife* (1984) is a harrowing account of the collapse and breakup of a ten-year marriage; it was shot, like *Man of Flowers,* by the gifted cinematographer Yuri Sokol. After his sensuous documentary on Egypt,

and Jeni Thornley (*For Love or Money*, 1983); Tom Zubrycki (*Kemira: Diary of a Strike*, 1984; *Friends and Enemies*, 1987); Dennis O'Rourke (*Half Life*, 1985); Graham Chase (*Democracy*, 1986); Tom Haydon (*Behind the Dam*, 1986); Richard Lowenstein (*Australian Made*, 1987); and Barbara A. Chobocky (*Witch Hunt*, 1987).

A younger wave of Australian filmmakers has recently announced itself in the work of Michael Pattinson (*Moving Out*, 1982; *Street Hero*, 1984; *Ground Zero*, 1987), Ken Cameron (*Monkey Grip*, 1982; *Fast Talking*, 1984; *The Good Wife*, 1987), music-video director Russell Mulcahy (*Razorback*, 1984; *Highlander*, 1985), Ray Lawrence (*Bliss*, 1985), and Barry Peak (*Future Schlock*, 1984; *The Big Hurt*, 1986). Other second-generation Australian filmmakers are Jane Oehr (*On the Loose*, 1985); Robyn Nevin (*The More Things Change*, 1985); Bill Bennett (*Backlash*, 1986); Nadia Tass (*Malcolm*, 1986); Brian Kavanagh (*Departure*, 1986); Neil Armfield (*Twelfth Night*, 1986); George Ogilve (*Short Changed*, 1986); Di Drew (*The Right Hand Man*, 1987); Virginia Rouse (*To Market, To Market*, 1987); Roger Scholes (*The Tale of Ruby Rose*, 1987); Sarah Gibson (*Landslides*, 1987); Pamela Gibbons (*Belinda*, 1987); Brian McKenzie (*With Love to the Person Next to Me*, 1987); Ian Munroe (*Custody*, 1987); Martha Ansara (*The Pursuit of Happiness*, 1987); Steve Jodrell (*Shame*, 1988); and Mark Joffe (*Grievous Bodily Harm*, 1988).

Death and Destiny (1985), Cox produced a clear masterpiece in *Cactus* (1986), easily the most *tactile* film made in Australia since *Picnic at Hanging Rock*. *Cactus* is about a love affair between two persons, one blind since childhood, the other threatened with blindness through an automobile accident after a lifetime of sight; it represents a complex blend of intense emotional drama, documentary technique, and abstract experimental form. Cox's *Vincent—the Life and Death of Vincent Van Gogh* (1987) is an experimental film that recreates the artist's subjective world and his uncompromising philosophy of art.

New Zealand (population 3.2 million), Australia's small island neighbor, sought to imitate that nation's success by establishing a Film Commission in 1978 to encourage the development of an independent film industry. New Zealand, whose topography is even more spectacularly varied than Australia's, had produced twenty-seven features between 1910 and 1930, but only seventeen from 1930 to 1970, owing to American domination after the coming of sound. When Roger Donaldson's futuristic political thriller *Sleeping Dogs* (1977) received international distribution, the government became convinced that an indigenous industry could be formed, and it threw the support of the new commission behind that director's second feature, *Smash Palace* (1981), a tense drama of marital discord which was a great critical success and New Zealand's highest-earning film to date. At about the same time, four other domestic features appeared from new directors trained in television—*Skin Deep* (Geoff Steven, 1979), *Beyond Reasonable Doubt* (John Laing, 1980), *Pictures* (Michael Black, 1981), and *Goodbye Pork Pie* (Geoff Murphy, 1981)—which confirmed the Film Commission's success in promoting New Zealand films on New Zealand subjects.

14.48 *Bliss* (Ray Lawrence, 1985): Barry Otto.

Since then, the country has regularly produced five to six features a year, as well as hosting such coproductions as *Bad Blood,* with the United Kingdom (Mike Newell, 1982), and *Mutiny on the Bounty,* with the United States (Roger Donaldson, 1984). Its Film Commission has assisted the work of a growing number of talented directors, including Donaldson (who has since left for Hollywood, where his first effort was the popular *film noir, No Way Out* [1987], and his second the awful, but undeniably popular, *Cocktail* [1988]); Geoff Steven (*Strata,* 1983); John Laing (*The Lost Tribe,* 1983; *Other Halves,* 1984; *Dangerous Orphans,* 1986); Geoff Murphy (*Utu,* 1983; *The Quiet Earth,* 1985; *Never Say Die,* 1988); Derek Morton (*Wild Horses,* 1983); Peter Sharp (*Trespasses,* 1983); Sam Pillsbury (*The Scarecrow,* 1982; *Starlight Hotel,* 1987); Melanie Read (*Trial Run,* 1984); Vincent Ward (the award-winning documentaries *A State of Siege* and *In Spring One Plants Alone; Vigil,* 1984; *The Navigator,* 1988); Michael Firth (*Heart of the Stag,* 1984; *Sylvia,* 1985); Bruce Morrison (*Constance,* 1984; *Shaker Run,* 1985; *Queen City Rocker,* 1987); Denis Lewiston (*Hot Target,* 1985); Grahame McLean (*Should I Be Good?,* 1985; *The Lie of the Land,* 1985); and Ian Mune (*Came a Hot Friday,* 1985; *Bridge to Nowhere,* 1986). New Zealand has also produced some distinctive documentary features in the work of Merata Mita (*Patu,* 1983; *Mauri,* 1988), Pat McGuire (*War Years,* 1983), and Barry Barclay (*The Neglected Miracle,* 1985).

14.49 *Sleeping Dogs* (Roger Donaldson, 1977): Sam Neill.

14.50 Donaldson's *Smash Palace* (1981): Bruno Lawrence, Greer Robson.

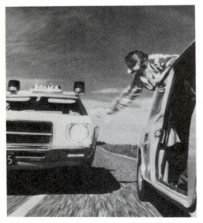

14.51 *Goodbye Pork Pie* (Geoff Murphy, 1981).

The latter director's *Ngati* (1987) is one of the nation's first Maori-focused theatrical films. Its first animated feature is Murray Ball's marvelous *Footrots Flats* (1986).

Despite recent successes, however, the fate of the world's youngest film industry is difficult to predict. Because of its size, New Zealand's main profit center lies in exports, whereas Australia, for example, is large enough to maintain a medium-sized industry on the strength of its domestic market alone. For the same reason, the government of New Zealand can fund only a small portion of domestic production budgets, with the rest coming from private investors. Thus, New Zealand will continue to be torn between producing films with significance mainly for New Zealanders and producing those that appeal primarily to an international mass market.

CANADA

Canada is another Commonwealth nation whose cinema has experienced sudden and unexpected growth. Although Canada is one of the largest and wealthiest countries in the world, its film market was dominated until very recently by American productions, much as British cinema had been during the thirties. Before 1978, film production in Canada was basically a cottage industry under the tight control of the National Film Board (NFB). Founded in 1939 by British documentary producer John Grierson, the NFB coordinated all government film activities in an attempt to end Hollywood dominance and establish a national cinema that would, in Grierson's words, "interpret Canada to Canadians and the world." For this purpose, Grierson gathered about him a group of talented documentarists (Stuart Legg, Stanley Hawes, Raymond Spottiswoode, Joris Ivens, John Fernhout, and Irving Jacoby). During World War II, Canada became the world's leading producer of Allied war propaganda films (the *World in Action* series, 1942–45, and *Canada Carries On*, 1940–45), as well as other types of nonfiction film. After the war, Grierson returned to England, but the NFB continued to produce distinguished documentaries and animated shorts, as in the brilliant experimental work of Norman McLaren* (b. 1914). With the arrival of television, Canadian filmmakers turned increasingly to *cinéma vérité* techniques (the *cinéma-direct* movement, in fact, was founded in the early sixties by French-Canadian filmmakers at the NFB, including Michel Brault, Pierre Perrault, and Claude Jutra, under the influence of Jean Rouch—see Chapter 13).

For all of Canada's success with documentary and animated cinema, feature filmmaking was left almost exclusively to the Americans until

---

* McLaren developed and perfected the technique of the cameraless film, originated by Len Lye (1901–80) in 1934. He works by painting and drawing his images directly on the celluloid, regardless of frame divisions. See Valliere T. Richard, *Norman McLaren: Manipulator of Movement: The National Film Board Years, 1947–1967* (Newark: University Press of Delaware, 1982).

1963, when the NFB produced two remarkable semidocumentaries. Don Haldane's *Drylanders* is an account of the harsh existence of a Canadian farming family during the first thirty years of the century, and Paul Perrault and Michel Brault's *Pour la suite du monde* (*So That the World Goes On*/*Moontrap*), about the attempt of the people of an isolated St. Lawrence River island to revive the hunting of Beluga whales. By 1964, the NFB was supporting feature production in both French (Gilles Groulx's *Le Chat dans le sac* (*The Cat in the Sack*) and English (Don Owen's *Nobody Waved Goodbye*). But Canadian feature production averaged only four films per year, and many Canadian directors (e.g., Norman Jewison, Sidney J. Furie, Arthur Hiller, Silvio Narizzano, Ted Kotcheff) and actors (Donald Sutherland, Christopher Plummer, Michael Sarrazin, Joanna Shimkus) migrated south to work in the American industry. And it was a rare Canadian feature indeed—such as Irvin Kershner's *The Luck of Ginger Coffey* (U.S.-Canada, 1964), shot on location in Montreal—that enjoyed even modest success beyond its own borders.

In an effort to reverse this trend, the Canadian Film Development Corporation (CFDC) was established by an Act of Parliament in 1967 with a fund of 10 million dollars (now a revolving annual fund of 4.5 million dollars) to promote the national feature industry through grants and guaranteed loans. By 1972, the annual feature output had risen to twelve and included such notable French- and English-language films as Michel Brault's *Entre la mer et l'eau douce* (*Between the Sea and the Still Waters*, 1968); Gilles Carle's *Le Viol d'une jeune fille douce* (*The Rape of a Sweet Young Girl*, 1968) and *La Vraie nature de Bernadette* (*The True Nature of Bernadette*, 1972); Gilles Groulx's *Entre tu et vous* (*Between Yourselves*, 1969); Claude Jutra's *Mon Oncle Antoine* (*My Uncle Antoine*, 1971) and *Kamouraska* (1973); Denys Arcand's *Réjeanne Padovani* (1972); Paul Almond's *Isabel* (1968); Don Owen's *The Ernie Game* (1968); Allan King's *Warrendale* (produced for the CBC) and *A Married Couple* (1969); Don Shebib's *Goin' Down the Road* (1970) and *Between Friends* (1973); Jean Chabot's *Mon Enfance à Montréal* (*My Childhood in Montreal*, 1972); William Fruet's *Wedding in White* (1972); and Eric Till's *A Fan's Notes* (1972). In 1974, the CFDC scored an unprecedented international success with Ted Kotcheff's *The Apprenticeship of Duddy Kravitz*. Nevertheless, by 1977 less than 6 million dollars in private funds were being invested in Canadian feature films.

But in 1978 two things occurred that radically changed the nature of the Canadian industry. The first was a policy change at the CFDC in which the seed money for Canadian feature projects was lent to producers rather than directors, increasing investment incentive within the business community. Second, and infinitely more important, the Canadian government enacted wide-ranging tax shelter legislation for film investment, which has rapidly become the second most popular form of tax relief in the country (after oil depletion allowances). The result has been a boom in the production of commercial features the like of which few countries have experienced in modern times: 6 million dollars was invested in Canadian feature production in 1977; over 150 million dollars in 1979; and 300 million dollars in 1980. At the same time, coproductions

14.52 *The Apprenticeship of Duddy Kravitz* (Ted Kotcheff, 1974), the first Canadian feature to achieve international distribution: Richard Dreyfuss, Micheline Lanctôt.

with the United States, France, Italy, and Japan, as well as domestic productions on a previously unthinkable big-budget scale, have combined to produce one of the most commercially lucrative production environments anywhere in the world today. Among the first big winners were Irving Reitman's *Meatballs,* with 40 million dollars in receipts for 1979, and Bob Clark's odious *Porky's,* 1981, which, though shot on location in Florida, has become the highest grossing "Canadian" film in the industry's brief history. That the environment and the films lack a specifically Canadian character has troubled some observers, but there can be no question that the kind of filmmaking activity being financed in Canada today represents a solid economic achievement.

Between 1977 and 1981, for example, Canada produced or coproduced all of the following films, among many others: *Why Shoot the Teacher* (Silvio Narizzano, 1977), *Who Has Seen the Wind?* (Allan King, 1977), *J. A. Martin, Photographe* (Jean Beaudin, 1977), *Outrageous* (Richard Brenner, 1977), *Skip Tracer* (Zale Dalen, 1977), *Le Soleil se leve en retard* (*The Sun Rises Late;* André Brassard, 1978), *Caro papa* (*Dear Papa;* Dino Risi, 1978), *Una giornata speciale* (*A Special Day;* Éttore Scola, 1978), *A Nous deux* (*Us Two;* Claude Lelouch, 1979), *A Man, a Woman, and a Bank* (Noel Black, 1979), *Silent Partner* (Daryl Duke, 1979), *Mourir à tue-tête* (English title: *Primal Fear;* Anne-Clair Poirier, 1979), *The Changeling* (Peter Medak, 1979), *Murder by Decree* (Bob Clark, 1979), *Agency* (George Kaczender, 1979), *Bear Island* (Don Sharp, 1979), *Out of the Blue* (Dennis Hopper, 1980), *Circle of Two* (Jules Dassin, 1980), *Atlantic City* (Louis Malle, 1980), *L'Affair Coffin* (*The Coffin Affair;* Jean-Claude Labrecque, 1980), *L'Arrache coeur* (*The Broken Heart;* Mireille Dancereau, 1980), *Les Bon débarras* (*Good Riddance;* Francis Mankiewicz, 1980), *The Lucky Star* (Max Fischer, 1980), *Fantastica* (Gilles Carle, 1980), *Keiko* (Claude Gagnon, 1980), *Shades of Silk* (Mary Stephen, 1980), *L'Homme à tout faire* (*The Handyman;* Micheline Lanctôt, 1980), *Scanners* (David Cronenberg, 1981), *The Hounds of Notre Dame* (Zale Dalen, 1981), *Ticket to Heaven* (R. L. Thomas, 1981), *Heartaches* (Don Shebib, 1981), *Quest for Fire* (Jean-Jacques Annaud, 1981), *Threshold* (Richard Pearce, 1981), *Improper Channels* (Eric Till, 1981), *Surfacing* (Claude Jutra, 1981), and *Les Plouffe* (Gilles Carle, 1981).

With twenty-four entries at the 1980 Cannes Festival, Canada announced its intention to become a "world class" force in cinema, but in fact its success in this arena has been limited at best. Although Canada has continued to produce a number of interesting films with uniquely Canadian content—e.g., *Suzanne* (Robin Spry, 1981), *The Grey Fox* (Phillip Borsos, 1982), *Unfinished Business* (Don Owen, 1984; a sequel to *Nobody Waved Goodbye,* twenty years after), *Big Meat Eater* (Chris Windsor, 1982), *The Terry Fox Story* (Ralph Thomas, 1983), *Videodrome* (David Cronenberg, 1983),* *Crime Wave* (John Paizs, 1985), *My American Cousin*

14.53 Anne-Claire Poirier's *Mourir à tue-tête,* Quebec's biggest commercial success of 1979.

---

* Other recent Canadian English-language features of note are *Alligator Shoes* (Clay Borris, 1981); *Running Brave* ("D. S. Everett," 1983); *Of Unknown Origin* (George Pan Cosmatos, 1983); *The Wars* (Robin Phillips, 1983); *Cross Country* (Paul Lynch, 1983); *Ups*

14.54 Micheline Lanctôt's *L'Homme à tout faire* (1980).

14.55 Hallucinated reception: David Cronenberg's *Video-drome* (1983): James Woods.

(Sandy Wilson, 1985), *Loyalties* (Anne Wheeler, 1986), *Dancing in the Dark* (Leon Marr, 1986), *Keeping Track* (Robin Spry, 1987), *Candy Mountain* (Robert Frank, 1987), *I've Heard the Mermaids Singing* (Patricia Rozeman, 1987), *Blindside* (Paul Lynch, 1988)—the majority of them are either shot out of the country with CFDC funding or use Canadian locales to represent other places entirely (particularly aggravating to

& Downs (Paul Almond, 1983); *Siege* (Maura O'Connell, 1983); *Music of the Spheres* (G. Phillip Jackson, 1984); *Bedroom Eyes* (William Fruet, 1984); *Bay Boy* (Daniel Petrie, 1984); *The Masculine Mystique* (John N. Smith and Giles Walker, 1984); *Low Visibility* (Patricia Gruben, 1984); *Night Magic* (Lewis Furey, 1985); *One Magic Christmas* (Phillip Borsos, 1985); *The Peanut Butter Solution* (Michael Rubbo, 1985); *Samuel Lount* (Laurence Keane, 1985); *The Adventures of Faustus Bidgood* (Michael Jones and Andy Jones, 1986); *Tramp at the Door* (Allan Krocker, 1986); *The Vindicator* (also known as *Frankenstein '88,* Jean-Claude Lord, 1986); and *The Gate* (Tibor Takacs, 1987).

In the documentary form, ever strong in Canada, the following titles are prominent: *A Private World* (Eric Saretzky, 1981); *Being Different* (Harry Raksy, 1981); Janis Cole and Holly Dale's *P4W: Prison for Women* (1981) and *Hookers on Davie Street* (1984); *Behind the Veil* (Gloria Demes, 1984); *Abortion: Stories from the North and South* (Gail Singer, 1985); *Dark Lullabies* (Irene Lilienheim, 1985); *Tears Are Not Enough* (John Zaritsky, 1985); *The Championship Part 3—The Final Battle* (Donald Brittain, 1986); *Prison Mother, Prison Daughter* (John Kastner, 1986); *Karsh: The Searching Eye* (Harry Rasky, 1986); *Sitting in Limbo* (John N. Smith, 1986); and *Passiflora* (Fernand Belanger, 1986). Within the documentary field, the Canadians have finely honed the subgenre of the concert film, of which the following are examples: *Ladies and Gentlemen The Fabulous Stains* (Lou Adler, 1982); *Rumours of Glory* (Martin Lavut, 1983); *Rock & Rule* (Clive A. Smith, 1983; animated); and *We Will Rock You* (Saul Swimmer, 1983).

See Gerald Pratley, *Torn Sprockets: The Uncertain Projection of the Canadian Film* (Newark: University of Delaware Press, 1987); Robert E. Miller, "The Canadian Feature Film Conundrum: 1894–1967," in *Current Research in Film: Audiences, Economics, and Law,* Vol. 4, ed. Bruce A. Austin (Norwood, N.J.: Ablex Publishing, 1988), pp. 125–46; Manjunath Pendakur, *Canadian Dreams and American Control: The Political Economy of the Canadian Feature Film Industry* (Detroit, Mich.: Wayne State University Press, 1988); and "The Internationalization of the Canadian Film Industry," in *Current Research in Film: Audiences, Economics, and Law,* Vol. 4, pp. 147–69.

Canadians in this regard are the hundreds of so-called "Stars and Stripes" films, which feature Canadian towns as cities or unidentified locations in the United States and employ mainly American actors).* In fact, according to Maurice Yacowar, in 1982 foreign-dominated—largely American—film and video distribution companies accounted for 73 percent of Canada's gross industry revenues; and non-Canadians also earned 95 percent of all royalties, rentals, and commissions.† In 1985 and 1986, however, the Canadian government restructured the CFDC to encourage local production and control and to eliminate certain tax incentives for foreign investment. Nevertheless, the Canadian film industry remains dominated today by the American majors, who by their own admission still control 80 percent of Canada's annual box-office receipts.

But while the country at large has become a major center for international production, a truly national Canadian cinema can be said to exist in the work of several young *québecois* directors, protégés of the somewhat older pathbreaking filmmaker Jean-Pierre Lefebvre (b. 1941)—*La Révolutionnaire* (*The Revolutionary*, 1965); *Las Dernières fiançailles* (*The Last Engagement*, 1973); *L'Amour blessé* (*Wounded Love*, 1975); *Le Vieux pays où Rimbaud est mort* (*The Old Country Where Rimbaud Died*, 1977); André Forcier—*Bar salon* (*Tavern*, 1974); Michel Brault—*Les Ordres* (*The Orders*, 1974); Denys Arcand—*La Maudite galette* (*Dirty Money*, 1971); *Gina* (1971); Jean Chabot—*Une Nuit en Amérique* (*A Night in America*, 1973); *La Fiction nucléaire* (*The Nuclear Lie*, 1979); Jean-Guy Noël—*Ti-cul Tougas* (1976); and Jacques Leduc—*La Tendresse ordinaire* (*Ordinary Tenderness*, 1975); *Chroniques de la vie quotidienne* (*Chronicles of Daily Life*, 1978). The question of whether *le cinéma québecois* could survive as a national entity in the face of CFDC's world class aspirations was answered affirmatively during the eighties in the work of a new generation of Francophone filmmakers—Robert Menard (*Une Journée en taxi* [*A Day in a Taxi*, 1982]); Bruno Carriére (*Lucien Brouillard*, 1983); Claude Fournier (*Bonheur d'occasion* [*The Tin Flute*, 1983]); François Bouvier (*Jacques et November*, 1985); Yves Simoneau (*Pouvoir intîme* [*Intimate Power*, 1986]); Léa Pool (*La Femme de l'hôtel* [*The woman in Transit*, 1984], *Anne Trister* [1986], *Les Fous de bassan* [*In the Shadow of the Wind*, 1987], *A Corps perdu* [*Straight to the Heart*, 1988]); Jean-Claude Lauzon (*Un Zoo la nuit* [*Night Zoo*, 1987]); and Hubert-Yves Rose (*La Ligne de chaleur* [*The Heat Line*, 1988]). In addition, more experienced directors continued to produce significant work in *Les Beaux souvenirs* (*Fond Memories* [Francis Mankiewicz, 1982]); *Au Clair de la lune* (*Moonshine Bowling* [André Forcier, 1983]; Jean-Pierre Lefebvre's *Au Rhythme de mon coeur* (*To the Rhythym of My Heart*, 1983) and *Le Jour "S"* ("*S*" *Day*, 1984); Claude Gagnon's *Larose, Pierrot, et la Luce* (1983), *Visage Pale* (*Pale Face*, 1985), and *The Kid Brother* (1987); Gilles Carle's *Maria Chapdelaine* (1983) and *La Guepe*

14.56 *Cinéma quebécois: On est au coton* (Denys Arcand, 1970), a feature-length documentary about the economic oppression of Canadian textile workers by American mill-owners, made for the National Film Board and suppressed by the government.

---

* On the body of Cronenberg's work, see the science fiction section of Chapter 12.

† Maurice Yacowar, "The Canadian as Ethnic Minority," *Film Quarterly* 60, 2 (Winter 1986–87): 13–19.

14.57 Archand in a different vein: *Le Déclin de l'empire Américain* (1986).

(*The Wasp*, 1986); Micheline Lanctôt's *Sonatine* (1984); *Les Années de rêves* (*Years of Dreams and Revolt* [Jean-Claude Labrecque, 1984]); *La Dame en coleurs* (*Our Lady of the Paints* [Claude Jutra, 1985]); *Sauve-toi, Lola* (*Run for Your Life, Lola* [Michel Drach, 1986]); and *Le Sourd dans la ville* (*Deaf to the City* [Mireille Dansereau, 1987]). Moreover, during this same period Quebec enjoyed major international hits by one of its most politically and socially committed filmmakers, Denys Arcand, in *Le Déclin de l'empire Americaine* (*The Decline of the American Empire*, 1986), an ironic study of contemporary sexual mores, and the audaciously conceived modern passion play *Jesus of Montréal* (1989).* In 1989, *le cinéma québecois* was riding higher than at any point since its founding, and the government of the province flexed its muscle by threatening to amend the Quebec Cinema Act to require that all non-French films be dubbed into that language before distribution, a move to protect the regional industry by hampering the operations of the American majors.

---

* Other notable examples of recent Quebec features are *Gapi* (Paul Blouin, 1982); *La Guerre des tugues* (*The Dog Who Stopped the War* [Andre Melancon, 1984]); *Hold-Up* (Alexandre Arcady, 1985); *Le Matou* (*The Alley Cat*, [Jean Beaudine, 1985]); *Le Dernièr glacier* (*The Last Glacier*, [Roger Frappier, 1985]); *Equinoxe* (Arthur Lamothe, 1986); *Henri* (François Labonte, 1986); *The Morning Man* (Daniel J. Suissa, 1987); *Flag* (*Flagrante Delicto*, [Jacques Santi, 1988]); and *Marie s'en va-t-en ville* (*Marie in the City*, [Marquise Lépage, 1988]). The *québecois* documentary is also well represented in such works as *Paroles du Québec* (*Quebec's Words*, [Jean-Claude Labrecque, 1981]); *Le Bête lumineuse* (*Shimmering Beast*, [Pierre Perrault, 1983]); *Mouvement-danse* (Gilles Pare and Celine Thibodeau, 1984); *Quel numero?* (*What Number?*, [Sophie Bissonette, 1985]); *10 jours . . . 48 heures* (Georges Dufax, 1986); and *Les Vidangeurs* (*Garbagemen*, [Jean-Claude Labreque, 1986]). It is worth noting that in 1979 the provincial government created the *Institut de Cinéma Québecois,* which subsidizes film projects, from script through production and distribution. The institute also operates the *Cinémathéque Quebécoise et Musée du Cinéma* in Montreal, modeled on the *Cinémathéque Française* in Paris. Montreal is also the home of a major competitive festival, the World Film Festival, held annually in late summer. The festival is unrelated to the *Institut.*

THE SECOND ITALIAN FILM RENAISSANCE

Like the American, French, and British cinemas, Italian cinema experienced a creative decline during the fifties as the neorealist impulse died out and the studios returned to the business of producing mass entertainment. Visconti, Rossellini, and De Sica (see Chapter 11) continued to make serious films, but, as elsewhere, the industry's emphasis was on spectacle and mildly titillating sex. The fifties was largely a period of "rosy realism" in the Italian film—a mode that might best be understood as a merging of *telefono bianco* and neorealism—and the decade witnessed the appearance of such international sex symbols as Sophia Loren, Gina Lollobrigida, and Marcello Mastroianni. But two figures were working within the domestic cinema at this time who would create the second postwar Italian film renaissance—Federico Fellini (b. 1920) and Michelangelo Antonioni (b. 1912).

Federico Fellini

Formerly a newspaper cartoonist, Fellini began his film career as a scriptwriter for Rossellini (*Roma, città aperta*, 1945; *Paisà*, 1946; *Il Miracolo*, 1948),* for Pietro Germi (*In nome della legge*, 1949; *Il cammino della speranza*, 1950), and for Alberto Lattuada (*Senza pietà*, 1948). His early films were very much in the orthodox neorealist tradition. *Luci del varietà* (*Variety Lights*, 1950), co-directed with Lattuada, provides an ironic portrait of a seedy itinerant vaudeville troupe. Fellini's first solo film, *Lo sceicco bianco* (*The White Sheik*, 1952), is a sardonic account of a young bride's infatuation with the hero of a *fumetto*, or popular photomagazine strip. But *I vitelloni* (*The Loafers* / *The Young and the Passionate*, 1953) was the first film to reveal the director's remarkable

---

* Released in the United States in 1950 as one of three episodes in a film distributed by Joseph Burstyn as *Ways of Love* (the other episodes were Marcel Pagnol's *Jofroi* [1933] and Jean Renoir's *Une Partie de campagne* [1936; 1946]). Fellini also starred in *Il miracolo* as the tramp who is mistaken by a peasant woman for St. Joseph. See Chapter 11.

15.1 *I vitelloni* (Federico Fellini, 1953): Vira Silenti, Franco Interlenghi, Alberto Sordi.

15.2 Fellini's *La strada* (1954): Giulietta Masina, Anthony Quinn.

feeling for character and atmosphere. This episodic study of aimless young loafers in the seaside resort town of Rimini, where Fellini grew up, contains semiautobiographical elements, and it remains one of his finest achievements.

With *La strada* (*The Road*, 1954), produced by Dino De Laurentiis and Carlo Ponti,* Fellini made a break with neorealism to tell the story of a simpleminded peasant girl who is sold to a circus strong man for a plate of pasta. He treats her brutally and, after a series of misadventures,

---

* De Laurentiis (b. 1919) and Ponti (b. 1910) both began their careers as producers during the neorealist period, the former with *Riso amaro* (1948), whose star, Silvana Mangano, De Laurentiis married in 1949, the latter with *Senza pietà* (1948) and *Il mulino del Po* (1949). In 1950 they formed Ponti–De Laurentiis Productions, which produced some of the most important Italian films of the decade—Rossellini's *Europa '51* (1952) and Fellini's *La strada* (1954) and *Le notti di Cabiria* (1956) among them—as well as the epic American / Italian coproduction *War and Peace* (King Vidor, 1956). The partnership was dissolved in 1957, when Ponti married Sophia Loren and began to produce films for her (*The Black Orchid,* Martin Ritt, 1958; *That Kind of Woman,* Sidney Lumet, 1959; *Heller in Pink Tights,* George Cukor, 1960; *Two Women,* Vittorio De Sica, 1960). In the sixties, De Laurentiis turned to the production of epic spectacles, such as *Barabbas* (Richard Fleischer, 1962), *The Bible* (John Huston, 1966), and *Waterloo* (Sergei Bondarchuk, 1970), at his vast studios near Rome (also producing Visconti's *Lo straniero* [1967] and Roger Vadim's *Barbarella* [1968]), but he liquidated the property and moved to the United States in the early seventies, where he has since produced such notable and / or infamous films as *Serpico* (Sidney Lumet, 1973), *Death Wish* (Michael Winner, 1974), *King Kong* (John Guillermin, 1976), *The Serpent's Egg* (Ingmar Bergman, 1977), and *King of the Gypsies* (Frank Pierson, 1979). During the same period, Ponti became a French citizen and produced for Godard, *Une Femme est une femme,* 1961 and *Les Carabiniers,* 1963; for Varda, *Cleo de cinq à sept,* 1962; for Demy, *Lola,* 1960; and for Chabrol, *Landru,* 1962. He also produced for David Lean, *Dr. Zhivago,* 1965; for Elio Petri, *La dècima vittima,* 1965; for Antonioni, *Blow-Up,* 1966, *Zabriskie Point,* 1970 and *The Passenger,* 1975; for Andy Warhol, *Andy Warhol's Frankenstein,* 1974, and *Andy Warhol's Dracula,* 1974, both directed by Paul Morrissey; and for Éttore Scola, *Brutti, sporchi, e cattivi,* 1976, and *Una giornata speciale,* 1977.

finally abandons her. Years later, he learns of her death and collapses in a fit of weeping. Realistic in form but essentially allegorical in content, *La strada* was attacked by leftist critics, including Zavattini (see Chapter 11), for betraying the social commitment of neorealism. But it attracted worldwide attention and won a Silver Lion, the second highest honor, at the prestigious Venice Film Festival in 1954. By the time he made *La strada,* Fellini had assembled about him the group of collaborators with whom he was to work for most of his career: his coscenarists, Ennio Flaiano and Tullio Pinelli; his director of photography, Otello Martelli; his composer, Nino Rota; and his leading lady, Giulietta Masina, who is also his wife. Fellini's next film was *Il bidone* (*The Swindle,* 1955); like *La strada,* it was realistic in style but symbolic in content. This tale of two-bit swindlers who victimize the poor has an aura of tragedy about it and contains a number of surreal touches which adumbrate Fellini's later concern with psychology and myth. *Le notti di Cabiria* (*Nights of Cabiria,* 1956), which Fellini wrote with the Marxist poet and future director Pier Paolo Pasolini, again has Giulietta Masina as the central figure. Here she plays a plucky, indomitable Roman prostitute who is betrayed and robbed by the young man she loves, but who nevertheless has the spirit to begin life anew.

After a hiatus of nearly four years, Fellini produced *La dolce vita* (1960), his first film in widescreen and a turning point in his work. This film concerns the life of a Roman journalist and press agent (Marcello Mastroianni) as he seeks sensational stories and hobnobs with the international jet set. Its superficially realistic milieu is corruption and decadence, and its visual extravagance borders on the fantastic. The film begins with a long traveling shot of a statue of Christ being flown by helicopter over the city and ends at the seashore with the capture of a monstrous dead fish. *La dolce vita* was a huge commercial success because of its sexual explicitness, but it nevertheless brought Fellini international recognition as a major artist and a new master of widescreen composition.

With *Otto e mezzo* (*8½,* 1963)—so named because it was his eighth-and-a-half film (the "half" having been his contributions to the anthology films *Amore in citta,* 1953, and *Boccaccio '70,* 1962)—Fellini moved directly into the world of self-reflexive fantasy. In *8½,* Guido (Mastroianni), a film director who represents Fellini himself, has undertaken a large-scale production but runs out of creative energy in the process. To escape, he lapses into a dreamworld of adolescent sexual fantasy and childhood memory, from which he ultimately emerges to accept defeat. In the film's final image, all of the major characters in his life (and in the film) link hands to dance around the rim of a circus ring as Guido—now a little boy—stands in the middle and directs them confidently through a megaphone. This surrealistic parable of the agony of artistic creation won many international awards; though it has been called a twentieth-century version of Dante's *Inferno,* *8½* is ultimately about the process of its own making.

In *Giulietta degli spiriti* (*Juliet of the Spirits,* 1965), his first feature in color, Fellini focused on a woman (played by Masina) who, like Guido in *8½,* collapses into a world of fantasy under the pressure of an unpleas-

15.3 Christ transported by helicopter in the opening shot of Fellini's *La dolce vita* (1960).

15.4 Fellini's *Otto e mezzo* (1963): Marcello Mastroianni, Edra Gale.

ant external reality (her husband's infidelity, the dominance of her glamorous mother and sisters) and who struggles out of it toward her own identity. Like *8½*, this basically nonnarrative film is concerned with the psychodynamics of memory, obsession, fantasy, and dream, and like Antonioni's *Il deserto rosso* the year before, it made highly expressive use of color. After contributing a characteristically haunting episode ("Toby Dammit") to the French anthology film *Histoires extraordinaires* (English title: *Spirits of the Dead*, 1968), Fellini embarked on his most ambitious project to date—*Fellini Satyricon* (1969), a flamboyant, personalized version of Petronius' epic paean to hedonism. In this lavish costume extravaganza based on a script by the director himself, he created a nightmarish portrait of the decadence of ancient Rome. Lacking any specific point of view or human reference, the film was felt by many critics to be purely a feast for the eye, as decadent and grotesque as its subject matter. But others maintained that Fellini had created a unique audiovisual language that transcended traditional narrative to suggest the continuity of depravity throughout human history.

I clowns (*The Clowns*, 1970) was a cinematic essay on the circus, a favorite Fellini metaphor, made on a low budget for Italian television, and it is a decidedly minor work. In *Fellini Roma* (1972), stunningly photographed by Giuseppe Rotunno, the director continued to explore his preoccupation with subjective history in an impressionistic study of Rome that combined stylized documentary with Fellini's own memories of the city as a youth. *Amarcord* (1974; the title is regional dialect for "I remember"), his next major work, is an autobiographical film about a young man growing up in the seaside town of Rimini some forty years ago. More directly autobiographical than *I vitelloni* and far less mannered and extravagant than its immediate predecessors, the film has been viewed by some critics as a return to Fellini's neorealist roots. It is actually a restrained and muted elegy for the director's youth, which provided Fellini with a breathing space before he undertook a spectacular English-language version of Casanova's *Memoirs* (*Casanova*, 1976)—a film more controversial with the critics for its glacially sumptuous tableaux than even *Fellini Satyricon*. *Prova d'orchèstra* (*Orchestra Rehearsal*, 1979), which uses the metaphor of a discordant symphony orchestra to comment on the dangerously chaotic state of modern democracy, has been widely praised for its cinematic beauty and intellectual depth. And the episodic *La città delle donne* (*City of Women*, 1980) offers an intelligent, if fanciful, vision of contemporary sexual warfare within the framework of its male protagonist's dreams. After a hiatus of two and a half years, Fellini returned to directing with *E la nava va* (*And the Ship Sails On*, 1983), a bizarre allegory on the nature of art (and, perhaps, the decline of the cinema) set in the context of a 1914 ocean voyage from Naples to Erimo Island, whose purpose is to scatter the ashes of a recently cremated opera diva. *Ginger e Fred* (*Ginger and Fred*, 1986) is a more conventional but equally hilarious satire on contemporary television and its cult of instant celebrity, while *Intervista* (*Federico Fellini's Interview*, 1987) is an entertaining personal documentary on the director's career at Cinecittà.

15.5 *Fellini Satyicon* (1969).

15.6 *E la nave va* (Federico Fellini, 1983): Peter Cellier, Norma West.

15.7 Fellini's *Ginger e Fred* (1986): Marcello Mastroianni, Giulietta Masina.

15.8 *Intervista* (1987).

Deeply influenced by neorealism in the formlessness and circularity of his narratives, Fellini structures his work through the sheer force of his own personality and obsessions. To use one of his favorite images, Fellini is first and foremost a great ringmaster whose circus is the human comedy as it exists both inside and outside himself. His theme is the mystery of identity (often his own or that of the characters played by Giulietta Masina), and he has learned to tap a large portion of the cinema's vast but generally unrealized potential to objectify subjective states, and vice versa. Fellini's rich frescoes and intoxicating images create a stylized world of mental fantasy in which reality is reinterpreted and made significant by the imagination of the artist. As Foster Hirsch has put it, "In his own way, [Fellini] combines the two strains that have always dominated Italian movies: the epic tradition, with its fondness for spectacle and operatic gesture, and the humanist tradition, with its deep feeling for the outcast and the oppressed."

Michelangelo Antonioni

Michelangelo Antonioni, like Fellini, began his career in film as a neo-realist. The son of a wealthy Ferrara businessman, he attended the Centro Sperimentale in Rome and wrote criticism for *Cinema*, after receiving a degree in political economy from the University of Bologna. In 1942 he collaborated on the script of Rossellini's *Un pilota ritorna* and served as an assistant to Marcel Carné on *Les visiteurs du soir*. His first films as a director were bleak and uncompromising neorealist documentary shorts like *Gente del Po* (*People of the Po*, 1943; 1947), *NU / Nettezza urbana* (*Dustmen*, 1948), and *La villa dei mostri* (*The House of Monsters*, 1950). But Antonioni's first features broke away from neorealist conventions to examine the middle-class milieu with which he was most familiar. *Cronaca du un amore* (*Story of a Love Affair*, 1950) depicts the consequences of an affair between a wealthy housewife and a car salesman. *I vinti* (*The Vanquished*, 1952) is an episodic film that examines violence among the restless youth of postwar Europe. *La signora senza camelie* (English title: *Camille Without Camellias*, 1953) concerns the rise and fall of a young movie star. All three films deal with social displacement and alienation, major themes in Antonioni's later work.

Antonioni continued to examine middle-class malaise in his first major feature, *Le amiche* (*The Girl Friends*, 1955), based on a novel by Cesare Pavese. In this pessimistic study of the alienated bourgeois women of Turin, Antonioni announced a new style, one which abandoned traditional plotting for a series of seemingly random events and which connected his characters intimately with their environment through the long take, or sequence shot, as opposed to montage. Use of the long take in *Le amiche,* which won the Silver Lion at Venice in 1955, enabled Antonioni to render the duration of real time on the screen and to emphasize the overwhelming importance of the material environment on the interior lives of his characters—the two major components of his mature style. In *Il grido* (*The Cry*, 1957), Antonioni turned briefly from the bourgeois milieu to portray the doomed journey of a factory worker and his daughter across the desolate wasteland of the Po Valley. Here, as in *Le amiche,* Antonioni used the physical environment of his film to express

15.9 Lost in space: Monica Vitti in *L'avventura* (Michelangelo Antonioni, 1959).

the psychology of the characters. But it was with *L'avventura* (*The Adventure,* 1959) that Antonioni achieved his first great masterpiece of *mise-en-scène.*

The first film in his brilliant trilogy about displacement and alienation in the modern world, and his first film in widescreen, *L'avventura* concerns a yachting party of rich Italians who land on a deserted volcanic island in the Mediterranean. A young woman, Anna, quarrels with her lover, Sandro, the leader of the party, and then mysteriously disappears. Anna's best fried, Claudia (played by Monica Vitti, who starred in Antonioni's next three films), and Sandro, both of whom have been marginal figures in the film up to this point, search the island for her and can find no trace. At Claudia's instigation, they return to mainland Sicily and continue their search, but they ultimately forget the missing woman and become lovers. The lack of final resolution and the seeming aimlessness of the narrative caused *L'avventura* to be jeered at the 1960 Cannes Festival, but it received the Jury Prize, and the impact of its revolutionary style was soon felt around the world.

For one thing, Antonioni used the sequence shot in *L'avventura* to equate film time with **real time**: every scene in the film, whether edited or not, takes the same amount of time to occur on the screen as it would in empirical reality. He also employed widescreen deep focus to link his characters inexorably with their oppressive surroundings. Both techniques have the effect of transferring the psychological experience of the characters to the audience since both groups are required to perceive time and space in precisely the same terms, unmediated by expressive montage. Thus, we experience the long and tedious search for Anna, first on the island and later on Sicily, very much as do Sandro and Claudia—at first with interest and anticipation, then with desperation, and finally with disgust and boredom, which leads us to forget the object of the search altogether and concentrate on the relationship of the searchers, just as do the searchers themselves. From one moment to the next, Antonioni never permits us to know any more about the mystery of Anna's disappearance (or about the mystery of their own relationship) than do Sandro and Claudia, and when the film ends with these mysteries unresolved, we realize that the psychological "adventure" of the characters has been made our own.

Antonioni continued his trilogy on what he calls "the great emotional sickness of our era" with *La notte* (*The Night,* 1960), a film about the growing estrangement of a successful novelist and his wife, and the alienation of both from the vacuous environment of modern industrial Milan. *L'eclisse* (*The Eclipse,* 1962), a brilliant conclusion to the trilogy, offered Antonioni's most sustained vision of the disorder and incoherence of modern existence. In Rome, two lovers conclude an affair, having "nothing left to say to each other," and the woman drifts into another affair with her mother's handsome young stockbroker. This affair, too, leads toward estrangement, and the film concludes with a seven-minute montage sequence of fifty-eight shots showing places in the city from late afternoon to nightfall where the lovers have met regularly during the

15.10 Ennui: Jeanne Moreau as the novelist's wife in Antonioni's *La notte* (1960).

15.11 Madness on the floor of the Milan stock exchange in Antonioni's *L'eclisse* (1962): Alain Delon.

15.12 A frame from the concluding sequence of *L'eclisse.*

course of the film, but in which neither of them now appears. Their unexplained disappearance (and our mute acceptance of it) is a chilling reminder of the fragility and impermanence of personal relationships and provides the perfect *coda* for a trilogy whose theme is the hopelessness of love in the modern age.

In *Il deserto rosso* (*Red Desert*, 1964) his first color film and winner of the Venice Golden Lion in 1964, Antonioni portrayed the neurotic wife of a wealthy engineer searching for meaning in the industrial wasteland of Ravena. Her sense of personal dislocation and the chaotic impingement of industry upon nature are both heightened by Antonioni's impressionist / expressionist use of color, the first of its kind in the history of film. Great poisonous clouds of yellow smoke billow from the factories, ships pass continuously in the background through the gray mists of the harbor, and chemical dyes give a nightmarish cast to the industrial wastes and slag heaps that intrude upon the natural landscape of the town. Antonioni created a foreshortened perspective for this nightmare world by using telephoto lenses (see below) in excess of 100mm to eliminate depth of field and heighten the film's abstraction.

Antonioni also used color symbolically in *Blow-Up* (1966), an abstract and mystifying film about a fashion photographer in "swinging" London who seems to have inadvertently photographed a murder in the background of some random shots he has taken of an anonymous woman in a park. As he "blows up" the telltale prints to greater and greater scale, objective reality becomes pure abstraction, and the film ends by suggesting that modern experience, even (or, perhaps, especially) when rendered visible on film, is not subject to interpretation and is therefore meaningless. *Blow-Up* was Antonioni's first film to reach a large popular audience, and its commercial success led to his filming of *Zabriskie Point* for MGM in America in 1969. Shot partly on location in Death Valley, this beautiful color film was an attempt to suggest the utter decadence of American society through the fantasies of the revolutionary young, but it failed due to Antonioni's misunderstanding of the American idiom and American culture. (Some critics had charged *Blow-Up* with a similar distortion of British society, but context was subordinate to concept in that particular film.) For a director to whom milieu is so crucial to meaning, a misunderstanding of this sort can be fatal.

After the commercial failure of *Zabriskie Point,* Antonioni went to China for five weeks to film a 220–minute documentary for Italian television. This poetic color film, entitled *Chung Kuo cina* (1972), is among Antonioni's finest documentary achievements, but it was attacked by the Chinese for denigrating their revolution (which it most certainly does not). For two years after his return from China, Antonioni worked on a project entitled *Technically Sweet* (*Tecnicamente dolce*), a feature film to be shot on location in the Amazon jungles with a new color telecamera system that would permit him to experiment still further with expressionistic color. The film's producer, Carlo Ponti, finally vetoed the project and asked Antonioni to consider filming a suspense thriller based on an original story by Mark Peploe about a man who changes his identity.

15.13 *Il deserto rosso* (Michelangelo Antonioni, 1964): Monica Vitti, Richard Harris.

15.14 David Hemmings takes the crucial photograph in Antonioni's *Blow-Up* (1966).

15.15 A scene from the conclusion of Antonioni's *The Passenger* (1975): Maria Schneider, Jenny Runacre, Angel del Pozo, José Maria Cafarel, and Jack Nicholson (partially off-frame) as the murdered reporter.

15.16 *Identificazione di una donna* (1982), Antonioni's last film. Tomas Milian, Christine Boisson.

The result was not a thriller at all but a despairing existential meditation on the uselessness of human individuality entitled *Professione: Reporter* (English title: *The Passenger,* 1975). Set in exotic international locations, *The Passenger* concerns a television news reporter at mid-life who finds a corpse in a Moroccan hotel and assumes the identity of the dead man. This desperate bid for self-liberation ends in disaster when the dead man turns out to have been a political operative dangerously involved in a Third World guerrilla war. Filmed as a series of long takes, and concluding with an elaborate seven-minute zoom-and-tracking shot in which the death of the reporter is obliquely implied rather than observed, *The Passenger* has been acclaimed as a masterpiece, although its clinical detachment from its subject verges on the inhuman. Antonioni has since adapted Jean Cocteau's *L'Aigle à deux têtes* (*The Eagle with Two Heads*) for Italian television as *Il mistero di Oberwald* (*The Mystery of Oberwald*), starring Monica Vitti, and has directed a final feature in *Identificazione di una donna* (*Identification of a Woman,* 1982), a film that encapsulates a lifetime of personal themes in a more or less straightforward narrative and won the Special Thirty-fifth Anniversary Prize at Cannes in the year of its release.

Now in his late seventies, Antonioni is one of the world's greatest living film artists, although a cerebral hemorrhage suffered in 1985 has prevented him from working since. He has tenaciously maintained his integrity and independence through a difficult career, to become a poet of the modern individual's estrangement from his environment and of his tragic inability to communicate with others and with himself. His films, from *L'avventura* (1959) through *The Passenger* (1975), contain little dialogue and less music, implying the virtual irrelevance of human communication, but they make brilliant use of naturalistic sound and silence to emphasize his characters' isolation in a seemingly random, if not hostile, universe. Antonioni has, by his own account, been concerned with behavior rather than story, and he lets the situations of his films grow out of the personalities and surroundings of his characters, rather than imposing situations through plot. His oblique and languorous narrative style, with its simultaneous capacity for distancing and involvement, has decisively influenced the development of the modern widescreen cinema. What he said of *L'avventura* after its Cannes premiere speaks for all that he has done since:

> I have rid myself of much unnecessary technical baggage, eliminating all the logical narrative transitions, all those connective links between sequences where one sequence served as a springboard for the one that followed. . . . Cinema today should be tied to the truth rather than logic. . . . The rhythm of life is not made up of one steady beat; it is, instead, a rhythm that is sometimes fast, sometimes slow. . . . There are times when it appears almost static. . . . I think that through these pauses, through this attempt to adhere to a definite reality—spiritual, internal, and even moral—there springs forth what today is more and more coming to be known as modern cinema, that is, a cinema which is not so much concerned with externals as it is with those forces that move us to act in a certain way and not in another.

Olmi, Pasolini, and Bertolucci

While Fellini and Antonioni were becoming acknowledged masters of the international cinema during the sixties, a second generation of postwar Italian directors was coming to prominence. Ermanno Olmi (b. 1931) was the young filmmaker most clearly in the neorealist tradition, though the slow-paced, elliptical style of his narratives brings him close to the later Antonioni. After making some forty documentaries in Milan between 1952 and 1959, Olmi established an international reputation in his narrative feature *Il pòsto* (*The Job / The Sound of Trumpets*, 1961). This sympathetic, insightful, and wistfully comic film concerns a young man from the provinces who takes a tedious job as a clerk with a large industrial firm in Milan. It contrasts the systematically dehumanizing nature of the job with his own naïve happiness at finding a place for himself in a complex, urbanized world. Like the films of Olmi's neorealist predecessors, *Il pòsto* was shot entirely on location with a cast of nonprofessional actors, and it is virtually plotless. *I fidanzati* (*The Fiancés*, 1963) confirmed Olmi's talent for the sympathetic and sophisticated treatment of the lives of ordinary working people. In it, an engaged couple is forced to separate so that the man can pursue his job in faraway Sicily, but they manage to endure and to sustain their relationship.

15.17 *Il pòsto* (Ermanno Olmi, 1961): Sandro Panzeri.

After an uncharacteristically pedestrian film about the life of Pope John XXIII, *E venne un uomo* (English title: *A Man Named John*, 1965), Olmi produced his finest work to date, *Un certo giorno* (*One Fine Day*, 1968). This film concerns a successful advertising executive who kills a man in an automobile accident and is forced to reexamine the course of his entire life in an attempt to make some sense of it. In the end, he is acquitted of his crime through the services of a smart lawyer and once more succumbs to bourgeois insensitivity. *I ricuperanti* (*The Scavengers*), made for Italian television in 1969, is about the vagrant life of battlefield scavengers in postwar Italy. But with *Durante l'estate* (*In the Summertime*, 1971), also made for television, Olmi moved toward romantic fantasy in the visually sumptuous tale of a forger whose rich inner life lends him dignity and significance. As always, Olmi's surface realism here is informed by a sense of the sad and absurd comedy of everyday life. His other films of the seventies are *La circostanza* (*The Circumstance*, 1974) and *L'albero degli zoccoli* (*The Tree of Wooden Clogs*, 1978). The latter, filmed as a three-part, 180-minute television series on peasant survival in the late nineteenth century, was produced, written, directed, photographed, and edited by Olmi himself. His *Camminacammina* (1983)—which he also wrote, designed, photographed, and edited, as well as directed—is a beautiful children's film about the coming of the Magi made for Italian television, Radiotelevisione Italiana (RAI). *Milano '83* (1984), a documentary on the cultural life of the city, was also funded by RAI. Olmi's recent theatrical feature, *Lunga vita alla Signora!* (*Long Live the Lady*, 1987), is a complex political allegory cast in the form of a gothic melodrama, while *La leggenda del santo bevitore* (*The Legend of the Holy Drinker*, 1988) is a religious parable set in 1920s Paris.

The Marxist poet, novelist, and essayist Pier Paolo Pasolini (1922–75),

15.18 *Il vangèlo secondo Matteo* (Pier Paolo Pasolini, 1964): Enrique Irazoqui, a non-professional actor, as Christ.

15.19 Pasolini's *Porcile* (1969): Pierre Clementi as the leader of the cannibals.

who had worked with Fellini on the script of *Le notti di Cabiria* (1956), made his first two films in the neorealist tradition but later rejected it in favor of what he called an "epical religious," or mythic, vision of experience. *Accattone* (*The Beggar*, 1961) and *Mama Roma* (1962) were tough, uncompromising studies of Roman low-life. Filmed on location with nonprofessional actors, they contained none of the sentimentality that sometimes marred the neorealist films of Rossellini and De Sica. The magnificent *Il vangèlo secondo Matteo* (*The Gospel According to St. Matthew*, 1964) was a semidocumentary reconstruction of the life of Christ from the Annunciation to the Resurrection that implicitly examined the relationship between the Marxist dialectic and Christian myth. This stark but brilliant work, shot in *cinéma vérité* style by Tonino Delli Colli (who would become Pasolini's regular cinematographer henceforth) with nonprofessional actors, stands today as the most dynamic version of the gospel story ever filmed.

As the sixties progressed, Pasolini turned more and more to allegory and myth. *Uccellacci e uccellini* (English title: *Hawks and Sparrows*, 1966) was, to use Pasolini's term, an "ideo-comic" film about the course of Italian Marxism. In *Edipo re* (*Oedipus Rex*, 1967), shot on location in Morocco, Pasolini set Sophocles' tragedy in a primitive region analogous to the unconscious mind and framed it with a contemporary Freudian prologue and epilogue in order "to project psychology onto myth." *Teorèma* (*Theorem*, 1968) and *Porcile* (*Pigsty*, 1969) were both major works in Pasolini's mythico-ideological mode, establishing him as a filmmaker of great intellectual importance. *Teorèma* is a mythical allegory set among the bourgeoisie that equates religious experience with sex: a bisexual, extraterrestrial Christ-figure visits an Italian middle-class family and causes it to disintegrate under the pressure of his mysterious sexual attraction. *Teorèma* scandalized the Catholic Church, but its companion piece, *Porcile*, goes even farther in its attack upon the religious and political hypocrisies of bourgeois culture. The film proceeds by intercutting two savage and revolting parables of capitalism—one about a band of medieval cannibals who live in the hills and eat the flesh of kidnapped travelers, the other about a wealthy contemporary West German industrialist who has made his fortune from the Holocaust and whose demented son loves intercourse with pigs. At the end of the film, the cannibals are ripped apart by wild dogs at the instigation of the local police authorities, and the German youth is eaten by his pigs.

After shooting an extraordinary version of Euripides' *Medea* (1969) in Turkey, Pasolini abandoned the surrealist satire of the sixties to make a "trilogy of life," as he called it, by adapting the world's three greatest works of omnibus literature: Boccaccio's *Decameron* (*Il decamerone*, 1971), Chaucer's *Canterbury Tales* (*I racconti di Canterbury*, 1972), and *A Thousand and One Nights / The Arabian Nights* (*Il fiore delle mille e una notte*, 1974), shot on location in Italy, England, and Persia, respectively. His last film was *Salò* (English title: *The 120 Days of Sodom*, 1975), a version of de Sade's bizarre pornographic epic, which Pasolini updated and set in the Salò Republic of Italy during the last days of

Fascist rule. An important theoretician of film in many published essays, as well as a brilliant director, Pasolini at his best succeeded in creating an intellectual cinema in which metaphor, myth, and narrative form all subserved materialist ideology. By a grim irony, given his vision of the human race as a "pigsty," Pasolini's remarkable career was cut short in the fall of 1975 when he was murdered by a young thug who claimed that the director had made sexual advances toward him.*

Bernardo Bertolucci (b. 1940), Pasolini's assistant on *Accattone*, has gone on to become the most significant new director to emerge from the Italian cinema in the sixties. His film *La commare secca* (*The Grim Reaper*, 1962), made from a script by Pasolini when Bertolucci was only twenty, is a documentary-style investigation into the murder of a prostitute which was extremely well received at the Venice Festival. But it was *Prima della rivoluzione* (*Before the Revolution*, 1964) that brought the young director to international attention. This visually complex and intelligent film concerns a young man's inability to break away from bourgeois values and fully commit himself to Marxist ideals. *Partner* (1968) is an uneven film, overtly derivative of Godard, about a modern intellectual who meets his double. But with his dense philosophical investigations into the roots of fascism—*La strategia del ragno* (*The Spider's Strategy*, 1970), adapted from the Borges fiction "Theme of the Traitor and Hero," and *Il conformista* (*The Conformist*, 1970)—Bertolucci forged a complex and elliptical visual style that bordered on surrealism but was still very much his own.†

In *La strategia del ragno*, produced for Italian television, a young man seeks to discover the truth behind his father's death during the Fascist period. *Il conformista*, from the novel by Alberto Moravia, explores the psychology of a young man who is hired by Italian fascists to assassinate his former professor in France, and it makes a remarkable equation between sexual disorder, social decadence, and the authoritarian personality. Both

15.20 *Il conformista* (Bernardo Bertolucci, 1970): Jean-Louis Trintignat, Dominique Sanda.

---

* When he died, Pasolini was his country's most prominent Marxist intellectual. He was well on his way toward making an accommodation with the Italian Communist Party, which had expelled him for scandals involving homosexuality in 1950, and rumors persist to this day that his murder was politically motivated. In addition to his work as a director, he was a prolific and highly respected author of poetry (in both standard Italian and his native Friulian dialect), fiction, and cultural criticism, as well as an important film theorist (see, e.g., his "The Cinema of Poetry" in Bill Nichols, ed., *Movies and Methods* [Berkeley: University of California Press, 1976]). Pasolini's poetry and cultural writings are still focal points of contemporary Italian thought. See Enzo Siciliano, *Pasolini*, trans. John Shepley (New York: Random House, 1982); and Pier Paolo Pasolini, *Roman Nights and Other Stories*, trans. John Shepley (Marlboro, Vt.: The Marlboro Press, 1986). See also Dutch documentarist Philo Bregstein's *Whoever Says the Truth Shall Die* (1984), a film biography of Pasolini that attempts to resolve the mysterious circumstances of his death.

† See Robert Phillip Kolker's provocative critical study *Bernardo Bertolucci* (New York: Oxford University Press, 1985); and T. Jefferson Kline, *Bertolucci's Dream Loom: A Psychoanalytic Study of Cinema* (Amherst: The University of Massachusetts Press, 1987). Bertolucci's cousin, Giovanni Bertolucci, often functions as his producer. His brother Giuseppe has collaborated with him as co-writer and is a director of some importance himself (e.g., *Segreti Segreti* [*Secrets Secrets*, 1985]).

15.21 Bertolucci's *Last Tango in Paris* (1972): Maria Schneider, Marlon Brando.

15.22 The fruits of political violence: *Novecento* (Bernardo Bertolucci, 1976). Donald Sutherland.

films employ intricate narrative structures that move freely back and forth through time, emphasizing its relativity. *Il conformista*, Bertolucci has said, is a film not of the past but of the present, because "however the world has changed, feelings remain the same." Bertolucci's controversial *Last Tango in Paris* (*Ultimo tango a Parigi*, 1972) is less complex than *Il conformista*, but like its predecessor it employs an expressionistic color scheme and a disjointed narrative style to take us into the mind of a man deranged by grief, where sex, pain, and death have all melded. The epic *Novecento* (*1900*, 1976)*—reputedly the most expensive feature ever made in Italy—employs a cast of international stars to tell the stories of two families, one rich and one poor, through the first fifty years of the twentieth century in a paean to the political consciousness of the Italian agricultural classes.

Influenced by Pasolini, Godard, and the later Visconti rather than the neorealist tradition, Bertolucci is clearly a filmmaker of major importance to the future of narrative cinema, and he has continued to produce increasingly sophisticated and significant work. Although *La luna* (*Luna*, 1979), his sensuous film about an incestuous mother-son relationship, disappointed some critics, *La tragedia di un uomo ridicolo* (*The Tragedy of a Ridiculous Man*, 1981) offered a brilliant dissection of contemporary Italian political and social life in the drama of a manufacturer attempting to deal with the enigmatic kidnapping of his son by terrorists. In 1987, Bertolucci directed a film of unique visual splendor in *The Last Emperor*, the winner of multiple international prizes, including nine

---

* There are two versions of *Novecento* in current release: a 320–minute European version and a 248–minute English-language version, which was edited by Bertolucci himself at the demand of the film's producer-distributor, Paramount. In the English-language version the principal actors speak in their own voices, whereas in the European version the voices are dubbed in Italian.

American Academy Awards. This Italian-Chinese-British coproduction, a biography of Pu Yi, the last imperial ruler of China, was sumptuously photographed by Vittorio Storaro, cost 25 million dollars, and employed some 19,000 extras.*

Other Italian *Auteurs*

Other important figures in the new Italian cinema are Marco Belloc-chio (b. 1940), Francesco Rosi (b. 1922), Vittorio De Seta (b. 1923), Elio Petri (1929–82), and Gillo Pontecorvo (b. 1919). Bellocchio's savage *I pugni in tasca* (*Fists in the Pocket*) shocked Italy in 1965 with its portrait of a young epileptic who makes a rational choice to murder off the members of his diseased bourgeois family. The director's complex and outrageously funny political satire *La Cina é vicina* (*China Is Near*, 1967) launched another frontal assault on bourgeois values and shared the Venice Jury Prize in 1967 with Godard's *La Chinoise*. With *Nel nom e del padre* (*In the Name of the Father*, 1971), Bellocchio offered a stylized autobiographical account of life in a provincial Jesuit college in the late fifties. Like Vigo in *Zéro de conduite* (1933) and Lindsay Anderson in *If . . .* (1968), Bellocchio uses school as a microcosm for the oppressive, joyless, and class-ridden society that creates and sustains it. Characteristically, his fourth feature, *Marcia trionfale* (*Triumphal March*, 1976), is set in a military academy, but as in several of Bellocchio's subsequent films (for example, *Il gabbiano* [*The Seagull,* 1977] and *Salto nel vuoto* [*Leap into the Void,* 1979]), its formal qualities are frequently obscured by a heavy overlay of Marxist ideology. With *Gli occhi, la bocca* (*The Eyes, the Mouth,* 1982), however, Bellocchio became less critical in his analysis of bourgeois family life in a sympathetic if labyrinthine study of the effects of a favorite son's suicide on his mother and brothers. In his adaptation of Pirandello's *Enrico IV* (*Henry IV,* 1984), Bellocchio returned to the theme of his 1974 documentary *Matil da slegare* (*Fit To Be Tied;* codirected with Silvano Agosti, Sandro Petrag, and Stefano Rulli) on the sanity of those socially defined—and institutionalized—as being mad. Here, Marcello Mastroianni gives a brilliant performance as a nobleman who is thrown from his horse on his way to a costume party—a trauma that apparently induces the delusion that he is the medieval monarch of the Holy Roman Empire and causes his family to isolate him in royal splendor in the ancestual castle for twenty years. More recently, Bellocchio has directed *Il diavolo in corpo* (1986), an erotic, apolitical version of Raymond Radiguet's novel *La Diable au corps* (*The Devil in the Flesh*), already adapted twice before.

---

* Storaro has been Bertolucci's regular cinematographer since *Il strategia del ragno* with the single exception of *La tragedia di un uomo ridicolo*, which was shot by the equally distinguished Carlo Di Palmi. Storaro also contributed the vibrant color to Franco Zeffirelli's *Romeo and Juliet* (1968), the sensuous surfaces of Visconti's *Morte a Venezia* (1971), and the desaturated images of 1938 Rome for Éttore Scola's *Un giornata speciale* (1977), as well as many others. His work on Francis Ford Coppola's *Apocalypse Now* (1979) won him an Academy Award, and he won again in 1987 for *The Last Emperor*.

15.23 *Salvatore Giuliano* (Francesco Rosi, 1962).

Francesco Rosi, a former assistant to both Visconti and Antonioni, came into his own with *Salvatore Giuliano* (1962), a semidocumentary account of the real-life career of a bandit and folkhero and his murder by the authorities in postwar Sicily. Shot on location with nonprofessional actors, the film has an extremely elliptical narrative structure that moves back and forth in time with the facility of Bertolucci's *Il conformista*. Rosi has since proven himself to be a director of great social commitment and a legitimate heir to neorealism. His *Le mani sulla città* (*Hands Over the City*, 1963) is a powerful political film shot on location in documentary style about the corrupt relationship between real-estate development and modern city planning. *Il momento della verità* (*Moment of Truth*, 1965) is a critical analysis of the collective psychology of bullfighting. Rosi's next films were *Uomini contro* (*Men Against*, 1970), a diatribe against Italy's involvement in World War I, and *Il caso Mattei* (*The Mattei Affair*, 1972), yet another documentary reconstruction of a historical event, in this case the mysterious murder of a government official. *A propòsito di Lucky* (English title: *Lucky Luciano*, 1973) attempts to show the link between American and Sicilian gangsters and governments, and *Cadaveri eccellenti* (*Illustrious Corpses*, 1976), a characteristic film of political murder and intrigue, won many international prizes. In 1980 Rosi completed work on a four-hour television film (which was also released as a two-and-a-half-hour theatrical feature) based on Carlo Levi's 1945 memoir of political exile *Cristo si e fermato ad Eboli* (*Christ Stopped at Eboli*; English title: *Eboli*, 1980). This award-winning film was followed by another, *Tre fratelli* (*Three Brothers*, 1981), in which three surviving sons return to their small village home for their mother's funeral and discuss the state of Italy today. Rosi's version of Bizet's opera *Carmen* (1984) was intelligent but unspectacular, while *Cronaca di una morte annunciata* (*Chronicle of a Death Foretold*, 1987) has been a stunning critical success. This adaptation of Gabriel García Márquez's fantastic novel of love and death in a sleepy Colombian river town circa 1950 was magnificently shot on location by Rosi's regular cinematographer Pasqualino De Santis* with newly improved Super-Techniscope cameras.

The Sicilian-born director Vittorio De Seta, who writes and photographs his own films, made independent documentaries before directing *Banditi a Orgosolo* (*Bandits of Orgosolo*, 1961), a semidocumentary feature shot on location with nonactors, about a Sardinian shepherd who joins a group of revolutionary bandits. The film influenced the development of *cinéma-vérité* camera styles in both Italy and France, but with the exeption of the four-hour semidocumentary *Diario d'un maestro* (*Diary of a Schoolmaster*, 1973), De Seta has done little significant work since.

Elio Petri began his career as a scriptwriter for Giuseppe De Santis and Carlo Lizzani during the last days of the neorealist movement, but he has since developed into a subtle filmmaker with a sensuous and elliptical visual style of his own. Petri is a Marxist, and his most characteristic

---

* Director of photography for Rosi's first four films was Gianni Di Venanzo; he died in 1964.

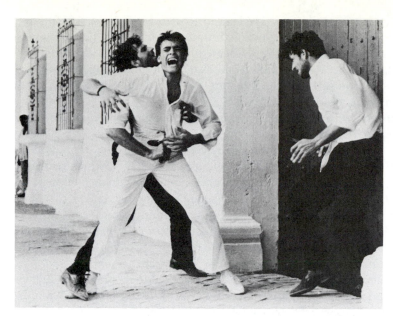

15.24 Rosi's *Cronaca di una morte annunciata* (1987).

films are social satires cast in the form of conventional genre pieces like *L'assassino* (*The Assassin*, 1961), *La dècima vittima* (*The Tenth Victim*, 1965), *Un tranquillo pòsto di campagna* (*A Quiet Place in the Country*, 1968), and his flamboyant analysis of the contemporary fascist personality, *Indagine su un cittadino al di sopra di ogni sospetto* (*Investigation of a Citizen Above Suspicion*, 1970). In the seventies Petri became more aggressively political, in films like *La classe operaia va in paradiso* (*The Working Class Goes to Heaven*, 1972), winner of the Cannes Grand Prix; *Todo modo* (*All Roads . . .* , 1976); and *Buone notizie* (*Good News*, 1979).

Gillo Pontecorvo was a film journalist and an assistant to Yves Allégret before turning to narrative cinema in 1960 with *Kapo,* a semidocumentary account of a young Jewish girl in Auschwitz who collaborates with the S.S. Since then, most of Pontecorvo's films have been scrupulously researched documentary reconstructions of historical events using authentic locations and nonactors. His most significant work to date is the remarkable *La battaglia di Algeri* (*The Battle of Algiers*, 1966), which employed the whole city and most of its population to reconstruct with complete verisimilitude the horrific events leading up to the liberation of Algeria. Financed by the Algerian government, the film won the Golden Lion at Venice in 1966. Impressive but less successful was *Queimada!* (*Burn!*, 1968), an attempt to probe the dynamics of colonial exploitation in the context of a nineteenth-century slave revolt on a Caribbean sugar plantation, and *The Tunnel* (1979), about the assassination of Spanish prime minister Carrero Blanco by Basque terrorists in 1973.

Finally, some note should be taken of the important role played by state-operated Italian television, RAI, in the production of major feature films. Since 1969, distinguished directors like Fellini (*I Clowns,* 1970), Antonioni (*Chung kuo Cina,* 1972), Bertolucci (*La strategia del ragno,*

15.25 *La battaglia di Algeri* (Gillo Pontecorvo, 1966): Mohamed Ben Kassen, Brahim Haggiag.

1970), Olmi (*I recuperanti*, 1969), and Rossellini (*Socrate*, 1970) have all made films for RAI, often in collaboration with foreign television networks, as in the eighties have Francesco Rosi, Paolo and Vittorio Taviani, and Éttore Scola. RAI also commissioned features during the seventies from such promising young directors as Nelo Risi, Giovanni Amico, Adriano Apra, and Liliana Cavani.

Cavani (b. 1936) emerged as a filmmaker of some importance with the notoriety of *Il portiere di notte* (*The Night Porter*, 1974), a sadomasochistic love story that attempts to dissect the culture of fascism, and *Al di là del bene e del male* (*Beyond Good and Evil*, 1977), which recreates the last, mad years of the German philosopher Friedrich Nietzsche in scatological detail. In the eighties, Cavani's work descended to *grand guignol* (*La pelle* [*The Skin*, 1981]) and melodramatic excess (*Oltre la porta* [*Beyond the Door*, 1982]), although *Interno Berlinese* (*The Berlin Affair*, 1985), her erotic account of a suicide pact *a trois* in Nazi Germany, earned critical respect.

Other notable Italian filmmakers who entered their major productive period during the seventies are Marco Ferreri (b. 1928), Éttore Scola (b. 1931), the Taviani brothers—Paolo (b. 1931) and Vittorio (b. 1929)—and Lina Wertmuller (b. 1928). Ferreri, who also works in France and the United States, is a surrealist social critic in the mode of Buñuel whose characters often end up committing unpremeditated murder (*Dillinger e morto* [*Dillinger Is Dead*, 1968]) or self-mutilation (*La Dernière femme* [*The Last Woman*, 1977]; *Chiòdo asilo* [*My Asylum*, 1979]). His most characteristic films of the decade were *La grande bouffe* (*Blow-Out*, 1973), in which four gourmets gorge themselves and die surrounded by their own excrement and vomit, and *Bye Bye Monkey* (1979), an allegory about the extinction of the human race set in New York. *Storie di ordinaria follia* (*Tales of Ordinary Madness*, 1981), adapted from stories by poet Charles Bukowski, depicts the 1960s Los Angeles counter-culture as a sleaze-pit of self-destructive impulse. *Storia di Piera* (*Story of Piera*, 1983) adapts the controversial autobiography of actress Piera Degli Esposita, whose childhood was allegedly sacrificed to incestuous relationships with both of her parents. Ferreri's other films of the eighties (*Il futuro e'donna* [*The Future Is Woman*, 1984]; *Y'a bon les blancs* [*Um, Good de White Folks*, 1988]) have not been successful, but *I Love You* (1986), about a young man who develops a fetish for a doll-like talking key-holder, shows that his anarchic spirit is nevertheless still intact.

Éttore Scola was a scriptwriter who began directing comedies in the sixties and achieved international critical acclaim with *C'eravamo tanto amati* (*We All Loved Each Other So Much*, 1975), an ambitious film that intertwines an examination of the myriad social and economic changes Italy has undergone since the end of World War II with a history of postwar Italian cinema as it has reflected and sometimes catalyzed those changes. *C'era vamo* is dedicated to Vittorio De Sica; and *Brutti, sporchi, e cattivi* (*Dirty, Mean, and Nasty / Down and Dirty*, 1976), a parody of that director's *Miracolo a Milano* (1950), shows the urban poor to be not a happy-go-lucky, socially cohesive group but hopelessly atomized

15.26 *La Nuit de Varennes* (Éttore Scola, 1982): Hanna Schygulla, Marcello Mastroianni, Harvey Keitel, *et al.*

and infected with capitalist greed. *Una giornata speciale* (*A Special Day*, 1977) recounts a chance meeting between two lonely outsiders—a weary housewife (Sophia Loren) and an antifascist homosexual journalist (Marcello Mastroianni)—on May 6, 1938, the occasion of Hitler's visit to Rome to sign the Axis alliance treaty with Mussolini. *La terraza* (*The Terrace*, 1980) is a film of comic vignettes that gently probes the relationship between Italian society and the cinema. *Passion d'amore* (1981) meticulously adapts a late-nineteenth-century novel about a strange liaison between a dashing young officer and an unattractive spinster. Scola's reputation as an international figure was resoundingly confirmed by *La Nuit de Varennes* (1982), a comedy of ideas that brings together Casanova, Thomas Paine, and Restif de la Bretonne on June 20, 1791, the day of the abortive flight of Louis XVI and Marie-Antoinette from the Tuileries. Since that time, Scola has directed *Le Bal* (*The Ball*, 1983), an adaptation of the Theatre du Campagnol's hit stage musical; the wistful comedy *Maccheroni* (*Macaroni*, 1985); *La famiglia* (*The Family*, 1987), a chronicle of the everyday life of a middle-class Roman family between 1906 and 1986; and *Splendor* (1989) a nostalgic salute to movie-going in the provinces in the immediate postwar years.

The Taviani brothers directed a number of openly political films during the sixties (*Un uomo da bruciare* [*A Man for Burning*, 1962]; *I sovversivi* [*The Subversives*, 1967]), before turning to a concern with the evolution of the "decent core" of society in the seventies. *Allonsanfan* (1974)—an Italian mispronunciation of the first two words of the French national anthem,"*Allons enfants . . .* "—is set in post-Napoleonic Italy where the Jacobins fight it out with the Freemasons over the purity of revolutionary ideals. *Padre Padrone* (*Father Master*, 1977), originally produced for Italian television, brought the Tavianis the Palm d'Or at Cannes, the New York Film Festival award, and international renown. This complex work, based on Gavino Ledda's autobiographical account of how he rose from the illiterate Sardinian peasantry to become a professor of linguistics, weaves fact and fiction, subjective sound and con-

15.27 *Padre, padrone* (Paolo and Vittorio Taviani, 1977): Omero Antonutti as Gavino Ledda, a Sardinian shepherd, raised in brutish isolation, who ultimately becomes a professor of linguistics.

15.28 *La notte di San Lorenzo* (Paolo and Vittorio Taviani, 1981).

crete image, to create a narrative that is at once emotionally satisfying and ideologically persuasive. After this stunning achievement, *Il prato* (*The Meadow*, 1979), about the social frustrations of a young Tuscan magistrate, was generally disappointing; but the Tavianis scored another triumph with *La notte di San Lorenzo* (*The Night of Shooting Stars*, 1981), which depicts the successful struggle of a small rural community to survive a massacre by the Germans in 1944. This film, which won a Special Jury Prize at Cannes, was written by the Tavianis and is narrated in flashback by a woman who was a six year old child at the time. Since then, the brothers have written and directed *Kaos* (*Chaos*, 1984), an anthology of five episodes adapted from the novels of Pirandello, and *Good Morning, Babilonia* (*Good Morning, Babylon*, 1987), an original film in which two Italian immigrant brothers impersonate master masons in order to get jobs as set designers on D. W. Griffith's epic spectacle *Intolerance* (1916).

Lina Wertmuller, who became something of a cult figure in the United States during the seventies, began her film career as an assistant to Fellini on *8 1/2* (1963). That year she directed her first feature, a socio-comedy of Italian provincial life entitled *I basilischi* (*The Lizards*). She continued to make intelligent comic films for the domestic market until she scored her first international success with *Film d'amore e d'anarchia* (*Love and Anarchy*, 1973), an ironic examination of sex and politics in Fascist Italy, focusing on the attempts of a bungling anarchist (played by Giancarlo Giannini—a Wertmuller regular) to assassinate Mussolini. *Mimi metallurgo ferito nell'onore* (*Mimi the Metalworker / The Seduction of Mimi*, 1972) and *Tutto a posto e niente in ordine* (*Everything's in Order But Nothing Works / All Screwed Up*, 1974) also deal with the situations of hopeless underdogs (both played by Giannini) pitted against the system, and both carry the connection between sex and politics one step further. The ultimate statement of that connection, however, is *Travolti da un insolito destino nell'azzurro mare d'Agosto* (*Swept Away by an Unusual*

Destiny in the Blue Sea of August / Swept Away, 1974), in which a wealthy woman and a deckhand are swept away by a storm from a pleasure yacht to a desert island, where their roles as master and slave are temporarily reversed. Eventually the two fall in love, but when they return to society their old roles reassert themselves. Many feminist critics were disturbed by the film's ironic balance, but such irony is precisely Wertmuller's stock in trade as an artist. As proof, we have *Pasqualino settebellezze* (English title: *Seven Beauties,* 1976), a physically sumptuous paean to survival ethics set largely in a Nazi concentration camp where the Giannini character, an Italian army deserter, spends the duration of World War II. This complex film is by turns beautiful and repellent, since we are asked to identify with a protagonist who possesses the moral sensibility of a cockroach as well as the knack of surviving like one. The moral relativism of *Seven Beauties* outraged as many liberal critics as *Swept Away* did feminists because both films seemed to endorse patriarchal fascism. Whatever their point ideologically, the last films made by Wertmuller in the seventies—*The End of the World in Our Usual Bed on a Night Full of Rain* (1978) and *Blood Feud* (1979)—failed at the box office. Wertmuller did not direct again until *Scherzo del destino in agguato deitro l'angola come un brigante di strada* (*A Joke of Destiny Lying in Wait Around the Corner Like a Robber,* 1983), a social allegory about a government minister getting locked up in his bullet-proof and soundproof limousine; *Camorra* (1986), a murder mystery with social themes set in the context of Neapolitan gang wars; and *Notte d'estate con profilo Greco, occhi a mandorla e odore di basilico* (*Summer Night with Greek Profile, Almond Eyes, and Scent of Basil,* 1986), a reworking of the class- and sex-war themes of *Swept Away,* set on a Sardinian isle.

15.29 *Swept Away* (Lina Wertmuller, 1974): Mariangela Melato, Giancarlo Giannini.

The most significant development for Italian cinema in the eighties was the emergence of a new generation of talented comedy directors whose roots reach back to the traditions of *commedia dell'arte* but whose social consciousness and filmic technique are firmly grounded in contemporary reality. This group includes Maurizio Nichetti (b. 1948), whose brilliant surrealist pantomime *Ratataplan* (the word imitates the sound of a drum roll to Italian ears) swept the awards at Venice in 1979. He followed with the equally hilarious send-up of contemporary advertising, *Ho fatto splash!* (*It Made a Splash!,* 1980), and the absurdist satires *Domani si balla* (*Tomorrow We Dance,* 1982) and *Il be e il ba* (*The Bi and the Ba,* 1986). Nanni Moretti (b. 1953) began making films in Super-8, and his first hit was the 16mm *Ecce Bomba* (1978), a parody of traditional Italian film comedy, which, like the work of Nichetti, owed much to American silent slapstick as well as to the satiric wit of Woody Allen and Mel Brooks. Moretti's next film, *Sogni d'oro* (*Golden Dreams,* 1981), about a Fellini-like director making a film on Freud's mother, won the Golden Lion at Venice. He continued to mine this vein of sardonic, irreverent social comedy in *Bianca* (1984) and *La messa e' finita* (*The Mass Is Over,* 1985).

Carlo Verdone (b. 1946) has been successful with such episodic film sketches in Roman dialect as *Un sacco bello* (*Life Is Beautiful,* 1980);

White, Red, and Verdone (1981, with the director's name replacing the *verde* of the Italian tricolored flag); *Acqua e sapone* (*Soap and Water,* 1983); and *I due carabinieri* (*The Two Cops,* 1985). Massimo Troisi (b. 1954), whose *Ricomincio da tra* (*I'm Starting from Three*) was a smash hit in 1981, makes low-budget films in the Neapolitan dialect; most recently he has teamed with the Tuscan dialect comic Roberto Benigni to produce *Non ci resta che piangere* (*Nothing Left to Do But Cry,* 1985) and *Le vie del Signore sono finite* (*The Ways of the Lord Are Finite,* 1987), a period comedy set in the early days of fascism. Like Nichetti, Moretti, and Verdone, Troisi not only writes and directs his films, but also plays leading roles in them. A final comic filmmaker of note is the prolific Bolognese director Pupi Avanti (b. 1938). Though of an older generation than the quartet discussed above, Avanti came to filmmaking relatively late. He is best known for the highly original musical about Italy's fascination with American culture *Aiutami a sognare* (*Help Me to Dream,* 1981), and such offbeat light comedies as *Una gita scolastica* (*A School Outing,* 1983); *Noi tre* (*We Three,* 1984); and *Festa di laurea* (*Graduation Party,* 1985); but he has also made serious contemporary dramas, such as *Regalo di natale* (*Christmas Present,* 1986) and *Ultimo momento* (*Last Moment,* 1987).

Two other new directors whose work has buoyed recent Italian cinema are Salvatore Piscicelli and the American-born Peter Del Monte. Piscicelli's sympathetic portrayal of a working-class lesbian love affair, *Immacolata e Concetta, l'altra gelosia* (*Immacolata and Concetta, the Other Jealousy,* 1980), was followed by *Le occasioni di rosa* (*Rosa's Chances,* 1981), an equally sensitive film on the same theme; a fast-paced rock film, *Blues Metropolitano* (*Metropolitan Blues,* 1985); and the brooding black-and-white melodrama *Regina* (1987). Del Monte had his first commercial successes with *Piso pisello* (*Sweet Pea,* 1981) and *Piccoli fuochi* (*Little Fires,* 1985), both filmed from the fantastic perspective of small children. He earned international accolades for his surrealistic *film noir, Julia e Julia* (*Julia and Julia,* 1987), shot in high-definition video and blown up for 35mm distribution.

CONTEMPARARY WIDESCREEN TECHNOLOGIES AND STYLES

The French and Italian film renaissances of the sixties paved the way for a new era of cinematic expression in the seventies and eighties, one in which narrative is no longer an end in itself but a medium for audiovisual essays in philosophy, psychology, ideology, and social criticism—essays, that is, on the human condition. In short, the cinema has become today at the level of general practice what it has always been for its greatest individual *auteurs,* regardless of their particular aesthetic: a form of audiovisual literature. But contemporary widescreen cinema is as formally distinct from the postwar sound film as the postwar sound film was from the silent film. Aesthetically, the new cinema is one of subjective involvement and *mise-en-scène* predicated upon the widescreen sequence shot.

This is the future cinema of the "integral style" announced by André Bazin before his death in 1958. Its predecessors were early masters of the long take—Feuillade, von Stroheim, and Murnau in the silent cinema; Renoir, Rossellini, and Welles in the sound film. These *mise-en-scène auteurs* had been forced to do their pioneer work within the black-and-white rectangle of the Academy frame and were recognizably eccentric to the mainstream tradition of narrative and expressive montage. The introduction of the widescreen processes and the improvement of color film stock in the fifties were the technological preconditions for a full-scale revolution in favor of *mise-en-scène* aesthetics, and Bazin recognized this in his last essays. But Bazin could not have foreseen two vastly significant technological developments of the sixties: 1) the perfection and widespread use of hand-held 35 mm cameras, which permit continuous and spontaneous on-location shooting, and 2) refinements achieved within the optical industries using computer technology, which include improved wide-angle and telephoto lenses and ultimately produced the modern zoom lens. This latter development was especially significant, since by the mid-sixties all three types of lenses were standard equipment for Western and Eastern filmmakers alike, and lens optics had become an essential component of the integral style.

The wide-angle lens is a lens of short **focal length,*** as low as 12.5mm, which covers a greater angle of vision than a conventional lens (the normal focal length for 35mm filmmaking is 35mm to 50mm). It is used by cinematographers to shoot relatively large subjects at short range, under the kinds of physical restrictions that obtain, for example, in small rooms and in automobiles. Since the wide-angle lens works like an inverted telescope, it gives its images an exaggerated depth of field. The **telephoto lens,** on the other hand, is a lens of great focal length, up to 500mm, and is capable of achieving a variety of long-distance, telescopic close-ups. As the optical opposite of the wide-angle lens, the telephoto produces images that have little or no depth of field. The **zoom** lens, finally, is a lens of variable focal length which can move continuously from an extreme wide-angle long shot to an extreme telephoto close-up, traversing all positions in between (optically, for example, from a focal length of 25mm to 250mm—a fairly standard zoom ratio of 10:1).†

---

* Focal length is the distance in millimeters from the optical center of the lens (a point midway between the front and rear elements) to the emulsion surface of the film stock when the lens is sharply focused on "infinity," that is, an extremely distant object. Focal lengths vary with the gauge of the film stock—e.g., a 25mm lens used with 16mm film gives the same results as a 50mm lens with 35mm stock.

† A lens of variable focal length—the Taylor-Hobson 40–120 mm "Varo," with a zoom ratio of 3:1—was introduced in Hollywood in 1932 and used in films intermittently through 1935. Its use can be noted, for example, in the opening scene of Rouben Mamoulian's *Love Me Tonight* (1932) and in the shipboard dance sequence in Harry Lachman's *Dante's Inferno* (1935). Cumbersome in size and shape, the "Varo" also had serious optical limitations that caused it to be abandoned. The "zoom" lens reappeared under its current name in 1955, but it was not sufficiently refined to maintain constant focus and *f*-stop (see Chapter 9 and Glossary) until the mid-sixties. The most striking use of the zoom lens before this time occurs in *Vertigo* (1958), where Hitchcock employed simultaneous tracking-out / zooming-in shots to convey the protagonist's acrophobia in the rooftop and staircase sequences.

15.30 Two wide-angle lens shots form *Barry Lyndon* (Stanley Kubrick, 1975); director of photography, John Alcott. Note the great depth of field.

15.31 An extreme wide-angle lens shot from *Barry Lyndon* and the same subject shot from head on through a telephoto lens (actually, a zoom lens which has moved from its wide-angle position to its telephoto position, so that these two stills are the beginning and end of the same shot). Note the loss of depth of field—the "flattening-out" of the image in the telephoto setting.

15.32 The conclusion of the optical tracking shot in *Bonnie and Clyde* (Arthur Penn, 1967); director of photography, Burnett Guffey.

The zoom lens introduced the important capacity for tracking *optically* without moving the camera. When such a lens is advanced toward its telephoto setting, the field of the image decreases radically and the camera seems to move toward its subject, and vice versa. Countless shots in Stanley Kubrick's *Barry Lyndon* (1975), for which a special 20:1 zoom lens was designed (the Cine-Pro T9 24–480mm), are structured according to this principle. Similarly, if the camera pans slightly in its telephoto setting, the effect on the screen will be that of a lateral tracking shot. An outstanding example of this latter technique occurs near the end of Arthur Penn's *Bonnie and Clyde* (1967), when the camera pans a long row of shops in slightly out-of-focus close-up before coming to rest and refocusing on C. W. Moss' father, as he betrays the two outlaws to a Texas Ranger through the window of an ice cream parlor. Visconti's *Morte a Venezia* (1971) is an excellent example of a film that consistently employs telephoto and zoom shots as a substitute for tracking, as are virtually all of the films of Robert Altman. But perhaps the most stunning use of optical traveling in recent cinema occurs at the end of Ján Kadár's *Adrift* (1971; see Chapter 16), when the anguished and apparently deranged protagonist, who has been standing under a tree outside his house at evening, attempts to return to the house. At the beginning of the shot, the camera is behind the man with the zoom lens in its telephoto setting, so that there seems to be very little distance between either him and the house or him and the camera. But as he starts to walk toward the house, the lens begins to zoom slowly backward toward its wide-angle position, putting ever greater distance between both man and house and man and camera. As he sees his house recede before him, the man starts to run wildly toward it, and the lens zooms backward at an ever-increasing pace, paralleling his headlong flight, until finally the runner is left optically adrift, hanging suspended in space as both camera and house recede toward infinity. This powerful image of madness and horror would have been impossible to achieve without a lens of variable focal length.

15.33 Optical hovering in *The Wild Bunch* (Sam Peckinpah, 1969); director of photography, Lucien Ballard.

Another effect of which the zoom lens is capable is that of hovering or searching, as if the camera were trying to decide which element of a scene to focus on from moment to moment—an especially valuable device for composing mass scenes like the mess hall sequences in Robert Altman's *M.A.S.H* (1970) or the outlaws' long walk through the teeming village of Agua Verde which precedes the final massacre in Sam Peckinpah's *The Wild Bunch* (1969). The zoom lens can also cause the camera to seem to leap backward or forward in space to isolate a significant detail in close-up without a cut. Thus, lenses of variable focal length permit a filmmaker to move back and forth—from long shot, to medium shot, to close-up—without the loss of continuity imposed by montage. It has even been suggested that Griffith would not have developed the syntax of narrative editing if zoom lenses had been available to him when he made his pioneering masterworks. This seems unlikely, since editing of some sort will always be an essential component of cinematic expression and since Griffith was too innovative a genius not to have recognized the fact; but in principle, at least, the suggestion is a valid one.

Of course, the possibilities for cutting on movement have been greatly increased by the cinema's new capacity for optical traveling, and the action sequences in Peckinpah's *The Wild Bunch* and *Junior Bonner* (1971) provide fine examples of the powerful kinetic impact that cutting on optical movement can achieve (see Chapter 18). Furthermore, unique visual effects can be obtained by intercutting telephoto and zoom shots with shots made through conventional lenses, which possess greater depth of field. This is because lenses of variable focal length have a distorting characteristic that makes optical movement qualitatively different from real camera movement; that is, they destroy depth of field. As Paul Joannides has written: "Unlike a tracking shot, a zoom represents a denial of perspective. The effect is not one of moving *through* space, but of space warping toward or away from the camera." For this reason, lenses of variable focal length can in some sense be said to eliminate the third dimension and to deny the reality of space by abstracting it. In Antonioni's *Il deserto rosso* (1964), for example, recurring telephoto close shots of the heroine depict a lone figure against an abstracted and flattened array of shapes, forms, and patterns—in reality the industrial landscape of Ravenna—that not only connects the character with her environment but emphasizes its meaninglessness.

This expressive effect could have been achieved only by shooting the

15.34 Giuliana (Monica Vitti) and her son in Antonioni's *Il deserto rosso* (1964); dirctor of photography, Carlo Di Palma. The diminished depth perspective of the telephoto lens forces the two humans into the same plane as the abstracted industrial landscape.

15.35 A shot composed for the variable-focus lens in *The Red and the White* (Miklós Jancsó, 1967); director of photography, Tamás Somló.

15.36 A frame from a zoom lens sequence shot in Jancsó's *Red Psalm* (1972); director of photography, János Kende.

scene through a wide-open telephoto or zoom lens, and it plainly illustrates how variable-focus lenses have become an important new aesthetic resource for contemporary filmmakers who practice the integral style. In fact, the recent refinement of lens optics, more than any technological development since the introduction of widescreen, has made possible the new cinema of subjective involvement and psychological affect—a cinema of *mise-en-scène,* whose surface is often as abstractly expressionistic as it is realistic. Writing of this future cinema in 1970, Paul Joannides noted: "The camera will . . . play a more passive role dramatically, but a more potent one visually. Rather than being placed to *construct* the scene, it will treat the scene as a formal entity. Thus observation and group composition will be more important than the dialectic of 'significant' detail which usually makes up drama. Dialogue will tend to be replaced by conversation and will be arranged differently, in set-pieces rather than by cross-cutting." Today, this cinema has arrived. As French and Italian films of the past few decades demonstrate, the world's most advanced filmmakers have for some time been composing for the lens rather than for the frame. It is wholly typical of this phenomenon that one of the most talented *auteurs* to emerge from Eastern Europe in the past twenty years, the Hungarian Miklós Jancsó (b. 1921)—*The Round-Up (Szegénylegények,* 1965); *The Red and the White (Csillagosok, katonák,* 1967); *Red Psalm (Még kér a nép,* 1972)—characteristically makes epic films of great visual complexity, some of which are composed of as few as a dozen long takes of ten minutes each (see Chapter 16).

INGMAR BERGMAN

Unassociated with a distinct aesthetic movement or technological trend, or even with a specifically defined period, are two European film artists whose bodies of work are so unique as to constitute "schools" unto themselves. Both Ingmar Bergman and Luis Buñuel were practicing directors whose careers spanned much of film history, and both were true *auteurs* long before that term had currency for the cinema. Bergman and Buñuel always attempted to exercise a high degree of control over the various components, technical and intellectual, that make up their films. Yet one has worked most of his life within the structure of a state-subsidized film industry where financial failure is virtually impossible, and the other has spent his entire career as an international free-lancer in commercial industries notoriously resistant to ideas. That both succeeded as artists on their own terms in such dissimilar environments testifies to the nearly limitless aesthetic potential of film.

Ingmar Bergman (b. 1918), the son of a Lutheran pastor to the royal court of Sweden, was trained in the Swedish theater and opera. Between 1940 and 1944 he worked on scripts for Svensk Filmindustri, the Swedish national film trust, and received his first screenplay credit for Alf Sjöberg's *Torment* (*Hets*, 1944), a film about a sadistic schoolmaster. Sjöberg (1903–80)—*The Road to Heaven* (*Himlaspelet*, 1942); *Miss Julie* (*Fröken Julie*, 1951 adapted from Strindberg) was a director very much in the Sjöstrom / Stiller tradition of poetic naturalism (see Chapter 4), and Bergman's earliest films reflect his influence. Between 1945 and 1955 Bergman wrote and directed thirteen somber films that explored the themes of loneliness, alienation, and the sheer difficulty of being alive, the best of which were *Thirst* (*Törst*, 1949), *Summer Interlude* (*Sommarlek*, 1951), *Monika / Summer with Monika* (*Sommaren med Monika*, 1952), and *Sawdust and Tinsel / The Naked Night* (*Gycklarnas afton*, 1953). It was during this apprenticeship that Bergman discovered a long-term collaborator, the cinematographer Gunnar Fischer (b. 1910), and built up his first stock company of distinguished performers: Max von Sydow, Gunnar Björnstrand, Ingrid Thulin, Gunnel Lindblom, Harriet Andersson, Bibi Andersson, and Eva Dahlbeck (Liv Ullmann and Erland Josephson joined him later). He also evolved his characteristic working method of

15.37 The Dance of Death at the conclusion of *The Seventh Seal* (Ingmar Bergman, 1956).

15.38 Victor Sjöstrom in Bergman's *Wild Strawberries* (1957).

first writing his films as novels and then distilling them into screenplays and, finally, audiovisual images.

It was *Smiles of a Summer Night* (*Sommarnattens leende*, 1955) that first brought Bergman to worldwide attention, although few critics recognized beneath the surface of this sophisticated farce a Swedish version of Renoir's *La Règle du jeu* (1939). In *The Seventh Seal* (*Det sjunde inseglet*, 1956), a poetic allegory of a medieval knight caught up in a losing chess match with Death, Bergman brilliantly evoked the Middle Ages and posed the first of a series of metaphysical questions about the relationship of man to God, a theme that was to occupy him for a decade. *The Seventh Seal* established Bergman as an important artist, but *Wild Strawberries* (*Smultronstället*, 1957), the film which followed, was clearly his greatest work of the fifties. This beautifully lyrical film is constructed around dreams and memories as they assail the elderly Isak Borg, a distinguished professor of science (superbly played by Bergman's greatest predecessor in Swedish cinema, Victor Sjöström) who is being driven across contemporary Sweden by his daughter-in-law to receive an honorary doctorate at the University of Lund. Borg's journey occasions a descent into the unconscious mind in which he is forced to confront all that he has been and become to his parents, his siblings, his children, and himself, in the course of his life. Structurally, Bergman makes his transitions from the present to the past and back again in single shots, so that one constantly has the impression of being in both time frames simultaneously. In its broad grasp of the basic philosophical problems of existence, *Wild Strawberries* is an even more important film than *The Seventh Seal*, and it holds a high place among Bergman's masterworks.

The Magician / The Face (*Ansiktet*, 1958) told a cryptic tale of a magic lanternist and prestidigitator (Bergman himself?) who dupes a bourgeois family (the audience?) into believing an elaborately contrived nightmare of murder and mayhem that has absolutely no substance. A stylistic tour-de-force, *The Magician* was somehow empty at the core. Bergman concluded his important work of the fifties with *The Virgin Spring* (*Jung-*

15.39 Bergman's *The Virgin Spring* (1959): Max von Sydow.

15.40 *Winter Light* (Ingmar Bergman, 1962): Gunnar Björnstrand, Ingrid Thulin.

frukällen, 1959), a powerful film based on a thirteenth-century ballad. In it, a beautiful young girl on her way to church is brutally raped and murdered in the woods by three herdsmen, who later seek refuge at her father's fortress. He discovers their guilt and butchers them like pigs in a sequence of nearly apocalyptic violence. When the girl's body is discovered later in the woods, the father vows to build a church on the spot, and in an ironic conclusion a spring wells up miraculously from the ground, signifying divine forgiveness. This devastating film concludes on an uncharacteristic note of hope (probably because Bergman was adapting someone else's material), but Bergman next made an austere trilogy about the difficulty of existing in a universe wholly unredeemed by the presence of God.

Through a Glass Darkly (*Sasom i en spegel,* 1961), the first work of what might be called a "religious" trilogy, is a starkly unappealing film about a schizophrenic woman living on a remote Baltic island with her physician husband, her father, and her teenage brother. When she comes to realize that her father is keeping a clinical journal of her breakdown for the purpose of writing a novel about it, she deteriorates altogether, commits incest with her brother, and is flown off the island by helicopter. In the plotless *Winter Light / The Communicants* (*Nattsvardsgästerna,* 1961), the austerity of Bergman's relentless spiritual probing becomes almost unbearable: a widowed village pastor celebrates communion regularly but can do nothing to assuage the real spiritual suffering of his communicants because he lacks literally what the Church gives him officially—the ability to make sense of a senseless universe by mediating between man and God. Much of *Winter Light* is constructed from extreme close-ups of the characters' faces, a technique that Bergman came to use more and more as a means of suggesting psychological torment. With the third film, *The Silence* (*Tystnaden,* 1963), Bergman succeeded in creating another masterpiece. In it, two sisters come to a Central European city accompanied by the youngest woman's small son. The language of the city's inhabitants and even the natural sounds on the brilliantly edited soundtrack are incomprehensible both to the travelers and to ourselves, and so—like most of us—they are forced to move through a meaningless world in relative isolation from their peers. Speech finally becomes irrelevant for the three travelers, as images of perverse eroticism and impending disaster come to dominate the film—visually the most striking of the trilogy. For Bergman, as for Antonioni, it seems that modern alienation has reduced human communication to a series of desperate sexual encounters that can only end in chaos.

The Silence was brilliantly photographed by Sven Nykvist (b. 1922), who had been Bergman's cinematographer since *The Virgin Spring,* the collaboration having begun when Nykvist was an assistant on *The Naked Night.* Working with Bergman from 1959 through the present, Nykvist has become one of the world's leading color cinematographers. Since the mid-sixties, Bergman and Nykvist have incorporated some of the more boldly experimental techniques of the French and Italian cinema into their work. This change in style signaled Bergman's new thematic con-

15.41 Bergman's *The Silence* (1963): Gunnel Lindblom, Ingrid Thulin.

15.42 Bergman's *Persona* (1966): Liv Ullmann, Bibi Andersson.

cern with the nature of human psychology, perception, and identity, explored in the director's second great trilogy of the sixties: *Persona* (1966), *Hour of the Wolf* (*Vargtimmen*, 1968), and *Shame* (*Skammen*, 1968).

Framed by sequences that seemingly depict the projection and photographing of the film itself, *Persona* collapses virtually every narrative convention of the cinema to suggest the illusory character of both the medium and the human personalities it seems so realistically to incarnate. The film is essentially about a transference of identity between nurse and patient to the point that their two faces merge, with perfect visual logic, into one. It is also about the different levels on which film, or media in general, can be said to represent the real. But its narrative style is so elliptical, disjointed, and self-reflexive that *Persona* ultimately suggests that the cinema is no more illusory than the reality that it pretends to record.

Hour of the Wolf is a hallucinatory parable of the agonies of artistic creation, reminiscent of Fellini at his most serious best. An artist and his wife live on a remote island and are one day invited to dinner at the castle of the island's owner, where the artist is humiliated by his host. The wife later discovers her husband's secret diary, which recounts trysts with his former mistress and the strange death of a boy. The artist goes mad and returns to the castle, where he finds his former mistress lying nude on a bier. He is invited to make love to her corpse, but she awakes and kisses him, to the raucous laughter of the ghoulish castle guests, and the artist flees madly into a swamp, where he is pursued by the entire company and finally done to death by a huge bird of prey. This bizarre but visually arresting allegory of a creative artist and his wife fallen into the ever-threatening grip of madness is less successful than *Persona*. But *Shame*, the final film of the second trilogy, is an utterly unique masterpiece.

Shame is about the hopelessness of maintaining human values and relationships in a state of perpetual war (which, Bergman seems to sug-

15.43 *Hour of the Wolf* (Ingmar Bergman, 1968).

15.44 *Shame* (Ingmar Bergman, 1968): Max von Sydow, Liv Ullmann.

gest, is the state of the modern world). In a nameless country, in the midst of a long and bloody civil war on the mainland, a childless husband and wife, both artists, have chosen to live an isolated existence on a relatively secure island off the coast. Former philharmonic musicians, they attempt to remain detached from the war that rages everywhere about them but are drawn irrevocably into it when their island is invaded and they are accused by both sides of collaborating with the enemy. The woman is strong and capable, but the husband proves himself to be a coward and, finally, a murderous turncoat. War devastates the beautiful island, turning it into a landscape of hell, and the couple—hating each other—escape together in a boat of refugees that drifts aimlessly in a sea of death. As the film concludes, the woman dreams hopelessly of having a child after the war, which we know will never end. Relying on close-ups of the faces of his protagonists, Bergman created in *Shame* a terrifying parable about the way war inevitably destroys all things valuable and human.

In *The Passion of Anna* (*En passion*, 1969), his first important color film, Bergman depicted the tense psychic interplay of four persons living on the small Swedish island of Farö where he himself resided (also the location for *Shame* and *Hour of the Wolf*). Characteristically, it is a drama of guilt, anguish, and finally rage, in which each of the four characters is caught up in his own unique kind of spiritual martyrdom. *The Passion of Anna* is unique in that it employs the Brechtian (and Godardian) distancing device of stopping the drama at moments of highest tension and having each of the four principals step briefly out of his role to discuss with the audience the character he is playing. The film is also brilliantly photographed by Nykvist and makes expressive use of color, sound, and the telephoto lens.

After filming a seventy-eight-minute *cinéma-vérité*–style documentary on his adopted home of Farö, entitled *Farö Document* (*Farö-Dokument*, 1970), Bergman made a theatrical feature for the newly organized ABC Pictures Corporation. *The Touch* (*Beroringen*, 1970) probed the disintegration of a middle-class marriage through the story of a model Swedish housewife who leaves her comfortable but conventional surroundings for a life with an unstable American archaeologist. The focal point of the film is the neurotic pathology of the conventionally "normal" housewife as oppposed to the relative emotional health of the "abnormal" archaeologist. To emphasize this conflict Bergman deliberately clogged his dialogue with the platitudes and clichés that make normal social intercourse as meaningless as the foreign speech of *The Silence*. *The Touch*, Bergman's first English-language film, was not generally regarded as a success due to the miscasting of Elliott Gould in the part of the archaeologist, but his next endeavor, *Cries and Whispers* (*Viskingar och rop*, 1972), was hailed as a masterpiece.

This highly stylized film about the nature of death and dying is a work of excruciating beauty in which reality, memory, and fantasy become one. Superbly photographed by Nykvist in rich autumnal hues, *Cries and Whispers* concerns the interrelationship of four women who are brought together by death in a gorgeously appointed manor house at the turn of the century. One is a spinster, dying slowly and painfully of cancer; two

15.45 Bergman's *Cries and Whispers* (1972): Ingrid Thulin, Harriet Andersson, Liv Ullmann, Lena Nyman.

15.46 Bergman's *Scenes from a Marriage* (1974): Erland Josephson, Liv Ullmann.

others are her wealthy married sisters, who have returned to their former home to attend her death; the fourth is the peasant servant, Anna, the only true "sister" of the dying woman because she can minister to her failing spirit with a warm, fleshly love. Eerie, enigmatic, and intense beyond measure, *Cries and Whispers* is constructed like a Strindberg dream play, but it is also quintessential Bergman, a brilliant distillation of his stylistic and thematic obsessions.

Bergman's next film, *Scenes from a Marriage* (*Scener ur ett aktenskap,* 1974), was originally made in six 50-minute installments for Swedish television but was cut to two hours and forty-eight minutes for theatrical release. (The six installments were shown uncut on American public television in 1977.) The theatrical version retains Bergman's original episodic structure: six scenes from a middle-class marriage spanning a decade. During this period, the relationship slowly disintegrates and ends in divorce, but the two individuals become progressively stronger in separation, and by the end of the film both are married to other people. As usual, Bergman relies heavily on the close-up to convey anguish (and also, of course, to make the film work on television), but his characteristic psychological realism is pursued with uncharacteristic verisimilitude in this film, minus fantasy, memory, and metaphor. Open-ended, slow-paced, and involving multiple dramatic climaxes, *Scenes from a Marriage* is actually structured like a soap opera but possesses a depth of feeling and intelligence usually alien to the form.

The Magic Flute (1975) is the triumphal realization of Bergman's life-long ambition to adapt the Mozart opera about the transcendent power of love and art. Lighthearted and exuberant, the film shows a playful, sprightly side of Bergman rarely seen in the decade of the trilogies, *The Passion of Anna,* and *Cries and Whispers.* Bergman mounted the film like an eighteenth-century stage production, and his obsession with the machinery of stage illusion in *The Magic Flute* links it implicitly with both *Persona* and *The Magician.** *Face to Face* (*Ansikte mot ansikte,* 1976), about the harrowing descent of a woman psychiatrist into mental illness, and *The Serpent's Egg* (1977), a film dealing with the psychological conflicts of a Jewish circus performer in pre-Nazi Germany shot in English in Berlin, were not critically successful. But with *Autumn Sonata* (*Herbstsonate,* 1978), an intense study of the relationship between a concert pianist and her middle-aged daughter, filmed on location in Norway, and *From the Life of the Marionettes* (1980), a searing account of psychosexual breakdown made in Germany, Bergman returned successfully to the tangled human relationships which he had illuminated so well in

---

* In 1976 Bergman emigrated from Sweden to France because of harassment by the Swedish government, which claimed that he owed hundreds of thousands of dollars in income taxes and even had him arrested and incarcerated briefly. Bergman and his supporters maintain that he was driven out of the country because of his implied criticisms of Swedish society in films like *The Touch* and *Scenes from a Marriage.* (Ironically, Swedish film critics had for decades attacked Bergman for his supposed detachment from contemporary Swedish life.) The tax dispute was settled almost entirely in his favor in late 1979, and he was welcomed back to a somewhat embarrassed Sweden to begin shooting *Fanny and Alexander* in Uppsala in the fall of 1981.

the past. In *Fanny and Alexander* (*Fanny och Alexander*, 1982), his most lavishly produced and accessible work and the winner of four American Academy Awards, Bergman recreated the magical world of his childhood in the university town of Uppsala in the early years of the century. Though not directly autobiographical, it is as close to a cinematic memoir as anything he ever produced, and on its release Bergman declared it to be his last film. In fact, he did shoot another film for Swedish television in 16mm, which was never intended for theatrical release. *After the Rehearsal* (*Efter repetitionen*, 1984) concerns the relationship between a middle-aged theater director and the actress daughter of his dead mistress, also an actress, and is essentially a one-act play for three characters. Bergman unsuccessfully tried to block the release of this telefilm when its producer, Jorn Donner, sold it to an American distributor, and he seems firm in his commitment to retire from "the world of cinema" and devote the rest of his life to the theater, which was, of course, his first love.

Bergman is an artist of vast and unusual talent, and he is clearly among the most important filmmakers in the history of Western cinema. His vision of the human condition is as gloomy as that of his great predecessors in Scandinavian cinema, the Swedes Mauritz Stiller and Victor Sjöström, and the Dane Carl-Theodor Dreyer (by whom he was profoundly influenced). His themes hark back, too, to those of the two Scandinavian giants of late-nineteenth-century drama, Ibsen and Strindberg (whose works *The Stranger* and *A Dream Play* stand behind *Persona* and *Fanny and Alexander,* respectively). But his pessimistic vision is not wholly unredeemed. Despite his cosmic nihilism, Bergman is essentially a religious artist whose films concern the fundamental questions of human existence: the meaning of suffering and pain, the inexplicability of death, the solitary nature of being, and the difficulty of locating meaning in a seemingly random and capricious universe. With the possible exception of *Persona,* Bergman has never been a great innovator in narrative form like Welles, Antonioni, or Godard, but he has been quick to assimilate the important innovations of others. His experiments have been intellectual and metaphysical rather than formal, for he has risked alienating his audiences time and again to ask difficult questions and to pursue inherently disturbing themes.

Bergman has been free to follow his dark vision of experience with integrity and independence largely due to the economic structure of Svensk Filmindustri, through which he has produced all but four of his forty features.* This organization guarantees to underwrite the production and distribution costs of any approved project that does not return a domestic profit, so it is fair to say that Bergman has rarely had to work under the extreme economic pressures that afflict most other filmmakers. But Bergman would surely have pursued his vision under any circumstances, no matter how difficult, because as he has declared many times, "To

15.47 *From the Life of the Marionettes* (Ingmar Bergman, 1980): Martin Benrath, Robert Atzorn.

15.48 *Fanny and Alexander* (Ingmar Bergman, 1982): Bertil Guve, Pernilla Allwin.

15.49 Bergman and cinematographer Sven Nykuist on location for *Fanny and Alexander*.

---

* The Swedish film industry is small, state subsidized, and oriented largely toward the domestic market of 8.4 million people. Bergman is its sole international giant, but other Swedish directors have recently achieved reputations outside their native land.

15.50 *Adalen 31* (Bo Widerberg, 1969).

15.51 *The Flight of the Eagle* (Jan Troell, 1982).

15.57 *My Life as a Dog* (Lasse Hallström, 1985).

15.53 *Black on White* (Jorn Donner, 1967).

15.54 *Earth is a Sinful Song* (Rauni Mollberg, 1973).

make films is for me a natural necessity, a need similar to hunger and thirst." Bergman has also maintained his independence by producing his films with a remarkable economy of means: he uses small casts and crews, and he shoots in natural locations whenever possible. Gunnar Fischer and Sven Nykvist, for instance, have between them photographed virtually all of his films, and Bergman often writes his scripts with specific actors from his stock company in mind. In a very important sense, Bergman views filmmaking as an essentially collective art form. He has often compared it to the process of building a medieval cathedral, in which each artisan dedicated the maximum skill of his craft anonymously to the greater glory of God; as he has written, "Regardless of whether I believe or not, whether I am Christian or not, I would play my part in the collective building of the cathedral." Ingmar Bergman is an artist of great moral integrity and spiritual courage whose long and productive career continues to affirm the necessity of being human in the face of death, disorder, and despair. He regards our darkness in an even darker universe and redeems them both through art.

LUIS BUÑUEL

After making the bitter and sardonic documentary *Las Hurdes* (1932; see Chapter 9)—which was banned by the Spanish Republican government of 1933–35 as "defamatory" but later released by the Popular Front government during the civil war—Buñuel (1900–83) did not direct another film for fifteen years. He worked sporadically as a producer in Paris, Hollywood, and Madrid before emigrating to America in 1938 to escape fascism. Here he edited war documentaries for the Museum of Modern Art (MoMA) in New York* and supervised the Spanish-language versions of films for Warner Bros. and MGM. In 1947 he was given a chance to direct two popular comedies for the Mexican producer Oscar Dancigers, *Gran casino* (*Grand Casino*, 1947) and *El gran calavera* (*The Great Madcap*, 1949), and on the strength of their commercial success he was permitted to make *Los olvidados* (*The Forgotten Ones* / *The Young and the Damned*, 1950), the film that restored his reputation as an important international artist.

Ostensibly a neorealist portrayal of juvenile delinquency in modern Mexico City, *Los olvidados* is actually a disturbing catalogue of man's darkest and most destructive impulses, as subversive in its way as Buñuel's earlier surrealist films. The corrupted slum youth of the city are condemned to live in a nightmarish world of violence, brutality, and degradation, not only because of the poverty imposed on them by bourgeois capitalism (whose image is ever-present in the rising skyscrapers that

---

* Buñuel was forced to resign from his position at MoMA in 1943 under pressure from the State Department, which was itself under pressure from the Catholic lobby in Washington because the filmmaker had been described as an atheist and a Marxist in Dali's *The Secret Life of Salvador Dali* (1942). See Buñuel's autobiography, *My Last Sigh,* trans. Abigail Israel (New York: Knopf, 1983).

dominate the film's background) but also because of the wretchedness of reality itself. Images of horror abound, all recorded with documentary-like objectivity: a limbless cripple is tipped off his cart and sent sprawling on his back like a turtle, a blind man is tormented and robbed by a gang of young thugs, a boy is bludgeoned to death with a rock by his companion, an old degenerate fondles the bare legs of a little girl, and finally the film's pathetic young protagonist is slashed to death and his body dumped on a garbage heap. Austerely photographed by the Mexican cinematographer Gabriel Figueroa (b. 1907), who was to work on all of Buñuel's Mexican masterpieces, *Los olvidados* achieves an almost hallucinatory quality through the relentless exposition of an external reality (not to mention a brilliant and terrifying Freudian dream sequence) that is literally hell on earth. The extraordinary quality of this film was recognized when it won Buñuel the Cannes Director's Prize in 1951. He continued to work within the Mexican commercial cinema for the next five years, producing a series of unique and expertly crafted films on low budgets and short production schedules.

Some of these films were neorealistic melodramas of sexual passion, like *Susana* (1951) and *El bruto* (*The Brute*, 1952); others were whimsical and sometimes fantastic comedies, like *Subida al cielo* (English title: *Mexican Bus Ride*, 1952) and *La ilusión viaja en tranvia* (*Illusion Travels by Streetcar*, 1954). Buñuel also made remarkable versions of two important English novels—an English-language *Robinson Crusoe* (1952), his first film in color, which turns Defoe on his ear to suggest the total uselessness of bourgeois civilization, and a Spanish-language *Wuthering Heights* (*Cumbres borrascosas / Abismos de pasión*, 1952), which ends with the Heathcliff character ripping open his beloved's recently interred coffin and attempting to make love to her corpse. Buñuel's most characteristic and personal films of this period, however, were *Él* (English titles: *This Strange Passion / Torment*, 1952) and *Ensayo de un crimen* (*Rehearsal for a Crime / The Criminal Life of Archibaldo de la Cruz*, 1955).

Él is a tale of pathological erotic obsession in which fantasy and reality, photographed from equally objective points of view, are constantly

15.55 *Los olvidados* (Luis Buñuel, 1950): Roberto Cobo (center).

15.57   *Cumbres borrascosas* (Luis Buñuel, 1952).

threatening to merge. A wealthy, repressed, middle-aged landowner, who is a pillar of society and a secret foot fetishist (a Buñuel trademark), woos and wins a beautiful girl. After the marriage, he turns his oppressive rococo villa into a hothouse of sexual neurosis, as his own impotence drives him to become insanely jealous of his perfectly innocent bride. The young woman begins to fear for her life, and one night she awakens to find her husband stealthily preparing to suture her vagina. She runs away and he goes totally mad, ultimately attempting to strangle his priest. But the Church takes him to her bosom and imprisons him in a monastery, where he becomes a monk. Years later, his former wife visits him and discovers that despite his external calm he is as lunatic as before. *Él* is among Buñuel's most savage attacks on the Catholic Church and the repressive mechanisms of bourgeois culture. It was booed from the screen at Cannes, but it was terrifically popular in Mexico, where audiences accepted it as a sympathetic study of a man driven crazy by jealousy.

15.56   Buñuel's *Subida al cielo* (1951): Lilia Prado.

Ensayo de un crimen is another film about a man in the grip of an overpowering erotic obsession. It is a black comedy—as, in some sense, are all of Buñuel's best films—but it is considerably lighter than *Él*. As a young boy, the film's hero has been told that his music box has the magical power to kill anyone he desires. The boy experiments on his governess, who is immediately shot dead by a stray bullet from a street riot, and he carries an erotic fascination with murder into adulthood. He attempts to become a sadistic murderer of young women but bungles every attempt, finally loses his obsession, and goes on to lead a normal life.

15.58   *Él* (Luis Buñuel, 1952): Arturo de Cordova, Delia Garces.

After 1955 Buñuel went to Paris, where he directed three international coproductions that are openly political in theme. As Raymond Durgnat observes, *Cela s'appelle l'aurore* (*It Is Called the Dawn,* Italy / France, 1955), *La Mort en ce jardin* (English title: *Evil Eden,* France / Mexico, 1956), and *La Fièvre mont à El Pao / Los ambiciosos* (English title: *Republic of Sin,* France / Mexico, 1959) together form a triptych that explores the morality of armed revolt against fascist dictatorships.

Buñuel returned to Mexico in 1958 to direct *Nazarín,* the masterpiece that marked the beginning of his greatest period. Based on a nineteenth-century Mexican novel set during the dictatorship of Porfirio Diaz, this

15.59 Buñuel's *Nazarín* (1958): Rita Macedo, Francisco Rabal.

film concerns the spiritual pilgrimage of a saintlike priest who makes the error of sincerely attempting to follow Christian doctrine and imitate the life of Christ. Cast out and reviled by his church, Father Nazarín journeys into the wilderness, followed by a band of female protégés whose attraction for him, it turns out, is less spiritual than fleshly. Like the biblical story of Jesus, the film has an episodic structure, and as Nazarín moves from one parabolic incident to the next, he becomes increasingly disillusioned with his mission. He is finally hunted down by police for his part in fomenting a workers' rebellion and is tossed into jail. The film ends with Nazarín chained to a wall between two thieves; but he is seemingly brought new hope when a peasant woman offers him a pomegranate. *Nazarín* was mistaken by many Catholic critics as signaling Buñuel's return to the fold, and in a fine irony the film was nearly awarded the prize of the International Catholic Cinema Office. But the point of this intentionally ambiguous film is that Nazarín, who undertakes his quest with sincerity, humility, and great moral courage, manages to achieve absolutely nothing in the course of it but his own destruction. As Buñuel said in another context, "One can be *relatively* Christian, but the absolutely pure being, the innocent, is condemned to defeat."

This attitude was given its most brilliant exposition in *Viridiana* (1961), an anti-Catholic, antifascist parable that Buñuel shot in Catholic Spain under the very noses of fascist censors, who approved the script.* Like *Nazarín*, *Viridiana* concerns a devout and saintly person whose attempts to lead a truly Christian life end in disaster for herself and everyone around her. Viridiana (the name derives from that of a little-known medieval saint), a beautiful young woman about to enter a convent, is advised by her mother superior to visit the country estate of an elderly uncle whom she barely knows. The uncle is overwhelmed by Viridiana's resemblance to his wife, who died years ago on their wedding night, and he falls madly in love with her. She gently rebuffs him, and finally (in a sequence highly reminiscent of *Él*), he has her drugged and laid out like a corpse in his

15.60 The parody of *The Last Supper* in Buñuel's *Viridiana* (1961).

---

* Between *Nazarín* and *Viridiana*, Buñuel made his second English-language film, *The Young One* (Mexico, 1960), a relatively light work (for Buñuel) about an American black man unjustly accused of rape, who flees to an offshore island to escape a lynch mob and becomes dangerously entangled there with a fourteen-year-old white girl and the man who loves her.

wife's wedding gown. He nearly rapes her, and the next day, as Viridiana is about to flee for the convent, she learns that her uncle has hanged himself with a jump rope. Feeling herself responsible for the old man's death, she stays on to help run the estate with her uncle's illegitimate son, Jorge; and in a Nazarín-like act of contrition she invites a group of diseased beggars from a nearby town to come live in some deserted cottages on her uncle's property. A famous montage sequence contrasts her futile efforts to save these villainous wretches through prayer with Jorge's strenuous practical endeavors to restore order to the estate. One day Viridiana and Jorge go to town on business, and the beggars break into the manor house and stage a riotous feast that Buñuel composed in grotesque parody of Leonardo da Vinci's fresco *The Last Supper*. The beggars' banquet ends in a frenzied orgy accompanied by the strains of Handel's *Messiah,* and when Jorge and Viridiana return, the girl is all but raped by a leper. This obscenity finally breaks her spiritual pride, and the final sequence of the film shows her joining Jorge and his mistress in a three-handed game of cards.

Blasphemous, ironic, and masterfully constructed, *Viridiana* is quintessential Buñuel—and all the more so for its being an outrageous practical joke on the fascist state that permitted its production. No sooner was the film released than Spanish authorities realized its subversive nature and attempted to destroy all copies. But it was too late: prints had already reached Cannes, where the film was accepted as the official Spanish entry in the festival and awarded the highest honors,* to the everlasting chagrin of the Franco regime. Moreover, there was so little ambiguity about the film's anticlericalism that it was officially denounced by the Vatican as "an insult to Christianity."

If *Viridiana* truly is Buñuel's ultimate insult to Christianity, then its successor, *El Ángel exterminador* (*The Exterminating Angel,* Mexico, 1962), is clearly his ultimate insult to conventional bourgeois morality. In this film, which many critics regard as Buñuel's greatest, a group of wealthy people gather at an elegant villa for a sumptuous dinner party. After the meal they retire to a drawing room, but when it is time to go home they find themselves mysteriously unable to leave the room—and, just as strangely, no one from outside can get in. The situation, initially humorous, persists for weeks and becomes a nightmare as the drawing-room is transformed into a miniature concentration camp. To eat, the inmates are forced to slaughter stray sheep that roam the villa in the aftermath of an elaborate practical joke. They cannot bathe, and they have no toilet facilities. When a old man dies and two lovers commit

15.61 *La caza* (Carlos Saura, 1965).

---

* The Palme d'Or—the first ever won by a Spanish film. With the exception of the work of Buñuel, which, of course, was done mainly outside of Spain, that country's cinema was badly retarded by the repressive, patriarchal nature of the Franco regime and its policies of official censorship. Under *El Caudillo,* the Spanish film industry remained state supported and paternalistic, although there was some hope of change in the early fifties, when the collaboration of Juan Antonio Bardem (b. 1922) and Luis García Berlanga (b. 1921) produced *Bienvenido, Mr. Marshall* (*Welcome Mr. Marshall!,* 1952), a satire about the enrichment of a small Spanish village as a result of the Marshall Plan.

15.62 *Cria cuervos* (Carlos Saura, 1975).

15.64 *El crimen de Cuenca* (Pilar Miro, 1979).

15.63 *El spiritu de la colmena* (Victor Erica, 1973).

suicide, their corpses are stuffed into a closet for possible future use, it is darkly hinted, should the supply of sheep run out. Filthy, foul-smelling, and driven to the brink of madness by their extreme situation, the prisoners finally attempt to reconstruct the circumstances leading up to their imprisonment. Miraculously, the tactic works, and they stumble out of the villa toward an anxiously waiting public like the emaciated survivors of a death camp. The film ends in a cathedral where the survivors have come to give thanks for their salvation. After a solemn *Te Deum*, the entire congregation finds itself unable to leave the church, and a flock of sheep suddenly enters the building, while anarchic violence erupts in the streets outside. As Raymond Durgnat has suggested, "the exterminating angel" of this film is the bourgeois ethos of conformity and convention that traps the dinner guests and, finally, everyone in the culture in their social roles. In this brilliant surrealist parable Buñuel suggests that bour-

15.65 *Francisca* (Manoel de Oliveira, 1981).

15.66 *L'univers concentrationnaire:* the trapped bourgeoisie of Buñuel's *El ángel exterminador* (1962).

geois concepts of self are as systematically delimiting and destructive of human freedom as the Nazi death camps, and that liberation can be achieved only by thinking ourselves back to the beginning of things.

With *Le Journal d'une femme de chambre* (*Diary of a Chambermaid,* 1964; also filmed by Renoir, 1946), Buñuel returned to France to make his most political film, and his first in widescreen. He transposed the setting of Octave Mirbeau's decadent novel of erotic obsession among the French upper classes from the turn of the century to 1928, a time when French fascism was gathering the force that would ultimately permit the collapse of the Third Republic and the Nazi Occupation. A Parisian chambermaid (Jeanne Moreau) quits her post to take a job in the manor house of a large provincial estate that proves to be a hotbed of reactionary politics and sexual pathology. Her elderly employer is a boot fetishist whose frigid married daughter is similarly obsessed with internal hygiene. The estate's gamekeeper, Joseph, a surly rightwinger committed to the "moral rebirth of France," is a psychopathic sadist who likes to torture the farm animals and who rapes and murders a little girl with whom the maid has become friends. The maid suspects Joseph immediately and has an affair with him in order to gather enough evidence to avenge her little friend. She does so, and finally denounces him to the police, for which she is fired. Joseph is not prosecuted, and the film ends years later in Marseille, with the former gamekeeper, now a prosperous cafe owner, shouting slogans in support of a large fascist rally. Buñuel cuts to a bolt of lightning rending the sky, an unequivocal reminder that brutality will continue to triumph over decency and innocence in the coming storm of war. Buñuel's equation of fascism, decadence, and sexual perversion in *Le Journal* is perfectly made, and it brings the film close in spirit to Bertolucci's *Il conformista* (1970).

Buñuel's next film, *Simón del desierto* (*Simon of the Desert,* Mexico, 1965) is a forty-two-minute feature based on the temptations of St. Simon Stylites, the fifth-century anchorite who spent his life perched atop a sixty-foot column in the desert, preaching and performing miracles for devout Christians who came to supplicate him. Written by the director himself and shot in Mexico in twenty-five days, the film is a jovial catalogue of Buñuelian obsessions and motifs: crowds of spectators rate Simon's miracles ("not bad"); local merchants attempt to corrupt him, while local priests try to do him in; Simon lavishes equal care on restoring the chopped-off hands of a convicted thief (who immediately uses them to beat his child) and on blessing a piece of food picked from between his teeth; the Devil appears to him as a little girl in a sailor suit and as a sexy young woman unconvincingly disguised as Christ. Finally, the Devil whisks him off to New York City on a jet-propelled coffin and leaves him sipping Coke in a discothèque crowded with teenagers doing a fashionable new dance ("the latest and the last," the Devil tells him) dubbed the "Radioactive Flesh." Subtly photographed in atonal black and white by Gabriel Figueroa and playfully pessimistic in mood, *Simón del desierto* won a special jury prize at Venice in 1965.

In 1967, at the age of sixty-seven, Buñuel returned to France to make *Belle de jour,* the film that he claimed would be his last (although he was

15.67   Buñuel's *Le journal d'une femme de chambre* (1964): Jeanne Moreau.

15.68   *Simón del desierto* (Luis Buñuel, 1965): Claudio Brook as Saint Simeon Stylites, tempted by Silvia Pinal in the guise of Christ the Good Shepherd.

15.69 Buñuel's *Belle de jour* (1967): Catherine Deneuve.

to direct five more unequivocal masterpieces). Exquisitely photographed in color by Sacha Vierny, *Belle de jour* is another Buñuelian classic of erotic obsession: Séverine, the beautiful wife of a successful surgeon who is also a kind husband, has a secret compulsion for sexual degradation. She attempts to realize her masochistic fantasies by working afternoons in Madame Anaïs's brothel, where she is christened "Belle de jour" (a play on *belle de nuit*, a French euphemism for prostitute). Here she caters to a whole range of perversions from simple fetishism to necrophilia, and her fantasy life grows apace. For Buñuel, the old surrealist, the brothel is a place of absolute freedom precisely because it *is* a region where fantasy interpenetrates reality. As the film progresses, it becomes increasingly difficult to distinguish Séverine's fantasies from the linear narrative, which now involves a sadistic young gangster who has fallen in love with Belle at the brothel. The gangster attempts to murder her husband and paralyzes him, we are told, for life. In an act of atonement, Séverine quits the brothel and becomes her husband's devoted nurse, until a jealous family friend tells him of her past existence as Belle de jour. At this, he first seems to die of shock and then rises from his wheelchair, miraculously cured. An empty black carriage with jingling bells, which has been associated with Séverine's fantasy world throughout the film, passes by in the park beneath the window of their fashionable apartment, and we are left to wonder whether the whole film has not been a dream or an extended fantasy in the mind of its heroine. *Belle de jour* is a hypnotically engaging film, as beautiful in its artistic intelligence as in its visually exquisite surface, and it was justly awarded the Golden Lion at the Venice Festival in 1967.

As if to contradict himself with all due haste, Buñuel turned to his next project immediately after the release of *Belle de jour*. *La Voie lactée* (*The Milky Way*, France, 1969) is a symbolic history of the Roman Catholic Church with all its heresies and schisms, told in the form of an episodic narrative about two tramps journeying from Paris to the shrine of the Apostle James at Santiago de Compostela ("St. James of the Field of Stars") in Spain. The road they follow is popularly known in Europe as "the Milky Way," but for Buñuel the term also signifies the supposedly celestial path of Christianity through the ages. Thus, in the course of their journey the tramps encounter figures from the past who either dramatize church history (for instance, an eighteenth-century Jansenist fencing with a Jesuit) or incarnate it (Christ, the Virgin Mary, the Devil). The film is less savage than impudently funny, although we are treated to the usual assortment of Buñuelian horrors: leprous blind beggars, the Marquis de Sade flogging a victim, a crucified nun, etc. Beautifully photographed in color by the veteran French cinematographer Christian Matras, *La Voie lactée* was not well received by some critics, who thought its exposition (and deflation) of Catholic theological doctrine too arcane.

About *Tristaña* (1970), however, there were no doubts at all. This French / Italian coproduction is set in the ancient Spanish city of Toledo in the twenties and concerns a decadent aristocrat, Don Lope, who systematically corrupts and enslaves his innocent young ward, Tristaña (from

15.70 *Tristaña* (Luis Buñuel, 1970): Fernando Rey, Lola Gaos, Catherine Deneuve.

15.71 Roused from a poker game in Buñuel's *Le fantôme de la liberté* (1974), two priests, two monks, and a nurse witness an act of sexual perversion: Paul Le Person, Milena Vukotic, Gilbert Montagne, Bernard Musson, Marcel Pérès.

triste, sad). Tristaña, for her part, attempts to resist by running away from her guardian with an artist who wishes to marry her. But she returns two years later with a crippling illness that has made it necessary for a leg to be amputated, confining her permanently to a wheelchair. Totally dependent now on Don Lope, Tristaña begins to internalize his perversity, taking as her own victims the half-witted deaf-mute who pushes her wheelchair, and finally Don Lope himself: the old man dies of a heart attack while she callously refuses to call a doctor. Subtly photographed by José Aguayo in autumnal hues, this film is as much about the decay of Spain as about the interrelationships of its characters. Tristaña is the victim not simply of Don Lope but of the corrupt and impotent moral code that he embodies and that was to be institutionalized by Franco (although Don Lope is himself a sort of liberal) after the civil war.

Buñuel's next film, *Le Charme discret de la bourgeoisie* (*The Discreet Charm of the Bourgeoisie,* France, 1973), is a legitimate successor to both *L'Âge d'or* (1930) and *El Ángel exterminador* (1962) but exchanges their savage bite for gently mocking irony. It is a buoyant satire about the foibles and follies of the privileged class, structured as an extended dream in the mind of Don Rafael, the ambassador to France from the Latin American country of Miranda, a military dictatorship which has the highest homicide rate in the world. Don Rafael's dream, which includes the dreams of others and dreams within dreams, concerns the constantly frustrated efforts of six friends to dine together in a civilized manner. Every time the attempt is made, the dinner is interrupted by some twist of dream logic or by another dream, which will in turn be interrupted by a dream or another attempted dinner party as soon as the situation has become engaging. The film, in fact, is one long pattern of interrupted episodes, and in this sense Buñuel has created a delightful parody of the mechanisms of narrative cinema. As soon as he draws us into a story, he cuts away to another, and the charming, civilized, self-indulgent bourgeoisie never do get to eat their dinner. A couple is overcome by sexual passion and has coitus on the table; a member of the party vomits just as the meal begins; the diners suddenly discover themselves upon a stage before a live audience and forget their lines; the whole group is arrested for being accomplices in a heroin-smuggling ring (an in-joke, since Fernando Rey, who plays Don Rafael, had played the heroin kingpin in William Friedkins' *The French Connection* a year before). Other dreams are darker and concern loss of identity and death, but the good bourgeoisie manage to meet most situations with composure and a kind of bemused tolerance toward the shallowness of their own existence. Buñuel himself seems uncharacteristically mellow toward the confusion of values embodied in his characters, as if a kind of serene compassion for a long-hated enemy had set in. *Le Charme discret de la bourgeoisie* is good-humored and frequently hilarious, and its technical virtuosity demonstrates Buñuel's mastery of his medium. As in many of his other films, notably *Belle de jour* and *Tristaña,* Buñuel uses no musical score, which contributes to the eerie surrealism of the piece.

Le Fantôme de la liberté (*The Phantom of Liberty,* France, 1974) continues the experiments begun in *Le Charme discret* and may well be Buñuel's most stylistically revolutionary work since *Un Chien andalou* and *L'Âge d'or.* In it, the director combines virtually every known story-telling device—narrative painting, the Gothic mode, the epistolary mode, omniscient narration, the flashback, the exemplary tale, the dream sequence, and dense patterns of allusion to other films—to create an episodic narrative that is simultaneously circular and self-reflexive. As Marsha Kinder has noted, *Le Fantôme de la liberté* is about the impossibility of escaping convention in society, politics, and art—and, ultimately, in the process of its own narrative, however radical that narrative may appear. There is no recurrent motif to bind together the separate episodes such as the dinner party in *Le Charme discret,* only the dream-logic of continuous interruption and circularity. By interweaving episodes from the past and present which constantly disappoint our narrative expectations, Buñuel has produced an authentically surrealist essay on the political violence, necrophilia, and sadism that underlie bourgeois cultural conventions and make an elusive phantom of personal freedom.

For his last film, Buñuel chose to adapt Pierre Louys' short novel *La Femme et le pantin* (1896), which was also the source of von Sternberg's *The Devil Is a Woman* (1935) and Duvivier's *A Woman Like Satan* (1958). *Cet obscur objet du desir* (*That Obscure Object of Desire,* 1977) is an urbane and coolly ironic film about a young Spanish girl who teases and ultimately fleeces a middle-aged French widower. Buñuel compounds the irony by having two actresses with distinctly different physical appearances play the single "object" of the title, as if to suggest the polymorphous nature of desire itself.

From *Un Chien andalou* to *Cet obscur objet du désir,* Buñuel proved himself to be the most experimental and anarchistic filmmaker in the history of the narrative cinema. He was fundamentally a brilliant satirist, comparable to Swift and Goya, who used sexual pathology as a metaphor for the distorting nature of bourgeois Christian culture. Necrophilia, sadomasochism, fetishism, cannibalism, and bestiality were for Buñuel at once both cause and effect of the mass psychosis that we call Western civilization. Like all great satirists, Buñuel was simultaneously a moralist, a humorist, and a savage social critic, who hoped that by exposing the nauseating inhumanity of human beings he would somehow make us more human. Until very near the end of his career, Buñuel employed a restrained and uncomplicated visual style, which led some critics to charge him with cinematic "indifference." We should remember, however, that for most of his career Buñuel was forced either to make films for other people on their terms, or to not make films at all. This often meant shooting on low budgets with production schedules as short as three or four weeks. It also meant that Buñuel could not make his first film in color until 1952 nor his first film in widescreen until 1964, and it would be fair to argue that, while an artist in Bergman's position can afford style, one in Buñuel's cannot.

But actually, of course, Buñuel's indifference to style is a style in itself. John Russell Taylor has written: "Style is for him the best and most economical way of saying a thing. . . . The highest tribute one can pay to Buñuel's direction is to say that one is hardly ever conscious of it." This is as it should be for an artist who deals so consistently in the blasphemous, sardonic, and perverse. The invisibility of Buñuel's style is the deliberate artistic strategy of a master ironist: what we see is so clearly what we get in Buñuel that we trust him not to dupe us, which enables him to dupe us every time. But he always dupes us for our own good, by forcing us to acknowledge what we really are instead of what we would like to be, and the jokes he makes at our expense are most often hilariously funny. Buñuel's ironic vision of human experience is perhaps best summed up in a statement he once made when asked if he had ever been a religious person. "I have always been an atheist," he responded, "thank God."

16

European Renaissance: East

All of the countries of Eastern Europe except for the Soviet Union were occupied by the Nazis or collaborated with them during World War II, and those that had strong national film industries at the time, such as Czechoslovakia and Hungary, saw them subverted for the purpose of propaganda. When the war ended, these countries were "liberated" by the Soviet army and found themselves once again occupied by a foreign totalitarian power. Gradually, but with much brutality, the Soviet government placed its own puppets at the heads of the Eastern European states, Stalinized the national governments, and forced the entire area into the Soviet bloc—a move formalized by the Warsaw Pact of 1955. Among the first acts of the new regimes was to nationalize the Eastern European film industries in order to use them, as the Nazis had, for the production of political propaganda. In Czechoslovakia and Poland, nationalization took place in conjunction with the establishment of state-supported film schools, repeating the pattern of the Soviet Union just after its revolution. The Czech film school, the Film and Television Faculty of the Academy of Dramatic Arts (FAMU) was founded in Prague in 1945; the Polish version, the Leon Schiller State Film School at Łódź, was established in 1948. Ultimately, each of the major Eastern European nations would have its own state-operated film school—Hungary its Academy for Dramatic and Cinematographic Art in Budapest (1947), Yugoslavia its Film Institutes in Belgrade and Zagreb (1950), Romania its Institute of Theater and Film Art (IATC, 1950) in Bucharest, and Bulgaria its Sofia Film and Television Academy (1973).* The thoroughness of the postwar nationalization meant that there would always be a close relationship between film and politics in Eastern Europe. Generally speaking, in times of oppression the Eastern European cinemas have been used for the purpose of political indoctrination; during periods of liberalization (Poland, 1954–63 and 1976–81; Czechoslovakia, 1963–68;

---

* Two Eastern European countries are omitted from this survey. The first is Albania, a small, extremely poor Balkan nation (population 3 million) that withdrew from the Warsaw Pact in 1968. Until recently, Albania was militantly closed to the West. The second is the German Democratic Republic (GDR; East Germany) which is treated with the Federal Republic of Germany (West Germany) in Chapter 18. Like its Warsaw Pact allies, the GDR has a thriving state-run film school, the Deutsche Hochschule für Filmkunst in Potsdam, established in 1954.

666

Hungary, 1963 to the present), the cinema has become a vehicle for social criticism and ideological debate. For this reason, the cinema has always been one of the most important arts for the Eastern European intelligentsia, while in the West this has only very recently become true.

During the repressive postwar years from 1945 to 1953, few Eastern European countries produced significant films. Most adopted official Soviet-style "socialist realism" as decreed at the first Congress of the Soviet Writers Union in 1934 (see Chapter 5), which demanded that the everyday life of the socialist worker be glorified at the expense of all thematic analysis and formal experiment. In the Soviet Union itself this policy had succeeded in effacing the great avant-garde heritage of the twenties, putting its creators either out of work (Vertov, Kuleshov) or under strict ideological control (Eisenstein, Pudovkin, Dovzhenko). After the war, the situation grew even worse as Andrei Zhdanov, the party boss in charge of ideological affairs, demanded rigid conformity to the style. When Stalin died in 1953, however, there was a brief period of liberalization, followed by an official policy of de-Stalinization which witnessed a distinct move away from the style of socialist realism in many Eastern European cinemas. The first to change was the cinema of Poland.

POLAND

The Polish School

Before World War II, the Polish cinema had been a rather modest affair. Perhaps the most significant prewar development was the founding in 1929 of the radical avant-garde film society, Society of the Devotees of the Artistic Film, or START, which included the future directors Wanda Jakubowska (b. 1907) and Aleksander Ford (b. 1908)—whose *Knights of the Teutonic Order* (*Krzyżacy,* 1960) was to become the first great Polish film epic—as well as the film historian Jerzy Toeplitz (b. 1909). During the war, the Nazis forbade domestic production, but the material base of Polish cinema was kept alive by the Polish Army Film Unit under the direction of Aleksander Ford. With the establishment of the socialist state after the war, the provisional government nationalized the film industry under a single centralized authority, Film Polski, in 1945. The first postwar films were about the horrors that the country had endured during the Nazi Occupation. Of these, the best were Jakubowska's *The Last Stage* (*Ostatni etap,* 1948), a semidocumentary account of her own experiences in Auschwitz, and Ford's *Border Street* (*Ulica Graniczna,* 1948), a fictionalized version of the Warsaw Ghetto uprising of 1943. Ford's neorealistic *Five Boys from Barska Street* (*Piątka z ulicy Barskiej,* 1952), the first major Polish color film, was also notable. But in general the rigid dogma of socialist realism kept the standards of Polish film at a relatively low level until after the death of Stalin in 1953. In 1954, things began to change. At a meeting of the Polish Association of Cinema and Theater, Jerzy Toeplitz, then director of the Łódź Film School, attacked

16.1 *Five Boys from Barska Street* (Aleksander Ford, 1953): Tadeusz Janczar.

the tenets of socialist realism and called for a new national cinema. A year later, Film Polski was reorganized as a confederation of individual, self-sustaining production units known collectively as the United Groups of Film Producers. (Even today the Polish film industry is organized as a series of ten mutually competitive production groups [*zespół*], each headed by a senior director, with its own unique identity.)* Simultaneously, the first generation of trained directors emerged from Łódź, and the Polish Communist Party chief, Władysław Gomułka, decreed a thorough de-Stalinization of Poland.† Thus the way was cleared for the Polish film movement known as the "Polish School," the influence of which was international in scope from 1954 to 1963.

The first major talents to rise from the Łódź Film School were Jerzy Kawalerowicz (b. 1922), Andrzej Munk (1921–61), and Andrzej Wajda (b. 1926). Kawalerowicz was the least characteristic of the group. His first films, *A Night to Remember* (*Celuloza*, 1953) and *Under the Phrygian Star* (*Pod gwiazdą frygijską*, 1954), comprised a two-part epic about the gradual radicalization of a young peasant between the wars. In *Night Train* (*Pociąg*, 1959), he turned what might have been a conventional murder mystery into an impressive parable of intolerance and mob violence. But his two most significant films are visually stylized historical dramas written by the director / writer Tadeusz Konwicki (b. 1926), which reveal a highly developed sense of compositional form. Based on the famous French case of the devils of Loudon—which also provided the raw material for Ken Russell's *The Devils* (1971)—*Mother Joan of the Angels* (*Matka Joanna od Aniołów*, 1961) is a tension-charged film about the demonic possession of a nun in a seventeenth-century Polish convent. *Pharoah* (*Faraon*, 1946) is an expensively produced spectacle set in the Egypt of Ramses XIII, whose underlying theme is the corrupting nature of political power. For a decade after *Pharoah*, Kawalerowicz made only two films, *Game* (*Gra*, 1965) and *Maddalena* (1970), neither of which

16.2 *Under the Phrygian Star* (Jerzy Kawalerowicz, 1952).

* Until 1984, these groups and their leaders were the following: "Aneks" (Grzegorz Królikiewicz), "Iluzjon" (Czesław Petelski), "Kadr" (Jerzy Kawalerowicz), "Perspektywa" (Janusz Morgenstern), "Profil" (Bohdan Poręba), "Rondo" (Wojciech Has), "Silesia" (Ernest Bryll), "Tor" (Krzysztof Zanussi), "Zodiak" (Jerzy Hoffman), "X" (Andrzej Wajda). In 1984, Wajda's Unit "X" was dissolved by the government for political reasons.

† Gomułka (1905–82), a popular Polish Workers' Party leader who had been purged and imprisoned by the Stalinists in 1951, was rehabilitated in the summer of 1956 when workers' rebellions in Poznan and other cities threatened the stability of the Communist government. This led directly to the so-called Polish Spring in October of that year, during which Gomulka faced down the threat of a Soviet invasion and was appointed first secretary by reformists within the party's Central Committee. Gomułka removed his conservative opposition, made some modest—mainly cosmetic—reforms (including easing the government's campaign against religion and releasing Cardinal Wyszńyski from jail), and in general preserved a veneer of liberalism for a few years. But as Chris Harman has observed: "Ten years after 'October,' people were receiving prison sentences for such heinous offences as tape recording satirical plays and reading forbidden books. Those who dared to express public sympathy with them were expelled from the party and later deprived of their jobs" (*Class Struggles in Eastern Europe, 1945–83* [London: Pluto Press, 1983], p. 118). In fact, in 1970 Gomułka was forced from office for the same illiberal excesses that had brought him to power in 1956.

was a critical success. But he was one of the most serious and influential artists of the Polish School during the height of its power, and his first film since 1970, *Death of the President* (*Śmierć prezydenta*, 1978), displayed a newly spontaneous style in probing the 1922 assassination of Poland's first elected president. Happily, Kawalerowicz continued to make important films well into the eighties, most notably *A Chance Meeting on the Ocean* (*Spotkanie na Atlantyku*, 1980) and *Austeria* (1983).

After graduating from Łódź, Andrzej Munk worked for several years in the documentary field and continued to do so often after he directed his first feature, *Man on the Track* (*Człowiek na torze*, 1955), which many critics believe to be his greatest finished film. Working closely with the scriptwriter Jerzy Stefan Stawiński (b. 1921), a cofounder of the Polish School, Munk completed only two other films before his death in an automobile accident in September 1961—the antiheroic war film *Eroica* (*Heroism*, 1957), which satirized the Polish national devotion to lost causes, and *Bad Luck* (*Zezowate szczęście*, 1959), an ironic look at opportunism in postwar Polish society. At the time of his death, Munk had nearly finished shooting *The Passenger* (*Pasażerka*), which would surely have been his masterpiece. In it, a former SS guard traveling on an ocean liner is forced to relive her relationship with a young Jewish woman in Auschwitz through a series of flashbacks. In the process, we come to see the death camp from the guard's point of view as well as from the prisoner's, and an extraordinary humanistic comment is made upon the nature of guilt and suffering. The film was released in 1963 in a sixty-two–minute version pieced together by Munk's assistant, Witold Lesiewicz, and it was hailed as a classic, giving Munk posthumous international status. Today, on the strength of four features and a score of documentaries, there can be no question that the cinema was impoverished by the loss of Munk.

Though his subject matter (unlike that of Kawalerowicz) was always Poland's present and her recent past, in his ironic and antiheroic attitude toward it Munk was outside the basically romantic vision of the Polish

16.3   Kawalerowicz's *Mother Joan of the Angels* (1961).

16.4   *Eroica* (**Andrzej Munk**, 1957): Josef Nowak.

16.5   Munk's *The Passenger* (1963).

16.6 *A Generation* (Andrzej Wajda, 1954): Roman Polański (center).

16.7 *Canal* (Andrzej Wajda, 1956): Wienczjslaw Glinski.

School as it finally evolved. Much more characteristic and formative was the work of Andrzej Wajda, the first Eastern European director whose films were widely shown in the West. The son of a Polish cavalry officer, Wajda studied painting at the Fine Arts Academy in Kraków before attending the Łódź Film School. After graduating, he assisted Aleksander Ford on *Five Boys from Barska Street*, and in 1954 he made his first feature, *A Generation* (*Pokolenie*). This film, the first in a trilogy about his country's horrific experience of the war, established Wajda as a major European director and brought Polish cinema to international attention.* An essentially romantic film in neorealist form, *A Generation* was about a group of teenagers who become radicalized during the Occupation, join a left-wing Resistance movement, and are ultimately tracked down by the Gestapo. Wajda meant it to capture the mood and attitudes of the "lost generation" of young Poles (his own) who had come of age in the crucible of World War II. The second part of the trilogy was the unrelievedly grim *Kanał* (*Canal*, 1956), adapted by Jerzy Stefan Stawiński from his own novel. The film deals with hundreds of Home Army Resistance fighters who find themselves trapped beneath the streets in the city's sewer system during the brutally suppressed Warsaw uprising of 1944. Utterly devoid of hope from the outset, they wander through a watery labyrinth of excrement and carrion while the Nazis leisurely pick them off from above with explosives and automatic weapons. Wajda's despairing vision of heroes doomed to die like sewer rats is the very prototype of the romantic fatalism that came to characterize the Polish School.

So too is the last and greatest film in Wajda's war trilogy, *Ashes and Diamonds* (*Popiół i diament*, 1958). It depicts a few hours in the life of a young Resistance fighter, Maciek Chełmicki, on May 9, 1945, the first day after the war. Maciek has been ordered by the military commander of his nationalist underground unit to go to a provincial city and assassinate the new Communist Party district secretary. He has no real political commitment to his mission, and he begins to vacillate when he discovers his victim to be only a tired and rather kindly old man. But he carries out his orders like a good soldier, is himself shot in reprisal, and dies in agony on a garbage dump, which he reaches by flailing his way through line after line of ghostly hanging laundry. The film's rich visual symbolism lends it universality of theme and should remind us that Wajda studied painting for four years before he entered the cinema. But *Ashes and Diamonds* also contains an implicit comment on some specific difficulties of a traditional society's adjustment to a revolution, and it offers Wajda's most disillusioned view of the futility of heroism in the modern world. Significantly, the part of Maciek was the first major role of Zbigniew Cybulski (1927–67), the brilliant and versatile young actor who became the icon of the Polish School's romantic pessimism from 1958 until his accidental death in 1967.

Wajda made two more films set in the war period and one with a

---

* The scripts of the film trilogy are now available in an excellent edition; see *Andrzej Wajda: Three Films* (London: Lorrimer Publishing, 1984), introduction by Bolislaw Sulik.

16.8 *Ashes and Diamonds* (Andrzej Wajda, 1958): Zbigniew Cybulski, Adam Pawlikowski.

16.9 Maciek's death in *Ashes and Diamonds*.

contemporary context before turning to historical themes in the sixties. *Lotna* (1959) deals with the suicidal charge of the Polish mounted cavalry against a German Panzer division during the Nazi invasion of September 1938; *Samson* (1960) is the story of a Jew who attempts to escape the Warsaw Ghetto. *Innocent Sorcerers* (*Niewinni czarodzieje*, 1960), written by the future New Wave director Jerzy Skolimowski (see p. 675), moved away from the wartime obsessions of the Polish School to examine the attitudes, problems, and values of the generation that succeeded Wajda's own. It is generally agreed that Wajda's historical films of the sixties constitute a falling-off from his previous level of achievement. *A Siberian Lady Macbeth* (*Sibirska Ledi Magbet*, 1962), shot in Yugoslavia with a Yugoslav cast and crew, was an uneven, stylized melodrama set in a nineteenth-century Russian village; *Ashes* (*Popioły*, 1965) was a large-scale epic account of the Polish involvement in the Napoleonic Wars; and *Gates of Paradise* (*Bramy raju*), also shot in Yugoslavia, was an unsuccessful (and, to date, unreleased) study of the moral issues surrounding the thirteenth-century Children's Crusade. The only totally satisfying work Wajda produced during this period was his short contribution to the French anthology film *L'Amour à vingt ans* (1962), which starred Zbigniew Cybulski as a former Resistance fighter who rescues a child from the bear pit at the Warsaw zoo.

16.10 Wajda's *A Siberian Lady Macbeth* (1962).

With *Everything for Sale* (*Wszystko na sprzedaż*, 1969), however, Wajda again hit his stride and made his most personal film. Like Fellini's *8½* (1963) and Truffaut's *Day for Night* (1973), *Everything for Sale* is about a filmmaker in the process of making a film and therefore about the relationship between cinematic illusion and reality, but it is more Pirandello-like than the other works that deal with this theme. The film was inspired by the gruesome death in January 1967 of the actor Cybulski, who was run over by a train that he was attempting to board. Cybulski was not only Wajda's close personal friend and Poland's most popular star, but—like James Dean in America—he was an important cultural symbol of a

16.11 *Everything for Sale* (Andrzej Wajda, 1969): the film within the film. Elzbieta Czyzewska.

16.12 Wajda's *Landscape after Battle* (1970): Daniel Olbrychski.

16.13 Wajda's *Wedding* (1972): Daniel Olbrychski.

16.14 *Man of Marble* (Andrzej Wajda, 1977).

whole generation's attitude toward life; his senseless death shocked the nation. *Everything for Sale* memorializes that death and poses some disturbing questions about the morality of art: A film crew has prepared itself to shoot a scene in which an actor is to fall under a train at the Wroclaw station (where Cybulski was killed), but the actor fails to arrive for the take. The crew searches for him and discovers that he has been accidentally killed. The director then makes the decision to finish the film using a stand-in, thereby committing crew members to killing their former friend and colleague on film in the same way that he has been killed in actuality. At times the reality of the film *Everything for Sale* and the film within the film overlap and merge, so that it is difficult for the viewer to distinguish between them. And this, of course, is played off against the "real" reality outside both films—the reality of Cybulski's horrible death and its impact upon the Polish film community. Ultimately, *Everything for Sale* asks the same question as that posed by the director, Ferrand (Truffaut), in *Day for Night*: "Are films [or art] more important than life?" Truffaut's answer was: "Yes, for film artists, they must be and they are"; in Wajda's case the answer is more ambivalent and more bitter.

Most of Wajda's films since 1968, except the lightweight sex comedy *Hunting Flies* (*Polowanie na muchy*, 1969), have been characterized by the kind of stylized impressionism announced in *Everything for Sale*. *Landscape after Battle* (*Krajobraz po bitwie*, 1970), *The Birch-Wood* (*Brzezina*, 1970), *Pilatus and Others* (*Pilatus und Andere*, 1972), and *Wedding* (*Wesele*, 1972) are all technically innovative, visually baroque meditations on the great themes of time, art, love, and death, without regard to historical context. But *The Promised Land* (*Ziemia obiecana*, 1976), which offers a vibrant account of the brutal industrialization of Poland by foreigners in the early twentieth century, marked a return to the political themes of the fifties. Both *Man of Marble* (*Człowiek z marmuru*, 1977),* a sweeping indictment of officially fabricated postwar Polish history, and *Without Anesthesia* (*Bez znieczulenia*, 1978) concern the political corruption of the Polish news media (and both films were threatened with official censorship but eventually reached the United States intact). Wajda completed two more nonpolitical films—*The Young Girls of Wilko* (*Panny z Wilka*, 1979; a Polish-French coproduction), a poetic film of love and memory set on a country estate in the period between the world wars, and *The Conductor* (*Dyrygent*, 1980), in which an internationally famous conductor (Sir John Gielgud) returns to his native Poland in pursuit of lost love and youth in the person of a former mistress' daughter. He then confronted Poland's government head-on in *Man of Iron* (*Człowiek z żelaza*, 1981), which became the standard-bearer for the new Solidarity movement and made Wajda himself, more than ever before, a symbol of the greatness and courage of Polish cinema. As a benefactor

---

* Regarded by Wajda, after *Ashes and Diamonds*, as his most important film, *Man of Marble* won the International Critics' Prize at Cannes in 1978 and became the most popular film in Polish box-office history. It is formally modeled on *Citizen Kane*, the film that Wajda says inspired his career.

of such younger directors as Feliks Falk (b. 1941), Agnieszka Holland (b. 1948), and Janusz Kijowski (b. 1948) in his Production Unit "X" and as a filmmaker in his own right (*Danton,* 1982; *A Love in Germany,* 1984; *Notes of Love,* 1985), Andrzej Wajda has established himself as both the aesthetic grand master and moral conscience of Polish film. After thirty years as a director in that industry, his international stature and influence have never been higher, as was demonstrated by *A Chronicle of Amorous Incidents* (*Kronika wypadków miłosnych,* 1987) and his masterful adaptation of Dostoevsky's *The Possessed* (*Les Possédés,* 1988), both shot on location in Poland.

The Second Generation

The so-called Polish School came to an end in the early sixties when the Gomułka regime began to attack the national cinema for presenting a negative view of everyday Polish life. At the Thirteenth Party Congress in July 1964, Wajda's *Innocent Sorcerers* (1960) and Roman Polański's *Knife in the Water* (*Nóż w wodzie,* 1962) were singled out for special abuse as examples of this tendency. The Łódź Film School came under fire too, since four-fifths of the country's forty-eight professional directors had been trained there. Thus, the generation of filmmakers that succeeded Wajda's made their first features in Poland, but as social and political conditions became increasingly repressive they left one by one to work in the West.

The two most prominent members of this generation are Roman Polański (b. 1933) and Jerzy Skolimowski (b. 1938), both of whom attended the Łódź Film School and were decisively influenced by the French New Wave. Polański began his career as an actor in Wajda's *A Generation* (1954), and his first films were the absurdist shorts *Two Men and a Wardrobe* (*Dwaj ludzie z szafą,* 1958), *The Fat and the Lean* (*Le Gros et le maigre,* shot in France, 1961), and *Mammals* (*Ssaki,* 1962), all of which contain dark undertones reminiscent of the plays of Samuel Beckett. Polański's first feature—and the only one of his features shot in Poland—was *Knife in the Water,* an economical, tension-charged account of sexual rivalry among a husband, a wife, and a young stranger during a weekend sailing trip on the husband's yacht. The stranger and the wife make love aboard the boat while the husband is gone, and an electrifying sense of repressed sexual violence is sustained throughout. *Knife in the Water* achieved widespread recognition as a brilliant feature debut,* and Polański subsequently made three films in England. *Repulsion* (1965) is a chillingly precise study of an individual's descent into madness under the pressure of sexual neurosis. In it, a beautiful young working girl, superbly played by Catherine Deneuve, is driven to murder by a combination of isolation and sexual repression. Polański's masterful evocation of the hallucinated

16.15 Wajda's *Without Anesthesia* (1978).

16.16 *Man of Iron* (Andrzej Wajda, 1981).

16.17 *Knife in the Water* (Roman Polański, 1962): Jolanta Umecka, Zygmunt Malanowicz.

---

* The film also received considerable hype: *Time* ran a still from the film on its cover in conjunction with an article about international cinema, and *Knife* was nominated by the Academy for its Best Foreign Film award in 1963.

16.18 Polański's *Repulsion* (1965): Catherine Deneuve.

16.19 *Chinatown* (Roman Polański, 1974): Jack Nicholson menaced by hoods (Polański at left).

16.20 *Tess* (Roman Polański, 1979): Natassia Kinski in the title role.

horror of psychosis, through both image and sound, makes *Repulsion* one of the classic studies of mental breakdown in modern cinema, comparable to Alain Jessua's *La Vie à l'envers* (*Life Upside Down*, 1964; see Chapter 13) and Ján Kadár's *Adrift* (1971; see p. 690). *Cul-de-sac* (1966) is a strangely engaging film about an eccentric married couple on a desolate Northumberland island whose life is dramatically altered by the arrival of two wounded gangsters from the mainland. A combination of Pinteresque black humor and forties *film noir, Cul-de-sac* is thought by many critics to be Polański's finest film, and it is the director's own favorite. *The Dance of the Vampires / The Fearless Vampire Killers* (1967), a stylish parody of the horror-film genre, is a much lighter affair but impressive nonetheless for its atmospheric evocation of Central Europe.

In 1968 Polański came to the United States to direct the most popular and commercially successful of all his films, *Rosemary's Baby,* based on the novel by Ira Levin. This tale of witchcraft and Satanism was shot on location in New York City for Paramount. The tension between its muted naturalistic style and its horrific material makes the film a classic of the genre of demonic possession. It far outdistances more contemporary manifestations like *The Exorcist* (William Friedkin, 1973) and *The Omen* (Richard Donner, 1976) in creating a sense of real evil beneath its sensationalist surface. Polański returned to England in 1971 to do a personalized, hyper-realistic version of *Macbeth* that was generally well received but was criticized in some quarters for excessive violence. While he was in Europe he also made the poorly distributed *Che?* (*What?*, 1972), a comic account of an American virgin's encounter with a cornucopia of sexual perversions on her first visit to Italy. Ultimately, Polański returned to America to direct *Chinatown* (1974), an extremely successful essay in *film noir* set in Los Angeles during the thirties. His most conventional film in terms of structure, *Chinatown* nevertheless conveys that sense of evil, menace, and sexual tension that has become the hallmark of Polański's work. In terms of intellectual influence, it is possible to speak of surrealism and the theater of the absurd—of Kafka, Ionesco, Beckett, and Pinter. In terms of cinematic influence, Buñuel and Hitchcock clearly come to mind. But Polański's thematic obsession with cruelty, violence, and the forces that produce them must also reflect the uniquely grim circumstances of his own life. In 1941, when he was eight years old, Polański's parents were both sent to concentration camps—his father to Matthausen, where he managed to survive; his mother to Auschwitz, where she died—and he was forced to live a wretched existence in hiding until the end of the war. In 1969, his pregnant wife, the actress Sharon Tate, along with several of her friends, was brutally murdered and mutilated by the Charles Manson gang in one of the most repugnant crimes of the decade. More recently, Polański himself was charged with the statutory rape of a thirteen-year-old girl in Los Angeles County and fled the country to avoid imprisonment. Since then, he has completed a superb version of *Tess of the d'Urbervilles* (*Tess*, 1979), Thomas Hardy's tragic novel of innocence destroyed, in England; directed stage versions of Peter Shaffer's *Amadeus* in Warsaw (1981) and Paris (1982); and written his autobiography

(*Roman*, 1984). His mock-heroic *Pirates* (1986), shot on location in Tunisia and the Seychelles, was not well received, but the perverse thriller *Frantic* (1988) returned Polański to critical favor. The nightmare vision of human experience set forth in Polański's films should hardly surprise us: in his own life the director has been intimately acquainted with the nightmarish and the horrific.

Jerzy Skolimowski began his career as an actor and as coscriptwriter for Wajda's *Innocent Sorcerers* (1961). He became a student at the Łódź Film School in 1961 and the same year collaborated with Polański on the script of *Knife in the Water*. Between matriculation and graduation in 1964, Skolimowski worked continuously on his first feature, which was released as *Identification Marks: None* (*Rysopis*, 1964). A loosely structured account of an expelled student's last ten hours of civilian life before entering the military, this film freely appropriated the stylistic devices of *cinéma-vérité* and the New Wave. Like other Skolimowski protagonists (usually played by Skolimowski himself), the student is an outsider whose alienated vision of his society is implicitly critical. In *Walkover* (*Walkower*, 1965), a feature film composed of only thirty-five long takes, an amateur boxer (Skolimowski) attempts to make it in the professional ring knowing full well that he will lose—although, ironically, he does not. Skolimowski characteristically represents this attempt as a form of rebellion against the prevailing social order. *Barrier* (*Bariera*, 1966) firmly established Skolimowski as the principal spokesman for his generation, as well as one of the most important Polish directors to emerge in the sixties. Influenced by Godard, this film is an intricately stylized account of a student's mythic journey through contemporary Poland, and its surrealist *mise-en-scène* makes it Skolimowski's most bizarre and poetic work to date. After shooting the mild black comedy *Le Départ* (*The Departure*, 1967) in Brussels, Skolimowski returned to Poland to make *Hands Up!* (*Ręce do góry*, 1967), his most scathing attack yet upon the enclosure and barrenness of modern Polish society, and the film that he personally regards as his best and most mature work. Unfortunately, the film was banned by Polish authorities on its completion, and at this point, Skolimowski—like Polański before him—became an émigré. (*Hands Up!* was finally shown at the 1981 Gdańsk Film Festival, edited by Skolimowski and with a new prologue shot by him in Beirut and London.) He has since made films in Czechoslovakia (*Dialogue 20–40–60*, 1968), Italy (*The Adventures of Gérard*, 1970), England (*Deep End*, 1970), and West Germany (*König, Dame, Bube,* 1972—an adaptation of Vladimir Nabokov's novel *King, Queen, Knave*). While much of his non-Polish work is impressive, the critical consensus is that Skolimowski must find a receptive, stable environment for his filmmaking activity if he is to continue to innovate new forms. He may have found that environment recently in England, where he made *The Shout* (1978), an expressionistic tale of aboriginal sorcery, sexual enslavement, and madness; it is narrated in flashback during a cricket match and makes brilliant use of Dolby sound. The film was chosen to represent Britain at Cannes in 1978 and won high praise in its general release. Similarly distinguished, Skolimowski's

16.21 Polański's *Frantic* (1988): Harrison Ford, Emmanuelle Seigner.

16.22 Jerzy Skolimowski (standing) as the young boxer in his *Walkover* (1965).

16.23 Skolimowski's *Barrier* (1966): Jan Nowicki, Joanna Szczerbic.

16.24 *Hands Up!* (Jerzy Skolimowski, 1967).

16.25 *The Shout* (Jerzy Skolimowski, 1978): John Hurt, Alan Bates.

16.26 Skolimowski's *Moonlighting* (1982): Jeremy Irons.

16.27 *The Structure of Crystal* (Krzysztof Zanussi, 1969): Andrzej Zarnecki, Jan Mislowicz.

Moonlighting (1982) is a dark political fable of four Polish workers who are sent to London by "the Boss" to renovate an expensive townhouse on a poverty-line budget. When they have finally completed the job at great personal sacrifice, they find that they cannot return to Poland because martial law has been declared, and they must adapt to ruthlessly exploitative capitalism or starve. After shooting *Success Is the Best Revenge* (1984), another drama of exile set in London, Skolimowski directed for CBS Productions, *The Lightship* (1986), a sort of metaphysical version of Hitchcock's *Lifeboat* (1944) set in the coastal waters off Virginia in 1955. He has also resumed his career as an actor in such films as Volker Schlöndorff's *Circle of Deceit* and Taylor Hackford's *White Nights* (1985). Skolimowski's most recent film is a sensuously photographed adaptation of the Ivan Turgenev short story *Torrents of Spring* (1989).

The Third Polish Cinema

Of the third postwar generation of Polish directors, sometimes called collectively the "Third Polish Cinema," the most important is Krzysztof Zanussi (b. 1939), who is today the only rival to Wajda among those filmmakers who are still regularly working in Poland. Trained as a physicist, Zanussi posits a deterministic social and biological order, while simultaneously offering the hope that human beings may somehow free themselves from it. His films tend to focus on a single contemporary problem and treat it in a highly analytic manner. In *The Structure of Crystals* (*Struktura kryształu*, 1969), for example, the focus is on the meeting of two former university classmates—one an extremely successful physicist, the other the manager of an isolated weather station. The film is a dissection of the two men's inability to communicate to one

16.28 Zanussi's *Illumination* (1973): Stanislaw Latallo as a young physicist plunged into confusion over the mysteries of life.

16.29 *Camouflage* (Krzysztof Zanussi, 1977).

16.30 Zanussi's *The Constant Factor* (1980).

another their separate visions and values. During the seventies, Zanussi made similarly provocative films: *Family Life* (*Życie rodzinne,* 1971); *Behind the Wall* (*Za ścianą,* 1971); *Illumination* (*Iluminacja,* 1973); *Quarterly Balance / A Woman's Decision* (*Bilans kwartalny,* 1975); *Camouflage* (*Barwy ochronne,* 1977); *Spiral* (*Spirala,* 1978); and *Night Paths* (*Wege in der Nacht,* West Germany, 1979). All use the multiple resources of cinema, drama, and language (including that of mathematics) to examine some aspect of contemporary Polish society and the individual's position within it. As head of Production Unit "Tor," however, Zanussi became closely identified with the "cinema of moral anxiety" in the Solidarity era, and his *The Constant Factor* (*Constans*), which won the Jury Prize at Cannes in 1980, was one of its primary documents. After the imposition of martial law, Zanussi became one of several directors who were forced to work outside of Poland for political reasons, although he has since returned to make such films as the controversial World War II drama *The Year of the Quiet Sun* (*Rok spokojnego słonca,* 1984), which won the Golden Lion at Venice and was given limited release at home, and *Wherever You Are* (1988), a British-Polish-West German coproduction on the same theme.

The last major Polish filmmaker who must be considered here is an internationally famous animator who has recently turned, with notable success, to the production of live-action features. Walerian Borowczyk (b. 1923) was trained as a painter and was already an established artist when he won the Polish National Prize for his graphic work in 1953. He made his first animated shorts in collaboration with Jan Lenica (b. 1928), one of the great modern innovators in the field. These films tended to be menacing surrealistic fables like *Dom* (*House,* 1958), which portrays the paranoid hallucinations of a young girl left alone overnight in her house. In 1959 Borowczyk emigrated to Paris (Lenica followed in 1963), where he produced a series of animated shorts projecting a world of absurd violence and private nightmare. Characteristic is *Renaissance* (1963), in

16.31 *Les Jeux des anges* (Walerian Borowczyk, 1964).

16.32 Jan Lenica's *Labyrinth* (*Labirynt*, 1962).

which a number of heaped-up disintegrated objects reconstitute themselves, only to reconstitute the source of their original destruction—a time bomb that duly explodes at the end of the film, returning the objects to their state of chaos. In the twelve-minute *Les Jeux des anges* (*Games of Angels,* 1964), Borowczyk takes us on an abstractionized tour of a concentration camp whose transmogrified horrors rival the images of Hieronymus Bosch.* In some twenty-five disquieting allegorical shorts and a single feature (*Le Théâtre de M. et Mme. Kabal,* 1967) made between 1959 and 1967, Borowcyk experimented with every known form of animation to project his vision of ironic, hallucinated horror. He has painted images directly on his film stock, combined live action with animation, and regularly employed collage, pixillation, and film loops.

When he turned to short live-action films in 1966 with *Rosalie* and *Gavotte,* Borowczyk remained essentially a graphic artist with a fine sense of the cruelty of modern existence. His first live-action feature, *Goto, l'île d'amour* (*Goto, Island of Love,* 1967), was an absurdist fable of a barbaric dictatorship on a paradisiacal tropical island, full of inane brutality and arbitrary destruction. Borowczyk then became preoccupied with sexual perversity as an image of modern disorder. His *Contes immoraux* (*Immoral Tales,* 1974), a visually lush anthology film containing four separate tales of sexual perversion, became the second most popular film in France in the year of its release. *The Story of Sin* (*Dzieje grzechu,* 1975), which Borowczyk made in his native Poland and which was the most popular domestic film of 1975, is a surrealistic allegory of an innocent young girl who is drawn down into a terrible vortex of crime, perversion, and murder. Borowczyk's most recent features are *La Bête* (*The Beast,* 1976), a parable of sexual obsession and insatiability concerning a hideous beast and a lovely maiden; *Zone de feu* (*Belt of Fire,* 1978), a comedy about the fifteenth-century mass murderer Gilles de Rais; and *Lulu* (1980), a graphic rendition of the Frank Wedekind sex tragedies of which Pabst's *Die Büchse der Pandora* (1928) remains the classic treatment. From both his live-action features and his animated films, it is clear

16.33 Borowczyk's *The Story of Sin* (Grazyna Dlugolecka, 1975).

---

* A Dutch painter (1450–1516) whose elaborate, hallucinatory depictions of the torments of the damned in Hell have made his work a landmark in the tradition of grotesque art.

that Borowczyk shares with many of his compatriots a fatalistic and absurdist vision of life. His work embodies a profound pessimism for the human heritage of dissolution, disorder, and decay. But pessimism is not cynicism and need not lead to despair. There is in Borowczyk's films a kind of affirmation in his utter outrage at human misery and in his sense of horror at the human stupidities that produce it. In his best work, in fact, Borowczyk has much more in common with the Buñuel of *Un Chien andalou, L'Âge d'or,* and *Las Hurdes* than he does with Wajda, Polański, Skolimowski, or Zanussi, yet in the eighties the director was reduced to making soft-core sex farces like *L'Art d'aimer (The Art of Love,* 1983) and *Emmanuelle 5* (1987). Nevertheless, with his four feature films of the seventies, Borowczyk is significantly responsible for bringing the Polish cinema to the position of international prominence that it has occupied since the war.

16.34 The Nazi Occupation as envisioned in *Third Part of a Night* (Andrzej Żulawski, 1971).

That position was temporarily weakened in the late sixties, during the political crisis that followed the student demonstrations of March 1968. In an attempt to forestall the kind of liberalization then sweeping Czechoslovakia, the Gomulka regime tightened censorship, increased police surveillance, and purged the leadership of the entire Polish film industry. The shake-up was blatantly anti-Semitic: Aleksander Ford was forced to emigrate to Israel; Jerzy Bossak, head of the highly respected Polish documentary production unit, was fired; and Jerzy Toeplitz, director of the Łódź Film School since 1949, was summarily dismissed. In 1968, Poland produced only twenty films, most of them officially sanctioned literary adaptations, and several older films, like Wajda's *Samson* (1961), were banned. By 1971, however, Gomułka had been forced from office by the more moderate Edward Gierek, who relaxed censorship and promoted the reorganization of the state production units to give them more autonomy, which in turn enabled new talents like Zanussi to appear. But in the late seventies, as the result of a steadily deteriorating economy, Poland was plunged into a social crisis of major proportions that ultimately led to the militant strikes of the summer of 1980 and to the formation of the free labor union movement Solidarity (*Solidarność*), 1980–81, under the leadership of Lech Wałęsa (b. 1943).

16.35 *Camera Buff* (Krzysztof Kieślowski, 1976).

Solidarity and the Polish Cinema

Like the Czech New Wave during the sixties, Polish cinema during the seventies played a crucial role in crystalizing public consciousness about the need for liberalization. Unlike the subtly allusive Czech films, however, the Polish films were often abrasive and directly confrontational in their social criticism. In works like Wajda's *Man of Marble* and *Without Anesthesia* and Zanussi's *Camouflage* and *The Constant Factor* (but also those of many newer directors, such as Krzysztof Kieślowski's *Camera Buff,* 1976; Janusz Kijowski's *Index,* 1977; Feliks Falk's *Top Dog,* 1978; Edward Żebrowski's *Transfiguration Hospital,* 1979; and Agnieszka Holland's *Provincial Actors,* 1980—see p. 680), the Poles created what they called *kino moralnego niepokoju*—a cinema of moral anxiety—whose central theme was the isolation experienced by persons of integrity in a

16.36 *Top Dog* (Feliks Falk, 1978).

16.37 *Provencial Actors* (Agnieszka Holland, 1980).

corrupt and dishonest society. Despite low budgets and a documentary-like austerity of means, these films were immensely popular with Polish audiences (whose contempt for the hypocrisies of the state-controlled broadcast and print media is nearly universal), and the films became closely identified with the nation's yearning for greater political and social freedom.* Thus, when Solidarity was set up in August 1980 in Gdańsk (formerly Danzig)—the site, appropriately, of both the historic Lenin Shipyard strikes and of Poland's major film festival—not only did most Polish filmmakers support its demands for economic and political reform but nine out of ten became members, founding their own self-governing union in September (the Cinematography Workers' Independent Trade Union, as distinct from the officially sanctioned Polish Filmmakers' Association [PFA]).

During the next sixteen months, Polish filmmakers enjoyed unprecedented creative and political freedom. Within a year, in fact, Poland had become one of the most talked about film-producing countries in the world, and the Eighth Gdańsk Festival of Polish Films, held in August 1981, was widely recognized to be a celebration of this fact. Its centerpiece was Andrzej Wajda's docudrama on the birth of Solidarity, *Man of Iron,* a sort of sequel to *Man of Marble* and winner of the 1981 Cannes Grand Prix. Equally compelling were two actual documentaries—Andrzej Piekutowski's *Peasants '81* (*Chłopi '81*), a heroic account of the creation of Rural Solidarity, and Tomasz Pobog-Malinowski's *100 Days* (*Sto dni*), a record of the construction and dedication of the Gdańsk Martyrs' Monument at the Lenin Shipyards on December 6, 1980.† Like the electrifying *Workers '80* (*Robotnicy '80,* Andrzej Zajaczkowski and Andrzej Chodakowski, 1980), documenting the shipyard strikes and the negotiations that followed, these films were intended as rallying cries for Solidarity and the newly won right to strike that it briefly guaranteed. Another notable category at Gdańsk in 1981 was comprised of four films previously banned by government censors and publicly screened for the first time: Jerzy Skolimowski's legendary *Hands Up!* (*Ręce do góry,* 1967; edited and partially reshot by Skolimowski, 1981), Antoni Krauze's *The*

---

* The standards of censorship for films in Communist Poland (and, indeed, in many Eastern bloc countries) have at times been more liberal than those for television, radio, books, or newspapers, which are perceived to be more dangerously influential since they enter the home. An official censorship handbook smuggled out of Poland in 1980 revealed a curious double standard under which controversial films may be shown in theaters but not mentioned in other media. In other words, publicity for Polish films is more carefully monitored than the films themselves. See *The Black Book of Polish Censorship,* ed. Jane L. Curry (New York: Random House, 1984).

†The monument, consisting of three gigantic iron crosses soaring ten stories above the shipyard gate, was erected by the Polish people in one hundred days to memorialize the dozens of civilian workers massacred there by the military during the Gdańsk uprising of December 16, 1970, on the tenth anniversary of that event. Another film about this remarkable achievement is the Finnish-Polish documentary *The Memorial in Gdańsk* (Jarmo Jaaskilaenan, 1982); two other notable documentary works on the Solidarity movement in general are the New York–based filmmaker Jill Godmilow's *Far from Poland* (1984) and Henrik Byrn's Danish–West German *Solidarnosc—The Hope from Gdańsk* (1985).

Pad (*Meta,* made for TV, 1971; 1974), Krzysztof Kieślowski's *The Calm Before the Storm* (*Spokój,* made for TV, 1976), and Janusz Kijowski's feature debut *Index* (*Indeks,* 1977). Among contemporary films at the festival were three ringing indictments of the repressive Stalinist era, Filip Bajon's *Shilly-Shally* (*Wahadelko*), Feliks Falk's *There Was Jazz* (*Był Jazz*), and Wojceich Marczewski's *Shivers* (*Dreszcze*—winner of the Silver Bear, Berlin, 1982). Further evidence of the stunning new vitality of Polish cinema was offered by Stanislaw Różewicz's *Lynx* (*Ryś*), Grzegorz Królikiewicz's *The Supreme Value of a Free Conscience* (*Klejnot wolnego sumienia*), Edward Żebrowski's *In Broad Daylight* (*W biały dzień*), Zanussi's *The Contract* (*Kontrakt,* made for TV), Piotr Szulkin's science-fiction allegory *The War of the Worlds—Next Century* (*Wojna swiatów-następne stulecie*), and Agnieszka Holland's drama of revolutionary violence, *Fever* (*Gorączka*). Appropriately, the First National Solidarity Congress ran concurrently with the Eighth Gdańsk Festival, and both concluded with a three-day program of twenty-six Solidarity-inspired documentaries entitled "A Document of Protest." Several months later, in the euphoria inspired by the new freedom, Wajda and nine other directors (Krzysztof Zanussi, Krzysztof Kieślowski, Feliks Falk, Agnieszka Holland, Filip Bajon, Janusz Zaorski, Edward Żebrowski, Wojciech Marzewski, and Tomasz Pobog-Malinowski) announced plans to hold their own festival in Warsaw in February 1982, with the expressed purpose of circumventing Film Polski and arranging coproduction with the West.

Then, suddenly, it was over. On the morning of December 13, 1981, Poland was invaded from within, as the military led by General Wojciech Jaruzelski abruptly replaced the civilian government and declared martial law with the moral and tactical support of the Soviet Union, which had its largest ally surrounded by fifty-nine armored divisions and garrisoned by four others when the coup took place. A curfew was imposed, assembly banned, travel restricted, and all telephone and telex lines cut; strikes were broken by armed force, Solidarity leaders arrested *en masse,* and the union itself brutally suppressed. The consequences for the film industry were immediate and grim. Undercapitalized and financially dependent by law upon the state, the Polish cinema found itself threatened with extinction through bankruptcy.* All of the nation's 1,180 film theaters were closed under the ban on public assembly, cutting the industry's immediate cash flow, and when the theaters reopened two months later Polish audiences discovered a significantly changed national cinema.

Conservatives like Ewa and Czesław Petelski, Bohdan Poręba, and Ryszard Filipski had been temporarily given control of the industry to make orthodox World War II epics and historical films. The Gdańsk

16.38 *The Contract* (Krzysztof Zanussi, 1980), made for Polish television.

---

* Despite its vitality and its size (over 30,000 workers), the Polish film industry has always operated on thin financial margins. Equipment comes at such a premium that a director generally works under a thirty-day production schedule and is fined for exceeding it; film stock is so scarce that directors are seldom allowed more than two takes per scene (compare Hollywood's fifteen to twenty); and actors and actresses are so underpaid that they routinely work in several films at once in order to make a living.

16.39 Wajda's *Danton* (1982), produced in Paris. Gerard Depardieu.

16.40 Wajda's *A Love in Germany* (1984), produced in Munich. Hanna Schygulla.

Festival was suppressed, and most films produced during the flowering of Solidarity were banned, many without ever having been released, including Antoni Krauze's *The Weather Forecast* (*Prognoza pogody*), Agnieszka Holland's *The Lonely Woman* (*Kobieta samotna*), Krzysztof Kieślowski's *Blind Chance* (*Przypadek*), Janusz Zaorski's *Mother of Kings* (*Matka królów*), Jerzy Domaradzki's *The Big Race* (*Wielki bieg*), Ryszard Bugajski's *The Interrogation* (*Przeszuchanie*)*, and two films seen at Gdańsk in 1981, Falk's *There Was Jazz* and Szulkin's *The War of the Worlds—Next Century*. In this climate, several of Poland's major filmmakers found it prudent to work abroad for a while—most notably Wajda, whose *Danton* (1982), a parable of counterrevolution adapted from Stanisława Przybyszewska's play *The Danton Affair,* was produced in Paris† and whose *A Love in Germany,* adapted from a Rolf Hochhuth novel of Nazi Germany, was produced in Munich; and Zanussi, who made his biography of Pope John Paul II,** *From a Far Country* (1982), in Italy and produced a number of dramatic films for French and West German television between 1982 and 1984.

In May 1983, Wajda was dismissed as head of Film Unit "X" by Jaruzelski's minister of culture, Kazimierz Zygulski, for having made films "which have nothing in common with the cultural policy of the state." At the same time, Unit "X" and Zanussi's Unit "Tor"—those most closely associated with the "cinema of moral anxiety" and, ironically, the two units with the greatest margin of success over costs—were denounced by the Central Committee of the Polish United Workers Party (PZPR) as "oppositional, demagogic, and existential." In December 1983, Wajda resigned as chairman of the Polish Filmmakers' Association (a position that he had held since 1978) along with the organization's entire governing board, and it seemed briefly as if the group might disintegrate, as had a number of other artists' unions under martial law. But the PFA reconstituted itself with virtually the same board as before (Krzysztof Zanussi, Kazimierz Kutz, Jerzy Kawalerowicz, Wojciech Has, Krzysztof Kieślowski, Jerzy Hoffman, Tadeusz Chmielewski, Feliks Falk, Andrzej Trzos-

---

* Still officially banned, *The Interrogation* became the most influential Polish film of 1985 when thousands of copies of it were distributed on videocassette by the cultural underground. Because the government did not initially control the diffusion of VCRs, Poland now has more per capita than any other country in the Eastern bloc, a situation that has opened a whole new sphere in the struggle to achieve a culture independent of the state and ultimately assisted in the restoration of civilian government in 1989. (But while Bugajski's harrowing film of Stalinist-style police tactics was being seen all over Poland, the director himself was forced into exile in Canada.)

† A Polish-French coproduction, *Danton* was originally to have been shot in Poland, but Wajda moved the project to France in the wake of the Jaruzelski coup. Films Polski's response was to slash its participation to less than 10 percent, leaving French Gaumont to put up the balance of funds and the Mitterand government to provide a grant of 500,000 dollars for postproduction. The film won France's prestigious Louis Delluc Prize for 1982, and the Onassis Foundation awarded Wajda its Athinai Prize "for his contribution to human dignity."

** Formerly Karol Cardinal Wojtyla, a supporter of the liberalization movement and archbishop of Kraków.

Rastawiecki, and Jerzy Toeplitz) and Wajda's close friend Janusz Majewski as chairman.

After 1984, when the Gdańsk Festival was reopened, a kind of uneasy truce existed between the film industry and the Jaruzelski regime. Just as many of the original strictures of martial law were lifted and most political prisoners freed, so were restrictions on the Polish cinema eased. Most of the exiled filmmakers have returned,* including Wajda who in 1985 directed a screen adaptation of Tadeusz Konwicki's *Notes of Love* in Warsaw—his first Polish film since *Man of Iron*. Most of the banned films from the early Solidarity era were released (some, like Wiesław Saniewski's *Custody* [*Nazdor*, 1981], with cuts), although several—e.g., Holland's *The Lonely Woman*, Bugajaki's *The Interrogation*, and Kieślowski's *A Short Day's Work* (*Krótki dzień pracy*, 1982)—are too political to see the light of day even now. Serious films with a contemporary setting became possible once more (e.g., Kieślowski's film of the grim year 1982, *Without End* [*Bez końca*, 1985]), but in general, social criticism was out and genre films were in, especially science fiction (Maciej Wojtyszko's *The Synthesis* [*Synteza*, 1984], Piotr Szulkin's *O-Bi, O-Ba—The End of Civilization* [*O-Bi, O-Ba—Koniec cywilizacji*, 1985]), horror (Marek Piestrak's *The She-Wolf* [*Wilczyca*, 1983], Marek Nowicki's *Phantom* [*Widziadło*, 1984]), comedy (Juliusz Machulski's *Sex Mission* [*Seksmisja*, 1984], Michal Dudziewicz's *The Job* [*Fucha*, 1985]), and historical drama (Tadeusz Konwicki's *The Issa Valley* [*Dolina Issy*, 1983], Janusz Majewski's *Epitaph for Barbara Radziwill* [1983], Stanislaw Różewicz's *Mrs. Latter's Pension* [*Pensja Pani Latter*, 1984], and Filip Bajon's *The Magnate* [*Magnat*, 1987]). Perhaps the most encouraging sign was the founding of a new experimental production collective, the Irzykowski Film Studio, modeled on the Béla Balász Studio in Hungary, from which Waldemar Dziki's shattering drama of the Holocaust, *Postcard from a Journey* (*Kartka z podróży*) emerged to international acclaim in 1984. The Film and Television School at Katowice also came forth as an important training ground for new talent, and there were indications everywhere that, despite continuing repression and internal subversion, the Polish film industry was bouncing back from its post-1981 crisis well before the restoration of a Solidarity-controlled civilian government in August 1989. Their thematic monotony notwithstanding, over thirty quality features were produced in 1985—an impressive 15 percent of which were made by first-time directors—and the Tenth Gdańsk Festival in August of that year gave ample proof of a revival, with the promise of better things to come. And, in fact, Polish films had become considerably more frank in the late eighties as is demonstrated by such work as Janusz Zaorski's *Lake Constance* (*Jezioro bodenskie*, 1986), Janusz Majewski's *The Deserters* (*C. K. Dezertenzy*, 1987), Feliks Falk's impressive sequel to *Top Dog*, *Hero of the Year* (*Bohater roke*, 1987), Robert Glinski's *Sunday Pranks* (*Niedzieine pgraszki*, 1987), and Krzysztof Kieślowski's *Blind Chance* (*Przypadek*, 1987), *A Short Film about Love* (*Krótki film*

---

*Polańsky, Skolimowski, and Andrzej Żulawski had chosen permanent exile before the events of 1980–81.

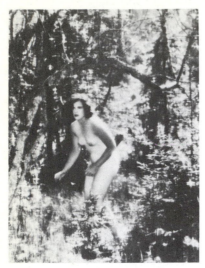

16.41 *Ecstasy* (Gustav Machatý, 1932): Hedy Lamarr).

16.42 *Jánošík* (Martin Frič, 1935).

o miłości, 1988), and *A Short Film about Killing* (*Krótki film o zabijaniu*, 1988), winner of the Best Film Prize at the first European Film Awards Festival in November 1988. (The last two are part of Kiéslowski's ten-film magnum opus *Dekalog* [*The Ten Commandments*], completed in 1989.)

CZECHOSLOVAKIA

The Postwar Period

Unlike Poland, Czechoslovakia had a distinguished cinematic tradition long before World War II. One of the major pioneers of camera technology, J. E. Purkyně (1787–1869), was from this region. Commercial production began in Prague in 1908, six years ahead of Berlin, and the city became a major continental film capital in the period just before World War I. By 1933 Prague had the most sophisticated production facilities in Europe, at the Barrandov studios. Between the wars, several Czech directors achieved international reputations—Karel Anton (b. 1898) for the first Czech sound film, *Tonka of the Gallows* (*Tonka šibenice*, 1930); Gustav Machatý (1901–63), who had worked as an assistant in Hollywood to both Griffith and von Stroheim, for his *Erotikon* (1929), *From Saturday to Sunday* (*Ze soboty na neděli*, 1931), and the sensational *Ecstasy* (*Extase*, 1932), which won a prize at Venice in 1933; Martin Frič (1902–68) for his Slovak folk epic *Jánošík* (1935); Josef Rovenský (1894–1937) for his lyrical film-poem *The River* (*Řeka*, 1934); and Otakar Vávra for *Guild of the Kutná Hora Maidens* (*Cech panen kutnohorských*, 1938), which won the Golden Lion at Venice in the year of its release. The Czech cinematographers Otto Heller (1896–1970) and Jan Stallich (b. 1907) also became internationally prominent during this period.* During the Occupation, domestic production slumped from forty films in 1940 to nine in 1944, as the Nazis appropriated the Barrandov studios and greatly expanded their production capacity in order to make German-language films (in fact, toward the end of the war, the Nazis planned to transfer their entire film industry to Prague). But during the same period, certain Czech filmmakers were already formulating plans

---

* In his important study *The Czechoslovak New Wave* (Berkeley: University of California Press, 1985), Peter Hames points out that many significant long-term developments for Czech cinema grew out of the avant-garde Devětsil movement of the thirties, which included among its members the poet Vitězslav Nezval, the novelist Vladislav Vančura, and the film director Martin Frič. Nezval wrote several important film scripts, Vančura directed five films before his execution by the Nazis as part of their retaliation for the Heydrich assassination in 1942, and Frič became Czechoslovakia's most popular director when he teamed fellow Devětsil members Jiří Voskovec and Jan Werich in the comedies *Heave Ho* (*Hej rup*, 1934) and *The World Belongs to Us* (*Svět patří nám*, 1937). It was no coincidence that Werich was featured in one of the first New Wave films, Vojtěch Jasný's *Cassandra Cat* (1963), or that some of the New Wave's most important works were adapted from Devětsil writers—e.g., František Vláčil's *Markéta Lazarová* (1967, from Vančura), Jiří Menzel's *Capricious Summer* (1968, from Vančura), and Jaromil Jireš's *Valerie and Her Week of Wonders* (1969, from Nezval).

for the nationalization of the industry when the Nazis withdrew. On August 11, 1945, the Czech President, Eduard Beneš,* signed a nationalization decree that established a new production system with three major components: (1) a specially equipped studio for the production of puppet and animation films, (2) the organization of collective production groups for live-action features, and (3) the foundation of a state film school— the Prague Film (and Television, after 1960) Faculty of the Academy of Dramatic Arts (FAMU). In 1947, a separate Slovak production system was organized, with its own documentary and feature studios in Bratislava (the Slovaks were at that time culturally and religiously separate from the Czechs). Czechoslovakia thus became the second country in Eastern Europe, after the Soviet Union, to totally and permanently nationalize its film industry.

Nationalization freed producers to concentrate on serious political themes, and the first postwar Czech films dealt with the historic struggle to create a communist state. Of these, the most impressive were Jiří Weiss' (b. 1913) *Stolen Frontier* (*Uloupená hranice*, 1947), which concerned Hitler's plundering of the Czech frontier in 1938; Karel Steklý's (b. 1903) *The Strike* (*Siréna*, 1947), a film about an 1889 miners' rebellion that won the Golden Lion at Venice in the year of its release; and Otakar Vávra's *Silent Barricade* (*Němá barikáda*, 1948), whose subject was the Prague uprising against the Nazis just prior to the Red Army's "liberation" of the city. All three bore the marked influence of Italian neorealism. Of more lasting significance were the first feature-length animated puppet films of Jiří Trnka (1912–69). His *The Czech Year* (*Špalíček*, 1947), a seven-part compilation film celebrating his country's rich folk tradition, won several festival prizes. He followed this with *Song of the*

---

* Beneš' postwar democratic government lasted less than three years. In 1948, it was replaced by a Communist dictatorship that became one of the most repressive in Eastern Europe, instituting mass purge trials and executions as early as 1949 that continued through 1954 and 1955.

16.43 *Old Czech Legends* (Jiří Trnka, 1953).

16.44 Trnka's later work: *The Hand* (1966).

Prairie (1949), a parody of American Westerns, then with a magical adaptation of a Hans Christian Andersen fairy tale, *The Emperor's Nightingale* (*Císařův slavík*, 1948), and *The Happy Circus* (*Veselý cirkus*, 1950), a short that employed the nearly forgotten technique of animating paper cutouts. Trnka made his two greatest puppet films in the fifties. *Old Czech Legends* (*Staré pověsti české*, 1953) was a folk epic comprised of seven distinct heroic tales, and it has been justly described as both *ciné*-ballet and *ciné*-opera. *A Midsummer Night's Dream* (*Sen noci svatojanské,* 1958) was an enchanting widescreen adaptation of the Shakespeare play which abandoned the text for mime and dance. Three years in production, this film is widely regarded as Trnka's masterpiece, but the English-language versions have, unfortunately, been dubbed with a voice-over narration and quotations from the play that run counter to the director's intentions. Karel Zeman (b. 1910), an early follower of Trnka, developed a unique style which combined graphics, live action, puppet animation, and special optical effects in four award-winning science fiction features, including *Prehistoric Journey* (*Cesta do pravěku,* 1954) and *The Invention of Destruction* (*Vynález zkázy,* 1958), which took the Grand Prix at the Brussels World's Fair.

With the exception of the films of Trnka and Zeman, the Czech cinema in the early fifties was one of doctrinaire socialist realism like that of the other Warsaw Pact nations, and the Czech film industry was rigidly centralized. Perhaps the most important event of the period was the formation in 1952 of the close association between the directors Elmar Klos (b. 1910) and Ján Kadár (1918–79), which would produce two of the greatest films of the Czech New Wave, *The Shop on Main Street* and *Adrift* (see p. 690). Klos and Kadár also collaborated on some of the most interesting Czech films of the fifties, culminating in the controversial *Three Wishes* (*Tři přání*, 1958), a veiled analysis of the mechanisms of social repression. By the year of the film's release, the post-Stalinist thaw had given Czech filmmakers greater freedom to explore both contemporary and historical themes, and the industry had been decentralized into five semiautonomous production groups according to the Polish model. But *Three Wishes* became the object of a neo-Stalinist attack on the industry at a conference at Bánska Bystrica in 1959, and, along with several other films, it was banned until 1963. This new and unexpected wave of repression caused directors to retreat to the perennially safe subject matter of the Nazi Occupation, but this time the Czech experience of the war was used as a vehicle for contemporary social comment. Jiří Weiss' *Romeo, Juliet, and the Darkness / Sweet Light in the Dark Room* (*Romeo, Julie a tma*, 1960) tells the story of a young Jewish girl sent to her death in a concentration camp through the indifference of her neighbors. Weiss' *The Coward* (*Zbabělec*, 1961) concerns a simple teacher in rural Slovakia who heroically supports his students in the face of Nazi terrorism. Vojtěch Jasný (b. 1925), an early FAMU graduate (1950) and a forerunner of the Czech New Wave, contributed *I Survived Certain Death* (*Přežil jsem svou smrt*, 1960), which deals with the courageous struggle of a concentration-camp prisoner to keep himself alive. But the most impor-

16.45 *The Invention of Destruction* (Karel Zeman, 1958), adapted from the writings of Jules Verne.

tant of the Occupation films of the early sixties were Zbyněk Brynych's (b. 1927) *Transport from Paradise* (*Transport z ráje*, 1963), a neorealistic account of the transfer of Jews from the "model" ghetto of Terezin (Teresienstadt) to the gas chambers of Auschwitz; and Klos and Kadár's *Death Is Called Engelschen* (*Smrt si říká Engelchen*, 1963), a formally innovative indictment of war as a corruptor of vanquished and victor alike.

Another haven from the neo-Stalinist assault on Czech film was formal experimentation. Jasný led the way with *Desire* (*Touha*, 1958), a film poem on the "four seasons" of life that used the camera as a metaphorical device. The art historian František Vláčil (b. 1924)* followed with *The White Dove* (*Bílá holubice*, 1960), a formalist allegory of repression, isolation, and entrapment in the guise of a tale about a sick boy who captures a dove. In Bratislava, the Slovak director Štefan Uher (b. 1930), whose first feature had been the unusual children's film *Grade 9A* (*My z deviatej A*, 1961), made *Sunshine in a Net* (*Slnko v sieti*, 1962), which many historians identify as the first film of the Czech New Wave. Technically unconventional and highly stylized, *Sunshine in a Net* deals primarily with the inner lives of its characters; it was attacked by the first secretary of the Slovak Communist Party for exalting subjective vision over socialist realism. Ultimately the film was banned in Bratislava, but Czech film critics organized a special premier showing in Prague and voted overwhelmingly for its artistic merit. At about the same time, a major reform of the Slovak Communist Party placed the liberal Alexander Dubček at its head and prepared the way for his subsequent challenge to Czech President and Party Secretary Novotný in January 1968 and the brief period of democratization that followed.

The Czech New Wave

The official vindication of *Sunshine in a Net* helped to clear the path for the Czech New Wave. So, too, did the extraordinary experimental films of Věra Chytilová (b. 1929), a former draftswoman and fashion model, who attended FAMU along with other future directors of the New Wave. Chytilová's medium-length graduation film, *Ceiling* (*Strop*), was distributed commercially with her second film, *A Bag of Fleas* (*Pytel blech*), in 1962, and they established her immediately as the chief formal innovator of the New Wave. Markedly influenced by French and American *cinéma-vérité* techniques, both of these films were stories of young women seeking self-actualization in the closed world of Czech urban society. Chytilová's first feature, for which she also wrote the screenplay, was *Something Else / Something Different* (*O něčem jiném*, 1963), a cin-

16.46 *Death Is Called Engelschen* (Ján Kadár and Elmar Klos, 1963).

16.47 *Night of the Bride* (Karel Kachyua, 1967).

16.48 *Sunshine in a Net* (Štefan Uher, 1962).

16.49 *Markéta Lazarová* (František Vláčil, 1967).

---

* Of all the First Wave and New Wave directors, Vláčil combined a concern for experimental form with a preference for historical subjects. His masterpiece is *Markéta Lazarová* (1967), a four-hour two-part adaptation of Vančura's novel of thirteenth-century Bohemia (1931). This violent and hypnotic widescreen spectacle took Vláčil four years to complete and has been compared to the epic films of Kurosawa, Eisenstein, and Griffith. To amortize the costs of its elaborate sets and costumes, Vláčil followed *Markéta* with *Valley of the Bees* (*Údolí včel*, 1967), a lesser but similarly stylized medieval film.

16.50 *Something Different* (Věra Chytilová, 1963).

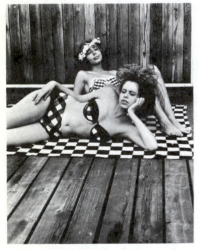

16.51 *Daisies* (Věra Chytilová, 1966): Jitka Čerhova, Ivana Karbanová.

éma-vérité portrait of the lives of two quite different women, an Olympic gymnast and a frustrated housewife. With *Daisies* (*Sedmikrásky*, 1966), however, Chytilová moved away from *cinéma-vérité* into the realm of surrealist fantasy and produced one of the outstanding works of the Czech New Wave. The film concerns two bored and self-indulgent girls (the "daisies" of the title) who embark upon an outrageous binge of destruction that ultimately destroys them as well. A bizarre and beautiful satire, *Daisies* was shot by Chytilová's husband, the brilliant cinematographer Jaroslav Kučera (b. 1929), who made free use of superimposition, collage, prismatic distortion, and expressive color to achieve dazzling visual effects for the film. It was designed and partially written by the versatile film artist Ester Krumbachová (b. 1923), a leading figure of the New Wave who has worked in close collaboration with Chytilová, Jan Němec, and Jaromil Jireš (see pp. 696–97; see below). Openly anarchic and subversive, *Daisies* was banned until 1967, when it won considerable critical acclaim both at home and abroad. Chytilová, however, was denied state funds to continue her filmmaking, and her next film, another collaboration with Kučera and Krumbachová, was financed by a Belgian production company. Her most surrealistic film to date, *The Fruit of Paradise* (*Ovoce stromů rajských jíme*, 1969) is a complicated parable about the fantasies of women trapped in a man's world; it won several international awards. But after 1970, Chytilová, who had chosen to remain and work in her homeland despite the Soviet invasion and the overthrow of the liberal Dubček regime in 1968, was forbidden by the government to make films altogether. The ban was lifted in 1975, and she produced *The Apple Game* (*Hra o jablko*, 1976), a furiously paced satire on the inefficiency and corruption of the Czech medical profession, followed by *Prefab Story* (*Panelstory*, 1978) and *Calamity* (*Kalamita*, 1979). Whatever her future as a filmmaker, Chytilová stands today as the most influential formal innovator of the Czech New Wave.

Another young formalist of note was Jaromil Jireš (b. 1935), who worked

16.52 and 16.53 Chytilová's *The Apple Game* (1976): Jiri Menzel and friends.

briefly with Chytilová on the script of *Daisies*. His first feature was a stylistically dazzling portrait of contemporary Czech society entitled *The First Cry* (*Křik*, 1963). It depicted a day in the life of a television repairman making his rounds from house to house while his wife lies in the hospital in labor. Clearly influenced by the French New Wave, Jireš cut back and forth with great precision among the repairman at work in a variety of social contexts (especially in the homes of the powerful, the only Czechs who could afford to own TV sets at this time), his wife in the hospital, and their memories of their past life together to suggest the nature of the world the child will be born into. Between 1963 and 1968 Jireš made no feature films because all of his scripts were rejected by the censors. But in the Prague Spring of 1968, the brief period of democratization fostered by the Dubček regime, he was able to produce a dark, ironic masterpiece, *The Joke* (*Žert*). Based on a contemporary novel by Milan Kundera, the film provides a savage indictment of the Stalinist system in the story of a postwar philosophy student who is unjustly expelled from school and sent to serve in one of the Czech army's notoriously brutal "black units" because he made a political joke. Stylistically restrained and harshly realistic, *The Joke* contrasts sharply with Jireš' later films. *Valérie and Her Week of Wonders* (*Valérie a týden divů*, 1969), adapted from a story by the Czech surrealist poet Vítězslav Nezval, is a beautifully photographed vampire film that alternates between the erotic and the grotesque. *And Give My Love to the Swallows* (*A pozdravují vlaštovky*, 1971) is a stylized version of the diaries of a young girl who was executed for aiding the Resistance during the Nazi Occupation, and *The Island of Silver Herons* (*Ostrov stříbrných volavek*, 1976) is a poetic meditation on honor and tradition as seen through the eyes of a young boy in a small German town at the close of World War I. (None of Jireš' more recent films have reached the West, but several have won domestic prizes.)

The films of Chytilová and Jireš signaled the beginning of the Czech New Wave, or the "Czech Film Miracle," as it has also been called. This movement was to have an impact on world cinema equivalent to that of Italian neorealism; it was political as well as artistic, in that its ultimate goal was to make the Czech people collectively aware that they were participants in a system of oppression and incompetence which had brutalized them all. The success of this consciousness-raising was nearly total, and there is little doubt today that the Czech cinema of 1963–68—like the Polish "cinema of moral anxiety," 1976–81—laid much of the groundwork for liberalization.* It also brought the Czech film industry into a position of international prominence once again.

16.54 *The First Cry* (Jaromil Jireš, 1963).

16.55 Jireš' *The Joke* (1968): Josef Somr.

16.56 Jireš' *Valérie and Her Week of Wonders* (1969).

---

* There was this significant difference, however: the Polish agitation for reform began with the working class and acquired the widespread support of Polish intellectuals only after the birth of Solidarity, but the Czechoslovak reform movement began within the intelligentsia and extended to the working class only during the Prague Spring of 1968. It is noteworthy in this regard that the Czech New Wave cinema was closely associated with concurrent experimental movements in literature and theater. In fact, at the Fourth Congress of the Czechoslovak Writers Union in 1971, Milan Kundera went so far as to describe the leading New Wave films as part of the history of Czechoslovak literature.

16.57 *The Shop on Main Street* (Jan Kadár and Elmar Klos, 1965): Ida Kamínska, Josef Kroner.

16.58 *The Shop on Main Street:* the round-up.

Though it was dominated by the youngest generation of FAMU-trained directors, the New Wave was a movement in which Czech filmmakers of all generations participated, precisely because it *was* a national political phenomenon. The veterans Klos and Kadár first contributed *The Defendant* (*Obžalovaný*, 1964), an unconventional courtroom drama about a man being tried for achieving economic success within the socialist system. They then produced an internationally acclaimed masterpiece, *The Shop on Main Street* (*Obchod na korze*, 1965), which won the American Academy Award as Best Foreign film of 1965. This film is about Tono, a carpenter in a small Slovak town, who becomes the "Aryan controller" of a button shop owned by an old Jewish woman during the early years of the Occupation. Because the woman is nearly deaf, Tono cannot explain his position to her, so for practical purposes he pretends to be her shop assistant. Initially the situation and film are gently comic, but as Tono gradually comes to pity the woman he recognizes the serious and potentially dangerous nature of his commitment. When the town's Jews are finally rounded up and deported to the death camps, he must choose between protecting the old lady and saving his own skin. He tries to conceal her but accidentally kills her in the process, after which he commits suicide. By making the tragedy of the Jews a metaphor for the multiple tragedies of modern Europe, Klos and Kadár evoked the collective responsibility of all Europeans for the existence and perpetuation of political oppression.

In 1968 Klos and Kadár began work on their greatest film, the Czech-American coproduction *Adrift* / *A Longing Called Anada* (*Touha zvaná Anada*, 1971), based on a novel by Lájos Zihály, from a screenplay by the Hungarian writer and future film director Imre Gyöngyössy. The shooting, in Kadár's native Slovakia, was interrupted by the Soviet-led invasion and finally completed after the interval of a year, during which Kadár came to the United States to direct *The Angel Levine* (1970), from a Bernard Malamud story. *Adrift* is an elaborately conceived parable of a man cutting himself loose from all traditional ties to his family, his culture, and his religion. Paradoxically, this liberation takes the form of madness, and its vehicle is sexual obsession. Catalyzed by his wife's apparently terminal illness, a simple middle-aged fisherman is overwhelmingly attracted by the image of a beautiful young woman whom he may or may not have pulled from the waters of the Danube. Except for its beginning and end—which recount the same action from different points of view—the whole film takes place in the mind of its protagonist as he stands on the brink of poisoning his sick wife and interrogates himself about the mental events that have led him to this pass. Its stylistic and structural complexity, which extends to a brilliantly modulated score by František Černý, caused many American critics to dismiss *Adrift* as incomprehensible. But the film has the circular logic of a fantasy or a dream, and to try to read it as a conventional narrative is to misconceive its intentions. After *Adrift*, Klos chose to remain in Czechoslovakia, but Kadár became a permanent resident of the United States, where he was made a Fellow of the American Film Institute. Kadár directed *Lies My*

Father Told Me (1975), a moving Canadian production about a Jewish boy growing up in a Montreal immigrant neighborhood, and he did some interesting work for American television (e.g., an adaptation of Steven Crane's short story, "The Blue Hotel" for PBS [1977], and the miniseries *Freedom Road* for NBC [1979]), before his death in 1979.

Vojtěch Jasný, the first director of importance to emerge from FAMU, made an important contribution to the New Wave with his highly stylized fantasy *Cassandra Cat* (*Až přijde kocour,* 1963) which helped to break a number of neo-Stalinist cinematic and social conventions. This balletic fable of a magic cat whose gaze makes everyone tell the truth was a modern political morality play masquerading as a fairy tale; its technical virtuosity won it a Special Jury Prize at Cannes. But Jasný's most significant film of the New Wave came at the very end of the period. This was the wistfully lyrical *All My Countrymen* (*Všichni dobři rodáci,* 1968), a bittersweet paean to the inhabitants of a small Moravian village who had worked together with Jasný since the war to achieve the reform of their society so recently and brutally crushed by the Soviet invasion.

16.59 *Cassandra Cat* (Vojtěch Jasný, 1963).

Most characteristic of the younger directors of the Czech New Wave, and ultimately the most famous, was Miloš Forman (b. 1932). Forman, who was orphaned by the Nazis during the Occupation, graduated from FAMU in 1955 as a scriptwriter and worked as an assistant to both Martin Frič and Alfred Radok (1914–76)* before making his first feature, *Black Peter / Peter and Pavla* (*Černý Petr,* 1963), which is generally considered to have marked the beginning of the New Wave. Clearly influenced by Olmi's *Il posto* (1961), this was an ironic film about generational conflict shot in *cinéma-vérité* fashion with nonactors and a deliberately functional camera style. A young man takes his first job as a detective in a supermarket, but he finds the work of spying on people so distasteful that it puts him at odds with his hidebound parents. The film, which won the Czech Film Critics' Prize, marked Forman's first association with his coscenarists, Ivan Passer (b. 1933) and Jaroslav Papoušek (b. 1929), and with the cinematographer Miroslav Ondříček (b. 1933), all of whom were to collaborate on his next two films. Like *Black Peter,* these were subtle behavioral studies built upon elaborated anecdotes rather than traditional plot structures, employing improvised dialogue, nonprofessional actors, and a "nonstudio" look (natural lighting, real locations, and so forth). And, like *Black Peter,* they were greeted with both popular acclaim and official disapproval. *Loves of a Blonde / A Blonde in Love* (*Lásky jedné plavovlásky,* 1965), which brought Forman to international attention, was the simple tale of a young factory girl who meets a touring piano player at a local dance and ends up going to bed with him. She

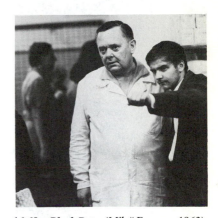

16.60 *Black Peter* (Miloš Forman, 1963).

---

* Radok was already one of Prague's most distinguished stage directors when he turned his energies to the cinema as an art consultant in 1947. In 1949, he directed his first feature, *The Long Journey* (*Daleká cesta,* 1949), an expressionistic portrait of life in the Terezín ghetto, which was the first Czech film to deal with the Nazis' extermination of the Jews. (The film was later ordered withdrawn by government censors for violating the canons of socialist realism.)

16.61 *Loves of a Blonde* (Miloš Forman, 1965): Hana Brejch-ová (right).

16.62 Forman's *Firemen's Ball* (1967).

16.63 *Taking Off* (Miloš Forman, 1971): Buck Henry, stoned.

later visits him in his hometown, to the acute embarrassment of the boy and his parents. The film is a sharply observed comedy of everyday life, and its superb sense of timing recalls the American screwball comedies of the thirties. But *Loves of a Blonde* also contained an implicit criticism of the banality of modern Czech society, its bureaucratic incompetence and ideological rigidity, which did not pass unnoticed by the authorities.

Firemen's Ball (*Hoří, má panenko,* 1967) went even farther in this direction—so far that its release was temporarily blocked by President Novotný himself. The film is a satire on Czechoslovakia's most sensitive contemporary political debate: What should be the official attitude toward the Stalinist brutality of the fifties (during the purges, 1949–55, some 190,000 victims were executed and imprisoned) and toward those still in power who perpetrated it? This issue is presented in the form of a comedy about a small town's commemorative celebration for its dying fire chief. The ball is interrupted by a fire, and the firemen return to discover that all of the food, gifts, and prizes have been stolen by the guests. Some are caught, and a great argument ensues over how the culprits should be treated. At the same time, *Firemen's Ball* is a slice-of-life comedy satirizing the stolidly heroic socialist realist melodramas made in the Soviet bloc countries during the 1940s and 1950s: The organizers of a pivotal beauty contest are totally disorganized, the contestants are all ugly, the narration is deflated and undramatic, and so forth. *Firemen's Ball* opened on December 15, 1967, just two weeks before the political crisis that overthrew Novotný and brought the liberal Alexander Dubček to power. When Dubček himself was ousted following the Soviet invasion, Forman, like so many of his colleagues, was forced to leave the country. With Ondříček, he came to the United States, where he directed *Taking Off* (1971), a social comedy about contemporary American mores in the *cinéma vérité* style of his Czech films.

After contributing *The Decathlon* to the omnibus film of the 1971 Berlin Olympics, *Visions of Eight* (1973; see pp. 366–67), Forman pro-

16.64 *One Flew Over the Cukoo's Nest* (Miloš Forman, 1975):
Jack Nicholson, a little nuts.

16.65 *Hair* (Miloš Forman, 1979): Don Dacus, Annie Golden,
Dorsey Wright, Treat Williams.

duced a highly acclaimed adaptation of Ken Kesey's novel *One Flew Over the Cuckoo's Nest* (1975) and a dynamic film version of the Broadway musical *Hair* (1979) shot on location in New York City. Although he stands today as a mainstream commercial talent in the West, Forman has never deserted the concrete visual poetry of his early work. In his concern for the texture of the everyday, Forman seems to have been influenced by Italian neorealism (and such latter-day exponents as Olmi) and also by British "Free Cinema" and social realism (see Chapter 14), as practiced by Lindsay Anderson (*This Sporting Life*, 1963) and Karel Reisz (*Saturday Night and Sunday Morning*, 1960). His nearly perfect sense of comic timing has been attributed to the influences of Chaplin, Keaton, and Hawks. But there is something uniquely Czech in the experiential quality of his shooting and lighting, and in the black humor of his satire. His adaptation of E. L. Doctorow's panoramic turn-of-the-century novel *Ragtime* (1975) confirmed Forman's status as a major figure; and in 1983, he returned triumphantly to Prague to film his sumptuous, much-heralded version of Peter Shaffer's *Amadeus* (1984), which makes brilliant use of Ondříček's widescreen color cinematography and Chris Newman's Dolby stereo sound.* The production reunited many former collaborators, and its technical credits read like an alumni roster of the New Wave.

Forman's influence upon his peers in Czechoslovak cinema was great. His coscenarists, Ivan Passer (*Intimate Lighting* [*Intimní osvětlení*, 1965]) and Jaroslav Papoušek (*The Most Beautiful Age* [*Nejkrásnější věk*, 1968]), both made plotless, anecdotal films in the manner of Forman during the New Wave. The FAMU-trained scriptwriter Pavel Juráček (b. 1935), who made the highly respected expressionistic *Josef Kilián* (*Postava k podpí-*

16.66 Forman's *Amadeus* (1984): Tom
Hulce in the title role.

16.67 *Intimate Lighting* (Ivan Passer,
1965): Jan Vostrčil.

* Critically short of convertible currencies, the Czechoslovak government permitted Forman's return to earn much-needed dollars for the Barrandov studios (the facility is regularly rented to foreign production companies). He had to promise not to visit former friends among the dissidents, and the authorities agreed not to harm friends who came to visit him on the set. (Forman had also returned to Czechoslovakia in 1980.)

16.68 *Josef Kilián* (Pavel Juráček and Jan Schmidt, 1963).

16.69 *Closely Watched Trains* (Jiří Menzel, 1966): Vaclav Neckář, Jitka Bendová.

16.70 Menzel in his film *Capricious Summer* (1967).

rání, 1963)* and the apocalyptic science fiction film *The End of August at the Hotel Ozone* (*Konec srpna v hotelu Ozón,* 1966) with Jan Schmidt (b. 1934), shot his first independent feature, *Every Young Man* (*Každý mladý muž,* 1965), in imitation of Forman. Juráček directed only one other film, *A Case for the Rookie Hangman* (*Případ pro začínajícího kata,* 1969), which was based on the third book of *Gulliver's Travels* and banned two months after its release; he emigrated to West Germany in 1978.

But the most important figure to adopt the antiheroic *cinéma-vérité* style developed by Forman was Jiří Menzel (b. 1938), although all of his films of the sixties were based on literary sources. Menzel graduated from FAMU in 1963 and spent the next two years working as an assistant to Věra Chytilová and as an actor for Evald Schorm (see p. 695). His first motion picture as a director was a contribution to the anthology film *Pearls of the Deep* (*Perličky na dně,* 1964), based on five short stories by Bohumil Hrabal. (Schorm, Jan Němec, Chytilová, and Jireš were the other contributors, making *Pearls of the Deep* a kind of omnibus of the Czech New Wave.) Menzel's first feature, *Closely Watched Trains* (*Ostře sledované vlaky,* 1966), was also adapted from Hrabal who ultimately preferred the film to his original; it brought Menzel international fame and became the second Czech film to win an American Academy Award (as Best Foreign Film of 1966). The film is an elliptical, Formanesque study of human attitudes and behavior set in a railway town during the Occupation. An awkward youth apprentices himself to the village railroad-station guard, whose sexual exploits he much admires. After failing miserably in his first sexual encounter, the young man makes a suicide attempt. He finally succeeds at sex with a beautiful Resistance fighter and, in a dramatic assertion of virility, blows up a Nazi ammunition train; during this act, he is killed by a German train guard's machine gun. *Closely Watched Trains* is both comic and deadly serious, often simultaneously, and in this regard it epitomizes an essential characteristic of Czech New Wave cinema—its ironic and often detached intermixing of dichotomous emotional responses. The film also owes a debt to surrealism in its subversive equation of sexual and political freedom. Menzel's other notable New Wave film is *Capricious Summer* (*Rozmarné léto,* 1967), a humorous but sometimes dark fable adapted from a Vančura novel about the sexual misadventures of three middle-aged friends in a small fishing village; it won the Grand Prix at Karlovy Vary in 1968. Menzel's reverential parody of American musical comedy, *Crime in the Nightclub* (*Zločin v šantánu,* 1968), was immensely popular in Czechoslovakia during the months that followed the invasion, but his *Skylarks on a String* (*Skřivánci na niti,* 1969), adapted from Hrabal, was banned, and Menzel was not permitted to make another film until the unremarkable *Who Looks for Gold?* (*Kdo hledá zlaté dno?,* 1975) and the routine

---

* *Josef Kilián* was written under the direct influence of Franz Kafka (1883–1924), whose literary reputation as a Czech (although he wrote in German) had been rehabilitated at the Liblice symposium in May 1963.

comedy *Seclusion Near a Forest* (*Na samotě u lesa*, 1976). Next he directed *Those Wonderful Movie Cranks* (*Báječní muži s klikou*, 1978), commemorating the seventieth anniversary of the film industry in Prague. It is a humorous and affectionate account of its beginnings in 1907, shot in the sepia tones of the era. For his next film, Menzel adapted another novel by Hrabal, *Cutting It Short* (*Postřižiny*, 1981), a lyrical comedy about life in a small provincial town just before the First World War.

The two most politically controversial and morally committed directors of the Czech New Wave were Evald Schorm (1931–89) and Jan Němec (b. 1936). Schorm, who is often called "the conscience of the New Wave," graduated from FAMU in 1962 and made eight documentary shorts before directing his first feature, *Everyday Courage / Courage for Every Day* (*Každý den odvadhu*) in 1964. In it he eschewed both the formal experiments of Chytilová and Jireš and the *cinéma-vérité* techniques of Forman, Passer, and Menzel to make a traditional dramatic film of uncompromisingly serious intent. *Everyday Courage* is the story of an idealistic communist organizer who gradually comes to recognize that his ideals are wrong and that they have caused much human misery. The official response to this allegory of de-Stalinization was violent condemnation. When *Everyday Courage* won the Czech Film Critics' Prize in 1965, the government refused to let Schorm accept it, and attempted to sabotage the film's distribution. International outcry finally forced official acceptance of *Everyday Courage,* but Schorm's next feature, *The Return of the Prodigal Son* (*Návrat ztraceného syna*, 1966), was banned outright for several months. This film, considered to be Schorm's masterpiece, is a parable of the fate of the individual in an authoritarian society. Its protagonist, Jan, is confined to a mental institution after a suicide attempt. Jan's failure to "adjust" to the existing social structure stems from his unwillingness to compromise his personal integrity, and he is hunted down by a mob that mistakes him for a rapist. Schorm's third film of contemporary social criticism, *Saddled with Five Girls* (*Pět holek na krku*, 1967), forms a kind of trilogy with *Everyday Courage* and *The Return of the Prodigal Son.* Less pessimistic than his earlier work, *Saddled* is a film of youthful love and alienation which juxtaposes its narrative with scenes from Weber's opera *Die Freischütz.* In *Pastor's End / The End of a Priest* (*Konec faráře*, 1968), Schorm and the scriptwriter Josef Škvorecký (b. 1924)—who has also worked with Menzel and other New Wave directors—collaborated on a farcical reworking of the Christ legend with pronounced political overtones. In a rural village, a sexton poses as a priest and accomplishes much good, but he is finally exposed and done to death by the repressive institutions of church and state. The release of *Pastor's End* was delayed by the authorities for a year, but it has now become generally available in the West. Schorm's next films, *The Seventh Day, the Eighth Night* (*Sedmý den, osmá noc*, 1969) and *Dogs and People* (*Psi a lidé*, 1970), were permanently banned in the spring of 1970, and Schorm was forbidden to work in the Czech film industry again. After that time, he made his living by directing operas in provincial theaters—like one of his own heroes, unwilling to compromise his moral integrity or his seriousness of purpose for the comfortable security of "fitting in." Schorm

16.71 *Return of the Prodigal Son* (Evald Schorm, 1966): Jan Kačer, Milan Morávec.

16.72 *Saddled with Five Girls* (Evald Schorm, 1967).

16.73 *Diamonds of the Night* (Jan Němec, 1964).

16.74 Němec's *The Party and the Guests* (1966), with Josef Škvorecký (wearing glasses) second from left.

emerged from internal exile to make his final film, *Killing with Kindness* (*Lastne se nic nestalo,* 1989), a parable of suffocating mother love that is highly reminiscent of his pre-1968 work. He died of heart failure in 1989.

Like Schorm, Jan Němec is an ethically committed filmmaker concerned with the survival of individual integrity in a repressive, regimented society. But unlike Schorm, he experiments boldly with form and has been on the cutting edge of the New Wave since his student days. His first feature, *Diamonds of the Night* (*Démanty noci,* 1964), was adapted by Němec and Arnošt Lustig from a novel by Lustig about two young Jews who escape from a Nazi death march. Němec turned the narrative into a nightmarish representation of the mental anguish of human beings under extreme physical and psychological stress. Documentarylike footage of the four-day hunt for the boys is intercut with images from their dreams, fantasies, and hallucinations as they become increasingly desperate. The film was a great domestic critical success and won several international awards.

Němec's next film began a brief but fruitful collaboration with the designer Ester Krumbachová and brought the wrath of officialdom down upon the heads of both. *The Party and the Guests / A Report on the Party and the Guests* (*O slavnosti a hostech,* 1966) was a stylized, Kafkaesque allegory about the mechanisms of repression in Czech society, and the most politically venomous film of the New Wave. The Host throws an elegant dinner party in a beautiful forest glade, assuring his guests throughout the evening that his only desire is to make them happy. As the party progresses, the guests assure The Host one by one that they are indeed supremely happy. Only one of them, The Guest Who Refused to Be Happy, resists being intimidated into contentment, and, significantly, he is played by the director Evald Schorm, whose *Return of the Prodigal Son* was then under a government ban. Eventually the unhappy guest discreetly slips away, and the crowd of remaining guests turns ugly. If a single guest refuses to join the merrymaking, it spoils the party for all, so the party takes to its feet and pursues the malcontent with dogs. This sinister parable of social conformity and political dissent was brilliantly designed by Krumbachová to achieve just the proper sense of strange beauty intermixed with menace. Many of the scenes were modeled on contemporary Czech paintings and media images, giving the film a rich subtext of visual allusion. Most of the roles were played by friends of the filmmaker's, so at yet another level of allusion the film stands as a collective political manifesto by Prague's artists and intellectuals. When President Novotný screened *The Party and the Guests,* he was outraged and is said to have remarked, "It's about the way we banned that fellow Schorm's film and then set the dogs on him, isn't it?" This time the dogs were set upon Němec and his friends. The film was banned for two full years and became the object of violent invective. Together with Chytilová's *Daisies,* it was used as an excuse for a denunciation of the entire New Wave in the Czechoslovak National Assembly in May 1967. Němec and Krumbachová, in the meantime, turned to the nonpolitical theme of sexual fantasy in the three-episode *Martyrs of Love* (*Mučedníci lásky,* 1967), which recalled the hypervisual, hallucinatory quality of *Diamonds of the Night.* When Dubček assumed power in January 1968, *The Party and the Guests* was finally released domestically, and that spring it was sent to Cannes as the official Czech entry. Němec was at work with Josef Škvorecký on a documentary about Prague when Soviet tanks entered the city on August 20–21. This film became *Oratorio for Prague* (1968), a melancholy account of the invasion which was smuggled out of Czechoslovakia for screening in the West. Němec was blacklisted immediately, and he was unable to make films from 1968 to 1974; in that year he was allowed to emigrate to France. He subsequently found work in West German television and completed *Czech Connection: Reflection of My Own Death* (1975), a forty-minute autobiographical film begun secretly in his homeland. Since 1977, Němec has lived in Santa Monica, California, where he remained virtually unknown until 1986, when he was contracted to direct a version of Japanese novelist Kobo Abe's *Friends* with Swedish and Japanese funding.

16.75 *Martyrs of Love* (Jan Němec, 1967).

"Banned Forever"

The Czech film miracle came to an abrupt end in 1968 with the Soviet-led invasion and the subsequent occupation of the country by Warsaw Pact troops. The liberalization of Czechoslovakia—the attempt to create a "socialism with a human face"—had threatened Soviet hegemony over Eastern Europe, and so it was suppressed by force. Party Secretary Dubček and his supporters were eased from office over the next eight months, to be replaced by a Novotný-like regime under Gustav Husák that undertook the "normalization" of Czechoslovakia.* Films in production were halted. Many already in release were withdrawn by party censors and

---

* In December 1987, Husák in turn was replaced by Miloš Jakeš.

16.76 *Deserters and Nomads* (Juraj Jakubisko, 1968).

16.77 *The Cremator* (Juraj Herz, 1968): Rudolf Hrusinksy.

banned. The managing directors of both the Barrandov studios and the Koliba studios in Bratislava were fired, and the director of the state distribution organization, Czechoslovak Film, was arrested and imprisoned for "antisocialist activities." The five autonomous production groups together with the Union of Czechoslovak Film and Television Artists (FITES) were dissolved, and every Czech filmmaker discussed in this chapter, except Jireš and Uher, was blacklisted and forbidden to work in the film industry indefinitely. Kadár, Jasný, Forman, Passer, and, ultimately, Němec and Juráček left the country for good, and a whole rising generation of new talent was permanently quashed. By 1973 virtually every important film of the previous decade lay buried in a vault in the cellar of the Barrandov studios, and four of these had been labeled "banned forever"—Forman's *Firemen's Ball*, Schorm's *Pastor's End*, Němec's *The Party and the Guests*, and Jasný's *All My Countrymen*. It was as if the New Wave and everything it had accomplished had never existed. What might have happened had the New Wave cinema been allowed to grow and prosper—and what that growth might have meant for the development of international cinema—is impossible to say. Surely its significance would have been great. But, instead, "normalization" left a huge vacuum that the Czech film industry has been unable to fill ever since.

Very few notable films came from Prague in the seventies, although there was recognition for the work of several Slovak directors: the films of the surrealist Juraj Jakubisko (b. 1938)—*Deserters and Nomads* (*Zbehovia a pútníci*, 1968); *Birds, Orphans, and Fools* (*Vtáčkovia, siroty a blázni*, 1969); *Build a House, Plant a Tree* (*Postav dom, zasad strom*, 1980); *The Millennial Bees* (*Tisícročna včela*, 1983); *Frau Holle* (1985)—which have been compared to those of Dovzhenko in their violent, elemental force; the baroque allegories of Juraj Herz (b. 1934)—*The Cremator* (*Spalovač mrtvol*, 1968); *Kerosene Lamps* (*Petrolejové lampy*, 1971); *Morgiana* (1972); *A Day for My Love* (*Den pro mou lásku*, 1977); *Beauty and the Beast* (1972); *Bulldogs and Cherries* (*Buldoci a třešně*, 1981); *The Ferat Vampire* (*Závody se smrtí*, 1982); and Dušan Hanák's lyrical gypsy romance *Rose-Tinted Dreams* (*Růšové sny*, 1976).* The comedies of Oldřich Lipský (b. 1924)—*Dinner for Adele* (*Adéla ještě nevečeřela*, 1978); *Long Live Ghosts* (*At' žijí duchové!*, 1979); *The Mysterious Castle in the Carpathians* (*Tajemství hrada v Karpatech*, 1984) have also enjoyed some international success. The years 1976–77 marked the return of several major directors and actors after years of enforced idleness, and recent Czech entries at the important Karlovy Vary festival give evidence of a gradual rapprochement between the film industry and the government. Examples would be Jiří Krejčík's *The Divine Emma* (*Božská Ema*, 1979); Karel Kachyňa's *Love Among the Raindrops* (*Laśki mesi kapkami deště*, 1980) and *Fandy* (1983); Jaromil Jireš' *The Rabbit Case* (*Causa králík*, 1980), *Escapes Home* (*Uteky domu*, 1981), *Opera*

* Only one of these features, Jakubisko's *Deserters and Nomads*, has been seen in the West; as Peter Hames points out, Slovak films traditionally receive little active support from the Czechoslovak export organization, which regards them as "regional" items (*The Czechoslovak New Wave*, p. 236).

in the Vineyard (Opera ve vinci, 1983), and *Partial Eclipse (Néupliné zatmění, 1983)*; František Vláčil's *Smoke on the Potato Fields (Dým bramborové natě, 1976)*, *Shadows of a Hot Summer Day (Stíny horkého leta, 1977)*, *Serpent's Poison (Hadí jed, 1982)*, and *Shepherd Boy from the Lowlands (Pasáček z doliny, 1984)*; Štefan Uher's *Concrete Pastures (Pásla kone na betóne)*; Jiří Menzel's Hrabal adaptation *Snowdrop Celebrations (Slavnõsti sněženek, 1984)*, and the documentary *Prague (1985)*, co-directed with Věra Chytilová; and Chytilová's own *The Very Late Afternoon of a Faun (Faunovo velmi pozdní odpoledne, 1984)*, her first collaboration with Ester Krumbachová since *Daisies* in 1966. Whether the Czech film miracle can come again under the democratic reform government led by Vaclav Pavel is uncertain, but during the Prague Spring a country with a population of 16 million, inhabiting a land mass no larger than the state of Tennessee, was able to produce over three hundred films that had a radical impact on its own sociopolitical structure and simultaneously changed the shape of international cinema.

16.78 *Rose-Tinted Dreams* (Dušan Hanák, 1976).

HUNGARY

Three Revolutions

Like Czechoslovakia, Hungary has had a long and distinguished cinematic tradition. The Hungarians, in fact, seem to have identified film as an art form before any other nationality in the world, including the French. From the beginning, they emphasized the literary and intellectual aspects of film, and most films were adapted from classical Hungarian novels and plays. For this reason, famous authors and actors from the legitimate stage had none of the qualms about working in film that afflicted their counterparts in the West. In 1912 the radical writer Sándor Korda* (who later worked in Britain as the producer-director Alexander Korda) founded *Pesti mozi* ("Pest† cinema"), the first Hungarian film journal, and by 1920 it had been joined by sixteen others. A strong tradition of advanced film theory was founded in the teens by the philosophers Jenö Török and Cecil Bognár, and passed on to Béla Balázs (pronounced "Ballázh"; 1884–1949), whose *Films—Werden und Wesen einer neuen Kunst*** became greatly influential. As in France, film attracted the avant-garde—the painter Laśzló Moholy-Nagy (1895–1946), for example, conducted numerous experiments with film's ability to transform space and light between 1923

---

* Hungarian names are given here with the surname last, although in Hungary the convention is the reverse.

† The present city of Budapest was formed in 1873 by the union of Buda and Óbuda, on the right bank of the Danube River, with Pest (pronounced "Pesht") on the left bank. Even today, many Hungarians refer to "Buda" or to "Pest" rather than to "Budapest," depending on which side of the river they live.

** The Balázs work was published in 1948 in Berlin; in English it appeared as *Theory of the Film: Character and Growth of a New Art*, trans. Edith Bone (London: Dobson, 1952; New York: Dover Books, 1972).

and 1928. Hungary also had the first nationalized film industry in history. Béla Kun's socialist revolution of March 1919 declared Hungary a "Red Republic of Councils" and the cinema was nationalized in April of that year—four months before Lenin nationalized the Soviet industry. This adventure lasted only until the rightest counter-revolution of Admiral Miklós Horthy, who installed himself as regent in August, but thirty-one films were produced in the interim. Hungary's first important director was Mihály Kertész (1888–1962), who studied filmmaking at Denmark's Nordisk studios, directed a number of films in Germany in the twenties, and settled in the United States, where he worked for Warner Bros. as Michael Curtiz. Other important figures were Pál Fejös (1898–1963) and Endre Tóth (b. 1900; also known as André de Toth), both of whom ultimately emigrated to America, with Fejös returning to Hungary in 1931 to make his internationally celebrated *Spring Shower* (*Tavazsi zápor,* 1932).

In 1920 the Horthy regime restored film production to the private sector, and during the twenties and thirties the Hungarian industry became commercialized along American lines. Most films of the period were made on an assembly-line basis in imitation of Hollywood; and after the conversion to sound in 1930, musicals like István Székely's *The Rákóczi March* (*Rákóczi-induló,* 1933) and Béla Gaál's *The Dream Car* (*Meseautó,* 1934) became extremely popular. Serious films appeared in the work of Fejös and in the Austrian director Georg Hoellering's *Hortobágy* (1935), a starkly realistic account of contemporary peasant life shot on location on the *puszta,* the great Hungarian plain. When World War II broke out, the Horthy government, which was allied with the Germans, took control of the industry through the National Film Committee and permitted it to produce only conformist entertainment and propaganda films. A notable exception was István Szőts' (b. 1912) anticapitalist *People on the Alps* (*Emberek a havason,* 1942), shot on location in the mountains of Transylvania, which won a prize at Venice in the year of its release and was hailed by the Italian journal *Cinema* as a model for neorealism. Unsure of the country's stability, the Nazis seized Hungary in March 1944, deposed Horthy, and set up their own government. The Soviet Union invaded in late 1944, and Hungary concluded an armistice with the Allies in January 1945. Almost immediately, the Academy for Dramatic and Cinematographic Art was founded, and hundreds of Soviet and American films were shown in Hungary for the first time. The most significant Hungarian film of this period was the privately produced *Somewhere in Europe* (*Valahol Európában,* 1947), a humanitarian fantasy about the reclamation of war orphans, written by Béla Balázs and directed by Géza Radványi (b. 1907). When a Communist government came to power early in 1948, the Hungarian film industry was nationalized for the second time. The first state-subsidized films, such as Frigyes Bán's (b. 1902) revolutionary peasant melodrama *The Soil Under Your Feet* (*Talpalatnyi föld,* 1948), were quite promising, but the political climate deteriorated rapidly under Stalinism, and the period 1949–53 was one of stolid socialist realism.

The death of Stalin in 1953 and the subsequent replacement of Mátyás

16.79 *Somewhere in Europe* (Géza Radványi, 1947): Miklós Gábor.

Rákosi as the Hungarian premier by Imre Nagy marked the beginning of the nation's "New Course," a brief era of liberalization. This period was one of high achievement for Hungarian cinema. It witnessed the emergence of a new generation of directors: Zoltán Fábri (b. 1917)—*Fourteen Lives in Danger* (*Életjel*, 1954), *Merry-Go-Round* (*Körhinta*, 1955), the anti-Stalinist parable *Professor Hannibal* (*Hannibal, tanár úr*, 1956; banned 1957); Károly Makk (b. 1925)—*Liliomfi* (1954); János Herskó (b. 1926)—*Under the City* (*A város alatt*, 1954); and Felix Máriássy (1919–76)—*Spring in Budapest* (*Budapesti tavász*, 1955); *A Glass of Beer* (*Egy pikoló világos*, 1955). Many of these filmmakers are still active in the Hungarian cinema today.* Their films expressed the increasingly liberal sentiments of the Hungarian workers and their yearning for a true social democracy. On October 23, 1956, this yearning began to manifest itself in demonstrations, street fighting, and, finally, armed violence in Budapest. As revolution spread swiftly throughout Hungary, workers' councils took control of most government functions, and on November 1, Nagy declared his intention to withdraw from the Warsaw Pact. Three days later the Soviet Union intervened—as it would do in Czechoslovakia in 1968 (but with considerably less brutality)—with 200,000 troops and 3,000 tanks under air cover. Over 25,000 Hungarian citizens died in the systematic tank bombardment of cities and industrial centers. Imre Nagy and about two thousand of his supporters were arrested and ultimately executed. Another ten thousand persons were deported to Soviet labor camps, an undetermined number were imprisoned for years without trial, and 200,000 fled into exile. The revolution was crushed, but the moderate Janos Kádár was installed as premier; he gradually embarked upon a realistic course of liberalization and economic growth (fostered by the New Economic Mechanism, or NEM, which injected free market elements into the predominately socialized system) that left Hungary substantially freer and more stable financially than any of its Warsaw Pact neighbors.

The effect of the revolt upon Hungarian cinema was to arrest its development. The films of 1954–56 had been notable primarily for their content, rather than for the kind of formal innovations which liberalization would produce in Poland and Czechoslovakia. In the matter of style and structure, Hungarian film was still essentially realist (or, at most, neorealist) when the revolution was put down. Afterward, it could evolve in neither form nor content until Kádár's steady process of liberalization had been realized. The films of 1957–61, therefore, were unremarkable. But between 1958 and 1961 the experimental Béla Balázs Studio was founded and put on a sound financial basis in order to give graduates of the state-operated Academy for Dramatic and Cinematographic Art in Budapest an opportunity to make their first films. The year 1961 saw the release of the studio's first batch of shorts and the reappearance of political themes in the work of Fábri (*Two Half-Times in Hell* [*Két félidő a*

16.80 *Merry-Go-Round* (Zoltán Fábri, 1955): Mari Töröcsik, Imre Sós.

16.81 *Catsplay* (Macskajáték, 1974), a film by Károly Makk: Margit Dayka.

---

* The contributions of both Fábri and Makk, for example, have been remarkably consistent to date and have helped to build an international audience for Hungarian cinema.

pokolban]) and Makk (*The Fanatics* [*Megszállottak*]). In 1962, Kádár unexpectedly declared a general amnesty, and the stage was set for a major resurgence of Hungarian cinema. The two figures of signal importance to this renaissance were András Kovács and Miklós Jancsó.

András Kovács

16.82   *Cold Days* (András Kovács, 1966).

András Kovács (pronounced "Kovach"; b. 1925) attended the Budapest Academy and made several features before undertaking a two-year period of study in Paris. There, Kovács fell under the influence of *cinéma vérité*, whose techniques he employed in *Difficult People* (*Nehéz emberek*, 1964) on his return to Hungary. This film examines the true cases of five Hungarian inventors whose work had been opposed or ignored through bureaucratic stupidity. *Difficult People* sparked a debate throughout the country, since it was the first time since 1955 that contemporary reality had been so directly confronted on the screen. Kovács' next film, *Cold Days* (*Hideg napok*, 1966), was a visually engaging account of the massacre of some three thousand Jews and Serbs in the town of Novi Sad (now part of Yugoslavia) by Hungarian troops in January 1942. The event is narrated in flashback by four participants who are in prison awaiting trial for the atrocity some years later. This film, too, provoked debate—this time about the collective nature of responsibility in both the national present and the national past. *Cold Days* appeared at several international festivals and attracted world attention to the new Hungarian cinema. In *Walls* (*Falak*, 1968) and *Relay Race* (*Staféta*, 1970), Kovács continued to probe the contradictions of contemporary Hungarian society with a degree of artistic freedom unprecedented in any other country in Eastern Europe. *Blindfold* (*Bekötött szemmel*, 1974) is close to *Cold Days* in its sober, black-and-white reconstruction of an actual incident from World War II—that of a priest brought before a military tribunal for having caused the "miracle" that saves a condemned soldier from execution; while *Labyrinth* (*Labirintus*, 1976) follows Truffaut, Wajda, and Fellini in creating a self-reflexive film about the process of filmmaking itself. Kovács returned to politics in *The Stud Farm* (*Ménesgazda*, 1979), a tale of political terror set during the first nervous months of the new Stalinist regime in 1950 and his first film in color, and *A Sunday in October* (*Októberi vasárnap*, 1980), an historical reconstruction of Admiral Horthy's secret attempt to abandon the Axis and negotiate a separate peace with the Soviet Union on October 15, 1944, near the end of World War II. Recent Kovács films include the romantic dramas *Temporary Paradise* (*Ideiglenes paradicsom*, 1981) and *An Afternoon Affair* (*Szeretok*, 1984); *The Red Countess* (*Vörös grófnő*, 1985), a richly mounted two-part biography of Count Mihály Károlyi and his wife, who were major political figures at the time of World War I and the socialist revolution of 1919 (Károlyi was, in fact, president of the short-lived First Republic of 1918); and *Rear Guard* (*Valahol Magyarországon*, 1988), a documentary-style drama about grass-roots party politics.

16.83   *Walls* (András Kovács, 1968).

Miklós Jancsó

The first major film of Miklós Jancsó (pronounced "Yahn-cho"; b. 1921), *Cantata* (*Oldas és kötés*, 1962), is also considered to be the first film of the Hungarian New Wave. Jancsó had studied law (in which he holds a doctorate), ethnography, and art history before he entered the Budapest Academy, from which he graduated in 1950. For eight years he made newsreels and documentaries that were fairly conventional in both form and content, as was his first feature, *The Bells Have Gone to Rome* (*A harangok Rómába mentek*, 1958). But *Cantata,* written by his perennial collaborator, Gyula Hernádi and shot in eleven days, revealed a striking talent for visual composition and psychological analysis. Photographed in the neutralized style of Antonioni, it concerns a young physician educated during the Stalin era who has risen to a favorable position within the socialist hierarchy and effectively isolated himself from the larger realities of Hungarian society. Returning after many years to the village of his birth, he is forced to confront his peasant origins in the person of his aged father and ultimately comes to realize his moral complicity in a system which, while offering him personal advancement, has ruined the lives of many others. It was *My Way Home* (*Igy jöttem*, 1964), however, which announced the style for which Jancsó would become famous—one based upon extended long takes sustained by rhythmic tracking movements of the camera and optical traveling through the zoom lens. The film is about a sixteen-year-old Hungarian conscript who has deserted the army and is attempting to make his way home across the western frontier during the last chaotic days of World War II. His life is threatened successively by Hungarian partisans, renegade Cossacks, the retreating Hungarian Fascists, and the advancing Red Army. He is finally captured by the latter and assigned to help a badly wounded Soviet soldier of about his own age tend some cows. Mutually distrustful at first, the two gradually become friends; and when the Russian dies of his wounds, the Hungarian sets off homeward again in his uniform, across the same landscape of murderously contending factions as before. *My Way Home* offers a pessimistic view of a hostile universe in a structure of great formal beauty—traits strikingly present in Jancsó's next film.

16.84 *My Way Home* (Miklós Jancsó, 1964).

The Round-Up / The Hopeless Ones (*Szegénylegények*, 1965), which brought Jancsó to international prominence when it was shown at Cannes in 1966, is a chilling account of a historical incident that occurred in 1868 and the first of many Jancsó films about great events from the Hungarian past. Under the commission of Count Gedeon Ráday, the political police of the Austro-Hungarian monarchy attempt to unmask Sándor Rózsa, the chief of a rebel army group during the 1848 Revolution, which was led by Lájos Kossuth,* who is now operating as a local *betyár,* or

---

* In 1848, as part of the revolutionary agitation then shaking all of Europe, Kossuth (1802–94) formed a government that declared his nation independent of Austria and of Hapsburg rule. The Austrians and their Russian allies succeeded in crushing the rebellion the follow-

16.85   Openness and closure in Jancsó's *The Round-Up* (1965).

bandit. The police round up several hundred peasants, herdsmen, and suspected outlaws—some of them former comrades-in-arms of Rózsa's, but most of them innocent civilians—into a prison stockade on the great Hungarian plain (*puszta*), where they employ sophisticated modern means of interrogation, torture, and political terror to force the inmates into mutual betrayal. A film of stark beauty and terrific force, *The Round-Up* introduced many of Jancsó's mature personal symbols and stylistic obsessions: the use of nudity to signify humiliation; the totally impersonal depiction of cruelty and violence; the menacing image of incessantly circling horsemen on the empty spaces of the plain; the balletic choreography of the camera and groups of actors within the frame; the replacement of characterization through dialogue with bureaucratic jargon, slogans, and songs; and a densely interwoven music track combining folk and classical melodies with incidental sound. The film also demonstrated that Jancsó was an absolute master of the new aesthetics whose cinematic structures are dependent upon widescreen composition, the long take, and the zoom lens. *The Round-Up* was shot by the cinematographer Tamás Somló (b. 1929), who worked with Jancsó on his next film as well.

Jancsó continued his bold stylistic experiments in a series of films whose symbolic subject was Hungary's past but whose real theme was Hungary's present and future. All were characterized by the abstract, mythographic, and sometimes theatrical quality visible in *The Round-Up,* but they tended to extend these modes to the very limits of coherence. *The Red and the White* (*Csillagosok, katonák,* 1967) was concerned with Hungarians fighting in the Red Army in 1918 during the civil war in

ing year, and Hungary again came under Hapsburg rule. But over the next two decades, Hapsburg power waned, and in 1867 the Emperor Franz Josef I of Austria agreed to give Hungary equal status with Austria in the Austro-Hungarian Empire, or Dual Monarchy, which lasted until Hungary became a republic after World War I. The events in Jancsó's film took place as part of a combined Austro-Hungarian attempt to quell continuing political unrest and banditry on the Great Plain in the Dual Monarchy's first year. (In contemporary Hungary, the national obsession with the 1848 Revolution has become a covert channel for anti-Soviet feelings, since the Russians participated in the revolt's suppression.)

Russia. It employed sustained lateral tracking and widescreen composition brilliantly to visualize the constantly shifting balance of power between two great armies massed against one another in empty space. *Silence and Cry* (*Csend és kiáltás,* 1968) was set in 1919 just after the fall of the Red Republic of Councils, at the time of the White Terror, when police were hunting down and punishing anyone suspected of radical sympathies. Like *The Round-Up,* it is a film about degradation, torture, alienation, and betrayal. *Silence and Cry* was also Jancsó's first film with the cinematographer János Kende (b. 1941), who has been his constant collaborator ever since. *The Confrontation* (*Fényes szelek,* 1969), Jancsó's first film in color, dealt with student disturbances in 1947 (procommunist students picketing, heckling, and bullying to force the closure of Catholic schools), but it had obvious reference to contemporary student unrest. Yet it was the director's most stylized film to date, a virtual ballet for camera and soundtrack in which every gesture had ritual significance.

In *Winter Wind* (*Sirokkó,* 1969), a film composed of only thirteen shots, some as long as ten minutes, a group of Croatian nationalists are being trained to assassinate King Alexander of Yugoslavia on the Hungarian-Yugoslav border. Again, Jancsó's theme is the destructive effects of political terror on the individual will. In *Agnus Dei* (*Égi bárány,* 1970), set like *Silence and Cry* during the defeat of the Republic of Councils, Jancsó went farther than ever before in the direction of symbolic abstraction. This beautiful color film is essentially a celebration of the revolutionary spirit; in it, all dialogue takes the form of quotations from the Bible or from national songs. With *Red Psalm* (*Még kér a nép,* 1972), Jancsó produced his masterpiece. Composed of fewer than thirty shots, this film is a stunning symbolic analysis of the revolutionary process, its psychological and social preconditions, and its ultimate, necessary failure. For eighty minutes, camera and lens move incessantly, circling and encircling the choric patricipants in the drama—historically, an abortive agrarian socialist rebellion in the late nineteenth century. Music and sound, color, focus—virtually every element in the film—work in concert to make *Red Psalm* a film of nearly perfect formal beauty, great humanity, and awesome cinematic power. Jancsó won the Golden Palm at Cannes for its

16.86   Symbolic use of nudity in Jancsó's *The Red and the White* (1967).

16.87   The aesthetics of widescreen space: Jancsó's *The Red and the White* (1967) and *Red Psalm* (1972).

16.88 A frame from one of the twelve sequence shots comprising Jancsó's *Elektreia* (1974).

16.89 *Allegro Barbaro* (Miklos Jancsó, 1979).

direction in 1972. Jancsó's twelve-shot *Elektreia* (*Szerelmem, Elektra,* 1974) extended his abstractionist vision into the realm of Greek myth, but not without his characteristic political subtext: the film is adapted from a play by László Gyurko that uses the Electra legend as an allegory of the Stalinist period to explore the morality of making reprisals against a tyrant's henchmen after his death.

After the Italian-Yugoslavian coproduction *Private Vices and Public Virtues* (*Vizi privati, pubbliche virtù,* 1976), loosely based on the Mayerling affair that had scandalized the Austro-Hungarian court in the last days of the empire, Jancsó returned to his national heritage and began work on an ambitious trilogy intended to represent Hungarian history from the turn of the century through World War II. Only two parts have so far been completed: *Hungarian Rhapsody* (*Magyar rapszódia,* 1979) and *Allegro Barbaro* (1979), which were shown as *Hungarian Rhapsody, Parts I* and *II* at Cannes in 1979, when Jancsó was awarded the Special Jury Prize for the entire body of his work. The films symbolically reconstruct the life of a single young man, István Zsdányi, based on the historical figure of Endre Bajcsy-Zsilinszky, who incarnated much of twentieth-century Hungarian politics. Bajcsy-Zsilinszky was the son of a minor aristocrat, who began his career as a counterrevolutionary terrorist under Horthy, became a leader of the radical peasant party during the thirties, and was executed by the Nazis in 1944 as the head of the Hungarian Resistance. Together the films represent the consummation of Jancsó's mature style (*Allegro Barbaro,* for example, is a masterpiece of widescreen choreography for camera containing only twenty-two shots), and afterward he began to experiment with drama on a more intimate scale. *The Tyrant's Heart, or Boccaccio in Hungary* (*A zsarnok szíve, abagy Boccaccio Magyarországon,* 1981), for example, is a Hamlet-like parable of royal intrigue confined to a fifteenth-century Hungarian palace and shot entirely in the studio. *L'Aube* (*Dawn,* 1986)*—a French-

---

* The film adapts the second novel in Elie Wiesel's Holocaust trilogy, consisting of *Night, Dawn,* and *The Accident.*

Israeli coproduction made for television and Jancsó's first color feature shot without János Kende—takes place in a single room in the course of one night in 1947 as Israeli freedom fighters debate the morality of killing a British hostage. Jancsó has also made two successful feature-length documentaries—*Music (Muzsika,* 1984), a striking portrait of Budapest, and *Omega, Omega* (1985), a record of a 1982 rock concert—as well as *Faustus, Faustus Faustus* (1985), the widely hailed nine-part adaptation of László Gyurkó's controversial novel on the past fifty years of Hungarian history entitled *The Blessed Descent to Hell of Dr. Faustus (Faustus Doktar beldogsagos pokaljarasa),* for national television. In 1987, Jancsó returned to theatrical feature-filmmaking with *Season of Monsters (Szörnyek evadja),* a surrealistic tale of contemporary suicide splendidly photographed by János Kende. More recently, Janscó directed *Jesus Christ's Horoscope (Jezus Krisztus horoszkopia,* 1989), a visually and aurally brilliant work—his most thematically challenging in years.

It has often been said of Jancsó that all of his films seem to be one and the same. But this criticism against consistency of vision might apply equally to Bergman, Antonioni, Ozu, and many other masters of contemporary cinema. The mysterious, mythopoeic qualities of Jancsó's images and structures, his symbolic use of song and ritual to embody his themes of human submission and domination, his seeming closeness to the earth, all remind one of Dovzhenko—but a Dovzhenko who has consciously and willfully rejected montage. Jancsó's mastery of widescreen composition and the extended long take alone would assure him a permanent place in the history of film. But Jancsó has always used this technical mastery to make films of hallucinatory beauty, profound feeling, and great intellectual depth. And it is this, above all else, that makes him one of the great artists of the modern cinema, as well as Hungary's greatest national film poet.

Gaál, Szabó, and Mészáros

Three other Hungarian filmmakers who have achieved international distinction within the past two decades are István Gaál (b. 1933), István

16.90 *Current* (István Gaál, 1964).

16.91   *The Falcons* (István Gaál, 1970): Iván Andonov, Gyórgy Bánffy.

16.92   Gaál's *Dead Landscape* (1971).

16.93   *Father* (István Szabó, 1966): Dániel Erdélyi.

Szabó (b. 1938), and Márta Mészáros (b. 1933). Gaál graduated from the Academy for Dramatic and Cinematographic Art in 1959 and studied for two years on an Italian State Scholarship at the Centro Sperimentale in Rome before returning to Budapest to join the experimental Béla Balázs Studio as one of its founding directors. There he made a series of shorts (for example, *Tisza—Autumn Sketch* [*Tisza—őszi vazlatok*, 1963]) before venturing the semiautobiographical trilogy, *Current* (*Sondrásban*, 1964), *The Green Years* (*Zöldár*, 1965), and *Baptism* (*Keresztelö*, 1967), which focuses on a recurring theme in new Hungarian cinema—the situation of the intellectual who comes from peasant origins, and the radical division between town and country in contemporary Hungary. *The Falcons* (*Magasiskola*, 1970), widely regarded as Gaál's masterpiece, is set on the Great Plain in a falconry camp which becomes a paradigm for Hungarian fascism and its retreat into the feudal past. This brilliant study of the authoritarian mentality, which took a prize at Cannes, creates a kind of concrete poetry in its Jancsó-like camera movement, relentlessly dynamic editing, and stunning manipulations of color and sound. Inspired by the actual case of the deserted village of Gyürüfü, *Dead Landscape* (*Holt vidék*, 1971) is an investigation of the ways in which people interact with their environment—here, three who have chosen to stay on in a small, decaying rural village after the rest of the population has moved away. At first, the lack of community seems a challenge to them, but it leads with mounting horror to loneliness, alienation, and psychological disintegration for all three. Though he now works slowly (having made only three theatrical features since 1971—*Legato* [1977], *Buffer Zone* [*Cserepek*, 1981], and a version of Gluck's opera *Orpheus and Eurydice* [*Orfeus és Eurydike*, 1985]), Gaál is very much a personal *auteur*, who has written all of his own scripts and edited all of his own films. He also has always worked with the same composer, András Szöllősy, one of Hungary's most prominent modernists. In addition, Gaál often functions as his own art director and sometimes collaborates on the camera work (as was the case in *The Falcons*).

István Szabó (pronounced "Shahbow") graduated from the Budapest Academy in 1961 and immediately joined the Béla Balázs Studio where he directed two acclaimed shorts, *Variations on a Theme* (*Variációk edgy témára*, 1961) and *You* (*Te*, 1963), the last of which has become a minor classic and the most-awarded short in Hungarian film history. His first feature, *The Age of Daydreaming* (*Álmodozások kora*, 1964), follows the fortunes of five newly graduated engineers as they set out to conquer the world in the optimistic sixties, and it bears the marked influence of the French New Wave, especially Truffaut, to whom it contains several explicit *hommages*. *Father* (*Apa*, 1966), a more tightly constructed and ambitious film, concerns a young man's attempts to come to terms with his dead father's reputation as a partisan hero of World War II in the context of his own involvement with the 1956 Revolution. In its concern with the impingement of the past on the present and future, *Father* is closer in theme to Resnais than to Truffaut, and Szabó's next two films actually employ many of Resnais' editing techniques: flashbacks cued by association, the repetition of significant scenes with slight variations, the steady integration of past and present through montage. These techniques characterize both *Love Film* (*Szerelmesfilm*, 1970), which focuses on a single couple separated by the events of 1956 who now seek reunion, and *25 Fireman's Street* (*Tüzoltó utca 25*, 1973), a stylistically and structurally difficult film about the "dreams" experienced by an old house in Budapest on the eve of its demolition. *Budapest Tales* (*Budapesti mesék*, 1976) is a picaresque work that provides an allegory of the Hungarian postwar condition as a group of survivors organize to push an abandoned streetcar from the outskirts of the city into Budapest. *Confidence* (*Bizalom*, 1979) is a restrained film shot in beautifully muted color by Lajos Koltai; it depicts a man and a woman living together in a Budapest suburb under false identities in the closing days of World War II; they begin in distrust but end as lovers.

16.94   *Love Film* (István Szabó, 1970).

With the Hungarian–West German coproduction *Mephisto* (1981), Szabó achieved his first great international success and reached a watershed in his career. Freely adapted by the director and Peter Dobai from Klaus Mann's 1936 novel (which itself was based on the career of the famous German actor Gustav Gründgens, who married Mann's sister), this uncharacteristically dark film chronicles the Machiavellian climb to fame of the provincial actor Hendrik Höfgen (Klaus Maria Brandauer) during the Nazi era. From playing with a leftwing theater troupe in Hamburg in 1929, he rises to the directorship of Berlin's National Theater by 1936 through a series of personal betrayals and artistic compromises which make him a favorite of the Nazi elite. At the pinnacle of his good fortune, however, Hendrik is forced to realize that he has made a truly Faustian bargain with the Nazis, who now own his soul. Distinguished by its superb performances, rich period detail, and Lajos Koltai's multitextured cinematography, *Mephisto* won many international awards, including the Cannes Jury Prize for Best Screenplay, the International Film Press Federation (FIPRESCI) Prize for Best Picture, and the American Academy Award for Best Foreign Film (all 1982). Szabó's next endeavor reunited the *Mephisto* team (Dobai, Koltai, Brandauer, and the producer Manfred Durnick) to create the Hungarian–West German–Austrian coproduction *Colonel Redl* (*Redl Ezredes* / *Oberst Redl*, 1985), based on the life of Alfred Redl, who was head of the Austro-Hungarian political police near the outbreak of World War I. An open homosexual, Redl was accused of being a Russian agent as well and was forced to commit suicide to smooth over his political and sexual indiscretions. Another dark study of the ravages of ambition and obsession, *Colonel Redl* stands as Szabó's most complex and impressively mounted film to date, and it took the Jury Prize at Cannes. *Hanussen* (1988)—similarly scripted by Szabó, shot by Koltai, and starring Brandauer—is also based on a real character, in this case a psychic who briefly became the darling of the National Socialists between the wars and was later murdered by them. Unlike Jancsó, who often improvises while on location from a basic outline of dialogue and action, Szabó works from a meticulously detailed—and almost always original—shooting script of his own device (*Mephisto* is his only film to

16.95   Szabó's *25 Fireman's Street* (1973).

16.96   *Mephisto* (István Szabó, 1981): Klaus Maria Brandauer behind the mask.

16.97 Szabó's *Colonel Redl* (1985): Klaus Maria Brandauer in the title role.

16.98 *Adoption* (Márta Mészáros, 1975).

16.99 Mészáros *Nine Months* (1976): Lili Monori.

date to be adapted from the work of another). This scrupulous preplanning has meant that each of his films has engaged Szabó for at least two years, but once in production, he seems capable of adapting to whatever circumstances are dictated by the shoot.

Márta Mészáros (pronounced "Messarowsh") was born in Budapest in 1931 but grew up in the Soviet Union where her leftist father, the noted sculptor László Mészáros, was forced to emigrate in 1936 (and where he later died in prison during the Stalinist purges). She attended the VGIK in Moscow on scholarship and worked briefly in the Romanian industry after graduating in 1956. In 1959 she returned to Budapest where she made some thirty documentary shorts before directing her first feature, *The Girl* (*Eltávozott nap*, 1968), which announced both the style and theme of her later features—a documentarylike flatness of presentation combined with a deep and abiding concern for the situation of women and children within contemporary Hungarian society. Like *The Girl,* in which a young woman raised in a state orphanage searches for her biological parents, most of Mészáros' films involve an independent woman who finds herself faced with making an important decision on her own, and they tend to be both intimate and open-ended. In *Binding Sentiments* (*A "holdudvar,"* 1969), for example, an alcoholic* mother and her son's fiancée play a cat-and-mouse game at a hillside villa overlooking Lake Balaton; and *Don't Cry, Pretty Girls* (*Szép lányok, ne sirjatok,* 1970) recounts a romance between a city-bred musician and a country girl at a youth hostel. After the documentary feature *Women at the Spinnery / At the Lörinc Spinnery* (*A Lörinci fonóban,* 1971), Mészáros made *Riddance / Free Breath* (*Szabad lélegzet,* 1973), which focuses on the struggles of a factory girl and her student lover to maintain their relationship against the prejudicial demands of his parents. *Adoption* (*Örökbefogadás,* 1975), winner of the Grand Prix at Berlin, is widely regarded as Mészáros' most aesthetically and psychologically satisfying feature to date. It concerns a middle-aged woman who wants to have a child by her mar-

* Hungary has inordinately high rates of alcoholism, suicide, and divorce.

ried lover. She befriends a young girl from a nearby community house, "adopts" her spiritually, and helps her toward marriage with her boyfriend. For this film, Mészáros adopted a fluid visual style to chart the changing emotional relationships between the two women.

In *Nine Months* (*Kilenc hónap*, 1976), winner of the FIPRESCI Prize at Cannes and Mészáros' first film in color, a factory woman with a child has an affair with a company engineer and becomes pregnant, but neither can compromise his or her individuality sufficiently to form a relationship; and the woman leaves him to bear her second child alone (Lili Monori, the Mészáros regular who played this part, was pregnant at the time, and the birth of her child was photographed for inclusion in the film). *Two of Them* (*Ők ketten*, 1977) deals with a cross-generational relationship similar to that of *Adoption*. Mari, the middle-aged director of a hostel for working women, is trapped in a dead marriage in an industrial town. Juli is a factory girl saddled with an alcoholic husband. The two women form a meaningful but troubled friendship in a world in which there are clearly no easy answers for either gender. In *Just Like at Home* (*Olyan, mint otthon*, 1978), whose strangely lyrical beauty owes much to the cinematography of Lajos Koltai, Mészáros shifts focus to study the male psyche from a female perspective in the haunting story of the relationship that develops between an alienated intellectual and a ten-year-old girl. With *The Heiresses* / *The Heritage* (*Örökség*, 1980), a French-Hungarian coproduction, she produced a period film that mirrored her contemporary themes. During the rise of nazism and World War II, a wealthy but sterile woman persuades a Jew to have a child by her husband in order to inherit her father's estate. The husband eventually falls in love with the surrogate wife, and his real wife responds by having the husband arrested for violating the Nuremberg Laws and the Jewish woman deported to Auschwitz. *Mother and Daughter* / *Anna* (*Anya és léanya*, 1981), Mészáros' second French-Hungarian film, concerns a middle-aged woman hunting in contemporary Budapest and Paris for her long-lost daughter, who disappeared in the wake of the 1956 uprising. More recently, *Land of Miracles* (*Delibabok országa*, 1983) is a version of Gogol's *The Inspector General*. *Diary for My Children* (*Napló gyermekeimnek*, 1984) is a small-scale but intensely personal autobiographical work about a young girl's coming of age during the grimmest years of Stalinism, 1947–53, which won the Special Jury Prize at Cannes.* Its sequel, *Diary for My Loves* (*Napló szerelmeimnek*, 1987), continues her story from 1949 through the fateful year of 1956. All three latter films are photographed in finely textured black and white by Mészáros' former stepson Miklós

16.100   *Just Like at Home* (Márta Mészáros, 1978): Zsuzsa Czinkóczy, Jan Nowicki.

16.101   Mészáros' *The Heiresses* (1980): Isabelle Huppert.

---

* *Diary* had originally included footage from the ludicrously stolid Soviet socialist realist films of the period, but Mészáros agreed to substitute clips from Hungarian films, so as not to irritate the Russians. Her comment on this matter illustrates the rather modest (by Eastern bloc standards) state of film censorship in Hungary: "The same point is made and I did not think this was a great compromise for me. If I insisted on the Soviet footage there would have been a conflict, and I didn't want that" (quoted in William Wolf, "Blue Danube Diary," *Film Comment* 10, 3 [May–June 1984], p. 4.) The fifty–year-old Mészáros intends *Diary* as the first of three films on her life.

Jancsó, Jr. (she was married to Miklós Jancsó in the sixties). Her most recent film is a rendition of a classic fairy tale—*Bye Bye, Red Riding Hood* (*Piroska és a farkas*, 1989)—with feminist overtones. On one level, Mészáros bears witness to Hungarian society from a consciously female perspective to confront issues usually ignored by Eastern European (and most other) cinema: the subjugation of women in a patriarchal system, the dissolution of traditional family structures, the plight of children raised without parental affection or control. But on another level, as Derek Elley has observed, her theme is the search by all people "for human warmth and companionship in a present-day, industrialized society,"* and she has created a body of work that shows remarkable stylistic consistency in pursuing it.

Other Hungarian Directors

Other Hungarian directors who have recently attracted world attention are Sándor Sára (b. 1933), Pál Gábor (1932–86), Péter Bacsó (b. 1928), Ferenc Kósa (b. 1937), Imre Gyöngyössy (b. 1930), Pál Sándor (b. 1939), Zsolt Kézdi-Kovács (b. 1936), Judit Elek (b. 1937), Livia Gyarmathy (b. 1932), István Dárday (b. 1940), János Rózsa (b. 1937), Ferenc Kardos (b. 1937), Zoltán Huszárik (1931–81), Pál Zolnay (b. 1928), Gábor Bódy (1947–85), and Péter Gothár (b. 1945). Sára, primarily a photographer and cameraman (for example, for Gaál's *Current,* Szabó's *Father* and *25 Fireman's Street,* Zoltán Huszárik's *Sindbad,* and for all but one of Ferenc Kósa's features), directed the famous Béla Balázs Studio short *Gypsies* (*Ciganyok*, 1963) before making a successful feature debut in *The Upthrown Stone* (*Feldobott kő*, 1968), which deals with the disillusionment of an idealistic intellectual under the dictatorial Rákosi government in the early fifties; in the end we learn that he has

---

* Derek Elley quoted in "Márta Mészáros," *World Film Directors, Volume Two, 1945–1985,* ed. John Wakeman (New York: H. W. Wilson, 1988), p. 682.

16.102 *The Upthrown Stone* (Sándor Sára, 1968).

16.103 Sára's *Eighty Hussars* (1978).

actually made the film we are watching in order to expose that regime's brutality. In the dark satire *Pheasant Tomorrow* (*Holnap lesz fácán*, 1974) a contemporary holiday camp for young people becomes a microcosm of totalitarian society, as a middle-aged "Leader" and his friends take control of the establishment and set up a miniature authoritarian state. *Eighty Hussars* (*80 Huszár*, 1978) makes a parable of a true episode from the 1848 Revolution: a squadron of hussars deserts the Imperial Army for home in order to fight with the rebels, but only a handful of the men make it back, rendering their heroic gesture futile. In *The Teachers* (*Neptanitok*, 1982) Sará took his camera to a reunion of the class of 1930 at the University of Pécs, where sixteen men talk of why they chose to become teachers, what the choice has meant to their lives, and how it involved them in the multiple upheavals of twentieth-century Hungarian history. *On the Crossroad* (*Keresztuton*, 1987) is a similarly engaging documentary about the experience of an expatriate Hungarian peasant Communist caught murderously between borders during World War II, while *Bábolna* (1986–88) is an ambitious attempt to trace the history of Hungary from 1945 to the present through a series of six feature-length documentaries on the fate of the cooperative farm Bábolna.

The features of Pál Gábor, whose debut *Forbidden Ground* (*Tiltott terület*) was the Hungarian entry at Venice in 1969, often take a documentary approach to the problems of modern life. *Horizon* (*Horizont*, 1970), for example, deals with the phenomenon of industrial alienation in a manner similar to that of British New Cinema (see Reisz's *Saturday Night and Sunday Morning*, 1960), a fact Gábor acknowledges by having his protagonist's antiestablishment rebellion sparked by watching Lindsay Anderson's *If . . .* (1968) several times. *Journey with Jacob* (*Utazás Jakabbal*, 1972) has two young men knocking about together among the small towns and villages of Hungary in their mindless jobs as fire equipment inspectors, and it bears the influence of such American "road" films as *Easy Rider* (Dennis Hopper, 1969). *Epidemic* (1976) is an uncharacteristic historical film set during the "cholera rebellion" that rocked northern Hungary in 1831, the first great peasant uprising since the 1500s. Gábor's most successful and widely distributed feature to date is *Angi Vera* (1978), set in 1948 as the Stalinists were asserting their control over the party machinery. The film's youthful heroine, Vera Angi,* touchingly portrayed by Veronika Papp, shows early "political consciousness" (that is, Communist leanings) by denouncing her former boss and is sent to a three-month training camp for aspiring party leaders. There, she has an affair with her married teacher István, which she later confesses out of political expediency, ruining him but advancing herself a step further up the party ladder. Written by Gábor and subtly photographed by the brilliant Lajos Koltai, *Angi Vera* is a deeply felt film: Vera's motivations are always ambiguous, at the very least, and her betrayal of István out of party loyalty has a tragic sincerity about it and a resonance for her future life that she can only vaguely understand. More

16.104 *Angi Vera* (Pál Gábor, 1978): Veronika Papp, Tamás Danai.

---

* In Hungarian, as mentioned previously, last names precede first names.

recently, Gábor has directed *Wasted Lives* (*Kettévált menny ezet,* 1982)—which is set during the shifting thaw of 1953–55 and also deals with the human consequences of a regime totally committed to politics—and *The Long Ride* (*Hosszú vágta,* 1985), a Hungarian–U.S. coproduction about a peasant boy who helps a downed American flyer escape from the Great Plain into Yugoslavia during World War II. Gábor died of a heart attack in October 1986, while participating in a forum on Hungarian film in Rome.

Péter Bacsó's work consists mainly of comedies with a sharp satirical edge. *Outbreak* (*Kitörés,* 1970) concerns a disgruntled factory worker who protests his working conditions, a local housing shortage, and other indignities, only to lose his girlfriend and his job for his pains. In *Present Indicative* (*Jelenidő,* 1971) a conscientious factory boss tries to instill his workers with a sense of pride in their jobs to no avail, and in *The Last Chance* (*Harmadik nekifutás,* 1973) a manager improbably decides to take responsibility for his plant's shortcomings and demotes himself to the ranks of the workers, who naturally regard him as a madman. In the mid-seventies Bacsó continued to follow his satirical bent in contemporary comedies like *Don't Pull My Beard!* (*Ereszd el a szakállamat!,* 1975) and the absurdist thriller *Alarm Shot* (*Riasztólövés,* 1976), but 1977 saw the release of his bristling satire of the Stalinist show trials, *The Witness* (*A tanú*), made in 1968 but suppressed due to the Warsaw Pact invasion of Czechoslovakia in that year (and not released abroad until 1981). Bacsó's *Electric Shock* (*Áramütés,* 1979) illuminates a contemporary brother-sister relationship, while *Let's Talk About Love* (*Kibeszél itt szerelemröl!?*) is a light satire on political opportunism. His film *The Man Who Went Up in Smoke* (*A svéd, akinek,* 1981) was a Hungarian-Swedish coproduction based on a Maj Sjöwall-Per Wahlöö *policier.* In *The Day Before Yesterday* (*Tegnapelött,* 1982), strikingly shot in color by János Zsombolyai (b. 1939), Bacsó returned to the period of *The Witness* with a film reminiscent of *Angi Vera* in its tale of a young woman whose revolutionary idealism turns to gall and wormwood when she gives false testimony against her lover; *Oh, Bloody Life!* (*Te rongyos élet . . . !,* 1984) treats the same kind of predicament in the same period, only here a popular young singing star is denounced as a "class enemy" (because she was once briefly married to an aristocrat) and she is sent to a rural labor camp in an isolated farming village. Bacsó returned triumphantly to black comedy with *What's the Time, Mr. Clock?* (*Hány az óra, Vekker Uro?,* 1985), set in the picturesque little village of Koszeg in 1944, where a popular Jewish watchmaker falls afoul of the invading Nazis but manages to save himself through his gift for split-second timing. *Banana Skin Waltz* (*Banánhéjkeringö,* 1987) is a tragicomedy about greed and corruption within contemporary Hungarian society, while *Titania, Titania* (1989) is a savage satire on the excesses of the Ceausescu dictatorship in neighboring Romania. For the past two decades, Péter Bacsó has been one of Hungary's most prolific directors, and he has remained remarkably consistent in his absurdist portrayal of horrendous events from recent history. His shooting style is documentarylike and involves great attention to the details of everyday life. Whenever possible he works with nonactors in real loca-

16.105 Péter Bacsó's *The Witness* (1968; released 1981).

tions, although he has also earned a reputation for his ability to evoke strong ensemble performances from professionals.

Ferenc Kósa graduated from the Budapest Academy in 1963 and completed his first feature in 1965, but its release was delayed for political reasons until 1967, when it was justly awarded the Grand Prix at Cannes. The result of years of documentary research, *Ten Thousand Suns* (*Tízezer nap*) traces the life of the peasant-born communist István Széles in flashback through all of the social changes that have overtaken Hungary in the thirty years from his birth through the 1956 Revolution. (The title refers both to the ten thousand days of its time frame and to István's vision of a new Utopia when he would see "ten thousand suns" bursting into flames above the sea.) In effect, the film is a complex meditation on whether the benefits brought to Hungary by communism (industrialization, urbanization, positive growth) can ever justify the brutal means used to achieve them. But it is also a richly poetic visual experience which has been compared to the work of Dovzhenko in its lyricism and of Eisenstein in its treatment of mass movement on the screen. Brilliantly photographed in widescreen black and white by Sándor Sára, *Ten Thousand Suns* was a landmark for the new Hungarian cinema both in terms of its political integrity and its striking compositional effects. *Judgment* (*Ítélet*, 1970) was a Romanian-Yugoslavian coproduction concerning a peasant uprising in 1514, and it was not well received critically; but *Beyond Time* (*Ninc idő*, 1972) proved a worthy successor to *Ten Thousand Suns*, and it was similarly controversial (though not suppressed). Set in a Hungarian prison in 1929, this intentionally baroque film charts the attempts of a weak but well-meaning governor to prevent a hunger strike among political prisoners, mainly communists; he fails in the end, and his job is turned over to the ruthless chief warden, a personification of the authoritarian mentality. In *Snowfall* (*Hószakadás*, 1974), a young soldier sets out across Transylvania with his peasant grandmother in search of his parents, who disappeared in the closing days of World War II. *Portrait of a Champion* (*Küldetés*, 1977), a great popular success with domestic

16.106 *Ten Thousand Suns* (Ferenc Kósa, 1965).

16.107 *Beyond Time* (Ferenc Kósa, 1972).

16.108   Kósa's *Snowfall* (1974).

audiences, provides a series of documentary interviews with a former Hungarian Olympic athlete who, in espousing meritocracy, is openly critical of the prevailing social system. *The Match* (*A mérkőzés,* 1981) is set during the tense summer of 1956 and, like Gábor's *Angi Vera* and Bacsó's *The Day After Yesterday,* is concerned with the acceptable limits of political expediency. In a provincial town, the police chief is also manager of the local soccer club; enraged over a miscall that costs his team a game, he kills the referee in a locker-room brawl and hastily conceals the crime. When a journalist attempts to investigate the cover-up, his family is threatened, he is arrested, and the district party boss whitewashes the whole affair. In *Guernica* (1982), the first Kósa film not shot by Sára, a young woman who works at a brick factory becomes obsessed with the prospect of nuclear war after watching some television programs on the East-West arms race. She eventually falls in love with an artist who has been moved by seeing Picasso's "Guernica" to devote his life to creating a gigantic sculpture representing the horrors of war in the granite hillside where his pacifist father was killed during World War II; the woman finally journeys to Spain to see the famous painting for herself, and the sculptor is murdered by her jealous boyfriend in her absence. Superbly photographed by Lajos Koltai, *Guernica* introduced a strain of hopelessness into Kósa's work that has remained ever since. His two-part historical drama, *The Other Person* (*A másik ember,* 1988) provided yet another impressive display of visual imagination and ideological praxis in two stories of a father's and a son's separate encounters with fascism—the father's as a soldier during World War II and the son's as a student insurgent during the 1956 Revolution, with each part filmed magnificently in a style appropriate to its theme.

Imre Gyöngyössy, scriptwriter for Gaál's *The Green Years,* Kósa's *Ten Thousand Suns,* and the Czechoslovak film *Adrift* (Jan Kadár, 1971), made his debut as a director with *Palm Sunday* (*Virágvasárnap,* 1969). Clearly influenced by Jancsó in its stylization of historical events, the film presents the violent demise of the Red Republic of Councils in 1919 as a kind of passion play in which the supporters of the revolution are collectively crucified. In *Legend About the Death and Resurrection of Two Young Men* (*Meztelen vagy,* 1971), Gyöngyössy created an intensely poetic film that works on both the literal level of narrative and the metaphorical level of ritual, symbol, and myth. A young gypsy returns with a friend to his native settlement determined to help his people rise above their poverty and squalor; but they turn against him, ultimately cutting out his tongue and drowning the friend in a vat of concrete. *Legend* is both an authentic documentary record of gypsy life and an attempt to recreate that life in the form of myth. As such, it is distinguished by its sophisticated, if ambiguous montage structure (constantly cutting forward to its own climax, for example, and providing the narrative with three separate conclusions) and the sensual, dreamlike cinematography of Janos Kende. *Sons of Fire* (*Szarvassá vált fiúk,* 1974), loosely based on the "Stag Boy" legend, concerns the attempted escape of a group of Communists from a Hungarian prison at the end of World War II. Once again, Gyöngyössy's

16.109   *A Quite Ordinary Life* (Imre Gyöngyössy, 1977).

provocative associative editing produced a complex, multileveled film that concludes with a tour-de-force montage sequence as the escapees are relentlessly hunted down and killed by local landowners amidst scenes of natural plentitude and splendor. The director's subsequent credits include numerous austere documentaries, such as *A Quite Ordinary Life* (*Két elhátarozás*, 1977), and the features *Expectations* (*Várakozók*, 1975), set in a large family mansion during the siege of Budapest, and *Glimpses of Life* (*Töredék az életröl*, 1982), concerning long-concealed tensions in a village to which a successful middle-aged woman returns to celebrate an award at work. Gyöngyössy's most distinguished and commercially successful achievement to date has been the Hungarian–West German coproduction *The Revolt of Job* (*Jób lazadása*, 1983), which he co-directed with Barna Kabay (b. 1949), his assistant since the mid-seventies, from a screenplay by the directors and Katalin Petenyi (Gyöngyössy's wife). Perhaps the most accessible of his features, this autobiographical work concerns an elderly Jewish couple—Job and Roza—who adopt a seven-year-old Christian boy, Lackó, in order to pass on their property and knowledge to him before the Holocaust consumes them.* Set in an East Hungarian village in 1943 and 1944, the film recreates the whole tapestry of Jewish life in a rural community through Lackó's eyes. From his child's perspective, the ominous portents of war and genocide are merely distant thunder until the village world is shattered by the coming of the Nazis. Shot in beautiful autumnal hues by Gábor Szabó, *The Revolt of Job* is finally a celebration of human dignity and courage in the face of impossible odds, as is *That Ye Inherit / In Memory of 450,000 Hungarian Peasant Jews* (*Add tudtul fiadnak*, 1985), a Hungarian–West German television documentary produced by the team of Gyöngyössy, Kabay, and Petenyi on the same subject. Made to commemorate the fortieth anniversary of the German defeat in World War II, this film has been praised as the best documentary ever made about the survivors of the Nazi camps. More recently the Gyöngyössy-Kabay-Petenyi group completed the Hungarian–West German–Canadian-British coproduction *Yerma*, an adaptation of a moody Garcia Lorca play filmed on location by Szabó in Andalusia.

Pál Sándor's first films, *Clowns on the Wall* (*Bohóc a falon*, 1967) and *Sarah, My Dear* (*Sarika drágám*, 1971), were New Wave–influenced works—full of mock *cinéma-vérité* interviews and trick photography—about generational conflict within contemporary Hungarian society. But *Football in the Good Old Days* (*Régi idők focija*, 1973) brilliantly combines technical experimentation with serious intentions in its tale of a Chaplinesque soccer manager attempting to field a winning team in Budapest in 1924. Deliberately imitative of American slapstick comedy,

---

* The Holocaust came late to Hungary: not until April 1944, after the Nazis had seized control of the Hungarian government. Aware that time was running out for them, the S.S. overlords streamlined the Hungarian extermination program, so that 565,000 of the country's 825,000 registered Jews perished within the eight months before January 1945, when Hungary concluded an armistice with the Allies. Hungarian deportation and killing operations were under the direct command of Adolph Eichmann.

16.110   *A Strange Role* (Pál Sándor, 1977).

which was at the height of its vogue in 1924, the film boasts detailed period reconstruction and is ever mindful of the political tensions seething just beneath the surface of everyday Hungarian life in the wake of 1919 and the counterrevolutionary terror. In *A Strange Role* (*Herkulesfärdöi emlék*, 1977) a young Communist boy, disguised as a girl, literally finds asylum in a sanatorium for women after the fall of the Red Republic of Councils. This moody and melancholic film, distributed in the United States as *Improperly Dressed*, won the Silver Bear at Berlin in 1978. *Deliver Us from Evil* (*Szabadits meg a gonosztól*, 1979) successfully blends pantomimic humor with a haunting evocation of Budapest in its final stages of wartime exhaustion in December 1944: the theft of a coat from a dancing-school cloakroom sends its attendant on a labyrinthine tour of the bombed-out city and its inhabitants in an effort to retrieve the stolen article. *Ham Actors* (*Ripacsok*, 1981) is a sort of madcap tragicomedy about the seamy side of contemporary show business that harks back stylistically to *Football in the Good Old Days*. Like *Deliver Us,* it is a character-rich fable, subtly photographed by Elemér Ragályi (b. 1939) in luminous Eastmancolor. More recently, Sándor has directed *Daniel Takes a Train* (*Szerencsés Dániel*, 1983—International Critics' Prize, Cannes), a controlled tale of two friends caught up in the stampede to leave Budapest in 1956, and *Just a Movie* (*Csak egy mozi*, 1985), a Truffaut-like film about a film director who finds himself stumped for creative ideas (and a purpose in life) in the midst of shooting a version of *Swan Lake*. Both films contain the Sándor trademarks of whimsy, bizarre characterization, and the stylized camera work and lighting of Ragályi. But *Miss Arizona* (1988) is a more serious affair—a romantic melodrama spanning the turbulent years 1920–45, and focusing on the fate of Hungary's middle-class Jews.

Zsolt Kézdi-Kovács graduated from the Budapest Academy and spent several years as an assistant to Jancsó before making his feature debut with *Temperate Zone* (*Mérsékelt égöv*, 1970), a chamber piece in which three contemporary characters try to come to terms with their respective Stalinist pasts in a series of complicated sequence shots. But it was the extraordinarily beautiful and quite different *Romanticism* (*Romantika*, 1972) that attracted international attention to his work. Set during the Enlightenment, this film concerns a young Hungarian nobleman who rejects his father's "civilized" material values for the philosophical ideal of the noble savage and ends as a kind of wild child, roaming the forests first with a band of local outlaws and finally with a pack of stags. Shot as a series of sustained long takes with zoom and telescopic lenses by János Kende, *Romanticism* bears the marked influence of Jancsó and has the visually rhapsodic quality of his greatest work. *When Joseph Returns* (*Ha megjön József*, 1976) is a probing psychodrama about the relationship that develops between the mother and the wife of a man during his long absence in the merchant marine, and *The Good Neighbor* (*A kedves szomszéd*, 1979) is a similar kind of film about the relationship between a man and his neighbors in an old tenement block. After the somewhat desultory *The Right to Hope* (*A remény joga*, 1982), dealing with a twelve-year-old boy's attempt to reconcile his estranged parents, Kézdi-Kovács staged a magnificent return to form with *Forbidden Relations* (*Visszaesők*, 1983). Based on the transcripts of a true case, the film gives a sensitive account of an incestuous affair that develops between a sister and her half-brother in a small rural village, and it is distinguished by its sensuous re-creation of country life and by János Kende's richly textured photography. Kéždi-Kovács and Kende also collaborated on the contemporary drama of divorce *The Absentee* (*A rejtözködő*, 1985) and *Cry and Cry Again* (*Kiattas és kialtas*, 1988), a love story set in the terror-filled postrevolutionary years.

Judit Elek, another Academy graduate from the banner year 1961, made numerous documentaries before directing her first feature, *The Lady from Constantinople* (*Sziget a szárazföldön*) in 1969. This closely observed portrait of an aging widow who must exchange apartments in Budapest was widely admired for its emotional authenticity and its resonant evocation of the old lady's lost world of memories, memorabilia, and faded dreams. Elek's next two films, *A Hungarian Village* (*Istenmezején*, 1974) and *A Simple Story* (*Egyszerű történet*, 1975), were politically engaged semidocumentaries on the quite different lives of two young girls working in the same contemporary mining town over a period of several years. Using nonprofessional actors, *cinéma-vérité*–style interviews, and elaborate montage, she demonstrates the generational conflicts between tradition and modernity lingering on just beneath the surface of the new social order, as well as the rootlessness of life in the new industrial towns. More recently Elek has made *Maybe Tomorrow* (*Majd holnap*, 1980), an unadorned story of two married lovers who can never quite bring themselves to make a permanent commitment to one another and leave their respective spouses, and *Mária's Day* (*Maria nap*, 1984), a Chekhovian account of the Szendrey family's reunion at a country house in September 1866 to celebrate the eldest daughter's name day. This woman had once been married to the revolutionary poet Sándor Petöfi, who was killed during the 1848 Revolution, and the film charts the various political and familial tensions proceeding from this circumstance—tensions that still are experienced by Hungarian society as a whole.

16.111   *The Lady from Constantinople* (Judit Elek, 1969).

Another woman director who uses *cinéma-vérité* techniques to deal with the social milieu of contemporary Hungary is Livia Gyarmathy. Trained as a chemical engineer, Gyarmathy's first feature, *Do You Know Sunday—Monday?* (*Ismeri a szandi mandit?*, 1968), was a sardonic, Formanesque comedy about worker alienation in a large chemical plant. She continued in this vein with *Stop the Music* (*Álljon meg a menet*, 1973), a collage of vignettes of blue-collar life. In the eighties, she made *Korportos* (1980), an adaptation of József Balázs's novel about an impoverished gypsy who returns to his village in an attempt to provide a decent burial for his bride, *Every Wednesday* (*Minden szerdán*, 1980), a film about the friendship that grows between an alienated teenager and a philosophical old man, and *Coexistence* (*Együttélés*, 1983), a portrait of a German-Hungarian community seen from the perspective of a couple's mixed marriage. *Now It's My Turn, Now It's Yours* (*Egy kicsit en . . . egy kicsit te . . .* , 1985) is a *cinéma-vérité*–style comedy of the domestic tensions between three generations of a family living together in a Budapest apartment, while *Blind Endeavor* (*Vakvilágban*, 1986) weaves together two separate stories of the frustrations of everyday life.

In 1974, another 1961 Academy graduate, István Dárday, pioneered a new genre mixing documentary and fiction in *Holiday in Britain* (*Jutalomutazás*). This satire concerns a peasant boy who wins a musical competition to travel with a government-sponsored youth group to Britain. His mother refuses to let him go, fearing that he will be "changed" by the experience (much as Hungarian rural life has been changed by collectivization), which puts her into direct conflict with the socialist bureaucracy. Shot on location with nonactors improvising from their own real-life roles, *Holiday* is a very funny film but also a markedly serious one in delineating the conflict betweeen a centuries-old peasant mentality and the attitudes of a modern bureaucratic state. Inspired by Dárday's success, the Béla Balázs Studio conducted a yearlong series of experiments on new ways of integrating the forms of documentary and feature films. The result was the genre of the "film-novel" (literally, *filmregény*, also known as "docudrama," "fiction-documentary," and "documentary play"), a kind of sociographic documentary as epitomized by Dárday's *Film Novel—Three Sisters* (*Filmregény—Három nővér*, 1979). This four-and-one-half hour feature follows the lives of three sisters between the ages of twenty and thirty over a period of two years in contemporary Budapest to provide an authentic portrait of Hungarian society today. Nonactors were cast in roles corresponding to those they play in real life and were then directed to flesh out fictional personalities according to a tightly constructed narrative line (written by Dárday and Györgyi Szalai), which is devised so as to encourage improvisation. This so-called "factional" technique was employed with similar success in the second Dárday-Szalai collaboration, *Point of Departure / Metamorphosis* (*Átváltozás*, 1984). Cut down from eight hours to two hours and thirty-five minutes, this film focuses entirely on the interaction between family members and friends within a two-story suburban home. Dárday's 215-minute *The Documentator* (*A dokumentator*, 1989) is a semidocumentary examination of the impact of Western-style media on Hungarians' social values and their daily lives. As a mode of analyzing contemporary social problems, the film-novel genre has become extremely popular with Hungarian audiences, and a new production group (Tarsulas) has been established to devote all of its activity to the form.

János Rózsa and Ferenc Kardos, who began their careers by co-directing the Truffaut-inspired film about schoolchildren, *Grimace* (*Gyermekbetegségek*), in 1965, have both made important individual contributions to the new Hungarian cinema. Rózsa's *Dreaming Youth* (*Álmodó ifjúság*, 1974) was based on an autobiographical novel by the great Hungarian film theorist Béla Balázs, while his *Spider Football* (*Pókfoci*, 1976) uses academic in-fighting at a newly opened technical school as a metaphor for Hungarian politics. *The Trumpeter* (*A trombitás*, 1979) is a violent but visually poetic epic about an anti-Hapsburg rebellion in the early seventeenth century, seductively photographed by Elemér Ragályi. Rozsa made two films of contemporary life: *Sunday Daughters* (*Vasárnapi szülők*, 1980), set in a girls' reformatory, and *Mascot* (*Kabala*, 1982), about a brother and sister's futile struggle to reconcile their divorced parents. Next he turned to the highly successful *Witches' Sabbath* (*Boszorkányszombat*, 1984), a lavish fantasy in which all of the famous fairy-tale characters—Little Red Riding Hood, Snow White and the Seven Dwarfs, Cinderella, and so forth—gather together to celebrate the awakening of Sleeping Beauty after her hundred-year slumber. Rózsa returned to contemporary problems in *Love, Mother* (*Csók, Anyu*, 1987), a film about middle-class family disintegration that focuses on the children and their neglect by their fast-track parents. Kardos' *Petőfi '73* (1973) was a stylized reconstruction of the 1848 Revolution in which the heroes of that revolt (among them, the poet Sándor Petőfi) are portrayed by contemporary young people dressed in jeans and T-shirts. His *Unruly Haiduks* (*Hajdúk*, 1974), concerns a cattle drive by Hungarian patriots during the seventeenth-century uprising also depicted in Rózsa's *The Trumpeter*; it features the magnificent cinematography of János Kende and ends with the Jancsó-like massacre of the peasants and their mercenaries (*haiduks*)* by the Austrian army. *The Accent* (*Ékezet*, 1977), by contrast, deals with a civil servant who attempts the hopeless task of bringing "cultural education" to a small factory town. After the relative failure of the contemporary *Once One* (*Egyszeregy*, 1979) and a long hiatus, Kardos returned to strength with the audaciously operatic *Heavenly Hosts* (*Mennyei seregek*, 1984). Set in 1664, when Hapsburg forces were driving the Turks from Hungary, this film concerns the effects on a small community of rescuing a wounded angel, and it is interpenetrated with the elemental symbolism of fire, smoke, light, and water, all heightened

16.112 *Grimace* (János Rózsa and Ferenc Kardos, 1965).

---

* The *haiduk*, or heroic bandit, is a figure of mythical signficance in the Hungarian and Balkan cinemas, with many of the attributes of the gunfighter in Hollywood Westerns and the *ronin* in Japanese samurai films. Especially in Balkan films, the *haiduk* is romanticized for his patriotic resistance to the Turks during the period of the Ottoman occupation, and in Yugoslavia, Romania, and Bulgaria the *haiduk* film has become a distinct popular genre.

by the celestial cinematography of Lajos Koltai and by György Selmeczy's otherworldly score.

Zoltán Huszárik, an eminent graphic artist and painter, entered the Budapest Academy in 1948 and was forced to leave for political reasons three years later. Through the intervention of Károly Makk, he was able to return in 1954, and he finally graduated with the "Béla Balázs generation" in 1961. All of Huszárik's films are extensions of his personal artistic vision which at the same time draw heavily on the native tradition of aestheticism in the fine arts. His internationally famous short, *Elegy* (*Elégia,* 1965), uses the life cycle of the horses of the Great Plain—the oldest of Magyar* cultural symbols—to create a lyrical meditation on life and death; and Huszárik's first feature, *Sindbad* (*Szindbád,* 1971), became one of the most highly praised Hungarian films of the decade. Sumptuously photographed by Sándor Sára, it presents the reveries, memories, and dreams of an aging sensualist in *fin-de-siècle* Budapest in images of astounding formal beauty. What begins as a hedonist's tour through the decadent splendors of the national capital gradually becomes a meditation on the transience of experience itself and the passing away of all things. Huszárik made only one other film before his death in 1981, and it was every bit as visionary as *Sindbad. Csontváry* (1980) contains dual narratives of the life of the turn-of-the-century "primitive" painter for whom the film is named and of a stage actor breaking down under the strain of playing Csontváry in the present. Huszárik and cinematographer Péter Jankura present both stories as a series of dazzling tableaux of light and color in an attempt to examine the sources of human creativity.

Several other Hungarian directors deserve mention here because at least one of their films has made a singular contribution to world cinema. Pál Zolnay's *Photography* (*Fotográfia*) caused a sensation in 1974 with its documentary account of two photographers who travel about the country soliciting orders for family photographs and inadvertently uncover a long concealed pair of murders. Shot in *cinéma-vérité* style by Elemér Ragályi, *Photography*'s power derives in no small part from Zolnay's actual discovery of the crime (an elderly couple having years ago killed their two daughters) in the process of making the film and his use of photographic evidence from the production to prove it. Zolany's *Embryos* (*Embriok,* 1986) is an equally successful dramatized documentary about a thirty-three-year-old obstetrician / gynecologist's tortured decision to have an abortion. In 1981, Gábor Bódy, one of the founders of the experimental Studio K3 of the Béla Balázs Studio and director of the award-winning short *American Fragment* (1976) delivered the elaborately stylized *Narcissus and Psyche* (*Psyché és Narcisz*). Based on Sándor Weöres' classic

---

* Although a number of other ethnic groups live in contemporary Hungary (including, for example, gypsies and Romanians), Magyars make up about 95 percent of the population. They are descended from the Magyar tribesmen who migrated to Hungary from the east in the late ninth century and who evolved the present-day Hungarian language (whose official designation is "Magyar").

novel-in-verse, it transfers the ancient Greek myth to nineteenth-century Central Europe, where Psyche becomes a revolutionary poetess and Narcissus an epicene dramatist. The film is presented as a series of richly staged widescreen tableaux with voice-over narration to simulate novelistic form, and it won wide acclaim for both Bódy and the Hungarian cinema. Péter Gothár's *Time Stands Still* (*Megáll az idő*, 1982), on the other hand, deals very specifically with the recent Hungarian past and also with the experience of an entire generation whose members were teenagers in the early 1960s. (The title refers to both a Hungarian hit song of the era and to the moment of the 1956 Revolution.) The film is about coming of age in the grim shadow of the failed uprising, when Hungarian society was being gradually reconstructed along Western lines. Even as the young men and women of this period begin to experience American rock and roll (which comprises most of the soundtrack), liberated sex, and Coca-Cola, the past weighs heavily upon them. The two young heroes are discriminated against because their father is an exiled freedom fighter; teachers appear and disappear at school according to the prevailing political climate; and there are strange unspoken tensions among neighbors who have betrayed other neighbors in the aftermath of the revolt. Charged with a nervous energy reminiscent of Truffaut's *Les Quatre-cents coups* (1959) and Malle's *Le Souffle au coeur* (1971), *Time Stands Still* focuses consistently on its adolescent protagonists; but their passage from youthful rebellion to social assimilation has obvious reference to the journey of the whole national body politic since 1956. In the background of their story, we witness Hungary growing progressively more affluent with every passing year, and when the film ends it is hard not to feel that these young people have been induced to "grow up"—in the same way that their parents' aspirations for freedom have been bought off—by the state with consumer goods. Like so many recent Hungarian films, *Time Stands Still* is notable for its subtle visual texture as well as for its intelligence and vitality of spirit. Lajos Koltai's cinematography achieves a strikingly expressive range of color (and black and white for the pretitle sequence in which we see the father defect in the last hours of fighting), and Gothar uses slow motion, dissolves, and freeze frames with both discretion and dramatic effect. Unfortunately, Gothar's subsequent films—*Time* (*Idő van*, 1985) and *Just Like America* (1987)—have not been able to equal his debut feature.

16.113 and 16.114   Péter Gothár's *Time Stands Still* (1982).

As the preceding account should make clear, the Hungarian cinema is one of the most politically acute and sensuously beautiful in the world today. And although it produces only twenty to twenty-five features per year on an average budget of 300,000 dollars per film, it is the only cinema in Eastern Europe to have *consistently* maintained an international standing since its inception, and especially since World War II. Scholastic standards for admission to the Academy of Dramatic and Cinematographic Art in Budapest are as rigorous as those of an American medical school—in 1978, for example, there were twenty-seven applicants for every position—and it is militantly craft-oriented. All prospective directors are required first to study screenwriting and cinematography, and the industry itself is notoriously exclusive. (Between 1978 and

1983, Hungary's 121 theatrical features were directed by only 70 persons.) As in other Eastern European countries, the state film monopoly, Mafilm, is divided into five semiautonomous production groups (including the Béla Balázs Studio) that turn out documentaries, animated shorts, children's films, film-novels, and regular features, which are marketed through the state distribution agency, Hungarofilm. Hungary also has the only Eastmancolor processing plant in the Eastern bloc, and has recently begun an aggressive campaign of coproduction with the West. In answer to its cinema's remarkable degree of refinement—and despite the country's small size (population 11 million; land mass 35,919 square miles)—Hungary has evolved an extraordinarily sophisticated national film culture, requiring, for example, four years of academic film study in all of its public high schools. Moreover, there are fewer constraints on filmmakers (and artists generally) in Hungary than in any other country in Eastern Europe, in part because the Hungarians have been committed to a policy of gradual liberalization since the failure of their premature rebellion in 1956. The nation's movement toward democratic socialism since the fall of 1989 guarantees even greater freedom of expression. As the director Imre Gyöngyössy has said so pointedly of his nation: "We are a small country . . . and we have a very, very difficult language and a very closed culture. Cinema has become for us a kind of international language, to open the doors and to make a dialogue between different cultures, sometimes different continents."

YUGOSLAVIA

The Yugoslavs in effect had no national film industry until after World War II, and their cinema did not attract attention abroad until fifteen years thereafter, when the "Zagreb school" of animation began piling up international awards. With the exception of Poland, no country in Eastern Europe suffered more wartime devastation than Yugolslavia. The nation known today as Yugoslavia was created at the end of World War I out of six separate regions corresponding to the historical boundaries of six Slavic nationality groups—the Bosnia Muslims, the Croatians, the Macedonians, the Montenegrins, the Serbs, and the Slovenes. Officially named the "Kingdom of the Serbs, Croats, and Slovenes," the country was founded on December 1, 1918, as a constitutional monarchy to be ruled by Alexander I of Serbia; but King Alexander abolished the constitution in 1929 and ruled as a dictator, changing the country's name to Yugoslavia, which means "land of the South Slavs." Alexander was assassinated by Croatian nationalists in 1934 (the subject of Jancsó's *Winter Wind* [1969]—see p. 705), but his policies were continued by his cousin Prince Paul, acting as regent for the eleven-year-old Peter II. When Paul attempted to ally Yugoslavia with the Axis on March 25, 1941, he was deposed by a military coup that briefly installed Peter II as monarch. The Nazis invaded on April 6 and forced an unconditional surrender within eleven days, after which Yugoslavia was dismembered and divided among the bordering Axis states. Resistance was quickly organized by two sep-

arate groups: the Chetniks, led by Colonel (later General) Draža Mihaj-
lović, and loyal to the government-in-exile of Peter II, and the Communist
Partisans, led by Marshal Tito. Cooperating at first, the two groups ended
by fighting each other and the brutal Croatian Ustashis (Praetorian Guard)
to the death in a savage civil war in which the Partisans, liberally assisted
by the Allies, were victorious over all factions. Politically, they won the
widespread support of the people and proclaimed Yugoslavia a federal
"People's Republic"—modeled on the U.S.S.R.—in November 1945, with
Tito as party secretary and president. In 1948, Tito broke with Stalin
over Yugoslavian self-determination, and the country was expelled from
the Cominform (an alliance of Communist countries) in June. Tito then
turned to the United States and other Western nations for aid; and even
though Yugoslavia resumed relations with the Soviet Union in 1955, it
developed in the interim an economic system based on worker self-management and regional autonomy quite different from the planned central
economies of the rest of the Eastern bloc (it also remained nonaligned in
the cold war, identifying itself, at Tito's behest, with the Third World in
international politics). The complexity of Yugoslavia's so-called socialist
market economy mirrors the diversity of a nation of 24 million people
comprised of six republics (Slovenia, Croatia, Bosnia and Herzegovina,
Serbia, Montenegro, and Macedonia) and two autonomous provinces
(Vojvodina and Kosovo), with three official languages (Serbo-Croatian,
Slovenian, and Macedonian), three major religions (Eastern Orthodox,
Roman Catholic, and Muslim), and two alphabets (Cyrillic, based on
Greek, which is generally used by the Serbs, as well as by the Bulgarians
and the Russians; and Latin, supplemented with diacritical marks, used
in Eastern Europe by the Croatians, the Poles, and the Czechs—as well
as by the author of this book).

The Yugoslav resistance against the Nazis plus a civil war, known collectively as the National War of Liberation, left 1.9 million of the country's 16 million people dead and its economic infrastructure nearly
destroyed. When Belgrade was liberated by the Red Army and the Yugoslav Partisans in October 1944, the country had virtually no material
base for film production or distribution, and most of its five hundred
theaters were badly damaged by war.

Partisan Cinema and Nationalist Realism

The new Communist government led by former Partisan commander
and marshal of Yugoslavia, Josip Broz, known as Tito (1892–1980),
quickly established a federal Committee for Cinematography, which in
turn established regional committees in each of the six republics. The
committee also began construction of a new studio complex, Film City
(*Filmski grad*), at Kosŭtnak on the outskirts of Belgrade, founded a state
film school (the Faculty of Dramatic Arts) at Belgrade, with separate
technical institutes at Belgrade and Zagreb, and established the monthly
journal *Film* as a forum for criticism, polemics and theoretical debate. By
1951, in spite of the economic dislocations that followed Tito's dramatic
break with Stalin and Yugoslavia's explusion from the Cominform in

June 1948, centrally administered subsidies from the State Film Fund had increased over ten times and the country had produced thirteen features. Most of these were patriotic Partisan war epics,* such as Vjekoslav Afríc's *Slavica* (1947, Yugoslavia's first dramatic feature) and France Štiglic's *On Their Own Ground* (*Na svojoj zemlji*, 1948), or dramas of socialist reconstruction like Vladimir Pogačić's *Story of a Factory* (*Priča o fabrici*, 1949), and they all followed the principles of "nationalist realism," Yugoslavia's more moderate variant of Zhdanovian socialist realism. (A notable exception was Radoš Novaković's *Sofka*, 1948, adapted from the classic nineteenth-century Serbian novel *Impure Blood* [*Nečista krv*] by Bora Stanković.) During this same period, however, Yugoslavia produced over five hundred compilation films, documentary shorts, and newsreel segments (known collectively as *kinokronika*) that graphically documented horrors of the National War of Liberation and early socialist efforts to rebuild the country. Finally, by 1951, central studios were in operation in all six of the republics, and the number of Yugoslav theaters had nearly doubled to some 920 (as had domestic ticket sales, from 31,520,000 in 1946 to 67,926,000 by the end of 1950).

On June 27, 1950, the National Assembly passed the "Basic Law on the Management of State Economic Enterprises and Higher Economic Associations by the Work Collectives," more commonly known as the law on workers' self-management, which, as Daniel J. Goulding points out, became the second founding myth of the postwar Yugoslav state (after the National War of Liberation). This legislation introduced Tito's unique concept of a socialist market economy, in which ownership was neither solely private nor public, but rather administered for the state through a trusteeship of autonomous workers' councils. For the fledgling film industry, this meant the dissolution of the Committee for Cinematography and the formation of the Union of Film Workers of Yugoslavia (*Savez filmskih radnika Jugoslavije*), whose production groups were theoretically free to raise their own funds through distribution contracts, leasing and rental fees, coproduction royalties, and the like, just as in the West. In practice, however, the industry was too underdeveloped for these arrangements, and the new system did not get off the ground until the passage of the Basic Law of Film in 1956, which replaced state subsidies with a tax on film admission tickets (17–20 percent), the lion's share of which went to finance new production. This mode of self-finance (*samofinansiranja*) enabled the rate of domestic production to rise from six films per year through 1954 to fourteen films annually from 1957 through 1960. During the same period, admissions for domestic films more than tripled, and for foreign films (mainly American, owing to Tito's tempo-

---

* Partisan films are popular not only in Yugoslavia, where the term designates an actual political faction during the National War of Liberation, but all over the Balkans and in the Soviet Union, where they are sometimes referred to by English-speaking critics as "Easterns" (i.e., eastern Westerns). They tell action-packed stories of heroic resistance to fascism during World War II, usually focusing on a small band of young guerrilla fighters operating out of isolated areas in the countryside. American critics, unfamiliar with this genre, failed to notice that John Milius' *Red Dawn* (1985) was a domestic version of the Eastern European Partisan film in almost every detail, including its reactionary politics.

rary break with Moscow) doubled. Furthermore, nineteen coproductions had been undertaken by the end of the decade, many of them with Western countries,* including Helmut Käutner's *The Last Bridge* (*Die letzte Brücke,* 1954), Giuseppe De Santis' *A One-Year Trip* (*Cesta duga godinu dana,* 1958), Gillo Pontecorvo's *The Great Blue Road* (*Veliki plavi put,* 1958), and Claude Autant-Lara's *Thou Shalt Not Kill* (*Tu ne tueras point,* 1961).

For Yugoslav film itself, the fifties witnessed a move away from nationalist realism and an expansion in the range of subject matter and genres. There were successful comedies, such as the Czech emigré director František Čap's *Vesna* (1953), and the debut of Yugoslavia's first woman director Soja Jovanović (b. 1922) with *Father Círa and Father Spira* (*Pop Círa i pop Spira,* 1957), the country's first color feature and winner of the first prize at the Pula Festival (inaugurated 1953 to showcase all new Yugoslav features). Literary-historical films—like Fedor Hanžeković's (b. 1913) version of Simo Matavulji's 1892 story *Monk Brne's Pupil* (*Bakonja Fra Brne,* 1951) and his adaptation of Slavko Kolar's play *Master of One's Own Body* (*Svoga tela gospodar,* 1956)—were also popular, as were the action-adventure films of the Serbian director Živorad Mitrović (b. 1921)—*Echelon of Dr. M* (*Ešalon Doktora M,* 1955), and *Captain Leši* (*Kapetan Leši,* 1960); the children's films of the Slovenian Jože Gale (b. 1913)—*Kekec,* 1951 (first prize in its category, Venice, 1952)—and those of the Croatian Branko Bauer (b. 1921)—*Grey Seagull* (*Sinji galeb,* 1953) and *Millions on an Island* (*Milijuni na otoku,* 1955). Yugoslavia's revolutionary past was by no means ignored, but it began to be treated with a new realism in such Partisan films as Radoš Novaković's (b. 1915) *The Sun Is Far Away* (*Daleko je sunce,* 1953), Vladimir Pogačić's *Big and Small* (*Veliki i mali,* 1956) and *Alone* (*Sam,* 1959), and the Serbian director Stole Janković's two-part *Partisan Stories* (*Partizanske priče,* 1960). Two films of Ustashi-occupied Zagreb—Branko Bauer's *Don't Turn Around, My Son* (*Ne okreći se, sine,* 1956) and the Slovenian France Štiglic's *The Ninth Circle* (*Deveti krug,* 1960)—also tapped the realistic vein, while Pogačić's anthology film *On Saturday Evening* (*Subotom uveče,* 1957) dealt in similar fashion with contemporary life. The direct influ-

16.115 *The Ninth Circle* (France Štiglic, 1960).

---

* Like southern California, Yugoslavia boasts a richly varied topography and has long been a favored site for foreign production and coproduction (one of the reasons, in fact, that the country was so long in developing an authentic national cinema). Within the space of 98,766 square miles—approximately the size of Wyoming—there are the alpine regions of Slovenia; the wooded farmlands of south Serbia; the plains of the Voivodina; the beautiful Adriatic coastline of Croatia; and, in Macedonia, areas reminiscent of the Pacific Northwest. Furthermore, as in other Eastern European countries, professional salaries and shooting costs are low by Western standards. Well-known "Western" films shot in Yugoslavia in whole or in part include J. Lee Thompson's *The Guns of Navarone* (1961), Orson Welles' *The Trial* (1962), Brian G. Hutton's *Kelly's Heroes* (1971), Norman Jewison's *Fiddler on the Roof* (1971), Sam Peckinpah's *Cross of Iron* (1975), Volker Schlöndorff's *The Tin Drum* (1979), Alan J. Pakula's *Sophie's Choice* (1982), Brian G. Hutton's *High Road to China* (1983), Rudy De Luca's *Transylvania 6–5000* (1985), and Jim Kaufman's *Race to the Bomb* (1987); also the "American" telefilms *Mussolini* (1985), *Guts and Glory* (1985), *Winds of War* (1985), *Wallenberg* (1986), *Escape from Sobibor* (1987), and *War and Remembrance* (1987).

ence of Italian neorealism was perceptible in the work of the Croatian Veljko Bulajić (b. 1928)—*Train Without a Schedule* (*Vlak bez voznog reda*, 1959); *City in Ferment* (*Uzavreli grad*, 1961)—who had studied at the Centro Sperimentale with Zavattini and worked as an assistant to De Santis.

In the late fifties and early sixties, a movement toward formal experimentation began to coalesce around several institutions outside of the mainstream feature cinema. One was the specialized animation studio Zagreb Film, founded in 1953, where the Croatian writer-director Vatroslav Mimica (b. 1923) and the Montenegrin Dušan Vukotić (b. 1927) pioneered an abstract, whimsical style that won international acclaim for the Yugoslavian cinema in such films as the former's *Alone* (*Samac*—Festival Prize, Venice, 1958) and the latter's *Ersatz* (*Surogat*—American Academy Award, 1961;* the first ever for a foreign animated film). Another realm of modernist experimentation was that of the documentary and short film, with "schools" centered in Belgrade, Zagreb, and Sarajevo, where future feature directors like Puriśa Djordjević (b. 1924) and Aleksander Petrović (b. 1929) were trained. Finally, there was a strong Yugoslav amateur film movement organized by the country's leading film theorist Dušan Stojanović around the Belgrade ("Beograd") *kino klub*. It was in this context that future leaders of the *novi film* movement, such as Dušan Makavejev (b. 1932), Živojin Pavlović (b. 1933), and Boštjan Hladnik (b. 1929), made their first shorts.

Novi Film

In the sixties, the Yugoslav cinema experienced a further decentralization of its production activities as studios were established in the two autonomous regions of Vojvodina and Kosovo, and it entered into its most richly creative period. The annual rate of production in 1961 was thirty-three features, double that of the previous decade, and in the years 1967 to 1969 it reached its zenith, averaging thirty-five features each year. Many of these were made under the rubric of *novi film* ("new film," or "open film"), an avant-garde movement closely associated with the wider agitation toward the democratization of Yugoslav society known

---

* As Mira and Antonín Liehm point out (*The Most Important Art* [Berkeley: University of California Press, 1977], p. 250), the development of children's and animated films was the great success story of the nationalization of the Eastern European cinemas in the fifties. Having no relationship with contemporary social and political realities, these kinds of films enjoyed a special creative mandate even in the worst years of Stalinism. In addition to the work of the Zagreb school, one thinks in this connection of the films of Jan Lenica and Walerian Borowczyk in Poland, the puppet films of Jiří Trnka and the animated features of Karel Zeman in Czechoslovakia, the cartoons of the Hungarians Attila Dargay (b. 1927) and Marcell Jankovics (b. 1941), the work of Todor Dinov in Bulgaria, Ion Popescu-Gopo in Romania, and Alexander Ptushko in the Soviet Union—all of whom are discussed in the text. See Ronald Holloway, *Z Is for Zagreb* (Cranbury, N.J.: A. S. Barnes, 1972); Ralph Stephenson, *The Animated Film* (Cranbury, N.J.: A. S. Barnes, 1973); and Bruno Edera, *Full Length Animated Feature Films* (New York: Hastings House, 1977).

as the Second Yugoslav Revolution.* Though *novi film* lacked a specific set of aesthetic principles, its advocates had as their goals a) the liberation of the filmmaking process from bureaucratic constraints and ideological dogma, b) the promotion of experiments with film as an audiovisual language along the lines of the French and Czech new waves, and c) the use of film to examine contemporary themes (*savremene teme*)—when necessary, from a critical perspective. Innovative in terms of means, *novi film* conceived of its practice firmly within the context of a Marxist-Leninist state and was not intent upon political subversion. But officials of the League of Communists of Yugoslavia (LCY), the country's ruling (and only) party, initially saw things in a different light.

In the vanguard of *novi film* were Aleksander Petrović's *Two* (*Dvoje*, 1961) and Boštjan Hladnik's *A Dance in the Rain* (*Ples v dežju*, 1961), both of which dispensed with conventional narrative structure in favor of visual metaphor and dealt pessimistically with contemporary themes. Their second films—Petrović's *Days* (*Dani*, 1963) and Hladnik's *Sand Castle* (*Peščani grad*, 1962)—followed these trends even further and were banned from official showing at the 1963 Pula Festival. At the same time, *The City* (*Grad*, 1963), the second film of the Belgrade *kino klub* associates Živojin Pavlović, Kokan Rakonjac, and Marko Babac, was seized and impounded in Sarajevo for portraying "a meaningless view of life . . . reduced to physical, senseless lust" and for presenting "a Yugoslav town in such a negative light that it raises the question whether it is worthwhile to live there." The famous Belgrade painter Miča Popović (b. 1908) was forced to re-edit his darkly brilliant first feature, *Man from the Oak Forest* (*Čovek iz hrastove šume*, 1963), because it made a Chetnik shepherd its major protagonist and gave him a credible psychology; while *The Return* (*Povratak*, 1963), Živojin Pavlović's first independent feature, was shelved until 1966 for showing the indifference of Yugoslav society to the plight of a former convict.

But the tide began to turn at the 1965 Pula Festival, where Petrović's third film, *Three* (*Tri*), won first prize, Puriša Djordjević inaugurated his surrealist tetralogy on the Partisan war and its aftermath with *Girl* (*Devojka*), Dušan Makavejev made his feature debut with *Man Is Not a Bird* (*Čovek nije tica*), and Rakonjac's *Horn* (*Klakson*) and Pavlović's *The Enemy* (*Neprijatelj*) were both well received. As if to confirm *novi film*'s ascendency, July 1966 witnessed the triumph of the League of Communists' most liberal wing, when the conservative Aleksander Ranković—founder and chief of the State Security Service (O.Z.N.A.†), party

16.116 *Three* (Aleksander Petrović, 1965).

---

* As should be obvious by this point, all of the Eastern European countries experienced changes in the period from 1961 to 1967, as the Stalinist system disintegrated and individual states began to introduce economic and political reforms that redefined their relationship with the Soviet Union. The changes in Yugoslavia were nearly extreme enough to warrant the term revolution, since the party's liberal wing took control in 1966 and turned Yugoslavia into the Eastern bloc's most market-oriented country in less than five years.

† An acronym for *Odeljenje za zaštitu norodna*, "Department for the Protection of the People," organized by Ranković in 1944 and fundamentally Stalinist in character.

16.117 *I Even Met Happy Gypsies* (Aleksander Petrović, 1967).

16.118 *When I am Pale and Dead* (Živojin Pavlović, 1967).

16.119 *Morning* (Puriša Djordjević, 1967).

secretary, and chosen successor to Tito—was forced from office for attempting a political coup.

At its height, *novi film* activity was centered in the country's two largest production sites, Belgrade and Zagreb. At Belgrade, Petrović followed *Three*, his multi-episode revaluation of the sacrosanct War of National Liberation, with *I Even Met Happy Gypsies* (*Skupljači perja*, 1967), an unromanticized portrait of gypsy life in the Vojvodina region filmed with nonactors and an authentic multilingual soundtrack (of Serbo-Croatian, Romany, and Slovak), which shared the Grand Prix at Cannes*. His *It Rains in My Village* (*Biče skoro propast sveta*, 1969) was a collage of motifs inspired by Dostoevsky's *The Possessed*, a contemporary news story, and the Soviet invasion of Czechoslovakia; while *The Master and Margarita* (*Majstor i Margarita*, 1972) is an ambitious adaptation of the Russian Mikhail Bulgakov's fantastic anti-Stalinist novel, which also implicitly attacks reactionism within the LCY. Pavlović's most important "new films" were often dark and brutally naturalistic: *Awakening of the Rats* (*Budjenje pacova*, 1966) is an account of degradation among slum-dwellers in contemporary Belgrade; *When I am Pale and Dead* (*Kad budem mrtav i beo*, 1967) is a bitter comedy about a pop musician, the human detritus of forced industrialization; *The Ambush* (*Zaseda*, 1969), which was banned shortly after release, was a deeply controversial film set in a Serbian village during the worst postwar excesses of O.Z.N.A.; and *The Red Wheat* (*Rdeče klasje*, 1971) concerned the failures of postwar collectivization of agriculture. During this same period in Belgrade, Puriša Djordjević completed his stylized tetralogy on the War of Liberation and its aftermath with *Dream* (*San*, 1966), *Morning* (*Jutro*, 1967—Grand Prix, Venice), and *Noon* (*Podne*, 1968).

But the most widely acclaimed director to emerge from the Belgrade *novi film* group by far was the Serbian Dušan Makavejev, who might best be described as an avant-garde satirist of great intellect. The forms of his films are experimental, and their subject is sexual and social repression, which he sees as intimately related phenomena. *Man Is Not a Bird* (*Čovek nije tica*, 1966) is a satirical romantic comedy set against the backdrop of an east Serbian copper mine which evokes the dehumanization of the socialist worker through regimentation. In *An Affair of the Heart, or The Tragedy of the Switchboard Operator* (*Ljubavni slučaj ili tragedija službenice PTT*, 1967), a film about the relationship between social structures, love, and sex, Makavejev inaugurated experiments in free association which culminated in the remarkable cinematic essay *WR— The Mysteries of the Organism* (*WR—Misterije organizma*, 1971). In between, he made the remarkable montage piece *Innocence Unprotected* (*Nevinost bez žastite*, 1968), which juxtaposes excerpts from the first Serbian "all-talking" film, made clandestinely by circus strongman Dragoljub Aleksić during the Nazi occupation in 1942, with documentary footage from the period, animation, and interviews with members of the

---

* Western awareness of *novi film* was high, even extending to the United States where *Three* and *Happy Gypsies* were both nominated for Academy Awards in 1967.

16.120 *Man Is Not a Bird* (Dušan Makavajev, 1965).

original production crew. *WR,* clearly influenced by the work of Věra Chytilová in Czechoslovakia (see pp. 687–88), is a surrealist collage that applies the radical theories of the Austrian psychoanalyst Wilhelm Reich (1897–1957) critically to both capitalist decadence and socialist authoritarianism. Like Reich, Makavejev ultimately equates social and sexual repression. The film won several international awards, including the Luis Buñuel Prize at Cannes, but it was banned in Yugoslavia and eventually forced Makavejev's emigration to the West.

In Zagreb the most important *novi film* figure was the former animator Vatroslav Mimica, whose films of the era include the abstractionist *Prometheus from Vishevica Island* (*Prometje sa otoka Viševice,* 1964), *Monday or Tuesday* (*Ponedeljak ili utorak,* 1966), *The Event* (*Dogadjaj,* 1969), and *The Adoptee* (*Hranjenik,* 1971). Mimica's most powerful "new film," however, was the radically experimental *Kaja, I'll Kill You* (*Kaja, ubit ću te,* 1967), which uses the Italian occupation of a Dalmatian coastal town during World War II to examine the psychopathology of fascism. Another Zagreb-based filmmaker, the documentarist Krsto Papić (b. 1933), won international acclaim for his feature *Handcuffs* (*Lisice,* 1970) on the brutal and random purging of Stalinists (uncharacteristically portrayed as victims) in a small Croatian village just after Yugoslavia's explusion from the Cominform (Soviet bloc) in the summer of 1948; and the musician-turned-scriptwriter Zvonimir Berković (b. 1928) made an impressive feature debut with *Rondo* (1966), a portrait of a love triangle cinematically structured on the variations of a Mozart piece. By the end of the decade, in fact, the influence of *novi film* had reached well beyond Belgrade and Zagreb to the provinces. At the newly established Neoplanta Film at Novi Sad, for example, Želimir Žilnik (b. 1942) made the archetypal "new film" in his debut feature *Early Works* (*Rani radovi,* 1969), a radically Godardian reflection on Marx's own *Early Works,* which won the Golden Bear at Berlin but was banned from domestic distribution. (Želnik's sequel, *Das Kapital,* 1971, has never seen the light of day.) At Bosna Film in Sarajevo, the documentarist Bata Čengić (b. 1931) followed his controversial antiwar film *Little Soldiers* (*Mali vojnici,* 1968) with the ideological satires *The Role of My Family in the World Revolution* (*Uloga moje*

16.121 *An Affair of the Heart, or the Tragedy of the Switchboard Operator* (Dušan Makavejev, 1967): Milena Dravić.

16.122 Makavejev's *WR—The Mysteries of the Organism* (1971): Milena Dravić.

16.123 *WR:* Makavejev arranging Dravić's severed head(s).

porodice u svetskoj revoluciji, 1971) and *Scenes from the Life of a Shock Worker* (*Slike iz života udarnika,* 1972), the latter focused on the political absurdities and human tragedies of Yugoslavia's postwar industrialization campaign. And in Slovenia, at Ljubljana, the film critic and former Godard assistant Matjaž Klopčić (b. 1934) directed *On Wings of Paper* (*Na papirnatih avionih,* 1967), a film about the transience of contemporary media and modern love.

Between 1969 and 1972, however, political events conspired to turn the tide against *novi film*. The June 1968 student demonstrations in Belgrade had alarmed Yugoslav authorities, and the Warsaw Pact invasion of Czechoslovakia in August had chastened them. More frightening yet, the Croatian nationalist-separatist movement erupted into anti-government terrorism in 1971, when Tito was 79 and still without a chosen successor. These circumstances pushed the League of Communists to the right once more and resulted in a purge of nonorthodox Marxists. Makavejev was expelled from the party and forced into exile in Paris; Petrović was dismissed from his faculty position at the film academy for "extreme political negligence" and also emigrated to France; Pavlović was similarly dismissed but reinstated without rank the following year. The term "new film" was officially replaced with "black film" (after a polemical essay by Vladimír Jovičić entitled "The Black Wave in Our Film" in *Borba,* the central daily of the LCY, in 1969) to condemn the movement's socially negative qualities, and ideologically unconventional films, such as Pavlović's *The Ambush* and Žilnik's *Early Works,* were once again seized and banned or drastically recut. The Twentieth National Pula Festival in 1973 told the tale: the awards were dominated by Stipe Delić's *Sutjeska,* a three-hour widescreen Partisan epic harking back to the days of nationalist realism that starred Richard Burton as Marshal Tito.

The "black film" counteroffensive was led by centrists rather than reactionaries and was in no way as brutal as, for example, the purge of the Czechoslovak New Wave following the Prague Spring. Nevertheless, the Yugoslav film industry was damaged by the crisis, and the period from 1973 to 1977 experienced the lowest annual rates of production since the early sixties, averaging fewer than eighteen films per year. Amidst a generally listless return to the time-honored genres of the heroic Partisan film, action-adventure, and light comedy, there were beacons of hope in Krsto Papić's *A Village Performance of Hamlet* (*Predstava Hamleta a selu Mrduša Donja,* 1973), adapted from Ivo Brešan's pungently satirical play; Pavlović's *The Flight of a Dead Bird* (*Let mrtve ptice,* 1974), a tale of rural decay filmed in northeast Slovenia; and Djordjević's *Pavle Pavlović* (1975), a satire on bureaucratic corruption that was banned from the Pula Festival even though Tito publicly defended it.

The "Prague Group"

Yugoslavian cinema did not make a real comeback until the late seventies and early eighties, when a new course was charted by five young

16.124 *Special Treatment* (Goran Paskaljević, 1980).

directors known as the "Prague Group" because they had all studied at FAMU in the years of the "black film" counterattack. As the Yugoslav heirs of Forman, Menzel, Passer, and Chytilová, the members of the Prague Group practice a kind of absurdist social satire, without the confrontational politics of their *novi film* predecessors. They have also formed the kind of close collaborative relationship among themselves and other young Yugoslav filmmakers that once characterized the French New Wave, and have won large domestic audiences and many international awards.

The members of the original Prague Group are the directors Goran Paskaljević (b. 1947), Goran Marković (b. 1946), Lordan Zafranović (b. 1944), Rajko Grlić (b. 1947), and Srđan Karanović (b. 1945), as well as the cinematographers Živko Zalar, Vilko Filač, and Miodrag Popovič. Paskaljević's most critically successful and popular films have been *The Beach Guard in Winter* (*Čuvar plaže u zimskom periodu,* 1976); *The Dog Who Liked Trains* (*Pas koji je voleo vozove,* 1978); *The Days Are Passing* (*Zemaljski dani teku,* 1979); and *Special Treatment* (*Poseban tretman,* 1980). More recently, his *Deceptive Summer of '68* (*Varljivo leto,* 1984) provides a deftly comic treatment of a Yugoslav student's sexual initiation by a young Czech girl in the latter days of Alexander Dubček's Prague Spring. The film, an *hommage* to FAMU, is deliberately evocative of both Forman's *Black Peter* (1963) and Menzel's *Closely Watched Trains* (1966). *Guardian Angel* (*Andjeo čuvar,* 1987; written and produced by the director), on the other hand, is a horrifying documentary-style exposé of the traffic in gypsy children between Yugoslavia and Italy, where they are exploited as virtual slaves. Marković is best known for his fast-paced comedies about contemporary Yugoslav youth in such films as *Special Education* (*Specijalno vaspitanje,* 1977—First Prize, Mannheim Festival), *National Class up to 26 Feet* (*Nacionalna klasa do 785 cm,* 1979), and *Teachers, Teachers* (*Majstori, majstori,* 1981), all bearing the marked influence of the Czech New Wave. His *Variola Vera* (1982—First Prize, Valencia Festiva) is a dark satire about the incompetence of medical and public-health officials during an outbreak of the fatal strain of smallpox named in the title, while *Taiwan Canasta* (*Tajvanska kanasta,* 1985) is an ironic comedy about an aging hippie unable to find a place in a society that, he feels, has betrayed his youthful idealism. *Déja Vu* (*Veo Videno*), winner of the Pula Festival's 1987 Grand Prix, is a stylish psychological thriller in the Hitchcock mode.

Lordan Zafranović is the most visionary filmmaker of the Prague Group, as demonstrated by his *Occupation in Twenty-Six Scenes* (*Okupacija u 26 slika,* 1978—First Prize, Pula Festival). This poetic re-creation of the Italian occupation of the ancient coastal city of Dubrovnik evokes the graciousness of prewar bourgeois life as well as the brutal smashing of that order by the Fascists and their bestial Ustashi collaborators. Zafranović's next film, which also won a Pula First Prize, was similarly concerned with the effects of the war on his native Dalmation coast and appeared to be the second work in a trilogy on the subject: *Fall of Italy* (*Pad Italije,* 1981; English title: *Island Chronicle*) is a stylized and often grimly beautiful account of Partisan fighting and Italian reprisals on a small Adriatic island. *Evening Bells* (*Večernja zvona,* 1986) is an adaptation of Mirko Kovać's prize-winning novel of the crucible of Yugoslavia's civil war; Zafranović won the director's award at Pula for it in the year of its release. Rajko Grlić's *Bravo Maestro* (1978), on the other hand, is set in the present and comments caustically on the rise of an ambitious young composer who manages to subvert the self-management system of the musical establishment by manipulating personal connections (*veze*), as so many contemporary Yugoslavs have learned to do. His next film, *The Melody Haunts My Revery* (*Samo jednom se ljubi,* 1981), whose English title translates a phrase from Hoagy Carmichael's popular forties song "Stardust," also has a political theme. It depicts the psychological disintegration of a dedicated young socialist leader under the pressures of Stalinism in a small Croatian village just after the war. No less philosophical, Grlić's *The Jaws of Life* (*U raljama života,* 1984) is a bittersweet comedy about the symbiotic relationship between a middle-aged woman filmmaker and the fictitious heroine of a television series she is directing. *Three's Happiness* (*Za sreću je pótrebno troje,* 1986), constructed around three overlapping love triangles, is also a witty comedy that won the Golden Palm at Valencia in 1986. More recently, Grlić directed the British-Yugoslav coproduction *The Summer of White Roses* (1989) about the delayed impact of World War II on an idyllic lakeside resort.

Šrđan Karanović is an important collaborator of Grlić's (the former FAMU classmates having reciprocated on each other's screenplays six times to date) and is a major Yugoslav director in his own right. His *The Scent of Wild Flowers* (*Miris poljskog cveća,* 1978), which shared the International Critics' Prize at Cannes, is a subtly ironic portrayal of an aging, world-famous actor who tries vainly to find some personal respite from the media's ravenous appetite for publicity, scandal, and "news." Considerably more dense and sober, *Petra's Wreath* (*Petrijin venac,* 1980—Director's Prize, Pula) is about the traumatized lifetime odyssey of an illiterate peasant before, during, and after the war, based on the experiences of a real woman. With *Something in Between* (*Nĕsto izmedju,* 1983), which took first prizes at both the Pula and Valencia festivals, Karanović

16.125 *Occupation in Twenty-Six Scenes* (**Lordan Zafranović, 1978**).

proved himself to be the leading intellectual filmmaker of his generation. Shot in English, with locations in New York, Belgrade, Dubrovnik, and Istanbul, this sophisticated comedy is on its surface about the whirlwind competition between two Yugoslav men, one a respected surgeon and the other a charming rogue, for the affections of an American female journalist on a six-week Eastern tour; on another level, however, the film is a social commentary on the contradictions inherent in Yugoslav daily life and the country's unique position "in between" East and West. More recently, Karanović has made *Caught in the Throat* (*Jagode u grlu,* 1985), a self-referential film about a reunion of the cast and crew of a thirteen-part serial he directed for Yugoslav television in 1974, and *Still Lacking a Good Title* (*Za sada bez dobrog naslova,* 1988), a multilevel satire about a TV crew attempting to document a contemporary Yugoslav-Albanian border incident, which intricately mixes film and video footage.

16.126 *Something in Between* (Srđan Karanović, 1983).

Closely associated with the Prague Group are the directors Miloš Radivojević, Bogdan Žižić, Slobodan Šijan (b. 1946), and Emir Kusturica (b. 1954). Radivojević's work tends toward the experimental and often deals with mental breakdown. His most significant films comprise an informal trilogy on the frustration of revolutionary idealism among the young: in *Breakdown* (*Kvar,* 1979) a successful television journalist comes apart when he realizes the false value system in which his career and his social life have become enmeshed; *Dreams, Life, and Death of Filip Filipović* (*Snovi, život, smrt Filipa Filipovića,* 1980) takes us into the mind of the first secretary of the Yugoslav Communist Party, who was killed in Stalin's purges in Russia in 1938, as he writes his memoirs while awaiting execution; and *Living Like the Rest of Us* (*Živeti kao sav normalan,* 1982) is a sharp satire on the elitist pretensions of contemporary students at the Belgrade Academy of Music when confronted with a working-class idealist as classmate. With *Una, My Love* (1986), Radivojević captured worldwide attention in a wildly erotic film about a sultry female student employed by the state to seduce her journalism professor and pump him for enough information to send him to jail. All of Radivojević's films are remarkably patterned in formal terms; *Filip Filipović,* for example, mixes archival period footage with distorted wide-angle images of the title character's reveries. Bogdan Žižić's reputation rests on two films with a single theme: the plight of exploited Yugoslav "guest-workers" (*Gastarbeiter*—immigrant blue-collar and service workers) in West Germany. *Don't Lean Out of the Window* (*Ne naginji se van,* 1977) is a fictional documentary on the wretched *demi-monde* of the provincial *Gastarbeiter* in Frankfurt, which won the Pula first prize; while *Early Snowfall in Munich* (*Rani snijeg u Münchenu,* 1984) portrays the cultural confusion of *Gastarbeiter* who have worked outside of Yugoslavia for so long that their sense of identity is divided between their native and their adoptive countries.

16.127 *Who's That Singing Over There?* (Slobodan Šijan, 1980).

Slobodan Šijan has become internationally famous for his black comedies of Serbian manners. *Who's That Singing Over There?* (*Ko to tamo peva?,* 1980) is an episodic account of a twenty-four-hour bus ride across the back roads of Serbia which delivers its passengers to Belgrade at the precise moment of the Nazi *blitzkrieg* on April 6, 1941, killing all aboard

16.128 *When Father Was Away on Business* (Emir Kusturica, 1985).

but two gypsies whose songs have connected the narrative. This film won prizes at Pula and Rotterdam, as well as France's coveted Georges Sadoul Award for best debut film by a foreign director. Šijan followed his success with *The Marathon Family* (*Maratonci trče počasni krug,* 1982), which deals in Formanesque fashion with a five-generation family of undertakers in the early thirties who must fight a gang war to maintain their ascendancy. More recently Šijan has produced *How I Was Systematically Destroyed by an Idiot* (*Kako sam sistematiski uništen od idiota,* 1983), a political satire about an aging revolutionary who becomes self-destructively involved in the 1968 student uprising at the University of Belgrade, and *Strangler vs. Strangler* (*Davitelja protiv davitelja,* 1984), a sophisticated *hommage* to Hitchcock's *Psycho* (1960), replete with allusions to other classics of the horror genre. But the rising star of Yugoslav cinema in the mid-eighties was clearly the Bosnian director Emir Kusturica, whose award-winning films *Do You Remember Dolly Bell?* (*Sjećaš li se Dolly Bell?,* 1981) and *When Father Was Away on Business* (*Otac na službenom putu,* 1985) have brought new prominence to Sarajevo as a production center. A recent graduate of FAMU (1978), where he studied under Jiří Menzel, Kusturica works in collaboration with the Bosnian poet Abdulah Sidran as screenwriter and the FAMU-trained Vilko Filač as cinematographer to mine a vein of ironic, even tragicomic, reminiscence from his region's recent past. *Dolly Bell,* which won the Golden Lion at Venice, for example, is an anecdotal story of a young boy's coming of age in a patriarchal Muslim family on the outskirts of Sarajevo in the early sixties; while *Father,* which won the Golden Palm Award at Cannes, assumes the perspective of an even younger child in the period 1947–52, when Tito had broken with Stalin and countless innocent Yugoslavs experienced arbitrary denunciation and imprisonment, in a Stalinist-style purge directed *against* suspected Stalinists. Like other films by members of the Prague Group and their associates discussed above, Kusturica's have been both critically successful and enormously popular with audiences at home and abroad (*Father,* for example, having done a brisk business in the United States and been nominated for an Academy Award for Best Foreign Film). Kusturica's *Time of the Gypsies* (*Dom za vesanje,* 1989), however, is much less mainstream than his earlier work in its poetic evocation of gypsy life and its occasionally experimental structure.

At the same time that the Prague Group and its followers were breathing new life into Yugoslav cinema and gaining great popularity with the domestic audience, many veterans of the *novi film* movement were forgiven their heresies and reintegrated with the mainstream industry. Among those who have returned are Puriša Djordjević (*Eight Kilos of Happiness* [*Osam kila sreće*, 1980]), Živojin Pavlović (*See You in the Next War* [*Nasvidenji u. naslednji vojni*, 1980]; *Body Scent* [*Zadah*, 1983]; *On the Road to Katanga* [*Na puta za Katangu*, 1987]), Vatroslav Mimica (*The Falcon* [*Banović Strahinja*, 1981]), Krsto Papić (*The Secret of Nikola Tesla* [*Tajna Nikole Tesle*, 1980]), Želimir Žilnik (*The Second Generation* [*Druga generacija*, 1983]; *Beautiful Women Walking About Town* [*Lijepe žene prolaze kroz grad*, 1986]), Bata Čengić (*Heads or Tails* [*Pismo-Glava*, 1983]), and Zvonimir Berković (*Love Letters with Intent* [*Ljubavna pisma s predumišljajem*, 1985]). Boštjan Hladnik returned indirectly through the 1983 release of his long shelved *Masquerade* (*Maskarada*, 1971), and Aleksander Petrović, who devotes himself now mainly to directing live theater, reappeared briefly to collaborate with Mimica on the screenplay for *The Falcon* (1981). Of the major *novi film* directors, only Dušan Makavejev has not participated in his country's cinema since the "black film" counteroffensive of the early seventies; all of his subsequent films were made abroad, until 1988.

Sweet Movie (1974), for example, was shot on location in the United States and Western Europe. Like *WR*, it uses the strategies of free association and, more especially, the manipulation of alternately attractive and repellent images to counterpose American commodity fetishism with the decadence of the Marxist ideal. Although it acquired a reputation for scandal, the film was a critical and commercial failure, and Makavejev has had difficulty funding his productions ever since. One effect has been to push him in the direction of more conventional narrative form, as the Swedish-British coproduction *Montenegro / Pigs and Pearls* (1981) demonstrates. Shot with English dialogue, the film concerns an American-born Swedish housewife (Susan Anspach), neglected by her businessman husband, who escapes into a world of anarchistic sexual pleasure at the Zanzibar, an underground club for transplanted Montenegrins in Stockholm. This linear plot contrasts sharply with an elaborate montage structure featuring graphic closeups of sexual activity and nudity in motion, plus Makavejev's characteristic psychoanalytic equation of violence, sex, blood, and death. Similarly, the Australian-financed *Coca-Cola Kid* (1985), a decade in preparation and two years in production, mixes eroticism and social satire with a more or less conventional plot: a corporate troubleshooter is sent from Atlanta to a remote part of Australia to discover why Coca-Cola sales have dried up and finds that a local land baron has enforced his own soft drink monopoly on the populace. The ensuing feud between the parties counterposes American and Australian attitudes toward everything from politics to sex (always equated in Makavejev, of course) and ends in a merger. Makavejev was an invited guest at the Pula Festival in 1982, and in 1988 he made his first film in Yugoslavia for twenty years, although it was produced by the American-based Cannon Group. Shot on location in the beautiful Slovenian village of Skofja Loka and adapted from a story by Zola, *Manifesto* (1988) is a comedy of political intrigue set in an unnamed central European country in 1920, and like all of Makavejev's work, it is ultimately about the relationship between sex and revolution.

Lacking the distinguished national traditions of Poland, Czechoslovakia, and Hungary, the Yugoslav cinema was spontaneously generated in the postwar era to become over the next several decades one of the most unusual in all of Eastern Europe. Not a little of its success was owed the vision of Josip Tito, who not only echoed Lenin on the importance of film for socialist society, saying, "Film is one of the most influential means of modern communication and its social, moral, and educational role is, therefore, great," but was himself an avid film buff who saw every feature film made in his country in his lifetime. His death on April 5, 1980, was mourned very specifically as a loss for Yugoslav cinema as well as for the country at large. It was Tito's vision that gave Yugoslavia its unique concept of worker self-management, which has meant for the film industry a level of autonomy and competition among its now twenty-seven production companies that very nearly resembles the American system.* Unlike Poland, Czechoslovakia, and Hungary, for example, where state subsidies guarantee the careers of critically successful filmmakers even when the box office doesn't, Yugoslavia must generate the lion's share of its film financing from the domestic audience. So it has been an event of major importance that the films of the Prague Group and its associates have managed to outdistance first-run American films at the Yugoslav box office in every year since 1978. In the years of their release, in fact, Karanović's *Something in Between* (1983) and Kusturica's *When Father Was Away on Business* (1985) outsold their nearest American competitors in the urban centers by three to one. At the same time, Yugoslavia Film—the national association of Yugoslav producers, distributors, and exhibitors—plans to mount an aggressive marketing campaign to ensure widespread distribution of its films to the West. There is little question that the world can expect both superb entertainment and critical distinction from the Yugoslav cinema for years to come.

BULGARIA

Some fifty-five feature films were produced in Bulgaria in the thirty-five years before Boris Borozanov's *Kalin the Eagle* (*Kalin Orelat*, 1950) appeared as the first fiction film of the recently nationalized film industry. Most of these films—such as Vassil Gendov's *Bai Ganiu* (1922), Nicolai Larin's *Under the Old Sky* (*Pod staroto nebe*, 1922), Peter Stoichev's

---

* An important difference, of course, is that salaries (and, therefore, production costs) are very low by American standards, with maximums ranging from two thousand dollars for writing a screenplay to ten thousand dollars for directing a film.

Land (*Zemia*, 1930) and *Song of the Mountains* (*Planinska pesen*, 1934), Alexander Vasov's *Cairn* (*Gramada*, 1936), and Iosip Novak's *Strahil the Voivoda* (*Strahil voivoda*, 1938)—were based on the rich literature of the Bulgarian National Revival which had occurred in the nineteenth century and reached its pinnacle with the country's liberation from nearly five hundred years of Turkish rule in 1876. Also notable were the films of Boris Grezhov—especially *Maiden Rock* (*Momina skala*, 1923), *After the Fire over Russia* (*Sled Pozhara v Russia*, 1929), and *Graves without Crosses* (*Beskrastini grobove*, 1931), the last a controversial elegy for the victims of the White Terror of 1923 and Bulgaria's first sound film—as well as the weekly newsreels of the Bulgarsko Dělo company, founded 1939, the organization that would later give birth to the anti-Fascist Resistance.

Bulgaria entered World War II on the side of the Germans in 1941 but, when defeated by the Soviet Union on September 10, 1944, became one of that country's staunchest allies. The Bulgarians and the Russians have always been close, owing to their shared Orthodox religion and Byzantine cultural heritage; furthermore, Russia helped to liberate Bulgaria from the Turks by joining its war of independence against the Ottoman Empire in 1876—an act precipitating the Russo-Turkish War of 1877–78. A People's Republic was established following World War II on September 15, 1946, and the film industry was nationalized in 1948. As noted above, the first official feature film of the new state was *Kalin the Eagle*, a wedding of traditional Bulgarian patriotism and Zhdanovian socialist realism in which an exiled *haiduk* turned freedom fighter returns to his homeland after the expulsion of the Turkish overlords to find his people newly oppressed by foreign capitalists. The second and more important film, *Alarm* (*Trevoga*, 1951), was the first feature of the well-known cinematographer and documentarist Zahari Zhandov (b. 1911). Scripted by Anzhel Vagenstein (b. 1922), a recent graduate of the Moscow State Film School (VGIK), this film was a semidocumentary story of the division of political loyalties within a single Bulgarian family during the last days of World War II. Zhandov and Vagenstein also collaborated on *Septembrists* (*Septemvriytsi*, 1954), an historically researched account of the 1923 uprising against the monarchy of King Ferdinand that generated the White Terror. Other landmarks of the era were Dako Dakovski's (1919–62) *Under the Yoke* (*Pod igoto*, 1952), an ambitious adaptation of a classic novel by the Bulgarian national poet Ivan Vazov that is set just before the 1876 rebellion; Todor Dinov's (b. 1919) *Brave Marko* (1953; released 1955), the first cartoon from the newly reorganized animation and puppet studio in Sofia; and the Russian director Sergei Vasiliev's *The Heroes at Shipka Pass* (*Geriote na Shipka*, 1955), a coproduction with the Soviet Union depicting an heroic battle from the Russo-Turkish War. By 1957, the new Bulgarian film industry had produced a total of twenty-six features, no small accomplishment for an enterprise that began in 1950 with (by Zahari Zhandov's account) two or three Arriflex cameras, antiquated sound equipment, and few laboratories or theaters.

A major turning point for Bulgarian cinema was Rangel Vulchanov's

16.129 *On a Small Island* (Rangel Vulchanov, 1958).

16.130 *We Were Young* (Binka Zheliazkova, 1961).

(b. 1928) *On a Small Island* (*Na malkiia ostrov,* 1958), scripted by the poet Valeri Petrov (b. 1920) and shot in thirty days by Dimo Kolarov (b. 1924) on the Black Sea island of Saint Anastasia. Set just after the September 1923 uprising, when the island was used as a prison camp for suspected rebels, the film describes the doomed escape attempt of four individuals—a fisherman, a student, a carpenter, and a doctor—who represent a cross-section of Bulgarian society and become in the film's stylization a metaphor for the destiny of the country as an independent state. The production team for *Island*—Vulchanov, Petrov, Kolarov, and the composer Simeon Pironkov (b. 1927)—made two more features to form a trilogy epitomizing the style of "poetic realism" then entering the Bulgarian cinema. This movement had affinities with French poetic realism and Italian neorealism but was more formally experimental than either of them, as demonstrated by *First Lesson* (*Parvi urok,* 1960), a tragic tale of young love set during the Resistance, and *Sun and Shadow* (*Slansteto i syankata,* 1962), which won a number of international awards. *Sun and Shadow* is an abstract statement on the cultural paranoia induced by living under the constant threat of a nuclear war between East and West. Another important film of the era was the German Democratic Republic–Bulgarian coproduction *Stars* (*Zvezdi / Sterne,* 1959), directed by the East German Konrad Wolf (1925–82) with the assistance of Rangel Vulchanov and written by Wolf's former VGIK classmate Anzhel Vagenstein. This extraordinary film about a love that grows between a German soldier and a Jewish girl during a transport to Auschwitz won the Special Jury Prize at Cannes in the year of its release and called world attention to the dynamic potential of Bulgarian cinema, as did Binka Zheliazkova's (b. 1923) *We Were Young* (*A biiahme mladi,* 1961), scripted by her husband Hristo Ganev (b. 1924).* Like Vulchanov, a graduate of the Sofia Academy of Dramatic Art,† Zheliazkova was the first woman director in the Balkans, and her feature debut was a lyrical story of love among Sofia Resistance fighters composed in the style of modern Bulgarian pictorial art.

Though it won a Gold Medal at the Moscow Festival, *When We Were Young* was criticized at home, and Zheliazkova didn't make another film for six years. Vulchanov, whose *Sun and Shadow* had also been attacked in Bulgaria (for "abstract humanism"), next carried poetic realism into the realm of *film noir* in two complicated psychological thrillers, *The Inspector and the Night* (*Inspektorat i noshta,* 1963) and *The She-Wolf* (*Valchitsata,* 1965), both admired at Cannes. Vulchanov then journeyed to North Africa to make the documentary *Between Two Shores* (*Mezhdu*

---

* An earlier Zheliazkova-Ganev collaboration, *Partisans / Life Flows Quietly By* (*Partizani / Zhivostat si teche tiho,* 1958), was officially suppressed due to its controversial subject of political careerism among former Partisan heroes. It has not been released to this day and remains a rare, though hardly unique, instance of state censorship of the Bulgarian film industry since the thaw of the late sixties.

† The Academy of Dramatic Art in Sofia maintained a small film department in one of its wings as the only domestic source of professional training until the establishment of the Sofia Film and Television Academy (VITIS) in 1973.

16.131 *The Peach Thief* (Vulo Radev, 1964).

dva briaga, 1967), and he settled briefly in Czechoslovakia where he made three films, the Czechoslovakian–Bulgarian historical tract *Aesop* (*Ezop,* 1968; released 1969) among them, before returning to Bulgaria in 1970. The pinnacle of poetic realism was reached in the directorial debut of the cinematographer Vulo Radev (b. 1923), *The Peach Thief* (*Kradetsut na praskovi,* 1964), a romantic story about a love triangle among a Bulgarian officer, his wife, and a Serbian POW set in the ancient fortress city of Turnovo during World War I and distinguished by its lush visual imagery. Radev practiced the same lyrical style in *Tsar and General* (*Tsar i general,* 1966), Bulgaria's first widescreen historical epic, which presents the conflict between King Boris III and General Zaimov, who heroically attempted to prevent the country's entry into World War II on the side of the Axis.

Zheliazkova returned to directing with the extraordinary *The Attached Balloon* (*Privarzaniiat balon,* 1966; released 1967), adapted by Zheliazkova and the brilliant satirist Iordan Radichkov from his own novella. Like its source, the film is an absurdist fantasy about a military dirigible that drifts into the vicinity of an isolated peasant village during World War II. The villagers see the balloon as a magical source of escape from their wretched daily lives and attempt to fly away in it, only to discover that it is tethered as firmly to the earth as they themselves are. Full of black humor and sardonic allusions to Stalinism, the film was released a year late and then quietly shelved, although it was transformed into a successful stage play entitled *Attempt to Fly* (after Radichkov's original) a decade later and presented at the Bulgarian Drama and Theater Festival in Sofia to great acclaim in 1979.

The cultural thaw that made such turnabouts possible occurred in Bulgaria much later than in other Eastern bloc countries, where its beginnings can generally be said to date from Khrushchev's "de-Stalinization" speech to the Twentieth Congress of the CPSU in February 1956. That year in Bulgaria, by contrast, Stalinist premier Vulko Chervenkov lost his title to one of his own lieutenants (Anton Iugov) and was made minister of culture, from which position he became the scourge of the intelligentsia and continued to control the government. His chief opponent, the more moderate Todor Zhivkov, had to bide his time as first secretary of

16.132 *Sidetrack* (Grisha Ostrovski and Todor Stoianov, 1967): Nevena Kokanova.

16.133 *Iconostasis* (Todor Dinov and Hristo Hristov, 1969).

16.134 *Iconostasis:* Dimiter Tashev.

the Communist Party of Bulgaria, until he was able to become premier himself in 1962, purge Chervenkov, and move cautiously, like Khrushchev, toward a policy of gradual reform. Even so, the new president of the Bulgarian Writers' Union proclaimed as late as 1964 the validity of Zhdanovian socialist realism, and it was not until the late sixties that signs of a real cultural thaw began to emerge in such films as Grisha Ostrovski and Todor Stoianov's *Sidetrack* (*Otklonenie,* 1967), Metodi Andonov's *The White Room* (*Bialata staia,* 1968), Georgi Stoianov's *Birds and Greyhounds* (*Ptitsi i hratki,* 1969), and Todor Dinov and Hristo Hristov's *Iconostasis* (*Ikonostasat,* 1969).

Ostrovski (b. 1918) and Todor Stoianov's (b. 1930)* *Sidetrack,* scripted by the poet Blaga Dimitrova, received international attention as the first Bulgarian film to deal openly with the Stalinist past. It is constructed as a series of Resnais-like flashbacks triggered by a chance meeting between two former lovers and party comrades, although its ultimate stylistic allegiance is to Antonioni. Andonov's (1932–74) *The White Room* focused on the dilemma of a nondogmatic scientist during the same era. Georgi Stoianov (b. 1939, Moscow), a 1964 graduate of the Institut des Hautes Études Cinématographiques (IDHEC) in Paris, founded by Marcel L'Herbier in 1943 (see Chapter 13), used elements of lyricism and grotesque black humor in *Birds and Greyhounds* to treat the subject of a group of young Partisans on trial for their lives in a small Bulgarian village during World War II. The high-water mark of Bulgarian cinema of the late sixties, however, was *Iconostasis,*† directed in 1969 by the distinguished animator Todor Dinov and by Hristo Hristov (b. 1926), recently graduated from the VGIK. Set at the height of the Bulgarian Renaissance, near the end of the Turkish occupation, this national epic has its literary source in Dimiter Talev's novel *The Iron Candlestick* (published 1952), but it also bears the obvious influences of Tarkovski's *Andrei Rublev* (1966) and Parajanov's *Shadows of Forgotten Ancestors* (1964). Filmed by Atanas Tasev in widescreen in austere black and white,** *Iconostasis* recounts the life, dreams, and visions of a late-nineteenth-century iconostasis wood-carver who draws upon the depth and breadth of the national folk culture for his inspiration.

The year of the release of *Iconostasis* marked the twenty-fifth anniversary of the Bulgarian People's Republic (BPR). Within that period its cinema had produced 160 features, 1,003 documentaries, 1,164 popular science films, and 144 cartoons. The number of theaters had increased exponentially from 165 in 1944 to 2,900, while total attendance had

---

* Among its other distinctions, *Sidetrack* was the first feature of its co-directors—Ostrovski was a gifted state director at the Sofia Satirical Theater and Stoianov a veteran cinematographer (for example, *The Peach Thief*). Despite the film's success, Ostrovski never worked in the cinema again, and Stoianov returned to directing only sporadically.

† An iconostasis is the elaborately decorated screen dividing the sanctuary from the laity in Eastern Orthodox churches. For Bulgarians, especially, the iconostasis has deep ritual and cultural significance.

** Color did not become general in Bulgarian cinema until 1973.

leaped from 13 million to over 100 million per year. The annual production rate had risen to fourteen features and two hundred shorts. As if to accelerate this progress, in 1971 a new general director was appointed for the Bulgarian State Cinematography Corporation in the person of Pavel Pisarev, who reorganized it into three independent production units (Haemus, Mladost [Youth], and Sredets, 1973–74, with a fourth, Suvremenik [Contemporary], added in 1978–79) and saw to the establishment of a Film and Television Academy in Sofia (VITIS) in 1973. In 1972 Vulchanov was named Honored Artist of the BPR, and Zheliazkova was permitted to make her first film in six years with *The Last Word* (*Poslednata duma,* 1973), a story of six women in a death cell awaiting execution for activities in the anti-Fascist Resistance. Obviously, things were poised for change.

The next breakthrough was the stunning box-office success of Metodi Andonov's *The Goat Horn* (*Koziiat rog,* 1972), which was seen by over 3 million Bulgarians in the year of its release. This revenge tragedy adapted by Nikolai Hatov from his own short story, was set in the seventeenth century when *haiduks* conducted a kind of guerrilla warfare against the occupying Turks. Nationalism was also a key element in Hristo Hristov's *Hammer or Anvil* (*Nakovalnia ili chuk,* 1972), a large-scale Soviet–East German–Bulgarian epic on the infamous Leipzig trial of Georgi Dmitrov, the Bulgarian patriot accused of setting the Reichstag fire in 1933. Other significant works of 1972 were Liudmil Kirkov's (b. 1933) satire on provincial life, *A Boy Becomes a Man* (*Momcheto si otiva*), the first of a two-part series scripted by the humorist Georgi Mishev (the second is *Don't Go Away* [*Ne si otivai,* 1976]); Georgi Stoianov's omnibus science fiction film (Bulgaria's first), *The Third Planet from the Sun* (*Treta sled slantseto*); and Liudmil Staikov's (b. 1937) feature debut, *Affection* (*Obich*), a film about the generation gap that probed the surface of contemporary Bulgarian society and won a Gold Medal at the Moscow Festival in 1973. But by far the most significant film to proceed from the reorganization was Hristov's *The Last Summer* (*Posledno liato*), completed in 1972 but

16.135 *The Goat Horn* (Metodi Andonov, 1972).

16.136 *Hare Census* (Eduard Zahariev, 1973).

not released until 1974. Adapted by Iordan Radichkov from his novel of the same title, it concerns the fate of a peasant who refuses to leave his home when his valley is evacuated for submersion as part of an industrial dam project. Widely admired as an avatar of Bulgarian surrealism, the film employs stream-of-consciousness techniques and fantasy sequences to evoke both the protagonist's private crisis and the submersion of traditional village life by the tide of modern progress.

In 1973, a new generation of filmmakers announced itself to the world in the first major work of Ivan Terziev (b. 1934), Eduard Zahariev (b. 1938, Moscow), and Georgi Djulgerov (b. 1943). Terziev's *Men Without Work* (*Mazhe bez rabota*) inaugurated a series of films about the ethical problems of workers and productivity in a socialist economy, of which Terziev's own *Strong Water* (*Silna voda*, 1975) and Todor Andreikov's *Sunday Games* (*Nedelnite machove*, 1975) were the most immediate successors. Zahariev's *Hare Census* (*Prebroiavane na divite zaitsi*), written in collaboration with Georgi Mishev, achieved a milestone for Bulgarian cinema in its absurdist satire of socialist bureaucracy: it recounts the story of an official statistician who is inexplicably sent to survey the number of hares near a small village, and it won several international awards. In *And the Day Came* (*I doide deniat*), Georgi Djulgerov inverted the standard formula for the "Eastern" (for Eastern Europeans, a Hollywood-style Western with a Resistance setting) to show Partisan warfare as it had really been—unheroic, inglorious, and tragically wasteful of the members of the "lost generation" who had waged it.

In 1974 and 1975, another problem endemic to Bulgarian society—and that of other Eastern European countries since World War II—became the subject of important films. This was the rapid migration of peasants from villages to towns and the radical changes imposed by urbanization on traditional ways of life. Hristov's *A Tree without Roots* (*Darvo bez koren*, 1974), Kirkov's *Peasant on a Bicycle* (*Selianinat s koleloto*, 1974), and Asen Shopov's *Eternal Times* (*Vechni vremena*, 1975) were all "migration films," but the most successful internationally was Zahariev and Mishev's *Villa Zone* (*Vilna zona*, 1975), a biting satire on the new urban class and its materialist values in the tale of a socially ambitious couple from the country trying to improve their status by giving a garden party. The actor and animator Ivan Andonov's (b. 1934) debut, *Fairy Dance* (*Samodivsko horo*, 1976), also written by Mishev, treated similar themes in its send-up of the art world and provincial consumerism. The other important films of 1976 dealt with historical subjects (for example, Borislav Sharaliev's *The Apostles* [*Apostolite*], commemorating the rebels who led the April 1876 uprising against the Turks; Liudmil Staikov's *Amendment to the Defense-of-State Act* [*Dopalnenie kam Zakona za zashtita*], a reconstruction of the terrorist bombing of Sofia's Holy Sunday Cathedral during a state funeral in 1925, written by Anzhel Vagenstein), or were *auteur* films (Hristov's metaphysical science fiction parable *Cyclops* [*Tsiklopat*], which he also wrote and designed,* and Georgi Sto-

16.137 *Villa Zone* (Eduard Zahariev, 1975).

---

* Hristov frequently writes his own screenplays, designs his own sets, and directs his films as complete artistic units.

ianov's *A Cricket in the Ear* [*Shturets v uhoto*], a sort of Bulgarian *Waiting for Godot*).

It was during the 1977–78 season that Bulgarian cinema achieved an international profile that rivaled that of its Eastern-bloc neighbors. Eight films that won major festival awards appeared in this time frame, announcing a new artistic maturity for Bulgarian film. In its story of a conman during the Stalinist era, Georgi Djulgerov's *Advantage* (*Avantazh*, 1977), scripted by Djulgerov and photographed by Radoslav Spasov, contained more information about national political history than any Bulgarian film ever made. It compares favorably with Pal Gabor's *Angi Vera* and took the Silver Bear for Direction at Berlin in 1978. Eduard Zahariev's *Manly Times* (*Muzhki vremena*, 1977), a Gold Medal winner at Teheran, was adapted by Nikolai Haitov from an ancient legend and brilliantly shot by Radislav Spasov on location in the Rhodophe Mountains. It tells the story of a peasant girl kidnapped for a rich suitor by a *haiduk;* she falls in love with her abductor during the course of their arduous journey across the mountains—with tragic results. Binka Zheliazkova's *The Swimming Pool* (*Basseinat*, 1977) was her first collaboration with her husband, the screenwriter Hristo Ganev, since *We Were Young* in 1961, and it won a Gold Medal at Moscow for its Proustian story of memories from the Stalinist past called up by a gathering of former friends and comrades around a luxurious swimming pool. Also reunited was the team of Vulchanov and Petrov (formerly of *Sun and Shadow*, 1962) for *With Love and Tenderness* (*S liubov i nezhnost*, 1978), a sophisticated study of a sculptor living in self-imposed exile on an island in the Black Sea.

Other important films were Ivan Nichev's (b. 1940) *Stars in Her Hair, Tears in Her Eyes* (*Zvezdi v kosite, salzi v ochite*, 1977), an affectionate but historically accurate account of an itinerant theater troupe during the height of the Bulgarian National Revival at the turn of the century, which was written by Anzhel Vagenstein and took a prize at the Anitalia Festival; and Georgi Stoianov's *Pantelei* (1978), a satire reminiscent of Pinter (or Chaplin) about a political innocent who loses his identification papers and is drawn into the murderous Partisan uprising of 1944—on both sides. Liudmil Kirkov's *Matriarch* (*Matriarhat*, 1977), scripted by Georgi Mishev, deals with a village collective inhabited exclusively by women whose men have been forced to seek industrial work in distant towns. (This increasingly common social problem was also the subject of *Agronomists,* made the same year by the distinguished documentarist Hristo Kovachev [b. 1929], which won the Golden Dove at Leipzig in 1978.) Stefan Dimitrov's *Hark to the Cock!* (*Chui petela!*, 1978) treats a similar theme in its portrait of old people in an abandoned village, while Ivan Andonov's *The Roof* (*Pokriv*, 1978) is a bittersweet love story that also analyzes the booming black market in illegally procured construction materials. The season was capped by Georgi Djulgerov's *Swap* (*Trampa*, 1978), a structurally complex drama about an eminent writer's return to the provincial town whose collectivization he had covered for Radio Sofia during the postwar years; the journey triggers flashbacks to the Bulgarian Stalinist past and his own participation in it, using actual newsreel foot-

16.138 *Advantage* (Georgi Djulgerov, 1977).

16.139 *Manly Times* (Eduard Zahariev, 1977).

age from the era. Finally, Kiran Kolarov (b. 1946), one of the first graduates of VITIS and a student of Hristov and Djulgerov, made a striking debut in *Status—Orderly* (*Sluzhebno polozhenie—ordinarets*, 1978), an ironic portrait of the lives of peasant military orderlies and their decadent officers in the royal barracks at the turn of the century.

As Bulgaria moved toward a jubilant celebration of its 1,300th anniversary as a nation (681–1981), the film industry was commissioned by the authorities of the State Cinematography Corporation to produce four superspectacles commemorating great events from the national past—Zahari Zhandov's *Master of Boiana* (*Boianskiiat maistor,* 1981), Liudmil Staikov's *Khan Asparukh* (1981), Georgi Stoianov's *Constantine the Philosopher* (*Konstantin Filosof,* 1983), and Borislav Sharaliev's *Boris the First* (*Boris Purvi,* 1984). Georgi Djulgerov's *Measure for Measure* (*Mera spored mera,* 1981), a three-part epic of the Macedonian struggle for liberation from the Ottoman Turks, was also produced for the celebration, as was Nikola Karabov's (b. 1929) documentary on the career of Bulgaria's world-famous operatic basso *Nikolai Ghiaurov—50* (1980). But while these films were in production, Bulgarian cinema continued to garner world attention in Rangel Vulchanov's *The Unknown Soldier's Patent Leather Shoes* (*Lachenite obuvko na neznaniia voin,* 1979), Hristo Hristov's *Barrier* (*Barierata,* 1979) and *The Truck* (*Kamionat,* 1980), Liudmil Staikov's *Illusion* (*Ilyuziya,* 1980), and Binka Zheliazkova's *The Big Night Bath* (*Goliamoto noshino kupane,* 1980).

The Unknown Soldier's Patent Leather Shoes, which opened the London Festival in the year of its release and won the Grand Prix at New Dehli in 1981, was based on a 1963 script by Vulchanov and had been fifteen years in the planning. Cast with nonprofessionals in the leading roles, lyrically photographed by Radoslav Spasov, and narrated by the director himself, it evokes the lost village culture of the era between the wars through a series of childhood memories, and many critics regard it as one of the most beautiful Bulgarian films ever made. Hristov's *Barrier* is a psychological fantasy about a composer on the brink of a nervous

16.140 *The Unknown Soldier's Patent Leather Shoes* (Rangel Vulchanov, 1979).

16.141 *Barrier* (Hristo Hristov, 1979).

breakdown who encounters a clairvoyant *anima* sprite and is taught "how to fly." The film, which ends with the protagonist's death "in flight," won first prize at the Moscow Festival in 1979, and its Chagall-like *mise-en-scène* brought cinematographer Atanas Tasev to international prominence. The following year, the same team produced *The Truck* (whose Bulgarian title, "Kamionat," literally means "burden-bearer"), a film about the tortuous journey of four companions through the mountains in the depths of winter to return the body of a dead comrade to his village for burial. Inspired by Clouzot's *The Wages of Fear* (1953), *The Truck* has all of that film's explosive tension, but it also provides a sharp metaphor for a society in the throes of profound social change, and it won the Grand Prix at Karlovy Vary in the year of its release. Staikov's *Illusion*—winner of the same prize in 1980—was an abstract philosophical "prequel" to his *Amendment to the Defense-of-State Act* (1976), set during the September uprising of 1923 which, when crushed, precipitated the two-year White Terror under the Fascist regime of Alexander Tsankov. Filmed as a succession of poetic images, some contextually related and others posing questions on the nature of social responsibility and revolutionary praxis, *Illusion* requires a knowledge of Bulgarian history for full comprehension but is visually and aurally absorbing in the same fashion as *Barrier*. Zheliazkova's *The Big Night Bath*, chosen to represent Bulgaria at Cannes, is an existential parable about a group of artists and bored vacationers at a Black Sea resort who, after an episode of night bathing, become involved in an ancient Thracian game.* As with *Illusion*, complete appreciation of the film is enhanced by a knowledge of Bulgaria's rich cultural heritage and its status as an archaeological treasure trove, but the themes of social responsibility and the burden of history become clear enough as the game proceeds from joke to deadly ritual and finally death for one of the players.

In the spring of 1981, the first of the superspectacles commissioned to celebrate the 1,300th anniversary of Bulgaria's founding as a state appeared in Zhandov's *Master of Boiana*, a fictionalized biography of the anonymous painter who did the world-famous egg-tempera frescoes at the Boiana Church on the outskirts of Sofia in 1259, a full half-century before Giotto introduced naturalism into religious painting in the West at the dawn of the Italian Renaissance. The film features vast sets duplicating the medieval village of Boiana and its church, which had recently been declared a cultural monument under UNESCO protection. The second celebration film to be released in 1981 was Staikov's monumental national epic *Khan*

---

* The Thracians were a savage Indo-European people who occupied the Balkan peninsula from approximately 3000 B.C. until it became part of the Roman Empire during the *Pax Romana*, 17 B.C.–A.D. 180. Racially, the Thracians were absorbed by the Slavs, who in turn bred with the Proto-Bulgars to become the Bulgarians. The Thracians, whom some historians credit with founding the music, mythology, and philosophy of ancient Greece, are thus the oldest identifiable descendants of the Bulgarian people—who are justly proud of this heritage. A Thracian art exhibit, a collection of one thousand gold and silver artifacts from the third and fourth centuries, toured the world's museums as part of Bulgaria's 1,300th anniversary celebration.

Asparukh, which depicts the mass migration of the Proto-Bulgars from the steppes of Central Asia to the Danube region between A.D. 679 and 681. This was an event in Bulgarian history comparable to the Norman invasion of the British Isles in 1066, since it resulted in the foundation of the Bulgarian state and its national culture. Running six hours and released as three separate features, *Khan Asparukh* took over a year to complete and employed some 50,000 extras from the Bulgarian army for its battle scenes. Part I, *Phanagoria,* is set on the plains of Azovian Great Bulgaria in what is now Soviet Kazakhstan, from which the title character (a relative of Attila the Hun) sets out to lead his people to a new homeland following the death of his father Khan Kubrat and the division of his kingdom. Part II, *Migration,* tells the story of the Bulgarian horde's two-decade trek westward across the Dnieper and the Danube to its friendly encounter with the Slavic tribes of the fertile Danube delta. Part III, *Land Forever,* recounts Asparukh's supreme accomplishment in his victory over the Byzantine army of Constantine IV Pogonatus in A.D. 680 against ten-to-one odds and the subsequent foundation of the Bulgarian state in partnership with the Slavs. Sumptuously costumed and superbly photographed by Boris Ianakiev in widescreen Technovision and Eastmancolor, *Khan Asparukh* was seen by 11 million people in its first six months of release, creating a national—and perhaps even a world—per capita attendance record, since the population of Bulgaria is only about 9 million. (A ninety-five-minute English-language version produced for a Warner Bros. release abroad as *681 A.D.: The Glory of Khan,* 1984, was truncated beyond the point of comprehension.) Staikov followed this trilogy in 1988 with *Time of Violence (Vreme razdelno),* a dazzling CinemaScope epic of the forced Islamization of a Bulgarian valley in the Rhodophe Mountains in the seventeenth century. This four-and-one-half-hour film was released domestically as two films and set new box-office records in its very first month, but a seamlessly edited 160-minute version was shown to wide acclaim at Cannes.

The last commissioned film to be completed in 1981 was Djulgerov's *Measure for Measure,* a three-part chronicle of Macedonia's struggle for liberation from the Ottoman Turks from 1878 to 1912, based on historical records and eyewitness accounts of survivors. Beautifully photographed in color by Radoslav Spasov and employing Macedonian dialect throughout, this five-hour* spectacle synthesizes the history of the troubled region into a dynamic blend of fact, metaphor, symbol, and myth. Part I deals with the origination of the "Macedonian question" (which still disturbs geopolitical relations among Yugoslavia, Bulgaria, and Greece today), when Bulgaria was liberated from the Turks in 1876 but the western part of its former empire, known as Macedonia, remained under Ottoman control. The period from 1878 to 1903 was one of awakening national identity for Macedonia, culminating in the bloody Ilinden Day uprising of August 2, 1903. Part II deals with the revolution that followed and the brutal counterinsurgency tactics of the Turkish army, from 1903 to 1906.

---

* A shortened three-hour "festival version" is available.

Part III covers the years 1906 to 1912, when the revolutionaries finally succeeded by aligning themselves with the Young Turks in their own revolt against the Ottoman Empire.*

The last two of the great historical epics produced to celebrate Bulgaria's 1,300th anniversary were completed in 1983 and 1984, respectively. Georgi Stoianov's three-part *Constantine the Philosopher* tells the story of Cyril (Constantine) and Methodius, the ninth-century brother-saints who, as missionaries from the Greek Christian Church in Constantinople to the Moravian Slavs, devised the Cyrillic alphabet still used in Eastern Orthodox countries today and who prepared their disciples for the conversion of the Bulgarians, A.D. 864–65. Borislav Sharaliev's *Boris the First,* an epic in two parts (*The Conversion to Christianity* and *Discourse on Letters*), scripted by Anzhel Vagenstein, deals with that conversion itself and with its impact upon Bulgarian history. King Boris ascended the throne in 852 and was converted in 864; he ruled for thirty-seven years, until 889, and was ultimately succeeded by his son Simeon, who heralded the "Golden Age" of the First Bulgarian Empire. By choosing the Christianity of Constantinople over that of Rome and by elevating Simeon, Boris set the course of the Eastern Orthodox Church in Bulgaria for the next thousand years. (Sharaliev's spectacle won the Golden Rose at the 1984 Varna Festival of Bulgarian Feature Films.) Taken together, the five films commissioned to celebrate Bulgaria's thirteenth centennial chronicle the history of the Bulgarian people from their first migration from the Central Asian steppes through early Christianity to the cataclysmic events of the twentieth century.† It would be difficult to find a comparable body of work in the history of Eastern European or indeed any other cinema, although Hungary's fascination with its own national past provides an obvious parallel.

Since the 1,300th anniversary celebration of 1981, New Bulgarian Cinema, as it is now known to international critics, has continued to grow and prosper, producing major contributions with, in 1981, Ianko Iankov's *The Queen of Turnovo* (*Turnovskaia tsaritsa*) and Ivan Pavlov's debut, *Mass Miracle* (*Massovo chudo*); in 1982, Hristo Hristov's *A Woman at Thirty-three* (*Edna Zhena na trideset i tri*), Eduard Zahariev's *Elegy* (*Elegiia*), the distinguished Spanish director Juan Antonio Bardem's version of the Leipzig trial, *The Warning* (*Preduprezhdenieto*; coproduced with the GDR), and Ivan Andonov's *White Magic* (*Biala magiia*), which

---

* In a tragic *coda* to its long war of liberation, Macedonia was simultaneously claimed by Serbia, Greece, and Bulgaria, resulting in the First (1912) and Second (1913) Balkan Wars and ultimately igniting World War I.

† The critical blanks in this chain were filled by two other films produced in conjunction with the anniversary, Borislav Sharaliev's *The Thrust* (*Udaret,* 1982) and Vladislav Ikonomov's *The Day of the Rulers* (*Deniat na vladetelite,* 1985). The former is a two-part chronicle of events in Sofia from August 26 to September 9, 1944, the date marking the liberation of the city by Soviet troops and the moment of victory for the Communist revolution. The latter, also in two parts, used sets left over from the major anniverary epics to recount the crucial years of A.D. 803–14, the reign of Khan Krum, who defeated the armies of the Byzantine Emperor Nicephorus I at Vurbishki Pass in 811 and expanded Bulgarian territory at the expense of the Greeks.

can be favorably compared with the work of Parajanov; in 1983, Rangel Vulchanov's *Last Wishes* (*Posledni zhelania*), the TV director Veselin Branev's *Hotel Central* (*Hotel Tsentral*), Ivanka Grubcheva's *The Golden River* (*Zlatnata reka*), Nikola Korabov's *Destiny* (*Orissia*), Liudmil Kirkov's *Balance* (*Ravnovesie;* his third collaboration with the scriptwriter Stanislav Stratiev and winner of the Silver Prize at Moscow), and Nikolai Volev's tribute to Balkan silent comedy at its best in *King for a Day* (*Gospodin za edin den*); in 1984, Kiran Kolarov's *Case No. 205 / 1913* (*Delo No. 205 / 1913*) and Hristov's *Question Time* (*Subesednik po zhelanie*) and in 1985, *Reference* (*Herakteristika*). More recently, Nikolai Volev's *All for Love* (*Da obichash na inat,* 1986) has explored official corruption, and Ivan Nichev's *Ivan and Alexandra* (*Ivan i Aleksandra,* 1989) demonstrates the influence of *glasnost* by recounting the horrifying use of children to denounce their parents during the Stalinist 1950s.

Today Bulgaria makes approximately twenty-five theatrical features and twenty-five features for television per year, in addition to twenty-five animated films and over two hundred shorts and documentaries—an astounding rate for an industry that averaged only one feature per year as late as 1953. All of these are produced under the authority of the Bulgarian State Cinematography Corporation, which has five separate components: the Boiana Feature Film Studio,* a vast production complex, or film city, located at the foot of Mt. Vitosha on the outskirts of Sofia; the Sofia Animation Film Studio, made world famous by the award-winning work of Todor Dinov during the sixties;† the Vreme Popular Science and Documentary Film Studio; the Film Laboratory, which currently has facilities for processing Eastmancolor, Sovcolor, Fugicolor, and Orwocolor, making Bulgaria an increasingly attractive site for foreign coproduction; and Bulgariafilm, the industry's foreign trade, cultural exchange, and public relations branch, which among its other functions,

---

*Until 1983, Boiana was made up of four production collectives, according to the Polish model. A filmmaker could join any group, which in turn had the right to final approval of story concepts and scenarios. In 1983, to increase the efficiency of the system, the four groups were disbanded and all feature production placed under the double management of industry veterans Zako Heskia and Liudmil Kirkov. Despite its highly centralized and hierarchical character, the Bulgarian film industry as a whole enjoys considerable autonomy from the government, a situation enhanced by the elimination of subsidies in 1968.

†Dinov developed what has come to be known as the "Bulgarian Animation School," whose hallmark is the philosophical parable in pen and ink (for example, *The Story of the Pinetree Branch* [1960], *Duet* [1961], *The Lightning Rod* [1962], *Jealousy* [1963], *The Apple* [1963], *The Daisy* [1965]). Dinov's major protégées are Donio Donev (b. 1929)— *Three Fools* (1970), *The Clever Village* (1972), *Three Foolish Hunters* (1972), *De Facto* (1973), *The Three Fools and the Cow* (1974), *The Musical Tree* (1976), and *Causa Perduta* (1977)—and Stoian Dukov (b. 1931)—*Houses Are Forts* (1967), *Mini* (1971), *En Passant* (1975), *A Musical Story* (1976), and *February* (1977). But Ivan Andonov (for example, *The Shooting Range* [1964] and *Trouble* [1967]) and Ivan Veselinov (*Tightrope Walker* [1969], *The Devil in the Church* [1969], and *The Heirs* [1970]) have also won many festival prizes. Recently, Sofia began the production of its first animated features in Rumen Petkov's *Treasure Planet* (*Planeta na sukrovishtata*, 1983), a science-fiction version of Robert Louis Stevenson's *Treasure Island*, and Donio Donev's *We Called Them Montagues and Capulets* (*Narekohme gi Monteki i Kapuleti*, 1985), loosely based on Shakespeare's *Romeo and Juliet*.

distributes a large number of feature, documentary, and animated films to Western television and video companies.* Bulgarian filmmakers—formerly trained abroad (usually at the VGIK or another Eastern-bloc academy) or at the small film department within the Academy of Dramatic Art in Sofia—since 1973 have been able to attend the Sofia Film and Television Academy (VITIS), which offers integrated degree programs in both cinema and theater. (Bulgarian cinema has always felt at home with its sister arts, with, for example, approximately 50 percent of its titles adapted from the national literature.) The Bulgarian film archive is one of the most sophisticated in the world, and attendance at the country's 3,600 theaters is among the highest in all of Europe—and, it should be noted, essential to the survival of the industry, since the government eliminated all forms of subsidy in 1968. Additionally, the Black Sea resort town of Varna has become the home of three major festivals—the National Feature Film Festival (October), the World Animated Film Festival (October), and the International Festival of Red Cross and Health Films (June)—each held every other year. All of this activity is quite remarkable for a country that barely had a cinema at all until the late 1950s. But the Bulgarians are clearly a remarkable people because in just three decades they have created out of the most primitive and archaic film industry in all of Eastern Europe (excepting, of course, Albania), a national cinema that is less cosmopolitan, perhaps, but every bit as rich as that of Czechoslovakia or Hungary. The ouster of Todor Zhivkov and the establishment of a reform government in November 1989 should enable it to flourish in the future.

ROMANIA

The Romanian film industry was initially more advanced than the Bulgarian by virtue of having its own film school, the Institute of Theater and Film (IATC), established in 1950, and an elaborate set of studios (completed in 1956) at Buftea, just outside of Bucharest. Romania produced about fifty full-length features even before World War II, many of them documentaries and travelogues funded by the Cinematographic Service of the National Tourism Office, established in 1936. After 1941, when the Cinematographic Service was transformed into the National Cinematographic Office (ONC), private production all but disappeared as a casualty of war. ONC dominated feature production until it too collapsed in 1943, after the failure of a joint filmmaking venture with the Italian government (CineRomIt). Nationalization of the industry began in 1948 with even less of a material base than that which existed in Yugoslavia, and the process was slowed by the Romanian Communist Party's close dependence upon the Soviet Union and its occupying forces. The

---

*For example, Iankov's *The Queen of Turnovo* (1981) was recently shown by TVS in England, Zhandov's *Master of Boiana* (1981) was broadcast by Irish Television, and TF1 and Antenne 2 in France and Swiss Television all regularly feature Bulgarian animation. Moreover, Bulgarian features are widely available on videocassette in the Scandinavian countries and Spain.

Romanian Communist Party had a scant record of wartime resistance and was never part of a popular political movement, as were the Communist parties in Yugoslavia and Poland. (Traditionally anti-Russian, Romania had allied itself closely with the Nazis under the leadership of the Fascist premier, Ion Antonescu, 1940–45.) The Communist Party was propped up by the presence of occupying Red Army troops from 1944 through 1958, during which time the USSR directed the Romanian economy through the creation of Soviet-Romanian corporations (SOV-ROM) and set its foreign policy. From the beginning of the sixties onward, the Romanians moved away from the Soviets, contracted economic and political relationships with the West, and became the only Warsaw Pact nation to maintain friendly relations with the People's Republic of China. But despite the adoption of a constitution calling for its complete independence in 1965, Romania has remained in practical terms very much part of the Soviet-dominated Eastern bloc.

The first Romanian postwar films were rural dramas like Paul Călinescu's (b. 1902) *The Valley Resounds* (*Rašună valea,* 1949) and Dinu Negreanu's (b. 1919) two-part chronicle of peasant life, *The Bugler's Grandsons* (*Nepoţii gornistului,* 1953) and *The Sun Rises* (*Răsare soarele,* 1954), constructed along strict Zhdanovian lines. There were also comedies adapting the farces of the world-famous Romanian playwright Ion Luca Caragiale (1852–1912), such as Jean Georgescu's *Chain of Weakness* (*Lanţul slăbiciunilor*), *The Visit* (*Vizita*), and *Romanian Farmer* (*Arendaşul român*), all 1952. But it wasn't until Premier Gheorghe Gheorghiu-Dei, drawing his inspiration from Tito, led a successful movement to break away from the Soviet Union and its policies in the early 1960s that a truly national cinema began to emerge in the work of the first generation of IATC graduates, including Mircea Drăgan (b. 1932)—*Thirst* (*Setea,* 1960; the first Romanian widescreen film); *Lupeni 29* (1962); *Golgotha* (*Golgota,* 1967); Liviu Ciulei (b. 1923)—*The Danube Waves* (*Valurile Dunării,* 1959); *The Forest of the Hanged* (*Pădurea spinzuratilor,* 1965; winner of the Best Director Prize at Cannes in that year); and Mircea Mureşan (b. 1930)—*Blazing Winter* (*Răscoala,* 1965). During this same period the work of Ion Popescu-Gopo (b. 1923)—*A Short History* (*Scurtă istorie,* 1957; Palme d'Or, Cannes); *The Seven Arts* (*Sapte arte,* 1958); *Homo Sapiens* (1960); *Hello! Hello!* (*Allo! Allo!,* 1962); *Sancta Simplicitas* (1968)—made Romania one of the world centers for animated film; since 1966, in fact, the International Festival of Animated Film has been held every second year in Mamaia (alternating with Annecy).*

As part of the new "Romanization of Romanian Culture"—which included the dropping of compulsory Russian from the public school curriculum and the elevation of such Romanian emigré artists as the sculptor Constantin Brancusi (1876–1957) and the playwright Eugène Ionesco (b. 1912), both naturalized French citizens—Romanian filmmakers turned

16.142 *The Forest of the Hanged* (Liviu Ciulei, 1965).

---

* After producing the antiwar fantasy *Stolen Bomb* (*S a furat o bombă,* 1961), Popescu-Gopo turned to making features combining animation and live action, usually in the fairy-tale or science fiction genres.

to the national historical tradition. They produced epics like Sergui Nico-laescu's (b. 1930) *The Dacians* (*Dacii,* 1966) and *Michael the Brave* (*Mihai viteazul,* 1971; an Oscar nominee), as well as the films of the swashbuck-ling *"haiduk"* cycle of Dinu Cocea (b. 1929). These latter works—*The Haiduks* (*Haiducii,* 1965), *The Revenge of the Haiduks* (*Răzbunarea haiducilor,* 1968), *The Haiduks of Captain Anghel* (*Haiducii lui Şapte-cai,* 1970), and others—translate the plots and techniques of Hollywood Westerns into romantic tales of *haiduks,* patriotic Romanian brigands doing battle with corrupt foreign overlords in the Carpathians. By 1965, the year in which Nicolae Ceausescu (1918–89) succeeded Gheorghiu-Dei as first secretary of the Romanian Communist Party, the country's film industry was in full swing, producing fifteen to eighteen features annually plus approximately 25 animated cartoons, and about a hundred newsreels.

16.143 *Sunday at Six* (Lucian Pintilie, 1965).

It was in this context that the first authentically Romanian *auteur* films appeared in the work of Lucian Pintilie (b. 1933), whose *Sunday at Six* (*Duminica lă ora 6,* 1965) and *Reconstruction* (*Reconstituirea,* 1969) both won an international following. The former was a Resnais-like evocation of an incident from the Resistance, skillfully directed and shot, and completely lacking in dogma, while the latter was a controversial allegory of social irresponsibility whose release was delayed for a year by Romaniafilm officials charging "evidence of Western influence." *Reconstruction* was in fact a profoundly Romanian film, focused on the peren-nial national traits of indifference to the fate of others and dereliction of duty, both encouraged by the consumption of enormous quantities of alcohol. It recounts the "reconstruction" of a crime by its original partic-ipants for an incompetent rural judge, all of whom couldn't care less about the event or its consequences. Strongly colored by Czech-inspired black humor, the film ends with a second and more serious crime being committed in the process of the reconstruction. Several of Pintilie's con-temporaries, for example, Gheorghe Vitanidis (b. 1929)—*A Woman for One Season* (*O femeie pentru un anotimp,* 1969)—and Nicolae Breban (b. 1934)—*Sick Animals* (*Animale bolnave,* 1971)—also made films of social criticism during this era, and for a while it seemed as if there might be a Romanian cultural breakthrough of the sort experienced concur-rently (however briefly) in Poland, Czechoslovakia, Hungary, and Yugo-slavia. This hope appeared to be crushed in the spring of 1971 when Ceausescu, now president, absorbed in the formation of a Stalin-like cult of personality, delivered a speech sharply critical of liberalizing tenden-cies among Romanian intelligentsia and creative artists. But in fact Ceau-sescu's attack was so stringent as to generate a strong wave of dissent, which resulted in an accommodation between Romanian politics and Romanian culture later in the year.

16.144 *Reconstruction* (Lucian Pintilie, 1969).

This left the way clear for the third generation of postwar Romanian filmmakers—"the Class of the 1970s," as it is called, since most of its members started working after the turn of the decade—to deal with themes that were formerly taboo in an atmosphere of increased tolerance for formal experimentation. Mircea Daneliuc (b. 1943) is the most promi-nent filmmaker of this generation, if not of all Romanian directors today,

16.145 *A Woman for One Season* (Gheorghe Vitanidis, 1969).

and he is followed closely by Dan Piţa (b. 1938), Mircea Veriou (b. 1941), and Alexandru Tatos (b. 1945). Daneliuc illuminated the generally dull landscape of the mid-seventies with *The Race / Long Drive* (*Cursa*, 1975), centering on the twenty-four–hour odyssey of two truck drivers and a pretty hitchhiker, and *Special Issue* (*Ediţie speciala*, 1978), an historical police thriller set in the context of the Romanian Fascist "Green Shirt" movement of the forties. The following year his *Microphone Test* (*Proba de microfon*, 1980) won enormous popular success and was nationally rated among the ten best Romanian films ever made. It employs *cinéma vérité* techniques to describe the hectic, if dispassionate, life of a TV news cameraman who tends to see reality in the terms of a filmic montage and who ultimately has a stormy romance with one of his interview subjects. The same kind of formal innovation characterizes *The Cruise* (*Croaziera*, 1981), in which a large group of workers from various companies and factories are treated to a weeklong outing on the Danube for their exceptional service to the state. The film becomes a parable of generational conflict in contemporary Romania, as the cruise's organizers and the younger cruisers lock horns over moral, political, and sexual attitudes. *Fox-Hunting* (*Vinetoarea de vulpi*, 1981), adapted by Dinu Săraru from his best-selling novel *Some Peasants* (*Nişte ţrani*), is Daneliuc's most controversial work to date. It uses flashbacks, flashforwards, and multiple points of view to tell the story of a group of peasants in the postwar years who stubbornly refuse to cede their land to the state, while party officials argue with them just as stubbornly for the historical necessity of collectivization. More recently, Daneliuc has attempted to create a metaphor for Romanian history itself in *Glissando* (1985), the title referring to a musical expression by violin and adapted from a short story by Cezar Petrescu. Set in the 1930s, this film follows the descent of a dissipated bourgeois intellectual into obsession and madness, and it concludes with a sustained Dantesque fantasy sequence that affirms the capacity for human dignity even in the grips of the most horrendous spiritual oppression. *Jacob* (1988), on the other hand, is a complicated parable about the oppression of gold miners and their families by a brutal—but unidentified—economic system, which might equally well be capitalism or communism. It is clear that in his films of the eighties Daneliuc has achieved the unique position of winning nearly unanimous praise from local and international critics, as well as enormous box-office success at home.

The best-known Romanian filmmaker after Daneliuc is Dan Piţa, who directed two award-winning medium-length features with Mircea Veriou about Carpathian peasant life—*The Stone Wedding* (*Nunta de piatra*, 1973) and its sequel, *Lust for Gold* (*Duhul aurului*, 1974)—before switching to contemporary issues in *Philip the Kind* (*Filip cel bun*, 1974), a realistic portrait of a young man's search for moral identity in the midst of rampant social change. He followed with a brilliant adaptation of the classic Romanian novel *Summer Tale* (*Tănase scatiu*, 1977) by Duilui Zamfirescu. Photographed in luxurious sequence shots by Călin Ghibu, this beautiful and elliptical film centers on the *fin-de-siècle* power struggle between the aristocracy and the bourgeoisie and is—from atmosphere, through music, to decor—highly reminiscent of late Visconti. Piţa next scored a smashing box-office success with his hilarious Romanian Western, *The Prophet, Gold, and the Transylvanians* (*Profetul, aurul, şi Ardelenii,* 1979), centering on a Transylvanian peasant family relocated in the trigger-happy American West of the 1800s. But he turned deeply serious, even metaphysical, in *Contest / Orientation Course* (*Concurs,* 1983; FIPRESCI Prize, New Delhi), the story of a group of alienated people running an obstacle course through the wilderness. In the manner of Tarkovski's *Stalker* (1979), the film becomes a dense parable about the failure of collectivity through indifference and is widely regarded as one of the most profound Romanian films ever made. *Chained Justice* (*Dreptate în lanţuri,* 1985; Special Jury Prize and Press Prize, Santarem) won similar praise in its tale of the real-life Pantelimon, a latter-day *haiduk* who fought against the oligarchy's police state circa 1910. More recently, Piţa directed the highly stylized *Pas in Doi* (*Paso doble,* 1986), in which a rather conventional love triangle becomes a vehicle for some incisive criticism of present-day Romanian society.

After co-directing *The Stone Wedding* and *Lust for Gold* with Dan Piţa, Mircea Veriou achieved a masterpiece in his adaptation of Ion Slavica's classic novel *Mara,* as *Beyond the Bridge* (*Dincolo de pod,* 1977). Set in a small town in Transylvania on the eve of the 1848 Revolution, this film tells a romantic love story in modern psychological terms, and its virtuoso photography by constant Veriou collaborator Călin Ghibu evokes the past in allusions to famous Flemish and other northern European Renaissance paintings. Veriou followed with *Mînia* (*Chronicle of the Barefoot Emperors,* 1978), an epic film based on the tragic peasant uprising of 1907 when over 11,000 rebels were shot down by the Romanian Army of King Carol I (also the subject of Muresan's *Blazing Winter*). Recent Veriou films include *To Die from Love of Life* (*Să mori rănit din dragoste de viaţă,* 1984), a sophisticated rendition of communist resistance to the Fascist "Green Shirts" in 1934, replete with stylish allusions to thirties' cinema, and *Adela* (1985), a sumptuously produced Chekhovian love story, set on a country estate in the lazy summer of 1899, which won the Gran Premio at San Remo.

Alexandru Tatos brought into the Romanian cinema a rich intellectual background from the theater. He dealt initially with contemporary themes in such films as *Red Apples* (*Mere rossi,* 1977) and *The Wandering* (*Rătăcire,* 1978). The former is a realistic exploration of a recently graduated surgeon in a rural hospital; while the latter concerns a young Romanian girl, attracted by the market economy's glittering prizes, who marries an ambitious West German, but finds herself unable to adapt to the culture of mass consumption. *The House in the Fields* (*Casa dintre cîmpuri,* 1980; originally made for television) tells the story of an idealistic agronomist who must battle corrupt and dishonest bureaucrats in the village where he is sent to work. But Tatos' most poetic film was *Anastasia Passed By / Gently Was Anastasia Passing* (*Duios Anastasia trecea,* 1980), adapted by Dumitreu Radu Popescu, one of the leading figures of contemporary Romania literature, from his own novella. It is a version of Sophocles' *Antigone,* set in a Nazi-occupied Danubian village, where a young schoolteacher defies a German edict not to bury a

Serbian partisan at the cost of her life. Tatos followed *Anastasia* with *Sequence* (*Secvente,* 1983), his most experimental film to date, which offers three original "short stories" in film about the relationship among cinematic illusion, history, and the quotidian real. More recently, Tatos has resumed his partnership with D. R. Popescu to produce *Forest Fruit* (*Fructe de padure,* 1984), a melancholy portrait of a seventeen-year-old country girl seduced and abandoned by her lover, which manages to become a lyrical testament to human dignity.

From a virtually nonexistent material base in the late forties, Romanian cinema in the eighties has grown into one of the more viable in Eastern Europe. Since the early seventies, the film industry has been decentralized and the production of feature films split into five groups, according to the Polish model. Since the 1978–79 season, these groups have produced an average of thirty features annually, with a high of thirty-six in 1984 and the declared goal of sixty by the end of the decade. (Furthermore, since 1971 the Romanian TV Film Studio, under the leadership of Victoria Marinescu, has produced or coproduced with the film industry fifteen serials, forty long- and medium-length features, thirty cartoons, and 562 medium and short documentaries or musicals, all in color.)* Because the Romanian is the only completely self-financing industry in the Eastern bloc, domestic box-office success is crucial to its survival. In a still developing country of 23 million people, it is no small accomplishment that since 1979 over one third of all admissions in the nation's 634 theaters have been for domestic films of an often high aesthetic and intellectual caliber. The effects on all this of the violent overthrow of the Cesausescu dictatorship during Christmas 1989 remain very much to be seen.

OTHER BALKAN COUNTRIES

Two other Balkan countries that have evolving film industries are Turkey (population 54.2 million) and Greece (population 10.5 million). The Turkish industry is large but erratic and geared mainly toward the production of domestic exploitation films. For example, 128 features were produced in 1978 and 195 in 1979, but only 70 in 1980 and 1981. This is because the industry is heavily dependent on the vicissitudes of the inflation-ridden national economy and, since the army seized control of

---

* Collaboration between the film and television industries in Romania is stronger than in any other Eastern European country and has resulted in some quite distinguished achievements. *August in Flames* (*August in flăcări,* 1974), for example, was a thirteen-part series directed by Dan Piţa, Alexandru Tatos, and Doru Năstase on the anti-Fascist uprising of August 23, 1944, which opened the floodgates of the revolution; *Independence War* (*Razboiul Independentei,* 1976–77), a colorful eight-part period piece directed by Sergui Nicolaescu, celebrated the centenary of the Romanian war of liberation against Turkey; while *Lights and Shadows* (*Lumini şi umbre,* 1981–82) is an ambitious thirty-three–part series on the activities of the Communist underground during World War II, directed by Andrei Blaier, Mihai Constantinescu, and Mircea Mureşan, which has been awarded the Prize of the Romanian Filmmakers Association.

the government in 1980, upon political whim as well. Nevertheless, Turkey has produced several filmmakers of great talent and at least one of legendary prominence since World War II. During the relatively liberal 1960s, a movement was born known as Young Turkish Cinema, or the National Cinema, which centered around the actor-writer Yilmaz Guney (1937–84), who had become a matinee idol early in the decade. Guney began directing from his own scripts in the late sixties, and in the early seventies he produced a significant body of politically motivated work through his own company, Guney-Filmcilik, focused on the everyday poverty and oppression of his people—*Hope* (*Umut*, 1970), *The Fugitives* (*Kacaklar*, 1971), *The Wrongdoers* (*Vurguncular*, 1971), *Tomorrow Is the Final Day* (*Yarin son gundur*, 1971), *The Hopeless Ones* (*Umutsuzlar*, 1971), *Pain* (*Aci*, 1971), *Elegy* (*Agit*, 1971), and *The Father* (*Baba*, 1971). The ironically titled *Hope* was banned by the Turkish government, which also forbade the film's entry in the Cannes Film Festival. A smuggled print of it was shown there in 1971, however, and attracted some attention. In 1972, in the midst of shooting *The Poor Ones* (*Zavallilar*, completed 1975), set in the underbelly of Istanbul, Guney was arrested, charged with harboring fugitive anarchists, and imprisoned without trial for twenty-six months. Released in 1974 under a general amnesty for political prisoners, Guney jumped immediately into producing *The Friend* (*Arkadas*, 1974), *Anxiety* (*Endise*, 1974), and completing *The Poor Ones* before being imprisoned again on trumped-up charges of murdering a right-wing judge (the initial sentence was twenty-four years of hard labor, later commuted to eighteen). In jail—owing to his popularity as an actor-director—Guney was permitted to screen films and continue to write scripts, which were directed by associates on the outside; these included *The Herd* (*Suru* [directed by Zeki Okten, 1978]), *The Enemy* (*Dusman* [Zeki Okten, 1979]), and his extraordinary masterpiece *Yol* (Serif Goren, director, 1982). This film, whose title literally means "the way," was shot by Goren but edited by Guney in France after his 1981 escape from Toptasi prison. It traces the fortunes of five men on one-week's leave from prison as they traverse the country from west to east and is a relentless, unflinching indictment of Turkey's patriarchal system of values. *Yol* shared the Golden Palm at Cannes in 1982 with Costa-Gavras' *Missing*, and Guney directed one last film—*Le Mur* (*The Wall*, 1983; France), based on a brutally suppressed prison revolt that occurred in Ankara in 1976—before dying of stomach cancer in Paris in 1984.

16.146 *Yol* (Yilmaz Guney, 1983). Turkey.

Guney's co-directors have since become important figures in Turkish cinema—Okten, for example, with *The Wrestler* (*Pehlivan*, 1985) and *The Voice* (*Ses*, 1987), and Goren with *Remedy* (*Derman*, 1984), *Germany, Bitter Land* (*Almanya, aci vatan*, 1985), *The Escape* (*Firar*, 1985), *The Frogs* (*Kurbagalar*, 1986), and *Blood* (*Kan*, 1986). Guney's teacher, the veteran director Atif Yilmaz (b. 1925), has also produced significant films in the eighties (for example, *Her Name Is Vasfiye* [*Adi Vasfiye*, 1986]; *Aah, Belinda!* [1987]; *The Mill* [*Degirmen*, 1987]; *My Dreams, My Love, and You* [*Hayallerim, askim ve sen*, 1988]). Guney's former assistant, Ali Ozgenturk, has made (*Horse, My Horse* [*At*, 1982], *The Guard* [*Bekci*, 1985], and *Water Also Burns* [1987]); and his former composer, Omer Zulfu, made *Iron Earth, Copper Sky* (*Yer demir, gok bakir*) in 1987. Other Turkish filmmakers of note are Eden Kiral (*On the Fertile Land* [*Bereketli topraklar uzerince,* 1980]; *Dilan* [1987]; *Hunting Time* [*Av zamani,* 1988]) and Omer Kavur, widely held to be the most European-style director in the country (*A Brokenhearted Love Story* [*Kirik bir ask hikayesi,* 1983]; *The Desperate Road* [*Amansiz yol,* 1986]; *Motherland Hotel* [*Anayurt oteli,* 1987]; *Night Journey* [*Gece Yoloulugu,* 1988]).

Because Greece was involved in a bloody civil war between Communist and loyalist factions for four years beyond the end of World War II, the film industry did not really revive itself until the 1950s when the output fluctuated between fifteen and thirty features per year, many of them broad *farsocomedies,* or so-called *foustanelas,* patriotic action films named after the traditional Greek male kilt. In 1951 the Lycourgos Stavrakos Film School was established in Athens, and most Greek filmmakers of the fifties and sixties received some training there. Serious films, such as Grigoris Grigoriou's *Bitter Bread* (*Picro psoume,* 1951) and Stelios Tatasopoulos' *Black Earth* (*Mavri yee,* 1952), were heavily influenced by Italian neorealism, but Michael Cacoyannis' *Stella* (1956), a film about a tavern singer played by Melina Mercouri, combined social criticism with Hollywood-style sex appeal to attract international attention at Cannes. During the sixties commercial cinema boomed as Greece became the site for such coproductions as *Never on Sunday* (Jules Dassin, 1960), *The Guns of Navarone* (J. Lee Thompson, 1961), and *Zorba the Greek* (Cacoyannis, 1965); and the domestic production rate reached nearly one hundred films per year, most of them blatantly commercial. With government backing, Thessalonika became the home of a major international and domestic festival; and Greek performers like Mercouri, Irene Papas, and Georges Foundas, and Greek composers like Manos Hadjidakas and Mikis Theodorakis gained international reputations.

But a truly national film culture did not emerge until after the colonels' coup of April 21, 1967, when the junta's attempts to stifle social change produced a cinema far more radical than anything Greece had experienced to date. Its founder and leader was Theodore Angelopoulos (b. 1935), whose first features, *Reconstruction* (*Anapatastassi,* 1970) and *Days of '36* (*Mere toy,* 1972), were both fairly direct critiques of the social system. But of Angelopoulos' later works, *Traveling Players* (*Thiassos,* 1975) is a formally complicated, multilayered tapestry of scenes tracing the performances of an itinerant theater troupe as it wanders the provinces during the crucial years of modern Greek history, 1939–50, while *The Hunters* [*I kynigi,* 1977]) is a densely symbolic meditation on the Civil War which consolidates the director's mature style of achronological narrative and extremely long, Jancsó-like takes, faintly resolved by cinematographer Giorgos Arvanitis. During the eighties Angelopoulos produced a series of demanding, impressive films—*Alexander the Great* (*O Megalexandros,* 1980; Golden Lion, Venice), *Voyage to Cythera* (*Taxidi sta Kithira,* 1984; Best Screenplay, Cannes), *The Beekeeper* (*O melissokomos,* 1986); and *Landscape in the Mist* (*Topio stin omihli,* 1988)—

16.147 *O Thiassos* (Theodore Angelopoulous, 1975).

that placed him among the front rank of world-class directors. His films inspired a generation of directors whose work in creating the New Greek Cinema began in earnest after the military dictatorship of George Papadopoulis ended in 1973, and flourished with the election of socialist Andreas Papandreou as prime minister in 1981. Papandreou appointed exiled dissident Melina Mercouri to the post of Minister of Culture with the mission to reinvigorate the government-funded Greek Film Center.

Among the more prominent figures in New Greek Cinema, directors who often write as well as produce their own films, are Nikos Panayotopoulos (b. 1941)—*The Colors of Iris* (*Ta chromata tis iridos*, 1974); *The Idlers of the Fertile Valley*, 1978; *The Woman Who Dreamed* (*I Yineka pou evlepe ta onira*, 1988); Pandelis Voulgaris (b. 1940)—*The Engagement of Anna* (*To proxento tis Annas*, 1972); *Great Love Song* (*O megalos erotikos*, 1973); *Happy Day* (1976); *Eleftherios Venizelos, 1910–1927* (1980); *Stone Years* (*Petrina chronia*, 1985); Pavlos Tassios (b. 1942)—*Yes, But* (*Nai men all*, 1972); *Special Request* (*Parangelia*, 1980); *Stigma* (1984); *Knock-Out* (1986); Nikos Koundouros—*Young Aphrodites* (*Mikres Afrodites*, 1963); *1922* (1978; released 1981); *Bordello* (1985); Frida Liappa—*The Roads of Love Are Night Roads* (*I dromi tis agape ine nykterini*, 1981); *A Quiet Death* (*Enas isichos thanatos*, 1986); Tonia Marketaki (b. 1942)—*The Price of Love* (*I timi tis agape*, 1984); Nikos Nikolaidis (b. 1939)—*Sweet Bunch* (*Glykia symmoria*, 1983); *Morning Patrol* (*Proini peripolis*, 1987); George Katakouzenos—*Angel* (*Anguelos*, 1982); *Absences* (*Apoussies*, 1987); Demos Avdeliodis—*The Tree We Were Hurting* (*To dendro pou pligoname*, 1986); Tassos Psarras (b. 1950)—*The Reason Why* (1974); *May* (1976); *Caravan Palace* (*Caravan sarai*, 1986); Nikos Papatakis—*Les Abysses* (1963); *The Photograph* (*I photographia*, 1986); and Costas Vretacos—*The Children of the Swallow* (*Ta pedia tis chelidonas*, 1987).

THE SOVIET UNION

The Soviet Union, whose political and military presence looms still so large over the other countries discussed in this chapter, has also produced some remarkably distinguished cinema since World War II. But before this could occur, the country went through a period of Stalinist repression even darker than that experienced by its satellites.

Stalinist Cinema

From 1934 onward the supreme arbiter of socialist realism had been Andrei A. Zhdanov (1896–1948), secretary of the Central Committee of the Communist Party of the Soviet Union (CPSU) and Stalin's chief lieutenant in the politburo. (Zhdanov is credited today, in fact, with creating many of the ideological components of Stalinism.) As party boss in charge of ideological affairs, Zhdanov's mission was to correct "aberrant" tendencies in Soviet art, especially as represented in the cinema by the avant-garde heritage of Vertov, Kuleshov, Eisenstein, Pudovkin, and Dovzhenko, which he set out systematically to discredit and destroy. In 1946, as part of a national crusade to "reestablish ideological conformity in the arts" (which had necessarily been relaxed during the war), Zhdanov embarked upon a course that nearly destroyed the Soviet film industry as a functioning entity. First came a dramatic decree from the Central Committee banning four current films—Leonid Lukov's *A Great Life, Part II* (*Bolshaia zhizń;* recut and rereleased 1958), Kozintsev and Trauberg's *Plain People* (*Prostie liudi;* recut and released 1956), Eisenstein's *Ivan the Terrible, Part II* (rereleased 1958), and Pudovkin's *Admiral Nakhimov* (reshot and rereleased 1947)—and sharply warning the industry to reform itself. Then a thinly veiled campaign of anti-Semitism was unleashed against "rootless cosmopolitanism" and "foreign influences" in the arts, followed by personal attacks on individual filmmakers, like Trauberg, in *Pravda.**

In the wake of such intimidation, only a handful of films were produced between 1948 and 1952, and the Central Committee demanded that two themes be portrayed in all of them: (1) that the CPSU was the motive force in all Soviet activities, foreign and domestic, and (2) that Stalin was personally involved in all decisions of consequence for the USSR, past and present. This latter dictate resulted in a virtual genre of what were called "artistic documentaries" (we would now call them "docudramas")—pseudohistorical epics deifying Stalin as the greatest ideologist, economic planner, and military strategist in recorded history (though a kindly, avuncular man of the people withal). Stalin had been heroically portrayed in Soviet films many times before (for example, in Mikhail Romm's *Lenin in October* [*Lenin v oktabre,* 1937] and *Lenin in 1918* [*Lenin v 1918-om godu,* 1939]; in the Vasilievs' *Defense of Tsaritsyn* [*Oborona Tsaritsyna,* 1941]; and, in passing, as early as Eisenstein's *October* [1927]), but these new films almost literally proposed Stalin as a god.

They combined documentary footage with fictional scenes to portray a charismatic Stalin (usually played by Mikhail Gelovani, a handsome lookalike who made a career of the part) carrying forth Lenin's putative mandate to develop the Soviet economy through a series of five-year plans (Mikhail Chiaureli's *The Vow* [*Kliatva,* 1946]), personally directing bril-

---

* Legal discrimination against the Jews—widely practiced in tsarist Russia—was officially prohibited by the Bolsheviks in setting up their new regime, but *de facto* discrimination persisted, especially in the professions. As an institution born of the October Revolution and closely identified with it, the Soviet cinema attracted many Jewish persons who had experienced discrimination in other fields. For this very reason, the film industry became a vulnerable target for Stalinist anti-Semitism in the general arsenal of state terrorism, 1927–53. When Zhdanov died under mysterious circumstances in August 1948, for example, his death was attributed to a conspiracy of prominent Moscow physicians—most of them Jewish—aimed at the destruction of the Soviet leadership. Publicly identified in December 1952 as the "Doctors' Plot," the conspiracy was declared a fake immediately after Stalin's death four months later. By this point, however, the terror engendered by charges of a plot had brought the film industry to a standstill. The talented scenarist Eugeni Gabrilovich (b. 1899) was one of several film workers blacklisted during this period; for his account of it, see his "Inquisition in the Other Eden," *Film Comment* 5, 1 (1968): 22–27.

liant military offensives (Igor Savchenko's *The Third Blow* [*Tretii udar*, 1948] and Chiaureli's *The Fall of Berlin* [*Padenie Berlina*]), defending the sacred Russian soil (Vladimir Petrov's *The Battle of Stalingrad* [*Stalingradskaia bitva*, 1950]), and crushing an anti-Bolshevik rebellion in Leningrad (Chiaureli's *The Unforgettable Year 1919* [*Nezabyvaemyi 1919-yi god*, 1952]).* As André Bazin wrote in "The Stalin Myth in Soviet Cinema" (1950), Stalin becomes in these films "History incarnate . . . omniscient, infallible, irresistible. . . ." It was a strange detour for a revolutionary cinema founded on the rejection of conventional narrative and individual heroes.

The "artistic documentaries" (most of which, with perfectly paranoid circularity, received the Stalin Prize for Artistic Merit) were in fact part of a larger propaganda effort to establish Stalin as a mythic figure in Soviet politics and culture that was undertaken in the last terror-filled years of his reign. To ensure this priority, the party in 1951 decreed that the film industry should produce "only masterpieces," to be directed only by "acknowledged masters of the art." The result was that by 1952 annual output had fallen to a record low of five films,† and no new graduates could be admitted to the industry from the VGIK (Soviet film workers later referred to this period as "the time of few films").

Cinema During the Khrushchev Thaw

Stalin's death on March 5, 1953, caused an immediate loosening of ideological criteria, and 1954 witnessed the production of forty Soviet features. But it was not until Nikita Khrushchev (1894–1972) became first secretary of the Central Committee and denounced Stalin's brutal despotism in his famous "secret speech" before the Twentieth Party Congress in February 1956 that the de-Stalinization process began in earnest. Khrushchev's charges against his former boss ranged from self-glorification to political mass murder, and he roundly indicted Stalin's promulgation of a "cult of personality" through the film. More striking still, perhaps, was his assertion that Stalin had lost touch with the reality of his country as he rose to power and that he eventually knew it only through the pseudorealistic film images mandated by his own cultural bureaucracy which, when he did not like the images, he caused to be ruthlessly

---

* Since Stalin's death and fall from grace, some of these films have been re-edited to eliminate or minimize his role in them—much as he had demanded the elimination of Trotski's part in *October*. See Alexander Sesonske, "Re-editing History: *Lenin in October*, Then and Now," *Sight and Sound* 53, 1 (Winter 1983 / 84): 56–58.

† By comparison, in 1951 the United States had produced 432 films; India, 250; and Japan, 215. Average annual output since 1956 in the Soviet Union has been around one hundred films. (See S. V. Utechin, *A Concise Encyclopedia of Russia* [New York: Doubleday, 1964], p. 111.) One type of Soviet film that saw a rise in production in the early fifties was the recorded stage play. Stalin considered himself a connoisseur of the theater but had grown increasingly fearful of appearing in public in his latter years. Accordingly, he ordered that favorite performances be filmed for "posterity," so that he could watch them privately in the Kremlin. Over twenty plays were transcribed at his mandate in the first two months of 1953 alone.

purged. In fact, Khrushchev declared that Stalin had not set foot in a village since 1928, adding:

> He knew the country and agriculture only from films. And these films had dressed up and beautified the existing situation. . . . . Many films so pictured *kolkhoz* life that the tables were bending from the weight of turkeys and geese. Evidently, Stalin thought it was actually so.

It is important to understand, however, that although Stalin was officially discredited, Zhdanov was not, and socialist realism as a doctrine was not then and never has been rescinded. It was simply interpreted with greater moderation than previously.

The Khrushchev regime's more flexible attitude toward the arts (initially, at least) produced a thaw in the Soviet film industry that started dramatically in 1956. In that year new films began to appear from recent graduates of the VGIK for the first time since the 1930s,* many of which had contemporary themes. Among them were Grigori Chukhrai's (b. 1921) *The Forty-first* (*Sorok pervyi*), Stanislav Rostotski's (b. 1921) *The Land and the People* (*Zemlia i liudi*), Samson Samsonov's (b. 1921) *The Grasshopper* (*Poprygunia*—from a Chekhov story), Marlen Khutsiev (b. 1925) and Felix Mironer's (b. 1927) *Spring on Zarechnaia Street* (*Vesna na Zarechnoi ulitse*), Eldar Riazanov's (b. 1927) musical comedy *Carnival Night* (*Karnavalnaia noch´*), Vasili Ordynski's (b. 1925) *A Man Is Born* (*Chelovek rodilsia*), Alexander Alov (b. 1928) and Vladimir Naumov's (b. 1927) *Pavel Korchagin* (based on Nikolai Ostrovski's *How Steel Was Tempered*), Lev Kulijanov (b. 1924) and Iakov Segel's *This Is How It Began* (*Eto nachinalos´ tak*), and the first non-Russian postwar film, *Magdana's Little Donkey* (*Lurdzha Magdany*), by the Georgian directors Tengiz Abuladze (b. 1924) and Revaz Chkheidze (b. 1926). Veteran directors were also productive in the early thaw—Sergei Iutkevich with *Othello* (1956), the first Soviet Shakespearean adaptation, and *Stories about Lenin* (*Rasskazy o Lenine*, 1957); Mark Donskoi with a remake of Pudovkin's *Mother* (*Mat´*, 1956); Alexander Ptushko (b. 1900) with the first Soviet widescreen film, the puppet-animation fairy tale *Ilia Muromets* (1957); and, most prominently, Mikhail Kalatozov with *The Cranes Are Flying* (*Letiat zhuravli*, 1957).

---

* Ironically, the artistic integrity of the Soviet cinema had been well preserved at the VGIK even during the worst years of the cult of personality owing to the Stalinist practice of compulsorily retiring "formalist" directors from the industry to the classroom during purges. Thus, Kuleshov had taught introductory courses from 1944 until his death in 1970; Eisenstein had designed the professional directing curriculum—the first of its kind in the world—between 1932 and 1935 and held the director's Chair from 1939 until his death in 1948; and Pudovkin, Dovzhenko, Tisse, Kosintsev, and Iutkevich had all held lectureships at the institute during the worst years of Stalin's regime. During the early years of the thaw, it was revealed that these and other VGIK teachers had kept the experimental impetus of the twenties alive for their students by cultivating a distinction between "production films" (orthodox films for public distribution) and "diploma films" (stylistically advanced films made within the institute that were required to demonstrate a working knowledge of contemporary innovations such as Italian neorealism). In this way, the old guard at the VGIK was able to infuse the rising generation of Soviet directors with a cinematically vital tradition during "the time of few films," so they were able to do significant work of their own during the thaw.

16.148 *Othello* (Sergei Iutkevich, 1956).

16.149 *The Cranes Are Flying* (Mikhail Kalatozov, 1957).

When the latter won the Grand Prix at Cannes in 1958, it announced to the world that some sort of revival was taking place within the Soviet cinema. Just over a year before, however, Soviet tanks had brutally crushed the Hungarian Revolution, and this produced a chilling effect on domestic culture. For a while, the safest subjects for films became literary adaptations, and the late fifties witnessed a glut of them, especially among directors of an older generation—for example, Sergei Gerasimov's (1907–85) three-part version of Mikhail Sholokhov's *And Quiet Flows the Don* (*Tikhii Don*, 1957); Ivan Pyriev's (1901–68) adaptations of Dostoevsky's *The Idiot* (*Idiot*, 1958) and *White Nights* (*Belye nochi*, 1959); Mark Donskoi's Gorki adaptation, *Foma Gordeev* (1959); Vladimir Petrov's (1896–1965) version of Turgenev's *On the Eve* (*Nakanune*, 1959); the actor Alexei Batalov's (b. 1928) adaptation of Gogol's *The Overcoat* (*Shinel'*, 1959—actually a remake of the Kozintsev and Trauberg 1926 version, but this time done in the Moscow Art Theater's naturalistic style); Iosif Heifitz's (b. 1906) adaptations from Chekhov, *The Lady with the Little Dog* (*Dama s sobachkoi*, 1960) and *In the Town of S* (*V gorode "S"*, 1966). Also notable in this category are the actor-director Sergei Bondarchuk's (b. 1920) version of *Fate of a Man* (*Sud'ba cheloveka*, 1959), adapted from Mikhail Sholokhov, and the four-part epic *War and Peace* (*Voina i mir*, 1965–67), adapted from Tolstoi; and Grigori Kozintsev's distinguished adaptations of *Don Quixote* (1956), *Hamlet* (1964), and *King Lear* (*Korol' Lir*, 1972).

16.150 *The Lady with the Little Dog* (Iosif Heifitz, 1960).

Yet Khrushchev was not Stalin, and advances in the industry continued to be made under his regime: by 1958 the annual output had reached 115 features, of which one third were in color (introduced to the Soviets in 1950); in 1959 the Moscow International Film Festival was inaugurated on a regular biennial basis; and, most significant perhaps, production was either renewed or begun on a full-time basis in all of the non-Russian republics in the period 1955–65. Furthermore, the bolder Soviet filmmakers continued to test the waters of social comment during this time with such works as Kulijanov and Segel's *The House I Live In* (*Dom v kotorom ia zhivu*, 1957); Chkheidze's *Our Courtyard* (*Nash*

16.151 Sergei Bondarchuk as Pierre in his adaptation of *War and Peace* (1965–67).

16.152 *King Lear* (Grigori Kozintsev, 1972): Yuri Zharvet as Lear, Valentina Shendrikova as Cordelia.

16.153 *Ballad of a Soldier* (Grigori Chukhrai, 1958): Shanna Prokhorenko, Vladimir Ivashov.

dvor, 1957) and *Father of a Soldier* (*Otets soldata*, 1964); Chukhrai's internationally acclaimed *Ballad of a Soldier* (*Ballada o soldate*, 1958)—a prizewinner at Cannes and San Francisco—and *Clear Skies* (*Chistoe nebo*, 1961); Kalatozov and Urusevski's (b. 1908) *The Letter That Wasn't Sent* (*Neopravlennoe pismo*, 1960) and *I Am Cuba* (*Ia Kuba*, 1965);* Iuli Raizman's *If This Is Love* (*A esli eto liubov*, 1961); Mikhail Romm's *Nine Days of One Year* (*Deviat´ dnei odnogo goda*, 1962); Andrei Tarkovski's debut, *Ivan's Childhood* (*Ivano vo detstvo*, 1962); Elem Klimov's *Welcome—or, No Trespassing* (*Dobro pozhalovat*, 1964), an anti-authoritarian satire in the guise of a children's comedy; and, most strikingly, Marlen Khutsiev's *Lenin's Guard* (also known as *Ilich Square* [*Zastva Ilicha*], produced 1962), which provoked a storm of official outrage and had to be reshot as *I'm Twenty* (*Mne dvadsat´ let*, released 1964) over the next eighteen months.

In December 1962, Khrushchev announced that liberalism in the arts had gone too far, and he issued a stinging indictment of Soviet modernist painting on the occasion of the exhibition "Thirty Years of Pictorial Art" in Moscow. This was followed by party-line attacks on *Nine Days in a Year* and *The Letter That Wasn't Sent*, making it clear that the basic tenets of socialist realism hadn't changed a bit. Caution immediately became the industry watchword, although remarkable debuts continued to be made—for example, by the Georgian directors Georgi Danelia (b. 1930)—*I Walk About Moscow* (*Ia shagaiu po Moskve*, 1963) and Eldar Shengelaia (b. 1933)—*White Caravan* (*Belyi karavan*, 1963), and by the actor-director Vasili Shukshin (1929–74)—*There Was a Lad* (*Zhivet takoi paren´*, 1964).

In October 1964, Khrushchev was removed from office by a conspiracy among his deputies, and a diumvirate was installed consisting of Leonid Brezhnev (1906–82) and Alexei N. Kosygin (1904–80) as first secretary of the Central Committee and chairman of the Council of Ministers, respectively. (Brezhnev became general secretary in 1966, and ultimately he superseded all of his comrades to become supreme leader of the coun-

*A dazzling realization of the concept of Eisenstein's Mexican project of 1930–32. See S. P. Hill, "Soviet Cinema Today," *Film Quarterly* 20, 4 (Summer 1967): 33–52.

16.154 *Nine Days in a Year* (Mikhail Romm, 1962).

try, a position he held until his death.) There followed a period of uncertainty and indecision for the arts that ended abruptly with the Warsaw Pact occupation of Czechoslovakia in August 1968 and a renewed domestic campaign against the liberalization of Soviet culture in 1969. Appropriately, however, the brief period of the Khrushchev thaw ended with the production of one of the most extraordinary and beautiful films ever made: Sergei Parajanov's *Shadows of Forgotten Ancestors* (*Teni zabytykh predkov*, 1964).

Sergei Parajanov and *Shadows of Forgotten Ancestors*

There was little in Parajanov's (b. 1924) early career to announce the remarkable sensibility displayed in *Shadows*. He attended the VGIK, where his major professor was the Ukrainian director Igor Savchenko (1906–51), who had studied under Dovzhenko, and where he was also tutored extensively by Lev Kuleshov and by Dovzhenko himself. Parajanov graduated from the Directing Department in 1951 and was assigned to the Dovzhenko Kiev Studio, where he made five Ukrainian-language films for regional consumption—all of them indifferent, by his own account—before undertaking the project that became *Shadows of Forgotten Ancestors*. Adapted by Parajanov and Ivan Chendei from a pre-Revolutionary novelette by the distinguished Ukrainian writer Mykhailo Kotsiubynsky to celebrate the centennial of his birth, the film retells an ancient Carpathian folk legend of universal resonance. Deep in the Carpathian mountains, at the farthest western reach of the Ukraine, a young man (Ivan) and a young woman (Marichka) become lovers despite a blood feud between their families. Marichka accidentally drowns one night searching for Ivan, and after a long period of bereavement, he marries another (Palagna). But Ivan is persistently haunted by the image of his first love and eventually chooses to join her in death.

Like the legends of Tristan and Isolde and Romeo and Juliet, *Shadows* offers a relatively familiar and uncomplicated tale of undying love that has variants in cultures all over the world. But in the telling of the tale, Parajanov created a vision of human experience so radical and unique as

16.155 *Shadows of Forgotten Ancestors* **(Sergei Parajanov, 1964).**

16.156 *Shadows of Forgotten Ancestors.*

to subvert all authority. To say that *Shadows* violates every narrative code and representational system known to the cinema is an understatement—at times, in fact, the film seems intent upon deconstructing the very process of representation itself. The relationship between narrative logic and cinematic space—between point of view inside and outside of the frame—is so consistently undermined that most critics on first viewing literally cannot describe what they've seen. Adjectives frequently used to characterize *Shadows* are "hallucinatory," "intoxicating," and "delirious"—terms that imply, however positively, confusion and incoherence. But the camera and editing techniques that elicit such comments are all part of Parajanov's deliberate aesthetic strategy to interrogate a whole set of historically evolved assumptions about the nature of cinematic space and the relationship between the spectator and the screen.

Parajanov proceeds by means of perceptual dislocation, so that it becomes impossible at any given moment to imagine a stable time-space continuum for the dramatic action. Often, for example, the viewer will be invited by conventional stylistic means to share a point of view that is suddenly ruptured by camera movement or some other disjunction in spatial logic; spaces that appear to be contiguous in one shot sequence are revealed to be miles apart in the next; surfaces that seem to be two-dimensional at the beginning of a shot will become richly textured in process by focal manipulation. Sometimes a shot will begin with a camera angle that encourages the viewer to misconstrue narrative space, as when a wall is momentarily made to resemble the surface of a roof. At other times, the camera assumes perspectives and executes maneuvers that appear to be *physically,* as well as dramatically, impossible: the camera looks down from the top of a falling tree, several hundred feet tall; it looks up through a pool with no optical distortion as Ivan drinks from its surface; it whirls 360 degrees on its axis for nearly a full minute, dissolving focus and color to abstraction; it turns corners and swoops down embankments with inhuman celerity. Finally, Parajanov and his cinematographer Iuri Ilenko (b. 1936) use a variety of lenses, including telephoto zoom and 180-degree wide angle, or "fish-eye," to warp the film's scenographic space to the outer limits of narrative comprehension—but never quite beyond it. The point of these techniques is not to confuse the spectator but to prevent him from constructing in his head the kind of comfortable, familiar, and logically continuous representational space associated with traditional narrative form. The reason is simply that the film posits a world that is neither comfortable, familiar, nor logically continuous, for *Shadows* exists most fully not in the realm of narrative but in the worlds of myth and the unconscious. It is above all else a deeply psychological film, rich in both Freudian and Jungian* imagery, and one whose sophistication makes the Pavlovian tactics of Eisenstein's montage seem almost primitive by comparison.

Shadows' psychological subtlety extends to its use of sound and color. It has been frequently noted that the film has an operatic, pageantlike quality; and Parajanov uses a complex variety of music—from atonal electronics, to lush orchestral romanticism, to hieratic religious chants, to vocal and instrumental folk music—to create leitmotifs for the film's various psychological atmospheres. Similarly, Parajanov employs color in a psychologically provocative way, having developed for *Shadows* what he called a "dramaturgy of color." When Ivan and Marichka are first drawn together as children, for example, the prevailing color is the white of the snow, corresponding to their innocence; the green of spring dominates their young love; monochrome and sepia tones are used to drain the world of color during the period of Ivan's grieving; but color returns riotously, if briefly, after he meets Palagna; as that relationship turns barren, the film is dominated by autumnal hues; monochrome returns during Ivan's death delirium; and at the moment of his death the natural universe is painted in surreal shades of red and blue. The ultimate effect of both the soundtrack and the color system, like that of the film's optical distortions and dislocations, is to destabilize the spectator perceptually, and therefore psychologically, in order to present a tale that operates at the level not of narrative but of myth, a tale that is an archetype of life itself: youth passes from innocence to experience to solitude and death in a recurring cycle, eons upon eons. This is the "shadow" of "forgotten ancestors": the archetypal pattern that outlasts and transcends individual identity.

When *Shadows of Forgotten Ancestors* appeared in the West in 1965, it was immediately recognized that the Soviet cinema had acquired a new genius on the order of Eisenstein and Dovzhenko. The film won sixteen foreign festival awards and was released in the United States and Europe to wide critical acclaim. Rarely since the triumph of *Potemkin*, in fact, had a Soviet motion picture enjoyed such international esteem. But at home the cultural situation had already begun to take its next nasty turn—

---

* The very title *Shadows of Forgotten Ancestors* resonates with Jung's "archetypes of the collective unconscious," and the film on one level is about experiences common to all humanity since the race evolved—love, despair, solitude, death. (American prints of the film also bear the title *Wild Horses of Fire*, added by its Chicago distributor in 1966.)

Shadows was variously accused of "formalism" and "Ukrainian nationalism," and it was deliberately underbooked in domestic theaters by officials of Sovkino (see chapters 5 and 9). Parajanov found himself personally attacked by the party secretary for "Ideological Problems," and when invitations to other countries began to pour in as the film's reputation spread, he was consistently denied permission to travel abroad. During the next ten years, Parajanov went on to write ten complete scenarios based on classical Russian literature and folk epics—all of which he was refused permission to shoot by Soviet authorities. He did make one more film—a visionary life of the Armenian poet Arutiun Sayadian (1712–95) entitled *The Color of Pomegranates (Sayat nova)*—which was banned on its release in 1969 and finally given limited distribution in a version "re-edited" by Sergei Iutkevitch in the early seventies (it was first seen in the United States at the 1980 New York Film Festival). Another project, *Kiev Frescoes (Kievskie freski)*, was approved but aborted after the first edited rushes were screened—the same kind of ritual humiliation accorded Eisenstein by the Stalinists during the production of *Bezhin Meadow (Bezhin lug, 1935)*. Then, while he was working on an adaptation of some fairy tales of Hans Christian Andersen for Soviet television in January 1974, Parajanov was arrested on a variety of specious charges and sentenced to six years at hard labor in the Gulag. An international petition campaign motivated the Soviets to release him in late 1977,* but he was not allowed to work in the film industry again until 1984, when he was exonerated and assigned to Georgia's Gruziafilm Studios. Parajanov's first film there, *The Legend of Suram Fortress (Legenda Suramskoi kreposti, 1985)*, co-directed with Dodo (David) Abashidze, was a return to the mythopoetic mode of *Shadows* that showed his remarkable cinematic sensibilities to be still very much intact. Similarly, *Asik Kerib* (Gruziafilm, 1988), a folklore-based adaptation of a Lermontov tale shot on location in Georgia, Armenia, and Azerbaijan, abounds in the ritualized tableaux and magical invention of Parajanov's earlier work.

Cinema Under Brezhnev

What happened to Parajanov during the Brezhnev years was extreme. More typical was the plight of Andrei Tarkovski (1932–86), the second major figure to emerge from the postwar Soviet cinema during the sixties. Son of the acclaimed Russian poet Arseni Tarkovski, Andrei studied at the VGIK under Mikhail Romm and had already won first prize at the New York Student Film Festival for his diploma project, *Steamroller and Violin (Katok i skripka,* co-directed with Andrei Mikhalkov-Konchalovski), when he graduated in 1960. His first feature, *Ivan's Childhood* (also

---

* According to Richard Grenier, the campaign's success was due largely to the relentless lobbying of Lili Brik (Maiakovski's former mistress, over ninety at the time) and the French Communist leader Louis Aragon (Brik's brother-in-law), who interceded personally with Leonid Brezhnev ("A Soviet 'New Wave'?," *Commentary* July 1981, pp. 62–67). See also Alan Stanbrook, "The Return of Paradjanov," *Sight & Sound* 55, 4 (Autumn 1986): 257–61.

known as *My Name Is Ivan*), which began his long collaborations with cinematographer Vadim Yusov and composer Viacheslav Ovchinnikov, won the Golden Lion at Venice in 1962. In content, this story of a heroic young orphan who becomes a frontline spy for the Soviet army during World War II follows the traditional pattern. But in terms of form, *Ivan's Childhood* approaches the avant-garde in its surreal rendition of the horrors of war; and Tarkovski's next film, *Andrei Rublev* (1966), from a script by Konchalovski, produced an official scandal. The title character is a historical figure, the Russian Orthodox monk who brought the art of religious icon painting to its zenith in the fifteenth century. Tarkovski used Rublev's life, reconstructed in loosely connected episodes, to symbolize the conflict between Russian barbarism and idealism. The film was banned in the Soviet Union on the grounds that it gave an inaccurate (that is, negative) account of medieval Russian history, although an edited version won the International Critics' Award at Cannes in 1969, and *Rublev* was ultimately given limited domestic release in a version further re-edited and cut by forty minutes.*

16.157 Tarkovski's *Andrei Rublev* (1966): Anatoli Solonitsyn in the title role.

Tarkovski's third feature was the metaphysical science fiction film *Solaris* (1971), adapted from a novel by the Polish writer Stanislaw Lem; it won the Special Jury Prize at Cannes in 1972 and was uncontroversial at home. But his autobiographical *A Mirror* (*Zerkalo*, 1974), reminiscent of Fellini's *Amarcord,* was much criticized for its labyrinthine structure and parabolic style; it was not suppressed, but neither was it offered for export until 1980. After directing an acclaimed stage version of *Hamlet* in Moscow in 1976, Tarkovski made *Stalker* (1979), a complex allegory of decay shot in Estonia and interpreted by many European critics as an indictment of the Soviet government's repression of intellectual freedom. In this gloomy film, a writer and a scientist are led by "the Stalker" on a journey through a wastelandlike "Zone" to a "Room" where all wishes may be fulfilled, but they fail in their quest through lack of will. By this point, Tarkovski had acquired an international reputation as the Soviet Union's most unorthodox filmmaker, and he soon became one of the few Soviet directors in many years to work outside of the country with official sanction.

16.158 *Solaris* (Andrei Tarkovski: 1971).

In 1982, Tarkovski began shooting *Nostalghia* (*Nostalgiia*, 1983) in Italy for Gaumont and RAI, with Soviet cooperation. Scripted by Tonino Guerra, a frequent collaborator of Antonioni and Francesco Rosi, *Nostalghia* portrays the memories, dreams, and waking experience of a Russian professor of architecture who has come to Italy for the first time, accompanied by a female interpreter of Botticelli-like beauty. It is perhaps Tarkovski's most mysterious and inaccessible film, but it was a great success at Cannes in 1983, where it shared a specially created Best Direction award with Robert Bresson's *L'Argent*, and also received the International Critics' Award. Largely on the strength of such prestige, Tarkovski continued working outside of the Soviet Union, in 1983 directing Mus-

---

*Tarkovski's original 185–minute version is now available in the United States from Corinth Films.

16.159 Tarkovski's *Nostalghia* (1983).

16.160 *A Nest of Gentlefolk* (Andrei Mikhalkov-Konchalovski, 1969).

16.161 *Uncle Vani* (Andrei Mikhalkov-Konchalovski, 1972): Vania (Innokenti Smoktunovski) is comforted by Sonya (Irina Kupchenko).

sorgsky's opera *Boris Godunov* for the London stage, and in 1985 completing the international coproduction *The Sacrifice* (*Zhertva*, 1986) in Sweden. Shot on location by the great cinematographer Sven Nykvist, this visionary work concerns the spiritual response of a small group of people on an isolated Baltic island to an imminent nuclear holocaust, and it won multiple international awards, including five at Cannes alone. Since *Andrei Rublev,* Tarkovski had won his creative freedom by remaining politically ambiguous, yet to many Western observers even his films made abroad bear the marks of careful, covert Soviet censorship. Fittingly, *The Sacrifice* showed no signs of reticence in providing a compendium of Tarkovski's lifelong themes and symbols. It was his last film; he died of lung cancer in Paris in December 1986.

A middle path is suggested by the work of Andrei Mikhalkov-Konchalovski. Konchalovski was born in 1937, a member of the Soviet artistic elite. His grandfather and great-grandfather were both famous painters; his mother and father are well-known writers; and his brother is the talented actor-director Nikita Mikhalkov (b. 1945). Konchalovski's first film as a director, *The First Teacher* (*Pervii uchitel´*, 1965), was a revisionist account of the conflict between revolutionary idealism and tradition in the Kirghiz mountains in the wake of October 1917, and it raised some eyebrows in official circles. But his second film, *Asya's Happiness* (*Asino schast´e,* 1966), was so critical of the poverty and backwardness of Soviet collective farms that it was damned and banned. (The public "damning" of films by party critics began in 1965 when Alov and Naumov's version of Dostoevsky's *Bad Joke* [*Skvernyi anekdot*] was pilloried; the practice continued for several years.) So Konchalovski prudently turned to the classics with subtle adaptations of Turgenev's *A Nest of Gentlefolk* (*Dvorianskoe gnezdo,* 1969) and Chekhov's *Uncle Vania* (*Diadia Vania,* 1970). Then he wrote some scripts for regional studios and directed the safely conformist modern musical romance *In Love* (*Vliublonnye,* 1974), before making the monumental *Siberiad* / *Sibiriana* (*Sibiriada,* 1979), which traces the histories of two Siberian families over a period of three generations from the Revolution to modern times. Widely regarded as the Soviet Union's greatest postwar epic, *Siberiad* was both a popular success at home and winner of the Special Jury Prize at Cannes in the year of its release. In 1980, Soviet authorities allowed Konchalovski to emigrate to the United States (with the very rare option of returning in the government's good graces), where he has made the downbeat, noncommercial *Maria's Lovers* (1983; released 1985) and *Runaway Train* (1985; screenplay by Akira Kurosawa) for the Cannon Group, which latter became a box-office and critical hit. More recently, he has directed an adaptation of Tom Kempinski's play *Duet for One* (1986) and a wild tale of survival in the backcountry Louisiana swamps ironically entitled *Shy People* (1987) for the same producers.

The various fates of Parajanov, Tarkovski, and Konchalovski notwithstanding, most Soviet directors remained at home in the post-Khrushchev era and adapted to the policy articulated by the new head of Soviet cinematography, Filip Yermash, in his 1972 Resolution of the Central Committee of the CPSU:

There are too many grey, formless works in which contemporary and historical themes are worked in a superficial manner, not finding any reflection of a fundamental social change taking place in Soviet society. . . . Persistent thematic planning will make possible the creation of films which will center on the positive hero of our time—man, for whom the struggle for the embodiment of the Communist ideal becomes the personal aim of his existence.

Clearly reminiscent of socialist realism, this new "pedagogic line," in fact, permitted greater technical innovation and complexity of expression. Typically, it was from the cinemas of the non-Russian republics, where a concentration on regional themes was tolerated and even encouraged, that some of the most extraordinary talent emerged in the seventies and eighties: from the Ukraine came the films of former cameraman Iuri Ilenko (b. 1936)—*On the Eve of Ivan Kupala* (that is, "Halloween Night"; *Noch´ nakanune Ivana Kupaly*, 1968), *White Bird with a Black Spot* (*Belaya ptitsa s chernoi otmetinoi*, 1971); and the extraordinary Larisa Shepitko, (1939–79)—*Heat* (*Znoi*, 1963); *Wings* (*Krillia*, 1966); *The Homeland of Electricity* (*Rodina electrichestva*, 1968); *You and I* (*Ty i ya*, 1971); *The Ascent* (*Voskhozhenie*, 1977; Golden Bear, Berlin). Armenia inspired Sergei Parajanov, of course, but also Frunze Dovlatian (b. 1927)—*Hello, It's Me* (*Alo, eto ya*, 1965), Genrikh Malian (b. 1925)—*Triangle* (*Treugolnik*, 1967), and subsequently, Albert Albert Mkrchian (*Tango of Our Childhood* (*Tango nashego detstva*, 1985), Bagrat Oganesian—*The Master* (*Khoziain*, 1986), Agasi Aivasian—*The Lit Lantern* (*Sashshennyi fonar*, 1986), and Dan Askarian—*Komitas* (1988; France). Meanwhile, Georgia, with its longstanding tradition of independence from the mainstream, produced something of a regional new wave in the work of Otar Ioseliani (b. 1934)—*When Leaves Fall* (*Listopad*, 1967); *There Lived a Singing Blackbird* (*Zhil pevchii drozd*, 1970), *Pastorale* (1976; shelved); *Les Favoris de la lune* (*Minions of the Moon*, 1984; France); Tengiz Abuladze (b. 1924)—*The Entreaty* (*Mol´ba*, 1968), *The Tree of Desire* [*Drevo zhelaniia*, 1977]; *Repentence* (*Pokaianie*, 1984; released 1987); Georgi Danelia (b. 1930)—*Cheer Up!* (*Ne goriui!*, 1969); *Mimino* (1976); *Autumn Marathon* (*Osennii maraton*, 1979); *Tears Are Flowing* (*Slezy kapali*, 1983); Georgi Shengelaia (b. 1937)—*Pirosmani* (1971); *Melodies of the Veri Neighborhood* (*Melodii Veriiskogo kvartala*, 1973); *The Journey of a Young Composer* [*Achalgazrda komozitoris mogazauroba*, 1986]—and his brother, Eldar (b. 1933)—*Odd Couple* [*Chudaki*]; *The Blue Mountains* [*Golubye gory*, 1985])—both sons of the Georgian pioneer director Nikolai Shengelaia (1903–43); and Lana Gogoberidze (b. 1928)—*Some Interviews on Personal Questions* (*Neskolko interviu po lichnym voprosam*, 1979), *The Day Longer Than the Night* (*Den´ dlinnee nochi*, 1984), *Succession of Events* (*Krugovorot*, 1987).

The cinema of Moldavia was distinguished mainly by the films of Emil Lotianu (b. 1936)—*Red Glades* [*Krasnye poliany*, 1966]; *The Leutary* [1972]; *The Shooting Party* (*Moi laskovyi i nezhnii zver*, 1979; adapted from Chekhov); *Pavlova* (1984)—but the cinemas of the neighboring Baltic republics all experienced notable growth at this time: Lithuania in the work of Vitautas Zhalakevichius (b. 1930)—*Nobody Wanted to Die*

16.162   Konchalovski's *Siberiad* (1979).

16.163   *Pirosmani* (Georgi Shengelaia, 1971).

16.164   *The Leutary* (Emil Lotianu, 1972).

(*Nikto ne khotel umirat'*, 1966); Algirdas Araminas (b. 1937)—*When I Was Young* (*Kogda byl malenkim*, 1969); Alamantas Grikiavcius (b. 1935)—*Ave Vita* (*Da budet zhizn*, 1970); Raymondas Vabalas (b. 1937)—*Stone on a Stone* (*Kamen' na kamen'*, 1972); Algimantas Puipa—*A Woman and Her Four Men* (*Zhenshchina i chetvero ee muzhchin*, 1984); Marionas Gedris (b. 1933)—*The Prodigal Son* (*Sunus palaidunas*, 1986); Latvia in the work of Gunars Piesis (b. 1931)—*In the Shadow of Death* (*Naves ena*, 1981); Aivars Freimanis (b. 1936)—*The Boy* (*Puika*, 1980); Herz Frank—*The Forbidden Zone* (*Aizlicqta zona*, 1975); and Ianas Streitch—*Other People's Passions* (*Svesas kaislibas*, 1986); and Estonia in the films of Kalja Kiisk (b. 1925)—*Madness* (*Hullumeelsus*, 1986); *Nipernaadi* (*Toomis Nipernaadi*, 1983); Olev Neuland—*Nest in the Wind* (*Gnezdo na vetru*, 1980); Peeter Simm—*Ideal Landscape* (*Ideaalmaastik*, 1986); Leida Laius—*Keep Smiling, Baby!* (*Naerata ometi*, 1986) and, with Arvo Icho, *Games for School Children* (*Igry dija detej skolnogo vozrasta*, 1987]). Finally the Soviet Asian republic of Kirghizia produced a vital cinema in the work of Bolobek Shamshiev (b. 1941)—*The Herdsman* (*Tshaban*, 1967); *The Gunshot in the Mountain Pass* (*Vystrel na perevale*, 1969); *The White Ship* (*Belyi parakhod*, 1977); *Among People* (*Sredi liudei*, 1979); *Early Cranes* (*Rannie zhuravli*, 1980), Irina Poplavskaia—*Jamila* (1968); *Vasilii i Vasilisa* (1981), Tolomush Okeev (b. 1934)—*The Sky of Our Childhood* (*Nebo nashego detstva*, 1967); *The Savage One* (*Liutyi*, 1974); *The Descendants of the Snow Leopard* [*Potomok belogo barsa*, 1985; Silver Bear, Berlin); *Mirages of Love* (*Mirazhi ljubvi*, 1988), as did the republic of Uzbekistan, in the films of Ali Khamraev (b. 1937)—*White, White Storks* (*Belye, belye aisty*, 1967); *Tryptych* (1978); *The Bodyguard* (1980); *A Hot Summer in Kabul* (1983); *The Garden of Desire* (*Sad zhlani*, 1988), and those of Eliör Ishmukhamedov (b. 1942)—*Tenderness* (*Nezhnost'*, 1966), *In Love* (*Zaliublennye*, 1969), *Youth of a Genius* (*Yunost' geniia*, 1983); and *Farewell, Green Summer* (*Proshal zelen leta*, 1987).

Among the Russians, this same period witnessed some progressive trends in the films of Vasili Shukshin (b. 1929)—*Strange People* (*Strannye liudi*, 1970); *The Red Snowball Bush* (*Kalina krasnaia*, 1974), and Gleb Panfilov (b. 1933)—*No Path Through the Flames* (*V ogne broda net*, 1968); *The Debut* (*Nachalo*, 1970); *May I Have the Floor?* (*Proshu slova?*, 1976); *Theme* (*Tema*, 1979; shelved until 1987); *Valentin, Valentina* (1981); *Vassa* (1983). Significant work was also done by Elem Klimov (b. 1935), the talented husband of Larisa Shepitko, in the comedy *Sport, Sport, Sport* (1971), the shelved historical drama *Agony* (*Agoniia,* also known as *Rasputin,* 1975; released recut, 1982; released in its original form, 1987); *Larisa* (1980; a moving documentary on his wife, who was killed with four members of her crew in an auto wreck in 1979); *Farewell* (*Proshchanie,* 1981); completed from the film Shepitko was working on when she died; and more recently, *Come and See* (*Idi i smotri,* 1985), a shattering film about the Nazi occupation of Byelorussia that won several international awards. Of course, Andrei Tarkovski and Andrei Mikhalkov-Konchalovski did most of their major work during this era, but it was a similarly fruitful period for Konchalovski's brother, Nikita Mikhalkov—*A Slave of Love* (*Raba liubvi,* 1976); *Unfinished Piece for a Player Piano* (*Neokonchennaia pesa dlia mekhanicheskogo,* 1977; based on Chekhov's play *Platonov*); *Five Evenings* (*Piat' vecherov,* 1979); *Oblomov* (1980; from the novel by Ivan Gonchov); *Kinfolk* (*Rodnia,* 1982); *Without Witnesses* (*Bez svidetelei,* 1983); *Dark Eyes* (*Oci cernye,* 1987; adapted from several Chekhov stories*); the youth director Dinara Asanova (1942–85)—*Woodpeckers Don't Get Headaches* (*Ne bolit golova u diatla,* 1975); *The Restricted Key* (*Kliuch bez prava peredachi,* 1977); *The Wife Has Left* (*Zhena ushla,* 1980); *Tough Kids* (*Patsany,* 1983); *Dear, Dearest, Beloved* . . . (*Milyi, dorogoi, liubimyi, edinstvennyi* . . . , 1984); and the director-writer team of Vadim Abdrashitov and Alexander Mindadze—*Fox Hunt* (*Okhota na lis,* 1980); *The Train Stopped* (*Ostanovilsia poezd,* 1982); *Parade of the Planets* (*Parad planet,* 1984). Older Russian directors still active in the eighties include Grigori Chukhrai—*Life Is Fine* (*Zhizn prekrasna,* 1980); Iosif Heifitz—*Married for the First Time* (*Vpervye zamuzhem,* 1980); *Asya* (1982; adapted from Turgenev); Iuli Raizman—*Private Life* (*Chastnaia zhizn,* 1983); *Time of Desires* (*Vremia zhelanii,* 1984); Alexander Zarkhi—*Chicherin* (1986); Andrei Khrzhanovski—*A Pushkin Trilogy* (1985; animated); Sergei Iutkevich—*Lenin in Paris* (*Lenin v Parizhie,* 1981); Sergei Bondarchuk—*Red Bells* (*Krasnye kolkola,* in two parts, 1982; 1983); *Boris Godunov* (1986; adapted from Pushkin's epic poem); Alexander Alov and Vladimir Naumov—*River Bank* (*Bereg,* 1984); and Sergei Gerasimov's swan song, *Lev Tolstoi,* (1984), in which the one-time actor played the lead role as well as writing and directing.

Contemporary Trends

In the seventies and eighties, film-going became an immensely popular activity in the Soviet Union. The average feature is seen by 17 million

* On Mikhalkov's *oeuvre,* see Karen Jaehne, "Rehabilitating the Superfluous Man: Films in the Life of Nikita Mikhalkov," *Film Quarterly* 34, 4 (Summer 1981): 14–21.

16.165 *Moscow Does Not Believe in Tears* (Vladmir Menshov, 1980).

people, tickets cost a dollar or less, and there are permanent theaters everywhere (5,257 of them in 1987) operating seven days a week. Even the country's most popular television show, "Film Panorama" (*"Kinopanorama"*), which is hosted by director Eldar Ryazanov and draws 140 million viewers per week, is about the movies. A recent trend in production has been toward the mildly satiric representation of contemporary life in films like Georgi Danelia's *Autumn Marathon* (1979), Ryazanov's *Garage* (*Garazh,* 1980) and *Station for Two* (*Vokzal dlia dvoikh,* 1983), Vladimir Menshov's *Moscow Does Not Believe in Tears* (*Moskva slezam ne verit,* 1980; the winner, unaccountably, of the American Academy Award for Best Foreign Film in that year); Peter Todorovsky's *The Beloved Woman of Mechanic Gavrilov* (*Liubimaia zenshchina mekhanika Gavrilova,* 1982); Vladimir Bortko's *The Blonde Around the Corner* [*Blondinka za uglom,* 1984); and Alla Surikova's *Sincerely Yours . . .* (*Iskrenne vash . . . ,* 1985). These films are called *bytovye,* after the Russian word for "everyday life," or "seamy side of life," and are sometimes risqué in their depiction of formerly forbidden subjects (*Station for Two,* for example, a comic blockbuster seen by 30 million Soviets, contains scenes of black-market activities and life in a forced labor camp). But many other areas, such as criticism of the party or the depiction of dissidents, remain taboo, and until the dawning of *glasnost,* the *bytovye* seemed ultimately to be escapist fare for a closed society in which the cinema, like every other aspect of public life, was still under tight state control.

In the late eighties there were twenty studios throughout the Soviet Union producing an average of 150 theatrical figures per year, plus 80 to 90 films for television. Each director, cinematographer, scriptwriter, set designer, and producer must graduate from the VGIK* or its equivalent

---

* The VGIK is today the world's largest film school. In addition to training students from thirty-six foreign countries, it provides the core of artistic personnel for the entire Soviet film industry through professional instruction in seven separate departments: directing, cinematography, acting, scriptwriting, film criticism and history, set design, and economics and organization (that is, production and distribution). At the Leningrad Institute of Cinema Engineers (LIKI, founded 1919), engineers and technicians are trained in such fields as acoustics, sound technology, camera and projection technology, and the technology of film processing, lighting, and optics. Research for the industry is conducted by the All-Union Scientific-Research Cinema-Photo-Institute in several locations. After successfully completing five years of training and writing a thesis, VGIK graduates are sent out to one of the twenty regional or specialized studios in the Soviet republics, according to the studios' needs. These are, in descending order of productivity: Mosfilm Studio (Moscow)—the largest, producing one-fourth of all films made in the country; Lenfilm Studio (Leningrad)—the oldest, founded by the Petrograd Cinema Committee in 1918; Gorki Central Studio of Children and Youth Films (Moscow); Kiev's Dovzhenko Film Studio (formerly Ukrainfilm); Armenfilm Studio (Erevan, Armenia); Byelarusfilm Studio (Minsk); Azerbaidzhanfilm Studio (Baku); Gruziafilm Studio (Tbilisi, Georgia); Kazakhfilm Studio (Alma-Ata); Kirghizfilm Studio (Frunze); Lithuanian Film Studio (Vilnius); Moldava-Film Studio (Kishinev); Odessa Film Studio; Yalta Film Studio (Yalta, Crimea); Riga's Latvian Film Studio; Tajikfilm Studio (Dushanbe); Tallinfilm Studio (Tallinn, Estonia); Turkmenfilm Studio (Ashkhabad); Uzbekfilm Studio (Tashkent); "Soiuzmultfilm" Film Studio ("All-Union Animated Cartoon Studio"—Moscow); and Sverdlovsk Film Studio (the film center for the Ural mountains). VGIK graduates may also be placed at two specialized facilities, "Filmexport" Film Studio, which prepares foreign-language versions of Soviet features, or "Tsentrnauch-

(such as FAMU) and be assigned to a specific studio in Russia or the non-Russian republics. Until 1987, scripts were subject to prior approval by the studio leadership, and films were rated by a national censorship commission after production; those not approved—like *Andrei Rublev* or, more recently, Elem Klimov's epic of the year 1917, *Agoniia* (1975; released recut 1982)—were either shelved or remade until they were acceptable to the censors (although some, like *Agoniia*, were sold abroad to return their investment).

With the succession of Mikhail Gorbachev (b. 1931) to the Soviet leadership in 1985, however, a more liberal policy was advanced by state film officials.* Several formerly banned films were released and offered for export for the first time, for example; and the much persecuted director Sergei Parajanov was rehabilitated and allowed to work again (indeed, Gorbachev chose as his first foreign minister Edward Shevardnadze, who as party secretary of Georgia has been an outspoken supporter of such "difficult" directors as Parajanov and Otar Ioseliani). Coproduction with Western countries was encouraged (for example, NBC's eight-hour mini-series *Peter the Great* [Marvin J. Chomsky and Lawrence Schiller, 1986] was shot on location in the Soviet Union), as was foreign-location shooting of Soviet films (such as Tarkovski's *The Sacrifice* [1986], produced in Sweden with British, Swedish, and Soviet capital). The Gorbachev regime even ended the freeze on VCRs imposed under Brezhnev in the late seventies, enabling Soviet citizens to see on cassette foreign films that are officially banned from public exhibition (Wajda's *Man of Iron* [1981] and Forman's *Amadeus* [1984], for instance, are extremely popular on video).

These were welcome changes, but they were thought to be largely cosmetic until 1986, which marked a major turning point for Soviet cinema. In that year, Gorbachev announced a serious bid to change the nature of Soviet society through a new *glasnost* ("openness") and *perestroika* ("restructuring"), and the Film Workers Union responded in May by ousting two-thirds of its leadership and replacing old-guard president Lev Kulijanov with the dynamic director Elem Klimov, whose films were

---

film" ("Central Studios for Popular-Science and Educational Films"), which produces classroom shorts for domestic use. Two other agencies of note are "Sovexportfilm" (established in 1937), the state monopoly in charge of exporting Soviet films and importing foreign ones (and thus the liaison to all international festivals), and "Gosfilmofond" (established in 1948), the state film archive housing over fifty-thousand titles. The average Soviet feature costs about 600,000 dollars to produce, with budgets scarcely ever rising above 1 million dollars. As in other Eastern European countries, both filmmakers and performers are modestly paid by Western standards, although Soviet directors are eligible to receive bonuses based on the quality of their completed productions, as determined by the national censorship panel mentioned above.

* Neither of Gorbachev's immediate predecessors—Yuri Andropov (1914–84), who replaced Leonid Brezhnev as secretary general of the Central Committee of the CPSU when he died in Novembver 1982, or Konstantin U. Chernenko (1911–85), who replaced Andropov when he died in February 1984—was in power long enough to have had much effect on the Soviet film industry, although a thaw of sorts was expected under Andropov, and Chernenko publicly called for a return to the rigid principles of socialist realism.

among the most shelved of any contemporary cineaste. In December the conservative Brezhnev-era bureaucrat Filip Yermash was replaced as head of Goskino, the state film committee, by the liberal Alexander Kamshalov; and calls to abolish the long-standing system of postproduction censorship finally met with success in 1987 when twenty-five shelved features were officially released in their homeland for the first time, many at the Moscow Film Festival for that year. These included the full version of Marlen Khutsiev's recut *I'm Twenty* (1963), Iuri Ilenko's *A Fountain for the Thirsty* (*Rodnik dlia zhazhdushchikh*, 1965), Konchalovski's *Asya's Happiness* (1966), Alexander Askodov's *The Commissar* (*Komissar*, 1966), Larisa Shepitko and Andrei Smirnov's *The Beginning of an Unknown Century* (*Nachalo nevedomogo veka*, 1967), Alexei German's *Trial on the Road* (*Proverka na dorogakh*, 1971) and *My Friend Ivan Lapshin* (*Moi drug Ivan Lapshin*, 1983), Alexander Sokurov's *A Lonely Man's Voice* (*Odinokii golos cheloveka*, 1978), Gleb Panfilov's *The Theme* (*Tema*, 1979; winner of the Berlin Golden Bear, 1987), Klimov's own *Agoniia* (1975) and *Farewell* (1981), and Tengiz Abuladze's hallucinatory satire *Repentence* (*Pokaianie*, 1984), the first Soviet film to be openly critical of Stalin. In addition to permitting the release of suppressed films, *glasnost* has encouraged the production of such outspoken and / or stylistically innovative new Russian features as Konstantin Lopushanski's postnuclear *Letters from a Dead Man* (*Pis'ma mertvogo cheloveka*, 1985), Viktor Ogorodnikov's *Burglar* (*Vzlomshik*, 1987), Iuri Mamin's *Neptune's Holiday* (1987), Aleksander Sokurov's *Heartless Grief* (*Skorbnoe beschuvstvie*, 1986; based on Shaw's *Heartbreak House*), Vadim Abdrashitov's *Plumbum, or a Dangerous Game* (*Pliumbum, ili opasnaia igra*, 1987), and Sergei Soloviov's extraordinary pop rock thriller *Assa* (1988), as well as the work of such new Ukrainian directors as Mikhail Belikov (*How Young We Were Then* [*Kak molodi mi byli*, 1986], the Georgians Nana Djordjadze (*Robinsoniad; Or, My English Grandfather* [*Robinzoniada, ili moi angliiskii dedushka*, 1986; winner of the 1987 Golden Camera award at Cannes]) and Timar Babluani (*The Sparrow's Flight* [*Perelet vorobiev*, 1987]), the documentaries *Trumpet Solo* (*Solo truby* [Alexander Ivankin, 1986]), *Risk* (Dmitri Barshtchevski, 1988), and *More Light* (Marina Babak [*Bol'she sveta!*, 1988]), an enthusiastic attempt to fill in some of the blank pages of Soviet history. The reform movement that has permitted this extraordinary liberalization of the Soviet cinema is deliberate, broad-ranging, and real; but the general contours of Soviet history and Soviet film history provide no guarantees that it will last.

As Lenin predicted in 1917, film for Eastern Europeans has become "the most important art." It has helped to support their revolutions and to transform their societies. And it has managed to attain for itself a sophistication of form unparalleled in any other part of the world. The reasons are many, but two stand out clearly. Culturally, the countries of Eastern Europe have always had an affinity for the kind of sensuous thinking that produces great films and creates new cinematic languages.

Their apprehension of art forms has historically been at once abstract and concretely structural. It is no coincidence that the same milieu that produced Franz Kafka, Karel Capek, Eugène Ionesco, and Stanislaw Lem also produced Věra Chytilová, Jan Němec, and Miklós Jancsó, for all of these artists fuse romanticism and cynicism into a strong sense of existential absurdity. Secondly, the countries of Eastern Europe have been plundered, colonized, occupied, and otherwise oppressed for most of their history. In periods of great social and political oppression, art often provides the only means of self-expression a culture can attain. And film art—"the most important art"—has traditionally served this function in Eastern Europe. As proof one has only to note the correlation between periods of political turbulence and great achievement in Eastern European film: Poland, 1954–63, for example, and Czechoslovakia, 1963–68. That so much greatness and beauty of expression should be the product of oppression is a tragedy. But that it exists at all—and has been permitted to influence the cinemas of the West—should renew our faith in the power of the human spirit not merely to survive but to prevail. And of the momentous changes sweeping the countries of Eastern Europe at present, one thing is certain: they will ultimately find expression in their national cinemas.

Wind from the East: Japan, India, and China

JAPAN

The Early Years

The Japanese cinema, like most other aspects of Japanese culture, evolved in nearly total isolation from the West until the end of World War II. The Edison Kinetograph was introduced into Japan as early as 1896, and movies almost immediately became a popular cultural form. But Japanese cinema went through a much longer "primitive" period than the cinemas of the West (roughly 1896–1926) because of the persistence of an older, more venerable cultural form: the *kabuki* theater. Ironically, it was *kabuki* that had stimulated Eisenstein in elaborating his radically innovative theory of montage.

Kabuki is a highly stylized and somewhat overwrought dramatic form deriving from the feudal Tokugawa period (1598–1867), and because of its perennial popularity in Japan, the earliest Japanese fiction films were versions of famous *kabuki* plays (there exist some 350 of them). As Japanese cinema grew into a large-scale domestic industry in the first two decades of this century, the stylized conventions of *kabuki* became the mainstream conventions of Japanese narrative film. This prohibited the kind of formal experimentation then going on in the West in the work of Griffith, Eisenstein, Feuillade, and Murnau, but allowed Japanese cinema to develop along its own path.

Two conventions of *kabuki* are especially unusual relative to Western films. First, all female roles until well into the twenties were played by professional female impersonators known as *onnagata* or *oyama*, which militated against even the simplest sort of photographic realism. Second, and much more formative in the development of Japanese cinema, was the convention of the *benshi*—an actor who stands at the side of the stage and narrates the action for the audience. In the earliest Japanese films, the *benshi* provided both voices for the characters and commentary on the action. After 1912, the *benshi* concentrated exclusively on dialogue in response to an influx of foreign films using intertitles, a practice quickly imitated by domestic producers. By 1920, however, the *benshi* had returned to the practice of mixing description/commentary with spoken dialogue—sometimes read from intertitles, sometimes interpolated from the action itself. As Donald Kirihara has pointed out, the effect on film form was immense: "[T]he presence of the *benshi* was a fact that filmmakers could assume during production, allowing them to make films with ambiguous spatial and temporal transitions or undermotivated plots with the knowledge that the *benshi* would be present to provide whatever narrative coherence was lacking."

In short, the presence of a human, *verbal* narrator permitted Japanese *cinematic* narrative to remain relatively diffuse. In 1923 an earthquake leveled the cities of Tokyo and Yokohama, including the physical facilities of the entire Japanese film industry.* After the quake, the industry, like much of Japan itself, had to be rebuilt from scratch, and one result was a turning away from the past and an increased receptivity to modern ideas, especially those from the West. The *oyama* rapidly disappeared, and Japanese films adopted nonnative styles, such as the newly discovered Western modes of naturalism (in Minoru Murata's† *The Street Juggler* [*Machi no tejinashi,* 1924]) and Expressionism (in Teinosuke Kinugasa's *A Page of Madness* [*Kurutta ippeiji,* 1926] and *Crossways* [*Jujiro,* 1928]). The *benshi,* however, many of whom had become stars in their own right, would remain a potent force in Japanese cinema until well after the introduction of sound. In 1927, there were 6,818 *benshi,* including only 180 women, who were licensed to practice throughout the Japanese Empire. Though their stranglehold on the industry was eventually broken by reorganization, there were still 1,295 of them—mostly unemployed—in 1940. Nevertheless, the coming of sound insured that directors could finally become the major creative force in Japanese film, as they already were in most countries of the West.

By 1925 the *kabuki*-oriented cinema had been replaced by a new director's cinema consciously divided into two large genres, or types, that persist to this day: the **jidai-geki,** or period film set before 1868 (the year marking the beginning of the Meiji Restoration and the abolition of feudal Japan), and the **gendai-geki,** or film of contemporary life. Both genres are obviously very broad, and each has come to contain a large number of subtypes. Currently, for example, the *jidai-geki* encompasses the *chanbara,* or sword-fight film,** which focuses on the figure of the masterless *samurai* ("warrior"), or *ronin;* the historical romance; and the ghost film. The *gendai-geki* includes such disparate types as the lower-middle-class comedy-drama (*shomin-geki*); the "children's film," in which the inanities and corruptions of the adult world are satirized by presenting them from a child's point of view; and the *yakuza-eiga,* or modern gangster film. The years 1926 to 1932 saw the appearance of the first major works of Japanese cinema in the beautiful period films of Teinosuke Kinugasa

17.1 *A Page of Madness* (Teinosuke Kinugasa, 1926): Masao Inoue.

---

* The great Kanto earthquake struck at noon on September 1, 1923, with shocks so violent that the seismographs at the Central Weather Bureau broke trying to record them. In the five ensuing tidal waves, 140,000 people were killed and 64 percent of standing structures in the two-city area were destroyed.

† Japanese names in this chapter are given in the Western style, with the surname last.

** For the Japanese the term *chanbara* is onomatopoeic, since it imitates the sound of two swords clashing together, as *"chan-chan, bara-bara."*

(1896–1982) and Kenji Mizoguchi (see pp. 792–94), and in the *shomin-geki* of Yasujiro Shimazu (1897–1945), Heinosuke Gosho (1902–81), Mikio Naruse (1905–69), and—above all—Yasujiro Ozu (see pp. 794–95). In careers that extended well into the postwar period, both Mizoguchi and Ozu became classical masters of the Japanese film; the third master was Akira Kurosawa (see pp. 784–92), whose career did not begin until the middle years of World War II.

Sound

17.2 *I Was Born, But . . .* (Yasujiro Ozu, 1932): Hideo Sugawara, Tokkan Kozo.

Sound entered the cinema in Japan more gradually and smoothly than it did in the countries of the West, because it was less of a novelty for both audiences and filmmakers. Japanese movies had always "talked" through the mediation of the *benshi,* and far from retarding the formal development of Japanese cinema (as it had for a brief period in the West), the coming of synchronously recorded sound actually accelerated it by permanently liberating films from subservience to a live narrator. The first successful talkie, Gosho's comic *shomin-geki, The Neighbor's Wife and Mine* (*Madamu to nyobo,* 1931), ranked very high in formal achievement among early sound films generally. But the addition of sound was a leisurely process in Japan. In 1932 only forty-five feature-length sound films were produced out of a total of four hundred, and silent features continued to be made until 1937 (the most important Japanese film of 1932, for example, was Ozu's silent "children's comedy" *I Was Born, but . . .* [*Umarete wa mita keredo*]). Other changes were swifter and ultimately more significant.

One important consequence of the reorganization was the complete monopolization of the Japanese film industry by three, and later five, major production companies, called *zaibatsu* ("conglomerates"), through the Japan Motion Picture Producers' Association (founded 1925) in a pattern remarkably similar to the American studio system. As in the American system, each of the three Japanese studios during the thirties (Nikkatsu, founded 1914; Shochiku, founded 1920; and Toho, founded 1932) had been formed by the ruthless absorption of smaller companies. And, as in the American system, they existed solely for the purpose of producing films for mass consumption through a highly efficient, rigidly structured production process. With some modification, this system still operates in Japan today, and until the recent economic recession it was the most productive in the world, averaging over four hundred features a year.

One aspect of the Japanese studio system that differed from the American, however—and that differs to this day as part of an ingrained cultural pattern—was the hierarchical master-pupil relationship between directors and their assistants. Aspiring young filmmakers had to apprentice themselves to older, more experienced directors and literally prove their worth (that is, their ability to turn a profit for the studio) before being permitted to direct on their own. Thus, Yasujiro Shimazu, who founded the *shomin-geki* in the early twenties, himself had been taught by the first-generation Shochiku director Kaoru Osanai, and in the course of his own long career trained ten younger directors, including the now prominent Keisuke Kinoshita (b. 1912), Masaki Kobayashi (b. 1916), and Kaneto Shindo (b. 1912). Another unique aspect of the Japanese studio system is the paternalistic relationship between the director and the entire cast and crew of a film. It seems clear that both the apprenticeship system and the familial organization of production recapitulate an element deeply rooted in Japanese society, which may be best described as feudalistic.

The Meiji Restoration of 1868–1912 had provided a brief respite of enlightenment after eight hundred years of feudal culture. In 1868, the fifteen-year-old Emperor Meiji abolished the Tokugawa *shogunate,* the military dictatorship that had ruled Japan in the legitimate emperor's stead since 1185, and outlawed the *samurai,* who had supported it. But these centuries-old feudal institutions did not disappear. Instead, the *samurai* translated themselves into a modern form and emerged in the late 1920s as the general staff and officer corps of a powerful military establishment. By the end of 1931, they had virtually reasserted their control of the government. As sound came to the Japanese cinema in the early thirties, militarism, patriotism, and xenophobia pervaded every segment of Japanese society. These factors led first to Japan's war of aggression against China in 1937 and ultimately to its catastrophic confrontation with the United States.

As ultranationalism gripped Japan, a new film genre appeared opposing it—the left-wing "tendency" film that, in either period or contemporary guise, was devoted to criticism of the established social order. The founder of the tendency film was Daisuke Ito (b. 1898), whose violently realistic *jidai-geki* of the late twenties—*Servant* (*Gero,* 1927), *Diary of Chuji's Travels* (*Chuji tabinikki,* 1927–28), *Ooka's Trial* (*Ooka seidan,* 1928), and the famous *Man-Slashing, Horse-Piercing Sword* (*Zanjin zamba ken,* 1930)—all attacked the feudalism of the Tokugawa period. Most tendency films, however, were *shomin-geki* that dealt with contemporary social problems and availed themselves of the heightened realism made possible by sound. The most important were Kinugasa's *Before Dawn* (*Reimei izen,* 1931); Shimazu's *O-Koto and Sasuke* (*O-Koto to Sasuke,* 1935); Gosho's *Everything That Lives* (*Ikitoshi ikerumono,* 1936); Shiro Toyoda's *Young People* (*Wakai hito,* 1937); Tomu Uchida's *The Naked Town* (*Hadaki no machi,* 1937); Ozu's first sound film, *The Only Son* (*Hitori musuko,* 1936); and Mizoguchi's two masterpieces, thought to be the greatest of Japanese prewar sound films, *Osaka Elegy* (*Naniwa ereji,* 1936) and *Sisters of the Gion* (*Gion no shimai,* 1936).

17.3 *Man-Slashing, Horse-Piercing Sword* (Daisuke Ito, 1930): Ryunosuke Tsukigata, Junichi Amano.

War

In response to the tendency film and other dissident elements in the culture, the government, through its Ministry of Propaganda, imposed a system of state censorship, the severity of which increased as the thirties wore on. In 1937, to the horror of the progressive filmmakers grouped

17.4 *Humanity and Paper Balloons* (Sadao Yamanaka, 1937): Sukezo Suketakaya, Chojuro Kawarazaki, Kanemon Nakamura.

17.5 *Five Scouts* (Tomotaka Tasaka, 1938): Isamu Kosugi (center).

17.6 Expert model work and special effects were used to simulate live battle action in *The War at Sea from Hawaii to Malaya* (Kajiro Yamamoto, 1942).

around Mizoguchi and Ozu, Sadao Yamanaka's (1907–38) humanistic film of life in the Tokugawa era, *Humanity and Paper Balloons* (*Ninjo kami-fusen,* 1937), was suppressed and its young director ordered to the Chinese front, where he was killed shortly after arriving. In addition to censoring what it did not like, the Ministry of Propaganda began to actively involve itself in production, demanding war films that showed Japanese military prowess in battle. Ironically, the first two films commissioned by the ministry—Tomotaka Tasaka's *Five Scouts* (*Go-nin no sekkohei,* 1938) and *Mud and Soldiers* (*Tsuchi to heitai,* 1939)—were profoundly humanistic accounts of men in battle that compare favorably with the great prewar pacifist films of the West, G. W. Pabst's *Westfront 1918* (1930) and Lewis Milestone's *All Quiet on the Western Front* (1930). Kimisaburo Yoshimura's (b. 1911) highly regarded *The Story of Tank Commander Nishizumi* (*Nishizumi senshacho-den,* 1940) was equally humane and individualistic in its outlook. It was almost as though Japanese directors had carried the banner of social realism into the war itself.

After the attack on Pearl Harbor in December 1941, the Japanese government issued strict guidelines and established quotas for the production of films on specific national policy themes. Then, following the example of Goebbels in Nazi Germany, Japanese government officials consolidated the ten existing studios into two large corporations under the Office of Public Information to insure that the guidelines would be adhered to. The result was a wave of conventional war propaganda films, both narrative and documentary, with titles like *Flaming Sky* (*Moyuru ozora,* Yutaka Abe, 1941), *The Suicide Troops of the Watch Tower* (*Boro no kesshitai,* Tadashi Imai, 1942), *The War at Sea from Hawaii to Malaya* (*Hawai-Marei oki kaisen,* Kajiro Yamamoto, 1942), and *Generals, Staff, and Soldiers* (*Shogun to sambo to hei,* Tetsu Taguchi, 1943). Since little battle footage was available from the Pacific at this point in the war, these films made remarkably sophisticated use of special effects and models to replicate battle action—a practice that became common in such films as the war progressed and that helps to explain the high quality of special effects in some of the better postwar Japanese science fiction films.

As the war grew more intense, virtually all genres, including the "children's" film (*Chocolate and Soldiers* [*Chokoreto to heitai,* Také Sado, 1942]) and the middle-class comedy-drama (*The Daily Battle* [*Nichijo no tatakai,* Yasujiro Shimazu, 1944]), were pressed into the service of national policy. Some directors, like Ozu (*The Brothers and Sisters of the Toda Family* [*Toda-ke no kyodai,* 1941]) and Gosho (*New Snow* [*Shinsetsu,* 1942]), protested the war by more or less ignoring it. Others, like Mizoguchi—*The Story of the Late Chrysanthemums* (*Zangiku monogatari,* 1939) and *Woman of Osaka* (*Naniwa onna,* 1940)—and Hiroshi Inagaki (b. 1905)—*The Rikisha Man / The Life of Matsu the Untamed* (*Muho Matsu no issho,* 1943)—avoided militaristic themes by turning to the *Meiji-mono* (historical dramas set in the enlightened Meiji era), but both were forced by the government to make *jidai-geki* set in the feudal Tokugawa period as well (Mizoguchi's *The Forty-seven Loyal Ronin, Part I* and *Part II* [*Genroku chushingura,* 1941–42] and Inagaki's *The*

Last Days of Edo [*Edo saigo no hi*, 1941]).* Akira Kurosawa began his career as a director with a *Meiji-mono* about the founder of judo, *The Judo Story* (*Sanshiro sugata*, 1943), which the Ministry of Propaganda liked so much (for the wrong reasons) that it sponsored a sequel, *The Judo Story, Part II* (*Zoku sanshiro sugata*, 1945).

Occupation

When World War II ended on August 14, 1945, much of Japan lay in ruins. The massive firebombing of its sixty major cities from March through June 1945 and the dropping of atomic bombs on Hiroshima and Naga-saki had resulted in some 900,000 casualties and the nearly total paral-ysis of civilian life. On the morning of August 15, when Emperor Hirohito broadcast to his subjects the news that the war had ended and that Japan had lost, there was widespread disbelief. Never in their history had the Japanese people been defeated or the nation occupied, and so the circum-stances of the American Occupation, 1945–52, were utterly unique.

The Occupation forces were led by General Douglas MacArthur, whose title, Supreme Commander for the Allied Powers, lent his administration the acronym SCAP. SCAP's primary objective was the "democratization" of Japan; to this end it imposed strict censorship through its Civil Infor-mation and Education Section (CI&E). Nearly half of Japan's movie the-aters had been destroyed by Allied bombing (there were only 845 in operation in October 1945), but most of the studios remained intact, and films continued to be produced. With the officially published vow that "Japan will never in the future disturb the peace of the world," CI&E demanded that these films do nothing to glorify feudalism, imperialism, or militarism—which necessarily eliminated the whole genre of *jidai-geki* and encouraged the production of *Meiji-mono* and films of contempo-rary life. Of the 554 wartime and postwar films confiscated by SCAP, 225 were banned on the grounds that they promoted antidemocratic ten-dencies, and many of them were destroyed.

Between 1946 and 1950, the Japanese could hardly have been said to control their own film industry. In an attempt at demonopolization, SCAP broke up the huge wartime *zaibatsu* in 1946 (they regrouped into five, later six, major corporations as soon as the Occupation ended). SCAP also attempted to ferret out war criminals within the industry, and CI&E dictated the subject matter of Japanese films. These phenomena were sig-nificant but short-lived; of more lasting consequence was the influx of American films into Japan for the first time since the beginning of the war—a time when domestic production was at a very low ebb (only sixty-seven indigenous films were released in 1946; the figure for 1927 had been over seven hundred). The influence of Frank Capra, John Ford,

* After the Occupation, however, Inagaki produced the masterful *chanbara* trilogy, *Samu-rai, Part I, Part II,* and *Part III* (*Miyamoto Musashi*, 1954; *Ichijoji no ketto*, 1955; *Ketto ganryujima*, 1956), based on the life of Musashi Miyamoto (c. 1584–1645), a warrior who rose from the peasantry to become a master swordsman in the service of Lord Tadotoshi Hosokawa.

17.7 Akira Kurosawa's post-war detective film *Stray Dog* (1949): Toshiro Mifune, Takashi Shimura.

17.8 *Rashomon* (Akira Kurosawa, 1950): the bandit (Toshiro Mifune), the husband (Masayuki Mori), the wife (Machiko Kyo).

Howard Hawks, and Orson Welles upon the first postwar generation of Japanese directors was comparable to their influence upon the *cinéastes* of the French New Wave. In any case, many Japanese studios during the Occupation found it politic to copy American styles and themes. The only domestic themes thoroughly endorsed by SCAP were those dealing with the new social freedoms made possible by democracy, especially the emancipation of women. Mizoguchi, Kinugasa, Kinoshita, Kurosawa, Gosho, Yoshimura, and Ozu all made fine films on this subject. During the Occupation, Akira Kurosawa (b. 1910) made four films—*The Men Who Tread on the Tiger's Tail* (*Tora no o o fumu otoko tachi*, 1945), *No Regrets for Our Youth* (*Waga seishun ni kuinashi*, 1946), *Drunken Angel* (*Yoidore tenshi*, 1948), and *Stray Dog* (*Nora inu*, 1949)—which established him as one of the great postwar directors. But it was not until his *Rashomon* (1950) unexpectedly won the Golden Lion at the Venice International Film Festival in 1951 that the real postwar renaissance of Japanese cinema began.

Rashomon, Kurosawa, and the Postwar Renaissance

Rashomon, based on two short stories by Ryunosuke Akutagawa (1892–1927), is a film about the relativity of truth in which four conflicting versions of the same event are offered by four equally credible (or equally incredible) narrators. In medieval Japan, three men take cover from a rainstorm under the crumbling Rashomon gate of the ancient capital, Kyoto. Two of them, a woodcutter and a priest, have just come from police headquarters, and they tell the third a strange tale which becomes the main portion of the film in flashback. The woodcutter explains how he had found the body of a nobleman in the woods; the man had been stabbed to death, but the weapon was missing. The priest says that he had encountered this same nobleman traveling with his wife on the road shortly before the murder.

While the woodcutter and the priest were at police headquarters, where both had come to give evidence, the police captured a bandit (played by Toshiro Mifune [b. 1920]—a brilliant actor and Kurosawa's constant collaborator) who confessed to killing the man and who gave the following account: The bandit was asleep in the woods when the nobleman passed by with his beautiful wife. Consumed with desire for her, he tricked the husband, tied him to a tree, and raped the wife. Afterward the woman forced the two men into a duel in which the husband was killed. Next, the wife was brought to police headquarters, where she gave her version of the truth. As she told the story, the bandit had left after the rape, and her husband then spurned her for being so easily dishonored. She had fainted from grief and awakened to find a dagger in her husband's breast. The priest and the woodcutter then inform the stranger that a third version was offered by the spirit of the dead husband, speaking through the lips of a medium. He testified that after the rape his wife had begged the bandit to kill her husband and carry her away. The bandit refused; the wife ran off into the woods; and her husband committed suicide with the dagger, which he felt someone remove from his body after his death. Finally, the woodcutter admits to the priest and the stranger that he had actually witnessed the whole sequence of events from a hiding place in the forest: "There was no dagger in that man's breast," he says. "He was killed by a sword thrust." The woodcutter's story is that both men were cowards and had to be goaded into the duel by the shrewish woman. In the event, he says, the bandit killed the husband almost by accident, and the woman ran off into the woods. But this "objective" account of things is called into question when the stranger accuses the woodcutter of having stolen the missing dagger.

Thus all four versions of the truth are shown to be relative to the perspectives and self-serving intentions of the individual participants. Even the woodcutter's detached account suggests the possibility of distortion. Kurosawa implies that reality or truth does not exist independent of human consciousness, identity, and perception. It is small wonder, then, that Alain Resnais claimed *Rashomon* as the inspiration for his own film about the enigmatic nature of reality, *L'Année dernière à Marienbad* (1961; see Chapter 13).

Cinematically, *Rashomon* is a masterpiece, and its release marked the emergence of Kurosawa as a major international figure. Each of the four tales has a unique style appropriate to the character of its teller, but the film as a whole is characterized by the many complicated tracking shots executed by cinematographer Kazuo Miyagawa (b. 1908), superbly paced editing, and thematically significant composition of the frame in depth. The camera seems to be almost constantly in motion, much of it violent, and Kurosawa uses many subjective shots to represent "reality" from the perspective of the individual narrators. Ironically, the Japanese had been somewhat reluctant to enter *Rashomon* in the Venice Festival, thinking that foreigners would misunderstand it. They were as amazed as they were pleased when the film won the Golden Lion, but their industry was quick to capitalize on its success. From 1951 through the present, the Japanese have consistently submitted entries to international film festivals, and they have achieved recognition and respect for their cinema all over the world. Between 1951 and 1965, as vast new export markets opened in the West and as Japanese films won prizes in festival after festival, Japanese cinema experienced a renaissance unprecedented in the history of any national cinema. Established figures like Mizoguchi and Ozu produced their greatest work during this period, and relatively new figures like Kurosawa, Shindo, Ichikawa, and Kobayashi all made films that stand among the classics of the international cinema.

Kurosawa became the most famous Japanese director in the West, perhaps because his films are more Western in construction than those of his peers. He followed *Rashomon* with an adaptation of Dostoevsky's *The Idiot* (*Hakuchi*, 1951) and the brilliant *shomin-geki Ikiru* (*Living / To Live*, 1952), a fatalistic yet ultimately affirmative account of the last months of a minor bureaucrat dying of cancer. In 1954 Kurosawa produced the epic *jidai-geki*, *Seven Samurai* (*Shichinin no samurai*), which many critics regard as his greatest work. Over eighteen months in production, this spectacular and deeply humanistic film tells the story of a small village that hires seven unemployed *samurai* to defend it against bandit raids in sixteenth-century Japan, an era in which the *samurai* as a class were rapidly dying out (in fact, the bandits are themselves unemployed *samurai*). As an epic, *Seven Samurai* clearly ranks with the greatest films of Griffith and Eisenstein, and cinematically it is a stunning achievement. As several critics have pointed out, the entire film is a tapestry of motion. Complicated tracking shots compete with equally elaborate and fast-paced editing to create a prevailing tempo which is like that of war punctuated by ever shorter intervals of peace. For the battle between bandits and *samurai* that concludes the film, Kurosawa created a montage sequence that rivals the massacre on the Odessa steps in *Potemkin* in its combination of rapid tracking shots and telephoto closeups of the action at various decelerated camera speeds. *Seven Samurai* was honored on a global scale, received the *Kinema Jumpo* award in Japan, the Silver Lion at Venice, and the Academy Award for Best Foreign Film in the United States. It was remade by John Sturges as *The Magnificent Seven* (1960), with its setting transposed to the American West, and it stands firmly behind the

17.9 *Ikiru* (Akira Kurosawa, 1952): Takashi Shimura, Miki Odagiri.

17.10 *Seven Samurai* (Akira Kurosawa, 1954): Toshiro Mifune, Yoshio Inaba, Takashi Shimura, Ko Kimura, Daisuke Kato, Seiji Miyaguchi, Minoru Chiaki.

17.11   The *samurai* enter the village.

17.12   The three peasants who had been sent to hire the *samurai* return to find the villagers terrified of their guests.

17.13   A lyrical interlude between a village girl and the youngest *samurai:* Keiko Tsushima, Ko Kimura.

17.14   Without waiting to be attacked, the *samurai* storm the bandits' river fortress and burn it to the ground.

17.15   In the attack, one of their number is killed and many of the bandits escape.

17.16   The remaining bandits launch an all-out attack on the village.

theme and style of Sam Peckinpah's classic anti-Western *The Wild Bunch* (1969; see Chapter 18).

Kurosawa's other masterpiece of the fifties was a brilliant adaptation of Shakespeare's *Macbeth* as a *jidai-geki* set in medieval Japan. Despite the cultural transposition, *Throne of Blood / Cobweb Castle* (*Kumono-sujo*, 1957) is perhaps the greatest version of Shakespeare on film. The supernatural element of the drama was enhanced by the sparing use of ritualized conventions from classical *noh* plays* and by the exteriors shot in the misty forests around Mount Fuji. Like *Seven Samurai*, *Throne of Blood* concludes with an elaborate montage sequence in which the Macbeth figure, Lord Washizu (Toshiro Mifune), is immolated by a hail of arrows.

In *Seven Samurai* and *Throne of Blood*, Kurosawa succeeded in elevating the *jidai-geki* from a simple action genre to an art form. After another literary adaptation, of Maxim Gorki's play *The Lower Depths* (*Donzoko*, 1957), he made three superb *chanbara*—*The Hidden Fortress* (*Kakushi toride no san-akunin*, 1958), *Yojimbo* (*The Bodyguard*, 1961), and *Sanjuro* (*Tsubaki sanjuro*, 1962). Though these films lack the thematic depth of his earlier *jidai-geki*, they are masterworks of widescreen composition and rival their predecessors in visual richness.

In 1960, Kurosawa was put in charge of his own production unit at Toho and given complete control of it. Kurosawa Productions' first effort was *The Bad Sleep Well* (*Warui yatsu hodo yoku nemuru*, 1960), a film

---

* Developed in medieval Japan, *noh* is a form of ritualized drama that treats mythic, historical, or literary themes. Whereas the more popular *kabuki* theater tends toward extravagance and relates events that are in the process of occurring, *noh* theater, for which about 250 plays exist, is more refined intellectually and always deals with events that occurred in the past. Its settings and gestures are symbolic, and its language is formal and highly allusive. Much use is made of mime and masks. Though *Throne of Blood* is his only film to employ *noh* elements throughout, many of Kurosawa's films use *noh* choruses (*The Men Who Tread on the Tiger's Tail*), music (*Seven Samurai*), and plot structure (*The Hidden Fortress*).

17.17   In the final battle in the rain all of the bandits are killed, but only three *samurai* survive. (Note the flattening of perspective produced by the telephoto lens.) On the following day, the *samurai* prepare to leave: "We've lost again . . . the farmers are the winners. Not us."

about corporate versus social responsibility in the form of a murder mystery. It was followed by *Yojimbo; Sanjuro; High and Low* (*Tengoku to jigoku*, 1963), a detective film based on a novel by Ed McBain; and *Red Beard* (*Aka hige*, 1965), the story of a young doctor's education in late-Tokugawa Japan. Although *Red Beard* was one of his most successful films financially, it was five years before Kurosawa produced another. In the interim, he wrote the screenplay for *Runaway Train*, based on a *Life* magazine article about an actual train accident in upstate New York, and contracted with 20th Century–Fox to shoot it in Rochester as his first color film. But bad weather on location forced cancellation of the project (it was eventually realized by Russian émigré director Andrei Konchalovsky for Cannon Films in 1985). Kurosawa was then invited by Fox to shoot the Japanese sequences of the Pearl Harbor battle epic *Tora! Tora! Tora!* (Richard Fleischer, 1970), an experience that ended bitterly for both parties when the director's footage was rejected.

Returning to Japan, Kurosawa finally made his first color film, the low-budget (albeit in Eastmancolor), independently produced *Dodes'kaden* (*Dodesukaden*, 1970), an unstructured narrative about the lives of the very poor in a Tokyo slum. This film failed at the box office, the first of Kurosawa's ever to do so, and in December 1971 the director, despondent over the state of his career, attempted suicide (a logical and culturally acceptable act for a Japanese who perceives the possibilities of his or her life to be exhausted). Fortunately he survived, and in 1976, after six years of silence, Kurosawa gave the cinema another masterpiece—*Dersu Uzala*, a Soviet-Japanese coproduction shot in 70mm with six-track sound. Set in the forests of eastern Siberia at the turn of the century, it is a portrait of the friendship between an aging hunter of the Goldi tribe and a young Russian surveyor. By 1977 the film had won the Grand Prize at the Moscow Festival and an Academy Award in America. In 1980 Kurosawa completed *Kagemusha* (*Shadow Warrior*), a tragic *jidai-geki* set during the sixteenth century civil wars; this film was cowinner of the Grand Prix at Cannes in the year of its release, but, as great as it was, *Kagemusha* was in many ways simply a test run for Kurosawa's masterpiece, *Ran* (literally, "Chaos"), in 1985. This 10-million-dollar Japanese-

17.18 The death of Lord Washizu in Kurosawa's *Throne of Blood* (1957): Toshiro Mifune.

17.19 Kurosawa's *Red Beard* (1965): Toshiro Mifune, Yuzo Kayama.

17.20 Masterful widescreen composition in Kurosawa's *The Hidden Fortress* (1958) and *Yojimbo* (1961). Compare the American and Italian-American Westerns of the same period (see Chapter 12).

17.21 The famous "explosion of blood" from the final sword-fight in Kurosawa's *Sanjuro* (1962): Toshiro Mifune, Tatsuya Nakadai.

French coproduction—the most expensive film ever made in Japan—was the culmination of a life's work: a stylized, epic version of *King Lear* set in the context of the same clan wars as those portrayed in *Kagemusha*. *Ran* was internationally recognized as the director's most brilliant, profound, and magisterial film. Kurosawa retired from directing in 1987, as if after making *Ran* there was little left to say.

Kurosawa is unquestionably a giant of the international cinema. Like Bergman and Antonioni, he is the true *auteur* of his films—he sets up his own shots, does his own editing, and writes his own scripts. He is probably more conscious of Western styles of filmmaking than any of his Japanese peers and always claimed a great stylistic debt to John Ford (American cinema's recent debt to Kurosawa has already been noted). Kurosawa was a professional student of Western painting before he entered the cinema, but it would be a mistake to assume that the Western "look" of his films betokens Western values. Sometimes mistakenly identified by Western critics as a humanist, he is, in fact, a fatalist, or at least an existentialist, in subtle but thoroughly Japanese terms. His vision of human experience is firmly rooted in the value system of feudal Japan. Zen Buddhism, the *samurai* code of *bushido* ("the way of the warrior"—loyalty and self-sacrifice), and the master-pupil relationship are all-important ethical components of his films. Because of his great universality of spirit, we can recognize ourselves in Kurosawa, but we would do well to remember that Kurosawa also shares many sympathies with Yukio Mishima (1925–70), the famous anti-intellectual novelist and right-wing militant who staged a raid on the Tokyo headquarters of the nation's "peacekeeping" forces on November 25, 1970, and committed a spectacular act of *seppuku* there to protest the decadence of contemporary Japan and the declining role of feudalism in its culture.*

17.22 Kurosawa's *Ran* (1985).

---

* Mishima, who also directed films and acted in them was the subject of a highly stylized, expressionistic film biography by Paul Schrader. Based on an assortment of the writer's semiautobiographical works, it was entitled *Mishima: A Life in Four Chapters* (1985). The film was barred from the 1985 Tokyo Festival and never distributed in Japan. Other Mishima adaptations are Kon Ichikawa's *Conflagration* (*Enjo*, 1958), adapted from the novel *Temple of the Golden Pavilion* (*Kinkaku-ji*, 1956); Senkichi Taniguchi's *The Sound of Waves* (*Shiosa*, 1959); based on the 1956 novel; and the British-produced *The Sailor Who Fell from Grace with the Sea* (John Lewis Carlino, 1976), based on the novel *Gogo no eiko*, 1983.

17.23 *Sisters of the Gion* (Kenji Mizoguchi, 1936): Isuzu Yamada, Yoko Umemura.

17.24 Mizoguchi's *Women of the Night* (1948): Kumeko Urabe, Kinuyo Tanaka. Note the dominance of diagonals relative to the borders of the frame.

Kenji Mizoguchi

More clearly Oriental in form than the work of Kurosawa is that of Kenji Mizoguchi (1898–1956), a director whose career spanned thirty-four years and encompassed ninety feature films. Like Kurosawa, Mizoguchi studied Western painting as a student, but his themes and visual style were purely Japanese. He began his career as an actor for the Nikkatsu studio and became a director there in 1922. Mizoguchi's first films were mainly thrillers and melodramas adapted from popular literature (such as *Harbor in the Fog* [*Kiri no minato*, 1923]), but in 1925 he began to make films dealing with the impact of urbanization on Japanese life (*Tokyo March* [*Tokyo koshin-kyoku*, 1929]; *Metropolitan Symphony* [*Tokai kokyogaku, 1929*]). Few of his silent films have survived, but those that do reveal an almost painterly evocation of atmosphere and mood. After a politically committed film about the urban working class, *Nevertheless, They Go On* (*Shikamo karera wa yuku,* 1931), Mizoguchi turned increasingly to period films to avoid government censorship. Yet his two greatest films of the thirties, *Osaka Elegy* (*Naniwa ereji,* 1936—banned in 1940) and *Sisters of the Gion* (*Gion no shimai,* 1936), both have contemporary settings and announce Mizoguchi's major thematic concern: the position of women within the social order and the redemptive power of their love. The films also contain Mizoguchi's first consistent use of the technique that would become the hallmark of his later films—the extended long take composed in depth for a static camera. Critics have compared *Osaka Elegy* and *Sisters of the Gion* with Jean Renoir's pre-war films (see Chapter 9) in terms of both their humanism and their *mise-en-scène*. Like Renoir, Mizoguchi constantly sought ways to portray internal states through external means, and he felt that in the long take he had discovered what he called "the most precise and specific expression for intense psychological moments." Diagonal composition leading the eye outward toward the world beyond the frame, fluid and thematically significant moving camera shots, luminous photography (often by Kazuo Miyagawa), and minimal cutting are other characteristics of Mizoguchi's mature style, which link him with the *mise-en-scène* tradition of the West.

During the war, Mizoguchi was forced to make a certain number of government-policy films, although he was able to confine them to *jidai-geki* like *The Forty-seven Loyal Ronin, Part I* and *Part II* (*Genroku chushingura,* 1941–42). After the surrender, he continued to examine the condition of Japanese women, in films like *Women of the Night* (*Yoru no onnatachi,* 1948), which concerns prostitution during the Occupation. But in the last six years of his life, with the Occupation ended, Mizoguchi produced his greatest masterpieces. In rapid succession he shot five films that many critics regard as among the most beautiful and haunting ever made. *The Life of Oharu* (*Saikaku ichidai onna,* 1952), winner of the International Director's Prize at the 1952 Venice Film Festival, is a humane critique of feudalism centered around the degraded life of a prostitute in seventeenth-century Kyoto. *Ugetsu* (*Ugetsu monogatari,* 1953), which won the Silver Lion at Venice in 1953, is set during the feudal

17.25 *Mise-en-scène* aesthetics in Mizoguchi's *Ugetsu* (1953): luminous photography, diagonal composition, the long take. Machiko Kyo, Masayuki Mori.

wars of the sixteenth century. Two ambitious young men leave their wives to seek wealth and glory. In the course of a long and picaresque pilgrimage, they both come to realize that nothing they have gained on their journey is worth the love of the women they have cast away. Simultaneously realistic, allegorical, and supernatural, *Ugetsu* is the most stylistically perfect of all Mizoguchi's works, and to some critics it is the greatest Japanese film ever made. *Gion Festival Music* (*Gion bayashi,* 1953) is a highly successful remake of *Sisters of the Gion;* but with *Sansho the Bailiff* (*Sansho dayu,* 1954), set in the eleventh century, and *Crucified Lovers / A Story from Chikamatsu* (*Chikamatsu monogatari,* 1954), set in the seventeenth century, Mizoguchi continued his concentrated scrutiny of the feudal social system and its impact upon women, although neither film was the equal of *The Life of Oharu* or *Ugetsu. The Empress Yang Kweifei* (*Yokihi,* 1955) and *New Tales of the Taira Clan* (*Shin heike monogatari,* 1955) were Mizoguchi's only films in color, and although both are decidedly "popular" in their content, they show a marvelously expressive sense of the medium. Characteristically, the last film Mizoguchi completed before his death in 1956 was *Street of Shame* (*Akasen chitai,* 1956), a fictionalized account of the lives of Tokyo prostitutes.

Mizoguchi is popularly perceived in the West, which has seen only about a tenth of his total opus, as a maker of period films. Indeed, as Kurosawa remarked when the elder director died, "Now that Mizoguchi is gone, there are very few directors left who can see the past clearly and realistically." But when Mizoguchi looked at the past, it was always as a mirror for the present. His lifelong critique of feudalism, his sympathetic concern for the social and psychological condition of women, his simple humanism in the face of a callous world are the thematic bridges uniting his period and his contemporary films. Furthermore, his absolute mastery of decor, the long take, and the moving camera make Mizoguchi one of the great *mise-en-scène* directors of the international cinema, a rival of Murnau, Ophüls, and Welles, to name only his contemporaries. Nevertheless, his nearly transcendental visual style finally makes Mizoguchi unique in the history of film. As the French New Wave director Jacques

Rivette said of him, "Mizoguchi, alone, imposes a feeling of a unique world and language, is answerable only to himself."

Yasujiro Ozu and the Use of Off-Screen Space

The Japanese director whose work most expresses traditional Japanese values is undeniably Yasujiro Ozu (1903–63); for that reason, he was the last of the three great masters of Japanese cinema to be discovered by the West. As a boy in Tokyo, Ozu spent much of his time in movie houses, entranced by Italian spectacles like *Quo vadis?* (1913), and by American comedy, melodrama, and romance (he particularly admired Lubitsch and Griffith). After briefly attending Waseda University, he became a scriptwriter at the Shochiku studio, where he was to work for the rest of his life. Here he soon became an assistant director under the tutelage of Tadamoto Okubo, a specialist in light comedies known as "nonsense-*mono,*" and by 1927 Ozu had directed his first feature, a *jidai-geki* entitled *The Sword of Penitence* (*Zange no yaiba*). This film was unremarkable, except for the fact that it was written by Kogo Noda, who was to become Ozu's lifelong collaborator and friend.

17.26 *Good Morning* (Yasujiro Ozu, 1959): Masahiro Shimazu, Koji Shidari, Yoshiko Kuga.

17.27 Ozu shooting a scene for *The Flavor of Green Tea over Rice* (1952). Note the low-angle, eye-level perspective.

For a time Ozu specialized in nonsense-*mono* in the manner of Okubo, but he soon turned his attention to the more serious genre of *shomin-geki,* social comedies that concentrate on the daily lives and interpersonal relationships of the members of lower-middle-class families. Ozu seems to have chosen this genre because he found in the routine lives of these people—in their necessary ability to cope with hardship—a "sympathetic sadness" at the harshness of the natural order that ultimately enables one to transcend it. In Western culture, the lower middle class has not been a traditional subject for art but rather, at best, for soap opera and low comedy. In Japan, however, the simple life-style necessarily practiced by the people of this class is highly regarded as the most authentic, valid, and human way to live, unencumbered as it is by false values, pretensions, and distortions. As Barbara Wolf has put it, "After all, what could possibly be so real as to be born, make a living, bring forth a new generation and then die?" Of Ozu's fifty-four films, nearly all deal with the life cycles and life crises of lower-middle-class family members. Often using the same actors, Ozu's films are, in a sense, all parts of one film that the director was driven to remake throughout his career.* Even the titles seem barely distinguishable from one another: *I Graduated, but . . .* (*Daigaku wa deta keredo,* 1929), *Life of an Office Worker* (*Kaishain seikatsu,* 1930), *I Flunked, but . . .* (*Rakudai wa shita keredo,* 1930), *The Chorus of Tokyo* (*Tokyo no gassho,* 1931), *I Was Born, but . . .* (*Umarete wa mita keredo,* 1932), *The Story of Floating Weeds* (*Ukigusa monogatari,* 1934), *Tokyo's a Nice Place* (*Tokyo yoi toko,* 1935), *College Is a Nice Place* (*Daigaku yoi toko,* 1936), *The Only Son* (*Hitori musuko,* 1936), *There Was a Father* (*Chichi ariki,* 1942), *Late Spring* (*Banshun,* 1949), *Early Summer* (*Bakushu,* 1951), *The Flavor of Green Tea over*

---

* In the fall of 1982, the Japan Society of New York sponsored the first American retrospective of Ozu's extant work, including many films never before seen in the United States.

17.28 Ozu's *Late Spring* (1949): Chishu Ryu, Setsuko Hara, Haruko Sugimura. Ozu's *Tokyo Story* (1953): Chishu Ryu, Cheiko Higashiyama. Note the low-angle horizontal composition, here and throughout the Ozu stills, as if the camera were a person seated on a *tatami* mat. Note also the reliance on off-screen space.

Rice (*O-chazuke no aji,* 1952), *Tokyo Story* (*Tokyo monogatari,* 1953), *Early Spring* (*Soshun,* 1956), *Tokyo Twilight* (*Tokyo boshoku,* 1957), *Equinox Flower* (*Higanbana,* 1958), *Good Morning* (*Ohayo,* 1959), *Floating Weeds* (*Ukigusa,* 1959), *Late Autumn* (*Akibiyori,* 1960), *The End of Summer* (*Kohayagawa-ke no aki,* 1961), *An Autumn Afternoon* (*Samma no aji,* 1962).

To these films of people living restrained and minimal lives, Ozu brought a restrained and minimal cinematic style. Most of the films he made from 1936 on take place within the confines of a typical Japanese home. His camera is often motionless, and it usually assumes the low-angle position of a person seated on a *tatami* mat whose eye level is about three feet above the floor, as if it were a guest or visitor in the household. Its attitude is one of calmness, quiescence, and repose. The composition of the frame is inevitably horizontal, and the editing style is spare, with no fades or dissolves but straight cuts only, and with little concern for traditionally fluid continuity. In fact, the characteristic Ozu film is composed of a series of static long takes in which the dialogue, always written by Ozu in close collaboration with Noda, sustains the drama. Sometimes, however, moments of stillness and stasis in which there are no human beings at all occur in Ozu's films. These are Ozu's famed "empty scenes" or "still lifes," and they are extremely important both to his aesthetic and to the international cinema at large.

It often happens in an Ozu film that the characters leave a room to eat or go to the bathroom or to bed, while the camera remains behind in its stationary position to record for a while the empty space that the actors have created by their departure. This preoccupation corresponds to a concept in Zen aesthetics known as *mu,* which, technically, designates the empty space between the flowers in the Japanese art of flower arrangement, but which more generally refers to the Zen doctrine that the spaces between the materials used to create a work of art are an integral part of the work. Will Peterson has put it this way: "The blank sheet of paper is perceived only as paper, and remains as paper. Only by filling the paper does it become empty." So Ozu's "still lifes," which appear in each of his major films, are an integral part of his transcendental vision of reality. But they are also of great importance to the formal evolution of narrative film. Through his use of the empty scene, Ozu became one of the first directors in the history of film to create **off-screen space.**

There are two ways of conceptualizing the cinema screen. In one, the outer edges of the screen become a framing device for the visual composition centered within it, like the frame of a painting or a still photograph. In this model, the reality of the film is contained entirely *within* the screen, and the edges of the screen are borders separating the film's reality from the categorically "real" reality outside. This way of regarding the screen and the method of composition it demands has, with a few notable exceptions (in the work of von Stroheim, Murnau, Renoir, Welles, Hitchcock, and Rossellini), dominated the narrative cinema of the West until very recently—perhaps the last twenty years. In the other mode of conceptualizing cinematic space, first formally articulated by André Bazin, the screen is conceived as a window on the world whose frame, if moved to the right or to the left, or up or down, would reveal more of the same spatial reality contained within the screen. Of course, the screen must contain most of the action most of the time, so this off-screen space must be revealed by camera movement (as in the lateral tracking shots of the films Godard made after 1968) or, more provocatively, by what can be termed off-center or noncentered framing. In this technique, the film frame is made to contain only part of the significant action, or sometimes, as in Ozu, no action at all.

Figure 17.29 on the opposite page shows two consecutive noncentered shots from Ozu's *Floating Weeds* (1959) which help to illustrate the concept. In traditional or centered framing, the force of the image is, in Bazin's terms, *centripetal:* the image is composed so that our eyes are drawn inward toward the vanishing point at the center of the frame. In antitraditional or off-center framing, the force of the image is *centrifugal:* our eyes are thrown out upon the world beyond the frame, a process that suggests the essential reality of that world. Centered framing has the effect of denying the reality of the world beyond the frame by isolating it from us; off-center framing has the effect of affirming the reality of the world beyond the frame by constantly calling our attention to it. In short, centered framing creates an illusion about the structure of reality that off-center framing seeks to destroy. Thus, the latter is an inherently more realistic technique in terms of the way we actually perceive reality. For this reason, off-center framing is increasingly favored by young Marxist directors on the Continent and in the Third World, since it promises to deconstruct what is for them an essentially deceptive, illusionist way of looking at the world and one's position in it.

Ozu's use of off-screen space was somewhat differently motivated. Many Ozu films exploit off-screen space by means of empty scenes in which the

17.29 Off-screen space can be created in front of the screen (and thus behind the camera) as well as beyond its linear borders. For example, classical Hollywood framing conceives an imaginary axis which positions the camera within a 180-degree semicircle vis-à-vis the action, cutting the viewer off from the 180 degrees of filmic space behind it. Anti-traditional framing often conceives filmic space as a full circle, breaking the imaginary axis of action and creating a totally new spatial paradigm. In the shot-reverse-shot sequence above, the same actor's feet extend into the frame first from the left and then from the right, making it clear that the camera has turned 180 degrees on its axis.

17.30 Ozu's *Late Autumn* (1960): (left) Yoko Tsukasa, Setsuko Hara, Keiji Sada, Shin Saburi, Nobuo Nakamura; (right) Setsuko Hara, Yoko Tsukasa, Nobuo Nakamura, Chishu Ryu.

motionless camera trains its attention for some time on dramatically insignificant objects—a vase on a nightstand, a ticking wall clock, an empty hallway—which, because they are themselves meaningless in terms of narrative and theme, draw our attention to the fact that they are surrounded by spaces containing meaningful objects and people off-screen. By showing us *nothing*, these shots draw our attention to the surrounding *something* in the same way—but much more emphatically—that off-center framing makes us aware of the world beyond the frame instead of denying its existence by isolating it from us. It is generally true that the longer the screen remains empty, the more our attention is drawn to off-screen as opposed to on-screen space, and Ozu was among the first directors anywhere to realize this. Another way that Ozu uses off-screen space is by training his stationary camera on some significant action while sig-

17.31 "Empty scenes" from the opening sequence of *Early Spring* (Yasujiro Ozu, 1956).

17.32 Ozu's *Floating Weeds* (1959): Hiroshi Kawaguchi, Ganjiro Nakamura.

17.33 *Twenty-Four Eyes* (Keisuke Kinoshita, 1954): Hideko Takamine.

nificant action is also in progress off-screen. This could be suggested by off-screen dialogue or naturalistic sound effects, or as in many of Ozu's later films, by having the action oscillate between off-screen and on-screen space. In *The End of Summer* (1960), for example, the static camera trains on a mother ironing a dress in full shot while her son and her father play catch, moving in and out of the frame at random as the game grows increasingly noisy and wild.

Yet, for all this, Yasujiro Ozu was an extremely conservative director. He did not make his first sound film until 1936 or his first color film until 1958, and he never used widescreen. His films employed only the most fundamental of stylistic devices—basically those that had been available since the "primitive" period of film history before 1914. Ozu's simplicity of style derives from the fact that his art is essentially religious in nature. It is an art predicated on the Zen Buddhist reverence for the mystery of the everyday. As Donald Richie has pointed out, it assumes that it is only through the mundane and the common that the transcendent can be expressed, and like much religious art, it is primitive in terms of technique. From this elementary base, however, Ozu made films of great emotional sophistication and subtlety, and he ranks today as one of the great *auteurs* of international cinema. From 1936 until his death in 1963 he kept the writing, casting, shooting, and editing of his films tightly under his control, building up his own repertory company of trusted performers and technicians. Although he was quintessentially Japanese, Ozu, like Shakespeare and Tolstoi, had a single universal subject: human nature. And in the course of his long career he became, as he was recently voted by the British Film Institute, "one of the greatest artists of the twentieth century in any medium and in any country."

The generation of Kurosawa, Mizoguchi, and Ozu also included Teinosuke Kinugasa (1896–1982), whose beautifully photographed *jidai-geki, Gate of Hell* (*Jigokumon*, 1953), is considered one of the finest color films ever made,* and Keisuke Kinoshita (b. 1912), whose humanistic *Twenty-four Eyes* (*Nijushi no hitomi*, 1954) traces the course of Japanese fascism from 1927 to 1946 through the eyes of a young schoolteacher and her pupils. Although he directed propaganda films for the government during the war, Tadashi Imai (b. 1912) became a politically committed critic of vestigial feudalism and a prolific exponent of neorealism. His three-part *Muddy Waters* (*Nigori*, 1953), for example, is an exposé of political and social repression during the "liberal" Meiji Restoration.†

---

* It is impossible, however, to experience *Gate of Hell* in its original form due to severe color fading of the negative. For more on this problem, see Chapter 12.

† Though Kinugasa retired in the late sixties and died in 1982, Kinoshita and Imai are both still working, the latter having delivered in the eighties *The Proper Way* (*Kosadate gokko*, 1980) and *Tower of Lilies* (*Himeyui no to*, 1982; a remake of his own 1953 film), and the former having produced *Children of Nagasaki/These Children Survive Me* (*Kono ko wo nokoshite*, 1983) and *Big Joys, Small Sorrows* (*Shin yorokobimo kanashimimo ikutoshitsuki*, 1986).

The Second Postwar Generation

The second generation of the postwar renaissance came to prominence in the fifties and sixties and was comprised primarily of Masaki Kobayashi (b. 1916), Kon Ichikawa (b. 1915), and Kaneto Shindo (b. 1912). The works of Kobayashi and Ichikawa are probably better known in the West than those of Shindo. Kobayashi was trained in philosophy at Waseda University, and his early films dealt mainly with social and political problems in a realistic vein. His first masterpiece was *The Human Condition* (*Ningen no joken*, 1959–61), a nine-and-one-half-hour antiwar epic depicting Japan's occupation and rape of Manchuria, 1943–45. Released in three parts, this humanistic but grimly realistic widescreen film tells the story of a young pacifist forced into the war and ultimately destroyed by it. Kobayashi's next important films were graphically violent *jidai-geki*—*Hara kiri* (*Seppuku*, 1962) and *Rebellion* (*Joi-uchi*, 1967)—both of which used the situation of an individual's doomed revolt against the authoritarian social system of the Tokugawa period to make serious comments on the survival of feudalism in modern technological Japan. In the uncharacteristic but strikingly beautiful film *Kwaidan* (*Kaidan*, 1964), Kobayashi made carefully controlled use of the widescreen format and expressive color to tell four haunting ghost stories adapted from the writings of Lafcadio Hearn (1850–1904), an American author who became a Japanese citizen. One of the tales, "Hoichi the Earless" ("Minimachi Hoichi") draws heavily on elements of the *noh* play. Among Kobayashi's more recent works are the period gangster film *Inn of Evil* (*Inochi bo ni furo*, 1971), and the thirteen-part television series, *Kaseki* (1975), a sensitive account of an elderly business executive who discovers that he is dying of cancer and must reassess his life. More recently, he has directed the intensely tactile erotic melodrama *Glowing Autumn* (*Moeru aki*, 1981), the Ozu-like domestic tragedy *Fate of a Family* (*Shokutaku no nai ie*, 1985), and the two-part 265–minute documentary *The Tokyo Trial* (*Tokyo saiban*, 1985), an extraordinary account of the war crimes trials held by the Allies from 1946 to 1948 of twenty-eight top Japanese officials charged with conspiracy and aggression in World War II.

Kon Ichikawa is widely acknowledged in the West as one of the Japanese cinema's most brilliant stylists. He began his career as an animator, but his first important film was *The Burmese Harp* (*Biruma no tategoto*, 1956), a lyrical epic about a Japanese soldier whose guilt at his complicity in the collective horrors of war drives him to become a saintly Buddhist monk. Ichikawa's other great pacifist film, *Fires on the Plain* (*Nobi*, 1959), is set during the last days of the Japanese occupation of the Philippines, when the remnants of the decimated Japanese army turned to murder and cannibalism in order to survive and face their final battle with "honor." The film offers a nightmarish vision of an inferno that goes far beyond its implicit social criticism of the feudal code of *bushido*. *Conflagration* (*Enjo*, 1958), adapted from a novel by Yukio Mishima, is a richly textured widescreen film that tells the true story of a young Buddhist novitiate who burns down the Temple of the Golden Pavilion at Kyoto in disgust at the worldly corruption that surrounds him. Other

17.34 The Human *Condition, Part I* (Masaki Kobayashi, 1959): Tatsuya Nakadai.

17.35 Kobayashi's *Hara kiri* (1962): Akira Ishihama.

17.36 *Fires on the Plain* (Kon Ichikawa, 1959): Eiji Funakoshi, Mickey Curtis.

Ichikawa films known in the West include *Odd Obsession / The Key* (*Kagi,* 1959), a disturbing tale of an elderly man's sexual perversion; *Alone in the Pacific* (*Taiheiyo hitoribochi,* 1963), based on the true story of a young man who sailed the Pacific from Osaka to San Francisco in three months; and the monumental documentary *Tokyo Olympiad* (1965), which compares favorably with Leni Riefenstahl's *Olympia* (1936). In 1973, Ichikawa produced *The Wanderers* (*Matatabi*), generically a nineteenth-century *chanbara,* which many critics saw as the consummation of his career to date in its combination of savage irony, technical mastery, and lush compositional beauty. After directing a series of overplotted potboilers for producer Haruki Kadokawa (e.g., *The Inugami Family* [*Inugami-ke no ichizoku,* 1976]; *The Devil's Bouncing Ball Song* [*Akuma no temari-uta,* 1977]; *Island of Horror* [*Gokumonto,* 1977]; *Queen Bee* [*Jobachi,* 1978]; *House of Hanging* [*Byoinzaka no kubikukuri no ie,* 1979]), Ichikawa returned to his formerly high standards. *Lonely Hearts* (*Kofuku,* 1982) is an adaptation of an Ed McBain crime thriller, shot by Ichikawa's regular cinematographer Kiyoshi Hasegawa in a filtering process midway between black-and-white and color, while *The Makioka Sisters* (*Sasame yuki,* 1983) is a rambling family epic set in the 1920s and based on the classic novel by Junichiro Tanizaki, and *Ohan* (1985), an old-fashioned domestic melodrama set in the same era. More characteristic of the main body of his work is the visually resplendent *Princess from the Moon* (*Taketori monogatari,* 1987), based on a ninth-century legend about a magical moon woman who is temporarily stranded on earth, and *Actress* (*Eiga joyu,* 1987), a fascinating biography of Japan's great female movie star Kinuyo Tanaka (1910–77), whose career spanned most of Japanese film history.

Kaneto Shindo began as a scriptwriter for Kurosawa, Ichikawa, and others. His status as a film artist is less secure than that of either Kobayashi or Ichikawa, but he has made a number of important films since the war. Shindo worked as an assistant to Mizoguchi on *The Life of Oharu* and *Ugetsu,** and in 1952 he made his first major film, *Children of Hiroshima* (*Genbaku no ko*), a stylized semidocumentary about the atomic holocaust and its effects upon the Japanese people. Shindo's reputation in the West rests on the international success of another semidocumentary, *The Island* (*Hadaka no shima,* 1960), which concerns the struggle of a peasant farming family to survive on a barren Pacific atoll. The film is poetic in the manner of Robert Flaherty's work—some consider it self-consciously beautiful—but it has obvious authenticity as a representation of human experience, which stems from the fact that it is largely autobiographical. Another Shindo film that is known outside of Japan is the folkloristic *jidai-geki Onibaba* (1964), which concerns a mother and daughter who survive the civil wars of the sixteenth century by killing wounded *samurai* and selling their armor for rice. This strange and brutal film blends gorgeous widescreen photography with sickening violence and graphic sex, and it never achieves the poetic quality Shindo appar-

---

* In 1979, Shindo produced and directed *Mizoguchi Kenji,* a documentary about the director's life and work.

ently sought for it. *Kuroneko* (1968), another ghost story, forms a pendant with *Onibaba,* and Shindo produced a final *jidai-geki* in *The Solitary Travels of Chikuzan* (*Chikuzan hitori tabi,* 1977), a film about the life of a wandering blind *shamisen* musician. Although some of his work has tended toward the sensational and melodramatic, Shindo is a prolific scriptwriter and remains a figure of importance in his nation's cinema. A recent notable Shindo film is *The Horizon* (*Chiheisen,* 1984), a chronicle of a Japanese woman who is fashioned after his own sister. She comes to San Francisco as the purchased bride of a Japanese farmer in 1920, raises a family, undergoes internment in an American concentration camp during World War II, and is ultimately reassimilated into American society after the war.

17.37 *Godzilla* (Ishiro Honda, 1954) and other Japanese monster films relied on a proficiency with models and special effects acquired in the production of domestic propaganda films during World War II.

The popular work of the director Ishiro (or Inoshiro) Honda (b. 1911), whose *Godzilla* (1954) started a twenty-year cycle of formulaic monster films, has demonstrated to the world the Japanese facility for special effects. Some typical Honda titles, in translation, are *Rodan* (1956), *The Mysterians* (1957), *Mothra* (1961), *King Kong vs. Godzilla* (1962), *Ghidrah, the Three-Headed Monster* (1965), and *Destroy All Monsters* (1968). Almost all of Honda's science fiction films are parabolic: the monster is unleashed through the careless explosion of an atomic bomb, and after wreaking havoc on the urban centers of the nation, it is finally destroyed by Japanese scientists. (See Chapter 11 for more on Japanese monster and science fiction films.)

The Japanese New Wave

The third postwar generation of Japanese filmmakers emerged during the late sixties and the seventies to form a kind of radical New Wave (*nuberu bagu*). Many of them began working for the studios (Shinoda, Yoshida, and Oshima, for example, worked for Shochiku) and for this reason did much of their early work in some form of CinemaScope, to which the studios had converted wholesale by 1960 in order to combat the threat of television. But ultimately, most of them moved away from the studios to form their own independent production companies. Some characteristic directors are Hiroshi Teshigahara (b. 1927), Susumu Hani (b. 1928), Masashiro Shinoda (b. 1931), Yasuzo Masumura (b. 1924), Yoshishige Yoshida (b. 1933), Seijun Suzuki, Koji Wakamatsu (b. 1936), Shohei Imamura (b. 1926), and Nagisa Oshima (b. 1932).

Teshigahara is an avant-garde abstractionist whose international reputation rests upon a single film, *Woman in the Dunes* (*Suna no onna,* 1964), based on a novel by Kobo Abé and produced for less than a hundred thousand dollars. Among the premier works of the Japanese New Wave, this film—which won the Cannes Special Jury Prize for the year of its release—is a complex allegory in which a young scientist becomes trapped in an isolated sand pit through the mysterious powers of a woman who apparently was condemned to shovel away the sand interminably by hand.

Susumu Hani began his career by making documentaries, which helped to shape his later *cinéma-vérité* style. Most of Hani's feature films are shot on location with nonactors, and they typically treat the problems of

17.38 *Woman in the Dunes* (Hiroshi Teshigahara, 1964): Kyoko Kishada, Eiji Okada.

the postwar generation—specifically, the problems of living in a once traditional culture disintegrating under the pressures of rapid social change. Hani has also made films about what it means to be Japanese in foreign lands—for example, the semidocumentary *Bwana Toshi* (Kenya, 1965) and *Bride of the Andes* (*Andesu no hanayome*, Peru, 1966). According to many critics, Hani's best and most characteristic film is *The Inferno of First Love* (*Hatsukoi jigoku-hen*, 1968), in which two teenagers attempt through physical love to cope with the social chaos that surrounds them, only to be destroyed. In 1978 Hani's former wife, Sachiko Hidari (b. 1930), one of Japan's finest actresses and the star of most of Hani's films, directed her own first feature, *The Far Road* (*Toi ippono michi*), which concerns the day-to-day life of an aging railroad worker, his wife, and his family. Hani himself subsequently made *A Tale of Africa* (*Afurika monogatari*, 1981), a symbolic drama about three people caught up alone in the wilds of Kenya.

Masashiro Shinoda is a New Wave director similarly committed to the younger generation's struggle against society, but unlike Hani, he is a supreme stylist whose sense of pictorial composition compares favorably with that of the "classical" directors of the fifties (and, in fact, he had worked as Ozu's assistant on *Tokyo Twilight*, 1957). He has made films on every major aspect of his country's history, as well as on contemporary life. Like the films of his peers, Shinoda's tend to be violent and nihilistic, but they are also ethically committed and formally precise. His most significant films of the New Wave and post–New Wave era are *Pale Flower* (*Kawaiba hana*, 1963), *Assassination* / *The Assassin* (*Ansatsu*, 1964), *Punishment Island* (*Shokei no shima*, 1966), *Double Suicide* / *The Love Suicide at Amijima* (*Shinju ten no amijima*, 1969), *The Scandalous Adventures of Buraikan* (*Buraikan*, 1970), *Banished Orin* (*Hanare goze Orin*, 1977), and *Demon Pond* (*Yashagaike*, 1979).

In the eighties, Shinoda produced two major mainstream works, both beautifully photographed by Kazuo Miyagawa, the foremost cinematographer in Japan (*Rashomon, Ugetsu*, etc.). *MacArthur's Children* (*Setouchi shonen yakudan*, 1984) treats the trauma of Japan's defeat in World War II and its five-year occupation by the American army as experienced in the microcosm of a rural island. *Gonza the Spearman* (*Yari no gonza*, 1986), a classical, if bloody, adaptation of an early-eighteenth-century play by Chikamatsu in the *bunraku* puppet theater tradition*, tells the story of a *samurai* trapped in the coils of his own implacable code of honor; it won the Silver Bear at Berlin in the year of its release.

17.39 The highly stylized *Double Suicide* (Masahiro Shinoda, 1969): Shima Iwashita, Kicheimon Nakamura. Shinoda's fatalism is perfectly embodied in this adaptation of a famous Chikamatsu *bunraku* play, which also entered the *kabuki* canon, by his mixing of the traditional puppets and human actors through match cutting until they become interchangeable. The *kuroko* (stagehands or puppeteers dressed in black) represent instruments of destiny for both groups, and the film's deliberate theatricality is balanced by Shinoda's brilliant manipulation of the CinemaScope frame, difficult to interpolate from this cropped still.

---

* In *bunraku* puppet theater, developed during the Tokugawa period (1616–1868), white-faced dolls, expressionless except for mobile eyelids, are manipulated by as many as three black-robed, masked, but fully visible puppeteers (*kuroko*); the musical narrative (*joruri*) is chanted by a reciter (*gidayu*) to the accompaniment of instruments. Many *bunraku* plays revolved around the theme of *shinju*, or lovers' suicide, motivated by the tension between *giri* (duty) and *ninjo* (human desires). Monzaemon Chikamatsu (1653–1725) was the greatest literary master of the form, and his work forms the basis of many significant Japanese films (e.g., Mizoguchi's *The Crucified Lovers* [*Chikamatsu monogatari*, 1954]). *The Love Suicides at Sonezaki* was filmed again in 1982 by Midori Kurisaki as an actual *bunraku* play, photographed by Kazuo Miyagawa.

Both of these films starred the popular Japanese rock singer Hiromi Go (b. 1956), for whom Shinoda filmed the phenomenally successful forty-five-minute music video *Allusion* in 1985.

Another New Wave directors of note is Yasuzo Masumura—*The Hoodlum Soldier* (*Heitai yakuza*, 1965); *Red Angel* (*Akai tenshi*, 1966); and the highly stylized *The Love Suicides at Sonezaki* (*Sonezaki shinju*, 1977), adapted from a Chikamatsu *bunraku* puppet play. Even more significant, however, is Yoshishige Yoshida—*Farewell to Summer Light* (*Saraba natsu no hikari*, 1968), and the important avant-garde trilogy about twentieth-century radicalism *Eros plus Massacre* (*Eros purasu gyakusatsu*, 1969), which focuses on both the Taisho-era anarchist Osugi Sakae and his female lovers (who were murdered by the military police [*kempei-tai*] in the aftermath of the 1923 Kanto earthquake) and their contemporary student counterparts. Yoshida's films of the seventies include *Heroic Purgatory* (*Rengoku eroica*, 1970), a densely symbolic analysis of student activism during the fifties; and *Martial Law* (*Kaigenrei*, 1973), an elliptical biography of Kita Ikki, whose writings inspired the abortive coup d'état of February 26, 1936, in which 1,400 young right-wing officers and troops briefly seized control of Tokyo and murdered a number of prominent civilian officials (and were in turn executed by the military police, along with Kita, when the rebellion was suppressed three days later). Yoshida did not make another feature for thirteen years, when *The Promise* (*Niguen no yakusoku*, 1986), a film that seems to plead for euthanasia, appeared at Cannes.

Seijun Suzuki, a comedy and action film director for Nikkatsu, produced a number of youth films (*seishun-eiga*), such as *Kanto Wanderer* (*Kanto mushuku*, 1963) and *Tokyo Drifter* (*Tokyo nagaremono*, 1966), that contained New Wave themes, but his major contribution to the movement was *Elegy to Violence / The Born Fighter* (*Kenka ereiji*, 1966), scripted by Kaneto Shindo, about a fighting youth from the provinces who becomes ensnared in the politics of the 1936 attempted coup d'état; after this, Suzuki became a prolific director of "pink" films (see p. 809), although his two beautifully decadent ghost films *Zigeunerweisen* (1980) and *Heat Shimmer Theater* (*Kageroza*, 1981), both independently produced, were critically acclaimed in the early eighties.

At the same time the former Nikkatsu contract director Koji Wakamatsu made a successful bid to raise the pink film to the level of New Wave abstraction with his *Secret Act Inside Walls* (*Kabe no naka himegoto*, 1965), for which he was fired from Nikkatsu, and his low-budget, independently produced *The Embryo Hunts in Secret* (*Taiji ga mitsuryo suru toki*, 1966) and *Violated Angels / Violated Women in White* (*Okasareta byakuri*, 1967), which was inspired by the mass murder of nine nurses in Chicago in 1964. Wakamatsu also produced the bizarre *Go, Go You Who Are a Virgin for the Second Time* (*Yuke, yuke nidome no shojo*, 1969)—whose point of reference is the Tate-LaBianca murders—and the revolutionary fantasy *Angelic Orgasm* (*Tenshi no kokot..*, 1970).

Another outstanding director of the New Wave is Shohei Imamura—*Pigs and Battleships* (*Buta to gunkan*, 1961); *Intentions of Murder / Unholy Desire* (*Akai satsui*, 1964); *The Insect Woman* (*Nippon konchuki*, 1964);

17.40 *The Pornographer* (Shohei Imamura, 1966).

The Pornographer (*Jinruigaku nyumon*, 1966); *A Man Vanishes* (*Ningen johatsu*, 1967); *The Profound Desire of the Gods/Kuragejima: Tales from a Southern Island* (*Kamkgami no fukaki yokubo*, 1968); *History of Postwar Japan as Told by a Bar Hostess* (*Nippon sengo-shi: Madamu Omboro no seikatsu*, 1970). The first four films, all photographed in high-contrast black and white by Shinsaku Himeda, deal, respectively, with the *yakuza* subculture living off the detritus of the American fleet in the Japanese port city of Yokusuka circa 1960; a housewife who becomes the willing victim and finally the accomplice of a rapist; a poor woman who achieves enormous success through prostitution in postwar Japan (her corruption clearly symbolizes that of her country during the same era); and a mild-mannered businessman who produces pornographic films to support his middle-class and classically Oedipal family. Characterized by a mixture of fiction and the documentarylike incrementation of sociological detail, and by a boldly experimental use of the anamorphic widescreen frame, Imamura's New Wave films have about them a kind of anthropological precision that prepared audiences for such essays in classical anthropology as *A Man Vanishes* and *The Profound Desire of the Gods,* the latter a narrative analysis of an incestuous family on a primitive southern island (the mythic origin of the story is an incestuous relationship between brother and sister gods).

A former assistant to Ozu, Imamura worked mainly in documentary television during the seventies (e.g., *History of Postwar Japan as Told by a Bar Hostess* [1970]; *The Making of a Prostitute* [*Karayuki-san*, 1975]), but emerged at the end of the decade as a truly major figure with *Vengeance Is Mine* (*Fukushu suru wa are ni ari*, 1979). A relentless, semidocumentary account of an actual seventy-eight-day murder spree, the film refuses to judge either society, the criminal, or his victims. *Eijanaika* (1980) is a drama about the culture shock involved in the opening of Japan to the West after two hundred years of self-imposed isolation (the title—*Why Not?* or *What the Hell?*—derives from the rallying cry of the bloody anarchist riots of 1867, which explode at the film's conclusion). Imamura's *The Ballad of Narayama* (*Narayamabushi-ko*, 1983), based on a story by Shichiro Fukazawa about a people in a remote section of Japan who traditionally take their aged to a high mountaintop to die,

17.41 *Eijanaika* (Shohei Imamura, 1980).

17.42 Imamura's *The Ballad of Narayama* (1983).

won the Golden Palm at Cannes in the year of its release (a 1958 version by Keisuke Kinoshita had adapted the narrative as if it were a Kabuki play). And his work *The Pimp* (*Zegen*, 1987), which links the rising fortunes of a pimp with the success of Japan's military adventures in creating the Greater Southeast Asia Coprosperity Sphere prior to World War II, was also critically acclaimed. Imamura's own production company also helped to make Japan's most controversial film since the New Wave— *The Emperor's Naked Army Marches On* (*Hara Yuki yukite shingun* [Kazuo Hara, 1987]), a two-hour documentary portrait of Kenzo Oku-zaki, an aging veteran who demands that Emperor Hirohito apologize publicly to the Japanese people for causing the horrors of World War II. More recently, Imamura has produced a restrained adaptation of Masuji Ibuse's novel on the atomic bombing of Hiroshima, *Black Rain* (*Kuroi ame*, 1989).

But by far the most influential filmmaker of the Japanese New Wave is Nagisa Oshima, a militantly radical intellectual who was trained at Kyoto University in political history and law. He joined the Shochiku studios as a scriptwriter in 1955 and began directing there in 1959. When one of his films, *Night and Fog in Japan* (*Nihon no yoru to kiri*, 1960), was withdrawn for political reasons, he left the studio to form his own production company, Sozosha (Creation), which is still in operation. Much of his early work was in the genre of the *yakuza-eiga*, or contemporary gangster film. It tended to be violent, sexually explicit, and politically radical, in that Oshima's criminals were figures in open revolt against modern Japanese society. The malaise of this society was to become Oshima's overriding theme, making him the first major postwar director to concentrate solely on the problems of being Japanese in the present. Appropriately, Oshima rejected his culture's cinematic past as well as its historical one, so that even his earliest films reveal the influence of the French New Wave rather than that of his great Japanese predecessors. The use of hand-held cameras, *cinéma-vérité* shooting techniques, and on-location sound recording is typical of Oshima's early work, although all of his films since 1960 have been made in widescreen and color. By the late sixties Oshima had moved away from narrative, and the influence of Godard and the Yugoslav avant-gardist Dušan Makavejev became

17.43 *The Man Who Left His Will on Film* (Nagisa Oshima, 1970).

apparent in his blending of fantasy and reality and in his use of printed chapter titles, voice-over narration, extreme long shots, and audience-alienation effects. As the Japanese critic Hideo Osabe puts it, the films of Oshima have become "provocations directed at the spectators." Like Godard's, Oshima's films are audiovisual polemics designed to generate in the audience indignation and rebellion at the state of contemporary society.

Japanese society, like our own, is one in which massive industrialization, urbanization, and technocratization have accelerated social change and caused the disintegration of traditional (and, in Japan's case, centuries-old) values without offering anything in their place. As Oshima sees it in films like *Death by Hanging* (*Koshikei,* 1968), *The Diary of a Shinjuku Thief* (*Shinjuku dorobo nikki,* 1968), *Boy* (*Shonen,* 1969), *The Man Who Left His Will on Film* (*Tokyo senso sengo hiwa,* 1970), and *The Ceremony* (*Gishiki,* 1972), the Japanese family structure so dear to Ozu has degenerated into a series of empty rituals; the giant corporations have destroyed the physical and psychological environment of the entire country; Japan's cities are sinks of pollution, overcrowding, and violent crime. In response, the Japanese state has become feudal once more—authoritarian, imperialistic, racist, and politically repressive. For Oshima, then, Japan is in the midst of a nightmare of social disorder that increasingly courts a rebirth of fascism. His films are works of aggressive, often violent, social protest. Frequently, the graphic, even pornographic, depiction of sex becomes a vehicle for his radical indictment of modern, technocratized Japan, as vividly demonstrated in his films of the late seventies, *Empire of the Senses / In the Realm of the Senses* (*Ai no corrida,* 1976) and *Empire of Passion / The Phantom of Love* (*Ai no borei,* 1978). Ultimately, ideas are more important to Oshima than visual surfaces, and he is frequently accused of having no consistent style. But critics often confuse inconsistency with versatility, and there can be no question that Oshima the social critic is also a great film artist and one of the foremost innovators of the international cinema today—a reputation confirmed in the eighties by *Merry Christmas, Mr. Lawrence* (1983), depicting the tragic results of cultural ambivalence between East and West in a Japanese prisoner-of-war camp on Java during World War II, and *Max, Mon Amour* (*Max, My Love,* 1986), a Buñuelian satire shot in Paris by Raoul Coutard about a British diplomat's wife who has an affair with a chimpanzee.

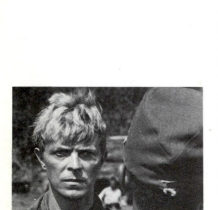

17.44 Oshima's *Merry Christmas, Mr. Lawrence* (1983): David Bowie in the title role.

Japanese Filmmaking After the New Wave

Of the post–New Wave generation, several filmmakers have already achieved international profiles, including Yoshimitsu Morita (b. 1950), Kohei Oguri (b. 1945), Mitsuo Yanagimachi (b. 1950), Shinji Somai (b. 1950), Ishii Sogo (b. 1957), and Juzo Itami. Morita became popular for cheaply made, breezy comedies such as *Something Like That* (*No yona-mono,* 1981) and *Boys and Girls* (*Boizu & gaaruzo*), but achieved his first major critical acclaim for *The Family Game* (*Kazoku geemu,* 1983)—a hilarious satire on contemporary Japanese family life and Ozu-style "home drama" films, as well as on the nation's educational system. Morita followed with *And Then* (*Sorekara*, 1986), an uncharacteristically serious adaptation of a period novel set in 1909.

Kohei Oguri achieved something of a coup when his first feature, *Muddy River* (*Doro no kawa*, 1981), was produced and distributed privately before being picked up by Toei and winning numerous Japanese awards, as well as an Oscar nomination and the silver prize at Moscow. This unsentimental black-and-white film depicts the friendship between two little boys of the underclass in 1956 Osaka, and it harks back to the postwar humanism of Mizoguchi and Ozu. Four years in production, Oguri's second feature, *For Kayako* (*Kayako no tameni*, 1985), is a visually exquisite, formally stylized story set in 1957 of a love affair between a Korean man (Koreans are notoriously subjected to racial discrimination in Japan) and a Japanese woman.

17.45   *Muddy River* (Kohei Oguri, 1981).

The focus of Mitsuo Yanagimachi's work to date has been the way in which rapid technological modernization has alienated the Japanese from nature, a major theme in a society that still practices a form of pantheism, which is associated with the religion of Shinto. His *A Nineteen Year Old's Map* (*Jikyusai no chizu*, 1979) concerns a deracinated student who wages guerrilla warfare against urban anomie through his paper route, while *A Farewell to the Land* (*Saraba itoshiki daichi*, 1982) is about a disaffected truck driver who descends to drug abuse and murder in reaction to the sterile industrial landscape that surrounds him. But Yanagimachi received worldwide recognition for *Fire Festival* (*Himatsuri*, 1985), based on an actual mass murder that occurred in 1980 in the Kumano region of southern Japan. There, in an area sacred to Shinto, where gods are believed to occupy both the mountains and the sea, land developers are attempting to build a tourist resort and marine park; the protagonist, a forty-year-old woodcutter and avid Shintoist, attempts to fight modernization of the region and, failing that, commits the ultimate self-declarative act by killing his family and himself with a shotgun.

17.46   *Fire Festival* (Mitsuo Vanagimachi, 1985).

Shinji Somai's first serious film was *A School of Fish* (*Cyoei no mure*, 1983), a documentary-style account of the life and work of an uncompromising Pacific coast tuna fisherman that employs extremely long takes. But his *Typhoon Club* (1985) brought him instant success when it shared the prize for the Young Cinema competition at the Tokyo International Festival for that year with Péter Gothár's *Time Stands Still* and Ali Ozenturk's *The Horse*. Characterized, like his earlier film, by magnificently revealing sequence shots, *Typhoon Club* concerns four junior high school students who are stranded inside their school building by a seasonal storm.

Ishii Sogo has parallel careers making films and directing rock videos and commercials. He produced several chaotic gang war fantasies—*Crazy Thunder Road* (*Kuruizaki Thunder Road*, 1980); *Burst City* (*Bakuretsu toshi*, 1981)—before scoring both commercially and critically with *The Crazy Family* (*Gyakufunsha-kazou* [literally, "Back-Jet Family"], a ferocious satire on contemporary Japanese consumerism.

Certainly the best known of the post–New Wave directors is Juzo Itami, a former actor whose black comedy *The Funeral* (*Ososhiki*, 1984) won a Japanese Academy Award for Best Picture and numerous festival prizes

17.47 *The Funeral* (Juzo Itami, 1984).

17.48 Juzo Itami's *Tampopo* (1986): Ken Watanabe, Ryutaro Otomo.

for its mordantly hilarious depiction of how the rising middle class handles one of its culture's most elaborate, expensive, and important social rituals. Itami, who also writes and produces his own work, continued in this vein with *Tampopo* (1986), a comic film about sex, food, and eating, and *A Taxing Woman* (*Marusa no onna*, 1987), a satire on the intricacies of the Japanese tax system.

Other promising directors of the post–New Wave generation are Yoichi Higashi (*Manon* [1981], and *Second Love* [*Sekando rabu*, 1983]), thought to be Japan's preeminent "women's director"; Kitchitaro Negishi (*Distant Thunder* [*En-rai*, 1982]) and *Our Wedding* [*Oretachi no wedding*, 1984]); Shuji Terayama (*Kusameikyu*, [1984] and *Farewell to the Ark* [*Saraba hakobune*, 1985]); Hideo Gosha (*Onimasa* [1982]; *A Life of Hanako Kiryuin* [*Kiryuin Hanako no shogai*, 1984]; and *Tokyo Bordello* [*Yoshiwara enjo*, 1987]); Kaizo Hayashi (*To Sleep so as to Dream* [*Yume miruyoni nemuritai*, 1986]); and Yojiro Takita (*Comic Magazine* [*Komikku zasshi nanka Irani*, 1986]).

Decline of the Studios

The rise of independent production and the New Wave was a consequence of the economic decline of the Japanese studio system. Multiple-channel color television was introduced in Japan in 1960, and ever since that time there has been a steady drop in film attendance (from one billion admissions in 1960, for example, to 150 million in 1980), paralleling the experience of the West. Two of the major studios—Shintoho and Daiei—have gone bankrupt, and the remaining four—Nikkatsu, Toei, Toho, and Shochiku—have become increasingly commercial and exploitative in their output.

The mid-sixties saw the rise of two new domestic exploitation genres which together came to constitute the mainstay of the declining film industry. The first was the *yakuza-eiga*, or contemporary gangster film, which has replaced the *samurai* film in popularity among Japanese audiences. The *yakuza* is in fact a kind of latter-day *samurai,* an outlaw swordsman in the urban jungle who nevertheless lives by a traditional code; this character type possesses considerable symbolic appeal for audiences whose traditional values have been eroded by a repressive technocracy. Moreover, *yakuza* films are invariably brutal and bloody, and they clearly provide audiences with a socially acceptable channel for their hostility and aggression—much of it directed toward society itself. In 1974, some one hundred *yakuza* films were produced by the Japanese studios, which constituted more than a third of the industry's output for that year.

The second exploitation genre to sweep Japan was the "eroduction," or "pink" film (*pinku-eiga*), a feature-length sex film with a high content of sadism. (Censorship in any form was illegal in Japan from 1966 to 1972.) Initially pure pornography, the eroduction has developed into a genre of some sophistication and, as is the case with the *yakuza-eiga,* has attracted some serious filmmakers. Among the most notable of these sado-erotic films are Takechi Tetsuji's *Black Snow* (*Kuroi yuki,* 1965), which contains explicit anti-American political elements; Adachi Masao's absurdist *Sexual Play* (*Seiyugi,* 1968); the previously mentioned work of Koji Wakamatsu (e.g., *Violated Women in White,* 1967), all of which is grounded in radical left-wing ideology; and Oshima's *In the Realm of the Senses* (1976). By the early seventies, the Japanese studio system was producing more pink films than any other kind. The situation changed slightly after censorship was reinstated in 1972, but between 1965 and 1975 the Japanese film industry devoted more than half of its total output to *yakuza-eiga* and eroductions, producing some sixteen hundred of these popular genre films in a single decade.

The box-office success of *Star Wars* (George Lucas, 1977) and *Close Encounters of the Third Kind* (Steven Spielberg, 1977) in Japan led to a glut of cheaply produced imitations, such as Toho's *Message from Space* (1978) and *War in Space* (1979), which recycle, with little imagination or style, the special-effects techniques of the *Godzilla / Rodan* films. By the mid-eighties, Japan had become the single largest export market for the major American producer-distributors, with Columbia's *Ghostbusters* and Warners' *Gremlins* breaking all-time box-office records there in 1984.

The Japanese cinema today is in flux. Though an economic recession in 1972 forced the government to grant subsidies to the industry to prevent its collapse, during the eighties production evolved completely in the private hands of the four studios—which form an oligopoly in the classical Hollywood sense—and a small but growing independent sector. In the seventies and eighties, the members of the first two generations of postwar filmmakers worked almost exclusively for the studios, if they worked at all, and even the most radical directors of the New Wave began to work for television or make studio films during the same period. Yet of the three hundred and fifty Japanese features produced a year, on average, Japanese film critic Tadao Sato estimates that two hundred are pornographic—either pink films or *"roman poruno"* (romance pornography). Film attendance has fallen at the steady rate of about 10 percent a year since the penetration of VCRs reach 42 percent of Japanese households in 1986. The hope of the future for Japanese cinema, then, would seem to lie in independent production, which in fact is the source of much of the post–New Wave work discussed above. Contemporary Japan has inarguably experienced the greatest economic miracle of the postwar world, but it has forfeited many things of cultural and spiritual value in the process. During the postwar period 1951–68, more than four hundred Japanese films won prizes at foreign film festivals, yet, as Westerners, we should not assume that even now we know a great deal about Japan or its cinema. As Tadao Sato wrote of such directors as Yoshimitsu Morita, Kohei Oguri, Mitsuo Yanagimachi, and Shinji Somai: "[They] have the ability to depict the subtle uneasiness that underlies Japan's superficial stability. They capture clearly the various contradictions: the confidence and fear, the timidity and pride, the traditional values that were upset in social revolution that followed World War II, and the simultaneous questioning of modernization and Westernization. Their achievement lies in highlighting the deeper meanings of this confusion."

INDIA

Because television does not yet exist as a mass medium in India, cinema is still the most popular form of entertainment. In the late eighties, the estimated weekly audience was 87 million for a population of nearly 800 million people,* and since 1971 India has been the largest film-producing nation in the world, accounting for fully one-fourth of the total global output each year. Its film industry—the country's tenth largest—is centered in Bombay (for Hindi-language films, which account for about 25 percent of the total), with substantial production facilities in Calcutta (for Bengali-language films) and Madras (for Tamil, Kannada, and Telugu films). India produces between eight and nine hundred features annually in more than sixteen different languages. But 90 percent of these films are rigidly conventionalized musicals† and mythological romances made for consumption by a largely uneducated and impoverished domestic audience. (Significant export markets for Indian films exist only in Indonesia, Malaysia, and the United Kingdom.) The formula has been described as "a star, six songs, and three dances"—usually about three hours long and in garish color. The Indian film industry is dominated today by a star system similar to that of Hollywood's early years, and the cinematic quality of the star vehicles matters little to either the producers or their unso-

---

* As compared, e.g., with Japan's 1988 population of 126 million, the USSR's of 285 million, and the Unites States' of 250 million. India's population is exceeded only by that of mainland China, which is 1 billion 100 million.

† The songs are not sung but lip-synchronized by the stars of the films. The singers—known as "playback singers"—often become stars in their own right by recording songs from current films and marketing the disks with their pictures on the jackets. The composers also sell records on the strength of their names, often recording their own songs.

phisticated audiences. Despite these conditions, India has managed to produce some filmmakers of extraordinary talent in the past few decades and in Satyajit Ray at least one contemporary director of major international stature.

The current structure of the mainstream Indian commercial film industry—the only major industry in the world to develop under colonial rule—was engendered by the coming of sound. The audience for Indian silent cinema had consisted of hundreds of thousands of Indians, Burmese, and Ceylonese, who spoke many different tongues. But with sound, production was initially forced to fragment into regional language groups, of which, within India alone, there were no less than twenty-six. Even the majority Hindi-speaking market of 140 million people had at least three separate dialects. Under these conditions, the first talking feature, the Hindi music drama *Alam Ara* (*Beauty of the World* [Ardeshir M. Irani, 1931]), might well have plunged the industry into chaos. But instead the film was a huge success—as indeed were all early Indian sound films—heralding an unprecedented boom. The reason was grounded deep in Indian culture: sound permitted a revival of the vastly popular folk-music drama of the nineteenth century (itself based on centuries-old religious myths), which had been, quite literally, "all-talking, all-singing, all-dancing." Between 1931 and 1932, the resurgence of this form on the screen played an enormous role in winning widespread acceptance for the Indian sound film despite language barriers. Although most Indian sound films were produced for domestic consumption and seemed to exist mainly as an excuse for musical performance and representation (as they still are and do), the Indian film industry nevertheless became a powerful entity during the transition to sound: from producing twenty-eight films in 1931—twenty-three of which were in Hindi, three in Bengali, and one each in Tamil and Telugu—it was producing 233 in 1935 in ten different languages.

As in the United States, the rapid diffusion of sound in India helped to consolidate a studio system that was already in place. But World War II saw the steady rise of independent production, initially as a means of laundering black market money. By the war's end, most of the major studios were bankrupt, and the vast majority of production was carried out on an *ad hoc* basis. After national independence was granted in 1947, however, the film industry came under increasing government supervision through the promulgation of official censorship codes, and independent production became the order of the day. With the arrival of color in the industry, there was an enormous boom in costume films and "mythologicals," both perfectly suited to the new technology. A very popular star of these lavish spectacles was Raj Kapoor (b. 1924). Kapoor became a producer-director himself during this period, and while the bulk of his work was romantic and popular, he also made films of social comment, or "socials," in the fifties, including *The Vagabond* (*Awara*, 1951; a smash hit in the Soviet Union in 1954); *Boot Polish* (1954); and *Mr. 420* (*Shri 420*, 1955). So, too, did his contemporary Bimal Roy (1912–66)—*Two Acres of Land* (*Do bigha zameen*, 1953; a prizewinner at Cannes and Karlovy Vary); *Madhumati* (1958); and *The Jew* (*Yahudi*, 1958). Other interesting filmmakers of the fifties were Guru Dutt (1925–64)—*Mr. and Mrs. 55* (1955); *Eternal Thirst* (*Pyaasa*, 1957); *Paper Flowers* (*Kaagaz ke phool*, 1959; India's first widescreen film) and Meboob Khan (*Savage Princess* [*Aan*, 1952]; *Mother India* [1957]). But the filmmaker who claimed international attention for the Indian cinema during the fifties, and still does, was Satyajit Ray (b. 1921).

Satyajit Ray

As a young man, Ray studied painting with the Bengali poet Rabindranath Tagore (1861–1941) and then worked for a while for the Calcutta branch of a British advertising agency as an illustrator. In 1947 he founded the Calcutta Film Society with his co-worker Chidananda Das Gupta (later a film critic), and its membership came to include many young Bengali intellectuals who would later become filmmakers, including Ritwik Ghatak and Mrinal Sen. Ray's job took him to London for six months in 1950; there he saw Vittorio De Sica's *Ladri di biciclette* (1948) and was tremendously impressed by the film and by the style of Italian neorealism. On his return to Calcutta, he met Jean Renoir and was able to observe him filming *The River* (1951). After many practical difficulties, Ray made his first film, a visualization of the first part of a long novel by the Bengali writer Bibhuttibhusan Bannerji entitled *The Song of the Road* (*Pather panchali*, 1955), which, to the astonishment of nearly everyone, won the Jury Prize at Cannes in 1956 in addition to becoming a box-office hit in Bengal. Ray followed with two more films, *The Unvanquished* (*Aparajito*, 1957) and *The World of Apu* (*Apur sansar*, 1958), which together completed his adaptation of the novel and form the Apu trilogy—a sensitive, humanistic story of the growth of a young Bengali boy from childhood to maturity. Ray's style was neorealistic in its simplicity and directness, and he made brilliant use of classical Indian music with a soundtrack composed and played by Ravi Shankar (Ray now composes his own scores). He acquired a large international following in the sixties based on his films *The Music Room* (*Jalsaghar*,

17.49 Family members in *Pather panchali* (Satyajit Ray, 1955): Karuna Bannerji, Runki Bannerji, Subir Bannerji.

1958; released 1963); *The Goddess* (*Devi*, 1960); *Two Daughters* (*Teen kanya*, 1961); *The Big City* (*Mahanagar*, 1963); *The Lonely Wife* (*Charulata*, 1964; adapted from a novel by Tagore); and *Days and Nights in the Forest* (*Aranyer din ratri*, 1970)—all of them studied accounts of some telling aspect of Bengali life.

Because his focus falls so frequently on personal relationships and the small intimacies of everyday life, Ray has sometimes been accused of ignoring India's pressingly serious problems of poverty, official corruption, and religious intolerance. In the seventies, however, he produced more politically conscious films such as *The Adversary* (*Pratidwandi*, 1971), which deals with unemployment among middle-class youth; *Distant Thunder* (*Ashanti sanket*, 1973), a depiction of the effects of famine on Bengal during World War II; *The Chess Players* (*Shatranj ke khilari*, 1978; Ray's first film in Urdu rather than Hindi), set during the British annexation of India's last independent princely state in 1856; and *The Middleman* (*Jana aranya*, 1979), a bitter satire about the Calcutta business world. During the eighties Ray wrote, directed, and scored the fifty-minute telefilm *Deliverance* (*Sadgati*, 1982), a stark depiction of the brutalities of the Hindu caste system adapted from a story by Munshi Premchand; the full-length theatrical feature *The Home and the World* (*Ghare baire*, 1984), based on a novel by Tagore set in 1905, when the British Viceroy Lord Curzon deliberately provoked antagonism between the Hindus and Muslims of Bengal to consolidate his rule; and an adaptation of Ibsen's socially conscious melodrama *An Enemy of the People* (*Ganashatru*, 1989). But whatever his status as a social critic, Ray is a serious film artist who has made the Indian cinema worthy of serious attention for the first time in its history.

Parallel Cinema

Ray's *Apu* trilogy also created the split in Indian cinema between commercial entertainment and art that persists to this day, and it generated great enthusiasm among other Bengali filmmakers, notably Ritwik Ghatak (1925–76) and Mrinal Sen (b. 1923). A radical Marxist intellectual, Ghatak made only eight films, the best known of which is *Pathetic Fallacy* (*Ajantrik*, 1958), a popular fable about a rural cabbie's love for his aging taxi. But Ghatak's true genius lay in the creation of an authentic alternative cinema. In his semiautobiographical trilogy on East Pakistani refugees—*The Cloud-Capped Star* (*Meghe dhaka tara*, 1960), *E Flat* (*Komal ghandhar*, 1961), and *River of Gold* (*Subarnarekha*, 1965)—brutal directness belies the rich mythic subtext. His masterpiece, *Reason, Debate and a Tale* (*Jukti takko aur gappo*, 1974), is an autobiographical account of an alcoholic intellectual who must come to terms with the decay of his own revolutionary idealism.

Sen was much more prolific, making films throughout the fifties and sixties (e.g., *The End of Night* [*Raat-bhor*, 1953] and *The Wedding Day* [*Baishay sravan*, 1960]), but his breakthrough film was *Bhuvan Shome* (*Mr. Shome*, 1969), which is generally considered to mark the beginning of New Indian Cinema, or "parallel cinema" (parallel, i.e., to the mainstream commercial industry). Inspired by the French *nouvelle vague*, specifically Truffaut's *Jules et Jim* (1961), *Bhuvan Shome* tells the story of a petty-minded railway official on holidiay who is humbled and then liberated by an uninhibited village girl, and it was financed by a small unsecured loan from the Indian Film Finance Corporation (FFC).

This agency had been founded by the government in 1960 as part of a constellation of institutions designed to enhance the quality of domestic films (the others were the Film Institute of India in Poona, established in 1961 to train aspiring directors, and the National Film Archive, founded in 1964), but until *Bhuvan Shome* it had only supported the work of established figures, like Ray. The critical and commercial success of Sen's film opened the FFC's doors to unknown directors of small- to medium-budget features. Over the next decade about fifty-five such films were produced under its auspices, including such extraordinary first works as Basu Chatterji's *The Whole Sky* (*Sara akaash*, 1969), Avtar Kaul's *27 Down* (1973), and M. S. Sathyu's Urdu-language saga *Scorching Wind* (*Garm hawa*, 1973). Kaul died in a drowning accident on the day his film won the Best Hindi Feature award, but Chatterji (*Tuberoses* [*Rajinigandha*, 1974]; *Just a Trifle* [*Choti si baat*, 1975]; *The Love Thief* [*Chitchor*, 1976]; *Sweet and Sour* [*Khatta meetha*, 1977]; *Mischief* [*Dillagi*, 1979]; etc.) and Sathyu (*The Legendary Outlaw* [*Kenneshwara rama*, 1977]; *The Restless Corpse* [*Chitegu chinte*, 1979]; *The Famine* [*Bara*, 1980]; etc.) both established careers as prolific directors within the Bengali industry.

Sen followed his success with the formally experimental *Interview* (1971) and *Calcutta '71* (1972); clearly influenced by Godard, these works mix third-person narrative with direct address to the audience. Next Sen produced a series of films—*The Guerrilla Fighter* (*Patidak*, 1973), *The Royal Hunt* (*Mrigaya*, 1976), *The Village Story / The Outsiders* (*Oka oorie katha*, 1977), *Man with the Axe* (*Parasuram*, 1978), and *In Search of Famine* (*Aakaler sandhane*, 1980)—that deal with the exploitation of the urban and the rual poor by multinational corporations, the British raj, Indian businessmen, and bourgeois leftist filmmakers, respectively. In the late seventies and eighties, Sen began a critique of middle-class hypocrisy in such films as *Quiet Rolls the Dawn* (*Ek din pratidin*, 1979), *Kaleidoscope* (*Chaalchitra*, 1981), *The Case Is Closed* (*Kharji*, 1982), *The Ruins* (*Khandaar*, 1983), and *Their Own Faces* (*Tasveer apni apni*, 1985). With the Indian-French-Belgian-Swiss coproduction *Genesis* (1986), a richly beautiful parable of the cyclical rise, decline, and fall of the human race, Sen achieved international status.

In the late sixties, the nonstar parallel cinema movement was basically Hindi-speaking and centered in Bombay, but during the seventies, regional industries in the southwest—especially Karnatka and Kerala—began to subsidize independent production, resulting in a "southern new wave." In Karnatka, whose Kannada-language industry is centered in Bangalor, Pattabhi Rama Reddy began the revival with *Last Rites* (*Samskara*, 1970), a film about the influence of Brahmins on village life, and it was sustained by his protégés Girish Karnad in *The Forest* (*Kaadu*, 1973), a brilliant film about two feuding villages as seen through a child's eyes, and B. B. Karanth in *Choma's Drum* (*Chomana dudi*, 1975), a chronicle of Harijan family life in the 1920s. Equally impressive are Karanth and Karnad's *The Cow-Dust Hour* (*Godhuli*, 1977); Girish Kasaravalli's *The Ritual* (*Ghatashraddha*, 1977), *The Siege* (*Akramana*, 1979), *The Three Paths* (*Mooru darigalu*, 1980), and *Tabara's Tale* (*Tabarana kathe*, 1986); and Karnad's *Once Upon a Time* (*Ondanondu kalladalli*, 1979), a lavish homage to Kurosawa that revitalizes a long forgotten native martial arts tradition, and *Festival* (*Utsav*, 1984), an erotic comedy based on a fourth-century Sanskrit play. In neighboring Kerala, India's most densely populated and literate state, where Malayalam is the principal language, the first major work was Adoor Gopalakrishna's *One's Own Choice* (*Swayamvharam*, 1972), a film about the grim consequences of a young couple's flaunting social convention. He followed this with the politically resonant *Ascent* (*Kodiyettam*, 1977), *The Rat Trap* (*Elippathayam*, 1981), and *Face to Face* (*Mukhamukham*, 1984), the latter a portrait of a disillusioned Keralese communist labor hero. Other notable Keralese directors are M. T. Vasudevan Nair (*Flower Offering* [*Nirmalyan*, 1973]) and G. Aravindan, known for such lyrically poetic works as *Throne of Capricorn* (*Uttarayanam*, 1974), *Golden Sita* (*Kanchana sita*, 1977), *The Tent* (*Thampu*, 1978), *The Bogeyman,* (*Kummatty* 1979), *Stephen (Esthappan*, 1980), *Twilight* (*Pokkuveyil*, 1981), *Chidambaram* (1986), and *There Was a Village Somewhere* (*Oridathu*, 1987).

In Bengal two former students of Ghatak, Mani Kaul (b. 1942) and Kumar Shahani, both graduates of the Poona Film Institute, carried on their teacher's tradition of uncompromising Marxist praxis. Kaul produced such Bressonian exercises as *Daily Bread* (*Uski roti*, 1969); *In Two Minds* (*Duvidha*, 1973); *Rising from the Surface* (*Satah se uthata aadmi*, 1981); *Dhrupad* (1982); a documentary about a medieval form of Indian classical music); and *Mind of Clay* (*Mati manas*, 1985). And Shahani made the epic narratives *Mirror of Illusion* (*Maya darpan*, 1972) and *Wages and Profits / Vibrations* (*Tarang*, 1984). The most commercially successful director of the parallel cinema, however, is indisputably Shyam Benegal (b. 1924), whose feature debut *The Seedling* (*Ankur*, 1974) provided a model for much of the New Cinema that followed. This stylistically polished film depicts the exploitation that underlies the landlord-serf relationship in a narrative that is at once realistic and dramatically satisfying. Benegal followed with *Night's End* (*Nishant*, 1975); *The Churning* (*Manthan*, 1976); and *The Boon,* (*Anugraham*, 1977), which underscore the link between entrenched feudal power and the sexual exploitation of women. He then delivered a sweeping and highly successful historical epic of the 1857 Sepoy rebellion in *The Obsession* (*Junoon*, 1978), and he moved even closer to the tastes of the popular audience with such spectacles as *The Machine Age* (*Kalyug*, 1981), *The Market Place* (*Mandi*, 1983), and *Past, Present, and Future* (*Trikal*, 1986). But Benegal's social commitment is still apparent in his two feature-length documentaries of 1985, *Pandit Nehru* and *Satyajit Ray,* and in such recent theatrical features as *The Essence* (*Susman*, 1987), about corruption in the hand-loom industry in his native Telugu-speaking state of Andhra Pradesh.

During the eighties, several young Marxist directors have become prominent in Bengali parallel cinema, especially Gautan Ghosh (*The Occupation* [*Dakhal*, 1982] and *The Crossing* [*Paar*, 1984]); Aparna Sen (*36 Chowringhee Lane* [1982] and *Paroma* [1986]); and Buddhadev Das Gupta (*Civil War* [*Grihayuddha*, 1982] and *The Return* [*Phera*, 1988]). But many observers feel that India may in fact be moving toward a so-called "middle cinema," patterned more or less on the work of Benegal—i.e., films whose political and social concerns are not at odds with audience accessibility and even entertainment. This tendency can be seen in the political thrillers of Benegal's former cameraman Govind Nihalani (*Cry of the Wounded* [*Aakrosh*, 1981], *Half Truth* [*Ardh satya*, 1983], and *Blood of Brothers* [*Aghaat*, 1986]); Ramesh Sharma (*New Delhi Times*, 1986); and Janu Barua (*The Catastrophe* [*Halodhia choraye baodham khai*, 1988); the fast-paced comedies of Kundan Shah (*Let It Pass, Boys* [*Jaane bhi do yaron*, 1983] and Saeed Mirza (*The Court Summons Joshi* [*Mohan Joshi hazir*, 1984]); and the more eclectic work of Ketan Mehta (*A Folk Tale* [*Bhavni bhavai*, 1981], *Festival of Fire* [*Holi*, 1985], and *A Touch of Spice* [*Mirch Masala*, 1987]).

CHINA

Motion pictures were introduced in China by European and American entrepreneurs at the same time as in the West, and the Chinese immediately loved them, calling them *ying she*, or "shadow play." The first indigenous films appeared in 1905, and by 1910 an industry centered mainly in the cities of the eastern coast began to form. Sound was introduced in 1929 and gained widespread acceptance, but the Japanese invasion of 1937 and the occupation of Shanghai forced the Chinese film industry to move south into the British Crown Colony of Hong Kong, where a large outpost was established, and into southeast Asia. When production resumed on the mainland in 1945, the focus was mainly on the traumas of the war and occupation in such epics as *Spring River Flows East* (*Yijiang chunshui xiang dong liu* [Cai Chusheng and Zheng Junli, 1947]) and *Eighty Thousand Miles of Clouds and the Moon* (*Bagianli lu yun he yue* [Shi Dongshan, 1947]). Meanwhile a civil war raged between Chiang Kai-shek's Nationalists and the Communist forces of Mao Ze-dong; when the latter won in 1949, he proclaimed the mainland as the People's Republic of China, and Chiang's government fled to Taiwan. Afterward, Chinese cinema, though unified by a single cultural heritage, developed in mainland China (People's Republic), Hong Kong, and Taiwan along separate paths.

The People's Republic of China

In the People's Republic, the period from 1949 to 1966 was one of nationalization and collectivization. The film industry was placed under the Minister of Culture and the government undertook to build ten major studios in each of the country's largest cities and to modernize the Northeast Film Studio in Changchun, a holdover from the Japanese invasion. Up to 1956 hundreds of socialist realist films that celebrated the revolution and the glories of life in the new socialist state were produced. The so-called "hundred flowers" movement of 1956 and 1957 invited constructive criticism of the Communist Party and briefly permitted the production of such mildly dissident films as Lü Ban's *Before the New Director Arrives* (*Xin juzhang daolai zhi qian,* 1956) and literary adaptations like Chen Xihe's *Family* (*Jia,* 1956).

This period was followed by a politically repressive "Anti-Rightist" movement and the launching in 1958 of the "Great Leap Forward" (China's second five-year plan, the first having been undertaken from 1953 to 1957). The Great Leap Forward was designed to increase national economic output, and from 1958 to 1959 the film industry was able to double production to 229 features and animated shorts, most of them—like Zhao Ming's *Loving the Factory as One's Home* (*Ai chang ru jia,* 1958) and Lu Ren's *Steel Man and Iron Horse* (*Gangren tiema,* 1958)—devoted to Great Leap themes. Between 1959 and 1964, however, the film industry was less subject to politicization, if not to ideology, and directors found themselves able to produce such stylistically interesting work as Zheng Junli's *Lin Zexu* (1959), based on Chinese poetry, and Xie Jin's *The Red Detachment of Women* (*Hongse niangzijun,* 1961). The early sixties witnessed the adaptation of a number of classic operas—Su Li's *Third Sister Liu* (*Liu sanjie,* 1960), Cui Wei's *Wild Boar Forest* (*Yezhe lin,* 1962), and Cen Fan's *Dream of the Red Chamber* (*Honglou meng,* 1962)—as well as novels, like Xie Tieli's *Early Spring in February* (*Zaochun eryue,* 1963, which had previously been forbidden as a "bourgeois" form). Also produced were such comedies of contemporary life as Xie Jin's *Fat Li, Young Li, and Old Li* (*Da Li, xiao Li, Li he lao Li,* 1962) and Yen Gong's *Satisfied or Not* (*Manyi bu manyi,* 1963). Three films of particular note made during this era were Lu Jen's popular comedy *Li Shuangshuang,* 1962); Xie jin's *Two Stage Sisters* (*Wutai jiemei,* 1965), a sensitive account of the relationship between two talented opera singers; and the Wan brothers' two-part animated feature *Uproar in Heaven* (1961; 1964).

In 1966 Mao unexpectedly swung his support to the ultraradicals within the Chinese Communist Party, bringing on the ten-year reign of terror known as the Cultural Revolution, during which every social and economic institution in the country was disrupted and many were destroyed. The impact on the film industry was enormous, as filmmakers, like most other Chinese professionals, were driven into the countryside for "re-education" by the peasants. Feature production ground to a halt between 1967 and 1969, and was resumed in 1970 largely by amateurs working in a single newly synthesized genre—*Geming Yangbanxi,* or "revolutionary model operas." This form, typified by Xie Tieli's *Taking Tiger Mountain by Strategy* (*Zhiqu Weihushan,* 1970), Cheng Yin's *The Red Lantern* (*Hongdeng ji,* 1970), and Pan Wenzhan and Fu Jie's *The Red Detach-*

17.50 *Battle Song of Taching* (Sun Yung Ping, 1966), one of the last films released before the Cultural Revolution.

ment of Women (*Hongse niangzijun*, 1971—a remake of Xie Jin's 1960 narrative feature) was characterized by melodramatic plots, stylized dances, acrobatics, and grandiose orchestral finales to create a kind of *circus maximus* of the revolution. They gave mainland Chinese cinema an unwarranted reputation for egregiousness from which it still suffers today. Professional filmmakers gradually returned from the reeducation camps between 1973 and 1976, but political conditions still were such that few films of quality could be made.

Party Chairman Mao and Premier Zhou En-lai both died in 1976, and a power struggle ensued between a group of moderates led by Hua Guofeng and Mao's widow, Jian Qing. Hua won and briefly succeeded Mao and Zhou, while Jian Qing and three of her followers (called the "Gang of Four")—now revealed as the real power behind the Cultural Revolution—were tried and imprisoned for treason. Hua was himself replaced by Deng Xiaoping in 1980, ushering in a period of moderation and relative liberalization for mainland China which ended abruptly with the Tiananmen Square massacre of Sunday, June 4, 1989, and the reign of terror that followed. After Mao's death the state distribution enterprise, the China Film Corporation, eliminated full subvention of production and required each of the country's twenty-two major studios to do its own financial planning.

The Chinese divide their filmmakers into generations: first, the pioneers; second, those who developed social realism in the thirties and forties; the third is comprised of those who were unable to study film formally because of the war and occupation, but who entered the industry shortly after the liberation; and the fourth is the generation that studied film before the Cultural Revolution but couldn't enter the industry until the Cultural Revolution had ended. The state film school, the Beijing Film Academy, reopened in 1978 after having been shut down since 1966 by the Cultural Revolution. In 1981 the academy graduated 2,100 students from the fourth generation in acting, directing, cinematography, sound recording, and graphic arts. The fifth generation of filmmakers is comprised of those who graduated from the academy after 1982. Because of their training, the fourth and fifth generations are sometimes grouped together as the "academic school." This fifth generation of Chinese filmmakers coalesced with the new, more market-oriented production context to produce a new kind of mainland cinema, much of it devoted initially to the trauma of individuals, regardless of class, during the Cultural Revolution. For example, Yang Yanjin and Deng Yimin's *Troubled Laughter* (*Ku'naoren de xiao*, 1979), Xie Jin's *Legend of Tianyun Mountain* (*Tianyunshan chuanqi*, 1980), and Wu Yigong's *Evening Rain* (*Bashan yeyu*, 1980), all were sympathetic to the plight of intellectuals, and Wang Qimin and Sun Yu's *At Middle Age* (*Ren doazhong nian*, 1982), Wu Tianming's *River Without Buoys* (*Meiyou hangbiao de heliu*, 1983) and *Life* (*Rensheng*, 1984) concern the suffering of professionals and intellectuals alike. Contemporary, even naturalistic, social commentary was also apparent in films like Chiang Liang's *Yamaha Fish Stall* (*Yamaha yu dang*, 1984) and *Juvenile Delinquents* (*Shaonian fan*, 1985) and Lu Xiaoya's *Girl in*

Red (*Hongye shaonu*, 1985), as well as Yan Xueshu's *Wild Mountains* (*Yeshan*, 1986), an ironic comedy on provincial wife-swapping. Tian Zhuanzhuang's Flaherty-like studies of Mongolian and Tibetan life, *On the Hunting Ground* (*Lie changzha sha*, 1985) and *Horse Thief* (*Dmazei*, 1986), Zhang Junzhao's *One and the Eight* (*Yige he bage*, 1984; released 1987), and Huangjian Zhong's *A Dead Man Visits the Living* (*Yigesizhe dul shengzhe de fanfwen*, 1988) are all impressive fifth generation contributions. But perhaps the most exciting figure to emerge in recent mainland cinema is Chen Kaige (b. 1953), whose *Yellow Earth* (*Huang tudi*, 1985) marked a critical and commercial breakthrough for Chinese film on the international distribution circuit. Chen followed this extraordinarily poetic rendition of the folk culture of the Yellow River plateau circa 1939, filmed in the style of Chinese scroll painting, with *The Big Parade* (*Dayue bing*, 1985) and *King of the Children* (*Haizi wang*, 1988), the former about military life in contemporary China and the latter about the mistakes of the Cultural Revolution. More recently, Chen's cinematographer Zhang Yimou directed a striking debut feature in *Red Sorghum* (*Hong gaoliang*, 1988), a film that begins as light comedy and ends with a horrendous evocation of Japanese wartime atrocities; it won the Golden Bear at Berlin in 1988. There has also been a considerable amount of coproduction with Hong Kong (e.g., Chang Hsin-yen's *Shaolin Temple* [*Shao-lin szu*, 1982] and its sequels, Ann Hui's *Boat People* [1982] and her two-part *Romance of Book and Sword* [1988]); with Japan (Junya Sato's *The Unfinished Chess Match* [*Mikan no taikyoku*, 1983] and *The Go Masters*, 1983); and with the West (NBC's Italian-produced miniseries *Marco Polo* [Guido Montaldi, 1983], Bertolucci's *The Last Emperor* [1986], and the first feature-length Chinese-American coproduction, Peter Wang's *A Great Wall Is a Great Wall* [1986]). Mainland films now must earn money at the domestic box office in order to justify their studio's continuing subsidies from the state, and so nearly all of the new films have an element of mass appeal, including the common use of widescreen and Technicolor (the People's Republic operates the only extant Technicolor dye-transfer printing plant in the world). Annual attendance hovers around 27 billion at 5,500 theaters nationwide, but television is now widely available (83 percent penetration in urban districts) and increasingly popular (the highest rating exceeds 100 million viewers). There is increasing competition from foreign films, which the China Film Corporation is empowered to import in an amount equivalent to one-third of the industry's annual domestic feature output, which has averaged about 120 for most of the eighties.

17.51 Chen Kaige's *Yellow Earth* (1985).

Hong Kong

In postwar Hong Kong, production was carried on throughout the fifties by a variety of small- to medium-sized companies that nevertheless managed to produce between 150 and 170 films per year in such popular genres as the family melodrama and the Cantonese-dialect swordplay (*wu xia*) and martial arts (*kung fu*) films. During the sixties these were replaced by comedies, urban musicals, and Mandarin-dialect swordplay films, characterized by greater violence and montage-style editing. At the same time, the Shaw Brothers Studio emerged as a vertically integrated major, with production facilities, laboratories, and dubbing studios in Hong Kong, and exhibition chains in Hong Kong, Singapore, and Malaysia. Shaw Brothers specialized in Mandarin swordplay films, turning out as many as fifty a year and giving birth to several major directorial talents: Li Hanxiang (b. 1926) who made *Magnificent Concubine* (*Yang guifei*, 1961), *Love Eternal* (*Liang shanbo yezhu yingtai*, 1963), and *The Happiest Moment* (*Yi le ye*, 1973); and King Hu (b. 1931), whose "Inn Trilogy" (*Come Drink with Me* [*Dazui xia*, 1966], *Dragon Gate Inn* [*Longmen kezhan*, 1967], and *The Fate of Lee Khan* [*Ying-ch'un qizhi feng-bo*, 1973]) combined the styles of Chinese opera and classical painting to elevate the swordplay genre to the level of art. Hu continued to inject the genre with philosophical mysticism in his "Buddhist Trilogy," produced outside of the Shaw system—*A Touch of Zen* (*Xia nu*, 1971), *Raining in the Mountain* (*Kong shanling yu*, 1979), and *Legend of the Mountain* (*Shanzhong chuanqi*, 1979)—the first of which won a prize for technique at Cannes in 1975. With the commercial success of such widescreen color sword epics in the mid- to late-sixties, Shaw Brothers was able to dominate the markets of Taiwan, Singapore, Malaysia, and Thailand.

The independent studio Golden Harvest had a similar experience in the early seventies with the Mandarin *kung fu* films of Bruce Lee (e.g., *The Big Boss* [*Tangshan da xiong*, 1971], *Fists of Fury* [*Jing wumen*, 1972], *The Way of the Dragon* [*Menglong guo jiang*, 1972]); but this bonanza ended with Lee's sudden death in 1974. Golden Harvest then turned to social satires starring and directed by popular variety show host Michael Hui (*Teppanyaki*, 1984, is a recent example) and to Keatonesque *kung fu* action-comedies with Jackie Chan (b. 1954—Samo Hung's *Winners and Sinners*, 1983; *Wheels on Meals*, 1984; *Heart of the Dragon*, 1985; *My Lucky Stars*, 1985; and Chan's self-directed *Project A* and *Project A, Part II*, 1984; *Armor of God*, 1986; *Police Force*, 1987).

Both Shaw Brothers and Golden Harvest continued to mass-produce cheap genre films during the seventies; approximately thirty smaller competitors produced even cheaper clones. In 1977 Hong Kong became the site of an annual domestic and international film festival of some standing that was held each April. Also, television became widespread and popular during this period, and introduced significant cross-fertilization to filmmaking when the first generation of television directors began working in cinema during the eighties. Notable among those who worked first in TV were Tsui Hark—*The Butterfly Murders* (*Tieh Pien*, 1979); *Don't Play with Fire* (*Diyi leixing weixian*, 1980); *Zu: Warriors of the Magic Mountain*, 1981; *Shanghai Blues*, 1984; *Working Class*, 1985; *Peking Opera Blues*, 1987; Allan Fong—*Father and Son* (*Fu zi qing*, 1981) and *Ah Ying*, 1983; Tan Jiaming (also known as Patrick Tam)—*The Sword*, 1980; *The Love Massacre*, 1980; *Nomad* (*Lie huo qingchun*, 1982); Kirk Wong—*The Club*, 1981; *Health Warning* (*Da leitai*, 1983);

Ann Hui—*The Secret* (*Feng jie,* 1979); *The Spooky Bunch* (*Zhuang dao zheng,* 1980); *The Story of Woo Viet* (*Hu yue de gushi,* 1981); *Boat People* (*Touibin hu hai,* 1982); *Love in a Fallen City,* 1984; Ching Sui Tung—*A Chinese Ghost Story,* 1987; Kwan Kan Pang—*Rouge,* 1987; and John Woo—*A Better Tomorrow,* 1987; *A Better Tomorrow—II,* 1988. These newcomers ultimately challenged Shaw Brothers' domination of the market, as did the films of the new independent Cinema City Company, whose slapstick *Aces Go Places* trilogy (Eric Tsang and Tsui Hark, 1982–84) became an all-time box-office champ. What will happen to the gritty vitality of Hong Kong's film industry when the British government cedes its former colony to the People's Republic in 1997 is unpredictable at this point, although the mainland's aggressive new "market communists" will surely put it to practical use.

Taiwan

The Taiwanese film industry was heavily imitative of Hong Kong's and dominated by it until very recently. During the sixties the government-owned Central Motion Picture Corporation (CMPC) sponsored the feature films of Li Hsing, widely regarded as the architect of Taiwanese cinema, which focused mainly on the problems of rural communities. As the island rapidly industrialized and its people became more affluent during the seventies, wave after wave of costume martial arts films (mostly Mandarin-dialect) and slick youth-oriented melodramas (mostly Taiwanese-dialect) appeared in a market that was largely dominated by Shaw Brothers product in any case. In the early eighties, however, a new generation of filmmakers, most of whom had studied abroad and had a clearer sense of their cultural identity, entered the industry. They created a distinctive "new wave" in low- to medium-budget films that dealt with day-to-day reality in Taiwan but were quite often stylistically experimental. The major figures of the Taiwan New Wave are generally agreed to be Edward Wang (*That Day on the Beach* [*Haitan de yitian,* 1983], *Tapei Story* [*Qingmei zhuma,* 1985], *The Terrorizers* [*Konbu finze,* 1987]); Chang Yi (*Jade Love* [*Yu Ch'ing sao,* 1985], *Hang-sheng, My Son* [*Wo erh hang-sheng,* 1986], *This Love of Mine* [*Wo-te ai,* 1986]; and Hou Hsiao-hsien (*The Boys from Fengkuei* [*Fengkuei lai de ren,* 1984], *A Summer at Grandpa's* [*Dongdong de jiagl,* 1985], *A Time to Live and a Time to Die* [*Tong nien wang shi,* 1986], *Dust in the Wind* [*Lienlin fung chen,* 1987], *Daughter of the Nile* [*Nilouhe nuer,* 1988]). In 1986, Taiwan released 106 domestic features, as compared to Hong Kong's 129.

18

The Seventies and the Eighties: Colonies of the Mind and Heart

The three most important historical developments of the seventies and eighties were the emergence of **Third World cinema** as an international movement, the spectacular renaissance of film in West Germany, and the conglomeration of the structure of the American film industry.

THIRD WORLD CINEMA

Vital national film cultures have gradually developed in the nations of Latin America and Africa collectively known as the Third World* in the past twenty-five years. By the mid-seventies, Third World cinema was widely recognized as one of the most important and innovative movements in contemporary filmmaking, as significant historically as were Italian neorealism and the French New Wave. The term covers a wide range of films produced on two continents, in countries most of which have long histories of exploitation and colonial oppression by Western powers. Only now are these countries emerging from centuries of underdevelopment,

---

* The term also includes large parts of Southeast Asia discussed in the previous chapter. Historically, the concept of a Third World is a post–World War II phenomenon in which the "developing nations"—most of them formerly colonies of various European countries—were counterposed to the "free world" of the Western democracies dominated by the United States, and to the "socialist world" of the communist countries dominated by the Soviet Union. Geopolitically, the postwar world came to be divided into developed countries with market economies (the United States; Canada; Western Europe, including Scandinavia; Japan; Australia; New Zealand; and, less clearly, Israel and South Africa), countries with centrally planned economies (the Soviet Union, Eastern Europe, the People's Republic of China, Mongolia, North Korea, and Vietnam), and developing countries with mixed or market economies (i.e., Latin America, the rest of Asia, and Africa, excepting South Africa). This latter group came to be called the "Third World" after the Bandung Conference of nonaligned nations in 1955. Economically, the developed countries account for one-fifth of the world's population and about 60 percent of the gross domestic product; and the Third World, which accounts for half of the world's land mass and half of its population, consumes around 12 percent of the gross product. In other words, the countries of the Third World are bound together by a level of poverty barely conceivable to the majority of inhabitants of the rest of the world.

and their struggle to do so has produced one of the most exciting creative impulses in cinema today.

Despite the ethnic and political diversity of Third World countries, their cinemas tend to have several common characteristics that identify them as parts of a coherent international movement. First, Third World filmmakers conceive of cinema not as an entertainment commodity produced to make a profit but as a compelling means of mass persuasion, cultural consolidation, and consciousness-raising. Second, Third World filmmakers often but not always operate from an independent production base outside of their countries' established (and usually Western-dominated) film industries. For this reason, Third World cinema is distinguished by its use of unconventional production modes, including collective production, secret or "underground" production, on-location shooting of guerrilla warfare, and non-Western extranational funding. Finally—and most important from an aesthetic standpoint—Third World cinema rejects the conventional narrative syntax of Hollywood and other Western film industries in an effort to extend the limits of film structure and provide audiences with new ways of seeing their sociopolitical reality. The ultimate goal of this process is the reclamation of authentic forms of national cultural expression long obscured by imposed foreign values. As the militant Argentine filmmakers Fernando Solanas and Octavio Getino—*La hora de los hornos* (*Hour of the Furnaces*, 1968)—put it, theirs is a "third cinema" that goes beyond conventional Hollywood narrative ("first cinema") or the auteurist cinema of personal expression ("second cinema"). To counter

a cinema of characters with a cinema of themes, one of individuals with one of the masses, one of *auteurs* with one of operative groups, a cinema of neocolonial misinformation with a cinema of information, one of escape with one that recaptures the truth, a cinema of passivity with one of aggression. To an institutionalized cinema, it counterposes a guerrilla cinema; to movies as shows or spectacles, it counterposes a film act or action; to a cinema of destruction, one that is both destructive and constructive; to a cinema made for and by the old kind of human beings, it counterposes a cinema *fit for a new kind of human being, for what each one of us has the possibility of becoming* [emphasis in the original].

LATIN AMERICA

Historically, the Latin American film industries have been dominated by large U.S.–based producer-distributors. In 1984, for example, American corporations controlled the largest shares of the film markets in all Latin American countries except Cuba, whose market is closed, and Brazil, which for the first time in history achieved a 50 percent share of its own market through the successful creation of a state-controlled monopoly. Typically, a Latin American country will harbor a strong and tightly knit group of American-based distribution companies which market major American and European productions in uneven competition with a handful of local distributors who market local productions and some minor

European and American product. The Americans are organized as branches of the U.S. Motion Picture Export Association (MPEA), and in general they function to oppose all forms of state protectionism for the local industries, including the placing of ceilings on the price of theater tickets, and any measures that would restrict the outward flow of foreign (i.e., American) currency. Furthermore, as Jorge Schnitman points out, the United States has always had the largest domestic film market in the capitalist world, a market where investments in production can be completely amortized before sending a film abroad.* This has meant that American films in foreign markets had only to recover local distribution costs before realizing a profit, while local films had to recover both production and distribution costs in the same market, with little hope of export.

Film as an entertainment commodity appeared in Latin America shortly after the first commercial projection by the Lumières in Paris in December 1895. There were projections in Brazil in July 1896 and in Argentina in September, and though film appeared much later in some of the smaller countries (in Bolivia, e.g., in 1909), exhibition facilities in general developed quite rapidly throughout Latin America—at first, as in the United States, mainly for working-class audiences. Latin American markets existed initially for both European and American films, but during World War I, the region was forced to rely exclusively on American products, and by 1916 American silent features dominated Latin American screens. At the same time (and about a decade after the United States), the Latin American distribution system changed from one of outright sale of prints to exhibitors to the leasing of prints to them for a percentage of the gross receipts, which favored the policy of American companies to establish their own local distributorships. By the early 1920s, the Latin American audience had expanded to include the middle and upper-middle class, and U.S. companies dominated distribution to the virtual exclusion of local and European competitors. American dominion remained unchanged even after the coming of sound, which in other parts of the world generally increased the muscle of local industries by creating a language barrier against the Hollywood product. Simply put, dependency on America had rendered the Latin American industries incapable of supplying their own markets—collectively estimated in 1920 to include 100 million people— even after the advent of sound created a demand for Spanish-language films. So Hollywood happily filled the gap by converting its studios to the production of features in Spanish and Portuguese, and later, by dubbing its own productions into the local languages. By 1935, for example, over 76 percent of the 504 feature films distributed in Argentina were brokered by American companies; and in Mexico three years later 80 percent of all films in release were American-made. The outbreak of war in Europe intensified the situation because it drastically decreased Hollywood's foreign film revenues. As explained elsewhere, Germany and

---

* Jorge A. Schnitman, *Film Industries in Latin America: Dependency and Development* (Norwood, N.J.: Ablex, 1984), p. 22.

the countries it occupied banned American films outright; other countries, like Britain and Australia, needed foreign exchange so badly that they imposed rigorous currency restrictions of their own. In fact, continental Europe, where the American majors had done over 25 percent of their international business in 1936, had practically vanished as a market by 1940, when the only business conducted there by American film companies was with neutral Switzerland and Sweden.

By 1941, only Central and South America remained major importers of American films, persuading Hollywood to recolonize its neighbors with a vengeance. The State Department aided the cause by creating the Office of the Coordinator of Inter-American Affairs (CIAA) in October 1940, whose objective was to promote the "Good Neighbor Policy" and combat pro-Axis sentiment in Latin America. The CIAA's Motion Picture Division was put under the directorship of John Hay Whitney, whose first goal was to eliminate unflattering Latin American stereotypes and misinformation from Hollywood features and to encourage the production of films employing authentic Latin stars. In short order, the war years would witness reverential biographies of nineteenth-century Mexican President Benito Juárez and continental liberator Simón Bolívar, as well as films with contemporary settings that differentiated, for the first time in American films, among various Latin American locales. Some examples of CIAA-influenced films are *Down Argentine Way* (Irving Cummings, 1940), *Weekend in Havana* (Walter Lang, 1941), *That Night in Rio* (Irving Cummings, 1941), and so on. There were also Latin American musical cycles from both RKO (e.g., *Too Many Girls* [George Abbott, 1940]; *They Met in Argentina* [Leslie Goodwins, 1941]; *Pan-Americana* [John H. Auer, 1945]) and 20th Century–Fox (e.g., *The Gang's All Here* [Busby Berkeley, 1943]). Finally, planeloads of Latin talent were imported into Hollywood during this era, acquainting American audiences with such performers as Lupe Velez, Carmen Miranda, Desi Arnez, and Cesar Romero, to name but a few. John Hay Whitney's second initiative was more overtly political and involved the neutralization of propaganda flowing into Argentina, Brazil, and Chile from Axis wire services, features, and documentaries. To this end, he created the Newsreel Section, and by 1943 the CIAA had shipped more than two hundred pro-American newsreels for free distribution in Latin American theaters. By the war's end, the United States' conquest of the Latin American film markets was as total as its geopolitical victory over the Axis. And, as Jorge Schnitman observes: "Although the U.S. film industry underwent remarkable transformations during the 1930–1980 period, for all practical purposes the problem of its overwhelming presence in Latin America remained throughout that period [with the obvious exception of Cuba after 1959], and only decreased somewhat whenever Latin American governments implemented consistent protectionist policies or when specific markets lost their appeal due to unfavorable exchange rates and similar problems."* Only three countries followed the protectionist path

---

* Schnitman, p. 26.

with any consistency—Argentina, Mexico, and Brazil—and of these only Mexico and Brazil have achieved even semiautonomy in their own markets.

Mexico

The less successful of the two has been Mexico, which attempted to model its industry on that of the United States and which, at its extraordinary best, could produce films like Buñuel's *Los olvidados* (1950; winner of the Best Direction prize at Cannes, 1951). At its worst, it churned out hundreds of low-budget quickies—known locally as *churros,* a popular fried dough confection of little nutritional value—the staple product of the sixties and beyond. The Mexican cinema's "golden age" occurred during the forties, which began with establishment in 1942 of the Banco Cinematográfico, a credit-granting agency for producers backed by the central government. By 1945, Mexico was producing a record eighty to ninety films a year, compared to Argentina's and Spain's fifty to sixty, and an oligarchic, star-based studio system was being consolidated along American lines. It was during this decade that the collaboration of the director Emilio "El Indio" Fernández (1904–83) and cinematographer Gabriel Figueroa (b. 1907)—e.g., *Flor silvestre* (*Wild Flower,* 1943; grand prize, Locarno, 1946); *María Candelaria* (1943; grand prize, Cannes, 1946); and *Río escondidô* (*Hidden River,* 1947)—became world famous, as did the work of the brilliant comic actor Cantinflas (Mario Moreno), and, less spectacularly, the working-class melodramas of Alejandro Galindo—*Campeón sin corona* (*Champion without a Crown,* 1945)—and Ismael Rodriguez—*Nosotros los pobres* (*We Poor Folks,* 1947). During the fifties and early sixties, locally popular genres were the ranch comedy (*comedia ranchera*) and the cabaret melodrama, while international attention was claimed by the Mexican films of Buñuel (see Chapter 15) and, to a lesser degree, those of his Spanish-born scriptwriter Luis Alcoriza—*Lôs jóvenes* (*The Young Ones,* 1960); *Tiburoneros* (*Shark Fishermen,* 1962); *Tarahumara* (1964). By the early sixties, however, the golden age was over. Production fell from an all-time high of 136 features in 1958 to a record low of 71 in 1961, and a wave of cheaply produced *churros* overwhelmed the industry.

In 1963, however, the country's first film school, Centro Universitario de Estudios Cinematográficos (CUEC) was established in Mexico City, and by the late sixties it was graduating young directors who turned for the first time to independent production in films that openly challenged the repressive regime of President Gustavo Díaz Ordaz. This generation included the Chilean-born Alexandro Jodorowsky, Jorge Fons, Felipe Cazals, Marcela Fernández Violante, Arturo Ripstein, Ariel Zuniga, and Jaime Humberto Hermosillo, as well as Paul Leduc and Sergio Olhovich, both trained abroad. From 1970 to 1976, the new filmmakers benefited from the pro-left policies of President Luis Echeverría Álvarez who encouraged them to make films of social criticism and revolutionary zeal that would at the same time upgrade the quality of Mexican cinema. To this end Echeverría virtually nationalized the film industry, and placed the administration of the Banco Cinematográfico in the hands of his brother Rodolfo. As a result, the seventies witnessed an extraordinary flourishing of Mexican film in such works as Jodorowsky's fabled cult classic *El Topo* (1970); Olhovich's *Muñeca reina* (1971); Leduc's *Reed: Mexico insurgente* (*Reed: Insurgent Mexico*, 1971) and *Etnocidio: Notas sobre el Mezquital* (*Ethnocide: Notes on the Mezquital*, 1976); Fons' *Fé, esperanza, y caridad* (*Faith, Hope, and Charity* 1974) and *Los albañiles* (*The Brick Layers*, 1975); Cazals' *Canoa* (1975), *El apando* (Solitary Confinement, 1975), and *Las Poquianchis* (1976); Violante's *De todos modos Juan te llamas* (English-language title: *The General's Daughter*, 1975); and Ripstein's *El castillo de la pureza* (*The Castle of Purity*, 1972), *El lugar sin límites* (*The Place without Limits*, 1977), and *Cadena perpetua* (*Life Term*, 1978); Zuniga's *Anacrusa* (1978); and Hermosillo's "Aguascalientes trilogy"—*La pasión según Berenice* (*The Passion According to Berenice*, 1975), *Matinee* (1976), and *Las apariences engañan* (*Deceitful Appearance*, 1977)—and his *Naufragio* (*Shipwreck*, 1977) and *María de mi corazón* (*My Dearest Maria*, 1979). But this renaissance did not survive the administration of President José López Portillo, 1976–82, who put his sister Margarita in charge of the film industry. In a disastrous attempt to return production to the private sector, she dissolved the Banco Cinematográfico and drove many of the independent artists fostered by Echeverría out of filmmaking altogether. At the same time, a fire in 1982 totally destroyed the Cineteca Nacional, Mexico's national film archive and the most important cinematheque in Latin America. In addition, Mexico—the Third World's second largest debtor nation, with a population of 88 million—began to experience one of the worst financial crises in its history. The establishment of the Mexican Film Institute by the new administration of President Miguel de la Madrid Hurtado in 1983 could do little to aid the film industry financially, and it has returned to the production of privately financed *churro*-like genre films—chiefly soft-core bordello comedies, gritty urban crime films, and borderline thrillers—at the rate of about seventy-five features per year. Still, there has been a handful of interesting films made since the crisis began, including Ariel Zuniga's *Uno entre muchos* (*One of Many*, 1981) and *El diablo y la dama* (*The Devil and the Lady*, 1983); Marcela Fernández Violante's *Misterio* (*Mystery*, 1983); Paul Leduc's *Frida* (1983) and *Como ves?* (*Waddya Think?*, 1987); Arturo Ripstein's *La seduction* (*The Seduction*, 1981), *El otro* (*The Other*, 1984), and *El imperio de la fortuna* (*The Realm of Fortune*, 1986); Jaime Humberto Hermosillo's *El corazón de la noche* (*The Heart of the Night*, 1983), *Doña Erlinda y su hijo* (*Dona Erlinda and Her Son*, 1985), and *Clandestinos destinos* (*Clandestine Destinies*, 1987); Felipe Cazals' *Bajo la metralla* (*At Gunpoint*, 1982) and *El tres de copas* (*Three of Hearts*, 1987); and the work of such recent film school graduates as Carlos Cruz and Carlos Mendoza—the documentary trilogy *Chapopote* (1979), *El Chahuistle* (1980), and *Charrotitlan* (1982); Gerardo Pardo—*De veras me atrapaste* (*You Really Got Me*, 1983); Luis Mandoki—*Motel* (1983); Jose Luis Garcia Agraz—*Nocaut* (*Knockout*, 1983); *Las noches del califas* (*Caliph's Nights*, 1986); and Juan de la Rivera—*Vidas errantes* (*Wandering Lives*, 1984).

18.1 *El castillo de la pureza* (Arturo Ripstein, 1972).

Brazil

Brazil has been more successful than Mexico in developing its own film industry. The country (population 162 million) initially adopted a Hollywood-style studio system but finally rejected it in favor of independent production. Despite an early attempt from 1908 to 1911 to organize a vertically integrated monopoly of national entrepreneurs, by 1924 the preponderance of films in the Brazilian market were from Hollywood, paralleling the situation in the rest of Latin America. Of 1,422 films presented for censorship that year, 1,268, or 86 percent, came from the United States. But in 1932, President Getúlio Vargas established the precedent of screen quotas for local film production. From that time until Vargas' death by suicide in 1954,* the model of state-directed, capitalist development of the national industry prevailed, although it hardly provided a serious threat to American hegemony. The most successful national genre during this period was a hybrid of musical revue and popular comedy called the *chanchada* (loosely translated as "cultural trash"), featuring comic performers from the radio and the Brazilian equivalent of cabaret. After Vargas' death, there was a decade of indecision during which continuing economic crises and a succession of weak governments raised the promise of radical social change, and it was in this context that Brazilian **cinema nova** ("new cinema") was born.

Cinema novo sought new approaches to the realities of underdevelopment, poverty, and exploitation that had gone unacknowledged in Brazilian films to date. Drawing on new links with the working class and a new focus on native folklore and tradition, *cinema novo* filmmakers modeled their practice on the improvisatory techniques of the Italian neorealists (e.g., the use of nonactors and location shooting) and the production strategies of the French New Wave (i.e., creative financing and low-budget, sometimes collective, production). As part of their Marxist ideology, these directors decried the colonization of Brazilian cinema by Hollywood and subverted classical narrative codes in their own work wherever possible. The clear leader of the movement was Glauber Rocha (1939–81), whose films and theoretical writings laid the foundation for a new Latin American cinema—one that would acknowledge the political and social realities of a land half of whose people were unemployed and half of whom were illiterate. Appropriately, Rocha's major work corresponds to each of the three recognized stages of *cinema novo*. The films of the first phase, 1960–64, drew on the history of proletarian revolt and were distinguished by radical optimism; to this period belong Rocha's *Deus e diabo na terra do sol* (*Black God, White Devil*, 1964); Ruy Guerra's (b. 1931) *Os fuzis* (*The Guns*, 1964); and Nelson Pereira dos Santos' (b. 1928) *Vidas secas* (*Barren Lives*, 1963); all three works were focused in various ways on peasant life in the *sertao*, Brazil's drought-ridden,

18.2 A peasant turned *cangaceiro* (rebel-bandit) in *Deus e o diabo na terra do sol* (Glauber Rocha, 1964), the first *cinema nôvo* feature to be widely seen outside Brazil.

18.3 Political violence in *Vidas sêcas* (Nelson Pereira dos Santos, 1963).

---

* Vargas ruled as a dictator from 1930 until 1945, when he was deposed by the military. Elected president again under a new constitution in 1950, he was forced from office by another coup in 1954, after which he killed himself.

impoverished northeastern plain. Also belonging to this first phase was Carlos Diegues' (b. 1940) *Ganga Zumba* (1963), a historical account of a successful slave revolt on a seventeenth-century surgarcane plantation. These films and their counterparts were extraordinarily successful on the international festival circuit, five of them winning major awards in 1962, when they represented 20 percent of the Brazilian industry's total output.

The second stage, 1964–68, marked a period of reassessment and, ultimately, disillusionment as the civilian government was overthrown by a military coup and the forms of democracy all but disappeared. This was the time of Paulo César Saraceni's *O desafio* (*The Challenge,* 1966) and Rocha's *Terra em transe* (*Land in Anguish,* 1967), whose protagonists are urban intellectuals consumed with self-doubt. In the movement's final, and in many ways its richest phase, 1968–72, corresponding to the imposition of the repressive Fifth Institutional Act, *cinema novo* filmmakers turned heavily to symbolism to circumvent military censorship. According to Randal Johnson and Robert Stam, this stage came to be known as the "cannibal-tropicalist" phase* because so many of its films were cast in the form of mythological allegories—like Rocha's *Antonio das Mortes* (1968) and Guerra's *Os deuses e os mortos* (*The Gods and the Dead,* 1969)—or anthropological documents—like Pereira dos Santos' *Como era gostoso meu frances* (*How Tasty Was My Little Frenchman,* 1970)—or gaudily grotesque celebrations of Brazil as a tropical paradise—like the work of Joaquim Pedro de Andrade (b. 1932—*Macunaíma,* 1969) and, in part at least, Diegues' *Os herdeiros* (*The Heirs,* 1969).

Despite their repressiveness, however, the military regimes of the sixties did attempt to support the expansion of Brazilian film production, creating the National Film Institute in 1966 and the state film trust Embrafilme in 1969. Strict sexual censorship was partially rescinded in the early seventies, although ideological censorship prevailed until the restoration of democracy in 1985. The immediate result was a wave of *pornochanchadas,* soft-core erotic comedies popular mainly with local audiences, but the eventual result of Embrafilme's mandate was the state-led vertical integration of the Brazilian industry. Distinguished *cinema novo* directors like Carlos Diegues and Nelson Pereira dos Santos returned at the virtual invitation of the government to enter mainstream production. Over the next fifteen years, the Brazilian industry produced at least a dozen international hits, most of them based on indigenous folklore, history, or literature, including Diegues' *Xica da Silva* (1976), Brazil's first worldwide box office success, and *Bye Bye Brazil* (1980); Bruno Barreto's *Dona Flor e seus dois maridos* (*Dona Flor and Her Two Husbands* (1976), which was so popular that it prompted the inferior 20th

---

* Randal Johnson and Robert Stam, *Brazilian Cinema* (Rutherford, N.J.: Fairleigh Dickinson University Press, 1982; repr. Austin: University of Texas Press, 1988), p. 37. *Cinema novo* filmmakers borrowed the cannibal metaphor from the Brazilian modernist writers of the twenties (e.g., Mario de Andrade, 1893–1945), who had used it to critique a world in which political, economic, and social relationships were fundamentally cannibalistic.

18.4 *Xica da Silva* (Carlos Diegues, 1976): Zeze Motta in the title role.

18.5 *Bye Bye Brazil* (Carlos Diegues, 1980): Betty Faria as "Salome the Rumba Queen."

18.6 Leon Hirzman's *Eles nao usam black-tie* (1981): Milton Goncalves.

18.7 *Memorias do carcere* (Nelson Pereira dos Santos, 1984).

18.8 Hector Babenco's *Pixote* (1981): Fernando Ramos da Silva, Marilia Pera.

18.9 *Erendira* (Ruy Guerra, 1983).

Century–Fox remake *Kiss Me Goodbye* (Robert Mulligan, 1982); Leon Hirszman's *Eles nao usam black-tie* (*They Don't Wear Black Tie,* 1981); Pereira dos Santos' *Tenda dos milagres* (*Tent of Miracles,* 1977) and *Memorias do carcere* (*Memories of Prison,* 1984), based on the memoirs of Graciliano Ramos, a political prisoner of the Vargas dictatorship and the author of *Vidas secas,* the source of the director's first film; Argentine-born Hector Babenco's *Pixote* (1981; winner of the New York Critics award for Best Foreign Film) and *O beijo da mulher aranha* (*Kiss of the Spider Woman,* 1985); and Ruy Guerra's *Erendira* (1983), *Opera do Malandro* (*Malandro,* 1986), and *Fábula de la bella palomeva* (*Fable of the Beautiful Pigeon Fancier,* 1988), all based on the work of Gabriel García Márquez. Other recent Brazilian films of note are Ana Carolina's *Mar de rosas* (*Sea of Roses,* 1977) and *Das tripas coracao* (*Bending over Backwards,* 1980); Glauber Rocha's controversial last work *A idade da terra* (*The Age of the Earth,* 1980); Carlos Alberto Prates Correia's *Cabaret Mineiro* (*Cabaret in Minas,* 1980) and *Noites de sertao* (*Sertao Nights,* 1984); Pereira dos Santos' *Estrada da vida* (*Road of Life,* 1980) and *Jubaiba* (1986); Tizuka Yamasaki's *Gaigin* (1980), *Paraiba, mulher macho* (1982), and *Patriamada* (1986); Suzana Amaral's *A hora da estrela* (*The Hour of the Star,* 1985); Sergio Rezende's *O homem da capa preta* (*The Man with the Black Cape,* 1986); Lauro Escorel Filho's *Sonno sem fim* (*Endless Dream,* 1986); Chico Botelho's *Cidade oculta* (*Hidden City,* 1986); Caetano Velsos's *Cinema falado* (*Talking Pictures,* 1986); Diegues' *Quilombo* (1984) and *Um trem para as estrelas* (*A Train for the Stars,* 1987); Bruno Barreto's *Romance da Empregada* (*The Story of Fausta,* 1988); Paulo César Saraceni's *Natal da portela* (*One-Armed Natal,* 1988); and Leon Hirszman's *Imagens do inconsciente* (*Pictures from the Unconscious,* 1988). By 1985, when democracy was restored and the country elected its first civilian president since 1964, Embrafilme had not only captured foreign attention for Brazilian cinema but also an unprecedented 50 percent share of its own market. From producing only twelve films in 1963, Brazil had become the sixth largest film producer in the world, with an average output of a hundred features per year since 1983. It seemed to be a triumph of capitalist initiative combined with state protectionism and politically committed talent. Unfortunately, the new government of Jose Sarney inherited from its predecessors an annual inflation rate of 800 percent and a staggering burden of foreign debt. As a result, Embrafilme production in the late eighties fell off by 30 to 40 percent, and rigorous new protectionist legislation was enacted. A wave of domestically produced pornographic films, both soft- and hard-core, has come to dominate the industry, although many films of international caliber continue to be made.

Argentina

Argentine cinema existed under various forms of state protectionism together with a rigorous system of pre- and postproduction censorship from the coming of sound until 1984. After the fall of the Peronist government in 1955, controls were relaxed and the studio system collapsed, but after 1957 new restrictions on imports were imposed, and domestic production was resumed on a film-by-film basis. It was at this time that the Argentine director Leopoldo Torre-Nilsson (1924–78) emerged as an international figure. The son of a Swedish mother and the Argentine director Leopoldo Torres-Rios (1899–1960), Torre-Nilsson's first independent production was an adaptation of a short story by Jorge Luis Borges, *Días de odio*, in 1954. The three films that brought him to the attention of European critics—*La casa del ángel* (*The House of the Angel*, 1957), *La caída* (*The Fall*, 1959), and *La mano en la trampa* (*The Hand in the Trap*, 1961)—were all adapted from novels by his wife and frequent collaborator, Beatriz Guido. Among Torre-Nilsson's later successes were *La Maffia* (*The Mafia*, 1972), *Los siete locos* (*The Seven Madmen*, 1973), and *Boquitas pintadas* (*Painted Lips*, 1974), a scathing criticism of the Argentine middle classes. Like Buñuel, with whom he is often compared, Torre-Nilsson deals with the hypocrisy and repressiveness of the bourgeoisie. A near contemporary of Torre-Nilsson is Fernando Birri (b. 1925), founder of the Documentary Film School of Santa Fe (La Escuela Documental de Santa Fe) at Argentina's National University of the Littoral in 1956 and a pioneer of what was to become the New Latin American Cinema movement. Birri, who studied at Rome's Centro Sperimentale, produced with his own students one of Latin America's first social documentaries in *Tire dié* (*Throw a Dime*, 1958), a short about the degrading poverty of Buenos Aires' slums, as well as the neorealistic feature *Los inundados* (*Flood Victims / Flooded Out*, 1962), a prizewinner at Venice in 1962. Living in exile since 1964, Birri has helped materially to develop the cinemas of Cuba, Mexico, and Venezuela, and in 1986 was named director of the newly established School of Film and Television (La Escuela de Cine y Televisión) in the suburbs of Havana.

In the early sixties there was some interesting activity among a group of young filmmakers who called themselves the "1960 generation" and practiced a European-style new cinema (*nuevo cine*). Most notable among them were Fernando Ayala—*El jefe* (*The Boss*, 1958); *El candidato* (*The Candidate*, 1959); Lautaro Murúa—*Shunko* (1960); *Alias Gardelito* (also known as *Little Gardel*, 1961); Manuel Antín—*La cifra impar* (*The Odd Number*, 1961; adapted by Julio Cortázar from his own story); and Leonardo Favio—*Crónica de un niño solo* (*Chronicle of a Boy Alone*, 1965); *El romance del Aniceto y la Francisca . . .* (*The Romance of Aniceto and Francisca . . .*, 1966). The influence of Brazilian *cinema novo* revealed itself in the birth of the *Cine Liberación* group in the late sixties, in response to both the doldrums of the Argentine commercial industry and the social upheavals of the era. Cine Liberación's most famous production was the three-part agit-prop documentary *La hora de los hornos* (*The Hour of the Furnaces*, 1968), directed by the group's founders, Fernando Solinas and Octavio Getino. This film combines newsreel and documentary footage with dramatic reenactments and printed slogans in a rapid-fire montage that is distinctly revolutionary (and nonrational) in its appeal. It is a classic example of "third cinema" in that its primary value is neither as entertainment nor art but rather as an agent of ideological

18.10 *La hora de los hornos* (Fernando Solanas and Octavio Getino, 1968): agitational cinema.

18.11 *La Patagonia rebelde* (Héctor Olivera, 1974).

praxis. Other work by members of Cine Liberación or influenced by it are Hugo Santiago *Invasión* (*Invasion*, 1968), adapted from a premonitory Borges story about a civil war in Buenos Aires; Gerardo Vallejo's *El camino hacia la muerte del viejos Reales* (*The Road Towards Death of the Old Reales*, 1969), a study of the exploitation of rural laborers; and Héctor Olivera's *La Patagonia rebelde* (*Rebellion in Patagonia*, 1974; Silver Bear, Berlin), based on an actual massacre by the army of southern Argentine farmhands at the behest of powerful British landowners during the twenties. Another important contemporary figure was Raúl de la Torre, whose thoughtful character studies of women—*Juan Lamaglia y señora* (*Juan Lamaglia and His Wife*, 1969), *Crónica de una señora* (*Story of a Lady*, 1971), *Heroíne* (*Heroine*, 1972), and *Sola* (*Alone*, 1976)—won critical acclaim for their intelligence and style, and are still a mainstay of Argentine cinema (for example, *Color escondido* [*Hidden Color*, 1988]).

In 1973 Juan Perón had returned to Argentina from exile in Spain and was elected president; when he died a year later his wife, Isabel, replaced him until she was removed by a military coup in 1976. The country then was plunged into an economic and political crisis of major proportion; inflation reached 100 percent, and the film industry was virtually paralyzed. Only one director of note emerged during this period: Adolfo Aristarain, whose compelling *films noir*—*La parte del leon* (*The Lion's Share*, 1978), *Tiempo de revancha* (*Time for Revenge*, 1981), and *Los ultimo días de la victima* (*The Last Days of the Victim*, 1982)—had submerged social themes. By 1982, domestic production had fallen to an all-time low of eighteen films per year, and under pressure from filmmakers the military government empowered the National Film Institute (INC, founded 1955) to make production loan guarantees and named director Manuel Antín as its head. Then came the disastrous Malvinas / Falkland Islands

18.12 *La historia oficial* (Luis Puenzo, 1985): Norma Aleandro.

18.13 *Camila* (Maria Luisa Bemberg, 1984).

war with Britain in 1982, the collapse of the Argentine dictatorship, and the restoration of democracy under President Raúl Alfonsín. Censorship was eliminated and exiled filmmakers returned from abroad. There followed a great wave of films examining the recent past, especially the fate of the 15,000 to 30,000 *desaparecidos** ("the disappeared") during the *guerra sucia* ("dirty war") of terror, torture, and murder conducted from 1976 to 1983 by the generals against suspected subversives. Into this category fall Héctor Olivera's *No habrá más penas ni olvido* (*Funny, Dirty Little War*, 1983; Silver Bear, Berlin); Fernando Ayala's *Pasajeros de una pesadilla* (*Passengers of a Nightmare*, 1984); Alejandro Doria's *Darse cuenta* (*Becoming Aware*, 1984); Luis Puenzo's Oscar-winning *La historia oficial* (The Official Story, 1985); and Carlos Lemos' *Los dueños del silencio* (*The Owners of Silence*, 1987). Other films deal with problems of exile—Fernando Solinas' *Tangos—el exilio de Gardel* (*Tangos—the Exile of Gardel*, 1985; Golden Lion, Venice) and *Sud* (*South*, 1988); Juan José Jusid's *Made in Argentina* (1987)—and with repression and terror in Argentine history—Manuel Antín's *La invitación* (*The Invitation*, 1982); Jusid's *Asesinato en el senado de la nación* (*Murder at the National Senate*, 1984); María Luisa Bemberg's *Camila* (1984) and *Miss Mary* (1986); and Raúl de la Torre's *Pobre mariposa* (*Poor Butterfly*, 1986). Recent manipulations of the Argentine economy by foreigners are considered in Ayala's *Plata dulce* (*Easy Money*, 1982), *El arreglo* (*The Deal*, 1983), and *El año del conejo* (*The Year of the Rabbit*, 1987). There have also been outstanding documentaries, such as Rodolfo Kuhn's *Todo es ausencia* (*Only Emptiness Remains*, 1983); Susana Munoz and Lourdes Portillo's *Las madres* (*The Mothers of the Plaza de Mayo*, 1986), both on the politically organized mothers of the *desaparecidos;* Miguel Perez's two-part history of Argentina, 1930–84, *La republica perdida* (*The Lost Republic*, 1983) and *La republica perdida II* (1986); and nonpolitical works by such talented new directors as Jorge Polaco (*Diapason*, 1986), Teo Kofman (*Perros de la noche* [*Dogs of the Night*, 1986]), Eliseo Subiela (*Hombre mirando al sudeste* [*Man Facing Southeast*, 1986]), Alejandro Agresti (*El hombre que gano la razón* [*The Man Who Gained Reason*, 1986]) and *El amor es una mujer gorda* ([*Love Is a Fat Woman*, 1987]).

Bolivia, Peru, and Chile

The Andean countries of Bolivia (population 7 million), Peru (22 million), and Chile (13 million) all experienced brief surges within their small domestic industries in the late sixties. Following the example of Brazilian *cinema novo*, Bolivia's Jorge Sanjinés and the Grupo Ukamau (a filmmaking collective named for *Ukamau* [1966], Sanjinés' award-winning first feature on Indian peasant life) produced the controversial *Yawar mallku* (*Blood of the Condor*, 1969), which became the most popular domestic feature made to date. Shot in neorealist fashion, the film shows the native Quechuan Indians being methodically wiped out through an involuntary sterilization program administered by the American "Prog-

---

* The 1988 population of Argentina was approximately 30 million.

ress Corps"; and it was ultimately responsible for the Peace Corps' expulsion from the country. *Coraje del pueblo* (*Courage of the People*), about a 1967 massacre of striking miners and their families by the army, was Sanjinés first film in color and was produced for Italian television in 1971.* In the same year, Bolivia experienced the right-wing coup that brought Colonel Hugo Banzer Suarez to power. Sanjinés and several members of Grupo Ukamau sought asylum first in Peru, where they made *El enemigo principal* (*The Principal Enemy,* 1974), and then Ecuador, where they produced *¡Fuera de aguí!* (*Out of Here!,* 1977). Meanwhile, Sanjinés' cinematographer, Antonio Equino, remained in Bolivia with the rest of the group and directed two successful features during the seventies—*Pueblo chico* (*Small Town,* 1974) and *Chuquiago* (1977), the latter a four-part analysis of the social structure of La Paz which became the biggest box-office hit in the nation's history. With another change of government in 1979, Sanjinés returned to Bolivia and produced *Las banderas del amanecer* (*The Flags of Dawn,* 1984), a feature-length documentary recording the nation's history from 1979 through 1984. In 1979, Equino also directed a film—*Amargo mar* (*Bitter Sea*), a fictionalized account of Chile's invasion of Bolivia in 1879, coproduced with Cuba, but few films have been made in the country since, owing to a 60 percent decrease in attendance—the result of the diffusion of television between 1985 and 1987. Nevertheless, the nation has both an active film institute, Instituto Cinematográfico Boliviano (ICB, founded 1953), and the necessary technical equipment to resume production when economic circumstances permit.

18.14 Quechua Indians exploited by the "Progress Corps" in *Vawar mallku* (Jorge Sanjines and the Grupo Ukamau, 1969).

In Peru, which had produced little but government-sponsored newsreels (*actualidades*) and the ethnographic features of the so-called "Cuzco School" (e.g., Eulogio Nishiyama, Luis Figueroa, and Cesar Villanueva's *Kukili* [1960] and *Jarawi* [1965]), there was little theatrical filmmaking activity until the work of Armando Robles Godoy, especially *La muralla verde* (*The Green Wall,* 1970), was recognized both at home and abroad. In 1972, the government passed legislation designed to encourage national film production, and independent companies began to form throughout the seventies and eighties to make both documentaries and commercial features. Especially notable in the latter category is the work of Francisco Jose Lombardi, whose *Muerte al amanecer* (*Death at Dawn,* 1977), *Maruja en el infierno* (*Maruja in Hell,* 1983), *La ciudad y los perros* (*The City and the Dogs,* 1985; adapted from the first novel of Maria Vargas Llosa), and *La boca del lobo* (*The Wolf's Den,* 1988) have all received international attention. Also well known are Jorge Reyes' neorealistic account of Peru's first labor organizer, *La familia Orozco* (*The Orozco Family,* 1982), and two Peruvian-Cuban coproductions dealing with political events

18.15 *Chuquiago* (Antonio Eguino, 1977).

---

* The miners, who were not insurrectionists but who had publicly declared their sympathies with the antigovernment guerrillas led by Ché Guevara in the south, were accused of fomenting revolution to justify the massacre. Guevara himself was killed by the Bolivian army shortly thereafter.

from the country's past—*Tupat Amaru* (Federico Garcia, 1985), based on a late-eighteenth-century Inca rebellion against Spanish rule, and *El socio de Dios* (*The Partner of God* [Federico Garcia Hurtado, 1987]). Another recent coproduction (with Cuba, West Germany's ZDF, and England's Channel Four) is *Malabrigo* (1986), Alberto Durant's atmospheric evocation of corruption in a small fishing port. The future of the small Peruvian industry, like that of the democratic government of center-left president Alan Garcia, is much in doubt. An escalating civil war between the army and the Maoist guerrillas of the *Sendero Luminoso* movement, the "Shining Path," threatens to tear the country apart.

From its earliest years through 1960, the Chilean film industry produced fewer than 160 films, half of them before the coming of sound. Yet the government had experimented with a national production company (Chile Films) in the forties, and in the fifties and sixties supported the development of university-based programs in both filmmaking and critical studies—e.g., the Film Institute of the Catholic University, founded 1955, and the Experimental Film Center of the University of Chile, founded 1957. The country also had a distinguished tradition of political documentary film production, especially in the work of Sergio Bravo—*Mimbre* (*Wicker*, 1957), *Trilla* (*Threshing*, 1958), *La marcha al carbon* (*Coal March*, 1963), *Las banderas del pueblo* (*The Banners of the People*, 1964)—which was influenced by that of Joris Ivens. With the election of Salvador Allende Gossens' socialist coalition ("Popular Unity") government in 1970, there was an explosion of cinematic expression as Miguel Littín, whose debut feature *El chacal de Nahueltoro* (*The Jackal of Nahueltoro*, 1969) had radicalized Chilean audiences the year before, was named to head the nation's film industry. The Allende regime was overthrown by a bloody CIA-backed coup in 1973, but its three years in power marked the most creative era in Chilean film history. This brief period witnessed the production of such extraordinary documentaries as *Venceremos* (*We Shall Win*, Pedro Chaskel and Héctor Ríos, 1970), *Compañero Presidente* (Miguel Littín, 1971), *No es hora de llorar* (*No Time for Tears*, Pedro Chaskel and Luis Alberto Sanz, 1971), *El primer año* (*The First Year*, Patricio Guzmán, 1971), *La respuesta de octubre* (*The Answer to October*, Guzmán and El Equipo Primes Año, 1972), and *Abastecimiento* (*Stocking Up*, Raúl Ruiz, 1973). Also produced were such features as Helvio Soto's *Voto + fusil* (*The Vote and the Gun*, 1970) and *Metamorfósis de un jefe de la policía política* (*Metamorphosis of a Political Police Chief*, 1973); Raúl Ruiz' *Nadie dijo nada* (*No One Said a Thing*, 1971); Aldo Francia's *Ya no basta con rezar* (*Praying is No Longer Enough*, 1971); and Littín's *La tierra prometida* (*The Promised Land*, 1973, unreleased in Chile).

After General Pinochet's junta seized control of the government, murdering Allende and many of his followers (see, e.g., Constantin Costa-Gavras' film *Missing* [1982]), most "Popular Unity" filmmakers went into exile—Littín to Mexico; Ruiz, Soto, and Guzmán and his El Equipo Primer Año associates to France—where they continued their political

18.16   *La tierra prometida* (Miguel Littin, 1973).

project. Guzmán's group produced *La batalla de Chile* (*The Battle of Chile*, 1975–79) in Paris and later Cuba (where it was edited at ICAIC with the assistance of Julio García Espinosa), as well as a remarkable three-part documentary on the final year of the Allende presidency—*La insurrección de la burguésia* (*The Insurrection of the Bourgeoisie*, 1975), *El golpe de estado* (*The Coup d'etat*, 1977), and *El poder populara* (*Popular Power*, 1979)—with the help of French documentarist Chris Marker. Marker also produced with the Chilean refugees his own account of the Allende years, the two-and-one-half-hour *La Spirale* (1975). Now living in Cuba, Guzmán has since directed the Cuban-Venezuelan coproduction *La ros de los vientos* (*The Rose of the Winds*, 1985), a poetic meditation on the survival of Latin American identity despite five hundred years of cultural colonization, and *En el nombre de Dios* (*In the Name of God*, 1987), a documentary for Spanish television about the role of the Roman Catholic Church in Chile in the years following the coup. Helvio Soto directed only two features in exile—*Llueve sobre Santiago* (*It Rains over Santiago*, 1976) and *La triple muerte tercer del personaje* (*The Triple Death of the Third Character*, 1979). But Raúl Ruiz (b. 1941) has become one of the world's most prolific and experimental directors. His *Diálogo de exilados* (*Dialogue of Exiles*, 1974) harks back ideologically to his radical first feature *Tres triste tigres* (*Three Sad Tigers*, 1968), but Ruiz has since become increasingly metaphysical in such films as *La Vocation suspendue* (*The Suspended Vocation*, 1977), *L'Hypothèse d'un tableau volé* (*Hypothesis of a Stolen Painting*, 1978), *Las tres coronas del marinero* (*The Sailor's Three Crowns*, 1982), *La Ville de pirate* (*City of Pirates*, 1983), *La Presence réele* (*The Real Presence*, 1983), and *Memoire des apparences* (*Memories of Appearances*, 1986), to name but a few of the more than fifty he has made since leaving Chile. Working mainly on commission in Portugal and France, Ruiz also directs documentaries, video essays, and children's films, all informed by his vaguely surrealist sensibility and all shot at lightning speed.

In Mexico, Miguel Littín produced *Actas de Marusia* (*Letters from Marusia*, 1976), which draws a historical parallel between a 1907 massacre of Chilean mineworkers and the 1973 coup d'etat. He also made *Viva el Presidente,* also known as *El recurso del metodo* (*The Discourse on Method,* 1978) and *Las viuda de Montiel* (*Montiel's Widow,* 1980), before directing *Alsino y el condor* (*Alsino and the Condor,* 1983) for Nicaragua's film institute, INCINE, and Cuba's ICAIC, but he never again achieved the stylistic complexity of his early work. In 1985, Littín returned secretly to Chile and spent six weeks incognito filming the Cuban-produced television documentary *Acta general de Chile* (*General Document on Chile,* 1986), a moving four-hour condemnation of the Pinochet dictatorship.

Early in the eighties many exiled filmmakers were able to return to Chile. They found an economy wrecked by the junta, barely able to finance a handful of cheaply made films each year, most of them shot in 16mm and blown up to 35mm. Examples are Sergio Bravo's first feature *No eran nadie* (*They Were Nobody,* 1981), shot in the archipelago of Chile for 115,000 dollars; Christian Sanchez' *Los deseos conceibidos* (*Conceived Desires,* 1982), made for 70,000 dollars; Alejo Alvarez' *Como aman los Chilenos* (*How Chileans Love,* 1984), made for 100,000 dollars; Luis R. Vera's *Hechos consumados* (*An Accomplished Fact,* 1985) shot in Santiago for 60,000 dollars; Cristian Lorca's *Nemesio* (1986) made for 50,000 dollars; and so on. In fact, since 1977 only thirty-odd films and videos have been produced in Chile, and these were shot under very difficult conditions. To this total must be added a number of militant anti-Pinochet documentaries made in Chile but smuggled out of the country for distribution abroad—the Cine-Oio collective's *Chile, no invoco tu nombre in vano* (*Chile, I Do Not Call Your Name in Vain,* 1984), Juan Andres Racz's *Dulce patria* (*Sweet Country,* 1986), and Gaston Ancelovici's *Memorias de una guerra cotidiana* (*Images of an Everyday War,* 1986)—and such features as Pablo Perelman's *Imagen latente* (*Latent Image,* 1987), a film about the Chilean disappeared edited in Canada and still awaiting domestic distribution. It is a sad—and, one hopes, temporary—conclusion for what was so recently Latin America's most politically and aesthetically vibrant film culture.

Venezuela, Colombia, and Central America

During the late sixties oil-rich Venezuela experienced a surge in documentary production with such works as Jesus Enrique Guedes' *La ciudad que nos ve* (*The City Which Sees Us,* 1967) and Carlos Rebolledo's *Pozo muerto* (*Dead Well,* 1968), and in 1973 the government embarked upon a program of developing a national cinema by guaranteeing production subsidies and regulating the distribution of foreign product. From 1975 to 1980, the state subsidized the production of nearly thirty films, including Mauricio Wallerstein's *Sagrado y obsenco* (*Sacred and Obscene,* 1975) and *La empresa perdona un momento de locura* (*The Company Excuses a Moment of Insanity,* 1977), Román Chalbaud's *El pez que fuma* (*The Fish That Smokes,* 1977), Carlos Rebolledo's *Alias, el rey del Joropo* (*Alias the Joropo King,* 1978), and Iván Feo and Antonio Llerandi's *País portátil* (*Portable Country*, 1978), the latter Venezuela's biggest box-office hit to date. *Variety* proclaimed Venezuela's the fastest-growing film industry in Latin America, which, in fact, it was. Various factors have since weakened government support for the film industry, but it is still producing a large number of well-made films, considering Venezuela's population of only 18 million. During the eighties these have most prominently included Thaelman Urgelles' *La boda* (*The Wedding*, 1982); Diego Risquez' *Bolívar* (1982), *Orinoko—neuvo mundo* (1984), and *Amerika, terra incognita* (*America, Unknown Land*, 1988); Antonio Llerandi's *Adiós Miami* (*Bye, Bye, Miami*, 1983); Freddy Siso's *Diles que no me maten* (*Tell Them Not to Kill Me*, 1984); Dominique Cassuto de Bonet/Salvador Bonet's *Tiznao* (1984); Jose Novoa's *Agonía* (*Agony*, 1985); Fina Torres' *Oriane* (*Oriana*, 1985); Olegario Barrera's *Pequeña revancha* (*Little Revenge*, 1985), Román Chalbaud's *Manon* (1986) and *La oveja negra* (*The Black Sheep*, 1987); and Mauricio Wallerstein's Venezuelan-Colombian coproduction *De mujer a mujer* (*Woman to Woman*, 1987).

Neighboring Colombia (population 27 million) also produced a number of interesting documentaries in the late sixties, especially Jorge Silva and Marta Rodríguez' *Chircales* (*Brickmakers*, 1968), Carlos Alvarez' *Asalto* (*Assault*, 1968), and Julia Alvarez' *Un día yo pregunté* (*One Day I Asked*, 1969). In 1971 the government attempted to protect its small industry by requiring the exhibition of Colombian shorts at all first-run domestic theaters and mandating an admission ticket surcharge to be rebated to producers. This had the effect of stimulating the production of shorts to the level of nearly one hundred per year by 1975, and in 1978 the government attempted to promote feature production by setting up the Film Development Company (FOCINE). Since that time, Colombia has seen the production of such theatrical films as Dunav Kuzmanich's semidocumentary *Canaguaro* (1981); Luis Ospina's *Pura sangre* (*Pure Blood*, 1983); Lisandro Duque Naranjo's *El escarabajo* (*The Bicycle Racer*, 1983) and *Visa U.S.A.* (1986; a Colombian-Cuban coproduction); Francisco Norden's *Condores no entierran todos los días* (*Condors Don't Die Every Day*, 1984); Carlos Mayolo's *Carne de tu carne* (*Flesh of Your Flesh*, 1984) and *La mansion de Araucaima* (*The Araucaima Mansion*, 1986); Leopoldo Pinzon's *Pisingana* (*Hopscotch*, 1985); Jorge Ali Triana's Colombian-Cuban coproduction *Tiempo de morir* (*A Time to Die*, 1985; based on an original screenplay by Gabriel García Márquez); Carlos Palau's *A la salida nos vemos* (*See You After School*, 1986); Pepe Sanchez' *San Antonito* (*Little Saint Anthony*, 1986); and Manuel Franco Posse's *La recompensa* (*The Reward*, 1988).

The Central American countries of Nicaragua (population 3 million) and El Salvador (population 5 million) were both the site of revolutionary filmmaking activity in the eighties despite the fact that neither is economically capable of producing more than a few films each year. The Nicaraguan Film Institute—Instituto Nicaraguense de Cine, or INCINE—was established by the Sandinista government shortly after the Somoza dictatorship was overthrown in 1979. Though its resources are extremely limited, INCINE has played host to numerous documentaries produced by filmmakers from other countries—the Finnish director Victoria Schultz's *Women in Arms* (1980), the Brazilian Helena Solberg's *Nicaragua: From the Ashes* (1981), the West German / Chilean Tercer Cine Collective's *Women in Nicaragua: the Second Revolution* (1983), the Australian David Bradbury's *Nicaragua—No Pasarán* (1984), the Americans Susan Meisalas' *Living at Risk: The Story of a Nicaraguan Family* (1985) and Anita Clearfield's *Vacation Nicaragua* (1986). In addition, there have been such ambitious features as Peter Lilienthal's *The Insurrection* (1980); *Alsino y el Condor* (*Alsino and the Condor* [Miguel Littín, 1983]), a Nicaraguan-Cuban-Mexican-Costa Rican coproduction about the friendship between an American military adviser and a peasant boy; the U.S.–backed *Walker* (Alex Cox, 1987), dealing with an American adventurer who installed himself as president of Nicaragua in 1855; and Nicaragua's first domestic theatrical release *Mujeres de la frontera* (*Women of the Frontier*, Ivan Arguello, 1987), coproduced with Cuba. Subsequent Nicaraguan-Cuban features, like *El espectro de la guerra* (*The Ghost of War*, Ramiro Lacayo Deshon, 1988), have dealt mainly with the vagaries of the Contra war.

Guerrilla cinema activities are even more tenuous in neighboring El Salvador, where revolutionary collectives like the Radio Venceremos film group have produced such documentaries as *La decisión de vencer* (*Decisions to Win*, 1981) and *Tiempo de audacio* (*A Time of Daring*, 1983), both filmed on the front lines of the guerrilla war. There have also been such Salvadorian–U.S. coproductions as Glenn Silber and Tete Vasconellos' Oscar-winning *El Savador: Another Vietnam* (1981) and Frank Christopher's *In the Name of the People* (1985), both documentaries, and Oliver Stone's controversial feature *Salvador* (1986). Other Central American countries producing militant cinema are Costa Rica (Valeria Sarmiento's *Un hombre, cuando es un hombre* [*A Man, When He Is a Man*, 1985]) and Guatemala (Gregory Nava's PBS-financed *El Norte* [*The North*, 1983]; Pamela Yates and Thomas Sigel's *When the Mountains Tremble* [1985]).

CUBA AND THE NEW LATIN AMERICAN CINEMA

A small colonial film industry in Cuba before 1959 produced approximately 150 features in its sixty-year history. Many were Mexican-Cuban coproductions, like Emilio Fernández' *La rosa blanca* (*The White Rose*, 1953), and yet prerevolutionary Cuba had the highest film attendance rates of any Latin American country. A foretaste of the future was provided in 1955 when Tomás Guitiérrez Alea (b. 1928) and Julio García Epinosa (b. 1925), both of whom had studied at Rome's Centro Sperimentale in the early fifties and would become major figures in Cuban cinema after the revolution, produced the neorealistic *El mégano* (*The Charcoal Worker*), an indictment of peasant exploitation under the corrupt regime of President Fulgencio Batista. These same directors were the leading lights of Cine Rebelde, the rebel army's film unit, which produced two documentary shorts—*Esta tierra nuestra* (*This Is Our Land,* Alea) and *La vivienda* (*Housing,* Espinosa)—for the National Board of Culture in 1959 before the unit became part of the revolutionary government's national film institute—Instituto Cubano del Arte e Industria Cinematograficos, or ICAIC.

Like other revolutionary leaders before him, Fidel Castro understood the potential of motion pictures as a medium for mass education and persuasion—especially among a poor and largely illiterate populace—and, according to Alfredo Guevera, the founding director of ICAIC, the development of an indigenous film industry was in fact a major priority of the new government, second only to the national literacy campaign of 1960–61. ICAIC was created on March 24, 1959—only three months after the overthrow of Batista—by an act of law declaring cinema to be a national art and mandating the "reeducation" of the Cuban people through its "fount of revolutionary inspiration, of culture, and of information."* On that day, the Cuban film industry consisted of a few offices, some old 35mm equipment, a black-and-white laboratory, and a small group of people with virtually no filmmaking experience beyond the limited forays of Alea and Espinosa. As the screenwriter Manuel Pereira has said, the Cuban cinema was born "without original sin."† Over the next twenty-four years, however, ICAIC managed to produce 112 features (both documentary and theatrical), approximately 900 documentary shorts, and over 1,300 weekly newsreels.**

The first films were brilliant, controversial documentaries—most prominently those of Santiago Alvarez (b. 1919)—e.g., *Hanoi martes 13* (*Hanoi, Tuesday the 13th,* 1967); *LBJ,* 1968; *79 primaveras* (*79 Springtimes,* 1969)—which experimented in early Soviet fashion with every known variety of montage. Then in the late sixties and early seventies

18.17 The dark comedy *La muerte de un burócrata* (Tomás Gutiérrez Alea, 1966), which the director dedicated to Laurel and Hardy, among others: Salvador Wood, Silvia Planas.

18.18 Alea's *Memorias del subdesarrollo* (1968): pre-revolutionary consciousness. Sergio Corriere.

---

* Quoted in Dennis West, "Cuba: Cuban Cinema before the Revolution and After," in *World Cinema Since 1945,* ed. William Luhr (New York: Ungar, 1987), p. 141.

† Quoted in Pat Aufderheide, "Red Harvest," *American Film* 9, 5 (March 1984): 29.

** Figures cited by Julianne Burton, "Film and Revolution in Cuba: The First Twenty-five Years," in Peter Steven, ed., *Jump Cut: Hollywood, Politics and Counter-Cinema* (New York: Praeger, 1985), p. 345.

18.19 Scenes from the three parts of *Lucia* (Humberto Solás, 1969): Raquel Revuelta, Eslinda Nuñez, Adela Legra.

18.20 *La primera carga al machete* (Manuel Octavio Gómez, 1969).

came fiction features like Alea's *La muerte de un burócrata* (*Death of a Bureaucrat,* 1966) and *Memorias del subdesarrollo* (*Memories of Underdevelopment,* 1968); Humberto Solás' (b. 1943) *Lucía* (1968); and Manuel Octavio Gómez' (b. 1939) *La primera carga al machete* (*The First Charge of the Machete,* 1969), all of which mixed documentary and narrative technique in startlingly innovative ways and claimed international attention for the new Cuban cinema. *Memories,* for example, is a collage evoking the prerevolutionary consciousness of the intellectual bourgeoisie set against the backdrop of the missile crisis of 1962, and *La primera carga* assumes the imaginary perspective of a news crew covering the 1868 war of independence. Perhaps the most formally original of all, *Lucía* tells the stories of three women by that name in three crucial periods in Cuban history, each in a filmic style that evokes its era. It provides a critique of Cuban society both before and after the revolution through an analysis of the changing roles of women. During the seventies, epic-scale documentary features—García Espinosa's *Tercer mundo, tercera guerra mundial* (*Third World, Third World War,* 1970), Pastor Vega's (b. 1940) *¡Viva la república!* (*Long Live the Republic!,* 1972), and Alvarez' *Abril de Vietnam en el año del gato* (*April in Vietnam in the Year of the Cat,* 1975)—began to appear, astonishing international audiences with their sophistication and stylistic versatility.

At the same time, ICAIC was educating its domestic audience by taking *cine-mobiles*—trucks, wagons, and even boats equipped with projection gear and revolutionary films, as well as films such as those of Charlie Chaplin—to the provinces, in the manner of the Bolshevik "agit-trains" of the twenties; see Octavio Cortázar's (b. 1935) award-winning short *Por primera vez* (*For the First Time,* 1967). Later, a full-scale film-education program for Cuba's 11 million people was established. Now fully institutionalized, this program involves the dissemination of ICAIC's own periodical *Cine cubano,* which features interviews, essays, and production information on Cuban and other Latin American cinema; mass screenings at the Cinemateca de Cuba for approximately 100,000 spectators per week; and two national television programs devoted to film education. (In the most popular, "24 por secondo" ["Twenty-four Frames a Second"], the host describes current films, shows clips from them, and discusses their history and structure.) As Cuba's audience has grown ever more sophisticated, so too has its already exciting cinema.* The seventies witnessed an explosion of genres and styles in such work as the black director Sergio Giral's *El otro Francisco* (*The Other Francisco*, 1975), a complex experimental film that attempts a Marxist critique of the bourgeois liberalism underlying Cuba's first antislavery novel, Anselmo Suarez y Romero's *Francisco* (1839); Alea's *La última cena* (*The Last Supper*, 1976), which uses the historical context of a late-eighteenth-century slave rebellion to fashion a hieratic confrontation between Christian and Afro-Cuban culture, and the same director's *Los sobrevivientes* (*The Survivors*, 1978), a darkly comic allegory of the bourgeoisie's descent from "civilization" through slaveholding to barbarism and finally cannibalism; Sara Gómez' (1943–75) *De cierta manera* (*One Way or Another*, 1974; released 1977), which interfuses a traditional Hollywood-style narrative about young lovers from different socioethnic backgrounds with *cinéma vérité* and agitational techniques to expose the vestiges of neocolonial racism and sexism still facing Cuba's new order. The same theme is developed in the more conventionally structured *Retrato de Teresa* (*Portrait of Teresa*, 1979), Pastor Vega's first theatrical feature, which shows the persistence of machismo and the double standard facing working women in Cuban daily life. One of the most formally innovative films of the era was Manuel Octavio Gómez' *Una mujer, un hombre, una ciudad* (*A Woman, a Man, a City*, 1978), whose structure in many ways resembles *Citizen Kane*, although Gómez' next film *El señor presidente* (*Mr. President*, 1983) was a more or less conventional adaptation of Miguel Angel Asturia's novel of life under the Guatemalan dictatorship.

The eighties marked the return to prominence of Humberto Solás, whose feature-length epic *Cantata de Chile* (1975) had been widely regarded as

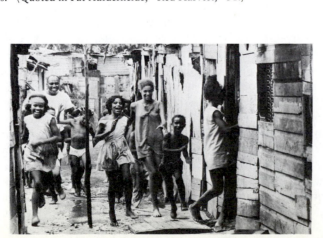

18.21 Alea's *La última cena* (1977): the count (Nelson Villagra) with one of the twelve slaves he has invited to his "last supper."

---

* As Alea has said of this film education project, "Filmmakers can't move faster than the audience. That's what happened to Godard. His analytical cinema attracted me, but the public didn't get it. You have to include in your considerations what the known cinematic language is." (Quoted in Pat Aufderheide, "Red Harvest," 31.)

18.22 *De cierta manera* (Sara Gómez, 1974), a critique of racism and sexism in contemporary Cuba.

18.23 *Cecilia* (Humberto Solás, 1981).

an ambitious failure. His subsequent work included the Cuban-Spanish coproduction *Cecilia* (1981; based on a novel by Cirilio Villaverde), an allegorical film of political intrigue among slaveholders in nineteenth-century Havana; *Amada* (1983), a stylized melodrama about a bourgeois wife who falls in love with an anarchist in 1914; and *Un hombre de exito* (*A Successful Man*, 1986), a chronicle tracing the very different lives of two Havana brothers from 1932 through the Cuban Revolution. The decade also witnessed the first dramatic feature of Santiago Alvarez, *Los refugiados de la cueva del muerto* (*The Fugitives of Dead Man's Cave*, 1983), a historical reconstruction of a guerrilla assault on the Moncada army barracks in 1953; and *Patakan!* (*Fable!* [Manuel Octavio Gómez, 1984]), a tongue-in-cheek Hollywood-style musical about contemporary life in the workers' paradise. Also of note were Alea's *Hasta cierto punto* (*Up to a Certain Point*, 1983), an attempt to renew the dialogue begun by Sara Gomez' *De cierta manera* at the level of the professional artist; Pastor Vega's *Habanera* (1984), an atypical European-style film of mid-life crisis among Cuba's intellectual professionals; Juan Carlos Tabio's *Se permuta* (1985), adapted from his own comic play about Cuba's housing shortage; Juan Padron's bawdy animated feature *Vampiros en la Habana* (*Vampires in Havana*, 1985); and two works by newcomer Jésus Díaz, *Polvo rojo* (*Red Dust*, 1981), an epic of postrevolutionary reconstruction, and *Lejanía* (*Distance*, 1985), a film about the irreconcilable differences between Cuban and American society. Ironically, Díaz' younger brother, Rolando, has developed a flair for American-style commercial comedy in such films as *Los pájaros a la escopeta* (*Birds Will Fly*, 1984) and *En tres y dos* (*Full Count*, 1985). The eighties ended eclectically in Cuba, with a literate historical romance, Alea's *Cartas del parque* (*Letters from the Park*, 1988); an agitational account of prerevolutionary terrorism, Fernando Perez' *Clandestinos* (*Living Dangerously*, 1988); a colorful adaptation from Gabriel García Márquez, Fernando Birri's *Un señor muy viejo con unas alas enormes* (*A Very Old Man with Enormous Wings*, 1988); and a raucous contemporary satire, Juan Carlos Tabio's *Plaff!* (1989), which lampoons all things Cuban, from the socialist bureaucracy to *santéria*.

In terms of production ICAIC operates as a collective, in which there is—amazingly—no government oversight and directors are free to choose their own subjects and write their own scripts. In the late eighties, the Cuban cinema continues to evolve on course, but the U.S. trade embargo and the country's endemic poverty make creative improvisation within the industry a way of life. There is, for example, a chronic shortage of raw film stock. Moreover, U.S. disapproval has a negative impact on international sales, and many distributors won't buy Cuban films for fear of boycotts by American producers. Furthermore, the United States freezes all profits from Cuban bookings within its borders, so that only a handful of Cuban films are known to American audiences, and Unifilm, ICAIC's main American distributor, was driven into bankruptcy in the early eighties by the squeeze. Yet, in a short span of time, Cuban cinema and Cuban spectators have come a long way, and they have provided enormous inspiration, not to mention valuable production and postproduction assistance, to militant film movements all over the hemisphere. The Festival of New Latin American Cinema held annually in Havana has been an event of increasing international importance since its inception in 1979, and it is now widely considered to be the most important Spanish-language festival in the world, surpassing both Barcelona and Madrid in attendance and market share. At the conclusion of the 1986 festival, Fidel Castro announced the creation of the New Latin American Cinema Foundation in Havana, under the direction of Nobel Prize–winning novelist Gabriel García Márquez, and the establishment of the International Film and Television School (La Escuela de Cine y Televisión), commonly known as "the School of the Three Worlds," just outside Havana, in San Antonio de las Baños (the location of Alea's *Los sobrevivientes*), under the direction of Argentine documentarist Fernando Birri, a pioneer of the New Latin American Cinema movement. The foundation's major goals will be the creation of an "information bank" on Latin American cinema, and the lobbying of local governments for economic support of the movement. The film school will replace Cuba's existing apprenticeship system and also train film- and video-makers from Africa, Asia, and the rest of Latin America to work, as its charter proclaims, "for the growing and effective solidarity of Latin American filmmakers within a framework of dignity, social justice, and the preservation of the cultural heritage of the Latin American peoples."*

AFRICA

As Clyde Taylor points out, over ninety African nations have gained independence since World War II—most of them since 1960—and yet the African film market is small by Western standards. It can logically be divided between North African and sub-Saharan cinema. In the north, the most prominent film-producing country is Algeria, whose film industry was nationalized shortly after the nation won its independence in a savage war of liberation with France that lasted from 1954 to 1962. Algeria's first films concerned that struggle and were collectively known as *cinema mudjahad*—"freedom fighter cinema." Several of these films, such as Ahmed Rachedi's (b. 1938) *L'Aube des damnés* (*Dawn of the Damned*, 1965) and Mohamed Lakhdar-Hamina's (b. 1935) *Le Vent des Aurés* (*The Wind of Aurés*, 1966; winner of the Cannes Camera d'or), were of superior quality, but it was not until the *cinema djidid* ("new cinema") movement of the seventies that Algeria established an authentic and sophisticated alternative cinema, especially in the work of Ali Ghalem—*Mektoub* (1970); Mohamed Bouamari (b. 1941)—*Le Charbonnier* (*The Coal-Miner,* 1973); Mohamed Slim Riad (b. 1932)—*Ryah el janoub* (*The South Wind,* 1975); and Mohamed Lakhdar-Hamina—*Chronique des années de braise* (*Chronicle of the Years of Embers,* 1975),

---

* Quoted in Dennis West, "A Film School for the Third World," *Cineaste* 15, 3 (1987): 37.

18.24 *Chronique des années de braise* (Mohamed Lakhdar-Hamina, 1975): reflections on the Algerian war of liberation. Leila Shenna (right).

an epic film about a family's coming to revolutionary consciousness in the crucial period from 1939 to 1954 which won the Grand Prix at Cannes. More recently, Ali Ghalem has returned with *Maraa le ibni* (*A Wife for My Son*, 1983), and Ahmed Rachedi, with *Tahounet al sayed Fabre* (*Mr. Fabre's Mill*, 1986), while Lakhdar-Hamina has directed the French-Algerian coproduction *Le Dernière image* (*The Last Image*, 1986). Algeria, whose population is approximately 23 million, currently produces about five or six features and sixty to eighty shorts a year, and it has also coproduced films with Italy (Gillo Pontecorvo's *La battaglia di Algeri* [*The Battle of Algiers,* 1966]) and Egypt (Youssef Chahine's *Al-asfour* [*The Sparrow,* 1973]). Moreover, there are a number of native Algerian filmmakers who live and work in France, including Mehdi Charef—*Le é au harem d'Archimede* (*Tea in the Harem,* 1985), *Miss Mona* (1987), *Camomille* (1988); and Merzak Allouache—*Un Amour à Paris* (*A Romance in Paris,* 1987).

Neighboring francophone Tunisia (population 8 million), which has been host of the Carthage Film Festival since 1966, has a small government-supported industry which has coproduced such notable features as *Dhil Al-ardh* (*Shadow on the Earth,* Taieb Louhichi, 1982; with France); *La Ballade de Mamlouk* (*The Ballad of Mamlouk,* Abdelhafidh Bouassida, 1982; with Czechoslovakia); and two documentaries of Ferid Boughedir—*Camera d'Afrique: 20 Years of African Cinema* (1983) and *Camera Arabe: The Young Arab Cinema* (1987), both with France. In 1986, an all-Tunisian production, Nouri Bouzid's *Rih al saad* (*Man of Ashes*) won the golden prize at the twenty-second Taormina Film Festival in Sicily, and its companion-piece *Sfayah min dhahab* (*The Golden Horseshoes,* 1989) was an official jury selection three years later at Cannes. Morocco (population 25 million), the other country of the *Maghreb* (liberally, "the sunset"—that region of northern Africa that extends most prominently into the Mediterranean and includes Algeria, Tunisia, and Morocco), made only about twenty features in the years from independence in 1956 to 1980, but these films were notably more experimental than those of Algeria and Tunisia, perhaps because of Morocco's relatively high cultural level and active *cine club* tradition. The success of such films as Latif Lahlou's *Soleil de printemps* (*Spring Sun*, 1970), Southel Ben Barka's (b. 1942) *Les Mille et une mains* (*The Thousand and One Hands*, 1972), Moumen Smihi's (b. 1945) *El cherqui* (*The Violent Silence*, 1975), and Ahmed al Maanouni's (b. 1944) *Alyam! Alyam!* (*Oh the Days! Oh the Days!*, 1978) created the grounds for a system of government support through the Centre Cinematographique Marocaine (CCM). Between 1980 and 1984, thirty new films were produced under its auspices; prominent among them were *Le Coiffeur du quartier des pauvres* (*The Neighborhood Barber*, Mohamed Reggab, 1982), *Amok* (Southel Ben Barka, 1983), *Cauchemar* (*Nightmare*, Ahmed Yasfine, 1984), and *Zeft* (*Concrete*, Tayeb Saddiki, 1984). Among recent Moroccan films notable for their formal stylization are Moumen Smihi's *44 ou les Rectis de la nuit* (*44 or Tales of the Night*, 1985), Mohamed Aboulouakar's *Hadda* (1986), and Najib Sefrioui's *Chams* (1986).

Egypt (population 49 million) is the other North African country with a sizable film industry, although it is by and large relentlessly commercial and star-oriented. (For example, actor Omar Sharif [b. 1932] was a product of the Egyptian star system.) Recently Egypt has turned out seventy to eighty features annually. Its filmmakers are capable of producing such complex individual films as Shadi Abdes-Salam's (b. 1930) *Al-momia* (*The Night of Counting the Years*, 1969), and it has a director of international standing in Youssef Chahine (b. 1926), whose major works have been *Bab al-hadid* (*Cairo Station*, 1958), *Al-ard* (*The Land*, 1969), and *The Sparrow* (an Algerian coproduction noted above). Chahine's cinematic autobiography, combined with a social history of modern Egypt, began with *Iskandariya . . . Lih?* (*Alexandria . . . Why?*, 1978) and continued in *Hadduta misriya* (*An Egyptian Story*, 1982) and *El Yom el sades* (*The Sixth Day*, 1986), a melodrama set during the 1947 cholera epidemic. Other Egyptian directors of note are veterans Salah Abou Seif— *El bedaya* (*Satan's Empire / The Beginning*, 1986); Kamal el Sheikh— *El-taous* (*The Peacock*, 1982); *Kaher el zaman* (*Conqueror of Time*, 1986); and the relative newcomer Mohamed Khan—*El harrif* (*Street Player*, 1983); *Awdat mowatin* (*Return of a Citizen*, 1986); and *Zawgat ragol mohim* (*Wife of an Important Man*, 1987).

The most important film-producing country in sub-Saharan Africa is Senegal (population 7 million), largely owing to the work of one director, Ousmane Sembène (b. 1923), who studied filmmaking in Moscow with Mark Donskoi and is also a distinguished writer of short stories and novels. Sembène made all of his films outside of the French Ministry of Cooperation program, which assisted production in its former sub-Saharan colonies from 1962 to 1980. Most historians identify his twenty-minute short *Borom Sarret* (1963), which won a prize at the International Festival of Tours, as the first indigenous black African film. Sembène followed this realistic account of a day in the life of an impoverished Dakar cartman with his sixty-minute *La Noire de . . .* (*Black Girl*, 1966; adapted from his own story). Arguably the first sub-Saharan feature and one of the first significant anticolonial documents of Africa, *La Noire de . . .*

18.25 *Xala* (Ousmane Sembène, 1974): a government official (Thierno Leye) caught between neo-colonialism and the ancient curse of impotence.

18.26 *Touki-Bouki* (Djibril Diop Mambety, 1973).

describes a young black woman who loses her cultural identity as a maid in service to a French family. *Mandabi* (*The Money Order*, 1968), Sembene's first full-length color feature, was shot in both French and Wolof, a language spoken by 90 percent of the Senegalese people. A muted social satire about the humiliating ordeal of an illiterate Dakar workingman trying to cash a check sent to him by his nephew in Paris, it took prizes at international festivals in Tashkent, New York, and Atlanta, and became the first Senegalese feature to be distributed commercially in its home country. His *Emitai* (1971) mixes epic and documentary aspirations in its rendition of a confrontation between a group of Diola villagers and French troops sent to requisition their harvest during World War II. The film, whose title means "god of thunder" in Diola, was shot almost entirely in that language and concludes with the brutal massacre of the villagers. Although it won major awards at Moscow and Tashkent, *Emitai* could not be distributed in Senegal because of pressure from the French government, which has maintained close economic and cultural ties with its former colony since independence was granted in 1959. Sembéne's next film, *Xala* (1974), was adapted from a short novel he published in French the same year. Its title, usually translated as *The Curse*, actually means "impotence" in Wolof, and the film is a ferocious satire on the black bourgeoisie of the new Senegalese republic. Its protagonist is a corrupt bureaucrat who is stricken by impotence on the night of wedding his third wife and must exorcise the curse by resorting to a degrading primitive ritual. Sembène then made *Ceddo* (1977), which he adapted from his own novel and produced himself with the profits from *Xala* and a government-sponsored loan. It collapses several centuries of colonial African history into the events of several days in the exemplary tale of an Islamic *imam* (spiritual teacher) who dethrones a village king and imposes his religion on the people. The *imam* ultimately is killed by the *ceddo* ("outsiders" in Wolof), who reject his claims. Richly stylized and highly controversial in a country which is 80 percent Muslim, *Ceddo* was banned by the Senegalese government for eight years. In the meantime, Sembéne pursued his career as a writer and planned his projected *magnum opus*— a six-hour epic on the life of Samori Toure, the nineteenth-century West African nationalist who resisted French imperialism. While seeking funding for *Samori*, Sembéne directed (with Thierno Faty Sow) the Senegalese-Tunisian-Algerian coproduction *Camp de Thiaroye* (*Camp Thiaroye*, 1988). This powerful anticolonial film is based upon an actual massacre ordered by the French army against black veterans returning to Senegal from World War II. Other Senegalese filmmakers are Djibril Diop Mambety (b. 1945), whose *Touki-Bouki* is widely regarded as Africa's first avant-garde film; Mahama Johnson Traore (b. 1942)—*Reou-takh* (*The Big City*, 1971) and *Njangaan* (1974); Safi Faye (b. 1943)—*Kaddu-beykat* (*Letter from a Village*, 1976); *Fad jal* (*Grandfather*, 1979); *Ambassades nourricières* (*Culinary Embassies*, 1984); Ben Diogaye Beye—*Sey seyeti* [*One Man, Many Women*, 1980); Ababakar Samb (b. 1934)—*Kodou* (1979) and *Jom* (1981); Paulin Soumanou Vieyra (b. 1925), a former documentarist whose collaborative short *Afrique sur Seine* (*Africa on the Seine,* 1955) is sometimes described as the foundation stone of African cinema—*En Residence surveillée* (*Under House Arrest,* 1982); and the Vietnamese documentarist Trinh T. Minh-ha—*Réassemblage* (1982); *Naked Spaces* (1985), who has recently been working in Africa. Between 1968 and 1983, Senegal produced twenty-six features, most of them with the assistance of the French Ministry of Cooperation, and the nation's solid, government-backed industry gives every indication that it will continue at this rate.

Other sub-Saharan film-producing countries are Mali, Burkina Faso (formerly Upper Volta), the Ivory Coast, Ghana, Nigeria, and Angola. Mali has two filmmakers whose work is becoming known in the West, both of whom produce, like Sembéne, outside the system of French assistance available to most of France's former colonies. They are Souleymane Cisse (b. 1940), trained in Moscow—*Den muso* (*The Girl,* 1975); *Baara* (*The Porter,* 1978); *Finye* (*The Wind,* 1982); *Yeelen* (*Brightness,* 1987); and Cheick Oumar Sissoko, whose *Nyamanton* (*The Garbage Boys,* 1986) attracted considerable international attention. In Burkina Faso (Upper Volta) the work of Gaston Kaboré (b. 1951)—*Wend kuuni* (*The Gift of God,* 1982); *Zan Boko* (1988); of Sanou Kollo—*Paweogo* (*The Emigrant,* 1983); of Paul Zoumbara—*Jours de tormentes* (*Days of Torment,* 1985); and of Idrissa Quedraogo—*Poko* (1981); *Yam daabo* (*The Choice,* 1987); *Yaaba* (*Grandmother,* 1989)—has received some attention. The nation's capital, Ouagadougou, has hosted the African Film Week and is the home of the African Film Institute. From the Ivory Coast have come such recent independent features as Kramo-Lanciné Fadika's *Djeli* (*The Girot,* 1981), Désiré Ecaré's *Visages de femmes* (*Faces of Women,* 1985), and M'Bala Roger Gnoan's *Ablakon* (1985). And from Ghana there have come Kwaw Ansah's *Love Brewed in the African Pot* (1980) and King Ampaw's *Kukurantum—The Road to Accra* (1983). In Nigeria, IDHEC-trained Ola Balogun (b. 1945) has produced ten features since 1972, most recently *Cry Freedom!* (1981), *Money Power* (1982), and *A deusa negra* (*Black Goddess,* 1983). Angola established a film institute in 1977, two years after liberation from Portugal, and has produced a major director in Rui Duarte de Caralho—*Faz la coragem, camarada!* (*Courage, Comrade!,* 1977); *Nelisita* (1983). There are also occasional films from Guinea-Bissau, Mozambique, Kenya, the Central African Republic, Cameroon, the Republic of Congo, and the eastern island of Madagascar.*

---

* South Africa is eliminated from this account of sub-Saharan cinema for the obvious reason that its industry, which produces about twenty-five features a year, is operated for the benefit of the ruling white minority. Exceptions exist in the trilogy of filmscripts by the distinguished playwright Athol Fugard (b. 1932)—*Boseman and Lena* (1974), *Marigolds in August* (1980), and *The Guest* (1984), all directed by Ross Devenish; the adaptations of eleven Nadine Gordimer (b. 1923) stories made by various film crews for West German television; and such occasional, courageous independent features as *Last Grave at Dimbaza* (Nana Mahomo, 1975) and *Place of Weeping* (Darrell Roodt, 1986). An important South African filmmaker in exile is documentarist Lionel Ngakane (b. 1928), whose feature-length *Vukani* (*Awake,* 1964), *Jemima and Johnny* (1975), *Once Upon a Time* (1975), and *Nel-*

More significant is the work of several African filmmakers living abroad. Especially notable is the Mauritanian Med Hondo (b. 1936), whose *Soleil-O* (*O Sun*, 1970), after a song sung by African slaves transported to the West Indies; *Les Bicots-nègres, vos voisins* (*The Negroes, Your Neighbors*, 1973); and *West Indies* (1979)* are vigorous indictments of slavery, racism, and the neocolonial mentality. For *Sarrounia* (1986), Med Hondo returned to Africa (Burkina Faso) to direct an epic account of a tribal queen's victory over French expeditionary forces in central Africa in 1898–99. Other exiles are UCLA-trained Haile Gerima (b. 1946), whose monumental documentary *Mirt sost shi amit* (*Harvest: 3,000 Years*, 1975) was shot on location in Ethiopia on the eve of the revolution there; and Sarah Maldoror (b. Sarah Ducades, 1929), a French resident, of Guadeloupe parentage, trained in Moscow, whose tense film of the Angolan liberation struggle, *Sambizanga* (1972), was shot secretly in the Republic of Congo and won many international awards.

GERMANY: *DAS NEUE KINO*

Postwar Origins

Related to the Third World cinema movement through its emphatic rejection of conventional narrative syntax and its Marxist ideological perspective, **das neue Kino** ("the new cinema") has made West German cinema among the most exciting in the world today, compensating for its long postwar eclipse. After World War II, German cinema, like the nation itself, was split into Western and Eastern parts which ultimately became the Federal Republic of Germany (FRG, population 61 million) and the German Democratic Republic (GDR, population 16.5 million). Most of the production equipment was under Soviet control in the Eastern zone, as were the former UFA studios at Neubabelsberg. In May 1946, all activities of these production facilities were nationalized under the Deutsche Film Aktiengesellschaft (German Film Company, or DEFA), which provided new production capital in the form of state subsidies. In the Western sector, the Americans installed the former UFA producer Erich Pommer (see Chapter 4) as film commissioner for that zone and

---

son Mandela (1985) have all been made abroad. See Keyan G. Tomaselli, "The Teaching of Film and Television Production in a Third World Context: The Case of South Africa," *Journal of the University Film and Video Association* 34, 4 (Fall 1982): 3–12, "Racism in South African Cinema," *Cineaste* 13, 1 (1983): 12–15, and *The Cinema of Apartheid: Class and Race in South African Cinema* (New York: Smyrna Press, 1988); Gary Crowdus, "South African Filmmaking in Exile: An Interview with Lionel Ngakane," *Cineaste* 15, 2 (1986): 16–17; Jo-Anne Collinge, "Under Fire," *American Film* (November 1985): 30–36.

* In the West Indies themselves, films have been produced in Jamaica—e.g., Perry Henzell's cult classic *The Harder They Come* (1973); *Countryman* (Dickie Jobson, 1982); *Cool Runnings* (Robert Mugge, 1983; released 1986); *Diggers* (Roman J. Foster, 1986); plus Brian Saint-Juste's *Children of Babylon* and *Smile Orange*; and Martinique—*Sugar Cane Alley / Street of Black Shacks* (*Rue cases negres*, 1983), directed by Euzhan Palcy.

insured, through various decartelization laws, that no centralized German film industry could emerge to compete with their own. Nevertheless, the Allies began to license individual production companies in 1946, and the years 1946–48 saw the release of several notable films dealing with immediate postwar social problems in both the Eastern and Western zones, among them *Die Mörder sind unter uns* (*The Murderers Are Among Us* [Wolfgang Staudte, East Germany, 1946]); *Freies Land* (*Free Land* [Milo Harbig, East Germany, 1946]); *Morituri* (Artur Brauner [West Germany, 1946]); *In jenen Tagen* (*In Former Days* [Helmut Käutner, West Germany, 1947]); and *Berliner Ballade* (*The Ballad of Berlin* [Robert Stemmle, West Germany, 1948]). These were known as *Trümmerfilme* ("rubble films") because of the devastated physical condition of the Germany they portrayed, and they gave some hope of a realist German film movement, similar to the one being born concurrently in Italy.* But as production rose to over seventy German films a year in 1949, currency reform brought the promise of prosperity to West Germany, and the films of that sector turned away from self-scrutiny toward lightweight entertainment.

Economic recovery proceeded rapidly through the fifties, and West Germany became the fifth largest producer of films in the world. Yet its increasingly escapist *Heimatfilme* ("homeland films") were directed exclusively at the domestic audience, and they compared unfavorably with the glossy Hollywood products which flowed ceaselessly into the market through American-owned distributors. (Although the Americans had prevented the reemergence of a centralized German film industry during the Occupation, they had supported the rebuilding of the exhibition and distribution sectors. After a series of monetary crises during the fifties, all but one of the major West German distributors, Constantin Film, had fallen into American hands.) In East Germany, the DEFA output remained relatively small and ideologically focused, attacking Nazism as the arch-enemy of the new socialist state.

When television and increased mobility began to change patterns of leisure activity in the late fifties, West German film attendance fell off dramatically, just as it did in the rest of Europe and in the United States. Between 1956 and 1968, in fact, it dropped from 900 million to 192 million annually. Domestic production was badly hurt, and the West German film industry had no alternative but to appeal to the federal government for subsidies. These were granted at first in the form of guaranteed credits (*Ausfallbürgschaften*) but were eliminated in 1961 when the Ministry of the Interior decided to help rejuvenate German cinema by awarding production grants for feature films.

Young German Cinema

The seeds of *das neue Kino* were sown at the Oberhausen Film Festival in 1962, when twenty-six writers and filmmakers who had accepted min-

18.27 *Die Mörder sind unter uns* (Wolfgang Staute, 1946).

18.28 *In jenen Tagen* (Helmut Käutner, 1947).

18.29 A typical *Heimatfilm: Ich denke oft an Piroschka* (*I Often Think of Piroschka*, Kurt Hoffmann, 1956): Liselotte Pulver.

---

* Roberto Rossellini's neorealist classic *Germania, anno zero.* (*Germany, Year Zero*, 1947) was shot on location in bombed-out Berlin (see Chapter 11).

istry grants called for the establishment of a *junger detuscher film*, a "young German cinema," in a manifesto that concluded as follows:

> The collapse of the commercial German film industry finally removes the economic basis for a mode of filmmaking whose attitude and practice we reject. With it, the new film has a chance to come to life. The success of German shorts at international festivals demonstrates that the future of the German cinema lies with those who have shown that they speak the international language of the cinema. This new cinema needs new forms of freedom: from the conventions and habits of the established industry, from intervention by commercial partners, and finally freedom from the tutelage of other vested interests. We have specific plans for the artistic, formal and economic realization of this new German cinema. We are collectively prepared to take the economic risks. The old cinema is dead. We believe in the new.

Through its spokesmen, the directors Alexander Kluge and Norbert Kückelmann, the Oberhausen group successfully lobbied the West German parliament (Bundestag) for the formation in 1965 of the Young German Film Board (Kuratorium Junger Deutscher Film), an institution charged with implementing the proposals of the Oberhausen manifesto. Specifically, drawing from the cultural budgets of the various federal states, the Kuratorium sponsored the first features of Kluge, Hans-Jürgen Pohland, and Werner Herzog, and seventeen other features, between 1965 and 1968. The Oberhausen group was also able to achieve the foundation of two professional film schools (at Munich and Berlin) and a German Film Archive in Berlin.

But by 1970 the successes of the "young German cinema" rang rather hollow. The passage of a Film Subsidies Bill by the Bundestag in 1967 had established a Film Subsidies Board (Filmförderungsanstalt, or FFA) that concentrated economic power in the hands of the commercial studios and distributors, and the result was a boom in the production of quick, shoddily made features that were foisted on a dwindling audience through block booking. Most of these productions were idiotic classroom comedies and soft-core pornographic films aimed at West Germany's two million immigrant workers. Theater owners were forced to book them as part of package deals with distributors, whether a local audience existed for the films or not. With West German production hitting an all-time high of 121 films per year in 1969 and film attendance slipping at the rate of one million per year, the late sixties and early seventies witnessed a wave of theater closings all over the country. The drivel produced by the first three years of FFA subsidies had alienated serious filmgoers, bored the general public, and brought the West German film industry to the brink of another financial crisis. As recently as 1971 the *New York Times* could write, "The persistently dismal situation of German film art is unique; a list of new films comprises a greater proportion of trash than anywhere else."

The New German Cinema

Nevertheless, a new German cinema was about to be born from the combined efforts of the Oberhausen group and a group of somewhat younger independent filmmakers who began their careers in West German television. In 1971 this group formed the Filmverlag der Autoren (literally, the "Authors' Film-Publishing Group") as a private company to distribute on a cooperative basis the films of its members, who quickly came to include Alexander Kluge, Rainer Werner Fassbinder, Bernhard Sinkel, Peter Lilienthal, Ulli Lommel, Edgar Reitz, Hans W. Geissendörfer, Hark Bohm, Reinhard Hauff, Uwe Brandner, and Wim Wenders. (In 1985, the Filmverlag was sold to the independent producer-distributor Futura Films.) The impetus of the Oberhausen group, the resources of West German television and the Kuratorium, and a liberalized FFA grant policy* have made possible the phenomenal rise of the New German Cinema. Although the films of the movement have only a small following in West Germany itself, they have created more excitement within the international cinema than anything comparable since the French New Wave. Although the young film artists whose work collectively comprises the New German Cinema are quite diverse, they do have some distinct stylistic traits in common. Thomas Elsaesser writes of

> an unusual degree of aesthetic closure towards formal beauty and abstraction, a refusal to be explicit on the level of argument and meaning. Sensuousness, color, and emotional luxuriance to the point of morbidity lure the viewer into accepting as valid discourse a social stance that is poignantly defensive and individualistic to a vulnerable extent. A style has evolved in the German cinema of the last five or six years that vacillates between satirical realism and symbolism of almost oppressive obliqueness, a style not unconnected with the cultural limbo affecting much of Germany's intellectual life today.

The last point is important, because West Germany is a country that has only just begun to come to terms with the nightmare of its own recent history, its *unbewältige Vergangenheit* ("unassimilated past"). The generation of young filmmakers represented by *das neue Kino* grew up in an Americanized, economically prospering Germany; they were only dimly aware of the Nazi past. Cultural historians point out that since the collapse of the "Thousand-Year Reich," the German people have suffered from a kind of collective amnesia about the "brown years" of Nazi rule, 1933–45. The shock and humiliation of defeat, the appalling devastation of the material environment, the partitioning of the country, and the collective guilt for the most terrible acts of barbarism and genocide ever committed—all conspired to rob Germany of its cultural identity by robbing it of access to its immediate past. The past was not discussed in postwar German households nor dwelled upon in postwar West German

---

* The FFA makes about 7.5 million dollars available for film production annually by levying a six-cent (0.15 Deutschmarks) tax on every ticket sold in West Germany's three thousand cinema theaters. (In 1979 a new law raised the tax by 50 percent.) Only directors whose previous films have returned at least 500,000 dollars may apply for funds, which gives the FFA a decidedly commercial bias. But since 1975, three million dollars annually have been earmarked for worthy independent projects selected by an eleven-man committee of critics and businessmen. The committee provided up to 80 percent funding for forty-one projects between 1975 and 1978.

schools.* Since the early seventies, however, when the postwar generation began demographically to displace the generation that had actually experienced Nazism, public curiosity and confusion about the past has steadily increased. Added to this is the fact that, through its lucrative postwar alliance with the United States, West Germany has traded off large chunks of its cultural identity to become one of the most highly technocratized countries in the world, surpassing perhaps even Japan and the United States itself in some sectors of the gross national product. This set of circumstances has produced in the postwar generation an acute sense of alienation and anomie (signs of which are apparent in Japan, the United States, and many other industrialized nations as well). Robbed of their past by the infamy of Nazism and of their future by American cultural imperialism, the filmmakers of *das neue Kino* express the sense of psychological and cultural dislocation described by the film critic Michael Covino as "a worldwide homesickness." Their films are unsettling and sometimes depressing, but there can be no question of their unique contribution to international cinema.

Volker Schlöndorff, Alexander Kluge, and Margarethe von Trotta

Historically, the New German Cinema movement can be said to date from the release of Volker Schlöndorff's independently produced *Der junge Törless* (*Young Törless*, 1966), a psychologically detailed adaptation of Robert Musil's antimilitarist novel set in a boy's school before

---

*In a survey of West German teenagers taken in 1970, an overwhelming majority could identify Hitler only as "the man who built the *Autobahn*." Indeed, the Bonn government expressed concern in 1978 that the lack of understanding of Nazism among West German youth could lead to a rekindling of it. As if to certify this concern, after *Holocaust* (the NBC-produced miniseries on the Nazis' extermination of the Jews) was shown on West German television in January 1979, national polls revealed that 70 percent of viewers between the ages of fourteen and nineteen felt that they had learned more about Nazism from the American television program than from all their years of studying German history.

That telecast, in fact, was the source of great emotional upheaval in West Germany and became a cultural phenomenon akin to the first broadcast of *Roots* in the United States. Initially opposed on the grounds that it would open old wounds—and denied national broadcast on the First German Network (WDR [Westdeutscher Rundfunk], Cologne)—*Holocaust* was finally aired regionally on the Third German Network (ZDF [Zweites Deutsches Fernsehen], Mainz). Over half of the adult population of the country (20 million viewers, or 48 percent of the West German audience of 61 million) saw all or part of it. Polls conducted by the Bonn government and the Marplan Institute in the months after the telecast indicated a profound and lasting effect. In one poll, 64 percent of the viewers said that they were "deeply shocked," and 21 percent had been moved to tears. The number of viewers who, after viewing the program, favored the 1944 plot to assassinate Hitler increased from 49 to 63 percent; over half of the viewers reported that they had learned something new about Nazi atrocities; 73 percent felt "very positive" about the experience of watching *Holocaust;* and over half of the adults and two-thirds of the teenagers said that they would like to see it again because the program was so informative. (*Variety,* May 23, 1979.) The miniseries was finally broadcast on the national West German network in the fall of 1982. Characteristically, the East German government refused to broadcast *Holocaust* on the grounds that its people had already been thoroughly schooled about Nazism and its crimes.

World War I, which won the International Critics' Prize at Cannes. Schlöndorff (b. 1939), who studied at IDHEC (Paris), had worked as an assistant to Louis Malle, Alain Resnais, and Jean-Pierre Melville before directing this feature. His next independent film* was *Baal* (1969), an adaptation of Bertolt Brecht's first play, which was followed by *Der plötzliche Reichtum der armen Leute von Kombach* (*The Sudden Wealth of the Poor People of Kombach,* 1971), a bizarre parody of the *Heimatfilm* tradition in which a group of nineteenth-century peasants rebel against the degradation of rural life by becoming bandits and are put to death by the state. Other notable Schlöndorff films are *Coup de grace* (*Der Fangschuss,* 1976), a psychological drama set among German volunteers in the Baltic states at the end of World War I, and *Nur zum Spass—nur zum Spiel, Kaleidoskop Valeska Gert* (1977), in which a famous cabaret artist, shortly before her death in 1978, reminisces about her more than sixty years in show business. In 1979 Schlöndorff's adaptation of Günter Grass' novel *The Tin Drum* (*Die Blechtrommel*) shared the Grand Prix at Cannes with the American director Francis Ford Coppola's *Apocalypse Now,* and in 1980 it won the American Academy Award for Best Foreign Film. Schlöndorff has worked frequently for the commercial studios, where he has collaborated with his wife, Margarethe von Trotta (b. 1942), the scenarist and actress, on a number of important films dealing with feminism and other social and political themes. Most notable among these have been *Strohfeuer* (*Summer Lightning / A Free Woman,* 1972), and *Die verlorene Ehre der Katharina Blum* (*The Lost Honor of Katharina Blum,* 1975; from the novel by Heinrich Böll [1917–85]). During the eighties, Schlöndorff produced *Die Faelschung* (*Circle of Deceit / The Forgery,* 1981), based on events in the Lebanese civil war, 1974–76, as they are experienced by a German photojournalist; *Un Amor de Swann* (*Swann in Love,* 1984), a lavish adaptation of the second part of the first volume of Proust's *A la recherche du temps perdu* (sixteen volumes, 1913–27), shot on location in Paris and environs by Sven Nykvist; and an unusual version of Arthur Miller's *Death of a Salesman* (1985), with Dustin Hoffman as Willy Loman, produced for American television.

Another founder of *das neue Kino* was Alexander Kluge (b. 1932), whose *Artisten unter der Zirkuskuppel: ratlos* (*Artists under the Big Top: Disoriented,* 1968) provided a metaphor for the plight of the serious film artist in Germany in the Godardian parable of a young woman who inherits a circus but cannot reform its deeply embedded traditions to create a new role for it in the "media world." Kluge, a practicing lawyer, novelist, legal scholar, and social theoretician, worked as an assistant to Fritz Lang (see Chapter 4) during Lang's brief return to Germany in the late fifties, and he is the intellectual father of New German Cinema. As spokesman

18.30 *Der junge Törless* (Volker Schlöndorff, 1966): Matthieu Carrière, Barbara Steele.

18.31 *Artisten unter der Zirkuskuppel: ratlos* (Alexander Kluge, 1968): Hannelore Hoger.

---

* Two commercial features intervened: a murder mystery entitled *Mord und Totschlag* (*A Degree of Death,* 1966) and the German-Czech-American coproduction *Michael Kohlhass—der Rebell* (1969), an epic of a sixteenth-century German political rebellion based on an 1808 story by Heinrich von Kleist (the same story was filmed as *Michael Kohlhass* in 1979 by the director Wolf Vollmar).

for the original Oberhausen *junger deutscher Film* group, he was responsible for convincing the federal government to establish the Kuratorium and the film schools in Munich and Berlin. Kluge's style is objective, coolly rational, and satirical. His films almost always involve the precise analysis of some social problem which besets contemporary Germany, focusing on a representative protagonist (often played by his younger sister, Alexandra Kluge). Kluge's most significant films of the seventies are *Gelegenheitsarbeit einer Sklavin* (*Part-Time Work of a Domestic Slave,* 1974), which examines the issue of women's liberation and political organizing, and *Strong Man Ferdinand* (*Der starke Ferdinand,* 1976), a satirical allegory of Fascism about an industrial security guard whose paranoid quest for order results in catastrophe for everyone around him. Kluge then brought together ten other New German filmmakers and the Nobel Prize–winning novelist Heinrich Böll to produce *Deutschland im Herbst* (*Germany in Autumn,* 1978) for the Filmverlag der Autoren. Highly reminiscent of SLON's *Loin de Vietnam* (1967), this semidocumentary cooperative feature is a rumination on the events of autumn 1977, when a public official was kidnapped and murdered by terrorists, and several of the terrorists later died under mysterious circumstances in prison. Kluge, expanding his contribution to *Deutschland im Herbst,* made *Die Patriotin* (*The Patriot,* 1980), a meditation on the teaching of German history both in and out of school. In other cooperative projects, Kluge, Schlöndorff, and two younger directors produced *Der Kandidat* (*The Candidate,* 1980), an ironic documentary portrait of Franz Josef Strauss, the right-wing challenger in the 1980 West German federal elections, and *Krieg und Frieden* (*War and Peace,* 1983), an omnibus work on the nation's peace movement. Kluge himself has produced and directed the documentary *Die Macht der Gefuehle* (*The Power of Emotion,* 1983), as well as *Der Angriff der Gengenwart au die übrige Zeit* (*The Assault of the Present upon the Rest of Time,* 1985) and *Vermischte Nachrichten* (*Odds and Ends,* 1987), the latter two composed of documentary-style vignettes about contemporary German life and attitudes.

Schlöndorff and Kluge remain important representatives of *das neu Kino;* in the late seventies and eighties their ranks were joined by Margarethe von Trotta as a major director in her own right with the appearance of *Das zweites Erwachen der Christa Klages* (*The Second Awakening of Christa Klage,* 1978) and *Schwestern oder die Bilanz des Glucks* (*Sisters, or the Balance of Happiness,* 1979), both concerned in different ways with the emergence of feminist consciousness. Von Trotta's breakthrough film, however, was *Die bleierne Zeit* (*The German Sisters/ The Leaden Time,* 1981), a film about the coming to political awareness of two siblings in the late sixties and the radically different paths chosen by each. Based on the true story of a member of the Baader-Meinhof terrorist gang, *Die bleierne Zeit* became the second film by a woman to win the Golden Lion at Venice in thirty-nine years (the first was, ironically, Leni Riefenstahl's *Olympia*), but von Trotta was not so successful with her subsequent *Frauenfilme* ("women's films") *Heller Wahn* (*Sheer Madness,* 1982) and *Paura e Amore* (*Fear and Love/ Three Sisters,* 1988), the latter vaguely adapted from Chekhov. On the other hand, von Trotta's

18.32 *Rosa Luxemburg* (Margarethe von Trotta, 1986).

Rosa Luxemburg (1986), a biography of the revolutionary socialist leader and cofounder of the Spartacus League who was murdered by Freikorps troops in 1919, is regarded as a major work. Von Trotta is the most visible of a large number of West German women directors whose work runs the gamut from traditional narrative to radical polemics. They include Heidi Genee (b.1938)—*1 + 1 = 3* (1980); *Stackel im Fleisch* (*Thorn in the Flesh*, 1981); *Kraftprobe* (*Test of Strength*, 1982); Dorris Dorrie (b. 1955)—*Mitten ins Herz* (*Straight to the Heart*, 1983); *Im innern des Wals* (*Inside the Whale*, 1985); *Männer* (*Men*, 1985); *Paradies* (*Paradise*, 1986); *Me and Him* (1989); Jutta Bruckner (b. 1941)—*Tue Recht und scheue niemand* (*Do Right and Fear No One*, 1978); *Hungerjahre* (1980); *Ein Blick—und die Liebe bricht aus* (*One Look—and Love Begins*, 1985); Ula Stockl (b. 1938)—*Der Schlaf der Vernunft* (*The Sleep of Reason*, 1984); Helke Sander (b. 1937), founder of the feminist film journal *Frauen und Film* (*Women and Film*) in 1974—*Der subjektive Faktor* (*The Subjective Factor*, 1981); and Helma Sanders-Brahams (b. 1940)—*Deutschland, bleiche Mutter* (*Germany, Pale Mother*, 1980); *Die Beruehrte* (*The Touched* / *No Exit, No Panic*, U.S.A. [*No Mercy, No Future*, U.K.], 1981); *L'Avenir de'Emilie* (*The Future of Emily*, 1984); *Laputa;* (1986); *Maneuvers* (1988). Outside of Germany itself, the work of three other filmmakers garnered international acclaim for *das neue Kino* during the seventies. They are Rainer Werner Fassbinder, Werner Herzog, and Wim Wenders.

Rainer Werner Fassbinder

Rainer Werner Fassbinder (1946–82) was extremely well known and very prolific, having completed forty-seven features between 1969 and 1982. Previously an actor, a playwright, and a theater director, he became the undisputed leader of the New German Cinema. Fassbinder began shooting low-budget features while he was still directing experimental theater in Munich, using a stock company of actors and technicians who stayed with him through his later work. Many of these early films were based on scenarios improvised by Fassbinder and concerned with the untreated malaise beneath the affluent surface of contemporary West German society. His film *Katzelmacher* (1969)—the term is Bavarian slang for a foreigner from the south who is possessed of great sexual potency—is about a Greek *Gastarbeiter*, or immigrant worker (played by Fassbinder), who is lynched by a group of young toughs because he is so attractive to their girls. *Warum läuft Herr R. amok?* (*Why Does Herr R. Run Amok?*, 1969) concerns a successful technical designer who one day murders his wife, their child, and a friend, and later commits suicide at his office by hanging himself over an open toilet. In *Der amerikanische Soldat* (*The American Soldier*, 1970), an extended *hommage* to the American gangster film, a young German who has just returned to Munich from service with the American Special Forces in Vietnam is hired by three cops to commit a series of murders; all of the principals, of course, have been killed by the end of the film.

18.33 *Warum läuft Herr R. amok?* (Rainer Werner Fassbinder, 1969): Kurt Raab.

If the plots of these films sound melodramatic, it is because Fassbinder intended them to be. He had a high regard for melodrama as a popular form, as evinced by his admiration for the films of Douglas Sirk (b. Detlef Sierck, 1900), the German émigré director who settled in Hollywood during the Nazi years and became master of the widescreen melodrama in the fifties (*Magnificent Obsession*, 1954; *All That Heaven Allows*, 1956; *Written on the Wind*, 1957; *Interlude*, 1957; *The Tarnished Angels*, 1958; *Imitation of Life*, 1959). Most of Fassbinder's films are about people who don't "make it," who have somehow failed to reap the material benefits of the German "economic miracle." For depicting the condition of these people, he saw melodrama as a form of heightened realism. He wrote: "I don't find melodrama 'unrealistic'; everyone has the desire to dramatize the things that go on around him . . . everyone has a mass of small anxieties that he tries to get around in order to avoid questioning himself; melodrama comes up hard against them. . . . The only reality that matters is in the viewer's head." Melodrama, in other words, is about real life. From this perspective, bourgeois culture despises melodrama because it has developed much more repressive forms of communication (for example, the high-culture forms of classical music and art, literature, and history) whose aim is to conceal process and function, and therefore to keep the bourgeoisie unaware of itself as a class in relationship to other classes. So it was as a Marxist that Fassbinder chose melodrama as his particular form, but it was as a humanist that he chose Marxism, and this is finally what he admired in Sirk: "Sirk has made the tenderest films I know; they are films of someone who loves people and doesn't despise them as we do."

The most obvious stylistic influence on Fassbinder's early films (some of which were shot in less than ten days) was Godard, but with *Der Händler der vier Jahreszeiten* (*The Merchant of Four Seasons*, 1971) he began to develop a style of his own. The melodrama, however—stripped bare of theatrics, mock-heroics, and sentimentality, but nearly always photographed in garish color—remained a constant in his work. In *Der*

18.34   Fassbinder's *Der Händler der vier Jahreszeiten* (1971): Irm Hermann, Hans Hirschmüller, Klaus Löwitsch.

18.35   *Die bitteren Tränen der Petra von Kant* (R. W. Fassbinder, 1972): Margit Carstensen, Hanna Schygulla.

Händler, which was extremely popular with German audiences, a failed engineer enters a loveless marriage and becomes a fruit vendor. Bullied by his wife and betrayed by his friends, he grows terminally depressed and finally drinks himself to death in a bar. In *Die bitteren Tränen der Petra von Kant* (*The Bitter Tears of Petra von Kant,* 1972), the title character has an affair with a younger woman who constantly betrays her and drives her to a nervous breakdown. *Wildwechsel* (*Wild Home,* 1972) deals with a sexual liaison between a fourteen-year-old girl and a nineteen-year-old boy. The boy is sent to prison for seducing a minor, and on his release the couple murders the girl's father. *Angst essen Seele auf* (*Fear Eats the Soul / Ali.* 1973), which won the International Critics' Prize at Cannes in 1974, is about the prejudice encountered by a widowed Munich charwoman when she marries a Moroccan immigrant worker some twenty years her junior. *Fontane Effi Briest* (*Effi Briest,* 1974), Fassbinder's least characteristic film, is an adaptation of a late-nineteenth-century novel by Theodor Fontane about a young middle-class woman destroyed by rigid social conventions because she is believed to have committed adultery. The film was shot in austere black and white, and Fassbinder used devices such as fades to white,* titles, and voice-over narration to replicate the narrative strategies of nineteenth-century fiction.

In *Faustrecht der Freiheit* (*Fist-Right of Freedom / Fox and His Friends,* 1975) a young working-class homosexual (Fassbinder) wins half a million Deutschmarks in the national lottery and is taken up by a group of corrupt bourgeois homosexuals who spend all of his money and abandon him, after which he takes an overdose of tranquilizers and dies on the floor of an ultramodern Frankfurt subway station. In *Mutter Küsters Fahrt zum Himmel* (*Mother Küster's Trip to Heaven,* 1975), the working-class husband of a sweet little old lady goes berserk at his factory, killing himself and his foreman. The widowed Mother Küster suddenly finds herself the center of attention, as her husband's former employers, the popular press, her careerist daughter, and assorted political groups attempt to use the scandal for their own ends. Ultimately, like so many of Fassbinder's protagonists, she is used shamelessly and abandoned. *Angst vor der Angst* (*Fear of Fear,* 1975) is a study of a happily married middle-class housewife who has a psychotic breakdown; the film, as Vincent Canby pointed out, dramatizes one possible end of capitalism, "when everything becomes

18.36 *Angst essen Seele auf* (R. W. Fassbinder, 1973): Brigitte Mira, El Hedi Ben Salem.

18.37 *Fontane Effi Briest* (R. W. Fassbinder, 1974): Hanna Schygulla.

---

* Of these unusual fades to white instead of black, Fassbinder has commented: "According to [Siegfried] Kracauer [in *Theory of Film*], when it gets black, the audience begins to fantasize, to dream, and I wanted to make them awake. It should not function like most films through the subconscious, but through the conscious. It's . . . the first time that I know of where the audience is supposed to have its own fantasy, like reading a novel—the first normal fiction film. . . . It's like a novel that one reads where you can have your own dreams and fantasies at the same time. When you read a book, a novel, you imagine your own characters. That's just what I wanted to do in this film. I didn't want to have predetermined characters made for the audience; rather, the audience should continue the work. . . ." (Quoted in Paul Thomas, "Fassbinder: Poetry of the Inarticulate," *Film Quarterly* 30, 2 [Winter 1977–78]: 6.)

18.38 *Faustrecht der Freiheit* (R. W. Fassbinder, 1975): Fox (Fassbinder) and his friend.

18.39 Fassbinder's *Die Ehe der Maria Braun* (1979): Günter Lamprecht, Gisela Uhlen, Gottfried John, Anton Schirsner, Hanna Schygulla, Elisabeth Trissenaar.

perfect and, suddenly, nothing works." *Die Reise ins Licht* (*Despair*, 1978), with a scenario by the British playwright Tom Stoppard, is a brilliant adaptation of Vladimir Nabokov's ironic novel about a man who tries to murder his double. Shot in Germany on a big budget (2.5 million dollars) and with a predominantly English cast, this film marked a departure from Fassbinder's usual, more improvisational, mode of production. But he returned to that mode in *Die Ehe der Maria Braun* (*The Marriage of Maria Braun*, 1979), a rambling melodrama set in wartime and postwar Berlin which was a great commercial success in both Germany and America; *Die dritte Generation* (*The Third Generation*, 1979), a film about the relationships among a group of young terrorists; and *In einem Jahr mit 13 Monden* (*In a Year of 13 Moons*, 1979), a portrait of the hellish life of a contemporary transsexual. Fassbinder also contributed to *Deutschland im Herbst* (see p. 856) and adapted Alfred Döblin's classic novel of working-class life, *Berlin Alexanderplatz* (1929—first filmed in 1930 by Piel Jutzi), as a fourteen-part* series for German television in 1980. He completed the features *Lili Marlene* (1981), *Lola* (1981), and *Veronica Voss* (1982)—all concerned with wartime and postwar German society—before his death from a drug overdose in 1982. His last film was *Querelle* (1982), a version of Jean Genêt's dark novel of homosexuality *Querelle de Brest* (1947).

Clearly, Fassbinder's is a cinema of the underdog, the exploited, and the oppressed. It is also a cinema of great formal beauty grounded in the expressive use of color, lighting, and decor. Again, Fassbinder's comments on Sirk are instructive:

> Sirk has said: you can't make films *about* things, you can only make films *with* things, with people, with light, with flowers, with mirrors, with blood, in fact with all the fantastic things that make life worth living. Sirk has also said: a director's philosophy is his lighting and

---

* Thirteen segments, totaling thirteen and a half hours, plus a two-hour epilogue.

camera angles. . . .* Sirk's lighting is always as unnatural as possible. Shadows where there shouldn't be any make feelings plausible which one would rather have left unacknowledged. In the same way, the camera angles in *Written on the Wind* are almost always tilted, mostly from below, so that the strange things in the story happen on the screen, not just in the spectator's head. Douglas Sirk's films liberate your head.

So Fassbinder was pictorial, even painterly, but not for the sake of pictorialism, any more than he was melodramatic for the sake of creating melodrama. Of his true ends, he said this: "I don't want to create realism the way it's usually done in films. It's a collision between film and the subconscious that creates a new realism. If my films are right, then a new realism comes about in the head, which changes the social reality." Fassbinder preeminently deserved his reputation as the most exciting young director of the seventies, as well as the most prolific, and he will probably be remembered as the most original talent to appear in the international cinema since Godard.

Werner Herzog

Werner Herzog (b. Werner H. Stipetic, 1942) studied literature and theater at the University of Pittsburgh and worked briefly in American television. When he returned to Germany, Herzog became a welder in order to finance his own short documentaries, of which he made four before shooting his first feature in 1967. Produced by the Kuratorium, this was *Lebenszeichen* (*Signs of Life*), the allegorical tale of a young German soldier on a Greek island during World War II who stages a one-man rebellion against the army. But it was the bizarre *Auch Zwerge haben klein angefangen* (*Even Dwarfs Started Small,* 1970), shot on location in the Canary Islands, that first brought Herzog to international attention. The film is a black, Buñuelesque fantasy, played entirely by dwarfs and midgets, about an abortive revolt staged by the inmates of a correctional institution. Its grotesque vision of human futility was matched by *Land des Schweigens und der Dunkelheit* (*Land of Silence and Darkness,* 1971), a feature-length documentary about a deaf and blind woman who attempts to liberate others similarly handicapped. Both films speak to the flawed nature of humanity itself rather than to the insufficiency of particular social institutions, and they emphasize the metaphysical, even mystical, nature of Herzog's central artistic concerns. To film *Fata Morgana* (1970), Herzog went to the Sahara Desert for what can only be described as a transcendental documentary about disintegration and alienation. The nearly hallucinatory camera style of this film, with its 360-degree pans and seemingly interminable tracking shots, is accompanied by sacred texts from Guatemalan Indian creation myths of the sixteenth century. It has no narrative line but proceeds on a poetic, visionary level to create from the material surfaces of reality images of total wreckage and decay. As Amos Vogel writes, the result is "an interior travelogue; an obsessive,

18.40 *Auch Zwerge haben klein ange-fangen* (Werner Herzog, 1970).

18.41 *Fata morgana* (Werner Herzog, 1970): images of cosmic desolation.

* Compare Godard's "The dolly shot is a moral statement."

18.42 Herzog's *Aguirre, der Zorn Gottes* (1972): Klaus Kinski, Cecilia Rivera.

18.43 *Jeder für sich und Gott gegen alle* (Werner Herzog, 1974): Bruno S.

hypnotic, and iconoclastic 'comment' on technology, sentimentality, and stupidity, filled with everyday objects that reveal their frightening secrets."

Aguirre, der Zorn Gottes (*Aguirre, the Wrath of God*, 1972), Herzog's most powerful film to date, was shot on location in the jungles of Brazil and Peru and was based on an actual historical incident of the sixteenth century. It concerns a detachment of Spanish conquistadors in search of El Dorado in the steaming rain forests of the Andes. The quest is suicidal from beginning to end, since the Spaniards insist on dragging the clumsy accoutrements of modern civilization into the tangled wilderness with them. The film opens with the very image of futility, as about fifty conquistadors in heavy battle dress attempt to maneuver a huge cannon down a plunging forest hillside to the river valley below. What we witness in this sequence is a concrete visualization of the characteristic that dooms all "civilized" peoples: their inability to surrender their dependence on technology in situations that render technology utterly useless.* But the folly of the Spaniards is protracted by Aguirre, a fanatical officer strikingly portrayed by Klaus Kinski, who usurps the crown of King Philip II, declaring himself to be "the Wrath of God," and drives the group ever deeper into the jungle in his mad obsession to establish a new order of civilization at El Dorado. As the quest ensues, it becomes increasingly pathological and ruthless, until it ends in the destruction of everyone but Aguirre himself, who in the final frames stands among the dead, on a drifting raft, shouting orders to the monkeys in the trees that line the river. The film, shot like most of Herzog's subsequent work by Thomas Mauch in splendidly evocative color, is a brilliant study of idealism turned to barbarism through zealotry, and the Nazi past clearly stands behind it. But so, too, does the European conquest of Africa in the late nineteenth century,† the American experience in Vietnam, and all other historical tragedies in which high-minded aspirations have ended in a welter of murder, madness, and despair.

Herzog's next film, *Jeder für sich und Gott gegen alle* (*Every Man for Himself and God Against All* / *The Mystery of Kaspar Hauser*, 1974), is an equally bizarre allegory of the human condition: as the prologue announces, it was based upon an actual event and treats "the sole known case in human history in which a man was born as an adult." In 1828, a young man who has been locked in a cellar since birth, without access to memory or speech, suddenly appears in a small German town, where he is at first treated as a freak and then gradually taught to live by the systems of rational men. His acquisition of language, logic, religion, and natural philosophy plunges him into despair, and he is finally murdered

---

* Western cultural historians used to point to the fact that the Peruvian Incas had not invented the wheel as proof that their civilization was not a highly advanced one. But it was subsequently observed that the technology of the wheel would have been completely inappropriate to the mountainous terrain of the Andes.

† As elaborated, say, in Joseph Conrad's novel *Heart of Darkness* (1898), to which *Aguirre* has been aptly compared (Aguirre = Kurtz, the Amazon = the Congo, etc.). Compare *Apocalypse Now* (Francis Ford Coppola, 1979).

by the man who had initially redeemed him from his brutish state. Reminiscent of Truffaut's *L'Enfant sauvage* (1969) in terms of theme and plot, *Kaspar Hauser* is considerably darker in its vision of the relationship between civilization and its discontents. Herzog employs a variety of unpredictable camera angles, awkward framing devices, and unusual lighting effects to transfer Kaspar's experience of perceptual disorientation to the audience. But Herzog achieves the film's most spectral and estranging effect by casting a former schizophrenic brought up in various institutions, the pseudonymous "Bruno S.," in the title role. The disaffected but strangely endearing Bruno S. also has the title role in Herzog's *Stroszek* (1977), a balladic tale of three oddly assorted losers—two street musicians and a prostitute—who become friends and set out from contemporary Berlin to find the Promised Land in the backwoods of northern Wisconsin; of course, what they discover there is something altogether different. But for all its bitter irony, the film is full of a spontaneous and sympathetic humor which, Herzog seems to suggest, may be our only conceivable means of survival.

18.44 Herzog's *Stroszek* (1977): Bruno S., Eva Mattes.

Herz aus Glas (*Heart of Glass*, 1977) is simultaneously Herzog's most beautiful and most enigmatic film. Shot in 1976 in Wyoming, Alaska, Utah, Bavaria, Switzerland, and the Skellig Islands off the coast of Ireland, it concerns (apparently) a small medieval village whose entire economy is based upon the production of a certain "ruby glass" by its glassworks. The secret of producing this strange crystal dies with an aged glassblower, and for the rest of the film every inhabitant of the town constructs and acts out fantastic hypotheses about the missing formula. A young man who is to inherit the glassworks becomes obsessed with the notion that the secret ingredient is blood, and he murders a young girl to obtain it. In the apocalypse that follows, he burns the factory to the ground, destroying all hope for the village and plunging its inhabitants into collective madness. If *Herz aus Glas* resists any concrete allegorical interpretation, it is because the film seems to be about the nature of mystery itself, in the same way that *Aguirre* is about the nature of idealism (and, possi-

18.45 Herzog's *Herz aus Glas* (1977): the glassworks owner's valet (Clemens Scheitz) foretells doom.

18.46 *Woyzeck* (Werner Herzog, 1979): Klaus Kinski, Willy Semmelrogge.

bly, of power). More than in other Herzog films, in *Herz aus Glas* the interpenetration of fantasy and reality is so thorough that we find it difficult to distinguish the two realms—perhaps because the people of the age he recreates did not themselves make that distinction. It is in fact this magical view of reality, so alien to the contemporary world, to which Herzog would recall us. He attempted to evoke it for *Herz aus Glas* by hypnotizing its cast every day in advance of shooting. "It was a stylistic effort," he has said. "I wanted this air of the floating, fluid movements, the rigidity of a culture caught in decline and superstition, the atmosphere of prophecy. . . . My heart is very close to the Middle Ages." Herzog's *Nosferatu* (1979), a U.S.-French-West German coproduction backed by 20th Century–Fox, is a studied remake of Murnau's 1922 classic (see Chapter 4) which uses exquisite European locations and rings some interesting changes on the vampire theme. But neither it nor the more modestly produced version of Georg Büchner's 1850 play *Woyzeck* (1979) enjoyed the critical esteem accorded Herzog's earlier films.

With *Fitzcarraldo* (1982), Herzog returned (literally) to the terrain of *Aguirre* in the fact-based tale of a Peruvian rubber baron, played by Kinski, who attempts in about 1894 to build an opera house in the Amazonian jungle—a project that involves the portage of a 320-ton riverboat across a mountainous, mile-wide isthmus by 500 Indians. The difficulties that plagued this film in production (including charges by human rights groups that Herzog had enslaved his Indian extras!) were legion and became the subject of Les Blank's fascinating documentary *Burden of Dreams* (1982). More recently, *Wo die grünen Ameisen traumen* (*Where the Green Ants Dream,* 1984), shot on location in Australia, pits aboriginals against a conglomerate that intends to violate one of their sacred places to mine uranium. *Cobre verde* (*Slave Coast,* 1988) casts Kinski once again as a European afflicted with tropical madness in an account of the legendary nineteenth-century Brazilian slave trader Francisco Manoel da Silva.

In addition to his major features, Herzog has made two extraordinary documentary shorts: *Die grosse Ekstase des Bildschnitzers Steiner* (*The Great Ecstasy of the Wood-Sculptor Steiner,* 1975), about a man so

18.47 Herzog's *Fitzcarraldo* (1982): Klaus Kinski.

obsessed with ski-jumping* that he constantly risks his life to break records, and *La Soufrière* (1977), a thirty-minute record of what happened on Guadeloupe in 1976 when the prediction of a dire volcanic eruption caused the mass evacuation of the Caribbean island's entire population of seventy-five thousand, except for a single old peasant who refused to leave, though he was warned of certain death. Despite absolute confirmation by a team of international scientists and meteorologists, the eruption failed to materialize, and *La Soufrière* ends with Herzog peering into the depths of the smoking volcanic crater and commenting, "This, then, is a report about an inescapable catastrophe that did not take place." *La Soufrière,* at least as much as *Aguirre* and *Herz aus Glas,* epitomizes Herzog's metaphysical vision of reality. As Amos Vogel has so acutely written,

> To reveal a metaphysical element in life or art without becoming a reactionary is one of the challenges of the day: and Herzog, compulsively, and whenever possible, rubs salt into this particular, festering wound. . . . He examines the Holy Fool . . . the person considered a fool because outsider and eccentric, the one who dares more than any human should, and who is therefore—and this is why Herzog is fascinated by him—closer to possible sources of deeper truth though not necessarily capable of reaching them.

Our twentieth-century technology and rationalism have become an infallible religion to us, Herzog warns us, no less than sixteenth-century technology and rationalism were an infallible religion to the conquistadors in Peru. And he suggests that we, no less than Aguirre, are engaged in a self-destructive process of dragging heavy artillery into jungles where there is no one to bombard but ourselves and the monkeys. As Herzog himself remarked:

> We are surrounded by worn-out images, and we deserve new ones. Perhaps I seek certain utopian things, space for human honor and respect, landscapes not yet offended, planets that do not exist yet, dreamed landscapes. Very few people seek these images today which correspond to the time we live, pictures that can make you understand yourself, your position today, our status of civilization. I am one of the ones who try to find those images.

As if to confirm his facility for new ways of seeing, Herzog's most recent documentary is the forty-five-minute *Ballad von kleinen Soldaten* (*Ballad of the Little Soldiers,* co-directed with Denis Reichle, 1984), which views the resettlement of the Miskito Indians by the Sandinista government of Nicaragua in such a way that he has been accused of being both procommunist and "an opportunistic lackey for the CIA."

Wim Wenders

Wim Wenders (b. 1945) is the newest director of *das neue Kino* to achieve an international reputation, largely on the basis of his 1976 film

---

* As Herzog himself is obsessed—his favorite photograph of himself shows him upside down in midair, in the midst of a jump.

Im Lauf der Zeit (see below), which won the International Critics' Prize at Cannes in the year of its release. While studying at the Munich Film School from 1962 to 1970, Wenders worked as a critic for cinema journals and newspapers. In 1971, after making several experimental shorts, he completed his first feature, a version of Peter Handke's novel *Die Angst des Tormanns beim Elfmeter* (*The Goalie's Anxiety at the Penalty Kick*), from a script which he had written with Handke. Ostensibly a murder mystery, *Die Angst des Tormanns* is in fact a film of psychological disintegration in which a soccer goalie goes quietly mad from the fragmentation and discontinuity of his existence. Through Ozu-like camera placement and a variety of unusual subjective shots, Wenders attempts to induce in the viewer a state of anxiety similar to that experienced by the goalie. After a liberal adaptation of Hawthorne's *The Scarlet Letter* in 1972, Wenders made *Alice in den Städten* (*Alice in the Cities,* 1974), another film of existential questing. In it, a down-and-out young journalist and an abandoned nine-year-old girl meet in New York City and begin a search for the girl's European relatives which takes them across West Germany. The search becomes a symbol of futility and dislocation, since the only clue to the whereabouts of Alice's relatives is a random, unmarked snapshot of her grandmother's house.

18.48 *Im Lauf der Zeit* (Wim Wenders, 1976): Hanns Zischler, Rudiger Vogler.

Covino has described Wenders' major theme as "a worldwide homesickness," the anxiety-ridden sense of psychological and geographical dislocation induced by living in the modern world. Wenders' next film, *Im Lauf der Zeit* (*In the Course of Time / As Time Goes By;* English title: *Kings of the Road,* 1976), provides his most brilliant exposition of this theme. It is a story of two men in their thirties who meet by accident on the road and begin an aimless journey across the desolate plains of northern Germany. Bruno lives in his van and survives by driving from one country town to another repairing broken movie projectors. Robert is a psycholinguist from Geneva whose wife has recently left him; he meets Bruno in the course of an absurd attempt to commit suicide by driving his Volkswagen into a shallow river. The two men tacitly agree to travel together, and the rest of the film chronicles their movement through the stark wastelands of the East-West border regions. Strikingly photographed in crisp black and white by Wenders' cinematographer, Robbie Müller, *Im Lauf der Zeit* is nearly three hours long (176 minutes), but the film is so carefully and uniquely composed that we barely notice the passage of time (which, as the original title announces, is what the film is really about). Nothing much happens to Bruno and Robert in the course of time, and very little is communicated between them, but Wenders has a genius for creating cinematic metaphors for the contemporary malaise afflicting the two men. Extremely long takes and slow traveling shots, unusual camera angles and framing devices, and, above all, the manipulation of off-screen space generate in the viewer a sense of perceptual dislocation corresponding to the spiritual disorientation of Bruno and Robert. In this sense, *Im Lauf der Zeit,* like other Wenders films, is extremely self-contained: it can be said to describe itself by calling into question conventional modes of film structure.

After *Falsche Bewegung* (*Wrong Move,* 1976), another film about rootlessness from a script by Handke, Wenders made his first (relatively) big-budget production,* a version of Patricia Highsmith's novel *Ripley's Game,* entitled *Der amerikanische Freund* (*The American Friend;* original title: *Regel ohne Ausnahme* [*Rule Without Exception*], 1977), which continued the theme of dislocation in the form of an international thriller. In 1980, Wenders collaborated with the late American director Nicholas Ray to produce *Lightning Over Water / Nick's Movie,* a sensitive film about Ray's attempt to continue his work while dying of cancer. The following year Wenders went to work on *Hammett* (1982), based on mystery writer Dashiel Hammett's early days in San Francisco, for the American producer Francis Ford Coppolla. Amid numerous delays in the scripting and shooting of this film, Wenders independently directed *Der Stand des Dinge* (*The State of Things,* 1982), a low-budget black-and-white feature on the difficulties of making an independent film. In contrast to *Hammett,* which was not particularly successful at interpreting the American experience, *Paris, Texas* (1984) is a brilliant American odyssey of self-recognition based on Sam Shepard's "Motel Chronicles" short stories, which confirmed Robbie Müller as one of the world's best cinematographers. After the ruminative *Tokyo-Ga* (1985), a self-described "filmed diary" of his search for the vanished Tokyo inscribed in the films of Yasujiro Ozu (1903–63), Herzog returned to Germany and produced a magical masterpiece in *Der Himmel über Berlin* (*The Sky over Berlin / Wings of Desire,* 1987), a film written in collaboration with Handke about angels watching over the people of Berlin, in the tradition of *Here Comes Mr. Jordan* (Alexander Hall, 1941), *It's a Wonderful Life* (Frank Capra, 1946), and *Heaven Can Wait* (Warren Beatty, 1978).

18.49 Wenders' *Die amerikanische Freund* (1977): Dennis Hopper.

18.50 *Paris, Texas* (Wim Wenders, 1984): Harry Dean Stanton.

Unlike many of his associates in the Filmverlag, Wenders is not openly political. Yet he has said that "film language is always political: it is either exploitation or it isn't exploitation . . . not only the story that is told, but the way it is told." In this regard, Wenders claims as his masters Yasujiro Ozu and the American action director Anthony Mann, both of whom had a brilliant facility for the creation of spatial metaphors. Clearly, Wenders has a similar gift, but there is something in the austerity of his vision which is reminiscent of Bresson and Dreyer. Like his frequent collaborator Peter Handke (now a director in his own right: *Die linkshandige Frau* [*The Left-Handed Woman,* 1978]; *Das Mal des Todes* [*The Malady of Death,* 1985]), Wenders seems to have a clear vision of the modern world's spiritual confusion and a tremendous talent for translating that confusion into the terms of his art.

Hans Jürgen Syberberg and Others

A fourth director of international stature, one associated with *das neue Kino* but not of it, is Hans Jürgen Syberberg (b. 1935). Originally from what is now East Germany, he escaped to the West when he was seven-

---

* 1.2 million dollars, or more than his first six films put together.

18.51 *Hitler: ein Film aus Deutschland* (Hans Jürgen Syberberg, 1977).

teen, ultimately studying theater at the University of Munich. After working for several years as a director for Bavarian television, he began making low-budget features in the late sixties and spent much of the seventies producing his "German trilogy" of fictionalized documentaries on the irrational in Teutonic history and myth. *Ludwig: Requiem fur einen jungfräulichen König* (*Ludwig: Requiem for a Virgin King*, 1972), shot in eleven days on a minuscule budget, constructs a Brechtian tour through the psyche of Ludwig II, the "mad" king of Bavaria who was Richard Wagner's patron and the primary architect, in a literal sense, of Germany's nineteenth-century romantic mythology. *Karl May* (1974) focuses on a crucial period in the life of its title character (1842–1912), an immensely popular writer of exotic / utopian fiction, most often adventure novels set on an imaginary American frontier. May's works were, astonishingly, favorites of Hitler's and also Einstein's. The last film in the trilogy was preceded by *Winifred Wagner und die geschichte des hauses wahnfried von 1914–1975* (*The Confessions of Winifred Wagner*, 1975), a five-hour interview with Wagner's English-born daughter-in-law, who became the director of the Bayreuth Festival and a close friend of Hitler's during the Nazi years. The culmination of these works was *Hitler: Ein Film aus Deutschland* (*Hitler: A Film from Germany*, 1977; distributed in the United States as *Our Hitler*), shot in twenty days after four years of planning on a budget of 500,000 dollars. This seven-hour film is a complex, multifaceted attempt to answer the central, agonizing question posed by the trilogy and by twentieth-century German history: "Why Hitler?" The answer is that Hitler became "the greatest filmmaker of all time," staging National Socialism, World War II, and the Holocaust; engaging the irrationalism of the German people; and finally fulfilling the promise of Ludwig, Wagner, and May to make Germany part of a grand, all-consuming myth. Syberberg continued his extraordinary critique of Germanic *angst* in a four-hour-and-fifteen-minute adaptation of Wagner's last opera *Parsifal* (1982), and *Die Nacht* (*The Night*, 1985), a six-hour pastiche of music from Bach and Wagner and text from the great nineteenth-century German poets described by the director as "the swansong of Europe."

During the late seventies and eighties a number of directors emerged from *das neue Kino* whose work has had less cumulative effect than that of Syberberg and his contemporaries but has nonetheless received international attention. In concert with his prison film *Die Verrohung des Franz Blum* (*The Brutalization of Franz Blum*, 1975) and its sequel, *Endstation Freiheit* (*Last Stop Freedom*, 1981), Reinhard Hauff (b. 1939) has been remarkably consistent in such features as the *Kasper Hauser*-like *Messer im Kopf* (*Knife in the Head*, 1978); *Der Mann auf der mauer* (*The Man on the Wall*, 1982), a metaphorical tale of a man who leaps across the East-West border blockade; his documentary portrait of Indian director Mrinal Sen, *10 Tage in Calcutta* (*10 Days in Calcutta*, 1984); *Stammheim* (1986), an extraordinary account of the trial of the Baader-Meinhof gang in the Stuttgart-Stammheim prison; and the witty musical *Linie 1* (*Line 1*, 1988). Niklaus Schilling (b. 1944), functioning as his own writer, designer, and cameraman (e.g., *Rheingold*, 1978), is an *auteur* in the complete sense of the term. He specializes in "border films" like *Der Willi-Busch Report* (*The Willy Busch Report*, 1979) and *Der Western Leuchtet!* (*Lite Trap*, 1982), and experimental works mixing film and video—e.g., *Zeichen und Wunder* (*Signs and Wonders*, 1982), *Die Frau ohne Korper und der Projektionist* (*The Woman without a Body and the Projectionist*, 1984), and *Dormire* (1985). The documentarylike features of Peter Lilienthal (b. 1929) often have a political theme, as in *Es herrscht Ruhe im Land* (*The Country Is Calm*, 1975), which evokes the Pinochet dictatorship in Chile; *David* (1978), about a young Jew struggling to survive in Nazi Germany; *Der Aufstand* (*The Insurrection*, 1980), filmed on location during the overthrow of the Somoza government in Nicaragua; *Dear Mr. Wonderful* (1982), shot on location in working-class neighborhoods in New York; *Das Autogram* (*The Autograph*, 1984), set in post–World War II Argentina; and *Das Schweigen des Dichters* (*The Silence of the Poets*, 1986), shot on location in Israel. More clearly in the art-film tradition is the work of Hans W. Geissendörfer (b. 1941), who has mounted impressive literary adaptations of Ibsen (*The Wild Duck*, 1977) and Thomas Mann (*Der Zauberberg* [*The Magic Mountain*, 1982]), as well as of such Patricia Highsmith thrillers as *Die glaserne Zelle* (*The Glass Cell*, 1977) and *Edith's Tagebuch* (*Edith's Diary*, 1983). Edgar Reitz (b. 1932), whose earlier work includes the television films *Stunde null* (*Zero Hour*, 1977) and *Der Schneider von Ulm* (*The Tailor from Ulm*, 1979), became world famous through a single remarkable work, the sixteen-hour *Heimat* (*Homeland*, 1984), which recounts the history of twentieth-century Germany as reflected in the lives of three families from the Rhineland village of Hunsruck; it took him over five years to complete and has been called "the fulfillment of all the hopes of the New German cinema over the past two decades," as well as a milestone in contemporary film history.*

The remarkably eclectic Werner Shroeter (b. 1945) moves with ease between the experimental underground—*Die Generalprobe* (*Dress Rehearsal*, 1981); *Tag der Idioten* (*Day of the Idiots*, 1982); *Der lachende Stern* (*The Laughing Star*, 1984); *De l'Argentine* (*About Argentina*, 1986); the historical epic—*Il regno di Napoli* (*The Kingdom of Naples*, 1978); contemporary social commentary—*Palermo oder Wolfsberg* (1980; winner of the Golden Bear at Berlin); and the art film—*Liebeskonzil* (*Council of Love*, 1982); *Der Rosenkönig* (*The Rose King*, 1986). The Bavarian humorist Herbert Achternbusch (b. 1938) makes dialogue-laden low-budget comedies in the tradition of the Marx brothers and W. C. Fields at the rate of about two a year, and he has acquired a committed following through such features as *Der Comanche* (*The Comanche*, 1979); *Der neger Erwin* (*Black Erwin*, 1981—a send-up of the film subsidy system that produced it); *Der Depp* (*The Blockhead*, 1982); *Die Olympiasiergerin* (*The Woman Olympic Winner*, 1984); *Blaue Blumen* (*Blue Flower*, 1985); and *Healt Hitler!* (*Heal Hitler!*, 1986). Like

---

* *Variety*, September 8, 1984, p. 14.

the comedies of the more visually inclined Walter Bockmayer (b. 1948) and Rolf Buermann—*Flammende Herzen* (*Flaming Hearts,* 1978), *Looping* (1981), *Salzstangen-Gefluester* (*Pretzel Whispers,* 1982), *Kiez* (*Hell's Kitchen,* 1983), and *Geierwally* (1988)—Achternbusch's are often shot in Super-8mm and blown up for exhibition to 16mm or 35mm. Far more sophisticated intellectually and cinematically are the films of Robert van Ackeren (b. 1946), whose rigorously stylized portraits of middle-class behavior often reveal a decadent underside combining sexual perversity and emotional paralysis. Such, at least, is the force of his best work— *Belcanto* (1977), an adaptation of Heinrich Mann's last Hollywood-written novel; *Die Reinheit des Herzens* (*Purity of Heart,* 1980), *Deutschland: Privat* (*Germany: Private,* 1981); *Die flambierte Frau* (*A Woman in Flames,* 1983, see below); and *Die Venusfalle* (*The Venus Trap,* 1988)— all produced with expertise and great formal precision. Sometimes associated with van Ackeren because of the latter's perverse sexual themes, but much less focused aesthetically, are members of the so-called "Berlin Underground," especially Rosa von Praunheim (b. Holgar Mischwitzky, 1942)—*Armee der Liebenden oder Aufstand der Perversen* (*Army of Lovers, or Revolt of the Perverts,* 1979); *Unsere Liechen Leben noch* (*Our Bodies Are Still Alive,* 1981); *Rote Liebe* (*Red Love,* 1982); *Stadt der verlorenen Seelen* (*City of Lost Souls,* 1983); *Horror Vacui* (1984); *Ein Virus kennt keine Moral* (*A Virus Knows No Morals,* 1986); *Anita— Tanze des Lasters* (*Anita—Dances of Vice,* 1984); *Dolly, Lotte, und Maria* (1988); Lothar Lambert—*Tiergarten* (*Zoo,* 1980); *Die Alptraumfrau* (*The Nightmare Lady,* 1981); *Verdammte Stadt* (*Damned City,* 1981); *Fraulein Berlin* (1983); *Paso Doble* (1983); *Die Liebeswuste* (*The Desert of Love,* 1986); *Der sexte Sinn* (*The Sixth Sense,* 1986); and Frank Ripploh—*Taxi zum Klo* (*Taxi to the Loo,* 1981) and its sequel *Taxi nach Cairo* (*Taxi to Cairo,* 1987). Such underground films are shot in 16mm on extremely low budgets and are often written, directed, photographed, and edited by an *auteur* who is also their star. As their titles imply, they usually feature protagonists who are sexual outlaws, and while some deal with serious subjects, such as AIDS, many are outrageously funny.

Jean-Marie Straub and Marxist Aesthetics

A final figure who must be mentioned as having inspired and influenced *das neue Kino*, although his own aesthetic concerns are independent of it, is the French-born Jean-Marie Straub (b. 1933). Straub, who has lived and worked in Germany since 1958, is the patron saint of minimalist cinema—cinema that involves minimal dependence on the technical conventions of the medium as a narrative form. Specifically, this means the consistent use of direct sound, natural lighting, nonnarrative editing and camera styles, and, of course, nonactors. (Straub worked as an assistant to Robert Bresson during the fifties* and was permanently

---

* During the same period, Straub also worked as an assistant to Abel Gance (*Tour de Nesle,* 1954); Jean Renoir (*French Cancan,* 1955, and *Eléna et les hommes,* 1956); Jacques Rivette (*Le Coup de berger,* 1956); and Alexander Astruc (*Une Vie,* 1958); see Chapters 9 and 13.

influenced by his austerity of technique, especially that of *Les Dames du Bois de Boulogne,* 1945.) Philosophically, Straub regards cinema as a material rather than narrative form. While narrative forms tell stories that encourage audience identification with fictitious characters and events, material forms can be said to create primary experiences for their audience rather than secondary or vicarious ones. It is the difference between being told a story about a madman or a "wild child" and being asked to participate in the experience of perceptual disorientation and disaffection which characterizes a state of madness or savagery. In a sense, it is the difference between Truffaut's *L'Enfant sauvage* (1970) and Herzog's *Kaspar Hauser* (1974), or between Dennis Hopper's *Easy Rider* (1969) and Wenders' *Im Lauf der Zeit* (1976).

In pursuing his own vision of materialist cinema, Straub has created (in collaboration with his wife, Danièle Huillet) a number of extraordinary films whose structures of light, space, and sound approach the mathematical precision of musical composition. These include *Nicht versöhnt* (*Not Reconciled,* 1965), a series of moving tableaux derived from Heinrich Böll's novel *Billiards at Half Past Nine* (1959); *Chronik der Anna Magdalena Bach* (*The Chronicle of Anna Magdalena Bach,* 1968)—a historical study whose viewpoint is that of Bach's wife; *Othon* (1970)—an intentionally static, ahistorical version of Pierre Corneille's most rigidly formalized verse tragedy; *Leçons d'histoire* (*History Lessons,* 1972), a narrative analysis of the mercantile system of ancient Rome borrowed from Brecht's novel *The Business Affairs of Mr. Julius Caesar; Moses und Aron* (1975)—a severe version of Arnold Schoenberg's modernist opera; *Fortini-Cani* (1977), the text of Franco Fortini's polemic on the Israel-Palestine conflict accompanied by contrapuntal imagery; *Klassenverhaltnisse* (*Class Relations,* 1984), an uncharacteristically faithful adaptation of Kafka's posthumous novel fragment *Amerika* (1927); and *Der Tod des Empedokles* (*The Death of Empedocles,* 1987), a self-described nonfilm based on Holderlins's 1798 verse play. As with musical composition, Straub / Huillet's films are "about" what happens to the viewer while watching them as much as they are "about" their ostensible content. That is, in their restraint these films create a vacuum that the viewer must fill with the primary experience of his or her own life, forcing introspection rather than encouraging vicarious identification with invented characters and plots.

18.52   Minimal / materialist cinema: the chorus in *Moses und Aron* (Jean-Marie Straub and Danièle Huillet, 1975).

It is this theoretical assumption that links Straub / Huillet with the young filmmakers of *das neue Kino,* although as individual artists they are more clearly members of the experimental avant-garde. Straub / Huillet and their followers take the Marxist position that perception is an ideological as well as a physiological phenomenon, or at least that perception is ideologically and culturally conditioned. Cinema is a communications medium whose basic signifying unit (the shot) is a discrete unit of perception: every shot, and every individual frame within a shot, offers a unique perceptual perspective on some event or object. But in the conventional narrative cinema of the Western capitalist countries, those perceptual perspectives have been ideologically appropriated to create fictions about life, and we, the audience, have been ideologically conditioned to expect and receive these fictions. From the Marxist perspective, fiction or narrative is defined as a bourgeois form whose purpose it is to propagate illusions about the real nature of our society and our lives within it. We must have illusions, the Marxists insist, to divert our attention from the exploitation, violence, and oppression that are the necessary by-products of our economic system; and therefore our cinema (and most of our other art forms) has traditionally been a narrative medium whose purpose is the creation of illusionist spectacle that serves the ideology of the ruling class.

What the new breed of radical filmmakers is attempting, in both Europe and the Third World, is the *deconstruction* of bourgeois perceptual ideology through a deconstruction of conventional cinematic language—language that has, since its inception and throughout its history (with notable exceptions during the periods of Soviet silent realism, Italian neorealism, and the French New Wave) been a bourgeois medium for the production of narrative pleasure. J. Dudley Andrew summarizes the Marxist position: "The Marxists call for a critical cinema which will 'deconstruct' itself at every moment. Instead of fabricating an illusion, this cinema will let the viewer see beneath the images and the story to the process of creation itself. . . . Every subject should be exposed for its socioeconomic underpinnings; every signification (every image and narrative relation) should expose its own work. This way we can strive toward the conscious reshaping of the world." In other words, the cinema's enslavement to a narrative code of vision has radically restricted its potential for the expression of new cultural realities. The vast range of ideas, feelings, perceptions, and experience that film is capable of communicating has barely been touched upon in the ninety-odd years of its history as a narrative form. But radical filmmakers like Straub / Huillet and the leaders of *das neue Kino* are now attempting to tap that potential as never before, and it is this effort—much of it successful—that lends the quality of strangeness and mystery and otherness to their films. They are groping toward a new cinematic language with which to express the formerly inexpressible, and the process demands that the audience feel, see, and think things formerly alien to the experience of film watching.

Unfortunately, this same process can anger an audience that *wants* to be diverted by illusion rather than to struggle to acquire new codes of vision and experience. And this process of audience disaffection is occurring in West Germany today, just as it occurred in France during the New Wave. With a few exceptions (such as Fassbinder's *Der Händler der vier Jahreszeiten* and Wenders' *Im Lauf der Zeit*), *das neue Kino* has not been popular with German audiences, who find the films obscure, depressing, and overly intellectual.* The largest markets are in France, Great Britain, and the United States, where many *das neue Kino* directors have won

---

* This is true for other forms as well. West Germany is currently the center of a European experimental avant-garde that extends from literature (Günter Grass, Jakov Lind, Peter Handke, Peter Weiss) to electronic rock (Brian Eno, Kraftwerk), and encompasses a broad spectrum of radical ideologies, sexual practices, and politics.

festival prizes and become fashionable cult figures among the intelligentsia. It is ironic that a cinema which aspires to create a new vision of the world cannot find a popular audience, while the illusionist spectacle it seeks to replace enjoys mass approval. In West Germany itself, the films with the biggest box-office receipts during the seventies were American superproductions like *The Godfather, Part II* (Francis Ford Coppola, 1974), *Jaws* (Steven Spielberg, 1975), and *Cross of Iron* (Sam Peckinpah, 1977—shot in Germany), which were followed in the eighties by *The Return of the Jedi* (Richard Marquand, 1983), *Ghostbusters* (Ivan Reitman, 1984), and *Out of Africa* (Sydney Pollack, 1985).* American distributors remain in control of 60 to 65 percent of the West German market, despite a continuing high level of government support for indigenous films.

Obviously, a major problem for the filmmakers of *das neue Kino* is that of distribution. While the Film Subsidies Board generously supports independent production of all sorts, the outlets for exhibition in West Germany are few because major distributors are unwilling to risk their capital on potentially unpopular films. A situation now exists in which the films of the New German cinema have grown too elaborate and too numerous for the exhibition outlets available to them, and many observers believe that this will ultimately sink the movement entirely. During the seventies, some *neue Kino* directors began to make films for large production companies in order to achieve blanket distribution. Fassbinder shot the 2.5-million-dollar international coproduction *Despair* (1978) for Bavaria Film; Herzog's *Nosferatu* (1979) was underwritten by Fox; Wenders' *Hammett* (1982) was finally produced for several million dollars after four years of fits and starts. During the eighties, budgets of 3 million dollars and more were not uncommon for period pieces like Herzog's *Fitzcarraldo* (1982) and Schlöndorff's *Un Amor de Swann* (1984); Geissendörfer's *Der Zauberberg* (1982) cost 10 million dollars; and coproduction with the ZDF television network and with other countries became routine. It may be that, like the French New Wave, the New German Cinema is doomed to expire from its own aesthetic success. At the height of the New Wave, almost anyone with the will to do so could find money to produce a low-budget film; state subsidies guarantee the same for *das neue Kino* today. As was formerly the case in France, so many films are being produced by aspiring new talents in West Germany

---

* Wolfgang Petersen (b. 1941), whose early films *Die Konsequenz* (*The Consequence*, 1977) and *Schwarz und weiss wie Tage und Nächte* (*Black and White Like Day and Night*, 1978) were associated with *das neue Kino*, produced West Germany's two domestic box-office hits of the eighties in *Das Boot* (*The Boat*, 1981) and *Die unendliche Geschichte* (*The Never-Ending Story*, 1984)—respectively, a World War II combat film set in a submarine and a fantastic children's adventure film. Petersen was subsequently successful with the American-produced science fiction film *Enemy Mine* (1985). Other domestic features that did well locally in the eighties were Ulrich Edel's *Problemfilm* ("problem film") *Christiane F.—Wir Kinder vom Bahnhof Zoo* (*Christiane F.—We Children of the Bahnhof Zoo*, 1981), focusing on heroin addiction among affluent Berlin teenagers, and Robert van Ackeren's *Die flambierte Frau* (*A Woman in Flames*, 1983), a coldly elegant account of a Berlin prostitute who caters to the sexual underground.

18.53 Joris Ivens' *Spanish Earth* (1937).

18.55 *Soldaat van Oranje* (Paul Verhoven): Rutger Hauer.

18.54 *Paranoia* (Adriaan Ditvoorst, 1967).

today that exhibition outlets are not sufficient to return the modest profits necessary to keep the movement going. As Jan Dawson remarked, "The New German Cinema is, for the seventies [and eighties], what the *nouvelle vague* was for the sixties: a questioning of received values, an intoxicating burst of energy, a love affair with the cinema, and a love-hate relationship with Hollywood." Whether that kind of relationship can avoid the fate of the New Wave is really a moot point; that *das neue Kino* has flourished for nearly two decades will be enough to change the form of film language for some time to come.

HOLLYWOOD, 1965–1970

In the sixties, for the first time in its history, Hollywood fell behind the rest of the world—aesthetically, commercially, and even technologically (the latter because of the conservatism of its unions). Its decline resulted from the American industry's obstinate refusal to face a single fact: that the composition of the weekly American film audience was changing as rapidly as the culture itself. Between the mid-fifties and the mid-sixties, that audience shifted from a predominantly middle-aged, modestly educated, middle- to lower-class group to a younger, better educated, more affluent, and predominantly middle-class group. The new audience in America, as all over the world, was formed by the postwar generation's coming of age. It was smaller than the previous audience, and its values were different. By the early sixties, the old audience had begun to stay home and watch television, venturing out occasionally for some spectacular family entertainment but generally staying away from movie theaters. As the size of audiences decreased, admission prices rose well above the rate of general inflation,* which had the effect of further decreasing

---

* Between 1956 and 1972, when the general cost of living in the United States rose 53.9 percent, theater admission prices rose 160 percent.

the demand for the traditional Hollywood product. Yet the industry continued to make films according to the stylistic conventions of the forties and fifties, as if its old constituency still existed, when only vestiges of it did.

The principal change in filmmaking during this period was the cost of production, which by 1966 averaged 3 million dollars per film due to both monetary inflation and the industry's own extravagant search for a winning box-office formula. The new audience was not interested in seeing these films any more than was the old one, because as long as American cinema simply duplicated the popular entertainment function of television on a larger scale, neither audience particularly needed it. By 1962, Hollywood's yearly box-office receipts had fallen to their lowest level in history—900 million dollars, or one-half of the immediate postwar figure. The studios were in serious financial trouble, which grew worse as they made increasingly desperate attempts to recapture the old audience with spectacular flops like 20th Century–Fox's *Cleopatra* (1963). In 1965, the unprecedented success of Fox's *The Sound of Music,* which grossed more than 135 million dollars nationwide, rekindled false hope in the spectacle formula, but a succession of stunning failures, such as 20th Century–Fox's *Star!* (1968), *Doctor Dolittle* (1970), and *Tora! Tora! Tora!* (1971), and Paramount's *Darling Lili* (1968), *The Molly Maguires* (1970), and *Paint Your Wagon* (1971), pushed the industry to the brink of catastrophe by the early seventies.

As Hollywood's financial troubles worsened throughout the sixties, several commercial forces coalesced to bring the new American audience into the theaters. For one thing, the French and Italian New Waves had demonstrated to producers all over the world that "art" films could make money—especially if they were shot rapidly on low budgets by young directors who were willing to work for less money than older, more established ones. This realization had two profound consequences for the American cinema. In the first place, there was an increased tolerance for independent production of the type being practiced in Europe by Godard, Truffaut, Antonioni, Fellini, and others. By the mid-sixties, independent producers like Roger Corman of New World Films were able to sponsor young directors like Francis Ford Coppola (b. 1939) and George Lucas (b. 1944), who were making their first features. Independent producer-directors like Stanley Kubrick (b. 1928) and Arthur Penn (b. 1922) found themselves for the first time able to control the financing of their own films and to achieve an unprecedented degree of creative freedom. In the second place, the studios, who were turning increasingly to television production to save themselves from financial ruin,* became the willing distributors of these independent productions—a thing they would never have considered several years before—because distribution provided them with a badly needed source of revenue. The studios also became large-

---

* Fifty percent of the approximately twenty-five thousand jobs in Hollywood today are in television production and distribution. At present, 90 percent of all prime-time programming is shot on film, although this situation will change as the quality of videotape improves.

scale domestic distributors of foreign films, whose circulation in the United States they had successfully managed to limit when they were powerful monopolies. By the mid-sixties, the work of Fellini, Antonioni, Bergman, and Buñuel, as well as that of French New Wave directors—which had previously been available in this country only in specialized "art houses" in major urban centers, if at all—suddenly began to appear regularly in first-run theaters all over America. By the seventies, foreign films were as readily available as American ones, not just in cities but even in many small towns.*

As the rigid structure of the studio system began to crumble, new talent entered the film industry in the late fifties and early sixties, and, between 1960 and 1966, a number of young directors from television made films. These included Irvin Kershner (b. 1923)—*The Hoodlum Priest,* 1961; *The Luck of Ginger Coffey,* 1964; *A Fine Madness,* 1966; John Frankenheimer (b. 1930)—*The Manchurian Candidate,* 1962; *The Train,* 1965; *Seconds,* 1966; Sidney Lumet (b. 1924)—*12 Angry Men,* 1957; *Long Day's Journey into Night,* 1962; *Fail-Safe,* 1964; *The Hill,* 1965; *The Pawnbroker,* 1965; *The Group,* 1966; Arthur Penn (b. 1926)—*The Miracle Worker,* 1962; *Mickey One,* 1965; *The Chase,* 1966; and Sam Peckinpah (1926–84)—*Ride the High Country,* 1962; *Major Dundee,* 1965. New cinematographers from the East Coast also entered the film industry, including Conrad Hall (b. 1926), Haskell Wexler (b. 1926), William Fraker (b. 1923), and the Hungarian émigrés Laszlo Kovacs (b. 1933) and Vilmos Zsigmond (b. 1930). As these new filmmakers, working with ever-increasing creative freedom and mobility, assimilated the French and Italian innovations, a new kind of American cinema was born for a new American audience.

This audience was composed of the first generation in history that had grown up with the visually, if not intellectually, sophisticated medium of television. Through hours of watching television as children and teenagers, its members knew the language of cinema implicitly, and when filmmakers like Frankenheimer, Lumet, Penn, and Peckinpah began to move out of the studios in the mid- to late-sixties and to employ the New Wave techniques of the French and Italian cinemas for the first time on the American screen, this young audience liked what it saw. A phenomenal increase in the number and quality of college and university film study courses simultaneously enabled many members of the new audience to *understand* what they saw as well as to enjoy it.† It is important to realize that the values of the new audience, like its life-styles, were radically

---

*The availablity of foreign films in this country has decreased in the past two decades owing to several international recessions and the constantly rising domestic costs of advertising, distribution, and dubbing.

†As the number of film studies courses continues to increase in the United States, more and more of the country's educated citizens are achieving a state of what could be called cinema or media literacy (Charles Eidsvik's useful term is "cineliteracy"—see his *Cineliteracy: Film Among the Arts* [New York: Viking, 1978]). The American Film Institute's *Guide to College Courses in Film and Television* for 1981 lists nearly eight thousand courses in film and television at over six hundred American colleges and universities. The majority of these schools offer programs leading to a degree in one subject or both.

different from those of the old. For better or worse, it had a generally permissive attitude toward such former cultural taboos as the explicit representation of sex, violence, and death. Thus, when censorship was completely abolished and replaced by a ratings system in November 1968, the content of American cinema, as well as its form, was revolutionized to permit the depiction of virtually everything under the sun, including graphic sex and violent death. That this liberalization has created some disgusting abuses is inarguable, but it was necessary before the American film could achieve full maturity of content. It is difficult, for example, to imagine a director like Robert Altman (*Nashville*, 1975; *Three Women*, 1977) working at his best in the moral climate that produced *The Sound of Music* in 1965.

The New American Cinema: The Impact of *Bonnie and Clyde*

A new American cinema and a new American film audience announced themselves emphatically with the release in 1967 of Arthur Penn's *Bonnie and Clyde*. This film, which was universally attacked by the critics when it opened in August, had by November become the most popular film of the year.* It would subsequently receive ten Academy Award nominations and win two awards (Best Cinematography: Burnett Guffey; Best Supporting Actress: Estelle Parsons), win the New York Film Critics' Award for Best Script (David Newman and Robert Benton), and be named the Best Film of 1967 by many of the critics who had originally panned it. Most triumphant of all, perhaps, *Bonnie and Clyde* is the only film ever to have forced the public retraction of a critical opinion by *Time* magazine, which dismissed the film in a summer issue and in its issue of

---

* The film was so popular at the time of its release that its protagonists became cult figures. Double-breasted suits and fedora hats of the type worn by Clyde were all the rage in men's clothing, and Bonnie's thirties hemlines temporarily banished the miniskirt from the world of women's fashion. You could even buy transparent decals with which to simulate bullet holes on the windshield of your car in imitation of a famous shot from the film.

18.56 Romantic revolutionaries: a touched-up publicity shot and an unretouched still from *Bonnie and Clyde* (Arthur Penn, 1967): Faye Dunaway, Warren Beatty.

December 8, 1967, ran a long cover story on its virtues. Indeed, the phenomenal success of *Bonnie and Clyde* caused many retractions on the part of veteran film critics who, on first viewing, had mistaken it for a conventional, if gratuitously bloody, gangster film. *Bonnie and Clyde* was in fact a sophisticated blend of comedy, violence, romance, and—symbolically, at least—politics, which borrowed freely from the techniques of the French New Wave (it was originally to have been directed by Truffaut and then Godard) and which perfectly captured the rebellious spirit of the times.

Based on the real-life career of Bonnie Parker and Clyde Barrow, the film tells the story of two young and attractive small-time criminals (Warren Beatty and Faye Dunaway) from the Midwest who during the Depression fall in love, go on a spree of robberies and killings, and become national folk heroes in the process. Their targets are not the common people but the avaricious banks and the armies of police that protect them—in other words, "the system." Bonnie and Clyde were thus prototypes of the antiestablishment heroes who have come to dominate so many American films since, and they resonated perfectly with the revolutionary tenor of the late sixties. ("They're young! They're in love! And they kill people!" the advertising copy proclaimed.) By mid-film the lovers are clearly doomed, but nothing could prepare audiences in 1967 for the apocalyptic violence of the ending, in which Bonnie and Clyde are ambushed after a romantic interlude and their bodies ripped apart by machine-gun slugs in a protracted ballet of agony and death. Penn shot this conclusion with four cameras running at different speeds and with different lenses, and intercut the footage into a complex montage sequence which gives the deaths a mythic, legendary quality: Bonnie and Clyde are not simply killed; they are destroyed. Even today the sequence has an almost unbearable intensity because our dramatic identification with the characters is so complete. In the social climate of the times, however, the new American audience identified with Bonnie and Clyde less as dramatic characters

17.39 Vulnerable revolutionaries: two botched jobs.

18.58 A new aesthetic of violence: shots from the montage sequence which concludes *Bonnie and Clyde*. By intercutting footage of the death scene from several separate cameras equipped with different lenses and running at different speeds, Penn and his collaborators created an unprecedented (though now widely imitated) effect.

than as types of romantic revolutionaries. And the tense, nervous texture of the film, with its unpredictable shifts in mood and its graphic, sensual depiction of violent death, was as revolutionary in 1967 as were its protagonists. The form of *Bonnie and Clyde* has been imitated so many times by hundreds of "criminal couple" and "road" pictures since 1967* that it is hard for contemporary audiences to comprehend the originality of the film when it was released. But in 1967 it was clearly subversive in both form and content, and the angry critical debate it caused in the United States was, in many ways, less about a pair of thirties gangsters

---

* In addition to relentlessly juvenile drive-in fare like *Dirty Mary, Crazy Larry* (Larry Hough, 1974) and *Aloha Bobby and Rose* (Floyd Mutrux, 1976), the "criminal couple" format has produced such interesting films as Sam Peckinpah's *The Getaway* (1972), Robert Altman's *Thieves Like Us* (1974), Terrence Malick's *Badlands* (1974), Steven Spielberg's *Sugarland Express* (1974), and Ted Kotcheff's *Fun with Dick and Jane* (1977). *Bonnie and Clyde* also had distinguished forebears in Fritz Lang's *You Only Live Once* (1937), Nicholas Ray's *They Live By Night* (1948), and Joseph H. Lewis' *Gun Crazy* (1950).

than about the morality of violent dissent against an oppressive social order.

2001: A Space Odyssey

Another film that caught the imagination of a generation in the late sixties was Stanley Kubrick's *2001: A Space Odyssey* (1968). Produced at a cost of 10.5 million dollars over a period of two and a half years, *2001* offered a mythic vision of the relationship between humanity and technology at a time when that relationship had crucial bearing on the future of American society and of the entire Western world. Like its Greek namesake, the film has an epic structure. In Section I, we watch a tribe of prehistoric ape-men learn how to use bones as instruments of destruction (our first technology being weaponry, preceding even language) shortly after they have encountered an enormous monolithic slab in the middle of the desert. Later, one ape-man crushes the skull of a rival with a bone and tosses the weapon jubilantly into the air, where it rotates in slow motion until an associative cut transforms it into the axis of a gigantic space station (actually a weapons platform) several million years later. In Section II, a shuttle is launched from this station carrying scientists who have discovered a similar monolith buried beneath the surface of the moon; it is emitting a radio signal in the direction of the planet Jupiter. Section III opens eighteen months later with a huge phallic spacecraft gliding toward Jupiter in empty space. Inside are a team of astronauts and a brand-new HAL 9000* talking computer, which guides the ship and controls all of its vital functions. The mission of this probe is unclear, but it is apparently to track the radio signal.

HAL, who seems more highly evolved in emotional terms than any of the humans, suffers a paranoid breakdown when he makes a miscalculation, and he sets about killing all of his human shipmates in the belief that they are botching the mission. He succeeds in terminating the life functions of three hibernating astronauts and in marooning another in deep space, but the lone human survivor destroys HAL as a thinking entity by disconnecting his memory bank, while HAL tries desperately to talk him out of it. As we witness the computer regress to its basic language programs and finally expire, we feel a disturbing sympathy for it— disturbing because we have been encouraged to feel so little for the coolly disaffected humans of this future world. Alone aboard the drifting spacecraft now, the final astronaut is drawn toward Jupiter and, abandoning ship in a pod, encounters a third monolith floating through space. Suddenly he is sucked into another dimension, where he experiences a hallucinatory trip through time and space in which all perceptual relationships are blurred. Arriving as an older man in a conventional, completely white bedroom suite furnished in Louis XVI style, the astronaut ages to decrepitude before our eyes and is reborn in the film's final frames as the lumi-

---

* "HAL" is an acronym derived from the terms for two systems of problem solving used in mathematics, computer science, and artificial intelligence—"*h*euristic" and "*al*gorithmic."

18.59 *2001: A Space Odyssey* (Stanley Kubrick, 1968): a space station transformed from a prehistoric bone; the discovery of the monolith on the moon; deep space.

nous, embryonic Star-Child—a new order of intelligence, beyond ape, man, and machine, moving through space toward the earth from which it began its evolution millions of years before.

Enigmatic, mystical, and profoundly sensuous, *2001* resists concrete logical interpretation because in a real sense its medium *is* its message. As Kubrick himself has pointed out, the film is "essentially a nonverbal experience. . . . It attempts to communicate more to the subconscious and to the feelings than it does to the intellect." Indeed, less than half of the film contains dialogue; the rest alternates between a brilliantly scored combination of classical and avant-garde electronic music and the silence of deep space. *2001* also broke new ground in photographic special effects (supervised by Douglas Trumbull and Con Pederson), particularly in the technique of **front projection,*** which it is credited with perfecting. It was shot by Geoffrey Unsworth (1914–78) in Super Panavision for presen-

---

* A more effective alternative to rear projection (see Glossary), in which action is shot against a glass-beaded reflective screen. The background image is projected onto this screen by means of a small semi-silvered mirror, which both transmits and reflects light, and which is placed at a forty-five-degree angle to the camera lens. Since this puts the projector and the camera in the same optical position, the camera does not record the shadows cast on the screen from the projection by actors and sets. Extremely bright studio lighting is used to drown out the background image as projected on actors and set. The process requires half the studio space of rear projection and is more convincing on screen.

The special effects for *2001* took eighteen months to produce and cost 6.5 million dollars, over 60 percent of the film's entire budget; they have never been equaled in verisimilitude, although the special effects of *Star Wars* and subsequent films have gone beyond them in scope. The fullest account of how the *2001* effects were accomplished is contained in John Brosnan, *Movie Magic: The Story of Special Effects in the Cinema* (New York: St. Martin's Press, 1974), pp. 218–29.

tation in Cinerama. Immensely popular in 1968, the film has a large cult following even today and is constantly revived. It has been ranked by the critic Fred Silva with *The Birth of a Nation* and *Citizen Kane* as an American landmark film—that is, a film that describes "a critical, unsettled area of American life"—in this case, the emptiness of technology in the form of a film that is itself a technological wonderment. From any perspective, *2001* is that most rare of cinematic achievements: a big-budget, nonnarrative spectacle of enormous technical sophistication which nevertheless makes an original and personal artistic statement about the human condition.*

The Wild Bunch: "Zapping the Cong"†

The years 1968 and 1969, perhaps the darkest in American history since the Civil War, witnessed some of the most original American films since the late forties. Like *Bonnie and Clyde,* many of them were aimed at the new youthful audience and were either covertly or overtly concerned with the political hysteria that had gripped the nation over the war in Vietnam. If *Bonnie and Clyde* was about the type of romantic rebel who would fight the military-industrial complex to end the war and usher in the greening of America, Sam Peckinpah's *The Wild Bunch* (1969) was about America's mercenary presence in Vietnam itself. In this film, which opens with the bloody massacre of an entire Texas town in the course of a payroll robbery, a gang of aging outlaws led by Pike Bishop (William Holden) finds itself increasingly confined by the closing of the American frontier and, pursued by bounty hunters, crosses the border into Mexico in search of greener pastures. The year is 1914, and the Mexican Civil War is in full swing, but the members of the Wild Bunch aren't looking for a cause, only some action. (As one of them comments after they have crossed the Rio Grande, "Just more of Texas, as far as I'm concerned.") The group falls in with Mapache, a brutish general who is leading federal troops in the fight against Pancho Villa and the insurgents. Brilliantly played by the Mexican director Emilio Fernández,

---

* Kubrick's best films have always been both technically and intellectually a decade ahead of their time. His classic antiwar statement *Paths of Glory* (1957), set in a French army unit during World War I, relentlessly exposed the type of military stupidity and callousness that would lead us into Vietnam. *Dr. Strangelove, or How I Learned to Stop Worrying and Love the Bomb* (1963) is an unsparing black comedy about the inevitablity of nuclear holocaust, produced amid the optimism of the New Frontier. And *A Clockwork Orange* (1971), liberally adapted from the novel by Anthony Burgess, projected a vision of the alienated, drug-ridden, ultra-violent future incarnated by "punk" culture in the late seventies and eighties. *The Shining* (1980) is less the conventional horror film it was initially thought to be than an account of America's long-concealed history of domestic violence and child abuse, while *Full Metal Jacket* (1987) seems to suggest that the country itself is a sort of distopic Disneyland in which the Vietnam War became one of the more elaborate rides.

† A common slang phrase from the war era that referred to the indiscriminate killing of Vietnamese, usually with automatic weapons fired at a distance.

18.60 Mercenaries as mythic heroes: *The Wild Bunch* (Sam Peckinpah, 1969). Ernest Borgnine, William Holden, Warren Oates. (Note the expertly balanced composition.)

18.61 Radical destruction: a shot from the massacre which concludes *The Wild Bunch*. William Holden.

Mapache is a sadistic thug who murders and tortures indiscriminately. His military base in the village of Agua Verde is a corrupt, barely competent dictatorship propped up by powerful foreign governments (in this case Germany and her allies) and their sophisticated weapons technology. The Bunch agrees to rob an American munitions train near the border for Mapache, who then attempts to seize the arms without paying for them. The gang outwits him, but Mapache captures one of their number—a Mexican Indian who has collaborated with the rebels—and tortures him to death before their eyes. In disgust, Pike and his men confront Mapache and kill him. The film ends in a sustained bloodbath as the outlaws seize the *federales'* machine gun and blast Agua Verde to pieces, all of them dying in the process.

The spectacular massacres which open and close *The Wild Bunch* are filmed in the style of the final ambush of *Bonnie and Clyde,* with a variety of lenses and different cameras running at different speeds, usually decelerated to depict the moment of death. With the death scene from Penn's film, they are among the most complex, kinetic, and shocking montage sequences in postwar American cinema, and they are balletically choreographed in a manner reminiscent of the battle scenes from Kukrosawa's *Seven Samurai.* The film is also a stunning piece of widescreen composition from beginning to end, skillfully photographed by Lucien Ballard in Panavision-70. Nevertheless, critics of the period were outraged at the extent and ferocity of the bloodshed. The final massacre has about it a sort of mad, orgasmic ecstasy, as the slaughter grows more and more intense until it reaches Eisensteinian (or Buñuelian) proportions: we see more people die than could possibly fill the small village; we see the same people die over and over again. Furthermore, the victims of this "heroic" violence are principally civilians caught in the crossfire. But a year before the revelation of the My Lai massacre, the outraged critics could not know that they were watching a mythic allegory of American intervention in Vietnam.*

As with *Bonnie and Clyde,* the violence of *The Wild Bunch was* revolutionary, *was* excessive for its time—a thing difficult to see today, when slow-motion bloodletting has passed from innovation to convention to cliché. Nevertheless, Penn and Peckinpah were committed filmmakers during the time of the war. Like their counterparts in the *film noir* movement of the late forties (see Chapter 11), they were interested in exposing their audience to certain dark realities of contemporary American life which the audience had itself largely chosen to ignore. Their films introduced conventions for the depiction of violence and carnage which others exploited ad nauseam in the seventies. But both directors insisted for the first time in American cinema that the human body is made of real flesh and blood; that arterial blood spurts rather than drips demurely; that bullet wounds leave not trim little pinpricks but big, gaping holes; and, in general, that violence has painful, unpretty, humanly destructive consequences. By bringing the American film closer to reality in its depiction of what high-powered modern weaponry can do to the human body, Penn and Peckinpah had overturned decades of polite filmic convention that the body has the resilience of rubber and that death is simply a state of terminal sleep. This was important new knowledge for the citizens of a nation whose government was waging a savage war of annihilation in Southeast Asia by remote control.†

---

* In 1969, the original release print of *The Wild Bunch* had more individual shots than any color film ever made—a difficult claim to substantiate today since the film was withdrawn by Warner Bros. after its debut and rereleased in several different versions, none of them as long or elaborate as Peckinpah had intended. For example, Warners cut an entire series of flashbacks establishing the prior relationship between Pike and his pursuer, Deke Thornton, which is crucial to the film's themes of honor and betrayal. Also cut was an elaborate sequence in which Mapache's troops are routed at a provincial railroad station by Villa's, which adds depth to the general's characterization and opens up the plot. During 1969, *The Wild Bunch* was shown in alternate versions of 190, 148, 145, 143, and 135 minutes. Only the 145- and 135-minute versions are available in 16mm today, although Warner Bros. still owns the master print and may someday restore it for public exhibition. In 1985, Warners released a 145-minute restored version on videocassette.

† What *Bonnie and Clyde* and *The Wild Bunch* did for violence, *The Graduate* (Mike Nichols, 1967), *I Am Curious—Yellow* (Vilgot Sjöman, 1967; U.S. release, 1969), *Midnight Cowboy* (John Schlesinger, 1969), and *Carnal Knowledge* (Nichols, 1971) did for sex. All four films were enormously popular with the youth market of the period, and all four dealt explicitly with human sexuality in ways unthinkable only a few years before. *The Graduate* concerned a sexual liaison between a recent college graduate and a middle-aged woman (his girlfriend's mother). *I Am Curious—Yellow,* which was confiscated by U.S. Customs authorities in 1967 but released by court order in 1969, contained male and female frontal nudity and simulated copulation. *Midnight Cowboy,* a fine dramatic feature which became the first X-rated film to win an Academy Award, dealt allusively with homosexual prostitution. While *Carnal Knowledge,* incisively scripted by Jules Feiffer, offered a candid analysis of the sexual—and sexist—obsessions of two male friends from college through middle age. These four films and inferior imitations opened the floodgates for the graphic representation of sex on American screens in the seventies, making possible everything from *Deep Throat* (Gerard Damiano, 1972) to *Last Tango in Paris* (Bernardo Bertolucci, 1972).

End of a Dream

In the years 1968 and 1969 the violence of our lives erupted onto our screens. The veteran cinematographer Haskell Wexler's *Medium Cool* 1969) was literally *about* media representations of violence in an America divided against itself by the war. Its main character is an alienated news cameraman who learns in the course of the film how easily the "detachment" of the media blends into distortion. As if to comment on itself, *Medium Cool* was shot in *cinéma vérité* fashion with a climax staged against the very real backdrop of the police riots at the 1968 Democratic National Convention in Chicago. *Easy Rider* (Dennis Hopper, 1969) also dealt openly with the violence and paranoia of an ideologically divided nation, although like other movies of the period it was praised for its radical social perspective far beyond its value as a film. In it, two hippies score a big drug deal and set off from California to Florida on their motorcycles "in search of America." But, as the ad copy read, "they couldn't find it anywhere." Treated with unmitigated contempt because of their appearance everywhere they go, the bikers are finally gunned down on a southern highway by some angry rednecks. A modestly competent synthesis of *Bonnie and Clyde* and the grade-B biker film, scored with good contemporary rock, *Easy Rider* shrewdly exploited the paranoia of a generation that felt itself at war with a hostile and increasingly belligerent establishment, and it became the box-office phenomenon of the decade. Produced for 375,000 dollars, it returned 50 million dollars and convinced old-guard Hollywood that a vast new youth market was ready to be tapped.

This conviction led to a spate of low-budget "youth culture" movies about protest, drugs, and the generation gap. *Getting Straight* (Richard Rush, 1970), *The Strawberry Statement* (Stuart Hagmann, 1970), *Move!* (Stuart Rosenberg, 1970), *Joe* (John G. Avildsen, 1970), *Little Fauss and Big Halsey* (Sidney J. Furie, 1970), and *Cisco Pike* (Bill L. Norton, 1971) were probably the best of this type, while most were so bad that they couldn't even be sold to television after their theatrical release. Perhaps the only youth-oriented dramatic feature of the era to achieve any real distinction—and this on a standard production budget—was Arthur Penn's

18.62 The illusion of freedom: *Easy Rider* (Dennis Hopper, 1969). Dennis Hopper, Peter Fonda, Jack Nicholson.

Black film was also born as a mainstream enterprise in the late sixties, with films like Robert Downey's bitter satire *Putney Swope* (1969), Gordon Parks' *The Learning Tree* (1969), Melvin Van Peebles' *Sweet Sweetback's Baadasssss Song* (1970), and Ossie Davis' *Cotton Comes to Harlem* (1970). The loosening up and subsequent disappearance from the American cinema of taboos about racial mixing on screen (and of *some* racial stereotypes)—probably stronger than those against sex and violence put together—produced both the black exploitation, or "blaxploitation," films of the seventies (*Shaft* [Gordon Parks, 1971]); *Super-Fly* [Gordon Parks, Jr., 1973]; *Hit-Man* [George Armitage, 1972]); *Slaughter* [Jack Starret, 1972]; *Trouble Man* [Ivan Dixon, 1972]; *Coffy* [Jack Hill, 1973]; *Black Caesar* [Larry Cohen, 1973]; *Blacula* [William Crain, 1972]), parodied so astutely in Keenan Ivory Wayans' 1988 *I'm Gonna Git You Sucka'*, and such interesting features as *Sounder* (Martin Ritt, 1972); *Black Girl* (Ossie Davis, 1972); *Lady Sings the Blues* (Sidney J. Furie, 1973); *Ganja and Hess* (Bill Gunn, 1973); *Claudine* (John Berry, 1974); *Bingo Long and the Traveling All-Stars and Motor Kings* (John Badham, 1977); and *Stony Island* (Andrew Davis, 1978). (See the sections on AIP and New World Pictures in Chapter 12.)

18.63 *Woodstock* (Michael Wadleigh, 1970).

18.64 *Gimme Shelter* (Albert and David Maysles, 1971).

extraordinary *Alice's Restaurant* (1969), a nearly plotless film about the failed idealism of the protest movement. There was, however, a good deal of vitality in another form calculated to appeal exclusively to the youth market, the rock documentary.* While films like *Monterey Pop* (D. A. Pennebaker, 1969) and *Mad Dogs and Englishmen* (Pierre Adidge, 1971) did a fine job of recreating the experience of a live rock concert for a movie audience, Michael Wadleigh's *Woodstock* (1970) and, especially, Albert and David Maysles' *Gimme Shelter* (1971) attempted to make serious statements about the nature of rock music by approaching their respective concerts as social metaphors.

The "youth-cult" bubble of 1969–70 was soon to burst as the youth movement itself became increasingly disoriented and confused, and Hollywood returned to more conventional modes of production. With so many important films like *Bonnie and Clyde, The Wild Bunch, 2001,* and *Medium Cool* clustered around the years 1967–69, it had seemed for a time that America was headed for a major cinematic (and social) renaissance. But neither came to pass. Significantly, not one of the directors mentioned above, with the clear exception of Stanley Kubrick, has since made a film that truly equals in stature his contribution to the late-sixties groundswell. Arthur Penn's *Little Big Man* (1970), *Night Moves* (1975), *The Missouri Breaks* (1976), and *Four Friends* (1981) are all serious, intelligent, and cinematically sophisticated films, but they do not compare in originality and vitality with *Bonnie and Clyde*. Peckinpah's genius for depicting mass slaughter moved from self-plagiarism (*Straw Dogs*, 1971) to self-parody (*The Getaway*, 1972; *The Killer Elite*, 1975; *Convoy*, 1978) in the seventies, although he continued to make interesting films (*Junior Bonner*, 1972; *Pat Garrett and Billy the Kid*, 1973; *Bring Me the Head of Alfredo Garcia*, 1974; *Cross of Iron*, 1977; *The*

* The rock concert film, or "rockumentary," is today a recognized genre around the world with roots in *Don't Look Back* (1967), D. A. Pennebaker's *cinéma direct* account of Bob Dylan's 1965 English tour, and such brilliant contemporary manifestations as *The Last Waltz* (Martin Scorsese, 1979—The Band) and *Stop Making Sense* (Jonathan Demme, 1984—Talking Heads).

Osterman Weekend, 1983)—when he could find the work—until he died in 1984. Even Kubrick, whose reputation as a major figure is assured, has not produced a film to rival *2001* in historical importance, although some critics feel that his lavish attempt to recreate the structures of the nineteenth-century novel in *Barry Lyndon* (1975; from the novel by Thackeray) comes close. His epic of domestic horror, *The Shining,* adapted from Stephen King, did little to alter the balance of critical opinion, although *Full Metal Jacket* (1987) is clearly the definitive statement of why we were in Vietnam. Haskell Wexler has worked mainly as a cinematographer since 1968, collaborating as director with Saul Landau on *Interview with President Allende* (1971) and *Report on Torture in Brazil* (1971), and with Emile De Antonio on *Underground* (1976), but finally returning to features with the hard-hitting *Latino* (1985), set in war-torn Nicaragua. Dennis Hopper, whose success as a filmmaker was purely circumstantial in the first place, has completed three features as a director since *Easy Rider: The Last Movie* (1971), *Out of the Blue* (1980), and *Colors* (1988), but none approaches the vitality of his first film. There was clearly something about the political and intellectual ferment of the late sixties that produced, however briefly, a period of great creativity in the American cinema and contributed to the sweeping away of time-honored conventions of both form and content. It was comparable in kind, if not in degree, to the Czech renaissance that preceded the Soviet invasion of 1968. The hope of liberalization released a surge of creative energy whose influence continued to be felt long after the hope was crushed.

HOLLYWOOD IN THE SEVENTIES AND EIGHTIES

Inflation and Conglomeration

The enormous popular success in 1970 of two conventional formula films, *Love Story* (Arthur Hiller) and *Airport* (George Seaton), restored Hollywood's faith in the big-budget, mass-appeal feature, and the seventies witnessed an inflation in the production costs of American films unparalleled in the industry's history. It was a decade of ever bigger hits— *The Poseidon Adventure* (Ronald Neame, 1972); *The Godfather* (Francis Ford Coppola, 1972); *The Exorcist* (William Friedkin, 1973); *The Sting* (George Roy Hill, 1973); *The Towering Inferno* (John Guillermin, 1974); *Jaws* (Steven Spielberg, 1975); *Star Wars* (George Lucas, 1977); *Saturday Night Fever* (John Badham, 1977); *Grease* (Randal Kleiser, 1978); *Superman* (Richard Donner, 1978)—and ever bigger flops—*Jesus Christ Superstar* (Norman Jewison, 1973); *Lucky Lady* (Stanely Donen, 1975); *The Hindenburg* (Robert Wise, 1975); *Gable and Lombard* (Sidney J. Furie, 1976); *Sorcerer* (William Friedkin, 1977); *The Wiz* (Sidney Lumet, 1978); *1941* (Steven Spielberg, 1979). Between 1972 and 1977 the average production budget for a single film increased by 178 percent, or nearly four times the general rate of inflation. By the end of 1979, average production costs were nearly double the 1977 figure, having reached the staggering sum of 7.5 million dollars per feature. Profits rose accordingly only if the film was a huge success,* so the financial risks of production were substantially multiplied. This caused a trend toward the production of fewer and fewer films with every year that passed, plus a steady increase in the amount spent on advertising and marketing campaigns designed to insure the films' success, these expenditures often rising as high as twice the production costs.

By 1975 it was not unusual for a single production company like Paramount or 20th Century–Fox to have all of its capital tied up in five or six films annually, every one a blockbuster with an average budget of 4 to 7 million dollars (compare this figure with MGM's average of forty-two features per year during the thirties). In 1977 at least one company (Columbia) had all of its capital, reportedly 20 million dollars, invested in a single film (*Close Encounters of the Third Kind*), and since that time, production budgets of 15 to 20 million dollars have not been uncommon. Francis Ford Coppola's *Apocalypse Now* (1979) and Robert Wise's *Star Trek* (1979) topped the list at 40 and 42 million, respectively. The combined production costs of *Superman, Parts I* and *II* (Richard Donner, 1978; Richard Lester, 1980) are estimated to have been more than 60 million dollars. The profits reaped by a success like *Jaws* or *Star Wars* are immense,† but a single big-budget flop can threaten the solvency of an entire studio. This condition has been seen as inhibiting the creative freedom of people working within the industry, especially since it has become common practice for producers, directors, writers, and stars to receive a percentage of the net profits of their films as well as a smaller fixed salary, or fee-for-service. It also creates a hit-or-miss mentality among

---

* A Hollywood rule of thumb equates a film's breaking even with returning two-and-a-half times its "negative cost" (literally, all costs required to produce the final cut of the master negative, excluding the costs of promotion, distribution, and exhibition). This break-even figure allows for advertising, studio overhead, and distribution prints (which cost about a thousand dollars apiece). Therefore, a low- to medium-budget film (750,000 to 3 million dollars in the mid-seventies) was once regarded as a success if it returned four times its negative cost. This calculation went haywire in the late seventies, with big-budget features like *Star Wars* recouping as much as two hundred times their initial investment. The gross that returns to the producer-distributor—which determines all profits—represents what remains after the exhibitors have taken their cut. According to *Variety* for October 22, 1980, the average production cost per feature rose to 10 million dollars, with another 6 million dollars in average marketing costs—this, exclusive of another 24 million dollars per feature in national distribution costs. In 1980, in other words, the average American film had to earn 40 million dollars simply to return its investment. By 1988, these figures had doubled.

† As of January 1, 1980, *Jaws* had grossed 133 million dollars and *Star Wars* 176 million dollars in the domestic market alone, making them the first and second top-grossing films of all time (and Fox estimates that over 500-million-dollars worth of *Star Wars* toys were sold between the film's opening on May 25, 1977, and January 1, 1980). The films were produced for 8 and 10 million dollars, respectively. Some idea of what this means financially to the filmmakers is provided by the fact that Richard Zanuck, the producer of *Jaws*, has made more money from his share of that film's profits than his father, the veteran producer Darryl F. Zanuck, made in his entire career.

film executives who, as Leo Janos writes, are "trapped between the need to reap huge, ever-increasing profits and the absence of any body of professional knowledge or skill that can guarantee a hit."* In this volatile fiscal environment, it is almost impossible for a new writer or director to be given a chance to work on an even modestly expensive, 7- to 10-million-dollar, film. The fact that in 1978 there were approximately three thousand filmmakers competing to make about seventy major films provides an index of the limitations this situation places upon contemporary American cinema.

Exacerbating these constraints is the fact that during the financial and social turbulence of the sixties most of the established Hollywood studios allowed themselves to be absorbed by huge conglomerates. Universal was acquired in 1962 by Music Corporation of America (MCA, Inc.); Paramount in 1966 by Gulf + Western Industries (whose holdings at the time included firms supplying natural resources, agricultural products, and financial services); United Artists in 1967 by Transamerica Corporation; Warner Bros. (later reincorporated as Warner Communications, Inc., or WCI) in 1969 by the vastly diversified Kinney Services; and MGM in 1970 by the Las Vegas financier Kirk Kerkorian, who liquidated much of the studio's real estate at a huge profit, which he reinvested in resort hotels. (MGM reemerged as a major force in the motion picture industry in 1981 when Kerkorian bought United Artists from Transamerica in the wake of the *Heaven's Gate* disaster, forming MGM/UA Entertainment in 1983.) For most of these conglomerates, film and television production initially accounted for only a small percentage of their annual revenues. In 1977, for example, the entire "Leisure Time" division of Gulf + Western—which then owned several publishing companies and major sports franchises, in addition to Paramount—accounted for less than 11 percent of total corporate income. But as Anthony Hoffman, entertainment analyst for the investment firm of Bache Halsey Stuart Shields, has remarked: "One thing that is obvious about this industry, and what has attracted the conglomerates to it in the first place, is that if you take any recent four- or five-year period, and you match total investment in production costs with pre-tax profits, it is not unusual to come up with average rates of return of 40 to 50 percent. ... No other industry has that rate of return, particularly one that has such a low asset base." Given this compelling reason for conglomeration, only 20th Century–Fox, Columbia Pictures Industries, and the family-owned Walt Disney Productions, together with its wholly owned distributor, Buena Vista, remained in the control of veteran film industry management at the end of the seventies.†

---

* More and more, however, production companies are resorting to the sophisticated demographic and psychographic techniques of contemporary market research to discover what the public wants to see and then to "pre-sell" it.

† Even before they were purchased by larger interests, both Columbia and Fox were rapidly diversifying. In 1977, Columbia drew 46 percent of its income from feature film production and the rest from television production and recording industry and broadcasting activities. During the same period, 20th Century–Fox earned 63 percent of its annual income from

But, continuing this trend, Fox was purchased in 1981 by the Denver oil millionaire Marvin Davis, who sold it to the international newspaper baron Rupert Murdoch in 1985; the following year Murdoch merged the studio with the Metromedia Television group to form Fox, Inc., and its subsidiary Fox Broadcasting Company. Columbia was acquired in 1982 by the Coca-Cola Company as part of its entertainment division, and in 1985 Turner Broadcasting Systems (TBS) bought MGM/UA from Kirk Kerkorian in order to acquire MGM's vast film library (which includes both the RKO and the pre-1949 Warners libraries) for its superstations. Turner then resold MGM/UA to Kerkorian and in 1986 sold the MGM Culver City studio and laboratory facilities to Lorimar-Telepictures. A final convulsion of merger mania took place at the decade's end, when in 1990 Kerkorian sold UA to the Australian media conglomerate Qintex Entertainment, retaining MGM as a separate but relatively small production operation; Warner Communications acquired Lorimar and merged with Time, Inc., owner of HBO, Cinemax, and many other holdings, to form Time Warner, Inc.—the world's largest communications company; Columbia merged with Tri-Star to become Columbia Pictures Entertainment (CPE), which was then acquired by Sony Corp. and Gulf + Western spun off its financial services unit in order to concentrate exclusively on Paramount Pictures and its publishing subsidiaries.

Hollywood is by no means dead; in fact, 1980—the watershed year of conglomeration—was also the most lucrative year in its history before 1987, and new producer / distributor organizations like Orion (1978), the Ladd Company (1979), and Tri-Star (1982) sprang up on either side of it. But during the seventies, fewer than eighty major films were produced each year out of an average total output of 160 (compared with a record 538 in 1937 and 513 in 1988 [many of these, however, for direct release to video]), and there arose serious questions about the creative vitality of the American cinema.

New Filmmakers of the Seventies

Yet some critics have claimed that Hollywood—far from declining in creativity—actually experienced a renaissance of creative talent in the seventies as a result of the many young directors then working in the industry who were professionally trained at American film schools. Most new directors of the sixties—Penn, Peckinpah, Irvin Kershner, John Frankenheimer, Sidney Lumet—had been trained in the medium of television, and the modes of teleproduction that they knew best emphasized economy, flexibility, and speed. As with the *cinéastes* of the French New Wave, some of their best films bore the mark of spontaneous improvisation. Many new directors of the seventies, on the other hand, had studied film history, aesthetics, and production as formal academic subjects in uni-

---

film production and the rest from similarly diversified acquisitions, including Coca-Cola Bottling Midwest and Aspen Skiing Corporation. In 1979, profits from *Star Wars* enabled Fox to acquire for 72 million dollars the Pebble Beach Corporation, which owns several fashionable resorts and golf courses on the Monterey peninsula.

18.65 The dark side of American business: *The Godfather* (Francis Ford Coppola, 1972). Robert Duvall, Marlon Brando.

18.66 High-tech fairy tale: *Star Wars* (George Lucas, 1977). Darth Vader (David Prowse) and Ben (Obi-Wan) Kenobi (Alec Guinness).

versity graduate school programs. Francis Ford Coppola (b. 1939) and the screenwriter / director Paul Schrader (b. 1946) went to film school at UCLA; George Lucas (b. 1944) and the screenwriter / director John Milius (b. 1944) graduated from the University of Southern California; Martin Scorsese (b. 1942) and Brian De Palma (b. 1940) attended New York University; Steven Spielberg (b. 1946) studied film and dramatic arts at California State; others, like Peter Bogdanovich (b. 1939) and William Friedkin (b. 1939), had been documentarists and critics before making their first features. This highly specialized training produced a generation of American filmmakers whose visual and technical sophistication is immense but whose films are sometimes so painstakingly calculated for effect as to lack spontaneity.

Coppola, for example, is unquestionably a major American filmmaker; the films that comprise his epic of organized crime in the United States, *The Godfather* (1972) and *The Godfather, Part II* (1974), are two of the most significant American films of the decade. But there is something about *The Conversation* (1974), like De Palma's *Blow Out* (1981), that makes it all too obviously a remake of Antonioni's *Blow-Up* (1966) in audio electronics terms. George Lucas' *Star Wars* (1977) is important historically because of its unprecedented use of computer technology to generate special photographic and auditory effects*, but it is also a film intensely manipulative of its audience's perception. There is no room for interpretation or speculation in *Star Wars:* everyone who sees it has more or less the same experience. The same might be said of Steven Spielberg's *Jaws* (1975) and *Close Encounters of the Third Kind* (1977), both technically polished, but so calculated in terms of effect that they have all the predictability of a Big Mac hamburger. Scorsese's *Mean Streets* (1973) is a strikingly original independent feature; but *Taxi Driver* (1976) exploits

---

* *Star Wars* was the first widely released film to be both recorded and exhibited in Dolby stereo-optical sound (see Glossary).

the paranoid alienation it pretends to examine; and *New York, New York* (1977), a meticulously studied effort to recreate the musicals of the Big Band era, seems more like a scholarly article than a feature film. Finally, Brian De Palma, who directed some of the most stylish and effective horror thrillers of the period (*Sisters*, 1973; *Phantom of the Paradise*, 1974; *Obsession*, 1975; *Carrie*, 1976; *The Fury*, 1978), admits that he approaches film from a scientific point of view and says that he tends to equate filmmaking with "building machines." All of these extremely talented film-school–trained directors have produced works of distinction—some of near genius. Yet even in their best work—say, Coppola's *Apocalypse Now* (1979), Scorsese's *Raging Bull* (1980), De Palma's *Dressed to Kill* (1980), or, more recently, Coppola's *Tucker: The Man and His Dream* (1988), Scorsese's *The Last Temptation of Christ* (1988), and DePalma's *Casualties of War* (1989)—there is at times an almost academic preoccupation with cinematic effect and audience response. This attitude was described by Vincent Canby when he wrote of "major contemporary American filmmakers who, more and more, tend to put films together with such deliberation you might think that instead of making movies they were building arks to save mankind."

18.67 The "last supper" for Painless the dentist in *M.A.S.H.* (Robert Altman, 1970): Carl Gottlieb, David Arkin, Tom Skerritt, John Schuck (Painless), Donald Sutherland (Hawkeye), and Elliott Gould (Trapper John).

Perhaps the most important filmmaker working within the American commercial system during the seventies—as his own producer, through Lion's Gate Films, since 1971—was Robert Altman (b. 1925). Altman came to film from television, where he directed episodes of *Alfred Hitchcock Presents, Combat, Bonanza,* and *Bus Stop.* His first major feature was *M*A*S*H* (1970), an iconoclastic comedy set in a mobile army surgical hospital during the Korean War, which became the basis for the popular television series. The film is characterized by a subversive combination of humor and gore, and it makes effective use of the wide-angle Panavision compositions and overlapping dialogue for which Altman has become justly famous. While *M*A*S*H* had a tough, absurdist edge and set new standards for the melding of cruelty, violence, and humor, it never pretended to be more than a hip service comedy. *Brewster McCloud* (1970), on the other hand, is a deliberate venture into social satire and Altman's personal favorite among his films. It concerns a young man who is preparing for a bird flight in the Houston Astrodome under the tutelage of a bird-woman mentor named Louise. McCloud must avoid sex, which binds him to earth, and must kill a number of reactionary characters in order to realize his dream of total freedom through flight, an equation perfectly made by Altman through subjective aerial photography. Some critics thought the film eccentric nonsense, but Andrew Sarris was closer to the mark when he called it "the first American film to apply an appropriate tone and style to the absurdist follies of our times."

McCabe and Mrs. Miller (1971), Altman's next film, has become increasingly interesting in light of his later work. Beautifully photographed on location in Washington State by Vilmos Zsigmond, it is about a small-time gambler and (by his own account) gunfighter near the turn of the century who founds the town of Presbyterian Church. With the aid of an enterprising brothel madam, he helps the town grow and prosper until representatives of a large mining conglomerate approach him and attempt to buy him out. Always something of a buffoon beneath his self-confident exterior, McCabe actually believes in the free enterprise system, and he refuses to sell his interest in the town. Naturally, agents are sent to kill him, and after a serio-comic gun battle he is shot to death in the snow. The film ends with a slow zoom into the constricted pupil of Mrs. Miller as she lies in bed stoned on opium after the murder, suggesting an option which many Americans have chosen, in order to avoid confronting the brutality of our economic system.

After *Images* (1972), an experimental feature that attempted rather unsuccessfully to probe the mind of a schizophrenic, Altman made his most cinematically elegant film, an updated version of Raymond Chandler's forties detective novel *The Long Goodbye* (1973). Shot by Zsigmond on location in Los Angeles and Malibu, the film is less a detective story than a sardonic comment on contemporary American narcissism drenched in the languid and decadent atmosphere of southern California. Philip Marlow, an unsuccessful private detective, helps a friend who is accused of murdering his wife and defends him staunchly, only to discover that the friend actually committed the crime and has used Marlow shamelessly to avoid detection. Marlow, whose throwaway line throughout the film has been "It's OK with me," is finally backed up against something that's not OK, not even in the modern Babylon of Los Angeles, and he tracks his friend to his hideaway in Mexico and shoots him. *The Long Goodbye* was Altman's most visually elaborate film before *Three Women* (1977), and it makes striking thematic use of Zsigmond's wide-angle and telephoto zoom shots.

Thieves Like Us (1974), Altman's entry in the *Bonnie and Clyde* category, is adapted from the same novel as Nicholas Ray's *They Live by Night* (1949). It deals with three prison escapees during the Depression who set out on a spree of bank robbing, become notorious, and are finally killed by the police. *California Split* (1974), Altman's first film to use wireless eight-track sound, is an episodic story about compulsive gambling set in Las Vegas which, like *Thieves Like Us,* is ultimately about American rootlessness. But it was in *Nashville* (1975) that Altman made his most telling comment on the nature of American society.

Nearly three hours long* and recorded in Dolby sound, *Nashville* is set in the present and has no plot in the traditional sense. It concerns the lives of twenty-four separate characters in the five-day period preceding a rally to be given at the city's Parthenon for the "Replacement Party" presidential candidate, Hal Philip Walker (whose ironic campaign slogan is "New Roots for the Nation"). The characters all come from different

18.68 *McCabe and Mrs. Miller* (Robert Altman, 1971): Warren Beatty (McCabe) in the final showdown.

18.69 Altman's *The Long Goodbye* (1973): Elliott Gould as Marlowe.

18.70 From the final frames of *The Long Goodbye* Marlowe does a soft-shoe down a dusty Mexican road as the soundtrack plays "Hooray for Hollywood."

---

* Various rough cuts of *Nashville* ran between six and eight hours. A four-hour version was released theatrically, withdrawn, and pared to 161 minutes. There were plans to show the eight-hour version as a miniseries on television, but as of 1990 only a heavily edited theatrical print had been aired (on "The ABC Sunday Night Movie"). *Nashville,* of course, is available on videocassette, as are most of the works discussed in this book.

18.71 The "gang" in Altman's *Thieves Like Us* (1974): T-Dub (Bert Remsen), Chickamaw (John Schuck), and Bowie (Keith Carradine).

18.72 *Nashville* (Robert Altman, 1975): Barbara Harris as Albuquerque.

18.73 Altman's *Three Women* (1977): Shelley Duvall as Millie Lammoreaux, Sissy Spacek as Pinky Rose.

walks of life, but they have one thing in common: all are seeking either to become or to remain celebrities in the world of country music and, by extension, of American mass-mediated culture at large. Their individual lives coalesce at the political rally that concludes the film, where a young assassin who has come there to kill Walker kills one of the celebrities instead. As Pauline Kael has remarked, *Nashville* is "a country-and-Western musical; a documentary essay on Nashville and American life; a meditation on the love affair between performers and audiences; and an Altman party." But *Nashville* is also a film about the ways in which our national entertainment media and our national politics—all but indistinguishable from one another—work constantly to distract us from the massive inequalities of our society and the violence of our recent national past. Altman finds many American virtues to admire, but the most important theme of *Nashville* is how quickly we forget and gloss over such things as the terrible public violence of the sixties and the human consequences of the war in Vietnam. Its most urgent comment is that we Americans, in our blind pursuit of success and our compulsive need for social change, are leading unexamined lives.

Nashville was Altman's bicentennial birthday present to the United States. Such was the high-risk mentality of Hollywood in the seventies that though the film returned 8.8 million dollars,* it nonetheless was deemed a commercial failure. But Altman continued to produce original and sophisticated films. *Buffalo Bill and the Indians* (1976) is, like *Nashville,* an attack on the hypocrisy and exploitativeness of American "show biz," as reflected in the way in which the title character sustains his own popular myth in his dealings with Chief Sitting Bull. From this completely plotless film, Altman moved confidently into the realm of dreams with *Three Women* (1977), which deals with the nature of the female psyche in surrealistic terms. The film begins as a social satire with a strong subtext of mythic imagery and becomes progressively more allusive and mysterious until it transforms itself completely in the concluding sequences, which are surely among the most unusual in contemporary American cinema.

From the irreverent humor of *M*A*S*H* to the film-dreaming of *Three Women,* Robert Altman proved himself to be one of the most innovative American filmmakers of the past thirty years. But near the end of this period he stumbled badly with *A Wedding* (1978), *Quintet* (1979), and *A Perfect Couple* (1979). He then made two highly original films—the political satire *H.E.A.L.T.H.* (1980) and the musical *Popeye* (1980), starring Robin Williams in the title role—both of which were savagely panned by the critics. At this point, Altman turned to theater, filming Ed Graczyk's *Come Back to the Five and Dime, Jimmy Dean, Jimmy Dean* (1982) in super 16mm; David Rabe's *Streamers* (1983) in 35mm; and both *Secret Honor* (a one-man show featuring the ravings of a post-resignation Richard M. Nixon, made while Altman was a visiting professor at the University of Michigan in 1984) and Marsha Norman's *The Laun-*

---

* The remarkably low production cost was 1.2 million dollars.

dromat (1985) in video for HBO. More recently, Altman directed theatrical adaptations of Sam Shepard's *Fool for Love* (1986) and Christopher Durang's *Beyond Therapy* (1987), and shot a series of unique political docudramas for HBO entitled *Tanner '88*, which followed an imaginary candidate for the Democratic presidential nomination (played by Michael Murphy) from month to month as the actual 1988 primaries were taking place. Although he is no longer popular with mass audiences, Altman's talents are still very much in demand. He works with more economy and discipline than most of his contemporaries, both in Europe and in the United States; and, as Gary Arnold remarks, by the time Altman retires, he may be the only major filmmaker of his generation with as many films to his credit as the directors who worked in Hollywood during its Golden Age.

Like many of his European counterparts during the seventies, Altman progressively abandoned conventional narrative to develop his own highly personal style. Certain hallmarks make an Altman film of the era easy to identify: the overlapping dialogue and experimental use of sound (see note, Chapter 10); the sardonic humor; the visual lushness and density based on an uncommonly perceptive use of the wide-angle and telephoto zoom lens; the intriguingly unusual faces of his repertory company (Shelley Duvall, Michael Murphy, Bert Remsen, etc.). It is argued that style sometimes takes precedence over substance in these films, but it seems more accurate to suggest that in works like *Three Women*, style and substance have finally become indistinguishable. In the seventies, Altman saw us with our raw nerves exposed at a time in American history when the conflicting demands of community and individual freedom were never more extreme, and he became an epic poet of that conflict. But in the eighties, he was out of step, making *H.E.A.L.T.H.* rather than *Terms of Endearment* (James L. Brooks, 1983), *Popeye* rather than *E.T.* (Steven Spielberg, 1982), and maintaining consistently that movies were for adults as well as teenagers. Problems of artistic consistency (and they do exist) notwithstanding, Altman in the seventies made the most intellectually honest films about the American experience of any director since Orson Welles. And, like Welles, he found himself left behind in an era when intellectual integrity went out of fashion.

The American Film Industry in the Age of "Kidpix"

The eighties began with the single largest financial disaster ever to hit a major studio when Michael Cimino's 40-million-dollar adult Western, *Heaven's Gate* (1980), was withdrawn from distribution immediately following its release, amid critics' charges of incomprehensibility. Actually one of the decade's better films, this three-hour-and-forty-minute epic about the destruction of America's frontier due to ruthless capitalism nevertheless went down to perdition itself, taking United Artists as a corporate entity with it. In this context, it was probably inevitable that an industry which during the seventies had enjoyed some of the greatest profits in its history from films targeted for children (*Star Wars*, 1977; *Close Encounters*, 1977; *Superman*, 1978) and teenagers (*Saturday Night Fever*, 1977; *Grease*, 1978) would turn nearly wholesale to such produc-

18.74 *Coming Home* (Hal Ashby, 1978): Jane Fonda, Bruce Dern.

18.75 *Harlan County, U.S.A.* (Babara Kopple, 1976).

18.76 *An Unmarried Woman* (Paul Mazursky, 1978): Alan Bates, Jill Clayburgh.

18.77 Michael Cimino's ruinous *Heaven's Gate* (1980): Christopher Walken.

18.78 John Carpenter's *Halloween* (1979).

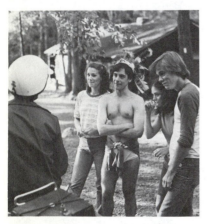

18.79 The "original" *Friday the Thirteenth* (Sean S. Cunningham, 1980): Kevin Bacon and others.

tions in the wake of *Heaven's Gate.* Furthermore, the industry was now being run by corporate attorneys and accountants who lacked the experience of industry veterans, and who tended to rely on vehicles with proven track records (thus, to date, three *Rambos,* four *Jaws,* four *Star Wars,* five *Rockys,* and at least two of almost everything else) and on the viscerally sensational (that is, films containing graphic sex, violence, or, preferably, both combined).

An alarming manifestation of sex and violence was the flood of "psycho-slasher" films that glutted the domestic market in the wake of John Carpenter's ultra-successful *Halloween* (1978), an artful low-budget chiller which returned 60 million dollars on an 800,000-dollar investment. The formula—confirmed by the record-breaking profits of the oafishly directed *Friday the Thirteenth* (Sean S. Cunningham, 1980)—involves the serial murder of teenagers by a ruthless, unstoppable psychotic, with plenty of gratuitous sex and mayhem, and with realistic gore provided by high-tech makeup and special effects artists like Dick Smith, Rob Bottin, and Tom Savini, who became stars in their own right. There were precedents for psycho-killer violence in Hitchcock's *Psycho* (1960) and Tobe Hooper's *The Texas Chainsaw Massacre* (1974), and the exploitation of gore had existed at the periphery of the industry for decades (for example, in the "splatter" movies of Herschell Gordon Lewis—*Blood Feast,* 1963; *2,000 Maniacs,* 1964; *Color Me Blood Red,* 1964; and others). But slasher films took it fully into the R-rated mainstream in literally hundreds of *Halloween* / *Friday the Thirteenth* spin-offs like *The Toolbox Murders* (Dennis Donnelly, 1979), *Driller Killer* (Abel Ferrara, 1979), *Prom Night* (Paul Lynch, 1980), *Terror Train* (Roger Spottiswoode, 1980), *Final Exam* (Jimmy Huston, 1981) *Hell Night* (Tom DeSimone, 1981), *Graduation Day* (Herb Freed, 1981), *My Bloody Valentine* (George Mihalka, 1981), *New Year's Evil* (Emmet Alston, 1981), *Deadly Blessing* (Wes Craven, 1981), *The Burning* (Tony Maylan, 1981), *Happy Birthday to Me* (J. Lee Tompson, 1981), *Night School* (Ken Hughes, 1981), *The Slumber Party Massacre* (Amy Jones, 1982), *Visiting Hours* (Jean-Claude Lord, 1982), *The Evil Dead* (Sam Raimi, 1983), *Nightmare on Elm Street* (Wes Craven, 1984), and, of course, the interminable sequels and imitations. In fact, *Variety* reported twenty-five slashers among the fifty top-grossing films of 1981, a year in which slashers accounted for nearly 60 percent of all domestic releases. The wave of popularity peaked shortly thereafter, but slasher films remain a regular feature of the annual production schedule, and their porno-violent chic has become obligatory for many first-rate horror films, such as *Poltergeist* (Tobe Hooper, 1982), *The Hunger* (Tony Scott, 1983), *Fright Night* (Tom Holland, 1985), *Poltergeist II* (Brian Gibson, 1986); *The Serpent and the Rainbow* (Wes Craven, 1987); for some science fiction films, like *Aliens* (James Cameron, 1986); and for many thrillers, such as *Body Double* (Brian De Palma, 1984), *Psycho III* (Tony Perkins, 1986), *Angel Heart* (Alan Parker, 1987), *The Believers* (John Schlesinger, 1987). Their grim social implications notwithstanding, slashers are now an important staple of the **videocas-**

sette and **cable television** markets, owing to the sheer number in which they were (and are) produced.

On a lighter note, science fiction / fantasy—which ran the gamut from Steven Spielberg's all-time box-office champ *E.T.: The Extra-Terrestrial* (1982) and the record-breaking *Ghostbusters* (Ivan Reitman, 1984) and *Gremlins* (Joe Dante, 1984), to Lucasfilm's 35-million-dollar fiasco *Howard the Duck* (William Hyuck, 1986)—was pervasively present in the eighties. So, too, was adventure / fantasy, in the vein of Spielberg's *Raiders of the Lost Ark* (1981) and *Indiana Jones and the Temple of Doom* (1984), as well as in the sword-and-sorcery genre, popularized by *Dragonslayer* (Matthew Robbins, 1981), *Conan the Barbarian* (John Milius, 1982), *The Sword and the Sorcerer* (Albert Pyun, 1982), *Krull* (Peter Yates, 1983), *The Dark Crystal* (Jim Henson, 1983), *The Beastmaster* (Don Coscarelli, 1983), and *Ladyhawke* (Richard Donner, 1985), a type that owed its appeal to the role-playing board game "Dungeons and Dragons." Most of these films were rated PG and relied heavily on action and special effects to attract an audience that cut across broad demographic groups. However, through a variety of tools, ranging from television to tie-ins, they were *marketed* mainly to young people. So, too, were the so-called "teenpix," a category of films created to exploit the PG-13 rating when it was instituted in 1984. This form had clear antecedents both during the eighties (for example, *Little Darlings* [Ronald F. Maxwell, 1980]; *Fast Times at Ridgemont High* [Amy Heckerling, 1982]; *Valley Girl* [Martha Coolidge, 1983], and in previous decades (for example, AIP's "Beach Blanket" cycle—see Chapter 12). Inspired by the financial success of the R-rated *Risky Business* (Paul Brickman) in 1983, filmmakers produced a glut of teen and preteen comedies with sexual / social themes over the next several years. Many were as forgettable as *The Revenge of the Nerds* (Jeff Carew, 1984), *Fraternity Vacation* (James Frawley, 1985), *Mischief* (Mel Damski, 1985), and *Better Off Dead* ("Savage" Steve Holland, 1985), but others were visually innovative, like *Tuff Turf* (Fritz Kiersch, 1985; shot by Willy Kurant, Godard's cinematographer on *Masculin Feminin*) and *St. Elmo's Fire* (Bob Schmacher, 1985), or thought-provoking, like *The Flamingo Kid* (Gary Marshall, 1984), *The Karate Kid* (John G. Avildsen, 1984), and *Just One of the Guys* (Lisa Gottlieb, 1985). The master of intelligent teenpix in the eighties was producer-director John Hughes, whose *Sixteen Candles* (1984), *The Breakfast Club* (1985), *Weird Science* (1985), *Pretty in Pink* (directed by Howard Deutch, 1986), *Ferris Bueller's Day Off* (1986), and *Some Kind of Wonderful* (directed by Deutch, 1987) all show a fine grasp of the social anxieties created by the rigid class stratifications of American high schools. Indeed, so lucrative was the teen market in the mid-eighties that films like *The Last Starfighter* (Nick Castle, 1984) and *Back to the Future* (Robert Zemeckis, 1985), which combined teen comedy with other genres (in both cases, science fiction), became instant hits. Perhaps the apex (or nadir) of age regression was reached in this era by *Pee Wee's Big Adventure* (Tim Burton, 1985)—an admittedly hilarious, even brilliant film—

18.80 Ur-slasher *The Texas Chainsaw Massacre* (Tobe Hooper, 1974).

18.81 *Poltergeist* (Tobe Hooper, 1982): Jobeth Williams, Oliver Robins.

18.82 Teenage wasteland: John Hugh's *The Breakfast Club:* Molly Ringwald, Anthony Michael Hall, Emilio Estevez, Ally Sheedy, Judd Nelson.

in which the infantile title character has a series of picaresque misadventures while searching for his stolen bicycle. Appropriately, the box-office smash of 1988 was Robert Zemeckis' *Who Framed Roger Rabbit?*, a technically dazzling blend of live action and animation that was fundamentally a feature-length cartoon.

The Effects of Video

While teenagers and their younger siblings were driving American box-office receipts toward an all-time high of 4.3 billion dollars in 1987, their parents were at home watching the same movies on what used to be called television, for during the eighties the fortunes of Hollywood were being affected by new technologies of video delivery and imaging as never before. Cable networks, direct broadcast satellites, and half-inch videocassettes provided unprecedented new means of motion picture distribution. In addition, **computer-generated graphics** provided new means of production, especially in the realm of special effects, forecasting the arrival of a fully automated "electronic cinema." Some studios, like Columbia and Universal, devote the majority of their schedules to the production of telefilm for the commercial networks, while nearly all the studios presell their theatrical features for cable and videocassette distribution. Indeed, Tri-Star, one of the industry's major producer/distributors, is a joint venture of CBS, Columbia Pictures, and Time, Inc.'s premium cable service, Home Box Office (HBO). And HBO and Showtime both function as producer/distributors themselves, by directly financing feature films and entertainment specials for transmission by cable. Starting in 1985, independent film producers released more motion pictures than the major studios for the first time since the early decades of this century, so voracious had the cable and home video markets become. In 1987, combined video rentals and sales totaled an astounding 7.2 billion dollars (4.4 billion dollars in rentals; 2.8 billion dollars in sales), or nearly twice that year's record-breaking income from theatrical rentals.

In terms of theatrical filmmaking, this penetration of video has meant a step toward the demise of the normative 35mm feature, as producers

18.83 *Flashdance* (Adrian Lyne, 1983): the original feature-length music video. Jennifer Beals.

18.84 *Aliens* (James Cameron, 1986): Sigourney Weaver and Carrie Henn in the egg chamber. Note the similarity with the shot in still 12.50 from *Them!* (Gordon Douglas, 1954).

sought properties on the one hand with video or "televisual" characteristics that would play well on the small screen or, on the other, that would draw audiences into the theaters with the promise of spectacular 70mm photography and multitrack Dolby sound. In the former category are such music-video–style films as *Flashdance* (Adrian Lyne, 1983), *Footloose* (Herbert Ross, 1984), *Streets of Fire* (Walter Hill, 1984), and *Dirty Dancing* (Emile Ardolino, 1987), all of which also cashed in on the teenpix phenomenon; and in the latter category are films like *Amadeus* (Milŏs Forman, 1984), *Runaway Train* (Andrei Konchalovski, 1985), *The Color Purple* (Steven Spielberg, 1985), *Aliens* (James Cameron, 1986), *The Untouchables* (Brian De Palma, 1987), *Empire of the Sun* (Steven Spielberg, 1987), and *The Last Emperor* (Bernardo Bertolucci, 1987), whose maximum effect derives from visual and aural spectacle. Films like *Top Gun* (Tony Scott, 1986), structured as a feature-length music video but full of breathtaking aerial cinematography that can only be fully appreciated on a wide screen, manage to have it both ways—which is probably why it has to date earned over 79 million dollars to become the nineteenth highest-grossing American film in history. *Top Gun* also had the canniness to be a military film at a time when that long-buried genre was coming back into fashion.

Repressed culturally by ambivalent feelings about the Vietnam War and commercially by the middling box-office performance of such earlier Vietnam-themed films as *Go Tell the Spartans* (Ted Post, 1978), *Coming Home* (Hal Ashby, 1978), *Apocalypse Now* (Francis Ford Coppola, 1979),* the war film reemerged like an exploding land mine when Oliver Stone's *Platoon* hit the screen in 1986. *Platoon* went on to become one of the highest-grossing American films of all times (twenty-sixth, in fact, in *Variety*'s 1988 survey). It was followed in rapid succession by a spate of Vietnam films of varying quality and political bias but obvious sincer-

18.85 *The Color Purple* (Steven Spielberg, 1985): Danny Glover, Whoopi Goldberg.

18.86 Brian De Palma's post-slasher period: *The Untouchables* (1987) pretending to be a classic Soviet film from 1925.

* Michael Cimino's *The Deerhunter* (1979) was a smash hit in 1979, but it wasn't really about Vietnam, as any veteran will testify.

18.87 *Top Gun* (Tony Scott, 1986): mixing music video, jingoism, and beefcake. Val Kilmer and Tom Cruise in the foreground, Rick Rossovich and Anthony Edwards to the rear.

18.88 *Platoon* (Oliver Stone, 1988): Tom Berenger, Mark Moses, Willem Dafoe.

18.89 *Full Metal Jacket* (Stanley Kubrick, 1987).

ity—*Gardens of Stone* (Francis Coppolla, 1987), *Hamburger Hill* (John Irvin, 1987), *Full Metal Jacket* (Stanley Kubrick, 1987), *Bat 21* (Peter Markle, 1988), *Good Morning, Vietnam* (Barry Levinson, 1988), *Off Limits* (Christopher Crowe, 1988), the HBO-produced *War Stories* (1987) and *Dear America: Letters Home from Vietnam* (1988), *84 Charlie Mopic* (Patrick Duncan, 1989), and Brian De Palma's horrific *Casualties of War* (1989). Some other military films seemed less sincere, however, (like *Top Gun,* for example) since the studios responded to the patriotic climate of the Reagan years by producing their most jingoistic works since the Korean War. There were films that endorsed the myth of political betrayal in Vietnam—*Uncommon Valor* (Ted Kotcheff, 1983); *Rambo: First Blood, Part II* (George Pan Cosmatos, 1985); *The Hanoi Hilton* (Lionel Chetwynd, 1987); that exploited fear of a Soviet invasion—*Invasion, U.S.A.* (Joseph Zito, 1985); *Red Dawn* (John Milius, 1985); and that glorified military vigilantism—*Born American* (Renny Harlin, 1986); *Iron Eagle* (Sidney J. Furie, 1986).

Perhaps because there was so little recognizably adult fare in the theaters, films with a "literary" quality, many of them British-made, were also popular in the American market during the eighties, as is typical of a period of political reaction—e.g., *Chariots of Fire* (Hugh Hudson, 1981); *Gandhi* (Richard Attenborough, 1982); *Passage to India* (David Lean, 1984); *A Room with a View* (James Ivory, 1985); *Out of Africa* (Sydney Pollack, 1985). Another adult genre that appeared in the second half of the decade was *film noir*. More generally characteristic of moral confusion than a specific political condition, this film type had its first eighties venue in the steamy and very nearly perfect *Body Heat* (1981), written and directed by Lawrence Kasdan, who would soon give America its first feature-length yuppie music video in *The Big Chill* (1983). After a lull of several years, *film noir* came back into its own in such well-made and intelligent films as *Black Widow* (Bob Rafelson, 1986), *Angel Heart* (Alan Parker, 1987), *Manhunter* (Michael Mann, 1987), *No Way Out* (Roger Donaldson, 1987), *Best Seller* (John Flynn, 1987), *Fatal Attraction* (Adrian Lyne, 1987), *Someone to Watch Over Me* (Ridley Scott, 1987), *House of Games* (David Mamet, 1987), *Frantic* (Roman Polanski, 1988), *Masquerade* (Bob Swaim, 1988), *The House on Carroll Street* (Peter Yates, 1988), *D.O.A.* (Rocky Morton, 1988), and *Into the Fire* (1989). Furthermore, as the decade neared its close independent filmmakers, resurgent under the new regime of video delivery, did some of the most unusual and interesting work the American cinema had seen for many years—for example, Joel and Ethan Coen's *Blood Simple* (1984) and *Raising Arizona* (1987), Jim Jarmusch's *Stranger than Paradise* (1984), *Down By Law* (1986), and *Mystery Train* (1989), Tim Hunter's *The River's Edge* (1986), James Foley's *At Close Range* (1986), Oliver Stone's *Salvador* (1986), *Wall Street* (1987), and *Talk Radio* (1988), and Steven Soderbergh's *Sex, lies, and videotape* (1989; Cannes Grand Prix). Many of these films are too original to have been made in the studio era and too eccentric for the mass market economies of the seventies and early eighties. They hark back, in a very real sense, to the vitality and integrity of the prestudio age—to the work of Griffith, Keaton, and von Stroheim—when everything was possible because everything was new. And in the sense that video distribution has broken every rule, everything *is* new again. It is possible to see in the prospect of a flourishing independent production sector the potential for a renewal of mainstream American cinema, a moving away from the arena of mechanized mass spectacle toward human

18.90 New *film noir: Angel Heart* (Alan Parker, 1987): Mickey Rourke.

18.91 *Manhunter* (Michael Mann, 1977): William Petersen.

18.92 *House of Games* (David Mamet, 1987): Joe Mantega and Lindsay Crouse.

18.93 *Fatal Attraction* (Adrian Lyne, 1987): Glenn Close, Michael Douglas, Anne Archer.

18.94 *Down by Law* (Jim Jarmusch, 1986): John Lurie, Tom Waits, Roberto Benigni.

18.95 *Raising Arizona* (Joel and Ethan Coen, 1987): Holly Hunter, Nicolas Cage.

drama and, perhaps, human values. Indeed, there is evidence of this trend in many films of the record-smashing "blockbuster summer" of 1989— e.g., *Indiana Jones and the Last Crusade* (Steven Spielberg), *Batman* (Tim Burton), and *The Abyss* (James Cameron)—despite their enormous budgets.

Colorization, Technology, and Film History

Since the late seventies, computer graphics technology has made it possible to "colorize" on videotape film shot in black and white. The process was first used to color documentary footage for the TV movies *King* (Abby Mann, 1978) and *Ike* (Boris Sagal and Melville Shavelson, 1979), and by the mid-eighties it was being used to colorize Hollywood feature films from the thirties and forties for distribution on television and videocassette. Colorization is essentially a sophisticated form of computer animation practiced by two companies—Color Systems Technology (CST), an independent Los Angeles firm, and Colorization, Inc. (originally Vidcolor Image), a Toronto-based facility owned by Hal Roach Studios. In recent years, CST, whose process results in an image texture akin to that of classical Technicolor, has colored *Miracle on 34th Street* (George Seaton, 1947), *Yankee Doodle Dandy* (Michael Curtiz, 1942), *The Absent-Minded Professor* (Robert Stevenson, 1961), a lost *Honeymooners* episode, and Alfred Hitchcock's introductions from his old TV series, to accompany its latter-day incarnation. Colorization, Inc., whose images look softer and tend toward the pastel palette of contemporary television shows like *Miami Vice*, has turned out colored versions of *Topper* (Norman Z. McLeod, 1937), the Laurel and Hardy feature *Way Out West* (James W. Horne, 1936), plus a number of Laurel and Hardy shorts, the Frank Sinatra vehicle *Suddenly* (Lewis Allen, 1954), *The Angel and the Badman* (James Edward Grant, 1947), and Frank Capra's *It's a Wonderful Life*

(1946). The results have been financially rewarding for both firms: when *Miracle on 34th Street* (whose black-and-white version has been in syndication for over twenty years) was shown in major television markets during the Christmas season of 1985, it produced Nielsens second only to the then top-rated *Dynasty;* and the colorized *Yankee Doodle Dandy* was the best-selling prerecorded videocassette of 1986.

The popularity of colorized movies has created a storm of controversy in Hollywood about the validity of the process. In January 1986, director Frank Capra and star Jimmy Stewart threatened to sue Colorization, Inc., for willfully ruining *It's a Wonderful Life,* and by the end of the year colorization had been publicly condemned by the Directors' Guild of America and by the American Film Institute, which sees it as destroying "our national film history and the rich heritage it represents." Earl Glick, chairman of Hal Roach Studios, and others have countered that colorized films have a better chance of being seen by today's color-oriented audiences than the black-and-white originals and that "a small group of people are *[sic]* saying that the public doesn't have constitutional choice to see those pictures in color." More recently, Ted Turner—owner of TBS, CNN, and, since July 1986, MGM-UA—announced plans to colorize that studio's entire library of 10,000 black-and-white classics, beginning with John Huston's *The Maltese Falcon* (1940), in order to make them competitive in program schedules with contemporary color films. This marketing ploy—pursued by Turner with near megalomania into the 1990s—has alarmed many persons in the creative end of the industry for several reasons.

In the first place, feature films shot in black and white were designed, lit, photographed, and edited to conform to the very specific demands of that medium. To "colorize" them by computer or any other means risks destroying their compositional values. Classical directors like Josef von Sternberg, Fritz Lang, Alfred Hitchcock, Howard Hawks, John Ford, Orson Welles, and Frank Capra conceived their films in black and white because that's the way they thought that present and future generations would experience them on the screen; to colorize their great black-and—white works would pervert their artistic intentions, to say the least. If Welles had shot *Citizen Kane* (1941) in color (or von Sternberg *Shanghai Express* [1932], or Ford *The Informer* [1935], or Hitchcock *Rebecca* [1940] or *Shadow of a Doubt* [1943]), he would have shot it quite differently. That is, if Welles had shot *Kane* in Technicolor in 1941, it would not look anything like a 1990 version of *Kane* colorized—he could never have achieved the chiaroscuro lighting effects and deep-focus photography so essential to that film's texture using pre–World War II Technicolor stock. Thus, the colorization of *Kane* would not only distort Welles' individual aesthetic intentions, but it would rewrite technological history by implying capabilities for Technicolor in the early 1940s that color stock did not possess for at least another fifteen years.

Directors whose work in black and white and whose place in film history would be significantly misrepresented by colorization would include F. W. Murnau, Robert Flaherty, Jean Renoir, von Sternberg, Lang, Hitchcock, Hawks, Ford, Welles, Capra, William Wyler, Kenji Mizoguchi, Max Ophüls, Luis Buñuel, Akira Kurosawa, Ingmar Bergman, and Alain Resnais, to name just the first rank. Add to this list all of the films of German Expressionism, French poetic realism, Italian neorealism, American *film noir,* and every important documentary movement before 1960—for all of which black and white was definitive of their very form—and you have an immense chunk of international film history. Since it is more probable than not that future generations will come to know this history largely through video, the colorization issue is crucial. In a free market economy like our own, the popularity of colorization could eventually lead to the disappearance of black and white from the classical repertoire. It's hardly likely, for example, that the studios will want to stock an inventory of both black-and-white *and* colorized versions of their classic films. The situation is liable to replicate that of the audio industry during the sixties when electronically reprocessed "stereo" versions of monaural recordings replaced the originals. Faced with these objections, colorizers reply that their films can be easily restored to black and white by muting the TV color control in playback, but this simply isn't so. Colorization heavily reworks the original black and white to accommodate its traveling matte process, and the decolorized result is less black and white than gray and pink.

We need to remind ourselves that films exist essentially as the product of a photochemical process. And if we value films, we really should not tamper with that process in any fundamental or permanent way. If colorization remains a pleasant novelty, then we should be prepared to accept and even to enjoy it as that. But if the practice becomes widespread, as it gives every indication of doing, then we must prevent it from distorting our cultural heritage by skewing the compositional values of the black-and-white medium and by suggesting technological imperatives (not to mention colors) that did not in fact exist.

THE SHAPE OF THE FUTURE

Whether or not the history of film and the history of television merge in the 1990s, it is certain that the technological evolution of the two media will continue to accelerate. It has been the main argument of this volume that film is a technological art form and that every revolution in its technology has produced and will continue to produce an essential change in the form itself. We have seen how the silent film is formally distinct from the sound film, and the widescreen film from them both—all on the basis of the technology available to filmmakers at any given point in time. The body of narrative conventions that Griffith worked a lifetime to discover is available today to anyone who can purchase a copy of *A Primer for Film-Making* or any of a score of similar instructional manuals. Eisensteinian montage can be found in every television commercial. Fluidity of camera movement, which once required all the brilliance of Murnau, Renoir, or Welles to achieve, can now be had for the rental fee of a Steadicam, the lightweight hand-held support camera that moves to record images as smoothly as if it were a crane or a dolly. In fact, by 1985 anyone with a thousand dollars could buy a half-inch video camcorder that would provide a fidelity of image and sound beyond anything available to the great American studios in their golden age. Technology obsolesces itself; art does not—that is the great paradox of a technological art form. To understand the true genius of Griffith, or Eisenstein, or Renoir, or Welles, or Hitchcock, or any other seminal figure in film history, we must think ourselves back to the technological limitations of their times, the limitations that they transcended to create an art of the moving photographic image. Otherwise, someday in the not-too-distant future, as we sit before our wall-sized holographic television screens and watch images of unprecedented sensory refinement dance before our eyes, we will be tempted to forget how very much we owe these pioneers—not only for creating and structuring our most technological of art forms, but for keeping that form meaningful, significative, and humane. Unless that commitment to the humane can be maintained by succeeding generations of film and video artists, the audiovisual environment of the future is likely to be as cold and alien as the landscape of the moon in *2001,* or the landscape of the soul in *The Shining.*

Academy aperture   The frame size established by the Academy of Motion Picture Arts and Sciences to standardize the sound film in 1932. It indicates an aspect ratio of 4:3, or 1.33:1. See **aspect ratio; widescreen.**

accelerated montage   A sequence made up of shots of increasingly shorter lengths that creates a psychological atmosphere of excitement and tension. See **montage; parallel action.**

accelerated motion   See **fast motion.**

aerial shot   A shot from above, usually made from a plane, helicopter, or crane. See **crane shot.**

"agit-Guignol"   Eisenstein's term for agitational effects involving shocking violence; derived from the Grand Guignol, a theater in Paris (1897–1962) that specialized in realistic depiction of murder and torture.

anamorphic lens   A lens that squeezes a wide image to fit the dimensions of a standard 35 mm film frame. In projection, an anamorphic lens on the projector reverses the process and redistributes the wide image on the screen. See **widescreen.**

animation   All techniques that make inanimate objects move on the screen, such as drawing directly on the film, individually photographing animation cells, and photographing the objects one frame at a time while adjusting their position between frames. See **pixillation; stop-motion photography.**

arc light   The source of high-energy illumination on the movie set and in the projector. It is produced by an electric current that arcs across the gap between two pieces of carbon.

Arriflex   A light, portable camera first used in the late fifties; it was essential to the mobile, hand-held photography of the New Wave and to most contemporary cinematography. Mitchell cameras, however, are the industry's workhorses.

art director   The person responsible for set design and graphics.

art houses   Small theaters that sprang up in the major cities of the United States during the 1950s to show "art films" (foreign films with intellectual and aesthetic aspirations) as opposed to "commercial films" (all American films except for occasional experimental productions like *Citizen Kane*)—a distinction that can no longer be made.

aspect ratio   The ratio of the width to the height of the cinematic image, or frame. The Academy aperture, standard through 1952, was 1.33:1. Contemporary widescreen ratios vary, but 1.66:1 is most common in Europe and 1.85:1 in the United States. Anamorphic processes such as CinemaScope can range from 2.00:1 to 2.55:1. See **widescreen.**

associative editing   The cutting together of shots to establish their metaphorical, or symbolic—as opposed to their narrative—relationship. The prehistoric bone that becomes a futuristic space station in Kubrick's *2001* (1968) is a prime example. See **match cut.**

asynchronous sound   Sound that does not proceed directly from the film image. See **contrapuntal sound.**

audion   Lee De Forest's vacuum tube, which first permitted amplification of audio signals for large audiences.

auteur   A director or other creative intelligence with a recognizable and distinctive style who is considered the prime "author" of a film. See *politique des auteurs.*

back-lighting   Lighting directed at the camera from behind the subject, thus silhouetting the subject. See **key light.**

back lots   Large tracts of open land owned by the studios and used to simulate various locations.

back projection   See **rear projection.**

biopic   A biographical film, especially the kind produced by Warner Bros. in the thirties and forties.

blimp   An awkward soundproofing cover for the camera first used in the early years of sound. Most cameras today are constructed with their own internal soundproofing.

blockbuster   A film that is enormously popular or one that was so costly to make that it must be enormously successful to make a profit. The first blockbusters were probably Italian superspectacles like *Cabiria* (Giovanni Pastrone, 1913), followed by the Griffith epics *The Birth of a Nation* (1915) and *Intolerance* (1916). During the twenties, films like *The Thief of Bagdad* (Raoul Walsh, 1924) and *Ben-Hur* (Fred Niblo, 1926) were conceived and marketed as blockbusters, as was David O. Selznick's *Gone with the Wind* (Victor Fleming, 1939) in the sound era. In the fifties and sixties, the epic-scale widescreen blockbuster (e.g., Cecil B. DeMille's *The Ten Commandments,* 1956) became a veritable genre. More recent examples include the record-breaking *Jaws* (Steven Spielberg, 1975), *Star Wars* (George Lucas, 1977), *Raiders of the Lost Ark* (Spielberg, 1981), and, of course, Warner Bros.' paradigmatic *Batman* (Tim Burton, 1989).

booking   Film rental.

boom The mobile arm that suspends the microphone above the actors and outside of the frame.

B-pictures Films that were made cheaply and quickly. They were used to fill the bottom half of a double bill when double features were standard.

broadcast The transmission of an electromagnetic signal over a widely dispersed area.

cable television The transmission of television signals via wire instead of broadcast radio waves. Although it was originally developed to permit television transmission to special geographical areas, it has become a popular alternative to broadcast television.

Cahiers du cinéma Paris-based film journal founded by André Bazin and Jacques Doniol-Valcroze in 1951 that featured important articles by future directors of the French New Wave. It is still being published.

camera angle The perspective that the camera takes on the subject being shot. Low angle, high angle, or tilt angle are the three most common.

calligraphism A term adopted by the neorealist director and critic Giuseppe De Sanits to designate a style of interwar Italian filmmaking devoted to the formally meticulous adaptation of late-nineteenth and early-twentieth century fiction; the neorealists associated it with the decadence of the Fascist cinema.

caméra-stylo Literally, "camera pen": a phrase first used by Alexandre Astruc in 1948 to suggest that cinema could be as multidimensional and personal as the older literary arts.

chanbara A Japanese sword-fight film.

chiaroscuro The artistic technique of arranging light and dark elements in pictorial composition.

cinéaste An artistically committed filmmaker.

Cinecittà The largest Italian studio complex; it is located in Rome.

cinema nôvo Literally, "new cinema": politically committed Brazilian cinema of the sixties.

CinemaScope The trade name used by 20th Century–Fox for its anamorphic widescreen process. The word is frequently used today to refer to all anamorphic processes.

Cinémathèque Française Established by Henri Langlois and Georges Franju in Paris in 1936, it is reputed to have the world's largest film library. By making older classics available to the public, it is also said to have influenced the style and themes of French films in the fifties and sixties.

Cinématographe The camera-projector-printer invented by the Lumière brothers in 1895.

cinematographer The "director of photography," or "lighting cameraman," who is responsible for the camera technique and the lighting of a film in production.

cinematography   Motion-picture photography.

cinéma vérité   Literally, "cinema truth", the French translation of Vertov's *Kino-pravda*: as originally used in postwar France, the term described a particular kind of cinema that utilized lightweight equipment, small crews, and direct interviews. The term is now used more casually to refer to any documentary technique. See **direct cinema** and **documentary.**

cinéphile   A person who loves cinema.

Cinerama   A widescreen process invented by Fred Waller that requires three electronically synchronized cameras; it was first used in the 1952 film *This Is Cinerama* and was abandoned in 1962 in favor of an anamorphic process marketed under the same name.

close-up   In its precise meaning, a shot of the subject's face or other object alone; more generally, any close shot.

compilation film   A film whose shots, scenes, and sequences come from other films, often archival newsreel footage. *The Fall of the Romanov Dynasty* (Esther Shub, 1927) is an early example.

computer graphics   Electronically generated animation, used since the late seventies to provide credit sequences (*Superman* [1978]) and special effects (*Star Wars*) [1977] for theatrical films. It is also used in television commercials and for network logos.

Constructivism   A movement in the theater arts closely related to **Futurism.** It advocated the use of architectural and/or mechanical set designs to give a 3-D effect.

continuity   The final editing structure of a completed film; also, arranging events as if they had occurred continuously when, in fact, they were shot out of sequence.

continuity editing   Editing shots together imperceptibly so that the action of a sequence appears to be continuous.

contract director   A director who works on projects from contract to contract, rather than on an annual salary as was common under the studio system.

contrapuntal sound   Sound used in counterpoint, or contrast, to the image.

crane shot   A shot taken from a mobile crane device. See **aerial shot.**

credits   The list of the writers, actors, technical personnel, and production staff of a film.

crosscutting   Intercutting shots from two or more sequences, actions, or stories to suggest **parallel action,** as D. W. Griffith did in *Intolerance* (1916).

cutting   Moving from one image or shot to another by editing.

day-for-night   The technique used to shoot night scenes during the day. The necessary effect is created by stopping down the lens aperture or by using special lens filters.

deep focus A technique that exploits **depth of field** to render subjects near the camera lens and far away with equal clarity and permits the composition of the image in depth. Orson Welles' *Citizen Kane* (1941) is one of the earliest and most famous films to use deep-focus shots as a basic structural element.

definition A term used to describe the facility of film stock to articulate the separate elements of an image. See **resolution.**

depth of field The varying range of distances from the camera at which an object remains in sharp focus.

diaphragm The mechanism that regulates the amount of light that passes through a lens; also *iris diaphragm.*

direct cinema Since the early sixties, the predominant documentary style in the United States. It is similar (to or, some argue, the same as) *cinéma vérité* in that it uses light, mobile equipment; but it stringently avoids narration or participation on the part of the filmmaker.

director of photography See **cinematographer.**

direct sound Sound that is recorded simultaneously with the image. With modern developments such as portable tape recorders and soundproofed cameras, direct sound has become common.

dissolve Frequently called a "lap dissolve": a transition that superimposes a fadeout over a fade-in.

documentary Coined by John Grierson in the thirties to describe formally structured nonfiction films like those of Robert Flaherty, the term has come to mean any film that is not entirely fictional.

Dolby A system (named for its inventor, Ray Dolby) for audio recording and playback that reduces background noise and improves frequency response, adding two-and-a-half octaves to the range. In motion picture exhibition, it can be used to produce multitrack stereophonic sound optically or magnetically—an advantage, since most exhibitors still use the less expensive optical playback equipment. Dolby was first used theatrically in rock concert documentaries and rock musicals (e.g., Ken Russell's *Tommy* [1975]). Francis Ford Coppola (*The Conversation*, 1974) and Robert Altman (*Nashville*, 1975) were the first directors to use it for strictly aesthetic ends, and *Star Wars* (1977) was the first widely released film recorded in Dolby throughout. Since 1977, Dolby sound has played an increasingly important role, in films.

dubbing The recording and **postsynchronization** of a dialogue or sound-effects track. For example, foreign-language dubbing.

editor The person who supervises the splicing or cutting together of the shots of a film into their final structure.

emulsion A thin, light-sensitive coating of chemicals covering the base of the film stock.

emulsion speed   A measure of a film stock's sensitivity to light. According to a scale established by the American Standards Association (ASA), the faster emulsion speeds are more sensitive to light and have a higher ASA number.

establishing shot   A shot, usually a long shot, that orients the audience in a film narrative by providing visual information (such as location) for the scene that follows.

exploitation film   A negative term for a film aimed at a particular audience and designed to succeed commercially by appealing to specific psychological traits in that audience.

exposure   The degree of light allowed to strike the surface of a film. Film can be underexposed to create dark, murky images, or overexposed to create light ones.

Expressionism   A literary or cinematic style that expresses the author's or director's private vision or offers a distorted perspective on reality. *Das Kabinett des Dr. Caligari* (1920) is an early Expressionist film.

extreme long shot   A shot made from a considerable distance, sometimes as far as a quarter of a mile. It provides a panoramic view of a location without camera movement. See **long shot** and **full shot.**

fade-in   A technique for beginning a scene whereby an image gradually appears on a blackened screen, finally brightening into full visibility.

fade-out   The opposite of **fade-in.**

fast motion   Action filmed at less than twenty-four frames per second (standard sound-film speed), so that when the processed film is projected at normal speed the action appears accelerated. Most silent films were shot at close to sixteen frames per second, and so they display unintentional fast motion when projected at sound speed, as they frequently are today.

feature   The main film in a program of several films, or any film over three reels (approximately 35 minutes) in length. Standard theatrical feature length is 90 to 120 minutes. See **short.**

fill light   A secondary light that illuminates the subject from the side or that lights areas not lit by the **key light.**

film clip   A short section of a film cut out of context, usually for the purpose of reviewing or previewing. Also used in making a **compilation film.**

film d'art   A movement in French cinema, started around 1908, that attempted to produce exact records of stage productions (minus, of course, the sound); it featured renowned dramatic personalities such as Sarah Bernhardt.

film gauge   The width of film stock, measured in millimeters: standard commercial film is 35mm, although 16mm is becoming more common; 70mm film produced from 65mm negative stock, is often used for epic productions; 16mm is standard for most other films; super 8mm is still basically the province of amateurs, and 8mm is now obsolete.

film noir A French term (literally, "black film") for a film set in a sordid urban atmosphere that deals with dark passions and violent crimes. Many American thrillers of the late forties and late eighties were of this type.

filmography A listing of films, their directors, and their dates, similar to a bibliography.

film plane The front surface of the film as it lies in the camera or projector gate (i.e., the film aperture).

film stock The basic material of film, made of cellulose triacetate and coated with photographic emulsions.

filter A plate of glass, plastic, or gelatin that alters the quality of light entering a lens.

final cut A film in its completed form. See **rough cut.**

first run The distribution of a new film to a limited number of showcase theaters. On its second run the film is usually distributed to a large number of theaters in less exclusive locations.

fish-eye lens A radically distorting wide-angle lens with an angle view of nearly 180 degrees.

flashback A shot, scene, sequence, or (sometimes) a major part of a film inserted into the narrative present in order to recapitulate the narrative past.

flash forward Like a flashback, a shot, scene, or sequence outside the narrative present, but projected into the narrative future.

focal length The distance in millimeters from the optical center of the lens (a point midway between the front and rear elements) to the emulsion surface of the film stock when the lens is sharply focused on "infinity," i.e., an extremely distant object. Short lenses are called **wide-angle lenses,** while long lenses are called **telephoto lenses.**

focus The clarity and sharpness of an image, limited to a certain range of distance from the camera. See **deep focus** and **shallow focus.**

focus plane The plane at which the lens forms an image when focused on a given scene, measured as the distance from the film plane. See **depth of field.**

Formalism The elevation of form over content. Formalism posits that meaning is a function of the strictly formal features of a discourse, and not the content or the referent of the content.

frame The smallest compositional unit of film structure, the frame is the individual photographic image both in projection and on the film strip. The term also designates the boundaries of the image as an anchor for composition.

Free Cinema An important documentary-style film movement in Britain started by Lindsay Anderson, Karel Reisz, and Tony Richardson in the mid-fifties.

freeze frame A shot that replicates a still photograph. The effect is achieved by printing a single frame many times in succession.

front projection An alternative to **rear projection**. While live action is filmed against a reflective backdrop, another image is projected on the backdrop by means of mirrors lying along the same axis as the camera lens. The lighting and reflective backdrop prevent shadows.

f-**stop** The lens aperture is the irislike diaphragm at the optical center of the lens, a point midway between the front and rear elements. Varying the diameter of this opening, which is measured in *f*-stops (e.g., *f*-1, *f*-1.4, *f*-2, *f*-2.8, *f*-4, *f*-5.6, *f*-8, *f*-11, *f*-16, *f*-22, *f*-32, *f*-45, *f*-64), determines how much light the lens will transmit to the emulsion surface of the film and therefore determines the visual quality of the image imprinted on the negative stock.

full shot A shot that includes the subject's entire body and often a three-fourths view of the set.

Futurism A revolutionary movement in the arts, closely allied with Constructivism, which glorified power, speed, technology, and the machine age at the expense of more traditional cultural forms. It had a natural affinity for the cinema and its mechanized apparatus.

gaffer The chief electrician and supervisor of all lighting on a set.

gendai-geki One of two major Japanese film genres, the *gendai-geki* deals with stories of contemporary life. A popular subtype is the *shomin-geki*, or comedy of middle-class and lower-middle-class family life. See *jidai-geki.*

genre A category used to classify a film in terms of certain general patterns of form and content, such as the Western, the horror film, or the gangster film.

glass shot A **special-effects** technique in which sections of a scene are painted on a glass plate which is then mounted in front of the camera for integration with live action.

grip The person who rigs up equipment, such as lights and props, and makes certain they function properly.

gross The total amount of money a film makes in rental and ticket receipts before deducting costs. The word is also used as a verb.

hand-held shot A type of shot made possible by portable, single-operator cameras. See **Arriflex.**

high key A lighting set-up in which the **key light** is particularly bright.

highlighting The use of extremely concentrated or fine light beams to accentuate certain parts of the subject.

holography A modern photographic technique that uses laser beams to replicate three-dimensionality.

intercutting See **crosscutting.**

intertitles Printed titles that appear within the main body of a film to convey dialogue and other narrative information. Intertitles are common in (but not essential to) the silent cinema.

iris shot A shot in which a circular, lens-masking device contracts or expands to isolate or reveal an area of the frame for symbolic or narrative visual effect.

jidai-geki One of two major Japanese film genres, the *jidai-geki* is a period film set before the Meiji Restoration of 1868. All *samurai* films are *jidai-geki*.

jump cut A cut that is made in the midst of a continuous shot, or a mismatched cut between shots (the opposite of a match cut's apparent seamlessness). Jump cuts create discontinuity in filmic time and space and draw attention to the medium itself, as opposed to its content.

key light The main light on a set, normally placed at a forty-five-degree angle to the camera-subject axis, mixed in a *contrast ratio* with fill light, depending on the desired effect. See **fill light** and **back-lighting.**

key-lighting In high-key lighting, the scene is almost entirely lit by the key light; in low-key lighting, little of the scene's illumination is provided by the key light.

Kinetograph The first viable motion picture camera, invented in 1889 by W. K. L. Dickson for the Thomas Edison Laboratories. See **Cinématographe; Kinetoscope.**

Kinetophone Edison's sound film system (never successfully marketed).

Kinetoscope Edison's peep-show device, in which short, primitive moving pictures could be seen before the invention of the projector.

kino-glaz Literally, "kino-eye": an early *cinéma-vérité* approach to film aesthetics conceived by Dziga Vertov in the twenties and best typified by his film *The Man with a Movie Camera* (1929).

lap dissolve See **dissolve.**

laser An acronym for "Light Amplification by Stimulated Emission of Radiation." Developed in 1960, lasers project concentrated beams of light whose different rays are coherent. Owing to its peculiar properties, laser light is a central factor in **holography.**

Latham loop A set of sprockets in early projection systems which looped the film to keep it from breaking as a result of its own inertia.

lens The optical device used in cameras and projectors to focus light rays by refraction.

lighting cameraman The British term for **cinematographer.**

linkage V. I. Pudovkin's description of **montage,** to which Sergei Eisenstein took exception.

location shooting Any shooting not done inside a studio.

long shot A shot that generally includes the whole figures of its subjects and a good deal of background. See **full shot** and **extreme long shot.**

long take A single unbroken shot, moving or stationary, which describes a complex action that might otherwise be represented through montage. It is essential to *mise-en-scène* aesthetics. See **sequence shot.**

mask A covering of some type placed before the camera lens to block off part of the photographed image. A mask can also refer to an aperture plate inserted behind a projector lens in order to obtain a desired aspect ratio. See **matte shot.**

master shot A shot, usually a long or full one, that establishes the spatial relationships among characters and objects within a dramatic scene before it is broken into closer, more discrete shots through editing.

match cut A cut in which two different shots are linked together by visual and/or aural, continuity. See **associative editing.**

matte shot A shot that is partially opaque in the frame area so that it can be printed together with another frame, masking unwanted content and allowing for the addition of another scene on a reverse matte. In a *traveling matte shot* the contours of the opaque areas can be varied from frame to frame.

medium shot A shot distanced midway between a **close-up** and a **full shot.**

microphotography Photographing or filming done through a microscope; also called photomicrography.

microphone A piece of electronic equipment that picks up sound waves and converts them into electrical signals for amplification.

minimal cinema A particularly stark, simplified kind of realism involving as little narrative manipulation as possible, associated with the films of Carl Dreyer, Robert Bresson, and, most recently, Jean-Marie Straub.

mirror shot A shot taken in a mirror, or a type of **glass shot.**

mise-en-scène Literally, "putting in the scene": a term that describes the action, lighting, decor, and other elements within the shot itself, as opposed to the effects created by cutting. Realists generally prefer the process of *mise-en-scène* to the more manipulative techniques of montage.

mix Optically, a **dissolve.** Aurally, the combination of several different soundtracks, such as dialogue and music.

mixing The work of the general sound editor, who refines, balances, and combines different soundtracks.

model shot A shot that uses miniatures instead of real locations, especially useful in disaster or science fiction films.

mogul Originally, a powerful conqueror; the word today designates the heads of the Hollywood studios in their heyday.

monogatari Japanese for "story" or "narrative." The word appears in many Japanese film titles.

monochromatic stock The earliest film stock, sensitive only to the blue area of the color spectrum but capable of great depth of field. Replaced by orthochromatic stock around 1918.

montage Its simplest meaning is "cutting." Sergei Eisenstein, however, developed an elaborate theory of montage based on the idea that contiguous shots relate to each other in a way that generates concepts not materially present in the content of the shots themselves. (**Montage** can also refer to the presentation of a great deal of narrative information through editing in a short period of time.)

narrative A story with a beginning, middle, and an end (though—to paraphrase Godard—not necessarily in that order).

narrative film A film whose structure follows a story-line of some sort. The mainstream of film history from the medium's birth through the present has been narrative.

naturalism A concept in literature and film that assumes that the lives of the characters are biologically, sociologically, or psychologically determined. Von Stroheim's *Greed* (1924) is a classic example of naturalism in film. (Frank Norris' *McTeague* [1899], the novel on which the film is based, is a classic of naturalism in fiction.)

negative Film that inversely records the light and dark areas of a photographed scene. **Positive** prints are produced from negatives.

negative cost The cost of producing a film, exclusive of advertising, studio overhead, and distribution prints.

neorealism A post—World War II movement in filmmaking associated primarily with the films of Roberto Rossellini, Luchino Visconti, and Vittorio De Sica in Italy. It was characterized by leftist political sympathies, location shooting, and the use of nonprofessional actors.

das neue Kino Literally, "the new cinema" of West Germany since 1968.

newsreel Filmed news reports shown along with the main feature in American theaters in the thirties, forties, and fifties; eclipsed by television news.

New Wave (*nouvelle vague*) Literally, "new wave": originally a school of French filmmakers who started their careers as critics for *Cahiers du cinéma* in the fifties. The year 1959 can be said to mark the beginning of this movement, since it was the release date of Truffaut's *Les quartre cents coups*, Godard's *À bout de souffle*, and Resnais' *Hiroshima, mon amour*. The phrase is also used to describe any new group of directors in any country whose approach to filmmaking is radically different from that of the established tradition, as in the Czech "New Wave."

nickelodeon The first permanent movie theaters, converted from storefronts. From *nickel* (the price of admission) plus *odeon* (Greek for "theater").

off-screen space The implied filmic space beyond the borders of the film frame at any given moment in projection. In conventional modes of representation (e.g., classical Hollywood narrative), off-screen space is treated as "dead," giving the borders the status of a compositional framing device beyond which filmic reality ceases to exist. Antitraditional modes of representation (e.g., in the films of Ozu or in contemporary materialist cinema) attempt to suggest the continuity of off-screen and on-screen space, giving the borders the status of a window frame beyond which there is more filmic reality. Off-screen space can also be created in front of the screen, as well as beyond its borders, if the camera traverses the 180-degree axis of action established by traditional practice and shoots what is, in effect, "behind" it.

optical printer   The machine that performs many postproduction optical processes, such as **dissolves,** color-balancing, and some **special effects.** Film prints are duplicated in a *contact printer.*

orthochromatic stock   A kind of black-and-white film stock that reacts particularly to the blue and green areas of the color spectrum rather than the red; widely replaced by **panchromatic stock** after 1926, but still used for special applications.

outtake   A **take** that is not included in the final print of the film.

pan   Any pivotal movement of the camera around an imaginary vertical axis running through it; from "panorama." See **roll; swish pan; tilt shot.**

Panavision   The anamorphic process most commonly used today; it replaced CinemaScope in the early sixties. Panavision-70 uses 70mm film stock without squeezing the image. In **Super-Panavision,** the original photography produces an unsqueezed negative which is reduced to 35 mm by anamorphic distorting. **Ultra-Panavision** produces a 65 mm negative anamorphically compressed in filming by a ratio of 1.25:1. Panavision is also the trade name of a widely used camera based on the design of the Mitchell.

panchromatic stock   Black-and-white film stock that is sensitive to all the colors of the spectrum, from red to blue, but is less capable of achieving great depth of field than the **orthochromatic stock** it replaced in 1927. The introduction of **widescreen** processes in the fifties greatly enhanced panchromatic **depth of field.**

parallel action   A narrative strategy that crosscuts between two or more separate actions in order to create the illusion that they are occurring simultaneously. See **accelerated montage.**

persistence of vision   The physiological foundation of the cinema: an image remains on the retina of the eye for a short period of time after it disappears from the actual field of vision; when a successive image replaces it immediately, as on a moving strip of film, the illusion of continuous motion is produced.

pixillation   A technique used for animating models by photographing them one frame at a time (as in *King Kong* [1933]). The technique can also be applied so that the illusion of continuous motion is disrupted. This effect is achieved either by stop-motion photography or by culling out particular frames from the negative of the film stock, as in work of Canadian filmmaker Norman McLauren (1914–84).

politique des auteurs   Literally, "authors' policy": the idea that a single person, most often the director, has the sole aesthetic responsibility for a film's form and content. François Truffaut first postulated the idea in his article *"Une certaine tendance du cinéma français,"* which appeared in the January 1954 issue of *Cahiers du cinéma.* Other prominent exponents of this theory of film have been André Bazin in France and Andrew Sarris in the United States.

positive   A print in which the light values of the film correspond to those of the scene recorded. Produced from a **negative.**

postsynchronization   Synchronization Synchronizing sound and image after the film has been shot—an important step forward in the liberation of the early sound film camera from its glass-paneled booth. Also called **dubbing.**

process shot   See **special effects.**

rack focus   A **shallow-focus** technique that forcibly directs the vision of the spectator from one subject to another. The **focus** is pulled and changed to shift the **focus plane.**

ratings   A system of film classification based on the amount of violence, sex, or "adult" language in a film. The British Board of Censors has three categories: U (universal); A (adult); and X (prohibited to children). The Motion Picture Association of America has five categories: G (general); PG (parental guidance suggested); PG-13 (parental guidance for children under 13); R (restricted to persons under seventeen unless accompanied by an adult); and X (prohibited to persons under seventeen).

reaction shot   A shot that cuts away from the central action to show a character's reaction to it.

realism   In cinema, realism describes a type of filming in which fidelity to the nature of the subject itself is more important than the director's attitude toward it. As opposed to expressionism, there is usually a minimum of montage and **special effects.** See **formalism; minimal cinema; neo-realism.**

real time   The actual time it would take for an event to occur in reality, outside of filmic time. In the works of modernist directors like Antonioni and Jancsó, real time and filmic time often coincide for long sequences, although not usually over the entire length of the film. In rare instances, however (Robert Wise's *The Set-Up* [1949], Agnès Varda's *Cleo de 5 à 7* [1962]), real time and filmic time coincide precisely.

rear projection   A technique in which a scene is projected onto a translucent screen located behind the actors, so that it appears that they are in a specific location.

reel   The casing and holder for the film or tape. The feed-reel supplies the film, and the take-up reel rewinds it. A 35mm reel holds up to 1,000 feet; a 16mm reel, 400 feet. At sound speed (twenty-four frames per second), a full 35mm reel runs about ten minutes; at silent speed (approximately sixteen frames per second), between fourteen and sixteen minutes.

release print   The final print used for screening and distribution.

resolution   The ability of a camera lens to define images in sharp detail.

reverse-angle shot   A shot taken at a 180-degree angle from the preceding shot—in practice rarely used. Instead, filmmakers have adopted shot / reverse-shot editing, in which the angle separating the two perspectives is usually between 120 degrees and 160 degrees. Two-party dialogue sequences are usually constructed through shot / reverse-shot editing, in a manner the French call *"champ-contra-champ"*: (visual) field against field.

reverse motion   Shooting a subject so that the action runs backward—achieved by turning the camera upside down (so long as the film is double-sprocketed), or by running it backward through an optical printer.

roll   The movement of the camera around the imaginary axis that runs between the lens and the subject.

rough cut   The first completed version of a film prepared by the editor. General polishing and the finer points of timing and continuity are accomplished later.

rushes   Also *dailies.* In production, the sound and image prints of each day's shooting, rapidly processed overnight, so that filmakers can evaluate the previous day's work before shooting begins again in the morning.

scenario   Either a part or the whole of a **screenplay.**

scene   A rather vague term that describes a unit of narration. In film, it may consist of a series of shots or of a single sequence that was shot in one location. See **shot; sequence.**

Schüfftan process   A process-photography technique that combines **mirror shots** and **model shots** to create a composite image. It was invented by the UFA cinematographer Eugen Schüfftan (later Schuftan) and was first used on a large scale by Fritz Lang to create the futuristic vistas of *Metropolis* (1926).

Scope   An abbreviation for **CinemaScope** or any other **anamorphic** process.

score   The musical **soundtrack** for a film. The word is also used as a verb.

screen   As a noun, the specially treated surface on which a film is projected; as a verb, the act of projecting or watching a film.

screenplay   The script of a film. It may be no more than a rough outline that the director fills in, or it may be detailed, complete with dialogue, continuity, and camera movements, as were most Hollywood studio scripts of the thirties and forties.

screwball comedy   A type of comedy popular in American films of the thirties; characterized by frantic action and a great deal of verbal wit. The focal point of the plot is usually a couple in a bizarre predicament, as in Capra's *It Happened One Night* (1934) and Hawks' *Bringing Up Baby* (1938).

second unit   In an elaborate production, a supplementary film crew that photographs routine scenes not shot by the first unit. Background and **establishing shots,** for instance, are usually shot by the second unit.

sequence   A unit of film structure made up of one or more **scenes** or **shots** that combine to form a larger unit.

sequence shot   A **long take** that usually requires sophisticated camera movement. Sometimes called by the French term *plan-séquence.*

set   The location where a scene is shot, often constructed on a **soundstage.**

set-up   The position of the camera, lights, sound equipment, actors, etc., for any given **shot.** The number of different set-ups that a film requires can be an important economic factor.

shallow focus   A technique that deliberately uses a shallow **depth of field** in order to direct the viewer's perception along a shallow **focus plane.** See **deep focus; rack focus.**

short   A film whose running time is less than thirty minutes.

shot   A continuously exposed, unedited piece of film of any length: the basic signifying unit of film structure. The average shot length (ASL) and the number of shots vary with every film.

shutter   The mechanism that opens and closes to obstruct light from individual film frames as they are moved into position for exposure in the camera and projection in the projector.

slapstick   A type of comedy that relies on acrobatic physical gags and exaggerated pantomine rather than on verbal humor. It was, obviously, the dominant comic form during the silent era.

slow motion   The camera is overcranked to film action at a speed faster than twenty-four frames per second. When the film is later projected at normal speed, the action appears much slower on the screen than it would in reality.

socialist realism   The aesthetic doctrine promulgated in the Soviet Union in the late twenties that insists that all art be rendered intelligible to the masses and subserve the purposes of the state. It has little to do with either socialism or realism.

soft focus   By means of lens filters, special lenses, or even vaseline smeared directly on a normal lens, the definition of a subject is blurred or softened, producing a dreamy or romantic effect (and, often, making an actor or actress appear younger).

sound effects   All sounds that are neither dialogue nor music.

soundstage   A specially designed soundproof building in which **sets** are constructed for filming.

soundtrack   There are two basic types of soundtrack in use today: optical and magnetic. Optical soundtracks encode information on a photographic light band that widens, narrows, or varies in density on the edge of the film strip. Magnetic soundtracks encode information electromagnetically on specially treated surfaces.

special effects   A term used to describe a range of artificial photographic processes or devices, such as **front projection, model shots, rear projection,** etc. It can also describe such **mechanical effects** as explosions, fires, the use of blood bags, etc.

split screen   Two or more images contained within a single frame which do not overlap. Abel Gance used the technique extensively in *Napoléon* (1927).

sprockets The evenly spaced holes on the edge of the film strip that allow it to be moved forward mechanically; also, the wheeled gears that engage these holes in the camera and projector.

stereophonic sound The use of two or more high-fidelity speakers and **soundtracks** to approximate the actual dimensionality of hearing with two ears.

still A production still shot for publicity purposes, or a single-frame enlargement from a film that looks like a photograph.

stock footage Film borrowed from a collection or library that consists of standard, often-used shots, such as of World War II combat or street crowds in New York City.

stop-motion photography A technique used for trick photography and **special effects,** in which one frame is exposed at a time so that the subject can be adjusted between frames; reputedly discovered by Georges Méliès. See **pixillation.**

subjective camera A technique that causes the viewer to observe events from the perspective of a character in the film, either empirically or psychologically.

subtitle A printed title superimposed over the images, usually at the bottom of the frame, to translate foreign dialogue, etc.

surrealism A movement in painting, film, and literature in the twenties; the term now suggests any fantastic style of representation.

swish pan A **pan** that moves from one scene to another so quickly that the intervening content is blurred.

synchronization The use of mechanical or electronic timing devices to keep sound and image in a precise relationship to each other. Also known as "sync."

synchronous sound Sound whose source is made clear by the image track. See **asynchronous sound; contrapuntal sound.**

take A director shoots one or more takes of each shot in a given **set-up,** only one of which appears in the final version of the film.

telephoto lens A lens with a long **focal length** that functions like a telescope to magnify distant objects. Because its angle of view is very narrow, it flattens the depth perspective.

television A system for the broadcast transmission of moving images and sound to home receivers, invented in the thirties but not available for mass marketing until after World War II. Since that time, television has usurped the cinema as America's dominant mass medium to the point that Hollywood is kept alive today less by theatrical filmmaking than by the production of telefilm. The word *television* derives from the Greek for "seeing at a distance."

theatrical distribution The distribution of films through normal commercial agencies and theaters.

theatrical film A film made primarily for viewing in a motion picture theater rather than for television or some other specialized delivery system.

Third World cinema A type of militant cinema now being produced in the countries of Latin America, Africa, and Asia. It is generally Marxist in ideology.

tilt shot   A shot made by turning the camera up and down so that it rotates on an axis running from left to right through the camera head. See **pan; roll.**

time-lapse photography   Used primarily as a scientific tool to photograph natural phenomena that occur too slowly for normal observation, it is a kind of extreme **fast-motion** shooting that compresses real time by photographing a subject at a rate (for example) of one frame every thirty seconds. The opposite type of time-lapse photography would rapidly expose film to capture movement that occurs too quickly to be seen by the naked eye.

track   A single recording channel on a **soundtrack** that can be mixed with others and modified to create a variety of effects.

tracking shot   A single continuous **shot** made on the ground with a moving camera that is also known as a traveling shot. **Aerial** and **crane** shots are also continuous.

two-reeler   A film running about thirty minutes, the standard length of silent comedies.

typage   A theory of casting actors and actresses that was used by Eisenstein: instead of professionals with individual characteristics, he sought "types" and representative characters.

undercrank   To run a camera at a speed of less than twenty-four frames per second. When the film is projected at normal speed, the subject appears in fast motion. See **slow motion.**

VCR   Abbreviation for "videocassette recorder" or "videocassette recording." See **videocassette.**

VHS   Abbreviation for "video home system." Any video system or combination of systems designed for home use, including VCRs, **videodisc** players, video games, and home computers with video display. More specifically, VHS is the technical designation for a popular half-inch videotape format (RCA, Panasonic, JVC, etc.) which competed on the consumer market with the Beta-format (Sony, Zenith, Toshiba, etc.) until it won the day in the mid-1980s. Since that time, only Sony (which invented the Beta format) has continued to manufacture Beta equipment, although many video professionals consider it to be technologically superior to VHS.

videocassette   A sealed two-reel system of three-quarter-inch or half-inch videotape generally used for private recording and viewing.

videodisc   A system for home video playback of prerecorded discs. Audiovisual information is encoded on plastic discs by a **laser** beam for decoding by a corresponding laser beam on the playback unit.

videotape   Magnetic tape for recording video images and sound; manufactured in two-inch (professional), three-quarter-inch, half-inch, and 8mm one-quarter-inch (amateur) formats.

VistaVision.   A nonanamorphic widescreen process developed by Paramount to compete with Fox's CinemaScope in 1954. It ran 35mm film stock through the camera horizontally rather than vertically to produce a double-frame image twice as wide as the conventional 35mm frame. The positive print could be projected horizontally with special equipment to cast a huge image on the screen, or it could be reduced anamorphically for standard vertical 35mm projection. The process was abandoned in 1961 because it was too expensive.

voice-over   A voice track laid over the other tracks in a film's sound mix to comment upon or narrate the action on screen.

VTR   Abbreviation for "videotape recorder" or "videotape recording," reel-to-reel or cassette.

wide-angle lens   A lens whose broad angle of view increases the illusion of depth but distorts the linear dimensions of the image. See **fish-eye lens; telephoto lens.**

widescreen   Any film format with an aspect ratio of 1.85:1, flat. Most widescreen processes are anamorphic, but some employ wide-gauge film (Panavision-70, Todd-AO) or multiple camera processes (Cinerama).

wild recording   Recording sound (usually to be used later as sound effects) independently of the visuals.

wild shooting   Shooting a film without simultaneously recording the soundtrack.

wild sound   See **wild recording.**

wipe   An optical process whereby one image appears to wipe the preceding image off the screen—a common transitional device in the thirties. See **dissolve; fade-out; iris-out.**

zoom   A variable-focus lens (one capable of focal lengths ranging from **wide-angle** to **telephoto**), often used to create optical motion without **tracking** the camera. Also used to describe a shot made with such a lens.

Selective Bibliography

What follows is the Bibliography as it appeared in the first edition. For a complete update, the reader is referred to the individual bibliographies as they appear in the footnotes and Instructor's Manual.

CHAPTER 1. *Origins*

Barnes, John. *The Beginnings of the Cinema in England.* New York: Barnes & Noble, 1976.
Benjamin, Walter. "A Short History of Photography." *Screen,* 13, 1 (Spring 1972), 5–26.
Ceram, C. W. *Archaeology of the Cinema.* London: Thames and Hudson, 1965.
Conot, Robert. *A Streak of Luck: The Life and Legend of Thomas Alva Edison.* New York: Seaview Books, 1979.
Cook, Olive. *Movement in Two Dimensions.* London: Hutchinson, 1963.
Dickson, W. K. L., and Dickson, Antonia. *History of the Kinetograph, Kinetoscope, and Kinetophone.* New York: S. Albert Bunn, 1895; reprinted, New York: Arno Press, 1970.
Gernsheim, Helmut. *The History of Photography.* New York: Oxford University Press, 1955.
Hammond, Paul. *Marvellous Méliès.* London: Gordon Fraser Gallery, 1974.
Hendricks, Gordon. *Eadweard Muybridge: The Father of the Motion Pictures.* New York: Grossman Publishers, 1965.
————. *Origins of the American Film.* New York: Arno Press, 1972. (Contains "The Edison Motion Picture Myth" [1961], "The Kinetoscope" [1966], and "Beginnings at Biograph" [1964].)
Hepworth, Cecil. *Came the Dawn: Memories of a Film Pioneer.* London: Phoenix House, 1961.
Josephson, Mathew. *Edison.* London: Eyre & Spottiswoode, 1961; New York: McGraw-Hill, 1963.
MacDonnell, Kevin. *Eadweard Muybridge.* Boston: Little, Brown, 1972.
Macgowan, Kenneth. *Behind the Screen.* New York: Delacorte Press, 1965.
Marey, E. J. *E. J. Marey, 1830–1904: La photographie du mouvement.* Paris: Musée National d'Art Moderne, 1977.
Muybridge, Eadweard. *Muybridge's Complete Human and Animal Locomotion: All 781 Plates from the 1887 "Animal Locomotion."* Introduction by Anita Ventura Mozley. 3 vols. New York: Dover Books, 1979.
Ramsaye, Terry. *A Million and One Nights: A History of the Motion Picture.* New York: Simon and Schuster, 1926; reprinted 1964.
Sanderson, Richard A. *A Historical Study of the Development of American Motion Picture Content and Techniques Prior to 1904.* New York: Arno Press, 1977.
Spehr, Paul C. *The Movies Begin: Making Movies in New Jersey, 1887–1920.* Newark, N.J.: The Newark Museum, 1977.
Wenden, D. J. *The Birth of the Movies.* New York: E. P. Dutton, 1974.

CHAPTER 2. *International Expansion 1907–1918*

Balshoffer, Fred J., and Miller, Arthur C. *One Reel a Week.* Berkeley: University of California Press, 1967.

Benjamin, Walter. "The Work of Art in the Age of Mechanical Reproduction." In *Illumina-tions*. New York: Schocken Books, 1969.

Everson, William K. *American Silent Film*. New York: Oxford University Press, 1978.

Fell, John L. *Film and the Narrative Tradition*. Norman: University of Oklahoma Press, 1974.

French, Philip. *The Movie Moguls*. London: Weidenfeld & Nicolson, 1969.

Hurt, James. *Focus on Film and Theatre*. Englewood Cliffs, N.J.: Prentice-Hall, 1974.

Jacobs, Lewis. *The Rise of the American Film*. New York: Harcourt, Brace, 1939; reprinted, New York: Teachers College Press, 1968.

Jarrat, Vernon. *The Italian Cinema*. New York: Falcon Press, 1951.

Lacassin, Francis. *Louis Feuillade*. Paris, 1964.

Lindsay, Vachel. *The Art of the Moving Picture*. New York: Macmillan, 1915; reprinted, New York: Liveright, 1970.

Macgowan, Kenneth. *The Living Stage*. Englewood Cliffs, N.J.: Prentice-Hall, 1955.

Pathé, Charles. *Souvenirs et conseils d'un parvenu*. Paris, 1926.

———. *De Pathé frères à Pathé cinéma*. Lyons, 1940.

Pratt, George C. *Spellbound in Darkness: A History of the Silent Film*. Rochester, N.Y.: University of Rochester Press, 1966; revised edition, Greenwich, Conn.: New York Graphic Society, 1973.

Rondi, Gian Luigi. *Italian Cinema Today*. London: Denis Dobson, 1966.

Slide, Anthony. *Aspects of American Film History Prior to 1920*. Metuchen, N.J.: Scarecrow Press, 1978.

———. *Early American Cinema*. Cranbury, N.J.: A. S. Barnes, 1969.

Tariol, Marcel. *Louis Delluc*. Paris, 1965.

Walker, Alexander. *Stardom*. New York: Stein & Day, 1970.

Zierold, Norman. *The Moguls*. New York: Coward-McCann, 1969.

CHAPTER 3. *D. W. Griffith and the Consummation of Narrative Form*

Aitken, Roy E. *"The Birth of a Nation."* Middleburg, Va.: William W. Denlinger, 1965.

Barry, Iris. *D. W. Griffith: American Film Master*. Edited by Eileen Bowser. New York: New York Graphic Society, 1965.

Bitzer, G. W. *Billy Bitzer: His Story*. New York: Farrar, Straus & Giroux, 1973.

Brown, Karl. *Adventures with D. W. Griffith*. New York: Farrar, Straus & Giroux, 1973.

Geduld, Harry M., ed. *Focus on D. W. Griffith*. Englewood Cliffs, N.J.: Prentice-Hall, 1971.

Griffith, D. W. *The Man Who Invented Hollywood: The Autobiography of D. W. Griffith*. Edited by James Hart. Louisville, Ky.: Touchstone, 1972.

Griffith, Linda Arvidson. *When the Movies Were Young*. New York: E. P. Dutton, 1925; reprinted, New York: Dover Books, 1969.

Henderson, Robert M. *D. W. Griffith: His Life and Work*. New York: Oxford University Press, 1972.

———. *D. W. Griffith: The Years at Biograph*. New York: Noonday Press, 1970.

Huff, Theodore. *"Intolerance": The Film by David Wark Griffith: Shot-by-Shot Analysis*. New York: Museum of Modern Art, 1966.

———. *A Shot Analysis of D. W. Griffith's "The Birth of a Nation."* New York: Museum of Modern Art Film Library, 1961.

Koszarski, Richard, ed. *The Rivals of D. W. Griffith: Alternate Auteurs 1913–1918*. Catalogue of exhibit at the Walker Art Center, Minneapolis, November–December 1976.

O'Dell, Paul. *Griffith and the Rise of Hollywood*. Cranbury, N.J.: A. S. Barnes, 1970.

Silva, Fred, ed. *Focus on "The Birth of a Nation."* Englewood Cliffs, N.J.: Prentice-Hall, 1971.

Thomas, Emory M. *The American "War and Peace."* Englewood Cliffs, N.J.: Prentice-Hall, 1973.

Wagenknecht, Edward, and Slide, Anthony. *The Films of D. W. Griffith*. New York: Crown Publishers, 1976.

Williams, Martin. *Griffith: First Artist of the Movies*. New York: Oxford University Press, 1980.

CHAPTER 4. *German Cinema of the Weimar Period, 1919–1929*

Amengual, Barthélemy. *G. W. Pabst*. Paris, 1966.
Atwell, Lee. *G. W. Pabst*. Boston: Twayne Publishers, 1977.
Baxter, John. *The Hollywood Exiles*. New York: Taplinger Publishers, 1967.
Béranger, Jean. *La grand aventure du cinéma suédois*. Paris, 1960.
Bogdanovich, Peter. *Fritz Lang in America*. New York: Frederick A. Praeger, 1967.
Bucher, Felix. *Germany: An Illustrated Guide*. Screen Series. London: A. Zwemmer, 1971.
Cowie, Peter. *Finnish Cinema*. Cranbury, N.J.: A. S. Barnes, 1977.
———. *Sweden*. Screen Series. 2 vols. Revised ed. Cranbury, N.J.: A. S. Barnes, 1969.
Eisner, Lotte H. *Fritz Lang*. New York: Oxford University Press, 1977.
———. *The Haunted Screen*. Berkeley: University of California Press, 1969.
———. *Murnau*. Berkeley: University of California Press, 1973.
Hardy, Forsyth. *Scandinavian Film*. London: Falcon Press, 1952.
Idestam-Almquist, Bengt. *Victor Sjöström*. Paris, 1965.
Jensen, Paul M. *The Cinema of Fritz Lang*. Cranbury, N.J.: A. S. Barnes, 1969.
Kracauer, Siegfried. *From Caligari to Hitler: A Psychological History of the German Film*. Princeton: Princeton University Press, 1947.
Milne, Tom. *The Cinema of Carl Dreyer*. Cranbury, N.J.: A. S. Barnes, 1971.
Neergaard, Ebbe. *The Story of Danish Film*. Copenhagen: Danish Institute, 1962.
Pensel, Hans. *Seastrom and Stiller in Hollywood*. New York: Vantage Press, 1969.
Phillips, M. S. "The Nazi Control of the German Film Industry." *Journal of European Studies* 1, 1 (1971), 37–68.
Skoller, Donald, ed. *Dreyer in Double Reflection*. New York: E. P. Dutton, 1973. (Translation of Dreyer's *Om Filmen*.)
Wollenberg, Hans H. *Fifty Years of German Film*. Edited by Roger Manvell. London: Falcon Press, 1948; reprinted, New York: Arno Press, 1972.

CHAPTER 5. *Soviet Silent Cinema and the Theory of Montage, 1917–1931*

Barna, Yon. *Eisenstein*. Boston: Little, Brown, 1973.
Bryher, W. *Film Problems of Soviet Russia*. Territet, Switzerland, 1929.
Constantine, Mildred, and Fern, Alan. *Revolutionary Soviet Film Posters*. Baltimore: Johns Hopkins University Press, 1974.
Dickinson, Thorold. *Soviet Cinema*. London: Falcon Press, 1948.
Dovzhenko, Alexander. *Alexander Dovzhenko: The Poet as Filmmaker*. Translated and edited by Marco Carynnyk. Cambridge, Mass.: MIT Press, 1973.
Eisenstein, Sergei. *The Complete Films of Eisenstein*. New York: E. P. Dutton, 1974.
———. *Film Form*. Translated and edited by Jay Leyda. New York: Harcourt Brace Jovanovich, 1969.
———. *The Film Sense*. Translated and edited by Jay Leyda. New York: Harcourt Brace Jovanovich, 1969.
———. *Notes of a Film Director*. New York: Dover Books, 1970.
Feldman, Seth R. *The Evolution of Style in the Early Work of Dziga Vertov*. New York: Arno Press, 1977.
Hough, Richard. *The Potemkin Mutiny*. Englewood Cliffs, N.J.: Prentice-Hall, 1960.
The Influence of Silent Soviet Cinema on World Cinema. Proceedings of the International Federation of Film Archives Symposium. Varna, Bulgaria, June 29–July 2, 1977.
Kuleshov, Lev. *Kuleshov on Film*. Translated and edited by Ronald Levaco. Berkeley: University of California Press, 1974.
Leyda, Jay. *Kino: A History of the Russian and Soviet Cinema*. London: George Allen & Unwin, 1960.
Marshall, Herbert, ed. *Sergei Eisenstein's "The Battleship Potemkin."* New York: Avon Books, 1978.
Mayer, David. *Eisenstein's "Potemkin."* New York: Grossman Publishers, 1972. (Shot-by-shot analysis.)

Moussinac, Léon. *Sergei Eisenstein.* Translated by D. Sandy Petrey. New York: Crown Publishers, 1970.

Nizhnii, Vladimir. *Lessons with Eisenstein.* Translated by Ivor Montagu. London: George Allen & Unwin, 1952; New York: Hill & Wang, 1962.

Pudovkin, V. I. *Film Technique and Film Acting.* London, 1929; reprinted, New York: Grove Press, 1970.

Sadoul, Georges. *Dziga Vertov.* Paris, 1971.

Schnitzer, Jean, ed. *Cinema in Revolution.* New York: Hill & Wang, 1973.

———, and Schnitzer, Luda. *Dovjenko.* Paris, 1966.

Seton, Marie. *Sergei M. Eisenstein.* New York: A. A. Wyn, 1953.

"Soviet Film." *Cinema Journal,* 17, 1 (Fall 1977 [special issue]).

Swallow, Norman. *Eisenstein: A Documentary Portrait.* London: George Allen & Unwin, 1976; New York: E. P. Dutton, 1977.

Taylor, Richard. *The Politics of the Soviet Cinema, 1917–1929.* London: Cambridge University Press, 1979.

CHAPTER 6. *Hollywood in the Twenties*

Asplund, Una. *Chaplin's Films.* Translated by Paul Britten Austin. London: David & Charles, 1971.

Barr, Charles. *Laurel and Hardy.* Berkeley: University of California Press, 1968.

Blesh, Rudi. *Keaton.* New York: Macmillan, 1966.

Brownlow, Kevin. *The Parade's Gone By.* New York: Alfred A. Knopf, 1968.

———, and Kobal, John. *Hollywood: The Pioneers.* New York: Alfred A. Knopf, 1979.

Brownlow, Kevin. *The Parade's Gone By.* New York: Alfred A. Knopf, 1968.

Byron, Stuart. *Movie Comedy.* New York: Grossman Publishers, 1977.

Calder-Marshall, Arthur. *The Innocent Eye.* New York: Harcourt, Brace, and World, 1963.

Carey, Gary. *Lost Films.* New York: Museum of Modern Art, 1970.

Carringer, Robert, and Sabath, Barry. *Ernst Lubitsch: A Guide to References and Resources.* Boston: G. K. Hall, 1978.

Chaplin, Charles. *My Autobiography.* New York: Pocket Books, 1966.

"Chaplin: Twelve Essays." *Film Comment,* 8, 3 (September–October 1972) [special issue]).

Cooke, Alistair. *Douglas Fairbanks: The Making of a Screen Character.* New York: Macmillan, 1940.

Curtis, Thomas Quinn. *Von Stroheim.* New York: Farrar, Straus & Giroux, 1971.

Dardis, Tom. *Keaton: The Man Who Wouldn't Lie Down.* New York: Charles Scribner's Sons, 1979.

Durgnat, Raymond. *The Crazy Mirror.* New York: Horizon Press, 1969.

Finler, Joel. *Stroheim.* Berkeley: University of California Press, 1968.

Gifford, Denis. *Chaplin.* Garden City. N.Y.: Doubleday, 1974.

Hall, Ben. *The Golden Age of the Movie Palace.* New York: Clarkson Potter, 1961.

Herndon, Booton. *Mary Pickford and Douglas Fairbanks.* New York: W. W. Norton, 1977.

Kerr, Walter. *The Silent Clowns.* New York: Alfred A. Knopf, 1975.

Lebel, J. P. *Buster Keaton.* Cranbury, N.J.: A. S. Barnes, 1967.

Lloyd, Harold. *An American Comedy.* New York: Dover Books, 1971.

McCabe, John. *Laurel and Hardy.* New York: E. P. Dutton, 1975.

McCaffrey, Donald W., ed. *Focus on Chaplin.* Englewood Cliffs, N.J.: Prentice-Hall, 1971.

Mast, Gerald. *The Comic Mind.* New York: Bobbs-Merrill, 1973.

Moews, Daniel. *Keaton: The Silent Features Close Up.* Berkeley: University of California Press, 1977.

Montgomery, John. *Comedy Films.* London: George Allen & Unwin, 1968.

Robinson, David. *Buster Keaton.* Bloomington: Indiana University Press, 1969.

———. *Hollywood in the Twenties.* Cranbury, N.J.: A. S. Barnes, 1968.

Rubinstein, E. *Filmguide to "The General."* Bloomington: Indiana University Press, 1973.

Schickel, Richard, and Fairbanks, Douglas, Jr. *The Fairbanks Album.* Boston: New York Graphic Society, 1975.
Sennett, Mack. *King of Comedy.* Garden City, N.Y.: Doubleday, 1954.
Sinclair, Upton. *Upton Sinclair Presents William Fox.* Los Angeles: Upton Sinclair, 1933.
Thomson, David. *Movie Man.* New York: Stein & Day, 1967.
Tyler, Parker. *Chaplin, Last of the Clowns.* New York: Horizon Press, 1972.
Wead, George. *The Film Career of Buster Keaton.* Boston: G. K. Hall, 1977.
Weinberg, Herman G. *The Complete "Greed."* New York: E. P. Dutton, 1972.
———. *The Lubitsch Touch.* New York: E. P. Dutton, 1971.
———. *Stroheim: A Pictorial Record of His Nine Films.* New York: Dover Books, 1975.

CHAPTER 7. *The Coming of Sound, 1926–1932*

Bergman, Andrew. *We're in the Money: Depression America and Its Films.* New York: New York University Press, 1971.
Cameron, Evan W., ed. *Sound and the Cinema: The Coming of Sound to American Film.* Pleasantville, N.Y.: Redgrave, 1979.
Geduld, Harry M. *The Birth of the Talkies: From Edison to Jolson.* Bloomington: Indiana University Press, 1975.
Hoffman, Charles. *Sounds for Silents.* New York: Museum of Modern Art, 1970.
Rosten, Leo C. *Hollywood: The Movie Colony, the Movie Makers.* New York: Harcourt, Brace, 1941.
Ryan, Roderick T. *A History of Motion Picture Color Technology.* New York: Focal Press, 1978.
Thorp, M. F. *America at the Movies.* New Haven: Yale University Press, 1939.
Thrasher, Frederic. *Okay for Sound.* New York: Duell, Sloan & Pierce, 1964.
Walker, Alexander. *The Shattered Silents: How the Talkies Came to Stay.* London: Elm Tree Books, 1978.

CHAPTER 8. *The Sound Film and the American Studio System*

Allen, Frederick Lewis. *Only Yesterday.* New York: Harper & Brothers, 1940.
Anderegg, Michael A. *William Wyler.* Boston: Twayne Publishers, 1979.
Balio, Tino. *United Artists.* Madison: University of Wisconsin Press, 1976.
Baxter, John. *The Cinema of John Ford.* London: Tantivy Press, 1971.
———. *The Cinema of Josef von Sternberg.* London: Tantivy Press, 1971.
———. *Hollywood in the Thirties.* Cranbury, N.J.: A. S. Barnes, 1968.
Behlmer, Rudy, ed. *Memo from David O. Selznick.* New York: Viking Press, 1972.
Benchley, Nathaniel. *Bogart.* Boston: Little, Brown, 1975.
Bogdanovich, Peter. *John Ford.* Berkeley: University of California Press, 1968.
Canham, Kingsley; Denton, Clive; Belton, John; et al. *The Hollywood Professionals,* vols. 1, 2, 3, and 4. Cranbury, N.J.: A. S. Barnes, 1974–78.
Capra, Frank. *The Name Above the Title.* New York: Bantam Books, 1971.
Croce, Arlene. *The Fred Astaire and Ginger Rogers Book.* New York: Vintage Books, 1977.
Durgnat, Raymond. *The Strange Case of Alfred Hitchcock.* Boston: M.I.T. Press, 1975.
Eames, John D. *The MGM Story: The Complete Story of Fifty Roaring Years.* New York: Crown Publishers, 1964.
Fernett, Gene. *Poverty Row.* Satellite Beach, Fla.: Coral Reef Publications, 1973.
Fielding, Raymond. *The March of Time.* New York: Oxford University Press, 1978.
Finch, Christopher. *The Art of Walt Disney.* New York: Harry N. Abrams, 1975.
French, Warren. *Filmguide to "The Grapes of Wrath."* Bloomington: Indiana University Press, 1973.
Glatner, Richard, ed. *Frank Capra.* Ann Arbor: University of Michigan Press, 1975.
Halliwell, Leslie. *Mountain of Dreams: The Golden Years of Paramount Pictures.* London: Hart-Davis, MacGibbon, 1978.

Harris, Robert A. *The Films of Alfred Hitchcock.* Secaucus, N.Y.: Citadel Press, 1976.

Higham, Charles. *Hollywood Cameramen.* Bloomington: Indiana University Press, 1970.

———. *Warner Brothers: A History of the Studio.* New York: Charles Scribner's Sons, 1975.

Hirschhorn, Clive. *The Warner Brothers Story.* New York: Crown Publishers, 1979.

Kempton, Murray. *Part of Our Time: Some Monuments and Ruins of the Thirties.* New York: Simon and Schuster, 1955.

Klingender, F. D., and Legg, Stuart. *Money Behind the Screen.* London: Lawrence & Wishart, 1937.

Koszarski, Richard. *Hollywood Directors, 1914–1940.* New York: Oxford University Press, 1976.

Lambert, Gavin. *On Cukor.* New York: Capricorn Books, 1973.

LaValley, Albert, ed. *Focus on Hitchcock.* Englewood Cliffs, N.J.: Prentice-Hall, 1972.

McBride, Joseph, ed. *Focus on Howard Hawks.* Englewood Cliffs, N.J.: Prentice-Hall, 1972.

McBride, Joseph, and Wilmington, Michael. *John Ford.* New York: DaCapo Press, 1975.

McCarthy, Todd, and Flynn, Charles. *Kings of the B's.* New York: E. P. Dutton, 1975.

Madsen, Axel. *William Wyler.* New York: Thomas Y. Crowell, 1973.

Marx, Arthur. *Goldwyn.* New York: W. W. Norton, 1976.

Marx, Samuel. *Mayer and Thalberg.* New York: Random House, 1975.

Miller, Don. *"B" Movies.* New York: Curtis Books, 1973.

Milne, Tom. *Rouben Mamoulian.* London: Thames and Hudson, 1969.

Naremore, James. *Filmguide to "Psycho."* Bloomington: Indiana University Press, 1973.

Parish, James R. *The Golden Era: The MGM Stock Company.* New Rochelle, N.Y.: Arlington House, 1974.

———. *The Great Gangster Pictures.* Metuchen, N.J.: Scarecrow Press, 1976.

Perlman, William. *The Movies on Trial.* New York: Macmillan, 1936.

Perry, George. *The Films of Alfred Hitchcock.* New York: E. P. Dutton, 1965.

Rohmer, Eric, and Chabrol, Claude. *Hitchcock: The First Forty-Four Films.* Translated and with an introduction by Stanley Hochman. New York: Frederick Ungar, 1979.

Sarris, Andrew. *The Films of Josef von Sternberg.* New York: Doubleday, 1966.

———. *The John Ford Movie Mystery.* Bloomington: Indiana University Press, 1975.

Schickel, Richard. *The Disney Version.* New York: Simon and Schuster, 1968.

Sennett, Ted. *Warner Brothers Presents.* New Rochelle, N.Y.: Arlington House, 1971.

Sinclair, Andrew. *John Ford.* New York: The Dial Press/James Wade, 1979.

Spoto, Donald. *The Art of Alfred Hitchcock: Fifty Years of His Motion Pictures.* New York: Hopkinson and Blake, 1976.

Taylor, John Russell. *Hitch: The Life and Times of Alfred Hitchcock.* New York: Pantheon Books, 1978.

Thomas, Bob. *Walt Disney.* New York: Simon and Schuster, 1976.

Thomas, Tony. *The Busby Berkeley Book.* Greenwich, Conn.: New York Graphic Society, 1969.

———, and Solomon, Aubrey. *The Films of Twentieth Century-Fox: A Pictorial History.* New York: Citadel Press, 1979.

Truffaut, François, and Scott, Helen. *Hitchcock.* New York: Simon and Schuster, 1966.

Tuska, Jon, ed. *Close Up: The Contract Director.* Metuchen, N.J.: Scarecrow Press, 1976.

———. *Close Up: The Hollywood Director.* Metuchen, N.J.: Scarecrow Press, 1978.

Vidor, King. *On Film Making.* New York: David McKay, 1972.

Weinberg, Herman G. *Josef von Sternberg.* New York: E. P. Dutton, 1967.

Willis, Donald C. *The Films of Frank Capra.* Metuchen, N.J.: Scarecrow Press, 1974.

———. *The Films of Howard Hawks.* Metuchen, N.J.: Scarecrow Press, 1975.

Wood, Robin. *Hitchcock's Films.* Cranbury, N.J.: A. S. Barnes, 1969.

———. *Howard Hawks.* Garden City, N.Y.: Doubleday, 1968.

Yacowar, Maurice. *Hitchcock's British Films.* Hamden, Conn.: Archon Books, 1977.

CHAPTER 9. *Europe in the Thirties*

Babitsky, Paul. *The Soviet Film Industry.* New York: Frederick A. Praeger, 1955.

Balcon, Michael. *Twenty Years of British Film.* London: Falcon Press, 1947.

Baxter, John. *The Hollywood Exiles.* New York: Taplinger Publishers, 1976. (European émigrés in Hollywood.)

Bazin, André. *Jean Renoir.* Edited by François Truffaut. New York: Simon and Schuster, 1973.

Birkos, Alexander S. *Soviet Cinema: Directors and Films.* Hamden, Conn.: Archon Books, 1976.

Bordwell, David. *Filmguide to "La Passion de Jeanne d'Arc."* Bloomington: Indiana University Press, 1973.

Braudy, Leo. *Jean Renoir.* Garden City, N.Y.: Doubleday, 1972.

Durgnat, Raymond. *Jean Renoir.* Berkeley: University of California Press, 1975.

Faulkner, Christopher. *Jean Renoir: A Guide to References and Resources.* Boston: G. K. Hall, 1979.

Fraigneau, André. *Cocteau on the Film.* 1954; reprinted, New York: Dover Books, 1972.

Geduld, Harry M., and Gottesman, Ronald, eds. *The Making and Unmaking of "Que Viva México!"* Bloomington: Indiana University Press, 1970.

Gilliatt, Penelope. *Jean Renoir: Essays, Conversations, Reviews.* New York: McGraw-Hill, 1975.

Gilson, René. *Jean Cocteau.* New York: Crown Publishers, 1974.

Infield, Glenn. *Leni Riefenstahl: The Fallen Film Goddess.* New York: Thomas Y. Crowell, 1976.

Ivens, Joris. *The Camera and I.* New York: International Publishers, 1969.

Hull, David Stewart. *Film in the Third Reich.* Berkeley: University of California Press, 1969.

Kulik, Karol. *Alexander Korda.* London: W. H. Allen, 1975.

Lawder, Standish D. *The Cubist Cinema.* New York: New York University Press, 1975.

Leiser, Erwin. *Nazi Cinema.* New York: Macmillan, 1974.

Leprohon, Pierre. *Jean Renoir.* New York: Crown Publishers, 1971.

Low, Rachel. *The History of the British Film, 1929–1939: Documentary and Educational Films of the 1930s.* London: George Allen & Unwin, 1979.

———. *The History of the British Film, 1929–1939: Films of Comment and Persuasion of the 1930s.* London: George Allen & Unwin, 1979.

Mast, Gerald. *Filmguide to "The Rules of the Game."* Bloomington: Indiana University Press, 1973.

Minton, David B. *The Films of Leni Riefenstahl.* Metuchen, N.J.: Scarecrow Press, 1978.

Montagu, Ivor. *With Eisenstein in Hollywood.* New York: International Publishers, 1967.

Ogle, Patrick. "Technological Influences Upon the Development of Deep Focus Photography in the United States," *Screen,* 13, 1 (Spring 1972), 45–72.

Perry, George. *The Great British Picture Show.* New York: Hill & Wang, 1974.

Petley, Julian. *Capital and Culture: German Cinema, 1933–45.* London: British Film Institute, 1979.

Renoir, Jean. *My Life and My Films.* Translated by Norman Denny. New York: Atheneum Publishers, 1974.

Sadoul, Georges. *French Film.* London: Falcon Press, 1953.

Salles Gomes, P. E. *Jean Vigo.* Berkeley: University of California Press, 1971.

Sesonske, Alexander. *Jean Renoir: The French Films, 1924–1939.* Cambridge, Mass.: Harvard University Press, 1980.

Smith, John M. *Jean Vigo.* New York: Frederick A. Praeger, 1972.

Taylor, Richard. *Film Propaganda: Soviet Russia and Nazi Germany.* New York: Barnes & Noble, 1979.

Wollenberg, Hans H. *Fifty Years of German Film.* London: Falcon Press, 1947; reprinted, New York: Arno Press, 1972.

CHAPTER 10. *Orson Welles and the Modern Sound Film*

Bazin, André. *Orson Welles: A Critical View.* Translated by Jonathan Rosenbaum. New York: Harper & Row, 1978.

Cowie, Peter. *A Ribbon of Dreams.* Cranbury, N.J.: A. S. Barnes, 1973.

France, Richard. *The Theatre of Orson Welles.* Lewisburg, Pa.: Bucknell University Press, 1977.

Gottesman, Ronald, ed. *Focus on "Citizen Kane."* Englewood Cliffs, N.J.: Prentice-Hall, 1971.

———. *Focus on Orson Welles.* Englewood Cliffs, N.J.: Prentice-Hall, 1975.

Higham, Charles. *The Films of Orson Welles.* Berkeley: University of California Press, 1970.

Kael, Pauline, ed. *The Citizen Kane Book.* Boston: Little, Brown, 1972.

Koch, Howard. *The Panic Broadcast.* Boston: Little, Brown, 1970.

McBride, Joseph. *Orson Welles.* New York: Viking Press, 1972.

Naremore, James. *The Magic World of Orson Welles.* New York: Oxford University Press, 1978.

———, ed. *Orson Welles: A Guide to References and Resources.* Boston: G. K. Hall, 1980.

CHAPTER 11. *War-Time and Post-War Cinema: Italy and America, 1940–1951*

Agel, Henri. *Romance américaine.* Paris: Éditions du Cerf, 1963.

Alloway, Lawrence. *Violent America: The Movies, 1946–1964.* New York: Museum of Modern Art, 1965.

Alton, John. *Painting with Light.* New York: Macmillan, 1950.

Armes, Roy. *Patterns of Realsim.* London: Tantivy Press, 1971.

Bohne, Luciana, ed. "Italian Neorealism." *Film Criticism,* 3, 2 (Winter 1979 [special issue]).

Calvocoressi, Peter. *Total War.* New York: Random House, 1972.

Guarner, José Luis. *Rossellini.* New York: Frederick A. Praeger, 1970.

Higham, Charles, and Greenberg, Joel. *Hollywood in the Forties.* Cranbury, N.J.: A. S. Barnes, 1968.

Hovald, P. G. *Néoréalisme.* Paris, 1959.

Huaco, George A. *The Sociology of Film Art.* New York: Basic Books, 1965.

Jones, Ken D., and McClure, Arthur F. *Hollywood at War.* Cranbury, N.J.: A. S. Barnes, 1973.

Kagan, Norman. *The War Film.* New York: Pyramid Publications, 1974.

Karimi, A. M. *Toward a Definition of the American Film Noir.* New York: Arno Press, 1976.

Leprohon, Pierre. *The Italian Cinema.* New York: Frederick A. Praeger, 1972.

Manvell, Roger. *Films and the Second World War.* Cranbury, N.J.: A. S. Barnes, 1974.

Morella, Joe, et al. *The Films of World War Two.* Secaucus, N.J.: Citadel Press, 1973.

Navasky, Victor. *Naming Names.* New York: Viking Press, 1980.

Nowell-Smith, Geoffrey. *Luchino Visconti.* Garden City, N.Y.: Doubleday, 1968.

Shindler, Colin. *Hollywood Goes to War: Films and American Society, 1939–52.* London: Routledge and Kegan Paul, 1979.

Stirling, Monica. *A Screen of Time: A Study of Luchino Visconti.* New York: Harcourt Brace Jovanovich, 1979.

Suid, Lawrence H. *Guts and Glory: Great American War Movies.* Reading, Mass.: Addison-Wesley, 1978.

Warshow, Robert. *The Immediate Experience.* Garden City, N.Y.: Doubleday, 1962; reprinted, New York: Atheneum Publishers, 1971.

Zavattini, Cesare. *Sequences from a Cinematic Life.* Translated by William Weaver. Englewood Cliffs, N.J.: Prentice-Hall, 1970.

CHAPTER 12. *Hollywood, 1952–1965*

Battcock, Gregory, ed. *The New American Cinema.* New York: E. P. Dutton, 1967.

Baxter, John. *Hollywood in the Sixties.* New York: Macmillan, 1972.

Casper, Joseph A. *Vincente Minnelli and the Film Musical*. London: Thomas Yoseloff, 1977.

Ceplair, Larry, and Englund, Steven. *The Inquisition in Hollywood: Politics in the Film Community, 1930–1960*. Garden City, N.Y.: Doubleday, 1980.

Ciment, Michel. *Kazan on Kazan*. New York: Viking Press, 1973.

Garnham, Nicholas. *Samuel Fuller*. New York: Viking Press, 1971.

Gow, Gordon. *Hollywood in the Fifties*. London: A. Zwemmer, 1971.

Halliday, Jon. *Sirk on Sirk*. New York: Viking Press, 1972.

Hardy, Phil. *Samuel Fuller*. New York: Frederick A. Praeger, 1970.

Kanfer, Stephan. *A Journal of the Plague Years*. New York: Antheneum Publishers, 1973. (Witch-hunts and blacklisting.)

Kreidl, John Francis. *Nicholas Ray*. Boston: Twayne Publishers, 1977.

Limbacher, James L. *Four Aspects of Film*. New York: Russell and Russell, 1975.

Madsen, Axel. *Billy Wilder*. Bloomington: Indiana University Press, 1969.

Manvell, Roger. *New Cinema in the U.S.A.* New York: E. P. Dutton, 1968.

Pratley, Gerald. *The Cinema of John Frankenheimer*. Cranbury, N.J.: A. S. Barnes, 1969.

———. *The Cinema of John Huston*. Cranbury, N.J.: A. S. Barnes, 1977.

———. *The Cinema of Otto Preminger*. Cranbury, N.J.: A. S. Barnes, 1971.

Ross, Lillian. *Picture*. New York: Avon Books, 1952. (On the filming of John Huston's *Red Badge of Courage*.)

Schumach, Murray. *The Face on the Cutting Room Floor*. New York: William Morrow, 1964.

Seidman, Steve. *The Film Career of Billy Wilder*. Boston: G. K. Hall, 1977.

Stern, Michael. *Douglas Sirk*. Boston: Twayne Publishers, 1979.

Sinyard, Neil, and Turner, Adrian. *Journey Down Sunset Boulevard: The Films of Billy Wilder*. London: BCW Publications, 1980.

Talbot, David, and Zheutlin, Barbara. *Creative Differences: Profiles of Hollywood Dissidents*. Boston: South End Press, 1978.

Vizzard, Jack. *See No Evil: Life Inside a Hollywood Censor*. New York: Pocket Books, 1971.

Wysotsky, Michael Z. *Wide-Screen Cinema and Stereophonic Sound*. New York: Hastings House, 1971.

Zolotow, Maurice. *Billy Wilder in Hollywood*. New York: G. P. Putnam's Sons, 1977.

CHAPTER 13. *The French New Wave and Its Native Context*

Allen, Don. *Truffaut*. New York: Viking Press, 1974.

Andrew, J. Dudley. *André Bazin*. New York: Oxford University Press, 1978.

Armes, Roy. *The Cinema of Alain Resnais*. Cranbury, N.J.: A. S. Barnes, 1968.

———. *French Cinema Since 1946*. 2 vols. Cranbury, N.J.: A. S. Barnes, 1970.

———. *French Film*. New York: E. P. Dutton, 1970.

Braudy, Leo, ed. *Focus on "Shoot the Piano Player."* Englewood Cliffs, N.J.: Prentice-Hall, 1972.

Brown, Royal S., ed. *Focus on Godard*. Englewood Cliffs, N.J.: Prentice-Hall, 1972.

Cameron Ian, ed. *Claude Chabrol*. New York: Frederick A. Praeger, 1970.

———. *The Films of Jean-Luc Godard*. New York: Frederick A. Praeger, 1969.

———. *The Films of Robert Bresson*. New York: Frederick A. Praeger, 1969.

Collet, Jean. *Jean-Luc Godard*. New York: Crown Publishers, 1968.

Crisp, C. G. *François Truffaut*. New York: Frederick A. Praeger, 1972.

Durgnat, Raymond. *Franju*. London: Studio Vista Books, 1967.

French, Philip, et al. *The Films of Jean-Luc Godard*. London: Blue Star House, 1967.

Giannetti, Louis D. *Godard and Others*. London: Tantivy Press, 1975.

Graham, Peter. *The New Wave*. Garden City, N.Y.: Doubleday, 1968.

Harvey, Sylvia. *May '68 and Film Culture*. London: British Film Institute, 1978.

Insdorf, Annette. *François Truffaut*. New York: William Morrow, 1979.

Kawin, Bruce F. *Mindscreen: Bergman, Godard, and First-Person Film.* Princeton, N.J.: Princeton University Press, 1978.

MacBean, James Roy. *Film and Revolution.* Bloomington: Indiana University Press, 1975.

Martin, Marcel. *France: Screen Guide.* New York: A. S. Barnes, 1971.

Monaco, James. *Alain Resnais.* New York: Oxford University Press, 1979.

———. *The New Wave: Truffaut, Godard, Chabrol, Rohmer, Rivette.* New York: Oxford University Press, 1976.

Mussman, Toby, ed. *Jean-Luc Godard.* New York: E. P. Dutton, 1968.

Nogueira, Rui. *Melville.* New York: Viking Press, 1971.

Petrie, Graham. *The Cinema of François Truffaut.* Cranbury, N.J.: A. S. Barnes, 1970.

Rosenbaum, Jonathan. *Rivette: Texts and Interviews.* London: British Film Institute, 1977.

Roud, Richard. *Jean-Luc Godard.* Bloomington: Indiana University Press, 1969.

Truffaut, François. *The Films in My Life.* New York: Simon and Schuster, 1979.

Van Wert, William F. *The Film Career of Alain Robbe-Grillet.* Boston: G. K. Hall, 1977.

Ward, John. *Alain Resnais or the Theme of Time.* New York: Doubleday, 1968.

Willemen, Paul, ed. *Ophüls.* London: British Film Institute, 1978.

Wood, Robin, and Walker, Michael. *Claude Chabrol.* New York: Frederick A. Praeger, 1970.

CHAPTER 14. *European Renaissance: West*

Aranda, Francisco. *Luis Buñuel.* London: Secker & Warburg, 1969.

Armes, Roy. *The Ambiguous Image: Narrative Style in Modern European Cinema.* Bloomington: Indiana University Press, 1976.

———. *A Critical History of British Cinema.* New York: Oxford University Press, 1978.

Barr, Charles. *Ealing Studios.* London: Cameron & Taylor, 1977.

Baxter, John. *An Appalling Talent: Ken Russell.* London: Michael Joseph, 1973.

———. *The Australian Cinema.* Sidney: Angus and Robertson, 1970.

Bergman, Ingmar. "Introduction: Bergman Discusses His Film-Making." In *Four Screenplays.* Translated from the Swedish by Lars Malstrom and David Kushner. New York: Simon and Schuster, 1960, p. xxii.

Bergom-Larsson, Maria. *Swedish Film: Ingmar Bergman and Society.* Cranbury, N.J.: A. S. Barnes, 1979.

Betti, Liliana. *Fellini: An Intimate Portrait.* Boston: Little, Brown, 1979.

Betts, Ernest. *The Film Business: A History of British Cinema 1896–1972.* London: George Allen & Unwin, 1973.

Björkman, Stig; Manns, Torsten; and Sima, Jonas. *Bergman on Bergman.* Translated by Paul Britten Austin. New York: Touchstone/Simon and Schuster, 1973.

Buache, Freddy. *The Cinema of Luis Buñuel.* Cranbury, N.J.: A. S. Barnes, 1973.

Butler, Ivan. *Cinema in Britain.* London: Tantivy Press, 1969.

Cameron, Ian. *Antonioni.* London: Studio Vista Books, 1969.

Christie, Ian, ed. *Powell, Pressburger, and Others.* London: British Film Institute, 1978.

Di Carlo, Carlo. *Michelangelo Antonioni.* Rome: Edizioni di Bianco e Nero, 1964.

Durgnat, Raymond. *Luis Buñuel.* Berkeley: University of California Press, 1970.

———. *A Mirror for England: British Movies from Austerity to Affluence.* New York: Frederick A. Praeger, 1971.

Feldman, Seth, and Nelson, Joyce. *Canadian Film Reader.* Toronto: Peter Martin Associates, 1977.

Fellini, Federico. *Fellini on Fellini.* Translated by Isabel Quigley. New York: Delacorte Press, 1976.

Foix-Molina, Vincente. *New Cinema in Spain.* London: British Film Institute, 1977.

Furhammar, Leif, and Isaksson, Folke. *Politics and Film.* Translated by Kersti French. New York: Frederick A. Praeger, 1971.

Gifford, Denis. *British Cinema.* Cranbury, N.J.: A. S. Barnes, 1968.

Gomez, Joseph A. *Peter Watkins.* Boston: Twayne Publishers, 1979.

Handling, Piers. *The Films of Don Shebib.* Ottawa: Canadian Film Institute, 1978.

Harcourt, Peter. *Six European Directors.* New York: Penguin Books, 1974.

Hillier, Jim. *Cinema in Finland.* London: British Film Institute, 1978.

Huss, Roy, ed. *Focus on "Blow-Up."* Englewood Cliffs, N.J.: Prentice-Hall, 1971.

Kaminsky, Stuart, and Hill, Joseph F., eds. *Ingmar Bergman: Essays in Criticism.* New York: Oxford University Press, 1975.

Krelman, Martin. *This Is Where We Came In: The Career and Character of Canadian Film.* Toronto: McClelland and Stewart, 1978.

Kulik, Karol. *Alexander Korda.* London: W. H. Allen, 1975.

Leahy, James. *The Cinema of Joseph Losey.* Cranbury, N.J.: A. S. Barnes, 1967.

Leprohon, Pierre. *Michelangelo Antonioni.* New York: Simon and Schuster, 1963.

Lyons, Robert J. *Michelangelo Antonioni's Neo-Realism.* New York: Arno Press, 1976.

Manvell, Roger. *New Cinema in Britain.* New York: E. P. Dutton, 1968.

———. *New Cinema in Europe.* New York: E. P. Dutton, 1966.

Mellen, Joan, ed. *The World of Luis Buñuel: Essays in Criticism.* New York: Oxford University Press, 1978.

Milne, Tom. *Losey on Losey.* New York: Doubleday, 1968.

Morris, Peter. *Embattled Shadows: A History of Canadian Cinema, 1895–1939.* Montreal: McGill–Queens University Press, 1979.

Murray, Edward. *Fellini the Artist.* New York: Frederick Ungar, 1976.

Perry, Ted. *Filmguide to "8½."* Bloomington: Indiana University Press, 1975.

Reade, Eric. *History and Heartburn: The Saga of Australian Film, 1896–1978.* East Brunswick, N.J.: Fairleigh Dickinson University Press, 1981.

Rosenthal, Stuart. *The Cinema of Federico Fellini.* Cranbury, N.J.: A. S. Barnes, 1976.

Salachas, Gilbert. *Federico Fellini.* New York: Crown Publishers, 1969.

Simon, John. *Ingmar Bergman Directs.* New York: Harcourt Brace Jovanovich, 1972.

Stack, Oswald, ed. *Pasolini on Pasolini.* Bloomington: Indiana University Press, 1969.

Steene, Birgitta, ed. *Focus on "The Seventh Seal."* Englewood Cliffs, N.J.: Prentice-Hall, 1972.

———. *Ingmar Bergman.* New York: Twayne Publishers, 1968.

Sussex, Elizabeth. *Lindsay Anderson.* New York: Frederick A. Praeger, 1970.

Taylor, John Russell. *Directors and Directions: Cinema for the Seventies.* New York: Hill & Wang, 1975.

Veroneau, Pierre, ed. *The Canadian Cinemas.* Ottawa: Canadian Film Institute, 1979.

Walker, Alexander. *Hollywood, U.K.* New York: Stein & Day, 1974.

Willemen, Paul, ed. *Pier Paolo Pasolini.* London: British Film Institute, 1977.

Wood, Robin. *Ingmar Bergman.* New York: Frederick A. Praeger, 1969.

Young, Vernon. *Cinema Borealis: Ingmar Bergman and the Swedish Ethos.* New York: Avon Books, 1971.

CHAPTER 15. *European Renaissance: East*

Banaszkiewicz, Wladyslaw. *Contemporary Polish Cinematography.* Warsaw: Polonia Publishing House, 1962.

Broz, Jarosław. *The Path of Fame of the Czechoslovak Film: A Short Outline of Its History.* Prague: Československý Filmexport, 1967.

Butler, Ivan. *The Cinema of Roman Polanski.* Cranbury, N.J.: A. S. Barnes, 1970.

Dolmatovskaya, Galina, and Shilova, Irina. *Who's Who in the Soviet Cinema.* Translated by Galina Dolmatovskaya. Moscow: Progress Publishers, 1979.

Estéve, Michel. *Miklós Jancsó.* Paris: Lettres Moderne, 1975.

Fuksiewicz, Jacek. *Film and Television in Poland.* Warsaw: Interpress Publishers, 1976.

Hibbin, Nina. *Eastern Europe: An Illustrated Guide.* Screen Series. Cranbury, N.J.: A. S. Barnes, 1969.

Holloway, Ronald. *Z Is for Zagreb.* Cranbury, N.J.: A. S. Barnes, 1972.

Kurzewski, Stanislaw. *Contemporary Polish Cinema.* London: Stephen Wischhusen, 1980.

Langdon, Dewey. *Outline of Czechoslovakian Cinema*. London: Informatics, 1971.

Liehm, Antonín J. *Closely Watched Films: The Czechoslovak Experience*. White Plains, N.Y.: International Arts and Sciences Press, 1974.

———. *The Miloš Forman Stories*. White Plains, N.Y.: International Arts and Sciences Press, 1975.

Liehm, Mira, and Liehm, Antonín J. *The Most Important Art: East European Film After 1945*. Berkeley: University of California Press, 1977.

Michalek, Boleslaw. *The Cinema of Andrzej Wajda*. Translated by Edward Rothert. Cranbury, N.J.: A. S. Barnes, 1973.

Nemeskürty, István. *Word and Image: History of the Hungarian Cinema*. Translated by Zsuzsanna Horn. Budapest: Corvina Press, 1968.

Petrie, Graham. *History Must Answer to Man: The Contemporary Hungarian Cinema*. London: Tantivy Press, 1979.

Škvorecký, Josef. *All the Bright Young Men and Women: A Personal History of the Czech Cinema*. Toronto: Peter Martin Associates, 1971.

Stoil, Michael. *Cinema Beyond the Danube: The Camera and Politics*. Metuchen, N.J.: Scarecrow Press, 1974.

Vronskaya, Jeanne. *Young Soviet Film-Makers*. London: George Allen & Unwin, 1972.

Whyte, Alistair. *New Cinema in Eastern Europe*. New York: E. P. Dutton, 1971.

Žalman, Jan. *Films and Film-Makers in Czechoslovakia*. Prague: Orbis, 1968.

CHAPTER 16. *Wind from the East: Japan and Elsewhere*

Anderson, Joseph L., and Richie, Donald. *The Japanese Film: Art and Industry*. Rutland, Vt.: Charles E. Tuttle, 1959.

Barnouw, Erik, and Krishnaswamy, Subramanyam. *Indian Film*. New York: Columbia University Press, 1963; second edition, New York: Oxford University Press, 1980.

Bock, Audi. *Japanese Film Directors*. New York: Kodansha International, 1978.

Burch, Noël. *Theory of Film Practice*. Translated by Helen R. Lane. New York: Frederick A. Praeger, 1973.

———. *To the Distant Observer: Form and Meaning in Japanese Cinema*. Revised and edited by Annette Michelson. Berkeley: University of California Press, 1979.

Castillon, Pierre de. *Le cinéma japonais*. Notes et études documentaire, nos. 4.158–4.159. Paris: Documentation Française, 1975.

Da Cunha, Uma. *Indian Film, '78/'79*. New Delhi: F. C. Rampal, 1979.

Eberhard, Wolfram. *The Chinese Silver Screen*. Taipei: The Oriental Cultural Service, 1972.

Iwazaki, Akira. *Kenji Mizoguchi*. Paris, 1967.

"Japanese Cinema." *Wide Angle*, 1, 4 (1977 [special issue]).

Leyda, Jay. *Dianying: Electric Shadows: An Account of Films and the Film Audience in China*. Cambridge, Mass.: MIT Press, 1972; revised edition, 1979.

Mellen, Joan. *Voices from the Japanese Cinema*. New York: Liveright, 1975.

———. *The Waves at Genji's Door*. New York: Pantheon Books, 1976.

Ray, Satyajit. *Our Films, Their Films*. Bombay: Orient Longmans, 1977.

Richie, Donald. *The Films of Akira Kurosawa*. Berkeley: University of California Press, 1965.

———. *Focus on "Rashomon."* Englewood Cliffs, N.J.: Prentice-Hall, 1972.

———. *Japanese Cinema*. Garden City, N.Y.: Anchor Books, 1971.

———. *The Japanese Movie*. Tokyo: Kodansha International, 1966.

———. *Ozu*. Berkeley: University of California Press, 1974.

Sato, Tadao. *The Art of Yasujiro Ozu*. Tokyo, 1974.

Tucker, Richard N. *Japan: Film Image*. London: Studio Vista Books, 1973.

Schrader, Paul. *Transcendental Style in Film: Ozu, Bresson, Dreyer*. Berkeley: University of California Press, 1972.

Seton, Marie. *Portrait of a Director: Satyajit Ray*. Bloomington: Indiana University Press, 1971.

Silver, Alain. *The Samurai Film*. Cranbury, N.J.: A. S. Barnes, 1977.

Svensson, Arne. *Japan: An Illustrated Guide.* Cranbury, N.J.: A. S. Barnes, 1971.

Tiedeman, Arthur E., ed. *An Introduction to Japanese Civilization.* New York: Columbia University Press, 1974.

Varley, H. Paul. *Samurai.* New York: Delacorte Press, 1970.

Vasuder, Aruna. *Liberty and License in the Indian Cinema.* New Delhi: Vikas, 1978.

Wood, Robin. *The Apu Trilogy.* New York: Frederick A. Praeger, 1971.

CHAPTER 17. *The Shape of the Seventies*

Agel, Jerome. *The Making of "2001."* New York: Signet Books, 1970.

Burton, Julianne. *The New Latin American Cinema: An Annotated Bibliography.* New York: Cineaste, 1976.

Cameron, Ian, et al. *Second Wave.* New York: Frederick A. Praeger, 1970.

Cawelti, John G., ed. *Focus on "Bonnie and Clyde."* Englewood Cliffs, N.J.: Prentice-Hall, 1972.

Chanan, Michael, ed. *Chilean Cinema.* London: British Film Institute, 1976.

Clarke, Arthur C. *Lost Worlds of "2001."* New York: Signet Books, 1972.

"Culture in the Age of Mass Media." *Latin American Perspectives,* 16, 5, 1 (Winter 1978 [special issue]).

Cyr, Helen W. *A Filmography of the Third World.* Metuchen, N.J.: Scarecrow Press, 1976.

The Education of the Film-Maker. Washington, D.C.: Unesco Press, 1975.

Geduld, Carolyn. *Filmguide to "2001: A Space Odyssey."* Bloomington: Indiana University Press, 1973.

Houston, Penelope. *The Contemporary Cinema.* Baltimore: Penguin Books, 1963; revised edition, 1971.

Jacobs, Diane. *Hollywood Renaissance.* Cranbury, N.J.: A. S. Barnes, 1977.

Johnson, Robert K. *Francis Ford Coppola.* Boston: Twayne Publishers, 1977.

Kagan, Norman. *The Cinema of Stanley Kubrick.* New York: Grove Press, 1975.

Kass, Judith. *Robert Altman: American Innovator.* New York: Popular Library, 1978.

Kolker, Robert Phillip. *A Cinema of Loneliness: Penn, Kubrick, Coppola, Scorsese, Altman.* New York: Oxford University Press, 1980.

Koszarski, Richard, ed. *Hollywood Directors, 1941–1976.* New York: Oxford University Press, 1977.

MacBean, James Roy. *Film and Revolution.* Bloomington: Indiana University Press, 1975.

Madsen, Axel. *The New Hollywood.* New York: Thomas Y. Crowell, 1975.

Manvell, Roger. *The German Cinema.* London: J. M. Dent, 1971.

McKinney, Doug. *Sam Peckinpah.* Boston: Twayne Publishers, 1979.

Monaco, James. *American Film Now: The People, the Power, the Money, the Movies.* New York: Oxford University Press, 1979.

Musun, Chris. *The Marketing of Motion Pictures.* Los Angeles: Chris Musun, 1969.

Nevares, B. R. *The Mexican Cinema.* Albuquerque: University of New Mexico Press, 1976.

Paul, William. "Hollywood *Harakiri.*" *Film Comment,* 13, 2 (March–April 1977), 40–43, 56–62.

Pye, Michael, and Myles, Linda. *The Movie Brats: How the Film Generation Took Over Hollywood.* New York: Holt, Rinehart, and Winston, 1979.

Roud, Richard. *Straub.* New York: Viking Press, 1972.

Salmane, Hala. *Algerian Cinema.* London: British Film Institute, 1977.

Sarris, Andrew. "After *The Graduate.*" *American Film,* 3, 9 (July–August 1978), 32–37.

Seydor, Paul. *Peckinpah: The Western Films.* Urbana: University of Illinois Press, 1980.

Smith, Julian. *Looking Away: Hollywood and Vietnam.* New York: Charles Scribner's Sons, 1975.

Toeplitz, Jerzy. *Hollywood and After: The Changing Face of Movies in America.* Translated by Boleslaw Sulik. Chicago: Henry Regnery, 1974.

Wake, Sandra, ed. *The "Bonnie and Clyde" Book.* London: Lorrimer, 1972.

Walker, Alexander. *Stanley Kubrick Directs*. New York: Harcourt Brace Jovanovich, 1971.

Wood, Robin. *Arthur Penn*. New York: Frederick A. Praeger, 1969.

Zuker, Joel S. *Arthur Penn: A Guide to References and Resources*. Boston: G. K. Hall, 1980.

World and American Film History

Bardèche, Maurice, and Brasillach, Robert. *A History of the Motion Pictures*. Translated and edited by Iris Barry. New York: W. W. Norton/Museum of Modern Art, 1938.

Bluem, William. *The Film Industries*. New York: Hastings House, 1973.

———. *The Movie Business*. New York: Hastings House, 1972.

Blum, Daniel. *A Pictorial History of the Silent Screen*. New York: G. P. Putnam's Sons, 1953.

Bohn, Thomas W., and Stromgren, Richard L. *Light and Shadows: A History of Motion Pictures*. 2nd edition. Sherman Oaks, Calif.: Alfred, 1978.

Brownlow, Kevin. *The Parade's Gone By*. New York: Alfred A. Knopf, 1968.

———. *The War, the West, and the Wilderness*. New York: Alfred A. Knopf, 1979.

———, and Kobal, John. *Hollywood: The Pioneers*. New York: Alfred A. Knopf, 1979.

Casty, Alan. *Development of the Film: An Interpretive History*. New York: Harcourt Brace Jovanovich, 1973.

Conant, Michael. *Antitrust in the Motion Picture Industry*. Berkeley: University of California Press, 1960.

Cowie, Peter. *A Concise History of the Cinema*. 2 vols. London: A. Zwemmer, 1971.

———. *Seventy Years of Cinema*. New York: Castle Books, 1969.

Dickinson, Thorold. *A Discovery of Cinema*. New York: Oxford University Press, 1971.

Earley, Steven C. *An Introduction to American Movies*. New York: New American Library, 1978.

Ellis, Jack C. *A History of Film*. Englewood Cliffs, N.J.: Prentice-Hall, 1979.

Fell, John L. *A History of Films*. New York: Holt, Rinehart, and Winston, 1978.

Fielding, Raymond. *A Technological History of Motion Pictures and Television*. Berkeley: University of California Press, 1967.

Fulton, A. R. *Motion Pictures: The Development of an Art from Silent Films to the Age of Television*. Norman: University of Oklahoma Press, 1960; revised edition, 1980.

Goodman, Ezra. *The Fifty Year Decline and Fall of Hollywood*. New York: Simon and Schuster, 1961.

Griffith, Richard, and Mayer, Arthur. *The Movies*. New York: Simon and Schuster, 1957; revised edition, 1970.

Hampton, Benjamin B. *A History of the American Film Industry from Its Beginnings to 1931*. Edited by Richard Griffith. New York: Covici, 1931; reprinted, New York: Dover Books, 1970. (Originally titled *A History of the Movies*.)

Hendricks, Gordon. *The Edison Motion Picture Myth*. Berkeley: University of California Press, 1961.

Hennebelle, Guy. *Quinze ans du cinéma mondial, 1960–1975*. Paris: Éditions Cerf, 1975.

Higham, Charles. *The Art of the American Film*. Garden City, N.Y.: Anchor Books, 1973.

Jacobs, Lewis, ed. *The Emergence of Film Art*. New York: Hopkinson and Blake, 1969; second edition, New York: W. W. Norton, 1979.

———. *The Rise of the American Film*. New York: Harcourt, Brace, 1939.

Jeanne, René, and Ford, Charles. *Histoire encyclopédique du cinéma*. Paris, 1947–68.

Jowett, Garth. *Film, the Democratic Art: A Social History of American Film*. Boston: Little, Brown, 1976.

Knight, Arthur. *The Liveliest Art: A Panoramic History of the Movies*. New York: Macmillan, 1957; revised edition, New York: Mentor Books, 1978.

Lacassin, Francis. *Pour une contre-histoire du cinéma*. Paris: Union Générale d'Éditions, 1972.

MacCann, Richard Dyer. *Hollywood in Transition*. Boston: Houghton Mifflin, 1962.

Macgowan, Kenneth. *Behind the Screen*. New York: Delacorte Press, 1965.

McClure, Arthur, ed. *The Movies: An American Idiom*. Rutherford, N.J.: Fairleigh Dickinson University Press, 1971.

Mast, Gerald. *A Short History of the Movies.* 3rd edition. Indianapolis: Bobbs-Merrill, 1981.

Mitry, Jean. *Histoire du cinéma: art et industrie.* Paris, 1967–73. (A three-volume account of the silent film.)

O'Connor, John E., and Jackson, Martin A., eds. *American History/American Film: Interpreting Hollywood Images.* New York: Frederick Ungar, 1979.

Pratt, George C. *Spellbound in Darkness: A History of the Silent Film.* Rochester, N.Y.: University of Rochester Press, 1966; revised edition, Greenwich, Conn.: New York Graphic Society, 1973.

Quigley, Martin. *Magic Shadows.* Washington, D.C.: Georgetown University Press, 1948.

Ramsaye, Terry. *A Million and One Nights: A History of the Motion Picture.* New York: Simon and Schuster, 1926.

Reader, Keith. *The Cinema: A History.* London: Hodder & Stoughton, 1979.

Rhode, Eric. *A History of the Cinema from Its Origins to 1970.* New York: Hill & Wang, 1976.

Robinson, David. *The History of World Cinema.* New York: Stein & Day, 1973.

Rotha, Paul, and Griffith, Richard. *The Film Till Now.* New York: Funk and Wagnalls, 1950.

Sadoul, Georges. *Histoire générale du cinéma.* Paris, 1946–54.

Schickel, Richard. *Movies: The History of an Art and an Institution.* New York: Basic Books, 1964.

Sklar, Robert. *Movie-Made America: A Cultural History of American Movies.* New York: Random House, 1975.

Taylor, Deems; Hale, Bryant; and Peterson, Marcelene. *A Pictorial History of the Movies.* New York: Simon and Schuster, 1950.

Thomson, David. *America in the Dark: The Impact of Hollywood Films on American Culture.* New York: William Morrow, 1979.

Tyler, Parker. *Classics of the Foreign Film.* New York: Citadel Press, 1962.

Vardac, Nicholas. *From Stage to Screen.* Cambridge: Harvard University Press, 1949.

Wagenknecht, Edward. *The Movies in the Age of Innocence.* Norman: University of Oklahoma Press, 1962.

Wright, Basil. *The Long View.* New York: Alfred A. Knopf, 1974.

Film History: Special Topics

Barsacq, Léon. *Caligari's Cabinet and Other Grand Illusions: A History of Film Design.* New York: New American Library, 1978.

Battcock, Gregory, ed. *The New American Cinema.* New York: E. P. Dutton, 1967.

Bazelon, Irwin. *Knowing the Score: Notes on Film Music.* New York: Van Nostrand Reinhold, 1972.

Bogle, Donald. *Toms, Coons, Mulattoes, Mammies, and Bucks.* New York: Bantam Books, 1974.

Brakhage, Stan. *Film Biographies.* Berkeley, Calif.: Turtle Island, 1977.

Brosnan, John. *Movie Magic: The Story of Special Effects.* New York: New American Library, 1976.

Cripps, Thomas. *Black Film as Genre.* Bloomington: Indiana University Press, 1978.

———. *Slow Fade to Black: The Negro in American Film.* New York: Oxford University Press, 1977.

Curtis, David. *Experimental Cinema.* New York: Universal Books, 1971.

"Film Music." *Cinema Journal,* 17, 2 (Spring 1978 [special issue]).

Gidal, Peter, ed. *Structural Film Anthology.* London: British Film Institute, 1976.

Haskell, Molly. *From Reverence to Rape: The Treatment of Women in the Movies.* Baltimore: Penguin Books, 1974.

"The Hollywood Cartoon." *Film Comment,* 11, 1 (January–February 1975 [special issue]).

Kay, Karyn, and Peary, Gerald. *Women and the Cinema.* New York: E. P. Dutton, 1977.

Klotman, Phyllis Rauch. *Frame by Frame—A Black Filmography.* Bloomington: Indiana University Press, 1979.

Limbacher, James L. *Film Music from Violins to Video.* Metuchen, N.J.: Scarecrow Press, 1974.

Matthews, J. H. *Surrealism and Film.* Ann Arbor: University of Michigan Press, 1971.

Murray, James. *To Find an Image: Black Films from Uncle Tom to Superfly.* Indianapolis: Bobbs-Merrill, 1973.

Prendergast, Roy M. *Film Music: A Neglected Art.* New York: W. W. Norton, 1977.

Renan, Sheldon. *An Introduction to the American Underground Film.* New York: E. P. Dutton, 1967.

Rosenblum, Ralph, and Karen, Robert. *When the Shooting Stops . . . the Cutting Begins.* New York: Viking Press, 1979.

Sitney, P. Adams. *Visionary Film: The American Avant-Garde.* New York: Oxford University Press, 1974; revised edition, 1979.

Stephenson, Ralph. *The Animated Film.* Cranbury, N.J.: A. S. Barnes, 1973.

General Reference Works and Bibliographies (Including Collections of Reviews and Essays)

Adler, Renata. *A Year in the Dark.* New York: Random House, 1969.

Agee, James. *Agee on Film.* Vol. 1: *Reviews and Comments.* Vol. 2: *Five Film Scripts.* Boston: Beacon Press, 1964.

The American Film Institute Catalogue of Motion Pictures Produced in the U.S. Part I: *Feature Films 1921–1930.* 2 vols. Part II: *Feature Films 1961–1970.* New York: R. R. Bowker, 1971, 1976.

Bawden, Liz-Anne, ed. *The Oxford Companion to Film.* New York: Oxford University Press, 1976.

Beattie, Eleanor. *The Handbook of Canadian Cinema.* 2nd edition. Toronto: Peter Martin, 1977.

Bellone, Julius, ed. *Renaissance of the Film.* London: Collier-Macmillan, 1970.

Bohnenkamp, Dennis R., and Grogg, Sam L., Jr., eds. *The American Film Institute Guide to College Courses in Film and Television.* Princeton, N.J.: Peterson's Guides, 1980.

Bowser, Eileen. *Film Notes.* New York: Museum of Modern Art, 1969.

Braudy, Leo, and Dickstein, Morris, eds. *Great Film Directors.* New York: Oxford University Press, 1978.

Bukalski, Peter J. *Film Research: A Critical Bibliography with Annotations and Essays.* Boston: G. K. Hall, 1972.

Cawkwell, Tim, and Smith, John, eds. *The World Encyclopedia of Film.* New York: A & W Visual Library, 1972.

Corliss, Richard. *Talking Pictures: Screenwriters in the American Cinema.* New York: Viking Press, 1973.

Cowie, Peter, ed. *Fifty Major Film Makers.* Cranbury, N.J.: A. S. Barnes, 1975.

———. *International Film Guide.* Cranbury, N.J.: A. S. Barnes, 1974–. (Issued annually.)

Crist, Judith. *The Private Eye, the Cowboy, and the Very Naked Girl.* New York: Holt, Rinehart and Winston, 1968.

Delson, Donn. *The Dictionary of Marketing and Related Terms in the Motion Picture Industry.* Thousand Oaks, Ca.: Brandson Press, 1979.

Directory of Films by and/or About Women. Berkeley: Women's Historical Research Center, 1972.

Dyment, Alan. *Literature of the Film.* London: White Lion Publishers, 1975.

Ellis, Jack D.; Derry, Charles; and Kern, Sharon, eds. *The Film Book Bibliography, 1940–1975.* Metuchen, N.J.: Scarecrow Press, 1979.

Farber, Manny. *Negative Space.* New York: Frederick A. Praeger, 1972.

Feinberg, Cobbett. *Reel Facts: The Movie Book of Records.* New York: Vintage Books, 1978.

Ferguson, Otis. *The Film Criticism of Otis Ferguson.* Edited by Robert Wilson. Philadelphia: Temple University Press, 1971.

Garbicz, Adam, and Klinowski, Jacek. *Cinema, the Magic Vehicle: A Guide to Its Achieve-*

ment. *Journey One: The Cinema Through 1949*. Metuchen, N.J.: Scarecrow Press, 1975.

—————. *Cinema, the Magic Vehicle: A Guide to Its Achievement. Journey Two: The Cinema in the Fifties*. Metuchen, N.J.: Scarecrow Press, 1980.

Gerlach, John C., and Gerlach, Lana, eds. *The Critical Index: A Bibliography of Articles on Film in English, 1946–1973*. New York: Teachers College Press, 1974.

Gifford, Denis. *The British Film Catalogue, 1895–1970: A Reference Guide*. 2 vols. New York: McGraw-Hill, 1973.

Gilliatt, Penelope. *Unholy Fools*. New York: Viking Press, 1973.

Gottesman, Ronald, and Geduld, Harry. *Guidebook to Film*. New York: Holt, Rinehart and Winston, 1972.

Graham, Peter, ed. *Dictionary of the Cinema*. London: Tantivy Press, 1964.

Guback, Thomas H. *The International Film Industry*. Bloomington: Indiana University Press, 1969.

Halliwell, Leslie. *The Filmgoer's Companion*. New York: Avon Books, 1978.

Halliwell, Leslie. *Halliwell's Film Guide*. New York: Charles Scribner's Sons, 1979.

Hecquet, Marie-Claude, and McNicoll, David. *A Guide to Film and Television Courses in Canada, 1978–79*. Ottawa: Canadian Film Institute, 1978.

Hedgecoe, John. *The Photographer's Handbook*. New York: Alfred A. Knopf, 1978.

Henshaw, Richard, ed. "Women Directors: 150 Filmographies." *Film Comment*, 8, 4 (November–December 1972), 33–45.

Hochman, Stanley, ed. *American Film Directors*. New York: Frederick Ungar, 1974.

International Index to Film Periodicals. Sponsored by Fédération Internationale des Archives du Film (FIAF). Yearly. Vol. 1: *1972*. Edited by Karen Jones. New York: R. R. Bowker, 1973. Vol. 2: *1973*. Edited by Michael Moulds. New York: R. R. Bowker, 1974. Vol. 3: *1974*. Edited by Karen Jones. London: Saint James Press; New York: St. Martin's Press, 1975. Vols. 4–6: *1975–77*. Edited by Frances Thorpe. New York: St. Martin's Press, 1976–78.

Jenkins, Bruce, ed. *Film Reader 3: Film Genre/Film and the Other Arts*. Evanston, Ill.: Northwestern University Press, 1978.

Jones, Karen, ed. *International Index to Film Periodicals, 1972* and *1974*. New York: R. R. Bowker, 1973, 1975.

Kael, Pauline. *Deeper into Movies*. Boston: Little, Brown, 1973.

—————. *Going Steady*. Boston: Little, Brown, 1970.

—————. *I Lost It at the Movies*. New York: Atlantic, Little, Brown, 1965.

—————. *Kiss Kiss, Bang Bang*. New York: Atlantic, Little, Brown, 1968.

—————. *Reeling*. Boston: Little, Brown, 1976.

Kauffmann, Stanley. *Before My Eyes*. New York: Harper & Row, 1980.

—————. *Living Images*. New York: Harper & Row, 1975.

—————. *When the Lights Go Down*. New York: Holt, Rinehart and Winston, 1980.

—————. *A World on Film*. New York: Harper & Row, 1966.

—————, and Henstell, Bruce, eds. *American Film Criticism: From the Beginnings to "Citizen Kane."* New York: Liveright, 1972.

Koszarski, Richard, ed. *Hollywood Directors, 1914–1940*. New York: Oxford University Press, 1977.

Leyda, Jay, ed. *Voices of Film Experience, 1894 to the Present*. New York: Macmillan, 1977.

Luboviski, Git. *Cinema Catalogue*. Hollywood: Larry Edmunds Cinema Bookshop, n.d.

Lyons, Timothy J., ed. *The Influence of the World Cinema Heritage on the Education and Training of Film/Television Directors and Communicators*. University Film Association Monograph No. 4, Fall 1979.

MacCann, Richard Dyer, ed. *The New Film Index: A Bibliography of Magazine Articles in English, 1930–1970*. New York: E. P. Dutton, 1975.

MacDonald, Dwight. *On Movies*. New York: Berkley, 1969.

McIlroy, Susan; Beard, David; and Maunder, T. C. *Cinebooks Catalogue*. Toronto: Cinebooks, 1976.

Maltin, Leonard, ed. *TV Movies.* 1981–82 revised edition. New York: Signet Books, 1980.

Manchel, Frank. *Film Study: A Resource Guide.* Rutherford, N.J.: Fairleigh Dickinson University Press, 1973.

Manvell, Roger. *The Film and the Public.* New York: Penguin Books, 1955.

———, and Jacobs, Lewis, eds. *International Encyclopedia of Film.* New York: Crown Publishers, 1972.

Mayer, Michael F., ed. *The Film Industries.* New York: Hastings House, 1978.

Mercer, John. *Glossary of Film Terms.* University Film Association Monograph No. 2, Summer 1978.

Michael, Paul, ed. *The American Movies Reference Book: The Sound Era.* Englewood Cliffs, N.J.: Prentice-Hall, 1969.

Mitry, Jean. *Dictionaire du cinéma.* Paris: Libraire Larousse, 1963.

Monaco, James, and Schenker, Susan. *Books About Film: A Bibliographical Checklist.* New York: New York Zoetrope, 1976.

Murray, Edward. *Nine American Film Critics.* New York: Frederick Ungar, 1975.

The New York Times Film Reviews, 1913–1970. 7 vols. New York: Arno Press, 1971.

Parish, James R., and Pitts, Michael R. *Film Directors: A Guide to Their American Films.* Metuchen, N.J.: Scarecrow Press, 1974.

Parish, James R., et al. *Film Directors Guide: Western Europe.* Metuchen, N.J.: Scarecrow Press, 1976.

Pechter, William S. *Twenty-Four Times a Second: Films and Film-Makers.* New York: Harper & Row, 1971.

Potamkin, Harry Alan. *The Compound Cinema: The Film Writings of Harry Alan Potamkin.* Edited by Lewis Jacobs. New York: Teachers College Press, 1977.

Rehrauer, George. *Cinema Booklist.* Metuchen, N.J.: Scarecrow Press, 1972. *Supplement One,* 1974; *Supplement Two,* 1976.

Roud, Richard, ed. *Cinema: A Critical Dictionary.* 2 vols. New York: Viking Press, 1980.

Sadoul, Georges. *Dictionary of Film Makers.* Translated and edited by Peter Morris. Berkeley: University of California Press, 1972.

———. *Dictionary of Films.* Translated and edited by Peter Morris. Berkeley: University of California Press, 1972.

Samples, Gordon. *The Drama Scholar's Index to Plays and Filmscripts.* Metuchen, N.J.: Scarecrow Press, 1974.

Sarris, Andrew. *The American Cinema: Directors and Directions, 1929–1968.* New York: E. P. Dutton, 1968.

———. *Confessions of a Cultist.* New York: Simon and Schuster, 1971.

———. *Politics and Cinema.* New York: Columbia University Press, 1978.

———. *The Primal Screen.* New York: Simon and Schuster, 1973.

Scheuer, Steven H. *Movies on TV.* 1978–79 revised edition. New York: Bantam Books, 1977.

Silva, Fred, et al., eds. *Film Literature Index,* Vols. 1–5, *1973–77.* New York: R. R. Bowker, 1975–79.

Silver, Alain, and Ward, Elizabeth. *Film Noir: An Encyclopedic Reference to the American Style.* New York: Overlook Press, 1979.

Simon, John. *Movies into Films: Film Criticism, 1967–70.* New York: Dial Press, 1971.

———. *Private Screenings.* New York: Berkley, 1967.

Slide, Anthony. *Films on Film History.* Metuchen, N.J.: Scarecrow Press, 1979.

Smith, Sharon. *Women Who Make Movies.* New York: Hopkinson and Blake, 1975.

Speed, F. Maurice. *Film Review.* London: W. H. Allen, 1966–.

Spottiswoode, Raymond, et al. *The Focal Encyclopedia of Film and Television Techniques.* New York: Hastings House, 1969.

Thomas, Bob, ed. *Directors in Action.* Indianapolis: Bobbs-Merrill, 1973.

Thomson, David. *A Biographical Dictionary of Film.* New York: William Morrow, 1976.

Weinberg, Herman G. *Saint Cinema.* New York: Dover Books, 1970.

Willis, John, ed. *John Willis' Screen World.* London: Frederick Muller, 1949–.

World Filmography. General editor, Peter Cowie. Vols. *1967* and *1968*. London: Tantivy Press, 1977. (An annual filmography of feature releases in 49 countries, projected at 70 volumes.)

Theory and Aesthetics

Alpert, Hollis. *The Dreams and the Dreamers*. New York: Macmillan, 1962.

Andrew, J. Dudley. *The Major Film Theories*. New York: Oxford University Press, 1976.

Armes, Roy. *Film and Reality*. New York: Penguin Books, 1974.

Arnheim, Rudolf. *Art and Visual Perception: A Psychology of the Creative Eye*. Berkeley: University of California Press, 1954.

———. *Film as Art*. Berkeley: University of California Press, 1957.

———. *Visual Thinking*. Berkeley: University of California Press, 1969.

Balázs, Béla. *Theory of the Film*. Translated by Edith Bone. New York: Roy, 1953; reprinted, New York: Dover Books, 1970.

Barr, Charles. "Cinemascope: Before and After." *Film Quarterly,* 16, 4 (1963), 4–24.

Bazin, André. *What Is Cinema?* 2 vols. Selected and translated by Hugh Gray. Berkeley: University of California Press, 1967; 1971.

Bluestone, George. *Novels into Film*. Baltimore: Johns Hopkins Press, 1957.

Bordwell, David, and Thompson, Kristin. *Film Art: An Introduction*. Reading, Mass.: Addison-Wesley, 1979.

Braudy, Leo. *The World in a Frame*. New York: Anchor Books, 1976.

Burch, Noël. *Theory of Film Practice*. Translated by Helen R. Lane. New York: Frederick A. Praeger, 1973.

Buscombe, Edward, ed. *Film Reader 4: Point of View/Metahistory of Film*. Evanston, Ill.: Northwestern University Press, 1979.

Cameron, Ian, ed. *Movie Reader*. New York: Frederick A. Praeger, 1972.

Cavell, Stanley. *The World Viewed: Reflections on the Ontology of Film*. New York: Viking Press, 1971; enlarged edition, Cambridge, Mass.: Harvard University Press, 1979.

Clair, René. *Reflections on the Cinema*. London: Kimber, 1953.

Cohen, Keith. *Film and Fiction*. New Haven: Yale University Press, 1979.

Dovzhenko, Alexander. *Alexander Dovzhenko: The Poet as Filmmaker*. Translated and edited by Marco Carynnyk. Cambridge, Mass.: MIT Press, 1973.

Eco, Umberto. *The Semiotic Threshhold*. The Hague: Mouton, 1973.

———. *A Theory of Semiotics*. Bloomington: University of Indiana Press, 1976.

Eisenstein, Sergei. *Film Essays and a Lecture*. Translated and edited by Jay Leyda. New York: Frederick A. Praeger, 1970.

———. *Film Form*. Translated and edited by Jay Leyda. New York: Harcourt Brace Jovanovich, 1969.

———. *The Film Sense*. Translated and edited by Jay Leyda. New York: Harcourt Brace Jovanovich, 1969.

Geduld, Harry M., ed. *Authors on Film*. Bloomington: Indiana University Press, 1972.

———, ed. *Filmmakers on Filmmaking*. Bloomington: Indiana University Press, 1967.

Gessner, Robert. *The Moving Image: A Guide to Cinematic Literacy*. New York: E. P. Dutton, 1970.

Giannetti, Louis. *Understanding Movies*. 2nd edition. Englewood Cliffs, N.J.: Prentice-Hall, 1976.

Godard, Jean-Luc. *Godard on Godard*. Edited by Tom Milne. New York: Viking Press, 1972.

Hauser, Arnold. *The Social History of Art*. Vol. 4. New York: Vintage Books, 1960.

Henderson, Brian. *A Critique of Film Theory*. New York: E. P. Dutton, 1980.

Houston, Beverle, ed. "Feminist and Ideological Criticism." *Quarterly Review of Film Studies,* 3,4 (fall 1978 [special issue]).

Huss, Roy, and Silverstein, Norman. *The Film Experience*. New York: Delta Books, 1968.

Jacobs, Lewis, ed. *Introduction to the Art of Movies.* New York: Farrar, Straus & Giroux, 1960.

———. *The Movies as Medium.* New York: Farrar, Straus & Giroux, 1970.

Johnson, Lincoln. *Film: Space, Time, Light and Sound.* New York: Holt, Rinehart and Winston, 1974.

Jowett, Garth and Linton, James M. *Movies as Mass Communication.* Beverly Hills: SAGE Publications, 1980.

Kracauer, Siegfried. *Theory of Film: The Redemption of Physical Reality.* New York: Oxford University Press, 1960.

Kuleshov, Lev. *Kuleshov on Film.* Translated and edited by Ronald Levaco. Berkeley: University of California Press, 1975.

Lawson, John Howard. *Film: The Creative Process.* New York: Hill & Wang, 1964.

Lindgren, Ernest. *The Art of the Film.* New York: Macmillan, 1948.

Lindsay, Vachel. *The Art of the Moving Picture.* New York: Macmillan, 1915; reprinted, New York: Liveright, 1970.

Lorentz, Pare. *Lorentz on Film.* New York: Harcourt Brace Jovanovich, 1975.

MacCann, Richard Dyer, ed. *Film: A Montage of Theories.* New York: E. P. Dutton, 1966.

Manvell, Roger. *Film.* Harmondsworth, Middlesex, England: Penguin Books, 1950.

Mast, Gerald, and Cohen, Marshall, eds. *Film Theory and Criticism.* New York: Oxford University Press, 1974; second edition, 1979.

Mekas, Jonas. *Movie Journal: Rise of the New American Cinema: 1969–1971.* New York: Macmillan, 1972.

Metz, Christian. *Film Language: A Semiotics of the Cinema.* Translated by Michael Taylor. New York: Oxford University Press, 1974.

———. *Language and Cinema.* Translated by Donna Jean Umiker-Sebeok. The Hague: Mouton, 1974.

Mitry, Jean. *Esthétique et psychologie du cinéma.* 2 vols. Paris: Éditions Universitaires, 1963.

Monaco, James. *How to Read a Film.* New York: Oxford University Press, 1977.

Montagu, Ivor. *Film World.* Baltimore: Penguin Books, 1964.

Münsterberg, Hugo. *The Film: A Psychological Study.* New York: D. Appleton, 1916; reprinted, New York: Dover Books, 1970.

Nichols, Bill, ed. *Movies and Methods.* Berkeley: University of California Press, 1977.

Nilsen, Vladimir. *Cinema as Graphic Art.* New York: Hill & Wang, 1973.

Perkins, V. F. *Film as Film: Understanding and Judging Movies.* New York: Penguin Books, 1972.

Pudovkin, V. I. *Film Technique and Film Acting.* London, 1929; reprinted, New York: Grove Press, 1970.

Sitney, P. Adams, ed. *The Avant-Garde Film: A Reader of Theory and Criticism.* New York: New York University Press, 1978.

———. *The Essential Cinema.* New York: New York University Press, 1975.

Solanas, Fernando, and Getino, Octavio. "Towards a Third Cinema." *Cinéaste,* 4, 3 (1970), 1–10.

Spottiswoode, Raymond R. *Film and Its Techniques.* Berkeley: University of California Press, 1951; reprinted, 1965.

Stephenson, Ralph, and Debrix, J. R. *The Cinema as Art.* New York: Penguin Books, 1965.

Talbot, Daniel, ed. *Film: An Anthology.* Berkeley: University of California Press, 1967.

Taylor, John Russell. *Cinema Eye, Cinema Ear.* New York: Hill & Wang, 1964.

Thomson, David. *Movie Man.* New York: Stein & Day, 1967.

Tudor, Andrew. *Theories of Film.* New York: Viking Press, 1973.

Tyler, Parker. *Hollywood Hallucination.* 1944; reprinted, New York: Simon and Schuster, 1970.

———. *Magic and Myth in the Movies.* 1947; reprinted, New York: Grove Press, 1970.

———. *Sex, Psyche, Etc., in the Film.* New York: Penguin Books, 1971.

———. *The Shadow of an Airplane Climbs the Empire State Building: A World Theory of Film.* Garden City, N.Y.: Doubleday, 1973.

———. *The Three Faces of the Film.* New York: Thomas Yoseloff, 1960.

———. *Underground Film.* New York: Grove Press, 1969.

Vogel, Amos. *Film as a Subversive Art.* New York: Random House, 1974.

Wollen, Peter. *Signs and Meaning in the Cinema.* 2nd edition. New York: Viking Press, 1972.

Wollenberg, H. H. *Anatomy of Film.* London: Marsland, 1947.

Wood, Robin. *Personal Views.* London: Gordon Fraser, 1976.

Young, Vernon. *On Film.* New York: Quadrangle Books, 1973.

Youngblood, Gene. *Expanded Cinema.* New York: E. P. Dutton, 1970.

Genre Studies

Baxter, John. *The Gangster Film.* Cranbury, N.J.: A. S. Barnes, 1970.

———. *Science Fiction in the Cinema.* Cranbury, N.J.: A. S. Barnes, 1970.

Brosnan, John. *Future Tense: The Cinema of Science Fiction.* New York: St. Martin's Press, 1978.

———. *The Horror People.* New York: St. Martin's Press, 1976.

Clarens, Carlos. *Crime Movies.* New York: W. W. Norton, 1980.

———. *An Illustrated History of the Horror Film.* New York: Capricorn Books, 1967.

Davis, Brian. *The Thriller.* New York: E. P. Dutton, 1973.

Dillard, Richard H. W. *Horror Films.* New York: Monarch Press, 1976.

Everson, William K. *The Bad Guys.* New York: Citadel Press, 1964.

———. *The Detective in Film.* New York: Citadel Press, 1972.

Eyles, Allen. *The Western.* Cranbury, N.J.: A. S. Barnes, 1975.

Fenin, George N., and Everson, William K. *The Western: From Silents to the Seventies.* 2nd edition. New York: Grossman Publishers, 1973.

Folsom, James K., ed. *The Western.* Englewood Cliffs, N.J.: Prentice-Hall, 1979.

French, Philip. *Westerns.* New York: Viking Press, 1973.

Gabree, John. *Gangsters: From Little Caesar to the Godfather.* New York: Pyramid Publications, 1973.

Gifford, Denis. *Science Fiction Film.* London: Studio Vista Books, 1951.

Glaessner, Verina. *Kung-Fu: Cinema of Vengeance.* New York: Bounty, 1973.

Gow, Gordon. *Suspense in the Cinema.* Cranbury, N.J.: A. S. Barnes, 1968.

Huss, Roy, ed. *Focus on the Horror Film.* Englewood Cliffs, N.J.: Prentice-Hall, 1972.

Johnson, William, ed. *Focus on the Science Fiction Film.* Englewood Cliffs, N.J.: Prentice-Hall, 1972.

Kaminsky, Stuart M. *American Film Genres: Approaches to a Critical Theory.* New York: Dell, 1974.

Karpf, Steven. *The Gangster Film: Emergence, Variation, and Decay of a Genre.* New York: Arno Press, 1973.

Kitses, Jim. *Horizons West.* Bloomington: Indiana University Press, 1970.

Kobal, John. *Gotta Sing Gotta Dance: A Pictorial History of Film Musicals.* London: Hamlyn, 1971.

McArthur, Colin. *Underworld U.S.A.* New York: Viking Press, 1972.

McVay, Douglas. *The Musical Film.* Cranbury, N.J.: A. S. Barnes, 1967.

Menville, Douglas. *A Historical and Critical Survey of the Science Fiction Film.* New York: Arno Press, 1975.

Nachbar, Jack, ed. *Focus on the Western.* Englewood Cliffs, N.J.: Prentice-Hall, 1974.

Parish, James R. *The Great Gangster Pictures.* Metuchen, N.J.: Scarecrow Press, 1976.

———. *The Great Science Fiction Pictures.* Metuchen, N.J.: Scarecrow Press, 1977.

———. *The Great Spy Pictures.* Metuchen, N.J.: Scarecrow Press, 1974.

———. *The Great Western Pictures*. Metuchen, N.J.: Scarecrow Press, 1974.

Pilkington, William T., ed. *Western Movies*. Albuquerque: University of New Mexico Press, 1979.

Pirie, David. *A Heritage of Horror: The English Gothic Cinema 1946–1972*. New York: Avon Books, 1973.

Rosow, Eugene. *Born to Lose: The Gangster Film in America*. New York: Avon Books, 1978.

Rovin, Jeff. *A Pictorial History of Science Fiction Films*. Secaucus, N.J.: Citadel Press, 1975.

Shadoian, Jack. *Dreams and Dead Ends: The American Gangster Film*. Cambridge, Mass.: MIT Press, 1977.

Solomon, Stanley J. *Beyond Formula: American Film Genres*. New York: Harcourt Brace Jovanovich, 1976.

Steinbrunner, Chris. *Cinema of the Fantastic*. New York: Saturday Review Press, 1972.

Sterne, Lee. E. *The Movie Musical*. New York: Pyramid Publications, 1974.

Taylor, John Russell, and Jackson, Arthur. *The Hollywood Musical*. New York: McGraw-Hill, 1971.

Turan, Kenneth, and Zito, Stephen F. *Sinema: American Pornographic Films and the People Who Make Them*. New York: Frederick A. Praeger, 1974.

Tuska, Jon. *The Detective in Hollywood*. Garden City, N.Y.: Doubleday, 1978.

———. *The Filming of the West*. Garden City, N.Y.: Doubleday, 1976.

Vallance, Tom. *The American Musical*. Cranbury, N.J.: A. S. Barnes, 1970.

Wright, Will. *Six Guns and Society: A Structural Study of the Western*. Berkeley: University of California Press, 1975.

The Documentary

Barnouw, Erik. *Documentary: A History of the Non-Fiction Film*. New York: Oxford University Press, 1974.

Barsam, Richard. *Non-Fiction Film: A Critical History*. New York: E. P. Dutton, 1973.

———, ed. *Non-Fiction Film Theory and Criticism*. New York: E. P. Dutton, 1976.

Beddeley, W. Hugh. *The Technique of Documentary Film Production*. New York: Hastings House, 1963.

Beveridge, James. *John Grierson: Film Master*. New York: Macmillan, 1978.

Calder-Marshall, Arthur. *The Innocent Eye: The Life of Robert Flaherty*. London: W. H. Allen, 1963; reprinted, New York: Penguin Books, 1970.

Fielding, Raymond. *The American Newsreel: 1911–1967*. Norman: University of Oklahoma Press, 1972.

Grierson, John. *Grierson on Documentary*. Edited by Forsyth Hardy. New York: Frederick A. Praeger, 1971.

Griffith, Richard. *The World of Robert Flaherty*. New York: Duell, Sloan, and Pearce, 1953.

Jacobs, Lewis, ed. *The Documentary Tradition*. New York: Hopkinson and Blake, 1971; second edition, New York: W. W. Norton, 1979.

Levin, G. Roy, ed. *Documentary Explorations*. Garden City, N.Y.: Doubleday, 1972.

Lovell, Alan, and Hillier, Jim. *Studies in Documentary*. New York: Viking Press, 1972.

Mamber, Stephen. *Cinéma Vérité in America*. Cambridge, Mass.: MIT Press, 1974.

Marcorelles, Louis. *Living Cinema*. New York: Frederick A. Praeger, 1973.

Rosenthal, Alan. *The New Documentary in Action*. Berkeley: University of California Press, 1971.

Sussex, Elizabeth. *The Rise and Fall of British Documentary*. Berkeley: University of California Press, 1976.